Societies and Cultures
IN WORLD HISTORY

Societies and Cultures
IN WORLD HISTORY
VOLUME II   1500 TO THE PRESENT

MARK KISHLANSKY
Harvard University

PATRICK GEARY
University of California, Los Angeles

PATRICIA O'BRIEN
University of California, Irvine

R. BIN WONG
University of California, Irvine

With

ROY MOTTAHEDEH
Harvard University

LEROY VAIL
Harvard University

ANN WALTNER
University of Minnesota

MARK WASSERMAN
Rutgers University

JAMES GELVIN
Massachusetts Institute
of Technology

HarperCollinsCollegePublishers

Executive Editor: Bruce Borland
Development Editor: Barbara Muller
Project Coordination: Ruttle, Shaw & Wetherill, Inc.
Cover Design: Mary McDonnell
Text Design: Anne O'Donnell
Photo Research: Sandy Schneider
Cartographer: Maps produced by Mapping Specialists, Inc.
Manufacturing Manager: Willie Lane
Compositor: Publication Services, Inc.
Printer and Binder: R.R. Donnelley & Sons Company
Cover Printer: The Lehigh Press, Inc.

Cover and Frontispiece: Scene from the Baghavat Purana with a swan.
Museum, New Delhi, India. Scala/Art Resource, NY.

Societies and Cultures in World History, Volume II 1500 to the Present

Library of Congress Cataloging-in-Publication Data
    Societies and cultures in world history / Mark Kishlansky ... [et al.]
        p.   cm.
    Includes indexes.
    Contents: v. 1. To 1715 — v. 2. 1500 to the present.
    ISBN 0-06-500351-9 (v. 1).—ISBN 0-06-500352-7 (v. 2)
    1. Civilization—History. I. Kishlansky, Mark A.
CB69.S632   1995
909—dc20   93-49368
                                                      CIP

96 97 9 8 7 6 5 4 3 2

BRIEF CONTENTS

DETAILED CONTENTS

CHAPTER 14

World Encounters, 1350–1700   *406*

CHAPTER 15

The Islamic World, 1400–1700   *440*

CHAPTER 16

Nation Building and War: Europe, 1450–1650   *472*

DOCUMENTS

Maps

CHARTS, TABLES, AND FIGURES

COLOR ESSAYS

PREFACE

There is no more difficult subject for an introductory textbook than world history. While textbook writers are always faced with the dilemma of what to include and what to leave out, for the authors of a world history text this choice usually involves entire civilizations across centuries. And now more than ever—with the explosion in scholarship on world societies over the past decade—there are no easy answers. Decisions once made on the basis of too little knowledge to reconstruct a story must now be made on other grounds. It is an extraordinarily daunting task.

In writing *Societies and Cultures in World History*, we first considered how the book would be used among the variety of courses currently taught under the title World Civilizations. We designed the book for courses that combine the teaching of Western and world civilizations. It devotes more space to the history of the West, broadly construed, than to that of any other civilization. This design will give students a base of knowledge from which to compare and contrast the experiences of other civilizations as well as to help them understand the impact (for good or ill) that the West has had on the rest of the world. In coverage of world civilizations, we have allocated most space to Asian civilizations and have attempted to treat equally Africa, the Middle East, and Latin America. Although this presentation conforms to the broad outlines of most world civilization courses, we recognize there are nearly as many configurations of the course as there are places where it is taught. We hope the strengths of our presentation will outweigh its shortcomings.

We believe our book offers two outstanding distinctions: an intellectual respect for the integrity of all civilizations and a concern for the demands placed on student users. In planning our world civilization text, we decided not to follow the well-beaten path of adding one or two specialists to the author team and requiring them to write about civilizations (or epochs) in which they had neither scholarly training nor teaching experience. Instead we have contributions from a diverse team of experts—specialists in African, Latin American, and Middle Eastern history, as well as in early and modern Asia. This means that *Societies and Cultures in World History* has the benefit of the most up-to-date knowledge of world societies presented by experts on those societies.

Ann Waltner of the University of Minnesota has written on early Asia for part or all of Chapters 1, 4, 8, and 11. Leroy Vail of Harvard University has written on Africa for part or all of Chapters 1, 7, 14, 18, 19, 27, and 33. Mark Wasserman of Rutgers University has written on Latin America for part or all of Chapters 1, 14, 28, and 33. Roy Mottahedeh of Harvard University has written on early Islamic civilization for part or all of Chapters 15, 19, and 33; and James Gelvin of the Massachusetts Institute of Technology has written on modern Islamic civilization for part or all of Chapters 19 and 33.

Secondly, we are acutely aware that studying world history can be as daunting as reconstructing it, and throughout the process we have been concerned that the book meet the diverse needs and abilities of the students who will study it. We have tried to write a book that students will want to read. A number of decisions contributed to our goal. First, we would not write an encyclopedia of world civilization. Information would never be included in a chapter unless it fit within the themes of that chapter. There would be no information for information's sake and we would need to defend the inclusion of names, dates, and events whenever we met to critique our chapters. To our surprise, we found that by adhering to the principle that information appear only to illustrate a particular point or a dominating theme, we included as much, if not more, than books that habitually listed names, places, and dates with no other context. In addition, we were committed to integrating the history of women and of ordinary people into the narrative. In this endeavor, we had the assistance of two reviewers who were assigned no other responsibilities than to evaluate our chapters for the inclusion and integration of these materials within our chapters.

To construct a book that students would want to read, we needed to develop fresh ideas about how to involve the readers with the material, how to transform them from passive recipients to active participants. From computer science we borrowed the concept of "user friendly." Seeking ways to stimulate the imagination of the student, we realized the most dynamic way to do this was visually. Thus we initiated the technique of the pictorial chapter opener. At the beginning of each chapter, we explore a picture, guiding students across a canvas or an artifact or a photograph, helping them see things that are not immediately apparent, unfolding both an image and a theme. In some chapters we highlight details in the manner of an art history course, pulling out a section of the original picture to take a closer look. In others we attempt to shock readers into recognition of horror or beauty. Some openers are designed to make students ask, "What was it like to be there?" All are chosen to illustrate a dominant theme within the chapter, and the lingering impression they make helps reinforce that theme. We believe the combination of words and images will actively involve our readers—grabbing their attention and drawing them into the narrative.

To reinforce our emphasis on involving readers through visual learning, we included eight color inserts, built around the single theme, "Gender and Culture." The images and essays were prepared by Debra Mancoff, Professor and Chair of the Art History Department at Beloit College. Professor Mancoff has contributed her scholarly expertise in writing and teaching about representations of women to a compelling set of images that students will be able to compare and contrast over time and across cultures. These pictorial essays are substantive—not merely decorative—text, and we hope instructors will build on students' experience in reading the chapter pictorial features to analyze these photographs.

Similarly, we have taken an image-based approach to our presentation of geography. When teachers of world civilization courses are surveyed, no single area of need is highlighted more often than geography. Students simply have no mental image of the world beyond its shape, no familiarity with the geophysical features that are a fundamental part of the realities of world history. No world civilization textbook is without maps and ancillary map programs, yet no survey of teachers shows satisfaction with the effectiveness of these presentations. In *Societies and Cultures in World History*, we have tried to ensure that each place identified in the text is also identified in a map located within the chapter. The second device we developed to engage students with historical subjects is the in-depth chapter feature. These two-page, illustrated essays focus on a single event or personality chosen to demonstrate or enhance the students' sense that history is as real and exciting as

life itself. They are written with more drama or sympathy or wonder than would be appropriate in the body of the text, and we believe they will captivate the imagination of their readers.

Finally, so that students can grasp the past firsthand, we have provided a wide variety of excerpts from primary source documents. Two criteria guided the selection of these excerpts: accessibility and immediacy. We believe students will be able to engage with these primary sources with no further introduction than that provided by the contextual headnotes that introduce each selection. In choosing these excerpts, we have tapped the widest variety of genres—literature, popular culture, philosophy, religion, and all manner of political accounts. For those instructors who wish to make primary materials more central to their course, *Societies and Cultures in World History* also comes with a two-volume supplementary source book, *Sources of World History*.

Although our text includes much that is new and out of the ordinary, we do not mean to suggest that we have attempted to appeal to students only by adding "whistles and bells." *Societies and Cultures in World History* is a mainstream text in which most of the authors' energies have been placed in developing a solid, readable narrative of world civilizations that integrates women and the masses into the traditional sequence of periods and major events. We have highlighted personalities while identifying trends. We have spotlighted social history while maintaining a firm grip on political developments. We hope there are many qualities in this book that every teacher of world civilization will find valuable. But we also hope that there are things here you will disagree with, themes you can develop better, arguments and ideas that will provoke you. A textbook is only one part of a course, and it is always less important than a teacher. We have attempted to produce a book that your students will read so that you will not need to read it to them. We hope that by doing our job successfully we have made your job easier and your students' job more enjoyable.

Mark Kishlansky
Patrick Geary
Patricia O'Brien
R. Bin Wong

ACKNOWLEDGMENTS

We wish to thank the many conscientious historians who reviewed our manuscript and gave generously of their time and knowledge. Their valuable critiques and suggestions have contributed greatly to the final product. We are grateful to the following:

Mark Bartusis
Northern State University

Doris L. Bergen
University of Vermont

Martin Berger
Youngstown State University

Timothy Brook
University of Toronto

Charles J. Bussey
Western Kentucky University

Lee Cassanelli
University of Pennsylvania

Weston F. Cook, Jr.
Kutztown University

Todd A. Diacon
University of Tennessee at Knoxville

Ross E. Dunn
San Diego State University

Ainslie T. Embree
Columbia University

Charles T. Evans
Northern Virginia Community College-Loudoun

William Edward Ezzell
DeKalb College-Central Campus

Jonathan Goldstein
West Georgia College

Joseph Gowaskie
Rider College

John Mason Hart
University of Houston

Kandice Hauf
Babson College

Gerald Herman
Northeastern University

Mark C. Herman
Edison Community College

Ira M. Lapidus
University of California, Berkeley

Alan LeBaron
Kennesaw State College

Geri H. Malandra
University of Minnesota

Jon E. Mandaville
Portland State University

Patrick Manning
Northeastern University

Thomas Metcalf
University of California, Berkeley

James A. Miller
Clemson University

Joseph C. Miller
University of Virginia

Barbara A. Moss
University of Georgia

On-cho Ng
Penn State University

Donathon C. Olliff
Auburn University

James B. Palais
Jackson School of International Studies at the University of Washington

Peter C. Perdue
Massachusetts Institute of Technology

Paul J. Smith
Haverford College

Alexander Sydorenko
Arkansas State University

Steven C. Topik
University of California, Irvine

Karen Turner
College of the Holy Cross

Anne Walthall
University of California, Irvine

Eric L. Wake
Cumberland College

Allen Wells
Bowdoin College

David L. White
Appalachian State University

Alexander Woodside
University of British Columbia

Madeline C. Zilfi
University of Maryland

SUPPLEMENTS

The following supplements are available for use in conjunction with this book:

For the Instructor

Instructor's Resource Guide, by George F. Jewsbury, Oklahoma State University. This unique Instructor's Resource Guide provides new materials not found in the text through the use of lecture modules, lecture launchers, critical thinking exercises relating to the text's primary documents, detailed chapter summaries, test questions, and listings of additional resources for videos and films. As a **special feature**, there are six essays by Dr. Robert Edgar, Professor of African History at Howard University which incorporate the African history portions of the text into the lectures and discuss many of the most important and controversial issues in the teaching of world history.

Discovering World History Through Maps and Views, by Gerald Danzer of the University of Illinois at Chicago, winner of the AHA's 1990 James Harvey Robinson Prize for his work in the development of map transparencies. This set of 100 four-color transparencies from selected sources is bound in a three-ring binder and available free

to adopters. It also contains an introduction on teaching history with maps and detailed commentary on each transparency. The collection includes cartographic and pictorial maps, views and photos, urban plans, building diagrams, classic maps, and works of art.

Test Bank, by John Paul Bischoff, Oklahoma State University. A total of 2000 questions, including 50 multiple-choice questions and five essay questions per text chapter. Each test item is referenced by topic, type, and text page number. Available in print and computerized format.

TestMaster Computerized Testing System. This flexible, easy-to-master computer test bank includes all the test items in the printed test bank. The TestMaster software allows you to edit existing questions and add your own items. Available for IBM and Macintosh computers.

QuizMaster. The new program enables you to design TestMaster generated tests that your students can take on a computer rather than in printed form. QuizMaster is available separate from TestMaster and can be obtained free through your sales representative.

Grades. A grade-keeping and classroom management software program that maintains data for up to 200 students.

Map Transparencies. A set of 40 transparencies of maps taken from the text.

The HarperCollins World Civilization Media Program. A wide variety of media enhancements for use in teaching world civilization courses. Offered to qualified adopters of HarperCollins world history texts.

For the Student

Study Guide, in two volumes. Volume I (Chapters 1 through 16) and Volume II (Chapters 14 through 35), prepared by John Paul Bischoff, Oklahoma State University. Includes chapter outlines; timeline; map exercises; lists of important terms, people and events; and sections on "Making Connections" and "Putting Larger Concepts Together."

World History Map Workbook: Geographic and Critical Thinking Exercises, in two volumes. Prepared by Glee Wilson of Kent State University, each volume of this workbook contains 40 maps accompanied by over 120 pages of exercises. Each of the two volumes is designed to teach the students the location of various countries and their relationship to one another and events. Also included are numerous exercises aimed at enhancing students' critical thinking abilities.

Sources of World History, by Mark Kishlansky, a collection of primary source documents available in two volumes. These volumes provide a balance among constitutional documents, political theory, philosophy, imaginative literature, and social description. Represented are examples of the works of each of the major civilization complexes, Asia, Africa, Latin America, and the Islamic world as well as the central works of Western Civilization. Each volume includes the introductory essay, "How to Read a Document," which leads students step by step through the experience of using historical documents.

SuperShell II Computerized Tutorial, prepared by John Paul Bischoff, Oklahoma State University. This interactive program for IBM computers helps students learn the major facts and concepts through drill and practice exercises and diagnostic feedback. SuperShell II provides immediate correct answers; the text page number on which the material is discussed, and a running score of the student's performance is maintained on the screen throughout the session. This free supplement is available to instructors through their sales representative.

TimeLink Computer Atlas of World History, by William Hamblin, Brigham Young University. This HyperCard Macintosh program presents three views of the world—Europe/Africa, Asia, and the Americas—on a simulated globe. Students can spin the globe, select a time period, and see a map of the world at that time, including the names of major political units. Special topics such as the conquests of Alexander the Great are shown through animated sequences that depict the dynamic changes in geopolitical history. A comprehensive index and quizzes are also included.

Mapping World History: Student Activities, a free student map workbook by Gerald Danzer of the University of Illinois at Chicago. It features numerous map skill exercises written to enhance students' basic geographical literacy. The exercises provide ample opportunities for interpreting maps and analyzing cartographic materials as historical documents. The instructor is entitled to one free copy of *Mapping World History* for each copy of the text purchased from HarperCollins.

ABOUT THE AUTHORS

MARK KISHLANSKY

Recently appointed Professor of History at Harvard University, Mark Kishlansky is among today's leading young scholars. Professor Kishlansky received his Ph.D. from Brown University and is a member of the Harvard University faculty. A Fellow of the Royal Historical Society, his primary area of expertise is seventeenth-century English political history. Among his main publications are *Parliamentary Selection: Social and Political Choice in Early Modern England* and *The Rise of the New Model Army.* He is the editor of the *Journal of British Studies* and the recipient of the 1989 Most Distinguished Alumnus Award from SUNY Stony Brook.

PATRICK GEARY

Holding a Ph.D. in Medieval Studies from Yale University, Patrick Geary is both a noted scholar and teacher. Professor Geary was named outstanding undergraduate history teacher for the 1986–87 year at the University of Florida. He currently teaches at the University of California, Los Angeles, where he is Director for the Center for Medieval and Renaissance Studies. He has also held academic positions at the École des Hautes Études en Sciences Sociales, Paris; the Universitat Wien; and Princeton University. His many publications include *Readings in Medieval History; Before France and Germany: The Creation and Transformation of the Merovingian World; Aristocracy in Provence: the Rhone Basin at the Dawn of the Carolingian Age;* and *Furta Sacra: Thefts of Relics in the Central Middle Ages.*

PATRICIA O'BRIEN

Professor O'Brien teaches at the University of California, Irvine, and is Associate Vice Chancellor in the Office of Research and Graduate Studies. Professor O'Brien holds a Ph.D. from Columbia University in modern European history. Among her many publications are *The Promise of Punishment: Prisons in 19th Century France; "l'Embastillement de Paris: The Fortification of Paris During the July Monarchy";* and *"Crime and Punishment as Historical Problems."*

R. BIN WONG

R. Bin Wong holds a Ph.D. from Harvard University where he studied both Chinese and European history. In addition to research publications in the United States, which include *Nourish the People: The State Civilian Granary System in China, 1650–1850* (with Pierre-Etienne Will), he has published articles in mainland China, Taiwan, Japan, France, and Holland. He has held a number of research and teaching positions, including ones in the Society of Fellows, the University of Michigan; the Institute of Economics, Chinese Academy of Social Sciences; Institute of Oriental Culture, University of Tokyo; and the École des Hautes Études en Sciences Sociales in Paris. Currently, Professor Wong teaches history and directs a research program in Asian Studies at the University of California, Irvine.

JAMES L. GELVIN

Holding a Ph.D. in History and Middle Eastern Studies from Harvard University, James L. Gelvin's particular field of interest is Syrian history during the late nineteenth and twentieth centuries. An award-winning teacher, Professor Gelvin has taught history and politics at Harvard University, Boston College, and Massachusetts Institute of Technology.

ROY P. MOTTAHEDEH

Professor of History at Harvard University, Roy Mottahedeh has served as Director of the Center for Middle Eastern Studies and is currently Chair of the Committee on Islamic Studies at that University. He received his B.A. and Ph.D. at Harvard University and taught for many years at Princeton University. His publications include *Loyalty and Leadership in an Early Islamic Society* and *The Mantle of the Prophet: Religion and Politics in Iran.*

LEROY VAIL

Professor of African History at Harvard University, Leroy Vail is a leading scholar of Africa. Having received his Ph.D. from the University of Wisconsin (Madison), he spent a dozen years in Africa, teaching at the Universities of Malawi and Zambia and carrying out research on the languages and history of southeast Africa. He is the author of numerous articles on the region's history and linguistics. In collaboration with Landeg White, he has written *Capitalism and Colonialism in Mozambique* and *Power and the Praise Poem: Southern African Voices in History*. He has also edited the important *The Creation of Tribalism in Southern Africa* and is currently editing a dictionary of Lakeside Tonga, a language of Malawi.

ANN WALTNER

An Associate Professor of History at the University of Minnesota and Director of Graduate Studies there, Professor Waltner holds a Ph.D. in Chinese history from the University of California at Berkeley. Her research interests center on the social and intellectual history of China in the sixteenth and seventeenth century, and include topics such as gender, kinship, and religion. She is presently completing a book on Tanyangzi, a young woman mystic who lived in south China in the sixteenth century. Her publications include numerous articles, as well as *Getting an Heir: Adoption and the Construction of Kinship in Late Imperial China*.

MARK WASSERMAN

With his Ph.D. from the University of Chicago, Mark Wasserman is professor of history at Rutgers, The State University of New Jersey. He has won prestigious post-doctoral fellowships from the Social Science Research Council, the Tinker Foundation, the American Philosophical Society, and the U.S. Department of Education. Among his main publications are *Capitalists, Caciques and Revolution: The Native Elite and Foreign Enterprise in Chihuahua, Mexico, 1854–1911*, *Persistent Oligarchs: Elites and Politics in Chihuahua, Mexico, 1910–1940*, *A History of Latin America*, and *Provinces of the Revolution: Essays on Regional Mexican History, 1910–1929*. He won the Arthur P. Whitaker Prize in 1984 from the Middle Atlantic Council of Latin American Studies for *Capitalists, Caciques, and Revolution*.

CHAPTER 14

World Encounters, 1350–1700

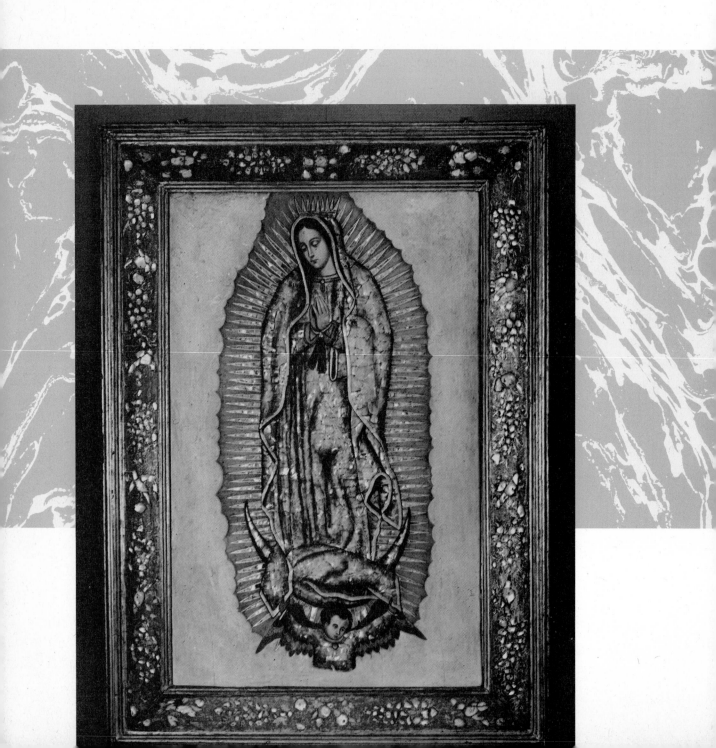

THE VIRGIN OF GUADALUPE

The Virgin of Guadalupe is perhaps the best known and the most important symbol of the Mexican nation. Her image reflects the complexity of the encounter between European and Indian cultures. Every year hundreds of thousands of people visit her shrine in Tepeyac just north of Mexico City. The most common version of the shrine's origin is that in 1531, barely a decade after the Spaniards had destroyed the Aztec capital of Tenochtitlán, the Virgin Mary appeared at Tepeyac to Juan Diego, a humble Indian, and spoke to him in his native language, Nahuatl. The Virgin ordered Juan Diego to tell the archbishop of Mexico that she desired a church to be built in her honor at Tepeyac. Of course, the Indian could not gain an audience with the great churchman. The Virgin then sent Juan Diego to gather roses in a place where only cactus grew, to put the roses in his cloak, and to present them to the archbishop. When the Indian unfolded his cloak, the image of the Virgin was stamped upon it. Acknowledging the miracle, the archbishop ordered the shrine built where Mary had appeared.

Over the following centuries the Virgin of Guadalupe was the subject of controversy, adoration, and manipulation. She came to illustrate much of the process and impact of colonial rule following the European encounters of the sixteenth century: the syncretization of folk religion and Catholicism; the flexibility of Spanish government; the conflicts within the Church over the plight of the Indian; the mestization, or mixture, of the native and European populations; and both the fierce and passive resistance of the Indians to the whites. The Virgin represented the "forging of the cosmic race," the Mexican people. It signified too the emergence of a sense of nationality among whites born in the New World. The Virgin became an important symbol of the new Mexican nation, and under her banner Father Miguel Hidalgo rallied the masses during the revolt for independence in 1810.

The site at Tepeyac exemplified the syncretic relation between native and Catholic religions, for it had previously been sacred to Tonantzin, the goddess of fertility. In the early years of the Christian shrine, the Indians may well have come to worship Tonantzin, and called out to her rather than to the Virgin Mary in their prayers. With the fusion of Indian and Spanish culture, the Virgin gradually integrated into the popular culture. The Virgin of Guadalupe may have served to restore the hope of salvation to the Indians, who had suffered in the conquest the death of all their old beliefs. The return of Tonantzin, through the Virgin of Guadalupe, rescued their gods.

The picture of the Virgin shown here from the seventeenth century is typical. She is usually represented standing on a crescent moon, surrounded by a crown of sunrays, which in turn is encompassed by clouds. She is clothed in a rich robe, ornamented with stars. Often a little cherub bears her on his head. The Virgin is dark-skinned.

Even before their encounters with the New World, the Virgin Mary, or Our Lady of the Immaculate Conception, was an important figure among Spaniards. One widely known version of her in Spain was the Virgin of Estremadura, which was coincidentally the birthplace of many of the *conquistadores*, or conquerors. Hernán Cortés's campaign banner carried a picture of Mary, who was a "symbol of Spanish power."

At first some clerics opposed the Virgin of Guadalupe cult. Their opposition ended, however, when during the first decades of the seventeenth century, the Virgin's intervention protected New Spain from desperate crises. Most notably, in 1629 displaying her image at the head of a procession protected Mexico City from inundation by floods. During the eighteenth century the Virgin became *patrona*, or patron saint, of New Spain.

The Guadalupe myth was important because it showed that Indians were capable of salvation; in other words, they could be Christians. This factor was crucial in the sixteenth-century debate over the humanity of the Indians. Some churchmen thought the Indian incapable of conversion and therefore rightfully exploited. Others maintained the Indians' humanity and resisted their oppression. For the Indian the most important aspect of the legend was that the Virgin appeared dark-skinned like an Indian. To rural Mexicans, the Virgin of Guadalupe was a "protectress" and an intermediary. In her were absorbed the ancient rites of agriculture. In the harshness of Christianity as it was imposed on the Indians by crusading clerics, the Virgin Mary, depicted as "the approachable little woman," mediated, praying for them to the Father and the Son. She was a "modest housewife," who as such eased the way to the acceptance of colonial authority. The Guadalupe myth also provided a place for the *mestizo* in the new order that emerged during the seventeenth century.

In one image, then, Indian, *mestizo*, and white were brought together. In their enthusiasm for her, they shunted aside class and racial differences. At a time when the Indians' world seemed destroyed by conquest and disease, when they were helpless and terrified, they gained comfort and hope in the Indian Virgin of Guadalupe. Later, when it was time to throw off the burden of Spanish colonial rule, Mexicans again called on the Virgin to unite and protect them.

Europe and the Encounters

In the history of the world, the fifteenth and sixteenth centuries were an age of encounters. Europeans, led by the Portuguese and the Spanish, set out to explore the world known to them in Africa and Asia and wound up discovering a world totally unknown to them—America. There were many reasons why this was the moment that Europeans would look beyond their own shores. Technological changes made long sea voyages possible, and the demands of commerce provided incentives. This was especially true in the trade for eastern spices, long dominated by Italian merchants but now gradually opening to traders along the Atlantic seaboard. Spices were rare and expensive, but they were not merely luxuries. Some acted as preservatives, others as flavorings to make palatable the rotting foodstuffs that were the fare of even the wealthiest Europeans. Some spices were used as perfumes to battle the noxious gases that rose from urban streets and invaded homes and workplaces. The drugs of the East, the nature of which we can only guess at, helped soothe chronic ill health. The demand for all of these "spices" continued to rise at a rate greater than their supply.

It was the Portuguese who made the first dramatic breakthroughs in exploration and colonization. In the early fifteenth century, they gained a foothold in northern Africa and used it to stage voyages along the continent's unexplored western coast. Like those of all explorers, the motives of the Portuguese were an unselfconscious mixture of faith and greed. Establishing bases there would enable them to surround their Muslim enemies while also giving them access to the

African bullion trade. The Portuguese navigator Bartolomeu Dias (ca. 1450–1500) summarized these goals succinctly: "To give light to those who are in darkness and to grow rich."

But those who were "in darkness" turned out to have rich cultures of their own. The cultures of the African peoples encountered by Dias and succeeding generations of Portuguese, Dutch, English, and French explorers and traders challenged many of the assumptions that Europeans made about non-Christians and initiated an encounter that transformed both European and African civilization. The Portuguese came to Africa seeking a passage to India and the gold that Africans were rumored to possess. Though they ultimately found both, they also found something that would prove more valuable still: slaves. At first, Europeans participated in the indigenous slave trade among the Africans, but soon they transformed it into an organized commercial activity that uprooted hundreds of thousands of black Africans to work plantations in the New World and on Atlantic and Indian Ocean islands.

While the Portuguese were the first Europeans to encounter African civilization, the Spaniards were the first to encounter the native populations of America. Queen Isabella of Castile was persuaded to take an interest in an expedition to the Indies led by a Genoese adventurer, Christopher Columbus (ca. 1446–1506). Like all well-informed people of his day, Columbus believed the world was round. By carefully calculating routes and distances, he concluded that a western track would be shorter and less expensive than the path the Portuguese were breaking around Africa. Because Columbus's conclusions were based on erroneous calculations, the land he reached on 12 October 1492 was not Japan, as he believed, but a hemisphere entirely unknown to Europeans.

Successive voyages by Columbus and others established that vast tracts of rich lands lay to the west of Europe. Indeed, in 1519 Ferdinand Magellan (ca. 1480–1521), a Portuguese mariner in the service of Spain, began a voyage that resulted in the circumnavigation of the globe. By then the globe had been divided between the Spanish and the Portuguese by the Treaty of Tordesillas (1494). The Portuguese were given the right to the eastern route to the Indies as well as to any undiscovered lands east of an imaginary Line of Demarcation fixed about 1,250 miles west of the Cape Verde Islands. This entitled Portugal to Brazil. The Spaniards received whatever lands lay west of the line.

Voyages of Discovery and World Empires

CHRISTOPHER COLUMBUS, LETTER FROM THE FIRST VOYAGE, 1493

■ *Christopher Columbus seemingly needs no introduction. His name has forever been associated with the European discovery of the New World, although the meaning of that discovery has been continually contested. In the summer of 1492 Columbus sailed west from the Canary Islands, believing that he would reach the coast of China. Instead he landed on an island in the Carribbean. This passage from a letter addressed to the royal treasurer of Spain contains his first impressions of the people he encountered.*

A Letter addressed to the noble Lord Raphael Sanchez, Treasurer to their most invincible Majesties, Ferdinand and Isabella, King and Queen of Spain, by Christopher Columbus, to whom our age is greatly indebted, treating of the islands of India recently discovered beyond the Ganges, to explore which he had been sent eight months before under the auspices and at the expense of their said Majesties.

The inhabitants of both sexes in this island, and in all the others which I have seen, or of which I have received information, go always naked as they were born, with the exception of some of the women, who use the covering of a leaf, or small bough, or an apron of cotton which they prepare for that purpose. None of them are possessed of any iron, neither have they weapons, being unacquainted with, and indeed incompetent to use them, not from any deformity of body (for they are well-formed), but because they are timid and full of fear.

They carry however in lieu of arms, canes dried in the sun, on the ends of which they fix heads of dried wood sharpened to a point, and even these they dare not use habitually; for it has often occurred when I have sent two or three of my men to any of the villages to speak with the natives, that they have come out in a disorderly troop, and have fled in such haste at the approach of our men, that the fathers forsook their children and the children their fathers. This timidity did not arise from any loss or injury that they had received from us; for, on the contrary, I gave to all I approached whatever articles I had about me, such as cloth and many other things, taking nothing of theirs in return: but they are naturally timid and fearful. As soon however as they see that they are safe, and have laid aside all fear, they are very simple and honest, and exceedingly liberal with all they have; none of them refusing any thing he may possess when he is asked for it, but on the contrary inviting us to ask them. They exhibit great love towards all others in preference to themselves: they also give objects of great value for trifles, and content themselves with very little or nothing in return.

Such are the events which I have briefly described. Farewell.

Lisbon, the 14th of March. Christopher Columbus, *Admiral of the Fleet of the Ocean.*

West of the line lay the ancient cultures of the Americas. The Spanish encounters with the Native Americans—the peoples they dubbed "Indians"—were no less momentous than were those of the Portuguese in Africa. Among the Aztecs and the Incas the Spanish beheld unimaginable marvels, at once appealing and repulsive. But the Spaniards came as conquerors and brought with them deadly microbes that took the lives of millions of native peoples. European diseases proved far more potent than European weapons in destroying the mighty American empires.

Africa and the Encounters

At the beginning of the fifteenth century two of sub-Saharan Africa's three "coasts" had long been frontiers of change. For centuries, Muslim traders and preachers had crossed to the Sahel, the southern shore of the Sahara, using camels as their "ships of the desert." Their influence, both economic and religious, had penetrated southward from the Sahel into the West African forest zone. Similarly, trade and Islam, borne on the

This woodcut of Christopher Columbus landing on the island of Hispaniola accompanied the first illustrated edition of a letter that Columbus wrote about his first voyage. The ship is inaccurately depicted as a Mediterranean galley.

The Portuguese Pursuit of African Pepper and Gold

Changes in the economy of northern Europe that occurred at the end of the fourteenth century prompted Portugal's early leadership in European explorations along Africa's Atlantic coast. Through its exports of fish and sugar Portugal had had commercial connections with northern Europe for some time. But northern Europe's economic recovery from the Black Death after 1380 stimulated demands for other commodities that Portugal's rulers felt Portugal might also fill. Northern Europeans, for example, were raising more animals for meat. Lacking fodder to feed all of them through the winter, however, they had to slaughter many more animals in the autumn than they could consume immediately. To prevent the meat from spoiling, they needed tremendous quantities of preservatives. One commonly used preservative was malagueta pepper, known at the time as "Grains of Paradise" and obtained from West Africa through the trans-Saharan trade. Europe's reviving economy also demanded more and more gold, another commodity long supplied through the trans-Saharan trade.

Portugal's rulers therefore decided to attempt to sail along the Atlantic coast of Africa to reach the actual sources of the pepper and gold south of the Sahara. Perhaps, they thought, they might even establish direct links with the fabled trading center of Timubuktu by striking overland from the west coast of Africa, eastward along the Sahel zone. If they succeeded in establishing such a direct trade link, they would both eliminate the North African middlemen from the profitable trade and, as Christians, also strike a blow against Islam by undermining the prosperity of Muslim states. They knew that Portugal was well placed to attempt such a strategy. Most obviously, its location at the edge of Europe, facing outward toward the Atlantic, had given Portuguese fishermen ample experience with its currents and winds, making them among Europe's best mariners. At the start of the fifteenth century Portugal also had a centralized government at a time when most other parts of Europe were politically fragmented, and hence the state could be directly involved in explorations. Moreover, it was a small country with a serious lack of land to provide estates for a group of fairly well-educated younger sons of the nobility, who were thus forced to search for new ways to make their fortunes. Finally, through earlier investments in Portugal, Genoese bankers had established links with it that ensured that capital would be available for profitable overseas ventures.

Indian Ocean's predictable monsoon winds, had affected the East Coast of Africa and helped create its Swahili culture. But the Atlantic coast had remained almost wholly unaffected by outsiders and almost purely African. This situation was soon to change.

After centuries of political disunity, by 1400 a new Europe was stirring. As a consequence, led by the Portuguese, but with Spanish, English, Dutch, and French merchants close behind, Europeans began to visit Africa's Atlantic coast. These visits began a process of change that affected large areas of Africa. They also created new kinds of relationships with Africans living along the west coast that gradually came to be overshadowed by a single factor: the growing need of New World plantation owners for African slaves.

Portuguese Explorations

As a small country in Europe, Portugal's future seemed to require overseas expansion. In 1415 this expansion began with the seizure of Ceuta, a wealthy Moroccan city on the Mediterranean coast, as the Portuguese sought access to Moroccan grain, cloth, and Berber slaves.

But very real technical problems had to be solved if Portuguese mariners were to overcome the barriers that had prevented them from sailing south of Cape Bojador, on the coast of the western Sahara, into the "Ocean Sea," as the Atlantic was then called. Northeast trade winds that blow in the same direction throughout the year dominate the ocean to the south of Cape Bojador. The Canary Current is strong and constant, and it flows in roughly the same direction as the winds. This meant that, while a vessel found it easy to sail south as it was pushed along by both currents and winds, it was almost impossible to sail back to Europe against these forces. Theoretically, mariners could sail into an adverse wind by tacking back and forth, but doing this was exceedingly difficult when they were opposed by a strong current as well.

Prince Henry, known as "the Navigator" (1394–1460), brother of the king of Portugal, was the person who sought to discover the solution to this technical problem and thereby open the way for serious Portuguese expansion. Henry's interests were many. He was

administrator of the Order of Christ, a religious order dedicated to anti-Muslim crusades, and he continued to make war on Morocco. He possessed plantations and other lands. He was closely linked to Portuguese trading interests and invested much of his and his order's money in overseas trading ventures. And every year after 1419 Prince Henry sponsored one or two expeditions to explore how to sail beyond Cape Bojador and return safely. The crucially important knowledge of tides, currents, and wind patterns he accumulated encouraged Henry to establish a formal center for his work on the south coast of Portugal in 1433. In 1434, Gil Eanes, a Portuguese sailor, ventured south past Cape Bojador and then, using the new understanding of the Atlantic's wind patterns, sailed westward into the Atlantic to return home, discovering the islands of Madeira on the way.

Eanes's discoveries encouraged the Portuguese to combine elements of navigational technology from around the world into a new synthesis. From the Arabs they learned about the compass and the lateen sail, a type of sail shaped so as to create a vacuum on its leeward side, effectively causing the vessel to be pulled along even when sailing very close to the wind. From northern Europe they took the single-piece keel and other elements of hull construction, changes that allowed the building of smaller shallow-draft boats known as caravels that were well suited to move into dangerous uncharted waters. These adaptations created almost limitless possibilities for exploration. And so, after 1433, the Portuguese, followed closely by Castilians from Spain, sailed farther and farther down the west coast of Africa, making steady progress toward their ultimate goal of gaining direct access to gold and pepper and other exotic products such as ivory. In the process they gathered additional valuable information about the lands and peoples they encountered.

Prince Henry died in 1460. But the decade after his death witnessed continuing Portuguese explorations along Africa's Guinea coasts, with the most promising discoveries coming at decade's end. In 1469, Portuguese navigators passed the bulge of West Africa and coasted southeastward to what later came to be known as the Ivory, Gold, and Slave Coasts. In 1471, the Portuguese discovered in the Gulf of Guinea two islands with rich volcanic soils, São Tomé and Principe. The warm and wet regions of the Guinea coasts had many more people living in them than did the desert coasts the Portuguese had encountered north of the Senegal River. The area's people produced pepper and hunted for ivory. But best of all, the people of the Gold Coast, known today as

Ghana, produced gold. At last, the Portuguese had reached a major source of the ancient trans-Saharan gold trade. In 1482 they built the fortress of São Jorge da Mina—Elmina—as a base for their trade there.

Sugar and the Rise of Plantation Slavery

In 1443, in the process of their trading explorations, the Portuguese had added a new commodity to their shopping list. Sailing one of the new lateen-rigged caravels, Nuno Tristão landed on Arguin, an island off the north coast of Mauritania, and, extending Portuguese practices in Morocco, he purchased some African slaves in the course of his trading. He sold them in Portugal. In 1444 six vessels set sail from Portugal specifically seeking slaves to be taken home as well as other items. So great were the profits of the new trade for human cargo that in 1445 no fewer that twenty-six ships participated in it as part of their larger trading enterprise. To dispel any doubts about its propriety, in 1452 Pope Nicholas V promulgated a bull, *Dum Diversas*, sanctioning the enslavement of pagans and infidels. While the slaves traded in the years before 1500 were of distinctly secondary importance in the context of the overall trade, numbering only about 1,800 to 2,000 annually, and while gold remained the primary interest for the Portuguese, the establishment of the new trade in slaves nonetheless inaugurated an activity that was to characterize for centuries European activities on Africa's Atlantic coast.

That there were slaves available for the Portuguese to purchase was hardly surprising. Virtually every precapitalist society in human history has used slaves to

The Portuguese fortress of São Jorge da Mina was built with labor and materials imported from Portugal.

perform arduous work for little cost. Those in Africa were no different. Significantly, a slave was defined as a person without relatives to protect him or her and, after being acquired, a slave was usually viewed as being in the process of being incorporated into the acquiring family as a subordinate relative. There were three basic categories of people who could find themselves "without relatives" and hence slaves. First, there were those given by one family to another as a way of redressing an injury. For example, if a man killed another man in a hunting accident, the dead man's family could be placated by the killer's family ceding a woman or young girl to the family of the dead man to compensate for his loss. Rather quickly, this slave would become a member of the new family, probably with a new name to signal her new social identity.

Second, families could sever ties of protection for criminals and other social misfits and then sell them into slavery. Disinheritance and the resulting status of slavery were mechanisms to punish serious criminal offenses or blatantly antisocial behavior in societies generally lacking prisons. Finally, and of special importance in the large states that were in time to become the main sources for the full-blown Atlantic slave trade, slaves were produced by warfare when enemies were captured. Such war captives might be treated badly and forced to do only menial work at first, but, if sold to a family, even they might be absorbed gradually into it. In short, considering the shortage of labor power in precapitalist Africa, it was quite natural that slavery was a social institution and that there were many ways of becoming a slave.

When the Portuguese appeared on the West African coast, therefore, they found Africans who were already slaves and who were available for purchase. But the destiny of those unfortunates was different from that which most slaves had experienced within Africa. In Africa there was a tendency to absorb slaves into the families that acquired them, but no such destiny awaited slaves purchased by the Portuguese and other European traders. For the most part, they became chattel slaves, who remained without kin and who were destined to labor long and hard on the plantations that were being developed in the Atlantic basin. The increase in the slave trade from West Africa and the development of the plantation as a system of production were linked inextricably. And it was sugar production that underlay both.

Sugar had had a long history. It was in India, around 500 C.E., that the discovery of a process for turning sugarcane juice into granulated sugar had made sugar

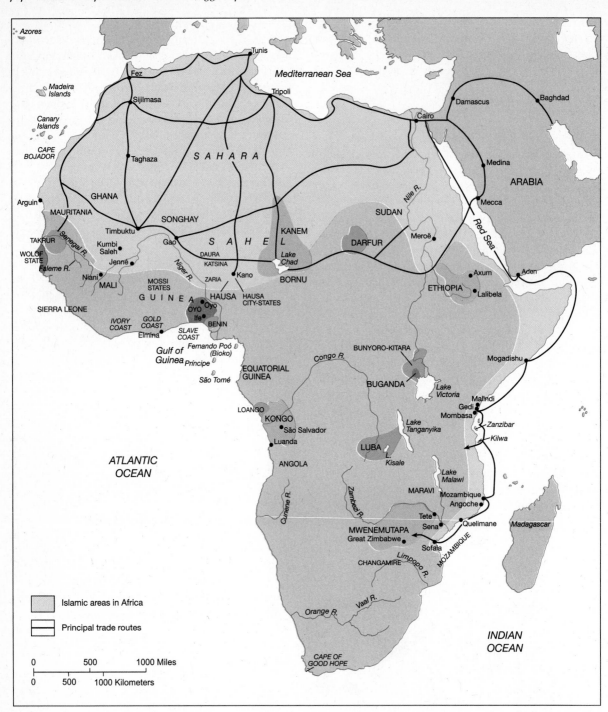

Africa, ca. 1400-1600

commercially important, for it could be stored indefinitely and traded over long distances. A luxury item valued widely for its many uses—medicinal, preservative, decorative, and as a sweetener—sugar was also highly profitable. Because all stages of its cultivation, harvesting, and processing required large numbers of highly disciplined workers, it was a crop ideal for production by slaves.

When the Crusaders from western Europe occupied Palestine in the eleventh century, they operated

Gender and Culture

VESPUCCI "DISCOVERING" AMERICA

Figure 1

The European encounter with the cultures of the western hemisphere posed a problem for visual artists. Prior to the voyages of discovery, the peoples of the world were represented according to Ovid's scheme of the *triplex mundus* or triple world, including Asia, Europe, and Africa. However, by the sixteenth century, the concept of a four or even five part world emerged, requiring a new and expanded symbolic mode. The allegory of the four continents first appeared in Abraham Ortelius's *Theatrum Orbis Terrarum*, published in Antwerp in 1570. Using the classical form of personification, a female figure bearing appropriate attributes signified a geographic location, and a new symbolic entity—America—was forged. The iconography confirmed fears about the strange new world, and long after Europe gained familiarity with the cultures of the indigenous peoples of America and elsewhere, the language of the arts retained the fantastic forms invented to describe the earliest encounters.

In the first depictions of new world allegories, "civilized" Europe contrasted with "savage" America. Theodor Galle's engraving *Vespucci "Discovering" America* (late sixteenth century, after a painting by Jan van der Street; Figure 1), seen on the preceding page, portrays the cartographer as a man of breeding, position, and science. He is stylishly dressed, and he holds the banner of the Southern Cross and an astrolabe. America, a massive woman, dressed in a scant feathered skirt and crowned with a feathered cap, springs from her hammock to greet him. Her domain is exotic and frightening. Odd animals, only the tapir and sloth can be identified, lurk in the lush foliage of her jungle home. In the distance, native people prepare a human leg on a spit. Cannibalism remained a persistent theme in the allegory; well into the seventeenth and eighteenth centuries, figures of America presided over grisly feasts, holding a severed head as an attribute.

The elegant interpretation of *America* by Giovanni Battista Tiepolo (1753, Italy; Figure 2) seems far removed from Galle's naive engraving. Painted in the stairwell of the Wurzburg Residenz of Prince-Bishop Carl Phillip von Greiffenklau, Tiepolo's handsome personification commands a procession of exotic people and extraordinary goods. She is presented with similar images of Africa and Asia, all bringing the wealth of their lands to Europe. Her trappings are magnificent. Decked in gold and multicolored feathers, she rides on the back of an alligator. Her tributes include powerful stags, bundles of brazil wood, and a cornucopia of ripe fruit. However, her savage heritage is not forgotten. Inconspicuously placed on

AMERICA

Figure 2

THE INDIAN WIDOW

Figure 3

the ground to the right of her retinue is a pile of severed heads, gruesomely pierced with arrows.

In the course of the eighteenth century, knowledge of the culture of the Americas increased. But, other inventions colored new world imagery. Rousseau's vision of the "Noble Savage," coupled with rising ethnographic interest about the beliefs and habits of the native Americans, informed a new ideal: the heroic Indian. Stories that proved the valor and nobility of the indigenous people provided the subjects for romantic painting. These works were a curious hybrid. Although often inspired by authentic lore, the artistic interpretation presented European values as Native American instinct. *The Indian Widow* by Joseph Wright of Derby (1783–85, England; Figure 3) praises the stoicism of indigenous women. According to tradition, on the first full moon after a chief is slain, his wife displays his war trophies and commemorates the day in silent reflection. Wright of Derby places the hero's widow in a potentially dangerous setting. Ominous clouds darken the sky, lightening crackles near the shore, and in the distance, smoke pours from an erupting volcano. Her quiet

BEAUTY ON A PALACE TERRACE

Figure 4

vigil becomes an act of bravery; she will fulfill her duties to her slain husband even at the risk of her own life.

Europe was not alone in projecting their ideas on other cultures. Asians and Americans similarly recorded the strange appearance and bizarre habits of the new people they encountered. A Moghul painting, *Beauty on a Palace Terrace* (late seventeenth century, Indian; Figure 4), depicts three European visitors, two women and a man, attended by an Indian serving girl. Their origins are distinguished by position and clothing rather than by facial features. But the daring necklines of the women's dresses, otherwise cut in a European fashion, are pure fantasy. Such decolletage would never be acceptable in Europe.

hundreds of sugar plantations using both free wage and slave labor. After the fall of their small Crusader kingdoms in the late twelfth century, Europeans moved sugar production onto Mediterranean islands such as Cyprus, again using a mixture of free and slave labor. It then moved steadily westward from island to island, often financed by Genoese bankers, until it finally reached Spain and Portugal. Sugar was, however, a crop that demanded special types of soils, which it quickly exhausted, as well as ample water. It was also a commodity that seemed to have an unlimited market in Europe. Therefore, while they continued their search for African gold, the Portuguese and their Castilian competitors also eagerly established new sugar plantations on the Atlantic islands of Madeira, which Portugal had claimed, and the Canaries, claimed by Castile. It was for these new sugar plantations that many African slaves were purchased, firming the link between plantation slavery and sugar production.

Clearly, the best sites for the Portuguese to obtain slaves were also best for them to trade for the other things they sought, places where African leaders had established states that could mobilize the labor needed for producing not only gold and ivory but also numbers of war captives. One should remember that the Portuguese were primarily traders in sub-Saharan Africa, not colonial settlers, and that they did not initially seek to obtain large pieces of territory. But they did need African partners to deliver the goods they wanted and to provide them with security while they were in the area. Quite naturally, therefore, they found it easiest to trade with powerful figures in large states. As a French visitor to the Lower Guinea coast reported, all aspects of the local slave trade were "the businesses of kings, rich men, and prime merchants exclusive of the lower sorts of blacks." Where powerful African states did not exist, trade could still be carried out, but only with greater difficulty and risk.

As they moved down the West African coast, the Portuguese found that the leaders of the peoples of the Lower Guinea coast were especially eager to deal with them. Not only did the Portuguese bring items from Europe that the rulers valued, such as hardware, alcohol, and cloth, but with their superior maritime skills, the Portuguese could also provide a useful service to the African elite by carrying a complex regional coastal trade on their caravels. Thus, for example, kola nuts were purchased for cloth and alcohol at Sierra Leone and then exchanged for slaves at the mouth of the Gambia River. Or, as the leaders of the Gold Coast sought labor to mine their gold, they became the annual purchasers of about

500 slaves whom the Portuguese obtained from the rulers of the states of Oyo and Benin, farther east, and whom they then exchanged for gold at the Portuguese trading post at Elmina.

In the process of their explorations and trading, the Portuguese also transplanted plantation agriculture to São Tomé. This occurred at the start of sixteenth century. Using African slaves obtained from nearby coastal areas of Africa, São Tomé became the world's largest single producer of sugar by the 1510s and 1520s. The combination of rich volcanic soils, disciplined slave labor, and the technological superiority of Portuguese transportation meant that sugar produced at this isolated outpost of empire could be delivered profitably to Lisbon and Genoa despite the long distance it had to be shipped.

Portuguese Success and Failure in the Indian Ocean Basin

Portugal's commercial successes along Africa's Guinea coasts inspired King John II (1455–95), the spiritual descendant of Henry the Navigator, to press on along the West African coast in search of yet greater successes. After a war between Portugal and Castile (1475–79) over the succession to the throne of Castile, the peace treaty recognized the Canary Islands as Castilian in exchange for the recognition of all African continental territory south of Cape Bojador as being within Portugal's commercial sphere. In the 1480s the Portuguese pressed onward to take advantage of this agreement. But by the 1480s it was really Asia, not Africa, that lay at the core of royal dreams. West Africa had been rewarding, but its trade was limited to a few commodities, and the amount of gold the Portuguese could obtain annually was stalled between 13,000 and 14,000 ounces. With the European economy improving steadily, Europeans more and more wanted to reach the fabulous riches of Asia directly, by sea, thereby eliminating middlemen located in eastern Europe and western Asia. In the context of the debate at the time over how best to reach Asia, John firmly believed the best route to Asia lay southward along the coast of Africa and was determined that his own fleets would pioneer it.

As part of this quest, in 1482, the explorer Diogo Cão arrived at the mouth of the Congo River and, somewhat surprisingly, was warmly welcomed by the leaders of the Kongo state, many of whom converted to Catholicism and asked for a Portuguese presence in their country.

THE NATURE OF THE PORTUGUESE PRESENCE IN WEST AFRICA: ELMINA, 1523

■ *King John III of Portugal well understood that Portugal was on the Guinea Coast to trade. The factory at Elmina, to which much West African gold gravitated, was crucially important for Portugal's success. By 1523 it had become a little city-state, with many local Africans having abandoned their earlier ties of loyalty and now living as Christian clients of the Portuguese governor. The governor had, however, expelled some people as punishment for alleged crimes. The king knew that successful trading required a contented population and peaceful conditions. In this letter he writes to the governor of Elmina admonishing him that his policy of harsh punishments is undermining the Portuguese's very purpose in being there to trade for gold.*

We have been informed that you are treating the knights of our village of Mina there harshly, in such a manner that the village is depopulated and men are going away to other parts; and we regard it as a matter very prejudicial to our interest and primarily to the welfare of that city and its trade. Since they are Christians and have received the water of baptism, they must be defended, protected and instructed, and not banished; and this also, since they are our vassals, and live there in obedience to us, serving in our name everything ordered them for our service, and with their people and their canoes conveying to the chiefs the wood for all our ships, and, furthermore, since many of them buy on a large scale in that factory, and all generally make purchases of old linen, which is bought by them and sold in their markets. Moreover, we are told that there are rich men among them, and that slaves may be had from them, and all of them are at our command, or may be, should they be treated well and protected with that moderation in punishment and also in instruction, which is meet and proper for our service and their security; then men tell us that for all their services, they neither have, nor expect, from us any other reward than we should protect them and command them to be maintained in justice. For this reason, it seems to us that you should not take it for granted that our interest would be promoted by your expelling them abroad. We command you, therefore, to treat them better and to dispense with banishments, otherwise, besides losing them and the service which we receive from them, the merchants will not come with similar new things [to trade].

From King John III to Affonso de Albuquerque, Governor of São Jorge da Mina, 13 October 1523.

(See Special Feature, "The Ambiguity of First Encounters: The Portuguese and the Kongo," pp. 418–419.) The Portuguese pressed onward, and in 1488 Bartholomeu Dias set sail from Portugal under orders to sail to the end of Africa to see if he could reach the Indian Ocean. Dias's ship was overtaken by a storm and blown far to the southwest. When the storm abated, Dias sailed eastward, expecting to strike the African coast. Without realizing it, he sailed past Africa into the Indian Ocean. At this point, however, his men mutinied and forced him to return to Portugal. As he sailed for home, he glimpsed the tip of South Africa and called it the Cape of Storms. When King John heard his story, the king aptly decided to rename it the Cape of Good Hope, for he saw it as a hopeful sign of future Portuguese successes in the Indian Ocean.

In 1492 Christopher Columbus, seeking Asia, discovered the New World of the Americas instead. In 1497, John's successor, King Manuel I (1495–1521), sent out the explorer Vasco da Gama (ca. 1460–1524) with four ships to enter the Indian Ocean and trade there. Engaging a Swahili pilot to guide him, da Gama succeeded in his venture, opening the Indian Ocean to Europeans for the first time. The Indian Ocean presented a far different situation from that which the Portuguese had been encountering for decades on the uncharted Atlantic coast of Africa. Romans, Persians, Arabs, Chinese, and others had sailed it for centuries and its sea-lanes were well mapped. Silks and spices, gold and jewels, ivory and slaves—all were available, and their presence seemed to testify to the wisdom of the Portuguese state's persisting with their explorations along the West

African coast. When Da Gama's ships returned home in 1499, the king was delighted, and he determined to use Portugal's naval power to try to dominate the Indian Ocean by force.

In the 1480s, after Spain had recognized Portugal's trading monopoly on the West Coast, Portugal became far more aggressive as they explored and traded. The king, for example, decreed that any non-Portuguese traders encountered along the coast were to be thrown into the ocean. When Vasco da Gama sailed into the Indian Ocean, he brought with him this new royal vision of a total Portuguese monopoly over important aspects of trade. In pursuit of this goal, he traumatically disrupted the region's flourishing trade, which was highly vulnerable to the superior Portuguese naval armaments. Portugal moved quickly to dominate the region's commercial life, trying to turn the trade in some items, such as pepper, ginger, cinnamon, and silk, into royal monopolies and charging merchants dealing in other commodities protection money. In 1505 the Portuguese captured the valuable flow of gold out of Zimbabwe from Swahili traders by seizing both the port of Sofala and the pivot of the gold trade, the city of Kilwa. In 1507, they constructed a fortress on Mozambique Island as their trading post in the area. In the following years the Portuguese continued their conquests and after defeating Muslim naval forces at the battle of Diu, off the coast of India, in 1509, the Portuguese ruled the seas, gradually adding to their list of fortified trading posts such places as Goa, in India (1510); Malacca, in Malaysia (1511); Hormuz, at the mouth of the Persian Gulf (1517); Macao, in China (1557); and Mombasa, in East Africa (1594).

But despite its striking naval successes, rather surprisingly the Portuguese state's share in the trade soon stagnated. This stagnation occurred for several reasons. First, its monopolies over the most lucrative trade items discouraged investments from private enterprises in Portugal because they could not legally trade in the commodities most likely to enrich them. Many individual Portuguese evaded the state's control by participating in a complex web of private deals that did the state little good. A second reason was fiscal. The Portuguese had few desirable manufactured goods to offer the sophisticated peoples of Asia in exchange for the commodities they sought. Forced, therefore, to purchase Asian products with gold and silver, Portugal soon found itself drained by a troubling balance of payments deficit to Asia. Finally, the Portuguese were never wholly unchallenged in their attempts to dominate the Indian Ocean. Their navies

had failed to take Aden, in southern Arabia, and this failure gave their Muslim rivals a base from which to attack Portuguese shipping in the Indian Ocean. The Portuguese usually responded effectively to such attacks, but their responses were costly and badly taxed their resources.

In short, while impressive for their rapid establishment, the series of trading posts that the Portuguese state established in the Indian Ocean was equally striking for their failure to transform or create much of anything new or enduring in the region. As a consequence of the growing problems in the middle of the sixteenth century, Portuguese leaders began to think of fresh and perhaps more satisfactory venues for their energies. Their thoughts turned to the New World.

Growing Links Between Africa and the New World

In 1494, soon after Columbus's first voyage, Spain and Portugal negotiated the Treaty of Tordesillas, formally dividing the world between themselves in order to forestall conflict. On one of Portugal's voyages of exploration, in 1500, Pedro Alvares Cabral (ca. 1468–1520) sailed out into the Atlantic far to the west and landed in Brazil. When he consulted his instruments, he discovered that this surprising piece of the New World was east of the line of division and hence belonged to Portugal. Aside from gathering some dyewoods there, however, the Portuguese largely ignored their new possession. Only in 1549 did the crown finally take direct control over some of Brazil's coastal areas and begin to send thousands of Portuguese settlers, government officials, and missionaries to occupy them.

The discovery that sugar grew extremely well in Brazil and that it could be the base of a prosperous economy motivated this change of policy. Gradually, a sugar industry was built up with Native Americans used as slave labor. But its major expansion occurred in the 1570s when an increase in Dutch investment and a decline in slave prices in Africa allowed large numbers of African slaves to be imported from across the Atlantic on the dreaded "Middle Passage." The new Brazilian sugar industry soon undercut the already established Spanish sugar industry on the island of Hispaniola as well as the older Portuguese industries on Madeira and São Tomé.

The success of Brazilian sugar affected West Africa greatly by demonstrating once again how profitable a plantation system based on highly disciplined slave labor could be. The specific parts of Africa to which the

An engraving of São Salvador (1686), illustrates an idealization of the capital of the Kingdom of Kongo.

The Ambiguity of First Encounters: The Portuguese and the Kongo

It is commonly believed that Europeans, with their superior military technology, have always been able to dominate Africans. Yet, in fact, before the late nineteenth century African leaders were generally able to act independently, in what they saw as their own best interests, when dealing with Europeans. It is in the revealing ambiguities embedded in such African dealings with Europeans that one can discover the contradictory self-interest and flawed humanity of all participants. None is more interesting than the Kongo welcome of the Portuguese between 1483 and 1543.

When the explorer Diogo Cão arrived at the mouth of the Congo River in 1482, he expected a cool reception similar to those his countrymen had earlier received from West African leaders farther north. But this was not the case. Instead, the Kongo king welcomed the Portuguese with startling enthusiasm. Over the next several decades, Kongo leaders converted to Roman Catholicism, took Christian names, made Catholi-cism a state religion, renamed their capital São Salvador, enthusiastically embraced reading and writing, gave rich gifts to the Portuguese, and clamored for westernization. One Kongo prince became a Catholic bishop.

Why? Some have suggested that the Kongo were overawed by the Portuguese and the magic of their technology. This answer is unconvincing for it ignores African motivation. Other African leaders encountered Europeans without acting as the Kongo did. Why were the Kongo different? The explanation lies in the nature of Kongo politics when Cão appeared on the scene.

The people of Kongo were typical of other African peoples. Although sharing a common culture, they had long been fragmented geographically and politically, with the local extended family being the main social unit. But, as among other peoples, a family's head, if powerful enough, was known as a "big man" because of his links of clientage with people not actually of his family. One such big man, who was situated at the crossroads of two important trade routes, had been able to levy tolls on the trade in cloth, salt, and copper, build up his power, and extend his authority over neighboring areas and fellow big men. Finally, he had assumed the title of *maniKongo* and become the "king" of all the Kongo.

Yet his position was not a dictator's, for he ruled within a complex system of checks and balances. His own family appointed influential counselors to advise him. The state's bureaucracy often acted independently. Religious leaders were prepared to oppose him. Groups on the fringe of the state sought opportunities to resist him or even secede from his control. In short, when Diogo Cão dropped anchor, the *maniKongo* was searching for allies, which would grant him greater independence, legitimacy, and freedom of action. When the Portuguese said that they wanted to be his friends, the *maniKongo* accepted them as allies who could supply him with European weapons. When Catholic missionaries arrived, the *maniKongo* also made them his allies, believing that they would give him a source of independent religious legitimacy he currently lacked.

The *maniKongo's* initial dependence on Portuguese support continued. When the *maniKongo* died in 1506, one of his sons,

Afonso, was ambitious to succeed him. According to Kongo custom, however, the kingship should have gone to a nephew. Convinced that European primogeniture was appropriate, the Portuguese supported Afonos, an old friend and ardent Catholic, and he was able to usurp the throne after a "miracle" enabled his army to defeat his rival's force and execute the rightful heir. Afonso rewarded the Portuguese by giving them access to the copper, ivory, cloth, and slaves that they sought.

Did the *maniKongo's* policies work? To the extent that the Portuguese strengthened his position, they clearly did. When Afonso died in 1543, the central government was still going strong and the economy was thriving.

Yet once established in Kongo territory, the Portuguese proved difficult to control. This was because they split into various factions, each with its own aims and strategies. Many of these Portuguese sought to expand slave trading for their own private benefit. Seeking slaves for sugar production on São Tomé, however the Portuguese crown tried to win Afonso's favor by sending him presents in 1508 and 1512. In response, he yielded to the crown a monopoly in buying war captives as slaves. The other Portuguese were outraged, for they wanted to participate in the lucrative trade, and they successfully pressured the crown to abandon its monopoly. All Portuguese in Kongo were then granted the right to trade for

slaves. But there were not enough war captives to supply the demand, and the Portuguese sought slaves wherever they could, trading arms to anyone who could provide them, legally or not, and ignoring Afonso and his interests. This situation endangered the *maniKongo's* position in two ways. First, ambitious local big men acquired arms from the Portuguese and, once they had established their own private armies, they pursued their own political goals. Second, the illegal enslavement of Kongo citizens led to popular discontent with Afonso's government for its inability to guarantee public safety. Ironically, then, only with the support he obtained from the Portuguese did he survive the problems precipitated by the Portuguese. In time, during the 1530s, the focus of the slave trade moved inland beyond the state's borders. This eased the pressures on the Kongo state and even permitted Afonso to increase his income by levying tolls on the new slave trade to the coast.

Clearly, the nature of the Kongo reception of the Portuguese can be explained only in terms of Kongo politics. But, as with most political initiatives, it was filled with ambiguities. The Portuguese shored up the *maniKongo* by supplying guns and bringing Catholicism. But they also brought the growing international slave trade, and, with its corrosive impact on society, it could not but lead to profound troubles in the long run not only for the Kongo leadership, but for the Kongo people as a whole.

View of a sugar mill in Pernambuco, Brazil. Sugar and tobacco were the two labor-intensive crops that fostered the growth of plantation agriculture and of slave labor in the New World.

Portuguese turned most for slaves for their Brazilian enterprises were Kongo and Angola, an area to the southwest of Kongo. The story of the new phase in the extraction of slaves from these areas is filled with contradictions.

After the 1540s, the *maniKongo* had ended relations with the Portuguese because of their interference in local affairs. During the 1560s and into the 1570s internal political problems had plagued the *maniKongo* Alvaro I, however, and it was only through accepting renewed Portuguese military support that he had survived the challenges from ambitious rival leaders within the state. The price tag for this military support was that the Portuguese be allowed to increase the level of slave trading from the Kongo region to supply labor to São Tomé and to Brazil's expanding plantations.

In later decades, the Brazilian demand grew more insistent as the plantation economy increased and as the slave population in Brazil did not reproduce itself. This was so for several reasons. The high mortality rate of slaves, plantation owners' discouragement of marriage and family life, psychological stress, the use of abortifacients, and being simply worked too hard all hindered tropical slave societies from reproducing themselves, and Brazil was no different. Furthermore, the trade was mostly in young men, with the number of women always far, far below that of men. As long as slaves could be obtained relatively cheaply in Africa, it made good economic sense for plantation owners to obtain young males, work them to death, and then replace them. If a slave lived for a minimum of four years, he had paid for the cost of his acquisition, transport, and food.

As elsewhere in Africa, despite the appalling sufferings of those enslaved, the burgeoning slave trade through Kongo and Angola greatly increased the power of the participating elites and, in the process, transformed the very nature of the Kongo state as it also changed the nature of slavery within the state. More and more societies of the interior, to the east beyond the Kongo state, became involved in catching people to supply the Portuguese demand. As a consequence, the *maniKongo* was able to increase his tolls on the trade from the interior to the coast. As the trade grew, the *maniKongo* invested much of the state's growing income from the tolls in acquiring slaves for his own state.

The state's leadership used these slaves in two wholly new ways. First, they provided the labor for large plantations established to grow food to be supplied to the Portuguese port of Luanda, founded in 1575 on the coast of Angola, and to the ships involved in the transatlantic slave trade. The introduction of maize and cassava (manioc), new crops from the New World, made this novel use of slave labor especially attractive. These crops yielded far more calories per unit of land than older native crops and hence produced far more income to plantation owners who grew them.

Second, the state also employed slaves as civil servants and, especially, as soldiers. In this way, the government of the *maniKongo* was able to reduce its former dependence upon subsidiary leaders for military support. With his own loyal army of an estimated 20,000 troops, the *maniKongo* effectively curtailed the independence of local big men and expanded the boundaries of his state. As a result of these changes, while in 1550, before the expansion of the slave trade to Brazil, there had been very few slaves in Kongo, by 1650 there were more slaves than free people.

But it was not only in the realms of economic prosperity and military power that the increased Portuguese presence aided the *maniKongo*. For example, literacy was used to strengthen bureaucratic efficiency in Kongo as written Arabic had done in the Sudanic region, with written records allowing for greater exactitude in levying taxes. The use of written letters also permitted the *maniKongo* to communicate directly with people both in his country and in Europe. And making Catholicism a state religion guaranteed that Catholic missionaries would become involved in the day-to-day administration of the state and helped to legitimize the power of the central government.

As a consequence of all this, between 1578, when Alvaro I received renewed support from the Portuguese

after the long period of estrangement, and 1614, when Alvaro II died, the Kongo state reached new heights of centralization and prosperity. The *maniKongo* skillfully used the Portuguese to overcome and blunt tendencies within the Kongo political structure to fragment and shatter. Yet support from the Portuguese had become an addiction for the *maniKongo*, and it, like all addictions, was dangerously unpredictable. This was so particularly as the Portuguese developed interests that conflicted with those of the *maniKongo*.

Such conflicting interests arose as a result of Portuguese activities in Angola, to the southwest of the Kongo state. In 1568 a Portuguese adventurer, Paulo Dias de Novais (d. 1589), had landed on Angola's coast. Sebastian (1557–78), the new Portuguese king, a romantic youth of fourteen, had ordered him to conquer the area, a radical departure from past Portuguese policy, which had relied upon cooperation with West African leaders and the maintenance of only small fortified posts such as Elmina. Novais's instructions were different because Portugal wanted direct access to two commodities thought to exist in the interior: silver and slaves. At the time of Novais's landing, there were a number of refugees also entering the area, fleeing the political instability in the Kongo state to the north. These refugees allied themselves with Novais and used Portuguese-supplied arms to raid for slaves for markets in Brazil, São Tomé, and elsewhere.

There was an element of perpetual motion in the slave raiding that came to typify the area, with new groups of people acquiring arms and carrying a slave-raiding frontier deeper and deeper into the interior. And with it came the Portuguese—some government officials and other adventurers working on their own—establishing their fortresses in the interior in the decades after 1600. By 1640 the interior of Angola had become an area of very real and expansive Portuguese military and economic activity, a situation up to then unknown on the West Coast of Africa.

This new situation to the south undermined the Kongo state in two ways. First, much of the earlier trade in slaves that had enriched the *maniKongo's* government for so long was drawn southward through Matamba, an area claimed by the Kongo, toward the Portuguese port of Luanda, on the Angolan coast. Using the income drawn from this new trade, the leaders of this area were able to break free from the overlordship of the Kongo and declare their independence under a remarkable queen, Nzinga. She then outfitted a strong army with Portuguese arms, and by the 1640s, virtually all 13,000 slaves annually exported to Brazil from Luanda were coming through Matamba, cutting off one of the *mani-Kongo's* main sources of income and enriching Nzinga's coffers.

A type of shell known as *nzimbu* was used in the region as a currency. Harvesting them from Luanda Bay, the Portuguese introduced immense quantities of these shells into the Kongo economy. The result was as if unlimited counterfeit money had been placed in circulation. A huge surge of inflation occurred at the very moment that the Kongo leadership was losing its control over the profitable slave trade from the interior. The inflation and the loss of control over its lucrative trade was a combination that the Kongo leadership could not long endure. When the Kongo state was challenged by Nsoyo, a rival coastal state to its west whose leaders had begun to strengthen themselves through trade with British and Dutch merchants challenging Portuguese commercial dominance in the region, the Kongo state entered upon a period of prolonged decline, defeat, and dismemberment. At last, in 1649, after a military defeat, the *maniKongo* surrendered his southern territories to the Portuguese, yielded them a trade monopoly, agreed to stop taxing the slave trade, and sent hostages to Lisbon as guarantors of his good behavior. The state of Kongo, long famous in Europe for its wealth and its adoption of many European customs, quickly collapsed. São Salvador, the Kongo capital, which had had tens of thousands of people living in it at the start of the century, was finally abandoned in 1678, with its people returning to the countryside.

A Portuguese delegation meets the formidable Queen Nzinga of Matamba. When the Portuguese governor refused her a chair, she sat down on one of her attendants.

Portuguese and Africans in Mozambique

During the sixteenth century the Portuguese also expanded their presence on the East Coast, in Mozambique, where gold was their main motivation. At the start of the century, they thought they could remain in their coastal settlements at Sofala and on Mozambique Island and that the gold trade would flow naturally down to them as it had long done in West Africa, at Elmina. These expectations were not fulfilled, however, and gradually the Portuguese felt that they had no choice but to intervene in the interior. One reason for such involvement was that they encountered stiff competition. Portuguese naval forces were too weak to prevent Swahili merchants from developing new inland trade routes for Zimbabwe's gold, bypassing the Portuguese settlements, and arriving at the coast at Angoche, a new Swahili port at which they offered better deals than the Portuguese did. The Portuguese quickly realized that if they were to prosper, they would have to compete by sending their own agents inland to seek direct access to the gold and cut out the Swahili competition.

Competition also came from individual Portuguese beyond official control. In establishing their empire, Portugal's rulers had largely relied upon a group of people whom they felt Portugal itself could well do without. Many of the foot soldiers of empire were criminals, not people from whom much loyalty to the Portuguese state could be expected. Once beyond Lisbon's direct control, these people often struck out on their own, seeking their fortunes by venturing beyond governmental control into the interior. As they pushed up into the hot and humid Zambezi valley in search of gold, they formed a second group of competitors to the official traders in coastal settlements. As time passed, more and more of these Portuguese adventurers traveled into the interior, married local African women, and settled down as Africanized *sertanejos*, or "backwoodsmen." As had happened earlier along the Guinea coast and was to happen later in Angola, an Africanized group of people of mixed race and culture developed in Mozambique after 1580.

That the Swahili merchants and Portuguese sertanejos were welcome in the interior was largely because of a situation there remarkably similar to that in Angola during the same period. Successors of the Great Zimbabwe state occupied the area, but none was as unified or powerful as its predecessor. Instead, several states competed with each other over access to gold and other resources. One of these was "Monomotapa," named after its ruler, the *Mwene Mutapa*. Other substantial states in the area included Changamire and a set of Maravi kingdoms north of the Zambezi River. Changamire posed an especially severe threat to the Mwene Mutapa, and so he welcomed outsiders to come into his area to trade and be his allies.

It was in this political context that Portuguese officials reluctantly moved up the Zambezi valley to compete more effectively for gold and other products. In the 1530s they established trading stations at Sena and Tete, both on the south bank of the Zambezi River. In 1544 they founded the coastal town of Quelimane as a commercial alternative to the Swahili port of Angoche. By 1560 the official Portuguese settlements were flourishing, but by then, too, their English, French, and Dutch rivals were beginning seriously to challenge the Portuguese naval dominance of the Indian Ocean basin.

A portrait of a Mwene Mutapa. *The Portuguese artist depicts the king with a European-style scepter and crown.*

The Portuguese began to think that it would be wise for them to consolidate their still tenuous position in Mozambique by taking direct control over the mines of the interior. Perhaps Mozambique was destined to become "the Brazil of Africa" and, if so, it should remain Portugal's.

During this period of reevaluation, in 1568, Sebastian, the new Portuguese king, became convinced that God had chosen him to lead a crusade against the Muslims. He decided that the Muslim Swahili traders competing with the Portuguese in Mozambique were ideal targets for his wrath. He dispatched an army to conquer the Mwene Mutapa and his Swahili allies and to seize Monomotapa's mines for Portugal. Things went well initially, and in 1569 the Portuguese handily defeated an African army and massacred Muslims they encountered. But soon malaria began to kill the Portuguese, sleeping sickness killed their horses, and the army gradually evaporated.

In the midst of this action, the Mwene Mutapa, both concerned with the Portuguese military advance into the interior and eager to gain their aid against his African enemies, especially the state of Changamire, executed several Muslim merchants at his capital to show his good intentions. In 1575 he concluded a treaty of friendship with the Portuguese. The treaty gave them the right to trade freely in his lands, to build churches, to mine gold, and to expel any Muslims that they might encounter. In subsequent years, as the Mwene Mutapa sought additional Portuguese arms, he made more concessions and further undermined the integrity of his state. As in the case of the Kongo, a situation was fast developing from which the African elite had no real escape. On the one hand, the Mwene Mutapa felt that Portuguese support was necessary for his campaigns against his local enemies. On the other hand, however, with the expulsion of the Muslims, he now had no one to balance against the Portuguese and their demands for concessions.

The dependency of the Mwene Mutapa on the Portuguese grew. In 1607 he signed a treaty that turned over to them the area's gold, copper, and iron mines and yielded five of his children as hostages, so that they might be trained as Catholics and educated as Portuguese. While these concessions kept the Portuguese state at bay, more and more unruly Portuguese sertanejos were coming to live in the interior beyond the reach of Portuguese officials and as laws unto themselves, frequently ignoring the Mwene Mutapa and his laws. At the death of the old Mwene Mutapa in 1624, a succession dispute occurred, which was marked by efforts by

Portugal and Africa, 1415–1650

1415	Seizure of the Moroccan city of Ceuta
1434	Discovery of the Madeira Islands in Atlantic Ocean
1444	First slaves traded from Argiun, on Mauritanian coast
1482	Fortified trading station built at Elmina, Guinea coast; Diogo Cão welcomed by the king of Kongo
1494	Treaty of Tordesillas divides the world between Spain and Portugal
1498	Vasco da Gama enters Indian Ocean
1509	Battle of Diu, near India, establishes Portugal as dominant naval power in Indian Ocean basin
1531	Portugal establishes trading station of Sena, in Mozambique's Zambezi valley
1549	Portugal decides to build sugar industry in Brazil
1568	Sebastian, an intense anti-Muslim, becomes king of Portugal
1569	Portugal's first serious invasion of inland Mozambique
1575	Establishment of colony at Luanda to facilitate slave trade from Angola
1629	*Mwene Mutapa* becomes "vassal" of Portuguese king and cedes concessions in Mozambique to Portugal
1649	*ManiKongo* cedes concessions of Portugal and Kongo state begins final collapse

a pretender, Kaparidze, to bring the Portuguese under control. He first seized some Portuguese trading stations and demanded tribute from the Portuguese government. In response, the Portuguese supported another pretender, whom they placed on the throne in 1629. He then signed an agreement with the Portu-

guese that formally made him a vassal of the Portuguese king and opened his country without any restriction to Portuguese traders and prospectors.

Monomotapa's people were unhappy to see their independence disappear in this way, and in 1631, Kaparidze organized a campaign of resistance to the Portuguese takeover. Missionaries, traders, prospectors, and Africans identified as collaborators with the Portuguese were killed, with the final death count reportedly running into the thousands. The Portuguese government sent an army to reestablish order, and through the army's successes in 1632 the Portuguese government secured a powerful position in the whole Zambezi valley. Once established there, the Portuguese went to work in succeeding decades to dismantle further the Mwene Mutapa's state as well as those of other Africans. Perhaps the greatest threat, however, came not from the Portuguese state itself but from the Portuguese sertanejos, who used slaves to create private mercenary armies that allowed them to rule over large tracts of the Zambezi valley utterly heedless of Lisbon and its laws and largely beyond the control of local Africans as well. In this way, large areas of Mozambique's interior experienced the same sort of changes then occurring in Angola's interior, with local Africans being drawn into an economic system largely dominated by Portuguese adventurers and with the Portuguese state laying the foundations of a colony destined to remain Portugal's until 1974.

The impact of Portuguese trade and intervention in the internal affairs of regions in the African hinterland was highly contradictory. Initially, for rulers who were able to supply what the Portuguese wanted, there were real benefits, and their governments were able to strengthen themselves. But one of Portugal's demands—for slaves to work sugar plantations—had especially negative consequences. It not only brought misery to the unfortunates who were enslaved and forced to experience the harrowing "Middle Passage" to the New World, but Portugal's demand for slaves also created extreme difficulties for African rulers, especially in places such as Kongo where the needs of the newly established Brazilian plantations prompted the Portuguese to intervene actively in the procurement of slaves. By the start of the seventeenth century, however, other European nations had decided to challenge Portugal's hegemony along all the coasts of Africa, beginning an era of far greater African contact with other European powers, far greater challenges for Africans, and far greater changes within Africa itself.

America and the Encounters

The regions of Mesoamerica and the central Andes underwent enormous changes during the half millennium between the mid-thirteenth and eighteenth centuries. Two powerful peoples, the Aztecs of the Valley of Mexico and the Incas of the Andean highlands, moved into the void left by the collapse of classic civilizations and constructed vast empires. At the zenith of their achievements they in turn fell before the Spanish *conquistadores* (conquerors).

The reaction of the peoples of Mesoamerica and the Andes to the Europeans framed the history of the succeeding two centuries. They resisted the imposition of European rule and the intrusion of European culture, particularly religion—fiercely and violently on occasion, passively and relentlessly most of the time. The conjunction of the two groups, combined with a third, the African peoples brought forcefully to work in the New World, forged a hybrid culture and produced new peoples of mixed blood (*mestizos*, the offspring of European and Indian; mulattos, or *pardos*, the progeny of European and African; *zambos*, the offspring of Indian and African).

The Spanish and Portuguese succeeded in controlling the vast territory from the Californias south to the Strait of Magellan at the tip of South America. Their success was due to a combination of their own administrative flexibility and the effects of the catastrophic decline in native population that resulted from the introduction of European diseases.

The Rise of the Aztec and Inca Empires

Mesoamerica and the Andes produced artistic, intellectual, and political accomplishments that rivaled and sometimes surpassed those of the Old World. (See Chapter 1.) The Olmec, Chavín, and Maya civilizations produced magnificent achievements. But these societies crumbled under circumstances that we only partially understand, leaving both the central Andes and Mesoamerica fragmented. After 200 to 300 years, in the fourteenth and fifteenth centuries, powerful new empires arose, the Aztec in Mesoamerica and the Inca in South America, unifying vast expanses of territory and millions of people. Both Aztecs and Incas rose meteorically; the Incas built their domain in the short span of thirty years. Neither had been in power long enough to consolidate and stabilize their conquered lands. Each faced the Europeans with a divided empire. Their vulnerabilities became all too apparent when they were confronted with the challenge of the Spaniards.

The Aztecs were one of the barbarian peoples called Chichimecas who migrated from the north to the Valley of Mexico. The Mexicas, as they were also known, arrived in the region and settled at Chapultepec on Lake Texcoco around 1250 C.E. Because of their extreme brutality, they were unwelcome neighbors, and in 1319 an alliance of city-states expelled them. The Mexica worked as mercenaries, eventually finding safe haven on an island in the middle of the lake, where in 1345 they founded what was to be Tenochtitlán. Borrowing the technology of the valley dwellers, they built an ingenious hydraulic farming system based on floating gardens, called *chinampas*, which enabled the city to grow to a population that exceeded 200,000 at its height.

The road to empire began between 1429 and 1433 when the Triple Alliance of Tenochtitlán and two neighboring city-states, Texcoco and Tlacopán, defeated the dominant power in the Valley of Mexico, Atzcapotzalco. The alliance conquered the Valley of Mexico and its neighboring regions, then set about to unify the high plateau under its rule and extend the empire south and east into what is now the state of Veracruz and then west to the Pacific Coast. To ensure the food supply, devastated in a four-year-long famine at mid-century, the alliance constructed an extensive system of irrigation and flood control for the lakes in the valley. The unprecedented series of military victories ended when the Aztecs attempted unsuccessfully to defeat the Tarascans in what is now Michoacán. Further defeats followed. In 1502 Moctezuma II (1466–1520) took power. He presided over the destruction of the empire by the Spanish.

Historians vary widely in their interpretations of the Aztec empire. The differing views focus on the nature of the relationship between the Aztecs and their subject peoples and on the extent of and the reasons for the practice of human sacrifice. There is substantial agreement that the Aztecs erected no significant bureaucracy, that they used marriage to link the city-states of the valley, and that they kept lesser local rulers in power as long as they paid the required tribute. The Aztecs maintained military control not by occupation but through threats and reconquest. No such consensus exists about the nature of the relations between the Aztecs and neighboring states. The nature of the "flowery wars" fought between the Triple Alliance and five city-states just over the mountains in the Puebla Valley, southeast of Tenochtitlán, is at the heart of the debate. Why did the Aztecs allow these states, most

NORTH
AMERICA

Gulf of Mexico

Caribbean Sea

M E S O A M E R I C A

Panama

ATLANTIC
OCEAN

PACIFIC
OCEAN

Orinoco R.

Pasto
Manta
Quito
ECUADOR
Tumbez

Amazon R.

Cajamarca
Chimú

ANDES
Chinchas

Moyobamba

SOUTH
AMERICA

Huanaco
Machu Picchu
Cuzco
Lake
Titicaca
Tiahuanaco

Arequipa
Cochabamba
Iquique
Atacama
Tarija

Copiapo

M O U N T A I N S

Coquimpu

C H I L E

Buenos Aires

Araucanians
A R G E N T I N A

ATLANTIC
OCEAN

Aztec Empire

Inca Empire

CHIHUAHUA

ZACATECAS

Gulf of Mexico

GUANAJUATO
Querétaro
MICHOACAN
Tarascan
Azcapotzalco
Texcoco
Tenochtitlán   Vera Cruz
Chapultepec   TLAXCALA   Coatza-
VERA CRUZ   coalcos
Petlatlán   Lake
Texcoco
Acapulco
Oaxaca
Mitla

Chichén Itzá
Uxmal
YUCATÁN

Mayas

Chiapas
Tikal

Copan

Caribbean Sea

PACIFIC
OCEAN

PANAMA

0   500 Miles
0   500 Kilometers

0   1000 Miles
0   1000 Kilometers

America, ca. 1300–1600

notably Tlaxcala, to maintain their autonomy, when Aztec military might should have brought easy victory over them? One possible answer is that these were phony wars used to provide a guaranteed supply of captives for human sacrifice. Another possible reason is that the Aztecs used these conflicts to furnish much-needed high-level military training for their young soldiers. The overall question of just how much control the Aztecs exerted over their empire is still only partially answered.

The extent of and motivation for human sacrifice by the Aztecs is perhaps the most controversial topic. Undoubtedly, human sacrifice was an integral part of Aztec religion. According to Aztec tradition, the world had gone through four previous stages or Suns, each destroyed by catastrophe. In order to maintain the Fifth Sun in place and ward off the predicted next disaster, the Aztecs sought to keep their deities satisfied. This required human blood obtained from bloodletting and sacrifice. Some observers see human sacrifice as an invention of imperial rule, aimed at terrorizing military foes into quick surrender and subject peoples into submission. The extent of the practice is also much debated. The Spanish chroniclers, who recorded the conquerors' exploits and who tried to compile a version of the Aztecs' history after their defeat, told of extensive sacrifice. At the dedication of a new temple in Tenochtitlán in the late fifteenth century, Aztec priests supposedly sacrificed tens of thousands of lives. Others believe the practice existed on a far more modest scale and that the chroniclers exaggerated the numbers to enhance the glory of the Aztec empire and, thus, the glory of its conquerors.

The Aztec capital, Tenochtitlán, rivaled the great cities of Europe. The city was laid out like Venice, and its canals furnished the major means of transportation. Although the chinampas were extremely productive, most supplies had to be brought in from the mainland on three causeways. Consequently, Tenochtitlán was a bustling commercial center. An extensive system of aqueducts transported drinking water. Large temples and palaces rose from the lake, forming a magnificent skyline.

The basic social unit of Aztec society was the *calpulli*, a kin-based community with landholding, religious, and military functions. At the top was the *tlatoani* or chief speaker (emperor). Originally elected by the calpulli, by the time of Moctezuma II the chief speaker reached the status of deity. As Aztec conquests expanded, society stratified; what began as bureaucratic and citizen military meritocracies became a hereditary nobility and a

The founding of Tenochtitlán, from Codex Mendoza. *The drawings at the bottom depict the early Aztec conquests of Colhuacan and Tenayucan.*

professional military. In the middle of the social scale were merchants and artisans. Merchants occupied perhaps the most precarious position in society, not only because they risked death as military spies for the Aztec armies, but because, if too successful and ostentatious in their display of wealth, they were subject to drastic punishment by their rulers. Artisans were assured an important status, for they crafted the gold and feather ornaments for the chief speaker and nobility, providing them with the necessary conspicuous consumption their exalted positions required. The common people, called *macehualtin*, were members of the calpulli and owned land. Beneath them were the *mayeques*, or bondsmen, who comprised perhaps as many as one-third of the population. We know very little about them other than that they were probably landless people attached to the lands of the nobility. The *tlacotin*, or slaves, made up roughly five percent of the population. One could become a slave by committing a crime, through debts, or by selling oneself. As society grew more hierarchical and social classes more stratified, women experienced less independence. Nonetheless, they could own their own property, conduct business such as trade (through traders), and practice quite autonomous professions like midwife, healer, or priestess. Women who died in childbirth were revered equally with those males who died in battle, the greatest glories an Aztec could attain.

There is little historical evidence about the rise of the other great American empire, the Incas. They had no writing, and archaeological discoveries in the Andes, especially in the environs of Cuzco, the Inca capital, are limited. Most likely, the Incas arrived in the region of Cuzco around 1250 C.E. For nearly two hundred years, they lived as one of numerous tribes in the region. They began their meteoric rise to mighty empire in 1438, when Inca Yupanqui, a disinherited son of the reigning Inca Viracocha, saved them from defeat by a local rival. Legend has it that, unable to gather enough recruits to battle, he turned stones into soldiers. The new ruler, now known as Pachacuti, began an unprecedented series of conquests. During the next thirty years, he and his successors carried the empire south to the region of Lake Titicaca and into what is now Argentina and Chile and north as far as Ecuador. They controlled the central Andean highlands and the Pacific Coast. Only the Amazonian jungles proved an impenetrable barrier.

In an extraordinarily short period, the Incas built an empire that rivaled in territory and population the great conquests of the Greeks and Romans. The expansion depended more on persuasion than on military prowess. Inca policies were meant to give subject peoples a stake in the empire and to foster loyalty to it. Whereas Aztec armies were composed of professional soldiers from the Triple Alliance, Inca armies consisted primarily of peasants from the most recently conquered states mobilized as part of their tribute obligations to the empire. Including subject peoples in the new military campaigns served two practical purposes. Since there were far too few Incas to carry out large-scale conquest, it furnished needed soldiers. In addition, it gave conquered people a stake in the empire. Local elites retained their power. The Incas also realized the need for at least the threat of coercion behind their persuasion. Consequently, they established a clear record of atrocities to back up their material incentives.

The Incas controlled their empire by means of a vast bureaucracy and tax system, more remarkable because they lacked a written language and because the Andes presented enormous difficulties in transportation and communication. They built their rule on existing polit-

An Inca "accountant." The Inca lacked writing, but they used the quipu, *knotted strings of different lengths and colors, to keep accurate and detailed records.*

ical structures. They were very flexible, treating small-scale chiefdoms differently from complex city-states. The Incas rewarded subject peoples with participation in the glory and spoils of new conquests, shrewdly taking advantage of regional rivalries, pitting a newly conquered people against an old, neighboring enemy. Moreover, the Incas provided other benefits, such as irrigation works, terraces, and roads.

The Incas closely administered conquered peoples. They resettled much of their subject population. The sons of the rulers of conquered states were sent to school in Cuzco, partly as hostages to assure cooperation, but also to indoctrinate them into Inca language and ideology. The Incas sought to spread their language, Quechua, and their religion. But they also absorbed other deities and beliefs into their pantheon. As always their inclusiveness and openness had a purpose. They often brought the idols of subject peoples to Cuzco to hold as hostages. The Incas' primary form of retribution against rebels was deportation, not death.

When they began their conquests, the Incas relied on peasant soldiers. As the empire grew, however, there evolved a professional military centered in specialized ethnic groups. Inca-led armies did not plunder or forage, but rather used provisions stored in warehouses along their famous road system.

By the early sixteenth century the Inca military campaigns slowed or ended. There was no method to maintain the satisfaction of peripheral subject peoples, and they frequently rebelled. When two rivals for leadership clashed in 1525, an underutilized military proved restless and dangerous and moved easily to civil war.

Inca social organization revolved around the family unit, called the *ayllu*. The ayllu distributed land among its members every two years. Its members cared for the old and infirm by working common lands. As in the case of the Aztecs, the social structure became more stratified as the empire grew. At the top of society was the Sapay-Inca, or emperor. By the time of the Spaniards' arrival, his position had evolved from tribal leader to god-king. Originally a council of ayllu elected the Sapay-Inca, but after the conquests, the ruler chose his successor. Below the Sapay-Inca was the hereditary nobility, the ruling Inca clan. Underneath them were the ayllus of Cuzco and the chieftains of conquered peoples. There was also a class of bondsmen called *yanacona*.

The Inca capital, Cuzco, was not nearly as elaborate as Tenochtitlán, but it had more than 100,000 residents. Each inhabitant had to wear the costume of his or her home tribe or city-state. Cuzco was an administrative and religious center, but unlike Tenochtitlán it was not a hub of commerce. The Inca state controlled trade in the Andes, and the medium of trade was barter.

Despite better administration and more benevolent rule, the Inca empire, like the Aztec, was in crisis in the years before the Spaniards arrived in Peru. The Inca Huayna Capac, who reigned from 1493 to 1525, had taken a number of measures that led to civil war. He moved his capital from Cuzco to Ecuador in the far northern reaches of the empire, which led to a geographic split between north and south. In addition, the emperor fostered rivalry between his legitimate heir and successor, Huáscar, and his son by a concubine, Atahuallpa. When Huayna Capac died, Atahuallpa refused to recognize his half-brother as Sapay-Inca and civil war ensued. With northern support, the rebel won. But the bloody civil war left wounds that never healed.

The Fall of the Aztec and Inca Empires

By the first decade of the sixteenth century the great empires were weakened and divided, having apparently reached their limits. The Aztecs had encountered the fierce resistance of western Tarascans and northern Chichimecs; bitter old enemies like Tlaxcala festered in their hate. There is evidence too that when slowed conquest diminished the supply of luxury items and sacrifice victims, internal dissension arose. Moreover, the population of the Valley of Mexico may have reached its ecological limits. In the mid-fifteenth century, when a massive famine struck, the Aztecs had trouble feeding a smaller version of the empire. Based on tribute, which often was in the form of sacrifice victims, the Aztec empire elicited no loyalty. Tlaxcalans, after a nasty defeat at the hands of the Spaniards, and imbued with old grudges against Tenochtitlán, allied with the newcomers. If the Aztec empire was held together by the terror of human sacrifice, it was not a lasting bond. The empire of the Incas tore itself apart by civil war between north and south. Hence, on the eve of the encounters, both empires were vulnerable.

The stories of the conquests of Mexico and Peru are epic tales told by the victors. Glorified by the chronicles of their companions, the *conquistadores*, or conquerors, especially Hernán Cortés (1485-1547), emerged as heroes larger than life. In 1517 the Spaniards sent a scouting expedition to the region of Veracruz. Cortés landed in the same region in 1519. He scuttled his ships and set off westward. After soundly thrashing a Tlaxcalan army and inducing the losers to join them against the Aztecs, the Spaniards marched to Tenochtitlán. They quickly captured and publicly humiliated Moctezuma, forcing him to rule as their puppet. Cortés had to return to the coast to head off an expedition led by Pánfilo de Narváez (ca. 1480-1528), sent to arrest him for insubordination to the governor of Cuba, under whose auspices the expedition had sailed. Cortés defeated Narváez, incorporating Narváez's remaining soldiers in his army, now numbering 1,300. While Cortés was away from Tenochtitlán, his second-in-command, Pedro de Alvarado (ca. 1485-1541), provoked a bloody confrontation with the Aztecs, leading to the overthrow of Moctezuma, who fell victim to a lethal stone thrown by one of his subjects. When Cortés returned, he realized he must retreat from the city. This he did on the night of 30 June 1520, known as *La Noche Triste*, the Night of Sorrows. The retreat cost the conquistador two-thirds of his men and most of his horses. The Aztecs, however, did not pursue the Spaniards, who fled to Tlaxcala. The Aztecs

THE MASSACRE AT THE CANAL OF THE TOLTECS

■ *The Aztecs and Incas did not relinquish their rule without persistent, fierce resistance to the Spaniards. As this passage from* The Broken Spears *indicates, the natives defeated the conquerors rather badly. If not for the ravages of disease on the population of Tenochtitlán, especially on the Aztec leadership, and the alliance of other cities once subordinated or allied with the Aztecs, the Spaniards might have perished.*

When the Spaniards reached the Canal of the Toltecs . . . they hurled themselves headlong into the water, as if they were leaping from a cliff . . .

The canal was soon choked with the bodies of men and horses; they filled the gap in the causeway with their own drowned bodies. Those who followed crossed to the other side by walking on the corpses . . .

The dawn was breaking as they entered the village. Their hearts were cheered by the brightening light of this new day: they thought the horrors of the retreat were all behind them. But suddenly they heard war cries and the Aztecs swarmed through the streets and surrounded them. They had come to capture the Tlaxcaltecas for their sacrifices. They also wanted to complete their revenge against the Spaniards.

---

remained in Tenochtitlán and reconstituted their forces. The Spaniards returned to besiege Tenochtitlán, now ruled by the emperor Cuauhtémoc. The Aztecs held out miraculously for nearly three months, during which time the city was almost completely destroyed by bombardment from ships on the lake and house-to-house fighting. The end of the siege came on 13 August 1521 with the capture of Cuauhtémoc. The resistance of native peoples did not end then, however.

Francisco Pizarro (ca. 1475–1541) arrived in Cajamarca, Peru, in November 1532. Like Cortés, he sought to capture the emperor, cutting off the head of the empire. This he did on 16 November, when the haughty Atahuallpa fatally miscalculated his military power. The Spaniards executed Atahuallpa and conducted an appalling slaughter of the Inca army. Pizarro needed a puppet to act as titular head of the Inca empire. Manco Capac, son of Huayna Capac, began as a collaborator. From 1533 to 1536 he acted as the Spaniards' stooge, humiliated and imprisoned. Finally, after the Europeans raped his wives in front of him, he escaped, gathered an army, and began the Inca resistance. Despite a numerically superior army—over 40,000 against 200 Spaniards—Manco was unable to successfully besiege Cuzco. When his army dissipated, Manco established a mountain retreat, from which he harassed the conquerors until betrayed by Spaniards to whom he had offered refuge. His son Sayri Tupac, only ten years old, succeeded him, only to surrender in 1555 to the enticements of a royal life under Spanish rule. When he died in 1560, another son of Manco, Titu Cusi, rekindled the resistance and ten years of guerrilla war ensued, ending with his death. The Spanish viceroy, Francisco de Toledo, penetrated the Inca redoubt, capturing the last Inca, Tupac Amarú, in 1572.

After the initial shocks of losing their leaders and their capitals, the Aztecs, Incas, and other native peoples fiercely resisted the Spaniards. They quickly learned how to fight against the guns and horses. Throughout the three hundred years of colonial rule, they resisted, if not by shedding blood then passively, day by day, to maintain their language and customs. Some fought into the twentieth century. Latin American culture today remains a testimony to their persistence.

The native population of Brazil was composed of nonsedentary and semisedentary peoples, who also fiercely resisted the incursions of the Europeans. Because of their mobility and the vastness and harshness of the land into which they could escape, they proved difficult to defeat permanently, though their numbers were decimated by disease.

The Portuguese in many ways obtained Brazil much as the British were later said to have acquired their empire—"in a fit of absence of mind." In 1500 Pedro Alvares Cabral, en route to Asia via the coast of Africa, was blown far off course across the Atlantic and landed

The Spanish attitude toward the Indians is demonstrated in this sixteenth-century drawing of a Spaniard kicking an Indian. Spanish colonial society was divided into classes on the basis of birthplace and race.

on the coast of what is now Brazil. He discovered, evidently to his surprise, that under the terms of the Treaty of Tordesillas, which was signed in 1494 by Spain and Portugal and divided the world between them, the territory he landed on belonged to Portugal. At the time, however, the Portuguese were preoccupied by trade with Asia. Aside from gathering brazilwood—from which the colony derived its name—for use in dyes, they largely ignored their new possession. Since no precious metals were readily available, there was no pressing need for attention.

Controversy as well as curiosity abounds about the reasons for the Spanish conquest, which was decisive and relatively swift. Vulnerable or not, the great Aztec and Inca empires were formidable foes and vastly outnumbered the Europeans. They had the advantage of knowing the land. They were brave, brilliant warriors.

How then did barely four hundred Spaniards under Hernán Cortés and perhaps one hundred with Francisco Pizarro destroy them?

The Spaniards recognized weakness and division and exploited both. Native soldiers comprised the preponderance of the army that Cortés led against Tenochtitlán. Pizarro allied with the losing side in the Inca civil war, the followers of Huáscar. Cortés and Pizarro provided brilliant leadership compared to the Aztecs and Incas. Early in the struggles the Spaniards captured both Moctezuma II and Atahuallpa, leaving a vacuum in these highly centralized empires.

The Spaniards had a number of advantages in the war against the Aztec and Inca empires. At first glance they appear to have enjoyed superior weaponry; they had guns, cannon, and metal armor. They also had horses, which added speed and mobility and frightened their opponents. Ultimately, though, their technology may not have been advantageous. The Spaniards quickly discarded their heavy armor, which in tropical climates or high altitudes was burdensome, and adopted the natives' woven cotton. Archers could reload faster than gunners. Although the noise of the cannon terrorized the native troops at first, they quickly got used to it. The initial advantage of the horses was soon lost, as they were a distinct hazard in closed spaces like Tenochtitlán.

The Spaniards' greatest advantage, perhaps, lay in their persistence and ruthlessness and in the profound cultural misunderstanding between them and their opponents, especially the Aztecs. The Spaniards, deeply motivated by greed and ambition, employed vicious tactics. Cortés's scuttling his ships in order to prevent any turning back clearly indicates the extent of the Spaniards' desperate motivation. The Spaniards also benefited from their view of warfare. To the Aztecs, war was a sacred undertaking, in which the goal was to capture the bravest, most capable opponents for sacrifice. At its utmost, war was one man against another, face to face. Aztec warriors did not retreat, did not hide behind walls or horses, did not kill civilians indiscriminately. The Spaniards did all of these, for their concept of war was quite different. To them, as to all Europeans, the goal of war was victory at any cost. This helps explain why the Spanish suffered so few casualties.

Another example of the radically different and mutually misunderstood worldviews of Aztecs and Spaniards was their respective perceptions of the gifts Aztec emperor Moctezuma II sent to Cortés after the latter landed in the region of Veracruz in 1519. These opulent presents were meant by the Aztecs as a haughty display

Aztec Indians suffering from smallpox during the conquest. The disease took a terrible toll among the inhabitants of Mexico, who had no immunity to the plagues of the Old World.

of their power; they were insults to the Spaniards. The Spaniards interpreted the gifts as a sign of Aztec weakness, attempted bribes to keep them from Tenochtitlán.

Perhaps the crucial factor in the defeat of the Aztec and Inca empires, however, was neither the military prowess of the Spaniards nor the internal weaknesses of the American empires, but rather the rapid spread of diseases like smallpox, measles, and plague, which devastated the native population. There is little question that disease preceded the arrival of the Spaniards to both Mesoamerica and Peru. Early landings had spread smallpox to Tenochtitlán. Several important leaders fell to the disease, weakening Aztec war-making power. In the Andes, half the population may have perished even before Pizarro arrived. So badly weakened, the Incas were easier prey for the Spaniards.

Spanish and Portuguese Colonial America, 1550–1700

Once the initial military victories in Mesoamerica and the Andes were complete, the Europeans, thousands of miles from their homelands across the Atlantic Ocean, confronted a vast extent of territory, with a population far larger than that of the Iberian Peninsula. The problems of ruling such an enormous domain were as vast and complex as the land and the people. The natives resisted fiercely, and rebellions punctuated the sixteenth century; some less sedentary peoples continued to fight for three hundred years to avoid the colonial yoke. Moreover, the New World colonies were constantly threatened by European rivals. English pirates, Dutch merchants, and French adventurers nibbled at Iberian hegemony. In Europe the Spanish crown engaged in continual warfare, with unfortunate consequences for its colonies.

The Spanish and Portuguese ruled their New World empires with utmost flexibility, bare-bones administration, and minimal use of force. The Spaniards, especially, centered their efforts on the extraction and removal of gold and silver, which the crown used to finance its European involvements.

A complex mixture of motivations, which historians have characterized as gold, glory, and God, comprised the psyche of the conquerors and colonists. They were exceptionally greedy and ruthless in their pursuit of riches and—particularly the earliest arrivals—fervent in their desire to Christianize the natives. They believed that military conquest and religious proselytization would bring honor to them and to the crown. To Ferdinand and Isabella, the first Spanish rulers of the New World, and their successors, Charles I and Philip II, the defense and spread of Christianity were paramount considerations. They were literally the defenders of the faith, second only to the pope. But it was enormously expensive to defend Christianity and the huge Spanish empire in Europe, which expanded when King Charles I of Spain became Holy Roman Emperor Charles V in the mid-sixteenth century. Spanish kings' demands for revenues from the New World were aggressive and unending. When faced with conflict between Christian virtue and treasure, the crown most assuredly chose the latter.

The administrative and economic complex of Spanish colonial rule evolved around the extraction of precious metals, such as gold and silver. For three hundred years the crown managed to walk a tightrope between meddling in the smallest matters involving revenue and

Spanish and Portuguese Colonial America

pushing the colonists to rebellion. Colonial administration functioned differently in the regions central to mining than in those in the periphery. The central mining regions were highly regulated, while the far regions were left for the most part to rule themselves. The entire economic system, including commerce, landholding, and labor organization, was based on a complex of mining center, city, and *hacienda* (a large landed estate). A similar situation existed in Brazil, where the Portuguese concentrated their efforts on the production of sugar, with interludes for gold and diamonds.

Two practical considerations shaped Iberian governance in the New World. First, the precipitous and catastrophic decline of the native population forced constant readjustments of Spanish policies. Demographic recovery resulting not only from increased immunities of the native peoples to European diseases after the mid-seventeenth century but also from the growing population of mixed-bloods (*mestizos* and mulattos) and white immigrants also forced important shifts. Second, the great distances between Spain and Portugal and their colonies and the inability of either to station large number of soldiers in the New World meant that flexibility was crucial. Colonists were in a favorable position to oppose onerous laws or policies.

The phrase *obedezco pero no cumplo*, which means "I obey but do not comply," aptly describes the ability of the colonists to refuse laws that they opposed.

There is considerable debate over the size of the population of the New World at the time of the arrival of the Europeans. For Mesoamerica in 1519, estimates range from 4.5 to 25.2 million, and for Peru from 3 to 32 million inhabitants. The best current estimates are probably 12 to 25 million for Mesoamerica, 9 million for Peru, and 2.4 million for Brazil. But there is no question that the population underwent a catastrophic decline. One estimate based on postconquest tribute (taxation) records posits that the population of Mesoamerica stood at 25.2 million in 1519 and then fell to 16.8 million in 1532; 6.3 million in 1548; 2.65 million in 1568; 1.9 million in 1580; 1.375 million in 1595; 1.075 million in 1605; 0.75 million in 1622. The destruction took place in successive epidemics, first of smallpox and measles, later influenza. In the mid-seventeenth century yellow fever and malaria arrived from Africa. By 1650 contact with Europeans had eliminated 90 to 95 percent of the native population. (Accepting the lower range of estimates for Mesoamerica in 1519, the percentage loss is over 80 percent for a population of 12 million.)

The demographic collapse changed landholding patterns, crop production, ecology, labor systems, and methods of administration. Formerly dense populations of native peoples disappeared, replaced by Europeans, Africans, and migrants from other regions. The decline was uneven, some areas were harder-hit than others. However, the devastating physical and psychological toll did not destroy the indigenous cultures.

Given the scarce resources and manpower and the vast distances between Spain and its empire, the first impulse of the Spanish was to merely take over the top ranks of the hierarchical indigenous societies. The native elite would remain in place, retaining most of its privileges, and ensuring that their subjects furnished tribute in the form of taxes and labor. However, the drop in population forced the Spaniards to involve themselves more extensively with the native people.

Because the revenues from Peru and New Spain, as the Spaniards named the Mesoamerican part of the empire, were so important, the crown constructed a large bureaucracy to administer them. These Spanish bureaucrats, with their propensity for paperwork, generated tons of laws, regulations, reports, and correspondence, which historians have used to study the period. Much of importance that happened was unrecorded, however.

At the top of the administrative pyramid, just below the Spanish king and based in Spain, was the Council of

III.
INDI, QVA ARTE AVRVM EX
MONTIBVS ERVANT.

X *Potossi montanis, aurifodinis omnium ditißimis per o-*
mnem Indiã, aurum Indi hac arte effodiunt, qua in nostris fere
regionibus itidem factitant. Næ ex rupibus excindenda omnia
sunt. Operarios in duos ordines dispescunt. Quorum hi de die la-
borantes, noctu quiescunt: illi noctu operis vacantes, interdiu dormiunt.
Quamuis nec diurnam nec nocturnam cæli facem videat, sed vniuersim suc-
censis cereis opus habeant: Cum vltrà 150. orgias infra terram sese demittant.
Nec tamen ista tàm immensa fodinarum profunditas impedit, quò minus
omne effossum es suis dorsis foras efferre cogantur. Quem in vsum scalas ad-
hibent, ita structas paratasq, vt bina sibi semper cõiuncta hæreant. Scalæ ve-
rò ex intortis boum coriis confectæ sunt, qua transuersis radiis lignies suffir-
mantur ita, vt ternis viris semper ex ordine descensu vno latere, altero verò
totidem ascensus sit. Cumq, in ascensu labore vtraq, manu scalas corripere
cogantur, ideo, qui illorum primus est, cereum ardentem de pollice religatum
gestat. Porrò, quia meta ascensuris nimis longa est, iccirco in media via sur-
recta quædã scamna sunt, quibus onera sua quadamtenus deponere possunt.

*A silver mine at Potosi, in Peru. The mine provided enormous wealth
for the Spaniards, but many of the Indian laborers lost their lives in
the harsh working conditions.*

the Indies. It was responsible for the legislative, judicial, and consultative functions of colonial administration, both recommending the appointment of officeholders and scrutinizing their work. Unfortunately, very few members of the Council had any experience in the colonies. The crown's ranking representatives in the Americas were the viceroys. Initially, there were two viceroys, one for New Spain and one for Peru. Each viceroy was responsible for general administration, tax revenues, public works, social order, defense, and protection of the native peoples. Although in theory they were substitute kings, in practice the viceroys were limited in power by the overlapping jurisdictions of the crown's financial officers and the Church. Because the viceroyalties proved far too large to administer, the crown divided them into smaller units known as *audiencias* (the equivalent of provinces). These in turn were divided into even smaller, local units known as *corregimientos*,

alcaldias mayores, and *gobernaciones* (the equivalent of districts). And finally, at the lowest level were the municipalities. The viceroy headed the audiencia in his capital; in the other regions they were headed by captain-generals. The *cabildo* (or city council) administered the municipalities. Each of these organizations had legislative and judicial as well as administrative functions.

The crown bureaucracy was meddlesome, corrupt, and inefficient. Because Spanish kings were always short of funds, they resorted to selling colonial offices. This practice had one positive and one negative effect. In the first instance, it enabled American-born Spaniards, known as *criollos* (creoles), to obtain offices, and thus presumably assured that colonial administration, especially at the municipal level, would be more responsive to local needs. In the second instance, however, the initial cost of acquiring office and the poor salaries offered forced officeholders to use their positions for profit-making enterprise. This situation ensured a high degree of corruption and suffering for subject people. The crown's colonial bureaucracy closely regulated all aspects of society and economy, often to the smallest detail. The rules and regulations were not always based on colonial realities and therefore were often widely ignored. The discrepancy between law and practice, then, became so large that it discredited law and government.

The introduction of sugar into Brazil made that colony a money-making enterprise and led to building permanent settlements. The native population, for the most part comprised of nonsedentary and semisedentary peoples, proved quite unwilling to subject themselves to the harsh labor conditions on sugar plantations. Resisting such work, they fled into the interior out of their tormentors' reach. Like their brethren in Spanish America, they lacked immunity to European diseases and died in great numbers. The Portuguese then turned to the importation of African slaves to work the sugar plantations and *engenhos*, or sugar mills.

The Portuguese were somewhat more relaxed in their governance than the Spanish. Their administration began as private enterprise in the form of vast grants of land by the crown, known as donatory captaincies. The recipients in turn had wide latitude to grant land to settlers and name officials, in return for which they were obligated to pay revenue to the crown. Most of the captaincies failed from the lack of capital, inability to attract enough colonists, or poor management. The danger of French intrusions in the mid-sixteenth century forced the crown to take a more formal role in the administration of Brazil. For this purpose, the Portuguese crown established the Overseas Council, which

LETTER OF VICEROY FRANCISCO DE BORJA TO HIS SUCCESSOR, 1621

■ *On the occasion of the completion of their term, the viceroys reviewed their terms in* memorias *or* memoirs *to their successors. This selection clearly indicates that Borja's priorities lay in the extraction of silver. It also reveals his deep-seated contempt for the native peoples. The Indians reported for work in the mines as part of a system of forced labor known as the* mita.

The Indians assigned for the labor [in the mines] are supposed to enter on Monday morning, and for this they assemble at a place called Guaina at the foot of the hill. Here the corregidor reviews them and delivers them to the recipients . . . and they work through the following Saturday. In fact, given their laziness and drunkeness that appears on holidays, it has always been difficult to get them rounded up before Monday afternoon, or even Tuesday morning . . . The holidays that they are supposed to observe are few . . . and the mineowners have tried to make them work on the holidays that the councils have left open, it has not seemed convenient to concede this. For they are miserable people and recently converted, and the labor of those few is hardly worth considering.

functioned like the Council of the Indies. The Portuguese equivalent of the viceroy in Spanish America was the governor-general. Both Spanish and Portuguese decentralized governance, with regions and localities operating quite independently in routine matters. Powerful family groups arose to rule over these geographic fragments.

Both crowns paid close attention to revenue-producing areas. In New Spain the central corridor extended from Parral in Chihuahua, through Zacatecas and Guanajuato into Mexico City, and then to Veracruz, the major Caribbean port. This corridor was intensely monitored because it included the most important mining camps and trading routes. The same was true for the highland mining centers in Peru. The Spanish crown demanded one-fifth of the value of all ores mined in its empire. It also maintained a monopoly over the production and supply of mercury, which was essential for silver extraction. Both Iberian colonial empires tried to limit their colonies' trade to the mother country. Spain went further, restricting New World trade to only one port in Spain, Seville, and two in the Americas, Veracruz and Panamá, and allowing goods to be transported on only one or two heavily guarded convoys sent back and forth across the Atlantic each year. (This was known as the *flota*, or fleet system.) Constructed to maximize crown revenues, the overbearing economic system added greatly to the cost of living in the colonies and resulted in widespread smuggling. The most notorious example of the adverse effects of the system was the prohibition of direct trade between Spain and Buenos Aires (in what is now Argentina). The colonial administration required goods to be shipped from Spain to Panamá, then to Peru, then across the Andes and Pampas to Buenos Aires on the Atlantic coast. The extra cost of this wayward route was large. Obviously, these rules were made to be broken. Crown customs officials were easily bribed, and smuggling in the vast underadministered territory was easy and rampant. Corruption and inefficiency made the system less onerous.

It was crucial for the Iberians to integrate the native peoples into their economic system, for without their labor, the colonies could not have survived. The two most important institutions for this acculturation were the Catholic church and the *hacienda*, or large landed estate.

The Church came early to the Americas to convert the native peoples to Christianity. A small number of regular clergy, composed of members of the Franciscan, Dominican, Augustinian, and later Jesuit orders, often heroically led the way into new territories. Initially, they tried to destroy the vestiges of the heathen religions. Unfortunately, in doing so, they erased much of the historical and cultural record of pre-Columbian times. But the friars quickly realized that they had to learn native cultures, religions, and languages in order to teach the people the word of their god. The regular clergy also sought to protect the native peoples from the rapacious European settlers. The resulting conflicts often led to violence. In one case in northern Brazil, several regular priests were forcefully put to sea in a raft;

the raft capsized and the passengers drowned, to the great satisfaction of the Portuguese settlers.

The most famous Spanish protector of the native peoples was friar Bartolomé de las Casas (1474–1566). In the early sixteenth century he gained the ear of the Spanish crown, who at his behest prohibited Indian slavery. Later in the colonial era the regular clergy were replaced by secular clergy, who were often American-born, far more pragmatic, and less solicitous of the native population. However, the crown itself was rarely willing to sacrifice mineral production for the spiritual well-being of the natives. In a choice between religion and the need for native labor, gold and silver took precedence.

By indoctrinating the native peoples into Catholicism, the priests taught them obedience and passivity. The misery of this world would be rewarded by heaven in the next. Any deviance from the norm was expurgated by the Inquisition, the Church's investigative arm.

Most native and mixed-blood (*mestizo*) people blended their folk culture and religion with Christianity to produce a unique form of Catholicism. Especially in the countryside, Catholicism was only imperfectly absorbed. There were never very many regular clergy. As a result, they touched the people of the periphery only lightly. The nomadic peoples fiercely resisted any incursions. In the cities many more priests presided and Catholicism was more conventional.

The Church also functioned as an important financial institution. It became enormously wealthy because many rich colonists bequeathed their funds and estates, others purchased penance in the form of indulgences, and the entire population was supposed to pay the tithe, usually a ten percent assessment on their income. Collectively, the Church was the largest rural property holder and urban landlord in New Spain and operated as the most important commercial and mortgage banker.

The hacienda evolved as a consequence of population decline in the demographic disaster, which caused a severe shortage of labor and the abandonment of large tracts of land. Originally the Spaniards adopted an institution from the Iberian Peninsula, later adapted to the Caribbean, the *encomienda*, which was a grant of tribute from the native people of a specified geographic entity, usually paid in the form of labor. The encomienda, however, presented serious problems for the Spanish crown. The owners of the encomiendas showed every indication of turning themselves into a New World hereditary nobility, a development the crown vigorously resisted. Most important, the decline in population wiped out the basis of the grant—people. Next the Spaniards turned to *repartimiento*, a forced labor system, but there

were not enough natives to fill the work quotas. The hacienda proved a solution to the shortage of labor, for it attracted native workers by offering to pay their tribute and church fees (for marriage, baptism, funeral). Hacienda laborers accumulated large debts that were passed on unpaid to their children. This system of debt peonage, however, offered some advantages, for it protected laborers from oppressive taxation or other obligations and provided an opportunity for security. In areas such as northern Mexico, indebtedness was more of an advance in wages than a burden. The evolution from encomienda to hacienda occurred unevenly. In some areas encomienda lasted centuries; in others different labor systems existed side by side.

The decline in native population caused both Spanish and Portuguese to turn to Africa to supply labor needed for New World plantations and mines. Large numbers of slaves were imported into Brazil, Mexico, and Peru. By 1800 2.5 million African slaves had been brought to the Americas, three-quarters of them to Brazil. The most profound impact was in Brazil. Because of a seemingly unending potential supply from Africa, the plantation owners of Brazil determined it was cheaper to work slaves to death than to feed or treat them well.

Life in Latin America Under Colonial Rule

The influx of Iberians, the loss of native population, and the realignment of landholding brought vast changes to life in the New World. The Europeans demanded different foods, most importantly wheat, olives, and wine. They brought with them new plants and animals. Their cattle, sheep, and goats required a completely altered pattern of land ownership and land usage. In an effort to better acculturate and administer the native peoples, the Spanish colonial government often tried to congregate or resettle them. Agriculture reorganized to supply markets in the mining camps and cities.

The great empires that preceded the Iberians were socially stratified, and colonial society was no different, but the Europeans added the new dimension of race. Under Spain and Portugal, whites were at the top of the social pyramid. Being white did not by any means assure one such an exalted position, however. There were poor and middle-class Spaniards. Moreover, there were two types of Spaniards, those born in the New World, known as *criollos* (creoles), and those born in Spain, *peninsulares*, or as they were known disparagingly, *gachupines* (greenhorns). Occupationally, the colonial elite were

This painted wooden beaker from Spanish colonial Peru is decorated with a multiracial portrait of a Spanish trumpeter, an African drummer, and a Native American official.

large landowners, miners, merchants, upper-level clergy, and government officials. These categories often overlapped, for example, when successful merchants and miners purchased large estates. In the middle were artisans, retail merchants, intermediate-level bureaucrats, and priests in the cities and, though their ranks were few in number, small farmers and ranchers in the countryside. Racially the middle comprised whites and some mixed-bloods, most likely *mestizos* or less often, *pardos*. The vast majority of the population, which included mestizos, pardos, Indians, and free Africans, was poor and lived in a continual state of deprivation. Most of the lower class lived in rural areas. At the very bottom were the African slaves, commodities to be bought and sold. Economically, urban and household slaves may have at times been better off than their mestizo or Indian counterparts, for their masters generally guaranteed them a minimal subsistence. Those who depended on market forces to determine their wages had no such guarantee. The distribution of wealth was extremely unequal, for the rich had almost all the resources and the poor virtually none. There was minimal chance for upward mobility. Mestizos and pardos were known to have purchased certificates of purity of blood that attested to their whiteness. Money could sometimes buy social standing, but rarely was the opportunity available.

The primary institution for the survival of Indian culture was the village, enduring through the demographic losses, the overbearance of the hacienda, and resettlement. It was most resilient in the regions on the periphery outside Spanish centralized rule. Communal landholding persisted, but most Indians had to work outside the village to obtain merchandise unavailable there. Hacienda and village developed a complex relationship, which was symbiotic when the hacienda needed labor and the villagers needed to supplement the subsistence yield of their individually or communally owned land, and which conflicted when the two fought over scarce land and water resources. Many Indians moved to towns and cities to escape tribute exactions. They earned a bare subsistence as day laborers or in textile factories.

In a society obsessed with matters such as honor and manhood, women were repressed by a double standard of behavior. There were, however, various ways to escape these constraints. Indeed, entrance into a convent was an important means for wealthy women to obtain their independence. Widows also obtained considerable autonomy, especially if they were beyond child-bearing age and thus free of pressure to remarry, because they were entitled to one-half their husbands' estates.

Rural and urban working-class women worked, for few families could survive without their income. In the countryside they planted and harvested. In the cities and towns the market vendors were often women. Other employment was available as domestic servants for the rich and as factory workers, particularly in the textile mills.

For men and women of the lower classes, life was a struggle to subsist. One of the most remarkable statistics of Latin American history is the fact that wages on the haciendas on the central plateau of Mexico stayed the same from 1650 to 1800, at a level that was not sufficient to provide the basics of food and shelter for a family. Wages rose only in areas such as the northern mining districts where labor was scarce.

The population of Latin America began to increase in the second half of the seventeenth century, when at last the Indian population, having developed immunities to European diseases, began to recover and the number of mixed-bloods and whites grew, the latter through immigration. This growth added to the general misery of the people and presented colonial rulers with a new set of difficulties. When these new pressures combined with a series of external events in Europe, they caused a crucial political realignment in the New World empires.

From 1519 to 1700 the great empires of the New World fell to the onslaught of internal dissension,

America and the Encounters

1325	Aztecs settle on Lake Texcoco
1427	Triple Alliance: Tenochtitlán, Tlacopán, Texcoco
1438–71	Reign of Sapay-Inca Pachacuti
1471–93	Reign of Sapay-Inca Topa Inca Yupanqui
1492	First voyage of Columbus
1493–1525	Reign of Sapay-Inca Huayna Capac
1500	Cabral discovers Brazilian coast
1516	Charles I ascends Spanish throne
1519	Hernán Cortés lands in Veracruz
1521	Tenochtitlán destroyed by Spanish-Tlaxcalan siege
1525	Civil war between Inca factions led by Huáscar and Atahuallpa
1527	First *Audiencia* and bishopric established in New Spain
1531	Francisco Pizarro reaches Peru
1555	Philip II succeeds to Spanish crown
1572	Execution of Tupac Amarú ends Inca resistance
1650	Low point of native population in Mexico, less than one million

Iberian arms, and European diseases. The new rulers, intolerant of the conquered, tried mightily to destroy indigenous culture and religion. They achieved only limited success. The vanquished did not succumb easily, fighting for centuries to preserve their ways. The Spanish and Portuguese never conquered all of Latin America, but rather succeeded only in occupying crucial areas. Flexible but authoritarian, meddlesome but inefficient, religious but ruthless, both Spanish and Portuguese colonial rule comprised a series of paradoxes.

The changes wrought by the encounter between Europeans and the native peoples of the Americas were extensive and profound. The very face of the land changed: where corn had once sprouted, wheat grew and cattle grazed. Where once the temples of Aztec gods had stood, Catholic churches dominated the skyline. But in many respects, life for most native people changed little with the coming of the Europeans. The Aztecs were feared and loathed throughout Mesoamerica. They were cruel conquerors, who at times demanded terrible tribute in the form of victims for human sacrifice, and who at the very least required the payment of luxury commodities while contributing little to their subjects. Though the Incas offered opportunity to share in the spoils of conquest and the benefits of tribute labor, such as roads and emergency food stores, they too exacted a high price from their subjects, who were forcibly resettled, held hostage, deprived of their gods, and forced to work for no recompense. The Spaniards who replaced the Aztecs and Incas were also takers. Those who defend the Iberians claim that religion, language, and peace were considerable contributions, but the Spaniards and Portuguese brought little to improve the lives of their subjects. They ruled for so long because the calamitous population decline of the native peoples made sustained resistance impossible for two centuries. But after the mid-seventeenth century, when the population began to recover, unrest recurred. As we will see (in Chapter 28), in the eighteenth century colonial rule became so burdensome to Latin America that it threw off its Iberian shackles.

In the centuries following the discovery of America and a passage to the East Indies by the Cape of Good Hope, a worldwide marketplace for the exchange of commodities emerged—a living symbol of the mixture these encounters had engendered. First the Dutch and then the English established monopoly companies to engage in exotic trades in Asia. First the Spanish and Portuguese, then the English and French established colonial dependencies in the Atlantic, which they carefully nurtured in hope of economic gain. Protected trade flourished beyond the wildest dreams of its promoters. Luxury commodities became staples; new commodities became luxuries. Trade enhanced the material life of all European peoples, though it came at great cost to the Asians, Africans, and Latin Americans whose labor and raw materials were converted into the new crazes of consumption. The consequences of black slavery and the destruction of native populations had as significant an impact on the modern world as the discoveries and encounters themselves.

SUGGESTIONS FOR FURTHER READING

EUROPE AND THE ENCOUNTERS

Felipe Fernández-Armesto, *Columbus* (Oxford: Oxford University Press, 1991). The best of the new studies. Reliable, stimulating, and up-to-date.

Felipe Fernández-Armesto, *Before Columbus: Exploration and Colonisation From the Mediterranean to the Atlantic 1229-1492* (London: Macmillan, 1987). A comprehensive survey. Difficult but rewarding.

C. R. Boxer, *The Portuguese Seaborne Empire 1415-1825* (London: Hutchison, 1968). A comprehensive history of the first of the explorer nations.

* Samuel Morrison, *Christopher Columbus, Mariner* (New York: New American Library, 1985). A biography by a historian who repeated the Columbian voyages.

* Dan O'Sullivan, *Age of Discovery 1400-1550* (London: Longman, 1984). Best short, synthetic work.

* J. H. Parry, *The Age of Reconnaissance* (New York: New American Library, 1963). A survey of technological and technical changes that made possible the European discovery of America.

* Eugene Rice, *The Foundations of Early Modern Europe 1460-1559* (New York: Norton, 1970). An outstanding synthesis.

AFRICA AND THE ENCOUNTERS

* Philip Curtin, *The Rise and Fall of the Plantation Complex: Essays in Atlantic History* (New York: Cambridge University Press, 1990). A highly readable survey of the context in which the African slave trade arose.

* Sidney W. Mintz, *Sweetness and Power: The Place of Sugar in Modern History* (New York: Viking Penguin, 1985). A fascinating history of sugar's impact on historical development.

* J. F. Ade Ajayi and Michael Crowder, eds., *History of West Africa*, 3d ed., Vol. I (New York: Longman, 1985). An encyclopedic treatment of all West African history.

A. F. C. Ryder, *Benin and the Europeans, 1485-1897* (New York: Humanities Press, 1969). A detailed discussion of one important West African state and its relationship with Europeans.

* David Birmingham and Phyllis Martin, eds., *History of Central Africa*, Vol. I (Harlow, UK: Longman, 1983). An edited survey of the history of a broadly defined central Africa in the precolonial era.

Anne Hilton, *The Kingdom of Kongo* (Oxford: Oxford University Press, 1985). A recent, comprehensive, but somewhat controversial analysis of the Kingdom of Kongo.

John Thornton, *The Kingdom of Kongo: Civil War and Transition, 1641-1718* (Madison, WI: University of Wisconsin Press, 1983). A standard survey of the decline of the Kongo state.

M. D. D. Newitt, *Portuguese Settlement on the Zambesi: Exploration, Land Tenure and Colonial Rule in East Africa* (London: Longman, 1973). A dense, extremely thorough analysis of Portuguese activity in Mozambique.

David Beach, *The Shona and Zimbabwe, 900-1850* (London: Heinemann, 1980). A historical analysis of the region of the Mwene Mutapa.

AMERICA AND THE ENCOUNTERS

Mark A. Burkholder and Lyman L. Johnson, *Colonial Latin America.* (New York: Oxford University Press, 1990). This comprehensive introduction to colonial history incorporates the latest research on social history.

Inga Clendinnen, *Ambivalent Conquests: Maya and Spaniard in Yucatan, 1517-1570* (New York: Cambridge University Press, 1987). Innovative look at the interaction of Spanish and Indian.

Inga Clendinnen, *Aztecs* (New York: Cambridge University Press, 1991). Broad interpretation using Aztec texts.

Hernán Cortés. *Five Letters of Cortes to the Emperor*, trans. J. Bayard Morris (New York: Norton, n.d.). Illuminating propaganda.

Alfred W. Crosby, Jr., *The Columbian Exchange: Biological and Cultural Consequences of 1492* (Westport, CT: Greenwood, 1972). Standard study of the plants, animals, and diseases exchanged by new world and old.

Charles Gibson, *Spain in America* (New York: Harper, 1966). Classic examination of the institutions of Spanish rule.

Ramon A. Gutierrez, *When Jesus Came, the Corn Mothers Went Away: Marriage, Sexuality, and Power in New Mexico, 1500-1846* (Stanford, CA: Stanford University Press, 1991). Brilliant and provocative view of the interchange of Spanish and native societies from the native perspective.

Miguel Leon-Portilla, *The Broken Spears: The Aztec Account of the Conquest of Mexico* (Boston: Beacon, 1969). Gripping story of the conquest from the Aztec side.

James Lockhart and Stuart B. Schwartz, *Early Latin America: A History of Colonial Spanish America and Brazil* (New York: Cambridge University Press, 1983). This is a sophisticated analysis of Iberian colonial rule.

Alfred Metraux, *The History of the Incas* (New York: Schocken Books, 1969). Comprehensive study.

R. C. Padden, *The Hummingbird and the Hawk* (New York: Harper, 1970). A provocative and controversial view of the Aztecs, it presents a brilliant picture of a terroristic state.

Thomas C. Patterson, *The Inca Empire* (New York: Berg, 1991). An up-to-date survey.

Caio Prado, Jr., *The Colonial Background of Modern Brazil*, trans. Suzette Macedo (Berkeley, CA: University of California Press, 1971). Standard introduction to Brazilian colonial history.

Jacques Soustelle, *Daily Life of the Aztecs*, trans. Patrick O'Brian (Stanford, CA: Stanford University Press, 1961). Thorough examination of life in the Aztec empire.

Stuart B. Schwartz, *Sugar Plantations in the Formation of Brazilian Society, 1550-1835* (New York: Cambridge University Press, 1985). Comprehensive study of the most important aspect of Brazilian economy during the colonial era.

Karen Spalding, *Huarochi: An Andean Society under Inca and Spanish Rule* (Stanford, CA: Stanford University Press, 1984). Insightful view of the interchange of conquerors and conquered.

Stanley J. and Barbara H. Stein, *The Colonial Heritage of Latin America* (New York: Oxford University Press, 1970). The classic exposition of the burden of colonial rule on the new nations of Latin America.

Steven J. Stern, *Peru's Indian Peoples and the Challenge of the Spanish Conquest* (Madison, WI: University of Wisconsin Press, 1982). Provocative examination of the ways in which the native people of Peru resisted their oppressors.

* Indicates paperback edition available.

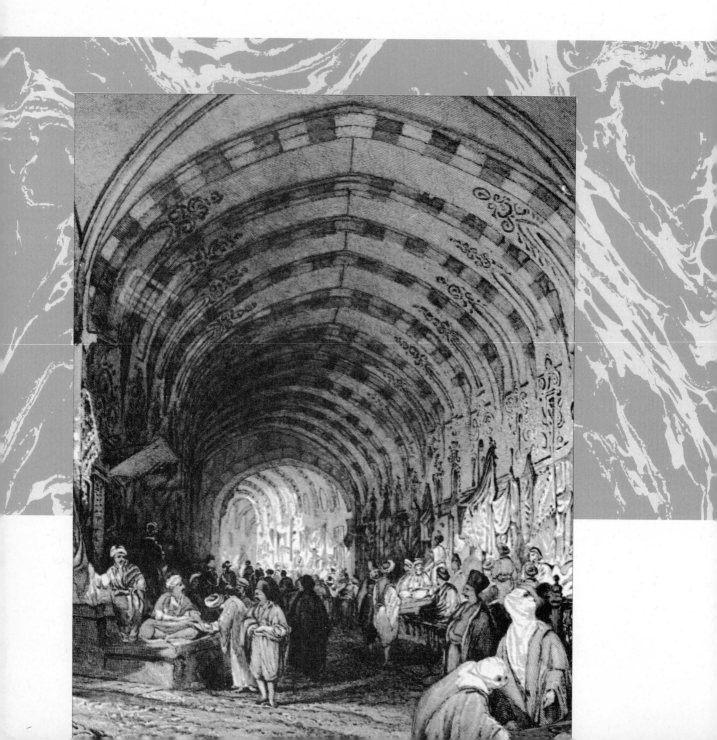

THE OLD *BEZESTAN*: MARKETS, MERCHANTS, AND PATRON SAINTS

Evliya Chelebi, a Turkish traveler born in 1611 in Istanbul, the capital of the Ottoman Empire, writes of the Old *Bezestan* (shown here), the oldest part of the central marketplace in his native city: "It is a great warehouse like a fortress, where the goods of all the military men and viziers are deposited . . . [with] six hundred shops." Evliya enumerates twenty-five kinds of merchants and artisans who work in the Old *Bezestan* or in the uncovered markets that surround it, which together employ several thousand people. An example of the professions enumerated are the satin merchants, of whom he says: "They are three hundred men, with one hundred and five shops. Their patron is Mansur, from Islamic Spain, who was girded [for his saintliness] by Salman [a companion of the Prophet Muhammad] . . . They are for the most part Jews."

With its lofty vaults and well-lit avenues, the Old *Bezestan*, built by the Ottoman sultan Mehmed the Conqueror after his acquisition of the Byzantine capital in 1453, was an impressive monument for the sultan's new seat of government. Evliya's description suggests areas of dependency between the market and the government. The market was used by government officials as a secure place to store goods and to deposit money with large merchants, who were the bankers of this world. Yet the government's attempts to control these merchants and artisans had limits. In the reign of the Ottoman sultan Murad III (1574–95), when the government's attempts to fix meat prices ran counter to all real economic conditions, wholesale butchers simply disappeared from Istanbul and the government was ultimately forced to relent.

The marketplace and mosque were the two breathing spaces of the Islamic town—large public spaces in which people gathered freely, exchanged information and formed public opinion. But the central mosque served this function principally on Friday when attendance at the noonday prayer was obligatory and men and women were separated, whereas the markets were open most or all days of the week, and in them men and women, and Muslims and non-Muslims, circulated freely, although certain sections of the market—or, in large cities, small separate markets such as the "thread market"—tended to be dominated by women.

The culture of the marketplace in the early modern Islamic empires—the Ottoman, Safavid, Sharifian, and Moghul empires—shows both continuity and change. As in earlier Islamic regimes, the area of the marketplace was considered a legal entity, although its boundaries were defined by custom, since there were distinctions between sales made in and outside the market. As in earlier centuries, the wholesale merchants rented or owned space in vast caravansaries, secure buildings on which the ground or lower floors had space for pack animals, offices, and storage, and the upper floors space for travelers and artisans. And, as in previous centuries, an official market inspector, an official sanctioned by Islamic law, supervised weights and measures.

Yet the changed functions of the market inspector in the Ottoman and Safavid empires show the ambitions of central governments to regulate society in these new empires much more closely. The tax system canonized in Islamic law was fairly rigid about taxes on agriculture but specified very few taxes on trade.

But, although the law forbade tolls within the Islamic world, in practice Islamic governments had always maintained toll stations to collect such noncanonical taxes.

The new empires owed their strength in significant part to an increased volume of world trade, and they used the market inspectors to organize the professions into guilds and to tax the guilds and the merchants. In the Safavid empire the market inspector was also supposed to fix prices on basic commodities such as food; the Ottomans did the same, more effectively, through other officials.

The early modern empires were not, however, very successful in acquiring deep commit-ment from the merchant community to their regimes. While some categories of merchants might be treated as a unit for tax purposes, they viewed their collective nature as coming from some saintly figure who, like the Mansur of the satin merchants, had practiced their profession in the past. In general, societies looked to themselves and not to their ruling centers for their identity. The merchants, like the religious experts, preserved their distance from the powerful ruling establishments of these new empires, and remained a truly international community in the premodern Islamic world.

The Islamic World Before the Early Modern Empires

By the end of the thirteenth century, Muslims had more reason than ever to regard their world, the Islamic world, as the center of civilization. Muslims inhabited and ruled a vast band of territory from Spain to northern India, prominently positioned between the other major land areas of the Old World—sub-Saharan Africa, East and Southeast Asia, and Europe. Throughout this vast territory the great majority of governments relied on elite slave soldiers to control their subjects and protect their interests. The populations they ruled adapted to this institution, nearly unique in world history. They did so partly because their more vivid loyalties were not to governments but to many overlapping groups, some of them truly international. These multiple group identities wove societies together and made them flexible enough to survive violent invasions and changes of regime. Two of the most important groups, the large merchants and the religiously learned, wove together the basic fabric of the entire Islamic world. The merchants created networks of trade, credit, and agreed forms of contract. The religiously learned interpreted the laws of contract and fostered the study and exchange of written culture, thereby giving the Islamic world a surprising degree of intellectual unity. Thanks largely to these groups, cultural life in the Islamic world flourished even in periods of political turmoil.

The Emergence of New Rulers: 1100–1400

For the Islamic world of the Middle East in the premodern world, there were two great physical and moral lineages: Muhammad, the prophet to whom the revelation of Islam came in the seventh century, and Genghis Khan, the Mongolian conqueror and military genius who convinced the peoples of Central Asia in the thirteenth century that he and his descendants had a mandate from heaven to rule all the known world. Of the two, lineage from the Prophet, his clan and his tribe, proved the more durable; and even today the royal families of Jordan and Morocco claim direct descent from Muhammad. But the later claim of Genghis Khan that he had a God-given grant of rulership was able not only to legitimize many lines of royal descent but also to create a style of rulership that survived from the thirteenth to the eighteenth century.

Central Asian people first entered the Middle East as slaves. By the eleventh century many of the people of Central Asia spoke Turkish languages. (While "Turkish" can be used in its modern political sense for things related to the nation of Turkey, it is used in this chapter for the family of closely related languages that includes modern Turkish and the peoples who speak them.) Like their ancestors—peoples such as the Huns—they were superb horsemen. The 'Abbasid caliphs, the descendants of Muhammad's uncle who ruled the Islamic empire from 750, began in the ninth century to buy young Turkish slaves to raise as the elite cavalry needed to control their vast territories. On the completion of their training, in the course of which they invariably converted to Islam, these slaves, somewhat like successful Roman gladiators, were freed. But rulers and commanders had strong personal bonds to their former slaves because freed slaves were legally clients of their former owners who had often acted as foster parents to them while young. Usually, these owners became their employers when they were freed.

In the long run, however, the Turkish soldiers of the 'Abbasids proved more interested in enriching themselves from the caliph's treasuries or in ruling the caliph's provinces as independent governors than in saving the empire. But they did not dare assume formal independence because, to their Muslim subjects, legitimacy came only from the governors' recognition of an overlord, such as a caliph, whose lineage was connected with the Prophet. Therefore, most such soldier-rulers, who were in effect kings of their own lands, acknowledged the nominal overlordship of the 'Abbasid caliphs. Consequently, though the 'Abbasids lost the last fragment of real power when a Turkish commander took over their capital city of Baghdad in the 930s, they were preserved for three more centuries because, like the emperors of Japan, the caliphs gave legitimacy to the dynasties that inherited their empire. Even as a fiction, the claim that most of the Islamic world remained united under a caliph meant that Muslims had freedom of movement within that world. And, more important, the contracts Muslims formed, for marriage or for sale of goods, were recognized throughout the Islamic world, regardless of the temporary borders and changes of regime created by the caliphs' nominal governors.

One of the most important dynasties descended from Turkish military slaves was the Ghaznavids, named after their capital Ghazna, in what would later become Afghanistan, overlooking the mountain passes to India. The Ghaznavid king Mahmud (998–1030) took advantage of his position to conquer over half of the Indian subcontinent. These conquests were rarely permanent, but they had many consequences. Mahmud, like future Muslim rulers, gained admiration and legitimacy by succeeding in his chosen role as a *ghazi*, a warrior who fought for Islam. He also opened the road for Muslim expansion into India. And the enormous amount of booty he brought back allowed him to be even more independent of his subjects than the kings before him. He even took the title *sultan*, which meant "dominion" or "authority" in Arabic; he was, literally, "Mr. Authority."

This separation between the people (often called the *ra'aya*, the "flocks") and a government headed by a military commander, was characteristic of most Middle Eastern Islamic regimes until the nineteenth century. The governments might be founded by tribes or, occasionally, even religious leaders, but they soon had to resort to slave and former slave soldiers as the mainstay of their rule. These slaves were expensive to buy, train, maintain, and equip in the most effective armor and weapons of the period. But, unlike tribes, they formed standing armies. Moreover, these military slaves were almost always from outside the Islamic world, not only because Islamic law forbade the enslaving of Muslims or protected peoples—such as the Christians and Jews—but also because rulers knew that outsiders were less likely to collude with the indigenous population.

The Arrival of The Turkish and Mongolian Tribes

Turks did not enter the Middle East only as slave soldiers. From the eleventh to the fifteenth centuries, whole tribes of Turkish nomads entered the Middle East in great waves of migration. The first wave entered in the eleventh century under the leadership of a royal clan called the Seljuqs. These Seljuq Turks, who were pious Muslims, preserved much of the social and cultural life of the area and created new forms of patronage, which in turn fostered Islamic Middle Eastern culture. They began using the developing Islamic law for pious endowments to found *madrasa*s (colleges), mosques, hospitals, and libraries.

Yet the foundations of Seljuq rule were far from stable. Despite their use of a large army of Turkish slave soldiers to rein in their unreliable army of Turkish tribes, they were defeated by these tribes in 1153. Disorder prevailed for about eighty years until a force appeared mightier than any seen in the Middle East since the Islamic conquests: the Mongols under Genghis

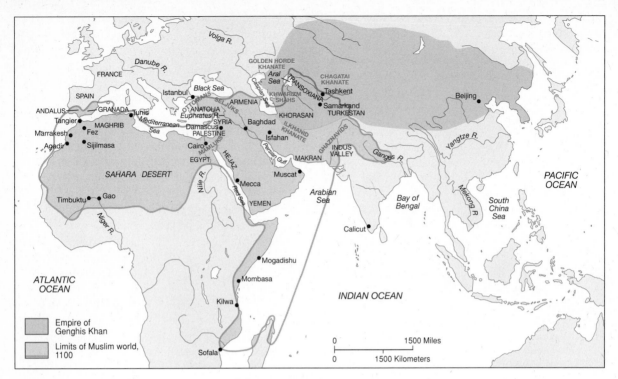

The Islamic World, 1100–1500

Khan. In 1219 Genghis launched an attack on the Islamic regime that ruled Transoxiana and Persia. His forces easily swept aside all Muslim opposition while they unleashed on many of the great cultural centers a wave of killing and destruction from which some never recovered; in Nishapur, for example, whose madrasas and men of learning were famous throughout the Islamic world, the Mongol troops carried out an order that neither a human of any age, nor "even cats and dogs should be left alive"; and the army returned several times to kill any inhabitants who might have survived in hiding.

As conquests continued under the descendants of Genghis Khan, who were, like him, not Muslims, the Mongol empire soon stretched from Hungary to Korea. But the real unity of the Mongol empire soon disappeared; and almost all of their Muslim subjects were ruled by the Mongols of Iran, the Il-Khans, or the Mongols of Russia, the Golden Horde. The Il-Khans ruled western Asia and their kingdom, whose rulers and troops eventually converted to Islam, lasted until the early fourteenth century. Toward the end of that century the Il-Khans were replaced by an empire that began with a wave of destruction rivaling the early Mongols: the em-

pire of Tamerlane. A Muslim of Mongolian descent, Tamerlane (1370–1405) reconstituted the empire of the Il-Khans, often with horrifying and very public demonstrations of his violence, such as the towers of skulls he made from the victims of his massacres. Tamerlane married a descendant of Genghis Khan and carried along a Genghisid puppet *khan* to give himself legitimacy. His far less warlike descendants ruled over dwindling kingdoms, as nomadic Turkish peoples divided the bulk of Tamerlane's lands between tribal rulers.

The influx of Turkish and Mongolian peoples had dramatic effects on the history of the Middle East. In their own historical tradition the people of the Middle East portrayed the Mongols as the villains of this great historical change, partly because most of the early Mongol rulers were hostile to Islam, now the religion of the overwhelming majority of the population. In contrast, the equally bloody conquests of the Muslim Tamerlane, who with few exceptions chose other Muslim powers as his victims, received a far better press.

The Mongols put a lasting stamp on the character of succeeding centuries of Turkish rule. Since so many of the troops the Mongols brought into or enlisted in the Middle East were Turks, the language of the Mongol ruling families of the Il-Khans and the Golden Horde soon became Turkish. And the long-term movement of the Slavic peoples south and east was halted for centuries as Turkish-speaking peoples dominated a great band of Asia from the area north of the Black Sea to the Pacific Ocean. Correspondingly, Turkish peoples regarded as nearly sacred descent from Genghis Khan and the customary law established by the Mongols. The universal mandate claimed by Genghis—"One sun in heaven, one lord on earth"—had such a dazzling effect both in creating the world's largest premodern empire and in momentarily uniting most of the Turks of Eurasia, that it was long remembered among Turkish peoples.

The Mongols had a strong tradition of unwritten law that originated in the decisions and maxims of tribal leaders. Genghis Khan's word weighed as that of no previous figure in Turco-Mongolian history had done, and gradually the story took hold that he had laid down a code called the Great Yasa. Before the Mongols, customary law and royal administrative law had existed uneasily alongside Islamic law. The Yasa was not fundamentally more acceptable to the specialists in Islamic law than any earlier form of customary law. However, it had greater authority than earlier non-Muslim law, and it was seen as a cumulative body of royal law that existed apart from the personality of the ruler, one that a ruler could change or amend but not cancel. Even Tamerlane, for all the authority he acquired as a world conqueror, reaffirmed the allegiance of his dynasty to the Yasa.

A fifteenth-century Egyptian painted leather figure in the form of a riverboat containing three archers. The figure was used in the shadow plays of the Mamluk period.

A Slave Aristocracy Rules Egypt and Syria

In Cairo in 1250, the freed slave soldiers of Saladin's much-weakened dynasty thrust aside their former masters and began to rule in their own right. They were called *Mamluks*, which literally means "those owned," and they represent a further step in the evolution of elite slave armies in the Middle East. Occasionally father-son successions appeared among these former slaves, but usually whichever Mamluk commander was most powerful would succeed his predecessor through persuasion or open warfare. This "slave" aristocracy bought its future commanders and sultans as boys from Turkish areas of Central Asia and from the Caucasus. The Mamluks recalled their Central Asian roots, even invoking the Yasa to settle disputes, although they remained free of Mongol rule.

In fact, the role of the Mamluks as champions of Islam against the Mongols was an important part of their success. In 1260 the Mamluk sultan handed the Mongols their first significant defeat in the Islamic world at a battle at Ain Jalut in Syria. Despite repeated attempts by the Mongol Il-Khans and their successors to conquer Syria, the Mamluks maintained control of Syria as well as Egypt for most of the next two and a half centuries. With non-Muslim Mongols ruling the Muslim east until 1295, Muslims came to see the Mamluk empire to their west both as a place of refuge and as a bastion of true belief. The Mamluks campaigned hard and successfully to drive the last Crusaders from the eastern Mediterranean. And, under the Mamluks, the emerging system of recognizing four schools of Islamic law as equally legitimate was established as a lasting element of orthodox Sunni Islam, the form of Islam accepted by the majority of Muslims.

People, Trade, and Culture in the Premodern Islamic World

The subjects of these Islamic regimes—perhaps half of whom had converted to Islam by the time of Mahmud of Ghazna—also found advantages in this system of military rule by outsiders, even though these military regimes often extorted heavy taxes in order to maintain themselves and sometimes acted like occupying armies. After the moral and military failure of the first two dynasties of caliphs, the Umayyads and 'Abbasids, Muslim subjects seldom felt committed to any regime; they settled for governments that at best kept violence restricted to fights within the military elite or against neighboring regimes.

Madrasa of the Shah's Mother in Isfahan, Iran.

The College with the Gilded Cage

In 1694, Shah Sultan Husayn (1694–1722) at age twenty-six emerged from the harem to rule the Safavid empire. Raised in the harem—where rulers sometimes kept their sons to prevent rebellions—Shah Sultan Husayn had little knowledge of the world. He was by nature quiet and studious, and when his mother built the college shown here he had a gilded cage prepared for himself so that he could take part in discussions among the religiously learned faculty who taught and studied at the college. Shah Sultan Husayn showed no aptitude for kingship and, while at first violently against the drinking of alcohol, soon became addicted to it. A weak man, he quickly found himself caught in a struggle between the court eunuchs and the specialists in religious learning, the ulama, who in the Safavid empire belonged to the Shi'ite branch of Islam. The empire more or less spontaneously disintegrated as subject peoples and neighbors became aware that no one was minding the throne, and in 1722 Shah Sultan Husayn gave his insignia of office to a former subject, an Afghan leader, who occupied the capital city of Isfahan.

Around the central courtyard of the *Madraseh-ye Madar-e Shah* (Madrasa of the Shah's Mother) are arcades of cells or rooms for students as well as rooms and recesses for classes. The *madrasa* contains a prayer hall and a library. Like many madrasas, it has nearby property, the income from which was dedicated by the founder to its upkeep. In this case, a building rented to merchants for offices, storage space, and even sleeping space helps maintain the college. It was not unusual for a woman to found a madrasa. Wealthy women, especially of royal families, often endowed madrasas and mosques, in part because of ties to leading religious figures.

Madrasas were colleges for training the ulama. With curricula centered on religious subjects, the madrasas are sometimes called theological colleges. But their curricula varied and might even include subjects such as astronomy, important for determining the time of prayer and its direction, since Muslims face Mecca to pray. Usually the terms of the endowment determined the curricula, although over time the number of subjects taught tended to increase and many subjects, such as philosophy were offered in private classes.

Even the public classes were not as formal as in modern schools. The students entered the madrasa with a basic literacy gained at a Qur'an school and sometimes, as in the Azhar, the major college of Cairo, memorization of the Qur'an was a prerequisite to entrance. Students in good standing could count on a bread ration to keep them alive during their years at the madrasa. Classes at the madrasa were largely based on reading and interpreting set texts until the highest levels of education, when the students engaged in open debate on subjects determined by the teacher. Students had a great deal of freedom, for there were seldom any formal degrees, only "permissions" granted by a reputable teacher for a student to teach a book or, at the highest level, to give a legal opinion.

Despite variations, in the thirteenth and fourteenth centuries a body of widely recognized classics on grammar, law, and kindred subjects began to emerge. After that time madrasa education gave a remarkable unity to the educated elite of the Islamic world. The ulama were not part of any church that could unify their opinions; but they wanted to prevent religious opinion from diverging in many directions, and the madrasas helped them. Ibn Battuta, probably the most traveled man in the world before the

fifteenth century, during the years between 1325 and 1349 found employment among Muslims as a judge or religious authority in many areas he visited—from sub-Saharan Africa to India, Central Asia, and even China—because Muslims recognized that the education he had received in his native Tangier in Morocco was similar to the education of Islamic learned men everywhere. Similarly, many of the bureaucracies of Islamic governments were staffed by men who had received some madrasa training and shared a common background.

In Persian and in many languages influenced by Persian, such as Urdu, the ulama were also called *mullahs*—one of whom is seen here entering a vestibule of the madrasa. The Shi'ite mullahs lived in an uneasy symbiosis with the Safavid monarchs. They were hungry for royal patrons but, at the same time, were never quite sure of the legitimacy of Safavid claims to rule. The proximity of this madrasa to the royal palace facilitated the Shah Sultan Husayn's participation and, at the same time, emphasized the building's royal patronage. The power of the Shi'ite mullahs at the end of the Safavid period encouraged them to develop the theory that they should run the government, a theory realized in the Iranian Revolution of 1978.

The nonmilitary elites also accommodated themselves to these regimes. The upper level of bureaucrats, among whom the vizier was most important as the public face of the sultan and the head of the civil bureaucracy, played a high-risk game in which they could become rich or lose their lives overnight. In contrast, the lower bureaucracy, as long as it remained appropriately faceless, often survived great upheavals in government unharmed. Like the upper level of bureaucrats, the wealthiest merchants were subject to arbitrary confiscation when governments had urgent need for money. But, as they were the only subjects of the sultan with large sums of cash the government could borrow, a sultan who was too greedy might lose all his credit in the marketplace and even be faced with the migration of his leading merchants. By and large the rest of the merchant community was left alone.

The situation of large landlords was more precarious. Like the lower bureaucrats, they were important to the governments because they often had a role in tax collection. But, unlike the lower bureaucrats, they were more exposed to the economic changes brought by the new regimes. From the tenth century the government began to assign land-tax revenues to soldiers, especially officers. This method of payment—in which the assignment was called *iqta'*—suited both soldiers and sultans so well that until the nineteenth century it was as characteristic of Islamic regimes as military slavery. Landlords were seldom directly harassed by the central government, but they were frequently harassed and sometimes replaced by the soldiers and their bailiffs who descended on the countryside to collect the revenues assigned to them. This system tended to discourage investment in improving the land, and most landlords chose to live in the cities to the further disadvantage of the countryside. The iqta' loosely resembled the European fief, but there was no hierarchy among fiefholders as in western Europe; and, while some iqta's did become hereditary, the government could always step in and reassign them to different holders.

Islam had no priesthood, but specialists in religious learning gradually became a semiprofessionalized elite and were collectively called *ulama*, "knowers" (See Special Feature, "The College With the Guilded Cage," pp. 446–447). But even after the foundation of special schools to train the ulama in the last half of the eleventh century, religious learning continued to be cultivated in various degrees by men who were also landlords, merchants, and bureaucrats.

In fact, almost all groupings in society overlapped: a craftsman who made silk brocade, lived in the quarter next to the citadel, subscribed to the Shafi'i version of Islamic law and the Ash'ari school of Islamic theology, and participated in the Qadiri order of Sufi mystics, would have a real loyalty to each of the groups to which he belonged. And each group would connect him with other groups: some makers of silk brocades might be Jews and some members of his Qadiri Sufi order might be wholesale grain merchants. Moreover, from the tenth to the nineteenth centuries in many Middle Eastern cities the population was also divided into two roughly equal factions that, although named after a profession such as the butchers or, more often, after a law school, included members of the community from other professions and law schools. The feuding between these factions became fierce at times when central government was weak, and it resembled the feuding between rival factions in some Italian city-states of the late Middle Ages. The majority of the population knew that if people did not maintain their multiple and overlapping identities they would become involved in factionalism of quarter, profession, or citywide groups to a degree that would inspire arson, murder, and other forms of destructive violence. This fear gave them yet another reason to want the rule of alien peoples such as slave-soldiers who, while commanding no vivid loyalty from their subjects, would act as arbiters generally more interested in order than in siding with any faction among the local population.

Middle Easterners were, more than ever, a "middle" people. An unwitting achievement of the Mongols was to bring to the Middle East a better knowledge of the Old World than any people had previously possessed. A vizier of the Il-Khans, Rashid ad-Din (1247–1318), wrote in Persian the most informed account of his time of all the cultures of Europe and Asia, including China. This was possible because the Pax Mongolica had for the first time created a continuous and busy overland traffic between the Mediterranean, the northeast European world, and East Asia. This overland trade continued with surprising vigor until the eighteenth century. Although western Europeans, especially Italians, continued to dominate merchant shipping in the Mediterranean, as they had since the eleventh century, Byzantine and Muslim participation in this trade was far from negligible.

The Indian Ocean was quite another matter. From the ninth century a network of Muslim traders spread all the way from East Africa to China. They came to dominate this area through daring, but they maintained their control through sound commercial practice. Islamic law had developed a sophisticated law of sale and partnership adaptable to a variety of market conditions. Thanks in significant part to a fairly uniform commercial law, Muslim traders knew what to expect of each other. The rise of Egypt under the Mamluks to preeminence among the centers of Islamic culture in the Arabic-speaking world owed a great deal to its position as an intermediary between the trade of the Indian Ocean and the Mediterranean.

In Islamic lands to the north and east of the Mamluks, an important feature of Turco-Mongolian rule was its cultural allegiance to the Persian tradition. Turkish tribes entered the Middle East through an area in which Persian was spoken. This meant that the leaders of these Turkish peoples saw Islamic Middle Eastern culture through a Persian filter. For many centuries the only major alternative to Arabic as a vehicle of written expression was Persian. Used principally in Iran, Afghanistan, and Central Asia, Persian appeared in the tenth century as a language of lyric poetry and became

in the eleventh century the language of epic poems, historical chronicles, and administrative correspondence, including most of the correspondence between Turkish-speaking rulers.

From India to Anatolia, Turkish-speaking rulers carried Persian court culture. This culture included a taste for long poems, unlike Arabic literature, which excelled in the short poem of praise and lamentation. Persian poetry was the vehicle for long imaginative epics on the semilegendary Iranian past, on romantic themes, and on mystical themes. These epics became the focus of a tradition of extraordinarily beautiful book illustration that spread to India, Anatolia, and Central Asia. Not only the descendants of Genghis Khan but also Tamerlane—who tried to save people of talent from the general slaughters he ordered—and his descendants were discriminating patrons of literature, the arts, and even the scholastic sciences (such as logic and jurisprudence), which were usually written about in Arabic.

Islamic lands west of the Mamluks—Arabic-speaking like Mamluk Egypt and Syria—were called by their inhabitants the Maghrib (roughly, Morocco, Algeria, Tunisia, and Libya) and Andalus (Islamic Spain and Portugal). Nowhere in the Muslim West did cultural life develop more brilliantly than in Andalus. Here, under tolerant Muslim rulers, Christians, Jews, and Muslims exchanged ideas freely. Europeans received their first extensive knowledge of Aristotle through Latin translations from the Arabic, along with the ingenious commentaries of the Muslim scholar Ibn Rushd (in Latin, Averroës, often called by the Europeans simply The Commentator). And here, as in many other places, Muslims brought about a "green revolution" by introducing crops such as cotton, sugarcane, and oranges (all three English words were borrowed from the Arabic). But Christian zeal for the reconquest of the Iberian Peninsula, officially considered to be a "crusade," proved too strong for the Muslim kingdoms; after the Muslim defeat at Las Navas de Tolosa in 1212, it was all downhill for the Muslims. Granada, the last Muslim kingdom in Spain, hung on until 1492. Its conquest was considered so important that the inscriptions around the tombs of Ferdinand and Isabella, which have no reference to the discovery of the New World, mention as their great achievement the capture of Granada and the expulsion of the Jews from Spain.

A curious complement to the history of the Iberian Peninsula of Spain and Portugal is the history of the Anatolian Peninsula, which was to become the backbone of the Ottoman Empire. In both peninsulas—one European, the other Asian—a holy war, waged by the

Life in the City, *a Persian watercolor miniature of the sixteenth-century by Mir Sayyid 'Ali, ca. 1540. The scene, showing preparations for a betrothal feast, was painted to illustrate a story.*

FROM THE *TRAVELS OF IBN BATTUTA*

■ *Ibn Battuta, the fourteenth-century Moroccan traveler who, by virtue of twenty-five years of travel in Asia, Africa, and Europe, was probably the most widely traveled person in premodern times, wrote a detailed account of his travels that is a fundamental source for its period. Here he relates an incident that began in the Turkish-speaking part of the Middle East and ended in China.*

My purpose in traveling to these mountains was to meet a notable saint who lives there, namely Sheikh Jalal al-Din of Tabriz. At a distance of two days journey from his abode I was met by four of his disciples, who told me that the Sheikh had said to his dervishes who were with him: "The traveler from the west has come to you: go out to welcome him." He had no knowledge whatever about me but this had been revealed to him. I went with them to the Sheikh and arrived at his hermitage, situated outside the cave. There is no cultivated land there, but the inhabitants of the country, both Muslim and infidel, come to visit him, bringing gifts and presents, and the dervishes and travelers live on these offerings. The Sheikh, however, limits himself to a single cow, with whose milk he breaks his fast every ten days. It was by his labors that the people of these mountains became converted to Islam, and that was the reason for his settling among them. When I came into his presence he rose to greet me and I embraced him. He asked me about my native land and my travels, and when I had given him an account of them he said to me: "You are the traveler of the Arabs." Those of his disciples who were there said: "And the non-Arabs, too, our Master." "And of the non-Arabs too," he repeated, "so show him honor." Then they took me to the hermitage and gave me hospitality for three days.

On the day when I visited the Sheikh I saw that he was wearing a wide mantle of goatshair. It took my fancy and I said to myself: "I wish the Sheikh could have given it to me." When I visited him to bid him farewell, he . . . took off the mantle and placed it upon me . . . The dervishes told me that the Sheikh was not in the habit of wearing this mantle and had put it on only when I arrived, saying to them: "This mantle will be asked for by the Moroccan, and it will be taken from him by an infidel king, who will give it to our brother Burhan al-Din of Sagharj, whose it is, for whom it was made."

Now it came about a long time afterwards that I visited China and eventually reached the city of Khansa . . . [The king summoned me and] questioned me about the Muslim sultans and when I replied to his questions, he looked at the mantle and took a liking to it. The *wazir* said to me: "Take it off," and I could not resist his order.

This incident roused my anger, but afterwards I recalled the Sheikh's saying that an infidel king would seize it and I was deeply amazed at the fulfillment of the prediction.

The following year I entered the palace of the king of China at Khan-Beliq [Beijing] and sought out the convent of the Sheikh Burhan al-Din of Sagharj. I found him reading and wearing that identical mantle . . . "This mantle," he went on, "was specially made for me by my brother Jalal al-Din, who wrote me saying: 'This mantle will reach you by the hand of so and so.' " Then he brought out the letter and I read it and marvelled at the Sheikh's perfect knowledge.

From *Travels of Ibn Battuta in Asia and Africa, 1325–1359.*

majority religion of the continent to which they were attached, eventually triumphed: Christianity in Iberia and Islam in Anatolia. In both peninsulas a sense of historical mission carried the conquerors far beyond their original homeland, and lent legitimacy to their ruling families. Both the Habsburgs, who succeeded Ferdinand and Isabella, and the Ottomans needed the economic and military resources of subject peoples to sustain their enterprise of expansion. By the second half of the sixteenth century the Habsburgs and the Ottomans were the two mightiest powers of the European and Mediterranean world.

The Islamic World Divides Into Four Empires

In the sixteenth century most of the Islamic world belonged to four empires, generally known after their ruling families: the Sharifians, the Ottomans, the Safavids, and the Moghuls. Morocco, the most westerly part of the Maghrib, was the seat of the Sharifian empire. The rest of the Maghrib and the lands immediately to its east, namely Egypt, Palestine, Syria, many parts of Arabia and Iraq, and the great peninsula known as Anatolia, or Asia Minor, belonged to the Asian part of the Ottoman Empire. Iran was the seat of the Safavid empire, which controlled much of what is modern Afghanistan as well as areas of the Caucasus, the knot of mountains to the west of the Caspian Sea, and areas further east that are now considered parts of Central Asia. The Indian subcontinent was the seat of the Moghul empire.

The Ottomans, Moghuls, Safavids, and Sharifians, often called the early modern Islamic empires, created a degree of order that the Islamic world had not known for some centuries, and for periods succeeded in controlling their realms more effectively and at deeper social levels than had any Islamic governments prior to them. In this respect the Ottomans were the most successful and the three other empires were influenced by their example. These empires (with the exception of the Moghuls) made new use of the established practice of creating slave elites, and they all got more use out of their (often non-Muslim) vassals. They represented themselves as warriors for Islam, whether fighting for the extension of their governments into non-Muslim areas or defending Islamic governments against an increasingly aggressive Europe. Their success was in part due to the ability of their populations to produce for—and act as middlemen in—a considerably intensified world trade. At their height, the stability and wealth of their central governments enabled the material culture of these areas to reach new heights.

The Ottomans: From Border State to Mightiest Empire of Islam

The Ottomans enter world history around 1300 as leaders of a small group of Turks in charge of the area of Anatolia closest to the Byzantines. As a border state fighting the most venerable opponent of Islam, they considered themselves *ghazi*s, fighters for Islam, and consequently were joined by volunteers who also wanted the honor of being ghazis. Like other border people they shared many cultural traits with their opponents so that, when they began to have modest success in acquiring nearby territory, Byzantine nobles often joined them. And, like many border peoples, they were not subject to the scrutiny of orthodox scholars of their religion and could take advantage of the enthusiasm of various slightly heterodox groups such as the Anatolian devotees of Sufism, the mystical tradition of Islam.

From very small beginnings the Ottomans expanded rapidly. By the 1350s they had a permanent foothold in Europe. Soon after, the Ottoman ruler assumed the style of Sultan. The reaction in western Europe to Ottoman success was mild, but in eastern Europe a coalition including Serbs, Hungarians, and Bulgarians took on the Ottomans at Kosovo Polje in Serbia in 1389. In the ensuing battle—famous in Serbian history for the heroism shown by their side—so many Serbs were killed that it was a foregone conclusion that the Ottomans would, as they did, soon occupy and control Serbia and the rest of the Balkans.

At the end of the fourteenth century, western Europeans woke up to the threat the Ottomans posed. With the support of the papacy a large army of crusaders, composed not only of the nobility of areas neighboring the Ottomans but also of the knighthood of England, France, and Germany, proceeded with great pomp under the leadership of the king of Hungary and Bohemia down the Danube toward the Ottomans. Despite their bravery, the crusaders were completely overwhelmed by the Ottoman sultan Bayazid, in 1396 at Nicopolis in Greece. The Ottomans now had the best ghazi credentials of any ruler since Mahmud of Ghazna.

Anatolia, however, still consisted of a welter of dynasties, most of them Turkish; and when the Ottoman sultan Bayazid annexed their territories, these rulers appealed to Tamerlane. Bayazid, known in Turkish as "the Lightningbolt," did not hesitate to face this latest world conqueror as he entered Anatolia. In 1402 at Ankara, Tamerlane dealt Bayazid a resounding defeat and—according to one story—after taking him prisoner carried him around in a cage until the hapless Ottoman died in captivity.

Defeat at the battle of Ankara showed the weaknesses and strengths of the Ottoman system. A major Ottoman weakness was dependence on an army that included many Turkish tribes, who could be fickle and undisciplined, and many troops led by Christian vassal rulers, some of whom would throw aside their allegiance to the Ottomans in the moment of the sultan's weakness. However, the anti-Catholic sentiment of the

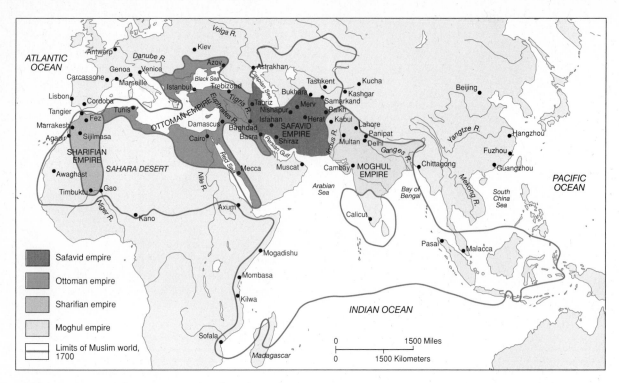

The Four Early Modern Islamic Empires, ca. 1700

Greek Orthodox church, which predominated in the Balkans, continued to help Ottoman rule and echoed the feeling of the Orthodox Patriarch, who said he would rather see in Constantinople the turban of the Turk than the mitre of the pope.

Nevertheless, the strengths of the Ottoman Empire were real enough to allow it to weather the storm. Very prominent among these strengths was the *timar* system, the Ottoman version of the Seljuk *iqta'*, upon which the Ottomans would increasingly depend after the defeat at Ankara. As they moved territory from vassalage to direct rule, they painstakingly recorded each region in registers listing the ownership of land and the number of households in the region. Then they assigned the tax revenues of the region to the sultan's loyal military supporters, including a fair number of Christians. These assignments or timars were at least large enough to support a single well-equipped mounted soldier, and sometimes large enough to support several other soldiers who fought alongside the timar-holder. Regional commanders had even larger assignments and acted both as provincial administrators and as field commanders. Timar-holders had a strong interest in keeping the Ottoman Empire a conquest state; for, as long as there was conquest, there were new territories to be divided into timars for relatives and retainers and new revenues to

keep the government from interfering with the income of timar-holders from existing timars.

By the reign of Bayazid's grandson, Murad II (1421–51), the Ottomans had developed significant new institutions that rendered them capable of creating the greatest Islamic empire in the Mediterranean since the early Caliphate of the eighth and ninth centuries. The Ottomans found that they needed, just as previous Islamic dynasties had needed, a standing army of freed slaves like the Mamluks; but in a bold innovation they domesticated the *mamluk* system. In contradiction to Islamic law, which guarantees the safety and possessions of Christians and Jews as long as they pay the taxes required of them, the Ottomans began a periodic levy of Christian boys inside their empire. They raised these boys as Muslims and trained them for service in the newly formed Janissary army corps and the Ottoman civil service. The prominence of this levy under Murad II opportunely fitted in with the new importance he gave to guns and artillery and his need to strengthen the central government against local heroes, especially renowned ghazis. The well-armed Janissary infantry protected the sultan in his palaces and surrounded him in battle; well-trained Janissary cannoneers gave his armies an advantage over Christian and Muslim opponents alike; and those in training for the Janissary corps who were spotted for administrative talent were separated and specially trained for high office in the sultan's administration. Gradually the training of the boys collected by the levy became the most elaborate and well-organized education ever created for soldiers and bureaucrats in Islamic history; and from 1453 most of the grand viziers, officials second only to the sultan, came from this background. Celibate until their "graduation" (usually in their twenties), slaves of the sultan and subject to his whim, the boys harvested by the levy were nevertheless offered a career with dazzling prospects. Bosnian Muslims were guaranteed a quota in the levies, and sometimes other Muslims tried to bribe levy officers to accept their children.

With its revived and new institutions, the Ottoman Empire saw over a century of nearly uninterrupted expansion. In 1453 Sultan Mehmed II, the son of Murad II, took Constantinople, the symbol of Christian resistance to Islamic conquest for seven centuries; and he rebuilt the city—usually called Istanbul by the Ottomans—with great splendor to give the empire a permanent capital worthy of his accomplishments. Mehmed gave to the Greek patriarch, the Grand Rabbi, and to other religious leaders theoretical and—often—real authority over the internal affairs of their people. The Ottomans not only tolerated religious diversity but also welcomed the Jews expelled from Spain.

On land the Ottomans carried all before them, and their European empire included Hungary, Croatia, Serbia, Bosnia, Albania, Greece, Bulgaria, Romania, and almost all of the districts of modern Russia and Ukraine adjacent to the Black Sea. In 1475, with the loss of Kaffa in the Crimea by the Genoese, the last route to Asia not in Muslim hands passed under Ottoman control. This loss contributed to the long-standing western European determination to reach East Asia by circumnavigating Africa (as Vasco da Gama did) or by finding a westerly

Venetian drawing of Suleiman the Magnificent leading a procession of Janissaries.

route (as Christopher Columbus attempted to do). The Ottomans acquired the largest segment of their Middle Eastern empire in one blow when they defeated the Mamluks in Syria at Marj Dabiq and then occupied Cairo in 1517. Not only did the Ottomans fall heir to the Mamluk role as guardian of the two holy places, Mecca and Medina, but they also gained responsibility as a sea power both on the Mediterranean and in the Indian Ocean, which had been newly invaded by the Portuguese. As rulers of the Arabic-speaking heartlands of the Middle East, the Ottomans inevitably came to see the Islamic tradition as much through Arab as Persian eyes.

The energies of the Spanish and Portuguese that had gone into the "reconquest" of the Iberian Peninsula were now fiercely directed toward North Africa, and a papal bull of 1494 required the faithful to help Spain in this "crusade." In 1497 the Spanish occupied the port of Malila in Morocco and subsequently took a whole string of ports including Algiers, which they occupied in 1510. Resistance to the Spaniards found its champions in an assortment of fearless North African sea captains, the most famous of whom was Khayr ad-Din Barbarossa (d. 1546). Barbarossa was by origin an Ottoman subject and a brilliant naval commander who lacked only the material support that the Ottomans could offer. With Barbarossa's help all of the North African coast except Morocco fell under Ottoman rule with its center at the recaptured port of Algiers. The interior, however, was seldom under Ottoman control and remained largely autonomous.

The acquisition of North Africa took place largely under Suleiman the Magnificent, whose reign from 1520 to 1566 has been considered the height of the empire. In Turkish Suleiman is known as Kanuni, the giver of *kanun*, or nonreligious law. Even the *shari'a*, the Islamic religious law, allowed some room for the ruler to dispense justice at his own discretion, and in practice most rulers in the Islamic world had taken a great deal of the law into their own hands and the hands of their officials rather than allowing it to remain in the hands of the *qadi*s, the judges appointed to adjudicate according to the shari'a. The Ottomans integrated the two systems of royal and religious law, and it was Suleiman who gave the combined system its fully mature form. The Ottomans even obliged the qadis to apply royal law alongside Islamic law in their courts.

This integration of royal and religious law reflects the degree to which the Ottomans penetrated and regulated society. The Ottomans were heirs to the Turco-Mongolian heritage of dynastic royal law and also to late-Roman traditions of law and bureaucracy preserved by the Byzantines. Like the Byzantines the Ottomans

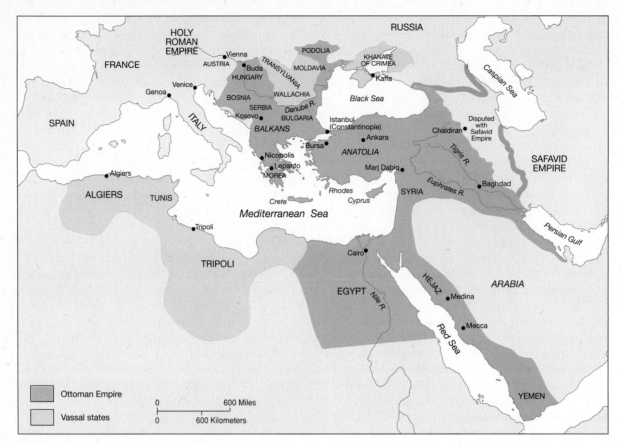

The Ottoman Empire at Its Peak in the 17th Century

organized the professions into guilds, counted house-holds, and established supreme religious officials in their capital. While the Ottomans very often failed to control society to the extent that they wished, they came nearer to achieving such control than had any previous Islamic regime.

By the end of Suleiman's reign the empire had reached its natural limits. The Ottomans were never as successful at sea as on land. With their conquest of Egypt in 1517 they inherited the Mamluk struggle to push the Portuguese out of the Indian Ocean. For a while the Ottoman navy kept open the old route through Egypt, although they could never decisively defeat the Portuguese; and in the seventeenth century, when the larger fleets of the Dutch and English entered the Indian Ocean, these routes too were lost, and con-sequently the eastern Arab provinces of the Ottoman Empire became impoverished.

In the Mediterranean the Ottomans did not have the commercial fleet that the major Christian powers pos-sessed; and they were dependent on the seafaring skills of such Ottoman subjects as Barbarossa in North Africa.

But the Ottomans had commercial interests, new prov-inces to protect and logistical needs to meet for further expansion in the Mediterranean, along which they con-trolled more than half the coast. They built a mighty navy and the Spaniards and Venetians, often enemies, allied themselves for a major confrontation. In 1571 at the battle of Lepanto off the coast of Greece in a fero-cious fight with over two hundred galleys on each side, the Ottomans were defeated. Although the Ottomans rebuilt their fleet with amazing rapidity and although the Spaniards and Venetians quarreled and were unable to build upon their success, Lepanto was one of the great victories in the history of Christian Europe. The Ottomans had reached the limits of their expansion at sea. After Lepanto, seaborne Ottoman conquest in the Mediterranean was limited to the conquest of islands off their territories. And, as a further consequence, the independence of Morocco, the most distant part of North Africa and the only part of the Arab world to remain free of Ottoman rule, was assured.

Ottoman land expansion in Europe also reached its limit at this time. The Ottomans were hampered by the overland distance between Istanbul and Vienna, in miles and in time. They were also trapped by the rise of a formidable power immediately to their east in Persia, the Safavids. The Ottomans could neither move their army's barracks westward toward Vienna nor concentrate on their western front. These weaknesses grew out of a more serious weakness in Ottoman government: the central government remained too narrowly based on personal loyalty to the sultan, and any vital initiative—military or otherwise—required the personal commitment and attention of the sultan or his public face, the grand vizier.

The Safavids: From Sufi Mystics to Persian Emperors

In less than a decade the Safavid family rose from relative obscurity to world prominence, largely due to their long-established role as spiritual leaders of a Sufi religious order in Azerbaijan, the Turkish-speaking northwestern province of Iran. The mystical tradition of Islam known as Sufism holds that disciples of organized Sufi orders achieve spiritual advancement through complete obedience to their spiritual masters, who were believed to be powerful intercessors in heaven for those venerating them or their tombs. Usually Safavid rule is dated from 1501 when Isma'il (1501–24), a handsome youth, assumed the title of Shah of Iran. But the seed of Safavid rule had been planted over two centuries earlier when a Sufi leader in Azerbaijan established a Sufi mystical order that grew in respect and influence under his descendants, called Safavids. Such orders had increased after the appearance of the Mongols, partly because they offered points of social cohesion in times of political disruption and partly because Turco-Mongolian rulers respected holy men as seers and welcomed Sufis into their courts.

The Safavids soon acquired authority as spiritual leaders beyond Azerbaijan. At some point in the largely unrecorded history of the Safavid leaders before 1500, a large number of Turkish—and a few Kurdish—tribes in eastern Anatolia, northern Iraq, and eastern Iran were converted by Safavid propagandists and became fervently devoted to the Safavid leadership. The Safavids, while remaining Sufi leaders, also gained credit as ghazis by leading expeditions against the Georgian Christians in the Caucasus. With the advent of Shah Isma'il, the Safavids emerged as a genuine government with an unexpectedly effective army.

Isma'il stepped forward with virtually all the cards of legitimacy in his hand: He was a ghazi; a mystical leader who was owed total obedience; a near-divine being who fulfilled the esoteric speculations of Turkish nomads and others who awaited a Messianic leader; and a supposed descendant of the Prophet through the Prophet's son-in-law 'Ali, who was seen as the font of all wisdom. He reunited the area of the Iranian plateau and became the "Shah of Iran" and therefore heir to the royal tradition most deeply respected in western Asia. Lastly—and to the ultimate unmaking of his dynasty—he was the actual heir of the working tradition of tribally oriented Turco-Mongolian administration, which had existed continuously in Iran, while the Ottomans had only inherited certain attitudes toward statecraft from this tradition.

With his army of devoted followers Isma'il soon united most of the area that had constituted the empire called Iran before the coming of Islam. A latent identification of the linguistically varied people of this area as Iranians worked in Isma'il's favor. Isma'il proclaimed Twelver Shi'ism the only publicly acceptable form of Islam in his empire; and he and his followers set about systematically imposing this form of Shi'ism in the parts of the Safavid realm most firmly under their control. Twelver Shi'ism holds that the leadership rests with a line of descent in the Prophet Muhammad's family, the first of whom was 'Ali and the twelfth of whom had disappeared in the ninth century and would reappear as the Messiah at the end of time. Under the Safavids, being an Iranian gradually became identified with being a Twelver Shi'ite. The identification was never complete, however: significant communities in the Arab world and India were (and remain) Twelver Shi'ites, and significant minorities in Iran clung to the Sunni version of Islam espoused by the majority of non-Iranian Muslims. Meanwhile, the Turkish nomadic followers of Isma'il devotedly believed their leader to be infallible, even though Twelver Shi'ite ulama were horrified at such a claim; and Isma'il's Turkish poetry, which found an audience among Turks everywhere, implied that Isma'il saw himself as more than human.

The rise of the Safavids posed a threat to the Ottomans very different from the threat of the European powers. Many elements in the Ottoman Empire, especially the Turkish tribesmen of Anatolia and Syria, admired Isma'il and shared some of the religious beliefs of his closest followers. Turkish-speaking tribes had played a role in earlier Ottoman conquests but were no longer a significant part of the Ottoman army. They were still, however, a warlike presence in central and eastern Anatolia, and the Ottomans could not afford to have them rally to the new Shi'ite power on their eastern flank. The Ottomans marched on Azerbaijan and in

1514 the two new empires of the Middle East faced each other in battle at Chaldiran. Shah Isma'il's smaller force of mounted archers, convinced of his invincibility, charged repeatedly at the Ottomans, shouting (in Turkish) the battle cry: "My spiritual leader and master, for whom I sacrifice myself"! The handguns of the Ottoman infantry were effective against these troops but even more so was the Ottoman artillery, for which the Safavids had no counterpart. It did not matter that the individual bravery of Safavid horsemen carried some of them through the Ottoman lines to hack at the chains that held the Ottoman gun carriages together: Ottoman numbers, discipline, and technological superiority carried the day.

The battle of Chaldiran was as least as decisive as the battle of Lepanto for the future of the Middle East. As befitted a power that was far wealthier and more experienced in the new technologies of war, the Ottomans kept the upper hand in their confrontations with the Safavids and the Iranian powers that would succeed them. And Shah Isma'il lost his aura of invincibility.

LETTER FROM THE SULTAN

■ *This letter was sent by the Ottoman sultan Selim shortly before the battle of Chalidiran in 1514 to the Safavid ruler, Shah Isma'il.*

I, sovereign chief of the Ottomans, master of the heroes of the age, who unites the force and power of Feridun [a legendary king of ancient Persia], the majesty and glory of Alexander the Great, the justice and clemency of Khusraw [the famous king of Persia, in whose reign the Prophet Muhammad was born]; I, the exterminator of idolators destroyer of the enemies of the true faith, the terror of the tyrants and pharaohs of the age; I, before whom proud and unjust kings have humbled themselves, and whose hand breaks the strongest sceptres; I, the great Sultan-Khan, son of Sultan Bayezid-Khan, son of Sultan Muhammad-Khan, son of Sultan Murad-Khan, I address myself graciously to you, Amir Isma'il, chief of the troops of Persia, comparable in tyranny to Zahhak and Afrasiab [legendary tyrants mentioned in the Persian national epic], and predestined to perish like the last Darius, in order to make known to you that . . . it is He [the Almighty] who has set up Caliphs on earth . . . it is then only by practicing the true religion that man will prosper in this world and merit eternal life in the other. As to you, Amir Isma'il, such a recompense will not be your lot; because you have denied the sanctity of the divine laws; because you have deserted the path of salvation and the sacred commandments; because you have impaired the purity of the dogmas of Islam; because you have dishonored, soiled and destroyed the altars of the Lord, usurped the sceptre of the East by unlawful and tyrannical means; because coming forth from the dust, you have raised yourself by odious devices to a place shining with splendor and magnificence; because you have opened to Muslims the gates of tyranny and oppression; because you have joined iniquity, perjury and blasphemy to your sectarian impiety; because under the cloak of the hypocrite, you have sowed everywhere trouble and sedition; because you have raised the standard of irreligion and heresy . . . you have dared . . . to permit the ill-treatment of the *ulama*, the doctors and amirs descended from the Prophet, the repudiation of the Koran, the cursing of the legitimate Caliphs. Now as the first duty of a Muslim and above all of a pious prince is to obey the commandment, "O, you faithful who believe, be the executors of the decrees of God!" the ulama and our doctors have pronounced sentence of death against you, perjurer and blasphemer, and have imposed on every Muslim the sacred obligation to arm in defense of religion and destroy heresy and impiety in your person and that of all your partisans.

Animated by the spirit of this *fetwa*, conforming to the Koran the code of divine laws, and wishing on one side to strengthen Islam, on the other to liberate the lands and peoples who writhe under your yoke, we have resolved to lay aside our imperial robes in order to put on the shield and coat of mail, to raise our ever-victorious banner, to assemble our invincible armies.

But the Safavids survived, and Ottoman occupation of parts of Iran after Chaldiran did the occupiers little good because of the scorched-earth policy of the retreating Safavids and the hostility of the local population. Moreover, the Ottoman troops, which included elements secretly sympathetic to the Safavids, disliked these campaigns and grumbled that they would prefer to fight non-Muslim powers in Europe. In any case, it took the Ottoman central army as long or longer to reach the Safavids as it did to reach Vienna. Ottoman expansion had reached its physical and its ideological limits in the east as well as in the west.

For the Safavids the consequences were even more dramatic. Isma'il was not invincible, and normative Twelver Shi'ism (which had regarded him as a mere human all along) increasingly set the religious tone for the Safavid court. The most devoted followers of Shah Isma'il commonly called him "the friend and representative" of God; and it was possible for ordinary Twelver Shi'ites to accept the more conservative claim of the Safavids to be the representative of the Messiah, a claim that still allowed them ample authority.

The Safavids wanted infantry troops on the Ottoman model; and, thanks to their efforts in the sixteenth century to increase the extent of crown lands, they were able by the seventeenth century to buy slaves from the Caucasus and create their own version of the Janissaries. In the seventeenth century, under the long reign of Shah Abbas I (1587–1629), the Safavid dynasty reached its political apogee. The Turkish tribal supporters of the Safavids were assigned to specific provinces where, somewhat in the style of the Seljuk *iqta'*, they received the revenue of the provinces in exchange for providing a tribal levy for major campaigns. A small force chosen from these tribes was the original element in the standing army, to which Shah Abbas added cavalry, infantry, and artillery. Some of these troops were of slave origin, but some were recruited from very diverse elements, including—most exceptionally in the history of the premodern Islamic Middle East—the Iranian peasantry.

In Abbas's stunningly beautiful new capital of Isfahan in the center of Iran, the court language changed from Turkish to Persian, and Persian-speaking bureaucrats directly supervised taxation and expenditure in the central provinces. The luxury products of the central provinces, especially silk textiles, had an avid market and gave the crown significant income. By the early seventeenth century Safavid Iran was acknowledged by its far larger and richer neighbors, in particular the Moghuls of India, to have a certain cultural hegemony within the Islamic world.

Miniature of Shah Abbas I as a young man by an unknown Moghul painter.

The Moghuls: Tamerlane's Descendants Seize India

The Moghuls of India were the true biological heirs of Genghis Khan and of Tamerlane. Babur, the founder of the Moghul dynasty, was a great-great grandson of Tamerlane and, on his mother's side, a direct descendent of Genghis Khan. Babur wandered through Central Asia and Afghanistan, winning and losing parts of the heartland of Tamerlane's empire until, having gained control of the Afghan city of Kabul, he found himself overlooking the passes to India. In his engaging—and amazingly candid—memoirs, he wrote: "India is a wonderful country . . . [for, while it] is a land of few charms . . . the pleasant things of India are that it is a large country and

has masses of gold and silver." At the battle of Pa-
nipat in 1526 Babur defeated the far more numerous
forces of the Muslim kings of Delhi with an Ottoman
tactic, placing a barrier of carts linked by chains behind
which musketeers fired at repeated cavalry charges.
Shortly afterward he defeated the leader of the Rajputs,
who formed a powerful Hindu military confederacy. His
grandson Akbar (1556–1605) continued his conquests,
uniting the greater part of India under one rule for the
first time since the Buddhist emperor Asoka in the
third century B.C.E. Indians used the term "Mongols" to
describe Central Asians, and they called the largely
Turkish dynasty of Babur the Moghuls, a Persian form of
the word *Mongols*.

India on the eve of the Moghul invasion was divided
into numerous kingdoms, very few of which were truly
centralized. In the fifth century Indian rulers had assigned hereditary rights to land in exchange for the services of the assignees in collecting taxes and keeping
order at a local level. As many of these assignees were
members of the Hindu religious elite called the Brahmans, they also controlled the extensive lands owned by
Hindu temples. This hereditary group worked, generally without much commitment, for the many changing
rulers of following centuries, who usually came from
low-caste groups—that is, groups of low social status—or from foreign invaders. Rulers were therefore not
considered to be divinely appointed; they were supposed to maintain the norms of society, which meant
maintaining the local control of traditional elites. As
long as they did so, they had more to fear from each
other than from the people they ruled; and, in fact,
they very often did not seek to replace each other but
only to become the head of confederacies of kingdoms, or the "great" king from whom lesser kings
derived their greatness.

This image of society and kingship was only slightly
altered by the invasion from the northwest of Turkish
and Afghan rulers from the Muslim world. Occasionally,
a Muslim ruler took the position that Hindus were poly-
theistic pagans and should be given a choice of Islam or
death. But the overwhelming majority of Muslim rulers
agreed with an early Muslim commander that Hindus
were a "people of the book" and therefore should be
tolerated just as Jews and Christians were. By and large,
the Muslims left local administration intact and welcomed the military support of warlike Hindu elites such
as the Rajputs. The Rajputs were a social category, or
caste, of northern and central India whose traditional
occupation was warfare and who exalted the virtues of a
courageous death on the battlefield.

*Akbar at the siege of the great Rajput fortress of Ranthambhor in
1568.*

The Moghuls immediately understood their situation: without the support of the Hindu Rajputs they
could never maintain an extensive empire in India.
Babur's grandson, Akbar, the true organizational
founder of the Moghul empire, married several Rajput
princesses (though only after defeating their fathers
and/or brothers), and used a Rajput stronghold as the
base from which his armies would establish a vast empire. By his death in 1605 the Moghul empire stretched
from the heart of Afghanistan on the west to the Bay of
Bengal on the east, and from The Himalaya on the
north to the center of the Deccan plateau. Under
Babur's successors, the Moghuls gained control of
almost all remaining parts of India.

The administration created by Akbar was remarkably
durable, and important aspects of it survived during the

period of direct British rule of India after 1858. Akbar gave all the great officials of the empire the title of *mansabdar*, meaning "holder of a position of rank," and arranged the mansabdars into a hierarchy of thirty-three grades. The mansabdars held their position at the pleasure of the emperor and received payment through *jagirs*, assignments of revenues, the Moghul equivalent of iqta's. In the time of a vigorous emperor like Akbar, much of the actual revenue collection was performed by treasury officials, who used surveys to control revenues down to the village level and who dispensed salaries to the mansabdars. The system was open to both talent and favoritism: Muslim warriors and administrators from other Islamic regions were welcomed, and of Indian-born officials and officers a very high percentage were Hindus.

The Sharifians: The Islamic "Far West" Becomes an Empire

Morocco also emerged as a reconstituted political unit at the time of the founding of the three larger early modern Islamic empires. In the late fifteenth and early sixteenth centuries the Portuguese acquired direct or indirect control of most of the Atlantic coast of Morocco, as well as such strategic Mediterranean ports as Tangier. The Portuguese not only tried to extract as much tax as they could from their Moroccan subjects and tributaries but also raided the interior for plunder and slaves. It is often forgotten that the North African seafarers depicted as "pirates" in the literature of early modern Europe were mirror images of many of their Christian European counterparts.

The Moroccans reacted violently, and an upswell of religious sentiment shaped the destiny of Morocco to the twentieth century. Much of this sentiment found its focus in Sufism. Moroccans of all classes showed greater devotion than Muslims in other parts of the Arab world to their local Sufi leaders, who were seen as healers and miracle workers. Thanks to the contributions they received and the trade routes they dominated, many of these Sufi leaders were more independent of sultans than the ulama.

In the eighth century a *sharif*, or descendant of the Prophet Muhammad, had fled the caliphs of the Islamic Middle East and founded a minor but long-lived dynasty in Morocco. Sharifian lineage acquired particular prestige in this area, and sharifs continued to emigrate to Morocco over the centuries. In 1511 one line of sharifs agreed to lead the people of southern Morocco against the Portuguese; and the Sufi leaders, greatly empowered by the new religiosity of Moroccans, rallied to support their cause. In 1550 Muhammad (who adopted the regnal title al-Mahdi, "the Messiah"), took the greatest town of the interior, Fez.

This line of Sharifians (as the rulers of Morocco are known up to the present day) reunified Morocco and gradually expelled the Europeans. Since an important goal of European expansion along the Atlantic coast was to trade for gold (and, later, slaves) from the sub-Saharan interior, to compete with them the Sharifians moved overland far to the south, conquering Timbuktu in 1590; and, for half a century, they were the predominant power in a vast region of Africa immediately to the south of Timbuktu.

The first line of Sharifians, the Sa'dians, created a government more centralized than Morocco had experienced in some centuries and added to their tribal support a standing army of European renegades—Muslims expelled from Spain, and black troops trained by Ottoman deserters. The new state apparatus, much influenced by the Ottoman example, managed to survive in spite of continually disputed successions, competing tribal powers, and, finally, the disaffection of the Sufi leaders.

The Early Modern Islamic Empires Compared

The great Islamic empires of the early modern period shared many points of origin and of ongoing contact. In their appeal for legitimacy they all looked back to sacred history or sanctified lineages. The Moroccan rulers used the titles "caliph" and "commanders of the faithful," implying that they were rightful successors to the Prophet in temporal affairs, because they were descendants of the Prophet through 'Ali. The early Ottomans such as Bayazid, used the title caliph, as well as sultan, as did the Ottomans of the eighteenth and nineteenth centuries. The Moghuls also called themselves caliphs. The Safavid claim—quite probably false—that they were descended from the Prophet through 'Ali was generally accepted. None of the dynasties turned its back on the longing among Muslims for a universal Islamic state led by a descendant of the Prophet and/or a rightful political successor to the revered caliph or caliphs that had directly succeeded the Prophet. In a sense, the Islamic world continued to be a unit within which intellectual, mercantile, and artisanal elites moved freely.

For all these dynasties except the Moroccans, succession to the Turco-Mongolian heritage was of immense importance. Naturally, they used the title sultan, which had represented authority ever since

Mahmud of Ghazna. The grandiose title *khaqan*, originally reserved for the leader of the descendants of Genghis Khan, was used very commonly by the Ottomans, who also designated the khans of the Crimea, direct descendants of Genghis Khan, as their successors in the unlikely event that all members of the Ottoman house should expire. The Safavids, who used few titles in addition to their regnal names, nevertheless constructed a hierarchy of military officials using the Central Asian Turkish titles *khan* and *beg*, as did the Moghuls and Ottomans—for these titles carried immediate authority with their Turkish-speaking troops. Just as distinctive as the titles used by the Safavids, Ottomans, and Moghuls was their use of the Persian title shah or padishah (king) or shahanshah (king of kings). Safavid territory closely corresponded to the territory of the Sassanian shahs who ruled Iran before Islam; hence their use of the title shah. The centuries-old Iranian tradition of court culture remained the archetype to which not only the Safavid dynasty but also the more distant Ottoman and Moghul dynasties looked back.

All four early modern Islamic dynasties gained as much or more from their reaction to the contemporary world as from their association with the great physical and spiritual lineages. All four gained legitimacy by their fight against non-Muslim powers and therefore proudly bore the title of ghazi. They arose at a time when European Christian powers were assuming control of the sea, and they survived into periods of vigorous European onslaughts by land; thus, their role as ghazis carried great respect.

All four empires made use of the Sufi orders, which had emerged as huge brotherhoods with endowed lodges and teaching institutions supervised by hierarchies of leadership. The Safavid dynasty sprang directly from Sufi leadership to imperial rule. The connection of the Sharifian dynasties of Morocco to local Sufi saints often provided their most vital link to the masses. In Ottoman society, all of the rulers as well as most of the elite were interested in or affiliated with a Sufi order. The Moghuls maintained Sufi leaders as favored members of their court; and Sufi mysticism acted as a bridge to the Hindu mysticism espoused by many of their non-Muslim subjects.

Why did so much of the early modern Islamic world compose itself into fairly stable empires around 1500? For the Ottomans, Safavids, and Moghuls a reinterpretation of the Turco-Mongolian heritage played an important role. All three governments aspired to give legal authority to royal commands and to control the traditional experts of religion more than previous Islamic dynasties. All three drew upon the tradition represented by the Yasa, ascribed to Genghis Khan, which gave a special aura to royal law. The Ottomans did this most successfully; their courts applied Islamic law as well as royal law. All three tried to standardize Islamic law (which ideologically resisted standardization because it accepted an established variety of interpretations). The Ottomans and the Safavids tried to supervise the affairs of the ulama. These attempts at organizing the religiously learned—their legal functions and their assets—did not always work; but they showed an ambition to control and standardize with few precedents in Islamic history.

This drive for central control manifested itself in other areas of government. All three empires, partly in the Mongol tradition, attempted extraordinarily careful surveys of their resources. Nevertheless, all three empires turned their backs on the fairly frequent Turco-Mongolian practice of dividing an empire between royal sons. But, ironically, the Safavids, inheriting the actual personnel and practices of the Turco-Mongolian tradition of administration, at first continued the tradition of assigning provinces to tribal peoples as hereditary "fiefs." Although they later attempted to suppress this system, they were unable to do so; and their failure severely undermined their attempts to build a central army and administration on the Ottoman model.

The Ottomans, Safavids, Moghuls, and Sharifians also owed their origins and ability to endure in part to the economic vitality of their greatest rivals, the Christian Europeans. The growing population and increasing sophistication of the European market gave an advantage to large centralized empires that controlled a significant part of the trade. It was no accident that Bursa, near the Sea of Marmara, a major depot for luxury goods crossing to the Mediterranean world, was for half a century the capital of the infant Ottoman government. The Sharifian dynasties of Morocco pushed hundreds of miles southward to control Timbuktu, the collection point for the gold from the rich West African mines. The Iranians controlled overland trade between the Persian Gulf and the Caspian Sea; in addition, their strong artisanal traditions made their products widely sought and gave them significant exports. The far more numerous Indians also had strong artisanal traditions and, from Roman times on, seem to have had a highly favorable balance of trade with areas to the west. As a result India, which has few sources of precious metal, was probably the most monetized large economy in the world in the sixteenth century; and truly astonishing sums of gold and silver passed through the Indian treasury. The new empires were fiscal empires, interested in enriching royal treasuries, as they sought to wring advantage out of a world market greatly increased by improvement in travel, growth of population, and the rise of Europe.

One European export proved essential to the centralizing activities of the later Islamic empires: guns. It is hard to imagine that the Ottoman Empire would have emerged as *the* Middle Eastern state without gunpowder weapons. The Mamluks were among the world's finest cavalry forces in the fifteenth century, and the Safavid Shah Isma'il had an army completely and selflessly devoted to him; but neither could stand up against Ottoman weapons. The Safavids and Moghuls learned to imitate the Ottoman tradition of gunnery. This achievement not only enabled them to withstand external threats but made them very different kinds of regimes internally. Thanks to guns, they subdued their own realms with unprecedented thoroughness. Whereas earlier empires had to come to terms with the local leaders in remote areas, the new empires could and often did gain direct rule, in some cases replacing small local dynasties whose origins dated back many centuries.

These empires also survived because they became emblematic of the cultural area they ruled. Their territories constituted a cultural area that their subjects felt would exist less fully or even disappear if their dynasties disappeared. Although far from modern nationalism, this sense of a culturally shared identity endured in both the Sharifian and Safavid empires. By the seventeenth century, the Ottoman-Safavid struggle had produced a border that has with small modification lasted to the present.

The Ottomans and Moghuls ruled empires far more ethnically and religiously diverse, but they nevertheless produced distinctive cultural styles, which their elites aspired to imitate. In the Ottoman case, this cultural style implied the knowledge of certain revered and/or admired classics of the Persian and Arabic traditions, the ability to speak and write the ornate form of Ottoman Turkish, and the observance of elaborate norms of polite behavior as defined by court culture. Properly trained, almost any people of the Ottoman Empire, Slavs, Arabs or Turks, could become "Ottomans." In the Moghul case, a distinctively Indian cultural synthesis emerged at the Moghul court. From this synthesis came Urdu, which is a northern Indian dialect written in characters like Persian and sprinkled with words borrowed from Persian, the official language of the Moghul court. Together with its sister language Hindi, essentially the same language but with an alphabet ultimately derived from Sanskrit and with somewhat fewer Persian words, Urdu was to become the most important intercommunal language of the Indian subcontinent.

Seventeenth-century allegorical representation of Shah Abbas I and Jahangir, emperor of India (1605–27). The two rulers embrace while standing on the symbols of peace on a globe of the world.

Artistic Refinement in the Early Modern Islamic Empires

The early modern Islamic dynasties were great patrons of culture, partly by individual whim and partly by political design. Court culture of this period shone most brilliantly in the production of material objects, both of practical and of aesthetic intent. Architecture throughout the region reached an astonishing refinement from the Sa'dian tombs in Morocco to the madrasas of Central Asia. In the central Islamic lands, above all Iran, color-tiled decoration gave buildings a visual brilliance and unity almost unrivaled to this day. The richer Ottomans and Moghuls were able to build enormous stone structures of great dignity, the best known of which is the Taj Mahal in India. Court patronage of painting brought the Persian miniature, with its slightly magical atmosphere, and Moghul painting, with its dramatic realism, to their highest points of perfection. Similarly, textiles such as brocades and rugs, some manufactured in royal workshops, became luxury items widely sought for their beauty on the international market.

The intellectual world did not flourish to the same degree. Practical items were imported and practical skills learned, but mainly to enhance existing cultural forms or to defend against European onslaught. Large numbers of grandfather clocks were imported for mosques, and European seafaring techniques were adopted; yet the more abstract sciences needed to understand and develop technologies were still cultivated largely along traditional Middle Eastern lines with little awareness of European developments. Ibn Khaldun (1332–1406), a North African Muslim scholar who was a highly original social thinker, reflects the difficulty faced in the Islamic world between about 1400 (when he wrote) and about 1800 by those persons curious about European thought and intellectual achievement: "We hear now that the philosophical sciences are greatly cultivated in western Europe . . . Existing systematic expositions of them are said to be comprehensive, the people who know them numerous and the students of them many. God knows best what exists there."

The Resilience of Islamic Societies

From the thirteenth to the eighteenth centuries Islam continued to spread as a world religion. In Central Asia it became the predominant religion, even among the Mongols, whose "paganism" had once seemed such a threat to the Islamic Middle East. Under the Moghuls the numbers of Muslims increased dramatically until Muslims accounted for over one-fifth of the inhabitants of the Indian subcontinent. The East Indies (modern Indonesia) became predominantly Muslim due to the continuing influence of Muslim traders in the Indian Ocean and to the persistence of Indian influence in Southeast Asia. The success of the Mamluks and Ottomans in controlling the Nile Valley and of the Moroccans in extending their state southward contributed to the conversion of a large area in sub-Saharan Africa. The presence of the Ottomans in the Balkans facilitated the conversion to Islam of Albania, Bosnia, and other areas.

The empires cared far more about the extraction of taxes than religious affiliation, however. Conversions were overwhelmingly the result of lay activity such as trade and, above all, the spread of the Sufi brotherhoods. The great majority of Muslims had some Sufi connection, whether they belonged to a Sufi order or merely visited the tombs of Sufi "saints," which existed throughout the Islamic world. Sufi themes dominated Islamic poetry. Sufism's success at directly reaching the masses also accounts for the use of writing in a host of hitherto largely unwritten languages, such as Pushtu in Afghanistan. And international Sufi orders, with chapter houses all the way from the Ottoman Empire to China, facilitated the movement of believers traveling throughout the Islamic world, who found likeminded Sufi "brothers" to give them shelter.

Local elites persisted, although religion often connected local life to much larger units. For example, the tomb of a Sufi saint might connect the villagers living nearby to more important saints' tombs around which yearly pilgrimages and organized Sufi life were centered. And the village Qur'an teacher might send humble boys of great talent to a distant madrasa, where they could rise to the top of the ulama hierarchy. The position of village headman, however, would most likely be hereditary in one of the richer families. As a rule, pastoralists and farmers remained interdependent. The pastoralists would use marginally cultivable land when regimes allowed them to do so, and often villages had longstanding agreements with tribal pastoralists in which food and seasonal land use was exchanged for protection of the village. In the Middle East proper a surprisingly large percentage of the population would alternate between full or part-time pastoralism and full or part-time farming according to political and ecological conditions. Pastoralists, particularly fully nomadic ones, could play an important role in the distribution of power.

In many parts of the Islamic world of this period members of the local elite were called *a'yan*, "notables." The notables usually consisted of landlords, prominent merchants, and locally distinguished religious scholars. This group tended to view themselves as hereditary; they intermarried and claimed ancient origins, but, in fact, people of new wealth became notables fairly easily. The notables had often played an important role as intermediaries between the government and the local community in earlier regimes, but when the new empires were at their strongest, the central governments often bypassed them and instead used bureaucrats assigned to local administrators. Nonetheless, the notables survived, their numbers often strengthened by the addition of former officials, civil and military, or their sons; and by the eighteenth century they had assumed the importance they once held under previous dynasties.

The life of cities was more volatile, reflecting the variety of their interest groups and the presence of government. Most cities were networks of narrow alleyways, overlooked by houses with grilled windows. Large cities were divided into quarters, often with their own

A sixteenth-century drawing of the Turkish city of Bitlis shows a typical Islamic townscape.

gates. The large and more open spaces regularly included the citadel or the governor's residence, the principal mosque (often called the Friday mosque, since Muslims of the region were all expected to gather at one specially designated mosque on Fridays) and the marketplaces. Outside many towns was an enormous area especially designated for the entire local community of Muslims to gather for such communal religious events as the yearly feast of sacrifice and the prayer for rain in times of extreme drought. Imperial cities also had parade grounds, some portion of which might be incorporated into the heart of the city as a central square and, upon occasion, as a royal polo field.

Town and city organization varied greatly, but a number of features recurred. Near the principal mosques, the ritually "cleanest" professions existed, such as the cloth trade; and since wholesale cloth sales were such an important element in big business, other professions that dealt with large sums, such as jewellers and money changers were located nearby. The madrasas and the court of the *qadi*, or judge, were also located near this more desirable part of the market quarter. Since ritual and physical cleanliness were obviously associated, the public baths were there as well. In contrast, professions involving the use of ritually unclean materials (such as animal dung for tanning leather) were placed on the outskirts of town, since these workers had to wash themselves in a specified way before they could pray.

The market inspector supervised the town market, enforcing a variety of rules considered essential to the proper function of the market, such as the use of proper weights or the wearing of proper garments. The market inspector could order summary punishments, some trivial and some intended to terrify, such as nailing a grossly

dishonest shopkeeper by his ear to his shop door. In general, the operation of market forces set prices, and the saying ascribed to Muhammad, that "God sets prices" was widely quoted. In fact, a customer could return goods within three days if she or he could prove that the object sold had hidden defects or that the price was above the prevailing market price. There were also very strict injunctions against hoarding, which amounted to a demand that all goods held by merchants for sale should be offered immediately so that no merchant gain an "unjust" profit margin. The merchant communities generally respected the market inspectors, and so valued their services that in formerly Muslim parts of Spain the Christian merchants perpetuated the office. The Ottomans and Safavids gave new functions to the market inspectors, and their governments tended more and more to control retail prices (see p. 466).

The legal official of highest prestige was the qadi. The qadi not only rendered judgments in his court but also acted as the eyes and ears of the sultan in the maintenance of all the major functions of government. In the case of the Ottomans this included the levy of boys and, in later centuries, the regulation of market prices. Usually a select group of local notables worked closely with the qadi and served as witness-notaries, attesting to important legal acts such as the signature of contracts, manumission of slaves, the establishment of *waqf*s (pious endowments) and the like.

Pious endowments were an enormously important instrument for the recirculation of wealth. They maintained street fountains, hospitals, libraries, madrasas, hostels, tomb gardens, baths, free kitchens, and often all manner of public and semipublic institutions. Through such endowments rulers memorialized their names on earth and won a place in heaven. The endowments also fulfilled the contract by which God gave them sovereignty in exchange for their good and just care of their subjects. In fact, people at all levels of society established endowments out of communal feeling. These pious endowments (guarded for perpetuity by the record in the qadi's court) helped keep social peace in large cities with extremes of wealth and poverty, such as Istanbul, which, in the seventeenth century, had a population of at least seven hundred thousand, larger than its nearest competitors in Europe—London and Paris.

The economic elites, however, held on tenaciously to the basic sources of their wealth, often using the waqf to set up family trusts and keep money in the family. The ranks of the ulama, although open to talented students of humble background, tended to form a hereditary class, who passed on judgeships and teaching positions to their more talented children and the supervision of waqfs to less talented children. Large merchants still maintained networks that reached around the world because—in a world without banks—they were the principal source of risk capital and could invest as silent partners with ship captains and other small traders, who would settle for a relatively limited percentage of the profit. These and other elites held their own and flourished as the empires flourished; but in the seventeenth and eighteenth centuries, when signs of imperial decay appeared and the price revolution disoriented the economies of many parts of the world, both the governments and the elites of the Islamic empires found themselves on the defensive.

Political Decline and Transformation in the Seventeenth and Eighteenth Centuries

The seventeenth and eighteenth centuries saw an end to the expansion of these empires and to their organization as conquest states. Not surprisingly, by the eighteenth century positions tended to become hereditary: the central governments lacked the income to buy and/or train military elites, and they also needed the continuity offered by groups willing to exchange loyalty for the prestige of imperial recognition. But that loyalty was weak, and rebellions were a chronic danger in all the empires. Moreover, the loss of transit trade to Europeans and other economic setbacks shrank the empires' economies. Increasingly, they lost territory to the more able European powers. Yet, despite losses and periods of chaos, the early modern Islamic empires or their successors retained their core territories, which formed the basic elements of later nation-states. Furthermore, the social categories through which they administered society retained a greater degree of institutionalization, even under weak imperial governments, than they had achieved under earlier regimes. The decline of these empires in military power did not necessarily imply the decline of their society and cultures.

The Sharifians and the Safavids Confront Turmoil

Both the Sharifians of Morocco and the Safavids of Iran owed their rule to Sufi backing, sanctified lineage, and a regional cultural identification. Both governments tried to imitate the Ottoman example; both were undone by tribal forces. Paradoxically, the Sharifians of Morocco, who were far less successful at creating central institutions, survived; the Safavids did not.

The first family of Sharifians, the Sa'dians, for all their success in reconstituting a Moroccan political unit between the Ottomans and the Spanish, were too weak to sustain their balancing act between the rivalries of the tribes, the cities, and even the different branches of their family. It was rare when the ulama of Fez and of Marrakech agreed on the successor to any Sa'dian ruler. And if the two most important internal cities of Morocco disagreed, the people on the periphery and even the Ottomans and the Spaniards found ways of interfering in nearly every succession. The weakness of the dynasty resulted in Christians gaining control of port cities, as the Spanish did in 1610. The Sufi holy men whose support had been so vital to the rise of the Sa'dians, now became hostile to them.

Finally, from this disorder, in the mid-seventeenth century, a Sharifian family called the Alawis reconstituted the empire. Their most powerful leader, Moulay Isma'il (1672–1727) created a large new army of black slaves. He also presided over the ejection of Europeans from several port cities, including Tangier, and gained prestige as a great defender of the faith. But ultimately his resources were so slender and the consequent weight of his taxation so heavy, that without his forceful leadership this centralizing process proved impossible to continue. Continual turmoil from Moulay Isma'il's death until the late eighteenth century limited the authority of the central government over its subjects and made the Sharifian the least powerful of the early modern Islamic empires.

The Safavids, as we have seen, succeeded in building an impressive imperial bureaucracy and army under Shah Abbas I. His successors were for the most part mediocre, and it is a tribute to the structures Shah Abbas created that the empire survived at all. After a century of struggle to keep southern Iraq, the Safavids lost this province more or less permanently to the Ottomans in 1638. In the center of the empire the Shi'ite ulama grew more powerful, while in the empire's outer provinces the tribes grew more independent. When Shah Sultan Husayn (1694–1722), who succeeded to the throne in 1694, tried to impose Shi'ism on his distant Sunni Afghan subjects, the Afghans defeated his armies and marched virtually unopposed to Isfahan, the Safavid capital in the heart of Iran, in 1722. A decade of disorder ensued, in which Peter the Great of Russia, the Ottomans, descendants of the Safavids, and Afghan leaders all attempted unsuccessfully to take over the remnants of the Safavid empire.

Then, in the 1730s a Turkish leader named Nader Shah not only reconstituted the empire but soundly beat the powers surrounding Iran. The Russians withdrew from the southern Caspian shores, both Turks and Russians lost hegemony over most of the Caucasus, the Uzbeks were driven from the nearer parts of Central Asia, and—most spectacular of all—Nader Shah in 1739 defeated the Moghuls, sacked Delhi, levied an indemnity of millions of gold pieces, and carried home the world's most elaborate throne—the Peacock Throne— and the world's most famous diamond, the Koh-i-noor. All of this did little to create a durable government because Nader Shah relied on tribal armies, whose loyalty was sustained only by success, and on extortionate taxation. When he was murdered by one of his own tribesmen, Iran again reverted to anarchy until the end of the eighteenth century, only briefly relieved by the benevolent rule of Karim Khan Zand, who controlled much of Iran from his southern capital of Shiraz from 1750 to 1779.

The Slow Decline of the Ottomans

At the death of Suleiman the Magnificent in 1566 it was far from clear to the Ottomans that they had reached the limits of their expansion; if the Ottoman Empire had failed to grow significantly for over a century, it had not shrunk. The Ottomans succeeded in capturing two important islands from the Venetians: Cyprus in 1571 and Crete in 1669. An Ottoman victory against the poorly organized Poles in 1676 made the Ottomans immediate neighbors to the growing power of eastern Europe— Russia. Most of these Ottoman victories were possible because their European opponents were locked in deadly struggles or were undergoing decline within the European system. Ottoman sultans seldom led their troops in battle anymore, and sometimes took little interest in the affairs of state. Fortunately, the grand viziers to whom they confided much of their power were often men of great ability, notably the Koprulu family, who ran the empire for much of the last half of the seventeenth century.

FROM A REGISTER OF PIOUS ENDOWMENTS

■ *The following passage is an entry in the register of the pious endowments of Tangier in Morocco, consisting in the most part of copies of deeds written in the second half of the eighteenth and throughout the nineteenth century.*

When Ahmad ibn Muhammad Al-Susi was named overseer of the pious endowments of the students [attached to] the Great Mosque, he did not find any document establishing these pious endowments. In fear that they might be confused with those of the Great Mosque he decided to make a list of them. The pious endowments of the students consist of a small hostel sharing a wall with the Great Mosque, consisting of fourteen rooms with a fig tree in the middle; the large weavers' workshop opposite the hostel; a room opposite the room for funerals; a room near the shops of the witness-notaries; another room above it; the house Khadda; the oven of the mosque, above which, two apartments; the house of Hajj Abdullah al-Katib; a weavers' workshop in the Aqbal quarters; a shop in the grocers' market; two shops in the perfumers' market; a shop above that of the sons of Ibn Jallul; [another] shop in the perfumers' market; the shop of Haddu; the oven of Zaghmuri; two shops opposite that of Haddu; a shop in the cobblers section; another shop at the end of the cobblers' section; a shop in which is found a shoeing smith and a maker of packsaddles, against the wall of the city; a shop on the small square; a little apartment in ruins at the same place . . . three-quarters of a weavers' workshop, called the workshop of Isa ibn Muqaddin; a weaving loom in the possession of Abd al-Qadir Misbah; a loom in the possession of Ali Azyad; three salt caves in the salt mines of [the district] old Tangier. First of the month Jumada ath-Thaniya 1183 [1769 C.E.]. Witnessed by two witness-notaries.

From *Archives Marocaines XXIII* (1914).

FROM A MANUAL ON SAFAVID ADMINISTRATION

■ The following passage is from a manual on Safavid administration written about 1726. The author is unknown to us but he was thoroughly acquainted with the tradition of later Safavid administration and compiled this manual to explain it to the Afghan leaders who had recently overthrown the Safavids.

The duties of the exalted Market Inspector of the Entire Kingdom. Every month [an official] obtains from the elders of each guild an undertaking concerning the prices of the goods [in which they deal]. Having satisfied himself [as to the accuracy of the document] he seals it and hands it to the Market Inspector of the Entire Kingdom. The latter must confirm every point of it and send it to the Overseer of the Royal Workshop. The latter too considers it and, if he feels satisfied, seals it and passes it on to the Heads of the Departments, in order that, in accordance with it, the Supervisors may draw up the documents for the goods to be bought.

As regards the pricing of the goods sold by guilds to the inhabitants of the town, if any of the artisan-merchants eludes the Market Inspector's regulations, the latter makes him wear a transportable pillory, that he may serve as an example to others.

The Market Inspector of the Entire Kingdom appoints Deputies everywhere in the God-protected provinces. In every place, the traders, month by month, sell goods to people in accordance with the Deputy's certificate [of prices], so that tranquility may reign among the people [the *ra'aya* or "flocks"] and the inhabitants and residents [of towns], and that the latter may pray for the most sacred person of the King.

The Ottoman system had entered a period of internal transformation which, by the seventeenth century, was apparent to intelligent Ottoman statesmen and thinkers. Officials of the empire were no longer devotees of the Ottoman house and the Ottoman way who owed their advancement to the favor of the sultan, but men who owed as much to their family as to their ruler. The Janissary corps had swollen in numbers from about 8,000 in 1527 to about 38,000 in 1609, in part because a larger infantry was needed to use increasingly heavy firearms. They had become unruly, extravagantly expensive, and—in part because of relaxation of the celibacy requirement—a partly hereditary and far less effective military force. A quick turn in Ottoman fortunes revealed their basic military weakness within a decade. In 1683, when the Ottomans marched on Vienna to stop the alliance of the Austrian Habsburgs, the Russians, and the Poles, they were repulsed and repeatedly defeated as they retreated to Istanbul. In 1687 the defeat of the Ottomans at Mohacs ended a century and a half of direct Ottoman rule of Hungary. Further defeats followed, and only the outbreak of war between France and Austria saved the Ottomans. In the landmark Treaty of Karlowitz in 1699, the Ottomans conceded a large part of the Balkans, almost all of Hungary, and even a part of Greece to their enemies. The initiative had passed into the hands of the Europeans, who were checked only by their own rivalries, the rivalries between the European Christian subjects of the Ottomans, and by a modest recovery of Ottoman abilities in the first half of the eighteenth century.

The second half of the eighteenth century was even less favorable to the Ottomans. Russia as the leading Eastern Orthodox power posed as the champion of the Christian population of the Ottomans and stirred up trouble inside the Ottoman Empire while attacking from outside. Ottoman control of local administration had grown so weak that even in Anatolia holders of timars had become semi-independent and these "lords of the valleys" had to be coerced to send the soldiers and taxes they owed the central government. An important point in the Ottoman-Russian duel was the Treaty of Kuchuk Kainarji in 1774, which established the Russians firmly on the Black Sea with rights to navigate past Istanbul to the Mediterranean. Just as important for the future was recognition in the treaty that the Russians had some kind of protectorate over certain Eastern Orthodox institutions in the Ottoman Empire in exchange

More than a century before the 1687 battle of Mohacs, an army of Janissaries led by Suleiman the Magnificent routed the Hungarians under their young king Louis II at the "first battle of Mohacs" in 1526. In this miniature of the battle, Suleiman directs the army from behind a row of cannon.

for a recognition of the Ottoman sultan as the "caliph" of the Muslims with some kind of protectorate over the Muslims of the Crimea. The new extraterritorial character of the Russian-Ottoman confrontation as well as the revival of a hitherto little-regarded Ottoman claim to the caliphate was to have dramatic consequences in the next century and a half.

The Costly Expansion of the Moghuls

After the death in 1605 of Akbar, the administrative founder of the empire, the Moghuls, unlike the Ottomans, had a series of able and energetic leaders. Of these the most militarily successful was Akbar's great-grandson, Aurangzeb. Early Moghul emperors had sparred with the Safavids over control of Qandahar, in what is now southwestern Afghanistan, or led campaigns toward Central Asia, with which—as descendants of Ta-

merlane and Genghis Khan—they felt a natural link. In his long reign from 1658 to 1707 Aurangzeb turned his attention southward and was able to conquer or reduce to vassalage virtually all of the Indian subcontinent, as well as the surrounding northern mountainous regions of the Hindu Kush and The Himalaya. Only Kerala at the southern tip of India and the strongholds of Marathas, warlike tribal people of central India who threw off Moghul rule, successfully resisted Aurangzeb's attacks.

The situation of the Moghuls was fundamentally different from that of the other Islamic empires in that they alone had a population that was overwhelmingly not Muslim. Of all the Moghul emperors, Akbar, a stocky, burly man with a hearty laugh but a regal presence, went the furthest toward making a synthesis of Islamic ideas and non-Islamic Indian culture and religion (much of which we loosely associate under the name of Hinduism). From early in his reign Akbar tried to remove all stigma from being non-Muslim. His only problem was that while a policy of tolerance made sense, and was followed by his son and grandson, it convinced almost none of the Hindu, Muslim, Zoroastrian, Jewish, Jain, and Jesuit holy men he brought to his court, who disliked each other as bitterly after Akbar as before.

Although both emperors were men of great military ability, Aurangzeb was markedly different from his celebrated great-grandfather. Whereas Akbar had a poor education (though an open and extremely keen mind) and was barely literate, Aurangzeb was well-educated and wrote a handsome Persian style, as befitted a Moghul monarch. Aurangzeb was thin and ascetic and had, as one Italian observer wrote, "a craze for being held a saint." He partly reversed Akbar's policy of toleration. He made some Hindus serving in his army pay the poll tax prescribed in Islamic law for non-Muslims in exchange for military exemption. He even showed intolerance for Muslims, such as Shi'ites, who did not fit his vision of religious orthodoxy. He was wise enough, however, to limit most of these acts of intolerance on the grounds of expediency. Through his gift of leadership and strategy, through his lavish bestowal of jagirs to buy the loyalty of his many hesitant vassals, and through sheer doggedness—he was carried in his litter to battles whenever possible right up to his death in his eighty-eighth year—he created an empire that under its surface unity had already begun to unravel.

Aurangzeb had given some of his most intractable enemies, the Maratha leaders, large *mansab*s, or assignments of revenues in order to buy their loyalty. As the empire stopped growing, however, and Aurangzeb spent fortunes to subdue rebels, there were fewer sources of

Portrait of a Great Mogol, *a drawing of Aurangzeb from a seventeenth-century English "Voyage to East India."*

revenue and the mansab holders found that the system could no longer work for them. Moreover, where the Moghul government maintained direct control, it reduced cultivators to misery by attempts to extract higher taxes. On Aurangzeb's death the mansab holders fell to quarreling with one another and supported rival Moghul pretenders.

Older Hindu lineages such as the Rajputs, Marathas, and Jats, and the newer non-Muslim adherents of the Sikh religion asserted their right to autonomy. Like the Muslim-ruled areas around Hyderabad and Oudh, they became self-contained governments. The breakdown of political unity led to disorder in the countryside, a situation that allowed European trading stations to become semi-independent states. By 1764 the British, who had driven the French and Dutch from most of

India a few years earlier, had uncontested control of the Bengal and Bihar, which they ruled as nominal governors of the powerless Moghuls. A surprising feature of this political scene was that many participants in the hurly-burly of Indian politics maintained the fiction that a Moghul empire still existed. This attitude continued right up to the great rebellion of 1857–1858, often called the Sepoy Rebellion, against the British, who were then in overwhelming control. During this uprising the Delhi rebels declared the Moghul ruler Bahadur Shah II emperor of India. The British consequently deposed him and put an end to all vestiges of Moghul rule. The Moghuls represented a claim that the subcontinent was an interrelated system with a center; they also represented the memory that the center had once been the carrier of a high court culture toward which all directed their gaze. That claim and that memory had sustained the twilight of Moghul rule for a remarkably long time.

Society and Culture in the Seventeenth and Eighteenth Centuries

The apparent decline of the four Islamic empires in the late seventeenth and eighteenth centuries can be explained only in part by the internal weaknesses of those empires. Earlier empires—even earlier phases of these early modern Islamic empires—had gone through periods of decentralization and then pulled themselves together. But the military and economic onslaught of Europe had brought about an altogether new situation. It was not only that Europeans were gobbling up the edges of Islamic regimes, but there was a growing awareness among Muslims that the Islamic world could no longer unthinkingly believe itself to be the central civilization of mankind. From the Treaty of Karlowitz in 1699 there were permanent European embassies in Istanbul. All Islamic powers became enmeshed in European patterns of diplomatic relations, hitherto alien, in large part so that they could use the rivalry of European powers to survive.

The Europeans used these diplomatic relations to good advantage in advancing European commercial penetration. Following a Byzantine custom, the Ottomans and other empires issued special rights to foreigners to trade and to govern their own traders abroad in treaties called "regimes of capitulation," which initiated a growing loss of trade to Europeans and—with the growth of foreign trader communities—a loss of sovereignty. Moreover, non-Muslim minorities often had trading partners of the same religious and ethnic affiliation throughout Europe and the Middle East. For example, the Armenians developed a network of trade in Persian

Suleiman receives the Austrian ambassador. Not until 1683 was the Turkish threat removed from Vienna.

silks that extended from India to Amsterdam. These minorities often knew European languages and acted as middle men in the trade between Europeans and the Islamic empires. By the eighteenth century European missionaries had come to educate Middle Eastern Christians, and the Greeks and Armenians of Istanbul often sent their children to the University of Padua in Italy. The rise of non-Muslim trading elites was yet another sign of the degree that the Islamic world was becoming enmeshed in a world economy.

This sense of no longer being in control of their destinies had a different effect on royal courts than it had on the ulama. The courts experienced a great vogue for European objects such as eyeglasses, telescopes, and pocket watches. But the growing gap in scientific development meant that technology could not be imported so easily. The Ottomans and Moghuls were still striving to make huge cannons at a time when Europeans were developing more mobile and accurate cannons. The trade in luxury objects was turning in favor of Europe.

Nevertheless, European objects were one of the important influences on many of the minor arts of the Islamic world, which reached their greatest sophistication in the seventeenth and eighteenth centuries.

Although taste in architecture and min often degenerated into a cloying cuteness a tality in the eighteenth century, the everyday of the wealthy—such as hair scissors, pen cases mal clothing—were of a sumptuous and yet no beauty. Similarly, some of the less-grandiose buildin the period, such as the summer houses of the Ottom nobility along the Bosporus, reflect a uniquely happy marriage of traditional Ottoman style with European rococo taste. Interestingly, while the older literatures of the Middle East, Arabic and Persian, produced few memorable works in this period, Ottoman Turkish poetry, as well as the poetry of newly written languages such as Pushtu and Urdu, produced lyrics of great beauty, in part because this poetry was closer to living vernaculars.

The ulama by and large reacted to European encirclement by becoming more hostile to European influence. In this they partly reflected the mood of the Muslim masses. They also reflected the disgust of many Muslims at the debauchery of the court. Selim II (1566–74), the son and successor of Suleiman the Magnificent, who bore the sobriquet "the Sot," was not the only drunkard among Muslim rulers. All four Safavid rulers who ruled from 1629 to 1722 were enthusiastically given to drinking—forbidden, of course, by Islamic law. Not only did they drink, but many of these seventeenth- and eighteenth-century rulers were patrons of miniature painting of great sensuality, which endeared them even less to the guardians of religion. When in 1727 an Ottoman statesman opened the first printing press owned by a Muslim in the Ottoman Empire, he wisely chose to print only books related to secular matters such as geography and the natural sciences. In the seventeenth century some of the Ottoman ulama waged a war against popular practices such as the use of tobacco and coffee, which was then becoming enshrined in the coffeehouses that would become a basic feature of local life in the Middle East. But in this instance the "consensus of the community," a principle of Islamic law, overwhelmed learned opposition and the ulama acquiesced.

Other influences, not necessarily related to European presence, also profoundly affected the orientation of Muslim religious thought in the eighteenth century. Many Muslims, both Sunni and Shi'ite, both ulama and lay believers, reacted against the highly scholastic Islamic sciences taught in madrasas and called for a renewal of direct imitation of the piety of the Prophet through a study of his sayings. Many Muslims also suggested the pious should take direct action to restore piety and not wait for governments to do so. One such movement to rid Islam of "false" accretions, called

...nth Centuries 469
...ature painting
...nd sentimen-
...possessions
...and for-
...gaudy
...gs of
...an

...nasties
... Empires

	...na raids over half ...continent
	...of Turkish nomads enter the Middle East
...th–14th c.	Mongol empire under Genghis Khan and his descendants, the Il-Khans in Iran and the Golden Horde in Russia
1212	Defeat of Muslims at Las Navas de Tolosa begins their loss of Iberia to the Spanish and Portuguese
1260	Mamluks defeat Mongols at Ain Jalut in Syria
end of 14th c.	Tamerlane reconstitutes empire of the Il-Khans
1389	Battle at Kosovo Polje in Serbia
1492	Fall of Granada; expulsion of Muslims and Jews from Spain
1453	Ottoman sultan Mehmed II takes Constantinople from the Byzantines
1501	Safavid ruler Isma'il assumes title Shah of Iran and later proclaims Twelver Shi'ism the only acceptable form of Islam in his empire
1516	Babur founds Moghul dynasty in India
1517	Ottomans defeat Mamluks at Marj Dabiq in Syria
1520–66	Height of the Ottoman Empire under Suleiman the Magnificent
1550	Sharifian leader Muhammad al-Mahdi captures Fez in Moroccan interior
1571	Spanish and Venetians defeat Ottomans at battle of Lepanto
1587–1629	Safavid dynasty reaches apogee under Shah Abbas I
1590	Sharifians conquer Timbuktu
1672–1727	Reign of Alawi Sharifian leader Moulay Isma'il, who expels Christian powers from port cities of Morocco
1683	Ottomans besiege Vienna but are repulsed
1722	Afghans march unopposed to the Safavid capital Isfahan
1699	Treaty of Karlowitz
1658–1707	Aurangzeb extends Moghul control to virtually all of the Indian subcontinent as well as the Hindu Kush and The Himalaya
1730s	Nader Shah reconstitutes Safavid empire, defeats Moghuls, sacks Delhi
1774	Treaty of Kuchuk Kainarji

Wahhabism after its leader Muhammad 'Abd al-Wahhab (1703–92), grew steadily in political power in Arabia and in intellectual influence throughout the Islamic world, where its austerity was seen as an answer to corruption and decline. Sufi leaders also adapted to the more activist climate of the eighteenth century and took a direct role in politics. The vigor and hope created by these pietistic movements was to persist well into the nineteenth century.

Broadly viewed, the decline of the great empires may have been accompanied by an impoverishment of their peoples and much local disorder, but this by no means meant a decay of the social order. Without doubt, in the eighteenth century the rulers of the great empires lost control of many of their provinces for long periods. Even the Ottomans, the stablest of the empires, had only a hazy control of Egypt and Iraq, which were effectively ruled by local Mamluks. However, all of these early modern Islamic empires, though not states in the modern sense, created or reinforced local structures that persisted through periods of weak central rule and maintained their collective existence even without government supervision. Somehow, the Islamic world emerged from the eighteenth century with its constituent social communities alive and intact.

The important changes that transformed the governments of the Middle Eastern and Islamic world in the period from the Mongol invasions in the thirteenth century to the eve of European colonization in the late eighteenth century were only partly responsible for changes in society and culture. Governments were more centralized, more accustomed to maintaining a body of royal law, more inclined to interfere in the application of Islamic law, and more prone to exact stock taking and exploitation of the resources of their domains. Governments moved toward creating institutions that might have an impersonal life apart from the ruler or his representatives. But government remained largely personal, and neither the reconfiguration of "fiefs" nor the restructuring of military slavery produced categories of people—even in the hearts of these empires—who felt permanently invested in maintaining the central governments' control.

Nevertheless, the empires helped define cultural areas that continued long after central governments failed. Moreover, many aspects of cultural life, in particular material culture, reached their highest development during this period. This high development was due not only to court patronage but also to the activity of certain categories of the population, such as traders and the ulama, who continued to form international elites. In this sense of belonging to an international community, they were joined by ordinary Muslims who felt less encapsulated in imperially defined "states" and more a part of a worldwide Islamic community. Therefore, while some aspects of what in Europe would be considered the "state" had emerged in these empires, by and large society looked to itself and not to its ruling centers for its identity. These early modern empires had respectably long lives—from two centuries among the Safavids to five centuries among the Ottomans. But even when the empires broke down, society proved remarkably resilient, perhaps because society and government, although closer in this period than in earlier periods of Islamic history, were still living together without being married.

SUGGESTIONS FOR FURTHER READING

GENERAL READING

* P. M. Holt, A. K. S. Lambton, and B. Lewis, eds., *Cambridge History of Islam* (Cambridge: Cambridge University Press, 1970). Excellent chapters on each of the early modern Islamic empires along with good surveys of major topics; a standard book in the field and a useful place to find basic historical facts.

* Ira M. Lapidus, *A History of Islamic Societies* (Cambridge: Cambridge University Press, 1988). A fine survey of Islamic history with good chapters on the early modern empires and thoughtful consideration of the role of Islam in shaping Islamic societies.

Francis Robinson, *Atlas of the Islamic World Since 1500* (New York: Facts on File, 1982). Not only an atlas but also a very imaginatively conceived social and cultural history of the period with magnificent illustrations.

THE ISLAMIC WORLD BEFORE THE EARLY MODERN EMPIRES

Ibn Battuta, *The Travels of Ibn Battuta* (Cambridge: Hakluyt Society, 1958–62). A translation—still not complete—of the memoirs of this fourteenth-century world traveler, which gives an unmatched view of the world of Islamic courts, colleges, holy men, and merchants.

* R. Stephen Humphreys, *Islamic History: A Framework For Inquiry* (Princeton: Princeton University Press, 1990). An astute guide to the major themes and problems facing historians of this subject with an expert review of bibliography of the field.

THE ISLAMIC WORLD DIVIDES INTO FOUR EMPIRES

R. M. Savory, *Iran Under the Safavids* (Cambridge: Cambridge University Press, 1980). The best book on the Safavids, with extensive treatment of cultural subjects such as literature.

S. A. A. Rizvi, *The Wonder That Was India*, Vol. II (London: Sidgwick and Jackson, 1987). While waiting for the new volume on the Moghuls in the *Cambridge History of Islam*, this study, which treats the entire subcontinent from 1200 to 1700, gives a useful panorama of most aspects of Moghul history.

Halil Inalcik, *The Ottoman Empire: The Classical Age 1300–1600* (London: Weidenfeld and Nicolson, 1973). A masterly treatment by the doyen of specialists on the Ottomans, strong on administration, trade, learning, and royal law.

* Jamil M. Abun-Nasr, *A History of the Maghrib* (Cambridge: Cambridge University Press, 1975). The standard history of the Maghrib and Andalus with good chapters on the Sa'dians, Alawis, and Ottoman provinces, and a helpful bibliography.

POLITICAL DECLINE AND TRANSFORMATION IN THE SEVENTEENTH AND EIGHTEENTH CENTURIES

Annemarie Schimmel, *The Mystical Dimension of Islam* (Chapel Hill: The University of North Carolina Press, 1975). The best general treatment of Sufism, which was probably the religious orientation of most Muslims during the period covered, with excellent chapters on its intellectual and literary traditions.

Thomas Naff and Roger Owen, eds., *Studies in Eighteenth Century Islamic Society* (Carbondale, IL: Southern Illinois University Press, 1987). A pioneering collection of articles that show that the old paradigm of decline does not fit the continuing vitality of Islamic society in the eighteenth century.

* Indicates paperback edition available.

CHAPTER 16

Nation Building and War: Europe, 1450–1650

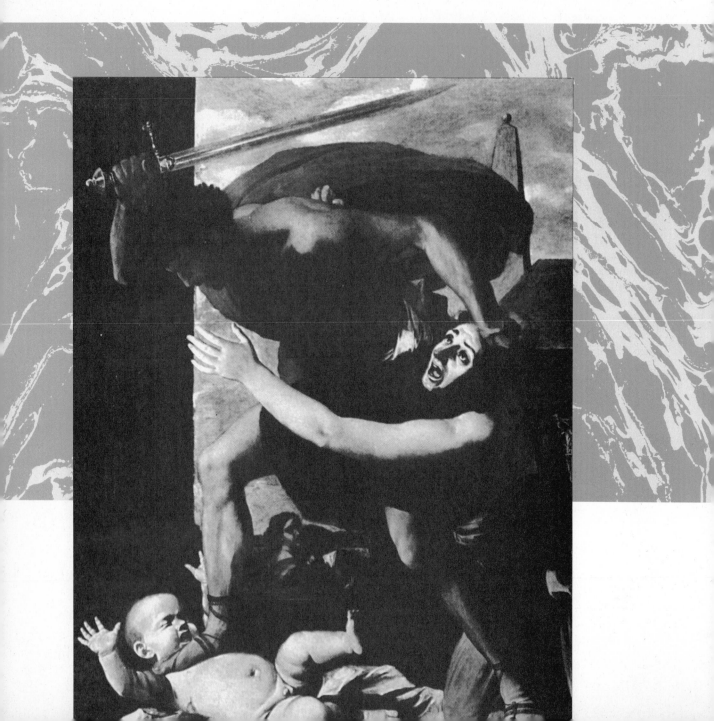

THE MASSACRE OF THE INNOCENTS

"War is one of the scourges with which it has pleased God to afflict men," wrote Cardinal Richelieu (1585-1642), the French minister who played no small part in spreading the scourge. War was a constant of European society and penetrated to its very core. It dominated all aspects of life. It enhanced the power of the state, it defined gender roles, it consumed lives and treasure and commodities ravenously. War affected every member of society from combatants to civilians. There were no innocent bystanders. Grain in the fields was destroyed because it was food for soldiers; houses were burned because they provided shelter for soldiers. Civilians were killed for aiding the enemy or holding out against demands for their treasure and supplies. Able-bodied men were taken forcibly to serve as conscripts, leaving women to plant and harvest as best as they could.

Neither the ancient temple nor the Roman costume can conceal the immediacy of the picture on the facing page. It is as painful to look at now as it was when it was created over 350 years ago. Painted by Nicolas Poussin (1594-1665) at the height of the Thirty Years' War, the *Massacre of the Innocents* remains a horrifying composition of power, terror, and despair. The cruel and senseless slaughter of the innocent baby that is about to take place is echoed throughout the canvas. Between the executioner's legs can be seen a mother clasping her own child tightly and anticipating the fall of the sword. In the background on the right another mother turns away from the scene and carries her infant to safety. In the foreground strides a mother holding her dead child. She tears at her hair and cries in anguish. To a culture in which the image of mother and child—of Mary and Jesus—was one of sublime peacefulness and inexpressible joy, the contrast could hardly be more shocking.

The picture graphically displays the cruelty of the soldier, the helplessness of the child, and the horror of the mother. By his grip on the mother's hair and his foot on the baby's throat, the warrior shows his brute power. The mother's futile effort to stop the sword illustrates her powerlessness. She scratches uselessly at the soldier's back. Naked, the baby boy raises his hands as if to surrender to the inevitable, as if to reinforce his innocence.

To study Europe at war, we must enter into a world of politics and diplomacy, of issues and principles, of judgment and error. There can be no doubt that the future of Europe was decisively shaped by the century of wholesale slaughter from 1555 to 1648, during which dynastic and religious fervor finally ran its course. The survival of Protestantism, the disintegration of the Spanish empire, the rise of Holland and Sweden, the collapse of Poland and Muscovy, the fragmentation of Germany—these were all vital transformations whose consequences would be felt for centuries. We cannot avoid telling this story, untangling its causes, narrating its course, revealing its outcome. But neither should we avoid facing its reality. Look again at the painting by Poussin.

The Formation of States

The early sixteenth century was the age of the prince, the first great stage of nation building that would last for the next three hundred years. The New Monarchies, as they are sometimes called, consolidated territories that were divided culturally, linguistically, and historically. The states of Europe are political units and they were forged by political means: by diplomacy, by marriage, and most commonly by war.

It was Machiavelli who identified the prince as the agent of change in the process of state formation. He believed that the successful prince could bring unity to his lands, security to his borders, and prosperity to his subjects. The unsuccessful prince brought nothing but ruin.

A process as long and as complex as the formation of nations is not subject to the will of individuals, even princes. Factors as diverse as geography, population, and natural resources are all decisive. So too are the structures of human activity. The ways in which families are organized and wealth is transmitted from generation to generation can result in large estates with similar customs or small estates with varying ones. The manner in which social groups are formed and controlled can mean that power is centralized or dispersed. The beliefs of ordinary people and the way they practice them can define who is a part of a community and who is apart from it. All these elements and many others influence the way European states began to develop from medieval monarchies at the end of the fifteenth century. Despite these complexities, we should not lose sight of the simple truth of Machiavelli's observations. In the first stages of the consolidation of European nations, the role of the prince was crucial.

Indeed, in the middle of the fifteenth century there were many factors working against the formation of large states in Europe. The most obvious involved simple things like transportation and communication. The distance that could be covered quickly was very small. In wet and cold seasons travel was nearly impossible. Large areas were difficult to control and to defend. Communication was subject not only to the hazards of travel but also to the distinct languages or dialects of small states. Separate languages meant separate cultures. Customary practices, common ancestry, and shared experiences helped define a sense of community through which small states defined themselves.

In addition to these natural forces that governed the existence of small units of government, there were in-

vented ones. To succeed, a prince had to establish supremacy over a number of rivals. For the most part, states were inherited. In some places it was customary to follow the rule of primogeniture, inheritance by the eldest son. In others, estates were split among sons, or among children of both sexes. Some traditions, like the French, excluded inheritance through women; others, like the Castilian, treated women's claims as equal to men's. Short lives meant prolonged disputes about inheritance. Rulers had to defend their thrones from rivals with strong claims to legitimacy.

So, too, did rulers have to defend themselves from the ambitions of their mightiest subjects. The constant warfare of the European nobility was one of the central features of the later Middle Ages. To avoid resort to arms, princes and peers entered into all manner of alliances, using their children as pawns and the marriage bed as the chessboard. Rulers also faced independent institutions within their states, powerful organizations that had to be won over or crushed. By the end of the fifteenth century, the long process of taming the Church was about to enter a new stage. Fortified towns presented a different problem. They possessed both the manpower and wealth necessary to raise and maintain armies. They also jealously guarded their privileges. Rulers who could not tax their towns could not rule their state. Finally, most kingdoms had assemblies representing the propertied classes, especially in matters of taxation. Some, like the English Parliament and the Spanish Cortes, were strong; others, like the Imperial Diet and the French Estates-General, were weak. But everywhere they posed an obstacle to the extension of the power of princes.

In combination, these factors slowed and shaped the process of state formation. But neither separately nor together were they powerful enough to overcome it. The fragmentation of Europe into so many small units of government made some consolidation inevitable. The practice of dynastic marriage meant that smaller states were continually being inherited by the rulers of larger ones. If the larger state was stable, it absorbed the smaller one. If not, the smaller state would split off again to await its next predator or protector. As the first large states took shape, the position of smaller neighbors grew ever more precarious.

This was especially true by the end of the fifteenth century because of the increase in the destructive power of warfare. Technological advances in cannonry and in the skills of gunners and engineers made medieval fortifications untenable. Gunpowder decisively changed battlefield tactics. It made heavy armor obsolete and allowed for the development of a different type of warfare. Lightly armored horses and riders could not only inflict more damage upon one another, but they were now mobile enough to be used against infantry. Infantry armed with long pikes or small muskets became the crucial components of armies that were growing ever larger. What could not be inherited, or married, could be conquered.

Eastern Configurations

The interplay of factors that encouraged and inhibited the formation of states is most easily observed in the eastern parts of Europe. There the different paths taken by Muscovy and Poland-Lithuania stand in contrast. At the beginning of the sixteenth century, the principality of Muscovy was the largest European political unit. Muscovy had established itself as the heir to the ancient state of Russia through conquest, shrewd political alli-

The sixteenth century saw the introduction of new and powerfully destructive weapons. Many felt that these "murderous engines" would destroy the virtues of chivalry. In this woodcut from 1521, the bows and arrows, lances, and heavy armor of the Middle Ages are challenged by the new cannon.

ances, and the good fortune of its princes to be blessed with long reigns. Muscovy's growth was phenomenal. Under Ivan III, "the Great" (1462–1505), Muscovy expanded to the north and west, annexing Novgorod and large parts of Livonia and Lithuania. Its military successes were almost unbroken, but so too were its diplomatic triumphs. Between 1460 and 1530, Muscovy increased its territory by 1.5 million square miles.

A number of factors led to the rise of Muscovy. The deterioration of the Mongol empire and the fall of Constantinople significantly diminished external threats. And internally, Ivan the Great was fortunate in having no competitors for his throne. He was able to extend power to others to administer the new Muscovite territories without fear of setting up rivals to power. Ivan expanded the privileges of his nobility and organized a military class who received land as a reward for their fidelity. He also extended his sovereignty to cover all lands to which there was an ancient Russian claim and combined it with the religious authority of the Orthodox church. Both he and his successors ruled with the aid of able Church leaders who were normally part of the prince's council.

What made the expansion of Muscovy so impressive is that land once gained was never lost. The military and political achievements of Ivan the Great were furthered by his son Vasili and his more famous grandson Ivan IV, "the Terrible" (1533–84). Ivan IV defeated the Mongols on his southeastern border and incorporated the entire Volga basin into Muscovy. But his greatest ambition was to gain a Livonian port on the Baltic Sea and establish a northern outlet for commerce. Nearly three decades of warfare between Muscovy and Poland-Lithuania, with whom Livonia had allied itself, resulted in large territorial gains, but never the prized Baltic port. And Ivan's northern campaigns seriously weakened the defense of the south. In 1571 the Crimean Tartars advanced on Muscovy's southwestern border and inflicted a powerful blow when they burned the city of Moscow. Although the Tartars were eventually driven off Muscovite soil, expansion in both north and south was at an end for the next seventy-five years.

By the reign of Ivan IV, Muscovite society was divided roughly into three groups: the hereditary landed nobility known as the boyars, the military service class, and the peasantry who were bound to the land. There was no large mercantile presence in Muscovy and its urban component remained small. The boyars inherited their lands and owed little to the tsar. Members of the military class, however, depended on the success of the crown for the possession of their estates, which were granted out of lands gained through territorial expansion.

Europe, ca. 1500

Gradually the new military service class grew in power and prestige, largely at the expense of the older boyars. Ivan IV used members of the military service class as legislative advisors and elevated them in his parliamentary council (the Zemsky Sobor), which also contained representatives of the nobility, clergy, and towns.

Unlike his grandfather, Ivan IV had an abiding mistrust of the boyars. They had held power when he was a child and it was rumored that they had poisoned his mother. It was in his treatment of the boyars that he earned the nickname "the Terrible." During his brutal suppression of supposed conspiracies, several thousand boyar families were massacred by Ivan's orders, and thousands more were forcibly relocated. This practice made the boyars' situation similar to that of the military service class, who owed their fortunes to the tsar.

All of these measures contributed to the breakdown of local networks of influence and power and to a disruption of local governance. But they also made possible a system of central administration, one of Ivan IV's most important achievements. He created departments of state to deal with the various tasks of administration, such as revenues and the military. He created new boyars, who owed their positions and loyalty to him. Both boyars and the military benefited from Ivan's policy of binding the great mass of people to the land. Russian

peasants had few political or economic rights in comparison to western peasants, but during the early sixteenth century even their meager rights were curtailed. Binding the peasants in serfdom to the land made possible the prolonged absence of military leaders from their estates and contributed to the creation of the military service class. But in the long term, serfdom retarded economic development by removing incentive from large landholders to make investments in commerce or to improve agricultural production.

Following the death of Ivan the Terrible in 1584, the Muscovite state began to disintegrate. Ivan had murdered his heir in a fit of anger and left his half-witted son to inherit the throne. This led to a vacuum of power at the center as well as a struggle for the spoils of government that lasted for thirty years. When Michael Romanov (1613–45) was chosen tsar by an assembly of landholders, he only gradually restored order.

The growth of an enlarged and centralized Muscovy stands in contrast to the experiences of Poland-Lithuania during the same period. At the end of the fifteenth century Casimir IV (1447–92) ruled the kingdom of Poland and the grand duchy of Lithuania. His son Vladislav II ruled Bohemia (1471–1516) and Hungary (1490–1516). Had the four states been permanently consolidated, they could have become an effective barrier to Ottoman

A delegation of Russian boyars bearing gifts visited the Holy Roman Emperor Maximilian II in 1576 to seek his aid against Poland-Lithuania.

expansion in the south and Russian expansion in the east. But the union of crowns had never been the union of states. It had taken place over the previous century by political alliances, diplomatic marriages, and the consent of the nobility. Such arrangements kept peace among the four neighbors, but it kept any one of them from becoming a dominant partner.

There were many reasons why a unified state did not appear in east central Europe as it did in Muscovy. In the first place, external forces disrupted territorial and political arrangements. Wars with the Ottomans and the Russians absorbed resources. Second, the princes faced internal rivals to their crowns. Though Casimir IV was able to place his son on the thrones of both Bohemia and Hungary, his success necessitated concessions to leading citizens, which decreased the ability of the princes to centralize their kingdoms or to effect real unification among them. The nobility of Hungary, Bohemia, and Poland-Lithuania all developed strong local interests that increased over time. In Bohemia, Vladislav II was king in name only, and even in Poland the nobility won confirmation of its rights and privileges from the monarchy.

Until the end of the sixteenth century, Poland-Lithuania was the dominant power in the eastern part of Europe. The permanent union of the two separate states in 1569 made it economically healthy and militarily powerful. Through its Baltic ports, especially Gdansk, Poland played a central role in international commerce and was a leader in the northern grain trade. Matters of war and peace, of taxation, and of reform were placed under the strict supervision of the Polish Diet, a parliamentary body that represented the landed elite. But the failure of the Jagiellon monarchy in Poland to produce an heir ended that nation's most successful line of kings and forced the Polish nobility and gentry to peddle their throne among the princes of Europe. Successively, a French duke, a Hungarian prince, and finally in 1587 the heir to the Swedish throne, Sigismund III (1587–1632), were elected. As in Muscovy, the absence of strong rule led to military and economic decline by the beginning of the seventeenth century.

The Western Powers

Just as in the east, there was no single pattern to the consolidation of the large western European states. They, too, were internally fragmented and externally imperiled. While England had to overcome the ruin of decades of civil war, France and Spain faced the challenges of invasion and occupation. Western European princes struggled against powerful institutions and individuals within their states. Some they conquered, others they absorbed. Each nation formed its state differently: England by administrative centralization, France by good fortune, and Spain by dynastic marriage. Yet in 1450 few imagined that any one of these states would succeed.

The Taming of England. England was the only European state that suffered no threat of foreign invasion during the fifteenth century. This island fortress might easily have become the first consolidated European state were it not for the ambitions of the nobility and the weakness of the Crown. For thirty years the English aristocracy fought over the spoils of a helpless monarch. The Wars of the Roses (1455–85), as they came to be called, were as much a free-for-all among the English peerage as they were a contest for the throne between the houses of Lancaster and York. At their center was an attempt by the dukes of York to wrest the crown from the mad and ineffective Lancastrian king Henry VI (1422–61). All around the edges was the continuation of local and family feuds that had little connection to the dynastic struggle.

Three decades of intermittent warfare virtually destroyed the houses of Lancaster and York. Edward IV (1461–83) succeeded in gaining the crown for the House of York, but he never wore it securely. When he died, his children, including his heir, Edward V (1483), were placed in the protection of their uncle Richard III (1483–85). The two boys disappeared, reputedly murdered in the Tower of London, and Richard declared himself king. Richard's usurpation led to civil war, and he was killed by the forces of Henry Tudor at the battle of Bosworth Field in 1485. By the end of the Wars of the Roses the monarchy had lost both revenue and prestige, and the aristocracy had stored up bitter memories for the future.

Henry Tudor picked up the pieces of the kingdom, as legend has it he picked up the crown off a bramble bush. The two chief obstacles to his determination to consolidate the English state were the power of the nobility and the poverty of the monarchy. No English monarch had held secure title to the throne for over a century. Henry Tudor, as Henry VII (1485–1509), put an end to this dynastic instability at once. He married Elizabeth of York, and their children were indisputable successors to the crown. He also began the long process of taming his overmighty subjects. Traitors were hung and turncoats rewarded. He and his son Henry VIII (1509–47) adroitly created a new peerage, who owed their titles and loyalty to the Tudors. They were favored with offices and spoils and were relied upon to suppress both popular and aristocratic rebellions.

The financial problems of the English monarchy were not so easily overcome. An English king was supposed to live "of his own," that is, off the revenues from his own estates. Only in extraordinary circumstances were the king's subjects required to contribute to the maintenance of government. This principle was defended through the representative institution, the Parliament. When the kings of England wanted to tax their subjects, they first had to gain the assent of Parliament. Though Parliaments did grant requests for extraordinary revenue, especially for national defense, they did so grudgingly. The English landed elites were not exempt from taxation, but they were able to control the amount of taxes they paid.

The inability of the Crown to extract its living from its subjects fostered the efficient management of the royal estates. Thus English state building depended upon the growth of centralized institutions that could oversee royal lands and collect royal customs. Gradually, medieval institutions like the Exchequer were supplanted by newer organs that were better able to adjust to modern methods of accounting, record keeping, and enforcement. Whether Henry's reputation for greed and rapacity was warranted, it was undeniable that he squeezed as much as possible from a not very juicy inheritance. His financial problems limited both domestic and foreign policy.

Not until the middle of the next reign was the English monarchy again solvent. As a result of his dispute with the papacy, Henry VIII confiscated the enormous wealth of the Catholic church, and with one stroke solved the Crown's monetary problems (see chapter 13). But the real contribution that Henry and his chief minister, Thomas Cromwell (ca. 1485–1540), made to forming an English state was the way in which this windfall was administered. Cromwell accelerated the centralization of government that had begun under Edward IV. He created separate departments of state to handle the various administrative functions—record keeping, revenue collection, law enforcement, etc. Each had a distinct jurisdiction and a permanent, trained staff. Cromwell coordinated the work of these departments by expanding the power of the Privy Council, which included the heads of these administrative bodies and which came to serve as the king's executive.

ANNE BOLEYN'S SPEECH FROM THE SCAFFOLD (1536)

■ *Anne Boleyn was the second wife of Henry VIII and the mother of Elizabeth I. Henry's desire to have a son and his passion for Anne resulted in his divorce from Catherine of Aragon and England's formal break with the Roman Catholic church. When Anne bore only a daughter she too became dispensable. She was convicted of adultery and incest and executed in 1536. Here are her last words.*

Good friends, I am not come here to excuse or to justify myself, for as much as I know full well that aught that I could say in my defense doth not appertain unto you, and that I could draw no hope of life from the same. But I come here only to die, and thus to yield myself humbly to the will of the King my Lord. And if in my life I did ever offend the King's grace, surely with my death I do now atone for the same. And I blame not my judges, nor any other manner of person, nor anything save the cruel law of the land by which I die. But be this, and be my faults as they may, I beseech you all, good friends, to pray for the life of the King my sovereign lord and yours, who is one of the best princes on the face of the earth, and who hath always treated me so well that better could not be; wherefore I submit to death and with a good will, humbly asking pardon of the world.

Holbein's last portrait of Henry VIII, 1542. Henry made England into one of the world's greatest naval powers but embroiled the kingdom in a series of costly foreign wars. He married six times in an effort to produce a legitimate male heir.

Cromwell also saw the importance of Parliament as a legislative body. Through Parliament, royal policy could be turned into statutes that had the assent of the political nation. If Parliament was well managed, issues that were potentially controversial could be defused. Laws passed by Parliament were more easily enforced locally than were proclamations issued by the king.

The Unification of France. Perhaps the most remarkable thing about the unification of France is that it took place at all. The forces working against the consolidation of a French state were formidable. France was surrounded by aggressive and powerful neighbors with whom it was frequently at war. Its greatest nobles were semi-independent princes who were constant rivals for the throne and consistent opponents of the extension of royal power. The French people were deeply suspicious

of the pretensions of the monarchy and fiercely loyal to their province and its local customs and institutions. And France was splintered by profound regional differences. The north and south were divided by culture and by language (the *langue d'oc* in the south and the *langue d'oïl* in the north).

The first obstacles that were overcome were the external threats to French security. For over a century the throne of France had been contested by the kings of England. The so-called Hundred Years' War (1337–1453) originated in a dispute over the inheritance of the French crown and English possessions in Gascony in southern France (see chapter 10).

The problems posed by the Hundred Years' War were not just those of victory and defeat. The struggle between the kings of England and the kings of France allowed French princes and dukes, who were nominally vassals of the king, to enhance their autonomy by making their own alliances with the highest bidder. When the English were finally driven out of France in the middle of the fifteenth century, the kings of France came into a weakened and divided inheritance.

Nor was England the only threat to the security of the French monarchy. On France's eastern border, in a long arching semicircle, were the estates of the dukes of Burgundy. The dukes of Burgundy and the kings of France shared a common ancestry; both were of the House of Valois. Still, the sons of brothers in one generation were only cousins in the next, and the two branches of the family grew apart. The original Burgundian inheritance was in the southeast, centered at Dijon. A good marriage and good fortune brought to the first duke the rich northern province of Flanders. For the next hundred years, by marriage and through force, the dukes of Burgundy managed to unite their divided estates in one long unbroken string. But it was a string stretched taut. The power of Burgundy threatened its neighbors in all directions. Both France and the Holy Roman Empire were too weak to resist its expansion, but the confederation of Swiss towns to the southwest of Burgundy was not. In a series of stunning military victories Swiss forces repelled the Burgundians from their lands and demolished their armies. Charles the Bold, the last Valois duke of Burgundy, fell at the battle of Nancy in 1477. His estates were quickly dismembered. France recovered its ancestral territories, including Burgundy itself, and through no effort of its own was now secure on its eastern border.

The king most associated with the consolidation of France was Louis XI (1461–83). He inherited an estate exhausted by warfare and civil strife. More by chance than by plan he vastly extended the territories under the dominion of the French crown and, more importantly, subdued the nobility. Louis XI was as cunning as he was peculiar. In an age in which royalty was expressed through magnificence, Louis sported an old felt hat and a well-worn coat. His enemies constantly underestimated his abilities, which earned him the nickname "the Spider." But gradually during the course of his reign, Louis XI won back what he had been forced to give away. Years of fighting both the English and each other depleted the ranks of the French aristocracy and the stocks of fathers and sons ran low. Estates with no male heirs fell forfeit to the king. In this manner the crown absorbed Anjou and Maine in the northwest and Provence in the south. And by brilliant political marriages for his son and daughter, Louis XI ultimately obtained control of the two greatest independent fiefs, Brittany and Orléans. When in 1527 the lands of the duke of Bourbon fell to the crown, the French monarch ruled a unified state.

The consolidation demonstrated how a state could be formed without the designs of a great leader. Neither Louis XI nor his son Charles VIII (1483–98) were nation builders. Louis's main objective was always to preserve his estate. And considerable good fortune saved him from the consequences of many ill-conceived policies. But no amount of luck could make up for Louis's failure to obtain the Burgundian Low Countries for France after the death of Charles the Bold in 1477. The marriage of his daughter and heir Mary of Burgundy to Maximilian of Habsburg initiated the struggle between France and Spain for control of the Low Countries that endured for over two centuries.

These long years of war established the principle of royal taxation, which was so essential to the process of state building in France. This enabled the monarchy to raise money for defense and for consolidation. Because of the strength of the nobles, most taxation fell only on the commoners, the so-called third estate. The *taille* was a direct tax on property, from which the nobility and clergy were exempt. The *gabelle* was a consumption tax on the purchase of salt in most parts of the kingdom, and the *aide* was a tax on a variety of commodities including meat and wine. These consumption taxes were paid by all members of the third estate no matter how poor they might be. In spite of complaints, the French monarchy established a broad base for taxation and a high degree of compliance long before any other European nation.

Along with money went soldiers, fighting men necessary to repel the English and to defend the crown against rebels and traitors. Again the French monarchy established a first, the principle of a national army,

raised and directed from the center but quartered and equipped regionally. Originally towns were required to provide artillery, but constant troubles with the nobility had led the kings of France to establish their own store of heavy guns. The towns supplied small arms, pikes, and swords and later pistols and muskets. By the beginning of the sixteenth century the French monarch could raise and equip an army of his own.

Taxation and military obligation demanded the creation and expansion of centralized institutions of government. This was the most difficult development in the period of state formation in France. The powers of royal agents were constantly challenged by the powers of regional nobles. It is easy to exaggerate the extent of the growth of central control and to underestimate the enduring hold of regional and provincial loyalties. Even the crown's absorption of estates did not always end local privileges and customs. But despite continued regional autonomy, a beginning had been made.

The Marriages of Spain.   Before the sixteenth century there was little prospect of a single nation emerging on the Iberian Peninsula. North African Muslims called Moors occupied the province of Granada in the south, while the stable kingdom of Portugal dominated the western coast. The Spanish peoples were divided among a number of separate states. The two most important were Castile and Aragon. Three religions and four languages (not including dialects) widened these political divisions. And the different states had different outlooks. Castile was, above all, determined to subjugate the last of Islamic Spain and to convert its large Jewish population to Christianity. Aragon played in the high-stakes game for power in the Mediterranean. It claimed sovereignty over Sicily and Naples and exercised it whenever it could.

A happy teenage marriage brought together the unhappy kingdoms of Castile and Aragon. When Ferdinand of Aragon and Isabella of Castile secretly exchanged wedding vows in 1469, both their homelands were rent by civil war. In Castile, Isabella's brother Henry IV (1454–74) struggled unsuccessfully against the powerful Castilian nobility. In Aragon, Ferdinand's father, John II (1458–79), faced a revolt by the rich province of Catalonia on one side and the territorial ambitions of Louis XI of France on the other. Joining the heirs together increased the resources of both kingdoms. Ferdinand took an active role in the pacification of Castile, while Castilian riches allowed him to defend Aragon from invasion. In 1479 the two crowns were united and the Catholic monarchs, as they were called,

An idealized portrait of Ferdinand and Isabella shows the Catholic monarchs reigning in Renaissance style surrounded by richly costumed courtiers.

ruled the two kingdoms jointly. But the unification of the crowns of Castile and Aragon was not the same as the formation of a single state. Local privileges were zealously guarded, especially in Aragon, where the representative institutions of the towns, the Cortes, were aggressively independent. The powerful Castilian nobility never accepted Ferdinand as their king and refused him the crown after Isabella's death.

But Ferdinand and Isabella (1479–1516) took the first steps toward forging a Spanish state. Their most notable achievement was the final recovery of the lands that had been conquered by the Moors. For centuries the Spanish kingdoms had fought against the North African Muslims who had conquered large areas of the southern peninsula. The *reconquista* was characterized by short bursts of warfare followed by long periods of wary coexistence. The final stages of the reconquista began in 1482 and lasted for a decade. It was waged as a holy war and was financed in part by grants from the pope and the Christian princes of Europe. It was a bloody undertaking, but in 1492 Granada, the only remaining Moorish stronghold, finally fell and the province was absorbed into Castile.

The reconquista helped create a national identity for the Christian peoples of Spain. In order to raise men and money for the war effort, Ferdinand and Isabella mobilized their nobility and town governments and created a central organization to oversee the invasion. The conquered territories were used to reward those who had aided the effort, though the crown maintained control and jurisdiction over most of the province. But the idea of the holy war also had a darker side and an unanticipated consequence. The Jewish population that had lived peacefully in both Castile and Aragon became another object of hostility. Many Jews had risen to prominence in government and in skilled professions. Others, who had accepted conversion to Christianity and were known as *conversos*, had become among the most powerful figures in the Church and the state.

Both groups were now attacked. The conversos fell prey to a special Church tribunal created to examine their sincere devotion to Catholicism. This was the Spanish Inquisition which, though it used traditional judicial practices—torture to gain confessions, public humiliation to show contrition, and burnings at the stake to maintain purity—used them on a scale never before seen. Thousands of conversos were killed and many more families had their wealth confiscated to be used for the reconquista. In 1492 the Jews themselves were expelled from Spain. Though the reconquista and the expulsion of the Jews inflicted great suffering upon victims and incalculable loss to the Castilian economy, both events enhanced the prestige of the Catholic monarchs.

In many ways, Ferdinand and Isabella trod the paths of the medieval monarchy. They relied upon personal contact with their people more than upon the use of a centralized administration. They frequently dispensed justice personally, sitting in court and accepting petitions from their subjects. Queen Isabella was venerated in Castile, where women's right to inheritance remained strong. Ferdinand's absences from Aragon were always a source of contention between him and the Cortes of the towns. Yet he was careful to provide regents to preside in his absence and regularly returned to visit his native kingdom.

Ferdinand and Isabella consciously sought to bring about a permanent union. Ferdinand made Castilian the official language of government in Aragon and even appointed Castilians to Aragonese posts. He and Isabella actively encouraged the intermarriage of the two aristocracies and the expansion of the number of wealthy nobles who held land in both kingdoms. Nevertheless, these measures did not unify Spain or erase the centuries-long tradition of hostility among the diverse Iberian peoples.

Heroic portrait of the Emperor Charles V by Titian, 1547. The emperor is shown at the battle of Mühlberg, which paved the way for the Peace of Augsburg of 1555.

Yet neither his personal efforts to rule as a Spanish monarch, nor those of his able administrators were the most important factor in uniting the Spanish kingdoms of Iberia. Rather it was the fact that Charles V brought Spain to the forefront of European affairs in the sixteenth century. Spanish prowess, whether in arms or in culture, became a source of national pride that helped erode regional identity. Gold and silver from the New World helped finance Charles's great empire. In Italy he prosecuted Aragonese claims to Sicily and Naples; in the north he held on firmly to the kingdom of Navarre, which had been annexed by Ferdinand and which secured Spain's border with France. In the south he blocked off Ottoman and Muslim expansion. The reign of Charles V ushered in the dawn of Spain's golden age.

The process by which European kingdoms became states was long and involved. The first steps were taken all over the continent at the end of the fifteenth century. Inheritance, dynastic marriages, and wars of conquest expanded territory under the domination of a single monarch. Bureaucracy, the spread of legal jurisdiction, and the extraction of resources through taxation expanded the monarch's internal control. In kingdoms as diverse as Muscovy and Spain, Poland-Lithuania, and England a similar process was under way, a process that would define European history for centuries to come.

It was left to the heirs of Ferdinand and Isabella to forge together the Spanish kingdoms, and the process was a painful one. The hostility to a foreign monarch increased dramatically at the accession of their grandson, who became the emperor Charles V (1516–56) and who had been born and raised in the Low Countries, where he ruled over Burgundy and the Netherlands. Through a series of dynastic accidents, Charles was heir to the Spanish crown with its possessions in the New World and to the vast Habsburg estates that included Austria. Charles established his rule in Spain gradually. For a time he was forced to share power in Castile and to suppress a disorganized aristocratic rebellion.

Because of his foreign obligations, Charles was frequently absent from Spain. During those periods he governed through regents and royal councils that helped centralize administration. Charles V realized the importance of Spain, especially of Castile, in his empire. He established a permanent bureaucratic court, modeled on that of Burgundy, and placed able Spaniards at the head of its departments. This smoothed over the long periods when Charles was abroad.

The Dynastic Struggles

The formation of large states throughout Europe led inevitably to conflicts among them. Thus the sixteenth century was a period of almost unrelieved warfare that took the whole Continent as its theater. Advances in technology made war more efficient and more expensive. They also made it more horrible. The use of artillery against infantry increased the number of deaths and maiming injuries, as did the replacement of the arrow by the bullet. As the size of armies increased, so did casualties.

Power and Glory

The frequency of offensive war in the sixteenth century raises a number of questions about the militaristic values of the age. Valor remained greatly prized—a Renaissance virtue inherited from the crusading zeal and chivalric ideals of the Middle Ages—and princes sought to do valiant deeds. Ferdinand of Aragon and Francis I

(1515–47) of France won fame for their exploits in war. Charles the Bold and Louis II of Hungary were less fortunate. Their battlefield deaths led to the breakup of their states. Wars were fought to further the interests of princes rather than the interests of national sovereignty or international Christianity. They were certainly not fought in the interests of their subjects. States were an extension of a prince's heritage; what rulers sought in battle was a part of their historical and familial rights, which defined themselves and their subjects. The wars of the sixteenth century were dynastic wars.

Along with desire came ability. The New Monarchs were capable of waging war. The very definition of their states involved accumulating and defending territories. Internal security depended upon locally raised forces or hired mercenaries. Both required money, which was becoming available in unprecedented quantities as a result of the increasing prosperity of the early sixteenth century and the windfall of gold and silver from the New World. Professional soldiers, of whom the Swiss and Germans were the most noteworthy, sold their services to the highest bidders. Developments in transport and supply meant campaigns could take place far from the center of a state. Finally, communications were improving. The need to know about potential rivals or allies strengthened the European system of diplomacy. Princes installed agents in all the European capitals, and their dispatches were the most reliable sources of information about the strengths of armies or the weaknesses of governments, about the birth of heirs or the death of princes.

Personality also influenced the international warfare of the early sixteenth century. The three most consistent protagonists, Charles V, Francis I, and Henry VIII, were of similar age and outlook. Each came unexpectedly to his throne in the full flush of youth, eager for combat and glory. The three were self-consciously rivals. Henry VIII and Francis I held wrestling bouts when they met in 1520. Francis I challenged Charles V to single combat after the French king's humiliating imprisonment in Madrid in 1526. As the three monarchs aged, their youthful wars of conquest matured into strategic warfare designed to maintain a Continental balance of power.

Habsburg and Valois

The struggle for supremacy in Europe in the sixteenth century pitted the French House of Valois against the far-flung estates of the Habsburg empire. In order for one house or the other to succeed, it was necessary to construct alliances among the various Italian city-states and most especially with England, whose aid both Charles and Francis sought in the early 1520s. Henry VIII was eager to reconquer France and cut a figure on the European scene. Despite the fact that his initial Continental adventures had emptied his treasury without fulfilling his dreams, Henry remained hungry for war. Charles V made two separate trips to London, while Henry crossed the Channel in 1520 to meet Francis I in one of the gaudiest displays of conspicuous consumption that the century would witness, appropriately known as the Field of the Cloth of Gold.

The result of these diplomatic intrigues was an alliance between England and the Holy Roman Empire. English and Burgundian forces would invade northern France while Spanish and German troops would attempt to dislodge the French forces from Italy. The strategy worked better than anyone could have imagined. In 1523 Charles's forces gained a foothold in Milan by taking the heavily fortified town of Pavia. Two years later Francis was ready to strike back. At the head of his own royal guards, he massed Swiss mercenaries and French infantry outside Pavia and made ready for a swift assault. Instead, a large imperial army arrived to relieve the town, and in the subsequent battle the French suffered a shattering defeat. Francis I was captured.

The Field of the Cloth of Gold, the lavish setting for the meeting between Henry VIII and Francis I in June 1520. The fountain in the foreground provides free wine for all.

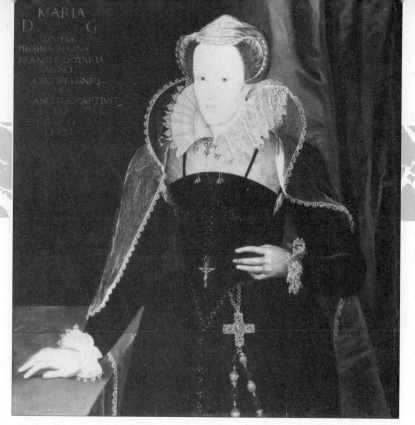

Portrait of Mary, Queen of Scots.

The Monstrous Regiment of Women

"To promote a woman to bear rule, superiority, dominion or empire above any realm, nation, or city is repugnant to nature, contumely to God, and the subversion of good order, of all equity and justice." So wrote the Scottish theologian John Knox (1513-72) in *The First Blast of the Trumpet Against the Monstrous Regiment of Women* (1558). Though he made his points more emphatically than many others, Knox was only repeating the commonplace notions of his day. He could quote Aristotle and Aquinas as well as a host of secular authorities to demonstrate female inadequacies:

"Nature, I say, doth paint them forth to be weak, frail, impatient, feeble, and foolish." He could quote Saint Paul along with the ancient Fathers of the Church to demonstrate the "proper" place of women—"Man is not of the woman, but the woman of the man."

But no stacking up of authorities, no matter how numerous or revered, could erase the fact that all over Europe in the sixteenth century women could and did rule. In the Netherlands Mary, Queen of Hungary (1531-52) and Margaret of Parma (1559-67) were successful regents. Jeanne d'Albret (1562-72) was queen of the tiny state of Navarre, territory claimed by both France and Spain but kept independent by this remarkable woman. Catherine de Médicis (1560-89), wife of one king of France and mother of three others, was the effective ruler of that nation for nearly thirty years. Mary, Queen of Scots (1542-87) was the nominal ruler of Scotland almost from her birth. England was ruled by two very different women, the Catholic Mary I (1553-58) and her Protestant half-sister Elizabeth I (1558-1603).

The problems faced by this long list of queens and regents were more than just the ordinary cares of government. The belief that women were inherently inferior in intelligence, strength, and character was so pervasive that for men like Knox, a woman ruler was almost a contradiction in terms.

Yet this was not the view taken by everyone, and female rule had its defenders as well as its detractors. One set of objections was overcome by the traditional medieval theory of the two bodies of the monarch. This argument was developed to reconcile the divine origins and functions of monarchs with their very real human frailties. In the theory of the two bodies, there was the body natural and the body politic. Both were joined together in the person of the ruler but the attributes of each could be separated. Rule of a woman did nothing to disrupt this notion. In fact, it made it easier to argue that the frailties of the body natural of a woman were in no way related to the strengths of the body politic of a monarch.

While such ideas might help a female ruler to be accepted by her subjects, they did little to invigorate her own sense of her role. Female rulers often strained against the straitjacket that definitions of gender placed them in. When angered, Elizabeth I would proclaim that she had more courage than her father, Henry VIII, "though I am only a woman." Mary, Queen of Scots, once revealed that her only regret was that she "was not a man to know what life it was to lie all night in the fields or to walk with a buckler and a broadsword." Some queens assumed masculine traits, riding in armor or leading forces to battle. Other women rulers mixed together characteristics that were usually separated by gender definitions. Margaret of Parma was considered one of the most accomplished horse riders of her day. After leading her courtiers through woods and fields at breakneck speed, she would then attend council meetings and work on her needlepoint. Mary, Queen of Scots, loved hawking, a traditional kingly sport in the Scottish wilds. After relishing the hawk's destruction of its prey, she liked to negotiate matters of state by beginning with tears and entreaties and ending with accusations and threats. The effect was more than discomforting.

Women were no more nor less successful as rulers than were men. Women's achievements, like men's, depended upon strength of character and the circumstances of the times. All the women rulers of the sixteenth century had received outstanding educations. Whether raised Catholic or Protestant, each was trained in Latin as well as modern languages, in the liberal arts, and in fine arts.

Mary, Queen of Scots, was the only one of these female rulers born to rule. She was the sole survivor of her father, who died shortly after her birth. Mary and Elizabeth Tudor came to their thrones after the death of their younger brother Edward VI; Mary of Hungary and Margaret of Parma came to theirs as princesses of the House of Habsburg. The rule of Catherine de Médicis was the most unexpected of all. Her vigorous husband, Henry II, died during a jousting tournament and her eldest son, Francis II, husband of Mary, Queen of Scots, died the following year. Instead of retirement as a respected queen dowager—the widow of a previous king—Catherine de Médicis was forced into the vortex of French politics to protect the rights of her ten-year-old son, Charles IX.

Unfortunately, the accomplishments of women rulers did little to dispel prejudices against women as a whole or to alter the definition of gender roles. Except for Mary, Queen of Scots, whose principal achievement was to provide an heir to the English throne, all the queens and regents of the sixteenth century were successful rulers. Margaret of Parma steered the careful middle course in the conflict between Spain and the Netherlands. She opposed the intervention of the Duke of Alba, and had her advice been followed, the eighty years of war between Spain and the Netherlands might have been avoided. Catherine de Médicis held the crown of France on the heads of her sons, navigated the treacherous waters of civil war, and provided the model for religious toleration that finally was adopted in the Edict of Nantes. Elizabeth I of England became one of the most beloved rulers in that nation's history. A crafty politician who learned to balance the factions at her court and who turned the aristocracy into a service class for the crown, she brought nearly a half-century of stability to England at a time when the rest of Europe was in flames.

The victory at Pavia in 1525 occurred on Charles V's twenty-fifth birthday and seemingly made him master of all of Europe. His ally Henry VIII urged an immediate invasion and dismemberment of France and began raising an army to spearhead the attack. But Charles's position was much less secure than it appeared. The Ottomans threatened his Hungarian territories, and the Protestants threatened his German lands. He could not afford a war of conquest in France. His hope now was to reach an agreement with Francis I for a lasting European peace, and for this purpose the French king was brought in captivity to Madrid.

It is doubtful that there was ever any real chance for peace between Habsburg and Valois after the battle of Pavia. Francis's personal humiliation and Charles's military position were both too strong to allow for a permanent settlement in which Habsburgs ruled in Milan and Naples. Charles demanded that Burgundy be returned to him. Though Francis was hardly in a position to bargain, he held out on this issue for as long as possible and he secretly prepared a disavowal of the final agreement before it was made. By the Treaty of Madrid in 1526, Francis I yielded Burgundy and recognized the Spanish conquest of Navarre and Spanish rule in Naples. The agreement was sealed by the marriage of

Francis to Charles's sister, Eleanor of Portugal. But marriage was not sufficient security for such a complete capitulation. To secure his release from Spain, Francis was required to leave behind as hostages his seven- and eight-year-old sons until the treaty was fulfilled. For three years the children languished in Spanish captivity.

No sooner had he set foot upon French soil than Francis I renounced the Treaty of Madrid. He even gained the sanction of the pope for violating his oath. Setting France on a war footing, he began seeking new allies. Henry VIII, disappointed with the meager spoils of his last venture, switched sides. Most importantly, Francis I entered into an alliance with the Ottoman sultan, Suleiman the Magnificent (1520–66), whose armies were pressing against the southeastern borders of the Holy Roman Empire. In the year following Pavia, the Ottomans secured an equally decisive triumph at Mohács, captured Budapest, and threatened Vienna, the eastern capital of the Habsburg lands. Almost overnight Charles V had been turned from hunter into hunted. The Ottoman threat demanded immediate attention in Germany, the French and English were preparing to strike in the Low Countries, and the Italian wars continued. In 1527 Charles's unpaid German mercenaries

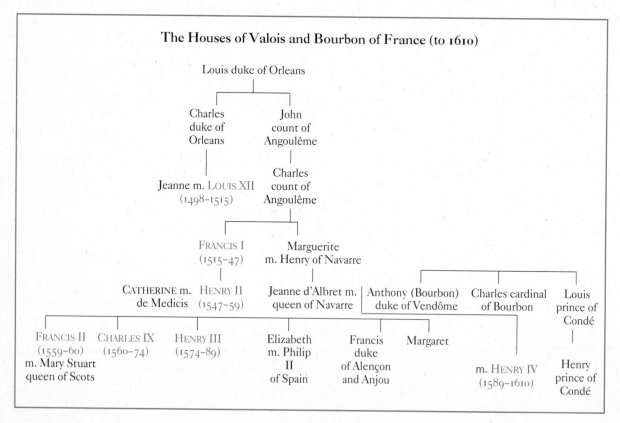

The Houses of Valois and Bourbon of France (to 1610)

stormed through Rome, sacked the papal capital, and captured the pope. Christian Europe was mortified.

The struggle for European mastery ground on for decades. The Treaty of Cateau-Cambrésis in 1559 brought to a close sixty years of conflict that had accomplished little. The great stores of silver that poured into Castile from the New World were consumed in the fires of Continental warfare. In 1557 both France and Spain declared bankruptcy to avoid foreclosures by their creditors. For the French, the Italian wars were disastrous. They seriously undermined the state's financial base, eroded confidence in the monarchy, thinned the ranks of the ruling nobility, and brought France nearly to ruin. The fiasco ended with fitting irony. After the death of Francis I, his son Henry II (1547–59) continued the struggle. Henry never forgave his father for abandoning him in Spain, and he sought revenge on Charles V, who had been his jailer. He celebrated the Treaty of Cateau-Cambrésis with great pomp and pageantry. Among the feasts and festivities were athletic competitions. Henry II entered the jousting tournament and there was killed.

In 1555 Charles abdicated all of his titles and retired to a monastery to live out his final days. He split apart his empire and granted to his brother, Ferdinand I (1558–64), the Austrian and German lands and the mantle of the Holy Roman Empire. To his son, Philip II (1556–98), he ceded the Low Countries, Spain and the New World, Naples, and his Italian conquests. The cares of an empire that once stretched from Peru to Vienna were lifted from his shoulders. On 21 September 1558, he died in his bed.

The wars for European supremacy between France and Spain dominated the politics of the first half of the sixteenth century. The quest for glory involved the Continent's two greatest kingdoms in unrelenting warfare, warfare that bankrupted both fiscally and emotionally. The humiliation of Francis I in prison in Madrid was ultimately matched by that of Charles V fleeing across the Alps as the Ottomans advanced on his German territories. For decades the two states poured all of their resources into warfare and made it a more deadly and more expensive venture than ever before.

The Crises of the European States

In the sixteenth century, society was an integrated whole, equally dependent upon monarchical, ecclesiastical, and civil authority for its effective survival. A Eu-

ropean state could no more tolerate the presence of two churches than it could the presence of two kings. But the Reformation had created two churches. The coexistence of both Catholics and Protestants in a single realm posed a stark challenge to accepted theory and traditional practice.

The problem proved intractable because it admitted only one solution: total victory. There could be no compromise for several reasons. Religious beliefs were profoundly held, and religious controversy was a struggle between everlasting life and eternal damnation. The practical solution of toleration was still unacceptable. To the modern mind, toleration seems so logical that it is difficult to understand why it took over a century of bloodshed before it came to be grudgingly accepted by those countries most bitterly divided. But toleration was not a practical solution in a society that admitted no principle of organization other than one king, one faith.

The French Wars of Religion

Protestantism came late to France. It was not until after Calvin reformed the church in Geneva and began to export his brand of Protestantism that French society began to divide along religious lines. By 1560 there were over two thousand Protestant congregations in France, whose membership totaled nearly 10 percent of the French population. Calvin and his successors had their greatest success among the middle ranks of urban society, merchants, traders, and craftsmen. They also found a receptive audience among aristocratic women, who eventually converted their husbands and their sons.

The wars of religion, however, were brought on by more than the rapid spread of Calvinism. Equally important was the vacuum of power that had been created when Henry II (1547–59) died in a jousting tournament. Surviving Henry were his extraordinary widow, Catherine de Médicis, three daughters, and four sons, the oldest of whom, Francis II (1559–60), was only fifteen. Under the influence of his beautiful young wife, Mary, Queen of Scots, Francis allowed the noble Guise family to dominate the great offices of state and to exclude their rivals from power. The Guises controlled the two most powerful institutions of the state—the army and the Church.

The Guises were staunchly Catholic and among their enemies were the Bourbons, a family with powerful Protestant members and a direct claim to the French throne. The revelation of a Protestant plot to remove the king from Paris provided the Guises with an opportunity to eliminate their most potent rivals. The Bourbon Duc de Condé, the leading Protestant peer of the realm, was sentenced to death. But five days before Condé's execution, Francis II died and Guise power evaporated. The new king, Charles IX (1560–74), was only ten years old and firmly under the grip of his mother, Catherine de Médicis, who now declared herself regent of France. (See Special Feature, "The Monstrous Regiment of Women," pp. 484–485.)

Condé's death sentence convinced him that the Guises would stop at nothing to gain their ambitions. Force would have to be met with force. Protestants and Catholics alike raised armies and in 1562 civil war ensued. Once the wars began, the leading Protestant peers fled the court, but the position of the Guises was not altogether secure. Henry Bourbon, king of Navarre, was the next in line to the throne should Charles IX and his two brothers die without male heirs. Henry had been raised in the Protestant faith by his mother, Jeanne d'Albret, whose own mother, Marguerite of Navarre, was among the earliest protectors of the Huguenots, as the French Calvinists came to be called.

The early battles were inconclusive, but the assassination of the Duc de Guise in 1563 by a Protestant fanatic added a personal vendetta to the religious passions of the Catholic leaders. They encouraged the slaughter of Huguenot congregations and the murder of Huguenot leaders. Protestants gave as good as they got. In open defiance of Valois dynastic interests, the Guises courted support from Spain, while the Huguenots imported Swiss and German mercenaries to fight in France. Noble factions and irreconcilable religious differences were together pulling the government apart.

By 1570 Catherine was ready for reconciliation. She announced her plans for a marriage between her daugh-

The French Wars of Religion

1559	Death of Henry II
1560	Protestant Duc de Condé sentenced to death
1562	First battle of wars of religion
1563	Catholic Duc de Guise assassinated
1572	Saint Bartholomew's Day massacre
1574	Accession of Henry III
1576	Formation of Catholic League
1584	Death of Duc d'Anjou makes Henry of Navarre heir to throne
1585	War of the three Henrys
1588	Henry Guise murdered by order of Henry III
1589	Catherine de Médicis dies; Henry III assassinated
1594	Henry IV crowned
1598	Edict of Nantes

ter Margaret and Henry of Navarre, a marriage that would symbolize the spirit of conciliation between the crown and the Huguenots. The marriage was to take place in Paris during August 1572. The arrival of Huguenot leaders from all over France to attend the marriage ceremony presented an opportunity of a different kind to the Guises and their supporters. If leading Huguenots could be assassinated in Paris, the Protestant cause might collapse and the truce that the wedding signified might be turned instead into a Catholic triumph.

Saint Bartholomew was the apostle that Jesus described as a man without guile. Ironically it was on his feast day that the Huguenots who had innocently come to celebrate Henry's marriage were led like lambs to the slaughter. On 24 August 1572 the streets of Paris ran red with Huguenot blood. Though frenzied, the slaughter was inefficient. Henry of Navarre and a number of other important Huguenots escaped the carnage and returned to their urban strongholds. In the following weeks the violence spread from Paris to the countryside and thousands of Protestants paid for their beliefs with their lives.

This scene depicts the mistreatment of French Catholics by the Protestants in the town of Angoulême. They were deprived of all nourishment, dragged over a taut rope, and then slowly roasted at the stake.

After Saint Bartholomew's Day, a genuine revulsion against the massacres swept the nation. A number of Catholic peers now joined with the Huguenots to protest the excesses of the crown and the Guises. These Catholics came to be called the *politiques* from their desire for a practical settlement of the wars. They were led by the Duc d'Anjou, next in line to the throne when Charles IX died in 1574 and Henry III (1574–89) became king. Against them, in Paris and a number of other towns, the Catholic League was formed, a society that pledged its first allegiance to religion. The League took up the slaughter of Huguenots where the Saint Bartholomew's Day massacre left off. Matters grew worse in 1584 when the Huguenot Henry of Navarre became next in line for the throne. Catholic Leaguers talked openly of altering the royal succession and began to develop theories of lawful resistance to monarchical power. By 1585, when the final civil war began—the war of the three Henrys, named for Henry III, Henry Guise, and Henry of Navarre—the crown was in the weakest possible position. Paris and the Catholic towns were controlled by the League, the Protestant strongholds by Henry of Navarre. King Henry III could not abandon his capital or his religion, but neither could he gain control of the Catholic party. The extremism of the Leaguers kept the politiques away from court, and without the politiques, there could be no settlement.

In December 1588 Henry III took matters into his own hands. He summoned Henry Guise and Guise's brother to a meeting in the royal bedchamber. There they were murdered in an attempt to destroy the League. The politiques were blamed for the murders—revenge was taken on a number of them—and Henry III was forced to flee his capital. He made a pact with Henry of Navarre and together royalist and Huguenot forces besieged Paris. Only the arrival of a Spanish army prevented its fall. In 1589 a fanatic priest avenged the murder of the Guises by assassinating Henry III.

Now Henry of Navarre came into his inheritance. But after nearly thirty years of continuous civil war it was certain that a Huguenot could never rule France. If Henry was to become king of all France, he would have to become a Catholic king. It is not clear when Henry made the decision to accept the Catholic faith—"Paris is worth a mass," he reportedly declared—but he did not announce his decision at once. Rather he strengthened his forces, tightened his bonds with the politiques, and urged his countrymen to expel the Spanish invaders. He finally made his conversion public and in 1594 was crowned Henry IV (1589–1610). In 1598 Henry proclaimed the Edict of Nantes, which granted limited toleration to the Huguenots. It was the culmination of decades of attempts to find a solution to the existence of two religions in one state.

The World of Philip II

By the middle of the sixteenth century Spain was the greatest power in Europe. The dominions of Philip II (1556–98) of Spain stretched from the Atlantic to the Pacific: his Continental territories included the Netherlands in the north and Milan and Naples in Italy. In 1580 Philip became king of Portugal, uniting all the states of the Iberian Peninsula. With the addition of Portugal's Atlantic ports and its sizable fleet, Spanish maritime power was now unsurpassed. Philip saw himself as a Catholic monarch fending off the spread of heresy. He was particularly hostile toward England,

FROM THE EDICT OF NANTES

■ *The Edict of Nantes (1598) was a milestone in the development of religious toleration in Europe. It was granted by King Henry IV to the Huguenots at the end of the French wars of religion. The Edict of Nantes established the rights of Protestants and was in effect for nearly a century.*

We ordain that the Catholic, Apostolic and Roman religion shall be restored and re-established in all places and districts of this our kingdom and the countries under our rule, where its practice has been interrupted, so that it can be peacefully and freely practiced there, without any disturbance or hindrance. We forbid very expressly all persons of whatever rank, quality or condition they may be, under the aforesaid penalties, to disturb, molest or cause annoyance to clerics in the celebration of the Divine worship.

where he had briefly been married to the Catholic Queen Mary I (1553–58). But her Protestant successor, Queen Elizabeth I (1558–1603), encouraged piracy against Spanish treasure ships and covertly aided both French and Dutch Protestants. Finally in 1588 Philip decided upon invasion.

He assembled a fleet of over 130 ships, many of them the pride of the Spanish and Portuguese navies. The ships of the Spanish Armada were bigger and stronger than anything possessed by the English, whose forces were largely merchant vessels hastily converted for battle. But the English ships were faster and more maneuverable in the unpredictable winds of the English Channel. They also contained guns that could readily be reloaded for multiple firings, while the Spanish guns were designed to discharge only one broadside before hand-to-hand combat ensued. With these advantages the English were able to prevent the Armada from reaching port in the Netherlands and to destroy many individual ships as they were blown off course. The

defeat of the Spanish Armada was less a military than a psychological blow to Philip II. He could more easily replace ships than restore confidence in Spanish power.

That confidence was to be shaken more thoroughly by the greatest crisis of his reign: the revolt of the Netherlands. Though Philip's father, Charles V, amassed a great empire, he had begun only as the duke of Burgundy. Charles's Burgundian inheritance encompassed a diverse territory in the northwestern corner of Europe. The seventeen separate provinces of this territory were called the Netherlands or the Low Countries because of the flooding that kept large portions of them under water. The Netherlands was one of the richest and most populous regions of Europe, an international leader in manufacturing, banking, and commerce. The heavy concentration of urban populations in the Low Countries provided the natural habitat for Calvinist preachers, who made converts across the entire social spectrum. As Holy Roman Emperor, Charles V may have made his peace with Protestants, but as king of Spain he

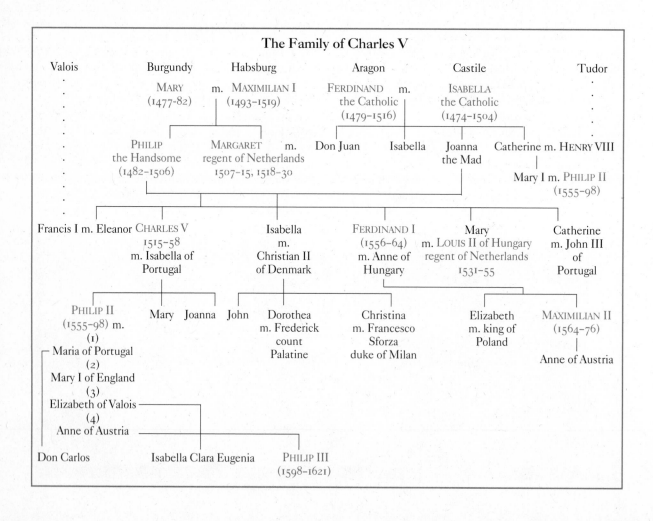

The Family of Charles V

Valois · Burgundy · Habsburg · Aragon · Castile · Tudor

MARY (1477-82) m. MAXIMILIAN I (1493-1519)

FERDINAND the Catholic (1479-1516) m. ISABELLA the Catholic (1474-1504)

PHILIP the Handsome (1482-1506) — MARGARET regent of Netherlands 1507-15, 1518-30 m.

Don Juan   Isabella   Joanna the Mad   Catherine m. HENRY VIII

Mary I m. PHILIP II (1555-98)

Francis I m. Eleanor   CHARLES V 1515-58 m. Isabella of Portugal

Isabella m. Christian II of Denmark

FERDINAND I (1556-64) m. Anne of Hungary

Mary m. LOUIS II of Hungary regent of Netherlands 1531-55

Catherine m. John III of Portugal

PHILIP II (1555-98) m.
(1) Maria of Portugal
(2) Mary I of England
(3) Elizabeth of Valois
(4) Anne of Austria

Mary   Joanna   John   Dorothea m. Frederick count Palatine

Christina m. Francesco Sforza duke of Milan

Elizabeth m. king of Poland

MAXIMILIAN II (1564-76)
Anne of Austria

Don Carlos   Isabella Clara Eugenia   PHILIP III (1598-1621)

The Spanish and the English Fleets Engaged, 1588, *by an unknown artist, ca. 1590. In the foreground, two English warships flank a Spanish ship bearing the standard of the pope.*

Protestants sought the protection of their local nobility who, Catholic or Protestant, had their own reasons for opposing the strict enforcement of heresy laws. Provincial nobility and magistrates resented both the substance of Philip's policies and the fact that they disregarded local autonomy. Town governors and noblemen refused to cooperate in implementing the new laws.

The Revolt of the Netherlands

The passive resistance of nobles and magistrates was soon matched by the active resistance of the Calvinists. Unable to enforce Philip's policy, Margaret of Parma, his half-sister, whom Philip had made regent, agreed to a limited toleration. But in the summer of 1566, before it could be put into effect, bands of Calvinists violently attacked Catholic property, breaking stained glass windows and statues of the Virgin and the saints, which they claimed were idolatrous. Local authorities could not protect Church property and open revolt ensued. Fearing social rebellion, even the leading Protestant noblemen helped suppress these riots.

In Spain, the events in the Netherlands were treated for what they were: open rebellion. Philip II was determined to punish the rebels and enforce the heresy laws. He sent a large military force from Spain under the

had not. Charles V had maintained the purity of the Spanish Catholic church through a sensible combination of reform and repression.

Philip II intended to pursue a similar policy in the Low Countries. With papal approval he initiated a scheme to reform the hierarchy of the Church by expanding the numbers of bishops, and he invited the Jesuits to establish schools for orthodox learning. The

The Revolt of the Netherlands

Revolt of the Netherlands

1559   Margaret of Parma named regent of the Netherlands

1566   Calvinist iconoclasm begins revolt

1567   Duke of Alba arrives in Netherlands

1572   Protestants capture Holland and Zeeland

1576   Sack of Antwerp
        Pacification of Ghent

1581   Catholic and Protestant provinces split

1609   Twelve Years' Truce

command of the Duke of Alba (1507–82). Alba fulfilled his mission with a vengeance, executing leading Protestant noblemen, harshly punishing participants in the rebellion, and destroying towns implicated in the revolt. As many as sixty thousand Protestants fled north beyond Alba's jurisdiction. By the end of 1568 royal policy had gained a sullen acceptance in the Netherlands, but for the next eighty years, with only occasional truces, Spain and the Netherlands were at war.

Alba's policies had driven Protestants into rebellion, and this forced the Spanish government to maintain its army by raising taxes from those southern provinces that had remained loyal. Soon the loyal provinces too were in revolt, not over religion, but over taxation and local autonomy. Alba was unprepared for the series of successful assaults Protestants launched in the northern provinces during 1572. The Protestant generals established a permanent base in the northwestern provinces of Holland and Zeeland. By 1575 they had gained a stronghold that they would never relinquish. Prince William of Orange assumed the leadership of the two provinces, which were now united against the tyranny of Philip's rule.

Spanish government was collapsing all over the Netherlands. William ruled in the north, and the States-General, a parliamentary body composed of representatives from the separate provinces, ruled in the south. No one was in control of the Spanish army. The soldiers, who had gone years with only partial pay, now roamed the southern provinces looking for plunder. Brussels and Ghent both were targets, and in 1576 the worst atrocities of all occurred when mutinous Spanish troops sacked Antwerp. Over seven thousand people were slaughtered and nearly a third of the city burned to the ground.

The "Spanish fury" in Antwerp effectively ended Philip's rule over his Burgundian inheritance. The Protestants had established a permanent home in the north. The States-General had established its ability to rule in the south, and Spanish policy had been totally discredited. To achieve a settlement, the Pacification of Ghent of 1576, the Spanish government conceded local autonomy in taxation, the central role of the States-General in legislation, and the immediate withdrawal of all Spanish troops from the Low Countries. This rift among the provinces was soon followed by a permanent split. In 1581 one group of provinces voted to depose Philip II while a second group decided to remain loyal to him. Philip II refused to accept the dismemberment of his inheritance and refused to recognize the independent

The House of Vasa of Sweden

Dutch state that now existed in Holland. Throughout the 1580s and 1590s military expeditions attempted to reunite the southern provinces and to conquer the northern ones. In 1609 Spain and the Netherlands concluded the Twelve Years' Truce, which tacitly recognized the existence of the state of Holland. By the beginning of the seventeenth century Holland was not only an independent state, it was one of the greatest rivals of Spain and Portugal.

The Thirty Years' War, 1618–1648

Though there was nothing new about warfare in Europe, the fighting that set the Continent ablaze from 1555 to 1648 brought together the worst of dynastic and religious conflicts. These wars were fought on a larger scale, were more brutal and more expensive, and claimed more victims, civilians and combatants alike. During this century war extended throughout the Continent. Dynastic strife, rebellion, and international rivalries joined together with the ongoing struggle over religion. Ambition and faith were an explosive mixture. The French endured forty years of civil war; the Spanish eighty years of fighting with the Dutch. The battle for hegemony in the east led to dynastic strife for decades on end, as Poles, Russians, and Swedes pressed their rival claims to each other's territory until the Swedes emerged victorious. Finally, in 1618, these separate theaters of war came together in one of the most brutal and terrifying episodes of destruction in European history, the Thirty Years' War.

The Rise of Sweden

Sweden's aggressive foreign policy began accidentally when the Baltic seaport of Reval requested Swedish protection. After some hesitation, Sweden fortified Reval in 1560. A decade later, Swedish forces captured Narva, farther to the east, and consolidated their hold on the Livonian coast, where they controlled a sizable portion of the Muscovite trade. As the Swedes secured the northern Livonian ports, more of the Muscovy trade moved to the south and passed through Riga, which would have to be captured or blockaded if the Swedes were to control commerce in the eastern Baltic. At the beginning of the seventeenth century the powerful Swedish navy blockaded Riga and entered into war against Poland.

A Livonian peasant. Livonia was conquered by Ivan the Terrible in his campaign of 1563, but was soon reclaimed by the Poles. In 1660 Livonia became part of the Swedish empire. Livonia was originally inhabited by the Livs, a Finnish people.

The blockade of Riga and the assembly of a large Swedish fleet in the Baltic threatened Denmark. The Danes claimed sovereignty over Sweden and now took the opportunity of the Polish-Swedish conflict to reassert it. In 1611, under the energetic leadership of the Danish king Christian IV (1588–1648), Denmark invaded Sweden from both the east and the west, threatening to take Stockholm. In the same year, during the Danish war, Sweden's king Charles IX died and was succeeded by his son Gustavus Adolphus (1611–32). Gustavus's greatest skills were military, and the calamitous wars inherited from his father occupied him during the early years of his reign. He was forced to conclude a humiliating peace with the Danes in 1613. For most of the next decade he rebuilt his armies and nursed his grievances. Then in 1621 he struck. He landed a force in Livonia and in two weeks he captured Riga, the capstone of Sweden's Baltic ambitions. Occupation of Riga increased Swedish control of the Muscovy trade and it deprived Denmark of a significant portion of its customs duties. Gustavus now claimed Riga as a Swedish port and successfully demanded that ships sailing from there pay tolls to Sweden rather than Denmark.

THE DESTRUCTION OF MAGDEBURG

■ No event of the Thirty Years' War had a greater effect on public opinion than the annihilation of the Protestant city of Magdeburg in 1631. Dozens of pamphlets and woodcuts detailed the slaughter of civilians and the devastation of property. It was commonly believed that neither a human nor an animal escaped the destruction.

Thus it came about that the city and all its inhabitants fell into the hands of the enemy, whose violence and cruelty were due in part to their common hatred of the adherents of the Augsburg Confession, and in part to their being imbittered by the chain shot which had been fired at them and by the derision and insults that the Magdeburgers had heaped upon them from the ramparts.

Then was there naught but beating and burning, plundering, torture, and murder. Most especially was every one of the enemy bent on securing much booty. When a marauding party entered a house, if its master had anything to give he might thereby purchase respite and protection for himself and his family till the next man, who also wanted something, should come along. . . .

Thus in a single day this noble and famous city, the pride of the whole country, went up in fire and smoke; and the remnant of its citizens, with their wives and children, were taken prisoners and driven away by the enemy with a noise of weeping and wailing that could be heard from afar, while the cinders and ashes from the town were carried by the wind to Wanzleben, Egeln, and still more distant places.

The rise of Sweden had two dramatic effects in the reorganization of power politics in northeastern Europe. In the first place, it signalled the permanent eclipse of Poland-Lithuania in the region. Once a territorial giant with pretensions of dominating all of eastern Europe, Poland-Lithuania now saw its territories shrink and its power diminish. With the Swedish capture of Riga, dominance over the Muscovy trade passed out of Polish hands, never to return. Secondly, and most importantly for the immediate future of Europe, the rise of Sweden created a Protestant counterbalance to the power of the Austrian Habsburgs. Sweden's domination of the Baltic ports placed its future firmly on German soil at just the moment that Germany was to explode into warfare.

Bohemia Revolts

The Peace of Augsburg had served the German states well. The principle that the religion of the ruler was the religion of the state complicated the political life of the Holy Roman Empire, but it also pacified it. Though rulers had the right to enforce uniformity on their subjects, in practice many of the larger states tolerated more than one religion. By the beginning of the seventeenth century Catholicism and Protestantism had achieved a rough equality within the German states, symbolized by the fact that of the seven electors who chose the Holy Roman Emperor, three were Catholic, three Protestant, and the seventh was the emperor himself, acting as king of Bohemia. This situation was not unwelcome to the leaders of the Austrian Habsburg family, who succeeded Emperor Charles V and who were more tolerant than their Spanish kinfolk. The head of their house was elected king of Bohemia and king of Hungary, both states with large Protestant populations.

In 1617 Mathias, the childless Holy Roman Emperor, began making plans for his cousin, Ferdinand Habsburg, to succeed him. Ferdinand was Catholic, very devout and very committed. In order to ensure a Catholic majority among the electors, the emperor relinquished his Bohemian title and pressed for Ferdinand's election as the new king of Bohemia. The Protestant nobles of Bohemia forced the new king to accept strict limitations upon his political and religious powers, but once elected Ferdinand had no intention of honoring them. His opponents were equally strong-willed. When Ferdinand violated Protestant religious liberties, a group of noblemen marched to the royal palace in Prague in May 1618, found two of the king's chief advisers, and hurled them out of an upper-story window.

The Defenestration of Prague, as this incident came to be known, initiated a Protestant counteroffensive throughout the Habsburg lands. Fear of Ferdinand's policies led to Protestant uprisings in Hungary as well as

Bohemia. Those who seized control of the government declared Ferdinand deposed and the throne vacant. But they had no candidate to accept their crown. When Emperor Mathias died in 1619, Ferdinand succeeded to the imperial title as Ferdinand II (1619–37) and Frederick V, one of the Protestant electors, accepted the Bohemian crown.

Frederick was a sincere but weak Calvinist whose credentials were much stronger than his abilities. He ruled a geographically divided German state known as the Palatinate. One hundred miles separated the two segments of his lands, but both were strategically important. The Lower Palatinate bordered on the Catholic Spanish Netherlands and the Upper Palatinate on Catholic Bavaria.

Once Frederick accepted the Bohemian crown, he was faced with a war on three fronts. Ferdinand II had no difficulty enlisting allies to recover the Bohemian crown, since he could pay them with the spoils of Frederick's lands. Spanish troops from the Netherlands occupied the Lower Palatinate, and Bavarian troops occupied the Upper Palatinate. Frederick, on the other hand, met rejection wherever he turned. Neither the Dutch nor the English would send more than token aid—both had advised him against breaking the imperial peace. The Lutheran princes of Germany would not enter into a war between Calvinists and Catholics, especially after Ferdinand II promised to protect the Bohemian Lutherans.

At the battle of the White Mountain in 1620, Ferdinand's Catholic forces annihilated Frederick's army. Frederick and his wife fled to Denmark, and Bohemia was left to face the wrath of Ferdinand, the victorious king and emperor. The retribution was horrible. Mercenaries who had fought for Ferdinand II were allowed to sack Prague for a week. Elective monarchy was abolished and Bohemia became part of the hereditary Habsburg lands. Free peasants were enserfed and subjected to imperial law. Those nobles who had supported Frederick lost their lands and their privileges. Calvinism was repressed and thoroughly rooted out, consolidating forever the Catholic character of Bohemia. Frederick's estates were carved up and his rights as elector transferred to the Catholic duke of Bavaria. The battle of the White Mountain was a turning point in the history of central Europe, for it forced all Protestant nations to arm for war.

The War Widens

For the Habsburgs, religious and dynastic interests were inseparable. Ferdinand II and Philip III of Spain (1598–1621) fought for their beliefs and for their patrimony. Their victory gave them more than they could have expected. Ferdinand swallowed up Bohemia and strengthened his position in the empire. Philip gained possession of a vital link in his supply route between Italy and the Netherlands. Spanish expansion threatened France. The occupation of the Lower Palatinate placed a ring of Spanish armies around France from the Pyrenees to the Low Countries.

Frederick, now in Holland, refused to accept the judgment of battle. He lobbied for a grand alliance to repel the Spaniards from the Lower Palatinate and to restore the religious balance in the empire. Though his personal cause met with little sympathy, his political logic was impeccable, especially after Spain again declared war upon the Dutch in 1621. A grand Protestant alliance—secretly supported by the French—brought together England, Holland, a number of German states, and Denmark. It was the Danes who led this potentially powerful coalition. In 1626 a large Danish army under the command of King Christian IV engaged imperial forces on German soil. But Danish forces could not match the superior numbers and the superior leadership of the Catholic mercenary forces under the command of the ruthless and brilliant Count Albrecht

The Rise of Sweden

von Wallenstein (1583–1634). In 1629 the Danes withdrew from the empire and sued for peace.

If the Catholic victory at the White Mountain in 1620 threatened the well-being of German Protestantism, the Catholic triumph over the Danes threatened its survival. More powerful than ever, Ferdinand II determined to turn the religious clock back to the state of affairs that had existed when the Peace of Augsburg was concluded in 1555. He demanded that all lands that had then been Catholic but had since become Protestant must now be returned to the fold. He also proclaimed that as the Peace of Augsburg made no provision for the toleration of Calvinists, they would no longer be tolerated in the empire. These policies together constituted a virtual revolution in the religious affairs of the German states, and they proved impossible to impose. Ferdinand succeeded in only one thing—he united Lutherans and Calvinists against him.

In 1630 King Gustavus Adolphus of Sweden decided to enter the German conflict to protect Swedish interests. While Gustavus Adolphus struggled to construct his alliance, imperial forces continued their triumphant progress. In 1631 they besieged, captured, and put to the torch the town of Magdeburg—a turning point in Protestant fortunes. Brandenburg and Saxony joined Gustavus Adolphus, not only enlarging his forces, but allowing him to open a second front in Bohemia. In the autumn of 1631 this combination overwhelmed the imperial armies. Gustavus won a decisive triumph at Breitenfeld, while the Saxons occupied Prague.

Gustavus Adolphus lost no time in pressing his advantage. The Swedes marched west to the Rhine, easily conquering the richest of the Catholic cities and retak-

The Thirty Years' War

1618	Defenestration of Prague
1619	Ferdinand Habsburg elected Holy Roman Emperor Frederick of the Palatinate accepts the crown of Bohemia
1620	Catholic victory at battle of the White Mountain
1621	End of Twelve Years' Truce; war between Spain and Netherlands
1626	Danes form Protestant alliance under Christian IV
1627	Spain declares bankruptcy
1630	Gustavus Adolphus leads Swedish forces into Germany
1631	Sack of Magdeburg Protestant victory at Breitenfeld
1632	Protestant victory at Lutzen; death of Gustavus Adolphus
1635	France declares war on Spain
1643	Battle of Rocroi; French forces repel Spaniards
1648	Peace of Westphalia

ing the Lower Palatinate. In early 1632 Protestant forces plundered Bavaria, but Wallenstein chose to chase the Saxons from Bohemia rather than the Swedes from Bavaria. Not until the winter of 1632 did the armies of Gustavus and Wallenstein finally meet. At the battle of Lutzen the Swedes won the field but lost their beloved king. In less than two years Gustavus Adolphus had decisively transformed the course of the war and the course of Europe's future. Protestant forces now occupied most of central and northern Germany.

The final stages of the war involved the resumption of the century-old struggle between France and Spain. When the Twelve Years' Truce expired in 1621, Spain again declared war upon the Dutch. Dutch naval power was considerable and the Dutch took the war to the far reaches of the globe, attacking Portuguese settlements in Brazil and in the East and harassing Spanish shipping on the high seas. In 1628 the Dutch captured the entire Spanish treasure fleet as it sailed from the New World. Spain had declared bankruptcy in 1627, and the loss of the whole of the next years' treasure from America exacerbated an already catastrophic situation.

The siege of Magdeburg, 1631. The sack of the city by the Imperial troops of Tilly's army was one of the most barbarous incidents of a brutal war.

Allegorical painting celebrating the Treaty of Westphalia. The shattered weapons of war lie in the foreground; at the right, the ship of peace carries the news to the capitals of Europe.

These reversals, combined with the continued successes of Habsburg forces in central Europe, convinced Louis XIII and his chief minister, Cardinal Richelieu, that the time for active involvement in European affairs was now at hand. Throughout the early stages of the war, France had secretly aided anti-Habsburg forces. Gustavus Adolphus's unexpected success dramatically altered French calculations. Now it was evident that the Habsburgs could no longer combine their might, and Spanish energies would be drained off in the Netherlands and in central Europe. The time had come to take an open stand. In 1635 France declared war on Spain.

France took the offensive first, invading the Spanish Netherlands. In 1636 a Spanish army struck back, pushing to within twenty-five miles of Paris before it was repelled. Both sides soon began to search for a settlement, but pride prevented them from laying down their arms. Spain toppled first. Its economy in shambles and its citizens in revolt over high prices and higher taxes, it could no longer maintain its many-fronted war. In 1643 Spain gambled once more on a knockout blow against the French. But at the battle of Rocroi, exhausted French troops held out and the Spanish invasion failed.

By now the desire for peace was universal. Most of the main combatants had long since perished: Philip III, ever optimistic, in 1621; Frederick V, an exile to the end, in 1632; Gustavus Adolphus, killed at Lutzen in the same year; Wallenstein, murdered by order of Ferdinand II in 1634; Ferdinand himself in 1637; and Louis XIII in 1643, five days before the French triumph at Rocroi. Those who succeeded them had not the same passions, and after so many decades the longing for peace was the strongest emotion on the Continent.

In 1648 a series of agreements, collectively known as the Peace of Westphalia, established the outlines of the political geography of Europe for the next century. Its focus was on the Holy Roman Empire and it reflected Protestant successes in the final two decades of war. Sweden gained further territories on the Baltic, making it master of the north German ports. France, too, gained

The Peace of Westphalia

THE HORRORS OF THE THIRTY YEARS' WAR

■ *No source has better captured the brutality of the Thirty Years' War than the novel* Simplisissimus. *In a series of loosely connected episodes, the hero (whose name means "the simplest of the simple") is snatched from his village to serve in marauding armies whose confrontations with local villagers are usually more horrifying than the episode narrated here.*

These troopers were even now ready to march, and had the pastor fastened by a rope to lead him away. Some cried, "Shoot him down, the rogue!" Others would have money from him. But he, lifting up his hands to heaven, begged, for the sake of the Last Judgment, for forbearance and Christian compassion, but in vain; for one of them rode him down and dealt him such a blow on the head that he fell flat, and commended his soul to God. Nor did the remainder of the captured peasants fare any better. But even when it seemed these troopers, in their cruel tyranny, had clean lost their wits, came such a swarm of armed peasants out of the wood, that it seemed a wasps'-nest had been stirred. And these began to yell so frightfully and so furiously to attack with sword and musket that all my hair stood on end; and never had I been at such a merry-making before: for the peasants of the Spessart and the Vogelsberg are as little wont as are the Hessians and men of the Sauerland and the Black Forest to let themselves be crowed over on their own dunghill. So away went the troopers, and not only left behind the cattle they had captured, but threw away bag and baggage also, and so cast all their booty to the winds lest themselves should become booty for the peasants: yet some of them fell into their hands. This sport took from me well-nigh all desire to see the world, for I thought, if 'tis all like this, then is the wilderness far more pleasant.

From Hans von Grimmelhausen, *Simplisissimus* (1669).

in territory and prestige. It kept the vital towns in the Lower Palatinate through which Spanish men and material had moved and, though it did not agree to come to terms with Spain immediately, France's fear of encirclement was at an end. The Dutch gained statehood through official recognition by Spain and through the power they had displayed in building and maintaining an overseas empire.

Territorial boundaries were reestablished as they had existed in 1624, giving the Habsburgs control of both Bohemia and Hungary. The independence of the Swiss cantons was now officially recognized as were the rights of Calvinists to the protection of the Peace of Augsburg, which again was to govern the religious affairs of the empire. Two of the larger German states were strengthened as a counterweight to the emperor's power. Bavaria was allowed to retain the Upper Palatinate, and Brandenburg, which ceded some of its coastal territory to Sweden, gained extensive territories in the east. The emperor's political control over the German states was also weakened. German rulers were given independent authority over their states and the imperial diet, rather than the emperor, was empowered to

settle disputes. Thus weakened, future emperors ruled in the Habsburg territorial lands with little ability to control, or influence, or even arbitrate German affairs. The judgment that the Holy Roman Empire was neither holy, Roman, nor an empire was now irrevocably true.

The Peace of Westphalia put back together the pieces of the map of European states. Protestantism and Catholicism now coexisted and there was to be little further change in the geography of religion. The northwest of Europe—England, Holland, Scandinavia, and the north German states—was Protestant; the south was Catholic. The empire of the German peoples was now at an end, the Austro-Hungarian empire at a beginning. Holland and Sweden had become international powers; Spain and Denmark faded from prominence. Muscovy began a long period of isolation from the west, attempting to restore a semblance of government to its people. But if the negotiators at Westphalia could resolve the political and religious ambitions that gave rise to a century of nearly continuous warfare, they could do nothing to eradicate the effects of war itself. The devastation of humanity in the name of God with which the reform of religion had begun was now exhausted. The costs were horrific. The population of Germany fell from 15 million in 1600 to 11 million in 1650. The armies brought destruction of all kinds in their wake. Plague again raged in Europe—the town of Augsburg lost 18,000 inhabitants in the early 1630s. Famine, too, returned to a continent that fifty years earlier had been self-sufficient in grain. The war played havoc with all of the economies that it touched. Inflation, devaluation of coinage, huge public and private debts were all directly attributable to the years of fighting. And the toll taken on the spirit of those generations that never knew peace is incalculable.

SUGGESTIONS FOR FURTHER READING

GENERAL READING

* J. H. Elliott, *Europe Divided 1559–1598* (New York: Harper & Row, 1968). An outstanding synthesis of European politics in the second half of the sixteenth century.

* Geoffrey Parker, *Europe in Crisis 1598–1648* (London: William Collins and Sons, 1979). The best introduction to the period.

* William Doyle, *The Old European Order* (Oxford: Oxford University Press, 1978). An important synthetic essay bristling with ideas.

* Jan de Vries, *The European Economy in an Age of Crisis* (Cambridge: Cambridge University Press, 1976). A comprehensive study of economic development, including long-distance trade and commercial change.

THE FORMATION OF STATES

J. H. Shennan, *The Origins of the Modern European State 1450–1725* (London: Hutchinson, 1974). An analytic account of the rise of the state.

Bernard Guenée, *States and Rulers in Later Medieval Europe* (London: Basil Blackwell, 1985). An engaging argument about the forces that helped shape the state system in Europe.

* Norman Davies, *God's Playground: A History of Poland, Vol. 1. The Origins to 1795* (New York: Columbia University Press, 1982). The best treatment in English of a complex history.

* Richard Pipes, *Russia Under the Old Regime* (London: Widenfeld and Nicolson, 1974). A magisterial account.

* Robert O. Crummey, *The Formation of Muscovy 1304–1613* (London: Longman, 1987). The best one-volume history.

* J. R. Lander, *Government and Community, England 1450–1509* (Cambridge, MA: Harvard University Press, 1980). A comprehensive survey of the late fifteenth century.

* S. B. Chrimes, *Henry VII* (Berkeley, CA: University of California Press, 1972). A traditional biography of the first Tudor king.

* C. D. Ross, *The Wars of the Roses* (London: Thames and Hudson, 1976). The best one-volume account.

* G. R. Elton, *Reform and Reformation, England 1509–1558* (Cambridge, MA: Harvard University Press, 1977). An up-to-date survey by the dean of Tudor historians.

Richard Vaughan, *Valois Burgundy* (Hampden, CT: Shoe String Press, 1975). An engaging history of a vanished state.

* Paul M. Kendall, *Louis XI: The Universal Spider* (New York: Norton, 1971). A highly entertaining account of an unusual monarch.

* R. J. Knecht, *French Renaissance Monarchy* (London: Longman, 1984). A study of the nature of the French monarchy and the way it was transformed in the early sixteenth century.

* J. H. Elliot, *Imperial Spain 1469–1716* (New York: Mentor, 1963). Still worth reading for its insights and examples.

THE DYNASTIC STRUGGLES

* J. R. Hale, *War and Society in Renaissance Europe* (Baltimore: Johns Hopkins University Press, 1986). Assesses the impact of war on the political and social history of early modern Europe.

M. E. Alvarez, *Charles V* (London: Thames and Hudson, 1975). An accessible biography of the most remarkable man of the age.

* R. J. Knecht, *Francis I* (Cambridge: Cambridge University Press, 1982). A compelling study by the leading scholar of sixteenth-century France.

* J. J. Scarisbrick, *Henry VIII* (Berkeley, CA: University of California Press, 1968). The definitive biography.

THE CRISES OF THE EUROPEAN STATES

J. H. M. Salmon, *Society in Crisis* (New York: St. Martin's Press, 1975). The best single-volume account of the French civil wars; difficult but rewarding.

Robert Kingdon, *Myths About the St. Bartholomew's Day Massacres 1572–76* (Cambridge, MA: Harvard University Press, 1988). A study of the impact of a central event in the history of France.

* Mark Greengrass, *France in the Age of Henri IV* (London: Longmans, 1984). An important synthesis of French history in the early seventeenth century.

Geoffrey Parker, *Philip II* (Boston: Little, Brown, 1978). The best introduction.

* Garrett Mattingly, *The Armada* (Boston: Houghton Mifflin, 1959). Still the classic account despite recent reinterpretations.

* Henry Kamen, *Spain 1469–1714* (London: Longmans, 1983). A recent survey with up-to-date interpretations.

* Geoffrey Parker, *The Dutch Revolt* (London: Penguin Books, 1977). An outstanding account of the tangle of events that comprised the revolts of the Netherlands.

W. E. Reddaway et al., eds., *The Cambridge History of Poland to 1696* (Cambridge: Cambridge University Press, 1950). A difficult but thorough narrative of Polish history.

Michael Roberts, *Gustavus Adolphus and the Rise of Sweden* (London: English Universities Press, 1973). A highly readable account of Sweden's rise to power.

THE THIRTY YEARS' WAR

* C. V. Wedgwood, *The Thirty Years' War* (New York: Doubleday, 1961). A heroic account; the best narrative history.

* Peter Limm, *The Thirty Years' War* (London: Longmans, 1984). An excellent brief survey with documents.

* Indicates paperback edition available.

CHAPTER 17

The Royal State System of Seventeenth-Century Europe

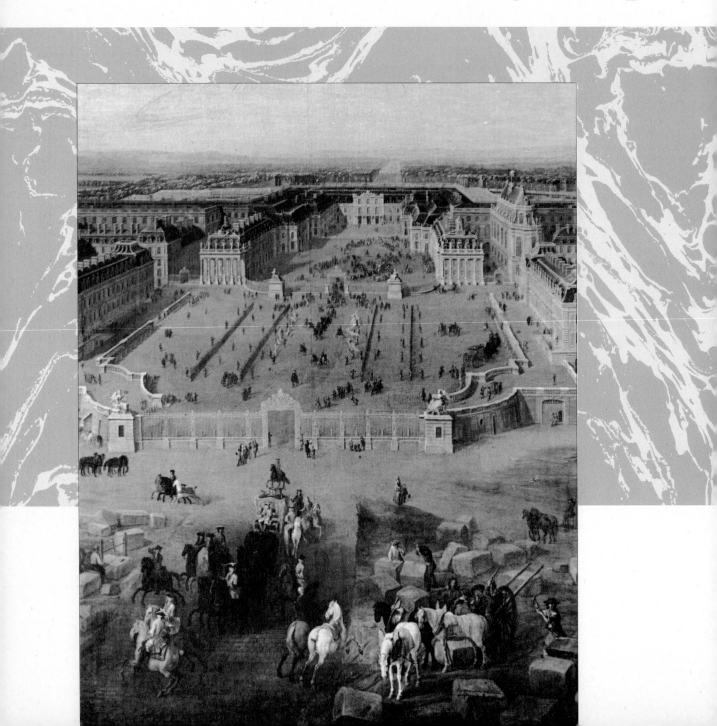

FIT FOR A KING

Behold Versailles: the greatest palace of the greatest king in seventeenth-century Europe. Everything about it was stupendous, a reflection of the grandeur of Louis XIV and of France. Sculptured gardens in dazzling geometric forms stretched for acres, scenting the air with exotic perfumes. Nearly as beautiful as the grounds were the 1,400 fountains, especially the circular basins of Apollo and Latona, the sun god and his mother. The hundreds of water jets that sprayed at Versailles defied nature as well as the senses, for the locale was not well irrigated and the water had to be pumped through elaborate mechanical works all the way from the Seine. Gardens and fountains provided the setting for the enormous palace with its hundreds of rooms for both use and show. Five thousand people, a tenth of whom served the king alone, inhabited the palace. Thousands of others flocked there daily. Most lived in the adjacent town, which had grown from a few hundred to over forty thousand in a single generation. The royal stables quartered twelve thousand horses and thousands of carriages. The cost of all of this magnificence was equally astounding. Fragmentary accounts indicate that construction costs were over 100 million French pounds. Louis XIV ordered the official receipts burned.

Like the marble of the palace, nature itself was chiseled to the requirements of the king. Forests were pared to make leafy avenues or trimmed to conform to the geometric patterns of the gardens. In spring and summer groves of orange trees grown in tubs were everywhere; in winter and fall they were housed indoors at great expense. Life-size statues and giant carved urns lined the carefully planned walkways that led out to breathtaking views or in to sheltered grottoes. A cross-shaped artificial canal, over a mile long, dominated the western end of the park. Italian gondolas skimmed along its surface, carrying visitors to the zoo and aviary on one side or to the king's private château on the other.

But this great pile of bricks and stone, of marble and precious metals expressed the contradictions of its age as well as its grandeur. The seventeenth century was a time when the monarchical state expanded its power and prestige even as it faced the grave challenge of balancing the monarch's right to rule with the subjects' duty to obey. As royal government wrapped itself in the mantle of the theory of absolute monarchy, it was challenged by civil wars and revolutions. Thus it was fitting that this prodigious monument was uncomfortable to live in, so unpleasant that Louis had a separate château built on the grounds as a quiet retreat. His wife and mistresses complained constantly of accommodations in which all interior comforts had been subordinated to the external facade of the building. Versailles was a seat of state as well as the home of the monarch, and it is revealing that the private was sacrificed to the public.

The Duc de Saint-Simon, who passed much of his time at Versailles, was well aware of the contradictions. "The beautiful and the ugly were sewn together, the vast and the constricted." Soldiers, tradesmen, and the merely curious clogged the three great avenues that led from Paris to the palace. When the king dined in public, hordes of Parisians drove out for the spectacle, filing past the monarch as if he were an exhibit at a museum. The site itself was poorly drained. "Its mud is black and stinking with a stench so penetrating that you can smell it for several leagues around." The orange groves and the stone urns filled with flower petals were more practical than beautiful: they masked the stench of sewage that was particularly noxious in the heat and rain. Even the gardens were too vast to be enjoyed. In the planted areas, the smell of flowers was overpowering while the acres of mown lawn were less than inviting to an aristocracy little given to physical exercise. "The gardens were admired and avoided," Saint-Simon observed acidly. In these contrasts of failure amid achievement Versailles stands as an apt symbol of its age: a gaudy mask to hide the wrinkles of the royal state.

The Rise of the Royal State

The religious and dynastic wars that dominated the early part of the seventeenth century had a profound impact upon the western European states. Not only did they cause terrible suffering and deprivation but they also demanded efficient and better-centralized states to conduct them. War was both a product of the European state system and a cause of its continued development. As armies grew in size, the resources necessary to maintain them grew in volume. As the battlefield spread from state to state, defense became government's most important function. More and more power was absorbed by the monarch and his chief advisers, more and more of the traditional privileges of aristocracy and of towns were eroded. At the center of these rising states, particularly in western Europe, were the king and his court. In the provinces were tax collectors and military recruiters.

Divine Kings

"There is a divinity that doth hedge a king," wrote Shakespeare. Never was that hedge more luxuriant than in the seventeenth century. In the early sixteenth century, monarchs treated their states and their subjects as personal property. Correspondingly, rulers were praised in personal terms, for their virtue, their wisdom, or their strength. By the early seventeenth century, the monarchy had been transformed into an office of state. Now rulers embodied their nation and, no matter what their personal characteristics, they were held in awe because they were monarchs.

Thus as rulers lost direct personal control over their patrimony, they gained indirect symbolic control over their nation. This symbolic power was everywhere to be seen. By the beginning of the seventeenth century, monarchs had permanent seats of government attended by vast courts of officials, place seekers, and servants. They no longer moved from place to place with their vast entourages. The idea of the capital city emerged, with Madrid, London, and Paris as the models. Here, the grandiose style of the ruler stood proxy for the wealth and glory of the nation. Great display bespoke great pride, and great pride was translated into great strength.

Portraits of rulers in action and in repose conveyed the central message. Elizabeth I was depicted bestriding a map of England or clutching a rainbow and wearing a gown woven of eyes and ears to signify her power to see and hear her subjects. The Flemish painter Sir Anthony van Dyck (1599–1641) created powerful images of three generations of Stuart kings of England. He was court painter to Charles I, whose qualities he portrayed with great sympathy and not a little exaggeration. Diego Velázquez (1599–1660) was court painter to Philip IV of Spain. His series of equestrian portraits of the Habsburgs—kings, queens, princes, and princesses—exude the spirit of the seventeenth-century monarchy, the grandeur and pomp, the power and self-assurance. Peter Paul Rubens (1577–1640) represented twenty-one separate episodes in the life of Marie de Médicis, queen regent of France.

Queen Elizabeth I of England. This portrait was commissioned by Sir Henry Lee to commemorate the Queen's visit to his estate at Ditchley. Here the queen is the very image of Gloriana—ageless and indomitable.

The themes of artists were no different from those of writers. Monarchy was glorified in a variety of forms of literary representation. National history, particularly of recent events, enjoyed wide popularity. Its avowed purpose was to draw the connection between the past and the present glories of the state. One of the most popular French histories of the period was entitled *On the Excellence of the Kings and the Kingdom of France*. Francis Bacon (1561–1626), who is remembered more as a philosopher and scientist, wrote a laudatory history of England's Henry VII, founder of the Tudor dynasty.

In England it was a period of renaissance. Poets, playwrights, historians, and philosophers by the dozens gravitated to the English court. One of the most remarkable of them was Ben Jonson (1572–1637). He began life as a bricklayer, fought against the Spanish in Flanders, and then turned to acting and writing. His wit and talent brought him to court, where he made his mark by writing and staging masques, light entertainment that included music, dance, pantomime, and acting. Jonson's masques were distinguished by their lavish productions and exotic costumes and the inventive set designs of the great architect Inigo Jones (1573–1652). They were frequently staged at Christmastime and starred members of the court as players. The masques took for their themes the grandeur of England and its rulers.

The role of William Shakespeare (1564–1616) in the celebration of monarchy was more ambiguous. Like Jonson, Shakespeare came from an ordinary family, had little formal education, and began his astonishing career as an actor and producer of theater. He soon began to write as well as direct his plays and his company, the King's Players, received royal patronage. He set many of his plays at the courts of princes and even comedies like *The Tempest* (1611) and *Measure for Measure* (1604) centered on the power of the ruler to dispense justice and to bring peace to his subjects. Both were staged at court. His history plays focused entirely on the character of kings. In *Richard II* (1597) and *Henry VI* (3 parts, 1591–94) Shakespeare exposed the harm that weak rulers inflicted on their states, while in *Henry IV* (2 parts, 1598–1600) and *Henry V* (1599) he highlighted the benefits to be derived from strong rulers. Shakespeare's tragedies made this point in a different way. The tragic flaw in the personality of rulers exposed the world around them to ruin. In *Macbeth* (1606) this flaw was ambition. Macbeth killed to become a king and had to keep on killing to remain one. In *Hamlet* (1602) the tragic flaw was irresolution. The inability of the "Prince of Denmark" to act decisively and reclaim the crown that was his by right brought his state to the brink of collapse. Shakespeare's plays were viewed in London theaters by members of all social classes, and his concentration on the affairs of rulers helped reinforce their dominating importance in the lives of all of their subjects.

The political theory of the divine right of kings further enhanced the importance of monarchs. This theory held that the institution of monarchy had been created by God, and the monarch functioned as God's representative on earth. One clear statement of divine right theory was actually written by a king, James VI of Scotland, who later became King James I of England (1603–25). In *The True Law of Free Monarchies* (1598) James reasoned that God had placed kings on earth to rule, and he would judge them in heaven for their transgressions.

The idea of divine origin of monarchy was uncontroversial, and it was espoused not only by kings. One of the few things that the French Estates-General actually agreed upon during its meeting in 1614—the last for over 175 years—was the statement that "the king is sovereign in France and holds his crown from God only." This sentiment echoed the commonplace view of French political theorists. The greatest writer on the subject, Jean Bodin (1530–96), called the king "God's image on earth." In *The Six Books of the Commonwealth* (1576), Bodin defined the essence of the monarch's power: "The principal mark of sovereign majesty is essentially the right to impose laws on subjects generally without their consent."

Though at first glance the theory of the divine right of kings appears to be a blueprint for arbitrary rule, in fact it was yoked together with a number of principles that restrained the conduct of the monarch. As James I pointed out, God had charged kings with the obligations "to minister justice; to establish good laws; and to procure peace."

Kings were bound by the law of nature and the law of nations. They could not deprive their subjects of their lives, their liberties, or their property without due cause established by law. As one French theorist held, "while the kingdom belongs to the king, the king also belongs to the kingdom." Wherever they turned, kings were instructed in the duties of kingship. In tracts, in letters, and in literature they were lectured on the obligations of their office. "A true king should be first in government, first in council, and first in all the offices of state."

The Court and the Courtiers

For all of the bravura of divine-right theory, far more was expected of kings than they could possibly deliver. The day-to-day affairs of government had grown beyond the capacity of any monarch to handle them. The expansion in the powers of the western states absorbed more officials than ever. At the beginning of the sixteenth century the French court of Francis I employed 622 officers; at the beginning of the seventeenth century the court of

THE DIVINE ORIGINS OF MONARCHY IN HUMAN SOCIETY

■ Sir Robert Filmer's Patriarcha *is one of the clearest statements of the divine origins of monarchy in human society. Filmer believed that Adam, the first father, was monarch of the universe and that his children owed him absolute obedience.* Patriarcha *was written a half century before it was published in 1680.*

In all kingdoms or commonwealths in the world, whether the prince be the supreme father of the people or but the true heir of such a father . . . there is, and always shall be continued to the end of the world, a natural right of a supreme father over every multitude, although, by the secret will of God, many at first do most unjustly obtain the exercise of it.

To confirm this natural right of regal power, we find in the decalogue that the law which enjoins obedience to kings is delivered in the terms of 'honour thy father' [Exodus, xx, 12] as if all power were originally in the father. If obedience to parents be immediately due by a natural law, and subjection to princes but by the mediation of an human ordinance, what reason is there that the law of nature should give place to the laws of men . . . ?

If we compare the natural duties of a father with those of a king, we find them to be all one, without any difference at all but only in the latitude or extent of them. As the father over one family, so the king, as father over many families, extends his care to preserve, feed, clothe, instruct and defend the whole commonwealth. His wars, his peace, his courts of justice and all his acts of sovereignty tend only to preserve and distribute to every subordinate and inferior father, and to their children, their rights and privileges, so that all the duties of a king are summed up in an universal fatherly care of his people.

From Sir Robert Filmer, *Patriarcha*, 1680.

LIFE AT VERSAILLES

■ *Louis de Rouvroy, Duc de Saint-Simon, spent much of his career at the court of Louis XIV. His* Memoires *provide a fascinating study of life at Versailles as well as poison-pen portraits of the king and his courtiers.*

He always took great pains to find out what was going on in public places, in society, in private houses, even family secrets, and maintained an immense number of spies and tale-bearers. These were of all sorts; some did not know that their reports were carried to him; others did know it; there were others, again, who used to write to him directly, through channels which he prescribed; others who were admitted by the backstairs and saw him in his private room. Many a man in all ranks of life was ruined by these methods, often very unjustly, without ever being able to discover the reason; and when the King had once taken a prejudice against a man, he hardly every got over it . . .

No one understood better than Louis XIV the art of enhancing the value of a favour by his manner of bestowing it; he knew how to make the most of a word, a smile, even of a glance. If he addressed any one, were it but to ask a trifling question or make some commonplace remark, all eyes were turned on the person so honored; it was a mark of favour which always gave rise to comment . . .

He loved splendour, magnificence, and profusion in all things, and encouraged similar tastes in his Court; to spend money freely on equipages and buildings, on feasting and at cards, was a sure way to gain his favour, perhaps to obtain the honour of a word from him. Motives of policy had something to do with this; by making expensive habits the fashion, and, for people in a certain position, a necessity, he compelled his courtiers to live beyond their income, and gradually reduced them to depend on his bounty for the means of subsistence.

From Duc de Saint-Simon, *Memoires.*

Henry IV employed over 1,500. Yet the difference was not only in size. Members of the seventeenth-century court were becoming servants of the state as well as of the monarch.

Expanding the court was one of the ways in which monarchs co-opted potential rivals within the aristocracy. In return, those who were favored enhanced their power by royal grants of titles, lands, and income. As the court expanded so did the political power of courtiers. Royal councils—a small group of leading officeholders who advised the monarch on state business—grew in significance. Not only did the council assume the management of government, it also began to advocate policies for the monarch to adopt.

Yet, like everything else in seventeenth-century government, the court revolved around the monarch. The monarch appointed, promoted, and dismissed officeholders at will. As befit this type of personal government, most monarchs chose a single individual to act as a funnel for private and public business. This was the "favorite," whose role combined varying proportions of

best friend, right-hand man, and hired gun. Some favorites, like the French Cardinal Richelieu and the Spanish Count-Duke Olivares, were able to transform themselves into chief ministers with a political philosophy and a vision of government. Others, like the English Duke of Buckingham, simply remained royal companions. Favorites walked a not very tight rope. They could retain their balance only as long as they retained their influence with the monarch. Richelieu claimed that it was "more difficult to dominate the four square feet of the king's study than the affairs of Europe." The parallel careers of Richelieu, Olivares, and Buckingham neatly illustrate the dangers and opportunities of the office.

Cardinal Richelieu (1585–1642) was born into a French noble family of minor importance. A younger son, he trained for the law and then for a position that his family owned in the Church; he was made a cardinal in 1622. After skillful participation in the meeting of the Estates-General of 1614, Richelieu was given a court post through the patronage of Queen Marie de Médicis, mother of Louis XIII. The two men made a good match. Louis XIII hated the work of ruling and Richelieu loved little else.

Though Richelieu received great favor from the king—he became a duke and amassed the largest private fortune in France—his position rested upon his managerial abilities. Richelieu never enjoyed a close personal relationship with his monarch, and he never felt that his position was secure. In 1630, Marie de Médicis turned against him and he was very nearly ousted from office. His last years were filled with suppressing plots to undermine his power or to take his life.

The Count-Duke Olivares (1587–1645) was a younger son of a lesser branch of a great Spanish noble family. By the time he was twenty he had become a courtier with a title, a large fortune, and most unusually, a university education. Olivares became the favorite of King Philip IV (1621–65). He was elevated to the highest rank of the nobility and lost no time consolidating his position.

Olivares used his closeness to the monarch to gain court appointments for his relatives and political supporters, but he was more interested in establishing political policy than in building a court faction. His objective was to maintain the greatness of Spain, whose fortunes, like the Count-Duke's moods, waxed and waned. Like Richelieu, Olivares attempted to further the process of centralizing royal power, which was not very advanced in Spain. Olivares's plans for a nationally recruited and financed army ended in disaster. His efforts at tax reform went unrewarded. He advocated the aggressive foreign policy that mired Spain in the Thirty Years' War and the eighty years of war in the Netherlands. As domestic and foreign crises mounted, Philip IV could not resist the pressure to dismiss his chief minister. In 1643 Olivares was removed from office and two years later, physically exhausted and mentally deranged, he died.

The Spanish master Diego Velázquez painted this portrait of the Count-Duke Olivares.

The Duke of Buckingham (1592–1628) was also a younger son, but not of the English nobility. He received the aimless education of a country gentleman, spending several years in France learning the graces of fashion and dancing. Reputedly one of the most handsome men in Europe, Buckingham hung about the fringes of the English court until his looks and charm brought him to the attention of Queen Anne, James I's wife. She recommended him for a minor office that gave him frequent access to the king. Buckingham quickly caught the eye of James I, and his rise was meteoric. In less than seven years he went from commoner to duke, the highest rank of the English nobility.

Along with his titles, Buckingham acquired political power. He assumed a large number of royal offices, among them Admiral of the Navy, and placed his relatives and dependents in many others. Buckingham took his obligations seriously. He began a reform of naval administration, for example, but his rise to power was so sudden that he found enemies at every turn. These increased dramatically when James I died in 1625. But he succeeded where so many others had failed by becoming the favorite and chief minister of the new king, Charles I (1625–49). His accumulation of power and patronage proceeded unabated, as did the enmity he aroused. But Charles I stood firmly behind him. In 1628 a discontented naval officer finally accomplished what the most powerful men in England could not: Buckingham was assassinated. While Charles I wept inconsolably at the news, ordinary Londoners drank to the health of his killer.

The Drive to Centralize Government

Richelieu, Olivares, and Buckingham met very different ends. Yet in their own ways they shared a common goal, to extend the authority of the monarch over his state and to centralize his control over the machinery of governance.

This portrait of Richelieu by Philippe de Champaigne shows the cardinal's intellectual power and controlled determination.

George Villiers, duke of Buckingham. The royal favorite virtually ruled the country between 1618 and 1628. The general rejoicing at his death embittered the king and helped bring about the eleven years' rule without Parliament.

One of the chief means by which kings and councilors attempted to expand the authority of the state was through the legal system. Administering justice was one of the sacred duties of the monarchy. The complexities of ecclesiastical, civil, and customary law gave trained lawyers an essential role in government. As legal experts and the demands for legal services increased, royal law courts multiplied and expanded. In France, the Parlement of Paris, the main law court of the state, became a powerful institution that contested with courtiers for the right to advise the monarch. In Spain the *letrados*—university-trained lawyers who were normally members of the nobility—were the backbone of royal govern-

ment. Formal legal training was a requirement for many of the administrative posts in the state. In Castile members of all social classes frequently used the royal courts to settle personal disputes. The expansion of a centralized system of justice thus joined the interests of subjects and the monarchy.

In England the legal system expanded differently. Central courts situated in the royal palace of Westminster grew and the lawyers and judges who practiced in them became a powerful profession. They were especially active in the House of Commons of the English Parliament, which along with the House of Lords had extensive advisory and legislative powers. More important than the rise of the central courts, however, was the rise of the local ones. The English Crown extended royal justice to the counties by granting legal authority to members of the local social elite. These justices of the peace, as they were known, became agents of the Crown in their own localities. Justices were given power to hear and settle minor cases and to imprison those who had committed serious offenses until the assizes, the semi-annual sessions of the county court.

Assizes combined the ceremony of rule with its process. Royal authority was displayed in a great procession to the courthouse that was led by the judge and the county justices, followed by the grand and petty juries of local citizens who would hear the cases, and finally by the carts carrying the prisoners to trial. Along with the legal business that was performed, assizes were occasions for edifying sermons, typically on the theme of obedience. Their solemnity, marked by the black robes of the judge, the Latin of the legal proceedings, and the public executions with which assizes invariably ended, all served to instill a sense of the power of the state in the throngs of ordinary people who witnessed them.

Efforts to integrate center and locality extended to more than the exercise of justice. The monarch also needed officials who could enforce royal policy in those localities where the special privileges of groups and individuals remained strong. The best strategy was to appoint local leaders to royal office. But with so much of the aristocracy resident at court, this was not always an effective course. By the beginning of the seventeenth century, the French monarchy began to rely on new central officials known as *intendants* to perform many of the tasks of the provincial governors. Cardinal Richelieu expanded the use of the intendants and by the middle of the century they had become a vital part of royal government.

The Lords Lieutenant were a parallel institution created in England. Unlike every other European state,

England had no national army. Every English county was required to raise, equip, and train its own militia. Lords Lieutenant were in charge of these trained bands. Since the aristocracy was the ancient military class in the state, the lieutenants were chosen from the greatest nobles of the realm. But they delegated their work to members of the gentry, large local landholders who took on their tasks as a matter of prestige rather than profit. Perhaps not surprisingly, the English military was among the weakest in Europe and nearly all its foreign adventures ended in disaster.

Efforts to centralize the affairs of the Spanish monarchy could not proceed so easily. The separate regions over which the king ruled maintained their own laws and privileges. Attempts to apply Castilian rules or implant Castilian officials always drew opposition from other regions. Olivares frequently complained that Philip IV was the king of Castile only and nothing but a thorough plan of unification would make him the king of Spain. This he proposed in 1625 to attempt to solve the dual problems of military manpower and military finance. After 1621, Spain was again deeply involved in European warfare. Fighting in the Netherlands and in Germany demanded large armies and larger sums of money. Olivares launched a plan for a Union of Arms to which all the separate regions of the empire, including Mexico and Peru in the west, Italy in the east, and the separate regions in Iberia would contribute. Not all of the Iberian provinces were persuaded to contribute. Catalonia stood upon its ancient privileges and refused to grant either troops or funds. But Olivares was able to establish at least the principle of unified cooperation.

The Taxing Demands of War

More than anything else, the consolidation of the state was propelled by war. Whether offensive or defensive, continuous or intermittent, successful or calamitous, war was the irresistible force of the seventeenth-century monarchy. War taxation was its immovable object. Perhaps half of all revenue of the western states went to finance war. To maintain its armies and navies, its fortresses and outposts, the state had to squeeze every penny from its subjects. Old taxes had to be collected more efficiently, new taxes had to be introduced and enforced. On the other side, the unprecedented demands for money on the part of the state were always resisted. The privileged challenged the legality of levying taxes, the unprivileged did whatever they could to avoid paying them.

The economic hardships caused by the ceaseless military activity touched everyone. Those in the direct path of battle had little left to feed themselves, let alone to provide to the state. The disruption of the delicate cycle of planting and harvesting devastated local communities. Armies plundered ripened grain and trampled seedlings as they moved through fields. The conscription of village men and boys removed vital skills from the community and upset the gender-based division of labor. Peasants were squeezed by the armies for crops, by the lords for rents, and by the state for taxes.

In fact, the inability of the lower orders of European society to finance a century of warfare was clear from the beginning. In Spain and France, the principal problem was that so much of the wealth of the nation was beyond the reach of traditional royal taxation. The nobility and many of the most important towns had long achieved exemption from basic taxes on consumption and wealth. European taxation was regressive, falling most heavily upon those least able to pay. Rulers and subjects alike recognized the inequities of the European system of taxation. Regime after regime began with plans to overhaul the national system of taxation

The oppression of the peasantry is the theme of this engraving published in the mid-seventeenth century: "This noble is the spider and the peasant the fly." The poor man is handing over goods and money to the fat milord, who says, "You must pay or serve." The peasant replies, "To all masters, all honors."

before settling for propping up new emergency levies against the rotting foundations of the old structure. Nevertheless, the fiscal crisis that the European wars provoked did result in an expansion of state taxation.

Though uninvolved in the European conflicts, England was not immune from military spending. War with Ireland in the 1590s and with Spain between 1588 and 1604 depleted the reserves that the crown had obtained when Henry VIII dissolved the monasteries. Disastrous wars against France and Spain in the 1620s provoked fiscal crisis for a monarchy that had few direct sources of revenue. While the great wealth of the kingdom was in land, the chief sources of revenue for the Crown were in trade. In the early seventeenth century customs duties, or impositions, became a lucrative source of income when the judges ruled that the king could determine which commodities could be taxed and at what rate.

Because so much of the Crown's revenues derived from commerce and because foreign invasion could only come from the sea, the most pressing military need of the English monarchy was for naval defense. Even during the Armada crisis, the largest part of the English fleet had been made up of private merchant ships pressed into service through the emergency tax of Ship Money. This was a tax on each port town to hire a merchant ship and fit it out for war. In the 1630s, Charles I revived Ship Money and extended it to all English localities.

War finance was like an all-consuming monster. No matter how much new revenue was fed into it, its appetite grew for more. New taxes and increased rates of traditional taxation created suffering and a sense of grievance throughout the western European states. Opposition to taxation was not based on greed. The state's right to tax was not yet an established principle. Monarchs received certain forms of revenue in return for grants of immunities and privileges to powerful groups in their state. The state's efforts to go beyond these restricted grants was viewed as theft of private property. In the Ship Money case challengers argued that the king had no right to what belonged to his subjects except in a case of national emergency. This was a claim that the king accepted, arguing that such an emergency existed in the presence of pirates who were attacking English shipping. But if Charles I did not make a convincing claim for national emergency, the monarchs of France and Spain, the princes of Germany, and the rulers of the states of eastern Europe all did.

Throughout the seventeenth century, monarchy solidified itself as a form of government. The king's authority came from God, but his power came from his people. By administering justice, assembling armies, and extracting resources through taxation, the monarch ruled as well as governed. The richer the king and the more powerful his might, the more potent was his state. Europeans began to identify themselves as citizens of a nation and to see themselves in distinction to other nations.

The Crises of the Royal State

The expansion of the functions, duties, and powers of the state in the early seventeenth century was not universally welcomed in European societies. The growth of central government came at the expense of local rights and privileges held by corporate bodies like the Church and the towns or by individuals like provincial officials and aristocrats. The state proved a powerful competitor, especially in the contest for the meager surplus produced on the land. As rents and prices stabilized in the early seventeenth century, after a long period of inflation, taxation increased, slowly at first and then at a pace with the gathering momentum of the Thirty Years' War. State exactions burdened all segments of society. Peasants lost the small benefit that rising prices had conferred upon producers. The surplus that parents had once passed on to children was now taken by the state. Local officials, never altogether popular, came to be seen as parasites and were easy targets for peasant rebellions. Larger landholders, whose prosperity depended upon rents and services from an increasingly impoverished peasantry, suffered along with their tenants. Even the great magnates were appalled by the state's insatiable appetite.

It was not only taxation that aroused opposition. Social and economic regulation meant more laws. More laws meant more lawyers and agents of enforcement. State regulation may have been more efficient—though many believed it was more efficient only for the state—but it was certainly disruptive. It was also expensive at a time when the fragile European economy was in a phase of decline. The early seventeenth century was a time of hunger in most of western Europe. Subtle changes in climate reduced the length of growing seasons and the size of crops. Bad harvests in the 1620s and 1640s left disease and starvation in their wake. And the wars ground on. Armies brought misery to those who were forcibly recruited to fight, those who were taxed into destitution, and those who simply had the misfortune to live in the path of destruction.

By the middle of the seventeenth century, a Europe-wide crisis was taking shape, though its timing and its forms differed from place to place. Rural protests, like grain riots and mob assaults on local institutions, had a long history in all of the European states. Popular revolt was not the product of mindless despair, but rather the natural form of political action for those who fell outside the institutionalized political process. Bread riots and tax revolts became increasingly common in the early seventeenth century. More importantly, as the focus of discontent moved from local institutions to the state, the forms of revolt changed. So, too, did the participants. Members of the political elite began to formulate their own grievances against the expansion of state power. If revolts were not new, their justification was. A theory of resistance, first developed in the French wars of religion, came to be applied to political tyranny, and posed a direct challenge to the idea of the divine right of kings. By the 1640s all of these forces converged and rebellion exploded across the Continent. In Spain the ancient kingdoms of Catalonia and Portugal asserted their independence from Castilian rule; in France members of the aristocracy rose against a child monarch and his regent. In Italy, revolts rocked Naples and Sicily. In England, a constitutional crisis gave way to civil war and then to the first political revolution in European history.

The Need to Resist

Europeans lived more precariously in the seventeenth century than in any period since the Black Death. One benchmark of crisis was population decline. In the Mediterranean, Spanish population fell from 8.5 to 7 million and Italian population from 13 to 11 million. The ravages of the Thirty Years' War were most clearly felt in central Europe. Germany lost nearly a third of its people, Bohemia nearly half. Northwestern Europe—that is, England, the Netherlands, and France—was hardest hit in the first half of the century and only gradually recovered by 1700. Population decline had many causes and, rather remarkably, direct casualties from warfare were a very small component. The indirect effects of war, the disruption of agriculture, and the spread of disease were far more devastating. Spain alone lost one half million people at the turn of the century and another half million between 1647 and 1652. Severe outbreaks in 1625 and in 1665 hit England, while France endured three consecutive years of epidemics from 1629 to 1631.

All sectors of the European economy from agriculture to trade stagnated or declined in the early seventeenth century. Not surprisingly, peasants were hardest

The Plague in Milan, *a painting by Caspar Crayer of the seventeenth-century Flemish school. The victims of the epidemic are shown being consoled by a priest.*

hit. The surplus from good harvests did not remain in rural communities to act as a buffer for bad ones. Tens of thousands died during the two great subsistence crises in the late 1620s and the late 1640s.

Predictably, acute economic crisis led to rural revolt. As the French peasants reeled from visitations of plague, frost, and floods, the French state was raising the *taille*, the tax on basic commodities that fell most heavily upon the lower orders. A series of French rural revolts in the late 1630s focused on opposition to tax increases. The Nu-Pieds—the barefooted—rose against changes in the salt tax, others rose against new levies on wine. These revolts began in the same way, with the murder of a local tax official, the organization of a peasant militia, and the recruitment of local clergy and notables. The rebels forced temporary concessions from local authorities, but they never achieved lasting reforms. Each revolt ended with the reimposition of order by the state. In England the largest rural protests, like the Midland Revolt of 1607, centered upon opposition to the enclosure of grain fields and their conversion to pasture.

The most spectacular popular uprisings occurred in Spanish-occupied Italy. In the spring of 1647 the Sicilian city of Palermo exploded under the pressure of a disastrous harvest, rising food prices, and relentless taxation. As grain prices rose, the city government subsidized the price of bread, running up huge debts in the process. When the town governors could no longer afford the subsidies, they decided to reduce the size of the loaf rather than increase its price. The women of the city rioted when the first undersized loaves were placed on sale, and soon the entire city was in revolt. Commoners who were not part of the urban power structure led the revolt, and for a time they achieved the abolition of Spanish taxes on basic foodstuffs. Their success provided the model for a similar uprising in Naples, the largest city in Europe. The revolt began in 1647 after the Spanish placed a tax on fruit. A crowd gathered to protest the new imposition, burned the customs house, and murdered several local officials. The protesters were led first by a fisherman and then by a blacksmith, and again the rebels achieved the temporary suspension of Spanish taxation. But neither of the Italian urban revolts could attract support from the local governors or the nobility. Both uprisings were eventually crushed.

The Right to Resist

Rural and urban revolts by members of the lower orders of European society were doomed to failure. Not only did the state control vast military resources, but it could count upon the loyalty of the governing classes to suppress local disorder. It was only when local elites rebelled and joined their social and political discontent to the economic grievances of the peasants that the state faced a genuine crisis. Traditionally, aristocratic rebellion centered upon the legitimacy rather than the power of the state. Claimants to the throne initiated civil wars for the prize of the crown. By the early seventeenth century, however, hereditary monarchy was too firmly entrenched to be threatened by aristocratic rebellions. When Elizabeth I of England died without an heir, the throne passed to her cousin, James I, without even a murmur of discontent. The assassination of Henry IV in 1610 left a child on the French throne, yet it provoked little more than intrigue over which aristocratic faction

would advise him. The principles of hereditary monarchy and the divine right of kings laid an unshakable foundation for royal legitimacy. But if the monarch's right to rule could no longer be challenged, was the method of rule equally unassailable? Were subjects bound to their sovereign in all cases whatsoever?

Luther and Calvin had preached a doctrine of passive obedience. Magistrates ruled by divine will and must be obeyed in all things, they argued. Both left a tiny crack in the door of absolute submission, however, by recognizing the right of lesser magistrates to resist their superiors if divine law was violated. It was during the French civil wars that a broader theory of resistance began to develop. In attempting to defend themselves from accusations that they were rebels, a number of Huguenot writers responded with an argument that accepted the divine right of kings but that limited royal power. They claimed that kings were placed on earth by God to uphold piety and justice. When they failed to do so, lesser magistrates were obliged to resist them. As God would not institute tyranny, oppressive monarchs could not be acting by divine right. Therefore, the king who violated divine law could be punished. In the most influential of these writings, *A Defense of Liberty Against Tyrants* (1579), Philippe Duplessis-Mornay (1549–1623) took the critical next step and argued that the king who violated the law of the land could also be resisted.

In the writings of both the French Huguenots and the Dutch Protestants there remained strict limits to this right to resist. These authors accepted all the premises of divine right theory and restricted resistance to other divinely ordained magistrates. Obedience tied society together at all levels. Loosening any of the knots might unravel everything. In fact, one crucial binding had already come loose when the arguments used to justify resistance in matters of religion came to be applied to matters of state. Logic soon drove the argument further. If it was the duty of lesser magistrates to resist monarchical tyranny, why was it not the duty of all citizens to do so? This was a question posed not by a Protestant rebel, but by a Jesuit professor, Juan de Mariana (1536–1624). In *The King and the Education of the King* (1598), Mariana described how human government developed from the need of individuals to have leaders to act for their convenience and well-being. These magistrates were first established by the people and then legitimated by God. Magistrates were nothing other than the people's representatives, and if it was the duty of magistrates to resist the tyranny of monarchs, then it must also be the duty of every individual citizen. "If the sacred fatherland is falling into ruins, he who tries to kill the tyrant will be acting in no ways unjustly."

In his defense of the English Revolution, the great English poet John Milton (1608–74) built upon traditional resistance theory as it had developed over the previous fifty years. Kings were instituted by the people to uphold piety and justice. Lesser magistrates had the right to resist monarchs. An unjust king forfeited his divine right and was to be punished as any ordinary citizen. In *The Tenure of Kings and Magistrates* (1649), Milton expanded upon the conventional idea that society was formed by a covenant, or contract, between ruler and ruled. The king in his coronation oath promised to uphold the laws of the land and to rule for the benefit of his subjects. The subjects promised to obey. Failure to meet obligations—by either side—broke the contract.

By the middle of the seventeenth century, resistance theory provided the intellectual justification for a number of quite different attacks upon monarchical authority. In 1640 simultaneous rebellions in the ancient kingdoms of Portugal and Catalonia threatened the Spanish monarchy. The Portuguese successfully dissolved the rather artificial bonds that had been created by Philip II and resumed their separate national identity. Catalonia, the easternmost province of Spain, which Ferdinand of Aragon had brought to the union of crowns in the fifteenth century, presented a more serious challenge. Throughout the 1620s, Catalonia, with its rich Mediterranean city of Barcelona, had consistently rebuffed Olivares's attempts to consolidate the Spanish provinces. The Catalan Cortes—the representative institution of the towns—refused to make even small contributions to the Union of Arms or to successive appeals for emergency tax increases. Catalonian leaders feared that these demands were only the thin edge of the wedge. They did not want their province to go the way of Castile, where taxation was as much an epidemic as was plague.

Catalonia relied upon its ancient laws to fend off demands for contributions to the Spanish military effort. But soon the province was embroiled in the French war and Olivares was forced to bring troops into Catalonia. The presence of the soldiers and their conduct inflamed the local population. In the spring of 1640 an unconnected series of peasant uprisings took place. Soldiers and royal officials were slain, and the Spanish viceroy of the province was murdered. But the violence was not only directed against outsiders. Attacks upon wealthy citizens raised the specter of social revolt.

It was at this point that a peasant uprising broadened into a provincial rebellion. The political leaders of Barcelona not only decided to sanction the rebellion, they decided to lead it. They declared that Philip IV had violated the fundamental laws of Catalonia and that in consequence their allegiance to the crown of Spain was dissolved. Instead they turned to Louis XIII of France, offering him sovereignty if he would preserve their liberties. In fact, the Catalonians simply exchanged a devil they knew for one they did not. The French happily sent troops into Barcelona to repel a Spanish attempt to crush the rebellion. Now two armies occupied Catalonia. The Catalan rebellion lasted for twelve years. When the Spanish finally took Barcelona in 1652, both rebels and ruler were exhausted from the struggle.

The revolt of the Catalans posed a greater external threat to the Spanish monarchy than it did an internal one. In contrast, the French Fronde, an aristocratic rebellion that began in 1648, was more directly a challenge to the underlying authority of the state. It too began in response to fiscal crises brought on by war. Throughout the 1640s the French state had tottered on the edge of bankruptcy. It had used every means of creative financing that its ministers could devise, mortgaging as much of the future as anyone would buy. Still it was necessary to raise traditional taxes and to institute new ones. The first tactic revived peasant revolts, especially in the early years of the decade; the second led to the Fronde.

The Fronde was a rebellion against the regency government of Louis XIV (1643–1715), who was only four years old when he inherited the French throne. His mother, Anne of Austria (1601–66), ruled as regent with the help of her Italian advisor, Cardinal Mazarin (1602–61). In the circumstances of war, agricultural crisis, and financial stringency, no regency government was going to be popular, but Anne and Mazarin made the worst of a bad situation. They initiated new taxes on officeholders, Parisian landowners, and the nobility. Soon all three united against them, led by the Parlement of Paris, the highest court in the land, in which new decrees of taxation had to be registered. When the Parlement refused to register a number of the new taxes proposed by the government and soon insisted upon the right to control the crown's financial policy, Anne and Mazarin struck back by arresting a number of leading members of the Parlement. But in 1648 barricades went up in Paris, and the court, along with the nine-year-old king, fled the capital. Quickly the Fronde—which took its name from the slingshots that children used to hurl stones at carriages—became an aristocratic revolt aimed not at the king, but at his advisers. Demands for Mazarin's resignation, the removal of the new taxes, and greater

An episode from the second Fronde, one of the two French civil wars that occurred during the minority of Louis XIV.

participation in government by nobles and Parlement were coupled with profuse statements of loyalty to the king.

The Duc de Condé, leader of the Parisian insurgents, courted Spanish aid against Mazarin's forces, and the cardinal was forced to make concessions to prevent a Spanish invasion of France. The leaders of the Fronde agreed that the crown must overhaul its finances and recognize the rights of the administrative nobility to participate in formulating royal policy. But they had no concrete proposals to accomplish either aim. Nor could they control the deteriorating political situation in Paris and a number of provincial capitals where urban and rural riots followed the upper-class attack upon the state. The catastrophic winter of 1652, with its combination of harvest failure, intense cold, and epidemic disease, brought the crisis to a head. Louis XIV was declared old enough to rule and his forces recaptured Paris, where he was welcomed as a savior. Born of frustration, fear, and greed, the Fronde accomplished little. It demonstrated only that the French aristocracy remained an independent force in politics. Like the Catalonian revolt, it revealed the fragility of the absolute state on the one hand, yet its underlying stability on the other.

The English Civil Wars

On the surface, it is difficult to understand why the most profound challenge to monarchical authority in the seventeenth century took place in England. Among the nations of Europe, England alone enjoyed peace in the early seventeenth century. Except for a brief period around 1620, the English economy sputtered along. The monarchy itself was stable. In 1603 James I had succeeded his cousin Elizabeth I without challenge and already had as many children as the Tudors had produced in nearly a century.

James I was not a lovable monarch but he was capable, astute, and generous. His principal difficulties were that he succeeded a legend and he was Scottish. There was little he could do about either. Elizabeth I had ruled England successfully for over forty years. As the economy soured and the state tilted toward bankruptcy in the 1590s, the queen remained above criticism. She sold off royal lands worth thousands of pounds and ran up huge debts at the turn of the century. Yet the gleaming myth of the glorious virgin queen tarnished not the least bit, and when she died, the general population wept openly.

At first, James I endeared himself to the English gentry and aristocracy by showering them with the gift of social elevation. On his way to London from Scotland, the first of the Stuart kings knighted thousands of gentlemen. But he showered favor equally on his own countrymen, members of his royal Scottish court who accompanied him to England. A strong strain of ethnic prejudice combined with the disappointed hopes of English courtiers to generate immediate hostility to the new regime. Though he relied upon Elizabeth's most trusted ministers to guide state business, James was soon plunged into financial and political difficulties. He never escaped from either.

His financial problems resulted directly from the fact that the tax base of the English monarchy was undervalued. For decades the monarchy had staved off a crisis by selling lands that had been confiscated from the Church in the mid-sixteenth century. But this solution reduced the Crown's long-term revenues and made it dependent upon extraordinary grants of taxation from Parliament. Royal demands for money were met by parliamentary demands for political reform. The most significant, in 1628, during the reign of Charles I, led to the formulation of the Petition of Right, which restated the traditional English freedoms from arbitrary arrest and imprisonment (habeas corpus), from nonparliamentary taxation, and from the confiscation of property by martial law.

Religious problems mounted on top of economic and political difficulties. Demands were made for thoroughgoing church reforms by groups and individuals who had little in common other than the name given to them by their detractors: Puritans. One of the most contentious issues raised by some Puritans was the survival in the Anglican church of the Catholic hierarchy of archbishops and bishops. These Puritans demanded the abolition of this episcopal form of government and its replacement with a presbyterial system similar to that in Scotland, in which congregations nominated their own representatives to a national assembly. Neither James I nor his son, Charles I, opposed religious reform, but to achieve their reforms they strengthened episcopal power. In the 1620s Archbishop William Laud (1573–1645) rose to power in the English church by espousing a Calvinism so moderate that many denied it was Calvinism at all. Laud preached the beauty of holiness and strove to reintroduce decoration in the church and a formal decorum in the service. One of Laud's first projects after he was appointed archbishop of Canterbury was to establish a consistent divine service in England and Scotland by creating new prayer books.

It fell to the unfortunate dean of St. Giles Cathedral in Edinburgh to introduce the new Scottish prayer book in 1637. The reaction was immediate: someone threw a stool at his head and dozens of women screamed that "popery" was being brought to Scotland. There were riots by citizens and resistance to the use of the new prayer book by clergy and the nobility. To Charles I the opposition was rebellion and he began to raise forces to suppress it. But Scottish soldiers were far more determined to preserve their religious practice than were English soldiers to impose the king's. By the end of 1640 an army of Charles's Scottish subjects had successfully invaded England.

Now the fiscal and political problems of the Stuart monarchs came into play. For eleven years Charles I had managed to do what he was in theory supposed to do, live from his own revenues. He had accomplished this by a combination of economy and the revival of ancient feudal rights that struck hard at the governing classes. He levied fines for unheard-of offenses, expanded traditional taxes, and added a brutal efficiency to the collection of revenue. While these expedients sufficed during peacetime, now that an army had to be raised and a war fought, Charles I was again dependent upon grants from Parliament, which he reluctantly summoned in 1640.

The Long Parliament, which met in November 1640 and sat for thirteen years, saw little urgency in levying taxes to repel the Scots. After all, the Scots were resisting Laud's religious innovations and there were many

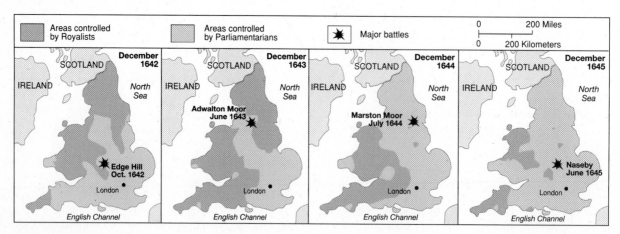

The English Civil War

Englishmen who believed that they should be resisted. Parliament proposed a number of constitutional reforms that Charles I reluctantly accepted. The Long Parliament would not be dismissed without its own consent. In the future Parliaments would be summoned once in every three years. Due process in common law would be observed, and the ancient taxes that the Crown had revived would be abolished.

At first Charles I could do nothing but bide his time and accept these assaults upon his power and authority. Once he had crushed the Scots he would be able to bargain from a position of strength. But as the months passed it became clear that Parliament had no intention of providing him with money or forces. Rather, the members sought to negotiate with the Scots themselves and to continue to demand concessions from the king as long as the Scottish threat remained. By the end of 1641 Charles's patience had worn thin. He bungled an attempt to arrest the leaders of the House of Commons, but he successfully spirited his wife and children out of London. Then he too left the capital and headed north where, in the summer of 1642, he raised the royal

AN EYEWITNESS ACCOUNT OF THE EXECUTION OF CHARLES I

■ *Charles I was executed at Westminster on a bitter January afternoon in 1649. This excerpt comes from an eyewitness account of his last moments. He was accompanied on the scaffold by the bishop of London and discovered that the chopping block was very short so that he could be held down if he resisted.*

And to the executioner he said, "I shall say but very short prayers, and when I thrust out my hands—"

Then he called to the bishop for his cap, and having put it on, asked the executioner, "Does my hair trouble you?" who desired him to put it all under his cap; which, as he was doing by the help of the bishop and the executioner, he turned to the bishop, and said, "I have a good cause, and a gracious God on my side."

The bishop said, "There is but one stage more, which, though turbulent and troublesome, yet is a very short one. You may consider it will soon carry you a very great way; it will carry you from earth to heaven; and there you shall find to your great joy the prize you hasten to, a crown of glory."

The king adjoins, "I go from a corruptible to an incorruptible crown; where no disturbance can be, no disturbance in the world."

The bishop. "You are exchanged from a temporal to an eternal crown,—a good exchange."

Then the king asked the executioner, "Is my hair well?" . . . and looking upon the block, said, "You must set it fast."

The executioner. "It is fast, sir."

King. "It might have been a little higher."

Executioner. "It can be no higher, sir."

King. "When I put out my hands this way, then—"

Then having said a few words to himself, as he stood, with hands and eyes lift up, immediately stooping down he laid his neck upon the block; and the executioner, again putting his hair under his cap, his Majesty, thinking he had been going to strike, bade him, "Stay for the sign."

Executioner. "Yes, I will, an it please your Majesty."

After a very short pause, his Majesty stretching forth his hands, the executioner at one blow severed his head from his body; which, being held up and showed to the people, was with his body put into a coffin covered with black velvet and carried into his lodging.

His blood was taken up by divers persons for different ends: by some as trophies of their villainy; by others as relics of a martry; and in some hath had the same effect, by the blessing of God, which was often found in his sacred touch when living.

A satirical print depicting Cromwell dissolving the Long Parliament in 1653. Symbolic animals include an owl that cannot see despite glasses and a candle, and a tiny dog mimicking the British lion. The sign on the wall says, "This House is to let."

standard and declared the leaders of Parliament rebels and traitors. England was plunged into civil war.

There were strong passions on both sides. Parliamentarians believed that they were fighting to defend their religion, their liberties, and the rule of law. Royalists believed they were fighting to defend their monarch, their church, and social stability. After nearly three years of inconclusive fighting, in June 1645 Parliament won a decisive victory at Naseby and brought the war to an end the following summer. The king was in captivity, bishops had been abolished, a Presbyterian church had been established, and limitations were placed on royal power. All that remained necessary to end three years of civil war was the king's agreement to abide by the judgment of battle.

But Charles I had no intention of surrendering either his religion or his authority. Despite the rebels' suc-

cesses, they could not rule without him, and he would concede nothing as long as opportunities to maneuver remained. In 1647 there were opportunities galore. The war had proved ruinously expensive to Parliament. It owed enormous sums to the Scots, to its own soldiers, and to the governors of London. Each of these elements had its own objectives in a final settlement of the war and they were not altogether compatible. London feared the parliamentary army, unpaid and camped dangerously close to the capital. The Scots and the English Presbyterians in Parliament feared that the religious settlement already made would be sacrificed by those known as Independents, who desired a more decentralized church. The Independents feared that they would be persecuted just as harshly by the Presbyterians as they had been by the king. In fact, the war had settled nothing.

The English Revolutions

Charles I happily played both ends against the middle until the army decisively ended the game. In June 1647 parliamentary soldiers kidnaped the king and demanded that Parliament pay their arrears, protect them from legal retribution, and recognize their service to the nation. Those in Parliament who opposed the army's intervention were impeached, and when London Presbyterians rose up against the army's show of force, troops moved in to occupy the city. The civil war, which had come so close to resolution in 1647, had now become a military revolution. Religious and political radicals flocked to the army and encouraged the soldiers to support their programs and to resist disbandment. New fighting broke out in 1648 as Charles encouraged his supporters to resume the war. But forces under the command of Sir Thomas Fairfax (1612–71) and Oliver Cromwell (1599–1658) easily crushed the royalist uprisings in England and Scotland. The army now demanded that Charles I be brought to justice for his treacherous conduct both before and during the war. When the majority in Parliament refused, still hoping against hope to reach an accommodation with the king, the soldiers again acted decisively. In December 1648 army regiments were sent to London to purge the two houses of Parliament of those who opposed the army's demands. The remaining members, contemptuously called the Rump Parliament, voted to bring the king to trial for his crimes against the liberties of his subjects. On 30 January 1649, Charles I was executed and England was declared to be a commonwealth. (See Special Feature, "King Charles's Head," pp. 518–519.) The monarchy and the House of Lords were abolished and the nation was to be governed by what was left of the membership of the House of Commons.

For four years the members of the Rump Parliament struggled with proposals for a new constitution while balancing the demands of moderate and radical reformers and an increasingly hostile army. It achieved little other than to raise the level of frustration. In 1653 Oliver Cromwell, with the support of the army's senior officers, forcibly dissolved the Rump and became the leader of the revolutionary government. At first he ruled along with a Parliament handpicked from among the supporters of the commonwealth. When Cromwell's Parliament proved no more capable of governing than had the Rump, a written constitution, The Instrument of Government (1653), established a new polity. Cromwell was given the title Lord Protector and he was to rule along with a freely elected Parliament and an administrative body known as the council of state.

Cromwell was able to hold the revolutionary cause together through the force of his own personality. A member of the lesser landed elite who had opposed the arbitrary policies of Charles I, he was a devout Puritan who believed in a large measure of religious toleration for Christians. As both a member of Parliament and a senior officer in the army, he had been able to temper the claims of each when they conflicted.

Though many urged him to accept the crown of England and begin a new monarchy, Cromwell steadfastly held out for a government in which fundamental authority resided in Parliament. Until his death he defended the achievements of the revolution and held its conflicting constituents together.

But a sense that only a single person could effectively rule a state remained too strong for the reforms of the revolutionary regimes to have much chance of success. When Cromwell died in 1658 his eldest son Richard was proposed as the new Lord Protector, but Richard had very little experience in either military or civil affairs. Nor did he have the sense of purpose that was his father's greatest source of strength. Without an individual to hold the movement together, the revolution fell apart. In 1659 the army again intervened in civil affairs, dismissing the recently elected Parliament and calling for the restoration of the monarchy, to provide stability to the state. After a period of negotiation in which the king agreed to a general amnesty with only a few exceptions, the Stuarts were restored when Charles II (1649–85) took the throne in 1660.

Twenty years of civil war and revolution had their effect. Parliament became a permanent part of civil government and now had to be managed rather than ignored. Royal power over taxation and religion was curtailed, though in fact Parliament proved more vigorous in suppressing religious dissent than the monarchy ever was. England was to be a reformed Protestant state, though there remained much dispute about what constituted reform. Absolute monarchy had become constitutional monarchy with the threat of revolution behind the power of Parliament and the threat of anarchy behind the power of the Crown.

Both threats proved potent in 1685 when James II (1685–88) came to the throne. A declared Catholic, James attempted to use his power of appointment to foil the constraints that Parliament imposed upon him. He elevated Catholics to leading posts in the military and in the central government and began a campaign to pack a

A fanciful rendition of the execution of Charles I by a contemporary Flemish painter. At the top are portraits of Charles and his executioner. Below are scenes of Charles on his way to execution and of people dipping their handkerchiefs in his blood after the beheading.

King Charles's Head

They could have killed him quietly: the executioners slipping away silently in the night, unauthorized, unknown. It was the quickest way and it would end all doubts. Since June 1647, Charles I had been a prisoner of the parliamentary army, and there had been more than one moment in which his elimination would have settled so many vexing problems. They could have let him escape. Let him live out his life in exile. Dangerous, perhaps, but still he would be gone and a new government in the name of the people could get on with creating a new order. They could have done it quietly.

Instead the leaders of Parliament and the army decided on a trial, a public presentation of charges against the king, a public judgment of his guilt. A high court of justice, enforcing the laws of England, would try its king for treason against the state. The logic was simple: if Parliament had fought for the preservation of the liberties of all Englishmen, then they could only proceed against the king by law. If they followed any other course, they were open to the charge that they were usurpers, that they ruled by the power of might rather than by the power of law. But if the logic was simple, everything else was hopelessly complex. English law was a system of precedents, one case stacking upon another to produce the weighty judgments of what was and was not lawful. Never had there been a treason case like this one. Indeed, how could the king commit treason, how could he violate his own allegiance? Always before, the king acted as prosecutor, the

king's judges had rendered decisions, and the king's executioner had carried out sentences. Not one of these precedents was now in the least way useful.

Nor was it clear what court had jurisdiction over this unprecedented case. The royal judges would have no part of it; neither would the House of Lords. The House of Commons was forced to create its own high court of justice, 135 supporters of the parliamentary cause drawn from its own members, from the army, and from among the leading citizens of London. Barely half attended any of the sessions. Judge John Bradshaw, who presided over two provincial royal courts, was chosen to preside at the king's trial after several of his more distinguished colleagues tactfully declined the post. Bradshaw took the precaution of lining his hat with lead against the chance that he would be shot from the galleries rather than the floor.

These shortcomings did not deter the leaders of the parliamentary cause. These were unprecedented times and the ossified procedures of lawyers and law courts could not be allowed to detract from the undeniable justice of their cause. Charles I had committed treason against his nation. He had declared war on his people. He had brought Irish and Scottish armies into England to repress Parliament, and when that had failed he had negotiated with French, Danish, and Dutch troops for the same purpose. Even when he had been defeated in battle, when the judgment of God was clear for all to see, even then he plotted and he tricked. His lies were revealed by his own hand, his captured correspondence detailing how he intended to double-cross those to whom he swore he would be faithful. Cromwell called him "a man against whom the Lord has witnessed," and the prosecution needed no better testimony than that. If there were no precedents, then this trial would set one.

Nevertheless, the makeshift nature of the court provided the king with his line of attack. If there was to be a public display, then Charles I was determined to turn it to his advantage. Even as his royal palace was being converted into a courtroom and an execution platform was being hastily erected on one of its balconies, even now the king could not conceive that the nation could be governed without him. Royal government had guided England for a millennium and for all he could see would do so for another. Rather he feared that he would be deposed and replaced, and against that eventuality he

had secured the escape of his two elder sons. They were safe in France and only his youngest child was in the hands of these savage parliamentarians.

About the trial itself, he worried not at all. There could be no court in the land that could try its king, no authority but his own that could determine a charge of treason. When it was read out that he was a tyrant and traitor, he burst out laughing. "Remember, I am your king, your lawful king and what sins you bring upon your heads and the judgment of God upon this land, think well upon it," he told his accusers.

The trial began on Saturday, 20 January 1649. Armed soldiers in battle dress cleared the floor of the large chamber. Curious onlookers packed the galleries. The king wore the enormous golden star of the Order of the Garter on his cloak but was allowed no other symbol of royalty to overawe his accusers.

The charge of "treason and high misdemeanors" had been carefully prepared. When the resounding indictment concluded, all eyes turned toward Charles I. Now he would have to answer the charge, guilty or not guilty. But rather than answer the charge, he questioned the authority of the court. "I would know by what power I am called hither, a king cannot be tried by any superior jurisdiction here on earth." This was the weakest point of the parliamentary strategy. Judge Bradshaw could only assert that the court represented the free people of England. But Charles was relentless. He demanded precedents and refused

to be silenced by the assertion that his objections were overruled.

In English law, a defendant who refused to plead was presumed guilty. Thus the king's trial ended as soon as it had begun. After three fruitless sessions and much behind-the-scenes maneuvering, it was decided that the king should be condemned and sentenced to die. On 27 January, Judge Bradshaw appeared in the scarlet robes of justice and issued the sentence. Charles had prepared a statement for maximum effect and waited patiently to deliver it. Now it was the king's turn to be surprised. After pronouncing sentence, Bradshaw and the commissioners rose from the bench. "Will you not hear me a word, sir," called a flustered Charles I. "No," replied the judge. "Guards, withdraw your prisoner."

Tuesday, 30 January, dawned cold and clear. Charles put on two shirts so that if he trembled from the cold it would not be interpreted as fear. In fact he made a very good end. The chopping block had been set very low and great iron staples were driven in the platform to pin down the king's arms if he attempted to resist his fate. But Charles was more than ready to accept his fate. He spoke briefly and to the point, denying he had acted against the true interests and rights of his subjects. Then he lay down on the platform, and prayed. As the axe fell, one witness recorded, "such a groan as I never heard and hope never to hear again," broke forth from the crowd. The English Revolution had begun.

new Parliament with his supporters. This proved too much for the governing classes, who entered into negotiations with William, Prince of Orange, husband of Mary Stuart, James's eldest daughter. In 1688 William landed in England with a small force. Without support, James II fled to France, the English throne was declared vacant, and William and Mary were proclaimed king and queen of England. There was little bloodshed in England and little threat of social disorder, and the event soon came to be called the Glorious Revolution. Its achievements were set down in the Declaration of Rights (1689), which was presented to William and Mary before they took the throne. The Declaration reasserted the fundamental principles of constitutional monarchy as they had developed over the previous half-century. Security of property and the regularity of Parliaments were guaranteed. The Toleration Act (1689) granted religious freedom to nearly all groups of Protestants. The liberties of the subject and the rights of the sovereign were to be in balance.

The events of 1688 in England reversed a trend toward increasing power on the part of the Stuarts. This second episode of resistance resulted in the development of a unique form of government which, a century later, spawned dozens of imitators. John Locke (1632–1704) was the theorist of the Revolution of 1688. He was heir to the century-old debate on resistance and he

carried the doctrine to a new plateau. In *Two Treatises on Civil Government* (1690), Locke developed the contract theory of government. Political society was a compact that individuals entered into freely for their own well-being. It was designed to maintain each person's natural rights—life, liberty, and property. Natural rights were inherent in individuals; they could not be given away. The contract between rulers and subjects was an agreement for the protection of natural rights. "Arbitrary power cannot consist with the ends of society and government. Men would not quit the freedom of the state of nature were it not to preserve their lives, liberties, and fortunes and by stated rules to secure their peace and happiness." When rulers acted arbitrarily, they were to be deposed by their subjects, preferably in the relatively peaceful manner in which James II had been replaced by William III.

The efforts of European monarchies to centralize their power came at the expense of the church, the aristocracy, and the localities. It was a struggle that took place over decades and was not accomplished easily. In France the Fronde was an aristocratic backlash; in Spain the revolt of the Catalans pitted the Castilian crown against a proud ethnic province. In England a civil war fought to prevent the encroachments of the Crown against the rights of the community gave way to a bloody revolution that combined religious and constitutional grievances. The excesses of monarchy were succeeded by the excesses of parliamentary rule. But the lesson learned by the English ruling elites was that for a nation to enjoy the benefits of a powerful central authority, it was necessary to restrain it. The Revolution of 1688 helped create a constitutional balance between ruler and ruled.

A 1689 engraving by de Hooghe and C. Allard shows William and Mary as the champions of parliamentary liberty and the Bill of Rights.

The Zenith of the Royal State

The mid-century crises tested the mettle of the royal states. Over the long term, the seventeenth-century crises had two different consequences. First they provided a check to the exercise of royal power. Fear of recurring rebellions had a chilling effect upon policy, especially taxation. Reforms of financial administration, long overdue, were one of the themes of the later seventeenth century. Even as royal government strengthened itself, it remained concerned about the impact of its policies. On the other hand, the memory of rebellion served to control the ambitions of factious noblemen and town oligarchies.

If nothing else, these episodes of opposition to the rising royal states made clear the universal desire for stable government, which was seen as the responsibility of both subjects and rulers. By the second half of the seventeenth century, effective government was the byword of the royal state. The natural advantages of monarchy had to be merged with the interests of the citizens of the state and their desires for wealth, safety, and honor. After so much chaos and instability, the monarchy had to be elevated above the fray of day-to-day politics, elevated to become a symbol of the power and glory of the nation.

In England, Holland, and Sweden a form of constitutional monarchy developed in which rulers shared power, in varying degrees, with other institutions of state. In England it was Parliament, in Holland the town oligarchies, and in Sweden the nobility. But in most other states in Europe there developed a pure form of royal government known as absolutism. Absolute monarchy revived the divine right theories of kingship and added to them a cult of the personality of the ruler. Absolutism was practiced in states as dissimilar as Denmark, Brandenburg-Prussia, and Russia. It reached its zenith in France under Louis XIV, the most powerful of the seventeenth-century monarchs.

The Nature of Absolute Monarchy

Locke's theory of contract provided one solution to the central problem of seventeenth-century government: how to balance the monarch's right to command and the subjects' duty to obey. By establishing a constitutional monarchy, in which power was shared between the ruler and a representative assembly of subjects, England found one path out of this thicket. But it was not a path that many others could follow.

The English solution was most suited to a state that was largely immune from invasion and land war. Constitutional government required a higher level of political participation of citizens than did an absolute monarchical one. Greater participation in turn meant greater freedom of expression, greater toleration of religious minorities, and greater openness in the institutions of government. All were dangerous. The price that England paid was a half-century of governmental instability.

The alternative to constitutional monarchy was absolute monarchy. It, too, found its greatest theorist in England. Thomas Hobbes (1588–1679) in his greatest work, *Leviathan* (1651), argued that before civil society had been formed, humans lived in a savage state of nature, "in a war of every man against every man." This

The title page of the first edition of Thomas Hobbes's Leviathan, *published in 1651. The huge figure composed of many tiny human beings symbolizes the surrender of individual human rights to those of the state.*

was a ghastly condition without morality or law—"the notions of right and wrong, of justice and injustice have there no place." People came together to form a government for the most basic of all purposes: for self-preservation. Without government they were condemned to a life that was "solitary, poor, nasty, brutish, and short." To escape the state of nature, individuals pooled their power and granted it to a ruler. The terms of the Hobbesian contract were simple. Rulers agreed to rule; subjects agreed to obey. When the contract was intact, people ceased to live in a state of nature. When it was broken, they returned to it. With revolts, rebellions, and revolutions erupting in all parts of Europe, Hobbes's state of nature never seemed very far away.

For most states of Europe in the later seventeenth century, absolute monarchy became not only a necessity but an ideal. The consolidation of power in the hands of the divinely ordained monarch who, nevertheless, ruled according to principles of law and justice, was seen as the perfect form of government.

The main features of absolute monarchy were all designed to extend royal control. As in the early seventeenth century, the person of the monarch was revered. Courts grew larger and more lavish in an effort to enhance the glory of the monarchy and thereby of the state. *L'etat, c'est moi*—"I am the state"—Louis XIV was supposed to have said. No idea better expresses absolutism's connection between governor and governed. As the king grew in stature, his competitors for power all shrank. Large numbers of nobles were herded together at court under the watchful eye of monarchs who now ruled rather than reigned. The king shed the cloak of his favorites and rolled up his own sleeves to manage state affairs. Representative institutions, especially those that laid claim to control over taxation, were weakened or cast aside for obstructing efficient government and endangering the welfare of the state. Monarchs needed standing armies, permanent forces that could be drilled and trained in the increasingly sophisticated arts of war. Thus the military was expanded and made an integral part of the machinery of government. The military profession developed within nations, gradually replacing mercenary adventurers who had fought for booty rather than for duty.

Yet the absolute state was never as powerful in practice as it was in theory. Nor did it ever exist in its ideal shape. Absolutism was always in the making, never quite made. Its success depended upon a strong monarch who knew his own will and could enforce it. It depended upon unity within the state, upon the absence or ruthless suppression of religious or political minorities. The absolute ruler needed to control information and ideas, to limit criticism of state policy. Ultimately, the absolute state rested upon the will of its citizens to support it. The seventeenth-century state remained a loose confederation of regions, many acquired by conquest and whose loyalty was practical rather than instinctive. There were no state police to control behavior or attitudes, no newspapers or mass communication to spread propaganda. Censorship might restrict the flow of forbidden books, but it could do little to dam up the current of ideas.

Absolutism in the East

Frederick William, the Great Elector of Brandenburg-Prussia (1640–88), was one of the European princes who made the most effective use of the techniques of absolutism. In 1640 he inherited a scattered and ungovern-

able collection of territories. The nobility, known as *die Junker*, enjoyed immunity from almost all forms of direct taxation, and the towns had no obligation to furnish either men or supplies for military operations beyond their walls.

When Frederick William attempted to introduce an excise—the commodity tax on consumption that had so successfully financed the Dutch Revolt and the English Revolution—he was initially rebuffed. But military emergency overcame legal precedents. By the 1650s Frederick William had established the excise in the towns though not on the land.

With the excise as a steady source of revenue, the Great Elector could now create one of the most capable standing armies of the age. The strictest discipline was maintained in the new army, and the Prussian army developed into a feared and efficient fighting machine. Frederick William organized one of the first departments of war to oversee all of the details of the creation of his army, from housing and supplies to the training of young officer candidates. This department was also responsible for the collection of taxes. By integrating military and civilian government, Frederick William was able to create an efficient state bureaucracy that was particularly responsive in times of crisis. The creation of the Prussian army was the force that led to the creation of the Prussian state.

The same materials that forged the Prussian state led to the transformation of Russia. Soon after the young Tsar Peter I, known later as "the Great" (1682–1725) came to the throne, he realized that he could compete with the western states only by learning to play their game.

Like those of Frederick William, Peter's greatest reforms were military. Peter realized that if Russia was to flourish in a world dominated by war and commerce it would have to reestablish its hold on the Baltic ports. This meant dislodging the Swedes from the Russian mainland and creating a fleet to protect Russian trade. Neither goal seemed likely. The Swedes were one of the great powers of the age, constant innovators in battlefield tactics and military organization. Peter studied their every campaign. His first wars against the Swedes ended in humiliating defeats, but with each failure came a sharper sense of what was needed to succeed.

First Peter introduced a system of conscription that resulted in the creation of a standing army. Conscripts were branded to inhibit desertion, and a strict discipline was introduced to prepare the soldiers for battle. Peter unified the military command at the top and stratified it in the field. He established promotion based on merit.

The Tsars of Russia 1462–1725

For the first time Russian officers were given particular responsibilities to fulfill during both training and battle. Peter created military schools to train cadets for the next generation of officers.

Finally in 1709 Peter realized his ambitions. At the battle of Poltava the Russian army routed the Swedes, wounding King Charles XII, annihilating his infantry, and capturing dozens of his leading officers. That night Peter toasted the captured Swedish generals. He claimed that everything he knew about warfare he had learned from them and he congratulated them on their success as teachers. After the battle of Poltava, Russia gradually replaced Sweden as the dominant power in the Baltic.

Like everything else about him, Peter the Great's absolutism was uniquely his own. But though Peter's power was unlimited, it was not uncontested. He secularized the Russian Orthodox church, subjecting it to the control of state power and confiscating much of its wealth in the process. He broke the old military service class, which attempted a coup d'etat when he was abroad in the 1690s. By the end of his reign, the Russian monarchy was among the strongest in Europe.

The Origins of French Absolutism

Nowhere was absolutism as successfully implanted as in France. Louis XIII (1610–43) was only eight years old when he came to the throne, and he grew slowly into his role under the tutelage of Cardinal Richelieu. It was Richelieu's vision that stabilized French government. As chief minister, Richelieu saw clearly that the prosperity and even the survival of France depended upon strengthening royal power. He preached a doctrine of *raison d'etat*—reason of state—in which he placed the needs of the nation above the privileges of its most important groups. Richelieu saw three threats to stable royal government, "the Huguenots shared the state, the nobles conducted themselves as if they were not subjects, and the most powerful governors in the provinces acted as if they were sovereign in their office."

Richelieu took measures to control all three. The power of the nobles was the most difficult to attack. The nobles' long tradition of independence from the crown had been enhanced by the wars of religion. Perhaps more importantly, the ancient aristocracy, the

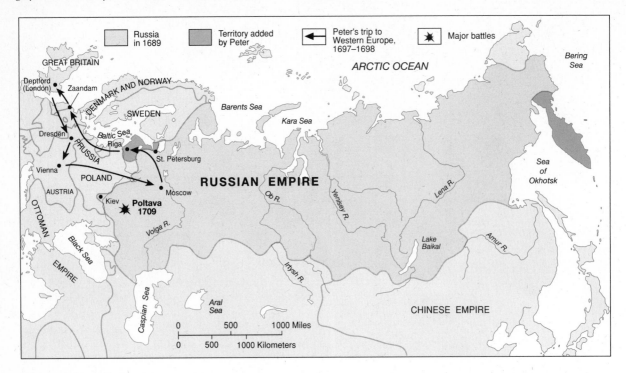

Russia Under Peter the Great

nobility of the sword, felt themselves in a particularly vulnerable position. Their world was changing and their traditional roles were becoming obsolete. Professional soldiers replaced them at war; professional administrators at government. Mercantile wealth threatened their economic superiority, the growth of the nobility of the robe—lawyers and state officials—threatened their social standing. They were hardly likely to take orders from a royal minister like Richelieu.

To limit the power of local officials, Richelieu used intendants to examine their conduct and to reform their administration. He made careful appointments of local governors and brought more regions under direct royal control. Against the Calvinists, who were called Huguenots in France, Richelieu's policy was more subtle. He was less interested in challenging their religion than their autonomy. In 1627 when the English sent a force to aid the Huguenots against the government, Richelieu and Louis XIII abolished the Huguenots' privileges altogether. They were allowed to maintain their religion but not their special status. Finally, in 1685 Louis XIV revoked the Edict of Nantes, which had guaranteed civil and religious rights to the Huguenots. All forms of Protestant worship were outlawed and the ministers who were not hunted down and killed were forced into exile. Despite a ban on Protestant emigration,

over two hundred thousand Huguenots fled the country, many of them carrying irreplaceable skills with them to Holland and England in the west and to Brandenburg in the east.

Richelieu's program was a vital prelude to the development of absolute monarchy in France. But the cardinal was not a king. While it is clear that Richelieu did not act without the full support of Louis XIII, and clear that the king initiated many reforms for which the cardinal received credit, there can be no doubt that Richelieu was the power behind the throne. Louis XIII hated the business of government and even neglected his principal responsibility of providing the state with an heir. For years he and his wife slept in separate palaces and only a freak rainstorm in Paris forced him to spend a night with the queen, Anne of Austria, in 1637. It was the night of the conception of Louis XIV. Louis XIII and Richelieu died within six months of each other in 1642–43, and the nation again endured the turmoil of a child king.

Louis le Grande

Not quite five years old when he came to the throne, Louis XIV was tutored by Cardinal Jules Mazarin (1602–61), Richelieu's successor as chief minister. If anything,

This Hyacinthe Rigaud portrait of Louis XIV in his coronation robes shows the splendor of the Roi Soleil (Sun King), who believed himself to be the center of France as the sun is the center of the solar system.

Mazarin was more ruthless and less popular than his predecessor. Like Richelieu, whom he emulated, Mazarin was an excellent administrator who had learned well the lessons of *raison d'etat*. At the conclusion of the Thirty Years' War, for example, Mazarin refused to make peace with Spain, believing that the time was ripe to deliver a knockout blow to the Spanish Habsburgs.

In order to pacify the rebellious nobility of the Fronde, who opposed Mazarin's power, Louis XIV was declared to have reached his majority at the age of thirteen. But it was not until Mazarin died ten years later in 1661 that the king began to rule. Louis was blessed with able and energetic ministers. The two central props of his state—money and might—were in the hands of dynamic men, Jean-Baptiste Colbert (1619–83) and the Marquis de Louvois (1639–91). Colbert, to whom credit belongs for the building of the French navy, the reform of French legal codes, and the establishment of national academies of culture, was Louis's chief minister for finance. Colbert's fiscal reforms were so successful that in less than six years a debt of 22 million French pounds

had become a surplus of 29 million. Colbert achieved this astonishing feat not by raising taxes but by increasing the efficiency of their collection. Until Louis embarked upon his wars, the French state was solvent.

To Louvois, Louis's minister of war, fell the task of reforming the French army. During the Fronde, royal troops were barely capable of defeating the makeshift forces of the nobility. By the end of the reign, the army had grown to 400,000 and its organization had been thoroughly reformed.

Louis XIV furthered the practice of relying upon professional administrators to supervise the main departments of state and to offer advice on matters of policy. He built upon the institution of the intendant that Richelieu had developed with so much success. Intendants were now a permanent part of government, and their duties expanded from their early responsibilities as coordinators and mediators into areas of policing and tax collection. It was through the intendants that the wishes of central government were made known in the provinces.

Though Louis XIV was well served, it was the king himself who set the tone for French absolutism. "If he was not the greatest king he was the best actor of majesty that ever filled the throne," wrote an English observer. The acting of majesty was central to Louis's rule. His residence at Versailles was the most glittering court of Europe, renowned for its beauty and splendor. It was built on a scale never before seen, and Louis took a personal interest in making sure it was fit for a king. When the court and king moved there permanently in 1682, Versailles became the envy of the Continent. But behind the imposing facade of Versailles stood a well-thought-out plan for domestic and international rule.

Louis XIV attempted to tame the French nobles by requiring their attendance at his court. Louis established a system of court etiquette so complex that constant study was necessary to prevent humiliation. While the nobility studied decorum, they could not plot rebellion. Leading noblemen of France rose at dawn so that they could watch Louis be awakened and hear him speak his first words. Dozens followed him from hall to gallery and from gallery to chamber as he washed, dressed, prayed, and ate. There was no greater concern than the king's health, unless it was the king's mood, which was as changeable as the weather.

During Louis's reign, France replaced Spain as the greatest nation in Europe. Massive royal patronage of art, science, and thought brought French culture to new heights. The French language replaced Latin as the universal European tongue. France was the richest and most populous European state, and Louis's absolute rule finally harnessed these resources to a single purpose. France became a commercial power rivaling the Netherlands, a naval power rivaling England, and a military power without peer. It was not only for effect that Louis took the image of the sun as his own. In court, in the nation, and throughout Europe everything revolved around him.

Louis XIV made his share of mistakes, which were magnified by the awe in which his opinions were held. His aggressive foreign policy ultimately bankrupted the crown. But without doubt, his greatest error was to persecute the Huguenots. As an absolute ruler, Louis believed that it was necessary to have absolute conformity and obedience. The existence of the Huguenots, with their separate communities and distinct forms of worship, seemed an affront to his authority.

Supporters of the monarchy celebrated the revocation of the Edict of Nantes in 1685 as an act of piety. Religious toleration in seventeenth-century Europe was still a policy of expediency rather than of principle. Even the English, who prided themselves on developing the concept, and the Dutch, who welcomed Jews to Amsterdam, would not officially tolerate Catholics. But the persecution of the Huguenots was a social and political disaster for France. Those who fled to other Protestant states spread the stories of atrocities that stiffened European resolve against Louis. Those who remained became an embittered minority who pulled at the fabric of the state at every chance. Nor did the official abolition of Protestantism have much effect upon its existence. Against these policies, the Huguenots held firm to their beliefs. There were well over one million French Protestants, undoubtedly the largest religious minority in any state. Huguenots simply went underground, practicing their religion secretly and gradually replacing their numbers. No absolutism, however powerful, could succeed in eradicating religious beliefs.

Louis XIV gave his name to the age that he and his nation dominated, but he was not its only towering figure. The Great Elector, Peter the Great, Louis the Great: so they were judged by posterity, kings who had forged nations for a new age. Their style of rule showed the royal state at its height, still revolving around the king but more and more dependent upon permanent institutions of government that followed their own imperatives. The absolute state harnessed the economic and intellectual resources of the nation to the political

will of the monarch. It did so to ensure survival in a dangerous world. But while monarchs ruled as well as reigned, they did so by incorporating vital elements of the state into the process of government. In England the importance of the landholding classes was recognized in the constitutional powers of Parliament. The rights of the monarch were balanced against the liberties of the subject. In Prussia the military power of *die Junker* was asserted through command in the army, the most important institution of the state. In France, Louis XIV co-opted many nobles at his court, while he made use of a talented pool of lawyers, clergymen, and administrators in his government. A delicate balance existed between the will of the king and the will of the state, a balance that would soon lead these Continental powers into economic competition and military confrontation.

SUGGESTIONS FOR FURTHER READING

GENERAL READING

* Thomas Munck, *Seventeenth Century Europe, 1598–1700* (New York: St. Martin's Press, 1990). The most up-to-date survey.

* William Doyle, *The Old European Order* (Oxford: Oxford University Press, 1978). An important synthetic essay bristling with ideas.

* Geoffrey Parker, *Europe in Crisis 1598–1648* (London: William Collins and Sons, 1979). The best introduction to the period.

Perry Anderson, *Lineages of the Absolutist State* (London: NLB Books, 1974). A sociological study of the role of absolutism in the development of the western world.

THE RISE OF THE ROYAL STATE

* Graham Parry, *The Golden Age Restor'd* (New York: St. Martin's Press, 1981). A study of English court culture in the reigns of James I and Charles I.

J. H. Elliott and Jonathan Brown, *A Palace for a King* (New Haven, CT: Yale University Press, 1980). An outstanding work on the building and decorating of a Spanish palace.

* J. N. Figgis, *The Divine Right of Kings* (Cambridge: Cambridge University Press, 1914). Still the classic study of this central doctrine of political thought.

* J. H. Elliott, *Richelieu and Olivares* (Cambridge: Cambridge University Press, 1984). A brilliant dual portrait.

* Roger Lockyer, *Buckingham* (London: Longman, 1984). A stylish biography of the favorite of two monarchs.

THE CRISES OF THE ROYAL STATE

* Quentin Skinner, *The Foundations of Modern Political Thought*, 2 vols. (Cambridge: Cambridge University Press, 1978). A seminal work on the history of ideas from Machiavelli to Calvin.

* Perez Zagoin, *Rebels and Rulers*, 2 vols. (Cambridge: Cambridge University Press, 1982). A good survey of revolutions, civil war, and popular protests throughout Europe.

* Trevor Aston, ed., *Crisis in Europe 1600–1660* (Garden City, NY: Doubleday, 1967). Essays on the theme of a general crisis in Europe by distinguished historians.

G. Parker and L. Smith, eds., *The General Crisis of the Seventeenth Century* (London: Routledge & Kegan Paul, 1978). A collection of essays on the problem of the general crisis.

* Lawrence Stone, *The Causes of the English Revolution* (New York: Harper & Row, 1972). A vigorously argued explanation of why England experienced a revolution in the mid-seventeenth century.

* Ann Hughes, *The Causes of the English Civil War* (New York: St. Martin's Press, 1991). A lucid introduction to the scholarship of a vast subject.

* D. E. Underdown, *Pride's Purge* (London: Allen and Unwin, 1985). The most important work on the politics of the English Revolution.

THE ZENITH OF THE ROYAL STATE

* H. W. Koch, *A History of Prussia* (London: Longman, 1978). A comprehensive study of Prussian history with an excellent chapter on the Great Elector.

* Paul Dukes, *The Making of Russian Absolutism* (London: Longman, 1982). A thorough survey of Russian history in the seventeenth and eighteenth centuries.

* Vasili Klyuchevsky, *Peter the Great* (Boston: Beacon Press, 1984). A classic work, still the best study of Peter.

* W. E. Brown, *The First Bourbon Century in France* (London: University of London Press, 1971). A good introduction to French political history.

* William Beik, *Absolutism and Society in Seventeenth Century France* (Cambridge: Cambridge University Press, 1985). The single best study of the government of a French province in the seventeenth century.

Peter Burke, *The Fabrication of Louis XIV* (New Haven, CT: Yale University Press, 1992). A compelling account of a man and a myth.

* John Wolf, *Louis XIV* (New York: Norton, 1968). An outstanding biography of the Sun King.

* Indicates paperback edition available.

REMBRANDT'S LESSONS

By the early seventeenth century interest in scientific investigation had spread out from narrow circles of specialists to embrace educated men and women. One of the more spectacular demonstrations of new knowledge was public dissection, by law performed only on the corpses of criminals. Here the secrets of the human body were revealed both for those who were in training as physicians and for those who had the requisite fee and strong stomach. Curiosity about the human body was becoming a mark of education. New publications, both scientific and popular, spread ancient wisdom as well as the controversial findings of the moderns. Pictures drawn on the basis of dissections filled the new medical texts like the one on the stand at the feet of the corpse in *The Anatomy Lesson of Dr. Nicolaes Tulp* (1632) by Rembrandt van Rijn (1606–69).

Dr. Tulp's anatomy lesson was not meant for the public. In fact, those gathered around him in various poses of concentration were not students at all. They were members of the Amsterdam company of surgeons, the physicians' guild of the early seventeenth century. The sitters had commissioned the picture, which was a celebration of themselves as well as of the noted Professor Tulp. They hired the young Rembrandt to compose the picture with the assurance that each of the sitters (whose names are written on the paper one of them holds in his hand) would appear as if he alone were the subject of a portrait. Rembrandt succeeded beyond expectation. Each individual was given his due. The expressions on their faces as much as their physical characteristics mark each one out from the group. Yet the portraits were only one part of the painting. The scene that Rembrandt depicted unified them. They became a group by their participation in the anatomy lesson. Rembrandt has chosen a moment of drama to stop the action. Dr. Tulp is demonstrating how the gesture he is making with his left hand looks in the dissected arm of the gruesome cadaver. The central figures of the group are rapt in attention though only one of them is actually observing the procedure of the anatomy. Each listens to Tulp, comparing his own experience and knowledge to that of the professor and the text that stands open.

The Anatomy Lesson established the twenty-five-year-old Rembrandt as one of the most gifted and fashionable painters in Amsterdam. If any people could be said to be consumers of art in seventeenth-century Europe, it was the Dutch. Artists flourished and pictures abounded. Travelers were struck by the presence of artwork in both public and private places and in the homes of even moderately prosperous people. The group portrait, which Rembrandt brought to new levels of expression, was becoming a favorite genre. It was used to celebrate the leaders of Dutch society who, unlike the leaders of most other European states, were not princes and aristocrats, but rather merchants, guild officials, and professionals. Rembrandt captured a spirit of civic pride in his group portraits. Here it was the surgeons' guild; later it would be the leaders of the cloth merchants' guild, another time a militia company.

Like the leaders of the surgeons' guild who commissioned their own portrait, which hung in their company's hall, the Dutch Republic swelled with pride in the seventeenth century. Its long war with Spain was finally over, and it was time to celebrate the birth of a new state. The Dutch were a trading people, and their trade flourished as much in times of war as in times of peace. Their ships traveled to all parts of the globe, and after a century of conflict they dominated the great luxury trades of the age. Bankers and merchants were the backbone of the Dutch Republic. Yet this republic of merchants was also one of the great cultural centers of the Continent. Intellectual creativity was cultivated in the same manner as was a trading partner. In the burgeoning port of Amsterdam, the fastest growing city in Europe, artists, philosophers, and mathematicians lived in close proximity. The free exchange of ideas made Amsterdam home to those exiled for their beliefs. The Dutch practiced religious toleration as did no one else. Catholics, Protestants, and Jews all were welcomed to the Republic and found that they could pursue their own paths without persecution. Freedom of thought and freedom of expression helped develop a new spirit of scientific inquiry, like that portrayed in *The Anatomy Lesson of Dr. Nicolaes Tulp.*

The New Science

"And new Philosophy calls all in doubt,/ The element of fire is quite put out;/ The sun is lost and the earth, and no man's wit/ Can well direct him where to look for it." So wrote the English poet John Donne (1572–1631) about one of the most astonishing yet perplexing moments in the history of Western thought: the emergence of the new science. It was astonishing because it seemed truly new. The discoveries of the stargazers, like those of the sea explorers, challenged people's most basic assumptions and beliefs. Men dropping balls from towers or peering at the skies through a glass claimed that they had disproved thousands of years of certainty about the nature of the universe. But it was perplexing because it seemed to loosen the moorings of everything that educated people thought they knew about their world. Nothing could be more disorienting than to challenge common sense. One needed to do little more than wake up in the morning to know that the sun moved from east to west while the earth stood still. But mathematics, experimentation, and deduction were needed to understand that the earth was in constant motion and that it revolved around the sun.

The scientific revolution was the opening of a new era in European history. After two centuries of classical revival, European thinkers had finally come against the limits of ancient knowledge. Ancient wisdom had served Europeans well, and it was not to be discarded lightly. But one by one, the certainties of the past were being called into question. The explanations of the universe and the natural world that had been advanced by Aristotle and codified by his followers no longer seemed adequate. There were too many contradictions between theory and observation, too many things that did not fit. Yet breaking the hold of Aristotelianism was no easy task. A full century was to pass before even learned people would accept the proofs that the earth revolved around the sun. Even then, the most famous of them —Galileo—had to recant these views or be condemned as a heretic.

The two essential characteristics of the new science were that it was materialistic and mathematical. Its materialism was contained in the realization that the universe is composed of matter in motion. This meant that the stars and planets were not made of some perfect ethereal substance but of the same matter that was found on earth. They were thus subject to the same rules of motion as were earthly objects. The mathematics of the new science was contained in the realization that calculation had to replace common sense as the basis for understanding the universe. Mathematics itself was transformed with the invention of logarithms, analytic geometry, and calculus. More importantly, scientific experimentation took the form of measuring repeatable phenomena. When Galileo attempted

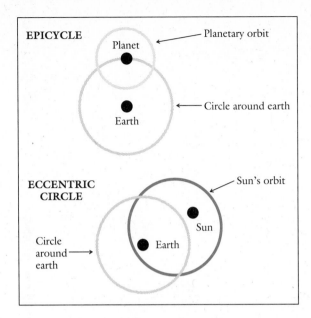

one. The heavens were unchangeable and therefore they were better than the earth. The sun, moon, and planets were all faultless spheres, unblemished and immune from decay. Their motion was circular because the circle was the perfect form of motion. The earth was at the center of the universe because it was the heaviest planet and because it was at the center of the great chain of being, between the underworld of spirits and the upperworld of gods. The second advantage to the Aristotelian worldview was that it was easily incorporated into Christianity. Aristotle's description of the heavens as being composed of a closed system of crystalline rings that held the sun, moon, and planets in their circular orbits around the earth left room for God and the angels to reside just beyond the last ring.

There were, of course, problems with Aristotle's explanation of the universe as it was preserved in the work of Ptolemy, the greatest of the Greek astronomers. For one thing if the sun revolved in a perfect circle around the earth, then why were the seasons not perfectly equal? If the planets all revolved around the earth in circles, then why did they look nearer or farther, brighter or darker at different times of the year? To solve these problems, a host of ingenious hypotheses were advanced. Perhaps the sun revolved around the earth in an eccentric circle, that is, a circle not centered on the earth. This would account for the differing lengths of seasons. Perhaps the planets revolved in circles that

to develop a theory of acceleration, he rolled a brass ball down an inclined plane and recorded the time and distance of its descent one hundred times before he was satisfied with his results.

The new science was also a Europe-wide movement. The spirit of scientific inquiry flourished everywhere. The main contributors to astronomy were a Pole, a Dane, a German, and an Italian. The founder of medical chemistry was Swiss, the best anatomist was Belgian. England contributed most of all—the founders of modern chemistry, biology, and physics. By and large, these scientists operated outside the traditional seats of learning at the universities. Though most were university-trained and not a few taught the traditional Aristotelian subjects, theirs was not an academic movement. Rather it was a public one made possible by the printing press. Once published, findings became building blocks for scientists throughout the Continent and from one generation to the next. Many discoveries were made in the search for practical solutions to ordinary problems, and what was learned fueled advances in technology and the natural sciences. The new science gave seventeenth-century Europeans a sense that they might finally master the forces of nature.

Heavenly Revolutions

There was much to be said for Aristotle's understanding of the world, for his cosmology. For one thing, it was harmonious. It incorporated a view of the physical world that coincided with a view of the spiritual and moral

This chart of the heavens was engraved by Andreas Cellarius in 1660. It portrays the heliocentric universe described by Nicolaus Copernicus and accepted by Galileo. Earth and Jupiter are shown with moons orbiting them.

COPERNICUS ON THE REVOLUTIONS OF HEAVENLY SPHERES

■ *Nicolaus Copernicus was born in Poland and educated at the University of Kraków, which had one of the greatest mathematics faculties of the age. He prepared for a career in the Church, but his abiding interest was the study of astronomy. Through observation and calculation, Copernicus worked out a heliocentric view of the universe in which Earth revolved on an axis and orbited the Sun. His path-breaking work was not published until the year of his death, and he was fully aware of the implications of his discovery.*

I was induced to think of a method of computing the motions of the spheres by nothing else than the knowledge that the Mathematicians are inconsistent in these investigations.

For, first, the mathematicians are so unsure of the movements of the Sun and Moon that they cannot even explain or observe the constant length of the seasonal year. Secondly, in determining the motions of these and of the other five planets, they use neither the same principles and hypotheses nor the same demonstrations of the apparent motions and revolutions. . . . Nor have they been able thereby to discern or deduce the principal thing—namely the shape of the Universe and the unchangeable symmetry of its parts . . .

Thus assuming motions, which in my work I ascribe to the Earth, by long and frequent observations I have at last discovered that, if the motions of the rest of the planets be brought into relation with the circulation of the Earth and be reckoned in proportion to the circles of each planet, not only do their phenomena presently ensue, but the orders and magnitudes of all stars and spheres, nay the heavens themselves, become so bound together that nothing in any part thereof could be moved from its place without producing confusion of all the other parts of the Universe as a whole.

rested on a circle around the earth. Then when the planet revolved within the larger circle, it would seem nearer and brighter, and when it revolved outside it, it would seem farther away and darker. This was the theory of epicycles.

In the 1490s, Nicolaus Copernicus (1473–1543) came to the Polish University of Kraków, which had one of the leading mathematical faculties in Europe. There they taught the latest astronomical theories and vigorously debated the existence of eccentric circles and epicycles. Copernicus came to Kraków for a liberal arts education before pursuing a degree in Church law. He became fascinated by astronomy and puzzled by the debate over planetary motion. Copernicus believed, like Aristotle, that the simplest explanations were the best. If the sun was at the center of the universe and the earth simply another planet in orbit, then many of the most elaborate explanations of planetary motion were unnecessary. "At rest, in the middle of everything is the sun," Copernicus wrote in *On the Revolutions of the Heavenly Spheres* (1543). "For in this most beautiful temple who would place this lamp in another or better position than that from which it can light up the whole thing at the same time?" Because Copernicus accepted most of the rest of the

traditional Aristotelian explanation, especially the belief that the planets moved in circles, his sun-centered universe was only slightly better at predicting the position of the planets than the traditional earth-centered one, but Copernicus's idea stimulated other astronomers to make new calculations.

Under the patronage of the king of Denmark, Tycho Brahe (1546–1601) built a large observatory to study planetary motion. In 1572, Brahe discovered a nova, a brightly burning star that was previously unknown. This discovery challenged the idea of an immutable universe composed of crystalline rings. In 1577 the appearance of a comet cutting through the supposedly impenetrable rings punched another hole into the old cosmology. Brahe's own views were a hybrid of old and new. He believed that all planets but the earth revolved around the sun and that the sun and the planets revolved around a fixed earth. To demonstrate this theory, Brahe and his students compiled the largest and most accurate mathematical tables of planetary motion yet known. From this research, Brahe's pupil, Johannes Kepler (1571–1630), one of the great mathematicians of the age, formulated laws of planetary motion. Kepler discovered that planets orbited the sun in an elliptical rather than a

THE STARRY MESSENGER

■ *No single individual is as much associated with the scientific revolution as Galileo. He made formative contributions to mathematics, physics, and astronomy, but he also served as a lightning rod for the dissemination of the newest ideas. He popularized the work of Copernicus and was condemned by the Catholic church for his views and publications. He ended his life under house arrest. Among his other accomplishments, Galileo was the first to use a telescope to make scientific observations.*

About ten months ago a report reached my ears that a certain Fleming had constructed a spyglass by means of which visible objects, though very distant from the eye of the observer, were distinctly seen as if nearby. Of this truly remarkable effect several experiences were related, to which some persons gave credence while others denied them. A few days later the report was confirmed to me in a letter from a noble Frenchman at Paris, Jacques Badovere, which caused me to apply myself wholeheartedly to inquire into the means by which I might arrive at the invention of a similar instrument. This I did shortly afterwards, my basis being the theory of refraction. First I prepared a tube of lead, at the ends of which I fitted two glass lenses, both plane on one side while on the other side one was spherically convex and the other concave. Then placing my eye near the concave lens I perceived objects satisfactorily large and near, for they appeared three times closer and nine times larger than when seen with the naked eye alone. Next I constructed another one, more accurate, which represented objects as enlarged more than sixty times. Finally, sparing neither labor nor expense, I succeeded in constructing for myself so excellent an instrument that objects seen by means of it appeared nearly one thousand times larger and over thirty times closer than when regarded with our natural vision.

It would be superfluous to enumerate the number and importance of the advantages of such an instrument at sea as well as on land. But forsaking terrestrial observations, I turned to celestial ones, and first I saw the moon from as near at hand as if it were scarcely two terrestrial radii . . . Let us speak first of that surface of the moon which faces us. For greater clarity I distinguish two parts of this surface, a lighter and a darker; the lighter part seems to surround and to pervade the whole hemisphere, while the darker part discolors the moon's surface like a kind of cloud, and makes it appear covered with spots . . . From observation of these spots repeated many times I have been led to the opinion and conviction that the surface of the moon is not smooth, uniform, and precisely spherical as a great number of philosophers believe it (and the other heavenly bodies) to be, but is uneven, rough, and full of cavities and prominences, being not unlike the face of the earth, relieved by chains of mountains and deep valleys.

From Galileo, *The Starry Messenger*.

---

circular path. This accounted for their movements nearer and farther from the earth. More importantly, he demonstrated that there was a precise mathematical relationship between the speed with which a planet revolved and its distance from the sun. Kepler's findings supported the view that the solar system was heliocentric and that the heavens, like the earth, were made of matter that was subject to physical laws.

What Kepler demonstrated mathematically, the Italian astronomer Galileo Galilei (1564–1642) confirmed by observation. Creating a telescope by using magnify-

ing lenses and a long tube, Galileo saw parts of the heavens that had never been dreamt of before. In 1610 he discovered four moons of Jupiter, proving conclusively that not all heavenly bodies revolved around the earth. He observed the landscape of the earth's moon and described it as full of mountains, valleys, and rivers. It was of the same imperfect form as the earth itself. He even found spots on the sun, which suggested that it, too, was composed of ordinary matter. Many of Galileo's scientific discoveries had to do with motion—he was the first to posit a law of inertia—but his greatest

These drawings of Galileo's moon observations accompanied the first draft of the Starry Messenger. *Galileo correctly interpreted the bright spots that appear on the dark part of the moon as mountain peaks.*

*T*he Trials of Galileo

For eight years he had held his peace. Since 1616 he had bided his time, waiting for a change in the attitudes of the Catholic authorities or, as he believed, waiting for reason to prevail. For a time he had even abandoned his astronomical investigations for the supposedly safer fields of motion and physics. Even there Aristotle had been wrong. No matter what he touched, his reason showed him that the conclusions of Aristotle, the conclusions adopted and supported by the Roman Catholic church, were wrong. Now finally, with the accession of Pope Urban VIII, old Cardinal Barbarini, who was himself a mathematician, Galileo felt confident that he could resume his writing and publishing.

Galileo's rebellion began early, when he decided to study mathematics rather than medicine. Galileo was fascinated with the manipulation of numbers and by the age of twenty-five was teaching at the University of Pisa. There he began to conduct experiments to measure rates of motion. Galileo was soon in trouble with his colleagues and was forced to leave Pisa for Padua.

It was in Padua that his real difficulties began. After seeing a small prototype made in Holland, Galileo developed a telescope that could magnify objects to thirty times their size, which made it possible to see clearly the stars and planets that had been only dimly perceptible before. In 1610 Galileo had looked at the moon and discovered that its properties were similar to those of the earth. He had seen four moons of Jupiter, the first conclusive proof that there were heavenly bodies that did not revolve around the earth. Even before he had gazed at the stars, Galileo was persuaded that Copernicus must be right in arguing that the earth revolved around the sun. Now he believed he had irrefutable proof, the proof of his own eyes. From the publication of the *Starry Messenger* in 1610, Galileo became the most active and best known advocate of the Copernican universe.

In 1616 he was called to Rome and warned about his opinions. Belief in the theories of Copernicus was heresy, he was told. If Galileo held or maintained them, he would incur a heavy penalty. The Church accepted unequivocally the Ptolemaic explanations of the structure of the universe and could cite innumerable passages in the Bible to support them. It was willful and stubborn to oppose official doctrine, doctrine that had been frequently and fully examined. At first it looked like Galileo would be silenced, but the erudite Cardinal Bellarmine, to whom the case had been assigned, wished only to caution him. Galileo might still examine the Copernican hypotheses, he might still discuss them with his learned colleagues, as long as he did not hold or maintain them to be true.

For eight years he kept his peace. When he decided to write again, it was with the belief that things were changing. He created a dialogue between a Ptolemaist and a Copernican. Let the one challenge the other on the most basic points just as if they were in formal academic dispute. How did each explain the most difficult things that there were to explain, the existence of spots on the sun or the movement of the tides. Especially the tides. If the earth stood still and the sun moved, why were there tides in the seas that moved with such regularity that they could be predicted?

Galileo was no heretic. He had no desire to challenge the Church. He would not print his tract anonymously in a Protestant country. Rather he would create a true dialogue, one with which not even the most narrow-minded censor of the Roman church could find fault. He submitted his book to the official censor in Rome for approval, then to the official censor in Florence. The censors struck out passages, changed some words, and deleted others. They demanded a new preface, even a new title: *A Dialogue Between the Two Great Systems of the World*. Finally, in 1632 the book went to press and it was an immediate success.

Indeed it was a success that could not be ignored. The Jesuits, who regarded learning and education as their special mission, demanded that action be taken against Galileo. Their teachings had been held up to ridicule; their official astronomers had been challenged; their doctrines had been repudiated. There was much at stake. Galileo's book had not been the vigorous academic dispute that he promised and it had not concluded with the triumph of Church doctrine over the speculations of Copernicus. No, it had been advocacy. Anyone could see where the author's true sympathies lay. The character chosen to speak the part of Aristotle was not named Simplicio for nothing. Though this was the name of an ancient Aristotelian, it was also a perfect description for the arguments that the speaker advanced. Especially in the matter of the tides, Galileo had reduced the Aristotelian position to nonsense. The Jesuits brought their case directly to the pope and won an investigation, an investigation that they knew would end with Galileo's condemnation.

Though initially Pope Urban VIII was reluctant to prosecute the seventy-year-old astronomer, "the light of Italy," ultimately he had no choice. The great war to stamp out heresy was going badly for the Church. The pope needed the support of the Jesuits in Vienna and in Madrid much more than he needed the support of a scientist who had seen the moons of Jupiter. Nevertheless, when the case was turned over to the Inquisition, it proved weak in law. Galileo had only to present the book itself to show that he had received the official sanction of not one, but two censors of the Roman Catholic church. If there was still anything in his book that offended, could the fault be his alone? The argument stymied the prosecutors, who were forced to find evidence where none existed. Resurrecting the agreement between Galileo and Bellarmine, they attempted to make it say that Galileo was under an absolute ban from even discussing the Copernican theories. Either Galileo would agree to recant his views, admit his errors, and beg the forgiveness of the Church or he would be tried and burned as a heretic. But though he could be forced to recant his view that the earth orbits the sun, Galileo could not be forced to change his mind.

After his recantation, Galileo was sentenced to live out his days under house arrest. Five years after his death in 1642, his greatest scientific work, *The Two New Sciences*, was smuggled out of Italy and printed anonymously in Holland in 1648.

contribution to the new science was his popularization of the Copernican theory.

As news of his experiments and discoveries spread, Galileo became famous throughout the Continent, and his support for heliocentrism became a celebrated cause. In 1616 the Roman Catholic church cautioned him against promoting his views. In 1633, a year after publishing his *A Dialogue Between the Two Great Systems of the World*, Galileo was tried by the Inquisition and forced specifically to recant the idea that the earth moves. He spent the rest of his life under house arrest. But Galileo insisted that there was nothing in the new science that was anti-Christian. He rejected the view that his discoveries refuted the Bible, arguing that the Bible was often difficult to interpret and that nature was another way in which God revealed himself. (See Special Feature, "The Trials of Galileo," pp. 534–535.)

The Natural World

The new science originated from a number of traditions that were anything but scientific. Inquiry into nature and the environment grew out of the discipline of natural philosophy and was nurtured by spiritual and mystical traditions. Much of the most useful medical knowledge had come from the studies of herbalists; the most reliable calculations of planetary motion had come from astrologers. Though the first laboratories and observatories were developed in aid of the new science, practice in them was as much magical as experimental. For those attempting to unlock the mysteries of the universe, there was no separation between magic and science. Some of the most characteristic features of modern science, such as the stress on experimentation and empirical observation, developed only gradually. What was new about the new science was the determination to develop systems of thought that could help humans understand and control their environment. Thus there was a greater openness and spirit of cooperation about discoveries than in the past, when experiments were conducted secretly and results were kept hidden away.

Aristotelianism was not the only philosophical system to explain the nature and composition of the universe. During the Renaissance the writings of Plato attracted a number of Italian humanists, most notably Marsilio Ficino (1433–99) and Pico della Mirandola (1463–94). In Florence, they taught Plato's theory that the world was composed of ideas and forms, which were hidden by the physical properties of objects. These Neoplatonic humanists believed that the architect of the universe possessed the spirit of a geometrician and

that the perfect disciplines were music and mathematics. These elements of Neoplatonism created an impetus for the mathematically based studies of the new scientists. They were especially important among the astronomers, who used both calculation and geometry in exploring the heavens. But they served as well to bolster the sciences of alchemy and astrology. Alchemy was the use of fire in the study of metals, an effort to find the essence of things through their purification. While medieval alchemists mostly attempted to find gold and silver as the essence of lead and iron, the new experimentation focused on the properties of metals in general. Astrology was the study of the influence of the stars on human behavior, calculated by planetary motion and the harmony of the heavenly spheres. Astrologers made careful calculations based on the movement of the planets and were deeply involved in the new astronomy. The Neoplatonic emphasis upon mathematics also accorded support for a variety of mystical sciences based on numerology. These were efforts to predict events from the combination of particular numbers.

The most influential of these mystical traditions was that associated with Hermes Trismegistus (Thrice Greatest), an Egyptian who was reputed to have lived in the second century C.E. and to have known the secrets of the universe. A body of writings mistakenly attributed to Hermes was discovered during the Renaissance and formed the basis of a Hermetic tradition. The core of Hermetic thinking centered on the idea of a universal spirit that was present in all objects and that spontaneously revealed itself. Kepler was one of many of the new scientists influenced by Hermeticism. His efforts to understand planetary motion derived from his search for a unifying spirit.

A combination of Neoplatonic and Hermetic traditions was central to the work of one of the most curious of the new scientists, the Swiss alchemist Paracelsus (1493–1541). Paracelsus studied with a leading German alchemist before following in his father's footsteps by becoming a physician. Though he worked as a doctor, his true vocation was alchemy, and he conducted innumerable experiments designed to extract the essence of particular metals. Paracelsus taught that all matter was composed of combinations of three principles: salt, sulfur, and mercury. This view replaced the traditional belief in the four elements of earth, water, fire, and air.

The Paracelsian system transformed ideas about chemistry and medicine. Paracelsus rejected the theory that disease was caused by an imbalance in the humors of the body, the standard view of Galen, the great Greek physician of the second century C.E. Instead, Paracelsus

Paracelsus devised this "anatomical furnace" in which a patient's urine was distilled in a measuring cylinder, the parts of which correspond in length and width to those of the human body. Thus the body was "chemically dissected" for the benefit of the patient.

gies to raising the study of medical chemistry above that of merely providing recipes for the cure of disease. He worked carefully and recorded each step in his experiments. Boyle's first important work, *The Sceptical Chymist* (1661), attacked both the Aristotelian and Paracelsian views of the basic components of the natural world. Boyle rejected both the four humors and the three principles. Instead he favored an atomic explanation in which matter "consisted of little particles of all sizes and shapes." Changes in these particles, which would later be identified as the chemical elements, resulted in changes in matter. Boyle's most important experiments were with gases—a word invented by Paracelsus. He formulated the relationship between the volume and pressure of a gas (Boyle's Law), and he invented the air pump.

The new spirit of scientific inquiry also affected medical studies. The study of anatomy through dissection had helped the new scientists reject many of the descriptive errors in Galen's texts. The Belgian doctor Andreas Vesalius (1514–64) published the first modern set of anatomical drawings in 1543. But accurate knowledge of the composition of the body did not mean better understanding of its operation. Dead bodies didn't easily yield the secrets of life. Much of what was known about matters as common as reproduction was an inadequate combination of ancient wisdom and the practical experiences of midwives and doctors.

One of the greatest mysteries was the method by which blood moved through the vital organs. It was generally believed that the blood originated in the liver, traveled to the right side of the heart, and then passed to the left side through invisible pores. William Harvey (1578–1657), an Englishman who had received his medical education in Italy, offered an entirely different explanation. Harvey's main interest was in studying the anatomy of the heart. He examined hearts in more than forty species before concluding that the heart worked like a pump or, as he put it, a water bellows. Harvey observed that the valves of the heart chambers allowed the blood to flow in only one direction. He thus concluded that the blood was pumped by the heart and circulated throughout the entire body.

The greatest of all English scientists was the mathematician and physicist Sir Isaac Newton (1642–1727). It was Newton who brought together the various strands of the new science. He made a great study of Hermetic writings and from them revived the mystical notions of attraction and repulsion. He merged the materialists and Hermeticists, the astronomers and astrologers, the chemists and alchemists. Newton was the first to

argued that each disease had its own cause, which could be diagnosed and remedied. Where traditional doctors treated disease by bloodletting or sweating to correct the imbalance of humors, Paracelsus prescribed the ingestion of particular chemicals, especially distilled metals like mercury, arsenic, and antimony, and he favored administering them at propitious astrological moments.

Although established physicians and medical faculties rejected Paracelsian cures and methods, his influence spread among ordinary practitioners. It ultimately had a profound impact on the studies of Robert Boyle (1627–91), an Englishman who helped establish the basis of the science of chemistry. Boyle devoted his ener-

DE HVMANI CORPORIS FABRICA LIBER II.   197
DECIMA
MVSCV·
LORVM TA·
BVLA·

Tenth "Muscle plate" from Andreas Vesalius's De Humani Corporis Fabrica (Concerning the Fabric of the Human Body), *published in 1543. The muscles of the back of the body are laid bare.*

understand the composition of light, the first to develop a calculus, the first to build a reflecting telescope. He made stunning contributions to the sciences of optics, physics, astronomy, and mathematics, and his magnum opus, *Mathematical Principles of Natural Philosophy* (1687), is one of a handful of the most important scientific works ever composed. Most importantly, Newton solved the single most perplexing problem: if the world was composed of matter in motion, what was motion?

Though Galileo had first developed a theory of inertia, the idea that a body at rest stays at rest, most materialists believed that motion was inherent in objects. In contrast, Newton believed that motion was the result of the interaction of objects and that it could be calculated mathematically. From his experiments he formu-

lated the concept of force and his famous laws of motion: (1) that objects at rest or in uniform linear motion remain in such a state unless acted upon by an external force; (2) that changes in motion are proportional to force; and (3) that for every action there is an equal and opposite reaction. From these laws of motion, Newton advanced one step further. If the world was no more than matter in motion and if all motion was subject to the same laws, then the movement of the planets could be explained in the same way as the movement of an apple falling from a tree. There was a mathematical relationship between attraction and repulsion, a universal gravitation as Newton called it, that governed the movement of all objects. Newton's theory of gravity joined Kepler's astronomy and Galileo's physics. The mathematical, materialistic world of the new science was now complete.

Science Enthroned

By the middle of the seventeenth century, the new science was firmly established throughout Europe. Royal and noble patrons supported the enterprise by paying some of the costs of equipment and experimentation. Royal observatories were created for the astronomers, colleges of physicians for the doctors, laboratories for the chemists. Both England and France established royal societies of learned scientists to meet together and discuss their discoveries. The French Académie des Sciences (1666) was composed of twenty salaried scientists and an equal number of students, divided among the different branches of scientific learning. The English Royal Society (1662) boasted some of the greatest minds of the age. It was there that Newton first made public his most important discoveries. Scientific bodies were also formed outside the traditional universities. These were the so-called mechanics colleges, like Gresham College in London, where the practical applications of mathematics and physics were taught.

The establishment of learned scientific societies and practical colleges fulfilled part of the program advocated by Sir Francis Bacon (1561–1626), one of the leading supporters of scientific research in England. In *The Advancement of Learning* (1605), Bacon proposed a scientific method through inductive, empirical experimentation. Bacon believed that experiments should be carefully recorded so that results were both reliable and repeatable, and in his numerous writings he stressed the practical impact of scientific discovery.

Bacon's support for the new science contrasts markedly with the stance taken by the Roman Catholic church. Embattled by the Reformation and the wars of religion, the Church had taken the offensive in preserving the core of its heritage. By the early seventeenth century the missionary work of the Jesuits had won many reconversions and had halted the advance of Protestantism. Now the new science appeared to be another heresy. Not only did it confound ancient wisdom and contradict Church teachings, but it was also a lay movement that was neither directed nor controlled from Rome. The trial of Galileo slowed the momentum of scientific investigation in Catholic countries and starkly posed the conflict between authority and knowledge. But the stand taken by the Church was based on more than narrow self-interest. Ever since Copernicus had published his views, a new skepticism had emerged among European intellectuals. Every year new theories competed with old ones, and dozens of contradictory explanations for the most common phenomena were advanced and debated. The skeptics concluded that nothing was known and nothing was knowable. Their position led inevitably to the most shocking of all possible views: atheism. But there was no necessary link between the new science and an attack upon established religion. So Galileo had argued all along. Few of the leading scientists saw a contradiction between their studies and their faith. Still by the middle of the century attacks upon the Church were increasing and some blamed the new science for them. Thus it was altogether fitting that one of the leading mathematicians of the day should provide the method for harmonizing faith and reason.

René Descartes (1596–1650) was trained in one of the best Jesuit schools in France before taking a law degree in 1616. He entered military service in the Dutch Republic and after the outbreak of the Thirty Years' War, in the Duke of Bavaria's army. Descartes was keenly interested in mathematics, and during his military travels he met and was tutored by a leading Dutch mathematician. For the first time he learned of the new scientific discoveries and of the advances made in mathematics. In 1619 he dreamt of discovering the scientific principles of universal knowledge. After this dream, Descartes returned to Holland and began to develop his system. He was on the verge of publishing his views when he learned of Galileo's condemnation. Reading Galileo's *Dialogue Between the Two Great Systems of the World* (1632), Descartes discovered that he shared many of the same opinions and had worked out mathematical proofs for them, but he refrained from publishing until 1637, when he brought out the *Discourse on Method*.

In the *Discourse on Method*, Descartes demonstrated how skepticism could be used to produce certainty. He began by declaring that he would reject everything that could not be clearly proven beyond doubt. Thus he rejected the material world, the testimony of his senses, all known or imagined opinions. He was left only with doubt. But what was doubt, if not thought, and what was thought, if not the workings of his mind? The only thing of which he could be certain, then, was that he had a mind. Thus, his famous formulation: "I think, therefore I am." From this first certainty came another, the knowledge of perfectibility. He knew that he was imperfect and that a perfect being had to have placed that knowledge within him. Therefore, a perfect being—God—existed.

Descartes's philosophy, known as Cartesianism, rested on the dual existence of matter and mind. Matter was the material world subject to the incontrovertible laws of mathematics. Mind was the spirit of the creator. Descartes was one of the leading mechanistic philosophers, believing that all objects operated in accord with natural laws. He invented analytic geometry and made important contributions to the sciences of optics and physics upon which Newton would later build. Yet it was in his proof that the new science could be harmonized with the old religion that Descartes made his greatest contribution.

Astronomy, chemistry, biology, and physics all had their modern origins in the seventeenth century. Because thinking about the natural world was integrated, the discoveries in one discipline made possible breakthroughs in another. The mathematical calculations of Kepler, the observational astronomy of Galileo, and the experimental biology of Harvey fed upon an atmosphere of intellectual curiosity and disciplined scientific enquiry. Though many of the breakthrough discoveries of the new scientists would not find practical use for centuries, the spirit of discovery was to have great impact in an age of commerce and capital. The quest for mathematical certainty and prime movers led directly to improvements in agriculture, mining, navigation, and industrial activity. The new sense of control over the material world provided a new optimism for generations of Europeans.

Empires of Goods

Under the watchful eye of the European states, a world-wide marketplace for the exchange of commodities had been created. First the Dutch and then the English had established monopoly companies to engage in exotic trades in the East. The Spanish and Portuguese, then the English and French had established colonial dependencies in the Atlantic, which they carefully nurtured in hope of economic gain. Protected trade had flourished beyond the wildest dreams of its promoters. Luxury commodities became staples; new commodities became luxuries. Trade enhanced the material life of all European peoples, though it came at great cost to the Asians, Africans, and Latin Americans whose labor and raw materials were converted into the new crazes of consumption.

Though long-distance trade was never as important to the European economy as was inland and intracontinental trade, its development in the seventeenth and eighteenth centuries had a profound impact upon lifestyles, economic policy, and ultimately on warfare. It was the Dutch who became the first great commercial power. Their achievements were based on innovative techniques, rational management, and a social and cultural environment that supported mercantile activities. Dutch society was freer than any other, open to new capital, new ventures, and new ideas. The Dutch innovated in the organization of trade by developing the concept of the entrepôt, a place where goods were brought for storage before being exchanged. They pioneered in finance by establishing the Bank of Amsterdam. They led in shipbuilding by developing the flyboat, a long flat-hulled vessel designed specifically to carry bulky cargoes like grain. They traded around the globe with the largest mercantile fleet yet known. It was not until the end of the seventeenth century that England and France surpassed the Dutch. This reversal owed less to new innovations than it did to restrictions on trade. Because the Dutch dominated the European economy, the French and English began to pass laws to eliminate Dutch competition. The English banned imports carried in Dutch ships; the French banned Dutch products. Both policies cut heavily into the Dutch superiority and both ultimately resulted in commercial warfare.

The Marketplace of the World

By the seventeenth century, long-distance trade had begun to integrate the regions of the world into a single marketplace. Slaves bought in Africa mined silver in South America. The bullion was shipped to Spain, where it was distributed across Europe. Most went to Amsterdam to settle Spanish debts, Dutch bankers having replaced the Italians as the paymasters of Europe. From Holland the silver traveled east to the Baltic Sea, the Dutch lifeline where vital stores of grain and timber were purchased for home consumption. By the 1630s over five hundred Dutch ships a year called at Gdansk,

The Geographer *by Jan Vermeer van Delft, 1669. a Dutch cartographer, holding dividers, is shown surrounded by charts, a globe, and other paraphernalia of his craft. Such cartographers combined the skills of artist and mathematician.*

the largest of the Baltic ports. From there the silver was transported to the interior of Poland and Russia, the great storehouses of European raw materials. Even more of this African-mined Spanish silver, traded by the Dutch, was carried to Asia to buy spices in the South Sea Islands, cottons in India, or silk in China. Millions of ounces flowed from America to Asia via the European trading routes. On the return voyage, brightly colored Indian cottons were traded in Africa to purchase slaves for the South American silver mines.

The remarkable fact about the expansion of European trade in the seventeenth and eighteenth centuries is that it took place as a result of the ingenuity of traders rather than because of technological or geographical discoveries. By the sixteenth century all the major trading routes had already been opened. The Spanish moved back and forth across the Atlantic; the Dutch and Portuguese sailed around the tip of Africa to the Indian Ocean. The Baltic trade connected the eastern and western parts of Europe as Danes, Swedes, and Dutch exchanged Polish and Russian raw materials for English and French manufactured goods. The Mediterranean, which had dominated world trade for centuries, was still a vital artery of intercontinental trade, but its role was

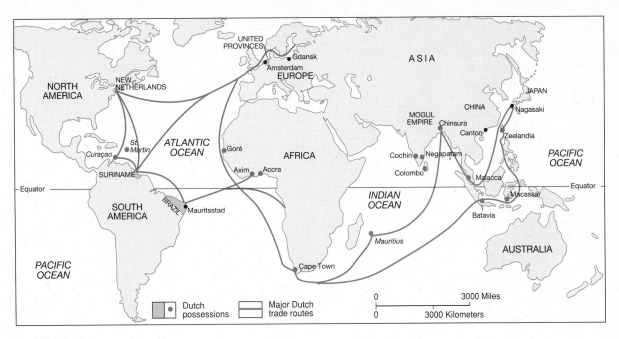

Dutch Trading Routes, ca. 1650

diminishing. In 1600 almost three-quarters of the Asian trade was still land-based, much of it carried through the Middle East to the Mediterranean. A century later nearly all Asian trade was carried directly to western Europe by Dutch and English vessels. Commercial power was shifting to the northern European states just as dramatically as was military and political power.

The technology associated with commerce achieved no breakthroughs to compare with the great transformations of the fifteenth century, when new techniques of navigation made transatlantic travel possible. It is certainly true that there continued to be improvements. The astronomical findings of the new science were a direct aid to navigation, as were the recorded experiences of so many practiced sea travelers. The materials used to make and maintain ships improved with the importation of pitch and tar from the east and with the greater availability of iron and copper from Scandinavia. It was the Dutch who made the single most important innovation in shipbuilding. To gain maximum profit from their journeys to the Baltic, the Dutch designed the so-called flyboats. Flyboats sacrificed speed and maneuverability, but they were cheap to build and could be manned by small crews. They carried no heavy armaments and were thus well adapted to the serene Baltic trade.

It was unspectacular developments like the flyboat that had such an impact on seventeenth- and eighteenth-century transcontinental trade. Innovation, organization, and efficient management were the principal elements of what historians have called the commercial revolution. Concerted efforts to maximize opportunities and advantages accounted for the phenomenal growth in the volume and value of commercial exchange. One of the least spectacular and most effective breakthroughs was the replacement of bilateral with triangular trade. In bilateral trade, the surplus commodities of one community were exchanged for those of another. This method, of course, restricted the range of trading partners to those with mutually desirable surplus production: England and Italy were unlikely to swap woolens or Sicily and Poland to trade grain. For those with few desirable commodities, bilateral trade meant the exchange of precious metals for goods, and throughout much of the sixteenth and early seventeenth centuries bullion was by far the most often traded commodity. Triangular trade created a larger pool of desirable goods. British manufactured goods could be traded to Africa for slaves, the slaves could be traded in the West Indies for sugar, and the sugar could be consumed in Britain. Moreover, the merchants involved in shifting these goods from place to place could achieve profits on each exchange. Indeed their motive in trading could now change from dumping surplus commodities to matching supply and demand.

Equally important were the changes made in the way trade was financed. As states, cities, and even individuals could stamp their own precious metal, there were hundreds of different European coins with different nominal and metallic values. The influx of American silver further destabilized an already unstable system of exchange. The Bank of Amsterdam was created in 1609 to establish a uniform rate of exchange for the various currencies traded in that city. From this useful function a second developed, transfer, or giro, banking, a system that had been invented in Italy. In giro banking, various merchant firms held money on account and issued bills of transfer from one to another. This transfer system meant that merchants in different cities did not have to transport their precious metals or endure long delays in having their accounts settled.

Giro banking also aided the development of bills of exchange, an early form of checking. Merchants could conclude trades by depositing money in a given bank or merchant house and then having a bill drawn for the sum they owed. Bills of exchange were especially important in international trade as they made large-scale shipments of precious metals to settle trade deficits unnecessary. By the end of the seventeenth century, bills of exchange had become negotiable, that is, they could pass from one merchant to another without being redeemed. Thus a Dutch merchant could buy French wines in Bordeaux with a bill of exchange drawn on an account in the Bank of Amsterdam. The Bordeaux merchant could then purchase Spanish oranges and use the same bill of exchange as payment. There were two disadvantages to this system: ultimately the bill had to return to Amsterdam for redemption, and when it

did the account on which it was drawn might be empty. The establishment of the Bank of England in 1694 overcame these difficulties. The Bank of England was licensed to issue its own bills of exchange, or bank notes, which were backed by the revenue from specific English taxes. This security of payment was widely sought after, and the Bank of England soon became a clearing house for all kinds of bills of exchange. The Bank would buy in bills at a discount, paying less than their face value, and pay out precious metal or their own notes in exchange.

The effects of these and many other small-scale changes in business practice helped fuel prolonged growth in European commerce. It was the European merchant who made this growth possible, accepting the risks of each individual transaction, building up small pools of capital from which successive transactions could take place. Most mercantile ventures were conducted by individuals or families and were based on the specialized trade of a single commodity. Trade offered high returns because it entailed high risks. The long delays in moving goods and their uncertain arrival, the unreliability of agents and the unscrupulousness of other traders, and the inefficiencies in transport and communication all weighed heavily against success. Those who succeeded did so less by luck than by hard work. They used family members to receive shipments. They lowered shipping costs by careful packaging. They lowered protection costs by securing their trade routes. Financial publications lowered the costs of information. Ultimately, lower costs meant lower prices. For centuries luxury goods dominated intercontinental trade. But by the eighteenth century European merchants had

Engraving of a Dutch flyboat by Salomon Savery, mid-seventeenth century.

created a world marketplace in which the luxuries of the past were the common fare of the present.

Consumption Choices

As long-distance trade became more sophisticated, merchants became more sensitive to consumer tastes. Low-volume, high-quality goods like spices and silks could not support the growing merchant communities in the European states. These goods were the preserve of the largest trading companies and, more importantly, they had reached saturation levels by the early seventeenth century. The price of pepper, the most used of all spices, fell nearly continuously after 1650. Moreover, triangular trade allowed merchants to provide a better match of supplies and demands. The result was the rise to prominence of a vast array of new commodities, which not only continued the expansion of trade but also reshaped diet, lifestyles, and patterns of consumption. New products came from both east and west. Dutch and English incursions into the Asian trade provoked competition with the Portuguese and expanded the range of commodities that were shipped back to Europe. An aggressive Asian triangle was created in which European bullion bought Indonesian spices that were exchanged for Persian silk and Chinese and Japanese finished goods. In the Atlantic, the English were quick to develop both home and export markets for a variety of new or newly available products.

The European trade with Asia had always been designed to satisfy consumer demand rather than to exchange surplus goods. Europeans manufactured little that was desired in Asia, and neither merchants nor governments saw fit to attempt to influence Asian tastes in the way they did those of Europeans. The chief commodity imported to the East was bullion, tons of South American silver, perhaps a third of all that was produced. In return came spices, silk, coffee, jewels, jade, porcelain, dyes, and a wide variety of other exotic goods. By the middle of the seventeenth century the Dutch dominated the spice trade, obtaining a virtual monopoly over cinnamon, cloves, nutmeg, and mace and carrying the largest share of pepper. Each year Europeans consumed perhaps one million pounds of the four great spices and seven million pounds of pepper. Both Dutch and English competed for preeminence in the silk trade. The Dutch concentrated on Chinese silk, which they used mostly in trade with Japan. The English established an interest in lower quality Indian silk spun in Bengal and even hired Italian silk masters to try to teach European techniques to the Indian spinners.

A Chinese porcelain copy of a vase from the famous pottery works at the Dutch town of Delft. The Delft vase itself had been copied from a Chinese original. The date is probably early eighteenth century.

The most important manufactured articles imported from the East to Europe were the lightweight, brightly colored Indian cottons known as calicoes. It was the Dutch who first realized the potential of the cotton market. Until the middle of the seventeenth century cotton and cotton blended with silk were used in Europe only for wall hangings and table coverings. Colorful Asian chintz contained floral patterns that Europeans still considered exotic. But the material was also soft and smooth to the touch, and it soon replaced linen for use as underwear and close-fitting garments among the well-to-do. The fashion quickly caught on and the Dutch began exporting calicoes throughout the Continent. The English and French followed suit, establishing their own trading houses in India and bringing European patterns and designs with them for the Asians to copy.

Along with the new apparel from the East came new beverages. Coffee, which was first drunk in northern Europe in the early seventeenth century, became a fashionable drink by the end of the century. Coffeehouses sprang up in the major urban areas of northern Europe.

Detail of an Indian textile from the Madras region, ca. 1650. Calicut gave its name to the cotton cloth called calico. This is an example of a "painted Calicut" wall hanging.

There political and intellectual conversation was as heady as the strong Middle Eastern brew that was served.

As popular as coffee became among the European elites, it paled in comparison to the importance of tea as both an import commodity and a basic beverage. While coffee drinking remained the preserve of the wealthy, tea consumption spread throughout European society. It was probably most important in England, where the combination of China tea and West Indian sugar created a virtual revolution in nutrition. The growth in tea consumption was phenomenal. In 1706 England imported 100,000 pounds of tea. By the end of the century the number had risen to over 15 million pounds. The English imported most of this tea directly from China, where an open port had been established at Canton. Originally just one of a number of commodities that was carried on an Asian voyage, tea soon became the dominant cargo of the large English merchant ships. Some manufactured goods would be brought to India on the outward voyage, to fill as much cargo space as possible, but once the ships had loaded the green and black teas, they sailed directly home. Almost all tea was purchased with bullion as the Chinese had even less use for Euro-

pean goods than did other Asians. It was not until the discovery that the Chinese consumed large quantities of opium, which was grown in India and Southeast Asia, that a triangular trade developed.

The success of tea was linked to the explosive growth in the development of sugar in Europe's Atlantic colonies. The Portuguese had attempted to cultivate sugar in the Azores at the end of the fifteenth century, but it was not until the settlement of Brazil, whose hot, humid climate was a natural habitat for the cane plants, that widespread cultivation began. The island of Barbados became the first English sugar colony. Barbados turned to sugar production accidentally when its first attempts to market tobacco failed. The planters modeled their development on Brazil, where African slaves were used to plant, tend, and cut the giant canes from which the sugar was extracted. Hot, sweet tea became a popular drink for the lower orders of English society, a drink that, unlike beer, provided a quick burst of energy. By 1700 the English were sending home over 50 million pounds of sugar besides what they were shipping directly to the North American colonies.

The triangular trade of manufactures—largely reexported calicoes—to Africa for slaves, who were exchanged in the West Indies for sugar, became the dominant form of English overseas trade. Colonial production depended upon the enforced labor of hundreds of thousands of Africans. Gold and silver, tobacco, sugar, rice, and indigo were all slave crops. Africans were enslaved by other Africans and then sold to Europeans to be used in the colonies. Over six million black slaves were imported into the Americas during the course of the eighteenth century. While rum and calicoes were the main commodities exchanged for slaves, the Africans that dominated the slave trade organized a highly competitive market. Every colonial power participated in this lucrative trade. Over three million slaves were imported into the Portuguese colony of Brazil; by the end of the eighteenth century there were 500,000 slaves and only 35,000 French inhabitants of the sugar island of Saint Domingue. But it was the English with their sugar colonies of Barbados and Jamaica and their tobacco colonies of Virginia and Maryland who ultimately came to control the slave trade. The prosperity of Newport, Rhode Island, in North America and the port of Liverpool in Lancashire were built entirely upon the slave trade, as were hundreds of plantation fortunes. The sweet tooth of Europe was fed by the sweat of black Africans.

Sugar was by far the dominant commodity of the colonial trade but was not the only one. Furs and fish

Nineteenth-century engraving of a tobacco plantation. Slaves labor while masters take their ease. In the background, ships wait to take the barrels of tobacco to far-off markets.

had first driven Europeans toward North America and both remained important commodities. Beaver and rabbit skins were the most common materials for making headgear in an age in which everyone wore a hat. The Canadian cod schools were among the richest in the world, and the catch was shipped back either salted ordried. The English established what amounted to a manufacturing industry on the Newfoundland coast, where they dried the tons of fish that they caught. In the eighteenth century, rice was grown for export in the southern American colonies, particularly South Carolina. Tobacco was the first new American product to come into widespread use in Europe, and its popularity—despite various official efforts to ban its use as dirty and unhealthy—grew steadily. American tobacco was grown principally in the colonies of Virginia and Maryland and shipped across the ocean, where it was frequently blended with European varieties. Although the English were the principal importers, it was the Dutch who dominated the European tobacco trade, making the most popular blends.

The new commodities flooded into Europe from all parts of the globe. By the middle of the eighteenth century tea, coffee, cocoa, gin, and rum were among the most popular beverages. These were all products that had been largely unknown a century earlier. New habits were created as new demands were satisfied. Tea and sugar passed from luxury to staple in little more than a generation and the demand for both products continued to increase. To meet it, the European trading powers

needed to create and maintain a powerful and efficient mercantile system.

Dutch Masters

For the nearly eighty years between 1565 and 1648 that the Dutch were at war, they grew ever more prosperous. While the economies of most other European nations were sapped by warfare, the Dutch seemed to draw strength from their interminable conflict with the Spanish empire. They did have the advantage of fighting defensively on land and offensively on sea. Land war was terribly costly to the aggressor, who had to raise large armies, transport them to the site of battles or sieges, and feed them while they were there. The defender simply had to fortify strong places, keep its water routes open to secure supplies, and wait for the weather to change. Sea war—or piracy, depending on one's viewpoint—required much smaller outlays for men and material and promised the rewards of captured prizes. The Dutch became expert at attacking the Spanish silver fleets, hunting like a lion against a herd by singling out the slower and smaller vessels for capture. The Dutch also benefited from the massive immigration into their provinces of Protestants who had lived and worked in the southern provinces. They brought with them vital skills in manufacturing and large reserves of capital for investment in Dutch commerce.

The Dutch East India Company's trading station on the Hooghly River in Bengal, 1665. The station was one of a network of bases the Company established throughout its eastern trading empire.

The Dutch grounded their prosperity on commerce. Excellent craftsmen, they took the lead in the skilled occupations necessary for finishing cloth, refining raw materials, and decorating consumer goods. They were also successful farmers, especially given the small amounts of land with which they had to work and the difficult ecological conditions in which they worked it. But their greatest abilities were in trade.

Though the Dutch Republic comprised seven separate political entities, with a total population of about two million, the province of Holland was preeminent among them. Holland contained more than a quarter of this population, and its trading port of Amsterdam was one of the great cities of Europe. The city had risen dramatically in the seventeenth century, growing from a mid-sized urban community of 65,000 in 1600 to a metropolis of 170,000 fifty years later. The port was one of the busiest in the world, for it was built to be an entrepôt. Vast warehouses and docks lined its canals. Visitors were impressed by the bustle, the cleanliness, and the businesslike appearance of Amsterdam. There were no great public squares and few recognizable monuments. The central buildings were the Bank and the Exchange, testimony to the dominant activities of the residents.

The Dutch dominated all types of European trade. They carried more English coal than England, more French wine than France, more Swedish iron than Sweden. Dutch ships outnumbered all others in every important port of Europe. Goods were brought to Amsterdam to be redistributed throughout the world. Dutch prosperity rested first upon the Baltic trade. Even after it ceased to expand in the middle of the seventeenth century, the Baltic trade composed over one quarter of all of Holland's commercial enterprise. The Dutch also were the leaders in the East Indian trade throughout the seventeenth century. They held a virtual monopoly on the sale of exotic spices and the largest share of the pepper trade. Their imports of cottons and especially of porcelain began new consumer fads that soon resulted in the development of European industries. Dutch potteries began to produce china, as lower quality ceramic goods came to be known. Dutch trade in the Atlantic was of less importance, but the Dutch did have a colonial presence in the New World, controlling a number of small islands and the rapidly growing mainland settlement of New Netherland. Yet the Dutch still dominated the secondary market in tobacco and sugar, becoming the largest processor and refiner of these important commodities.

In all of these activities the Dutch acted as merchants rather than as consumers. Unlike most other Europeans they regarded precious metal as a commodity like any other and took no interest in accumulating it for its own sake. This attitude enabled them to pioneer triangular trading and develop the crucial financial institutions necessary to expand their overseas commerce. The Dutch were not so much innovators as improvers. They saw the practical value in Italian accounting and banking methods and raised them to new levels of efficiency. They made use of marine insurance to help diminish the risks of mercantile activity. Their legal system favored the creation of small trading companies by protecting individual investments. The European stock and commodity markets were centered in Amsterdam. By the 1670s over 500 commodities were traded on the Amsterdam exchange, and even a primitive futures market evolved for those who wished to speculate.

There were many explanations for the unparalleled growth of this small maritime state into one of the greatest of European trading empires. Geography and climate provided one impetus, the lack of sufficient foodstuffs another. Yet there were cultural characteristics as well. One was the openness of Dutch society. Even before the struggle with Spain, the northern provinces had shown a greater inclination toward religious toleration than had most parts of Europe. Amsterdam became a unique center for religious and intellectual exchange. European Jews flocked there, as did Catholic dissidents like Descartes. They brought with them a wide range of skills and knowledge along with capital that could be invested in trade. There was no real social nobility among the Dutch and certainly no set of values that prized investment in land over investment in trade. The French and Spanish nobility looked with scorn upon their mercantile classes and shunned any form of commercial investment, and the English, though more open to industry and trade, sank as much of their capital as possible into landed estates and country houses. The Dutch economic elite invested in trade. By the middle of the seventeenth century the Dutch Republic enjoyed a reputation for cultural creativity that was the envy of the Continent. A truly extraordinary school of Dutch artists led by Rembrandt celebrated this new state born of commerce with vivid portrayals of its people and its prosperity.

Mercantile Organization

Elsewhere in Europe, trade was the king's business. The wealth of the nation was part of the prestige of the monarch and its rise or fall part of the crown's power. Power and prestige were far more important to absolute rulers than was the profit of merchants. Indeed, in all European states except the Dutch Republic, the activities of merchants were scorned by both the landed elite and the salaried bureaucrats. Leisure was valued by the one and royal service by the other. The pursuit of wealth by buying and selling somehow lacked dignity. Yet the activities of the mercantile classes took on increasing importance for the state for two reasons. First, imported goods, especially luxuries, were a noncontroversial target for taxation. Customs duties and excise taxes grew all over Europe. Representative assemblies composed of landed elites were usually happy to grant them to the monarch, and merchants could pass them on to consumers in higher prices. Secondly, the competition for trade was seen as a competition between states rather than individual merchants. Trading privileges involved special arrangements with foreign powers, arrangements that recognized the sovereign power of European monarchs. In this way, trade could bring glory to the state.

The competition for power and glory derived from the theory of mercantilism, a set of assumptions about economic activity that were commonly held throughout Europe and that guided the policies of almost every government. There were two interrelated ideas. One was that the wealth of a nation resided in its stock of precious metal, and the other was that economic activity was a zero-sum game. There was thought to be a fixed amount of money, a fixed amount of commodities, and a fixed amount of consumption. Thus what one country gained, another lost. If England bought wine from France and paid £100,000 in precious metal for it, then England was £100,000 poorer and France £100,000 richer. If one was to trade profitably, it was absolutely necessary to wind up with a surplus of precious metal. Therefore it was imperative that governments regulate trade so that the stocks of precious metal were protected from the greed of the merchants. The first and most obvious measure of protection, then, was to prohibit the export of coin except by license, a prohibition that was absolutely unenforceable and was violated more often by government officials than by merchants.

These ideas about economic activity led to a variety of forms of economic regulation. The most common was the monopoly, a grant of special privileges in return for both financial considerations and an agreement to abide by the rules set out by the state. In the context of the seventeenth-century economy, there were a number of advantages to monopolies. First, of course, were those that accrued to the crown. There were direct and indirect revenues: monopolists usually paid considerable fees for their rights, and their activities were easy to monitor for purposes of taxation. The crown could use the grant of monopoly to reward past favors or to purchase future support from powerful individuals. There were also advantages for the monopolists. They could make capital investments with the expectation of long-term gains. This advantage was especially important in attracting investors for risky and expensive ventures like long-distance trade. Indeed, there were even benefits for the economy as a whole, as monopolies increased productive investment at a time when most capital was being used to purchase land, luxury goods, or offices.

Two monopoly companies, the English and the Dutch East India companies, dominated the Asian trade. The English East India Company, founded in 1600 with a capital of £30,000, was given the exclusive

EARLY HISTORY OF THE DUTCH EAST INDIA COMPANY

■ The Dutch East India Company was the most important of the monopoly trading companies that were founded in the early seventeenth century. It was organized as a stock company and its shares traded on the Amsterdam bourse. Merchants could purchase portions of its ships' cargoes for both imports and exports, and the company was given total control over the eastern spice trade. It was also given political and diplomatic powers in the areas in which it traded, and its overseas members behaved as much as foreign ambassadors as merchants. This excerpt is from an early history of the company and provides details of its original charter.

After various private merchants joined with others in the 1590s and after the turn of the century to form companies, first in Amsterdam and then in other cities of Holland and Zeeland, to open up and undertake travel and trade with the East Indies, and from time to time equipped and sent out many ships, which returned, on the average, with no small success, the States General came to the conclusion that it would be more useful and profitable not only for the country as a whole but also for its inhabitants individually, especially all those who had undertaken and shared in navigation and trade, that these companies should be combined and this navigation and trade be placed and maintained on a firm footing, with order and political guidance. After much argument and persuasion, this union was worked out by Their High Mightinesses [the government of the United Provinces], in their own words, to advance the prosperity of the United Netherlands, to conserve and increase its industry and to bring profit to the Company and to the people of the country.

The Company's charter authorized it to make alliances with princes and potentates east of the Cape of Good Hope and beyond the Straits of Magellan, to make contracts build fortresses and strongholds, name governors, raise troops, appoint officers of justice, and perform other necessary services for the advancement of trade; to dismiss the said governors and officers of justice if their conduct was found to be harmful and disloyal, provided that these governors or officers could not be prevented from returning here to present such grievances or complaints as they think they might have.

The inhabitants of this country were permitted to invest as much or as little as they pleased in shares of the Company.

The subscription had to be made before September 1, 1602. . . .

. . . When the time for this investment or subscription had expired, various competent persons in different places presented requests in person or by sealed letter to the assembly of the XVII, asking that they be permitted to join the Company with the investment of certain sums of money; it was decided that no one else should be permitted to join in violation of the charter and to the detriment of the shareholders who had paid in their subscriptions before the expiration of the date fixed, and that the subscribed capital should be neither increased nor reduced.

right to the Asian trade and immediately established itself throughout the Indian Ocean. The Dutch East India Company was formed two years later with ten times the capital of its English counterpart. By the end of the century the Dutch company employed over twelve thousand people. Both companies were known as joint-stock companies, an innovation in the way in which businesses were organized. Subscribers owned a percentage of the total value of the company, based on the number of shares they bought, and were entitled to a distribution of profits on the same basis. Initially, the English company determined profits on single voyages and was to distribute all of its assets to its shareholders after a given period. But changes in legal practice gave the company an identity separate from the individuals that held the shares. Now shares could be exchanged without the breakup of the company as a whole. Both Amsterdam and London soon developed stock markets to trade the shares of monopoly companies.

Both East India companies were remarkably good investments. The Dutch East India Company paid an average dividend of 18 percent for over two hundred years. The value of English East India Company shares rose fivefold in the second half of the seventeenth century alone. Few other monopoly companies achieved a record comparable to that of the East India companies. The English Royal African Company, founded in 1672 to provide slaves for the Spanish colonies, barely recouped costs and was soon superseded by private trade. Even the French East Indian and African companies, which were modeled on the Dutch and English, were forced to abandon their monopolies. The Dutch and English companies were successful not because of their special privileges but because they were able to lower the costs of protecting their ships and cargoes.

Monopolies were not the only form of regulation in which seventeenth-century government engaged. For those states with Atlantic colonies, regulation took the form of restricting markets rather than traders. In the 1660s the English government, alarmed at the growth of Dutch mercantile activity in the New World, passed a series of Navigation Acts designed to protect English shipping. Colonial goods—primarily tobacco and sugar—could be shipped to and from England only in English boats. If the French wanted to purchase West Indian sugar, they could not simply send a ship to the English colony of Barbados loaded with French goods and exchange them for sugar. Rather, they had to make their purchases from an English import-export merchant and the goods had to be unloaded in an English port before they could be reloaded to be shipped to France. As a result, the English reexport trade skyrocketed. In the year 1700 reexports amounted to nearly 40 percent of all English commerce. With such a dramatic increase in trading, all moved in English ships, shipbuilding boomed. English coastal towns enjoyed heightened prosperity as did the great colonial ports of Bristol and Liverpool. For a time, colonial protection proved effective.

French protectionism was as much internal as colonial. The French entered the intercontinental trade later than their North Atlantic rivals, and they were less dependent upon trade for their subsistence. Of all the states of Europe, only France could satisfy its needs from its own resources. But to achieve such self-sufficiency required coordination and leadership. In the 1670s Louis XIV's finance minister, Jean-Baptiste Colbert (1619-83) developed a plan to bolster the French economy by protecting it against European imports. First Colbert followed the English example of restricting the reexport trade by requiring that imports come to France either in French ships or in the ships of the country from which the goods originated. In addition, he used tariffs to make imported goods unattractive in France. He sponsored a drive to increase French manufacturing, especially of textiles, tapestries, linens, glass, and furniture. To protect the investments in French manufacturing, enormous duties were placed on the import of similar goods manufactured elsewhere. The Venetian glass industry, for example, suffered a serious blow from Colbert's tariffs. English woolen manufacturers were also damaged and the English sought retaliatory measures. But in fact, the English had already begun to imitate this form of protection. In the early eighteenth century England attempted to limit the importation of cotton goods from India to prevent the collapse of the domestic clothing industry.

The Navigation Acts and Colbert's program of protective tariffs were directed specifically against Dutch reexporters. The Dutch were the acknowledged leaders in all branches of commerce in the seventeenth century. There were many summers when there were more Dutch vessels in London Harbor than there were English ships. In the 1670s the Dutch merchant fleet was probably larger than the English, French, Spanish, Portuguese, and German fleets combined. Restrictive navigation practices were one way to combat an advantage that the Dutch had built through heavy capital investment and by breaking away from the prevailing theories about the relationship between wealth and precious metals. The English and French Navigation Acts cut heavily into the Dutch trade and ultimately both the English and French overtook them. But protectionism had its price. Just as the dynastic wars were succeeded by the wars of religion, so were the wars of religion succeeded by the wars of commerce.

"The discovery of America and that of a passage to the East Indies by the Cape of Good Hope are the two greatest and most important events in the history of mankind." So wrote the great Scottish economist Adam Smith (1723-90) in *The Wealth of Nations* (1776). For Smith and his generation, the first great age of commerce was coming to an end. The innovations of the Dutch had given way to a settled pattern of international long-distance trade. States now viewed commerce as a part of their national self-interest. They developed overseas empires, which they protected as markets for their goods and sources for their raw materials. These were justified by the theory of mercantilism and the demands of a generation of consumers who saw the luxuries of the past as the necessities of the present.

The Wars of Commerce

The belief that there was a fixed amount of trade in the world was still strong in the late seventeenth century. One country's gains in trade were another's losses. There was not more than enough to go around and it could not be easily understood how the expansion of one country's trade could benefit all countries. Competition for trade was the same as competition for territory or subjects, part of the struggle by which the state grew powerful. It was not inevitable that economic competition would lead to warfare, only that restrictive competition would.

Thus the scramble for colonies in the seventeenth century led to commercial warfare in the eighteenth. As the English gradually replaced the Dutch as the leading commercial nation, so the French replaced the English as the leading competitor. Hostility between the English and the French had existed for centuries, and it was not without cause that the commercial wars of the eighteenth century should be likened to the territorial wars of the Middle Ages. The greed of merchants and the glory of princes fueled a struggle for the dominance of world markets that brought European warfare to every corner of the globe.

The Mercantile Wars

Commercial warfare in Europe began between the English and the Dutch in the middle of the seventeenth century. Both had established aggressive overseas trading companies in the Atlantic and in Asia. In the early seventeenth century the Dutch were the undisputed leaders, their carrying capacity and trade monopolies the greatest in the world. But the English were rising quickly. Their Atlantic colonies began to produce valuable new commodities like tobacco and sugar, and theirAsian trade was expanding decade after decade. Conflict was inevitable, and the result was a series of three naval wars fought between 1652 and 1674.

The Dutch had little choice but to strike out against English policy, but they also had little chance of overall success. Their spectacular naval victory in 1667, when the Dutch fleet surprised many English warships at port and burned both ships and docks at Chatham, obscured the fact that Dutch commercial superiority was slipping. In 1664 the English conquered New Netherland on the North American mainland and renamed it New York. With this defeat, the Dutch lost their largest colonial possession. The wars were costly to both states, nearly bankrupting the English Crown in 1672. Anglo-Dutch rivalry was finally laid to rest after 1688, when William of Orange, stadtholder of Holland, became William III (1689-1702), king of England.

The Anglo-Dutch commercial wars were just one part of a larger European conflict. Dutch commerce was as threatening to France as it was to England, though in a different way. Under Colbert, France pursued a policy of economic independence. The state supported internal industrial activity through the financing of large workshops and the encouragement of new manufacturing techniques. To protect French products, Colbert levied a series of punitive tariffs on Dutch imports, which severely depressed both trade and manufacture in Holland. Though the Dutch retaliated with restrictive tariffs of their own—in 1672 they banned the import of all French goods for an entire year—the Dutch economy depended upon free trade. The Dutch had much more to lose than did France in a battle of protective tariffs.

But the battle that Louis XIV had in mind was to be more deadly than one of tariffs. Greedily he eyed the Spanish Netherlands—to which he had a weak claim through his Habsburg wife—and believed that the Dutch stood in the way of his plans. The Dutch had entered into an alliance with the English and Swedes in 1668 to counter French policy, and Louis was determined to crush them in retaliation. He successfully bought off both of Holland's supposed allies, providing cash pensions to the kings of England and Sweden in return for England's active participation and Sweden's passive neutrality in the impending war. In 1672 Louis's army, over one hundred thousand strong, invaded the Low Countries and swept all before them. Only the opening of the dikes prevented the French from entering the province of Holland itself.

The French invasion coincided with the third Anglo-Dutch war, and the United Provinces found themselves besieged on land and sea. Their international trade was disrupted, their manufacturing industries were in ruins,

ADAM SMITH, *THE WEALTH OF NATIONS*

■ *Adam Smith was a Scottish political theorist whose* The Wealth of Nations *was the first great work of economic analysis in European history. Smith had wide-ranging interests and wrote with equal authority about manufacturing, population, and trade. He was the first to develop the doctrine of free trade, which he called "laissez-faire." Smith argued that the government that governed least governed best, and he was an early critic of protective tariffs and monopolies.*

Every individual necessarily labours to render the annual revenue of the society as great as he can. He generally, indeed, neither intends to promote the public interest, nor knows how much he is promoting it. By preferring the support of domestic to that of foreign industry, he intends only his own security; and by directing that industry in such a manner as its produce may be of the greatest value, he intends only his own gain, and he is in this, as in many other cases, led by an invisible hand to promote an end which was no part of his intention. Nor is it always the worse for the society that it was no part of it. By pursuing his own interest he frequently promotes that of the society more effectually than when he really intends to promote it. I have never known much good done by those who affected to trade for the public good . . .

Each nation has been made to look with an invidious eye upon the prosperity of all the nations with which it trades, and to consider their gain as its own loss. Commerce, which ought naturally to be, among nations as among individuals, a bond of union and friendship, has become the most fertile source of discord and animosity. The capricious ambition of kings and ministers has not, during the present and the preceding century, been more fatal to the repose of Europe, than the impertinent jealousy of merchants and manufacturers. The violence and injustice of the rulers of mankind is an ancient evil, for which, I am afraid, the nature of human affairs can scarce admit of a remedy. But the mean rapacity, the monopolizing spirit of merchants and manufacturers, who neither are, nor ought to be, the rulers of mankind, though it cannot perhaps be corrected, may very easily be prevented from disturbing the tranquillity of anybody but themselves . . .

The natural advantages which one country has over another in producing particular commodities are sometimes so great, that it is acknowledged by all the world to be in vain to struggle with them . . . Very good grapes can be raised in Scotland, and very good wine too can be made of them at about thirty times the expense for which at least equally good can be brought from foreign countries. Would it be a reasonable law to prohibit the importation of all foreign wines merely to encourage the making of claret and burgundy in Scotland?

From Adam Smith, *The Wealth of Nations,* 1776.

and their military budget skyrocketed. Only able diplomacy and skillful military leadership prevented total Dutch demise. A separate peace was made with England, and Spain, whose sovereign territory had been invaded, entered the war on the side of the Dutch as did a number of German states. Louis's hope for a lightning victory faded, and the war settled into a series of interminable sieges and reliefs of fortified towns. The Dutch finally persuaded France to come to terms in the Treaty of Nijmegen (1678–79). While Louis XIV retained a number of the territories he had taken from Spain, his armies withdrew from the United Provinces and he agreed to lift most of the commercial sanctions against Dutch goods. The first phase of mercantile warfare was over.

The Wars of Louis XIV

It was Louis XIV's ambition to restore the ancient Burgundian territories to the French crown and to provide secure northern and eastern borders for his state. Pursuit of these aims involved him in conflicts with nearly every other European state. Spain had fought for eighty years to preserve the Burgundian inheritance in the Low

Countries. By the Peace of Westphalia (1648), the northern portion of this territory became the United Provinces, while the southern portion remained loyal to the crown and became the Spanish Netherlands. This territory provided a barrier between Holland and France that both states attempted to strengthen by establishing fortresses and bridgeheads at strategic places. In the east, Louis eyed the duchies of Lorraine and Alsace and the large swath of territory farther south known as Franche-Comté. The Peace of Westphalia had granted France control of a number of imperial cities in these duchies, and Louis aimed to link them together. All of these territories were ruled by Habsburgs: Alsace and Lorraine by the Austrian Holy Roman Emperor, Franche-Comté by the Spanish king.

In the late seventeenth century, ambassadors and ministers of state began to develop the theory of a balance of power in Europe. This was a belief that no state or combination of states should be allowed to become so powerful that its existence threatened the peace of the others. Behind this purely political idea of the balance of power lay a theory of collective security that knit together the European state system. French expansion in either direction not only threatened the other states directly involved but also posed a threat to European security in general.

Louis showed his hand clearly enough in the Franco-Dutch war that had ended in 1679. Though he withdrew his forces from the United Provinces and evacuated most of the territories he had conquered, by the Treaty of Nijmegen France absorbed Franche-Comté as well as portions of the Spanish Netherlands. Louis began plotting his next adventure almost as soon as the treaty was signed. Over the next several years, French troops advanced steadily into Alsace, ultimately forcing the city of Strasbourg, a vital bridgehead on the Rhine, to recognize French sovereignty. Expansion into northern Italy was similarly calculated. Everywhere Louis looked, French engineers rushed to construct fortresses and magazines in preparation for another war.

It finally came in 1688 when French troops poured across the Rhine to seize Cologne. A united German empire led by Leopold I, archduke of Austria, combined with the maritime powers of England and Holland, led by William III, to form the Grand Alliance, the first of the great balance of power coalitions. In fact, the two sides proved so evenly matched that the Nine Years' War (1688–97) settled very little, but it demonstrated that a successful European coalition could be formed against France. It also signified the permanent shift in alliances that resulted from the Revolution of 1688 in England. Although the English had allied with France against the Dutch in 1672, after William became king he persuaded the English Parliament that the real enemy was France. Louis's greatest objective, to secure the borders of his state, had withstood its greatest test. He might have rested satisfied but for the vagaries of births, marriages, and deaths.

Like his father, Louis XIV had married a daughter of the king of Spain. Philip IV had married his eldest

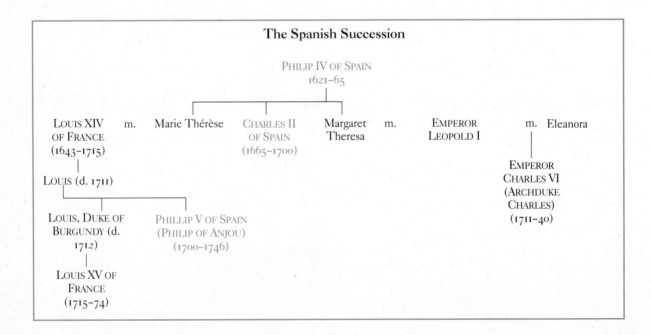

The Spanish Succession

PHILIP IV OF SPAIN
1621–65

LOUIS XIV OF FRANCE (1643–1715) m. Marie Thérèse — CHARLES II OF SPAIN (1665–1700) — Margaret Theresa m. EMPEROR LEOPOLD I m. Eleanora

LOUIS (d. 1711)

EMPEROR CHARLES VI (ARCHDUKE CHARLES) (1711–40)

LOUIS, DUKE OF BURGUNDY (d. 1712) — PHILLIP V OF SPAIN (PHILIP OF ANJOU) (1700–1746)

LOUIS XV OF FRANCE (1715–74)

War and Peace, 1648–1763

1648	Peace of Westphalia
1652–54	First Anglo-Dutch War
1665–67	Second Anglo-Dutch War
1672	Franco-Dutch war
1672–74	Third Anglo-Dutch war
1678–79	Treaty of Nijmegen
1688	Revolution of 1688; William of Orange becomes William III of England Grand Alliance formed
1688–97	Nine Years' War (France vs. Grand Alliance)
1702–14	War of the Spanish Succession
1713–14	Treaty of Utrecht
1756–63	Seven Years' War
1763	Peace of Paris

daughter to Louis XIV and a younger one to Leopold I of Austria, who subsequently became the Holy Roman Emperor (1658–1705). Before he died, Philip finally fathered a son, Charles II (1665–1700), who attained the Spanish crown at the age of four but was mentally and physically incapable of ruling his vast empire. For decades it was apparent that there would be no direct Habsburg successor to an empire which, despite its recent losses, still contained Spain, South America, the Spanish Netherlands, and most of Italy. Louis XIV and Leopold I both had legitimate claims to an inheritance that would have irreversibly tipped the European balance of power.

As Charles II grew increasingly feeble, efforts to find a suitable compromise to the problem of the Spanish succession were led by William III who, as stadtholder of Holland, was vitally interested in the fate of the Spanish Netherlands and, as king of England, in the fate of the Spanish American colonies. In the 1690s two treaties of partition were drawn up. The first achieved near universal agreement but was nullified by the death of the German prince who was to inherit the Spanish crown. The second, which would have given Italy to Louis's son and everything else to Leopold's son, was opposed by Leopold, who had neither naval nor commercial interests and who claimed most of the Italian territories as imperial fiefs.

All of these plans had been made without consulting the Spanish. If it was the aim of the European powers to partition the Spanish empire in order to prevent any one state from inheriting too much of it, it was the aim of the Spanish to maintain their empire intact. To this end, they devised a brilliant plan. Charles II bequeathed his entire empire to Philip of Anjou, the younger grandson of Louis XIV, with two stipulations. First that Philip renounce his claim to the French throne, and second that he accept the empire intact, without partition. If he—or more to the point, if his grandfather Louis XIV—did not accept these conditions then the empire would pass to Archduke Charles, the younger son of Leopold I. Such provisions virtually assured war between France and the empire unless compromise between the two powers could be reached. But before terms could even be suggested, Charles II died and Philip V (1700–46) was proclaimed king of Spain and its empire.

Thus the eighteenth century opened with the War of the Spanish Succession (1702–14). Emperor Leopold rejected the provisions of Charles's will and sent his troops to occupy Italy. Louis XIV confirmed the worst fears of William III when he provided his grandson with French troops to "defend" the Spanish Netherlands. William III revived the Grand Alliance and initiated a massive land war against the combined might of France and Spain. The allied objectives were twofold: to prevent the unification of the French and Spanish thrones and to partition the Spanish empire so that both Italy and the Netherlands were ceded to Austria. The objective of Louis XIV was simply to preserve as much as possible of the Spanish inheritance for the house of Bourbon.

William III died in 1702 and was succeeded by Anne (1702–14). John Churchill (1650–1722), duke of Marlborough and commander in chief of the army, continued William's policy. England and Holland again provided most of the finance and sea power, but in addition the English also provided a land army nearly seventy thousand strong. Prussia joined the Grand Alliance, and disciplined Prussian troops helped offset the addition of the Spanish army to Louis's forces. In 1704 Churchill defeated French forces at Blenheim in Germany and in 1706 at Ramillies in the Spanish Netherlands. France's military ascendancy was over.

Efforts to negotiate a peace settlement took longer than the war itself. The Austrians had taken control of Italy, the English and Dutch had secured the Spanish Netherlands, and the French had been driven back beyond the Rhine. The Allies believed that they could now enforce any treaty they pleased upon Louis XIV and

An eighteenth-century English playing card showing Philip of Anjou, the grandson of Louis XIV, stealing the Spanish crown.

in the Nine Years' War and the War of the Spanish Succession did not result in large territorial gains but it did result in an enormous increase in English power and prestige. Over the next thirty years England would assert its own imperial claims.

The Colonial Wars

The Treaty of Utrecht (1713–14) ushered in almost a quarter century of peace in western Europe. Austrian rule in the Netherlands and Italy remained a major irritant to the Spanish but Spain was too weak to do more than sulk and snarl. The death of Louis XIV in 1715 quelled French ambitions for a time and even led to an Anglo-French accord, which guaranteed the preservation of the settlement reached at Utrecht. Peace allowed Europe to rebuild its shattered economy and resume the international trade that had been so severely disrupted over the last forty years. The Treaty of Utrecht had resolved a number of important trading issues, all in favor of Great Britain, as England was known after its union with Scotland in 1707. In addition to receiving Gibraltar and Minorca from Spain, Britain was also granted the monopoly to provide slaves to the Spanish American colonies and the right to send

along with concessions from France attempted to oust his grandson, Philip V, from the Spanish throne. This proved impossible to achieve though it took more than five years to learn the lesson. By then the European situation had taken another strange twist. Both the Emperor Leopold and his eldest son had died. Now Leopold's younger son, Archduke Charles, inherited the empire as Charles VI (1711–40) and raised the prospect of an equally dangerous combined Austrian-Spanish state. Between 1713 and 1714 a series of treaties at Utrecht settled the War of the Spanish Succession. Spanish possessions in Italy and the Netherlands were ceded to Austria; France abandoned all its territorial gains east of the Rhine and ceded its North American territories of Nova Scotia and Newfoundland to England. England also acquired from Spain Gibraltar on the southern coast of Spain and the island of Minorca in the Mediterranean. Both were strategically important to English commercial interests. English intervention

Treaty of Utrecht

The storming of Quebec by British forces in 1759. The capture of the first city of New France was a major British victory in the North American theater of the Seven Years' War.

one trading ship a year to them. In east and west, Britain was becoming the dominant commercial power in the world.

At least some of the reason for Britain's preeminence was the remarkable growth of the Atlantic colonies. The colonial economy was booming and consumer goods that were in demand in London, Paris, and Amsterdam were also in demand in Boston, Philadelphia, and New York. Like every other colonial power, the British held a monopoly on their colonial trade. They were far less successful than were the Spanish and French in enforcing the notion that colonies existed only for the benefit of the parent country, but the English Parliament continued to pass legislation aimed at restricting colonial trade with other nations and other nations' colonies. Like almost all other mercantile restrictions, these efforts were stronger in theory than in practice. Tariffs on imports and customs duties on British goods provided a double incentive for smuggling.

France emerged as Britain's true colonial rival. In the Caribbean, the French had the largest and most profitable of the West Indian sugar islands, Saint Domingue (modern-day Haiti). In North America France held not

only Canada but laid claim to the entire continent west of the Ohio River. The French did not so much settle their colonial territory as occupy it. They surveyed the land, established trading relations with the Native Americans, and built forts at strategic locations. The English, in contrast, had developed fixed communities, which grew larger and more prosperous by the decade. France determined to defend its colonies by establishing an overseas military presence. Regular French troops were shipped to Canada and installed in Louisburg, Montreal, and Quebec. The British responded with troops of their own and sent an expeditionary force to clear the French from the Ohio River Valley. This action was the immediate cause of the Seven Years' War (1756–63).

Although the Seven Years' War had a bitter Continental phase, it was essentially a war for empire between the English and the French. There were three main theaters: the North American mainland, the West Indian sugar plantations, and the eastern coast of India. All over the globe, the British won smashing victories. The British navy blockaded the water route to Canada, inflicting severe hardship on French settlers in

Seven Years' War

Montreal and Quebec. British forces ultimately captured both towns. After some initial successes, the French were driven back west across the Mississippi River and their line of fortresses in the Ohio Valley fell into English hands. The English also succeeded in taking all the French sugar islands except Saint Domingue. British success in India was equally complete. The French were chased from their major trading zone and English dominance was secured.

By the end of the Seven Years' War, Britain had become a global imperial power. In the Peace of Paris (1763) France ceded all of Canada in exchange for the return of its West Indian islands. British dominion in the East Indian trade was recognized and led ultimately to British dominion of India itself. In less than a century the ascendancy of France was broken and Europe's first modern imperial power had been created.

European commercial expansion was the first step in a long process that would ultimately transform the material life of all human beings. The quest for new commodities led to the sophistication of transportation, marketing, and distribution, all vital developments for agricultural changes in the future. The ability to move large quantities of goods from place to place and to exchange them between different parts of the globe laid the foundation for organized manufacturing. The practical impact of scientific discovery, as yet only dimly glimpsed, would soon spur the transformation of handicrafts into industries. In the eighteenth century the material world was still being conquered and the most unattractive features of this conquest were all too plainly visible. Luxuries for the rich were won by the labors of the poor. The pleasures of sugar and tobacco were purchased at the price of slavery for millions of Africans. The greed of merchants and the glory of princes was an unholy alliance that resulted in warfare around the globe. But it was a shrinking globe, one whose peoples were becoming increasingly interdependent, tied together by the goods and services that they could provide to each other.

SUGGESTIONS FOR FURTHER READING

GENERAL READING

* A. Rupert Hall, *The Revolution in Science 1500–1750* (London: Longman, 1983). The best introduction to the varieties of scientific thought in the early modern period. Detailed and complex.

* Jan de Vries, *The European Economy in an Age of Crisis* (Cambridge: Cambridge University Press, 1976). A comprehensive study of economic development, including long-distance trade and commercial change.

* K. H. D. Haley, *The Dutch in the Seventeenth Century* (London: Thames and Hudson, 1972). A well-written and illustrated history of the golden age of Holland.

* Derek McKay and H. M. Scott, *The Rise of the Great Powers 1648–1815* (London: Longman, 1983). An outstanding survey of diplomacy and warfare.

* Jeremy Black, *The Rise of the European Powers 1679–1793* (New York: Edward Arnold, 1990). A new look at diplomatic history from an English point of view.

THE NEW SCIENCE

* Margaret C. Jacob, *The Cultural Meaning of the Scientific Revolution* (New York: Knopf, 1988). Scientific thought portrayed in its social context.

* Stillman Drake, *Galileo* (New York: Hill and Wang, 1980). A short but engaging study of the great Italian scientist.

* Allen Debus, *Man and Nature in the Renaissance* (Cambridge: Cambridge University Press, 1978). An especially good account of the intellectual roots of scientific thought.

Charles Webster, *The Great Instauration: Science, Medicine, and Reform* (London: Duckworth, 1975). A complicated but rewarding analysis of experimental science and the origins of scientific medicine.

* Frank E. Manuel, *Sir Isaac Newton: A Portrait* (Cambridge, MA: Harvard University Press, 1968). A readable account of one of the most complex intellects in European history.

Empires of Goods

* Ralph Davis, *The Rise of the Atlantic Economies* (Ithaca, NY: Cornell University Press, 1973). A nation-by-nation survey of the colonial powers.

K. N. Chaudhuri, *The Trading World of Asia and the English East India Company* (Cambridge: Cambridge University Press, 1978). A brilliant account of the impact of the Indian trade on both Europeans and Asians.

* Sidney Mintz, *Sweetness and Power* (New York: Viking Press, 1985). An anthropological examination of the lure of sugar and its impact upon Western society.

* Philip Curtin, *The Atlantic Slave Trade* (Madison, WI: University of Wisconsin Press, 1969). A study of the importation of African slaves into the New World with the best estimates of the numbers of slaves and their destinations.

* Simon Schama, *The Embarrassment of Riches* (New York: Knopf, 1987). A social history of the Dutch Republic, which explores the meaning of commerce in Dutch society.

* Holden Furber, *Rival Empires of Trade in the Orient 1600–1800* (Minneapolis: University of Minnesota Press, 1976). A comprehensive survey of the battle for control of the Asian trade in the seventeenth and eighteenth centuries.

The Wars of Commerce

A. C. Carter, *Neutrality or Commitment: The Evolution of Dutch Foreign Policy 1667-1795* (London: Edward Arnold, 1975). A tightly written study of the objectives and course of Dutch diplomacy.

Charles Wilson, *Profit and Power* (London: Longman, 1957). Still the best study of the Anglo-Dutch wars of the mid-seventeenth century.

Paul Langford, *The Eighteenth Century 1688-1815* (New York: St. Martin's Press, 1976). A reliable guide to the growth of British power.

Ragnhild Hatton, ed., *Louis XIV and Europe* (London: Macmillan, 1976). An important collection of essays on French foreign policy in its most aggressive posture.

Richard Pares, *War and Trade in the West Indies 1739-63* (Oxford: Oxford University Press, 1936). A blow-by-blow account of the struggle for colonial supremacy in the sugar islands.

* Indicates paperback edition available.

CHAPTER 19

Africa and the Middle East, 1600–1800

A Surprise from Benin

It is 18 February 1897 in Benin City, in the southwestern part of Nigeria. A British force under Admiral Sir Harry Rawson has just entered the abandoned city. By now the colonial takeover of Africa is in its last stages, and this action is seen as something of a mopping-up operation. But this campaign turns out to be somewhat different. Upon entering the palace of the king (*oba*) of Benin, the British troops encounter something that perplexes and astonishes them. All around them, in every corner of the palace, are over two thousand plaques and statues made of brass, ivory, iron, and wood. Although doubtful that Africans could have made such striking artifacts, Rawson is nonetheless pleased to have some curios to send back to the British Museum as spoils of war and to parcel out to his men as souvenirs of their participation in the campaign. Two days after the fall of the city, on 20 February, a fire sweeps through Benin City, a fittingly apt symbol for the end of Benin's independence.

The dynasty that was overthrown by the British on that February day in 1897 was extraordinary. Occupying a strategically important position in the coastal hinterland, the obas, local big men, had been able to expand their small city-state gradually before 1300. Between 1325 and 1380 they began to have themselves memorialized in brass and ivory. In subsequent decades the power of the obas' state increased with its expansion, and the obas themselves became increasingly regarded as powerful rulers.

As kings, they realized that there were always tendencies for states in Africa to disintegrate. Therefore, they did everything possible to ensure that this fate did not befall Benin. Control was the essence of continued power, and the obas established control wherever possible. Religious ceremonies gave the oba spiritual control, and whenever the oba appeared in public, he was surrounded by the trappings of majesty and power. Guilds of artisans were all headed by the oba, thereby giving him economic control. The army was expanded, giving the oba political control. The thrust for control extended to the arts as well, and all artists who worked in brass were forbidden, under threat of death, to work for anyone outside the royal court. By 1485, under the oba's rule, Benin City had become one of Africa's largest and most prosperous cities.

While Benin was a strictly African phenomenon, based on trade within the region and on specifically African political and religious ideas and institutions, it was drawn into the wider world economy after 1485, initially through trade with the Portuguese. The obas of Benin, like many other African leaders, were wise enough not to equate independence with isolation from strangers, realizing that the powers they already had could be increased through contacts with the world beyond Africa. And so the obas vigorously encouraged Europeans to establish trading centers in Benin's territory, making sure all the time, however, that they monopolized the trade. Local people traded ivory, beads, pepper, cloth, and slaves to the Europeans. In return, the obas received various European luxury goods, brass and iron, and, most importantly, guns and ammunition, and even, at times, cavalry horses. With a steady supply of Western imports, the obas were able to expand their state and maintain their independence until the fateful British attack on 18 February 1897.

Throughout this long period of over five hundred years, the obas decorated their palace with brass plaques, such as the one illustrated here, both because they were beautiful in themselves and because they attested to their power. In this plaque, dating from the last half of the sixteenth century, power is the central theme. The oba is much bigger than his retainers. He carries a shield and a spear, symbols of military power. A naked retainer carries a huge sword. The oba wears the royal crown and the distinctive collar, or choker, made of coral. This coral was imported to Benin over the trans-Saharan trade routes from the Balearic Islands and its use was restricted to the powerful. Significantly, in the upper corners there are two floating figures depicting Portuguese traders with whom the oba dealt. It is appropriate that they appear on the plaque, for they represent another source of the oba's powers, this drawn from beyond Africa and fittingly symbolized by their lack of local roots.

When the British troops returned home from Africa in 1897, some sold the curios they had acquired. Some of the most elaborate plaques fetched a price of about $100. During the twentieth century, however, things began to change. The racism of the nineteenth century, which devalued all things made by Africans, began to erode. Great Western artists such as Pablo Picasso began to draw inspiration from African art. Art critics began to take African creativity seriously. And the price of Benin plaques responded, starting to rise in the 1930s and continuing upward. Were the descendants of one of the British troops in the campaign of 1897 to find a "souvenir" such as the one depicted in an attic trunk today, they would be lucky indeed. At auction, the plaque that sold for $100 in 1900 would today probably go for $500,000. The obas clearly had good artistic taste as well as political and economic power.

Africa in the Era of Rising European Capitalism

In the seventeenth century, several increasingly powerful competitors successfully challenged the Portuguese's position as the principal Europeans dealing with Africa. Seeking both a part of the profits made from supplying slaves to the expanding plantations of America and a share of the Indian Ocean trade, English, Dutch, and French traders increased European involvement with Africa and brought ever wider areas of it into deeper relations with the world economy. Such intervention contributed to changes in many African societies, especially in West Africa, where Europeans functioned primarily as traders, and in South Africa, where they settled.

During the last third of the eighteenth century, at the very height of the slave trade, criticism of it grew, especially in Britain, which was entering the first stages of the Industrial Revolution. Abolitionists not only demanded the end of the slave trade but also called for the establishment of a new relationship between Europe and Africa to be based solely on a trade in commodities other than slaves. The effort to expand this so-called "legitimate trade" was a slow and uncertain process and was marred by the persistence of the slave trade. By 1860, however, the West African slave trade had largely ended and the region entered into a new type of relationship with Europeans.

European Mercantilism and the Growth of Sugar Consumption

In 1580 Spain invaded Portugal and brought it under the Spanish crown, apparently confirming itself as the world's most powerful state. By 1600, however, the unified Iberian monarchy was in decline for two important reasons. The first was a shift in fiscal and economic power to the cities of Antwerp and Amsterdam because of Portugal's balance of payments deficit with its Asian trading partners and the persistent inflation in Spain caused by the inflow of large amounts of silver from America. The second reason for the decline of the Iberian monarchy was a parallel shift in political balance toward the countries of northwest Europe at a time when Holland, England, and France were emerging as nation-states able to challenge Spanish hegemony. The well-known destruction of the Spanish Armada in 1588 was, for example, merely one incident in a long conflict between Elizabethan England and Spain that lasted from 1585 to 1604. This rivalry between the new nation-states and Spain led to Spain's gradual defeat.

With Spain's decline and its conclusion in 1609 of the Twelve Years' Truce with the United Provinces, a new world power, Holland, came into prominence, growing ever stronger as the seventeenth century passed. The Dutch economy was based on a wide range of activities ranging from fishing and shipbuilding to sugar refining and agriculture, and its rulers sought to play an active role in world trade. Holland's rise to power coincided with important structural changes in Europe's economy. During the fifteenth and sixteenth centuries the European economy as a whole had expanded rapidly, drawing Africa, the Caribbean, Brazil, and the Indian Ocean basin more and more deeply into its orbit. At

the start of the seventeenth century, however, much of the economy entered a period of sluggishness that continued until 1750 and brought a declining standard of living to rural Europe and a slowing of industrial growth.

After 1600, then, the combination of the growing Dutch political and economic threat and the persistent economic lethargy of the rest of Europe severely challenged the states of western Europe. In response, a new economic ideology known as mercantilism became widely accepted. Put simply, this was the idea that every nation-state should have its own colonies and that these would exchange their raw materials for manufactured goods from the home country. Mercantilism's aim was to create a closed system that would help insulate the home country's economy from outside influences. Between 1600 and 1750, mercantilism came to be the established economic orthodoxy for most of Europe's leaders, prompting them to build navies and seek colonies throughout the world, especially those already in Spanish and Portuguese control. In the wild scramble for colonies that occurred in the first half of the seventeenth century, the French seized Guadeloupe and Martinique and the English occupied many of the Caribbean islands, including Barbados, and also British Guiana (now Guyana), on the coast of South America. The Dutch seized Curaçao, Aruba, and Dutch Guiana (now Suriname), which remained Dutch until the twentieth century, as well as briefly occupying the

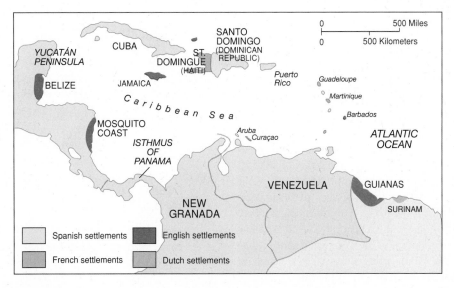

Caribbean Colonies, 17th Century

thriving Portuguese sugar colony of Brazil. In Africa, the Dutch for a short while also occupied Angola, from which most slaves for America's plantations were then obtained, and seized the old Portuguese trading fortress of Elmina, on the Lower Guinea Coast, where gold was still traded.

To the disappointment of their new owners, many of the Caribbean colonies initially seemed useless, with failed early attempts to grow cotton and tobacco with white European indentured laborers. Gradually, however, the new colonial powers decided that sugar, the one major crop that had already proven a success in America's tropics, might be suitable for their Caribbean colonies. This changeover to sugar production prompted a shift to using black African slaves, for it was widely believed that only slaves could provide the large, cheap, and disciplined workforce the plantation owners required. A 40 per cent drop in the prices of slaves from the Kongo-Angola area in the middle decades of the seventeenth century because of chronic warfare there encouraged them to expand this use of slaves.

Changing patterns of sugar consumption soon ratified the shift to sugar production in the Caribbean. For the most part, sugar had been used mostly as a medicine, condiment, and preservative. Between 1650 and 1675, however, just as increased production in America was lowering its price, its use as a sweetener sharply increased. At that time three new beverages—chocolate, tea, and coffee—were coming into fashion. All are naturally bitter and benefit from the addition of sugar. The growing middle classes of Europe particularly relished the new beverages, especially when sweetened, and provided a ready market for all four commodities as their prices fell. In short, a situation developed in which all the sugar that could be produced in the world would be consumed. In the third quarter of the seventeenth century sugar consumption accelerated with each passing year, ensuring both the further expansion of America's sugar plantations and fresh demands for African slaves.

In effect, then, the combination of mercantilist economic policies that demanded the creation of colonial empires and a seemingly unrelievable European sweet tooth that demanded endless supplies of sugar drew Africa ever more firmly into the world economy. Many areas of Africa—and most especially West Africa—became locked into economic relations that centered on the trade of slaves from Africa to America, the trade of sugar from America to Europe, and the trade of manufactured goods from Europe to Africa and America.

The New World's Demands on Africa: The West African Slave Trade

In the last half of the sixteenth century, English and Dutch merchants had sporadically challenged Portuguese domination of the West African trade. Although mortality rates from disease were high among Europeans, profits were also high, and, to the great disappointment of the Portuguese, in the seventeenth century British and Dutch companies established permanent trading stations along the West African coast. These companies enthusiastically traded for gold, pepper, ivory, gums, and other tropical products as well as for slaves.

After 1650, this situation gradually changed. Now possessing their own colonies in America and having improved their trade links with Asia, Europeans could obtain tropical products cheaper and with less loss of life from disease than thay could from Africa. As a result, an African trade deficit with Europe began to become evident along the West African coast. Africans were now being asked to pay gold, a commodity rare outside the Gold Coast, for the imported goods they purchased, not trade other items they produced. This change presented a dilemma to African traders and politicians who depended on the import-export trade. How could they obtain the cloth and metal goods from Europe upon which they had come to depend? The question boiled

The Lower Guinea Coast

down to whether or not they could find a substitute for gold that would satisfy European traders.

Certain powerful Africans in certain areas responded to their fiscal problems by marketing the one remaining item that Europeans were eager to purchase from Africa in larger and larger quantities. That item was slaves. The worldwide demand for slaves was growing with the plantation system, and these West African leaders believed that, if they were to maintain their positions of power and wealth, they had no choice but to increase the supply of slaves. As they increased their efforts to meet the demand, and during the eighteenth century especially, armaments became more important in the mix of imports from Europe as certain leaders consolidated their military power and turned it on less powerful neighbors specifically to produce war captives whom they could then sell.

As demand grew, the main source of African slaves gradually shifted from the Portuguese-dominated Kongo-Angola area northward to the Lower Guinea Coast. During the late eighteenth century, at the height of the transatlantic slave trade, the great majority of slaves—as many as 65 per cent in any one year—came from this relatively small stretch of territory. This was so for two reasons. First, this region had dense populations near the coast from which slaves could be drawn. Second, sturdy trading infrastructures were already in place that could increase the numbers of slaves available as fast as demand rose.

In the western part of the Lower Guinea Coast it was the leaders of such powerful states as Benin, Asante, Oyo, and Dahomey who, at different times, became active in the trade. They had access to coastal trading ports and were also strong enough to dominate the trade routes to the interior, from which most slaves were obtained.

Oyo, a Yoruba-speaking state located in the south central area of Nigeria, provides one example of how the trade worked. Oyo had long traded salt, kola nuts, and high quality cotton cloth produced in its own cities northward to the Sudanic region. In exchange it received horses, which it used to outfit a cavalry corps. Using this powerful cavalry, in the late seventeenth century Oyo's leaders expanded to the south and southwest, through a tsetse-free corridor of land, all the way to the coast, defeating neighboring Yoruba- and Aja-speaking peoples whom they encountered and taking many prisoners. These war captives were then sold into the ever receptive Atlantic slave trade, with many of the manufactured items acquired from Europe then traded north to the Sudanic zone for more horses. By building up its cavalry in this way, in the early eighteenth century

This drawing of the oba *in great state was published in 1668 in a report of a visit to Benin by the Dutch traveler O. Dapper.*

Oyo came to dominate the inland zones of a large part of the Lower Guinea Coast, using the Portuguese fortress of Ouidah (Whydah) as its main coastal outlet for slaves.

The eastern part of the Lower Guinea Coast, the Niger Delta and Bight of Biafra areas, produced slaves in a manner different from the western sector's. Here slaves were seldom captured in warfare or raiding carried out by states but rather came from kidnapping, small-scale skirmishing, and through the manipulation of judicial and religious institutions. The political organization of the area's Igbo and Ibibio speakers was on a small scale, taking the form of city-states or even villages. Nonetheless, big men whose fortune and power rested on trade were powerful in these societies, and they had formed alliances among themselves to create merchant castes protected by mercenaries. Religious leaders who supervised the oracles that adjudicated disputes and prophesied the future worked with these castes to produce slaves. False accusations of witchcraft became common, and religious officials demanded human sacrifices as compensation. Payments to the oracle for foretelling the future could also be made in the form of human beings. The victims so obtained were delivered to the merchants, who then disposed of them into the transatlantic trading system.

By employing existing legal and religious institutions, the violence of warfare and raiding common to the west was largely avoided. Yet the area's silent violence, which was so effective at producing slaves, sorely tested the ideology of kinship, with "family" becoming defined in ever more restricted terms and with the former assimilation of pawns, criminals, and war captives into the extended family largely forgotten. The turmoil that resulted as leaders sought to meet the increased demand for slaves in America could not but erode old cultural values and stimulate new ones.

Clearly, the slave-producing systems that operated on the Lower Guinea Coast in the late seventeenth and eighteenth centuries were complex. But there was also a unity of purpose evident. Throughout the area slaves were produced for the single overriding reason that powerful political leaders and wealthy merchants saw the trade as essential to maintaining themselves in their positions of power, especially when rising prices for slaves encouraged more exports. It was the work of an elite and its agents, not of the ordinary people, who remained for the most part engaged in subsistence production at the village level and who were not major consumers of the goods obtained from abroad. While important overall, the slave trade had few direct links with the village-level local economy.

An African slave is immobilized by a heavy forked log as he awaits shipment to the New World.

Several questions arise from the existence of the slave trade. First, how many people were transported across the Atlantic? For the entire period of trade across the Atlantic, from 1444, when the Portuguese began it at Arguin, to the late nineteenth century, scholars estimate that some 13 to 14 million Africans from all parts of Africa were transported, with, of course, substantial numbers of war captives and other victims dying either before leaving Africa or on shipboard during the dreaded "Middle Passage." During the period of the peak of the trade, between 1700 and 1810, West Africa alone exported 3,250,000 slaves, most of whom were carried in British, French, and Portuguese vessels.

That such large numbers of people were removed raises the further question of how Africa could, with its chronic labor shortage, "afford" to send away so many millions of its young and productive men and women. In trying to answer this question one must take certain facts into account. First, since a free market in labor did not exist, Africa was exporting a commodity that had already been ideologically devalued. Most victims of the trade were war captives from outside the society that actually traded them and were considered "surplus." As a consequence, at times of great availability of supply, prices for slaves reached astonishingly low figures on the coast.

Moreover, the draining of people does not seem to have depopulated Africa as a whole. This may have been because the population was growing naturally. Or it may have been because most people taken were young men, with women left behind to bear children in Africa. Scholars have also suggested that the introduction from

A Slave's Experience of the Middle Passage, 1755

■ *Although the slave trade was a central factor in relations between Europeans and Africans for centuries, there are few descriptions by those enslaved of their experiences. One exception is the autobiography of Olaudah Equiano, an Igbo boy sold into slavery at the age of ten, transported to Barbados, and eventually freed in 1766. His book was published in 1789 as part of the Abolitionist campaign to end the slave trade. This passage describes his experiences on the slave ship that took him from Africa.*

The stench of the hold while we were on the coast was so intolerably loathsome that it was dangerous to remain there for any time, and some of us had been permitted to stay on the deck for fresh air; but now that the whole ship's cargo were confined together it became absolutely pestilential. The closeness of the place and the heat of the climate, added to the number in the ship, which was so crowded that each had scarcely room to turn himself, almost suffocated us. This produced copious perspirations, so that the air became unfit for respiration from a variety of loathsome smells, and brought on a sickness among the slaves, of which many died, thus falling victim to the improvident avarice of their purchasers. This wretched situation was again aggravated by the galling of the chains, now become insupportable, and the filth of the necessary tubs, into which the children often fell and were almost suffocated. The shrieks of the women and the groans of the dying rendered the scene of horror almost inconceivable.

One day, when we had a smooth sea and moderate wind, two of my wearied countrymen who were chained together, preferring death to such a life of misery, somehow made through the nettings and jumped into the sea: immediately another quite dejected fellow, who on account of his illness was suffered to be out of irons, also followed their example; and I believe many more would soon have done the same if they had not been prevented by the ship's crew, who were instantly alarmed.

America of maize and cassava, crops that could feed more people per unit of land than earlier ones had done, supported a population growing enough to match the drain of the slave trade. In any case, however, had the slave trade never occurred, Africa's population would probably have been substantially greater than it was at the time the trade was finally ended.

Yet statements regarding the impact of the slave trade on Africa as a whole are largely irrelevant. In terms of the trade, Africa was *not* a whole, but a set of parts and regions and peoples, each with its own experience. When the trade affected a single area for a short and intense period—which was usual, since warfare was one of the major ways slaves were produced—then that area suffered greatly, not merely because slaves were taken from it, but because the violence destroyed local infrastructure and drove away people as refugees.

Finally, there is the issue of the extent to which the slave trade injured the underlying social structures in the affected areas. As we have seen, most African societies involved in the slave trade had already become differentiated into rulers and governed, rich and poor, powerful and powerless during the period when the luxury trade in gold and spices and other commodities was in its heyday, from the fifteenth through the mid-seventeenth centuries. Clearly, the slave trade benefited the rich and powerful who participated in it and who viewed it as a necessary, if regrettable, part of economic and political life once European traders decided that they did not want other African products. Clearly also, it injured the defeated or raided societies, such as the Aja or Yoruba, and greatly victimized people who were kidnapped within societies such as the Igbo.

The Abolitionist Movement and the Decline of Slavery's Viability

In 1800, the transatlantic slave trade raged stronger than ever. The American plantation economies that had originally sparked it had grown, and slaves were working now to produce not only sugar, but tobacco and cotton, with coffee soon to be added to the list. Yet by 1860 the

This diagram shows how slaves were packed into cargo holds for the notorious Middle Passage to the Americas. The plan was a model of efficiency as slave traders sought to maximize profits.

slave trade had virtually ended, and Africa was poised to enter a new phase of its history having little to do with that trade. The ending of the slave trade was not merely a natural occurrence brought about by changes in the world economy. Rather, it was also directly due to the success of the Abolitionist movement, which grew up in many countries in the last third of the eighteenth century.

Until the 1760s, most Europeans—indeed, most societies—felt that slavery was both normal and acceptable. Periodic criticisms of it were regarded as little more than manifestations of crankiness. Yet major changes occurred in the late eighteenth century that, when combined, undermined the slave trade's acceptability. The first was a complex change in ideas about the nature of humanity that occurred throughout all western Europe. Some of these ideas arose from the French Enlightenment and proclaimed the revolutionary message that all people were created equal at birth and should have equal opportunity in this life. Intellectuals such as the Baron Montesquieu (1689–1755) and Jean-Jacques Rousseau (1712–78) specifically argued that Western civilization had been basically corrupted

by its pursuit of profits from such endeavors as growing sugar on plantations with slave labor and its denial of equality to slaves. The literature of the time depicted slaves as people who, although enslaved, preserved their original human dignity and their love of liberty in a world almost wholly corrupted by European greed and selfishness.

Buttressing the French Enlightenment's critique were arguments made by Scottish intellectuals, who argued against slavery from two perspectives. First, they said that it was immoral because of the suffering it caused and that no amount of reasonable, logical argumentation demonstrating its economic rationality could justify slavery. Adam Smith (1723–90), perhaps the most famous of Scottish intellectuals of the time, went further, arguing that slavery was not only morally repugnant but also economically irrational because free laborers worked harder than slaves. Slavery and the slave trade were, then, both ethically evil and economically stupid.

Finally, changes in Christianity also prompted attacks on the slave trade. Most Christians had long accepted that it was natural to have slaves at the bottom of the social hierarchy. Yet in the seventeenth and eighteenth centuries many Protestants began to make the radical claim that human equality in heaven should somehow be reflected by equality on earth, and they singled out slavery as an inherently sinful phenomenon because it denied human equality. Quakers and Methodists especially equated slavery with sin and asserted that slaveholders and slave traders were the very agents of Satan. Atonement for this sin required the ending of slavery and the slave trade. By the 1780s these three strains of criticism had merged to provide people with the intellectual ammunition for a generalized attack on both evils. The campaign that followed was known as Abolitionism.

As early as 1772 Britain's chief justice had declared that any slave who walked on English soil automatically became free. Then, in 1783, a group of Quakers organized a committee to petition the British Parliament to end the slave trade abroad. This initiative occurred simulataneously with great public shock and rage about one of the most hideous atrocities in the trade's whole atrocious history. The owners of the slave ship *Zong* had filed an insurance claim for a payment for lost property for 132 slaves who had been thrown into the Atlantic because, they claimed, the ship's provisions were running out. Such an action was legal, because slaves were viewed as property. At the enquiry, however, it was discovered that dysentery had broken out on the ship and that the 132 slaves who were thrown overboard were actually ill. Because insurance did not cover loss through illness, the owners fabricated the story about food running out as they sought to have their insurance cover their losses.

The inhumanity demonstrated by the *Zong* incident galvanized British opinion, and the Quakers soon found themselves with many allies. In 1787 the Quaker committee became the Society for the Abolition of the Slave Trade. In 1788 Parliament established a committee to investigate the slave trade, and in 1789 Olaudah Equiano published his *Travels* as part of the ongoing campaign against it. The British slave trade's seemingly imminent day of reckoning was postponed, however. The uncertainties produced by the French Revolution of 1789 and the horror of social chaos that the British felt when the slaves of Haiti, led by Toussaint L'Ouverture (ca. 1743–1803), successfully rebelled in 1791 and expelled the French colonial masters from the country, made British leaders reluctant to tamper with any type of property relations for some twenty years.

By the first years of the nineteenth century, however, the economic situation within the British Empire had altered, and those with vested interests in the slave trade had become too weak to mount an effective resistance to the Abolitionist arguments. British colonial sugar plantation owners, undercut in the mid- and late eighteenth century by competition from Martinique, Guadeloupe, and Haiti, had advocated tariff protection in keeping with the mercantilist notions of the time. By the start of the next century, however, leading figures in British economic life were moving to end mercantilist protectionism. As industrialization took hold in Britain, free trade became more and more attractive and mercantilism was seen as little more than an anachronistic excuse for sugar tariffs, slavery, and other evils. Protection seemed all the more pointless now that Britain had seized from France West Indian islands, such as Dominica, that produced cheaper sugar than Trinidad or British Guiana. The slave trade, an intrinsic part of the mercantilist system, came to be viewed as having outlived its usefulness, and it was accepted that both slavery and the slave trade, the immoral enemies of progress, should end. This was the age of liberalism (see chapter 25), and to be liberal meant to be against slavery.

In 1805 Britain outlawed the slave trade to its newly acquired colonies; in 1806 the ban was extended to include colonies of foreign countries; and in 1807 all slave trading by British subjects was outlawed. In the following year the United States passed a similar law. In 1814 the Netherlands acted similarly, and in 1815 France followed suit. Britain pressured Portugal, whose nationals were among those most deeply involved in the trade, to outlaw the trade as well. But, as ideas of liberalism and free trade had not yet penetrated to mercantilist Portugal, it refused. Only under great pressure did it agree to restrict the trade to areas south of the equator. To enforce these laws and agreements, the British established an anti-slave-trade patrol to arrest any ships caught in the trade, with special attention given to the main area of the trade, the West African coast.

Settler Society in South Africa

The impact of an expansive Europe after 1600 was by no means restricted to West Africa. In the process of meeting the growing seventeenth-century European demand for tea, coffee, and the various products of Asia, the Dutch East India Company, almost accidentally and certainly without intention, drastically changed the history of South Africa. The company's ships, sailing from Holland to the Far East, needed places to stop for fresh provisions. One such strategically important place had been the Cape of Good Hope, at the southern tip of Africa, where they took on fresh water and traded iron

This romanticized version of the partnership between England and the African kingdoms was rendered after the Congress of Vienna condemned the slave trade in 1815.

for meat. The Africans with whom the Dutch dealt there were the Khoi people, descendants of the hunters and gatherers who had once inhabited all of Africa south of the equator and who had been largely displaced when Bantu speakers occupied the subcontinent. As the Cape had a Mediterranean-type climate, however, it was unsuitable for the crops the Bantu grew and they had, therefore, left the Khoi in possession of the land, on which they raised sheep and cattle.

In the middle of the seventeenth century the Dutch East India Company decided that the Cape could also produce fresh fruit and vegetables for passing ships as well as supply water and meat. Having had good relations with the Khoi for decades and having recently been expelled by the Portuguese from their occupancy of Angola, in 1652 the company established a much-needed station at the Cape. As it was a private, capitalist company, its aim was to trade, not to govern people, and the very last thing it wanted was to have warfare eat up its profits. A small way station with well-defined boundaries and peaceful relations with the Khoi was the company's aim when it established Cape Town.

Unlike tropical Africa, where Europeans lacked immunity to local fevers and draft animals died, the Cape had neither malaria nor tsetse fly. Its climate was pleasant and its soils were good. The Khoi, sparsely settled on the land, did not threaten. As a consequence, in 1657, the company made a decision, the effects of which are still present in southern Africa. It released a group of its employees from their contracts, assigned them land, and told them to start producing food. These people came to be known as "free burghers." In response, the Khoi attempted to drive the Dutch out by waging guerrilla wars in 1659–60 and between 1673 and 1677. One by one, however, the Dutch forced the Khoi groups to come to terms. Many became propertyless laborers in Cape Town, working for the free burghers, and many others disappeared into the interior to join other groups of Khoi. After 1670 the company's representatives, seeking more meat and draft animals, pushed deeper into the interior and forced the Khoi there to trade their animals at prices the company set. Coming at a time of recurrent drought and cattle diseases, the company's persistent new demands pushed the Khoi into a pattern of social disintegration by the 1690s. Cattle, the wealth of the Khoi, were disappearing from their society and they were going bankrupt.

By 1713, just sixty years after Cape Town was founded, the majority of the Khoi had become manual laborers in the colony. Then fell the final blow. In February 1713 a ship carrying smallpox put into the harbor. By April an epidemic had broken out in the town. The Khoi died in large numbers. To escape the epidemic, many fled to seek refuge with their relatives in the interior. As a result, they carried smallpox into the interior. Over half the Khoi population died. The Khoi never recovered from this catastrophe, and after 1713 they gradually faded away, with their genes becoming merged in a general "coloured" population, which also included slaves imported from east Africa and Malaysia to do manual labor for the white settlers. By the end of the eighteenth century, the Khoi had lost their own specific identity.

While such changes were destroying Khoi society, other changes affecting the free burghers were making them into a wholly new one. In the first thirty years of their agriculturally oriented settlement, which was based on production carried out largely by slaves and Khoi workers, the European population had grown only slowly. Then, in 1685, in far-distant France, King Louis XIV revoked the Edict of Nantes, which had guaranteed religious freedom to French Protestants. Many thousands of Protestant Huguenots fled France and many of these came to the Cape, bringing with them the specialized skills needed to make local society viable. With wheelwrights, carpenters, engineers, glassmakers, and other skilled artisans now present, it became a largely self-sufficient society based on wheat and wine production and vegetable growing.

By 1700 it was clear that the increased settler population was exceeding the company's own limited requirements. Yet, with its mercantilist attitudes, it refused to allow the settlers to produce commodities for the wider world market. Finding themselves at an economic dead-end, many settlers decided to abandon farming, move away from Cape Town, and become cattle and sheep ranchers, occupying the niche that the now-fading Khoi had occupied in the local economy and forcibly displacing the San hunters and gatherers from the land onto which they moved. As the company wanted meat, it granted these settlers so-called loan farms on which to raise animals. Most of these loan farms were situated in dry areas of the interior, where the number of animals a unit of land could support was

limited. As there was no shortage of land, the loan farms tended to be very large, in the neighborhood of 6,000 acres or even more. Because the farms and ranches were so large, European expansion eastward across South Africa proceeded quickly.

During this period of expansion, the free burghers formed a new rural society. Sometimes called the Boers ("farmers"), they differed greatly from their cousins who had remained as farmers in the western Cape area, near Cape Town and even more greatly from their distant cousins in faraway Holland. Theirs was a semisubsistence pastoral existence and they depended for their survival on their cattle and sheep, trading meat, cattle hides, or wool when they needed to purchase goods. Wealth for them came to be seen as cattle and sheep, not as money or land. In religion they were all Calvinist Protestants and remained far from the leavening influence of the Enlightenment. The settlers founded no real cities as they expanded eastward nor did they produce intellectuals. Although they generally could read and write some Dutch, their spoken language began to change, picking up words and terms from local Khoi or from their slaves, gradually becoming a new language which was later to be called Afrikaans.

Significantly, their society was organized on strictly hierarchical lines that were congruent with race. On top were whites, the possessors of wealth. Below them were low-paid Khoi and "coloured" farm laborers who were considered dependents of the settlers. Finally, at the bottom, almost every Afrikaner had a slave or two, imported either from the East Indies or from East Africa. The perpetuation of this racial hierarchy entrenched among settlers attitudes of disdain and exploitation towards people of color.

As they left Cape Town farther and farther behind, these settlers became increasingly independent of the Dutch East India Company and developed their own distinct goals that conflicted with the company's. Their rapid eastward expansion continued until, in the 1770s, they reached the Bantu-speaking, black-skinned, cattle-raising agriculturalists who lived in the Eastern Cape. These were people who spoke the Xhosa language. Initially, in the late 1760 and early 1770s, the Xhosa and the settlers traded peacefully with one another. When missionaries ventured into Xhosa country, they were usually allowed to remain and some Xhosa even converted to Christianity. Some Xhosa worked on Afrikaner ranches. Some settlers went to dwell in Xhosa society, marry Xhosa women, become part of the group, and raise families.

A seventeenth-century engraving shows an idyllic scene of peaceful, mutually beneficial trade between the Khoi people and European sailors. In reality, the Europeans more often killed the Khoi and took what they wanted.

By the late 1770s, however, the westernmost Xhosa and the leading edge of the expanding population of settlers found themselves in increased competition for limited summer pasture lands. Cattle rustling on both sides further soured relations. As competition grew, the earlier peaceful relationships between settlers and Xhosa deteriorated and the first of a series of frontier wars broke out (1779–81). Unlike the Khoi, however, the Xhosa did not crumble or fade away.

These problems caused the Dutch East India Company great apprehensions. Its purpose was to make money, not fight wars. And so it promulgated a series of laws intended to keep the European settlers away from the Africans and thus reduce friction. The settlers ignored the company's efforts, however, and conflict grew. Finally, in 1793, after a great drought had made summer pastureland even more valuable, the Second Frontier War broke out. The company rushed troops to the area, but, instead of attacking the Xhosa, its troops forced the settlers to withdraw westward, hoping that physical separation would produce peace in the Eastern Cape. In February 1795 some settlers rebelled against the company, justifiably claiming that it was preoccupied with its profits and unconcerned with their interests. They demanded the right to administer local affairs and to have unlimited access to guns and ammunition.

The British Takeover of the Cape and the Great Trek

It was at this point, in 1795, that European events caught up with the settlers. Engaged in the early stages of the Napoleonic wars, Britain wanted to strangle France's world trade. Because France had occupied the Netherlands, the British seized the Cape of Good Hope from the Dutch East India Company in 1795. The new British administration was uncertain as to how long it would remain. The British wanted to keep Cape Town because of its strategic importance on the route to India and were willing to administer the Western Cape area because it was peaceful, but they feared involvement in costly wars with the Xhosa in the Eastern Cape for the sake of a scattering of settler stock raisers. Repeated British attempts to fix a firm boundary line between Xhosa and settlers, including the Third Frontier War (1799–1803), all failed, and the uncertainties of the Eastern Cape continued as before.

In 1811, however, this situation, which had dragged on for some thirty-five years or so, changed suddenly. The British, increasingly aware that the economic power given to them by the Industrial Revolution at home and the political power garnered by successive defeats of the French abroad had made them the world's most powerful nation, decided to use their power to establish order in the Eastern Cape. The British victory in the Fourth Frontier War (1811–12) ended the balance

The Great Trek

THE DUTCH EAST INDIA COMPANY'S ATTITUDE TO THE XHOSA, 1794

■ *In business to make profits, not war, the Dutch East India Company desired peace with the Xhosa people on the Eastern Cape frontier. After the war of 1793 between the Xhosa and the Afrikaner settlers, the company asked for a report of its causes. In this report, the company's agent in the Eastern Cape suggests how the Xhosa should be treated if peace is to be maintained.*

Whoever has even an average knowledge of our country and the nature of the [Xhosa] nation will quickly understand that the discord with them must bring about the most disastrous consequences for the colony and its inhabitants. The colony is already being plagued by the vexations of the Bushmen (San people) who have now eventually been reduced to a wild and savage nation, staying alive through theft alone, so that the inhabitants of the colony are hardly able to protect themselves and their possessions against them. And who does not then realize that hostilities with the [Xhosa], who are so powerful people and of whom—as experience has taught—even a small part can throw the country into tumult, will produce the most fatal consequences for this colony.

I am convinced that these consequences cannot be countered, nor can peace and quiet be preserved, by other means than by lenient and moderate measures. Such measures, as I have often found, can have a great influence on the [Xhosa] nation, as a people susceptible to reason and jealous of their freedom. Yet these are also measures so alien to the way of thinking of many of our inhabitants that I must add, though it grieves me greatly to do so, that in continuing with these measures, I am meeting with the most extreme opposition and have difficulty in keeping some of the inhabitants from violence against this nation . . . [D]iscord with these [Xhosa] should at all times be counteracted with the most lenient measures. At the least, one should in no cases resort to extreme measures, but only do so when it is essential as a means of defence, and all other more humane measures have been tried without success.

From Report of H. C. D. Maynier to Commissary A. J. Sluysken, 31 March 1794.

that had existed between settlers and Xhosa and resulted in the expulsion eastward of some 8,000 Xhosa people, with many killed in the process. From that time the military advantage was unmistakably on the side of the Europeans.

The British determined to act against the white settlers as well. Intent upon introducing a wholly new form of colonialism based on bureaucratic efficiency and concern for due process of law, they soon gave the settlers a full catalog of grievances. One area of contention was labor relations. The large group of mixed-race offspring of the settlers and Khoi, San, Malay, Xhosa, or slave concubines were not themselves slaves, but settler law curtailed their rights to own property, compelled them to carry identity documents known as "passes," and forced them to work for the settlers for low wages. The British asserted that anyone not a slave was free and should have the rights of a free man. As a consequence,

the British took a series of steps to liberate the settlers' dependents, culminating in 1828 with the promulgation of Ordinance 50. This law reinforced earlier laws, ended peonage absolutely, and freed people from the obligation of having to carry passes. It also permitted them to own land in their own right, and it regulated working conditions for the first time. In effect, the British had dissolved the ties of dependency between the settlers and their clients.

A wide-ranging British attack on settler culture and institutions also provoked resentment. Pursuing a policy of anglicization, the British decreed that only English was to be used in the courts. English was also encouraged in the schools, and the British even found a group of Scottish Calvinist clergymen to fill the pulpits of the Calvinist Dutch Reformed Church, the settlers' church. In 1820 over 5,000 British settlers were introduced to the Eastern Cape to dilute the

Dutch presence. The cultural assault was increased in 1827, when the British replaced the system of local government and courts that the settlers had established with new English-speaking local magistrates and new British-staffed courts. Local political power was, thus, finally removed from local settlers to Cape Town.

Another grievance focused on the economy. Although the economy had grown after the British take-over, the major beneficiaries were the new English settlers, with the Dutch settlers remaining embedded in a sleepy subsistence economy. They felt that the British were unfairly dominating the economy and that they had been left behind in poverty. Finally, the straw

A young man of mixed Khoi and European ancestry poses in Western garb. African children of mixed blood often adopted Western manners and dress.

that broke the camel's back was the British policy on slavery. In 1834 slavery was abolished throughout the British Empire. The settlers were embittered both by what they saw as a violation of their property rights and by an inadequate compensation for their lost property.

Chafing under such policies, a group of settlers decided that if they were to remain true to their cultural heritage, they would have to leave British control. In 1835 some 4,000 of them, together with several thousand of their African and mixed-race retainers, left the Cape Colony on what became known as the Great Trek, moving north of the Orange River into the interior to escape the British. The interior had been affected during the 1820s by a series of wars known as the *Mfecane*, and many of its Tswana- and Sotho-speaking inhabitants were too weak to resist the migrants effectively. The powerful Zulu state, the one power that might have blocked their invasion of the interior, was itself defeated in 1838 at the battle of Blood River, one of the turning points in the history of South Africa, and the settlers were able to establish their new societies.

The Great Trek became the defining event in the history of Dutch settlement in South Africa. The settlers staked out huge ranches and farms of between 6,000 and 12,000 acres, forced defeated Africans to become farm laborers, and set up their own independent governments. Seeing them occupying only the barren interior, the British decided not to expend the money or effort that would be required to undo this movement of settler independence. Locked away in the interior, the British believed, the settlers could do little harm and they were thus given the opportunity to develop further into a unique people that came to be known as the Afrikaners.

"Legitimate Trade" and the Slave Trade in West Africa After 1807

At the end of the eighteenth century approximately 90 per cent of the value of the exports from sub-Saharan Africa was in the form of slaves. The outlawing of the slave trade could not but change radically the structure of African societies and their economies. What the British hoped was that the slave trade, now considered evil and illegitimate, would be replaced by a major expansion of what they termed the "legitimate trade." The expansion of European industrialization had produced a growing demand for vegetable oils to lubricate industrial machinery, to be manufactured into candles by which the newly literate classes could read, and, especially, to be made into soap. Peanuts grew well along the

Upper Guinea Coast, while along the Lower Guinea Coast palm trees produced palm nuts and palm oil in abundance. Traders eager to purchase these products soon arrived on the West Coast in ever larger numbers.

The expansion of this "legitimate trade" brought important changes to the coastal societies. First, new classes were given the opportunity to participate in the trade. While the production of slaves had been mostly controlled by large-scale merchants, aristocrats, and kings, producing peanuts and palm oil could be done by ordinary people using family labor and traditional tools. The new trade gave ordinary people the opportunity to earn money and brought about the creation of a new African peasantry willing and even eager to produce for the world economy.

At the same time, it opened the way for new middle classes to emerge by prompting a change in the system of labor mobilization. Up to then labor for subsistence cultivation had been mobilized either through kinship or, where possible, domestic slavery. These old ways were, however, inadequate to meet growing demands for oil products. The result was a commercialization of labor in West Africa, with certain people using the money they obtained from the new trade to hire either local poor people or migrant workers from the north for

A Xhosa fighter armed with traditonal weapons. The Xhosa were the first Bantu speakers to clash with the British and the Boers in southern Africa.

more production or even to purchase people as slaves to work locally. These increasingly well-off people, with their own ideas about progress, joined the social structure between the elite above and the poor peasants, subsistence producers, and slaves below.

The nature of imports also changed. The slave trade had involved imports of textiles, tobacco, rum, luxury goods for the elite, guns, and gunpowder. Ordinary people were uninterested in large quantities of guns and gunpowder, and traders now brought larger quantities of textiles, tobacco, hardware, salt, and other goods intended for mass consumption, thereby developing a mass market in West Africa for the first time.

Changes in pricing in the decades before 1860 greatly strengthened the growth of the new type of trade. As competition to buy African vegetable oils increased, their prices rose by over 100 per cent in forty years. At the same time, the prices of imported manufactured goods decreased steadily because of technological strides in Europe. This meant that producers were able to obtain more and more manufactured goods per unit of their oil products. In other words, between 1810 and 1860, the terms of trade were very much in Africa's favor, improving with each decade and stimulating even more production.

Yet despite these remarkable changes, the slave trade from West Africa continued. The Portuguese legally traded slaves south of the equator, using Angola and Mozambique as principal sources. Yet even in the parts of West Africa where the new "legitimate trade" was taking root and growing, those with vested interests in the slave trade on both sides of the Atlantic resisted British attempts to suppress it. In Cuba and Brazil, for example, as well as in areas of the American South, the importance of slaves in plantation agriculture increased in the early nineteenth century as demand for sugar, coffee, and cotton grew steadily. Thus, when Brazil became independent from Portugal in 1822, it renounced even Portugal's half-hearted restrictions on the slave trade and vigorously continued it. Slavery endured in Brazil until 1888.

When the British moved to abolish the trade in 1807, African rulers and merchants were astonished that Europeans should suddenly be denouncing what they had been clamoring for for so many centuries. Once they had recovered from their astonishment, however, most determined that they would continue the trade if at all possible. It had been the source of the arms and luxury goods that they had come to depend upon for their political and economic survival, and they would not willingly let it die. The income from peanut and palm oil production seemed a poor substitute for the wealth derived from the slave trade, particularly as it was difficult to tax peasant producers.

But the African leaders needed partners, and with demand for slaves still strong in America, people eager to take up that role soon appeared. European nationals generally obeyed their countries' laws and abandoned the slave trade. But when the price of slaves on the West African coast fell to about half of what it had been before 1807, a group of Brazilians moved to the Bight of Benin to handle the trade. By 1820, it had revived and an estimated 80,000 slaves, many drawn illegally from West Africa, were shipped annually across the Atlantic.

This reinvigorated trade was clandestine and illegal but it was nonetheless real. British attempts at blockading it were far from effective. The nearness of the Lower Guinea Coast to the equator meant that a ship flying the Portuguese or Brazilian flag could drop quickly into the Southern Hemisphere, where the trade was still legal in international law. Also, the limitations of poor communications in the days before radio and the slow sail-powered ships in the British antislavery patrol resulted in the British being simply unable to stop slavers even when they detected them north of the equator, for the slave traders used the most advanced American-built ships, which could outrun the antiquated British naval vessels. The West African coast itself also had many lagoons and estuaries in which the slave traders' ships could hide until their cargo was completed, at which time they would make a break when signals were given that, literally, the coast was clear of the British navy. Finally, the Portuguese rented their flag to the ships of other nations, thereby protecting them from seizure. As Britain's foreign minister in the mid-1830s, Lord Palmerston, aptly remarked, "The ships of Portugal now prowl about the oceans, pandering to the crimes of other nations; and, where her own ships are not sufficiently numerous for the purpose, her flag is lent as a shield to protect the misdeeds of foreign pirates."

So successfully had the Brazilians been in eluding the British that in 1850 the commander of the British anti-slave-trade squadron reported that the profits of the traders were as high as ever and that the export of slaves from the Bight of Benin area was actually increasing to meet the demand for slaves that a recent expansion of Cuban sugar production and Brazilian coffee production had produced. As a result of all these problems, it is estimated that only one out of every sixteen slaves—or 160,000 people in all—sent across the Atlantic after 1807 were actually rescued and freed by the British patrols.

The Development of South African Society to 1852

1652	Dutch East India Company establishes Cape Town as a way station between Holland and the East Indies
1657	The company releases workers from their contracts, creating a class of European settlers known as "free burghers"
ca. 1700	Expansion of European settlement eastward from Cape Town as free burghers become sheep farmers and cattle ranchers on "loan farms"
1713	Smallpox epidemic destroys over half of Khoi people
ca. 1770	Settlers expanding eastward encounter Xhosa people in Eastern Cape in neighborhood of the Great Fish River
1795	Britain takes over the Cape from the Dutch during Napoleonic wars
1811	British military expels Xhosa beyond the Great Fish River in effort to establish a border
1818	Shaka becomes leader of Mthethwa and begins Zulu expansion
1820	Arrival of 5,000 British settlers in the Eastern Cape
1828	Ordinance 50 restructures relationships between Afrikaners and their dependents
1834	British abolition of slavery in the Cape angers Afrikaners
1835–38	Many Afrikaners leave Cape on their Great Trek into the interior, where they create their own states beyond British control
1838	Battle of Blood River, in which Afrikaners defeat the Zulu armies
1852–54	Britain grants level recognition to Afrikaner republics in the interior

The final end of the transatlantic slave trade came abruptly. In 1856, accepting the argument that the trade was a crime against humanity, the British government threatened war against Brazil. Brazil capitulated immediately. Once the demand was turned off, the trade that had characterized relations between Europe and Africa to a lesser or greater extent since 1444 trickled out speedily.

Mid-nineteenth-century Africa was very different from the Africa of 1600. In large measure this difference was the result of the impact that Europeans had as Africa entered into an expanding world economy through the nexus of trade. Aside from the intensive white settlements in South Africa and the far weaker influence of the Portuguese in Angola and Mozambique, Africa was still politically independent, with many states having profited from the centuries of trade with Europe and strengthened themselves. In 1860 there seemed to be no reason why this independence should not continue. Yet within two decades a new era had begun. It was to be far more exploitative than the one that had ended in around 1860. This was the era of imperialism and colonial takeover.

The Middle East and the World System

Tsar Nicholas II of Russia called it the "sick man of Europe"; British prime minister William Gladstone referred to it as "the unspeakable Turk." Indeed, to most nineteenth-century European observers, the Ottoman Empire appeared to be an empire in decline, a petrified shell of its former grand self.

The evidence for such a view of not only the Ottoman Empire, but also of Egypt (which, although autonomous during this century, was legally a part of the Ottoman Empire), and of Persia was clearly discernible to contemporary observers. Although during the nineteenth century the leaders of these states attempted to build the infrastructure necessary to maintain their territorial integrity and transform their societies, the boundaries that separated the Ottoman Empire and Persia from Europe were continuously pushed back. By the first decades of the twentieth century, the Ottoman Empire would be forced out of most of its European territories, French and Italian settlers and armies would be entrenched in North Africa, and Great Britain would occupy Egypt, where its troops would remain until 1956.

In terms of economics, over the course of the nineteenth century the Ottoman Empire, Egypt, and Persia became increasingly dependent on international markets, which set the prices for the agricultural goods they sold: Cotton from Egypt fed the mills of Lancashire, while raw silk from Lebanon was exported to France. In return, the empires of the Middle East imported manufactured goods and borrowed money from Europe to finance internal improvements. The trade imbalances and debts became so severe that both the Ottoman Empire and Egypt were forced to declare bankruptcy in 1876.

Integration of the Middle East into the World Economy

The relationship between the Middle East and Europe in the nineteenth century was the culmination of a process that had begun three centuries earlier when European voyages of discovery, the commercial revolution, and the rise of the Atlantic economies placed western Europe at the center of a new world economic and political system, integrating other regions of the world into the system in a subordinate role.

The discovery of large quantities of gold and silver in the Americas in the sixteenth century affected the Middle East as well as Africa. The influx of precious metals inflated prices in Europe, so Europeans turned to the Ottoman Empire for agricultural products and raw materials such as wheat, wool, raw silk, and metals. Further, to offset their trade deficits, governments of European trading states encouraged their merchants

The European Great Powers, especially Russia, had designs on Ottoman territory. This cartoon shows the British lion, the German and Austrian eagles, and the Russian bear closing in on a hapless turkey, which represents the "sick man of Europe."

to produce and export manufactured goods, such as textiles, for overseas markets. Such goods, sold in Middle Eastern markets, undercut local craftsmen and crippled local production. By the mid-eighteenth century, imports into the Ottoman Empire exceeded exports.

If the Ottoman Empire, Egypt, or Persia had been able to raise the level of import tariffs or create monopolies to guarantee local production, perhaps they could have resisted the subordination of the Middle East to the Atlantic economies. But because of their political and military weakness, neither the Ottoman Empire, Egypt, nor Persia was able to do so. Thus, an unequal trade relationship developed and continued between Europe and the Middle East, a relationship not without its ironies. Between 1840 and 1914, for example, cotton textiles represented about one-third of the Middle East's imports, while during the first decade of the twentieth century raw cotton made up 90 percent of Egypt's exports and about 20 percent of the exports from the Ottoman Empire and Persia.

Thus, during the nineteenth century, the pace and scope of the political and economic incorporation of the Middle East into the world system accelerated and widened. This process affected all aspects of social, economic, and political life in the region.

The Near Eastern Question

The Treaty of Kuchuk Kainarji in 1774 between Russia and the Ottoman Empire marked a turning point in the history of Ottoman-European relations. The Ottoman state was clearly no longer, in the words of one seventeenth-century English observer, "the present terror of the world." As the eighteenth and nineteenth centuries progressed, European statesmen no longer worried about how to defend against Ottoman expansion. Instead, they pondered how to deal with the problem of an increasingly enfeebled Ottoman state whose decay threatened to create a power vacuum in southeastern Europe and the eastern Mediterranean—a power vacuum that would threaten the balance of power in Europe. This problem became known as the Near Eastern Question.

There were two parts to the Near Eastern Question in the nineteenth century—one external to the region, one internal. After the Russian state had been consolidated under Tsar Peter the Great in the eighteenth century, it began to expand southward, threatening the Ottoman Empire in the southwest and Persia in the southeast. The Russian advance south in search of a warm-water outlet to the sea could be made only at the expense of the Ottoman Empire.

At the same time, to protect its lifeline to India and to ensure a European balance of power favorable to its interests, Great Britain had to prevent the Russian advance. British foreign secretary Lord Palmerston, reacting to one in a series of Middle Eastern crises that focused the attention of his nation on the region, enunciated a policy to which British governments adhered until 1914: "His majesty's government attach great importance to the maintenance of the integrity of the Ottoman Empire, considering that state to be a material element in the general balance of power in Europe." Britain and Russia remained at loggerheads over the Ottoman Empire throughout the century. Farther east, the Russian attempt to expand at the expense of Persia threatened British India and sparked a rivalry between the two powers that was called by Rudyard Kipling the Great Game.

Over the course of the nineteenth century, the Near Eastern Question was complicated by the activities of other European powers, which frequently intervened in the region to protect their interests. After France lost control of the Atlantic to the British in the Seven Years' War (1756–63), for example, it turned to the Mediterranean as an area from which to sell manufactured goods. French economic and strategic concerns in the region led to their invasion of Egypt in 1798 and conquest of Algeria in 1830. After unification, Germany also looked to the Middle East as an area for commercial expansion, and became a major promoter of Ottoman railroad construction, even proposing a line from Berlin to Baghdad.

The integrity of the Ottoman Empire was further threatened by two internal factors. The first factor was the rise of nationalism among the Balkan peoples of the Ottoman Empire, who desired independence and often sought the assistance of their fellow Orthodox Christians in Russia to obtain it. The second factor was the inability of the Ottoman government to control local governors in the Middle East and North Africa, such as Muhammad 'Ali, the viceroy of Egypt, who sought autonomy or independence with increasing success.

Defensive Modernization

Confronted by both foreign and internal challenges, Middle Eastern leaders responded by attempting to centralize and expand their authority in order to strengthen their states and make them more efficient. In the Ottoman Empire, Egypt, and Persia, leaders concentrated their first efforts on military matters. To

The Decline of the Ottoman Empire

resist foreign encroachment, they sought to reconstruct their armies along Western lines. Military reform was expensive, however, and to support these new armies they encouraged the cultivation of cash crops and tried to rationalize taxation and increase tax revenues. The Ottoman Empire eliminated middlemen such as tax farmers—private individuals who purchased from the state the right to collect and pocket taxes from the local peasantry. Further, staffing the modern armies and government bureaus required educated personnel. This meant building new educational institutions and teaching subjects such as mathematics, engineering, and foreign languages. This process is known as defensive modernization.

The most striking example of defensive modernization took place in Egypt, where a dynasty established in 1807 by a former Albanian soldier in the Ottoman service, Muhammad 'Ali, took power during the chaos that followed the French invasion. For Muhammad 'Ali, military reform was essential for two reasons: not only did he want to maintain internal stability and protect Egypt's near total autonomy in the Ottoman Empire, but he wanted to expand the area under his control to ensure the supply of essential raw materials and to monopolize east-west trade routes.

Thus, in 1831, Muhammad 'Ali's son, Ibrahim, led a military expedition into Syria to gain access to trade routes that passed through the eastern Mediterranean

LAMENT ON THE FRENCH CONQUEST OF ALGIERS

■ *The following is an excerpt from a lament written by Shaykh 'Abd al-Qadir, a witness to the French conquest of Algiers in 1830. It later became a part of Algerian oral tradition.*

May your servants regain peace, may all their grief be ended
And may this oppression which crushes the Muslims cease!
Let us cry over the *muftis*, over the *qadis*,
Over the *ulama* of the city, those guides of the religion.
Let us cry over the mosques and their sermons
And over their pulpits of elevated marble.
Let us weep over their *minarets*[1] and the calls of the *muezzins*;[2]
and over the classes of their teachers and over their cantors of the Qur'an.
Let us lament the private chapels whose doors have been locked
And which have sunk today, yes Sir, into oblivion.
Alas where are the precious trinkets of the city, where are its houses?
Where are their low apartments and the elevated rooms for the eunuchs?
They are no longer but a parade ground and their traces have disappeared.
So much does that cursed one breathe to plague us!
The Christians have installed themselves in the city;
Its appearance has changed;
It no longer has seen anything but impure people.
The *janissaries'* houses! They have razed their walls;
They have torn down its marble and its sculptured balustrades,
The iron grills which protected the windows
Have been put to pieces by those impious ones, enemies of the Religion.
Likewise, they have named that Qaisariya "the Square",
Where the Books and their binders were formerly found.
The Magnificent Mosque which was next to it
Has been destroyed by them simply in order to spite the Muslims.

[1]*Minaret:* slender tower attached to mosques. Balconies on the minaret are the place from where people are called to prayer.
[2]*Muezzin:* Muslim official who calls the faithful to prayer (from the minaret).

region, acquire raw materials such as timber, and monopolize the Syrian silk trade. Egypt continued to occupy this area for ten years until the Ottoman government, with British assistance, was able to reassert control. During that time, the Egyptians introduced policies into the region typical of defensive modernizers: conscription, direct taxation, public works, the cultivation of cash crops that could be sold abroad to earn foreign exchange, and measures to increase public security and expand trade.

To support his military adventures abroad, Muhammad 'Ali undertook new economic policies at home. He confiscated lands that had been held by the previous Mamluk rulers of Egypt. He placed lands that had been under the control of tax farmers directly under the control of the Egyptian government. His government attempted to control all aspects of agriculture. The government encouraged the planting of cash crops, particularly cotton. It set up a monopoly that bought cotton from cultivators to sell to European agents, and it invested in industries associated with cotton, such as ginning and spinning. These changes had important social consequences: They put women to work spinning and weaving in factories while their husbands were recruited to the corvee (forced labor) digging irrigation ditches.

Muhammad 'Ali, shown here meeting with the British colonel Patrick Campbell and French engineers, called upon foreign experts to help in the modernization of Egypt.

Muhammad 'Ali's encouragement of cotton cultivation further integrated Egypt into the world economic system, and Egyptian revenues became directly dependent on the price of cotton in the international marketplace. In 1800, for example, more than 50 percent of Egypt's trade was with the Ottoman Empire, and 14 percent was with Europe; by 1823, these figures were reversed.

Cotton production proved to be both a blessing and a curse for Egypt. During the American Civil War, the Northern blockade of Southern ports cut off Europe's supply of Confederate cotton and drove cotton prices up. As a result, both Egyptian revenues and dependency on cotton cultivation increased. Muhammad 'Ali's successors, anticipating a lasting boom, borrowed heavily from European bankers to finance internal improvements and prestige projects, such as an opera house in Cairo. When the American crop went on the market again, the price of cotton plummeted, Egyptian revenues collapsed, and the government was forced to declare bankruptcy.

It is ironic that the policy originally intended to ensure political and economic independence had the opposite effect. For Egypt, defensive modernization led to borrowing, borrowing led to bankruptcy, and bankruptcy led in 1882 to a British occupation that would last more than three-quarters of a century. While in Egypt, the British encouraged the continued cultivation of cotton to feed their mills and discouraged investment in industries that might compete with those in Britain. British direction hindered the social and political development of Egypt as well. For example, the first British consul general, Lord Cromer, discouraged expenditures on education because he feared the creation of a class of disaffected, unmanageable intellectuals.

In other parts of the Middle East, defensive modernization, called by the Ottomans the *Tanzimat* ("reorderings"), also had mixed results. The Ottoman Empire of the eighteenth century had been virtually decentralized; instead of power being concentrated in Istanbul, local notables ruled their provinces with little control from the central government. Even in those regions where the state could exercise power, however, it often did not do so, allowing the population to organize its own affairs through guilds and informal networks of authority.

Under the nineteenth-century Tanzimat sultans, the state not only attempted to curb the powers of local leaders, but it also expanded its own authority into areas where governments had never before intruded, such as education and social welfare. The Tanzimat sultans abolished the Janissary corps and replaced it with a conscript army. They legislated against tax-farming, restructured the central bureaucracy along European lines, and established provincial councils based on representative principles. They extended the authority of secular law. In an attempt to unify the empire, they built railroads and established *rushdiyye* schools, which took children after Qur'an training and prepared them for Western-style colleges.

The effects of the Tanzimat, however, were uneven. As in the case of Egypt, the cost of defensive modernization eventually led to bankruptcy and to European supervision of Ottoman finances. The size and diversity of the empire also complicated the centralization and rationalization of the government and the economy. Whereas, by contrast, the homogeneity of the land and population of Egypt made the mandating of a cotton-based economy relatively easy, such was not the case in the Ottoman Empire, which included the Balkans, North Africa, and the Arab Middle East.

Furthermore, the traditional Ottoman state had been built on informal networks, the predominance of Islamic institutions, and local autonomy. Many groups resisted centralization. For peasants, the restructuring often meant the potential for more efficient taxation and conscription; for ulama who were not attached to the central bureaucracy, it meant loss of prestige and limitations on their educational and judicial functions; for local notables, it meant loss of power.

Because of this local resistance, many of the regulations had effects different from those intended. For

INAUGURATION DU CANAL DE SUEZ. — *Te Deum* chanté à Port-Saïd en présence de LL. MM. l'Empereur d'Autriche et l'Impératrice des Français. — D'après un croquis de M. Auguste Marc.

The ceremony for the opening of the Suez Canal in 1869.

*L*inking the Seas

Building a canal to link the Mediterranean Sea with the Red Sea and Indian Ocean had been a dream since the times of the Egyptian pharaohs. With the shift in the center of the European economy away from the Mediterranean toward the Atlantic, beginning in the sixteenth century, the benefits to be derived from such a canal increased. A canal, cut through the Isthmus of Suez, would reduce by half the distance that merchant ships traveled from London to Bombay.

According to an apocryphal story still told in Egypt, history owes the construction of the Suez Canal to macaroni. Muhammad 'Ali, the founder of a dynasty that ruled Egypt for more than 150 years, was a soldier who hated the corpulence of his son, Sa'id. Muhammad 'Ali forced Sa'id to take exercise every

morning, but while out riding, Sa'id would meet up with Ferdinand de Lesseps, a junior member of the French diplomatic mission in Egypt, and the two would return to the embassy to lunch on pasta. When, years later, de Lesseps returned to Egypt with a plan to dig the Suez Canal, Sa'id could not refuse him.

Whatever the truth to this story, it is well-known that Sa'id had a passion for grand public works and was very susceptible to the flattery of anyone who had a project to promote. He could hardly have been unmoved by de Lesseps' memorandum in which the wily promoter wrote,

The names of the Egyptian sovereigns who erected the pyramids, those monuments of human pride, remain unknown. The name of the

Prince who opens the great maritime canal will be blessed from century to century, down to the most distant posterity.

De Lesseps thus acquired the backing of the viceroy for his project.

Sa'id obligated the Egyptian government to purchase 64,000 of the 400,000 public shares of de Lesseps' Suez Canal Company. When, by 1858, only half the stock issue had been sold, de Lesseps persuaded the Egyptian government to take up the remainder. In addition, Sa'id promised de Lesseps that he would provide a corvee (forced labor) of 20,000 laborers each year to dig the canal. At times, the number of forced laborers exceeded 40,000, contributing the equivalent of over 1 million days of labor. The conditions under which these laborers worked, equated by the British press to the worst conditions of slavery, caused a furor in Europe. In a public exchange of letters, an outraged de Lesseps accused the British of hypocrisy, comparing, without any hint of irony, conditions among the laborers on the canal to that of the unemployed poor of London or the lowest classes in British India.

De Lesseps understood that the British government based its concern for the plight of the Egyptian fellah (peasant) on the fact that it felt that "Egypt is the key to our house in India." Because of this, the British naturally opposed a French-initiated canal project straddling the route to their most important colony. If a canal was to be built, Britain would have to control it. As Prime Minister Lord Palmerston put it,

We do not want Egypt or wish it for ourselves, any more than any rational man with an estate in the north of England and a residence in the south would have wished to possess the inns on the road. All he could want would have been that the inns should be well-kept, always accessible, and furnishing him, when he came, with mutton-chops and post-horses.

Thus, in 1875, with the canal an established fact, the British government purchased the Suez Canal Company stock owned by an Egyptian government which, in the wake of the collapse of cotton prices, was heavily in debt and facing bankruptcy. With this purchase, the British government became the largest single shareholder of the canal company's stock. The protection of this vital interest became a major British strategic concern and was one of the reasons for the British invasion and occupation of Egypt in 1882.

Canal construction continued for ten years. Sa'id's successor, Isma'il, planned a huge celebration for the opening of the canal in 1869: a procession of ships, led by Empress Eugénie of France aboard the imperial yacht, sailed down the canal. The viceroy commissioned the Italian composer Giuseppe Verdi to write an opera with an Egyptian theme, *Aida*, for the event. When one Egyptian minister complained to a European guest about the cost of the festivities, saying "We are eating up the Pyramids stone by stone," his guest summed up European relations with Egypt by replying, "Never mind, Your Excellency, you can borrow money from us and then you can buy from us the cement to replace them."

The opening to the Suez Canal had major repercussions for international and regional trade. The cost of shipping goods from Europe to India and vice versa was substantially cut, and the opening of the canal proved to be a boon to fragile steamboats, which could not weather the Cape route. The canal had major repercussions for the Middle Eastern economy as well. While trade between Iraq and Europe grew, and the value of Iraqi exports, such as grain and wool, increased by 350 percent during the period 1870–75, the importance of cities dependent on the overland caravan trade, such as Damascus, declined. Ironically, with the opening of the canal, the Egyptian government lost revenues from the overland transit of goods and mail from Alexandria, on the Mediterranean, to the Red Sea ports.

In 1876, the Turkish statesman Midhat Pasha (1822–83) proclaimed a constitution for the Ottoman Empire, culminating an era of reform based on western European ideas. However, the constitution did not survive the succession of the Sultan Abdülhamid II (1876).

example, the 1858 Ottoman Land Code was designed to increase agricultural production and end tax farming by giving peasants the right to register the lands they were working in their own names. Peasants were often suspicious of the motives of the Ottoman government. Fearing that this "gift" of land was made merely to increase their tax burden and that registration would lead to conscription, many either fled their land or signed it over to urban-based notables, becoming, in the process, tenant farmers.

In Persia, the effects of defensive modernization were different from either Egypt or the rest of the Ottoman Empire. Three situations explain this difference. First, the dynasty that governed the country, the Qajar dynasty, did not have strong roots among the population and, having little effective control outside the capital of Tehran, ruled indirectly through tribal leaders, local families, and the indigenous bureaucracy. Second, as a result of the Great Game, both Britain and Russia discouraged the Persian government from seeking technical assistance or loans from its rival. Finally,

the Shi'i ulama of Persia, who conceived of themselves as defenders of Persian Shi'i tradition against foreign domination and autocratic rule, were not only well organized and financially independent, but they also were allied with other urban-based strata, such as merchants, an alliance that increased their influence in society.

After half-hearted attempts at military reform early in the century had failed, and after only limited success in fostering institutions necessary for defensive modernization, successive Persian governments attempted to generate revenues and hasten development by granting concessions to European financiers—that is, selling them the right to produce, market, and export a commodity or commodities. For example, in 1872 the Persian shah granted to Julius de Reuter, a British subject, the exclusive right to build streetcars and railroads, extract minerals, establish a national bank, and exploit the national forests in exchange for a modest down payment and the promise of future royalties. A similar concession in 1889 to the Imperial Tobacco Company allowed the company to control the cultivation, sales, distribution, and export of all Persian tobacco and tobacco products. In the wake of protests led by ulama, both of these agreements had to be cancelled.

The overall effects of the attempts at defensive modernization in Egypt, the Ottoman Empire, and Persia were ambiguous. If measured by the success in centralization and the spread of governmental authority into previously unregulated areas of society, then it is possible to claim that defensive modernization succeeded in Egypt, had mixed results in the Ottoman Empire, and had very modest success in Persia. But the purpose of defensive modernization was to defend Middle Eastern states from Western political and economic intrusion, and this effort failed. During the nineteenth century, the Ottoman Empire lost most of its Balkan and North African territories, Britain occupied Egypt, and, in 1907, Britain and Russia announced plans to divide Persia into spheres of influence. Economically, some measures actually facilitated Western economic penetration of the region. Among these were the encouragement of cultivation of cash crops, foreign borrowing, and the construction of networks of communication and transportation, as well as educational and governmental institutions that more closely corresponded with those of Europe.

Overall, integration of the Middle East into the world system and changes brought about as a result of defensive modernization affected, either directly or indirectly, almost every aspect of life in the region. As a result, both social institutions and the relationship between state and society in the Middle East were substantially different at the close of the nineteenth century from those at the beginning of the century.

The Transformation of Society and Culture in the Middle East

In the nineteenth century, the Middle East was defined to a great extent by its integration into the world system and by the reaction of national leaders to this integration. However, to view Middle Eastern history in this era as only decline and subordination to Europe would be a mistake. Dramatic changes took place: new social classes were created, urban centers were reconstructed, and the responsibilities of government and citizenry were redefined.

Accompanying the institutional changes that transformed the Middle East in the nineteenth century were corresponding cultural changes. European penetration of the region influenced the content of the intellectual movements, both directly and indirectly, while defensive modernization fostered a stratum of intellectuals who would be both the primary producers and primary consumers of many of the new intellectual trends.

The Reconstruction of Urban Life

Urban-based civilizations have inhabited the Middle East for thousands of years. Indeed, the residents of such cities as Damascus and Jericho still demonstrate civic pride by claiming that their cities are the oldest continuously inhabited places on earth. Until the nineteenth century, however, Middle Eastern cities had differed from European and American cities in several ways. Unlike their Western counterparts, for example, Middle eastern cities were not independent, corporate entities, nor did they foster such entities. Autonomous municipal governments with responsibility for providing public services simply did not exist. Instead, residents themselves took responsibility for endowing public works such as fountains, parks, and mosques, and for providing the limited public services, such as the policing of residential areas.

In the nineteenth century, European economic penetration and defensive modernization transformed urban life and municipal structures in several ways. First, as the Middle East became more tightly integrated into the world economic system, coastal cities such as Alexandria in Egypt, Jaffa in Palestine, and Beirut in Lebanon became the centers for the export of agricultural products and the import of manufactured goods from Europe. These cities grew dramatically over the course of the nineteenth century. In 1800, the population of Beirut was approximately 6,000; on the eve of World War I, the population had reached 130,000. Moreover, cities such as Ismailia on the Suez Canal were founded in response to new trade routes, population shifts, and new export products.

To ensure rapid and widespread shipment of goods, railroads linked coastal cities to the interior. Rail networks were constructed connecting Beirut and Damascus, Alexandria and Cairo, Jaffa and Jerusalem, spreading the economic and social transformation inland. Interior towns such as Zahle along the Beirut-Damascus rail line took on new importance, while farmers in the grain-producing Hauran region that had supplied Damascus began cultivating crops for foreign consumption. In Iraq, new steam-powered riverboats plying the Tigris and Euphrates rivers served the same function as railroads did in other parts of the empire and proved to have such potential for transporting grain that, on the eve of the First World War, British planners envisioned using Mesopotamia as a huge plantation to supply India with agricultural products.

Cities were rebuilt as a result of new technologies, foreign investment, or imported conceptions of municipal order. The new city of Ismailia was laid out according to a checkerboard pattern, and the viceroy of Egypt, Isma'il, and the shah of Persia, Nasr ed-Din, were so impressed by late nineteenth-century Paris that they rebuilt parts of their capitals in imitation, with wide boulevards, public parks, and landscaped roads.

The destruction of old quarters, the leveling of narrow cul-de-sacs, and the construction of wide streets and public transportation fostered a new civic identity among the populace, whose lives were no longer confined to a bounded quarter. This civic sense was further enhanced by new civic institutions. By the late nineteenth century, cities such as Damascus, which had been governed by a single locally-chosen governor, were governed by municipal councils that dealt with local administrative, financial, and judicial affairs. The new councils were neither autonomous nor democratically elected; members were appointed by the Ottoman government from among various notable families. Nonetheless, they represented an important step in the integration of the city as a whole.

The integration of the Middle East into the world economy, compounded by Ottoman attempts to strengthen centralized control over the population, sparked the transformation of other urban institutions as well. For centuries associations of artisans of the same profession, called guilds, had been influential urban structures. At times their functions included everything from providing for the welfare of their members and their members' families to ensuring high standards of artisanal production. By the nineteenth century, however, locally produced goods could not compete with mass-produced European goods, and the guild system began to decay. To fill the void, the Ottoman state itself assumed responsibility for many of the guilds' social welfare functions.

Economic integration and defensive modernization affected social relations in other ways. A new class of Christian merchants, based in coastal cities such as Beirut and Alexandria, acted as middlemen between European companies and Middle Eastern consumers or producers. These merchants, who were familiar with European commercial practices and European languages, and who frequently had connections abroad, were often granted special status by European consulates. This status enabled them to engage in foreign trade while paying the same low tariffs as foreign nationals. Their privileges gave them an advantage over Muslim merchants, and, as a result, the evolution of the Christian communities in the Middle East often followed a different path from that of their Muslim neighbors, sometimes precipitating tension or violence between the two communities.

Defensive modernization was the most important factor behind the emergence of another stratum in Middle Eastern society, one that would have far more political importance than the Christian merchant class. These were the professionals, trained military officers and intellectuals who were graduates of modern, secular educational systems that had been established as a result of defensive modernization. As the product of societies in which government responsibilities had expanded dramatically in the previous half century, these professionals generally shared the attitude that deficiencies in society could be overcome by the intervention of an activist government.

By the early twentieth century, individuals from the professional stratum would lead the agitation for constitutional rule in the Ottoman Empire, participate in the Iranian Constitutional Revolution of 1906, and found the first political parties in Egypt. Their agitation for constitutional and parliamentary rule was not rooted in a belief in democracy, but rather in the fact that they were part of an emergent, yet unrepresented, social group seeking access to political participation. It would be from this group that much of the post-World War I leadership in the Middle East would arise.

Cities and Countryside: Connections and Conflicts

In the Middle East, city and hinterland had always been interconnected. In the nineteenth century, advances in transportation, the cultivation of cash crops for export, the spread of the use of money and usury, and changing patterns of land tenure all contributed further to binding the two areas together.

As mentioned, urban notables in the Ottoman Empire increasingly took control over surrounding lands,

A study of Syrian Bedouins by Bonfils, a French photographer.

sometimes as an unforeseen result of the 1858 Ottoman Land Code, sometimes as a result of peasants defaulting on loans, sometimes merely because land provided a profitable opportunity for investment. The holdings were often quite extensive; by the first decade of the twentieth century, for example, each of the wealthiest families of the cities of Homs and Hama in Syria owned from forty-five to sixty villages in the surrounding plain. Thus, urban notables dominated the grain trade, frequently set grain prices, and had the power to dictate which crops would be cultivated. Similarly, in Egypt, agriculture was dominated by wealthy landlords, often descendants of the family and retainers of Muhammad ʿAli. Having confiscated lands that had been held by the Mamluk rulers of Egypt, Muhammad ʿAli distributed them to his family and associates, sometimes forcing the beneficiaries to pay "back taxes" in exchange.

The boundaries between city and village were permeable, and during periods of rural insecurity and famine, peasants frequently sought shelter in nearby cities. Because artisanal trades in Ottoman cities at the beginning of the nineteenth century were regulated by guilds, and because guilds attempted to keep prices high by restricting production, most peasants found it difficult to enter the trades and so ended up in lower-class quarters, frequently outside the city wall, where they engaged in husbandry and "unclean" professions such as tanning.

Migration also took place in the opposite direction. During the first half of the nineteenth century, many peasants living in Damascus and Aleppo returned to their original villages. There were two causes for this migration: not only was the Ottoman government temporarily able to ensure rural security, but employment opportunities in the important weaving industry declined as a result of the importation of cheap, European-made textiles. During this period, the populations of Damascus and Aleppo dropped from highs of approximately 120,000 and 150,000, respectively, to 80,000 each. In addition to migration, temporary labor exchanges also took place. In times of emergency, a city's population might be mobilized to help with the harvest or to beat off infestations of locusts, a situation that occurred in Palestine and Syria during the First World War.

The immediate countryside around most urban concentrations in the Ottoman Empire stretched no further than about thirty miles. The area outside this limit was often the equivalent of a frontier, sometimes inhabited by Bedouin. The romantic image of Bedouin life is that of independent nomads grouped together into small family-based units. This image is mistaken on several counts. Bedouin were not necessarily isolated groups of primitives. Indeed, during the nineteenth century, tribal confederations sometimes contained as many as 250,000 members. Tribes were often made up of settled cultivators, or seasonal cultivators, or even migrant workers who hired out to work fields during harvest or planting seasons. Bedouin depended on the cities for certain commodities, sometimes sought permanent or semipermanent employment in urban areas, and borrowed money from urban-based usurers. Thus, the cities, the surrounding agricultural hinterland, and the deserts were linked demographically and economically, and the relationship between tribe and village or tribe and city ran the gamut from hostile to interdependent.

While the states in the Fertile Crescent that had preceded the Ottoman state had often attempted to integrate the Bedouin by granting tribal leaders land in exchange for tribute or loyalty, by the end of the sixteenth century the Ottoman government felt strong enough to attempt to crowd the Bedouin out—both by using force and by placing economic embargoes on the tribes. In the seventeenth century, large-scale tribal migrations into the Fertile Crescent foiled the Ottoman plan. As a result, the Ottoman government changed its strategy, hoping to integrate tribes into the Ottoman system by settling them along major communication routes, or by employing them to escort and/or provision both commercial caravans and the yearly Hajj caravan to Mecca.

Throughout the eighteenth and nineteenth centuries, the balance between the state and the Bedouin in frontier areas tipped first in one direction, then the other. In the period following the Crimean War (1854–56), the Ottoman government implemented a policy of forced settlement of the Bedouin throughout the Fertile Crescent. By the late nineteenth century, children of Bedouin *sheikhs* could attend a special school set up for them in Istanbul.

Because of the widespread cultivation of cash crops and advances in land reclamation, Bedouin leaders and urban notables could work together profitably. Tribal leaders offered their tribes as cheap agricultural labor to work on marginal lands, while the urban notables provided financial backing. Marriages were even arranged among the families of urban notables and those of tribal leaders.

The relationship between the central authority and the Bedouin varied from place to place throughout the Middle East. In Egypt, where life can be sustained only in a small area on the banks of the Nile River, Muhammad 'Ali had little trouble settling large numbers of indigenous Bedouin. In Iraq, on the other hand, the "Bedouin problem" was not resolved until well into the twentieth century, when the Iraqi government was able to call on the technical assistance of the British Royal Air Force to forcibly settle tribes that resisted control by the state.

Moral Reconstruction: Purifying Islam

The eighteenth century was marked by political and social turmoil in the Ottoman Empire. Local notables effectively challenged the authority of the central government. European armies consistently pushed back the boundaries of the empire. Peasants, who could no longer count on the government to ensure rural security, fled to the cities. Artisans were displaced as a result of the sale of cheap European manufactured products.

These circumstances engendered a feeling of malaise and a yearning for moral reconstruction among both intellectuals and the urban masses. There was a feeling that something had gone drastically wrong, and this feeling was accompanied by the search for the causes of the decline and for a model upon which society could be reconstructed. That model—one readily accessible to Muslims—was the original Islamic community in Medina, which had been founded and guided by Muhammad in the year 622.

The desire for reconstruction was combined with a form of organization that could overcome the feeling of rootlessness of the displaced peasant, artisan, or merchant—the Sufi *tariqa* (literally, "path"). Sufism has been previously described as Islamic mysticism. Like Western mysticism, most Sufi paths tended toward pantheism, the loss of the individual identity and its absorption into God. In the eighteenth century, however, many Sufi *turuq* (the plural of *tariqa*) focused on providing guidance for individuals who did not seek to escape the world. These turuq emphasized the need for individuals to live their lives in accord with the rules and regulations established by Muhammad and his companions in the original Islamic community.

Sufi turuq proliferated and spread throughout the Middle East. These organizations took diverse forms. They might be informal clubs organized by merchants to study the pronouncements of the Prophet about the rules of trade, or they might be more formal. They were very popular: by the beginning of the nineteenth century almost every male of every social class in Cairo, for example, belonged to a tariqa.

Increasingly, in the eighteenth century, turuq became the vehicles for purification and renewal. Since different turuq or Sufi masters might be based in different cities, merchants and ulama traveled from city to city, cross-fertilizing ideas from one part of the Middle East with ideas from another—from Istanbul to Damascus to Mecca and Medina to, of course, Cairo, with its great Islamic university, al-Azhar.

In outlying areas of the empire, movements associated with moral reconstruction—either associated with turuq or organized along other lines—took openly political forms. The most famous of these movements, Wahhabism, has already been discussed (see Chapter 15). In the heart of the empire, movements took a less political form, but the message was the same—moral reconstruction based on the principles of a purified Islam, an Islam without the accretions of eleven hundred years of local custom and medieval scholasticism.

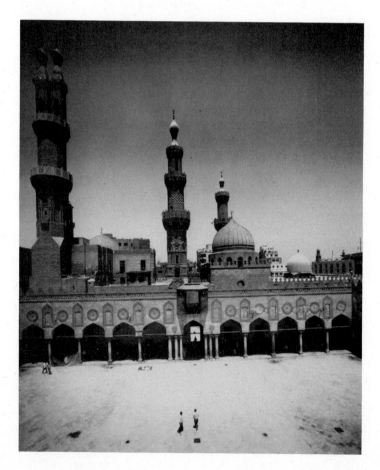

The university of al-Azhar in Cairo, founded in the tenth century, is one of the world's oldest.

Islamic Modernism: Reinterpreting Islam

Thus, an overwhelming majority of Muslims in the Ottoman Empire found indigenous Islamic answers to problems raised by the events of the eighteenth and early nineteenth centuries. Among the ruling elites, however, successive military defeats brought a different response, a response engendered by the educational policies associated with defensive modernization.

Middle Eastern leaders such as Muhammad 'Ali sent students to Europe to learn Western science and technology. Although these students and elites recognized the need to restructure the Ottoman Empire or Egypt by adopting certain mechanical, military, or administrative techniques, they were equally certain that Islamic/Ottoman culture was inherently superior to the culture of Christian Europe. But as the century progressed and the West pulled further ahead of the Middle East, that confidence was shaken.

Whereas at the beginning of the nineteenth century intellectuals might merely assert Muslim superiority, by 1850 they increasingly took up the cause of moral reconstruction. In reply to Western polemics, intellectuals argued from two premises. First, they argued that the Islam of their day *was* in a deplorable state. This had occurred because pure, true Islam, which had once inspired the conquest of the area between Afghanistan and Spain, had been corrupted and was therefore inadequate to maintain order even in the heart of the empire.

This argument was not new. But these intellectuals added a new twist to moral reconstructionism. They argued that the Islam that had preserved Greek philosophy during Europe's Dark Ages was not incompatible with science and reason. If Islam would shed its superstitious additions and root itself in reason, it could act as the foundation for a Middle Eastern scientific and industrial revolution.

Those who argued that true Islam was compatible with Western progress and modern ideas were called "Islamic modernists." Islamic modernists had usually been exposed to Western ideas and frequently were acquainted with either English or French. In addition, they usually advocated reform through education, not through direct political confrontation. Although they were united by the same general ideas and tactical

ISLAMIC MODERNIST STATEMENT ON THE UNIVERSALITY OF SCIENCE

■ *In a speech delivered at Albert Hall, Calcutta, India, in 1882, the Islamic modernist Jamal ad-Din al-Afghani stated the following:*

The strangest thing of all is that our ulama these days have divided science into two parts. One they call Muslim science, and one European science. Because of this they forbid others to teach some of the useful sciences. They have not understood that science is that noble thing that has no connection with any nation, and is not distinguished by anything but itself. Rather, everything that is known is known by science, and every nation that becomes renowned becomes renowned through science. Men must be related to science, not science to men.

How very strange it is that the Muslims study those sciences that are ascribed to Aristotle with the greatest delight, as if Aristotle were one of the pillars of the Muslims. However, if the discussion relates to Galileo, Newton, and Kepler, they consider them infidels. The father and mother of science is proof, and proof is neither Aristotle nor Galileo. The truth is where there is proof, and those who forbid science and knowledge in the belief that they are safeguarding the Islamic religion are really the enemies of that religion. The Islamic religion is the closest of religions to science and knowledge, and there is no incompatibility between science and knowledge and the foundation of the Islamic faith.

approaches for changing society and although sharing many of the same experiences, details of the programs of groups of Islamic modernists differed according to time and place.

An illuminating example of Islamic modernism lay in the heart of the Ottoman Empire. There, a diffuse group of intellectuals known as the Young Ottomans argued that the Tanzimat had failed—that while it strengthened the powers of the sultan, it did not stop the European penetration of the Ottoman Empire. What was needed, they argued, was a political system that could guarantee and inspire the loyalty of all citizens of the empire. Such a system should be based on authentic Islamic principles, particularly the principle of *shura*, government by consultation. The Young Ottoman message thus laid the ideological groundwork for the Ottoman constitution of 1876.

In other parts of the Ottoman Empire, Islamic modernism took different forms. One of the first important propagators of the Islamic modernist message was Jamal ad-Din al-Afghani (1838–97). As a teenager, al-Afghani had spent time in India during the Indian Mutiny of 1857. The mutiny, actually a revolt against British rule, was endorsed by Muslim leaders as *jihad* (holy war). From this experience, according to his biographers, al-Afghani took three ideas. First, he developed a fierce hatred of imperialism, particularly British imperialism. Second, because of the strength of the West, he believed that the battle against imperialism would be successful only if it involved all Muslims. Because he called for the unity of all Muslims against the West, al-Afghani has been considered the father of modern pan-Islamism. Finally, al-Afghani believed that to defeat imperialism, Muslims would have to adopt both the technology of the West and the method to obtain that technology— the scientific method. Like the moral reconstructionists and Wahhabis before him, he argued that Muslims had to stop following the dictates of the medieval scholastics, who were ignorant of the world around them, and instead apply reason to solve modern problems. Muslims must base their moral lives on the first generation of Muslims, the salaf-al-salih (*pious ancestors*). Because he took his inspiration from this period, the Islamic modernist movement which al-Afghani founded has been called the Salafiyya movement.

Al-Afghani's influence was spread by his students. His students, however, borrowed selectively from their teacher's ideas. For example, Muhammad 'Abduh (1849–1905), who would hold the highest judicial post in Egypt, Grand Mufti, and who also was rector of al-Azhar, borrowed al-Afghani's passion for reason and re-

The Transformation of the Middle East in the Nineteenth Century

1774	Treaty of Kuchuk Kainarji between Russia and the Ottoman Empire
1798	Invasion of Egypt by Napoleon Bonaparte
1805–49	Rule of Muhammad 'Ali in Egypt
1830	French conquest of Algeria
1831–41	Egyptian occupation of Syria
1839–76	Era of the Tanzimat reforms of the Ottoman Empire
1858	Ottoman Land Code grants peasants right to register in their own names the land they work
1826	End of the Ottoman Janissary Corps
1838–97	Jamal ad-Din al-Afghani, the father of modern pan-Islamism
1856–80	Forced settlement of Bedouin by Ottoman government
1866	Founding of Syrian Protestant College in Beirut, later renamed American University
1869	Opening of the Suez Canal
1872	Persian shah grants railroad, mineral, banking, and forestry concession to Julius de Reuter
1876	Ottoman constitution
1882	Declaration of bankruptcy by Egyptian government leads to British occupation of Egypt

form, ignoring his teacher's political radicalism. One of 'Abduh's students, the Syrian-born Rashid Rida (1865–1935), followed a different path. He, like al-Afghani, was a political activist who believed in pan-Islamism. He therefore encouraged the Ottoman sultan to stand at the head of the international Islamic community as caliph, the spiritual leader of the Muslims, and to lead a united Islam in the struggle against the West. Like 'Abduh, Rida also held high office, becoming the president of the Syrian General Congress in the immediate aftermath of the First World War.

The Revival of Arabic Culture

While Islamic modernists attempted to reinterpret Islamic symbols and values to conform to the aspirations of their social class and to modern conditions, other mid- to late-nineteenth-century intellectuals propounded secular modernist ideas. These intellectuals, mainly Syrian and Lebanese Christians from Beirut and Damascus, and Syrian and Lebanese émigrés in such far-flung places as Europe and the Americas, participated in a literary revival to resurrect the Arabic language and culture. This emerging stratum of intellectuals undertook language reform and often adopted Western literary forms to write Arabic-language poetry, short stories, and even, in one case, epics to be used as libretti for Arabic-language opera. Typical of these intellectuals were the activities of playwrights and theatrical producers in Egypt and Syria during the latter half of the nineteenth century. Writers such as Farah Antun and Khalil Matran translated into Arabic the works of Sophocles, Molière, and Shakespeare and produced them on stage in an effort to forge a new Arabic literary culture. Others disseminated their ideas and works through newspapers and literary salons that proliferated in Beirut, Cairo, and Istanbul. Both newspapers and literary salons became increasingly common when censorship was lifted in the wake of the Ottoman Constitutional Restoration of 1908.

It should come as no surprise that westernized Christians, members of the aforementioned rising Christian bourgeoisie, would prefer to adopt modernism in a secular rather than Islamic form. Many of these Christians were trained in Western mission schools, such as the American missionary-sponsored Syrian Protestant College in Beirut, now called the American University in Beirut, founded in 1866. These Arab Christians saw in an Arabic language and cultural rebirth a means of forging a common secular Arab identity with their Muslim neighbors.

Also participating in a cultural revival were young Arab Muslims who had graduated from one of the centers of higher education in Istanbul or one of the preparatory schools in the Arab provinces of the empire. Their abandonment of Islamic themes was in part rooted in their secular training and in the declining status and opportunities for those trained in the religious sciences in a post-Tanzimat Ottoman Empire—an Ottoman Empire in which education and judicial affairs had increasingly come under secular authority.

The economic and political changes that took place in the Middle East in the nineteenth century affected every aspect of life, from the creation of new social classes and the redefinition of urban space to the evolution of new intellectual and literary movements. These changes set the course for the twentieth century as well, for those Arabs, Turks, and Persians who came of age in the late nineteenth century would be the state builders in the aftermath of the First World War.

SUGGESTIONS FOR FURTHER READING

AFRICA IN THE ERA OF RISING EUROPEAN CAPITALISM

Philip D. Curtin, *The Atlantic Slave Trade: A Census* (Madison, WI: University of Wisconsin Press, 1969). A classic, seminal work on the question of how many people were sent to the New World as slaves.

Joseph C. Miller, *Way of Death: Merchant Capitalism and the Angolan Slave Trade, 1730–1830* (Madison, WI: University of Wisconsin Press, 1988). A magisterial study of the Angolan slave trade to Brazil.

* Paul E. Lovejoy, *Transformations in Slavery: A History of Slavery in Africa* (New York: Cambridge University Press, 1983). A comprehensive survey of the place slavery and the slave trade have held in African history.

* Patrick Manning, *Slavery and African Life: Occidental, Oriental, and African Slave Trades* (New York: Cambridge University Press, 1990). A recent summary of what is known about the trade and stimulating suggestions as to its impact on African societies.

Roger Anstey, *The Atlantic Slave Trade and British Abolition, 1760–1810* (London: Macmillan, 1975). An old but still useful analysis of the British abolitionist movement in the late eighteenth century.

* David Eltis, *Economic Growth and the Ending of the Transatlantic Slave Trade* (New York: Oxford University Press, 1987). A dense and closely argued analysis of the motives, costs, and effects of the British Abolitionist effort down to 1860.

* A. G. Hopkins, *An Economic History of West Africa* (London: Longman, 1973). A controversial but immensely stimulating assessment of changes in West African trade patterns.

* Leonard Thompson, *A History of South Africa* (New Haven, CT: Yale University Press, 1990). A comprehensive overview of South African history.

Richard Elphick, *Kraal and Castle: Khoikhoi and the Founding of White South Africa* (New Haven, CT: Yale University Press, 1977). A classic discussion of the downfall of Khoi society in the Cape of Good Hope.

* Richard Elphick and Hermann Giliomee, eds., *The Shaping of South African Society, 1652–1840* (Middletown, CT: Wesleyan University Press, 1989). A lengthy and highly detailed discussion of South Africa's development before 1840.

Gender and Culture

DEPARTURE FROM THE ISLE OF CYTHERA

Figure 1

The recognition of love and the pursuit of affection are standard subjects in the visual arts. They also offer insight into the codes of culture and the habits of society. Images of courtship and flirtation have remarkable similarities that span time and location, misleading us to think that love is expressed in a universal language. The characteristic actions—the exchange of glances, the holding of hands, the sharing of kisses—are easy to identify in a work of art. However, these seemingly natural gestures have ritual importance that varies from culture to culture. Similarly, there seem to be set roles for men and women. The active male pursues his love, while the passive female serves as the inspiration for his affection. Yet these are nuanced roles, given to subtle reversals. Interpreting the imagery of romantic love is simultaneously easy and complex, for it represents a message of culturally specific ideas in a deceptively familiar language.

Antoine Watteau's *Departure From the Isle of Cythera* (1717, France; Figure 1) idealizes romantic love. On the island of Venus, elegant couples meet, exchange their vows, and share their affections in an atmosphere of peace and pleasure. The men carry staffs and traveler's pouches, revealing that this journey is a pilgrimage, to pay tribute to the goddess of love. But, details of the painting reveal that this perfect moment will soon end. At the far right, is a statue of Venus, adorned with rose garlands. It takes the form of a "term," a

LOVERS ENTERTAINED BY MUSICIANS AND DANCERS

Figure 2

pedestal topped with a half-length statue, traditionally used to mark the termination of a road. The three couples in the foreground rise to join their companions for the journey home. Their gestures and responses tell a poignant story. In each case, the man leads the woman back to the mundane life and, in each case, she is reluctant to go. Watteau's golden vision is fleeting, revealing that the perfect moment of love always passes and it is always bittersweet.

The Persian miniature painting *Lovers Entertained by Musicians and Dancers*, attributed to Sultan-Muhammad (ca. 1533, Persia; Figure 2), offers an intimate glimpse of royal courtship. One of five illustrations in the Diwan of Hafiz manuscript, it is believed to depict the son of Shah Isma'l, a notable patron of the arts. He has spared no expense to please his graceful lover. Seated in the shade of a fine, brocade canopy, they watch lithe dancers play castanets and move to the rhythm of drums and tambourines. They are serenaded by singers and served tea by a silent servant. Courtly love is an elaborate affair, involving gifts and rituals, available only to the privileged few.

In another Persian painting, the roles of pursuer and pursued seem to be reversed. The beautiful women depicted in this miniature from the *Anthology of Iskandar Sultan* (1410, Persia; Figure 3), beckon to the men on the shore to join them in their frolic in the water. Their gestures are bold. Lifting their hands above the waves, they reach out to the objects of their desire. One man has taken the challenge, and embraces the woman as he joins her in the water. The other men keep to the shore, but are drawn to the irresistible call. These are not natural women, but sirens, and like Ulysses and his mariners, Iskandar and his men are enchanted by the unearthly song and risk their lives for a glance at a beautiful femme fatal.

ANTHOLOGY OF ISKANDAR SULTAN   *Figure 3*

THE SWING

Figure 4

The Swing, by Jean Honoré Fragonard (1766, France; Figure 4), portrays a lively and flirtatious young woman. She is the picture of energy and joy, delighting in the simple, vigorous activity. Her girlish hat, her flushed cheeks, and the way she kicks off her shoe suggest a childlike ingenuity. In actuality, the subtext of this picture is anything but innocent. The Baron de Saint-Julien commissioned this painting directly from the artist and dictated its particular content. He requested a portrait of his mistress, amusing herself on a swing. He instructed Fragonard to paint him as well, positioned "to observe the legs of this charming girl." The Baron even used the scene to make fun of the clergy. A bishop works the pulls of the swing in the background, unaware of the flirtation he facilitates. Fragonard inserted his own joke. The little statue of Cupid, based on a well-known work by Falconet, presses his finger to his lips, warning the viewer not to reveal the secret.

THE MIDDLE EAST AND THE WORLD SYSTEM

S. N. Fisher, *The Middle East: A History* (New York: Alfred A. Knopf, 1959). Good overview; a bit simplistic.

J. C. Hurewitz, *The Middle East and North Africa in World Politics*, Vol. 1: 1535–1914 (New Haven, CT: Yale University Press, 1975). Collection of source documents in diplomatic history.

Charles Issawi, *The Economic History of the Middle East 1800–1914* (London: Methuen, 1981). An interesting selection of source documents in economic history.

Peter Mansfield, *A History of the Middle East* (New York: Penguin Books, 1991). Similar to S. N. Fisher's book but more up-to-date.

M. E. Yapp, *The Making of the Modern Near East, 1792–1923* (London: Longman, 1987). The most detailed and probably the best of the general histories on this list.

THE TRANSFORMATION OF SOCIETY AND CULTURE IN THE MIDDLE EAST

M. S. Anderson, *The Eastern Question, 1774–1923* (New York: St. Martin's Press, 1966). Perhaps the best general survey of international diplomacy in the Middle East.

Niyazi Berkes, *The Development of Secularism in Turkey* (Montreal: McGill University Press, 1961). Account of defensive modernization in Turkey from the eighteenth century through the establishment of the republic.

L. Carl Brown, *International Politics and the Middle East* (Princeton, NJ: Princeton University Press, 1984). Traces the Near Eastern Question from its inception to the present day.

Moshe Ma'oz, *Ottoman Reform in Syria and Palestine* (Oxford: Oxford University Press, 1968). Study of the local effects of defensive modernization.

Afaf Lutfi as-Sayyid Marsot, *Egypt in the Reign of Mohammad 'Ali* (Cambridge: Cambridge University Press, 1984). Well-written narrative of life and policies of Egypt's first defensive modernizer.

Roger Owen, *The Middle East in the World Economy, 1800–1914* (London: Methuen, 1981). The standard work on political economy in the nineteenth century.

Sevket Pamuk, *The Ottoman Empire and European Capitalism, 1820–1913* (Cambridge: Cambridge University Press, 1987). Detailed study of the effects of integration and peripheralization on the Middle East.

W. R. Polk and R. L. Chambers, *The Beginnings of Modernization in the Middle East* (Chicago: University of Chicago Press, 1968). A strong collection of essays on the Tanzimat.

Hamid Algar, *Religion and State in Iran 1785–1906* (Berkeley, CA: University of California Press, 1969). Emphasizes the role of the Shi'i ulama in shaping modern Iran.

Gabriel Baer, *Fellah and Townsman in the Middle East* (London: Frank Cass and Co., 1982). Collection of essays, including superlative essays on urban history from the sixteenth to twentieth centuries, urban and rural revolts, and Turkish guilds.

Gabriel Baer, *Studies in the Social History of Modern Egypt* (Chicago: University of Chicago Press, 1969). Excellent collection on selected topics in Egyptian social history.

Edmond Bosworth and Carole Hillenbrand, *Qajar Iran* (Costa Mesa, CA: Mazda Publishers, 1992). Contains more than twenty essays, divided into sections on political and cultural history.

Nikki R. Keddie, *Scholars, Saints, and Sufis* (Berkeley, CA: University of California Press, 1972). Essays on the role of the ulama in Middle Eastern society.

Donald Quataert, *Social Disintegration and Popular Resistance in the Ottoman Empire, 1881–1908* (New York: New York University Press, 1983). Innovative study of social/political movements in the late Ottoman Empire.

Linda Schilcher, *Families in Politics* (Stuttgart: Franz Steiner Verlag Wiesbaden GMBH, 1985). Detailed account of elite family politics in Damascus, Syria, in the eighteenth and nineteenth centuries.

David Dean Commins, *Islamic Reform* (New York: Oxford University Press, 1990). Study of the intellectual origins of the Salafiyya movement in Syria.

Albert Hourani, *Arabic Thought in the Liberal Age, 1798–1939* (Cambridge: Cambridge University Press, 1962). Best introduction to modernist thinking in the Middle East.

Nikki R. Keddie, *An Islamic Response to Imperialism* (Berkeley, CA: University of California Press, 1968). Good introduction to the life and works of Jamal ad-Din al-Afghani, including his writings.

Bernard Lewis, *The Emergence of Modern Turkey* (London: Oxford University Press, 1961). Although the book covers all aspects of Ottoman/Turkish history, it is strongest when describing intellectual life.

Serif Mardin, *The Genesis of Young Ottoman Thought* (Princeton, NJ: Princeton University Press, 1962). A detailed study of the doctrines and members of the Young Ottoman movement.

John Obert Voll, *Islam: Continuity and Change in the Modern World* (Boulder, CO: Westview Press, 1982). Traces Islamic responses to economic, political, and social changes from the eighteenth through twentieth centuries.

* Indicates paperback edition available.

CHAPTER 20

The Balance of Power in Eighteenth-Century Europe

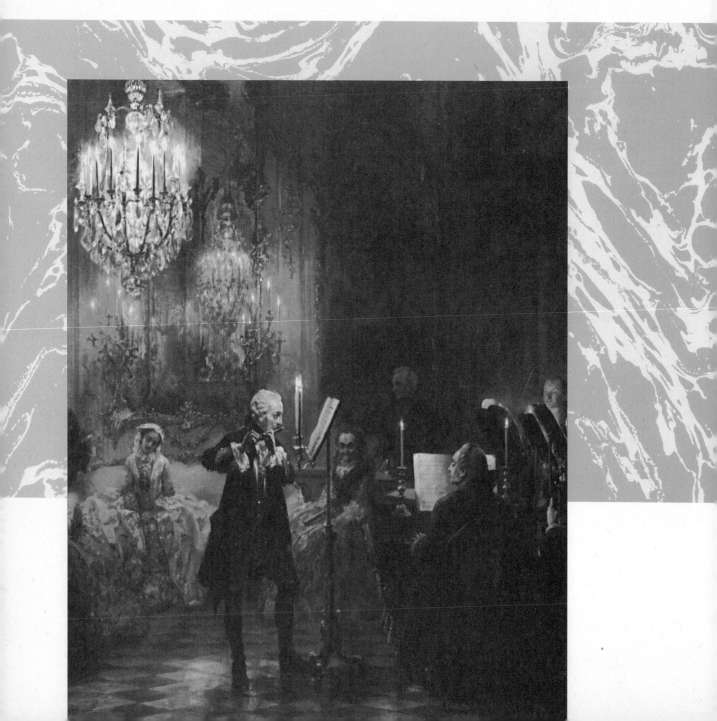

CALLING THE TUNE

Frederick the Great loved music. During his youth it was one of his private passions that so infuriated his father. Mathematics, political economy, modern languages, even dreaded French—these were the subjects that a future king of Prussia should learn. But music, never. Rather the boy should be at the hunt watching the dogs tear apart a stag, or on maneuvers with the Potsdam guards, a troop of soldiers all nearly seven feet tall. This was the regimen King Frederick William I prescribed for his son. It was no longer enough to reign over one's subjects; to be a successful monarch in the power politics of the eighteenth century, a king had to be a soldier.

But Frederick the Great loved music. He secretly collected all the books and manuscripts he could find on the subject, outspending his tiny allowance in the process. He had Johann Quantz (1697–1773), the greatest flutist of the day, placed on his staff to teach him and to conspire with him against his father. At night, while the old king drank himself into a stupor—an activity he warmly recommended to his son—Frederick powdered his hair, put on a jacket of the latest French style, and regaled his friends with his newest compositions. A lookout guarded the door in case the king wandered by unexpectedly. Once the musicians were almost discovered and Frederick's fine new jacket was tossed on the fire, but the flutes and musical scores remained safely hidden.

After he became king Frederick the Great could indulge his passion more openly. Yet he preferred to hold his concerts, usually small gatherings, at the Palace of San Souci, which he built in Potsdam. A special music room was designed for the king's use and he lavished attention on it. The great chandelier, lit by a circle of candles, illuminated the center of the room and highlighted the soloist. The entire palace reflected Frederick's personal taste. Unlike most great palaces of state, it was small, functional, and beautiful. Here Frederick could escape the mounting cares of governing one of the most powerful states in Europe by reading, corresponding with eminent French intellectuals, and playing the flute. In this picture, *Das Flötenkonzert* (the Flute Concert), Frederick is portrayed performing in his great music room. Before a small audience of courtiers and intimates, he plays to the accompaniment of cello, violins, and piano.

Frederick's talent was real enough. A British visitor to Sans Souci, who had little reason to flatter the king, reported: "I was much pleased and surprised with the neatness of his execution. His performance surpassed anything I had ever heard among the dilettanti or even professors." This judgment is reinforced when one studies the expressions of the three men in the left-hand corner of the painting. They are taking genuine pleasure in the music they are hearing (all the more genuine in that the king's back is to them). So, too, are the musicians who are accompanying the king. There is as much joy as concentration upon their faces.

Frederick's musical accomplishment was not unique among eighteenth-century monarchs. Joseph II of Austria was also a skilled flutist. But it was not so much music as accomplishment that was coming to be valued among the monarchs of the new European powers. Catherine the Great of Russia corresponded with philosophers; Frederick the Great brought the great French intellectual Voltaire (1698–1778) to his court—though they quickly took a dislike to each other. The acquisition of culture seemed to matter more and more as the century wore on. Museums, opera houses, great art collections were established all over the Continent. The Hermitage in Saint Petersburg was stocked with the works of Dutch and English masters. The British Museum was founded in London with the support of King George II, who deposited his great library there. Whether this veneer of culture did anything to lessen the brutality of warfare and power politics is a matter of opinion. But as a veneer it was as highly polished as the flute that Frederick the Great is so delicately pressing to his mouth.

Europe in 1714

Within a relatively short span of time at the beginning of the eighteenth century, two treaties brought about a considerable reorganization of the political geography of Europe. The Treaty of Utrecht (1713–14) created a new Europe in the west. The Treaty of Nystad (1721) created a new Europe in the east. Both agreements reflected the dynamics of change that had taken place over the previous century. The rise of France on the Continent and of Britain's colonial empire around the globe were facts that could no longer be ignored. The decline of Sweden and Poland and the emergence of Russia as a great power were the beginning of a long-term process that would continue to dominate European history.

All of this could be seen on a map of Europe in the early eighteenth century. France's absorption of Alsace and encroachments into Lorraine would be bones of contention between the French and Germans for two centuries and ultimately contributed to the outbreak of World Wars I and II. The political footballs of the Spanish Netherlands and Spanish Italy, now temporarily Austrian, continued to be kicked about until the nationalist movements of the nineteenth century gave birth to Belgium, Luxembourg, and a united Italy. The emergence of Brandenburg-Prussia on the north German coast and the gradual decline in the power of the Holy Roman Emperor were both vital to the process that created a unified Germany and a separate Austria. In the southeast, the slow but steady reconquest of the Balkans from Ottoman dominion restored the historic southern border of the Continent. The inexorable expansion of Russia was also already apparent.

Expansion in the West

Perhaps the most obvious transformation in the political geography of western Europe was the expansion of European power around the globe. In the Atlantic, Spain remained the largest colonial power. Through its viceroyalty system it controlled all of Mexico and Central America, the largest and most numerous of the Caribbean islands, North America from Colorado to California (as well as Florida), and most of South America. The other major colonial power in the region was Portugal, which shared dominion over the South American continent. In the Portuguese colony of Brazil, production of sugar, dyestuffs, timbers, and exotic commodities amply repaid the meager investment the Portuguese had made.

In North America the French and British shared the eastern half of the continent. The French controlled most of it. They had landed first in Canada and then slowly made their way down the Saint Lawrence River. New France, as their colonial empire was called, was a trading territory and it expanded along the greatest of the waterways, the Great Lakes, and the Ohio, Missouri, and Mississippi rivers. French settlements had sprung up as far south as the Gulf of Mexico. France also claimed the territory of Louisiana, named for Louis XIV, which stretched from New Orleans to Montana. The British settlements were all coastal, stretching from

Europe, ca. 1714

Maine to Georgia on the Atlantic seaboard. Unlike the French, the British settled their territory and were only interested in expansion when their population, which was doubling every twenty-five years, outgrew its resources. By the early eighteenth century the ports of Boston, New York, Philadelphia, and Charleston were thriving commercial centers.

Europeans managed their eastern colonial territories differently than they did those in the Atlantic. Initially the Portuguese and the Dutch had been satisfied with establishing trading factories—coastal fortresses in Africa and Asia that could be used as warehouses and defended against attack. But in the seventeenth century, the European states began to take control of vital ports and lucrative islands. Here the Dutch were the acknowledged leaders, replacing the Portuguese who had begun the process at the end of the sixteenth cen-

tury. Holland held by force or in conjunction with local leaders all the Spice Islands in the Pacific. The Dutch also occupied both sides of the Malay Peninsula and nearly all the coastal areas of the islands in the Java Sea. Dutch control of Ceylon was strategically important for its Indian trade. Compared to the Dutch Republic, all other European states had only a minor territorial presence in the East, with the exception of Spain, which still controlled the Philippines. The British had limited their eastern outposts to trading establishments. Through these they maintained a significant presence in India. During the eighteenth century the British began to colonize the Indian subcontinent directly.

Imperial expansion was the most obvious change in the geopolitical boundaries of Europe, but it was not the only one. A brief tour of the western states after the Treaty of Utrecht reveals some others. In 1707 England

European Colonial Powers in America

Since the accession of Louis XIV, France had plucked small pieces from the territories that had been contested between France and Spain since the fifteenth century. Between French aggression and the Dutch occupation of such important places as Ghent and Ypres, the ability of the southern provinces to maintain a separate identity suffered a grave blow. But not as grave as that formalized at Utrecht, when sovereignty over this territory was assigned to Austria, ostensibly because the emperor was a Habsburg, but really because the balance of power in western Europe demanded it.

To the south lay France, still the most powerful nation in Europe despite its losses in the War of the Spanish Succession. By 1714 Louis XIV had broken forever the danger of Spanish encirclement that had been the worry of every French king since Francis I in the early sixteenth century. Louis had methodically set out to occupy those territories that were strategically necessary to defend his state from invasion by the Dutch, the Spanish, the British, or the emperor. In the northeast he absorbed the Duchy of Bar. In the north he absorbed a healthy portion of Flanders including Dunkirk on the English Channel and the prosperous clothing town of Lille. He pushed the eastern boundary of his state to the Rhine by overrunning Alsace and parts of Lorraine. Strasbourg remained French under the settlement of 1714, testimony to the fact that it was possible to hold France only at the western banks of the Rhine. Finally, farther to the south Louis had won and held Franche-Comté, once the center of Burgundy. In 1714 France was larger, stronger, and better able to defend its borders than ever before. It was also exhausted.

and Scotland formally joined together to form Great Britain. In addition to its eastern and western colonies, Britain had also gained control of Gibraltar at the foot of Spain and the island of Minorca in the Mediterranean. Both territories were strategically important to British commerce.

Across the English Channel were the Low Countries, now permanently divided between the United Provinces in the north, led by Holland, and those provinces in the south that had remained loyal to the Spanish crown in the sixteenth century. By 1714 the golden age of the Dutch was over. Though the Dutch continued as a colonial and maritime power, their small numbers and meager natural resources eventually outweighed their abilities as innovators and managers. They lost their eastern empire to Britain, their predominance in European trade to France. What the Dutch gained at Utrecht was the right to maintain their forces in the towns along the border between France and the old Spanish Netherlands. The Spanish Netherlands, the original Burgundian inheritance, were now being slowly dismembered.

European Colonial Powers in the East Indies

As France expanded, so Spain contracted. Less than two centuries earlier a Spanish king had dreamed of being monarch over all of Europe. Now a French Bourbon sat on the great Habsburg throne and Spain was slowly being sliced to pieces. By 1714 the European territories of the Spanish empire had been reduced to Iberia itself. But the loss of its European empire was to prove a blessing in disguise for Spain, which now entered upon a new and unexpected phase of growth and influence.

The center of Europe remained occupied by the agglomeration of cities, bishoprics, principalities, and small states known collectively as the Holy Roman Empire, but now more accurately called the German empire. There were still over three hundred separate jurisdictions, most of them vulnerable to preying neighbors such as Louis XIV. Bavaria in the south, and Saxony, Brandenburg, and Hanover in the north were among the most important of the large states with the added twist that Hanover was now ruled by the king of Great Britain. The emperor, now officially prohibited from interference in the internal administration of the large states, was less dominant in German affairs than he had been before the Thirty Years' War.

Increasingly, Habsburg power centered on Austria, Bohemia, and Hungary. This was especially true during the reign of Leopold I (1655–1705). Withstanding threats on all sides, Leopold was able to expand his state both to the west and to the south and to bring Austria into the ranks of the great European powers. Such an outcome could hardly have been foreseen in the middle of the seventeenth century, when the Ottomans made their last great thrust into the interior of Europe. In 1683 the Ottomans besieged Vienna itself, and only the arrival of seventy thousand Polish-led troops saved it from falling. But from that time forward, Austrian forces scored stunning victories. By 1699 almost all of Hungary had been retaken by Austria; with the Treaty of Passarowitz in 1718 Austria gained the rest of Hungary and Serbia. When the Treaty of Utrecht granted Austria control of the Netherlands, Lombardy, and Naples, the Austrian Habsburgs became rulers of a European empire.

Austria's Italian possessions included the vast southern territories of Naples (including Sicily after 1720) and the rich industrial area surrounding Milan in the north. Alongside the Austrian territories a number of independent city-states continued to flourish on the Italian peninsula. Both Venice and Genoa remained prosperous and independent. The Grand Duchy of Tuscany, with its great city of Florence, and the Papal States had expanded over the course of the seventeenth century, absorbing their smaller neighbors until both were

Composite view of the siege of Vienna, 1683, when the invading Turks were repelled in this, their last great advance in Europe.

large consolidated territories. To the west of the Italian states was the Duchy of Savoy. Savoy had pursued a flexible foreign policy, pleasing whichever of its powerful neighbors was most dangerous and accepting the patronage of whichever seemed most friendly. Client of the Spanish, French, and Austrians, Savoy grew and prospered. After the War of the Spanish Succession Savoy was counted among the victors, though it fought on both sides. Duke Victor Amadeus II became a king when he received the island of Sicily, which he exchanged with Austria for Sardinia in 1720.

Thus the Treaty of Utrecht signaled a new configuration of political power. England, France, Prussia, and Austria were the ascending powers, Holland and Spain the declining ones. Italy and the southern Netherlands were the bones over which the biggest dogs fought, sometimes playfully, sometimes in deadly earnest.

Realignment in the East

This was western Europe in 1714. In the east, it was the Treaty of Nystad (1721) ending the Great Northern War (1700–21) that fixed the political geography. Here the emerging powers were Russia and Prussia, those in decline were Sweden and Poland. The critical factor in eastern European politics remained access to the sea. Outlets to the Baltic Sea in the north and the Black Sea in the south were the vital lifeline for this part of the Continent, and control of these outlets was the central motivation for the long years of war fought among the eastern states.

The expansion of Russia is one of the central events in European history, and the early eighteenth century is its pivotal period. During the long years of social and economic recovery after the death of Ivan the Terrible in 1584, Russia had been easy prey for its powerful neighbors Sweden and Poland. Through a series of wars and political pacts, Russia had ceded most of its Baltic territories to Sweden while it had relinquished land and population in the west to Poland. Peter the Great (1682–1725) set out to reclaim what had been lost. As a result of the Great Northern War, Russia regained the eastern Baltic coastline from the southeastern end of Finland to Riga in the west. Russia now controlled all of the vital Baltic ports in the east. Peter built a new capital on the Gulf of Finland. In this new city, named Saint Petersburg, he laid the foundation for the Russian navy.

What Russia gained, Sweden lost. At the height of its power in the middle of the seventeenth century, Sweden had dominated the Baltic. It occupied all of Finland, controlled the important eastern coast of Norway, and had gained a foothold in Germany. Most importantly, Sweden had captured the southern tip of its own peninsula from the Danes, making the mainland portion of its state whole. But Sweden's century-long rise to power was followed by a rapid period of decline. The small and relatively poor population could not long succeed in governing an empire. The Great Northern War ended whatever pretensions Sweden had left. It lost all of its German territories: those on the North Sea went to Hanover, those on the Baltic to Prussia. Livonia, Estonia, and the eastern provinces were returned to Russia, but Sweden was able to hold on to its vital gains from the Danes. Sweden had built its own window to the west at Göteborg on the North Sea, and from there it could carry on a direct trade with Britain and the Netherlands.

Since the end of the Thirty Years' War, Brandenburg-Prussia had been steadily growing. A strange configuration of a state with its geographical heart in Brandenburg, it was one of the domains of the Holy Roman Empire. From the capital at Berlin the princes of Brandenburg directed the accumulation of small neighboring German lands: Magdeburg and Halle to the southwest, a piece of Pomerania to the northeast. But while Brandenburg expanded in every direction, it could do little to join itself to the kingdom of Prussia. A huge swath of Poland, cutting between the two, stood in the way. This division of Brandenburg-Prussia was its most important geopolitical feature. In the eighteenth century, the determination to expand to the east dominated Prussian history.

This aim meant, of course, eventual conflict with Poland. Despite its political weakness, Poland was one of the largest landmasses in Europe. On its southern

This portrait of Peter the Great by his court painter Louis Caravaque pays homage to Peter's intense interest in naval matters. Ships flying English, Dutch, Danish, and Russian flags prepare for maneuvers under his command.

border it held back Ottoman expansion, on its eastern border it held back the Russians. Its great port of Gdansk on the Baltic dominated the grain and timber trade with northern Europe as well as local Baltic commerce between Scandinavia and the mainland. Sweden and Russia, the eastern powers, controlled Poland politically, helping nominate its elected kings and ensuring that its decentralized form of aristocratic government kept Poland weak. Poland served as a useful counterweight in the balance of power in eastern Europe. Except for its Baltic territories, Poland was not yet seen as a great prize to be fought over. But by the beginning of the eighteenth century it was a helpless giant ready to be toppled.

Thus a potent Prussia and Russia and a prostrate Poland characterized the realignment of the eastern portion of Europe. Most importantly, the separation between east and west was narrowing. Prussia's German orientation and the westernization of Russia led to closer ties with the west.

The Rise of Russia

At the beginning of the eighteenth century, Russia was scarcely known about or cared about in the rest of Europe. Peter the Great changed all that. The Treaty of Nystad had confirmed the magnitude of his victory over the Swedes in the Great Northern War, both in territory and prestige. The change created consternation in the courts of Europe. Just a quarter century before, no one had cared very much what the king of Russia called himself. In fact, little was known for sure about the Russian ruler or his state. What little mercantile contact there was between Russia and the west was conducted entirely by westerners. Foreign merchants were allowed to live in Moscow in a separate ghetto called "Germantown." Their letters were the main source of western knowledge about the vast Muscovite empire.

Peter the Great brought Europe to Russia and Russia to Europe. Twice he visited Europe to discover the secrets of western prosperity and might. He arranged marriages between the closest heirs to his throne, including his son Alexis, and the sons and daughters of German princes and dukes. By 1721 he had established twenty-one separate foreign embassies. The sons of the Russian gentry and nobility were sent west—sometimes forcibly—to further their education and to learn to adapt to western outlooks. Peter recruited Europeans to fill the most important skilled positions in the state: foreign engineers and gunners to serve in the army; foreign architects to build the new capital at Saint Petersburg; foreign scholars to head the new state schools; foreign administrators to oversee the new departments of state. Peter borrowed freely and adapted sensibly. If necessary, he would drag his countrymen kicking and screaming into the modern world.

By 1721 Russia was recognized all over Europe as an emerging power. The military defeat of the seemingly invincible Swedes had made monarchs from Louis XIV to William III sit up and take notice. And the great Russian victory over Sweden at Poltava in 1709 was no fluke. Peter's forces followed it up with several strong campaigns which proved that Russia could organize, equip, finance, and train an up-to-date military force. Moreover, Peter's absorption of Sweden's Baltic territories made Russia a power in the north. The Russian navy, built mostly by foreigners, was now capable of protecting Russian interests and defending important ports such as Riga and Saint Petersburg. Even the Dutch, who had long plotted the decline of Swedish

might, now became nervous. Thus it was unsettling that Peter wished to be recognized as emperor.

The Reforms of Peter the Great

Peter the Great was not the first Russian tsar to attempt to borrow from western developments. The process had been under way for decades. The opening of the northern port of Archangel in 1584 led to direct contact with British and Dutch traders, who brought with them new ideas and useful products, which were adapted to Russian needs and conditions. Russia was a vast state and Europe was only one of its neighbors. Its religion had come from Byzantium rather than Rome, thus giving Russian Christianity an eastern flavor. Its Asian territories mixed the influence of Mongols and Ottomans; its southern borders met Tartars and Cossacks. While most European states were racially and ethnically homogeneous, Russia was a loose confederation of diverse peoples. Yet it was the western states that posed the greatest threat to Russia in the seventeenth century, and it was to the west that Peter, like his father before him, turned his attention.

It would be wrong to see Peter's westernizing innovation as a systematic program. More to the point, nearly all of his reforms—economic, educational, administrative, social, military—were done to enhance military efficiency rather than civil progress. In his thirty years of active rule there was only one year—1724—during which he was not at war. Vital reforms like the poll tax (1724), which changed the basis of taxation from the household to the individual adult male, had enormous social consequences. The new policy of taxing individuals officially erased whole social classes. A strict census taken (and retaken) to inhibit tax evasion became the basis for further governmental encroachments on the tsar's subjects. Yet the poll tax was not designed for any of these purposes. It was instituted to increase tax revenue for war. Similarly, the establishment of compulsory, lifetime military service required of the landowning classes (the nobility and gentry) was undertaken to provide officers and state servants for an expanding military machine.

Yet if Peter's reforms were not systematic and developed from little other than military necessity, nevertheless they constituted a fundamental transformation in the life of all Russian people. The creation of a gigantic standing army and an entirely new navy meant conscription of the Russian peasantry on a grand scale. In a ten-year period of the Great Northern War the army absorbed 330,000 conscripts, most of whom never returned to their homes. Military service was not confined to the peasantry. Traditionally, the rural gentry raised and equipped the local conscript forces and gave them what training they could. Most gentry lived on estates that had been granted to them along with the resident peasants as a reward for their military contributions. Peter the Great intensified the obligations of the gentry. Not only were they to serve the state for life, but they were to accompany their regiments to the field and lead them in battle. When too old for active military service, they were to perform administrative service in the new departments of state.

The expansion of military forces necessitated an expansion of military administration as well. Peter's first innovation was the creation of the Senate, a group of nine senior administrators who were to oversee all aspects of military and civil government. The Senate became a permanent institution of government led by an entirely new official, the Procurator-General, who presided over its sessions and could propose legislation as well as oversee administration. From the Senate emanated five hundred officials known as the fiscals, who traveled throughout the state looking for irregularities in tax assessment and collection. They quickly developed into a hated and feared internal police force.

Peter's efforts to reorganize his government went a step further in 1722, when he issued the Table of Ranks. This was an official hierarchy of the state that established the social position or rank of individuals. It was divided into three categories—military service, civil service, and owners of landed estates. Each category contained fourteen ranks, and it was decreed that every person who entered the hierarchy did so at the bottom and worked his way up. The creation of the Table of Ranks was significant in a number of ways. It demonstrated Peter's continued commitment to merit as a criterion for advancement. This standard had been shown in the military, where officers were promoted on the basis of service and experience rather than birth or background. Equally important was Peter's decision to make the military service the highest of the three categories. This reversed the centuries-old position of the landed aristocracy and the military service class. Though the old nobility also served in the military and continued to dominate state service, the Table of Ranks opened the way for the infusion of new elements into the Russian elite.

Many of those who were able to advance in the Table of Ranks did so through attendance at the new institutions of higher learning that Peter founded. His initial

Peter the Great was a precocious child. He began his education at the age of two, using a book similar to the illustrated Russian speller whose "Z" page is seen above.

educational establishments were created to further the military might of the state. The colleges of Mathematics, Engineering, and Artillery, which became the training grounds for his army officers, were all founded during the Great Northern War. But Peter was interested in liberal education as well. He had scores of western books translated into Russian. He had a press established in Moscow to print original works, including the first Russian newspaper. He decreed that a new, more westernized alphabet replace that used by the Russian Orthodox church and that books be written in the language that the people spoke rather than in the formal literary language of religious writers. He also introduced Arabic numerals into official accounting records.

Peter's reforms of government and society were matched by his efforts to energize the economy. No state in Europe had as many natural resources as did

Russia, yet manufacturing barely existed there. As with everything else he did, Peter took a direct hand in establishing factories for the production of textiles, glass, leather, and most importantly, iron and copper. The state directly owned about half of these establishments, most of them on a larger scale than any known in the west. By 1726 more than half of all Russian exports were manufactured goods and Russia had become the largest producer of iron and copper in the world.

In all of these ways and more, Peter the Great transformed Russia. But the changes Peter wrought did not come without cost. The traditions of centuries were not easily broken. Intrigue against Peter led first to confrontation with the old military elite and later to conflict with his only son, Alexis. It remains unclear if the plot with which Alexis was connected actually existed or was a figment of Peter's imagination, but it is abundantly clear that Alexis's death from torture plunged the state into a succession crisis in 1725. Finally, the great costs of westernization were paid by the masses of people who benefited little from the improvement in Russia's international standing or from the social and economic changes that affected the elites.

Life in Rural Russia

At the beginning of the eighteenth century nearly 97 percent of the Russian people lived on the land and practiced agriculture. Farming techniques and agrarian lifestyles had changed little for centuries. Most of the country's soil was poor. Harsh climate and low yields characterized Russian agriculture. Thirty-four of the one hundred Russian harvests during the eighteenth century can be termed poor or disastrous, yet throughout the century state taxation was making larger and larger demands upon the peasantry. During Peter's reign alone, direct taxation increased by 500 percent.

The theory of the Russian state was one of service, and the role of Russian peasants was to serve their master. Beginning in the mid-seventeenth century, the peasantry had undergone a change in status. The law code of 1649 formalized a process that had been under way for over a century whereby peasants were turned into the property of their landlords. During the next century laws curtailed the ability of peasants to move freely from one place to another, eliminated their right to hold private property, and abolished their freedom to petition the tsar against their masters. At the same time that landlords increased their hold over peasants, the state increased its hold over landlords. They were made responsible for the payment of taxes owed by their peasants and for the military service due from them. By the middle of the eighteenth century over half of all peasants—6.7 million adult males by 1782—had thus become serfs, the property of their masters, without any significant rights or legal protection.

Private landlords reckoned their wealth in the number of serfs they owned. But in fact most owned only a small number, fewer than fifty in the middle of the eighteenth century. This resulted from the common practice whereby a father divided his estate among all of his surviving sons. Most gentry were small landholders, constantly in debt and rarely able to meet their financial and service obligations to the state. This life of poverty at the top was, of course, magnified at the bottom. The vast majority of serfs lived in small villages where they divided up their meager surplus to pay their taxes and drew lots to see who would be sent for military service. When the debts of their lords became too heavy, it was the serfs who were foreclosed upon.

If serfs made up the bottom half of the Russian peasantry, there were few advantages to being in the top half among the state peasants. State peasants lived on lands owned by the monarchy itself. Like the serfs, they were subject to the needs of the state for soldiers and workers. The use of forced labor was a feature of each of Peter's grandiose projects. Saint Petersburg was built by the backbreaking labor of peasant conscripts. From 1709, when the project began, perhaps as many as 40,000 laborers a year were forced to work on the various sites. The unhealthy conditions of the swampy environment from which the new capital rose claimed the lives of thousands of these workers, as did the appalling conditions of overwork and undernourishment in which they lived.

Many Russian peasants developed a philosophy of submission and a rich folk culture that valued a stubborn determination to endure. For those who would no longer bend to the knout—the heavy leather whip that was the omnipresent enforcer of obedience—there was only flight or rebellion. Hundreds of thousands of serfs fled to state-owned lands in hope of escaping the cruelties of individual landlords. Although severe penalties were imposed for aiding runaway serfs, in fact most state overseers and many private landlords encouraged runaways to settle on their lands. In their social and economic conditions, eighteenth-century Russian peasants were hardly distinguishable from medieval European serfs.

The Enlightened Empress Catherine

Of all the legacies of Peter the Great, perhaps the one of most immediate consequence was that government could go on without him. During the next thirty-seven years, six tsars ruled Russia, "three women, a boy of twelve, an infant, and a mental weakling," as one commentator acidly observed. More to the point, each succession was contested, as there were no direct male heirs to the throne in this period. Nevertheless, despite turmoil at the top, government continued to function smoothly and Peter's territorial conquests were largely maintained. Russia also experienced a remarkable increase in numbers during this period. Between 1725 and 1762 the population increased from 13 to 19 million, a jump of nearly one-third in a single generation. This explosion of people dramatically increased the wealth of the landholding class, who reckoned their status by the number of serfs they owned.

The expansion of the economic resources of the nobility was matched by a rise in legal status and political power. This was the period sarcastically dubbed "the emancipation of the nobility," a phrase that captures not only the irony of the growing gap between rich and poor but also the contrast between the social structures of Russia and those of western Europe. In return for their privileges and status, Peter the Great extended the duties the landowning classes owed to the state. By granting unique rights, like the ownership of serfs, to the descendants of the old military service class, Peter had forged a Russian nobility. Lifetime service, however, was the price of nobility.

In order to gain and hold the throne, each succeeding tsar had to make concessions to the nobility to gain their loyalty. At first it was a few simple adjustments. The sons of wealthy landowners who completed a course of education at one of the state academies were allowed to enter the Table of Ranks in the middle of the hierarchy rather than at the bottom. Then life service was commuted to a term of twenty-five years, still a long time in a world of short lives and sudden deaths. But these concessions were not enough.

Twenty-five years of service did not solve the problem of estate management, especially as the tasks of management grew along with the population of serfs. Thus the next capitulation was that a single son could remain on the estate and escape service altogether. The births of younger sons were concealed; owners of multiple estates claimed the exemption of one son for each. Most decisively, the talented remained at home to serve the family while the wastrels were sent to serve the

state. Finally in 1762, the obligation for state service by the nobility was abolished entirely.

The abolition of compulsory service was not the same as the abolition of service itself. In fact the end of compulsory service enabled Catherine II, the Great (1762–96), to enact some of the most important reforms of her reign. (See Special Feature, "Catherine Before She Was Great," pp. 604–605.) At first, Catherine's accession seemed nothing more than a continuation of monarchical instability—her first two acts were to have her husband Peter III murdered and to lower the salt tax. Each bought her a measure of security.

Catherine was a dynamic personality who alternately captivated and terrified those with whom she came into contact. Her policies were as complex as her personality, influenced on the one hand by the new French ideas of social justice and the nobility of the human race and on the other by the traditional Russian ideas of absolute rule over an enserfed and subhuman population. Catherine handled these contrasting dimensions of her rule masterfully, gaining abroad the reputation as the most enlightened of European monarchs and at home the sincere devotion of her people.

The most important event in the early years of Catherine's reign was the establishment of a legislative commission to review the laws of Russia. Catherine herself wrote the *Instruction* (1767) by which the elected commissioners were to operate. She borrowed her theory of law from the French jurist Baron de Montesquieu (1689–1755) and her theory of punishment from the Italian reformer Cesare Beccaria (1738–94). Among other things, Catherine advocated the abolition of capital punishment, torture, serf auctions, and the breakup of serf families by sale. Few of these radical reforms were ever put into practice.

But in 1775 Catherine did restructure local government. Russia was divided into fifty provincial districts, each with a population of between 300,000 and 400,000 inhabitants. Each district was to be governed by both a central official and elected local noblemen. This reform was modeled upon the English system of justices of the peace. Previous local reforms had failed because of the absence of a resident local nobility. The abolition of compulsory service finally made possible the establishment of local institutions. In 1785, Catherine issued the Charter of the Nobility, a formal statement of the rights and privileges of the noble class. The Charter incorporated all the gains the nobility had made since the death of Peter the Great, but it also instituted the requirements for local service that had been the basis of Catherine's reforms. District councils with the

MEMOIRS OF THE EARLY YEARS OF CATHERINE THE GREAT

■ *Catherine the Great has left a fascinating account of her early years that is in sharp contrast to her reputation for ruthlessness as a ruler.*

My father, whom I saw very seldom, considered me to be an angel, my mother did not bother much about me. She had had, eighteen months after my birth, a son whom she passionately loved, whereas I was merely tolerated and often repulsed with violence and temper, not always with justice. I was aware of all this, but not always able to understand what I really felt about it.

At the age of seven I was suddenly seized with a violent cough. It was the custom that we should kneel every night and every morning to say our prayers. One night as I knelt and prayed I began to cough so violently that the strain caused me to fall on my left side, and I had such sharp pains in my chest that they almost took my breath away.

Finally, after much suffering, I was well enough to get up and it was discovered, as they started to put on my clothes, that I had in the meantime assumed the shape of the letter Z; my right shoulder was much higher than the left, the backbone running in zigzag and the left side falling in.

right to petition directly to the tsar became the centerpiece of Russian provincial government.

In order to train the local nobility for government service, Catherine introduced educational reforms. Peter had established military schools for the nobility and had staffed them with foreigners. The University of Moscow had been founded in 1755, and its faculty too was dominated by European emigrants. Catherine saw the need to broaden the educational system. Borrowing from the Austrian system, she established provincial elementary schools to train the sons and daughters of the local nobility. To staff these, Catherine created teachers' colleges so that the state would have its own educators. Though the program called for the equal educationof women, except in Saint Petersburg and Moscow few women attended either elementary or high schools.

Catherine's reforms did little to enhance the lives of the vast majority of her people. Though she often spoke in the terms of the French philosophers who saw the enserfment of fellow humans as a blot on civilization, Catherine took no effective action either to end serfdom or to soften its rigors. In fact, by grants of state land Catherine gave away 800,000 state peasants, who became serfs. So, too, did millions of Poles who became her subjects after the partition of Poland in 1793 and 1795.

The most significant uprising of the century, Pugachev's revolt (1773–75), took place during Catherine's reign. Emelyan Pugachev (1726–75) was a Cossack who in his youth had been a military adventurer.

Chained but undaunted, Emelyan Pugachev awaits punishment for leading a peasant rebellion in the southern Urals.

Portrait of Catherine the Great.

Catherine Before She Was Great

Catherine the Great wasn't always called the Empress of all the Russias. In fact, she wasn't always called Catherine. Sophie of Anhalt-Zerbst was the daughter of a petty German prince whose estates were too poor to provide for his family. He hired himself out as a military officer to the kings of Prussia and became governor of the dreary Baltic port of Stettin. Here Sophie passed her childhood.

By far the most significant event of Sophie's childhood was the sudden sickness that overtook her at the age of seven. She was seized by coughing, fevers, and fits that incapacitated her for weeks. For a time her life was in danger. Then one morning she awoke without fever and without the racking cough that had seared through her body. But in its place had come a physical change. Weeks of lying on her side had deformed her physique: "I had assumed the shape of a letter Z," she later recalled. Doctors were sought for advice, but none could help until at last a veterinarian who practiced on the limbs of horses and cows built a body frame for Sophie that was designed to reshape her deformity. She wore this for four years until she regained her former posture.

Sophie's father was a strict Lutheran who prescribed a regimen for the education of his children that was to be precisely followed. At the age of seven, just after her recovery, tutors were brought in to teach Sophie history and geography, and a Lutheran minister was deputed to train her in religion. Though Sophie did not have a close relationship with her mother—in later years they quarreled incessantly—it was her mother who showed her the world outside Stettin. Joanna of Holstein-Gottorp had grown up surrounded by courtly pomp rather than military rigor, and every year she visited her relations in Brunswick. When Sophie began to accompany her mother on these trips, they became for her the principal means to escape the boredom of life in Stettin. On one visit to Berlin she was introduced to Frederick William I, king of Prussia. These trips to Brunswick and Berlin opened Sophie's eyes to the possibility of a life different than the one she had expected, the possibility of life with one of the crown princes of Europe.

As it happened, Sophie had little need to wish. By a strange twist of fate, another of her mother's innumerable cousins had recently been declared heir to the throne of Russia. This was Peter, soon to be duke of Holstein-Gottorp and ultimately to be Peter III of Russia. Empress Elizabeth of Russia was childless and Peter was her nearest relative. She determined to have him married to an eligible German princess, and after much casting about, the choice fell on Sophie. In 1744 Sophie was summoned to Russia.

Princely marriages were matters of international diplomacy. In the case of Russia, Frederick the Great of Prussia took more than a neighborly interest. It was he who pushed the claims of a daughter of one of his own military dependents and it was he who enlisted Joanna to become an agent of Prussia at the Russian court. No one asked Sophie what she thought, since her opinion hardly mattered.

The journey to Russia was a trip that Sophie would never forget. On the journey to the east, carriages gave way to sleighs, and her heavy cloth clothing to sable. Sophie and Joanna huddled together for warmth, covering their faces and hands from the bitter arctic winds. It took nearly four weeks to reach Saint Petersburg, and when they arrived they were informed that they must hurry to join the royal court at

Moscow. There they were received with unusual warmth as it was the sixteenth birthday of the new heir to the throne and all of Russian society was eager to see his bride-to-be.

Sophie's earliest meetings with her fiancé were not entirely satisfactory. In a strange land she might have expected strange customs, but Peter was a German like herself. Thus she was unprepared for their first interview, in which Peter professed his passionate love for one of the ladies of the court. Sophie was only fifteen and, by her own account at least, innocent in sexual matters. Peter's frank confession, which was accompanied by assurances that he would marry Sophie anyhow, caused her as much confusion as it did anger and resentment. She resolved to keep her own counsel and to attempt to please the empress if not the heir. Sophie spent the days before her marriage learning both the Russian language and the Eastern Orthodox religion. She would have to convert to the old faith before she could be betrothed. As part of her conversion, she had to take a Russian name and thus she came to be called Catherine. Whether her change of religion was sincere or not, it was required. Sophie was shrewd enough to realize the importance of the Church, and she won many admirers at court when, after being taken ill, she asked for an Ortho-

dox priest rather than a Lutheran minister or a doctor.

Sophie's marriage took place in 1745. By then she knew that she was alone in the world. She had fought bitterly with her mother, who had become a political liability after she bungled her role as an agent for Frederick the Great. Sophie shared nothing with her new husband—including the marriage bed. The household set up for her was composed entirely of spies for the empress and even her correspondence was monitored. She spent the next fifteen years supplementing the education that she had received as a child. She read everything that she could get. She devoured the classics, especially history and philosophy, and for the first time became acquainted with the works of the new European writers whose reputations had reached as far as Russia.

She also developed a passion for the handsome guardsmen who inhabited the palace. Perhaps in revenge for her husband's conduct, perhaps in return for his neglect, she took the first of more than twenty lovers. When she became pregnant in 1754, it was almost certainly not Peter's child. Eight years later the private life of Sophie of Anhalt-Zerbst ended. Then Empress Elizabeth died, the half-mad Peter III acceded to the throne, and Sophie, now known to the world as Catherine, began her remarkable public career.

Disappointed in his career, he made his way to the Ural mountains, where he recruited Asian tribesmen and laborers forced to work in the mines. By promising freedom and land ownership, he drew peasants to his cause. In 1773 Pugachev declared himself to be Tsar Peter III, the murdered husband of Catherine II. He began with small raiding parties against local landlords and military outposts and soon had gained the allegiance of tens of thousands of peasants. In 1774, with an army of nearly twenty thousand, Pugachev took the city of Kazan and threatened to advance on Moscow. It was another year before state forces could effectively control the rebellion. Finally, Pugachev was betrayed by his own followers and sent to Moscow, where he was executed.

During the reigns of Peter and Catherine the Great, Russia was transformed into an international power. Saint Petersburg, a window to the west, was a capital worthy of a potent monarch, and during the course of the eighteenth century it attracted many of Europe's leading luminaries. At court French was spoken, the latest fashions were worn, and the newest ideas for economic and educational reform were aired. The Russian nobility mingled comfortably with its European counterparts, while the military service class developed into bureaucrats and administrators. But if life glittered at court, it remained the same dull regimen in the country. Millions of peasants were owned either by the state or by private landlords, and their quality of life was no different at the end of the campaign of westernization than it had been at the beginning.

The Two Germanies

The Thirty Years' War, which ended in 1648, initiated a profound transformation of the Holy Roman Empire. Warfare had devastated imperial territory. It was decades before the rich imperial lands recovered, and then the political consequences of the war had taken effect. There were now two empires, a German and an Austrian, though both were ruled by the same person. In the German territories, whether Catholic or Protestant, the Holy Roman Emperor was more a constitutional monarch than the absolute ruler he was in Austria. The larger states like Saxony, Bavaria, and Hanover made their own political alliances despite the jurisdictional control that the emperor claimed to exercise. Most decisively, so did Brandenburg-Prussia. By the beginning of the eigh-

teenth century, the electors of Brandenburg had become the kings of Prussia, and Prussia's military power and efficient administrative structure became the envy of its German neighbors.

The Austrian empire was composed of Austria and Bohemia, the Habsburg hereditary lands, and as much of Hungary as could be controlled. In Austria, the Habsburgs clung tightly to their power. For decades Austria was the center of the still-flourishing Counter-Reformation, and the power and influence of the Jesuits was as strong here as it was in Spain. The War of the Spanish Succession, which gave the Habsburgs control of the southern Netherlands and parts of Italy, brought Austria an enhanced role in European affairs. Austria remained one of the great powers of Europe and the leading power in the Holy Roman Empire despite the rise of Prussia. Indeed from the middle of the eighteenth century the conflict between Prussia and Austria was the defining characteristic of central European politics.

The Rise of Prussia

The transformation of Brandenburg-Prussia from a petty German principality to a great European power was one of the most significant and least expected developments of the eighteenth century. Frederick William, the Great Elector (1640–88), had begun the process of forging Brandenburg-Prussia into a power in its own right by building a large and efficient military machine. At the beginning of the eighteenth century Prussia was on the winning side in both the War of the Spanish Succession and the Great Northern War. When the battlefield dust had settled, Prussia found itself in possession of Pomerania and the Baltic port of Stettin. It was now a recognized power in eastern Europe.

Frederick William I (1713–40) and his son Frederick II, the Great (1740–86), turned this promising beginning into an astounding success. A devout Calvinist, Frederick William I deplored waste and display as much on moral as on fiscal grounds. The reforms he initiated were intended to subordinate both aristocracy and peasantry to the needs of the state and to subordinate the needs of the state to the demands of the military.

Because of its geographical position, Prussia's major problem was to maintain an efficient and well-trained army during peacetime. Defense of its exposed territories required a constant state of military preparedness, yet the relaxation of military discipline and the desertion of troops to their homes inevitably followed the cessation of hostilities. Frederick William I solved this problem by integrating the economic and military structures of his state. First he appointed only German officers to command his troops, eliminating the mercenaries who sold their services to the highest bidders. Then he placed these noblemen at the head of locally recruited regiments. Each adult male in every district was required to register for military service in the regiment of the local landlord. These reforms dramatically increased the effectiveness of the army by shifting the burden of recruitment and training to the localities.

Yet despite all the attention that Frederick William I lavished on the military—by the end of his reign nearly 70 percent of state expenditures went to the army—his foreign policy was largely pacific. In fact, his greatest achievements were in civil affairs, reforming the bureaucracy, establishing a sound economy, and raising state revenues. Through generous settlement schemes and by welcoming Protestant and Jewish refugees, Frederick William was able to expand the economic potential of these eastern territories. Frederick William I pursued an aggressive policy of land purchase to expand the royal domain, and the addition of so many new inhabitants in Prussia further increased his wealth. While the major western European powers were discovering deficit financing and the national debt, Prussia was running a surplus.

Financial security was vital to the success of Frederick the Great. Father and son had quarreled bitterly throughout Frederick's youth—not only about music—and most observers expected that out of spite Frederick would tear down all that his father had built up. In fact father and son were cast in the same mold, with the unexpected difference that the son was the more ruthless and ambitious. With his throne, Frederick II inherited the fourth largest army in Europe and the richest treasury. He wasted no time in putting both to use. His two objectives were to acquire the Polish corridor of West Prussia that separated his German and Prussian territories and the agriculturally and industrially rich Austrian province of Silesia to the southeast of Berlin. Just months after his coronation, Frederick conquered Silesia, increasing the size of Prussia by nearly a quarter. Within a decade the province dominated the Prussian economy, outproducing and outconsuming all other areas of Frederick's state.

It was Frederick's military prowess that earned him the title "the Great." But this was only a part of his

DEFINITION OF AN ENLIGHTENED DESPOT

■ *Frederick the Great wrote philosophical and military tracts and composed dozens of compositions for the flute. Here is his definition of the enlightened despot.*

The sovereign is attached by indissoluble ties to the body of the state; hence it follows that he, by repercussion, is sensible to all the ills which afflict his subjects; and the people, in like manner, suffer from the misfortunes which affect their sovereign. There is but one general good, which is that of the state. . . . The sovereign represents the state; he and his people form but one body, which can only be happy as far as united by concord. The prince is to the nation he governs what the head is to the man; it is his duty to see, to think, and act for the whole community, so that he may procure it every advantage of which it is capable. . . . Such are in general the duties imposed upon a prince, from which, in order that he may never depart, he ought often to recollect that he himself is but a man, like the least of his subjects. If he be the first general, the first minister of the realm, it is not so that he should shelter in the shadow of authority, but that he should fulfil the duties of such titles. He is only the first servant of the state, who is obliged to act with probity and prudence; and to remain as totally disinterested as if he were each moment liable to render an account of his administration to his fellow citizens.

From: Frederick the Great, *An Essay on Forms of Government.*

Prussian infantry officers display their uniforms in this painting from the late eighteenth century. Distinctive, colorful, and elaborate uniforms, different for each regiment, were common in European armies before the field-gray and khaki era of the twentieth century.

achievement. More than his father, Frederick II forged an alliance with the Prussian nobility, integrating them into a unified state. A tightly organized central administration, which depended upon the cooperation of the local nobility, directed both military and bureaucratic affairs. At the center, Frederick worked tirelessly to oversee his government. Where Louis XIV had proclaimed, "I am the state," Frederick the Great announced "I am the first servant of the state." He codified the laws of Prussia, abolished torture and capital punishment, and instituted agricultural techniques imported from the states of western Europe. By the end of Frederick's reign, Prussia had become a model for bureaucratic organization, military reform, and enlightened rule.

Austria Survives

Austria was the great territorial victor in the War of the Spanish Succession, acquiring both the Netherlands and parts of Italy. Austrian forces recaptured a large part of Hungary from the Turks, thereby expanding their territory to the south and the east. Hereditary ruler of Austria and Bohemia, king of Hungary, and Holy Roman Emperor of the German nation, Charles VI (1711–40) was recognized as one of Europe's most potent rulers. But appearances were deceptive. The apex of Austrian power and prestige had already passed. Austria had benefited from balance-of-power politics, not so much from its own strength as from the leverage it could give to others. With the rise of Russia and Prussia there was now more than one fulcrum to power in eastern Europe.

The difficulties facing Austria ran deep. The Thirty Years' War had made the emperor more an Austrian monarch than an imperial German ruler. On the Austrian hereditary estates, the Catholic Counter-Reformation continued unabated, bringing with it the benefits of Jesuit education, cultural revival, and the religious unity necessary to motivate warfare against the Ottomans. But these benefits came at a price. Perhaps as many as two hundred thousand Protestants fled Austria and Bohemia, taking with them their skills and capital. For centuries the vision of empire had dominated Habsburg rule. This meant that the Austrian monarchy was a multiethnic confederation of lands loosely tied together by loyalty to a single head. The components preserved a high degree of autonomy: Hungary elected the Habsburg emperor its king in a separate ceremony. Local autonomy continually restricted the imposition of central policy, and never were the localities more autonomous than in the matter of taxation. Thus it was hard for Austria to centralize in the same way as had Prussia.

Austria was predominantly rural and agricultural. Less than 5 percent of the population lived in towns of ten thousand or more; less than 15 percent lived in towns at all. On the land the local aristocracy, whether nobility or gentry, exploited serfs to the maximum. Not only were serfs required to give labor service three days a week (and up to six during planting and harvest times), but the nobility maintained a full array of feudal privileges including the right to mill all grain and brew all beer. When serfs married, when they transferred property, even when they died, they paid taxes to their lord. As a result they had little left to give the state. In consequence, the Austrian army was among the smallest and the poorest of the major powers despite the fact that it had the most active enemies along its borders.

REVERIES UPON THE ART OF WAR

■ *Herman Maurice de Saxe was the illegitimate son of the king of Poland. He had extensive military experience in both eastern and western Europe. He ultimately achieved the office of Marshal of France, where he was celebrated as a military reformer. He modeled many of his reforms on the Prussian army.*

Would it not be much better to establish a law obliging men of all conditions of life to serve their king and country for the space of five years? A law, which could not reasonably be objected against, as it is both natural and just for people to be engaged in the defense of that state of which they constitute a part, and in choosing them between the years of twenty and thirty, no manner of inconvenience can possibly be the result; for those are years devoted, as it were, to libertinism; which are spent in adventures and travels, and, in general, productive of but small comfort to parents. An expedient of this kind could not come under the denomination of a public calamity, because every man, at the expiration of his five years service, would be discharged. It would also create an inexhaustible fund of good recruits, and such as would not be subject to desertion. In course of time, everyone would regard it as an honor rather than a duty to perform his task; but to produce this effect upon a people, it is necessary that no sort of distinction should be admitted, no rank or degree whatsoever excluded, and the nobles and rich rendered, in a principal manner, subservient to it. This would effectually prevent all murmur and repining, for those who had served their time, would look upon such, as betrayed any reluctance, or dissatisfaction at it, with contempt; by which means, the grievance would vanish insensibly, and every man at length esteem it an honor to serve his term. The poor would be comforted by the example of the rich; and the rich could not with decency complain, seeing themselves on a footing with the nobles.

Lack of finance, lack of human resources, and lack of governmental control were the underlying problems of Austria, but they were not the most immediate difficulties facing Charles VI. With no sons to succeed him, Charles feared that his hereditary and elective states would go their separate ways after his death and that the great Habsburg monarchy would end. For twenty years his abiding ambition was to gain recognition for the principle that his empire would pass intact to his daughter, Maria Theresa. He expressed the principle in a document known as the Pragmatic Sanction, which stated that all Habsburg lands would pass intact to the eldest heir, male or female. Charles VI made concession after concession to gain acceptance of the Pragmatic Sanction. But the leaders of Europe licked their lips at the prospect of a dismembered Austrian empire.

Maria Theresa (1740–80) inherited the imperial throne in 1740 and quickly discovered what it was like to be a woman in a man's world. In 1740 Frederick of Prussia invaded the rich Austrian province of Silesia and attracted allies for an assault upon Vienna. Faced with Bavarian, Saxon, and Prussian armies, Maria Theresa might well have lost her inheritance had she not shown her remarkable capacities so early in her reign. She appeared before the Hungarian estates, accepted their crown, and persuaded them to provide her with an army capable of halting the allied advance. Though she was unable to reconquer Silesia, Hungarian aid helped her hold the line against her enemies.

The loss of Silesia, the most prosperous part of the Austrian domains, signaled the need for fundamental reform. The new eighteenth-century idea of building a state replaced the traditional Habsburg concern with maintaining an empire. Maria Theresa and her son Joseph II (1780–90) began the process of transformation. For Austria, state building meant first the reorganization of the military and civil bureaucracy to clear the way for fiscal reform. As in Prussia, a central directory was created to oversee the collection of taxes and the disbursement of funds. Maria Theresa personally persuaded her provincial estates both to increase taxation and to extend it to the nobles and the clergy. While her success was limited, she finally established royal control over the raising and collection of taxes.

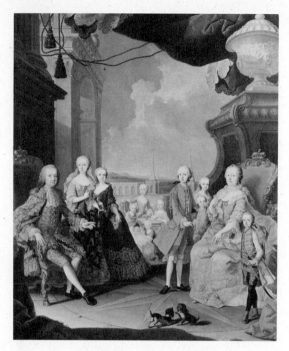

Maria Theresa and her family. Eleven of Maria Theresa's sixteen children are posed with the empress and her husband, Francis of Lorraine. Standing next to his mother is the future emperor Joseph II.

The second element in Maria Theresa's reform program involved the condition of the Austrian peasantry. Maria Theresa established the doctrine that the "peasant must be able to support himself and his family and pay his taxes in time of peace and war." She limited labor service to two days per week and abolished the most burdensome feudal dues. Joseph II ended serfdom altogether. The new Austrian law codes guaranteed peasants' legal rights and established their ability to seek redress through the law. Joseph II hoped to extend reform even further. In the last years of his life he abolished obligatory labor service and ensured that all peasants kept one-half of their income before paying local and state taxes. Such a radical reform met a storm of opposition and was ultimately abandoned at the end of the reign.

The reorganization of the bureaucracy, the increase in taxation, and the social reforms that created a more productive peasantry revitalized the Austrian state. The efforts of Maria Theresa and Joseph II to overcome provincial autonomy worked better in Austria and Bohemia than in Hungary. The Hungarians declined to contribute at all to state revenues, and Joseph II took the unusual step of refusing to be crowned king of Hungary so that he would not have to make any concessions to Hungarian autonomy. He even imposed a tariff on Hungarian goods sold in Austria. More seriously, parts of the empire already had been lost before the process of reform could begin. Prussia's seizure of Silesia was the hardest blow of all. Yet in 1740, when Frederick the Great and his allies swept down from the north, few would have predicted that Austria would survive.

The Politics of Power

Frederick the Great's invasion of Silesia in 1740 was callous and cynical. Since the Pragmatic Sanction bound him to recognize Maria Theresa's succession, Frederick cynically offered her a defensive alliance in return for which she would simply hand over Silesia. It was an offer she should not have refused. Though Frederick's action initiated the War of the Austrian Succession, he was not alone in his desire to shake loose parts of Austria's territory. Soon nearly the entire Continent became embroiled in the conflict.

The War of the Austrian Succession (1740–48) resembled a pack of wolves stalking its injured prey. It quickly became a major international conflict involving Prussia, France, and Spain on one side and Austria, Britain, and Holland on the other. Spain joined the fighting to recover its Italian possessions, Saxony claimed Moravia, France entered Bohemia, and the Bavarians moved into Austria from the south. With France and Prussia allied, it was vital that Britain join with Austria to maintain the balance of power. Initially the British did little more than subsidize Maria Theresa's forces, but once France renewed its efforts to conquer the Netherlands, both Britain and the Dutch Republic joined in the fray. That the British cared little about the fate of the Habsburg empire was clear from the terms of the treaty that they dictated at Aix-la-Chapelle (Aachen) in 1748. Austria recognized Frederick's conquest of Silesia, as well as the loss of parts of its Italian territories to Spain. France, which the British had always regarded as the real enemy, withdrew from the Netherlands in return for the restoration of a number of colonial possessions. The War of the Austrian Succession made Austria and Prussia permanent enemies and gave Maria Theresa a crash course in international diplomacy. She learned firsthand that self-interest rather than loyalty underlay power politics. This lesson was reinforced in 1756 when Britain and Prussia entered into a military accord at the beginning of the Seven Years' War (1756–63). Prussian expansion and duplicity had already alarmed both Russia and France, and Frederick II feared that he would be squeezed from east and west. He could hardly expect help from Maria Theresa, so he extended overtures to the British, whose interests in protecting Hanover, the hereditary estates of their German-born king, outweighed their prior commitments to Austria. Frederick's actions drove France into the arms of both the Austrians and the Russians, and an alliance that included the German state of Saxony was formed in defense. Thus was initiated a diplomatic revolution in which France and Austria became allies after three hundred years as enemies.

Once again, Frederick the Great took the offensive and once again, he won his risk against the odds. His attack on Saxony and Austria in 1756 brought a vigorous response from the Russians, who interceded on Austria's behalf with a massive army. Three years later, at the battle of Kunersdorf, Frederick suffered the worst military defeat of his career when the Russians shattered his armies. In 1760 his forces were barely a third of the size of those massed by his opponents, and it was only a matter of time before he was fighting defensively from within Prussia.

In 1762 Empress Elizabeth died. She was succeeded by her nephew, the childlike Peter III, a German by birth who worshiped Frederick the Great. When Peter came to the throne, he immediately negotiated peace with Frederick, abandoning not only his allies but also the substantial territorial gains that the Russian forces had made within Prussia. It was small wonder that the Russian military leadership joined in the coup d'état that brought Peter's wife, Catherine, to the throne in 1762. With Russia out of the war, Frederick was able to fend off further Austrian offensives and to emerge with his state, including Silesia, intact.

The Seven Years' War did little to change the boundaries of the German states, but it had two important political results. The first was to establish beyond doubt the status of Prussia as a major power and a counterbalance to Austria in central Europe. The existence of the dual Germanies, one led by Prussia and the other by Austria, was to have serious consequences for German unification in the nineteenth century and for the two world wars in the twentieth. The second result of the Seven Years' War was to initiate a long period of peace in eastern Europe. Both Prussia and Austria were financially exhausted from two decades of fighting. Both states needed a breathing spell to initiate administrative and economic improvements, and the period following the Seven Years' War witnessed the sustained programs of internal reforms for which Frederick the Great, Maria Theresa, and Joseph II were famous in the decades following 1763.

Peace among the eastern European powers did not mean that they abandoned their territorial ambitions.

Partition of Poland

All over Europe absolute rulers reformed their bureaucracies, streamlined their administrations, increased their sources of revenue, and built enormous standing armies. All over Europe except in Poland. There the autonomous power of the nobility remained as strong as ever. No monarchical dynasty was ever established, and each elected ruler not only confirmed the privileges of the nobility but usually was forced to extend them. In the Diet, the Polish representative assembly, small special-interest groups could bring legislative business to a halt by exercising their veto power. Given the size of Poland's borders, its army was pathetically inadequate for the task it had to face. The Polish monarchy was helpless to defend its subjects from the destruction on all sides.

In 1764 Catherine the Great and Frederick the Great combined to place one of Catherine's former lovers on

This engraving by Le Mire is called The Cake of the Kings: First Partition of Poland, 1773. *The monarchs of Russia, Austria, and Prussia join in carving up Poland. The Polish king is clutching his tottering crown.*

of northeast Poland, which included over one million people, while Frederick would unite his lands by seizing West Prussia. Austria gained both the largest territories, including Galicia, and the greatest number of people, nearly two million Polish subjects.

In half a century the balance of power in central Europe had shifted decisively. Prussia's absorption of Silesia and parts of Poland made it a single geographical entity as well as a great economic and military power. Austria, despite its lost territory, proved capable of surviving the accession of a female ruler and of fighting off an attempt to dismember its empire. Its participation in the partition of Poland strengthened its role in the politics of the eastern powers, while its alliance with France fortified its role in the west. From one empire there were now two states, and the relationship between Prussia and Austria would dominate central Europe for the next century.

The Greatness of Great Britain

By the middle of the eighteenth century, Great Britain had become the leading power of Europe. It had won its spurs in Continental and colonial wars. Britain was unsurpassed as a naval power, able to protect its far-flung trading empire and to make a show of force in almost any part of the world. Perhaps more impressively for a nation that did not support a large standing army, British soldiers had won decisive victories in the European land wars. Until the American Revolution, Britain came up a winner in every military venture it undertook. But might was only one part of British success. Economic preeminence was every bit as important. British colonial possessions in the Atlantic and Indian oceans poured consumer products into Britain for export to the European marketplaces. Growth in overseas trade was matched by growth in home production. British advances in agricultural technique had transformed Britain from an importer to an exporter of grain. The manufacturing industries that other European states attempted to create with huge government subsidies flourished in Britain through private enterprise.

British military and economic power was supported by a unique system of government. In Britain the nobility served the state through government. The British constitutional system, devised in the seventeenth century and refined in the eighteenth, shared power between the monarchy and the ruling elite through the

the Polish throne and to turn Poland into a weak dependent. Russia and Prussia had different interests in Poland's fate. For Russia, Poland represented a vast buffer state that kept the German powers at a distance from Russia's borders. It was more in Russia's interest to dominate Polish foreign policy than to conquer its territory. For Prussia, Poland looked like another helpless flower, "to be picked off leaf by leaf," as Frederick observed. Poland seemed especially appealing because Polish territory, including the Baltic port of Gdansk, separated the Prussian and Brandenburg portions of Frederick's state.

By the 1770s the idea of carving up Poland was being actively discussed in Berlin, Saint Petersburg, and Vienna. Austria, too, had an interest in a Polish partition, especially to maintain its power and status with the other two states, and perhaps to use Polish territory as a potential bargaining chip for the return of Silesia. Finally, in 1772, the three great eastern powers struck a deal. Russia would take a large swath of the grain fields institution of Parliament. Central government integrated monarch and ministers with chosen representatives from the localities. Such integration not only provided the Crown with the vital information necessary to formulate national policy, but it eased acceptance and enforcement of government decisions. Government was seen as the rule of law which, however imperfect, was believed to operate for the benefit of all.

The parliamentary system gave Britain some of its particular strengths, but they came at a cost. Politics was a national pastime rather than the business of an elite of administrators and state servants. Decentralization of decision making led to half-measures designed to placate competing interests. Appeals to public opinion, especially by candidates for Parliament, often played upon fears and prejudices that divided rather than united the nation. Moreover, the relative openness of the British system hindered diplomatic and colonial affairs, in which secrecy and rapid changes of direction were often the monarch's most potent weapons. These weaknesses came to light most dramatically during the struggle for independence waged by Britain's North American colonists. There the clash of principle and power was most extreme and the strengths and weaknesses of parliamentary rule were ruthlessly exposed.

The British Constitution

The British Constitution was a patchwork of laws and customs that was gradually sewn together to form a workable system of government. Many of its greatest innovations came about through circumstance rather than design, and circumstance continued to play an essential role in its development in the eighteenth century. At the apex of the government stood the king, not an absolute monarch like his European counterparts, but not necessarily less powerful for having less arbitrary power. The British people revered monarchy and the monarch. The theory of mixed government depended upon the balance of interests represented by the monarchy in the Crown, the aristocracy in the House of Lords, and the people in the House of Commons. Less abstractly, the monarch was still regarded as divinely ordained and a special gift to the nation. The monarch was the actual and symbolic leader of the nation as well as the "Supreme Head" of the Church of England. Allegiance to the Anglican church, whether as a political creed among the elite or as a simple matter of devotion among the populace, intensified allegiance to the king.

The partnership between Crown and representative body was best expressed in the idea that the British government was composed of King-in-Parliament. Parliament consisted of three separate organs: monarch, lords, and commons. Though each existed separately as a check upon the potential excesses of the others, it was only when the three functioned together that parliamentary government could operate. The king was charged with selecting ministers, initiating policy, and supervising administration. The two houses of Parliament were charged with raising revenue, making laws, and presenting the grievances of subjects to the Crown.

There were 558 members of the House of Commons after the union with Scotland in 1707. Most members of the lower house were nominated to their seats. The largest number of seats were located in small towns where a local oligarchy, or neighboring patron, had a customary right to make nominations that were invariably accepted by the electorate. Even in the largest cities, influential citizens made arrangements for nominating members in order to avoid the cost and confusion of an actual election. Campaigns were ruinously expensive for the candidates—an election in 1754 cost the losing candidates £40,000—and potentially dangerous to the local community, where bitter social and political divisions boiled just below the surface.

The British gentry dominated the Commons, occupying over 80 percent of the seats in any session. Most of these members also served as unpaid local officials in the counties, as justices of the peace, captains of the local militias, or collectors of local taxes. They came to Parliament not only as representatives of the interests of their class, but as experienced local governors who understood the needs of both Crown and subject.

Nevertheless, the Crown had to develop methods to coordinate the work of the two houses of Parliament and facilitate the passage of governmental programs. The king and his ministers began to use the deep royal pockets of offices and favors to bolster their friends in Parliament. Not only were those employed by the Crown encouraged to find a place in the House of Commons, but those who had a place in Parliament were encouraged to take employment from the Crown. Despite its potential for abuse, this was a political process that integrated center and locality, and at first it worked rather well. Those with local standing were brought into central offices. There they could influence central policy making while protecting their local constituents. These officeholders, who came to be called *placemen*, never constituted a majority of the members of Parliament.

The interior of the British House of Commons in the 1700s. The arrangement of the benches and galleries is much the same as that seen today in the London parliamentary chamber.

They formed the core around which eighteenth-century governments operated but it was a core that needed direction and cohesion. It was such leadership and organization that was the essential contribution of eighteenth-century politics to the British Constitution.

Parties and Ministers

Though parliamentary management was vital to the Crown, it was not the Crown that developed the basic tools of management. Rather these techniques originated within the political community itself and their usefulness was only slowly grasped by the monarchy. The first and, in the long term, most important tool was the party system. Political parties initially developed in the late seventeenth century around the issue of the Protestant succession. Those who opposed James II because he was a Catholic attempted to exclude him

from inheriting the crown. They came to be called by their opponents Whigs, which meant "Scottish horse thieves." Those who supported James's hereditary rights but who also supported the Anglican church came to be called by their opponents Tories, which meant "Irish cattle rustlers." The Tories cooperated in the Revolution of 1688 that placed William and Mary on the throne because James had threatened the Anglican church by tolerating Catholics and because Mary had a legitimate hereditary right to be queen. After the death of Queen Anne in 1714, the Tories supported the succession of James III, James II's Catholic son who had been raised in France, rather than of George I (1714–27), prince of Hanover and Protestant great-grandson of James I. An unsuccessful rebellion to place James III on the throne in 1715 discredited the leadership of the Tory party, but did not weaken its importance in both local and parliamentary politics.

The Whigs supported the Protestant succession and a broad-based Protestantism. They attracted the allegiance of large numbers of dissenters, heirs to the Puritans of the seventeenth century who practiced forms of Protestantism different from the Anglican church. The struggle between Whigs and Tories was less a struggle for power than it was for loyalty to their opposing viewpoints. As the Tories opposed the Hanoverian succession and the Whigs supported it, it was no mystery which party would find favor with George I. Moreover, as long as there was a pretender to the British throne—another rebellion took place in Scotland in 1745 led by the grandson of James II—the Tories continued to be tarred with the brush of disloyalty.

The division of political sympathies between Whigs and Tories helped create a set of groupings to which parliamentary leadership could be applied. A national, rather than a local or regional outlook, could be used to organize support for royal policy as long as royal policy conformed to that national outlook. The ascendancy of the Whigs enabled George I and his son George II (1727–60) to govern effectively through Parliament, but at the price of dependence upon the Whig leaders. Though the monarch had the constitutional freedom to choose his ministers, realistically he could choose only Whigs, and practically none but the Whig leaders of the House of Commons. Happily for the first two Georges, they found a man who was able to manage Parliament but desired only to serve the Crown.

Sir Robert Walpole (1676–1745) came from a long-established gentry family in Norfolk. Walpole was an early supporter of the Hanoverian succession and an early victim of party warfare. But once George I was

Sir Robert Walpole addressing the cabinet.

securely on the throne, Walpole became an indispensable leader of the House of Commons. His success rested upon his extraordinary abilities: he was an excellent public speaker; he relished long working days and the details of government; and he understood better than anyone else the intricacies of state finance. Walpole became First Lord of the Treasury, a post that he transformed into first minister of state. From his treasury post, Walpole assiduously built a Whig parliamentary party. He carefully dispensed jobs and offices, using them as bait to lure parliamentary supporters. Walpole's organization paid off both in the passage of legislation desired by the Crown and at the polls, where Whigs were returned to Parliament time and again.

From 1721 to 1742 Walpole was the most powerful man in the British government. He refused an offer of a peerage so that he could continue to lead the House of Commons. Walpole's long tenure in office was as much a result of his policies as of his methods of governing. He brought a measure of fiscal responsibility to government by establishing a fund to pay off the national debt. In foreign policy he pursued peace with the same fervor that both his predecessors and successors pursued war. The long years of peace brought prosperity to both the landed and merchant classes, but they also brought crit-

icism of Walpole's methods. The way in which he used government patronage to build his parliamentary party was attacked as corruption. So too were the ways in which the pockets of Whig officeholders were lined. During his last decade in office Walpole struggled to survive. His attempt to extend the excise tax on colonial goods nearly led to his loss of office in 1733. His refusal to respond to the clamor for continued war with Spain in 1741 finally led to his downfall.

Walpole's twenty-year rule established the pattern of parliamentary government. The Crown needed a "prime" minister who was able to steer legislation through the House of Commons. It also needed a patronage broker who could take control of the treasury and dispense its largess in return for parliamentary backing. Walpole's personality and talents had combined these two roles. Hereafter they were divided. Those who had grown up under Walpole had learned their lessons well. The Whig monopoly of power continued unchallenged for nearly another twenty years. The patronage network Walpole had created was vastly extended by his Whig successors. Even minor posts in the customs or the excise offices were now exchanged for political favor, and only those approved by the Whig leadership could claim them. The cries of corruption grew louder not only in the country houses of the long-disenfranchised Tories, but in the streets of London, where a popular radicalism developed in opposition to the Whig oligarchy. They were taken up as well in the North American colonies, where two million British subjects champed at the bit of imperial rule.

America Revolts

Britain's triumph in the Seven Years' War (1756–63) had come at great financial cost to the nation. At the beginning of the eighteenth century, the national debt stood at £14 million; in 1763 it had risen to £130 million despite the fact that Walpole's government had been paying off some of it. Then, as now, the cost of world domination was staggering. George III (1760–1820) came to the throne with a taste for reform and a desire to break the Whig stranglehold on government. He was to have limited success on both counts, though not for want of trying. In 1763 the king and his ministers agreed that reform of colonial administration was long overdue. Such reform would have the twin benefit of shifting part of the burden of taxation from Britain to North America and of making the commercial side of colonization pay.

This was sound thinking all around, and in due course Parliament passed a series of duties on goods imported into the colonies, including glass, wine, coffee, tea, and most notably sugar. The so-called Sugar Act (1764) was followed by the Stamp Act (1765), a tax on printed papers such as newspapers, deeds, and court documents. Both acts imposed taxes in the colonies similar to those that already existed in Britain. Accompanying the acts were administrative orders designed to cut into the lucrative black market trade. The government instituted new rules for searching ships and transferred authority over smuggling from the local colonial courts to Britain's Admiralty courts. Though British officials could only guess at the value of the new duties imposed, it was believed that with effective enforcement £150,000 would be raised. All this would go to pay the vastly greater costs of colonial administration and security.

British officials were more than perplexed when these mild measures met with a ferocious response. Assemblies of nearly every colony officially protested the Sugar Act. They sent petitions to Parliament begging for repeal and warning of dire economic and political consequences. Riots followed passage of the Stamp Act. Tax collectors were hounded out of office, their resignations precipitated by threats and acts of physical violence. In Massachusetts mobs that included political leaders in the colony razed the homes of the collector and the lieutenant-governor. However much the colonists might have regretted the violence that was

done, they believed that an essential political principle was at stake. It was a principle of the freedom of an Englishman.

At their core, the protests of the American colonists underscored the vitality of the British political system. The Americans argued that they could not be taxed without their consent and that their consent could come only through representation in Parliament. Since there were no colonists in Parliament, Parliament had no jurisdiction over the property of the colonists. Taxation without representation was tyranny. There were a number of subtleties to this argument that were quickly lost as political rhetoric and political action heated up. In the first place, the colonists did tax themselves through their own legislatures and much of that money paid the costs of administration and defense. Secondly, as a number of pamphleteers pointed out, no one in the colonies had asked the British government to send regiments of the army into North America. The colonists had little reason to put their faith in British protection. Hard-fought colonial victories were tossed away at European negotiating tables, while the British policy of defending Indian rights in the Ohio Valley ran counter to the interests of the settlers. When defense was necessary, the colonists had proven themselves both able and cooperative in providing it. A permanent tax meant a permanent army, and a standing army was as loathed in Britain as it was in the colonies.

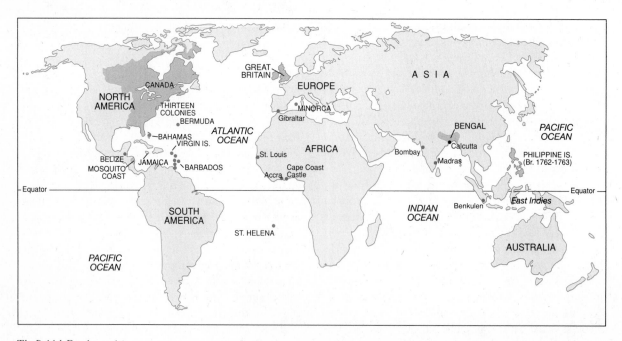

The British Empire, 1763

FROM *THE DECLARATION OF INDEPENDENCE*

■ *The* Declaration of Independence *succinctly summarized the principles upon which the American colonists were to build a new form of democratic government. It was written by Thomas Jefferson.*

We hold these truths to be self-evident, that all men are created equal, that they are endowed by their Creator with certain inalienable Rights, that among these are Life, Liberty and the pursuit of Happiness. That to secure these rights, Governments are instituted among Men, deriving their just powers from the consent of the governed, That whenever any Form of Government becomes destructive of these ends, it is the Right of the People to alter or to abolish it, and to institute new Government, laying its foundation on such principles and organizing its powers in such form, as to them shall seem most likely to effect their Safety and Happiness. Prudence, indeed, will dictate that Governments long established should not be changed for light and transient causes; and accordingly all experience hath shown, that mankind are more disposed to suffer, while evils are sufferable, than to right themselves by abolishing the forms to which they are accustomed. But when a long train of abuses and usurpations, pursuing invariably the same Object, evinces a design to reduce them under absolute Despotism, it is their right, it is their duty, to throw off such Government, and to provide new Guards for their future security.

Colonists also tried to draw a distinction between internal and external taxation in opposing the Stamp Act. They deemed regulation of overseas commerce a legitimate power of Parliament but argued that the regulation of internal exchange was not. But this distinction was lost once the issue of parliamentary representation was raised. If the colonists had not consented to British taxation, then it made no difference whether taxation was internal or external. The passion generated in the colonies was probably no greater than that generated in Britain. The British government also saw the confrontation as a matter of principle, but for Britain the principle was parliamentary sovereignty. This, above all, was the rock upon which the British Constitution had been built over the last century. Parliament had entered into a partnership with the Crown. The Crown had surrendered—willingly or not—many of its prerogatives. In return, Parliament had bound the people to obedience. There were well-established means by which British subjects could petition Parliament for redress of grievances against the monarch, but there were no channels by which they could question the sovereignty of Parliament.

Once the terms of debate had been so defined, it was difficult for either side to find a middle ground. Parliamentary moderates managed repeal of the Stamp Act and most of the clauses of the Sugar Act, but they also joined in passing the Declaratory Act (1766), which stated unequivocally that Parliament held sovereign jurisdiction over the colonies "in all cases whatsoever." This was a claim that became more and more difficult to sustain as colonial leaders began to cite the elements of resistance theory that had justified the Revolution of 1688. Then the protest had been against the tyranny of the king, now it was against the tyranny of Parliament. American propagandists claimed that a conspiracy existed to deprive the colonists of their property and rights, to enslave them for the benefit of special interests and corrupt politicians.

The techniques of London radicals who opposed parliamentary policy were imported into the colonies. Newspapers were used to whip up public support; boycotts brought ordinary people into the political arena; public demonstrations like the Boston Tea Party (1774) were carefully designed to intimidate; mobs were occasionally given free rein. Though the government had faced down these tactics when they were used in London to support John Wilkes (1725–97), an ardent critic of royal policy, they were less successful when the crisis lay an ocean away. When, in 1770, British troops fired upon a Boston mob, American propagandists were provided with empirical evidence that Britain intended to enslave the colonies. Violence was met by violence, passion by passion. In 1775 full-scale fighting was under

An engraving by Paul Revere showing the Boston Massacre on March 5, 1770, in which five rioters were killed by British soldiers sent to Boston to enforce British tax laws. This incident became one of the landmark events on the way to revolution in the British North American colonies.

way. Eight years later Britain withdrew from a war it could not win, and the American colonies were left to govern themselves.

By the end of the third quarter of the eighteenth century, Europe had a new political configuration. A continent once dominated by a single power—Spain in the sixteenth century and France in the seventeenth—was now dominated by a state system in which alliances among several great powers held the balance. Despite the loss of its American colonies, Great Britain had proved the most potent of the states. Its victories over the French in the Seven Years' War and over France and Prussia in the War of the Austrian Succession secured its position. But it was a position that could be maintained only through alliances with the German states, either with Prussia or Austria. The rise of Prussia provided a counterweight to French domination of the Continent. Though these two states became allies in the middle of the century, the ambitions of their rulers made them natural enemies, and it would not be long before French and Prussian armies were again pitted against each other. France, still the wealthiest and most populous of European states, had slumbered through the eighteenth-century reorganization. The legacies of Louis XIV took a long time to reach fruition. He had claimed glory for his state, giving the French people a sense of national identity and national destiny, but mak-

The New European Powers

1707	England and Scotland unite to form Great Britain
1713–14	Treaty of Utrecht ends War of the Spanish Succession (1702–14)
1714	British crown passes to House of Hanover
1721	Treaty of Nystad ends Great Northern War (1700–21)
1721–42	Sir Robert Walpole leads British House of Commons
1722	Peter the Great of Russia creates Table of Ranks
1740	Frederick the Great of Prussia invades Austrian province of Silesia
1748	Treaty of Aix-la-Chapelle ends War of the Austrian Succession (1740–48)
1756–63	Seven Years' War pits Prussia and Britain against Austria, France, and Russia
1773–75	Pugachev's Revolt in Russia
1774	Boston Tea Party
1775	American Revolution begins
1786	Catherine the Great of Russia issues Charter of the Nobility

ing them pay an enormous price in social and economic dislocation. Thus the mid-eighteenth century was to be an age of the greatest literary and philosophical achievement for France, but the late eighteenth century was to be an age of the greatest social upheaval that Europe had ever known.

SUGGESTIONS FOR FURTHER READING

GENERAL READING

* Olwen Hufton, *Europe: Privilege and Protest 1730-1789* (Ithaca, NY: Cornell University Press, 1980). An excellent survey of the political and social history of the mid-eighteenth century.

* Leonard Krieger, *Kings and Philosophers 1689-1789* (New York: Norton, 1970). A brilliant depiction of the personalities and ideas of eighteenth-century Europe.

* M. S. Anderson, *Europe in the Eighteenth Century 1713-1783* (London: Longman, 1976). A country-by-country survey of political developments.

Nicholas Riasanovsky, *A History of Russia* (New York: Oxford University Press, 1984). The best one-volume history of Russia.

EUROPE IN 1714

* Derek McKay and H. M. Scott, *The Rise of the Great Powers* (London: Longman, 1983). An outstanding survey of diplomacy and warfare.

THE RISE OF RUSSIA

* Paul Dukes, *The Making of Russian Absolutism 1613-1801* (London: Longman, 1982). An extensive survey of the Russian monarchy in its greatest period.

* B. H. Sumner, *Peter the Great and the Emergence of Russia* (New York: Collier Books, 1962). A short and readable study; the best introduction.

* M. S. Anderson, *Peter the Great* (London: Thames and Hudson, 1978). A well-constructed, comprehensive biography.

* Jerome Blum, *Lord and Peasant in Russia* (New York: Columbia University Press, 1961). The best work on the social life of Russians.

* Isabel de Madariaga, *Catherine the Great, a Short History* (New Haven, CT: Yale University Press, 1990). The best brief life.

THE TWO GERMANIES

* H. W. Koch, *A History of Prussia* (London: Longman, 1978). An up-to-date study of the factors that led to Prussian dominance of Germany.

* Gerhard Ritter, *Frederick the Great* (Berkeley: University of California Press, 1974). A classic biography; short and readable.

* Walther Hubatsch, *Frederick the Great of Prussia* (London: Thames and Hudson, 1975). A full account of the reign of Prussia's greatest leader.

* Ernst Wangermann, *The Austrian Achievement* (New York: Harcourt Brace Jovanovich, 1973). The most readable study of Austrian politics, culture, and society in the eighteenth century.

* T. C. W. Blanning, *Joseph II and Enlightened Despotism* (London: Longman, 1970). Displays the relationship between new ideas, reform policies, and the practical necessities of government.

C. A. Macartney, *Maria Theresa and the House of Austria* (Mystic, CT: Verry Inc., 1969). Still the best introductory study.

THE GREATNESS OF GREAT BRITAIN

*J. C. D. Clark, *English Society 1688-1832* (Cambridge: Cambridge University Press, 1985). A bold reinterpretation of the most important features of English society.

* J. H. Plumb, *The Origins of Political Stability, England 1675-1725* (Boston: Houghton Mifflin, 1967). A comprehensive account of the contributions of Walpole to the establishment of the British Constitution.

Ragnhild Hatton, *George I Elector and King* (Cambridge, MA: Harvard University Press, 1978). An outstanding biography that shows the German side of a British monarch.

* John Brewer, *The Sinews of Power* (New York: Alfred A. Knopf, 1989). A brilliant account of the rise of Britain.

* Ian Christie and Benjamin W. Labaree, *Empire or Independence 1760-1777* (New York: Norton, 1977). Surveys the American troubles from the British point of view.

* Bernard Bailyn, *The Ideological Origins of the American Revolution* (Cambridge, MA: Harvard University Press, 1967). A brilliant interpretation of the underlying causes of the break between Britain and the North American colonies.

* Edward Countryman, *The American Revolution* (New York: Hill & Wang, 1985). A readable, up-to-date narrative of the events of the American Revolution.

* Indicates paperback edition available.

CHAPTER 21
Culture and Society in Eighteenth-Century Europe

HAPPY FAMILIES

"Happy families are all alike," wrote Lev Tolstoy in the nineteenth century when the idea of a happy family was already a cliché. Such an idea would never have occurred to his eighteenth-century forebears. For them the happy family was doubly new—new in the change in the relationships within the family, new in the stress upon happiness itself. Personal happiness was an invention of the Enlightenment, the result of novel attitudes about human aspirations and human capabilities. "Happiness is a new idea in Europe," wrote Louis de Saint-Just (1767–94). It emerged in response to the belief that what was good brought pleasure and what was evil brought pain. Happiness, both individual and collective, became the yardstick by which life was measured. This meant a reorientation in personal conduct and most of all a reorientation of family life. Especially for those with an economic cushion, a pleasurable family life was essential. Husbands and wives were to become companions, filled with romantic love for each other and devoted to domestic bliss. Children, the product of their affection, were to be doted upon, treated not as miniature adults to be lectured and beaten, but as unfilled vessels into which all that was good was to be poured.

Were ever a couple more in love than the husband and wife depicted in *A Visit to the Wet Nurse* by Jean-Honoré Fragonard (1732–1806)? The man clasps his wife's arm to his cheek, she lays her hand on his shoulder. Their sighs are almost audible! Together they admire the fruit of their love, the baby asleep in the cradle. It is hard to guess which parent dotes more, the mother with her rapturous expression or the father with his intensity. He kneels on a cushion in almost religious devotion, his hands folded as if in prayer. Who can doubt their companionship or their love for their babe? They have come together to see how the wet nurse is caring for their child. Doubtless it was they who provided the rather opulent bassinet, which contrasts sharply with the other furniture in the room, and the linens and pillows into which the baby has nestled.

At the beginning of the eighteenth century, the use of a wet nurse was still common among the families of the French bourgeoisie, the class to which this couple—judging from their clothes—undoubtedly belongs. As time moved on, however, more and more mothers began to nurse their babies themselves. In part this change was a response to the higher mortality rate among infants sent out to wet nurses. The unsanitary environment of the towns ran a close race with the neglect that many wet nurses showed their charges. But a wet nurse who could be supervised, that is one who lived near enough to be visited, but far enough away from the town to enjoy wholesome air, might be the best of both worlds. This is just what the couple here has found, and today they come, with their other child (the boy in the hat), to see their baby sleeping peacefully, the wet nurse sitting attentively at the infant's side.

But there are two families in this picture, and they are hardly alike. At first glance, the wet nurse looks like an old woman, perhaps even an aging nanny. She sits with her distaff in her hand, for the arrival of her clients has interrupted her spinning. It is shocking to realize that she cannot be much older than thirty, an age beyond which wealthy families would not hire her for fear either she would not have much milk or that it would be sour. The two younger children are undoubtedly hers, the youngest probably just weaned so that all of her milk would go to the baby. No adoring husband sits beside the wet nurse. Her husband, if he is still alive, is hard at work with no leisure time for visits. Not only does the wet nurse have to sell her milk, but she also spins, to keep her family clothed and to earn a little extra to put away for hard times. The newest fads of the age have passed her family by. While the child in the cradle will be spoiled by toys manufactured especially for children—puzzles, games, rocking horses and balls—the children of the wet nurse must make do with household objects and their own imagination. A ball of yarn thrown to the cat helps the elder child while away the hours. Like much else in the eighteenth century, the world of the family was divided between high and low.

The Nobility

Eighteenth-century society was a hybrid of old and new. It remained highly stratified. Birth and occupation determined wealth, privilege, and quality of life as much as they had in the past. There were now more paths toward the middle and upper classes, more wealth to be distributed among those above the level of subsistence, but at the top of society the nobility remained the privileged order in every European state.

Nobles were defined by their legal rights. They had the right to bear arms, the right to special judicial treatment, the right to tax exemptions. In Russia only nobles could own serfs; in Poland only nobles could hold government office. In France and Britain the highest court positions were always reserved for noblemen. Nobles dominated the Prussian army. The Spanish nobility rich or poor, shunned all labor as a right of their heritage. Swedish and Hungarian noblemen had their own legislative chambers, just as the British had the House of Lords.

Though all who enjoyed these special rights were noble, not all nobles were equal. In many states the noble order was subdivided into easily identifiable groups. The Spanish grandees, the upper nobility, were numbered in the thousands; the Spanish *hidalgos*, the lower nobility, in the hundreds of thousands. In Hungary out of 400,000 noblemen only about 15,000 belonged to the "landed" nobility who held titles and were exempt from taxes. In England the elite class was divided between the peerage and the gentry. The peerage held titles, were members of the House of Lords, and had a limited range of judicial and fiscal privileges. In the mid-eighteenth century there were only 190 British peers. The gentry, which numbered over 20,000, dominated the House of Commons and local legal offices but were not strictly members of the nobility. The French nobility was informally distinguished among the small group of peers known as the *Grandes*, whose ancient lineage, wealth, and power set them apart from all others; a rather larger service nobility whose privileges derived in one way or another from municipal or judicial service; and what might be called the country nobility, whose small estates and local outlook made their exemption from taxes vital to their survival.

These distinctions among the nobilities of the European states masked a more important one: wealth. As the saying went, "all who were truly noble were not wealthy, but all who were truly wealthy were noble." In the eighteenth century, despite the phenomenal increase in mercantile activity, wealth was still calculated in profits from the ownership of land, and it was the wealthy landed nobility who set the tone of elite life in Europe.

All That Glitters

For the wealthy, aristocracy was becoming an international status. The influence of Louis XIV and the court of Versailles lasted for well over a century and spread to town and country life. Most nobles maintained multiple residences. The new style of aristocratic entertainment required more public space on the first floor, while the increasing demand for personal and familial privacy necessitated more space in the upper stories. The result was larger and more opulent homes. Here the British elite led all others. Over one hundred fifty country houses were built in the early eighteenth century alone, including Blenheim Palace, which was built for John Churchill, duke of Marlborough, at a cost of £300,000. To the expense of architecture was added the expense of decoration. New materials, like West Indian mahogany, occasioned new styles, and both drove up costs. The high-quality woodwork and plastering made fashionable by the English Adam brothers was quickly imitated on the Continent. Only the Spanish nobility shunned country estates, preferring to reside permanently in towns.

The building of country houses was only one part of the conspicuous consumption of the privileged orders. Improvements in travel, both in transport and roads, permitted increased contact between members of the national elites. The stagecoach linked towns, and canals linked waterways. Both made travel quicker and more enjoyable. The grand tour of historical sites continued to be used as a substitute for formal education. The grand tour was a means of introducing the European aristocracies to each other and also a means of communicating taste and fashion among them. Whether it was a Russian noble in Germany, or a Briton in Prussia, all spoke French and shared a common cultural outlook.

Decorative architecture, especially interior design, reflected the increasing sociability of the aristocracy. Entertainment became a central part of aristocratic life, losing its previous formality. In this atmosphere music became one of the passions of noble culture. The string quartet made its first appearance in the eighteenth century and chamber music enjoyed unparalleled popularity.

Musical entertainments in European country houses were matched by the literary and philosophical entertainments of the urban salons. The salons, especially in Paris, blended the aristocracy and bourgeoisie with the leading intellectuals of the age. At formal meetings, papers on scientific or philosophical topics were read and discussed. At informal gatherings new ideas were examined and exchanged. There were to be found the most influential thinkers of the day presenting the ideas of the Enlightenment, a new European outlook on religion, society, and politics. The Enlightenment was not an aristocratic movement; indeed, many Enlightenment ideas were profoundly anti-aristocratic. But it was

the nobility who had the leisure to read, write, and discuss, and many of the nobility were actively engaged in the intellectual and social changes that the Enlightenment brought in its wake. Though enlightened thinkers sought the improvement of life for the many, they pitched their appeal to the few. "Taste is thus like philosophy," Voltaire opined. "It belongs to a very small number of privileged souls."

The Enlightenment

The Enlightenment was less a set of ideas than it was a set of attitudes. At its core was criticism, a questioning of traditional institutions, customs, and morals. In 1762 the French philosopher Jean-Jacques Rousseau (1712–78) published one of the most important works on social theory, *The Social Contract*, which opened with the gripping maxim "Man is born free and everywhere he is in chains." But most of the great thinkers of the Enlightenment were not so much philosophers as savants, knowledgeable popularizers whose skills were in simplifying and publicizing a hodgepodge of new views.

In France Enlightenment intellectuals were called *philosophes* and claimed all the arts and sciences as their purview. The *Encyclopedia* (35 volumes, 1751–80), edited by Denis Diderot (1713–84), was one of the greatest achievements of the age. Entitled the *Systematic Dictionary of the Sciences, Arts, and Crafts*, it attempted to summarize all acquired knowledge and to dispel all imposed superstitions. There was no better definition of a *philosophe* than that given them by one of their enemies. "Just what is a *philosophe?* A kind of monster in society who feels under no obligation towards its manners and morals, its proprieties, its politics, or its religion. One may expect anything from men of their ilk."

The influence of French counterculture on enlightened thought was great, but the Enlightenment was by no means a strictly French phenomenon. Its greatest figures included the Scottish economist Adam Smith (1723–90), the Italian legal reformer Cesare Beccaria (1738–94), and the German philosopher Immanuel Kant (1724–1804). In France it began among anti-establishment critics; in Scotland and the German states it flourished in the universities; and in Prussia, Austria, and Russia it was propagated by the monarchy. The Enlightenment began in the 1730s and was still going strong a half-century later when its attitudes had been absorbed into the mainstream of European thought.

No brief summary can do justice to the diversity of enlightened thought in eighteenth-century Europe.

THE PURPOSE OF AN ENCYCLOPEDIA

■ *The* Encyclopedia *was one of the great collaborative ventures of the new spirit of reason that so characterized the Enlightenment. Following is the* Encyclopedia's *entry on itself, the purpose of compiling human knowledge in book form.*

Encyclopedia . . . In truth, the aim of an *encyclopedia* is to collect all the knowledge scattered over the face of the earth, to present its general outlines and structure to the men with whom we live, and to transmit this to those who will come after us, so that the work of past centuries may be useful to the following centuries, that our children, by becoming more educated, may at the same time become more virtuous and happier, and that we may not die without having deserved well of the human race . . .

　　I have said that it could only belong to a philosophical age to attempt an *encyclopedia;* and I have said this because such a work constantly demands more intellectual daring than is commonly found in [less courageous periods]. All things must be examined, debated, investigated without exception and without regard for anyone's feelings . . . We must ride roughshod over all these ancient puerilities, overturn the barriers that reason never erected, give back to the arts and sciences the liberty that is so precious to them . . . We have for quite some time needed a reasoning age when men would no longer seek the rules in classical authors but in nature.

From Denis Diderot, *The Encyclopedia* (1751–72).

Because it was an attitude of mind rather than a set of shared beliefs, there are many contradictory strains to follow. In his famous essay *What Is Enlightenment?* (1784) Immanuel Kant described it simply as freedom to use one's own intelligence. "I hear people clamor on all sides: Don't argue! The officer says: Don't argue, drill! The tax collector says: Don't argue, pay. The pastor says: Don't argue, believe." To all of them Kant replied: "Dare to know! Have the courage to use your own intelligence."

The Spirit of the Enlightenment.　In 1734 there appeared in France a small book entitled *Philosophical Letters Concerning the English Nation*. Its author, Voltaire (1694–1778) had spent two years in Britain and while there he made it his business to study the differences between the peoples of the two nations. In a simple but forceful style Voltaire demonstrated time and again the superiority of the British. They practiced religious toleration and were not held under the sway of a venal clergy. They valued people for their merits rather than their birth. Their political constitution was a marvel— "The English nation is the only one on earth that has succeeded in controlling the power of kings by resisting

them." They made national heroes of their scientists, their poets, and their philosophers. In all of this Voltaire contrasted British virtue with French vice. He attacked the French clergy and nobility directly, the French monarchy implicitly. Not only did he praise the genius and accomplishments of Sir Isaac Newton above those of René Descartes, but he also graphically contrasted the Catholic church's persecution of Descartes with the British state's celebration of Newton. "England, where men think free and noble thoughts," Voltaire enthused.

　　It is difficult now to recapture the psychological impact that the *Philosophical Letters* had on the generation of educated Frenchmen who first read them. The book was officially banned and publicly burned, and a warrant was issued for Voltaire's arrest. The *Letters* dropped like a bombshell upon the moribund intellectual culture of the Church and the universities and burst open the complacent, self-satisfied Cartesian worldview. The book ignited in France a movement that would soon be found in nearly every corner of Europe.

　　Born in Paris in 1694 into a bourgeois family with court office, François-Marie Arouet, who later took the pen name Voltaire, was educated by the Jesuits, who encouraged his poetic talents and instilled in him an enduring love of literature. He was a difficult student, especially as he had already rejected the core of the Jesuits' religious doctrine. He was no less difficult as he grew and began a career as a poet and playwright. It was not long before he was imprisoned in the Bastille for penning verses that maligned the honor of the regent of France. Released from prison, he insulted a nobleman, who retaliated by having his servants publicly beat Voltaire. Voltaire issued a challenge for a duel, a greater insult than the first, given his low birth. Again he was sent to the Bastille and was only released on the promise that he would leave the country immediately.

Thus Voltaire found himself in Britain, where he spent two years learning English, writing plays, and enjoying his celebrity free from the dangers that celebrity entailed in France. When he returned to Paris in 1728, it was with the intention of popularizing Britain to Frenchmen. He wrote and produced a number of plays and began writing the *Philosophical Letters*, a work that not only secured his reputation but also forced him into

exile at the village of Cirey, where he moved in with the Marquise du Châtelet (1706–49).

The Marquise du Châtelet, though only twenty-seven at the time of her liaison with Voltaire, was one of the leading advocates of Newtonian science in France. She built a laboratory in her home and introduced Voltaire to experimental science. While she undertook the immense challenge of translating Newton into French, Voltaire worked on innumerable projects: poems, plays, philosophical and anti-religious tracts (which she wisely kept him from publishing), and histories. It was one of the most productive periods of his life, and when the Marquise du Châtelet died in 1749, Voltaire was crushed.

Now past 50 years old, Voltaire began his travels. He was invited to Berlin by Frederick the Great, who admired him most of all the intellectuals of the age. The relationship between these two great egotists was predictably stormy and resulted in Voltaire's arrest in Frankfurt. Finally allowed to leave Prussia, Voltaire eventually settled in Geneva, where he quickly became

Painting of a lively conversation among philosophers, who are conveniently identified by number. Voltaire, with raised arm, is shown seated to the left of Diderot.

This illustration from Diderot's Encyclopedia *details the many types of wigs and tonsorial accessories worn by men in the eighteenth century. The tradition of wig-wearing lingers on in British law courts.*

questioned his own paternity and the morals of his mother; he lived openly with the Marquise du Châtelet and her husband; and he spoke as slightingly of kings and aristocrats as he did of his numerous critics. At the height of the French Revolution, Voltaire's body was removed from its resting place in Champagne and taken in great pomp to Paris, where it was interred in the Panthéon, where the heroes of the nation were put to rest. "Voltaire taught us to be free," was the slogan that the Parisian masses chanted during the funeral procession. It was an ending perhaps too solemn and conventional for one as irreverent as Voltaire. When the monarchy was restored after 1815, his bones were unceremoniously dumped in a lime pit.

Some enlightened thinkers based their critical outlook on skepticism, the belief that nothing could be known for certain. When the Scottish philosopher David Hume (1711–76) was accused of being an atheist, he countered the charge by saying he was too skeptical to be certain that God did not exist. Hume's first major philosophical work, *A Treatise of Human Nature* (1739), made absolutely no impression upon his contemporaries. For a time he took a post as a merchant's clerk; then he served as a tutor; and finally he found a position as a private secretary. During the course of these various employments he continued to write, publishing a series of essays on the subject of morality and rewriting his treatise into *An Enquiry Concerning Human Understanding* (1748), his greatest philosophical work.

embroiled in local politics and was none too politely asked to leave. He was tired of wandering and tired of being chased. His youthful gaiety and high spirits, which remained in Voltaire long past youth, were dealt a serious blow by the tragic earthquake in Lisbon in 1755, when thousands of people attending church services were killed.

Optimism in the face of such a senseless tragedy was no longer possible. His black mood was revealed in *Candide* (1759), which was to become his enduring legacy. *Candide* introduced the ivory-tower intellectual Dr. Pangloss, the overly optimistic Candide, and the very practical philosophy, "everyone must cultivate their own garden." It was Voltaire's capacity to challenge all authority that was probably his greatest contribution to Enlightenment attitudes. He held nothing sacred. He

Voltaire.

David Hume.

Hume made two seminal contributions to Enlightenment thought. He exploded the synthesis of Descartes by arguing that neither matter nor mind could be proved to exist with any certainty. Only perceptions existed, either as impressions of material objects or as ideas. If human understanding was based on sensory perception rather than on reason, then there could be no certainty in the universe. Hume's second point launched a frontal attack upon established religion. If there could be no certainty, then the revealed truths of Christian religion could have no basis. In his historical analysis of the origins of religion Hume argued that "religion grows out of hope or fear." He attacked the core of Christian explanations based on either Providence or miracles by arguing that to anyone who understood the basis of human perception it would take a miracle to believe in miracles.

In 1749 Hume received in the mail a work from an admiring Frenchman, entitled *The Spirit of the Laws*. The sender was Charles-Louis de Secondat, Baron Montesquieu (1689–1755). Born in Bordeaux, he ultimately inherited both a large landed estate and the office of president of the Parlement of Bordeaux. His novel *Persian Letters* (1721) was a brilliant satire of Parisian morals, French society, and European religion all bound together by the story of a Persian despot who leaves his harem to learn about the ways of the world. The use of the Persian outsider allowed Montesquieu to comment on the absurdity of European customs in general and French practices in particular. The device of the harem allowed him to titillate his audience with exotic sexuality.

After this success, Montesquieu decided to sell his office and make the grand tour. He spent nearly two years in England for which, like Voltaire, he came to have the greatest admiration. Back in Bordeaux, Montesquieu began to assemble his thoughts for what he believed would be a great work of political theory. The two societies that he most admired were ancient Rome and present-day Britain, and he studied the forms of their government and the principles that animated them. *The Spirit of the Laws* was published in 1748, and despite its gargantuan size and densely packed examples, it was immediately recognized as a masterpiece. Catherine the Great of Russia kept it at her bedside, and it was the single most influential work for the framers of the United States Constitution.

In both the *Persian Letters* and *The Spirit of the Laws* Montesquieu explored how liberty could be achieved and despotism avoided. He divided all forms of government into republics, monarchies, and despotisms. Each form had its own peculiar spirit: virtue and moderation in republics, honor in monarchies, and fear in despotisms. Like each form, each spirit was prone to abuse and had to be restrained if republics were not to give way to vice and excess, monarchies to corruption, and despotisms to repression. Montesquieu classified regimes as either moderate or immoderate, and through the use of extensive historical examples attempted to demonstrate how moderation could be maintained through rules and restraints, through the spirit of the law.

For Montesquieu, a successful government was one in which powers were separated and checks and balances existed within the institutions of the state. As befit a provincial magistrate, he insisted upon the absolute separation of the judiciary from all other branches of government. The law needed to be independent and impartial and it needed to be just. Montesquieu advocated that law codes be reformed and reduced mainly to regulate crimes against persons and property. Punishment should fit the crime but should be humane. He was one of the first to advocate the abolition of torture. Like most Europeans of his age, he saw monarchy as the only realistic form of government, but he argued that for

VOLTAIRE'S DEFINITION OF EVIL

■ More than anyone, Voltaire symbolized the new thinking of the Enlightenment. Witty, ironic, irreverent, and penetrating, his writings provoked howls of protest and squeals of delight. Among the most widely read was his philosophical dictionary, from which this definition of evil is drawn.

People clamor that human nature is essentially perverse, that man is born the child of the devil, and of evil. Nothing is more ill-advised; for, my friend, in preaching at me that everybody is born perverse, you warn me that you were born that way, that I must distrust you as I would a fox or a crocodile . . . It would be much more reasonable, much nobler, to say to me: "You were all born good; see how frightful it would be to corrupt the purity of your being." We should treat mankind as we should treat all men individually . . .

Man is not born evil; he becomes evil, as he becomes sick . . . Gather together all the children of the universe; you will see in them nothing but innocence, gentleness, and fear . . .

If men were essentially evil, if they were all born the subjects of a being as malevolent as it is unhappy, who inspired them with all this frenzy to avenge his own torment, we would see husbands murdered by their wives, and fathers by their children every morning.

From Voltaire, *The Philosophical Dictionary* (1764).

---

a monarchy to be successful, it needed a strong and independent aristocracy to restrain its tendency toward corruption and despotism. He based his arguments on what he believed was the case in Britain, which he praised as the only state in Europe in which liberty resided.

Enlightened thinkers attacked established institutions, above all the Church. Most were deists who believed in the existence of God on rational grounds only. Following the materialistic ideas of the new science, deists believed that nature conformed to its own material laws and operated without divine intervention. God, in a popular Enlightenment image, was like a clock-maker who constructed the elaborate mechanism, wound it, and gave the pendulum its first swing. After that the clock worked by itself. Deists were accused of being anti-Christian and they certainly opposed the ritual forms of both Catholic and Protestant worship. They also opposed the role of the Church in education, for education was the key to an enlightened view of the future. This meant, above all, conflict with the Jesuits. "Let's eat a Jesuit," was Voltaire's half-facetious comment.

Jean-Jacques Rousseau attacked the educational system. His tract on education, disguised as the romantic novel *Emile* (1762), argued that children should be taught by appealing to their interests rather than with strict discipline. Education was crucial because the Enlightenment was dominated by the idea of the British philosopher John Locke (1632–1704) that the mind was blank at birth, a *tabula rasa*—"white paper void of all characters"—and that it was filled up by experience. Contrary to the arguments of Descartes, Locke wrote in *An Essay Concerning Human Understanding* (1690) that there were no innate ideas and no good or evil that was not conditioned by experience. For Locke, as for a host of thinkers after him, good and evil were defined as pleasure and pain. We do good because it is pleasurable and we avoid evil because it is painful. Morality was a sense experience rather than a theological one. It was also relative rather than absolute. This was an observation that derived from increased interest in non-European cultures. The *Persian Letters* of Baron Montesquieu was the most popular of a genre that described non-European societies that knew nothing of Christian morality.

By the middle of the eighteenth century the pleasure/pain principle enunciated by Locke had come to be applied to the foundations of social organization. If personal good was pleasure, then social good was happiness. The object of government, in the words of the Scottish moral philosopher Francis Hutcheson (1694–1746), was "the greatest happiness of the greatest number." This

The frontispiece from Montesquieu's The Spirit of the Laws *has a medallion of the author surrounded by allegorical figures, including blind justice. In the lower left corner are copies of the authors works.*

of liberation from the weight of centuries of traditions. "This is the best of all possible worlds and all things turn out for the best," was the satirical slogan of Voltaire's *Candide.* But if Voltaire believed that enlightened thinkers had taken optimism too far, others believed that it had to be taken further still.

Progress, an idea that not all enlightened thinkers shared, was another invention of the age. It was expressed most cogently by the French philosopher the Marquis de Condorcet (1743–94) in *The Progress of the Human Mind* (1795), in which he developed an almost evolutionary view of human development from a savage state of nature to a future of harmony and international peace.

The Impact of the Enlightenment. As there was no single set of Enlightenment beliefs, so there was no single impact of the Enlightenment. Its general influence was felt everywhere, even seeping to the lowest strata of society. Its specific influence is harder to gauge. Paradoxically, enlightened political reform took firmer root in eastern Europe, where the ideas were imported, than in western Europe, where they originated. It was absolute rulers who were most successful in borrowing Enlightenment reforms.

It is impossible to determine what part enlightened ideas and what part practical necessities played in the

principle was at the core of *Crimes and Punishments* (1764), Cesare Beccaria's pioneering work of legal reform. Laws were instituted to promote happiness within society. They had to be formulated equitably for both criminal and victim. Punishment was to act as a deterrent to crime rather than as retribution. Therefore Beccaria advocated the abolition of torture to gain confessions, the end of capital punishment, and the rehabilitation of criminals through the improvement of penal institutions. By 1776 happiness was established as one of the basic rights of man, enshrined in the American Declaration of Independence as "life, liberty, and the pursuit of happiness."

It was in refashioning the world through education and social reform that the Enlightenment revealed its orientation toward the future. *Optimism* was a word invented in the eighteenth century to express this feeling

Jean-Jacques Rousseau.

THE STRENGTHS OF REPUBLICAN GOVERNMENT

■ *Baron de Montesquieu's* Spirit of the Laws *was one of the most important political works of the Enlightenment. It analyzed the various forms of government and estimated their strengths and weaknesses. Montesquieu provided inspiration for the American Declaration of Independence and the Constitution.*

OF THE REPUBLICAN GOVERNMENT, AND THE LAWS IN RELATION TO DEMOCRACY

In a democracy the people are in some respects the sovereign, and in others the subject. There can be no exercise of sovereignty but by their suffrages, which are . . . fundamental to this government. And indeed it is as important to regulate in a republic, in what manner, by whom, to whom, and concerning what suffrages are to be given, as it is in a monarchy to know who is the prince, and after what manner he ought to govern . . .

The people are extremely well qualified for choosing those whom they are to intrust with part of their authority . . . They can tell when a person has fought many battles, and been crowned with success . . . They can tell when a judge is assiduous in his office, gives general satisfaction, and has never been charged with bribery . . . But are they capable of conducting an intricate affair, of seizing and improving the opportunity and critical moment of action? No; this surpasses their abilities . . .

As most citizens have sufficient ability to choose, though unqualified to be chosen, so the people, though capable of calling others to an account for their administration, are incapable of conducting the administration themselves.

From Montesquieu, *Spirit of the Laws* (1750).

eastern European reform movement that began around mid-century. In at least three areas the coincidence between ideas and actions was especially strong: law, education, and the extension of religious toleration. Law was the basis of Enlightenment views of social interaction, and the influence of Montesquieu and Beccaria spread quickly. In Prussia and Russia the movement to codify and simplify the legal system did not reach fruition in the eighteenth century, but in both places it was well under way. The Prussian jurist Samuel von Cocceji (1679–1755) initiated the reform of Prussian law and legal administration. Cocceji's project was to make the enforcement of law uniform throughout the realm, to prevent judicial corruption, and to produce a single code of Prussian law. The code, finally completed in the 1790s, reflected the principles of criminal justice articulated by Beccaria. In Russia, the Law Commission summoned by Catherine the Great in 1767 never did complete its work. Nevertheless, profoundly influenced by Montesquieu, Catherine attempted to abolish torture and to introduce the Beccarian principle that the accused was innocent until proven guilty. In Austria, Joseph II presided over a wholesale

reorganization of the legal system. Courts were centralized, laws codified, and torture and capital punishment abolished.

Enlightenment ideas also underlay the efforts to improve education in eastern Europe. The religious orders, especially the Jesuits, were the most influential educators of the age, and the Enlightenment attack upon them created a void that had to be filled by the state. Efforts at compulsory education were first undertaken in Russia under Peter the Great, but these were aimed at the compulsory education of the nobility. It was Catherine who extended the effort to the provinces, attempting to educate a generation of Russian teachers. She was especially eager that women receive primary schooling, although the prejudice against educating women was too strong to overcome. Austrian and Prussian reforms were more successful in extending the reach of primary education, even if its content remained weak.

Religious toleration was the area in which the Enlightenment had its greatest impact in Europe, though again it was in the eastern countries that this was most visible. Freedom of worship for Catholics was barely whispered about in Britain, while neither France nor Spain were moved to tolerate Protestants. Nevertheless, within these parameters there were some important changes in the religious makeup of the western European states. In Britain, Protestant dissenters were no longer persecuted for their beliefs. By the end of the eighteenth century the number of Protestants outside the Church of England was growing, and by the early nineteenth century discrimination against Protestants was all but eliminated. In France and Spain relations between the national church and the papacy were undergoing a reorientation. Both states were asserting more independence—both theologically and financially—from Rome. The shift was symbolized by disputes over the role of the Jesuits, who were finally expelled from France in 1764 and from Spain in 1767.

In eastern Europe, enlightened ideas about religious toleration did take effect. Catherine the Great abandoned persecution of a Russian Orthodox sect known as the Old Believers. Prussia had always tolerated various Protestant groups, and with the conquest of Silesia it acquired a large Catholic population. Catholics were guaranteed freedom of worship, and Frederick the Great even built a Catholic church in Berlin to symbolize this policy. Austria extended furthest enlightened ideas about toleration. Maria Theresa was a devout Catholic and actually increased religious persecution in her realm. But Joseph II rejected his mother's dogmatic position. In 1781 he issued the Patent of Toleration, which granted freedom of worship to Protestants and members of the Eastern Orthodox church. The following year he extended this toleration to Jews. Joseph's attitude toward toleration was as practical as it was enlightened. He believed that the revocation of the Edict of Nantes—which had granted limited toleration to Protestants—at the end of the seventeenth century had been an economic disaster for France, and he encouraged religious toleration as a means to economic progress.

A science of economics was first articulated during the Enlightenment. A group of French thinkers known as the *physiocrats* subscribed to the view that land was wealth and thus argued that agricultural activity, especially improved means of farming and livestock breeding, should take first priority in state reforms. As wealth came from land, taxation should be based only on land ownership, a principle that was coming into increased prominence, despite the opposition of the landowning class. Physiocratic ideas combined a belief in the sanctity of private property with the need for the state to increase agricultural output. Ultimately the physiocrats, like the great Scottish economic theorist Adam Smith, came to believe that government should cease to interfere with private economic activity. They articulated the doctrine *laissez faire, laissez passer*—"let it be,

THE INDESTRUCTIBILITY OF THE GENERAL WILL

■ *Jean-Jacques Rousseau's* The Social Contract *was one of the greatest visionary tracts of the eighteenth century. In it Rousseau envisioned a harmonious society capable of eliminating want and controlling evil. Here he discusses his famous idea of the general will.*

As long as men united together look upon themselves as a single body, they have but one will relating to the common preservation and general welfare. Then all the energies of the state are vigorous and simple; its maxims are clear and luminous; there are no mixed contradictory interests; the common prosperity shows itself everywhere, and requires only good sense to be appreciated. Peace, union, and equality are enemies of political subtleties. Upright, honest men are difficult to deceive, because of their simplicity; decoys and pretexts do not impose upon them, they are not cunning enough to be dupes. When we see among the happiest people in the world troops of peasants regulating the affairs of state under an oak, and conducting themselves wisely, can we help despising the refinements of other nations, who make themselves illustrious and miserable with so much art and mystery?

From Jean-Jacques Rousseau, *The Social Contract* (1762).

Major Works of the Enlightenment

1690	*An Essay Concerning Human Understanding* (Locke)
1721	*Persian Letters* (Baron Montesquieu)
1734	*Philosophical Letters Concerning the English Nation* (Voltaire)
1739	*A Treatise of Human Nature* (Hume)
1740	*Pamela* (Richardson)
1748	*An Enquiry Concerning Human Understanding* (Hume) *The Spirit of the Laws* (Baron Montesquieu)
1751–80	*Encyclopedia* (Diderot)
1759	*Candide* (Voltaire)
1762	*Emile; The Social Contract* (Rousseau)
1764	*Crimes and Punishments* (Beccaria)
1784	*What Is Enlightenment?* (Kant)
1795	*The Progress of the Human Mind* (Marquis de Condorcet)
1798	*An Essay on the Principles of Population* (Malthus)

let it go." The ideas of Adam Smith and the physiocrats ultimately formed the basis for nineteenth-century economic reform.

If the Enlightenment did not initiate a new era, it did offer a new vision, whether in Hume's psychology, Montesquieu's political science, Rousseau's sociology, or Smith's economic theory. All of these subjects, which have such a powerful impact on contemporary life, had their modern origins in the Enlightenment. As the British poet Alexander Pope (1688–1744) put it: "Know then thyself, presume not God to scan/ The proper study of mankind is man." Enlightened thinkers challenged existing ideas and existing institutions. A new emphasis on self and on pleasure led to a new emphasis on happiness. All three fed into the distinctively Enlightenment idea of self-interest. Happiness and self-interest were values that would inevitably corrode the old social order, which was based upon principles of self-sacrifice and corporate identity. It was only a matter of time.

The Bourgeoisie

Bourgeois is a French word, and it carried the same tone of derision in the eighteenth century that it does today. The bourgeois was a man on the make, scrambling after money or office or title. He was neither well born nor well bred, or so said the nobility. Yet the bourgeoisie served vital functions in all European societies. They dominated trade, both nationally and internationally. They made their homes in cities and did much to improve the quality of urban life. They were the civilizing influence in urban culture, for unlike the nobility they were permanent denizens of the city. Perhaps most importantly, the bourgeoisie provided the safety valve between the nobility and those who were acquiring wealth and power but who lacked the advantages of birth and position. By developing their own culture and class identity, the bourgeoisie provided successful individuals with their own sense of pride and achievement and eased the explosive buildup of social resentments.

In the eighteenth century the bourgeoisie was growing in both numbers and importance. An active commercial and urban life gave many members of this group new social and political opportunities and many of them passed into the nobility through the purchase of land or office. But for those whose aspirations or abilities were different, this social group began to define its own values, which centered on the family and the home. A new interest in domestic affairs touched both men and women of the European bourgeoisie. Their homes became a social center for kin and neighbors and their outlook on family life reflected new personal relationships.

Marriages were made for companionship as much as for economic advantage. Romantic love between husbands and wives was newly valued. So were children, whose futures came to dominate familial concern. Childhood was recognized as a separate stage of life and the education of children as one of the most important of parental concerns. The image of the affectionate father replaced that of the hard-bitten businessman; the image of the doting mother replaced that of the domestic drudge.

The Dutton Family *by John Zoffany. This eighteenth-century painting shows the comforts enjoyed by the British upper middle class.*

Urban Elites

In the society of orders, nobility was the acid test. The world was divided into the small number of those who had it and the large number of those who did not. At the apex of the non-noble pyramid was the bourgeoisie, the elites of urban Europe whose place in the society of orders was ambiguous. Bourgeois, or burgher, simply meant "town dweller," but as a social group it had come to mean "wealthy town dweller." The bourgeoisie was strongest where towns were strongest: in western rather than in eastern Europe, in northern rather than southern Europe, with the notable exception of Italy. Holland was the exemplar of a bourgeois republic. More than half of the Dutch population lived in towns and there was no significant aristocratic class to compete for power. The Regents of Amsterdam were the equivalent of a European court nobility in wealth, power, and prestige, though not in the way in which they had accumulated their fortunes. The size of the bourgeoisie in various European states cannot be absolutely determined. At the end of the eighteenth century the British middle classes probably constituted around 15 percent of the population, the French bourgeoisie less than 10 percent. By contrast, the Russian or Hungarian urban elites were less than 2 percent of the population of those states.

Like the nobility, the bourgeoisie constituted a diverse group. At the top were great commercial families engaged in the expanding international marketplace and reaping the profits of trade. In wealth and power they were barely distinguishable from the nobility. At the bottom were the so-called petit-bourgeois; shopkeepers, craftsmen, and industrial employers. The solid core of the bourgeoisie was employed in trade, exchange, and service. Most were engaged in local or national commerce. Trade was the lifeblood of the city, for by itself the city could neither feed nor clothe its inhabitants. Most bourgeois fortunes were first acquired in trade. Finance was the natural outgrowth of commerce, and another segment of the bourgeoisie accumulated or preserved their capital through the sophisticated financial instruments of the eighteenth century. While the very wealthy loaned directly to the central government or bought shares in overseas trading companies, most bourgeois participated in government credit markets. They purchased state bonds or lifetime annuities and lived on the interest. The costs of war flooded the urban credit markets with high-yielding and generally stable financial instruments. Finally, the bourgeoisie were members of the burgeoning professions that provided services for the rich. Medicine, law, education, and the bureaucracy were all bourgeois professions, for the cost of acquiring the necessary skills could be borne only by those already wealthy.

During the course of the eighteenth century, this combination of occupational groups was expanding both in numbers and in importance all over Europe. So was the bourgeois habitat. The urbanization of Europe continued steadily throughout the eighteenth century. A greater percentage of the European population were living in towns and a greater percentage were living in large towns of over 10,000 inhabitants which, of necessity, were developing complex socioeconomic structures. In France alone there were probably over a hundred such towns, each requiring the services of the bourgeoisie and providing opportunities for their expansion. And the larger the metropolis the greater the need. In 1600 only twenty European cities contained as many as 50,000 people; in 1700 that number had risen to thirty-two; and by 1800 to forty-eight. London, the largest city, had grown to 865,000, a remarkable feat considering that in 1665 over a quarter of the London population died in the Great Plague. In such cities the demand for lawyers and doctors, for merchants and shopkeepers was almost insatiable.

Besides wealth, the urban bourgeoisie shared another characteristic: mobility. The aspiration of the bourgeoisie was to become noble, either through office or by acquiring rural estates. In Britain, a gentleman was still defined by lifestyle. "All are accounted gentlemen in England who maintain themselves without manual labor." Many trading families left their wharves and countinghouses to acquire rural estates, live off rents, and practice the openhanded hospitality of a gentleman. In France and Spain, nobility could still be purchased, though the price was constantly going up. For the greater bourgeoisie, the transition was easy; for the lesser, the failure to move up was all the more frustrating for being just beyond their grasp. The bourgeoisie did not only imagine their discomfort, they were made to feel it at every turn. They were the butt of jokes, of theater, and of popular songs. They were the first victims in the shady financial dealings of the crown and court, the first casualties in urban riots. Despised from above, envied from below, the bourgeoisie were uncomfortable with the present yet profoundly conservative about the future. The one consolation to their perpetual misery was that as a group they got richer and richer. And as a group they began to develop a distinctive culture that reflected their qualities and aspirations.

Bourgeois Values

Many bourgeoisie viewed their condition as temporary and accepted the pejorative connotations of the word itself. They had little desire to defend a social group out of which they fervently longed to pass. Others, whose aspirations were lower, were nevertheless uncomfortable with the status that they had already achieved. They had no ambition to wear the silks and furs reserved for the nobility or to attend the opening night at the opera decked in jewels and finery. In fact, such ostentation was alien to their existence and to the success that they had achieved. There was a real tension between the values of noble and bourgeois. The ideal noble was idle, wasteful, and ostentatious; the ideal bourgeois was industrious, frugal, and sober. Voltaire, who made his fortune as a financial speculator rather than a man of letters, aped the lifestyle of the nobility. But he could never allow himself to be cheated by a tradesman, a mark of his origins. When Louis XVI tried to make household economies in the wake of a financial crisis, critics said that "he acts like a bourgeois."

Even if the bourgeoisie did not constitute a class, they did share certain attitudes that constituted a culture. The wealthy among them participated in the new world of consumption, whether they did so lavishly or frugally. For those who aspired to more than their birth allowed, there was a loosening of the strict codes of dress that reserved certain fabrics, decorative materials, and styles to the nobility. Merchants and bankers could now be seen in colored suits or with pipings made of cloth of gold; their wives could be seen in furs and silks. They might acquire silverware, even if they did not go so far as the nobility and have a coat of arms engraved upon it. Coaches and carriages were also becoming common among the bourgeoisie, to take them on the Sunday rides through the town gardens or to their weekend retreats in the suburbs. Parisian merchants, even master

The Marriage Contract from "Marriage à la Mode," a series of satirical paintings by the English artist William Hogarth (1697–1764). The contract is between the daughter of a rich but lowborn merchant and the son of an impoverished noble.

craftsmen like clockmakers, were now acquiring suburban homes although they could not afford to retire to them for the summer months.

But more and more, the bourgeoisie was beginning to travel. In Britain whole towns were established to cater to leisure travelers. The southwestern town of Bath, which was rebuilt in the eighteenth century, was the most popular of all European resort towns, famous since Roman times for the soothing qualities of its waters. Bath was soon a social center as notable for its marriage market as for its recreations. Brighton, a seaside resort on the south coast, quadrupled in size in the second half of the eighteenth century. Bathing—what we would call swimming—either for health or recreation, became a middle-class fad, displacing traditional fears of the sea.

The leisure that wealth bestowed on the bourgeoisie quickly became, in good bourgeois fashion, commercialized. Theater and music halls for both light and serious productions proliferated. Voltaire's plays were performed before packed houses in Paris, with the author himself frequently in attendance to bask in the adulation of the largely bourgeois audiences who attended them. In Venice it was estimated that over 1,200 operas were produced in the eighteenth century. Public concerts were a mark of bourgeois culture, for the court nobility was entertained at the royal palaces or at great country houses.

Theater and concert going were part of the new attitude toward socializing that was one of the greatest contributions of the Enlightenment. Enlightened thinkers spread their views in the salons, and the salons soon spawned the academies, local scientific societies which, though led and patronized by provincial nobles, included large numbers of bourgeois members. The academies sponsored essay competitions, built up libraries, and became the local center for intellectual interchange. A less structured form of sociability took place in the coffeehouses and tearooms that came to be a feature of even small provincial towns. In the early eighteenth century there were over two thousand London coffee shops where men—for the coffeehouse was largely a male preserve—could talk politics, read the latest newspapers and magazines, and indulge their taste for this still-exotic beverage. Parisian clubs, called *sociétés*, covered a multitude of diverse interests. Literary *sociétés* were the most popular, maintaining their purpose by forbidding drinking, eating, and gambling on their premises.

Above all, bourgeois culture was literate culture. Wealth and leisure led to mental pursuits—if not always to intellectual ones. The proliferation of relatively cheap printed material had an enormous impact on the lives of those who were able to afford it. Holland and Britain were the most literate European societies and

A caricature by an unknown artist shows Lloyd's, the famous London coffeehouse, in the 1790s.

also, because of the absence of censorship, the centers of European printing. This was the first great period of the newspaper and the magazine. The first daily newspaper appeared in London in 1702; eighty years later, thirty-seven provincial towns had their own newspapers, while the London papers were read all over Britain. Then as now, the newspaper was as much a vehicle for advertisement as for news. News reports tended to be bland, avoiding controversy and concentrating on general national and international events. Advertising, on the other hand, tended to be lurid, promising cures for incurable ills, and the most exquisite commodities at the most reasonable prices.

For entertainment and serious political commentary, the British reading public turned to magazines, of which there were over 150 separate titles by the 1780s. The most famous were *The Spectator*, which ran in the early part of the century and did much to set the tone for a cultured middle-class life, and the *Gentleman's Magazine*, which ran in the mid-century and was said to have had a circulation of nearly fifteen thousand. The longest-lived of all British magazines was *The Ladies Diary*, which continued in existence from 1704 to 1871 and doled out self-improvement, practical advice, and fictional romances in equal proportion.

The Ladies Diary was not the only literature aimed at the growing number of leisured and lettered bourgeois woman. Though enlightened thinkers could be ambivalent about the place of women in the new social order, they generally stressed the importance of female education and welcomed women's participation in intellectual pursuits. Whether it was new ideas about women or simply the fact that more women had leisure, a growing body of both domestic literature and light entertainment was available to them. This included a vast number of teach-yourself books aimed at instructing women how best to organize domestic life or how to navigate the perils of polite society. Moral instruction, particularly on the themes of obedience and sexual fidelity, was also popular. But the greatest output directed toward women was in the form of fanciful romances, from which a new genre emerged. The novel first appeared in its modern form in the 1740s. Samuel Richardson (1689–1761) wrote *Pamela* (1740), the story of a maidservant who successfully resisted the advances of her master until he finally married her. It was composed in long episodes, or chapters, that developed Pamela's character and told her story at the expense of the overt moral message that was Richardson's original intention.

Family Life

In the eighteenth century a remarkable transformation in home life was under way, one that the bourgeoisie shared with the nobility. In the pursuit of happiness encouraged by the Enlightenment, one of the newest joys was domesticity. The image—and sometimes the reality—of the happy home, where love was the bond between husband and wife and care between parents and children, came to dominate both the literary and visual arts. Only those wealthy enough to afford to dispense with women's work could partake of the new domesticity, only those touched by Enlightenment ideas could attempt to make the change. But where it occurred, the transformation in the nature of family life

Lady leaving a lending library with a book, a colored mezzotint by J. R. Smith, 1781.

was one of the most profound alterations in eighteenth-century culture.

The first step toward the transformation of family relationships was in centering the conjugal family in the home. In the past, the family was a less important structure for most people than the social groups to which they belonged or the neighborhood in which they lived. Marriage was an economic partnership at one end and a means to carry on lineage at the other. Individual fulfillment was not an object of marriage and this attitude could be seen among the elites in the high level of arranged marriages, the speed with which surviving spouses remarried, and the formal and often brutal personal relationships between husbands and wives.

Patriarchy was the dominant value within the family. Husbands ruled over wives and children, making all of the crucial decisions that affected both the quality of their lives and their futures. As late as the middle of the eighteenth century a British judge established the "rule of thumb," which asserted that a husband had a legal right to beat his wife with a stick, but the stick should be no thicker than a man's thumb. It was believed that children were stained with the sin of Adam at birth and that only the severest upbringing could clean some of it away. Children were sent out first for wet-nursing, then at around the age of seven for boarding, either at school or in a trade, and finally into their own marriages.

There can be no doubt that this profile of family life began to change, especially in western Europe, during the second half of the eighteenth century. Though the economic elements of marriage remained strong—newspapers actually advertised the availability of partners and the dowries or annual income that they would bring to the marriage—other elements now appeared. Fed by an unending stream of stories and novels and a new desire for individual happiness, romantic and sexual attraction developed into a factor in marriage. Potential marriage partners were no longer kept away from each other or smothered by chaperons. Perhaps more importantly, the role of potential spouses in choosing a partner appears to have increased. Even in earlier centuries parents did not simply assign a spouse to their children, but by the eighteenth century adolescents themselves searched for their own marriage partners and exercised a strong negative voice in identifying unsuitable ones.

The quest for compatibility, no less than the quest for romantic love, led to a change in personal relationships between spouses. The extreme formality of the

Motherhood, *an oil painting by Marguerite Gérard (1761–1837).*

past was gradually breaking down. Husbands and wives began spending more time with each other, developing common interests and pastimes. Their personal life began to change. For the first time houses were built to afford the couple privacy from their children, their servants, and their guests. Rooms were designed for specific functions and were set off by hallways. This new design allowed for an intimate life that earlier generations did not find necessary and which they could not, in any case, put into practice.

Couples had more time for each other because they were beginning to limit the size of their families. There were a number of reasons for this development, which again pertained only to the upper classes. For one thing, child mortality rates were declining among wealthy social groups. Virulent epidemic diseases like the plague, which knew no class lines, were gradually disappearing. Moreover, though there were few medical breakthroughs in this period, sanitation was improving. Bearing fewer children had an enormous impact on the lives of women, reducing the danger of death and disablement in childbirth and giving them leisure time to pursue domestic tasks. This is not to say that the early part of a woman's marriage was not dominated by children; in fact, because of new attitudes toward child rearing it may have been so dominated more than ever. Many couples appear to have made a conscious decision to space births, though success was limited by the fact that the most common technique of birth control was *coitus interruptus*, or withdrawal.

The transformation in the quality of relationships between spouses was mirrored by an even greater transformation in attitudes toward children. There were many reasons why childhood now took on a new importance. Decline in mortality rates had a profound psychological impact. Parents could feel that their emotional investment in their children had a greater chance of fulfillment. But equally important were the new ideas about education, especially Locke's belief that the child enters into the world a blank slate whose personality is created through early education. This view not only placed a new responsibility upon parents but also gave them the concept of childhood as a stage through which individuals passed. This idea could be seen in the commercial sphere as well as in any other. In 1700 there was not a single shop in London that sold children's toys exclusively; by the 1780s there were toyshops everywhere. There were also shops that sold clothes specifically designed for children, no longer simply adult clothes in miniature. Most important of all was the development of materials for the education of children. This took place in two stages. At first so-called children's books were books whose purpose was to help adults teach children. Later came books directed at children themselves with large print, entertaining illustrations, and nonsensical characters, usually animals who taught moral lessons.

The commercialization of childhood was, of course, directed at adults. The new books and games that were designed to enhance a child's education not only had to be purchased by parents but had to be used by them as well. More and more mothers were devoting their time to their children. Among the upper classes the practice of wet nursing began to decline. Mothers wanted to nurture their infants both literally by breast-feeding and figuratively by teaching them. Children became companions to be taken on outings to the increasing number of museums or shows of curiosities.

The emergence of the bourgeoisie was one of the central social developments of the eighteenth century. Their culture, which emphasized a fulfilling homelife, leisure pursuits, and literacy, soon came to dominate the values of society in general. But this transformation of family life could not be shared by the population at large. Working women could afford neither the cost of instructional materials for their children nor the time to use them. Ironically, they now began using wet nurses,

once the privilege of the wealthy, for increasingly a working woman's labor was the margin of survival for her family. Working women enjoyed no privacy in the hovels in which they lived with large families in single rooms. Wives and children were still beaten by husbands and fathers and were unacquainted with enlightened ideas of the worth of the individual and the innocence of the child. By the end of the eighteenth century two distinct family cultures coexisted in Europe, one based on companionate marriage and the affective bonds of parents and children, the other based on patriarchal dominance and the family as an economic unit.

The Masses

The paradox of the eighteenth century was that for the masses life was getting better by getting worse. More Europeans were surviving than ever before, more food was available to feed them; there was more housing, better sanitation, even better charities. Yet for all of this, there was more misery. Those who would have succumbed to disease or starvation a century before now survived from day to day, beneficiaries—or victims—of increased farm production and improved agricultural marketing. The market economy organized a more effective use of land, but it created a widespread social problem. The landless agrarian laborer of the eighteenth century was the counterpart of the sixteenth-century wandering beggar. In the cities, the plight of the poor was as desperate as ever. Even the most open-hearted charitable institutions were unable to cope with the massive increase in the poor. Thousands of mothers abandoned their children to the foundling hospitals, hoping they would have a better chance of survival, even though hospital death rates were near 80 percent.

Not all members of the lower orders succumbed to poverty or despair. In fact, many were able to benefit from existing conditions to lead a more fulfilling life than ever before. The richness of popular culture, signified by a spread of literacy into the lower reaches of European society, was one indication of this change. So too were the reforms urged by enlightened thinkers to improve basic education and to improve the quality of life in the cities. For that segment of the lower orders that could keep its head above water, the eighteenth century offered new opportunities and new challenges.

Beggar Feeding a Child, *by Giacomo Ceruti. Every eighteenth-century European city had its legion of beggars. This man has done well enough to be able to feed himself and his little daughter for one more day.*

Breaking the Cycle

Of all the legacies of the eighteenth century, none was more fundamental than the steady increase in European population that began around 1740. This was not the first time that Europe had experienced sustained population growth, but it was the first time that such growth was not checked by a demographic crisis. Breaking the cycle of population growth and crisis was a momentous event in European history despite the fact that it went unrecorded at the time and unappreciated for centuries after.

The figures tell one part of the story. In 1700 European population is estimated to have been 120 million. By 1800 it had grown 50 percent to over 180 million. And the aggregate hides significant regional variations. While France, Spain, and Italy expanded between 30 and 40 percent, Prussia doubled and Russia and Hungary may have tripled in number. Britain increased by 80 percent from about 5 to 9 million, but the rate of growth was accelerating. In 1695 the English population stood

at 5 million. It took 62 years to add the next million and 24 years to add the million after that. In 1781 the population was 7 million, but it took only 13 years to reach 8 million and only 10 more years to reach 9 million. Steady population growth had continued without significant checks for well over half a century.

Ironically, the traditional pattern of European population found its theorist at the very moment that it was about to disappear. In 1798 Thomas Malthus (1766–1834) published *An Essay on the Principles of Population.* Reflecting on the history of European population, Malthus observed the cyclical pattern by which growth over one or two generations was checked by a crisis that significantly reduced population. From these lower levels new growth began until it was checked and the cycle repeated itself. Because people increased more quickly than did food supplies, the land could sustain only a certain level of population. When that level was near, population became prone to a demographic check. Malthus divided population checks into two categories, positive and preventive. Positive checks were war, disease, and famine, all of which Malthus believed were natural, although brutal, means of population control. Famine was the obvious result of the failure of food supplies to keep pace with demand; war was the competition for scarce resources; and disease often accompanied both. It was preventive checks that most interested Malthus. These were the means by which societies could limit their growth to avoid the devastating consequences of positive checks. Celibacy, late marriages, and sexual abstinence were among the choices of which Malthus approved, though abortion, infanticide, and contraception were also commonly practiced.

In the sixteenth and seventeenth centuries, the dominant pattern of the life cycle was high infant and child mortality, late marriages, and early death. All controlled population growth. Infant and child mortality rates were staggering: only half of all those born reached the age of ten. Late marriage was the only effective form of birth control—given the strong social taboos against sexual relations outside marriage—for a late marriage reduced a woman's childbearing years. Women in western Europe generally married between the ages of twenty-four and twenty-six; they normally ceased bearing children at the age of forty. But not all marriages lasted this fourteen or sixteen-year span, as one or the other partner died. On average, the childbearing period for most women was between ten and twelve years, long enough to endure six pregnancies, which would result in three surviving children. (See Special Feature, "Giving Birth to the Eighteenth Century," pp. 640–641.)

A woman being delivered by a man midwife is covered by a sheet to protect her modesty. The inset is a model drawing showing a delivery using forceps.

Giving Birth to the Eighteenth Century

"In sorrow thou shalt bring forth children." Such was Eve's punishment for eating of the forbidden tree, and that sorrow continued for numberless generations. Childbirth was painful, dangerous, and all too often, deadly. Though successful childbirth needed no outside intervention whatsoever—there were no obstetricians in caves—without the accumulated wisdom of the ages, babies and mothers routinely perished. That wisdom was passed from mother to daughter and finally was accumulated by skilled women who practiced the craft of midwifery. Every village, no matter how small, had women who were capable of assisting others in childbirth.

Midwives, who until the late seventeenth century were always women, were part of the support group that attended a woman during her labor. Typically, childbirth was a social occasion for women. Along with the midwife would be a wet nurse and female kin and neighbors, who would offer encouragement, bring refreshments, and tend to the ordinary chores that the pregnant woman would otherwise have performed herself. Without chemicals to induce contractions and without the ability to intervene in the delivery, labor was usually a long-drawn-out affair. Ordinarily it did not take place in bed, but rather in a room or a part of a room set aside for the occasion. By the eighteenth century, at least in larger urban areas, poor women, who had no separate space for labor, could give birth in lying-in hospitals. Within the birthing room, the conclave of women was much like a social gathering. The pregnant woman was advised to adopt any positions that made her feel comfortable; standing and walking were favored in the belief that the effects of gravity helped the baby move downward. The woman might sit on a neighbor's lap or on a birthing stool, a chair open at the bottom, during contractions and delivery.

By the seventeenth century manuals for midwives began to be published, some of them written by women, but most by male doctors whose surgical experiences provided them with ideas and information that were valuable to childbearing. Midwives and doctors were always at daggers drawn. No matter how skilled, midwives were denied access to medical training that might have enabled them to develop lucrative practices on their own. Thus they had no intention of letting male doctors into their trade. For a time the compromise was the handbooks, which contained guides to anatomy, descriptions of the most common complications, and the direst warnings to call trained physicians when serious problems arose.

By the beginning of the eighteenth century the "man-midwife," medically trained and usually experienced in other forms of surgery, had made his appearance in western Europe. The emergence of the man-midwife led to a number of breakthroughs in increasing the safety of childbirth. But at the same time, the social experience of childbirth changed dramatically. What had been a female rite of passage, experienced by and with other women, now became a private event experienced by an individual woman and her male doctor. As female midwives were still excluded from medical training and licensing, their ability to practice their trade eroded in the face of new techniques and information to which they were denied access.

The man-midwife's first task was to ascertain that the fetus was in the proper position to descend. In order to do this, however, he had to make an examination that was socially objectionable. Though advanced thinkers could face their man-midwife with the attitude "I considered that through modesty I was not to give up my life"—as one English noblewoman reasoned—many women and more husbands were unprepared for the actual practice of a man. Thus students were taught that they were not to examine the patient unless there was another person present in the room. They were not to ask direct questions, and they were not to face the patient during any of their procedures. They were taught to keep a linen cloth on top of the woman's abdomen and to make the examination only by touch. If the fetus was in the correct position, nothing further would be done until the delivery itself. It was only when the fetus was in what was labeled an "unnatural" position that the skill of the physician came into play.

For the most part, a child that could not be delivered head first and face down was in serious risk of being stillborn, and the mother was in serious risk of dying in labor. This was the problem to which physicians addressed themselves in the eighteenth century and for

which they found remarkable solutions. The first advance was the realization that the fetus could be turned while still in the womb. Pressure applied on the outside of the stomach, especially in the early stages of labor, could help the fetus drop down correctly. A baby who emerged feet first had to be turned face down before it was pulled through the birth canal.

For babies who could not be manually manipulated, the greatest advance of the eighteenth century was the invention of the forceps. or the *tire-tête* as the French called them. With forceps the physician could pull the baby by force when the mother was incapable of delivery. Forceps were used mostly in breech births but were also a vital tool when the baby was too large to pass through the cervix by contraction. The forceps were invented in Britain in the middle of the seventeenth century. In the eighteenth century they came into general use when the Scotsman William Smellie (1697–1765) developed a short, leather-covered instrument that enabled the physician to do as little damage as possible to either mother or child. Obstetrics now emerged as a specialized branch of medical practice. If neither the pain nor the sorrow of childbirth could be eliminated, its dangers could be lessened.

Three surviving children for every two adults would, of course, have resulted in a 50 percent rise in population in every generation. Celibacy was one limiting factor, cities were another. Perhaps as much as 15 percent of the population in western Europe remained celibate either by entering religious orders that imposed celibacy or by lacking the personal or financial attributes necessary to make a match. Rural migrants accounted for the appallingly high urban death rates in cities. When we remember that the largest European cities were continuously growing—London from 200,000 in 1600 to 675,000 in 1750; Paris from 220,000 to 576,000; Rome from 105,000 to 156,000; Madrid from 49,000 to 109,000; Vienna from 50,000 to 175,000—then we can appreciate how many countless thousands of immigrants perished from disease, famine, and exposure before marriage. If urban perils were not enough, there were still the positive checks. Plagues carried away hundreds of thousands, wars halved populations of places in their path, and famine overwhelmed the weak and the poor.

The late seventeenth and early eighteenth centuries was a period of population stagnation if not actual decline. It was not until the third or fourth decade of the eighteenth century that another growth cycle began. It rapidly gained momentum throughout the Continent and showed no signs of abating after two full generations. More importantly, this upward cycle revealed unusual characteristics. In the first place fertility was increasing. This had several causes. In a few areas, most notably in Britain, women were marrying younger, thereby increasing their childbearing years. This pattern was also true in eastern Europe where women traditionally married younger. Sexual activity outside marriage was also rising. Illegitimacy rates, especially in the last decades of the century, were spurting everywhere.

But increasing fertility was only part of the picture. More significant was decreasing mortality. The positive checks of the past were no longer as potent. European warfare not only diminished in scale after the middle of the century, it changed location as well. Rivalry for colonial empires removed the theater of conflict from European communities. So did the increase in naval warfare. The damage caused by war had always been more by aftershock than by actual fighting. The destruction and pillage of crops and the wholesale slaughter of livestock created food shortages that weakened local populations for the diseases that came in train with the armies. As the virulence of warfare abated, so did that of epidemic disease. The plague had all but disappeared from western Europe by the middle of the eighteenth century. The widespread practice of quarantine, especially in Hungary, which had been the crucial bridge between eastern and western epidemics, went far to eradicate the scourge of centuries.

Without severe demographic crises to maintain the cyclical pattern, the European population began a gentle but continuous rise. Urban sanitation, at least for permanent city dwellers, was becoming more effective. Clean water supplies, organized waste and sewage disposal, and strict quarantines were increasingly part of urban regulations. The use of doctors and trained midwives helped lower the incidence of stillbirth and decreased the number of women who died in childbirth. Almost everywhere levels of infant and child mortality were decreasing. More people were being born, more were surviving the first ten dangerous years, and thus more were marrying and reproducing. Increased fertility and decreased mortality could have only one result: renewed population growth. No wonder Malthus was worried.

Daily Bread

In the past, if warfare or epidemic diseases failed to check population growth, famine would have done the job. How the European economy conquered famine in the eighteenth century is a complicated story. There was no single breakthrough that accounts for the ability to feed the tens of millions of additional people who now inhabited the Continent. Holland and Britain, at the cutting edge of agricultural improvement, employed dynamic new techniques that would ultimately provide the means to support continued growth, but most European agriculture was still mired in the time-honored practices that had endured for centuries. Still,

Agricultural techniques are illustrated in this plate from Diderot's Encyclopedia. *In the foreground, a man steers a high-wheeled, horse-drawn plow while a woman operates a hopper device to sow seeds.*

not everyone could be fed or fed adequately. Widespread famine might have disappeared, but slow starvation and chronic undernourishment had not. It is certainly the case that hunger was more common at the end of the eighteenth century than at the beginning and that the nutritional content of a typical diet may have reached its lowest point in European history.

Nevertheless, the capacity to sustain rising levels of population can be explained only in terms of agricultural improvement. Quite simply, European farmers were now producing more food and marketing it better. In the most advanced societies this was a result of conscious efforts to make agriculture more efficient. In traditional open-field agriculture, communities quickly ran up against insurmountable obstacles to growth. The three-field crop rotation system left a significant proportion of land fallow each year, while the concentration on subsistence cereal crops progressively eroded the land that was in production. Common farming was only as strong as the weakest member of the community. There was little incentive for successful individuals to plow profits back into the land, either through the purchase of equipment or the increase of livestock.

Livestock was a crucial variable in agricultural improvement. As long as there was only enough food for humans to eat, only essential livestock could be kept

alive over the winter. Oxen, which were still the ordinary beasts of burden, and pigs and poultry, which required only minimal feed, were the most common. But few animals meant little manure and without manure the soil could not easily be regenerated.

It was not until the middle of the seventeenth century that solutions to these problems began to appear. The first change was consolidation of landholdings so that traditional crop rotations could be abandoned. A second innovation was the introduction of fodder crops, some of which—like clover—added nutrients to the soil, while others—like turnips—were used to feed livestock. Better grazing and better winter feed increased the size of herds, while new techniques of animal husbandry, particularly crossbreeding, produced hardier strains. It was quite clear that the key to increased production lay in better fertilization, and by the eighteenth century some European farmers had broken through the "manure barrier." Larger herds, the introduction of clover crops, the use of human waste from towns, and even the first experiments with lime as an artificial fertilizer were all part of the new agricultural methods.

Along with the new crops that helped nourish both soil and animals came new crops that helped nourish people. Indian corn, or maize, was a staple crop for Native Americans and gradually came to be grown in most parts of western Europe. Maize not only had higher nutritional value than most other cereals, it also yielded more food per acre than traditional grains. So, too, did the potato, which also entered the European diet from the New World. The potato grew in poor soil, required less labor, and yielded an abundant and nutritious harvest. It rapidly took hold in Ireland and parts of Prussia, from which it spread into eastern Europe. The potato allowed families to subsist on smaller amounts of land and with less capital outlay.

It must be stressed, however, that these new developments involved only a very narrow range of producers. The new techniques were expensive and knowledge of the new crops spread slowly. Change had to overcome both inertia and intransigence. With more mouths to feed, profits from agriculture soared without landowners having to lift a finger. Only the most ambitious were interested in improvement. At the other end, peasant farmers were more concerned with failure than success. An experiment that did not work could devastate a community; one that did only meant higher taxes. Thus the most important improvements in agricultural production were more traditional ones. Basically, there was an increase in the amount of land that was utilized for

Cereal Crops

growing. In Russia, Prussia, and Hungary hundreds of thousands of new acres came under the plow, while in the west, drainage schemes and forest clearance expanded productive capacity.

There was also an upswing in the efficiency with which agricultural products were marketed. From the seventeenth century onward, market agriculture was gradually replacing subsistence agriculture in most parts of Europe. Market agriculture had the advantage of allowing specialization on farms. Single-crop farming enabled farmers to benefit from the peculiarities of their own soil and climate. They could then exchange their surplus for the range of crops they needed to subsist. Market exchange was facilitated by improved transportation and communication and above all by the increase in the population of towns, which provided demand. The new national and international trade in large quantities of grain evened out regional variations in harvests and went a long way toward reducing local grain shortages. The upkeep of roads, the building of canals, and the clearing of waterways created a national lifeline for the movement of grain.

Finally, it is believed that the increase in agricultural productivity owed something to a change in climate that took place in the late eighteenth century. The European climate is thought to have been unusually cold and wet during the seventeenth century, and it seems to have gradually warmed during the eighteenth century. Even moderate climatic change, when combined with new techniques, new crops, expanded cultivation, and improved marketing, would go a long way toward explaining how so many more people were being fed at the end of the eighteenth century.

The Plight of the Poor

"Of every ten men one is a beggar, five are too poor to give him alms, three more are ill at ease, embarrassed by debts and lawsuits, and the tenth does not represent a hundred thousand families." So observed an eighteenth-century Frenchman about the distribution of wealth in his country. There can be no doubt that the most serious social problem of the eighteenth century centered on the dramatic population increase of poor people throughout Europe. There was grim irony in the fact that advances in the production and distribution of food and the retreat of war and plague allowed more people to survive from hand to mouth than ever before. Where their ancestors had succumbed to quick death from disease or starvation, they eked out a miserable

existence of constant hunger and chronic pain with death at the end of a seemingly endless corridor.

It is impossible to gauge the number of European poor or to separate them into categories of greater and greatest misery. The truly indigent, the starving poor, probably composed 10 to 15 percent of most societies, perhaps as many as 20 million people throughout the Continent. They were most prevalent in towns but were an increasing burden on the countryside, where they wandered in search of agricultural employment. The wandering poor had no counterpart in eastern Europe, where serfdom kept everyone tied to the land, but the hungry and unsheltered certainly did. Yet the problem of poverty was not to be seen only among the destitute. In fact, the uniqueness of the poor in the eighteenth century is that they were drawn from social groups that even in the hungry times of the early seventeenth century had been successful subsistence producers.

It was easy to see why poverty was increasing. The relentless advance of population drove up the price of food and drove down the price of wages. In the second half of the eighteenth century, the cost of living in France rose by over 60 percent while wages rose only by 25 percent. In Spain the cost of living increased by 100 percent while wages rose only 20 percent. Only in Britain did wages nearly keep pace with prices. Rising prices made land more valuable. At the beginning of the eighteenth century, as the first wave of population expansion hit western Europe, smallholdings began to decrease in size. The custom of partible inheritance, by which each son received a share of land, shrank the average size of a peasant holding below that necessary to sustain an average-size family, let alone one that was growing larger. In one part of France it was estimated that thirty acres was a survival plot of land in good times. At the end of the seventeenth century 80 percent of the peasants there owned less than twenty-five acres.

As holdings contracted, the portion of the family income derived from wage labor expanded. In such circumstances males were more valuable than females, either as farmers or laborers, and there is incontrovertible evidence that European rural communities practiced female infanticide. In the end, however, it became increasingly difficult for the peasant family to remain on the land. Small freeholders were forced to borrow against future crops until a bad harvest led to foreclosure. Many were allowed to lease back their own lands, on short terms and at high rents, but most swelled the ranks of agricultural laborers, migrating during the planting and harvest seasons, suffering cruelly during winter and summer.

Emigration was the first logical consequence of poverty. In places where rural misery was greatest, like Ireland, whole communities pulled up stakes and moved to America. Frederick the Great attracted hundreds of thousands of emigrants to Prussia by offering them land. But most rural migrants did not move to new rural environments. Rather they followed the well-trodden paths to the cities. Many traditional domestic crafts were evolving into industrial activities. In the past, peasants supplemented their family income by processing raw materials in the home. Spinning, weaving, and sewing were common cottage industries in which the workers took in the work, supplied their own equipment, and were paid by the piece. Now, especially in the cloth trades, a new form of industrial activity was being organized. Factories, usually located in towns or larger villages, assembled workers together, set them at larger and more efficient machines, and paid them for their time rather than for their output. Families unable to support themselves from the land had no choice but to follow the movement of jobs.

Neither state nor private charities could cope with the flood of poor immigrants. Hospitals, workhouses, and more ominously, prisons were established or expanded to deal with them. Hospitals were residential asylums rather than places for health care. They took in the old, the incapacitated, and increasingly, the orphaned young. Workhouses existed for those who were capable of work but incapable of finding it. They were supposed to improve the values of the idle by keeping them busy, though in most places they served only to improve the profits of the industrialists, who rented out workhouse inmates at below-market wages. Prisons grew with crime. There were spectacular increases in crimes against property in all eighteenth-century cities and despite severe penalties that could include hanging for petty theft, more criminals were incarcerated than executed. Enlightened arguments for the reform of prisons and punishment tacitly acknowledged the social basis of most crime. As always, the victims of crime were mostly drawn from the same social backgrounds as the perpetrators. Along with all of their other troubles, it was the poor who were most commonly robbed, beaten, and abused.

Popular Culture

However depressing is this story of the unrelieved misery of the poor, we should not think of the masses of eighteenth-century society only as the downtrodden victims of social and economic forces beyond their control. For the peasant farmer about to lose his land or the urban artisan without a job, security was an overwhelming concern. While many were to endure such fates, many others lived comfortably by the standards of the age and almost everyone believed that things were better now than they had ever been before. Popular culture was a rich mixture of family and community activities that provided outlets from the pressures of work and the vagaries of fortune. It was no less sustaining to the population at large than was the purely literate culture of the elite, no less vital as a means of explanation for everyday events than the theories of the philosophers or the programs of the *philosophes*.

In fact, the line between elite and popular culture in the eighteenth century is a thin one. For one thing, there was still much mixing of social classes in both rural and urban environments. Occasions of display, like festivals, village fairs, or religious holidays, brought entire communities together and reinforced their collective identities. Moreover, there were many shared elements between the two cultures. All over Europe, literacy was increasing, the result of primary education, of new business techniques, and of the millions of books that were available in editions tailored to even the most modest purse. Nearly half of the inhabitants of France were literate by the end of the eighteenth century, perhaps 60 percent of those in Britain. Men were more likely to have learned to read than women, as were those who lived in urban areas. More than a quarter of French women could read, a number that had doubled over the century. As the rates of female literacy rose, so did overall rates, for women took the lead in teaching children.

Popular literacy spawned popular literature in remarkable variety. Religious tracts aimed at the populace were found throughout Europe. They contained stories of the saints in Catholic countries or of the martyrs in Protestant ones, proverbs intended to increase spirituality, and prayers to be offered for all occasions. Romances were the staple of lending libraries, which were also becoming a common feature of even small towns. These books were usually published in inexpensive installments spaced according to the time working families needed to save the pennies to purchase them. Yet the best-selling popular fiction, at least in western Europe, was melodramatic tales of knights and ladies from the age of chivalry. These themes had seeped into popular consciousness after having fallen out of favor among the elites.

Nevertheless, literate culture was not the dominant form of popular culture. Traditional social activities continued to reflect the violent and even brutal nature of day-to-day existence. Village festivals were still the safety valve of youth gangs who enforced sexual morals by shaming husbands whose wives were unfaithful or women whose reputations were sullied. Many holidays were celebrated by sporting events that pitted inhabitants of one village against those of another. These almost always turned into free-for-alls in which broken bones were common and deaths not unknown.

Even more popular were the so-called blood sports, which continued to be the most common form of popular recreation. These were brutal competitions in which, in one way or another, animals were maimed or slaughtered. Dog- and cock-fighting are among those that still survive today. Less attractive to the modern mind were bearbaiting or bullrunning, in which the object was the slaughter of a large beast over a prolonged period of time. Blood sports were certainly not confined to the masses—foxhunting and bullfighting were pastimes for the very rich—but they formed a significant part of local social activity.

So too did the tavern or alehouse, which in town or country was the site for local communication and recreation, where staggering amounts of alcohol were consumed. The increased use of spirits—gin, brandy, rum, and vodka—changed the nature of alcohol consumption in Europe. Wine and beer had always been drunk in quantities that we would find astounding, but these beverages were also an important part of diet. The nutritional content of spirits was negligible. People drank spirits to get drunk. The level to which drunkenness rose in the eighteenth century speaks volumes about the changes in social and economic life that the masses of European society were now experiencing.

Eighteenth-century Europe was a society of orders gradually transforming itself into a society of classes. At the top, as vigorous as ever, was the nobility. But the bourgeoisie was growing in both numbers and importance. An active commercial and urban life gave many members of this group new social and political opportunities and many of them passed into the nobility through the purchase of land or office. Opulence and poverty increased in step as the fruits of commerce and land enriched the upper orders while rising population impoverished the lower ones. The rise of the new science and of Enlightenment ideas highlighted the contradictions. The attack on traditional authority, especially the Roman Catholic church, was an attack on a conservative, static worldview. Enlightenment thinkers looked to the future, to a new world shaped by reason and knowledge, a world ruled benevolently for the benefit of all human beings. Government, society, the individual—all could be improved if only the rubble of the past was cleared away. They could hardly imagine how potent their vision would become.

The Cockpit *(ca. 1759) by William Hogarth. The central figure is a blind nobleman who was said never to have missed an important cockfight. The steel spurs on the birds' legs enabled them to inflict serious damage in the heat of battle.*

SUGGESTIONS FOR FURTHER READING

GENERAL READING

* Olwen Hufton, *Europe: Privilege and Protest 1730-1789* (Ithaca, NY: Cornell University Press, 1980). An excellent survey of the political and social history of the mid-eighteenth century.
* Leonard Krieger, *Kings and Philosophers 1689-1789* (New York: Norton, 1970). A brilliant depiction of the personalities and ideas of eighteenth-century Europe.
* Isser Woloch, *Eighteenth Century Europe, Tradition and Progress, 1715-89* (New York: Norton, 1982). Especially strong on social movements and popular culture.
* William Doyle, *The Old European Order 1660-1800* (Oxford: Oxford University Press, 1978). An important essay on the structure of European societies and the ways in which they held together.

* Raymond Birn, *Crisis, Absolutism, Revolution: Europe 1648-1789/91* (New York: Dryden Press, 1977). A reliable survey with especially good chapters on the Enlightenment.

THE NOBILITY

Michael Bush, *Noble Privilege* (New York: Holmes & Meier, 1983). A good analytic survey of the rights of European nobles.

J. V. Beckett, *The Aristocracy in England* (London: Basil Blackwell, 1986). A comprehensive study of a tightly knit national aristocracy.

* Albert Goodwin, ed., *The European Nobility in the Eighteenth Century* (New York: Harper & Row, 1967). Separate essays on national nobilities, including those of Sweden, Poland, and Spain.

* Norman Hampson, *The Enlightenment* (London: Penguin Books, 1982). The best one-volume survey.

* Peter Gay, *The Enlightenment: An Interpretation*, 2 vols. (New York: Knopf, 1966–69). A difficult but rewarding study by one of the leading historians of the subject.

Carolyn Lougee, *Le Paradis des Femmes: Women, Salons, and Social Stratification* (Princeton, NJ: Princeton University Press, 1976). A study of the foundation of the French salons and the role of women in it.

* Judith Sklar, *Montesquieu* (Oxford: Oxford University Press, 1987). A concise, readable study of the man and his work.

Theodore Besterman, *Voltaire* (Chicago: University of Chicago Press, 1976). The best of many biographies of an all-too-full life.

* John G. Gagliardo, *Enlightened Despotism* (New York: Thomas Y. Crowell, 1967). A sound exploration of the impact of Enlightenment ideas on the rulers of Europe, with most emphasis on the east.

THE BOURGEOISIE

Jan de Vries, *European Urbanization 1500-1800* (Cambridge, MA: Harvard University Press, 1984). An important, though difficult study of the transformation of towns into cities with the most reliable estimates of size and rates of growth.

* P. J. Corfield, *The Impact of English Towns 1700-1800* (Oxford: Oxford University Press, 1982). A thorough survey of the role of towns in English social and economic life.

* Elinor Barber, *The Bourgeoisie in Eighteenth Century France* (Princeton, NJ: Princeton University Press, 1955). Still the best study of the French bourgeoisie.

* Simon Schama, *The Embarrassment of Riches* (Berkeley: University of California Press, 1987). The social life of Dutch burghers richly portrayed.

* Ian Watt, *The Rise of the Novel* (Berkeley: University of California Press, 1957). An important essay on the relationship between literature and society in the eighteenth century.

David Garrioch, *Neighborhood and Community in Paris, 1740-90* (Cambridge: Cambridge University Press, 1986). A good microstudy of Parisian neighborhoods and of the people who inhabited them.

George Sussman, *Selling Mothers' Milk: The Wet-Nursing Business* (Bloomington: Indiana University Press, 1982). A study of buyers and sellers in this important social marketplace.

Samia Spencer, *French Women and the Age of Enlightenment* (Bloomington, IN: Indiana University Press, 1984). A survey of the role of women in French high culture.

* Lawrence Stone, *The Family, Sex and Marriage in England 1500-1800* (New York: Harper & Row, 1979). A controversial but extremely important argument about the changing nature of family life.

* Jean Louis Flandrin, *Families in Former Times* (Cambridge: Cambridge University Press, 1979). Strong on family and household organization.

THE MASSES

* Michael W. Flinn, *The European Demographic System* (Baltimore: Johns Hopkins University Press, 1981). The best single-volume study, especially for the nonspecialist reader.

E. A. Wrigley and R. S. Schofield, *The Population History of England* (Cambridge, MA: Harvard University Press, 1981). The most important reconstruction of a national population by a team of researchers.

Olwen Hufton, *The Poor in Eighteenth Century France* (Oxford: Oxford University Press, 1974). A compelling study of the life of the poor.

* Roy Porter, *English Society in the Eighteenth Century* (London: Penguin Books, 1982). A breezy, entertaining survey of English social life.

* J. M. Beattie, *Crime and the Courts in England* (Princeton, NJ: Princeton University Press, 1986). A difficult but sensitive analysis of crime and criminal justice.

* Peter Burke, *Popular Culture in Early Modern Europe* (New York: Harper & Row, 1978). A wide survey of practices throughout the Continent.

Robert Muchembled, *Popular Culture and Elite Culture in France, 1400-1750* (Baton Rouge, LA: Louisiana State University Press, 1985). A complex but richly textured argument about the relationship between two cultures.

* Robert Malcolmson, *Popular Recreation in English Society, 1700-1850* (Cambridge: Cambridge University Press, 1973). Sport and its role in society.

* Indicates paperback edition available.

CHAPTER 22

The French Revolution and the Napoleonic Era, 1750–1815

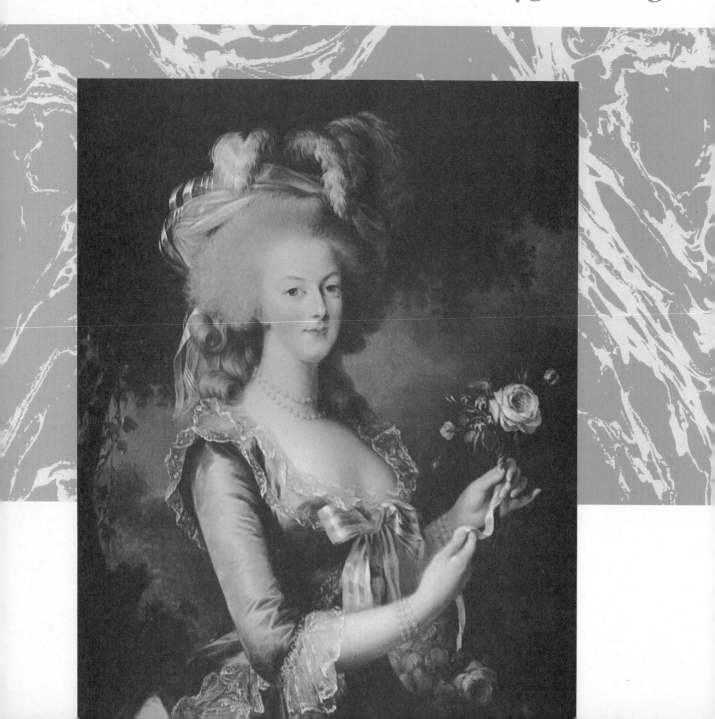

"Let Them Eat Cake"

The Queen of France was bored. Try as she might, Marie Antoinette (1755–93) found insufficient diversion in her life at the great court of Versailles. When she was fourteen, she had married the heir to the French throne, the future Louis XVI. By the age of nineteen, she was queen of the most prosperous state in continental Europe. Still she was bored. Her life, she complained to her mother, Empress Maria Theresa of Austria, was futile and meaningless. Maria Theresa advised the unhappy queen to suffer in silence or risk unpleasant consequences. Sometimes mothers know best.

Unpopular as a foreigner from the time she arrived in France, Marie Antoinette suffered a further decline in her reputation as gossip spread about her gambling and affairs at court. The public heard exaggerated accounts of the fortunes she spent on clothing and jewelry. In 1785 she was linked to a cardinal in a nasty scandal over a gift of a diamond necklace. In spite of her innocence, rumors of corruption and infidelity surrounded her name. Dubbed "Madame Deficit," she came to represent all that was considered decadent in royal rule.

She continued to insist, "I am afraid of being bored." To amuse herself, she ordered a life-size play village built on the grounds of Versailles, complete with cottages, a chapel, a mill, and a running stream. Then, dressed in the silks and muslins intended as the royal approximation of a milkmaid's garb, she whiled away whole days with her friends and children, all pretending they were inhabitants of this picturesque "hamlet." Her romantic view of country life helped pass the time, but it did little to bring her closer to the struggling peasants who made up the majority of French subjects.

Marie Antoinette's problems need not have mattered much. Monarchs before her had been considered weak and extravagant. The difference was that her foibles became public in an age when the opinion of the people affected political life. Rulers, even those believed to be divinely appointed, were subjected to a public scrutiny all the more powerful because of the growth of the popular press. Kings, their ministers, and their spouses were held accountable—a dangerous phenomenon for an absolute monarchy.

This Austrian-born queen may not have been more shallow or spendthrift than other queens, but it mattered that people came to see her that way. The queen's reputation sank to its nadir when it was reported that she dismissed the suffering of her starving subjects with the haughty retort: "Let them eat cake." What better evidence could there be of the queen's insensitivity than this heartless remark?

Marie Antoinette never said, "Let them eat cake," but everyone thought she did. This was the kind of callousness that people expected from the monarchy in 1789. Marie Antoinette understood the plight of her starving subjects, as her correspondence indicates. Probably a courtier at Versailles was the real source of the brutal retort, but the truth didn't matter. Marie Antoinette and her husband were being indicted by the public for all the political, social, and fiscal crises that plagued France.

In October 1793, Marie Antoinette was put on trial by the Revolutionary Tribunal and found guilty of treason. She was stripped of all the trappings of monarchy and forced to don another costume. Dressed as a poor working woman, her hair shorn, the former queen mounted the guillotine, following in the footsteps of her husband, who had been executed earlier that year. The monarchy did not fall because of a spendthrift queen with too much time on her hands. Nor did it fall because of the mistakes of the well-meaning but inept king. The monarchy had ceased to be responsive to the profound changes that shook France. It fell because of a new concern in the land for royal accountability in words and deeds. A rising democratic tide carried with it ideas about political representation, participation, and equality. If a queen could change places with a milkmaid, why should not a milkmaid be able to change places with a queen?

The Crisis of the Old Regime in France, 1715–1788

France in the eighteenth century, the age of the Enlightenment, was a state invigorated by new ideas. It was also a world dominated by tradition. The traditional institutions of monarchy, Church, and aristocracy defined power and status. Talk of reform, progress, and perfectibility coexisted with the social realities of privileges and obligations determined by birth. The eighteenth century was a time when old ways prevailed even as a new view of the world was taking shape.

The tensions generated by the clash of continuity and change made the end of the eighteenth century an exciting and complex period in both Britain and France. In France, reformers talked of progress while peasants still used wooden plows. The *philosophes* glorified reason in a world of violence, superstition, and fear. The great crisis of eighteenth-century France, the French Revolution, destroyed the *ancien régime* (old regime). But the Revolution was as much a product of continuities and traditions as it was a product of change and the challenge of new ideas.

Louis XV's France

When Louis XV (1715–74) died, he was a hated man. His legacy was well captured in the expression erroneously attributed to him, *aprés moi le déluge*—"after me, the flood." In his fifty-nine-year reign, he managed to turn the public against him. He was denounced as a tyrant who was trying to starve his people, a slave to the mistresses who ruled his court, and a pleasure-seeker dominated by evil ministers. Louis XV's apathy and ineptitude contributed to his poor image. The declining fortunes and the damaged prestige of the monarchy, however, reflected more than the personality traits of an ineffectual king: they reflected structural challenges to fiscal solvency and absolutist rule that the monarchy was unable to meet.

Louis XV, like his great-grandfather Louis XIV, laid claim to rule as an absolute monarch. He insisted that "the rights and interests of the nation . . . are of necessity one with my own, and lie in my hands only." Such claims failed to mask the weaknesses of royal rule. Louis XV lacked a sufficiently developed bureaucracy to administer and tax the nation in an evenhanded fashion. By the beginning of the eighteenth century, the absolute monarchy had extended royal influence into the new areas of policing, administration, lawmaking, and taxation. But none of this proved sufficient to meet the growing needs of the state.

The growing tensions between the monarch and the aristocracy found expression in various institutions, especially the *parlements*, the thirteen sovereign courts in the French judicial system, with their seats in Paris and a dozen provincial centers. The magistrates of each parlement were members of the nobility, some of them nobles of recent origin and others of long standing, depending on the locale. The king needed the parlements to record royal decrees before they could become law.

This recording process conferred real political power on the parlements, which could withhold approval for the king's policies by refusing to register his decrees. When the king attempted to make new laws, the magistrates could refuse to endorse them. When decrees involved taxation, they often did. Because magistrates purchased their offices in the parlements, the king found it difficult to control the courts. His fiscal difficulties prevented him from buying up the increasingly valuable offices in order to appoint his own men. Stripping magistrates of their positions was considered tantamount to the theft of property. By successfully challenging the king, the parlements became a battleground between the elite, who claimed that they represented the nation, and the king, who said the nation was himself.

The king repeatedly attempted to neutralize the power of the parlements by relying instead on his own state bureaucracy. His agents in the provinces, called *intendants*, were accountable directly to the central government. The intendants, as the king's men, and the magistrates who presided in the parlements represented contradictory claims to power. As the king's needs increased in the second half of the eighteenth century, the situation was becoming intolerable for those exercising power and those aspiring to rule in the name and for the good of the nation.

The nadir of Louis XV's reign came in 1763 with the French defeat in the Seven Years' War on the Continent and in the French and Indian War in the American colonies. In the Treaty of Paris, France ceded territory, including its Canadian holdings, to Great Britain. France lost more than lands; it lost its footing in the competition with its chief rival Great Britain, which had been pulling ahead of France in international affairs since the early eighteenth century. The war was also a financial debacle, paid for by loans secured against the guarantee of victory. The defeat not only left France barren of funds, it also promoted further expenditures for strengthening the French navy against the superior British fleet. New taxation was the way out of the financial trap in which the king now found himself.

Louis XV's revenue problem was not easily solved. In order to raise taxes, the king had to turn to the recording function of the parlements. Following the costly Seven Years' War, the parlements chose to exercise the power of refusal by blocking a proportional tax to be imposed on nobles and commoners alike. The magistrates resisted taxation with an argument that confused liberty with privilege: the king, the magistrates asserted, was attacking the liberty of his subjects by attempting to tax those who were exempt by virtue of their privileged status.

René Nicolas Charles Augustin de Maupeou (1714-92), Louis XV's chancellor from 1768 to 1774, decided that the political power of the parlements had to be curbed. In 1770, in an attempt to coerce the magistrates into compliance with the king's wishes, he engineered the overthrow of the Parlement of Paris, the most important of the high courts. Those magistrates who remained obdurate were sent into exile. New courts whose membership was based on appointment instead of the sale of offices took their place amid much public criticism. Ultimately, Maupeou's attempt did nothing to improve the monarch's image, and it did less to solve the fiscal problems of the regime.

In 1774 Louis XV died suddenly of smallpox. His unprepared twenty-year-old grandson, Louis XVI (1774-92), a young man who amused himself by hunting and pursuing his hobby as an amateur locksmith, was left to try to stanch the flood.

Louis XVI and the National Debt

Louis XV left to his heir Louis XVI the legacy of a disastrous deficit. From the beginning of his reign, Louis XVI was caught in the vicious circle of excessive state spending—above all, military spending—followed by bouts of heavy borrowing. Borrowing at high rates required the government to pay out huge sums in interest and service fees on the loans that were keeping it afloat. These outlays in turn piled the state's indebtedness ever higher, requiring more loans, and threatening to topple the whole financial structure and the regime itself.

In inheriting this trouble-ridden fiscal structure, Louis XVI made his own contribution to it. Following in the footsteps of his grandfather, Louis XVI involved France in a costly war, the War of American Independence (1775-83), by supporting the thirteen colonies in their revolt against Great Britain. The involvement brought the French monarchy to the brink of bankruptcy. Contrary to public opinion, most of the state's expenditures did not go toward lavishing luxuries on the royal court and the royal family at Versailles. They went to pay off loans. More than half of the state budget in the 1780s represented interest on loans taken to pay for foreign military ventures.

As one of the first acts of his reign, in 1775 Louis XVI had restored the magistrates to their posts in the

This cartoon from 1789 depicts Necker (at left) showing the king how to conceal the size of the deficit from the estates. On the wall, a list of royal loans is headed "New ways to revive France"—but the total is "Deficit."

more than a drop compared to the vast ocean of debt that threatened to engulf the state.

The existing tax structure proved hopelessly inadequate to meet the state's needs. The *taille*, a direct tax, was levied, either on persons or on land, according to region. Except for those locales where the taille was attached to land, the nobility was always exempt from direct taxation. Members of the bourgeoisie could also avoid the direct tax as citizens of towns enjoying exemption. That meant that the wealthy, those best able to pay, were often exempt. Indirect taxes, like those on salt (the *gabelle)* and on food and drink (the *aide*), and internal and external customs taxes were regressive taxes that hit hardest those least able to pay. The peasantry bore the brunt of the nation's tax burden, and Louis XVI knew all too well that a peasantry too weighted down would collapse—or rebel.

Louis XVI appointed Anne-Robert-Jacques Turgot (1727–81) as his first controller-general. Turgot's reformist economic ideas were influenced by Enlightenment *philosophes*. In order to generate revenues, Turgot reasoned, France needed to prosper economically. The government was in a position to stimulate economic growth by eliminating regulations, by economizing at court, and by improving the network of roads through a tax on landowners. Each of Turgot's reforms offended established interests, thereby ensuring his early defeat. Emphasis on a laissez-faire economy outraged the guilds; doing away with the forced labor of peasants on the roads (the *corvée*) threatened privileged groups who had never before been taxed. As the king was discovering, divine right did not bring with it absolute authority or fiscal solvency.

As he floundered about for a solution to his economic difficulties, the king turned to a new adviser, Jacques Necker (1732–1804), a Swiss-born Protestant banker. Necker applied his accounting skills to measuring—for the first time—the total income and expenditures of the French state. Instead of raising taxes, Necker committed his ministry to eliminating costly inefficiencies. He promised to abolish venal offices that drained revenues from the crown. He next set his sights on the contracts of the farmers-general, collectors of the indirect salt taxes. But the budget that Necker produced was based on disastrous miscalculations, and he was forced to resign in 1781.

Charles Alexandre de Calonne (1734–1802), appointed controller-general in 1783, had his own ideas of how to bail out the ship of state. He authored a program of reforms that would have shifted the tax burden off those least able to pay and onto those best able to

parlements, treating their offices as a form of property of which they had been deprived. By 1776 the Parlement of Paris was again obstructing royal decrees. The privileged elite persisted in rejecting the crown's attempts to tax them. But to those who could afford to purchase them, the king continued to sell offices that carried with them titles, revenues, and privileges. He also relied on the sale of annuities that paid high interest rates and that attracted speculators, large and small. The crown had leased out its rights to collect the salt tax in return for large lump-sum advances from the Royal General Farms, a syndicate of about one hundred wealthy financier families. But the combined revenues collected by the king through these various stratagems were little support the state. He proposed a tax on land proportional to land values, a measure that would have most seriously affected the land-rich nobility. In addition, taxes that affected the peasantry were to be lightened or eliminated. Finally, Calonne proposed the sale of Church lands for revenues. In an attempt to bypass the recalcitrant parlements, Calonne advised the crown in 1787 to convene an Assembly of Notables made up of 150 individuals from the magistracy, the Church hierarchy, the titled nobility, and municipal bodies, for the purpose of enlisting their support for reforms. Louis listened to Calonne, who was denounced by the Assembly of Notables for attacking the rights of the privileged. He too was forced to resign. All of Louis XVI's attempts to persuade the nobility to agree to tax reforms had failed.

In the 1780s, almost 50 percent of annual expenditures went to servicing the accumulated national debt of 4 billion livres and paying interest. The new controller-general, Archbishop Loménie de Brienne (1727–94) recommended emergency loans. The crown once again disbanded the Parlement of Paris, which was now threatening to block loans as well as taxes. Aristocratic magistrates now insisted on a constitution, in which their own right to govern would be safeguarded and the accountability of the king would be defined. In opposing the royal reforms, nobles spoke of the "rights of man" and used the term *citizen*. The nobility had no sympathy for tax programs that would have resulted in a loss of privilege and what some nobles were beginning to consider an attack on individual freedom.

Louis XVI was a desperate man in 1788, so desperate that he yielded to the condition placed on him by the Parlement of Paris: he agreed to convene the Estates-General, a medieval body that had not met since 1614 and that had been considered obsolete with the rise of a centralized bureaucratic government. In the 1614 voting of the Estates-General, the three orders—clergy, nobility, commoners—were equally weighted. This arrangement favored the nobility, who controlled the first two estates and thus were not worried by the prospect of the Estates-General deciding the tax reform program. Many were sure that a new age of liberty was at hand.

The Three Estates

The Estates-General included representatives from the three "estates" of the clergy, nobility, and commoners. About two hundred thousand subjects belonged to the

first two estates. The Third Estate was composed of all those members of the realm who enjoyed a common identity only in their lack of privilege—over 23 million French people. In the second half of the eighteenth century, these traditional groups no longer reflected social realities—a situation that proved to be a source of serious problems for the Estates-General. The piety of the first order had been called into doubt as religious leaders were criticized for using the vast wealth of the Church for personal benefit instead of public worship. The protective military function of the second order had ceased to exist with the rise of the state and the changing nature of war. The bourgeoisie, those who worked with their heads, not their hands, shared privileges with the nobility and aspired to a noble lifestyle, in spite of their legal and customary presence in the ranks of the Third Estate.

The vast majority of French subjects who constituted the Third Estate certainly were identified by

Cartoon showing the plight of the French peasants. An old farmer is bowed down under the weight of the privileged aristocracy and clergy while birds and rabbits, protected by unfair game laws, eat his crops.

work, but the vast array of mental and physical labor—and lack of work—splintered the estate into myriad occupations, aspirations, and identities. All power flowed upward in this arrangement, with the First and Second Estates dominating the social and political universe.

The king continued to stand at the pinnacle of the eighteenth-century social pyramid. Traditionally revered as the "father" of his subjects, he claimed to be divinely appointed by God. Kingship in this era had a dual nature. The king was both supreme overlord from feudal times, and he was absolute monarch. As supreme overlord he dominated the aristocracy and the court. As absolute monarch he stood at the head of the state and society. Absolutism required a weakened nobility and a bureaucracy strong enough to help the monarchy to adjust to changes. After the death of Louis XIV in 1715, Louis XV and Louis XVI faced a resurgent aristocracy without the support of a state bureaucracy capable of successfully challenging aristocratic privilege or of solving fiscal problems.

While the system of orders set clear boundaries of social status, distinctions within estates created new hierarchies. The clergy, a privileged order, contained both commoners and nobles, but leadership in the Church depended on social rank. The aristocracy retained control of the bishoprics, even as an activist element among the lower clergy agitated for reforms and better salaries. In a state in which the king claimed to rule by God's will, Catholicism, virtually the state religion, was important in legitimizing the divine claims of the monarchy.

The nobility experienced its own internal tensions, generated by two groups: the older nobility of the sword, who claimed descent from medieval times; and the more recent nobility of the robe, who had acquired their position through the purchase of offices that conferred noble status. By increasing the numbers of the nobility of the robe, Louis XIV hoped to undermine the power of the aristocracy as a whole and to decrease its political influence. But aristocrats rallied and closed ranks against the dilution of their power. As a result, both Louis XV and Louis XVI faced a reviving rather than a declining aristocracy. Nobles had succeeded in restoring their economic and social power. A growing segment of the aristocracy, influenced by Enlightenment ideas and the example of English institutions, was intent on increasing the political dominance of the aristocracy too.

The nobility strengthened their powers in two ways. First, they monopolized high offices and closed access to nonnobles. They took over posts in ministries, the Church, and the army. Second, the nobility benefited greatly from the doubling in land values brought on by the increase in the value of crops. Those aristocrats who controlled sizable holdings profited greatly from higher dues paid to them, as they reaped increased incomes from crops. In addition, many aristocrats revived feudal claims to ancient seigneurial, or lordly, privileges. They hired lawyers to unearth old claims and hired agents to collect dues.

Although technically prevented from participating in trade by virtue of their titles and privileges, an active group among the nobility succeeded in making fortunes in metallurgy, glassmaking, and mining. These nobles were an economically dynamic and innovative segment of the aristocracy. In spite of the obsolete aspect of their privileges, aristocrats were often responsible for the introduction of modern ideas and techniques in the management of estates and in the bookkeeping involved with collection of rents. These nobles formed an elite partnership with forward-looking members of the bourgeoisie.

Common people, that is, those who did not enjoy the privileges of the nobility, embraced a broad range of the French populace. The peasantry was by far the largest group, joined in the designation as "commoners" by the middle class, or bourgeoisie, and by workers in both cities and rural areas. Most French peasants were free, no longer attached to the soil as serfs were in a feudal system. Yet all peasants endured common obligations placed on them by the crown and the privileged classes. Peasants owed the tithe to the Church, land taxes to the state, and seigneurial dues and rents to the landlord. A bewildering array of taxes afflicted peasants. Dues affected almost every aspect of rural life, including harvests and the sale of property. In addition, indirect taxes like that on salt (the hated gabelle) were a serious burden for the peasantry.

The precariousness of rural life and the increase in population in the countryside contributed to the permanent displacement and destitution of a growing sector of rural society. Without savings and destroyed by poor harvests, impoverished rural inhabitants wandered the countryside looking for odd jobs and eventually begging to survive. Many peasants with small plots were able to work for wages. Peasant women sought employment in towns and cities as seamstresses and servants in order to send money back home. Children, too, added their earnings to the family pot. But in spite of various strategies for survival, more and more families were disrupted by the end of the eighteenth century.

Bourgeoisie—as the term was used in the eighteenth century—meant those members of the middle class who lived on income from investments. Yet the term really embraced within it a whole hierarchy of professions from bankers and financiers to businessmen, merchants, entrepreneurs, lawyers, shopkeepers, and craftsmen. Along with the nobility, wealthy bourgeois formed the urban elites that administered cities and towns. Prestigious service to the state or the purchase of offices that carried with them noble status enabled the wealthiest members of the bourgeoisie to move into the ranks of the nobility.

Like the rest of the social universe, the world of artisans and workers was shaded with various gradations of wealth and status. Those who owned their own shops and perhaps employed other workers stood as an elite among the working class. In spite of their physical proximity, there was a vast difference between those who owned their own shops and those who earned wages or were paid by the piece. Wage earners represented about 30 percent of the population of cities and towns. And their numbers were swelling, as craftsmen were pushed out of their guilds and peasants were pushed off their land.

Those who worked in crafts were a labor elite, and guilds were intended to protect the corporations of masters, journeymen, and apprentices through monopolistic measures. Guilds insisted that they were best able to ensure the quality of goods. But the emphasis on free trade and the expansion of markets in the eighteenth century weakened the hold of the guilds. Merchants often took them over and paid workers by the piece. The effect was a reduction in the wages of skilled workers. By the 1780s, most journeymen who hoped to be masters knew that their dream would never be realized. Frustration and discontent touched workers in towns and cities who may not have shared a common work experience. But they did share a common anger about the high cost of bread.

In August 1788 Louis XVI announced that the Estates-General would meet in May 1789. In desperate straits, the king hoped that the clergy, nobility, and commoners from the three estates who were to assemble at Versailles would solve all of his problems. The Estates-General was to achieve what the king's ministers could not—fiscal solvency and a strengthened monarchy. Yet each of the estates had its own ideas about proper solutions and its own grievances. The stage was set for a confrontation of social groups whose political values were riven by conflicting ideas about justice, social status, and economic well-being.

The First Stage of the French Revolution, 1789–1792

The French Revolution, or the Great Revolution, as it was known to contemporaries, was a time of creation and discovery. The ten years from 1789 to 1799 were punctuated by genuine euphoria and democratic transformations. From the privileged elites who initiated the overthrow of the existing order to peasants and workers, women and men, who united against tyranny, the Revolution touched every segment of society.

The Revolution achieved most in the area of politics. The overthrow of absolutist monarchy brought with it new social theories, new symbols, and new behavior. The excitement of anarchy was matched by the terror of repression. Revolutionary France had to contend with a Europe-wide war. The Revolution had its dark side of violence and instability, and in its wake came internal discord, civil war, and violent repression. In the search for a new order, political forms followed one upon the other in rapid succession: constitutional monarchy, republic, oligarchy. The creation of Napoleon's dictatorship at the end of the century was the act that signified that the Revolution had come to an end.

Revolutionary incidents flared up throughout Europe in the second half of the eighteenth century—in the Netherlands, Belgium, and Ireland. Absolute authority was challenged and sometimes modified. Across the Atlantic, American colonists concerned with the principle of self-rule had thrown off the yoke of the British in the War of Independence. But none of these events, including the American Revolution, was so violent in breaking with the old order, so extensive in involving millions of men and women in political action, and so consequential for the political futures of other European states, as was the French Revolution. The triumphs and contradictions of the revolutionary experiment in democracy mark the end of the old order and the beginning of modern history. Politics would never be the same.

Taking Politics to the People

Choosing representatives for the Estates-General in March and April 1789 stirred up hope and excitement in every corner of France. The call for national elections set in motion a politicizing process the king could not control. From the very beginning, there were warning signs that a more astute monarch might have noticed.

Members of the Third Estate, traditionally excluded from political and social power, were presented with the opportunity of expressing their opinions on the state of government and society. In an increasingly literate age, pamphlets, broadsides, and political tracts representing every political persuasion blanketed France. Farmhands and urban laborers realized that they were participating in the same process as their social betters. And they believed they had a right to speak and be heard. Taxes could be discussed and changed; the state bureaucracy could be reformed—or better, abolished.

Intellectuals discussed political alternatives in the salons of the wealthy. Nobles and bourgeois met in philosophical societies dedicated to enlightened thought. Commoners gathered in cafes to drink and debate. The poor fell outside this network of communication, but they were not immune to the ideas that emerged. In the end, people of all classes had opinions, and they were more certain than ever of their right to express their ideas. Absolutism was in trouble, although Louis XVI did not know it, as people began to forge a shared idea of politics. People now had a forum—the Estates-General—and a focus—the politics of taxation. But most important, they had the elections. The message of the elections,

and of the representative principle on which they were based, was that one could compete for power.

In competing for power, some members of the Third Estate were well aware of their vast numerical superiority over the nobility. Because of it, they demanded greater representation than the three hundred members per estate defined according to the practices of 1614. At the very least, they argued, the number of representatives of the Third Estate should be doubled to six hundred members, giving commoners equality in numbers with nobles and priests together. Necker, recalled as director-general of finance in August 1788, agreed to the doubling in the size of the Third Estate as a compromise but left unresolved the additional demand of vote by head rather than by order. If voting was to be left as it was, in accordance with the procedures of 1614, the nobility who controlled the First and Second Estates would determine all outcomes. With a voting procedure by head instead of by order, however, the deputies of the Third Estate could easily dominate the Estates-General.

In conjunction with this political activity and in scheduled meetings, members of all three estates drew up statements of their problems. This took place in a variety of forums, including guilds and village and town meetings. The people of France set down their grievances in notebooks—known as *cahiers de doléances*—that were then carried to Versailles by the deputies elected to the Estates-General. This was the first national poll of opinion commissioned by the crown, and it involved every level of society. It was a tool of political education as the mass of French people were being given the impression for the first time that they were part of the policy-making process.

The cahiers expressed the particular grievances of each estate. These notebooks contained a collective outpouring of problems and they are important for two major reasons. First, they made clear the similarity of grievances shared throughout France. Second, they indicated the extent to which a common political culture, based on a concern with political reform, had permeated different levels of French society. Both the privileged and the nonprivileged identified a common enemy in the system of state bureaucracy to which the monarch was so strongly tied. Although the king was still addressed with respect, new concerns with liberty, equality, property, and the rule of law were voiced. People were questioning their traditional roles and now had elected deputies who would represent them before the king. In the spring of 1789 a severe economic crisis swept through France heightening

Revolutionary France

political uncertainty. For a king expected to save the situation, time was running out.

Convening the Estates-General

The elected deputies arrived at Versailles at the beginning of May 1789, carrying in their valises and trunks the grievances of their estates. The opening session of the Estates-General took place in a great hall especially constructed for the event. The 1,248 deputies presented a grand spectacle as they filed to their assigned places to hear speeches by the king and his ministers. Contrasts among the participants were immediately apparent. Seated on a raised throne under a canopy at one end of the hall, Louis XVI was vested in full kingly regalia. On his right sat the archbishops and cardinals of the First Estate, dramatically clad in the pinks and purples of their offices. On his left were the richly and decorously attired nobility. Facing the stage sat the 648 deputies of the Third Estate, dressed in plain black suits, stark against the colorful and costly costumes of the privileged. Fired by the hope of equal treatment and an equal share of power, they had come to Versailles to make a constitution.

The tension between commoners and privileged was aggravated by the unresolved issue of how the voting was to proceed. The Third Estate was adamant in its demand for vote by head. The privileged orders were equally adamant in insisting on vote by order. Paralysis set in, as days dragged into weeks and the Estates were unable to act. The body that was to save France from fiscal collapse was hopelessly deadlocked.

Two men in particular, whose backgrounds made them unlikely heroes, emerged as leaders of the Third Estate. One, the Abbé Emmanuel-Joseph Sieyès (1748–1836), was a member of the clergy who frequented Parisian salons. The other, the comte Honoré Gabriel Victor de Mirabeau (1749–91), a black sheep among the nobility, had spent time in prison because of his father's charges that he was a defiant son who led a misspent, debauched, and profligate youth. In spite of his nobility, Mirabeau appeared at Versailles as a deputy for Aix and Marseilles to the Third Estate. His oratory and presence commanded attention from the start. As a consummate politician, Mirabeau combined forces with Sieyès, who had already established his reputation as a firebrand reformer with his eloquent pamphlet, "What Is the Third Estate?"

Sieyès and Mirabeau reminded members of the Third Estate of the reformist consensus that characterized their ranks. Under their influence, the Third

The French Revolution

August 1788	Louis XVI announces meeting of Estates-General to be held in May 1789
5 May 1789	Estates-General convenes
17 June 1789	Third Estate declares itself the National Assembly
20 June 1789	Oath of the Tennis Court
14 July 1789	Storming of the Bastille
20 July 1789	Revolution of peasantry begins
26 August 1789	*Declaration of the Rights of Man and Citizen*
5 October 1789	Parisian women march to Versailles; force Louis XVI to return to Paris
November 1789	Church property nationalized
February 1790	Monasteries, convents dissolved
July 1790	Civil Constitution of the Clergy
June 1791	Louis XVI and family attempt to flee Paris; are captured and returned
June 1791	*Declaration of Rights of Woman and Citizen*
April 1792	France declares war on Austria
10 August 1792	Storming of the Tuileries
21 September 1792	Abolition of monarchy
22 September 1792	Creation of the First Republic; day one of revolutionary calendar (implemented in 1793)
January 1793	Louis XVI executed
July 1793	Robespierre assumes leadership of Committee of Public Safety
1793–94	Reign of Terror
1794	Robespierre guillotined
1794–95	Thermidorian Reaction
1795–99	Directory
1799	Napoleon overthrows the Directory and seizes power

"WHAT IS THE THIRD ESTATE?"

■ As an ambitious clergyman from Chartres, the site of one of France's most stunning Gothic cathedrals, the Abbé Sieyès was a member of the First Estate. In the elections for the Estates-General, Sieyès was elected a deputy from the Third Estate on the basis of his attacks on aristocratic privilege. He participated in the writing and editing of the great documents of the early Revolution: the Oath of the Tennis Court and the Declaration of the Rights of Man and Citizen. His most famous revolutionary document, the pamphlet for which he is immortalized in revolutionary lore, was his daring "What Is the Third Estate?" Written in January 1789, it boldly confronted the bankruptcy of the system of privilege of the Old Regime and threw down the gauntlet to those who ruled France. In this document the Revolution found its rallying point.

1st. What is the third estate? Everything.
2nd. What has it been heretofore in the political order? Nothing.
3rd. What does it demand? To become something therein.

Who, then, would dare to say that the third estate has not within itself all that is necessary to constitute a complete nation? It is the strong and robust man whose one arm remains enchained. If the privileged order were abolished, the nation would not be something less but something more. Thus, what is the third estate? Everything; but an everything shackled and oppressed. What would it be without the privileged order? Everything; but an everything free and flourishing. Nothing can progress without it; everything would proceed infinitely better without the others. It is not sufficient to have demonstrated that the privileged classes, far from being useful to the nation, can only enfeeble and injure it; it is necessary, moreover, to prove that the nobility does not belong to the social organization at all; that, indeed, it may be a *burden* upon the nation, but that it would not know how to constitute a part thereof.

The third estate, then, comprises everything appertaining to the nation; and whatever is not the third estate may not be regarded as being of the nation. What is the third estate? Everything!

From Abbé Emmanuel-Joseph Sieyès, "What Is the Third Estate?"

Estate decided to proceed with its own meetings. On 17 June 1789, the Third Estate, joined by some sympathetic clergy, changed its name to the National Assembly as an assertion of its true representation of the French nation. Three days later, members of the new National Assembly found themselves locked out of their regular meeting room by the king's guard. Outraged by this insult, they moved to a nearby indoor tennis court, where they vowed to stay together for the purpose of writing a constitution. This event, known as the Oath of the Tennis Court, marked the end of the absolutist monarchy and the beginning of a new concept of the state that power resided in the people. The Revolution had begun.

The drama of Versailles, a staged play of gestures, manners, oaths, and attire, also marked the beginning of a far-reaching political revolution. Although it was a drama that took place behind closed doors, it was not one unknown to the general public. Throughout

May and June 1789, Parisians trekked to Versailles to watch the deliberations. Then they brought news back to the capital. Deputies wrote home to their constituents to keep them abreast of events. Newspapers that reported daily on these wranglings and pamphleteers who analyzed them spread the news throughout the nation. Information, often conflicting, stirred up anxiety; news of conflict encouraged action.

The frustration and the stalemate of the Estates-General threatened to put the spark to the kindling of urban unrest. The people of Paris had suffered through a harsh winter and spring under the burdens of high prices (especially of bread), limited supplies, and relentless tax demands. The rioting of the spring had for the moment ceased, as people waited for their problems to be solved by the deputies of the Estates-General. The suffering of the urban poor was not new, but their ability to connect economic hardships with the politics at Versailles and to blame the government was. As hopes began to dim with the news of political stalemate, news broke of the creation of the National Assembly.

The Storming of the Bastille

The king, who had temporarily withdrawn from sight following the death of his son at the beginning of June, reemerged to meet with the representatives of each of the three estates and propose reforms, including a constitutional monarchy. But Louis XVI refused to accept the now popularly supported National Assembly as a legitimate body, choosing instead to rely on the three estates for advice. He simply did not understand that the choice was no longer his to make. He summoned troops to Versailles and began concentrating soldiers in Paris. Urban dwellers recognized the threat of repression that the troops represented, and crowds decided to meet force with force. To do so, they needed arms themselves, and they knew where to get them.

On 14 July 1789, irate citizens of Paris stormed the Bastille, a royal armory that also served as a prison for a handful of debtors. The storming of the Bastille has become the great symbol in the revolutionary legend of the overthrow of the tyranny and oppression of the old regime. But it is significant for another reason. It was an expression of the power of the people to take politics into their own hands. Parisians were following the lead of their deputies in Versailles. They had formed a citizen militia, known as the National Guard, and were prepared to defend their concept of justice and law.

The people who stormed the Bastille were not the poor, the unemployed, the criminals, or the urban rabble, as they were portrayed by their detractors. They were bourgeois and petit bourgeois, shopkeepers, guild members, family men and women, who considered it their right to seize arms to protect their interests. The Marquis de Lafayette (1757–1834), a noble beloved of the people because of his participation in the American Revolution, helped organize the National Guard. Under his direction, the militia adopted the tricolor flag as their standard, replacing the fleur-de-lis of the Bourbons.

The king could no longer dictate the terms of the constitution. By their actions, the people in arms had ratified the National Assembly. Louis XVI was forced to yield. Similar uprisings erupted in cities and towns throughout France. National guards in provincial cities modeled themselves after the Parisian militia. Government officials fled their posts and abandoned their responsibilities. Commoners stood ready to fill the power

This painting of the Oath of the Tennis Court is by the Revolution's leading artist, Jacques Louis David. Sieyès sits at a table on which Bailly stands reading the oath. Robespierre is seen clutching his breast in the group behind Sieyès.

This lively amateur painting of the fall of the Bastille is by Claude Cholat, one of the attackers. Tradition has it that Cholat is manning the cannon in the background. The inscription proclaims that the painting is by one of the "Conquerors of the Bastille."

vacuum that now existed. But the Revolution was not just an urban phenomenon. The peasantry had their own grievances and their own way of making a revolution.

The Revolution of the Peasantry

In the spring and early summer of 1789, food shortages drove bands of armed peasants to attack manor houses throughout France. In the areas surrounding Paris and Versailles, peasants destroyed game and devastated the forests where the king and his nobles hunted. The anger reflected in these seemingly isolated events was suspended as the hope grew that the proceedings at Versailles would produce results. Remote as peasant involvement in the drawing up of the cahiers might have been, peasants everywhere expected that aid was at hand.

News of the events of Versailles and then of the revolutionary action in Paris did not reassure rural inhabitants. By the end of June the hope of deliverance from crippling taxes and dues was rapidly fading. The news of the Oath of the Tennis Court and the storming of the Bastille terrified country folk, who saw the actions as evidence of an aristocratic plot that threatened sorely needed reforms. As information moved along postal routes in letters from delegates to their supporters, or news was repeated in the Sunday market gatherings, distortions and exaggerations crept in. It seemed to rural inhabitants that their world was falling apart. Some peasants believed that Paris was in the hands of brigands and that the king and the Estates-General were victims of an aristocratic plot.

This state of affairs was aggravated as increasing numbers of peasants had been pushed off the land to seek employment as transient farm laborers, moving from one area to another with the cycles of sowing and harvesting. Throughout the 1780s the number of peasants without land was increasing steadily. Filthy, poorly dressed, and starving men, women, and children were frightening figures to villagers who feared that the same fate would befall them with the next bad harvest.

Hope gave way to fear. Beginning on 20 July 1789, peasants in different areas of France reacted with a kind of collective hysteria, spreading false rumors of a great conspiracy. Fear gripped whole villages, and in some areas spawned revolt. Just as urban workers had connected their economic hardships to politics, so too did desperate peasants see their plight in political terms. They banded together and marched to the residences of the local nobility, breaking into the chateaus with a single mission in mind: to destroy all legal documents by which nobles claimed payments, dues, and services from local peasants. They drove out the lords and in some cases burned their chateaus, putting an end to the tyranny of the privileged over the countryside.

The overthrow of privileges rooted in a feudal past was not as easy as that. Members of the National Assembly were aghast at the eruption of rural violence. They knew that to stay in power they had to maintain peace. They also knew that to be credible they had to protect property. Peasant destruction of seigneurial claims posed a real dilemma for the bourgeois deputies directing the Revolution. If they gave in to peasant demands, they risked losing aristocratic support and undermining their own ability to control events. If they gave in to the aristocracy, they risked a social revolution in the countryside, which they could not police or repress. Liberal members of the aristocracy cooperated with the bourgeois leaders in finding a solution.

In a dramatic meeting that lasted through the night of 4-5 August 1789, the National Assembly agreed to abolish the principle of privilege. The peasants had won—or thought they had. In the weeks and months ahead, rural people learned they had lost their own prerogatives—the rights to common grazing and gathering—and were expected to buy their way out of their feudal services.

Women on the March

Women participated with men in both urban and rural revolutionary actions. Acting on their own, women were responsible for the most dramatic event of the early years of the Revolution: in October 1789 they forced the king and the royal family to leave Versailles for Paris to deal in person with the problems of the bread supply, high prices, and starvation. Women milling about in the marketplaces of Paris on the morning of 5 October were complaining bitterly about the high cost and shortages of bread. The National Assembly was in session and the National Guards were patrolling the streets of Paris. But these trappings of political change had no impact on the brutal realities of the marketplace.

On the morning of 5 October 1789, six thousand Parisian women marched out of the city toward Versailles. Women, who were in charge of buying food for their families, were most directly in touch with the state of provisioning the capital. When they were unable to buy bread because of shortages or high prices, the situation became intolerable. They were taking their problem to the king with the demand that he solve it. Later in the day, Lafayette, sympathetic to the women's cause, led the Parisian National Guard to Versailles to mediate events. The women were armed with pikes, the simple weapon available to the poorest defender of the Revolution, and they were prepared to use them.

The battle came early the next morning, when the women, tired and cold from waiting all night at the gates of the palace, invaded the royal apartments and chased Marie Antoinette from her bedroom. Several members of the royal guards, hated by the people of Paris for

This engraving from the late eighteenth century shows French country houses ablaze while speeding carriages carry their frightened owners to safety. The peasants attacked and looted the houses of the gentry and burned the rolls of feudal duties.

A contemporary print of the women of Paris advancing on Versailles. The determined marchers are shown waving pikes and dragging an artillery piece. The women were hailed as heroines of the Revolution.

alleged insults against the tricolor cockade, were killed by the angry women, who decapitated them and mounted their heads on pikes. A shocked Louis XVI agreed to return with the crowd to Paris. The crowd cheered Louis' decision, which briefly reestablished his personal popularity. But as monarch, he had been humiliated at the hands of women of the capital. "The baker, the baker's wife, and the baker's son" were forced to return to Paris that very day. Louis XVI was now captive to the Revolution, whose efforts to form a constitutional monarchy he purported to support.

The Revolution Threatened

The disciplined deliberations of committees intent on fashioning a constitutional monarchy replaced the passion and fervor of revolutionary oratory. The National, or Constituent, Assembly divided France into new administrative units—*départements*—for the purpose of establishing better control over municipal governments. Along with new administrative trappings, the government promoted its own rituals. On 14 July 1790, militias

from each of the newly created eighty-three départements of France came together in Paris to celebrate the first anniversary of the storming of the Bastille. A new national holiday was born and with it a sense of devotion and patriotism for the new France liberated by the Revolution. In spite of these unifying elements, however, the newly achieved revolutionary consensus showed signs of breaking down.

On 2 November 1798 Church lands were nationalized. Three months later, legislation dissolved all monasteries and convents, except for those that provided aid to the poor or that served as educational institutions. As the French church was stripped of its lands, Pope Pius VI (1775–99) denounced the principles of the Revolution. In July 1790 the government approved the Civil Constitution of the Clergy: priests now became the equivalent of paid agents of the state. By requiring an oath of loyalty to the state from all practicing priests, the National Assembly created a new arena for dissent: Catholics were forced to choose to embrace or reject the Revolution. Many "nonjuring" priests who refused to take the oath went into hiding.

The wedge driven between the Catholic church and revolutionary France allowed a mass-based counterrevolution to emerge. Aristocratic émigrés who had fled the country because of their opposition to the Revolution were languishing because of lack of a popular base. From his headquarters in Turin, the king's younger brother, the comte d'Artois, was attempting to incite a civil war in France. When the revolutionaries decided to attack the Church, not just as a landed and privileged institution but also as a religious one, the counterrevolution rapidly expanded.

The Constitution of 1791, completed after over two years of deliberations, established a constitutional monarchy with a ministerial executive power answerable to a legislative assembly. Louis XVI, formerly the divinely anointed ruler of France, was now "Louis, by the grace of God and the constitutional law of the state, King of the French." In proclaiming his acceptance of the constitution, Louis expressed the sentiments of many when he said, "The end of the revolution is come. It is time that order be reestablished so that the constitution may receive the support now most necessary to it; it is time to settle the opinion of Europe concerning the destiny of France, and to show that French men are worthy of being free."

The Constitution of 1791 marked the triumph of the principles of the Revolution. But months before the ink was dry on the final document, the actions of the king doomed the new constitution to failure. To be successful, constitutional monarchy required a king worthy of honor and respect. Louis XVI seemed to be giving the revolutionaries what they wanted by cooperating with the framers of the constitution. Yet late one night in June 1791, Louis XVI, Marie Antoinette, and their children disguised themselves as commoners, crept out of the royal apartments in the Tuileries Palace, and fled Paris. Louis intended to leave France to join foreign forces opposing the Revolution at Metz. He got as far as Varennes, where he was captured by soldiers of the National Guards and brought back to a shocked Paris. The king had abandoned the Revolution. Although he was not put to death for another year and a half, he was more than ever a prisoner of the Revolution. The monarchy was effectively finished as part of a political solution and with its demise went liberal hopes for a constitutional settlement. The defection of the king was certainly serious, but other problems plagued the revolutionary government, notably the fiscal crisis coupled with inflation, and foreign war.

In order to establish its seriousness and legitimacy, the National Assembly had been willing in 1789 to absorb the debts of the old regime. The new government could not sell titles and offices, as the king had done to deal with financial problems, but it did confiscate

The fleeing Louis XVI and his family were apprehended at Varennes in June 1791.

Church property. In addition, it issued treasury bonds in the form of *assignats* in order to raise money. The assignats soon assumed the status of banknotes, and by spring 1790 they became compulsory legal tender. Initially they were to be backed by land confiscated from the Church and now being sold by the state. But the need for money soon outran the value of the land available and the government continued to print assignats according to its needs. Depreciation of French currency in international markets and inflation at home resulted. The revolutionary government found itself in a situation that in certain respects was worse than that experienced by Louis XVI before the calling of the Estates-General. Assignat-induced inflation produced a sharp decline in the fortunes of bourgeois investors living on fixed incomes. Rising prices meant increased misery for workers and peasants.

New counterrevolutionary groups were becoming frustrated with revolutionary policies. Throughout the winter and spring of 1791–92 people rioted and demanded that prices be fixed, as the assignat dropped to less than half of its face value. Peasants refused to sell their crops for the worthless paper. Hoarding further drove up prices. Angry crowds turned to pillaging, rioting, and murders, which became more frequent as the value of the currency declined and prices rose.

Foreign war beginning in the fall of 1791 also challenged stability. Some moderate political leaders welcomed war as a blessing in disguise, since it could divert the attention of the masses away from problems at home and could promote loyalty to the Revolution. Others envisioned war as a great crusade to bring revolutionary principles to oppressed peoples throughout Europe. The king and queen, trapped by the Revolution, saw war as their only hope of liberation. Louis XVI could be rightfully restored as the leader of a France defeated by the sovereigns of Europe. Others opposed the war, believing it would destabilize the Revolution. France must solve its problems at home, they argued, before fighting a foreign enemy. Louis, however, encouraged those ministers and advisers eager for battle. In April 1792, France declared war against Austria.

The first stage of the French Revolution ended in the summer of 1792 with the prospect of increased violence both from abroad in international war and at home in mounting civil strife. In its first three years, however, the Revolution had accomplished great things by abolishing aristocratic privilege, by affirming the political principles of liberty, equality, and fraternity, and by asserting constitutional prerogatives of royal accountability. The attempt at constitutional monarchy had failed, but the contours of a new political universe took shape according to bourgeois definitions of political participation, property, and civil liberties. As women and men of all classes discovered between 1789 and 1792, there was little certainty about what political solutions lay ahead, but there was no doubt there could be no turning back.

Experimenting with Democracy: The Revolution's Second Stage, 1792–1799

The French Revolution was a school for the French nation. A political universe populated by individual citizens replaced the eighteenth-century world of subjects loyal to their king. This new construction of politics in which all individuals were equal ran counter to prevailing ideas about collective identities defined in guilds and orders. People on all levels of society learned politics by doing it. In the beginning, experience helped. The elites, both noble and bourgeois, had served in government and administration. But the rules of the game under the old regime had been very different, with birth determining power.

After 1789, all men were declared free and equal, in opportunity if not in rights. Men of ability and talent, who had served as middlemen for the privileged elite under the old regime, now claimed power as their due. Many of them were lawyers, educated in the rules and regulations of the society of orders. They experienced firsthand the problems of the exercise of power in the old regime and had their own ideas about reform. But the school of the Revolution did not remain the domain of a special class. Women demanded their places. Workers seized their rights. And because of the inherent contradictions of representation and participation, experimenting with democracy led to outcomes that did not look very democratic at all.

Declaring Political Rights

The Constitution of 1791 was a statement of faith in a progressive constitutional monarchy. A king accountable to an elected parliamentary body would lead France into a prosperous and just age. The constitution acknowledged the people's sovereignty as the source of political power. It also enshrined the principle of property by making voting rights dependent on property ownership. All men might be equal before the law, but by the Constitution of 1791 only wealthy men had the right to vote for representatives and hold office.

All titles of nobility were abolished. In the early period of the Revolution, civil liberties were extended to Protestants and Jews, who had been persecuted under the old regime. Previously excluded groups were granted freedom of thought and worship and full civil liberties. More reluctantly, slavery in the colonies was outlawed in 1794. Slave unrest in Saint Domingue (modern-day Haiti) had coincided with the political conflicts of the Revolution and exploded in rebellion in 1791, driving the revolutionaries in Paris to support black independence although it was at odds with French colonial interests. Led by Toussaint L'Ouverture (1743–1803), black rebels worked to found an independent Haitian state, which was declared in 1804. But the concept of equality with regard to race remained incompletely integrated with revolutionary principles, and Napoleon reestablished slavery in the French colonies in 1802.

Men were the subject of these newly defined rights. No references to women or their rights appear in the constitutions or the official Declaration of Rights. But women were critical actors in the Revolution from its very inception, and their presence shaped and directed the outcome of events, as the women's march to Versailles in 1789 made clear. The Marquis de Condorcet (1743–94), elected to the Legislative Assembly in 1791, was one of the first to chastise the revolutionaries for overlooking the political rights of women who, he pointedly observed, were half of the human race. "Either no individual of the human race has genuine rights, or else all have the same; and he who votes against the right of

another, whatever the religion, color, or sex of that other, has henceforth abjured his own." Condorcet argued forcefully but unsuccessfully for the right of women to be educated. Women's talents, he warned, were slumbering under the ignorance of neglect.

The revolutionaries had declared that liberty was a natural and inviolable right, a universal right that was extended to all with the overthrow of a despotic monarch and a privileged elite. The principle triumphed in religious toleration. Yet the revolutionary concept of liberty foundered on the divergent claims of excluded groups of workers, women, and slaves, who demanded full participation in the world of politics. In 1792 revolutionaries confronted the contradictions inherent in their political beliefs of liberty and equality now challenged in the midst of social upheaval and foreign war. In response, the Revolution turned to more radical measures in order to survive.

The Second Revolution: The Revolution of the People

The first revolution of 1789 through the beginning of 1792 was based on liberty—the liberty to compete, to own, and to succeed. The second revolution, which began in 1792, took equality as its rallying cry. This was the revolution of the working people of French cities. The popular movement that spearheaded political action in 1792 was committed to equality of rights in a way not characteristic of the leaders of the Revolution of 1789. Urban workers were not benefiting from the Revolution, but they had come to believe in their own power as political beings. Organized on the local level into sections, craft workers in cities identified themselves as

Slaves revolting against the French in Saint Domingue in 1791. Napoleon sent an army to restore colonial rule in 1799, but yellow fever decimated the French soldiers and the rebels defeated the weakened French army in 1803.

DECLARATION OF THE RIGHTS OF MAN AND CITIZEN

■ Sounding a refrain similar to the American Declaration of Independence (1776), the Declaration of the Rights of Man and Citizen was adopted by the National Assembly on 26 August 1789. The document amalgamated a variety of Enlightenment ideas drawn from the works of political philosophy, including those of Locke and Montesquieu. The attention to property, which was defined as "sacred and inviolable," rivaled liberty as a "natural" and "imprescriptible" right of man.

1. Men are born and remain free and equal in rights. Social distinctions may be founded only upon the general good.

2. The aim of all political association is the preservation of the natural and imprescriptible rights of man. These rights are liberty, property, security, and resistance to oppression.

3. The principle of all sovereignty resides essentially in the nation. No body nor individual may exercise any authority which does not proceed directly from the nation.

4. Liberty consists in the freedom to do everything which injures no one else; hence the exercise of the natural rights of each man has no limits except those which assure to the other members of the society the enjoyment of the same rights. These limits can only be determined by law.

5. Law can only prohibit such actions as are hurtful to society. Nothing may be prevented which is not forbidden by law, and no one may be forced to do anything not provided for by law.

6. Law is the expression of the general will. Every citizen has a right to participate personally, or through his representative, in its formation. It must be the same for all, whether it protects or punishes. All citizens, being equal in the eyes of the law, are equally eligible to all dignities and to all public positions and occupations, according to their abilities, and without distinction except that of their virtues and talents.

7. No person shall be accused, arrested, or imprisoned except in the cases and according to the forms prescribed by law. Any one soliciting, transmitting, executing, or causing to be executed, any arbitrary order, shall be punished. But any citizen summoned or arrested in virtue of the law shall submit without delay, as resistance constitutes an offense.

8. The law shall provide for such punishments only as are strictly and obviously necessary . . .

9. As all persons are held innocent until they shall have been declared guilty, if arrest shall be deemed indispensable, all harshness not essential to the securing of the prisoner's person shall be severely repressed by law.

10. No one shall be disquieted on account of his opinions, including his religious views, provided their manifestation does not disturb the public order established by law.

11. The free communication of ideas and opinions is one of the most precious of the rights of man. Every citizen may, accordingly, speak, write, and print with freedom, but shall be responsible for such abuses of this freedom as shall be defined by law.

12. The security of the rights of man and of the citizen requires public military forces. These forces are, therefore, established for the good of all and not for the personal advantage of those to whom they shall be intrusted.

13. A common contribution is essential for the maintenance of the public forces and for the cost of administration. This should be equitably distributed among all the citizens in proportion to their means.

14. All the citizens have a right to decide, either personally or by their representatives, as to the necessity of the public contribution; to grant this freely; to know to what uses it is put; and to fix the proportion, the mode of assessment and of collection and the duration of the taxes.

15. Society has the right to require of every public agent an account of his administration.

DECLARATION OF THE RIGHTS OF MAN AND CITIZEN

16. A society in which the observance of the law is not assured, nor the separation of powers defined, has no constitution at all.

17. Since property is an inviolable and sacred right, no one shall be deprived thereof except where public necessity, legally determined, shall clearly demand it, and then only on condition that the owner shall have been previously and equitably indemnified.

sans-culottes, literally those who did not wear knee breeches, to distinguish themselves from the privileged elite.

On 10 August 1792, the people of Paris invaded the Tuileries Palace, chanting their demands for "Equality!" and "Nation!" Love and respect for the king had vanished. What the people of Paris demanded now was universal manhood suffrage and participation in a popular democracy. The self-designated sans-culottes were the working men and women of Paris. Some were wealthier than others, some were wage earners, but all shared a common identity as consumers in the marketplace. They wanted government power to be decentralized, with neighborhoods ruling themselves through sectional organizations. When they invaded the Tuileries, the sans-culottes did so in the name of the people. They saw themselves as patriots whose duty it was to brush the monarchy aside. The people were now a force to be reckoned with and feared.

"Terror Is the Order of the Day"

Political factions characterized revolutionary politics from the start. The terms *Left* and *Right*, which came to represent opposite ends of the political spectrum, originated in a description of where people sat in the Assembly in relation to the podium. Political designations were refined in successive parliamentary bodies. The Convention was the legislative body elected in September 1792, which succeeded the Legislative Assembly by the latter's own decree and had as its charge determining the best form of government after the collapse of the monarchy. On 21 September 1792, monarchy was abolished in France; the following day the Republic, France's first, came into being. Members of the Convention conducted the trial of Louis XVI for treason and

pronounced the death sentence for his execution on the guillotine in January 1793.

The various political factions of the Convention were described in terms borrowed from geography. The Mountain, sitting in the upper benches on the left, was made up of members of the Jacobin Club (named for its meeting place in an abandoned monastery). The Jacobins were the most radical element, supporting democratic solutions and speaking in favor of the cause of people in the streets. The Plain held the moderates, who were concerned with maintaining public order against popular unrest. Many members of the Plain came to be called Girondins in the mistaken belief that they originated in the Gironde département of France.

Both Girondins and Jacobins were from the middle ranks of the bourgeoisie, and both groups were dedicated to the principles of the Revolution. At first the two groups were more similar than different. Although controlling the ministries, the Girondins began to lose their hold on the Revolution and the war. The renewed European war fragmented the democratic movement, and the Girondins, unable to control violence at home, saw political control slipping away. They became prisoners of the Revolution when eighty thousand armed Parisians surrounded the National Convention in June 1793.

Girondin power had been eroding in the critical months between August 1792 and June 1793. A new leader was working quietly and effectively behind the scenes to weld a partnership between the popular movement of sans-culottes and the Jacobins. He was Maximilien Robespierre (1758–94), leader of the Mountain and the Jacobin Club. Robespierre was typical of the new breed of revolutionary politicians. Only 31 years old in 1789, he wrote mediocre poems and attended the local provincial academy to discuss the latest

DECLARATION OF THE RIGHTS OF WOMAN AND CITIZEN

■ *"Woman, wake up!" In such a manner did Olympe de Gouges (d. 1793), the daughter of a butcher and a self-educated playwright, address French women in 1791. Aware that women were being denied the new rights of liberty and property extended to all men by the* Declaration of the Rights of Man and Citizen, *Gouges composed her own* Declaration of the Rights of Woman and Citizen, *modeled article for article on the 1789 document. In addition to defending the political rights of women, Gouges spoke out for the freedom of slaves. Persecuted for her political beliefs, she foreshadowed her own demise at the hands of revolutionary justice in article 10 of her* Declaration: *". . . woman has the right to mount the scaffold; she must equally have the right to mount the rostrum, provided her demonstrations do not disturb the legally established public order." The Declaration of the Rights of Woman and Citizen became an important document in women's demands for political rights in the nineteenth century, and Gouges herself became a feminist hero.*

Article I

Woman is born free and lives equal to man in her rights. Social distinctions can be based only on the common utility.

Article II

The purpose of any political association is the conservation of the natural and imprescriptible rights of woman and man; these rights are liberty, property, security, and especially resistance to oppression.

Article III

The principle of all sovereignty rests essentially with the nation, which is nothing but the union of woman and man; no body and no individual can exercise any authority which does not come expressly from it [the nation].

Article IV

Liberty and justice consist of restoring all that belongs to others; thus, the only limits on the exercise of the natural rights of woman are perpetual male tyranny; these limits are to be reformed by the laws of nature and reason.

Article V

Laws of nature and reason proscribe all acts harmful to society; everything which is not prohibited by these wise and divine laws cannot be prevented, and no one can be constrained to do what they do not command.

Article VI

The law must be the expression of the general will; all female and male citizens must contribute either personally or through their representatives to its formation; it must be the same for all: male and female citizens, being equal in the eyes of the law, must be equally admitted to all honors, positions, and public employment according to their capacity and without other distinctions besides those of their virtues and talents.

Article VII

No woman is an exception; she is accused, arrested, and detained in cases determined by law. Women, like men, obey this rigorous law.

Article VIII

The law must establish only those penalties that are strictly and obviously necessary. . . .

Article IX

Once any woman is declared guilty, complete rigor is [to be] exercised by the law.

Article X

No one is to be disquieted for his very basic opinions; woman has the right to mount the scaffold; she must equally have the right to mount the rostrum, provided that her demonstrations do not disturb the legally established public order.

Article XI

The free communication of thoughts and opinions is one of the most precious rights of woman, since that liberty assures the recognition of children by their fathers. Any female citizen thus may say freely, I am the mother of a child which belongs to you, without being forced by a barbarous prejudice to hide the truth; [an exception may be made] to respond to the abuse of this liberty in cases determined by the law.

DECLARATION OF THE RIGHTS OF WOMAN AND CITIZEN

Article XII

The guarantee of the rights of woman and the female citizen implies a major benefit; this guarantee must be instituted for the advantage of all, and not for the particular benefit of those to whom it is entrusted.

Article XIII

For the support of the public force and the expenses of administration, the contributions of woman and man are equal; she shares all the duties [*corvées*] and all the painful tasks; therefore, she must have the same share in the distribution of positions, employment, offices, honors and jobs [*industrie*].

Article XIV

Female and male citizens have the right to verify, either by themselves or through their representatives, the necessity of the public contribution. This can only apply to women if they are granted an equal share, not only of wealth, but also of public administration, and in the determination of the proportion, the base, the collection, and the duration of the tax.

Article XV

The collectivity of women, joined for tax purposes to the aggregate of men, has the right to demand an accounting of his administration from any public agent.

Article XVI

No society has a constitution without the guarantee of rights and the separation of powers; the constitution is null if the majority of individuals comprising the nation have not cooperated in drafting it.

Article XVII

Property belongs to both sexes whether united or separate; for each it is an inviolable and sacred right; no one can be deprived of it, since it is the true patrimony of nature, unless the legally determined public need obviously dictates it, and then only with a just and prior indemnity.

ideas, when he was not practicing law in his hometown of Arras. Elected to the Estates-General, he joined the Jacobin Club and quickly rose to become its leader. He was willing to take controversial stands on issues. Unlike most of his fellow members of the Mountain, including his rival, the popular orator Georges-Jacques Danton (1759–94), he opposed the war in 1792. Although neither an original thinker nor a compelling orator, Robespierre discovered with the Revolution that he was a stunning political tactician. He gained a following and learned how to manipulate it. It was he who engineered the Jacobin replacement of the Girondins as leaders of the government.

Robespierre's chance for real power came when he assumed leadership of the Committee of Public Safety in July 1793. Due to the threat of internal anarchy and external war, the elected body, the National Convention, yielded political control to the twelve-man Committee of Public Safety that ruled dictatorially under Robespierre's direction. The Great Committee, as it was known at the time, orchestrated the Reign of Terror (1793–94), a period of systematic state repres-

sion that meted out justice in the people's name. Summary trials by specially created revolutionary tribunals were followed by the swift execution of the guilty under the blade of the guillotine. (See Special Feature, "The Guillotine and Revolutionary Justice," pp. 670–671.)

Influenced by the *Social Contract* (1762) and other writings of Jean-Jacques Rousseau, Robespierre believed that sovereignty resided with the people. For him individual wills and even individual rights did not matter when faced with the will of the nation. As head of the Great Committee, Robespierre oversaw a revolutionary machinery dedicated to economic regulation, massive military mobilization, and a punitive system of revolutionary justice characterized by the slogan, "Terror is the Order of the Day." Militant revolutionary committees and revolutionary tribunals were established in the départements to identify traitors and to mete out the harsh justice that struck hardest against those members of the bourgeoisie who were perceived as opponents of the government. The civil war, which raged most violently in the Vendée in the west of France, consisted often of primitive massacres that sent

In this portrayal of the execution of Louis XVI, one of the executioners displays the erstwhile king's severed head to the crowd.

The Guillotine and Revolutionary Justice

In the sultry summer days of 1792, Parisians found a new way to entertain themselves. They attended executions. French men, women, and children were long accustomed to watching criminals being tortured and put to death in public view. During the old regime, spectators could enjoy the variety of a number of methods: drawing and quartering, strangling, or hanging. Decapitation, reputedly a less painful death, was a privilege reserved for nobles sentenced for capital crimes. The Revolution extended this formerly aristocratic privilege to all criminals condemned to death. What especially attracted people into public squares in the third year of the Revolution was the introduction of a novel method of decapitation. In 1792 the new instrument of death, the guillotine, became the center of the spectacle of revolutionary justice.

The guillotine promised to eliminate the suffering of its victims. Axes, swords, and sabers—the traditional tools of decapitation and dismemberment—were messy and undependable, producing slow and bloody ordeals when inept and drunken executioners missed their mark or victims flinched at the fatal moment. The design of the guillotine took all of this into account. On its easel-like wooden structure, victims, lying on their stomachs, were held in place with straps and a pillory. Heavy pulleys guaranteed that the sharp blade would fall efficiently from its great height. A basket was placed at the base of the blade to catch the severed head; another was used to slide the headless body for removal through the base of the scaffolding. In place of unintended torture and gore, the guillotine was devised as a humanitarian instrument to guarantee swift and painless death.

It should have been called the Louisette, after its inventor, Dr. Antoine Louis. In what now seems a dubious honor, the new machine was named instead after its greatest supporter, Dr. Joseph Ignace Guillotin, a delegate to the National Assembly. Both Guillotin and Louis were medical doctors, men of science influenced by Enlightenment ideas and committed to the Revolution's elimination of the cruelty of older forms of punishment. In the spirit of scientific experimentation, Louis' invention was tested on sheep, cadavers, and then convicted thieves. In 1792 it was used for the first time against another class of offenders, political prisoners.

Early in the Revolution, the Marquis de Condorcet, philosophe and mathematician, had opposed capital punishment with the argument that the state did not have the right to take life. Ironically, Maximilien Robespierre, future architect of the Reign of Terror, was one of the few revolutionaries who agreed with Condorcet. But those who favored justice by execution of the state's enemies prevailed. The revolutionary hero and associate of the radical Jacobins, Jean Paul Marat (1743–93), who was himself stabbed to death in his bathtub, advocated the state's use of violence against its enemies: "In order to ensure public tranquillity, 200,000 heads must be cut off." By the end of 1792, as revolution and civil war swept over France, eighty-three identical guillotines were constructed and installed in each of the départements of France. For the next two years, the guillotine's great blade was rhythmically raised and lowered daily in public squares all over France. In the name of the Revolution, the "axe of the people" dispatched over 50,000 victims.

Although intended as a humanitarian instrument, the guillotine became the symbol of all that was arbitrary and repressive about a revolution run amok. Day and night in Paris, the Revolutionary Tribunal delivered the death sentence to the "enemies of the people." Most of those executed were members of what had been the Third Estate: members of the bourgeoisie, workers, peasants. Only 15 percent of the condemned were nobles and priests. During the Terror, the guillotine was sometimes used to settle old scores. Sans-culottes turned in their neighbors, sometimes over long-standing grievances that owed more to spite than politics. The most fanatical revolutionaries had fantasies that guillotines were about to be erected on every street corner to dispense with hoarders and traitors. Others suggested that guillotines be made portable so that by putting justice on wheels, it could be taken directly to the people.

As usual, Paris set the style. The most famous of the guillotines stood on the Place du Carrousel, deliberately placed in front of the royal palace of the Tuileries. It was eventually moved to the larger Place de la Révolution in order to accommodate the growing numbers of spectators. Famous victims drew especially large crowds. The revolutionary drama took on the trappings of a spectacle, as hawkers sold toy guillotines, miniature pikes, and liberty caps as souvenirs, along with the usual food and drink. Troops attended these events, but not to control the crowd. Members of the National Guard in formation, their backs to the people, faced the stage of the scaffold. They, like the citizenry, were there to witness the birth of a new nation and, by their presence, to give legitimacy to the event. The crowd entered into the ritual, cheering the victim's last words and demanding that the executioner hold high the severed head. In the new political culture death was a festival.

For two centuries, Western societies have debated the legitimacy of the death sentence and have periodically considered the relative merits of the guillotine, the gas chamber, and the electric chair. For the French, the controversy temporarily ceased in 1794, when people were convinced that justice had gotten out of hand and that they had had enough. For the time being, the government put an end to capital punishment. The guillotine would return. But at the height of its use between 1792 and 1794, it had played a unique role in forging a new system of justice: the guillotine had been the great leveler. In the ideology of democracy, people were equal—in death as well as in life. The guillotine came to be popularly known as the "scythe of equality." It killed king and commoner alike.

probably a quarter of a million people to their deaths. The bureaucratized Reign of Terror was responsible for about forty thousand executions in a nine-month period.

The Cult of the Supreme Being, a civic religion without priests or churches and influenced by Rousseau's ideas about nature, followed dechristianization. The cathedral of Notre Dame de Paris was turned into the Temple of Reason, and the new religion established its own festivals to undermine the persistence of Catholicism. The cult was one indication of the Reign of Terror's attempt to create a new moral universe of revolutionary values.

Conspicuously absent from the summit of political power were women. After 1793 Jacobin revolutionaries, who were willing to empower the popular movement of workers, turned against women's participation and denounced it. Women's associations were outlawed and the Society of Revolutionary Republican Women was disbanded. Olympe de Gouges was guillotined. Women were made unfit for political participation, the Jacobins declared, by their biological functions of reproduction and child-rearing. Rousseau's ideas about family policy were probably more influential than his political doctrines. His best-selling books, *La Nouvelle Héloïse* (1761) and *Émile* (1762), were moral works that transformed people's ideas about family life. Under his influence, the reading public came to value a separate and private sphere of domestic and conjugal values. Following Rousseau's lead, Robespierre and the Jacobins insisted that the role of women as mothers was incompatible with women's participation in the political realm.

Robespierre attacked his critics to the Left and to the Right, thereby undermining the support he needed to stay in power. He abandoned the alliance with the popular movement that had been so important in bringing him to power. Using the Terror, Robespierre eliminated his enemies and purged the Jacobins of those who might pose a threat to his control. Charges of conspiracy were leveled against Danton and his followers, who were all guillotined. Robespierre's enemies—and he had many—were able to break the identification between political power and the will of the people that Robespierre had cultivated. As a result, he was branded a traitor by the same process that he had enforced against many of his own enemies and friends. He saved France from foreign occupation and internal collapse but he could not save democracy through terror. In the summer of 1794, Robespierre was guillotined. The Reign of Terror ceased with his death in the revolutionary month of Thermidor 1794.

The Revolution did not end with the Thermidorian Reaction, as the fall of Robespierre came to be known, but his execution initiated a new phase. For some, democracy lost its legitimacy. The popular movement was reviled and sans-culotte became a term of derision. Jacobins were forced underground. Price controls were abolished, resulting in extreme hardship for most urban residents. Out of desperation in April 1795, the Jacobins and the sans-culottes renewed their alliance and united to demand "Bread and the Constitution of 1793." The politics of bread had never been more accurately captured in slogan. But their demands went unheeded and the popular revolution was suppressed.

*Robespierre, having executed everyone else ("Toute la France")
during the Reign of Terror, turns the guillotine on the executioner.*

The End of the Revolution

In the four years after Robespierre's fall, a new government by committee, called the Directory, appeared to offer mediocrity, caution, and opportunism in place of the idealism and action of the early years of the Revolution. No successor to Robespierre stepped forward to command center stage; there were no heroes like Lafayette or the great Jacobin orator Danton to inspire patriotic fervor. Nor were there women like Olympe de Gouges to demand in the public arena equal rights for women. Most people, numbed after years of change, barely noticed that the Revolution was over. Ordinary men in parliamentary institutions effectively did the day-to-day job of running the government. They tried to steer a middle path between royalist resurgence and popular insurrection. This nearly forgotten period in the history of the French Revolution was the fulfillment of the liberal hopes of 1789 for a stable, constitutional rule.

The Directory, however, continued to be dogged by European war. A mass army of conscripts and volunteers had successfully extended France's power and frontiers. France expelled foreign invaders and annexed territories, including Belgium, while increasing its control in Holland, Switzerland, and Italy. But the expansion of revolutionary France was expensive and increasingly unpopular. Military defeats and the corruption of the Directory undermined government control. The Directory might have succeeded in the slow accretion of a parliamentary tradition. But reinstatement of conscription in 1798 met with widespread protest and resistance. No matter what their political leanings, people were weary. They turned to those who promised stability and peace.

In the democratic experiment at the heart of the second stage of the French Revolution, the sovereign will of the people permanently replaced the monarch's claim to the divine right to rule. Yet with democracy came tyranny. The severe repression of the Terror revealed the pressures that external war and civil unrest created for the new Republic. The Thermidorian Reaction and the elimination of Robespierre as the legitimate interpreter of the people's will opened a time of conciliation, opportunism, and a search for stability. Ironically, the savior that France found to answer its needs for peace and a just government was a man of war and a dictator.

The Reign of Napoleon, 1799–1815

The great debate that rages to this day about Napoleon revolves around the question of whether he fulfilled the aims of the Revolution or perverted them. In his return to a monarchical model, Napoleon resembled the enlightened despots of eighteenth-century Europe. In a modern sense, he was also a dictator, manipulating the French people through a highly centralized administrative apparatus. He locked French society into a program of military expansion that depleted its human and material resources. Yet, in spite of destruction and war, he dedicated his reign to building a French state according to the principles of the Revolution.

Bonaparte Seizes Power

In Paris in 1795 a young, penniless, and unknown military officer moved among the wealthy and the beautiful of Parisian society and longed for fame. Already nicknamed at school "the Little Corporal" on account of his short stature, he was snubbed because of his background and ridiculed for his foreign accent. His story is typical of all stories of thwarted ambition. Yet the outcome of this story is unique. Within four years this young man had become ruler of France.

Napoleon Bonaparte (1769–1821) was a true child of the eighteenth century. He shared the philosophes' belief in a rational and progressive world. Napoleon was born into an Italian noble family in Corsica, which until a few months before his birth was part of the Republic of Genoa. He secured a scholarship to the French military school at Brienne, graduating in 1784. He then spent a

Cartoon, published in 1792, showing Louis XVI wearing the red hat of the sans-culottes and drinking to the health of the nation.

In this German caricature (1814), called the "Corpse Head," Napoleon's face is composed of his prisoners, living and slain. The epaulet is his own blood-stained hand.

year at the Military Academy in Paris, and received a commission as a second lieutenant of artillery in January 1786.

The Revolution changed everything for him. It made new posts available when aristocratic generals defected and crossed over to the enemy side both before and after the execution of the king. The Revolution also created great opportunities for military men to test their mettle.

Foreign war and civil war required military leaders devoted to the Revolution. Forced to flee Corsica because he had sided with the Jacobins, Bonaparte crushed Parisian protesters who rioted against the Directory in 1795. The revolutionary wars had begun in 1792 as wars to liberate humanity in the name of liberty, equality, and fraternity. Yet concerns for power, territory, and riches replaced earlier French concerns with defense of the nation and of the Revolution. This aggrandizement was nowhere more evident than in the Egyptian campaign of 1798, in which Napoleon Bon-

aparte headed an expedition whose goal was to enrich France by hastening the collapse of the Turkish Empire, crippling British trade routes, and handicapping Russian interests in the region. With Napoleon's highly publicized campaigns in Egypt and Syria, the war left the European theater and moved to the east, leaving behind the original revolutionary ideals.

The Egyptian campaign, which was in reality a disaster, made Napoleon a hero at home. Above all, his victories in the Italian campaign in 1796–97 launched his political career. As he extended French rule into central Italy, he became the embodiment of revolutionary values and energy. In 1799 he readily joined a conspiracy that pulled down the Directory, the government he had earlier preserved, and became the First Consul of a triumvirate of consuls.

Napoleon set out to secure his position of power by eliminating his enemies on the Left and weakening those on the Right. He guaranteed the security of property acquired in the Revolution, a move that undercut the royalists, who wanted to return property to its original owners. Through policing forces and special criminal courts, law and order prevailed and civil war subsided. The First Consul promised a balanced budget and appeared to deliver it. Bonaparte spoke of healing the nation's wounds, especially those opened by religious grievances caused by dechristianization during the Revolution. Realizing the importance of religion in maintaining domestic peace, Napoleon reestablished relations with the pope in 1801 in the Concordat, which recognized Catholicism as the religion of the French and restored the Roman Catholic hierarchy.

Napoleon's popularity as First Consul flowed from his military and political successes and his religious reconciliation. He had come to power in 1799 by appealing for the support of the army. In 1802 Napoleon decided to extend his power by calling for a plebiscite in which he asked the electorate to vote him First Consul for life. Public support was overwhelming. An electoral landslide gave Napoleon greater political power than any of his Bourbon predecessors.

War and More War

Napoleon was at war or preparing for war during his entire reign. His military successes, real and apparent, before 1799 had been crucial in his bid for political power. By 1802, he had signed favorable treaties with both Austria and Great Britain. He appeared to deliver a lasting peace and to establish France as the dominant power in Europe. But the peace was short-lived. In 1803 France embarked on an eleven-year period of continuous war. Under Napoleon's command, the French army delivered defeat after defeat to the European powers. Austria fell in 1805, Prussia in 1806, and the Russian armies of Alexander I were defeated at Friedland in 1807. In 1808 Napoleon invaded Spain in order to drive out British expeditionary forces intent on invading France. Spain became a satellite kingdom of France although the conflict continued.

Britain was the one exception to the string of Napoleonic victories. Napoleon initially considered sending a French fleet to invade the island nation. Lacking the strength necessary to achieve this, he turned to economic warfare and blockaded European ports against British trade. Beginning in 1806, the Continental System, as the blockade was known, erected a structure of protection for French manufactures in all continental European markets. The British responded to the tariff walls and boycotts with a naval blockade that succeeded in cutting French commerce off from its Atlantic markets. The Continental System did not prove to be the decisive policy that Napoleon had planned: the British economy was not broken and the French economy did not flourish when faced with restricted resources and the persistence of a black market in smuggled goods.

Still, by 1810 the French leader was master of the Continent. French armies had extended revolutionary reforms and legal codes outside France and brought with them civil equality and religious toleration. They had also drained defeated countries of their resources and had inflicted the horrors of war with armies of occupation, forced billeting, and pillage. Napoleon's empire extended across Europe, with only a diminished Austria, Prussia, and Russia remaining independent. He placed his relatives and friends on the thrones of the new satellite kingdoms of Italy, Naples, Westphalia, Holland, and Spain.

This engraving, from the series "Disasters of War" by Francisco Goya, depicts the horrors of war. The series was inspired by Napoleon's invasion and occupation of Spain from 1808 to 1813.

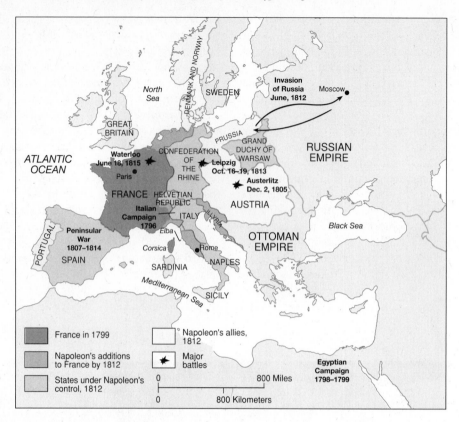

Napoleon's Empire

Peace at Home

Napoleon measured domestic prosperity in terms of the stability of his reign. Through the 1802 plebiscite that voted him First Consul for life, he maintained the charade of constitutional rule, while he ruled as virtual dictator. In 1804, he abandoned all pretense and had himself proclaimed emperor of the French. He staged his own coronation and that of his wife Josephine at the cathedral of Notre Dame de Paris.

Secure in his regime, surrounded by a new nobility that he created based on military achievement and talent, and that he rewarded with honors, Napoleon set about implementing sweeping reforms in every area of government. He recognized the importance of science for both industry and war. The Revolution had removed an impediment to the development of a national market by creating a uniform system of weights and measures—the metric system, which was established by 1799. But Napoleon felt the need to go further. To assure French predominance in scientific research and application, Napoleon became a patron of science, supporting important work in the areas of physics and

chemistry. Building for the future, Napoleon made science a pillar in the new structure of higher education.

The Directory had restored French prosperity through stabilization of the currency, fiscal reform, and support of industry. Napoleon's contribution to the French economy was the much needed reform of the tax system. He authorized the creation of a central banking system. French industries flourished under the protection of the state. The blockade forced the development of new domestic crops like beet-sugar and indigo, which became substitutes for colonial products. Napoleon extended the infrastructure of roads so necessary for the expansion of national and European markets.

Perhaps his greatest achievement was the codification of law, a task begun under the Revolution. Combined with economic reforms, the new Napoleonic Code facilitated trade and the development of commerce by regularizing contractual relations and protecting property rights and equality before the law. The civil laws of the new code carved out a family policy characterized by hierarchy and subordination.

Married women were neither independent nor equal to men in ownership of property, custody of children, and access to divorce. Women also lacked political rights. In the Napoleonic Code, women, like children, were subjected to paternal authority. The Napoleonic philosophy of woman's place is well captured in an anecdote told by Madame Germaine de Staël (1766–1817), a leading intellectual of her day. As the daughter of Jacques Necker, the Swiss financier and adviser to Louis XVI at the time of the Revolution, she had been educated in Enlightenment ideas from an early age. On finding herself seated next to Napoleon at a dinner party, she asked him what was very likely a self-interested question: whom did he consider the greatest woman, alive or dead? Napoleon had no name to give her but he responded without pausing, "The one who has had the most children."

Napoleon turned his prodigious energies to every aspect of French life. He encouraged the arts, while creating a police force. He had monuments built but did not forget about sewers. He organized French administrative life in a fashion that has endured. In place of the popular democratic movement, he offered his own singular authority. In place of elections, clubs, and free associations, he gave France plebiscites and army service. To be sure, Napoleon believed in constitutions but he thought they should be "short and obscure." For Napoleon the great problem of democracy was its unpredictability. His regime solved that problem by eliminating choices.

Decline and Fall

Militarily, Napoleon went too far. The first cracks in the French facade began to show in the Peninsular War (1808–14) with Spain, as Spanish guerrilla tactics proved costly for French troops. But Napoleon's biggest mistake, the one that shattered the myth of his invincibility, occurred when he decided to invade Russia in June 1812. Having decisively defeated Russian forces in 1807, Napoleon entered into a peace treaty with Tsar Alexander I that guaranteed Russian allegiance to French policies. But Alexander repudiated the Continental System in 1810 and appeared to be preparing for his own war against France. Napoleon seized the initiative, sure that he could defeat Russian forces once again. With an army of 500,000 men, Napoleon moved deep into Russia in the summer of 1812. The tsar's troops fell back in retreat, and when Napoleon and his men entered Moscow in September, they found a city in flames. The people of Moscow had destroyed their own city to de-

prive the French troops of winter quarters. Napoleon's men found themselves facing a severe Russian winter without overcoats, without supplies, and without food. The starving and frostbitten French army was forced into retreat. Fewer than 100,000 men made it back to France.

The empire began to crumble. Britain, unbowed by the Continental System, remained Napoleon's sworn enemy. Prussia joined Great Britain, Sweden, Russia, and Austria in opposing France anew. In the Battle of Nations at Leipzig in October 1813, France was forced to retreat. Napoleon refused a negotiated peace and fought on until the following March, when the victorious allies marched down the streets of Paris and occupied the French capital. Deserted by his allies, Napoleon abdicated in April 1814, in favor of his young son, the titular king of Rome (1811–32). When the allies

The Reign of Napoleon

1799	Napoleon establishes consulate; becomes First Consul
1801	Napoleon reestablishes relations with pope; restores Roman Catholic hierarchy
1802	Plebiscite declares Napoleon First Consul for life
1804	Napoleon proclaims himself Emperor of the French
1806	Continental System implemented
1808–14	France engaged in Peninsular War with Spain
June 1812	Napoleon invades Russia
September 1812	French army reaches Moscow, is trapped by Russian winter
October 1813	Napoleon defeated at Battle of Nations at Leipzig
March 1814	Napoleon abdicates and goes into exile on island of Elba
March 1815	Napoleon escapes Elba and attempts to reclaim power
15 June 1815	Napoleon is defeated at Waterloo and exiled to island of Saint Helena

This 1835 painting by De Boisdenier depicts the suffering of Napoleon's Grand Army on the retreat from Moscow. The Germans were to meet a similar fate over one hundred years later when they invaded Russia without adequate supplies for the harsh winter.

refused to accept the young "Napoleon II," the French called upon the Bourbon Louis XVIII and crowned him king. Napoleon was then exiled to the Mediterranean island of Elba.

Still it was not quite the end for Napoleon. While the European heads of state sat in Vienna trying to determine the future of Europe and France's place in it, Napoleon returned from his exile on Elba. On 15 June 1815, Napoleon once again and for the final time confronted the European powers in one of the most famous battles in history—Waterloo. With 125,000 loyal French forces, Napoleon seemed within hours of reestablishing the French empire in Europe, but the defeat of his forces was decisive. Napoleon's return proved brief—it lasted only one hundred days. He was exiled to the island of Saint Helena in the South Atlantic. For the next six years, Napoleon wrote his memoirs under the watchful eyes of his British jailors. He died on 5 May 1821.

The period of revolution and empire from 1789 to 1815 radically changed the face of France. A new, more cohesive elite of bourgeois and nobles emerged, sharing power based on wealth and status. Ownership of land remained a defining characteristic of both old and new elites. A new state bureaucracy, built on the foundations of the old, expanded and centralized state power.

The people as sovereign now legitimated political power. Napoleon at his most imperial never doubted that he owed his existence to the people. In this sense, Napoleon was the king of the Revolution—an apparently contradictory fusion of old forms and new ideology. Napoleon channeled democratic forces into enthusiasm for empire. He learned his lessons from the failure of the Bourbon monarchy and the politicians of the Revolution. For sixteen years Napoleon successfully reconciled the old regime with the new France. Yet he could not resolve the essential problem of democracy: the relationship between the will of the people and the exercise of political power. The picture in 1815 was not dramatically different from the situation in 1789. The Revolution might be over, but changes fueled by the revolutionary tradition were just beginning. The struggle for a workable democratic culture recurred in France for another century and elsewhere in Europe through the twentieth century.

SUGGESTIONS FOR FURTHER READING

THE CRISIS OF THE OLD REGIME IN FRANCE, 1715-1788

C. B. A. Behrens, *Society, Government, and the Enlightenment* (New York: Harper & Row, 1985). A comparative study of eighteenth-century France and Prussia, focusing on the relationship between government and the ruling classes, that explains how pressures for change in both countries led to different outcomes, revolution in France, and reform in Prussia.

* Roger Chartier, *The Cultural Origins of the French Revolution*, trans. Lydia G. Cochrane (Durham, NC: Duke University Press, 1991). Argues for the importance of the rise of critical modes of thinking in the public sphere in the eighteenth century and of long-term dechristianization in shaping the desire for change in society and politics.

Olwen Hufton, *The Poor in Eighteenth-Century France, 1750-1789* (Oxford: Clarendon, 1974). Examines the lives of the poor before the Revolution and the institutions that attempted to deal with the problem of poverty.

* Daniel Roche, *The People of Paris* (Berkeley, CA: University of California Press, 1987). An essay on popular culture in the eighteenth century, in which the author surveys the lives of the Parisian popular classes—servants, laborers, and artisans—and examines their housing, furnishing, dress, and leisure activities.

Isser Woloch, *Eighteenth-Century Europe: Tradition and Progress, 1715-1789* (New York: Norton, 1982). A discussion of eighteenth-century Europe, comparing social, economic, political, and intellectual developments elsewhere in Europe to the French experience, with special attention to cultural aspects, such as popular beliefs and religion.

THE FIRST STAGE OF THE FRENCH REVOLUTION, 1789-1792

* Georges Lefebvre, *The Great Fear of 1789* (New York: Pantheon Books, 1973). This classic study analyzes the rural panic that swept through parts of France in the summer of 1789. The Great Fear is presented as a distinct episode in the opening months of the Revolution, with its own internal logic.

François Furet and Denis Richet, *The French Revolution* (New York: Macmillan, 1970). Two experts on the French Revolution present a detailed overview of the period from 1789 to 1798, when Bonaparte returned to Paris.

Colin Lucas, ed., *Rewriting the French Revolution* (Oxford: Clarendon Press, 1991). Responding to the historiographic challenge of the bicentenary of the French Revolution, eight scholars present new interpretations in the areas of social development, ideas, politics, and religion.

* Michel Vovelle, *The Fall of the French Monarchy* (Cambridge: Cambridge University Press, 1984). A social history of the origins and early years of the Revolution, beginning with a brief examination of the old regime and paying special attention to social and economic changes initiated by the Revolution, the role of the popular classes, and the creation of revolutionary culture.

EXPERIMENTING WITH DEMOCRACY: THE REVOLUTION'S SECOND STAGE, 1792-1799

* François Furet, *Interpreting the French Revolution* (Cambridge: Cambridge University Press, 1981). A series of essays challenging many of the assumptions concerning the causes and outcome of the Revolution and reviewing the historiography of the Revolution. The author argues that political crisis, not class conflict, was the Revolution's primary cause and that revolutionary ideas concerning democracy are central to an understanding of the Terror.

Carla Hesse, *Publishing and Cultural Politics in Revolutionary Paris, 1789-1810* (Berkeley, CA: University of California Press, 1991). Reconstructs the publishing world that emerged from the revolutionary struggles of publishers and printers of Paris; and examines the political, legal, and socioeconomic forces shaping the new cultural politics between 1789 and 1810.

* Lynn Hunt, *Politics, Culture, and Class in the French Revolution* (Berkeley, CA: University of California Press, 1984). A study of the Revolution as the locus of the creation of modern political culture. The second half of the book examines the social composition and cultural experiences of the new political class that emerged in the Revolution.

* Lynn Hunt, *The Family Romance of the French Revolution* (Berkeley, CA: University of California Press, 1992). Studies recurrent images of the family in French revolutionary politics to understand the gendered nature of revolutionary and republican politics.

* Joan B. Landes, *Women and the Public Sphere* (Ithaca, NY: Cornell University Press, 1988). Landes examines the genesis of the modern notion of the public sphere from a feminist perspective and argues that within the revolutionary process women were relegated to the private sphere of the domestic world.

* Sara E. Melzer and Leslie W. Rabine, eds., *Rebel Daughters: Women and the French Revolution* (New York: Oxford University Press, 1992). Contributors from a variety of disciplines examine the integral relationship of women and the French Revolution, with special attention to the political exclusion of women from the new politics.

* Albert Soboul, *The Sans-Culottes* (New York: Anchor, 1972). An exhaustive study of the artisans who composed the core of popular political activism in revolutionary Paris. The political demands and ideology of the sans-culottes are examined with the composition, culture, and actions of the popular movement during the Revolution.

THE REIGN OF NAPOLEON, 1799-1815

* Louis Bergeron, *France Under Napoleon* (Princeton, NJ: Princeton University Press, 1981). An analysis of the structure of Napoleon's regime, its social bases of support, and its opponents.

Isser Woloch, *The French Veteran From the Revolution to the Restoration* (Chapel Hill, NC: University of North Carolina Press, 1979). Examines the social impact of revolutionary and Napoleonic policies by concentrating on the changing fortunes of war veterans.

* Indicates paperback edition available.

CHAPTER 23

States and Societies in East Asia, 1600–1800

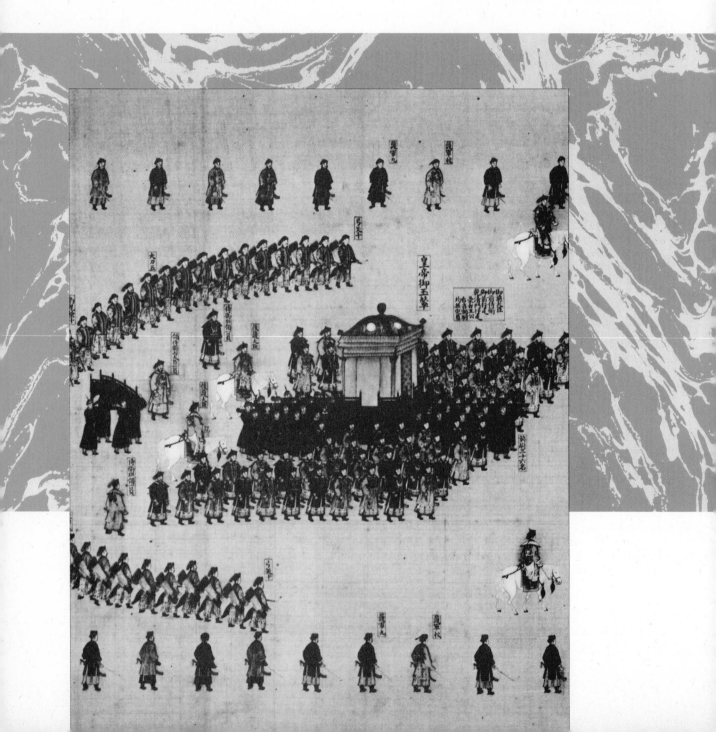

RITUALS AND REALITIES OF CHINESE IMPERIAL RULE

Hidden from view in his palanquin, shouldered by thirty-six soldiers, the Qianlong emperor (1736–95) took his place in the stately procession from his palace to the Temple of Heaven. There he, like Ming (1368–1643) and Qing (1644–1911) emperors before him, annually made sacrifices to Heaven at the winter solstice. Flanked by swordsmen with a rear guard of archers, the emperor's palanquin came near the end of a magnificent display that included carriages drawn by teams of white horses and others pulled by elephants. Colorful banners and flags identified different officials who walked alongside.

Whenever the emperor moved from his palace chambers on a formal occasion, he was accompanied by an armed honor guard. The Song emperor Shenzong (1067–85) reportedly had some 22,000 attendants accompany him on the most important occasions. In contrast, the early Qing emperors kept very small honor guards. At times only fourteen people were in attendance—six men carrying banners, two with parasols, and six armed guards. In 1748 the Qianlong emperor announced new regulations to expand his honor guard, the size of the entourage growing with the importance of the ceremony from 104 to 660 attendants.

The annual sacrifices at the Temple of Heaven required the most lavish presentation of imperial grandeur to affirm the emperor's august authority. His 660 attendants were part of a much larger procession painted on the scroll we view here, which measures a majestic 56 feet in length. From this scroll of the 1748 sacrifices, we know that more than 3,700 participants to this event witnessed the emperor perform his solemn duty of informing Heaven of the past year's important events.

The grandeur depicted here does not tell the whole story of imperial rule, however, for the observance of ritual occasions was but one important part of the emperor's duties. Equally crucial during this period were the bureaucracy's administrative duties, which some emperors guided more effectively than others. In contrast to the late Ming emperors, who ruled before the Manchu takeover, three early Qing emperors— the Kangxi emperor (1661–1722), the Yongzheng emperor (1723–35), and the Qianlong emperor (1736–95)—fulfilled ritual functions as well as promoting active bureaucratic rule of the empire. The Kangxi emperor personally led military campaigns to consolidate the empire's expanded borders; for civilian administration, he approved new procedures for evaluating official performance and for managing state finances. His son, the Yongzheng emperor, allocated more resources to local officials to help them meet the challenges of maintaining local social order; he also streamlined bureaucratic communication among different levels of the administration, and centralized imperial control over important decision making.

In his early years, the Qianlong emperor continued to implement policies that promoted popular welfare—for example, a vast granary system provided famine relief, and river and canal maintenance reduced flooding possibilities and improved transportation. By the 1780s, however, the limitations of the bureaucracy became increasingly evident. Officials often had too few fiscal and human resources to meet their responsibilities. By the late eighteenth century, toward the end of the Qianlong emperor's long reign, the expansion of the empire—territorially, demographically, and economically—greatly complicated the bureaucratic task of sustaining political order. As a result, the limits to China's imperial rule, not apparent in the ritual performances of this scroll, were becoming clearer to officials of the day. But these problems were themselves the products of political successes. Without the creation of major institutions to promote popular welfare and social stability, their maintenance could not have become an issue.

This century of rule stands out in late imperial Chinese history, not simply for the grandeur of its rituals, but more importantly for its political successes. These were more imposing than those of their late Ming predecessors in the seventeenth century but less obvious than the political failures of their late Qing successors in the nineteenth century.

Late Imperial China, 1600–1800

In 1600 China was the world's most populous country, as it had been for centuries and has continued to be until the present. With an expanding commercial economy based on agricultural and rural handicraft production, the society had as strong an economic foundation as any across Eurasia. But the imperial state revealed growing weaknesses domestically and in foreign relations, leading the country into a period of turmoil similar in some ways to the crises challenging European states and societies during this same century.

For China, the resolution of political conflicts and social unrest was the fall of the Ming dynasty (1368–1644) and its replacement by the Qing dynasty (1644–1911). After consolidating its domestic rule by the 1680s, the Qing guided the country through a century of general social stability and relative material security. The empire's territory and population virtually doubled, and the agrarian commercial economy expanded dramatically. The state attempted to guide these processes of change.

The Experience of Daily Life in Late Imperial China

Most of the 150 million to 175 million people alive in China in 1600 lived in villages and spent much of their time working the land. These peasants exceeded in numbers the total population of all of Europe, which at the time numbered roughly 100 million people. Beneath the massive weight of the numbers, we can discover dramatic variety in the local conditions of Chinese peasant life. Speaking mutually unintelligible dialects, peasants in north China could not understand those in the area along the Yangzi River. Those living along the southeast coast spoke dialects different from those in north China and Guangdong. Living in very different ecologies, ranging from semitropical forest in the southwest to semiarid plateaus in the northwest, China's peasants planted different crops to meet the possibilities and limitations of distinct environments. South of the Yangzi River, the areas of paddy rice agriculture were gradually extended; in the north, dry fields planted in some combination of wheat, buckwheat, and millet provided the staple grains, which were often made into noodles or porridge. In China's northwest, peasants fashioned homes out of the caves in the windswept hillsides of a dry and difficult terrain; on the North China Plain, surrounding the capital city of Beijing, peasants built their homes of bricks fired in small kilns. To provide heat during the chilly winters, these homes in the north relied upon the *kang*, an elevated bed platform made of earthen bricks that radiated heat supplied by the flues connected to cooking stoves. To the south of the Yangzi River, peasants enjoyed a broader variety of building materials, including timber and bamboo. Throughout China, rural homes were usually rectangular and their layouts had a strong sense of symmetry.

The Chinese family ideal was to have many generations living under a single roof. This goal led to the addition of rooms to form courtyards to house married sons and their families. With the great importance attached to filial piety and respect for the ancestors, most rural life centered on the family household. In some villages of seventeenth-century China, families belonged to larger kinship groups, or lineages, that traced their origins to a common male ancestor of several generations before. But extended families and lineages were more important as a Confucian ideal than as a common social reality. Most families were in fact small and many did not belong to lineages.

Women generally left their villages of birth to live with their husbands. In only a few parts of seventeenth-century China did many women routinely get beyond the household gate or the fields. Their social horizon was bounded by kinship relations. For peasant men the social universe was a bit larger, often extending to a nearby market town, where peasants sold their cash crops and handicrafts, sipped tea in teahouses, and discussed local social affairs. More prominent in the market towns were the gentry, who achieved high social status by earning degrees from passing civil service examinations. They were joined by other literati who were equally educated but less successful at the exams. Some of the gentry, many of whom were large landowners, lived in the market towns alongside other rich landlords and merchants, while others continued to live in the countryside. The gentry met in teahouses as well as at each others' homes, to discuss local politics, to learn about prices in distant markets, to write each other poetry, and to enjoy fine food and wine. While there were certainly differences in wealth and status in late imperial China, there was no sharp separation of urban and rural classes or between rich and poor. All pursued their lives in a society increasingly influenced by a cash economy.

Commercialization in an Agrarian Society

In late imperial China market exchange played some role in virtually everyone's life. Few people lived in households where all their food, clothing, and other daily needs were met solely by their own family's efforts. The region along the lower reaches of the Yangzi River made the most dramatic advances in cash cropping, handicrafts, and trade, sustaining its position as China's most prosperous area, an achievement it has largely maintained from the tenth century to the present day. The expansion of cash crops and handicrafts—cotton and silk textiles, tobacco, indigo for dyeing cotton cloth blue, paper products, straw mats—spread along the Yangzi River, creating new markets and agricultural centers of production in both the middle and upper Yangzi regions. Beyond the Yangzi watershed, significant agricultural and handicraft developments took place in Guangdong and along the southeast coast. In north China, less favored by nature with riverine transportation possibilities, commercialization was most pronounced along the Grand Canal and in the hinterlands of larger cities.

By 1600 the lower Yangzi region had developed a considerable network of specialized market towns.

Farmer operating a combination plow and seeder pulled by a water buffalo.

Other parts of the empire had less sophisticated networks, but trade itself continued to expand. These urban developments continued in the eighteenth century. But China's overall population did not become more urbanized, as was the case in Europe beginning in the late eighteenth century, because the countryside's population also continued to grow. Rural areas supported continued commercialization, making much of the Chinese countryside among the most market-oriented in the world.

Two major merchant groups dominated trade between the sixteenth and eighteenth centuries. First were the Shanxi merchants, who initially made their money in the Ming dynasty from government contracts to provision troops stationed along China's north and northwest borders. In exchange for supplying grain to the frontiers they received licenses to sell salt, a commodity with state-determined prices from which merchants could make large profits. Salt was an easy commodity for the state to control because its production was limited to a few places and it was important to everyone's food supply, both to preserve and to season food. Shanxi merchants entered other trades, developed a financial network, and dominated commerce in the northern half of the empire. The second group, the Huizhou merchants, initially made their money in grain, cloth, and timber. They established commercial operations in all the major cities and market towns in the southern half of the empire, much as Shanxi merchants did in the north.

Merchants never developed an exclusively urban orientation. They were city sojourners who usually maintained agricultural lands in their native places. Some of their sons managed those lands, while others helped out with the urban businesses. But the most prestigious work was to study successfully for the civil service examinations. Status was based on ideals defined by the political system and the landowning elite. As a consequence, the urban lifestyle developed by Chinese merchants, unlike those in Japan and Europe, never achieved much autonomy from the ideals typical of other social groups. Chinese merchant wealth could support sumptuous feasts, the collection of pottery and painting, and new themes in literature, but it did not generate a distinctive view of the material and social worlds that would displace older visions of political and social order. Gentry and landed elites nevertheless worried that the profits from trade would entice too many people with extravagant lifestyles. But the value of owning land and living in a restrained manner retained its attractions.

Official fears that merchant wealth would lure people away from agriculture were exaggerated. Vulnerability to poor harvests was a more constant possibility than the dangers of extravagant living. Along with their counterparts across Eurasia, Chinese peasants shared a basic dependence on weather and climate that made their lives intimately enmeshed with the seasons. In any one year, flood and drought could spell disaster, and a series of harsh years made survival extremely tenuous. When human disruptions—peasant rebellions or war—compounded the impact of natural disasters, peasant life was in great peril indeed. Such circumstances seriously threatened the political life of the dynasty, as happened in the first half of the seventeenth century.

From the Ming Dynasty to the Qing Dynasty

Traditional Chinese historians believed in a dynastic cycle. When a dynasty was young and vigorous, the emperor ruled benevolently and the people prospered. As a dynasty grew old, corruption crept into the bureaucracy and emperors became feeble leaders. The seventeenth-century political scene conforms to many elements of this belief. For decades a faction-ridden bureaucracy had made decisions without meaningful guidance or even participation by the emperors. Struggle in the government raged between two factions—one led by eunuchs who served in large numbers in the Imperial Household Administration, the other led by a group of officials known as the Donglin ("Eastern Forest"), movement. These officials criticized the eunuchs' control over the government and proposed reforms to give themselves more power. Nonetheless, factionalism proved easier to deal with than the mounting fiscal problems. In spite of tax reform begun in the sixteenth century, the need for additional resources grew steadily because of military expenditures along the northern border, where China was vulnerable to attack by the Manchus. To raise additional funds, the government levied new taxes, which prompted popular protests. In one dramatic instance in 1601, the imposition of a tax on Suzhou weavers brought the industry to a halt as weavers protested what they perceived to be unwarranted and illegitimate taxes. The government quelled the disturbance and made arrests. But when one of the leaders was released more than a decade later he was still remembered as a local hero.

In the seventeenth century, the Chinese state, like its European counterparts, had difficulties raising revenues to meet crises, often of military origin. Domestic

Zhang Ying's Advice to His Son

■ *"Remarks on real estate" by Zhang Ying (1638–1708) was initially addressed to this official's six sons during a home leave from Court, probably around 1697. In this long essay filled with historical allusions and contemporary anecdotes, Zhang stresses the importance of investing in land. Land does not depreciate in value, nor can it be stolen. It can, however, be passed on to one's descendants and form the basis of family security for generations into the future. Zhang recognizes that higher returns can be made from investments in usury or commerce, but he believes the dangers of losing profits kept in cash through poor investment or extravagant spending make the lower returns from landownership more prudent. In a period of increasing commercialization and the pursuit of material pleasures in market towns and cities, Zhang promoted the virtues of scholarship and frugal living in the countryside.*

Only land is a commodity which even after a hundred or a thousand years is always as good as new. Even if agricultural labour is not intensive, if the land is poor and the produce meagre, as soon as it is manured and irrigated it will be renewed. Even if the land is gone to waste and the homestead is covered with weeds, once it is reclaimed it will be renewed. If you construct many ponds, poor land can be enriched, and if you vigorously uproot the weeds then barren soil can be made fertile. From ancient times to the present day there has never been any fear that it will decay or fall into ruin, nor anxiety lest it abscond or suffer attrition. This is really something to be treasured!

In the present age the young men in a family have elegant clothing and spirited horses and are always dancing and carousing . . .

If the young men have a modicum of good sense they will not tolerate things being thrown away extravagantly. How can they live sheltered lives knowing what it is like to have full stomachs and warm clothing, but paying no attention whatever to the conservation of resources and indeed casting them away in the mire?

Thus failure to regulate expenditure is undoubtedly the major reason for incurring debts and selling property. Apart from this, however, gambling, depravity and wastefulness also lead unquestionably to ruin. Again, there are those who sell their property because of marriage expenses, which is absolutely ridiculous. As long as there are men and women there will always be marriages, but you should measure your resources and regulate the style of the affair on the basis of a good year's savings. Why should you sell something which has been the mainstay of the family for generations in order to make a fine show on one particular occasion?

For a family the two words 'wealth' and 'honour' signify merely transient glory. To raise their sons and grandsons they rely ultimately on agriculture and study.

When finally you succeed in your studies and are given an official appointment you may live in the city. Thus you move back to the city, but after one or two generations it is proper once more to live in the country, so you again move to the country to live. In this way agriculture and study, country and city life succeed each other in cycles and may be great and long-lasting. What a fine and auspicious thing this is!

disorder compounded state fiscal problems and led to profound political uncertainty. The Ming Court faced the double challenge of the Manchus poised for attack from the north and domestic peasant rebellions. Between 1627 and 1631, Li Zicheng, an unemployed post-station attendant who had previously served as an iron-worker's apprentice and worked in a wineshop, organized peasants for raiding in the northwestern province of Shanxi. The scale of raiding grew in a second period between 1631 and 1636, as rebel groups roamed

East Asia, ca. 1800

the forested border areas of Hubei, Henan, and Shanxi. In a third stage, Li Zicheng and a second major rebel leader, Zhang Xianzhong, organized more formal armies, and after 1641 these armies seriously challenged the state and brought down the government. In the fourth and final stage, marked by Li's entrance into Beijing, the Manchus quickly followed his rebel armies to proclaim themselves the restorers of social order. They routed the rebels and defeated the Ming dynasty. As the Manchus proclaimed their Qing dynasty in 1644, they made their appeal to Beijing residents in the language and logic of earlier Chinese rulers, not as some northern barbarians ignorant of Chinese ways. They were able to do so because for many decades the Manchus had been building their power in the northeast and preparing for the day they might enter China proper.

The Manchus were one of two different kinds of people living to the north of the Great Wall. The first, of whom the most famous were the Mongols, were nomadic and seminomadic peoples who lived on the steppe and depended on livestock grazing and trade

with sedentary peoples. The second, represented by the Manchus, lived to the northeast in heavily forested areas and depended upon hunting, agriculture, and trade. Their hunting tradition provided the Manchus with the martial values and skills to conquer other peoples in the northeast. To consolidate their rule in this region, the Manchus developed new forms of organization; from Chinese institutions they borrowed certain principles that they combined with their own to form a government that centralized Manchu forces. Thus, before even entering China proper, the Manchus had a far better sense of China than had the Mongols who preceded them in forming a Chinese dynasty some four hundred years earlier. But Manchu understanding of Chinese customs did not make important elites any friendlier to them. In order to gain their support and help with local rule, the new regime had to accommodate elite interests on subjects like tax reform.

Creating domestic order through a combination of intimidation and accommodation proved less dramatic a challenge than facing the military power of generals farther south, who had been rewarded for their service to the Manchus during the defeat of the Ming with large estates of land and control over bureaucratic appointments. The most famous of these was Wu Sangui (1612–78), the general who had let the Manchus through the Shanhaiguan pass to enter China proper. As the Qing moved to reduce their power, Wu and his colleagues mounted a counteroffensive known as the Revolt of the Three Feudatories, which lasted from 1673 to 1681, when Qing troops defeated the rebel generals. Two years later the last rebels, who had fled to the island of Taiwan, were defeated and the island was incorporated into the southeast coastal province of Fujian. In contrast to conventional images of a peaceful government, the Qing state in fact continued to be an active military power for the next century, giving battle to groups across the northern and northwestern frontiers as well as making forays into Southeast Asia. Qing defeats by the Vietnamese and Burmese in the 1780s marked the end of a century of military successes.

As they established their dynasty, the Qing adopted most of the bureaucratic institutions of the Ming, with the central government divided into Six Boards and a vertically integrated territorial administration of provinces, prefectures, and counties. To the Ming system of government the Qing added a system to register all Manchus, as well as some Chinese and Mongolians. Known in English as the banner system, this organizational format was the basis for the Qing's military forces. In addition, even Manchus who were not actively serving in military service were organized into banners through which they were allotted land to cultivate. The Qing made other changes, including streamlined bureaucratic communication with the throne, and the creation of a new high-level body known as the Grand Council to handle the most important reports or memorials.

As a minority, the Manchus were acutely aware that China proper contained a diverse population. The Han Chinese dominated as the principal ethnic group, but many other small populations of ethnically or culturally distinct people were important in different areas. Some groups were ethnically and linguistically related to populations in Southeast Asia such as the Miao (Hmong) and Tai. In the northwest and southwest, there was a considerable religious minority of ethnic Han who had converted to Islam, mostly after the sixteenth century. Finally, there were groups of Han Chinese who suffered friction with local Han Chinese residents. The largest such group, called Hakka, or "guest people," was in south China and had a distinct dialect, customs, and cuisine. Qing rulers were sensitive to the problems of minorities. Often the government regulated Han settlement in minority areas to protect minority people's livelihoods. At the same time, however, the government sought to incorporate the minority groups politically. Through a shift from native chieftain rule to standard bureaucratic administration during the Yongzheng reign, the government began to incorporate remote areas with indigenous ethnic minorities.

The Hall of Prayer for Good Harvests in Beijing, built originally in 1420 on the spot where Ming emperors came to pray for good harvests. The complex was enlarged and rebuilt by the Qianlong emperor, and it remains an emblem of China's enduring civilization to this day.

Complementing political integration was sinification, the effort to make the entire population thoroughly Chinese. The government insisted that Chinese language and customs were the standard for civilization and created the category of "Chinese" as a cultural rather than a racial designation. A "Chinese" was someone who spoke, dressed, and ate in the manner of a Chinese; a "Chinese" was one who was married and buried according to Chinese customs. One could become Chinese, and conversely one could potentially become "barbarian" by adopting the customs of some minority people. To achieve stability across an agrarian empire, the Qing sought to create a Chinese cultural order. An expanding empire with a distinctive agrarian political economy supported this goal.

The Political Economy of Eighteenth-Century China

The initial establishment of Qing political control was quickly followed by the resettlement of lands abandoned during the peasant rebellions of the late Ming. Resettlement of fertile areas was followed by migration to ecologically less favored frontier regions in the southwest and northwest. The government supported these movements through a homesteading policy that granted tax holidays of three to five years to peasants opening unclaimed land. In some cases the government made loans of seed grain and provided help with buying draft animals. By the eighteenth century more than seven million acres of newly reclaimed land were added to the tax registers, and the total amount of reclaimed land was even greater due to new fields that escaped registration. This expansion supported the growth of China's population from 175 million to 350 million during the eighteenth century.

This dramatic population growth was also stimulated by continued intensification of land use and expanded commercial exchange. Increased use of organic fertilizers, coupled with seed improvements and expanded irrigation facilities, made higher yields possible in many locales across China. New trade patterns—such as north China soybean fertilizer exchanged for cloth produced in the lower Yangzi region—were established. Peasant families also turned to handicraft production to create new sources of income. In addition to expanding cotton textile production, activities like mat weaving

The Grand Canal, shown here winding through farmland, is one of the world's longest artificial waterways, extending 1200 miles from Beijing to Hangzhou.

or silkworm raising involved members of the household in different agricultural and handicraft activities—all carried out within the family's dwelling.

Unlike European states, which paid little attention to peasants other than as a source of tax revenues, the Qing state demonstrated considerable concern for peasant welfare, motivated by the Confucian belief that a starving peasantry would rise up in rebellion and bring down the dynasty. Officials monitored market prices, and bought and sold grain to dampen seasonal and annual fluctuations in harvest supplies. These policies complemented efforts to promote agricultural production and migration to frontiers.

Contrary to stereotypes, the Chinese state was not anticommercial in any serious sense. The state actively supported merchants' movement of goods over long distances and envisioned its own role as most important in those areas of the empire most poorly served by the commercial economy. In other words, the state was most active in storing grain, promoting land clearance, and creating infrastructure for the agrarian economy in areas where commerce mattered relatively little. Officials were committed to the policies of "practical learning," or the statecraft necessary to sustain these efforts successfully.

The eighteenth-century Chinese state's achievements were remarkable. Chinese grain prices fluctuated far less than European prices in the same centuries, while life expectancy in China was at least as high as in Europe. Dwarfing efforts made by European states to affect the economic conditions of peasants, the Qing dynasty was able to oversee a dramatic demographic expansion supported by economic developments that confirmed China's position of preeminence in Asia. Taking advantage of the positive functions that merchants and literati elites could perform, the state succeeded in managing a broad and diverse empire. The state's capacity to span varied scenarios and integrate them into an agrarian empire depended in part upon the state's promotion and control over a common culture.

Chinese Culture and the State

For centuries the Chinese state took an active role in defining acceptable belief and behavior. In Europe organized religion was the institutional source of moral belief and guidelines for proper behavior. Compared to the Chinese state, European states had much less to say about such matters in the seventeenth and eighteenth centuries. At the center of the Chinese state's influence over elite perspectives was the examination system. Study for the civil service examinations committed would-be degree holders to mastering a canon of general beliefs about politics and society, more specific strategies for good government, and concrete methods to deal with particular problems. But literati culture, the culture of the educated elite, extended well beyond studying for exams. To live up to the amateur ideal of someone skilled in the cultural arts, for example, a proper gentleman would always be able to compose a poem at a fine banquet or upon parting from friends.

Fiction and drama appealed to the tastes and curiosities of a broader audience. Martial heroes, heartless lovers, reunited couples, thieves and tricksters filled romances and stories of court cases. Other tales were filled with ghosts and spirits. Dramas were performed for a variety of occasions. Some were held during annual festivals to honor local gods. Other plays were performed at larger market towns, where beggars, gamblers, and fortune tellers gathered. Itinerant troupes performed different kinds of plays according to the kind of sponsor and type of audience in attendance. Lineage heads and village leaders favored plays celebrating proper Confucian virtues, while the plays designed to attract people to a temple fair were more likely to appeal to popular preferences for the supernatural, romances, or martial exploits, themes that lay beyond those actively promoted by Confucianism.

Late Ming elites, like the common people, were attracted to ideas beyond Confucianism. Disenchanted with state service, which was becoming more difficult to secure as qualified individuals increasingly outnumbered vacant positions, the gentry patronized local Buddhist monasteries and created for themselves a cultural space separate from the Confucian state. Eighteenth-century literati continued to be disenchanted with the civil service system. But instead of dissatisfaction with Confucianism leading to its further rejection, many believed that the Ming dynasty fell because intellectuals had become too interested in Buddhist-inspired metaphysics and had paid too little attention to more practical matters. Eighteenth-century literati championed a Confucian social order, in part because they were able to define career alternatives to state service. Nourished by the intellectual excitement of *kaozheng*, "evidential research," a movement to study the classics and other earlier texts with an eye to establishing authenticity, scholars avoided the pressures of bureaucratic life by becoming associated with academies that were havens

Nineteenth-century leather shadow puppet from Shanxi province. The character is a child with supernatural ability, pouring swords from a magical gourd.

outside state control. To be educated no longer necessarily meant a strong commitment to government service. Literati could gain employment teaching in local schools, writing inscriptions to commemorate major events or new buildings, and compiling records of a locale for publication as a gazetteer. These roles outside government continued to fit political definitions of acceptable cultural activity. Literati disaffection did not generate a serious critique of the state, let alone lead to a major political challenge.

Women's place in the hierarchical structure of Chinese society was reaffirmed amid the social changes of the seventeenth and eighteenth centuries. In popular stories, Chinese courtesans became heroines when they exhibited the proper virtues of loyalty to their lovers. The good courtesan ultimately married her lover, allowing her to become a good Confucian wife. Of course, most women did not live in the world of popular fiction; they were instead peasants who worked at making handicrafts and managing their households. Among the most socially vulnerable women were widows, whose chastity was promoted by officials and elites during the eighteenth century. At the same time, however, there were often great pressures on women to remarry; a dead husband's kin often wanted to repossess the widow's land,

an act more easily accomplished if the woman remarried. For peasant women generally, the economic pressures of survival dictated remarriage whenever possible, especially if the children were not yet old enough to help support her. The Qing state promoted widow chastity to demonstrate its commitment to the values stressed by Confucian elites. This commitment represented simply one feature of a much larger effort to shape popular cultural beliefs.

The state supervised China's temples, which were filled with a multitude of deities who performed a variety of functions. The state recognized a continuum between beliefs that were officially sanctioned and those that were dangerous and heterodox. So-called heterodox beliefs were prominent in the White Lotus Rebellion of 1796–1804, many of whose initial participants subscribed to a belief in a millennial age when a new social order would bring peace and prosperity to true believers. Orthodox belief, in contrast, was marked by state acceptance of deities. The state promoted a celestial bureaucracy that paralleled earthly arrangements. But officials could not force all deities into this bureaucratically inspired structure and ultimately accepted considerable diversity in local beliefs to fill in the space between the strictly orthodox and the decidedly not. Unable to patrol or even monitor local religious practices, the eighteenth-century state relied on local elites to keep popular beliefs confined within the boundaries etched out by Confucianism.

To promote actively moral indoctrination, the Qing state implemented a village lecture system modeled on earlier practices in which local elites gave moral presentations that were elaborations upon themes set out in imperial edicts. The Kangxi emperor's "Sacred Edict" offered sixteen maxims, which counseled the people in such matters as diligence, frugality, and proper treatment of relatives and friends. The Yongzheng emperor penned a set of amplified instructions that went beyond the terse classical language used by his father. Though never uniformly implemented across all of China, the lectures represented the state's interest in molding popular beliefs. The overlap of elite and official visions of acceptable cultural practices and beliefs added stability and harmony that might otherwise have been difficult to sustain. Educated elites responded to state expectations that local leaders had the power and responsibility to create and sustain social order. The more local leaders succeeded in this effort, the less the state intervened in local affairs. The bond joining state and elites was a common commitment to Confucian beliefs.

The state exercised considerable influence over the world of cultural expression. If a new vision of society was to emerge anywhere during the seventeenth and eighteenth centuries to challenge the prevailing Confucian cultural orthodoxy, it would be in the cities. But cities, which in Europe were the settings within which new attitudes were expressed about commerce, politics, and social order, remained in China under central government control and closely tied to the countryside. Shared cultural perspectives—of urban and rural sectors as well as among different classes—enabled the state to shape significantly the overall content of beliefs and preferences. Not only was the state alert to potential heterodox beliefs at the popular level, but it was vigilant about elite expression as well. During the mid-eighteenth century it launched an inquisition that led to the burning of thousands of books in Beijing, an event similar to ones that also took place in eighteenth-century Europe.

The Chinese state's success at ruling an agrarian empire depended upon its abilities to control the emergence of groups and ideas that might challenge its capacities and authority to rule. Amid commercialization, demographic growth, and a doubling of the empire's territory, the Qing state joined Chinese and Manchu elements to create a stable agrarian empire that was the widely acknowledged political center of East Asia. No stagnant society, no homogeneous country, no ineffectual and irrelevant imperial government, China was a dynamic economy and a diverse society led by a strong government that could oppress as well as promote.

The Chinese World Order

As heirs to an imperial tradition of rule, the Ming and Qing emperors conceived a world order with the emperor at the political center. All local authorities, wherever they might be, were subordinated to the emperor and expressed their understanding of this relationship through the presentation of tribute. Beyond the sphere of China's domestic government were peoples toward whom Ming and Qing rulers adopted various strategies to persuade, bribe, or coerce them to accept their places in a Chinese view of the world. Non-Chinese agreed not to challenge the empire even if they did not always agree with the Chinese view.

For China's world order, tribute relations were a key component helping to structure China's relations with peoples within and beyond its cultural orbit. The tribute system was both a political system and an economic system. The presentation of tribute by peoples from afar affirmed to the Chinese Court the centrality of their own position in the world. Through elaborate rituals of investiture, the Chinese symbolically recognized the authority of other leaders. To show their gracious recognition of tribute presentations, the Chinese offered gifts in return. Tribute presentations themselves were a kind of gift trade. Other trade often followed the presentation of tribute. In some cases—for example, Russia—the Chinese permitted trade in Beijing without tribute presentations. They also allowed this practice at some officially recognized frontier markets. These forms of administered trade were far more common than any sort of free-market trade that characterized domestic transactions. Strictly economic considerations, important though they could be, were usually secondary to the political.

Inner Asia and China: Formation of the Qing Union

For centuries the Chinese empire had a complex relationship with peoples to the north of the Great Wall. But before the Qing, no dynasty brought much territory beyond the Great Wall under formal imperial rule. It comes as no surprise that the Manchus included their own northeastern homeland in the empire, but they also subjugated other groups in Inner Asia. From what became Manchuria in the northeast through Mongolia, Xinjiang, and Tibet to the west, the Qing virtually doubled the territory of the Chinese empire and made the eighteenth-century Chinese state an impressive land-based empire flexing its military muscles in regions of interest to the Russians and British as well as the Chinese. To handle its affairs with the peoples of Inner Asia, the Qing established a specific institution, the Lifan Yuan, or Office of Border Affairs.

The Manchus divided their ancestral homeland into three provinces administered by a set of bureaucratic offices paralleling those used to rule China proper. Formally closed off to general Han immigration in order to protect the area from Chinese influence and thus protect Manchu identity, the area's fertile lands were nevertheless opened up by Han immigration. As the Qing state grew increasingly focused on China proper, the maintenance of a homeland untainted by Han influence

Pastoral Mongols live in felt-covered houses called yurts. The economy of these nomads is based on herds of cattle, horses, sheep, and goats. Their animals supply them with milk, meat, hair, and wool.

became less necessary, especially when Russian interest in territory around the Amur River, beginning in the eighteenth century, could be countered by Han settlement.

Well before the Manchus entered China proper, they had adopted the Tibetan Buddhism of the Mongols. Several eastern Mongolian tribes became attached to the Manchus; they could accept their position in an East Asian empire in which China was at the center but over which their allies the Manchus ruled. While the eastern Mongols became allied with the Manchus, others to the west remained their enemies, and the Qing had to subjugate them. The Kangxi emperor personally led the campaign against the western Mongol leader Galdan in order to destroy any lingering challenge the Mongols posed to Qing power.

In China's northwest, three distinct civilizations joined the Chinese to form the most culturally complex corner of the empire. Tibetan civilization was distinct in its origins from the Mongols, who owed their roots to Turks who dominated the steppe in the sixth century C.E. Tibetans live not only in what became Tibet under the Qing but also in western Sichuan, Yunnan, Gansu, and Xinjiang. Economically the region depended on a combination of high plateau agriculture, pastoralism, and trade. The central social institution was monasticism, which organized a large portion of the population. A Tibetanized form of Buddhism dominated their cultural life.

Along with Han Chinese, Turco-Mongolian, and Tibetan civilizations, Islam was the fourth important culture to meet in China's northwestern frontier in the eighteenth century. China contained two major groups of Islamic believers. Chinese-speaking Muslims, known as Hui, were mainly descended from Han who converted to Islam beginning in the sixteenth century. Turkic-speaking Uighurs, who generally had uneasy relations with the Hui, formed the second major group. Together with smaller groups of Muslim believers, these two groups accounted for several million people in eighteenth-century China.

The incorporation of an Inner Asian frontier into China was a Qing achievement. The administrative format adopted in different parts of Inner Asia varied considerably, but all were tied in one way or another to the Chinese imperial system, the same system whose tribute framework embraced the diverse peoples of Southeast Asia.

THE KANGXI EMPEROR'S MILITARY STRATEGY

■ *The Kangxi emperor (1662–1722) understood the solemn importance of ritual displays and the bureaucratic implications of his pronouncements to officials. Under his rule, China's agrarian economy recovered from the disruptions of the Ming-Qing transition, and state control was secured across China proper. But the Kangxi emperor was also a Manchu warrior, adept at martial skills and fond of the challenges that pursuit of a mounted enemy offered, so very different from the difficulties of creating and maintaining civilian bureaucratic rule of the agrarian empire. In this excerpt from his own writings, Kangxi recounts some of the preparations taken as he moved against the western Mongol chieftain Galdan, who represented one of the last major threats to Qing security in Inner Asia.*

Twenty years before, General Chang Yung had made secret inquiries about Galdan, and assessed his impetuous yet indecisive character, his age and family situation, his problems with the Moslems, and his love of wine and women. Since then I had observed Galdan's cunning and delight in feinting, his overconfidence, his gullibility and inability to think far ahead. After we sent the envoys, our scouts watched for the smoke of his campfires and assessed his army's movements on the evidence of hoofprints and horse dung. And as Galdan began to flee we moved into pursuit, first strengthening a base camp in which to leave the sick horses and the servants who had been marching on foot, then leaving behind the slower Green Standard Infantry, then abandoning the cannon, and finally sending Maska on ahead as commander of a flying column.

Before we moved against Galdan in 1696 I told the senior officers—Manchu, Mongol, and Chinese—to meet together by Banner and discuss how we might anticipate Galdan's movements and how we should deploy our own troops. . . . After the basic strategy of a western strike from Ninghsia and a central strike from Peking across the Gobi was agreed upon, the Council of Princes and High Officials worked out the details of rations for soldiers and servants, fodder for camels, the number of carts, and so on, basing their figures on an estimated 10,790 troops in the western army, and 8,130 in the center . . .

Again Galdan eluded us, and the following spring I pursued him for a third time, marching west to Ninghsia. The Shansi censor Chou Shih-huang tried to dissuade me, saying, "The despicable wretch is in desperate straits, and will be dead in a few days," . . . But I said that Galdan had to be finished off like Wu San-kuei . . . Then General Wang Hua-hsing also tried to divert me, suggesting that we all ride up to the Lake Hua-ma hunting grounds, and I told him: "Galdan is not yet destroyed, and the question of horses is a crucial one . . .

For in war it's experience of action that matters. The so-called *Seven Military Classics* are full of nonsense about water and fire, lucky omens and advice on the weather, all at random and contradicting each other. I told my officials once that if you followed these books, you'd never win a battle. Li Kuang-ti said that in that case, at least, you should study classical texts like the *Tso-chuan*, but I told him no, that too is high-flown but empty. All one needs is an inflexible will and careful planning. And so it was that, in the far northwest on the bend of the Yellow River in the early summer of 1697, I heard the news that Galdan, abandoned by nearly all his followers, had committed suicide.

Southeast Asia: World Religions in the Chinese World Order

The same Chinese tribute-system framework that defined the proper display of ritual relationships between the Middle Kingdom and the various peoples of Inner Asia also defined the relations between China and the polities of Southeast Asia. The Vietnamese, Thai, and Burmese all made tribute missions to the Chinese in the eighteenth and early nineteenth centuries. Relations with these countries were handled by the Ministry of

Rites, the organization also responsible for all ritual matters within the empire, such as Court ceremonials and festivals. The placement of tribute relations within the larger realm of ritual underscored the importance to the Chinese state of symbolic affirmations of the Chinese world order within and beyond China's borders.

The peoples of Southeast Asia were mostly peasants who lived in village settlements and for whom the politics linking their rulers to China were of little, if any, consequence. In Vietnam and some parts of the Philippines, family ties and broader kinship relations organized village life. For lowland peasants in Cambodia and in the Thai and Burman areas of control, the Buddhist temple was the focus of communal life. In the delta areas of the main rivers—the Red River, the Mekong, the Chao Phraya, the Salween, and the Irrawaddy—paddy rice agriculture produced the major staple. In most areas the mountains and plateaus were too dry to allow anything more than slash-and-burn agriculture. Other parts of the region were dense forest. Southeast

Asia was sparsely settled in the seventeenth and eighteenth centuries, with roughly 20 million people clustered in those places supporting either rice agriculture or maritime trading ports.

In those locales permitting permanent settlement, people formed peasant villages more similar to society in China than to the pastoralism of the steppe. Most houses were built on wooden poles to protect against flooding in the monsoon season. With thatched roofs, walls made of matting, and split bamboo flooring, houses lasted roughly ten years before being replaced. Meat and vegetable consumption was modest, but abundant fruits compensated for the limited vegetables. People suffered few famines, except those caused by war.

The mainland peninsula is divided into a series of isolated river valleys, and the archipelago is a string of islands, often with their own distinctive local variations. Spanning these diverse areas were the world's great religions—Buddhism, Islam, and Christianity.

Buddhism has two major traditions. The northern school, known as Mahayana Buddhism, spread

Southeast Asia, ca. 1800

The Potala, a palatial monastery at Lhasa, Tibet, was the home of the Dalai Lama.

historically from India to Nepal, Tibet, Mongolia, China, Japan, Korea, and northern Vietnam. In each area Buddhism underwent a distinctive transformation. Sometimes it gradually dominated local religious culture, as in Tibet and Mongolia. In other places, such as China, Japan, and Korea, it became one of several important religious influences. For most of Southeast Asia, Theravada Buddhism, the so-called southern school, held great influence after the thirteenth century. Every village had a monastery for its monks, and the monastery's core was a group of celibate monks clad in saffron robes who took vows of poverty and devotion to religious study. The monastery offered all village males a time and space to receive religious training and hence rudimentary literacy. The abbots and monks of each village monastery were part of an ecclesiastical hierarchy.

In contrast to Buddhism's land-centered agrarian social base, the religion of Islam followed the maritime routes weaving through the archipelago, to establish itself along the coast, a geographical and cultural area known as the *pasisir* in Indonesian. *Pasisir* Islam was rather narrowly defined and had no hierarchical religious structure. Religious life was focused at the village level, and religious sentiment was rarely mobilized to buttress or challenge secular government. Small Islamic states and societies existed all along the archipelago. Across tropical terrains inhospitable to human settlement, river-mouth cities were established as trading ports and political centers. These cities formed a political system of their own, into which the Portuguese entered in the

sixteenth century, the Dutch in the seventeenth, and the English in the eighteenth. Over time, the European presence began to grow and to weaken the powers of the Islamic port polities. During the fifteenth and sixteenth centuries the pasisir looked outward rather than toward the agrarian interior. But in the early seventeenth century a new dynasty, the Mataram, conquered all Java and absorbed the pasisir. With a hereditary king and local lords, the Javanese political system lay lightly over a myriad of local economies, some of which became tied to international trade through the Dutch East India Company. Java and the Malay sultanates, like the Spanish Philippines, lay beyond the furthest reaches of the Chinese empire. With the exception of Sulu in the Philippines, they lacked formal tributary relations with the Chinese. They did not exist in the formal political world order of the Chinese state, but they became the bases for the many migrating Chinese who engaged in trade throughout Southeast Asia.

In the Philippine Islands the competing interests of a secular government led by the Spanish and the two major religious forces of Christianity and Islam made for an unstable political situation. Christianity was actively promoted by the Spanish, whose religious zeal led them to combine the duties of priests and bureaucrats in complex ways. Priests became salaried officials, but the crown could intervene in ecclesiastical business when its interests were at stake. The governor of the Philippines was the king's personal representative and vice-patron of the Roman Catholic church. He sat atop an unresponsive bureaucracy, whose provincial governors ignored him and established virtually autonomous control over their territories. The only potentially effective link the governor had with the peasants was through the native priests recruited to serve in the villages, but tensions developed when these priests demanded more power. The Spanish governor's authority was also repeatedly tested through warfare with Muslim sultanates in Mindanao and Sulu during the eighteenth century. Making peace with the sultans could bring the governor into conflict with the Catholic church.

Closer to the Chinese political world order were the mainland polities, many of which were Theravada Buddhist monarchies. The two most prominent Buddhist monarchies of the seventeenth and eighteenth centuries were the Burmese monarchy of Ava and the Thai kingdom of Ayudhya. The Ava kings tried to control some important non-Burman peoples, such as the Mons in the south, linguistically related to the Cambodians, and the Thai-speaking people known to them as the Shan (a corruption of the word *Siam*) in the northeast; a shared Buddhism made this possible. The Thai and Burman courts became major competitors, each claiming vassal states. Their vassals reached from the Lao and Shan in the north to the peoples of the Malay Peninsula in the south. For Cambodia, the seventeenth and eighteenth centuries was a period of domination by outsiders, when monarchs sponsored by Vietnamese or Thai were often installed. When the Ayudhya state was defeated by the Burmese in 1767, a new Thai government under Rama I (1782–1809) rose to replace it.

Thai leaders, like many other leaders in Southeast Asia, could accept their minor roles in China's world order because China was not very important to them. The spread of Chinese influence in Southeast Asia had been halted by Vietnam. Vietnamese struggles to maintain independence from China meant that Chinese could not reach other parts of Southeast Asia by land and with military forces, but only by sea as peaceful traders.

Vietnam: Chinese Institutions Beyond China's Borders

Today Vietnam is a long, thin country dominated by two major river valleys, the Red River valley in the north and the Mekong Delta in the south. It was created by southern frontier expansion beginning in the fifteenth century, when the Vietnamese moved south from the Red River valley to defeat the Cham, a seafaring people influenced by Indian and Islamic cultures. In the seventeenth century Vietnamese settlers moved into the Mekong Delta, where Cambodia had previously claimed authority. With status as a Chinese tributary state, the Vietnamese used Confucian principles to strengthen their bureaucracy and systematize their legal code as they developed their political institutions. But unity was difficult to achieve. Real power rested in the hands of two families, the Trinh in the north and the Nguyen in the south. Each formed a government with Chinese-style bureaucracies. Between 1620 and 1673 they fought with each other, and the Nguyen won recognition from the Trinh as independent rulers. The Trinh held effective power in the north and the Nguyen continued a gradual expansion in the south. For the next century there was sporadic conflict but no major wars or rebellions. This peace was broken in 1771 by a peasant rebellion in Binh Dinh province. The three Tay-son brothers sought to control central Vietnam. By 1778 Vietnam was no longer divided into two regions; now there were three. In 1786–87 Tay-son armies attacked the north, and the Trinh called upon the Qing for assistance. When Qing armies responded by invading Vietnam in order to increase their power in the region, the Tay-son declared the most gifted brother, Quang-trung, as emperor in 1788. Quang-trung initiated a program of change that was cut short by his death in 1792. His young son proved ineffective, and the exiled Nguyen leader, Phuc Anh, returned to defeat Tay-son generals between 1799 and 1801. Anh then recovered north Vietnam and proclaimed himself emperor of a united Vietnam.

The Vietnamese political and social order was centered on the three relationships borrowed from China: subject-ruler, son-father, and wife-husband. The Vietnamese subscribed to a Chinese ideology and created Chinese institutions to implement this political vision. They held Chinese-style examinations to test knowledge of the Confucian Four Books and Five Classics. In art, architecture, and literature the Vietnamese adopted Chinese models and forms with certain distinctive differences. Compared to China, Buddhism in Vietnam achieved a more prominent position, Vietnamese women's social status was a bit higher, and Vietnamese literati were more conservative in their Confucian views. The content of great literary works spoke of Vietnamese experiences, even when borrowing themes from Chinese literature, much as Shakespeare addressed his own English society in plays taken from foreign stories like the Italian *Romeo and Juliet*. During the seventeenth and eighteenth centuries, Chinese characters were adapted for the Vietnamese written language, further deepening the Chinese cultural influence. In foreign relations as well the Vietnamese modeled themselves on Chinese practices, styling themselves the "central country" to which others paid political homage and economic tribute. Envoys from Laotian and Cambodian states honored the Vietnamese just as the Vietnamese emperor recognized himself to be a tribute-bearing vassal of the Chinese.

The Chinese realized that there were peoples in Southeast Asia who lived well beyond the civilizing force of their culture, but such peoples seemed unimportant compared to the threats that peoples on the steppe could pose. With Vietnam on its southwestern border firmly within its political and cultural orbit, the Chinese empire of the seventeenth and eighteenth centuries could rest secure in the knowledge that challenges to its view of the world would not likely come from this quarter.

Europe in China's World Order

Europeans entered China's world order in two roles—as merchants and as missionaries. The Portuguese and Dutch reached China after having established trade relations in Southeast Asian ports. By the early seventeenth century the Portuguese were active in the trade between China and Japan, taking Chinese silks to Japan and returning to China with silver. The transition from the Ming dynasty to the Qing dynasty disrupted European trade relations in China and Southeast Asia. But Dutch trade relations, like those of the Portuguese, survived the dynastic change. Sino-Dutch trade declined by the late seventeenth century as the English began to assert themselves. This shift took place as the Qing government in 1685 began to regulate some foreign trade for fiscal purposes rather than as a part of the tribute system.

The so-called Canton trade system regulated China's European trade between 1760 and 1834. This system subordinated foreign traders to licensed Chinese monopolists known as the Cohong; in turn the Cohong were subordinated to the imperially appointed superintendent of maritime customs at Canton (now Guangzhou), called by the Europeans the Hoppo. The Cohong made profits by selling tea and textiles to monopoly trading firms like the British East India Company. Located at the periphery of the empire, European merchants were part of a maritime world that the Chinese state considered of little importance economically or politically. More important to the seventeenth- and eighteenth-century rulers were the Catholic missionaries.

Matteo Ricci and Ly Paulus, one of his Chinese converts. Though Ricci was held in great respect by the Chinese, he failed to make many converts to Christianity.

The most famous Jesuit pioneer, Matteo Ricci (1552–1610) reached China in 1582, where he and his colleagues tailored their Christian message to be understood in Chinese terms. To facilitate their credibility and acceptance, they adopted the Chinese scholar's gown. They captured the attention of officials and the Court by giving demonstrations of practical objects like clocks and presenting knowledge about astronomy and geography. Ricci and his seventeenth-century successors proved their worth to the Ming and Qing courts, serving as astronomers, cartographers, interpreters, architects, engineers, painters, and engravers. Their success was ended not by Chinese reactions to them so much as by criticism leveled at them by other Christian missionaries, who believed the Jesuits had gone too far in accommodating Chinese practices. The Jesuits had clearly outdistanced their Christian rivals in winning the trust and friendship of Chinese leaders.

At issue was how the Church should view several Chinese practices. Was ancestor worship simply a "civil rite" and therefore compatible with Christianity? Or was it "pagan worship" and therefore unacceptable?

What about officials praying for rain or the state's veneration of Confucius? These questions were posed to the pope by Dominicans and Franciscans who reached southeast China fresh from their successes in the Philippines, where no state power had stopped them from reaching the common people. They hoped, vainly as it turned out, to employ the same methods in China. For a century (1640–1742) the disagreements continued. In 1700 the Kangxi emperor wrote in support of the Jesuit view of Chinese rites—an outrage to the Church, which could hardly consider the Kangxi emperor an appropriate authority on matters of Christian doctrine. When the Yongzheng emperor came to power, he turned against the missionaries, who had been drawn into palace politics. In 1724 he declared Christianity a heterodox sect.

In 1742 the Catholic church closed the controversy with a papal bull forbidding all Catholics to practice the "rites and ceremonies of China." After promising beginnings, the missionaries became as unimportant as foreign merchants in eighteenth-century China. Nineteenth-century events would dramatically change this eclipse of the missionaries and the modest role of merchants. But in the seventeenth and eighteenth centuries, Europeans were but a marginal presence in the Chinese world order.

Korea and the Ryukyu Islands: Competition in China's World Order

More troubling to the Chinese government's sense of its power and authority than the European presence were events in Korea and the Ryukyu Islands, where Japanese advances challenged the centrality of the Son of Heaven. Like Vietnam, Korea experienced a period of direct Chinese control, after which a tributary relationship became the historical norm. Korea, again like Vietnam, modeled its political system on Chinese practices. From the perspective of administrative structure, political ideology, and its relationship to China, Korea appeared to be well within the Chinese world order. But Korea was also quite different from China in social and economic terms.

Korea's social system was based on a hereditary class structure. The upper class was composed of families allowed to own land, who served as either civil or military officials. They had a virtual monopoly on the right to take the civil service examinations. Below the upper class was a small group who served as petty government functionaries. Far more numerous were the commoners, who comprised the economic base of the state, working government lands and paying taxes and labor service. A final group, perhaps accounting for as much as a quarter of the population in 1600, was the lowest class of base people, who were slaves, actors, female entertainers, and other people with despised occupations.

As the year 1600 approached, Korea found itself in a difficult political situation. In 1592 the Japanese invaded Korea on their way to attack China. The Chinese met the Japanese invasion on Korean soil and achieved a military stalemate. Another major Japanese campaign of 1597 was ended in 1598 by the death of Hideyoshi, the Japanese leader responsible for the ill-fated military campaigns. In 1600, the Tokugawa family came to power in Japan; in 1609 they established friendly relations with Korea, which lasted until the second half of the nineteenth century. But before the Koreans could fully recover from the Japanese invasions, the Manchus began attacks to secure their flanks in upcoming struggles with the Ming dynasty. A 1627 incursion was followed by an invasion of 100,000 soldiers in 1637, which forced the Korean Yi dynasty to switch allegiance from the Ming to the Qing in advance of the Manchu conquest of China.

Once political relations became settled again, Korea's economy and society underwent major changes in the seventeenth and eighteenth centuries. New lands were opened and commerce expanded. The extension of irrigation facilitated double cropping rice in the south, while cotton and the potato were introduced in different parts of the country. Government land-tax collection in money rather than in kind helped to stimulate commercial activities, which broke out of the framework of licensed government monopolies. Socially, the relaxation of government regulations on slave status generally permitted more people to achieve commoner status; the manumission of all slaves in government service came in 1801. These domestic developments were joined by the spread of Christianity, about which Koreans learned from their contacts with Jesuits in Beijing. The Korean government became sufficiently anxious about the inroads made by this alien religion that it banned Christianity in 1785. While Christian influence was thereby limited, elements of Western scientific knowledge—also acquired by the Koreans from Jesuits in Beijing and from Chinese books—was not as controversial.

Chinese models clearly shaped the development of Korean statecraft in the seventeenth and eighteenth centuries. But it would be misguided to expect the simple replication of Chinese ideas and institutions on

China and the Chinese World Order, 1600–1800

1350–1767	Ayudhya begins as small Thai principality, becomes leader of Thai kingdom
1565	First permanent Spanish settlement in the Philippines
1598–1610	Jesuit missionary Matteo Ricci serves the Ming imperial court
1559–1626	Manchu state established
1604–26	Donglin Academy scholars oppose corruption in Chinese government
1630–47	Rebellions widespread across China
1644	Li Zicheng invades Beijing, overthrows Ming dynasty, Manchus invade and defeat Li Zicheng, establish Qing dynasty
1644–80	Ming loyalists resist Manchu rule
1662–1722	Reign of Kangxi emperor
1670–1750	Manchus conquer Xinjiang and Tibet
1673–81	Revolt of the Three Feudatories led by Wu Sangui
1683	Taiwan falls to the Manchus
1722–35	Reign of the Yongzheng emperor; period of autocratic control and bureaucratic reform
1736–95	Reign of the Qianlong emperor
1760–1834	Canton trade system in place to regulate China's European trade
1771	Vietnamese peasant rebellion leading to Tay-son regime
1796–1804	White Lotus Rebellion

Korea's position between China and Japan was paralleled on a far smaller scale by the uncertain status of the Ryukyu Islands to the south of Japan. The Ryukyus were once an independent kingdom, but the arrival of Chinese, Japanese, and Portuguese traders in the sixteenth century transformed the islands into an intermediary between China and Japan. While already in tributary relations with the Ming state, the Ryukyu Islands were invaded in 1603 by the feudal Japanese lord of Satsuma. With the approval of the central Japanese government, Satsuma leaders divided the Ryukyu Islands into a northern group under their direct administration and a southern group under a country administrator. But throughout the Qing dynasty, the Ryukyu kings continued to petition the Chinese emperor for investiture according to the Chinese tributary system. The ability of the Ryukyu islanders to play the Chinese and Japanese off against each other by recognizing their loyalty to each underscores the definite limits to China's world order.

As the largest state, boasting the most people, greatest territory, and most advanced economy, China in the seventeenth and eighteenth centuries, not surprisingly, had a clear vision of itself at the center of the political universe. For the Ming state there were basically two kinds of foreign governments—those modeled on Chinese principles, like the Korean or the Vietnamese, and those that had some other method of rule. The Qing dynasty recognized a third group composed of Inner Asian peoples whose ways were closer to their own than those of Southeast Asian countries, where political practices were shaped by Buddhist, Islamic, and Christian influences. European trading groups and missionaries occupied minor roles in the Chinese world order, representing peoples even more removed from the center of China's world than the most distant Southeast Asian kingdom. The Chinese could hardly be expected to be anxious about this minor presence. Japan's unification under the Tokugawa and its refusal to affirm its earlier tributary status was a more immediate potential problem to China's vision of itself and the world.

Korean soil. Korean social values, for instance, clashed with Confucian norms for family organization. Even though the Korean state was modeled upon the Chinese, its actual functioning was significantly different because the monarchy was very weak. As a result the bureaucracy enjoyed more power. Government battles raged among bureaucratic factions, which became hereditary groups, each with its own academies to train scholar-officials.

Tokugawa Japan, 1600–1800

The Tokugawa consolidation of national rule in 1600 created a new political system for a country that had been torn by a century of fighting. The leaders succeeded in constructing new institutions to govern society and a new ideology to explain their purposes and their power. Blending ideas from native Shinto with elements from both Buddhism and Confucianism, political and social leaders created a new vision of their country. For peasants, the first two centuries of Tokugawa rule brought major changes to village life. The warriors, known as samurai, who had fought in the preceding decades of civil strife, were sent to castle towns by the government. Villages of peasants became more tightly organized as communities, in which households gradually shifted from subsistence production to crop and craft production for the market. In the cities, samurai became civil administrators served by merchants who forged new trading networks. Commercial wealth funded the development of an urban popular culture animated by new kinds of theater, fiction, and painting. Whether viewed in political, cultural, or economic terms, Tokugawa Japan was a dynamic society.

Tokugawa State Making

By the year 1600 Japan was emerging from a century of civil war. For the preceding forty years the country had been subject to unification efforts by two talented leaders, Oda Nobunaga (1534–82) and Toyotomi Hideyoshi (1536–98). The ultimate beneficiary of this process was Tokugawa Ieyasu (1542–1616), who came to power in 1600, decisively defeating his rivals at the battle of Sekigahara.

Under the Tokugawa structure, the shogun, who was the leader of the Tokugawa ruling family, directly controlled roughly one-fifth of the arable land in Japan. His administration was called the *bakufu*. The balance of the land was divided among some 245 to 295 lords with their own smaller collections of land. Their number fluctuated as new domains, or *daimyo*, were awarded to families who had aided the Tokugawa in their rise to power and older ones lacking heirs were dissolved. There were three kinds of daimyo. First were those in the hands of the ruler's collateral family. A second group included so-called house daimyo belonging to those families who had been rewarded by the Tokugawa for their service; and a third group was composed of established lords known as outside daimyo.

The bakufu and daimyo both found advantages in the political system developed in the seventeenth century. The bakufu first made several moves to strengthen itself. In the sixteenth century Japan's landscape had

been dotted with imposing castles constructed by warriors seeking to fortify their territories. The Tokugawa shogun demanded that the lords give up all castles but the ones in which they lived, and he made his own castle in the city of Edo the most spectacular and intimidating. To assert his power over the daimyo, the Tokugawa shogun also demanded that the lords personally live half their time in Edo and maintain their capital residences with other family members and staff at all times. First applied to outside daimyo, the policy was later extended to include house daimyo. During the eighteenth century, the daimyo maintained about 1,000 residences in Edo with a total of some 250,000 to 300,000 people, of whom one-half to two-thirds lived in the capital permanently, most as staff to relatives of the lord.

In many ways the bakufu was as dependent on the daimyo as the many daimyo were on the bakufu. While the bakufu set limits on daimyo authority, it was the daimyo governments that actually reached down to the village level to monitor local life across most of the country. The daimyo government collected taxes, prevented people from leaving their villages, and enforced the regulations on clothing and food that differentiated peasants, samurai, priests, and merchants. Perhaps the

Himeji Castle in Japan. During the age of the Japanese warlords such formidable fortresses dominated the countryside.

most important service the bakufu rendered the daimyo was the knowledge that they did not have to worry about violent competition among themselves because all were parts of a system stabilized by the bakufu. In the absence of military conflicts the daimyo did compete economically. By tapping the land reclamation projects for new revenues, some daimyo expanded their fiscal bases as the bakufu's income remained roughly constant.

A key component of Tokugawa state making was the transformation of the samurai from warriors into administrators. (See Special Feature, "Samurai: Warrior, Administrator, National Hero," pp. 702–703.) Rather than displacing a military elite with a civilian one, the Japanese samurai left behind his military exploits for the new challenges of civilian administration. The warrior class supplied officials for both the bakufu and daimyo administrations. Not all samurai, however, could gain employment in government. Those without any government job relied heavily on the stipends they received in recognition of their elite status, but for many of them this income was inadequate. Others were not well suited for civilian government. Nonetheless they remained the country's status elite even as their role in society was transformed and their economic security was undermined.

The bakufu closely controlled relations with other countries. The nineteenth-century Japanese view of these policies, subsequently adopted by most twentieth-century accounts, viewed the Tokugawa as isolationist. However, the concept of isolation is not one the Tokugawa leaders themselves would have understood. Instead, they first pursued a diplomacy for normalizing relations in northeast Asia after Hideyoshi's failed Korean invasions. Reestablishing peaceful relations with Korea was a means of presenting themselves as the center of their own world order, which was quite distinct from that constructed by the Chinese.

The Japanese assertion of their divine descent— making Japan a land of the gods—was made first in a diplomatic context. These beliefs allowed the Japanese to claim, at least implicitly, a kind of parity with the Chinese. As already noted in the previous section on the Chinese world order, the Ryukyu kingdom found it wise to play its part in both the Chinese and Japanese systems of foreign relations. In fact, in 1715 the Japanese persuaded Chinese merchants to acknowledge Japanese superiority, the same kind of acceptance typically demanded by the Chinese of Japanese merchants three hundred years before. The ability of the bakufu to limit

and control foreign relations was a way to distinguish its broader range of powers and authority from those of the daimyo. Foreign relations thus served to strengthen the central government's hand with respect to local governments.

The Tokugawa had been able to initiate several centralizing efforts in the seventeenth century and maintain most of them in the eighteenth. First, by 1640, the Buddhist church was subordinated to the state and Christianity eradicated; the potential for a religious threat to the Tokugawa was thereby removed. Second, the Tokugawa regulated commerce and the economy to promote economic expansion and its own security. Third, they kept the daimyo lords from becoming a challenge through effective regulation. Fourth, they sustained revenues on a routine basis even if these funds were at times insufficient and the power to levy taxes was shared with the daimyo. These successes have tempted scholars to compare the Tokugawa state with absolutist states in Europe. But there were significant differences between Japan and Europe. Japan had no political equivalent to France's Third Estate. In Japan the samurai were the ruling class; the bonds of obligation they shared with their superiors were based on a feeling of loyalty, not on a notion of contractual obligation. Beyond the state there were other major differences. Japan lacked free cities with politically independent and powerful merchants; the society was closed off economically to much of the outside world, making foreign trade a negligible factor in economic change. Nevertheless, many political and social changes in early modern Japan resonate more closely with Europe's developments than they do with conditions in China.

Political and Social Thought

When the Tokugawa established their regime, they invented a vision of their state and its relationship to society that would gain the agreement of the daimyo lords and the common people. Their goal was to transform warlord power into a form of authority that would not be challenged. The strategy adopted by Tokugawa Ieyasu and followed by later shoguns was to elevate themselves as leaders in religious terms, to seek self-deification through the Shinto religion. Using this policy, the Tokugawa could not only elevate themselves with respect to the common people and daimyo leaders but also displace the emperor from his position as the ritual center of the society. They diverted to

Japanese actors Toshiro Mifune (left) and Tatsuya Nakadai portrayed samurai in the film Joiuchi (Rebellion). *The film is an attack on the abuse of individuals under the feudal code.*

Samurai: Warrior, Administrator, National Hero

Over the common Japanese kimono, a loose-fitting robe with wide sleeves, the samurai put on a matching jacket and trousers of dark blue, dull brown, or sedate gray. Tucked into a sash beneath his jacket on his left side rested his two swords. The samurai of the Tokugawa period was easily recognized by these two swords, for only members of his hereditary class were permitted to carry both the long and the short swords. Swords had been used by many people during the war-torn sixteenth century. But by the beginning of the seventeenth century, the Tokugawa pacification had dis-

armed the peasants; swords became more important as a symbol of the samurai's status rather than as a practical weapon. Samurai made the transition from violence to peace, many of them becoming civilian administrators who served the shogun and daimyo in positions of power and authority. Others, however, who did not hold any official position, depended on modest stipends and faced economic hardships.

Whether rich or poor, samurai lived in towns and cities where the development of an urban merchant culture created luxuries and temptations that the former warriors

theoretically were not allowed to indulge in. Many of them nevertheless were attracted to the pleasure quarters, where some took on multiple mistresses and others became mired in family feuds. Not all of them could live according to the ideal code of the samurai, which combined a stress on Confucian virtues of loyalty and frugality with a Zen Buddhist approach of giving up desires and attachment to material things in order to face death easily.

Confucian loyalty and Buddhist resignation figure at the center of "Chushingura," the famous tale of forty-seven faithful samurai. When their daimyo lord is humiliated by a shogunate official in the Edo castle, he draws his sword—an offense so serious that he is ordered to commit suicide, after which his domain is confiscated. This foul act turned his many samurai retainers into *ronin*, or masterless samurai. Forty-seven of them chose to avenge his death. The shogunate, fearing that the ronin would avenge their deceased lord, monitored their leaders closely. To diminish official anxieties, the ronin leaders cleverly adopted a wild lifestyle as if wishing to escape the pain of losing their lord by losing themselves in drunken pleasures. For two years they did nothing to cause suspicion. Once the court had relaxed a bit, they planned their attack and fulfilled their bond of loyalty to their lord by assassinating the official responsible for his death.

The public was thrilled by this display of righteous loyalty and revenge. Even the government valued the virtue of loyalty the ronin's actions expressed. But the government could not allow the violation of social order that the assassination of the official represented without undermining their own authority. The government therefore forced the forty-seven ronin to commit suicide. By this action, the government transformed the forty-seven into heroic figures who have lived on in the popular imagination.

In the twentieth century few stories are as well-known. Between 1907 and 1962 the "Chushingura" story was made into a movie more than eighty times. The feudal virtues of loyalty and sacrifice have been adapted to other, more modern sensibilities in more recent films, as the forty-seven are celebrated for their sincerity, integrity, or bravery. Like the American cowboy, the samurai has become a cultural symbol with many dimensions of meaning. Outstanding examples of samurai swords are still made today according to techniques used in the Tokugawa period. The best craftsmen are honored by the government as "national living treasures" and pursue their craft subsidized by the government. More than a century after the samurai were dismantled as a class, Japanese society continues to be inspired by their heroics, and the state honors those who can still supply the finely crafted swords that these dead warriors can no longer use.

themselves the religious attention previously given the emperor.

A crucial part of the Tokugawa political vision was based on adapting Confucian thought to create a stable social order. The state promoted a four-class ideal, with samurai as the elite, followed in Confucian perspective by peasants, artisans, and merchants. Based on the Chinese idealized hierarchy, the Japanese gentleman had much more martial spirit than his Chinese counterpart. The state articulated codes for different social groups to define rules of proper behavior. The state also promoted a spatial separation of the status groups, with the samurai, merchants, and artisans living in different quarters of the cities and the peasants in the villages. Social stratification was reinforced by making samurai status hereditary. Creating a predictable and stable social order was a basic component of the Tokugawa's political logic for securing their rule. Thus, Chinese Confucian concepts were adapted to a different social situation in Japan, as they had been in Korea.

Confucianism entered Japan from China as an outside force in a culture already possessing well-developed Shinto and Buddhist traditions. In fact Confucianism was spread by Zen priests who studied Confucianism as part of acquiring a general familiarity with Chinese culture. Buddhism and Shinto had long enjoyed a division of religious labor. Shinto with its many deities and spirits was a religion for this world. Buddhism prepared one for the next, and in the Japanese context became fused with ancestor worship. The social thought of Tokugawa culture was thus composed of interwoven strands of Buddhism and Shinto, with a new prominence given to Confucianism. The state's appeal to the Confucian categories of benevolent rule and the loyalty of subjects offered a philosophy separate from the ideology associated with the emperor or the samurai warriors of the previous century.

It is easy to oversimplify the role of Confucianism in Tokugawa thought and to imagine that its influence was limited to the politics of a Tokugawa state at work crafting a new vision of political and social order. But an interest in Confucian ideas developed as well among intellectuals who lived on the margins of the ideal four-class system. Confucian ideas were also studied by merchants. In their own academies of scholarship, merchants used the Confucian category of virtue to valorize their own behavior. For them, seeking profit was the businessman's form of righteous behavior. Japanese merchants explained economics in Confucian terms. They believed that it was the duty of officials to help

nourish the people, to promote their livelihoods, and reduce the inequalities among them. Unfortunately, in many merchant eyes, the government was not strong enough to undertake many of the policies needed to reach these ends. Instead, the government often meddled in the market to squeeze resources from merchants to support the poor samurai. This kind of intervention was harmful because government attempts to regulate prices artificially in order to benefit one group undermined the economy's natural operations.

In the late seventeenth and eighteenth centuries the synthesis of Confucianism with Shinto and Buddhism was challenged by a nativist reaction to imported systems of thought. Nativist thinkers began by promoting Japanese literature as a major source from which to gain knowledge. They then broadened their efforts to include Japanese historical chronicles. Intellectuals and political leaders surveying the government's weaknesses after a century of Tokugawa rule—modest control over the domain governments, worrisome limitations to fiscal resources, difficulties in keeping stable a social order based on rigid distinctions and separations among the classes—associated the country's problems with the importance of foreign concepts in governmental practice. They urged a return to native ideas, which they distinguished from Chinese principles and practices whenever possible. Reverence for the emperor, who was believed to be part of an unbroken line of rulers descended from the gods, contrasted with the scorn nativists heaped upon the Chinese practice of ruling houses rising and falling in dynastic cycles. The Japanese emperor united political, religious, and familialistic ideas about a "national body" that nativists considered uniquely Japanese.

The stress on native elements in Japanese culture made its mark in politics in the eighteenth century, but did not by any means eradicate the deep influences of Buddhism and Confucianism in society more generally. Intellectuals synthesized imported ideas with native sensibilities to create cultural norms meaningful to peasants in the countryside and samurai, merchants, and artisans in the city.

Rural Life

Few farmhouses of the style common in the Tokugawa period remain in rural Japan today. Unlike China, where the vast majority of the population still lives in the countryside, most of Japan's population has now become urban. In Tokugawa times, peasant houses had wooden supports with walls made of loosely woven mats covered with mud and straw. Roofs were made of thatch or of wooden shingles held down by rocks. The floors were made of a straw matting known as *tatami*, still used in traditional homes today.

The management of day-to-day activities in the peasant household was usually the wife's responsibility, much as it was in China. Before reaching her position of authority, she was first a daughter-in-law to her husband's mother and before that a daughter in her own family's household. While waiting a considerable length of time before having major responsibilities and authority of their own, Japanese peasant women in the seventeenth and eighteenth centuries came to enjoy positions of importance within the family economy that would later become eroded by the development of urban industrial society and the creation of more-limited domestic roles for women as wives and mothers.

Within the Tokugawa village, landholdings varied. The rich served as village headmen to deal with higher authorities. The village itself formed a corporate unit tied politically to the outside through agricultural taxes that were levied on the village as a unit. Though this tax system placed a premium on rice production, cash crops did spread and farmers who did not grow rice bought it on the market to pay their taxes. Tokugawa Japan's household-level, labor-intensive agriculture using family labor was in many ways similar to Chinese agrarian organization. By the eighteenth century, the mix of cash crops in Japan also resembled that in China—cotton, tea, hemp, mulberry, indigo, vegetables, and tobacco made their way to markets, with a regional spread of production in major cash crops.

Sekiya-no-sato on the Sumida River, one of the "Thirty-six Views of Mount Fuji," by the nineteenth-century artist Hokusai. Three samurai ride to Edo along a winding path between rice paddies, with Mount Fuji towering in the background. Today, this area is a bustling district of Tokyo.

In eighteenth-century Japan, handicraft industries developed in the countryside, much as they had begun to two centuries earlier in China. The earlier expansion of trade in seventeenth-century Japan had been controlled by larger merchants serving the bakufu and daimyo governments. By the second half of the eighteenth century this pattern of production and trade was challenged by the expansion of rural industries. Rural producers of silk and cotton cloth, soy sauce, and cooking oil competed with the older, established shops in Kyoto and Osaka. Handicraft production gave rural people a new source of income, one that escaped the taxation levied on the rice fields. Peasants also increased agricultural yields through heavily fertilizing their land with mulch and livestock manure. A new rural elite emerged as commerce penetrated rural society. Evidence of agricultural improvements without any major population increases suggests that living standards improved. But even if the average standard of living moved upward, growing disparities between rich and poor meant that many peasants continued to confront the chronic threats of poor harvests and increased taxation.

Peasants expected the daimyo to provide emergency relief and to assess moderate taxes. During the seventeenth century, before commercialization created economic linkages between peasants and the cities, most villages were largely subsistence-oriented. Families consumed locally whatever they did not forward to the daimyo as tax. Because taxes were levied on the village as a community, peasants shared a common interest in protesting what they saw as too heavy a burden. Even after commercialization created opportunities for peasants as individual families, they retained a collective interest in opposing new taxes and petitioning for aid in times of natural disasters. In the seventeenth century, villages usually communicated their dissatisfactions through their headmen, who supervised as many as ten or twenty villages and were expected by the government to manage dissent within the villages and keep the number of petitions expressing grievances to a minimum. To persuade rural elites to fill these roles, the daimyo granted them partial tax exemptions, small stipends, and ceremonial swords. By the eighteenth century more nonelite peasants entered as major actors; at times they revolted against the village headman, who was often the largest landlord and moneylender and therefore became an easy target for dissatisfaction.

Conflicts became particularly widespread during the 1780s in response to a series of poor harvests and difficult conditions. Inspired by religious visions of world renewal, peasants actively challenged authorities they believed had failed to meet obligations to the communities. Peasants also moved beyond mere appeals for relief and aid to make proposals for reform that would help them in the marketplace with merchants as well as with the government. When their petitions and requests for aid were unmet, violence often occurred. Protests became visible moments of disturbance that were part of a larger structure of dialogue in which the government often compromised with peasant points of view. Peasant protest wasn't driven simply by the anger and fear of starvation amidst poverty. It developed as a form of action to express in forceful ways popular demands and expectations of elites and government.

Peasant protests became part of the popular culture in the form of oral and written accounts. Through protests, peasants engaged elites in a dialogue about how society should be run. In each community's oral tradition were stories associated with local temples and shrines that formed important public spaces in the seventeenth and eighteenth centuries. Stories of strange events and brave people were told over the decades and the centuries to create rich local traditions. Within this rural world the community complemented the family-centered vision of social order that the state sought to achieve. With the residential segregation practiced by the government, these villages were very distant from the cities of Tokugawa Japan.

Urban Society and Economy

Japanese towns and cities of the Tokugawa period had come into existence for one of three reasons. First were the towns centered on the castle of a daimyo, with separate areas for warriors and townspeople; these numbered some two hundred in the Tokugawa period. Second were the temple towns centered on a cluster of major Buddhist temples and monasteries; before the Tokugawa unification and subordination of these towns, they had often been largely self-governing. Third and finally were the trading cities, which grew up to handle the expanding trade of the Tokugawa period. Tokugawa Japan's three great cities, Osaka, Kyoto, and Edo (now Tokyo) each represented one of these urban types. Osaka became the great commercial center, Kyoto the temple city, and Edo the city of samurai.

Osaka was Tokugawa Japan's commercial and financial center. Here was the center of Japan's largest rice market, forged during the seventeenth and eighteenth

HOW THE FOUR ORDERS OF PEOPLE IN MIMASAKA RAN RIOT

■ *In 1727, thousands of peasants in the Tsuyama domain of Mimasaka province of western Japan rose to protest changes in domanial taxation policies. Within months an account, "A Record of How the Four Orders of People in Mimasaka Ran Riot," from which the following excerpt is taken, was penned by an unknown writer whose text shows him to be knowledgeable about the Japanese historical tradition and even educated enough to quote, sometimes inaccurately, the Chinese classics. Perhaps a masterless samurai, a doctor or itinerant priest, the author locates the reasons for the peasants' unjust suffering in the evil manipulations of one Kubo Chikahira, who takes people's money by levying special taxes, which he then advances to higher retainers in Mimasaka. In the following passage peasants have assembled to air their grievances with officials who only appear to be sympathetic. Later on in the narrative the peasants are defeated, their protest is crushed, and their leaders executed. The "four orders" in the story's title is a reference to Confucian categories of officials, peasants, craftsmen, and merchants. The author's Confucian outrage at evil and demands for justice from those in power are tempered by his Buddhist resignation to the fate of these failed peasant rebels who were not meant to succeed.*

"First, we do not understand why you tacked a supplementary notice onto this year's tax bill, raising taxes 4 percent, or why we have to pay our taxes in full by the end of the year. When the previous ruler was still alive, his benevolence was so widely known in other provinces that even people from the shogun's domains aspired to live in Tsuyama. Nevertheless, after Kubo got himself put in charge, he did much wrong. It is because of Chikahira and his allies among the country samurai that the first sowing of wheat in autumn was suspended and seals were attached to ox and horse plows.

"It is unlikely that the central administration ordered us to pay the land tax as soon as possible. Rather it was the district and deputy district headmen who issued these instructions. They threatened those who paid late with manacles, and the way they have made the peasants suffer through their ordeals is indescribable . . .

"Are the authorities really unaware of how the district headmen show their contempt for the peasants by subtracting the loans owed them from the tax rice, then deceiving the authorities by pretending the peasants have not paid their taxes? Herein lies the source of peasants' accumulated frustrations," they argued as shrewdly as they could.

The two magistrates listened to them. "You're absolutely right. As you have requested, we will retract the supplementary notice raising taxes, and we will allow you to pay 86 percent of the regular taxes demanded in this year's tax bill. We will abolish the district and deputy district headmen, replace the village headmen, and leave it up to you to choose whomever you please for messenger service. Debtors and creditors will negotiate their terms face to face. We will cancel your obligation to repay the rice you borrowed from the domanial authorities. Right now we will distribute to every peasant present a day's ration of rice. The former village headmen are to let us know how many there are." Since they were talking about over thirteen thousand peasants who would each receive five *go*, they realized that even 120 bales of rice would not be enough.

The poor peasants each returned to his own district, leaving behind those ordinary peasants who had become the new messengers and those who had taken the lead in being the spokesmen. The spokesmen and the magistrates then exchanged written promises, but this was all a plot on the part of the magistrates to learn the names of the leaders for the future.

centuries. The country's major rice wine, or sake, makers as well as soy sauce producers were in the area. Between 1620 and 1660 two major lines began maritime transport linking Osaka and Edo. Though goods shifted to sea transport, the roadway linking Edo and Osaka continued to bear increased traffic. Daimyo in procession to take up residence in Edo or on their return journeys offered a vivid sight, while messengers for merchants and samurai made their way with vital information for both. Merchant houses might owe their

A traditional Kabuki performance at Edo's Nakamura-za theater in 1745. The hand-colored woodblock print is by Okumura Masanobu.

origins to some smaller town, but to become successful in a major way they developed bases of operation in either Osaka or at least one of the other two major cities of Kyoto and Edo.

Kyoto was the center of learning and high culture. It was home to the country's most famous Buddhist temples and Shinto shrines, and scenes of Kyoto were celebrated in painted screens that made the city's pleasures more generally known through the country. So numerous were the visitors to Japan's capital city that by the seventeenth century guidebooks were available that detailed the shrines and temples, the palace, and other famous sights. City maps helped visitors navigate during their stays and became souvenirs when they returned home. Kyoto's aesthetic atmosphere was heavily infused with the presence of the emperor and his court. Those who served the emperor pursued pastimes like viewing flowers, reciting poetry, and appreciating the distinct odors of different incense woods. Kyoto's great Buddhist temples housed large religious communities. Shinto shrines were the sites for major festivals like the Gion festival, which climaxed two weeks of summertime celebration with a parade of colorful floats.

Edo was where the Tokugawa established their base of power. In the late eighteenth century it was probably the largest city in the world, with a population well over one million. The largest European city, London, had yet to reach a million. Commercial and artisan classes were drawn to Edo to serve the bureaucracy, which was very large because it included not only the shogun's staff but also the Edo residences of the provincial lords. The merchants and artisans accounted for roughly half a million, with the samurai warriors and provincial lords making up most of the rest. Buddhist and Shinto priests with their families numbered as many as 100,000. Finally, there were the lowlifes—indigents, transients, and entertainers. Despite their low social status, actors were a vital component of Edo society, for the merchants spent lavishly on their leisure and amusements.

Popular Culture

The theater world of Edo, as well as that found in Kyoto and Osaka, grew up near rivers, where popular entertainers of an earlier period lived. Known as "riverbank folk," entertainers were located in marginal urban spaces that reflected their marginal social status.

Stages were set up to show kabuki performances as well as puppet shows. There were also places for sumo wrestling and sideshows with dance, music, storytellers, jugglers, acrobats, tightrope walkers, and fortune-tellers.

The word *kabuki* originally meant "inclined," to suggest off-center or wild behavior. The term then became associated with the dance performances of female troupes whose skits included music and suggestive dancing. Excitement and competition over kabuki women incited brawls and duels. To avoid such incidents, the government banned women from the stage in 1629. Techniques were developed through which men could play women's roles; key aspects of a woman's gestures and speech were given exaggerated emphasis to create a formalized elegance. The themes of kabuki transformed the vision of woman in Tokugawa society—men playing women's roles portrayed the Confucian virtues of fidelity and modesty.

Puppet theater grew out of literary narratives more than plays. The performances were initially a kind of accompaniment to the recitation of texts. These texts began to utilize more dialogue and take advantage of theatrical recitation. Puppet plays mainly took as their themes heroes of earlier times, drawn from military epics, theater texts, and folktales. The gifted writer Chikamatsu developed a three-act genre that was added to a five-act period piece to form an all-day performance. These three-act plays took as their protagonists common people—shopkeepers, farmers, and courtesans. The theme that captures one central element in popular urban culture of the seventeenth and eighteenth centuries focuses on the hopeless love between a courtesan and her lover, who is a merchant or tradesman unable to purchase her freedom. The difficulties of the young man meeting his business responsibilities and of the couple creating a life together lead them to the fatal belief that they can kill themselves and be reborn together in the Amida Buddha's Western Paradise. The tension of the story centers on the conflict between duty, or *giri*, and personal feelings, or *ninjō*. The young man has duties to his family and business, but he has feelings of love for his courtesan. The impossibility of creating a relationship that supports both social obligation and private passion leads to the tragedy of double suicide.

The new popular culture was also the subject of *ukiyo-e* prints, pictures of the floating world, a new style of painting that took as its subject matter both intimate moments and public scenes of city life. "Floating world" was a Buddhist expression in medieval Japan. It referred to the pain and suffering of this world, from which followed the idea of this as a transient and uncertain world. But by the late sixteenth century the term came to refer to the culture of townsmen, whose efforts to satisfy earthly desires gave a different meaning to fleeting moments. The preface to the novel *Ukiyo monogatari* (*Tales of the floating world*), which appeared around 1665, suggests, "In this world everything is a source of interest. And yet just one step ahead lies darkness. So we should cast off all gloomy thought about our earthly lot and enjoy the pleasures of snow, moon, flowers, and autumn leaves, singing songs and drinking wine; living our lives like a gourd bobbing buoyantly downstream. This is the floating world."

Ukiyo-e depicted the world of courtesans, at rest, at play, in the company of other courtesans, or with their lovers; whether the subjects were stepping into a bath, admiring bonsai (dwarf trees) in the snow, boating across a lake, or admiring cherry blossoms, these ukiyo-e evoked images of Japanese beauty. Kabuki actors in colorful costumes with brightly painted faces were another common theme; sometimes with the actors posed in dramatic scenes, in other cases with just their faces framed, kabuki was vividly evoked by ukiyo-e prints. Landscapes were another major theme; various views of Mt. Fuji at different times of day and in different seasons were made famous by the artist Hokusai. Other landscapes depicted winter snows or summer rains,

Japan, 1600–1800

1600	Tokugawa established power following victory at Sekigahara
1637	Beginning of promotion of Neo-Confucianism
1639–40	Portuguese expelled from Japan; persecution of Christians continues
1688–1703	Growth of Kabuki and puppet theater; *ukiyo-e*; growth of Edo, Osaka, and castle towns
1701–02	The affair of the forty-seven *ronin*
1730–1800	National learning movement
1781–88	Temmei famine; great hardship in villages; peasant uprisings and urban riots

The seated courtesan by Baiooken Eishun, ca. 1725, is an example of an ukiyo-e, *or "floating world," print.*

ethic. Schooled in loyalty and frugality with a strong sense of propriety and sober reason, the samurai was expected to distance himself from the merchant's many amusements. In fact, many samurai could not resist the pleasure quarters, where they attended the theater and visited courtesans. Samurai and merchant views of the world were also linked by a common interest in Confucianism. Just as rulers could govern with Confucian benevolence and virtue, merchants could engage in trade at fair prices and seek their virtue through honest effort. Unlike China, where merchants adapted to the Confucian culture defined by scholars and gentry, in Japan merchants were able to create their own kind of Confucian purpose and social meaning.

The first two centuries of Tokugawa rule were filled with successes. The government first turned samurai warriors into virtuous rulers acceptable in Confucian terms. It then divided society into four orders, again modeled on Confucian categories, and assigned them to separate places in the social order. Within this structure there were dramatic differences. The loud and gaudy urban pleasures of the Tokugawa period contrast sharply with the peaceful and simple elegance of Zen gardens. Japanese society of the seventeenth and eighteenth centuries embraced a diversity of lifestyles and worldviews, each associated with a particular class. Social order was created and reinforced through state supervision of both the economy and popular culture. A balance of different forces, Confucian and nativist ideas, bakufu and daimyo administrations, samurai status and merchant wealth, created Tokugawa Japan's political, cultural, and social stability. This equilibrium proved fragile but sustainable through the eighteenth century. This achievement through two centuries of political, social, and economic change would become threatened by events of the first half of the nineteenth century.

SUGGESTIONS FOR FURTHER READING

LATE IMPERIAL CHINA

* Pierre-Etienne Will and R. Bin Wong, *Nourish the People: The State Civilian Granary System in China, 1650–1850* (Ann Arbor, MI: University of Michigan Center for Chinese Studies, 1991). A temporal, spatial, structural, and comparative analysis of a major Qing institution affecting the lives of peasants gives a concrete sense of the capacities and commitments of the state.

moonlit bridges, or birds perched on delicate tree branches. Ukiyo-e originated in the Kyoto-Osaka area, but during the eighteenth century the center of urban cultural life passed to Edo and ukiyo-e was considered a special product of Edo. Townspeople bought prints and rented books with ukiyo-e from shops for a small fee.

The popular urban culture of Tokugawa Japan stands at a great distance from the ruling samurai class's ideal

Frederic Wakeman, Jr. *The Great Enterprise: The Manchu Reconstruction of Imperial Order in Seventeenth-Century China* (Berkeley, CA: University of California Press, 1985). A grand narrative of the Manchu conquest, through which much of the foundation for modern China was laid.

Philip Kuhn, *Soulstealers: The Chinese Sorcery Scare of 1768* (Cambridge, MA: Harvard University Press, 1990). An engrossing story about sorcery that reveals much about popular culture and official views of the society they ruled.

* Jonathan Spence and John Wills, eds., *From Ming to Ch'ing: Conquest, Region and Continuity in Seventeenth-Century China* (New Haven, CT: Yale University Press, 1979). A fine collection of essays on different aspects of late Ming and early Qing China.

THE CHINESE WORLD ORDER

* John Fairbank, ed., *The Chinese World Order: Traditional China's Foreign Relations* (Cambridge, MA: Harvard University Press, 1968). An excellent survey of China's relations with its neighbors, especially in the late imperial period.

Joseph Fletcher, "Ch'ing Inner Asia c. 1800," in John Fairbank, ed., *Cambridge History of China*, Vol. 10 (Cambridge: Cambridge University Press, 1978). The finest essay on Qing Inner Asia.

Morris Rossabi, *China and Inner Asia: From 1368 to the Present Day* (London: Thames and Hudson, 1975). Part One gives a good overview of Ming dynasty Inner Asia relations.

* David Joel Steinberg, ed., *In Search of Southeast Asia: A Modern History*, rev. ed. (Honolulu: University of Hawaii Press, 1986). Parts I and II give excellent thematic and country-specific accounts of Southeast Asia in the eighteenth century.

TOKUGAWA JAPAN

* Herman Ooms, *Tokugawa Ideology: Early Constructs, 1570–1680* (Princeton, NJ: Princeton University Press, 1985). A subtle study of how different kinds of Shinto and Neo-Confucian ideas were combined by different thinkers to create an ideology of rule for the early Tokugawa state.

* Stephen Vlastos, *Peasant Protests and Uprisings in Tokugawa Japan* (Berkeley, CA: University of California Press, 1986). A clear analysis of the social contexts and logic responsible for peasant conflicts.

* Tetsuo Najita, *Visions of Virtue in Tokugawa Japan: The Kaitokudō Merchant Academy of Osaka* (Chicago: University of Chicago Press, 1987). An important demonstration of the capacity of Japanese merchants to develop a positive place for themselves within a Confucian view of the world.

* Chie Nakane and Shinzaburoo Ooishi, eds., *Tokugawa Japan: The Social and Economic Antecedents of Modern Japan* (Tokyo: University of Tokyo Press, 1990). A useful set of essays by Japanese scholars on different aspects of Tokugawa Japan, including political institutions and popular culture as well as social and economic phenomena.

* Indicates paperback edition available.

PORTRAIT OF AN AGE

The Normandy train has reached Paris. The coast and the capital are once again connected. Passengers in their city finery disembark and are greeted by others who have awaited their scheduled arrival. Workmen stand ready to unload freight, porters to carry luggage. Steam billows forth from the resting engine, which is the object of all human activity. The engine stares at us as enigmatically as any character in a Renaissance portrait. We hardly think to ask what lies behind the round, black face with its headlight for an eye and chimney for a snout. Yet the train that has arrived in *La Gare Saint-Lazarre* by Claude Monet (1840–1926) is as much the central character in this portrait of the industrial age as was any individual in portraits of ages past.

The train's iron bulk dwarfs the people around it. Indeed, iron dominates our attention. Tons of it are in view. The rails, the lampposts, the massive frame of the station, no less than the train itself, are all formed from iron—pliable, durable, inexpensive iron, the miracle product of industrialization. The iron station with its glass panels became as central a feature of nineteenth-century cities as were stone cathedrals in the Middle Ages. Railway stations changed the shape of urban settings just as railway travel changed the lives of millions of people.

There had never been anything like it before. Ancient Romans had hitched four horses to their chariots; nineteenth-century Europeans hitched four horses to their stagecoaches. The technology of overland transportation had hardly changed in two thousand years. Coach journeys were long, uncomfortable, and expensive. They were governed by the elements and the muddy, rutted roads, which caused injuries to humans and horses with alarming regularity. First-class passengers rode inside, where they were jostled against one another and breathed the dust that the horses kicked up in front of them. Second-class passengers rode on top, braving the elements and risking life and limb in an accident.

Railway travel was a quantum leap forward. It was faster, cheaper, and safer. Overnight it changed conceptions of time, space, and, above all, of speed. People could journey to what once were distant places in a single day. Voyages became trips, and the travel holiday was born. Commerce was transformed, as was the way in which it was conducted. Large quantities of goods could be shipped quickly from place to place, orders could be instantly filled. The whole notion of locality changed, as salesmen could board a morning train for what only recently had been an unreachable market. Branch offices could be overseen by regional directors, services and products could be standardized, and the gap between great and small cities and between town and countryside could be narrowed. Wherever they went, the railroads created links that had never been forged before. In Britain, the railroad schedule became the source of the creation of official time. Trains that left London were scheduled to arrive at their destinations according to London time, which came to be kept at the royal observatory in Greenwich. Trains carried fresh fish inland from the coasts and fresh vegetables from rural farms to city tables. Mail moved farther and more quickly; news spread more evenly. Fashionable ideas from the capital cities of Europe circulated everywhere, as did new knowledge and discoveries. The railroads brought both diversity and uniformity.

They also brought wonderment. The engine seemed to propel itself with unimaginable power and at breathtaking speed. The English actress Fanny Kemble (1809–93) captured the sensation memorably: "You can't imagine how strange it seemed to be journeying on thus, without any visible cause of progress other than the magical machine, with its flying white breath and rhythmical, unvarying pace. I felt no fairy tale was ever half so wonderful as what I saw." For many the railroad symbolized the genius of the age in which they were living, an age in which invention, novelty, and progress were everywhere to be seen. It combined the great innovations of steam, coal, and iron that were transforming nearly every aspect of ordinary life. But for others, the railway was just as centrally a symbol of disquiet, of the passing of a way of life that was easier to understand and to control. "Seated in the old mail-coach we needed no evidence out of ourselves to indicate the velocity," wrote the English author Thomas De Quincey (1785–1859) in his obituary for the passing of horse travel. "We heard our speed, we saw it, we felt it. This speed was not the product of blind, insensate agencies, that had no sympathy to give, but was incarnated in the fiery eyeballs of the noblest among brutes."

The fruits of the railways, like the fruits of industrialization, were not all sweet. As the nineteenth century progressed, there could be no doubt that year by year one way of life was being replaced by another. More and more laborers were leaving the farms for the factories, and more and more products were being made by machines. Everywhere there was change, but it was not always or everywhere for the better. Millions of people poured into cities that mushroomed up without plan or intention. Population growth, factory labor, and ultimately the grinding poverty that they produced overwhelmed traditional means of social control. Families and communities split apart, the expectations of ordinary people were no longer predictable. Life was spinning out of control for individuals, for groups, for whole societies, an engine racing down a track that only occasionally ended as placidly as did the Normandy train at the Gare Saint-Lazarre.

The Traditional Economy

For generation after generation, age after age, economic life was dominated by toil. Every activity was labor intensive. Wood for shelter or fuel was chopped with thick, blunt axes. Water was drawn from deep wells by the long slow turn of a crank or dragged in buckets from the nearest stream. Everything that was consumed was pulled or pushed or lifted. French women carried soil and water up steep terraces in journeys that could take as long as seven hours. The capital that was invested in the traditional economy was human capital, and by the middle of the eighteenth century nearly eight out of ten Europeans still tilled the soil.

Though the traditional economy was dominated by agriculture, an increasing amount of labor was devoted to manufacture. The development of a secure and expanding overseas trade created a worldwide demand for consumer goods. In the countryside, small domestic textile industries grew up. Families would take in wool for spinning and weaving to supplement their income from agriculture. When times were good they would expend proportionately less effort in manufacturing; when times were bad, they would expend more. Their tasks were set by an entrepreneur who provided raw materials and paid the workers by the piece. Wages paid to rural workers were lower than those paid to urban laborers because they were not subject to guild restrictions and because they supplemented farm income.

Though domestic industry increased the supply of manufactures, it demanded even more labor from an already overworked sector of the traditional economy.

By the eighteenth century the process that would ultimately transform the traditional economy was already under way. It began with the Agricultural Revolution, one of the great turning points in human history. Before it occurred, the life of every community and of every citizen was always held hostage to nature. The struggle to secure an adequate food supply was the dominant fact of life to which nearly all productive labor was dedicated. After the Agricultural Revolution, an inadequate food supply was a political rather than an economic fact of life. Fewer and fewer farmers were required to feed more and more people. In Britain, where nearly 70 percent of the population was engaged in agriculture at the end of the seventeenth century, less than 2 percent worked on farms at the end of the twentieth century. By the middle of the nineteenth century, the most advanced economies were capable of producing vast surpluses of basic commodities. The Agricultural Revolution was not an event, and it did not happen suddenly. It would not deserve the label *revolution* at all were it not for its momentous consequences: Europe's escape from the shackles of the traditional economy.

Rural Manufacture

By the end of the eighteenth century the European population was reaching the point at which another check upon its growth might be expected. Between 1700 and 1800 total European population had increased by nearly 50 percent, and the rate of growth was continuing to accelerate. This vast expansion of rural population placed a grave strain upon agricultural production. Decade by decade more families attempted to eke out an existence from the same amount of land. The gains made by intensive cultivation were now lost to overpopulation.

The crisis of overpopulation meant that not only were there more mouths to feed, there were more bodies to clothe. This increased the need for spun and woven cloth, and thus for spinners and weavers. Traditionally, commercial cloth production was the work of urban artisans, but the expansion of the marketplace and the introduction of new fabrics, especially cotton and silk, had eroded the monopoly of most of the clothing guilds. Merchants could sell as much finished product as they could find, and the teeming rural population provided a tempting pool of inexpensive labor for anyone willing to risk the capital to purchase raw materials. Initially, farming families took manufacturing work into their homes to supplement their income. Spinning and weaving were the most common occupations, and they were treated as occasional work, reserved for the slow times in the agricultural cycle. This was known as cottage industry. It was by-employment, less important and less valuable than the vital agricultural labor that all members of the family undertook.

But by the middle of the eighteenth century, cottage industry was developing in a new direction. As landholdings grew smaller, even good harvests did not promise subsistence to many families. This oversupply of labor was soon organized into the putting-out system, which mobilized the resources of the rural labor force for commercial production of large quantities of manufactured goods. The characteristics of the putting-out system were similar throughout Europe, whether it was undertaken by individual entrepreneurs or lords of the manor,

Linen making is the subject of an engraving from Nuremberg by Franz Philipp Florin, 1705. The flax stems were soaked to soften the tough outer fibers, which were then removed by beating. The inner fibers were spun into linen on hand looms.

or even sponsored by the state. The process began with the capital of the entrepreneur, which was used to purchase raw materials. These materials were "put out" to the homes of workers where the manufacture took place, most commonly spinning or weaving. The finished goods were returned to the entrepreneur, who sold them at a profit, with which he bought raw materials to begin the process anew.

Putting-out required only a low level of skill and inexpensive, common tools. Rural families did their own spinning and rural villages their own weaving. Thus putting-out demanded little investment, either in plant, equipment, or education. Nor did it inevitably disrupt traditional gender-based tasks in the family economy. Spinning was women's work, weaving was done by men, and children helped at whichever task was under way.

As long as rural manufacture supplemented agricultural income, it was seen as a benefit for everyone involved—the entrepreneur, the individual worker, and the village community. But gradually the putting-out system came to dominate the lives of many rural families. Spinning and weaving became full-time occupations for families that kept no more than a small garden. But without agricultural earnings, piecework rates became starvation wages, and families unable to purchase their subsistence were forced to rely upon loans from the entrepreneurs who set them at work. Long hours in dank cottages performing endlessly repetitive tasks became the lot of millions of rural inhabitants. And their numbers increased annually. While the sons of farmers waited to inherit land before they formed their families, the sons of cottage weavers needed only a loom to begin theirs. They could afford to marry younger and to have more children, for children could contribute to manufacturing from an early age. Consequently, the expansion of the putting-out system, like the expansion of traditional agriculture, contributed to overpopulation. The putting-out system was labor- rather than capital-intensive, and as long as there were ready hands to employ, there was little incentive to seek better methods or more efficient techniques.

The Agricultural Revolution

The continued growth of Europe's population necessitated an expansion of agricultural output. In most places this was achieved by intensifying traditional practices, bringing more land into production and more labor to work the land. But in the most advanced European economies, first in Holland and then in England, traditional agriculture underwent a long but dynamic transformation, an agricultural revolution. It was a revolution of technique rather than technology. Humans were not replaced by machines nor were new forms of energy substituted for human and animal muscle. Indeed, many of the methods that were to increase crop yields had been known for centuries and practiced during periods of population pressure. But they had never been practiced as systematically as they came to be from the seventeenth century onward, and they were never combined with a commercial attitude toward farming. It was the willingness and ability of owners to invest capital in their land that transformed subsistence farming into commercial agriculture.

As long as farming was practiced in open fields, there was little incentive for individual landowners to invest in improvements to their scattered strips. But commercial agriculture was more suited to large rather than small estates and was more successful when the land could be utilized in response to market conditions rather than the necessities of subsistence. The consolidation of estates and the enclosure of fields was thus the initial step toward change. Single crops were sown in large enclosed fields and exchanged at market for the mixture of goods that previously had been grown in the village. Market production turned attention from producing a balance of commodities to increasing the yield of a single one.

The first innovation was the widespread cultivation of fodder crops such as clover and turnips. Crops like clover restore nutrients to the soil as they grow, shortening the period in which land has to lie fallow. In the late seventeenth century, Viscount Charles "Turnip" Townshend (1675–1738) made turnip cultivation popular. Townshend and other large Norfolk landowners developed a new system of planting known as the four-course rotation, in which wheat, turnips, barley, and clover succeeded one another. This method kept the land in productive use, and both the turnip and clover crops were used to feed larger herds of animals.

The ability of farmers to increase their livestock was as important as their ability to grow more grain. Horses and oxen were more productive than humans, and the animals also refertilized the land as they worked. But animals competed with humans for food, especially during the winter months when little grazing was possible. To conserve grain for human consumption, lambs were led to the slaughter and the fatted calf was killed in the autumn. Thus the development of the technique of meadow floating was a remarkable breakthrough. By flooding low-lying land near streams in the winter, English and Dutch farmers could prevent the ground from freezing during their generally mild winters. When the water was drained, the

The Colliery *by Leonard Defrance, 1778. Coal fueled the Industrial Revolution. The painting shows the pithead of a Belgian colliery in the late eighteenth century.*

land beneath it would produce an early grass crop on which the beasts could graze. This meant that more animals could be kept alive during the winter.

The relationship between animal husbandry and grain growing became another feature of commercial agriculture. In many areas farmers could choose between growing grain and pasturing animals. When prices for wool or meat were relatively higher than those for grain, fields could be left in grass for grazing. When grain prices rose, the same fields could be plowed. Consolidated enclosed estates made this convertible husbandry possible. Farmers who could convert their production in tune to the market could not only maximize their profits, they could also prevent shortages of raw materials for domestic manufacturers or of foodstuffs for urban and rural workers.

Convertible husbandry was but the first step in the development of a true system of regional specialization in agriculture. Different soils and climates favored different use of the land. In southern and eastern England the soil was thin and easily depleted by grain growing. Traditionally, these light soil areas had been used almost exclusively for sheep rearing. On the other hand, the clay soils of central England, though poorly drained and hard to work, were more suited to grain growing. The new agricultural techniques reversed the pattern. The introduction of fodder crops and increased fertilization rejuvenated thin soils, and southeastern England became the nation's breadbasket. Similarly, the midland clays became the location of great sheep runs and cattle herds. Experiments in herd management, crossbreeding and fattening all resulted in increased production of wool, milk, meat, leather, soap, and tallow for candles.

There can be no doubt about the benefits of the transformation of agricultural practices that began in Holland and England in the seventeenth century and spread slowly to all corners of the Continent over the next two hundred years. Millions more mouths were fed at lower cost than ever before. Cheaper food allowed more discretionary spending, which fueled the demand for consumer goods, which in turn employed more rural manufacturers. But there are no benefits without costs. The transformation of agriculture was also a transformation in a way of life. The open-field village was a community; the enclosed estate was a business. The plight of the rural poor was tragic enough in villages of kin and neighbors, where face-to-face charity might be returned from one generation to the next. With their scrap of land and their common rights, even the poorest villagers laid claim to a place of their own. But as landless laborers, either on farms or in rural manufacturing, they could no longer make that claim. They would soon be fodder for the factories, the "dark satanic mills" that came to disfigure the land once tilled in open-field villages. For the destitute, charity was now visited upon them in anonymous parish workhouses or in the good works of the comfortable middle class.

The Industrial Revolution in Britain

Like the changes in agriculture, the changes in manufacturing that began in Britain during the eighteenth century were more revolutionary in consequence than in development. A workforce that was predominantly agricultural in 1750 had become predominantly industrial a century later. A population that for centuries had centered on the south and east was now concentrated in the north and west. Liverpool, Manchester, Glasgow, and Birmingham mushroomed into giant cities. While the population of England grew by 100 percent between 1801 and 1851, from about 8.5 million to over 17 million, the populations of Liverpool and Manchester grew by over 1,000 percent.

It was the replacement of animal muscle by hydraulic and mineral energy that made this continued population growth possible. Water and coal drove machinery that dramatically increased human productivity. In 1812 one woman could spin as much thread as had two hundred women in 1770. What was most revolutionary about the Industrial Revolution was the wave after wave of technological innovation, a constant tinkering and improving of the ways in which things were made, which could have the simultaneous effects of cutting costs and improving quality. It was not just the great breakthrough inventions like the steam engine, the smelting of iron with coke, and the spinning jenny that were important, but also the hundreds of adjustments in technique that applied new ideas in one industry to another, that opened bottlenecks and solved problems.

The Industrial Revolution was a sustained period of economic growth and change brought about by the application of mineral energy and technological innovations to the process of manufacturing. It took place during the century between 1750 and 1850, though different industries moved at different paces, and sustained economic growth continued in Britain until the First World War. It is difficult to define the timing of the Industrial Revolution with any great precision because,

unlike a political event, an economic transformation does not happen all at once. Nor are new systems and inventions ever really new. Coal miners had been using rails and wheeled carriages to move ore since the seventeenth century; in the sixteenth century "Jack of Newbury" had housed his cloth workers in a large shed. The one was the precursor of the railroad and the other the precursor of the factory, but each preceded the Industrial Revolution by more than a century. Before 1750 innovations made their way slowly into general use, and after 1850 the pace of growth slowed appreciably. By then, Britain had a manufacturing economy. Less than a quarter of its labor force was engaged in agriculture and nearly 60 percent was involved in industry, trade, and transport.

Britain First

The Industrial Revolution occurred first in Britain, but even in Britain industrialization was a regional rather than a national phenomenon. There were many areas of Britain that remained untouched by innovations in manufacturing methods and agricultural techniques, though no one remained unaffected by the prosperity that industrialization brought. This was the result of both national conditions and historical developments. When industrialization spread to the Continent it took hold—as it had in Britain—in regions where mineral resources were abundant or where domestic manufacturing was a traditional activity. There was no single model for European industrialization, however much contemporaries looked toward Britain for the key to unlock the power of economic growth. There was as much technological innovation in France, as much capital for investment in Holland. Belgium was rich in coal, while eastern Europe enjoyed an agricultural surplus that sustained an increase in population. The finest

Canals and Rivers

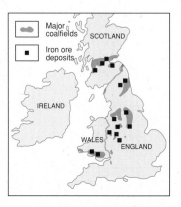

Coal and Iron Ore

Gender and Culture

THE IRON FORGE

Figure 1

The Industrial Revolution transformed the social structure of Europe. The economic base switched from agricultural work to mechanized production. The population traveled from the rural districts to the urban centers. Even the structure of the family changed. The extended, patriarchal community, based on the domestic and productive unity of several generations in a single household, gave way to the immediate family that sought separate employment outside the home. The dispersal of the family and the abandonment of the traditional homestead proved a rich topic in literature. Charles Dickens's novels *Hard Times* and *David Copperfield* offer two examples of a social critique encoded in the popular arts. But the visual arts proved hesitant to embrace these new subjects, preferring to preserve an idealized, pre-Industrial Europe or to glorify the changes through the lens of romanticism. Old conventions were used to celebrate and disguise new ideas. In some cases this worked, suggesting the new order extended, and at the same time, improved upon the old. But in

ON STRIKE

Figure 2

other cases, the traditional symbols clashed with their modern message, reflecting the cultural upheaval brought by social change.

Joseph Wright of Derby evokes the heroic tradition in his portrayal of a blacksmith in *The Iron Forge* (1772, England; Figure 1), seen on the preceding page. Presiding over home, work, and family, the head of the household dominates the center of the composition. His athletic physique and proud stance unites him with a construct of symbolic manhood dating back to ancient Greece. By placing his wife behind him with her back turned to the viewer, Wright of Derby defines her position in the family. Her life is devoted to caring for their children. The old man, seated and inactive in the left foreground, represents the passing of the extended family work force. The huge drum in front of the forge is powered by water rather than muscle, allowing the blacksmith/hero to reign as the sole family support.

Over a century later Hubert von Herkomer exposed the harsh reality of industry's effect on the family. In *On Strike* (1891, England; Figure 2), the head of the household is helpless. In the second half of the nineteenth century, workers sought new ways to consolidate and exercise power to protect themselves against low wages and dangerous conditions. But every gain demanded sacrifice. Here, the factory worker stands idle in his doorway, waiting for the results of the negotiations. Twisting his hat nervously, he worries about his safety, his future, and he wonders how he will feed his family if the strike continues. His gaunt wife tries to comfort him, but her own grief and fear cannot be disguised. Herkomer exposes the myth of the new industrial age. It has brought dependency rather than freedom; the factory worker is the new serf rather than the new hero, indentured to his employer with no alternative for security.

Other forms of social upheaval raged in the Industrial Age. In the nineteenth century political revolutions erupted throughout Europe. The struggles against ancient entitlements and the quest for new enfranchisement flamed for over a century in France. The July

LIBERTY LEADING THE PEOPLE

Figure 3

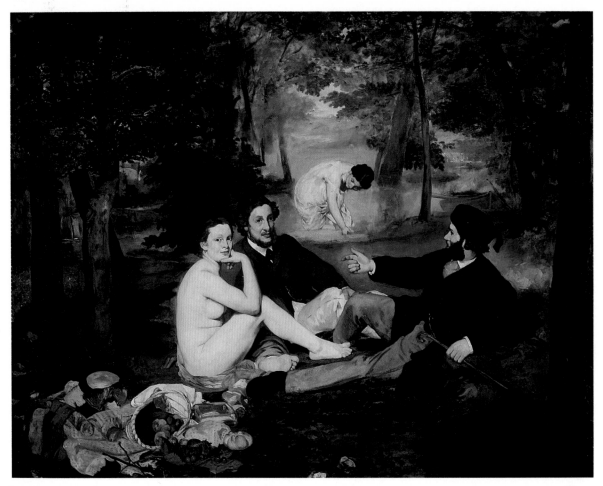

Figure 4

Revolution of 1830 sought to end the decadence of the restored Bourbon kings and replace their rule by privilege with a constitutional government. Although the reign of Louis Philippe, the self-styled "Citizen King," proved as corrupt as that of his predecessors, the force that brought him to power was fueled with optimism. Eugène Delacroix captured this spirit in *Liberty Leading the People* (1830, France; Figure 3), seen on the preceding page. Combining a traditional figure to personify liberty with real representatives of every social class, Delacroix's painting encodes a new message in a traditional configuration, praising the people's cause as heroic and enduring.

When Edouard Manet attempted to fuse old forms with new meaning, he caused a revolution in the arts. Like Delacroix, he counterposed real, modern male figures with the traditional form for personification, a nude or half clad woman. In his painting *Luncheon on the Grass* (1863, France; Figure 4), however, the role of the woman in the foreground is ambiguous. While Delacroix left no doubt that his female figure served to personify an idea, Manet's figure confronts the viewer with unnerving reality. Although this painting drew hostile criticism, wreaking disaster on Manet's career, it severed the dependency of contemporary art on past convention and inspired a new generation of artists, the Impressionists, to seek their own imagery, as well as their ideas, in their own world.

The Worsley-Manchester Canal, as shown in Arthur Young's Six Months' Tour Through the North of England, *1770. This view shows the mouth of the subterranean tunnel at Worsley, where the canal was driven underground to a mine.*

cotton in the world was made in India, the best iron was made in Sweden. Each of these factors was in some way a precondition for industrialization, but none by itself proved sufficient. Only in Britain did these circumstances meld together.

Among Britain's blessings, water was foremost. Water was its best defense, protecting the island from foreign invasion and making it unnecessary to invest in a costly standing army. Rather, Britain invested heavily in its navy to maintain its commercial preeminence around the globe. The navy protected British interests in times of war and transported British wares in times of peace. Britain's position in the Asian trade made it the leading importer of cottons, ceramics, and teas. Its colonies, especially in North America, not only provided sugar and tobacco, but also formed a rich market for British manufacturing.

But the commercial advantages that water brought were not confined to oceanic trade. Britain was favored by an internal water system that tied inland communities together. In the eighteenth century, no place in Britain was more than 70 miles from the sea or more than 30 miles from a navigable river. Water transport was far cheaper than hauling goods overland; a packhorse could carry 250 pounds of goods on its back or it could move 100,000 pounds by walking alongside a river pulling a barge. Small wonder that river transport was one of the principal interests of merchants and traders. Beginning in the 1760s private concerns began to invest in the construction of canals, first to move coal from inland locations to major arteries and then to connect the great rivers themselves. Over the next fifty years several hundred miles of canals were built by authority of Navigation Acts, which allowed for the sale of shares to raise capital. In 1760 the Duke of Bridgewater (1736–1803) completed the first great canal.

Coal was the second of Britain's natural blessings on which it improved. Britain's reserves of wood were nearly depleted by the eighteenth century, especially those near centers of population. Coal had been in use as a fuel for several centuries, and the coal trade between London and the northern coal pits had been essential to the growth of the capital. Coal was abundant, much of it almost at surface level along the northeastern coast, and easily transported on water. The location of large coalfields along waterways was a vital condition of its early use. As canals and roadways improved, more inland coal was brought into production for domestic use. Yet it was in industry that coal was put to its greatest use. Here again Britain was favored, for large seams of coal were also located near large seams of iron.

The factors that contributed to Britain's early industrialization were not only those of natural advantage. Over the course of years, Britain had developed an infrastructure for economic advancement. The transformation of domestic handicrafts to industrial production depended as much upon the abilities of merchants as on those of manufacturers. The markets for domestic manufacturing had largely been overseas, where British merchants built up relationships over generations. Export markets were vital to the success of industrialization as production grew dynamically and most ventures needed a quick turnaround of sales to reinvest their profits in continued growth. Equally important, increased production meant increased demand for raw materials: Swedish bar iron for casting, Egyptian and American cotton for textiles, Oriental silk for luxuries. The expansion of shipping mirrored the expansion of the economy, tripling during the eighteenth century to over one million tons of cargo capacity.

The expansion of shipping, of agriculture, of investment in machines, plant, and raw material all required capital. Not only did capital have to exist, but it had to be made productive. Profits in agriculture, especially in the south and east, had somehow to be shifted to investment in industry in the north and west. The wealth of merchants, which flowed into London, had to be redistributed throughout the economy. More importantly, short-term investments had to give way to long-term financing. At the end of the seventeenth century, the creation of the Bank of England had begun the process of constructing a reliable banking system. The Bank of England dealt almost entirely with government securities, but it also served as a bill broker. It bought the debts of reputable merchants at a discount in exchange for Bank of England notes. Bank of England notes could then be exchanged between merchants, and this increased the liquidity of the English economy, especially in London. It also became the model for provincial banking by the middle of the eighteenth century. In 1700 there were just twelve provincial banks; by 1790 there were nearly three hundred.

Though the banking system was vital to large enterprises, in fact the capital for most industry was raised locally, from kin and neighbors, and grew by plowing back profits into the business. At least at the beginning, manufacturers were willing to take risks and to work for small returns to ensure the survival and growth of their business.

Minerals and Metals

There could have been no Industrial Revolution without coal. It was the black gold of the eighteenth century, the fuel that fed the furnaces and turned the engines of industrial expansion. The coal produced by one miner generated as much energy as twenty horses. Coal was the first capital-intensive industry in Britain, already well developed by the seventeenth century. Only the very wealthy could afford to invest in coal mining, and the largest English coalfields were owned by landed families of means who were able to invest agricultural profits in mining.

By far the most difficult mining problem was water. As pits were sunk deeper they reached pools of groundwater, which enlarged as the coal was stripped away from the earth. The pit acted like a riverbed and was quickly filled. Water drainage presented the greatest obstacle to deep-shaft mining. Women and children could carry the water out in large skin-lined baskets, which were attached to a winding wheel and pulled up by horses. Primitive pumps, also horse powered, had been devised for the same purpose. Neither method was effi-

cient or effective when shafts sank deeper. In 1709 Thomas Newcomen (1663–1729) introduced a steam-driven pump, which enabled water to be sucked through a pipe directly from the pit bottom to the surface. Though the engine was expensive to build and needed tons of coal to create the steam, it could raise the same amount of water in a day as 2,500 humans, and within twenty years of its introduction there were seventy-eight engines draining coal and metal mines in England.

Innovations like Newcomen's engine helped increase output of coal at just the time that it became needed as an industrial fuel. Between 1700 and 1830 coal production increased tenfold despite the fact that deeper and more difficult seams were being worked. Eventually, the largest demand for coal came from the iron industry. In 1793 just two ironworks consumed as much coal as the entire population of Edinburgh. Like mining coal, making iron was both capital- and labor-intensive, requiring expensive furnaces, water-powered bellows, and mills in which forged iron could be slit into rods or rolled into sheets. Iron making depended upon an abundance of wood, for it took the charcoal derived from ten acres of trees to refine one ton of iron ore. Because each process in the making of iron was separate, furnaces, forges, and mills were located near their own supplies of wood. The shipping of the bulky ore, pig iron, and bar iron added substantially to its cost.

The great innovations in the production of iron came with the development of techniques that allowed for the use of coke—coal from which most of the gas has been burned off—rather than wood charcoal in smelting and forging. Iron coking greatly reduced the cost of fuel in the first stages of production, but because most ironworks were located in woodlands rather than near coal pits, the method was not widely adopted. Moreover, although coke made from coal was cheaper than charcoal made from wood, coke added its own impurities to the iron ore. Nor could it provide the intense heat needed for smelting without a large bellows. The cost of the bellows offset the savings from the coke until James Watt (1736–1819) invented a new form of steam engine in 1775.

Like most innovations of the Industrial Revolution, Watt's steam engine was an adaptation of existing technology made possible by the sophistication of techniques in a variety of fields. Although James Watt is credited with the invention of the condensing steam engine, one of the seminal creations in human history, the success of his work depended upon the achievements of numerous others. An instrument maker in Glasgow, Watt was asked to repair a model of a Newcomen engine and immediately realized that it would work more efficiently if there were a separate chamber for the condensation of the steam. Though his idea was sound, Watt spent years attempting to implement it. He was continually frustrated that poor quality valves and cylinders never fit well enough together to prevent steam escaping from the engine. Watt was unable to translate his idea into a practical invention until he became partners with the Birmingham iron maker and manufacturer Matthew Boulton (1728–1809). At Boulton's works, Watt found craftsmen who could make precision engine valves, and at the foundries of John Wilkinson (1728–1808) he found workers who could bore the cylinders of his engine to exact specifications. Watt later designed the mechanism to convert the traditional up-and-down motion of the pumping engine into rotary motion, which could be used for machines and ultimately for locomotion.

Watt's engine received its first practical application in the iron industry. Wilkinson became one of the largest customers for steam engines, using them for pumping, moving wheels, and ultimately increasing the power of the blast of air in the forge. Increasing the heat provided by coke in the smelting and forging of iron led to the transformation of the industry. In the 1780s Henry Cort (1740–1800), a naval contractor, experimented with a technique for using coke as fuel in removing the impurities from pig iron. The iron was melted into puddles and stirred with rods. The gaseous carbon that was brought to the surface burned off, leaving a purer and more malleable iron than even charcoal could produce. Because the iron had been purified in a molten state, Cort reasoned that it could be rolled directly into sheets rather than first made into bars. He erected a rolling mill adjacent to his forge and combined two separate processes into one.

Puddling and rolling had an immediate impact upon iron production. There was no longer any need to use charcoal in the stages of forging and rolling. From mineral to workable sheets, iron could be made entirely with coke. Ironworks moved to the coalfields, where the economies of transporting fuel and finished product were great. Forges, furnaces, and rolling machines were brought together and powered by steam engines. By 1808 output of pig iron had grown from 68,000 to 250,000 tons and of bar iron from 32,000 to 100,000 tons.

Cotton Is King

Traditionally British commerce was dominated by the woolen cloth trade, in which techniques of production had not changed for hundreds of years. During the course of the seventeenth century new fabrics appeared on the domestic market, particularly linen, silk, and cotton. And it was cotton that captured the imagination of the eighteenth-century consumer, especially brightly colored, finely spun Indian cotton.

Spinning and weaving were organized as domestic industries. Work was done in the home on small inexpensive machines to supplement the income from farming. Even the widespread development of full-time domestic manufacturers did not satisfy the increased demand for cloth. Limited output and variable quality characterized British textile production throughout the early part of the eighteenth century. The breakthrough came with technological innovation. Beginning in the mid-eighteenth century a series of new machines dramatically increased output and finally allowed English textiles to compete with Indian imports.

The first innovation was the flying shuttle, invented by John Kay (1704–64) in the 1730s. A series of hammers drove the shuttle, which held the weft, through the stretched warp on the loom. The flying shuttle allowed weavers to work alone rather than in pairs, but it was adopted slowly for it increased the demand for spun thread, which was already in short supply. The spinning bottleneck was opened by James Hargreaves (d. 1778), who devised a machine known as the jenny. The jenny was a wooden frame containing a number of spindles around which thread was drawn by means of a hand-turned wheel. The first jennies allowed for the spinning

This hand-colored engraving shows the interior of a German weaver's shop around 1850. Two men are weaving at looms and two women are winding bobbins. The scene is bordered with details of tools such as shuttles and quills.

of eight threads at once, and improvements brought the number to over one hundred. Jennies replaced spinning wheels by the tens of thousands. The jenny was a crucial breakthrough in redressing the balance between spinning and weaving, though it did not solve all problems. Jenny-spun thread was not strong enough to be used as warp, which continued to be wheel spun.

The need to provide stronger warp threads posed by the introduction of the jenny was ultimately solved by the development of the water frame. It was created in 1769 by Richard Arkwright (1732–92), whose name was also to be associated with the founding of the modern factory system. Arkwright's frame consisted of a series of water-power-driven rollers, which stretched the cotton before spinning. These stronger fibers could be spun into threads suitable for warp, and English manufacturers could finally produce an all-cotton fabric. It was not

long before another innovator realized that the water frame and the jenny could be combined into a single machine, one that would produce an even finer cotton yarn than that made in India. The mule, so named because it was a cross between a frame and a jenny, was invented by Samuel Crompton (1753–1827). It was the decisive innovation in cotton production. By 1811 ten times as many threads were being spun on mules as on water frames and jennies combined.

The original mules were small machines that, like the jennies, could be used for domestic manufactures. But increasingly, the mule followed the water frame into purposely built factories, where it became larger and more expensive. The need for large rooms to house the equipment and for a ready source of running water to power it provided an incentive for the creation of factories, where manufacturers could maintain control over

COTTON MANUFACTURES IN GREAT BRITAIN

■ *Cotton manufactures was the first of the new industries that led to British economic domination in the nineteenth century. In producing cotton cloth, new inventions like the spinning jenny and the water frame revolutionized manufacture and the factory system was born. Britain's domination of cotton production impressed contemporaries. In this excerpt a contemporary tries to explain why Britain took the lead in industrialization.*

In comparing the advantages of England for manufactures with those of other countries, we can by no means overlook the excellent commercial position of the country—intermediate between the north and south of Europe; and its insular situation, which, combined with the command of the seas, secures our territory from invasion or annoyance. The German ocean, the Baltic, and the Mediterranean are the regular highways for our ships; and our western ports command an unobstructed passage to the Atlantic, and to every quarter of the world.

A temperate climate, and a hardy race of men, have also greatly contributed to promote the manufacturing industry of England.

The political and moral advantages of this country, as a seat of manufactures, are not less remarkable than its physical advantages. The arts are the daughters of peace and liberty. In no country have these blessings been enjoyed in so high a degree, or for so long a continuance, as in England. Under the reign of just laws, personal liberty and property have been secure; mercantile enterprise has been allowed to reap its reward; capital has accumulated in safety; the workman has "gone forth to his work and to his labour until the evening;" and, thus protected and favoured, the manufacturing prosperity of the country has struck its roots deep, and spread forth its branches to the ends of the earth.

England has also gained by the calamities of other countries, and the intolerance of other governments. At different periods, the Flemish and French protestants, expelled from their native lands, have taken refuge in England, and have repaid the protection given them by practising and teaching branches of industry, in which the English were then less expert than their neighbours.

From Edward Baines, *The History of the Cotton Manufacturers in Great Britain* (1835).

the quality of products through strict supervision of the workforce. Richard Arkwright built the first cotton factories in Britain, all of which were designed to house water frames.

The organization of the cotton industry into factories was one of the pivotal transformations in economic life. Domestic spinning and weaving took place in agricultural villages, factory production took place in mill towns. The location of the factory determined movements of population, and from the first quarter of the eighteenth century onward a great shift toward the northeast of England was under way. Moreover, the character of the work itself changed. The operation of heavy machinery reversed the traditional gender-based tasks. Mule spinning became men's work, while hand-loom weaving was taken over by women. The mechanization of weaving took longer than that of spinning, both because of difficulties in perfecting a power loom and because of opposition to its introduction by workers known as Luddites, who organized machine-breaking riots in the 1810s. The Luddites attempted to maintain the traditional organization of their industry and the independence of their labor. For a time, hand-loom weavers managed to survive by accepting lower and lower piece rates. But their competition was like that of a horse against an automobile. In 1820 there were over 250,000 hand-loom weavers in Britain; by 1850 the number was less than 50,000.

The transformation of cotton manufacture had a profound effect upon the overall growth of the British economy. It increased shipping since the raw material had to be imported, first from the Mediterranean and then from America. American cotton, especially after 1794 when American inventor Eli Whitney (1765–1825) patented his cotton gin, fed a nearly insatiable demand. In 1750 Britain imported less than 5 million pounds of raw cotton; a century later the volume had grown to 588 million pounds. And to each pound of raw cotton, British manufacturers added the value of their technology and of their labor. By the mid-nineteenth century nearly half a million people earned their living from cotton, which alone accounted for over 40 percent of the value of all British exports.

The Iron Horse

The first stage of the Industrial Revolution in Britain was driven by the production of consumer goods. Pottery, cast-iron tools, clocks, toys, and textiles, especially cottons, all were manufactured in quantities unknown in the early eighteenth century. These products fed a ravenous market at home and abroad. The greatest complaint of industrialists was that they could not get enough raw materials or fuel, nor could they ship their finished products fast enough to keep up with demand. Transportation was becoming a serious stumbling block to continued economic growth. Even with the completion of the canal network that linked the major rivers and improvement in highways and tollways, raw materials and finished goods moved slowly.

It was the need to ship increasing amounts of coal to foundries and factories that provided the spur for the development of a new form of transportation. Ever since the seventeenth century, coal had been moved from the seam to the pit on rails, first constructed of wood and later of iron. Broad-wheeled carts hitched to horses were as much dragged as rolled, but this still represented the most efficient form of hauling and these railways ultimately ran from the seam to the dock. By 1800 there was perhaps as much as three hundred miles of iron rail in British mines. In the same year, Watt's patent on the

Textile Centers

Railroads, ca. 1850

Manufacturing Centers

The railroads changed the whole pattern of living during the Industrial Revolution. On this circular track, Richard Trevithick displayed his high-pressure steam locomotive, the "Catch-me-who-can," to a marveling London public in 1808.

steam engine expired, and inventors began to apply the engine to a variety of mechanical tasks.

Richard Trevithick (1771–1833) was the first to experiment with a steam-driven carriage. George Stephenson (1781–1848), who is generally recognized as the father of the modern railroad, made a vital improvement in engine power by increasing the steam pressure in the boiler and exhausting the smoke through a chimney. In 1829 he won a £500 prize with his engine "The Rocket," which pulled a load three times its own weight at a speed of 30 miles per hour and could actually outrun a horse.

In 1830 the first modern railway, the Manchester to Liverpool line, was opened. Like the Duke of Bridgewater's canal, it was designed to move coal and bulk goods, but surprisingly its most important function came to be moving people. In its first year the Manchester-Liverpool line carried over 400,000 passengers, which generated double the revenue derived from freight. Investors in the Manchester-Liverpool line learned quickly that links between population centers were as important as those between industrial sites, and the London to Birmingham and London to Bristol lines were both designed with passenger traffic in mind. Railway building was one of the great boom activities of British industrialization. By 1835 Parliament had passed 54 separate acts establishing over 750 miles of railways. In 1845 over 6,000 miles had been sanctioned and over 2,500 miles built; by 1852 over 7,500 miles of track were in use.

By the 1850s, coal was the dominant cargo shipped by rail and the speedy, efficient service continued to drive down prices. The iron and steel industries were modernized on the back of demand for rails, engines, and cast-iron seats and fittings. In peak periods—and railway building was a boom-and-bust affair—as much as a quarter of the output of the rolling mills went into domestic railroads and much more into Continental systems. The railways were also a massive consumer of bricks for beddings, sidings, and especially bridges, tunnels, and stations. Finally, the railways were a leading employer of labor, surpassing the textile mills in peak periods.

Most of all, the railroads changed the nature of people's lives. Whole new concepts of time, space, and speed emerged to govern daily activities. The cheap railway excursion was born to provide short holidays or even daily returns. Over six million people visited London by train to view the Crystal Palace exhibition in 1851, a number equivalent to a third of the population of England and Wales. The railways did more than link places; they brought people together and helped develop a sense of national identity by speeding all forms of communication.

Entrepreneurs and Managers

The Industrial Revolution in Britain was not simply invented. Too much credit is given to a few breakthroughs and too little to the ways in which they were improved and dispersed. The Industrial Revolution was an age of gadgets when people believed that new was better than old and that there was always room for improvement. "The age is running mad after innovation," the English moralist Dr. Johnson wrote. "All the business of the world is done in a new way; men are hanged in a new way." Societies for the advancement of knowledge sprang up all over Britain. Journals and magazines promoted new ideas and techniques. Competitions were held for the best invention of the year; prizes were awarded for agricultural achievements. Practical rather than pure science was the hallmark of industrial development.

Yet technological innovation was not the same as industrialization. A vital change in economic activity took place in the organization of industry. Putters-out with their circulating capital and hired laborers could never make the economies necessary to increase output and quality while simultaneously lowering costs. This was the achievement of industrialists, producers who owned workplace, machinery, and raw materials and who invested fixed capital by plowing back their profits. Industrial enterprises came in all sizes and shapes. A cotton mill could be started with as little as £300, or as much as £10,000. As late as 1840 less than 10 percent of the mills employed over 500 workers. Most were family concerns with under 100 employees, and many of them failed. For every story with a happy ending there was another with a sad one. When Major John Cartwright (1740–1824) erected a cotton mill, he was offered a Watt steam engine built for a distiller who had gone bankrupt. He acquired his machinery at the auction of another bankrupt. Cartwright's mill, engine, and machinery ended on the auction block less than three years later. There were over 30,000 bankruptcies in the eighteenth century, testimony both to the risks of business and the willingness of people to take them.

To survive against these odds, successful industrialists had to be both entrepreneur and manager. As entrepreneurs they raised capital, almost always locally from relatives, friends, or members of their church. Quakers were especially active in financing each other's enterprises. The industrial entrepreneur also had to understand the latest methods for building and powering machinery and the most up-to-date techniques for performing the work. One early manufacturer claimed "a practical knowledge of every process from the cotton-bag to the piece of cloth." Finally, entrepreneurs had to know how to market their goods. In these functions, industrial entrepreneurs developed logically from putters-out.

But industrialists also had to be managers. The most difficult task was organization of the workplace. Most gains in productivity were achieved through the specialization of function. The processes of production were divided and subdivided until workers performed a basic task over and over. The education of the workforce was the industrial manager's greatest challenge. Workers had to be taught how to use and maintain their machines and disciplined to apply themselves continuously. At least at the beginning, it was difficult to staff the factories. Many employed children as young as seven from workhouses or orphanages who, though cheap to pay, were difficult to train and discipline. It was the task of the manager to break old habits of intermittent work, indifference to quality, and petty theft of materials. Families were preferred to individuals, for then parents could instruct and supervise their children. There is no reason to believe that industrial managers were more brutal masters than farmers or that children were treated better in workhouses than in mills. Labor was a business asset, what was sometimes called "living machinery," and its control was the chief concern of the industrial manager.

Who were the industrialists who transformed the traditional economy? Because British society was relatively open, they came from every conceivable background; dukes and orphans, merchants and salesmen, inventors and improvers. Though some went from rags to riches, like Richard Arkwright, who was the thirteenth child of a poor barber, it was extremely difficult for a laborer to acquire the capital necessary to set up a business. Wealthy landowners were prominent in capital-intensive aspects of industries, for example, owning ironworks and mines, but few established factories. Most industrialists came from the middle classes, which while comprising a third of the British population, provided as much as two-thirds of the first generation of industrialists. These included lawyers, bankers, merchants, and those already engaged in manufacturing, as well as tradesmen, shopkeepers, and self-employed craftsmen. The career of every industrialist was different, as a look at two, Josiah Wedgwood and Robert Owen, will show.

Josiah Wedgwood (1730–95) was the thirteenth child of a long-established English potting family. He worked in the potteries from childhood but a deformed leg made it difficult for him to turn the wheel. Instead he studied the structure of the business. His head teemed with ideas for improving ceramic manufacturing, but it was not until he was thirty that he could set up on his own and introduce his innovations. These encompassed both technique and organization, the entrepreneurial and managerial sides of his business.

Wedgwood developed new mixtures of clays that took brilliant colors in the kiln and new glazes for both "useful" and "ornamental" ware. He was repelled by the disorder of the traditional pottery with its waste of materials, uneven quality, and slow output. When he began his first works he divided the making of pottery into distinct tasks and separated his workers among them. He invested in schools to help train young artists, in canals to transport his products, and in London shops to sell them. Wedgwood was a marketing genius. He named his famed cream-colored pottery Queen's ware and made special coffee and tea services for leading aristocratic families. He would then sell replicas by the thousands. In less than twenty years Wedgwood pottery was prized all over Europe, and Wedgwood's potting works were the standard of the industry.

Robert Owen (1771–1858) did not have a family business to develop. The son of a small tradesman, he was apprenticed to a clothier at the age of ten. As a teenager he worked as a shop assistant in Manchester, where he audaciously applied for a job as a manager of a cotton

Jasperware copy of the Portland vase by Josiah Wedgwood. The Portland vase is one of the most famous ancient vases. It was found near Rome in the seventeenth century in a tomb believed to be that of Alexander Severus.

mill. At nineteen he was supervising five hundred workers and learning the cotton trade. Owen was immediately successful, increasing the output of his workers and introducing new materials to the mill. In 1816 he entered a partnership to purchase the New Lanark mill in Scotland. Owen found conditions in Scotland much worse than those in Manchester. Over five hundred workhouse children were employed at New Lanark, where drunkenness and theft were endemic. Owen believed that to improve the quality of work one had to improve the quality of the workplace. He replaced old machinery with new, reduced working hours, and instituted a monitoring system to check theft. To enhance life outside the factory, he established a high-quality company-run store, which plowed its profits into a school for village children.

Owen was struck by the irony that in the mills machines were better cared for than were humans. He thought that with the same attention to detail that had so improved the quality of commodities he could make even greater improvements in the quality of life. He prohibited children under ten from mill work and instituted a ten-hour day for child labor. His local school took infants from a year old, freeing women to work and ensuring each child an education. Owen instituted old-age and disability pensions, funded by mandatory contributions from worker's wages. Taverns were closed and workers were fined for drunkenness and sexual offenses. In the factory and the village Owen established a principle of communal regulation to improve both the work and the character of his employees. New Lanark became the model of the world of the future, and each year thousands made an industrial pilgrimage to visit it.

The Wages of Progress

Robert Owen ended his life as a social reformer. His efforts to improve the lot of his workers at New Lanark led to experiments to create ideal industrial communities throughout the world. He founded cooperative societies, in which all members shared in the profits of the business, and supported trade unions in which workers could better their lives. His followers planted colonies where goods were held in common and the fruits of labor belonged to the laborers. Owen's agitation for social reform was part of a movement that produced results of lasting consequence. The Factory Act (1833) prohibited factory work by children under nine, provided two hours of daily education, and effectively created a twelve-hour day in the mills until the Ten Hours Act (1847). The Mines Act (1842) prohibited women and children from working underground.

Nor was Owen alone in dedicating time and money to the improvement of workers' lives. The rapid growth of unplanned cities exacerbated the plight of those too poor and overworked to help themselves. Conditions of housing and sanitation were appalling even by nineteenth-century standards. *The Report on the Sanitary Condition of the Laboring Population in Britain* (1842), written by Edwin Chadwick (1800–90) so shocked Parliament and the nation that it helped to shift the burden of social reform to government. The Public Health Act (1848) established boards of health and the office of medical examiner while the Vaccination Act (1853) and the Contagious Diseases Act (1864) attempted to control epidemics. (See Special Feature, "Industry and the Environment," pp. 730–731.)

The movement for social reform began almost as soon as industrialization. The Industrial Revolution initiated profound changes in the organization of British society. Cities sprang up from grain fields almost overnight. The lure of steady work and high wages prompted an exodus from rural Britain and spurred an unremitting boom in population. In 1750 about 15 percent of the

A view of the New Lanark mills and village in Scotland in 1818, at the time of Robert Owen's social experiments. The buildings included a school and a community center, which attracted many influential visitors from overseas.

population lived in urban areas, by 1850 about 60 percent did. Industrial workers married younger and produced more children than their agricultural counterparts. For centuries women had married in their middle twenties, but by 1800 age at first marriage had dropped to twenty-three for the female population as a whole and to nearly twenty in the industrial areas. This was in part because factory hands did not have to wait until they inherited land or money, and in part because they did not have to serve an apprenticeship. But early marriage and large families were also a bet on the future, a belief that things were better now and would be even better soon.

It is difficult to calculate the benefits of the Industrial Revolution or to weigh them against the costs. What is certain is that there was a vast expansion of wealth as well as a vast expansion of people to share it. Agricultural and industrial change made it possible to support comfortably a population over three times that of the seventeenth century, when it was widely believed that England had reached the limits of expansion. Despite the fact that population doubled between 1801 and

1851, per capita income rose by 75 percent. That means that had the population remained stable, per capita income would have increased by a staggering 350 percent. At the same time, untold millions of pounds had been sunk into canals, roads, railways, factories, mines, and mills.

But the expansion of wealth is not the same as the improvement in the quality of life, for wealth is not equally distributed. An increase in the level of wealth may mean only that the rich are getting richer more quickly than the poor are getting poorer. Similarly, economic growth over a century involved the lives of several generations, which experienced different standards of living. One set of parents may have sacrificed for the future of their children, another may have mortgaged it. Moreover, economic activity is cyclical. Trade depressions, like those induced by the War of 1812 and the American Civil War, which interrupted cotton supplies, could have disastrous short-term effects. The "Great Hunger" of the 1840s was a time of agrarian crisis and industrial slump. The downturn of 1842 threw 60 percent of the factory workers in the town of Bolton out of

OBSERVATIONS ON THE EFFECT OF THE MANUFACTURING SYSTEM

■ *Robert Owen was both a successful manufacturer and a leading philanthropist. He believed that economic advance had to take place in step with the improvement of the moral and physical well-being of the workers. He organized schools, company shops, and ultimately utopian communities in an effort to improve the lives of industrial laborers. Owen was one of the first social commentators to argue that industrialism threatened the fabric of family and community life.*

The acquisition of wealth, and the desire which it naturally creates for a continued increase, have introduced a fondness for essentially injurious luxuries among a numerous class of individuals who formerly never thought of them, and they have also generated a disposition which strongly impels its possessors to sacrifice the best feelings of human nature to this love of accumulation. To succeed in this career, the industry of the lower orders, from whose labour this wealth is now drawn, has been carried by new competitors striving against those of longer standing, to a point of real oppression, reducing them by successive changes, as the spirit of competition increased and the ease of acquiring wealth diminished, to a state more wretched than can be imagined by those who have not attentively observed the changes as they have gradually occurred. In consequence, they are at present in a situation infinitely more degraded and miserable than they were before the introduction of these manufactories, upon the success of which their bare subsistence now depends . . .

The inhabitants of every country are trained and formed by its great leading existing circumstances, and the character of the lower orders in Britain is now formed chiefly by circumstances arising from trade, manufactures, and commerce; and the governing principle of trade, manufactures, and commerce is immediate pecuniary gain, to which on the great scale every other is made to give way. All are sedulously trained to buy cheap and to sell dear; and to succeed in this art, the parties must be taught to acquire strong powers of deception; and thus a spirit is generated through every class of traders, destructive of that open, honest sincerity, without which man cannot make others happy, nor enjoy happiness himself.

---

work at a time when there was neither unemployment insurance nor a welfare system. Finally, quality of life cannot simply be measured in economic terms. People with more money to spend may still be worse off than their ancestors, who may have preferred leisure to wealth or independence to the discipline of the clock.

Thus there are no easy answers to the quality-of-life question. In the first stages of industrialization it seems clear that only the wealthy benefited economically, though much of their increased wealth was reinvested in expansion. Under the impact of population growth, the Napoleonic wars, and regional harvest failure, real wages seem to have fallen from the levels reached in the 1730s. Industrial workers were not substantially better off than agricultural laborers when the high cost of food and rent is considered. But beginning around 1820 there is convincing evidence that the real wages of industrial workers were rising despite the fact that more and more work

was semi- and unskilled machine-minding and more of it was being done by women, who were generally paid only two-thirds the wages of men. Thus in the second half of the Industrial Revolution, both employers and workers saw a bettering of their economic situation. This was one reason why rural workers flocked to the cities to work the lowest paid and least desirable jobs in the factories.

But economic gain had social costs. The first was the decline of the family as a labor unit. In both agricultural and early industrial activity families labored together. Workers would not move to mill towns without the guarantee of a job for all members of their family and initially they could drive a hard bargain. The early factories preferred family labor to workhouse conscripts and it was traditional for children to work beside their parents, cleaning, fetching, or assisting in minding the machines. Children provided an essential part of family income, and youngest children were the agency of care

CHILD LABOR IN THE COAL MINES

■ *The condition of child laborers was a concern of English legislators and social reformers from the beginning of industrialization. Most of the attention was given to factory workers and most legislation attempted to regulate the age at which children could begin work, the number of hours they could be made to work, and the provision of schooling and religious education during their leisure. It was not until the mid-1840s that a parliamentary commission was formed to investigate the condition of child labor in the mines. In this extract the testimony of the child is confirmed by the observations of one of the commissioners.*

Ellison Jack, 11-years-old girl coal-bearer at Loanhead colliery, Scotland:

I have been working below three years on my father's account; he takes me down at two in the morning, and I come up at one and two next afternoon. I go to bed at six at night to be ready for work next morning: the part of the pit I bear in the seams are much on the edge. I have to bear my burthen up four traps, or ladders, before I get to the main road which leads to the pit bottom. My task is four or five tubs: each tub holds 4¼ cwt. I fill five tubs in twenty journeys.

I have had the strap when I did not do my bidding. Am very glad when my task is wrought, as it sore fatigues. I can read, and was learning the writing; can do a little; not been at school for two years; go to kirk occasionally, over to Lasswade: don't know much about the Bible, so long since read.

R.H. Franks, Esq., the sub-commissioner: A brief description of this child's place of work will illustrate her evidence. She has first to descend a nine-ladder pit to the first rest, even to which a shaft is sunk, to draw up the baskets or tubs of coals filled by the bearers; she then takes her creel (a basket formed to the back, not unlike a cockle-shell flattened towards the neck, so as to allow lumps of coal to rest on the back of the neck and shoulders), and pursues her journey to the wall-face, or as it is called here, the room of work. She then lays down her basket, into which the coal is rolled, and it is frequently more than one man can do to lift the burden on her back. The tugs or straps are placed over the forehead, and the body bent in a semicircular form, in order to stiffen the arch.

From Testimony to the Parliamentary Investigative Committee, 1842.

Children's Labor in Coal Mines, *an engraving that appeared in the report of the Children's Employment Commission of 1842. As a result of the report, employment of women and of children under ten in the mines was banned by the 1842 Mines Act.*

London's inadequate sewers were enlarged in the 1840s, but until the 1860s wastewater was discharged into the Thames, giving rise to epidemics of cholera and other waterborne diseases.

Industry and the Environment

The Industrial Revolution changed the landscape of Britain. Small villages grew into vast metropolises seemingly overnight. The rates of growth were absolutely staggering: in 1801 there were 75,000 people in Manchester; by 1851 the number had more than quadrupled. This unremitting boom in population did more than strain the resources of local authorities. It broke them apart. It was not that the new industrial cities were unplanned; they were beyond the capacity of planning. Every essential requirement for human survival became scarce and expensive. Shortages of food, water, and basic accommodation were commonplace.

Shantytowns sprang up wherever space would allow, making the flimsily built habitations of construction profiteers seem like palaces. There was loud complaint about these nineteenth-century rip-off artists, but in truth the need for housing was so desperate that people willingly lived anywhere that provided shelter. Houses were built back to back and side by side, with only narrow alleyways to provide sunlight and air. In Edinburgh one could step through the window of one house into the window of the adjoining one. Whole families occupied single rooms where members slept as they worked, in shifts. In Liverpool over 38,000 people were estimated to be living in cellars—windowless, underground accommodations that flooded with the rains and the tides.

Most cities lacked both running water and toilet facilities. Districts were provided with either pumps or capped pipes through which private companies ran water for a few hours each day. The water was collected in buckets and brought to the home, where it would stand for the rest of the day and serve indifferently for washing, drinking, and cooking. Outhouse toilets were an extravagant luxury; in one Manchester district 33 outhouses had to accommodate 7,095 people. They were a mixed blessing even in the middle-class districts where they were more plentiful, as there was no system of drainage to flush the waste away. It simply accumulated in cesspools, which were emptied manually about every two years. The thing that most impressed visitors as they approached an industrial city was the smoke; what impressed them most when they arrived was the smell.

The quality of life experienced by most of the urban poor who lived in these squalid conditions has been recorded by a number of contemporary observers. Friedrich Engels was a German socialist who was sent to England to learn the cotton trade. He lived in Manchester for two years and spent much of his time exploring the working-class areas of the city. "In this district I found a man, apparently about sixty years old, living in a cow stable," Engels recounted from one of his walking tours in *The Condition of the Working Class in England in 1844.* "He had constructed a sort of chimney for his square pen, which had neither windows, floor, nor ceiling, had obtained a bedstead and lived there, though the rain dripped through his rotten roof. This man was too old and weak for regular work, and supported himself by removing manure with a hand-cart; the dungheaps lay next door to his palace!" From his own observations Engels concluded that "in such dwellings only a physically degenerate race, robbed of all humanity, degraded, reduced morally and physically to bestiality, could feel comfortable and at home." And as he was quick to point out, his own observations were no different from those of parliamentary commissioners, medical officers, or civic authorities who had seen conditions firsthand.

Among these observers, the most influential by far was Sir Edwin Chadwick (1800–90), who began his government career as a commissioner for the poor law and ended it as the founder of a national system of public health. Chadwick wrote the report of a parliamentary commission, *The Sanitary Condition of the Laboring Population of Britain* (1842), which caused a sensation among the governing classes. Building on the work of physicians, overseers of the poor, and the most technical scholarship available, Chadwick not only painted the same grim picture of urban life as did Engels, he proposed a comprehensive solution to one of its greatest problems, waste management.

Chadwick was a civil servant and he believed that problems were solved by government on the basis of conclusions of experts. He had heard doctors argue their theories about the causes of disease, some believing in fluxes that resulted from combinations of foul air, water, and refuse; others believing disease was spread by the diseased, in this case Irish immigrants who settled in the poorest parts of English industrial towns. Though medical research had not yet detected the existence of germs, it was widely held that lack of ventilation, stagnant pools of water, and the accumulation of human and animal waste in proximity to people's dwellings all contributed to the increasing incidence of disease. Chadwick fixed upon this last element as crucial. Not even in middle-class districts was there an effective system for the removal of waste. Chamber pots and primitive toilets were emptied into ditches, which were used to drain rain off into local waterways. The few underground sewers that existed were square containers without outlets, which were simply emptied once filled. Chadwick's vision was for a sanitation system, one that would carry waste out of the city quickly and deposit it in outlying fields where it could be used as fertilizer.

Chadwick realized that the key to disposing of waste was a constant supply of running water piped through the system. Traditionally, only heavy rainstorms cleared the waste ditches in most cities, and these were too infrequent to be effective. The river had to be the beginning of the sewerage system as well as its end. River water had to be pumped through an underground construction of sewage pits that were built to facilitate the water's flow. Civil engineers had already demonstrated that pits with rounded rather than angular edges were far more effective, and Chadwick advocated the construction of a system of oval-shaped tunnels, built on an incline beneath the city. Water pumped from one part of the river would rush through the tunnels, which would empty into pipes that would carry the waste to nearby farms.

Chadwick's vision took years to implement. He had all of the zeal of a reformer and none of the tact of a politician. He offended nearly everyone with whom he came into contact, because he believed that his program was the only workable one and because he believed that it must be implemented whatever the price. He was uninterested in who was to pay the enormous costs of laying underground tunnels and building pumping stations and insisted only that the work begin immediately. In the end, he won his point. Sanitation systems became one of the first great public-works projects of the industrial age.

for infirm parents. Paradoxically, it was the agitation for improvement in the conditions of child labor that spelled the end of the family work unit. At first young children were barred from the factories and older ones allowed to work only a partial adult shift. Though reformers intended that schooling and leisure be substituted for work, the separation of children from parents in the workplace ultimately made possible the substitution of teenagers for adults, especially as machines replaced skilled human labor. The individual worker now became the unit of labor and during economic downturns it was adult males with their higher salaries who were laid off first.

The decline of the family as a labor unit was matched by other changes in living conditions when rural dwellers migrated to cities. Many rural habits were unsuited to both factory work and urban living. The tradition of "Saint Monday," for example, was one that was deeply rooted in the pattern of agricultural life. Little effort was expended at the beginning of the work week and progressively more at the end. Sunday leisure was followed by Monday recovery, a slow start to renewed labor. The factory demanded constant application six days a week. Strict rules were enforced to keep workers at their stations and their minds on their jobs. More than efficiency was at stake. Early machines were not only crude, they were dangerous, with no safety features to cover moving parts. Maiming accidents were common in the early factories and they were the fault of both workers and machines. Similarly, industrial workers entered a world of the cash economy. Most agricultural workers were used to being paid in kind and to barter exchange. Money was an unusual luxury that was associated with binges of food, drink, and frivolities. This made adjustment to the wage packet as difficult as adjustment to the clock. Cash had to be set aside for provisions, rent, and clothing. On the farm the time of a bountiful harvest was the time to buy durable goods; in the factory "harvest time" was always the same.

Such adjustments were not easy, and during the course of the nineteenth century a way of life passed forever from England. For some its departure caused profound sorrow; for others it was an occasion of good riddance. A vertically integrated society in which lord of the manor, village worthies, independent farmers, workers, and servants lived together interdependently was replaced by a society of segregated social classes. By the middle decades of the nineteenth century a class of capitalists and a class of workers had begun to form and had begun to clash. The middle classes abandoned the city centers, building exclusive suburban communities in which to raise their children and insulate their families. Conditions in the cities deteriorated under the pressure of overcrowding, lack of sanitation, and the absence of private investment. The loss of interaction between these different segments of society had profound consequences for the struggle to improve the quality of life for everyone. Leaders of labor saw themselves fighting against profits, greed, and apathy; leaders of capital against drunkenness, sloth, and ignorance. Between these two stereotypes there was little middle ground.

The Industrialization of the Continent

Though Britain took the first steps along the road to an industrial economy, it was not long before other European nations followed. There was intense interest in the British miracle, as it was dubbed by contemporaries. European ministers, entrepreneurs, even heads of state, visited British factories and mines in hope of learning the key industrial secrets that would unlock the prosperity of a new age. The Crystal Palace exhibition of manufacturing and industry held in London in 1851 was the occasion for a Continent-wide celebration of the benefits of technology and a chance for ambitious Europeans to measure themselves against the mighty British. By then many European nations had begun the transformation of their own economies and had entered a period of sustained growth.

There was no single model for the industrialization of the Continental states. Contemporaries continually made comparisons with Britain, but in truth the process of British industrialization was not well suited to any but the coal-rich regions in Belgium and the Rhineland. Nevertheless, all of Europe benefited from the British experience. No one else had to invent the jenny, the mule, or the steam engine. Although the British government banned the export of technology, none of these path-breaking inventions remained a secret for long. Britain had demonstrated a way to make cheap, durable goods in factories, and every other state in Europe was able to skip the long stages of discovery and improvement. Thus while industrialization began later on the Continent, it could progress more quickly. France and Germany were building a railroad system within years of Britain despite the fact that they had to import most of the technology, raw materials, and engineers.

Britain shaped European industrialization in another way. Its head start made it very difficult for follower nations to compete against British commodities in the world market. This meant that European industrialization would be directed first and foremost to home markets where tariffs and import quotas could protect fledgling industries. Though European states were willing to import vital British products, they placed high duties on British-made consumer goods and encouraged higher-cost domestic production. Britain's competitive advantage demanded that European governments become involved in the industrialization of their countries, financing capital-intensive industries, backing the railroads, and favoring the establishment of factories.

European industrialization was therefore not the thunderclap that occurred in Britain. In France it was a slow, accretive development that took advantage of traditional skills and occupations and gradually modernized the marketplace. In Germany industrialization had to overcome the political divisions of the empire, the economic isolation of the petty states, and the wide dispersion of vital resources. Regions rather than states industrialized in the early nineteenth century and parts of Austria, Italy, and Spain imported machinery and techniques and modernized their traditional crafts. But most of these states and most of the eastern part of Europe remained tied to a traditional agrarian-based economy that provided neither labor for industrial production nor purchasing power for industrial goods. These areas quickly became sources for raw materials and primary products for their industrial neighbors.

Industrialization Without Revolution

The experience of France in the nineteenth century demonstrates that there was no single path to industrialization. Each state blended together its natural resources, historical experiences, and forms of economic organization in unique combinations. While some mixtures resulted in explosive growth, as in Britain, others made for steady development, as in France.

French industrialization was keyed to domestic rather than export markets and to the application of new technology to a vast array of traditional crafts. The French profited, as did all of the Continental states, from British inventions, but they also benefited from the distinct features of their own economy. France possessed a pool of highly skilled and highly productive labor, a manufacturing tradition oriented toward the creation of high-quality goods, and consumers who valued taste and fashion over cost and function. Thus while the British dominated the new mass market for inexpensive cottons and cast-iron goods, a market with high sales but low profit margins, the French were producing luxury items whose scarcity kept both prices and profits high.

Two decisive factors determined the nature of French industrialization: population growth and the French Revolution. From the early eighteenth to the mid-nineteenth centuries, France grew slowly. In 1700 French population stood at just under 20 million; in 1850 it was just under 36 million, a growth rate of 80 percent. In contrast, Germany grew 135 percent, from 15 to 34 million, and England 300 percent, from 5 to 20

A French steelworks, Manufacture Nationale, in Paris, 1800. At that time this was the only French steelworks that compared with those in Sheffield, England.

million, during the same period. Nevertheless, France remained the most populous nation in western Europe, second on the Continent only to Russia. There is no simple explanation for France's relatively sluggish population growth. The French had been hit particularly hard by subsistence crises in the seventeenth century, and there is reliable evidence that the rural population consciously attempted to limit family size by methods of birth control as well as by delaying marriages. Moreover, France urbanized slowly at a time when city dwellers were marrying younger and producing larger families. As late as the 1860s a majority of French workers were farmers. Whatever the cause of this moderate population growth, its consequences were clear. France was not pressured by the force of numbers to abandon its traditional agricultural methods, nor did it face a shortage of traditional supplies of energy. Except during crop failures, French agriculture could produce to meet French needs, and there remained more than enough wood for domestic and industrial use.

The consequences of the French Revolution are less clear. Throughout the eighteenth century, the French economy performed at least as well as had the British and in many areas better. French overseas trade had grown spectacularly until checked by military defeat in the Seven Years' War (1756–63). French agriculture steadily increased output while French rural manufactures flourished. A strong guild tradition still dominated urban industries, and although it restricted competition and limited growth, it also helped maintain the standards for the production of high-quality goods that made French commodities so highly prized throughout the world. The Revolution disrupted every aspect of economic life. Some of its outcomes were unforeseen and unwelcome. For example, Napoleon's Continental System, which attempted to close European markets to Britain, resulted in a shipping war, which the British won decisively and which eliminated France as a competitor for overseas trade in the mid-nineteenth century. But other outcomes were the result of direct policies, even if their impact could not have been entirely predicted. Urban guilds and corporations were abolished, opening trades to newcomers but destroying the close-knit groups that trained skilled artisans and introduced innovative products. Similarly, the breakup of both feudal and common lands to satisfy the hunger of the peasantry had the effect of maintaining a large rural population for decades.

Despite the efforts of the central government, there had been little change in the techniques used by French farmers over the course of the eighteenth century. French peasants clung tenaciously to traditional rights that gave even the smallest landholder a vital say in community agriculture. Landlords were predominantly absentees, less interested in the organization of their estates than in the dues and taxes that could be extracted from them. Thus the policies of successive Revolutionary governments strengthened the hold of small peasants on the land. With the abolition of many feudal dues and with careful family planning, smallholders could survive and pass a meager inheritance on to their children. French agriculture was able to supply the nation's need for food, but it could not release large numbers of workers for purely industrial activity.

Thus French industrial growth was constrained on the one hand by the relatively small numbers of workers who could engage in manufacturing and on the other by the fact that a large portion of the population remained subsistence producers, cash-poor and linked only to small rural markets. Throughout the eighteenth century the French economy continued to be regionally segregated rather than nationally integrated. The size of the state inhibited a highly organized internal trade, and there was little improvement of the infrastructure of transportation. Though some British-style canals were built, it must be remembered that canals in Britain were built to move coal rather than staple goods and France did not have much coal to move. Manufacturing concerns were still predominantly family businesses whose primary markets were regional rather than international. Roads that connected the short distances between producers and consumers were of greater importance to these producers than arterial routes that served the markets of others. Similarly, there was no national capital market until the mid-nineteenth century and precious few regional ones. Though French producers were as thrifty and profit-oriented as any others, they found it more difficult to raise the large amounts of capital necessary to purchase the most expensive new machinery and build the most up-to-date factories. Ironworks, coal mines, and railroads, the three capital-intensive ventures of industrialization, were financed either by government subsidy or by foreign investment.

It was not until mid-century that sustained industrial growth became evident in France. This was largely the result of the construction of railroads on a national plan, financed in large part by the central government. Whereas in Britain the railways took advantage of a national market, in France they created one. They also gave the essential stimulation to the modernization of the iron industry, of machine making, and of the capital markets.

The disadvantages of being on the trailing edge of economic change were mitigated for a time by conventional practices of protectionism. Except in specialty goods, agricultural produce, and luxury products, French manufactures could not compete with either British or German commodities. Had France maintained its position as a world trader, this comparative disadvantage would have been devastating. But defeat in the wars of commerce had led to a drawing inward of French economic effort. Marseilles and Bordeaux, once bustling centers of European trade, became provincial backwaters in the nineteenth century. But the internal market was still strong enough to support industrial growth, and domestic commodities could be protected by prohibitive tariffs, especially against British textiles, iron, and ironically, coal.

While France achieved industrialization without an industrial revolution, it also achieved economic growth within the context of its traditional values. Agriculture may not have modernized, but the ancient village communities escaped the devastation modernization would bring. The orderly progression of generations of farming families characterized rural France until the shattering experiences of the Franco-Prussian War (1870) and the First World War (1914–18). Nor did France experience the mushroom growth of new cities with all of their problems of poverty, squalor, and homelessness. Slow population growth ameliorated the worst of the social diseases of industrialization while traditional rural manufacturing softened the transformation of a way of life.

Industrialization and Union

The process of industrialization in Germany was dominated by the historic divisions of the empire of the German peoples. Before 1815 there were over three hundred separate jurisdictional units within the empire, and after 1815 there were still more than thirty. These included large advanced states like Prussia, Austria, and Saxony as well as small free cities and the personal enclaves of petty nobles who had guessed right during the Napoleonic wars. Political divisions had more than political impact. Each state clung tenaciously to its local laws and customs, which favored its citizens over outsiders. Merchants who lived near the intersection of separate jurisdictions could find themselves liable for several sets of tolls to move their goods and several sets of customs duties for importing and exporting them.

These would have to be paid in different currencies at different rates of exchange according to the different regulations of each state. Small wonder that German merchants exhibited an intense localism, preferring to trade with members of their own state and supporting trade barriers against others. Such obstacles had a depressing effect on the economies of all German states, but pushed with greatest weight against the manufacturing regions of Saxony, Silesia, and the Rhineland.

Most of imperial Germany was agricultural land suited to a diversity of uses. The mountainous regions of Bavaria and the Austrian alpine communities practiced animal husbandry; there was a grain belt in Prussia, where the soil was poor but the land plentiful, and one in central Germany in which the soil was fertile and the land densely occupied. The Rhine Valley was one of the richest in all of Europe and was the center of German wine production. While English farmers were turning farms into commercial estates, German peasants were learning how to make do with less land.

Agricultural estates were organized differently in different parts of Germany. In the east, serfdom still prevailed. Peasants were tied to the land and its lord and were responsible for labor service during much of the week. Methods of cultivation were traditional, and neither peasants nor lords had much incentive to adopt new techniques. In central Germany, the long process of commuting labor service into rents was nearly completed by the end of the eighteenth century. The peasantry was not yet free, as a series of manorial relationships still tied them to the land, but they were no longer mere serfs. Finally, western Germany was dominated by free farmers who either owned or leased their lands and who had a purely economic relationship with their landlords. The restriction of peasant mobility in much of Germany posed difficulties for the creation of an industrial workforce. As late as 1800 over 80 percent of the German population was engaged in agriculture, a proportion that would drop slowly over the next half-century.

Though Germany was well endowed with natural resources and skilled labor in a number of trades, it had not taken part in the expansion of world trade during the seventeenth century, and the once bustling Hanseatic ports had been far outdistanced by the rise of the Atlantic economies. The principal exported manufacture was linen, which was expertly spun and woven in Saxony and the Prussian province of Silesia. The linen industry was organized traditionally, with a mixture of domestic production managed on the putting-out system and some factory spinning, especially after the introduction of

British mechanical innovations. But even the most advanced factories were still being powered by water, and thus they were located in mountainous regions where rapidly running streams could turn the wheels. Neither linens nor traditional German metal crafts could compete on the international markets, but they could find a wider market within Germany if only the problems of political division could be resolved.

These were especially acute for Prussia after the reorganization of European boundaries in 1815 (see chapter 25). Prussian territory now included the coal- and iron-rich Rhineland provinces, but a number of smaller states separated these areas from Prussia's eastern domain. Each small state exacted its own tolls and customs duties whenever Prussian merchants wanted to move goods from one part of Prussia to the other. Such movement became more common in the nineteenth century as German manufacturing began to grow in step with its rising population. Between 1815 and 1865 the population of Germany grew by 60 percent to over 36 million. This was an enormous internal market, nearly as large as France, and the Prussians resolved to make it a unified trading zone by creating a series of alliances with smaller states known as the Zollverein (1834). The Zollverein was not a free-trade zone, as was the British empire, but rather a customs union in which member states adopted the liberal Prussian customs regulations. Every state was paid an annual portion of receipts based upon its population, and every state—except Prussia—increased its revenues as a result. The crucial advantage the Prussians received was the ability to move goods and materials from east to west, but Prussia reaped political profits as well. It forced Hanover and Saxony into the Zollverein and kept its powerful rival Austria out. Prussia's economic union soon proved to be the basis for the union of the German states.

The creation of the Zollverein was vital to German industrialization. It permitted the exploitation of natural advantages, like plentiful supplies of coal and iron, and it provided a basis for the building of railroads. Germany was a follower nation in the process of industrialization. It started late and it self-consciously modeled its success upon the British experience. British equipment and engineers were brought to Germany to attempt to plant the seeds of an industrial economy. German manufacturers sent their children to England to learn the latest techniques in industrial management. Friedrich Engels (1820–95) worked in a Manchester cotton factory, where he observed the appalling conditions of the industrial labor force and wrote *The Condition Of the Working Class in England* (1845). Steam en-

The train from Nuremberg to Fürth. This Bavarian train ran for the first time in 1835. Passengers rode the seven kilometers between Nuremburg and Fürth in coaches that closely resembled their horse-drawn predecessors.

gines were installed in coal mines, if not in factories, and the process of puddling revolutionized iron making, though most iron was still smelted with charcoal rather than coke. Though coal was plentiful in Prussia, it was to be found at the eastern and western extremities of Germany. Even with the lowering of tolls and duties, it was still too expensive to move over rudimentary roads and an uncompleted system of canals. Thus the railroads were the key to tapping the industrial potential of Germany. Here they were a cause rather than a result of industrialization. The agreements hammered out in the creation of the Zollverein made possible the planning necessary to build single lines across the boundaries of numerous states.

Germany imported most of its engines directly from Britain and thus adopted standard British gauge for its system. As early as 1850 there were over 3,500 miles of rail in Germany, with important roads linking the manufacturing districts of Saxony and the coal and iron deposits of the Ruhr. Twenty years later Germany was second only to Britain in the amount of track that had been laid and opened. By then it was no longer simply a follower. German engineers and machinists, trained in Europe's best schools of technology, were turning out engines and rolling stock second to none. And the railroads transported a host of high-quality manufactures, especially durable metal goods that came to carry the most prestigious mark of the late nineteenth century: made in Germany.

The Lands That Time Forgot

Nothing better demonstrates the point that industrialization was a regional rather than a national process than a survey of those states that did not develop industrial economies by the middle of the nineteenth century. These states ranged from the Netherlands, which was still one of the richest areas in Europe, to Spain and Russia, which were the poorest. Also included were Austria-Hungary, the states of the Italian peninsula, and Poland. In all of these nations there was some industrial progress. The Bohemian lands of Austria contained a highly developed spinning industry; the Spanish province of Catalonia produced more cotton than did Belgium, and the Basque region was rich in iron and coal. Northern Italy mechanized its textile production, particularly silk spinning, while in the regions around both Moscow and Saint Petersburg factories were run on serf labor. Nevertheless, the economies of all these states remained nonindustrial and, with the exception of the Netherlands, dominated by subsistence agriculture.

There were many reasons why these states were unable to develop their industrial potential. Some, like Naples and Poland, were simply underendowed with resources; others, like Austria-Hungary and Spain, faced difficulties of transport and communications that could not easily be overcome. Spain's modest resources were located on its northern and eastern edges while a vast, arid plain dominated the center. To move raw materials and finished products from one end of the country to the other was a daunting task, made more difficult by lack of waterways and the rudimentary condition of Spanish roads. Two-thirds of Austria-Hungary is either mountains or hills, a geographic feature that presented obstacles that not even the railroads could easily solve. But there was far more than natural disadvantage behind the

THE CONDITION OF THE WORKING CLASS IN ENGLAND

■ *Though born in Germany, Engels witnessed industrialization in England firsthand. His father owned a factory in Manchester of which Engels was put in charge. By day he oversaw industrial production and by night he wandered the city streets overwhelmed by the suffering of the working classes. His analysis of industrialization developed from his own observations. He became first a socialist and then, with Karl Marx, a founder of communism.*

Capital is the all-important weapon in the class war. Power lies in the hands of those who own, directly or indirectly, foodstuffs and the means of production. The poor, having no capital, inevitably bear the consequences of defeat in the struggle. Nobody troubles about the poor as they struggle helplessly in the whirlpool of modern industrial life. The working man may be lucky enough to find employment, if by his labour he can enrich some member of the middle classes. But his wages are so low that they hardly keep body and soul together. If he cannot find work, he can steal, unless he is afraid of the police; or he can go hungry and then the police will see to it that he will die of hunger in such a way as not to disturb the equanimity of the middle classes . . .

The only difference between the old-fashioned slavery and the new is that while the former was openly acknowledged the latter is disguised. The worker *appears* to be free, because he is not bought and sold outright. He is sold piecemeal by the day, the week, or the year. Moreover he is not sold by one owner to another, but he is forced to sell himself in this fashion. He is not the slave of a single individual, but of the whole capitalist class. As far as the worker is concerned, however, there can be no doubt as to his servile status. It is true that the apparent liberty which the worker enjoys does give him some *real* freedom. Even this genuine freedom has the disadvantage that no one is responsible for providing him with food and shelter. His real masters, the middle-class capitalists, can discard him at any moment and leave him to starve, if they have no further use for his services and no further interest in his survival.

From Friedrich Engels, *The Condition of the Working Class in England,* 1844.

Industrialization on the Continent

failure of these parts of Europe to move in step with the industrializing states. Their social structure, agricultural organization, and commercial policies all hindered the adoption of new methods, machines, and modes of production.

The leaders of traditional economies maintained tariff systems that insulated their own producers from competition. But protection was sensible only when it protected rather than isolated. Inefficiently produced goods of inferior quality were the chief results of the protectionist policies of the follower nations. Failure to adopt steam-powered machines made traditionally produced linens and silks so expensive that smuggling occurred on an international scale. Though these goods might find buyers in domestic markets, they could not compete in international trade, and one by one the industries of the follower nations atrophied. Those economies that remained traditionally organized came to be exploited for their resources by those that had industrialized. Traditional agriculture could not produce the necessary surplus of either labor or capital to support industry, and industry could not economize sufficiently to make manufactured goods cheap enough for a poor peasantry.

There was more than irony in the fact that one of the first railroads built on the Continent was built in Austria, but it was built to be powered by horses rather than engines. The first railways in Italy linked royal palaces to capital cities; those in Spain radiated from Madrid and bypassed most centers of natural resources. In these states the railroads were built to move the military rather than passengers or goods. They were state-financed, occasionally state-owned, and almost always lost money. They were symbols of the industrial age, but in these states they were symbols without substance.

The industrialization of Europe in the eighteenth century was an epochal event in human history. The constraints on daily life imposed by nature were loosened for the first time. No longer did population growth in one generation mean famine in the next; no longer was it necessary for the great majority of people to toil in the fields to earn their daily bread. Manufacture replaced agriculture as humanity's primary activity, though the change was longer and slower than the burst of industrialization that took place in the first half of the nineteenth century. For the leaders, Britain especially, industrialization brought international eminence. British achievements were envied, British inventors celebrated, Britain's constitutional and social organization lauded. A comparatively small island nation had become the greatest economic power in Europe. Industrialization had profound consequences for economic life, but its effects ran deeper than that. The search for new markets would result in the conquest of continents; the power of productivity unleashed by coal and iron would result in the first great arms race. Both would reach fruition in World War I, the first industrial war. For better or worse we still live in the industrial era that began in Britain in the middle of the eighteenth century.

Suggestions for Further Reading

General Reading

* Carlo Cipolla, ed., *The Fontana Economic History of Europe: The Emergence of Industrial Societies*, 2 vols. (London: Fontana Books, 1973). Country-by-country survey of Continental European industrialization.

* David Landes, *The Unbound Prometheus* (Cambridge: Cambridge University Press, 1969). Vigorously argued study of the impact of technology on British and European society from the eighteenth to the twentieth century.

* E. L. Jones, *The European Miracle*, 2d ed. (Cambridge: Cambridge University Press, 1987). A comparative study of the acquisition of technology in Europe and Asia and the impact that industrialization had upon the two continents.

* T. S. Ashton, *The Industrial Revolution* (Oxford: Oxford University Press, 1969). A brief, compelling account of the traditional view of industrialization.

The Traditional Economy

* E. A. Wrigley, *Continuity, Chance and Change* (Cambridge: Cambridge University Press, 1988). Explores the nature of the traditional economy and the way in which Britain escaped from it.

* L. A. Clarkson, *Proto-Industrialization: The First Phase of Industrialization?* (London: Macmillan, 1985). Study of domestic manufacturing and its connection to the process of industrialization.

J. D. Chambers and G. E. Mingay, *The Agricultural Revolution* (London: Batsford, 1966). The classic survey of the changes in British agriculture.

E. L. Jones, *Agriculture and the Industrial Revolution* (New York: John Wiley and Sons, 1974). Detailed study of the relationship between agricultural innovations and the coming of industrialization in Britain.

The Industrial Revolution in Britain

* Peter Mathias, *The First Industrial Nation*, 2d ed. (London: Methuen, 1983). Up-to-date general survey of British industrialization.

* Phyllis Deane, *The First Industrial Revolution*, 2d ed. (Cambridge: Cambridge University Press, 1979). The best introduction to the technological changes in Britain.

A. E. Musson, *The Growth of British Industry* (New York: Holmes & Meier, 1978). In-depth survey of British industrialization that is especially strong on technology.

* John Rule, *The Vital Century: England's Developing Economy, 1714-1815* (London: Longman, 1992). The most up-to-date survey on the British economy.

N. F. R. Crafts, *British Economic Growth During the Industrial Revolution* (Oxford: Oxford University Press, 1985). Study by a new economic historian arguing the case for slow economic growth in the early nineteenth century. Highly quantitative.

T. S. Ashton, *Iron and Steel in the Industrial Revolution* (Manchester: Manchester University Press, 1963). Lucid account of the transformation of iron making, including the story of James Watt.

Philip Bagwell, *The Transport Revolution from 1770* (London: Batsford, 1974). Thorough survey of the development of canals, highways, and railroads in Britain.

* Francois Crouzet, *The First Industrialists* (Cambridge: Cambridge University Press, 1985). Analysis of the social background of the first generation of British entrepreneurs.

* Harold Perkin, *The Origins of Modern English Society 1780-1880* (London: Routledge & Kegan Paul, 1969). Outstanding survey of British social history in the industrial era.

* E. P. Thompson, *The Making of the English Working Class* (New York: Random House, 1966). Brilliant and passionate study of the ways in which laborers responded to the changes brought about by the industrial economy.

Friedrich Engels, *The Condition of the Working Class in England in 1844* (London: Allen and Unwin, 1952). The classic eyewitness account of the horrors of the industrial city.

The Industrialization of the Continent

* Tom Kemp, *Industrialization in Nineteenth-Century Europe*, 2d ed. (London: Longman, 1985). Survey of the process of industrialization in the major European states.

* Clive Trebilcock, *The Industrialization of the Continental Powers 1780-1914* (London: Longman, 1981). Complex study of Germany, France, and Russia.

Sidney Pollard, *Peaceful Conquest* (Oxford: Oxford University Press, 1981). Argues for the regional nature of industrialization throughout western Europe.

Roger Price, *The Economic Transformation of France* (London: Croom Helm, 1975). Study of French society before and during the process of industrialization.

W. O. Henderson, *The Rise of German Industrial Power* (Berkeley, CA: University of California Press, 1975). Chronological study of German industrialization that centers on Prussia.

* Wolfgang Schivelbusch, *The Railway Journey* (Berkeley, CA: University of California Press, 1986). Social history of the impact of railways, drawn from French and German sources.

* Indicates paperback edition available.

CHAPTER 25

Ideas and Culture in Europe, 1815–1850

POTATO POLITICS

Vegetables have histories too. But none has a more interesting history in the West than the humble potato. First introduced to northern Europe from the Andean highlands of South America at the end of the sixteenth century, it rapidly became a staple of peasant diets from Ireland to Russia. The potato's vitamins, minerals, and high carbohydrate content provided a rich source of energy to Europe's rural poor. It was simple to plant, it required little or no cultivation, and it did well in damp, cool climates. Best of all, it could be grown successfully on the smallest plots of land. One acre could support a family of four for a year.

The French painter Jean-François Millet (1814–75) provides a view of the peasant labor involved in *Planting Potatoes*. Millet, the son of a wealthy peasant family, understood well the importance of the potato in the peasant family diet. The man and woman in this canvas plant their potatoes as a reverent act, bowing as field laborers might in prayer (as they do in Millet's more sentimental work, *The Angelus*). The primitive nature of the process is striking: the man uses a short hoe to scrape at what seems to be most unyielding soil. The peasants seem part of the nature that surrounds them, patient as the beast that waits in the shade, bent and gnarled and lovely as the tree that arches in the background.

The fleshy root not only guaranteed health, it also affected social life. Traditionally, peasants had delayed marrying and starting families because of the unavailability of land. The potato changed that behavior. Now the potato allowed peasants with only a little land to marry and have children earlier. Millet's depiction of the man and woman working together in the field resonates with the simple fact that potato cultivation aided in the formation of the couple. Millet's couple are parents whose baby sleeps swaddled in a basket and shaded by the tree. In those peasant homes where family members did putting-out work for local entrepreneurs, potato cultivation drew little labor away from the spinning wheel and loom. It permitted prosperous farmers to devote more land to cash crops, since only a small portion was required to feed a family. Most commonly, however, the potato was the single crop grown by most Irish farmworkers. As the sole item of diet, it provided life-sustaining nutrients and a significant amount of the protein so necessary for heavy labor. The Irish adult male ate an average of twelve to fourteen pounds of cooked potatoes a day—a figure that may seem preposterous to us today.

Proverbs warned peasants against putting all their eggs in one basket, but no folk wisdom prepared the Irish for the potato disaster that struck them. In 1845 a fungus from America destroyed the new potato crop. Although peasants were certainly accustomed to bad harvests and crop failures, they had no precedent for the years of blight that followed. From 1846 to 1850, famine and the diseases resulting from it—scurvy, dysentery, cholera, and typhus fever—killed over a million people in what became known as the Great Hunger. Another million people emigrated, many to the United States. Total dependence on the potato reaped its grim harvest, devastating all levels of Irish society. Within five years the Irish population was reduced by almost 25 percent.

The Irish potato famine has been called the last great European *natural* disaster, to distinguish it from the man-made horrors of war and revolution. But it was as much a social disaster as a natural one. Food was the most political of issues. Many argued that the disaster could have been averted. The United Kingdom of Great Britain and Ireland had been created in 1801, and this political unit, which also included England, Scotland, and Wales, constituted one of the world's most prosperous states. The British government expected that the free market would solve the problems caused by famine once trade barriers had been removed. The British Corn Laws, which had been enacted to protect domestic growers from foreign competition, were repealed in 1846. But the famine hit the Irish so hard that they simply did not have the money to buy what grains might be available. Emergency work relief was established and soup kitchens were opened in the spring of 1847, but even this meager assistance was withdrawn because the famine coincided with a banking crisis in England.

There is little to indicate that the continuation of work relief and soup kitchens could have reversed the death rates. In 1847 the problem was handed over to the Irish Poor Law system, a system Britain had imposed on Ireland in 1838. The workhouses created by the recent law were not intended to deal with disasters. Poor and starving Irish peasants were expected to support themselves. Mass deaths and mass graves were the inevitable result.

As the wealth of Western societies expanded, so did the numbers of those who lived on the edge, poised between unemployment and starvation. The Irish Great Hunger was only the most striking example of the one problem that plagued all Western societies in the first half of the nineteenth century: what to do with the poor.

Politicians grappled with devising ways to control the politically destabilizing consequences of poverty. Indigence was most visible in Europe's cities, which served as laboratories for social thinking and reform. Critics of the status quo felt that good government, in guaranteeing the liberty and happiness of its citizens, had to limit social inequities. Others disagreed, arguing that the poor were masters of their own fate. Ideologues of all stripes, from conservatives to liberals to socialists, developed theories of the state that took into account new ideas about public welfare and social responsibility.

Poverty was by no means a new social phenomenon, but the scale of impoverishment and its potential to destabilize whole societies were. In the case of the Irish famine, the British government was unable to handle an extreme crisis that was different in degree if not in kind from the cyclical economic challenges faced by other Western nations. The question of poverty, the social question, lay at the heart of social experience and new ideas about government in the first half of the nineteenth century. It also fueled the fire storm of protest and revolution that swept across Europe after 1830 and, most notably, in 1848. In the context of poverty and the politics of food, Millet's melancholy painting of *Planting Potatoes* is not a pretty picture.

Europe After 1815

In his quest for empire, Napoleon had given Europe a geography lesson. Because no one state had been able to defeat him, Napoleon had made clear the territorial and political interdependence of the European powers. This lesson was not lost on the Great Powers as they sat down to redraw the map of Europe in 1815. The leaders of Russia, Austria, Prussia, and France shared with the British foreign secretary Lord Castlereagh (1769–1822) the vision of Europe as a machine that must be kept in running order. They looked on the whole of Europe as one entity and conceived of peace in terms of a general European security.

The primary goal of the European leaders who met in 1815 was to devise the most stable territorial arrangement possible. The settlement that emerged from their meeting was not simply a reaction to the ideological challenges of the French Revolution, nor was it a restoration of the European state system that had existed before Napoleon. During the negotiations, traditional claims of the right to rule came head to head with new ideas about stabilization. The equilibrium established in 1815 made possible a century-long European peace. To be sure, conflicts erupted, but they too took on the characteristics of the new system that was constructed at Vienna in 1815.

The Congress of Vienna

Because of the concern with establishing harmony at the time of Napoleon's defeat, the peace enforced against France was not a punitive one. After Napoleon's abdication in 1814, the Four Powers decided that leniency was the best way to support the restored Bourbon monarchy. After 1793 royalist émigrés referred to the young son of the executed Louis XVI as Louis XVII, although the child died in captivity and never reigned. In 1814 the Great Powers designated the elder of the two surviving brothers of Louis XVI as the appropriate candidate for the restored monarchy. Because of the circumstances of his restoration, the new king, Louis XVIII (1814–15; 1815–24), bore the ignominious image of returning "in the baggage car of the Allies." Every effort was made not to weigh Louis XVIII down with a harsh settlement. The First Peace of Paris, signed by the Allies with France in May 1814, had established French frontiers at the 1792 boundaries, which included Avignon, Venaissin, parts of Savoy, and German and Flemish territories, none of which had belonged to France in 1789.

After the hundred-day return of Napoleon, the "usurper," the Second Peace of Paris of November 1815 somewhat less generously declared French frontiers restricted to the boundaries of 1790 and exacted from France an indemnity of 700 million francs. An army of occupation consisting of 150,000 troops was also placed on French soil at French expense but was removed ahead of schedule in 1818. As part of the first peace treaty, representatives of the victorious Allies agreed to convene in the Austrian capital of Vienna in September 1814 to mop up the mess created in Europe by French rule and to restore order to European monarchies.

The central actors whose personalities dominated the Congress of Vienna were the Austrian minister of foreign affairs Prince Klemens von Metternich (1773–1859), British foreign secretary Viscount Castlereagh (1769–1822), French minister of foreign affairs Charles Maurice de Talleyrand (1754–1838), the Russian tsar Alexander I (1801–25), and the Prussian king Frederick William III (1797–1840). In spite of personal eccentricities and occasionally outright hostilities among Europe's leaders, all shared a common concern with reestablishing harmony in Europe.

In La Balance Politique, *a cartoon of the Congress of Vienna, Wellington places money on a scales opposite Metternich and the King of Prussia, while Tsar Alexander confers with Talleyrand at the right.*

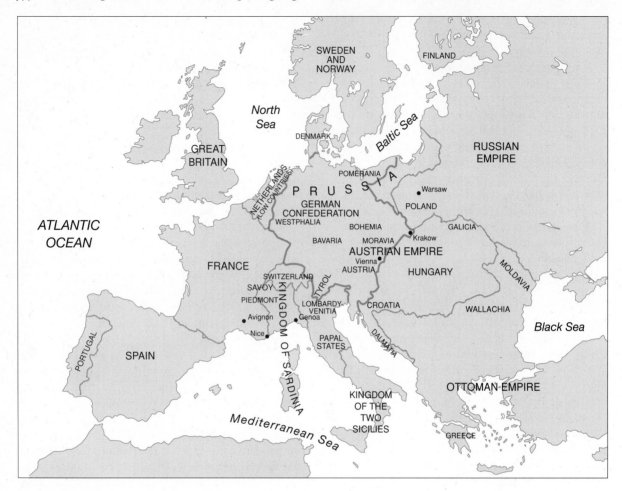

Europe in 1815

The dominant partnership of Austria and Britain at the Congress of Vienna resulted in treaty arrangements that served to restrain the ambitions of Russia and Prussia. No country was to receive territory without giving up something in return, and no one country was to receive enough territory to make it a present or future threat to the peace of Europe. To contain France, some steps taken prior to the Congress were ratified or expanded. In June 1814 the Low Countries had been set up as a unitary state as a buffer against future French expansion on the Continent and a block to the revival of French sea power. The new Kingdom of the Netherlands had been created out of the former Dutch Republic and the Austrian Netherlands and placed under the rule of William I of Orange (1815–40). The Catholic southern provinces were thus uneasily reunited with the Protestant northern provinces, regions that had been separated since the Peace of Westphalia in 1648. Lest there be any doubt about the

intended purpose of this new kingdom, Great Britain gave William I of the Netherlands 2 million pounds to fortify his frontier against France. The reestablishment of a monarchy that united the island kingdom of Sardinia with Piedmont and that included Savoy, Nice, and part of Genoa, contained France on its southeast border. To the east, Prussia was given control of the left bank of the Rhine. Switzerland was reestablished as an independent confederation of cantons. Bourbon rule was restored in Spain on France's southwestern border.

Austria's power was firmly established in Italy, either through outright territorial control or influence over independent states. The Papal States were returned to Pope Pius VII (1800–23), along with territories that had been Napoleon's Cisalpine Republic and the Kingdom of Italy. The Republic of Venice was absorbed into the Austrian empire. Lombardy and the Illyrian provinces on the Dalmatian coast were likewise restored to

Austria. The Italian duchies of Tuscany, Parma, and Modena were placed under the rule of Habsburg princes.

After the fall of Napoleon, the Allies made no attempt to restore the Holy Roman Empire. Napoleon's Confederation of the Rhine, which organized the majority of German territory under French auspices in 1806, was dissolved. In its place the German Confederation was created by reorganizing the three hundred petty states into thirty-eight. The German Confederation was intended as a bulwark against France and not to serve any nationalist or parliamentary function. The thirty-eight states, along with Austria as the thirty-ninth, were represented in a new Federal Diet at Frankfurt, dominated by Austrian influence.

All of these changes were the result of carefully discussed but fairly noncontroversial negotiations. The question of Poland was another matter indeed. Successive partitions by Russia, Austria, and Prussia in 1772, 1793, and 1795 had completely dismembered the land that had been Poland. Napoleon had reconstituted a small portion of Poland as the Grand Duchy of Warsaw. The dilemma of the Congress was what to do with this Napoleonic creation and with Polish territory in general. Fierce debate over Poland threatened to shatter congressional harmony.

Tsar Alexander I of Russia argued for a large Poland that he intended to be fully under his influence and that would extend Russian-controlled territories to the banks of the Oder. He also envisioned extending Russian dominance farther into central and eastern Europe. He based his claim on the significant contribution the Russian army had made to Napoleon's defeat. But such thinking conflicted with Austrian minister Metternich's pursuit of equilibrium.

Frederick William III of Prussia contended that if a large Poland was to be created, Prussia would expect compensation by absorbing Saxony. Both Great Britain and France distrusted Russian and Prussian territorial aims. Talleyrand, the wily and brilliant French negotiator, was able to take advantage of his position of nothing to lose to work out a compromise. As a bishop under the old regime, a revolutionary who managed to keep his head, an exile in America during the Terror, Napoleon's chief minister, and now the representative of a Bourbon monarchy at the Congress, Talleyrand knew something about survival and taking advantage of opportunities. Talleyrand was also a shrewd and experienced diplomat who managed to convince the Allies to accept France, their defeated enemy, as an equal partner in negotia-

tions. In the midst of the crisis over Poland, he persuaded Britain and Austria to sign a secret treaty with France to preserve an independent Polish territory. He then deliberately leaked news of the secret agreement of these powers to go to war, if necessary, to block Russian and Prussian aims. Alexander I and Frederick William III immediately backed down.

In the final arrangement, Prussia retained the Polish territory of Posen, and Austria kept the Polish province of Galicia. Kraków, with its population of 95,000, was declared a free city. Finally, a kingdom of Poland, nominally independent but in fact under the tutelage of Russia, emerged from what remained of the Grand Duchy of Warsaw.

In addition to receiving Polish territories, Prussia gained two-fifths of the kingdom of Saxony. Prussia also received territory on the left bank of the Rhine, the Duchy of Westphalia, and Swedish Pomerania. With these acquisitions Prussia doubled its population to around 11 million people. The Junkers, the landed class of east Prussia, reversed many of the reforms of the Napoleonic period. The new territories that Prussia gained were rich in waterways and resources but geographically fragmented. The dispersal of holdings that was intended to contain Prussian power in central Europe spurred Prussia to find new ways of uniting its markets. In this endeavor, Prussia constituted a future threat to Austrian power over the German Confederation.

In Scandinavia, Russia's conquest of Finland was acknowledged by the members of the Congress and, in return, Sweden acquired Norway from Denmark. Unlike Austria, Prussia, and Russia, Great Britain made no claim to territories at the Congress. Having achieved its aim of containing France, its greatest rival for dominance on the seas, Britain returned the French colonies it had seized in war. The redrawing of the territorial map of Europe had achieved its pragmatic aim of guaranteeing the peace. It was now left to a system of alliances to preserve that peace.

The Alliance System

Only by joining forces had the European powers been able to defeat Napoleon, and the necessity of a system of alliances was recognized even after the battles were over. Two alliance pacts dominated the post-Napoleonic era: the renewed Quadruple Alliance and the Holy Alliance. The Quadruple Alliance, signed by the victorious powers of Great Britain, Austria, Russia, and Prussia in November 1815, was intended to protect Europe against future French aggression and to preserve the status quo. In 1818 France, having completed its payment of war indemnities, joined the pact, which now became the Quintuple Alliance. The five powers promised to meet periodically over the next twenty years to discuss common problems and to ensure the peace.

The Holy Alliance, very different in tone and intent, was the brainchild of Alexander I and was heavily influenced by his mystical view of international politics. In this pact the monarchs of Prussia, Austria, and Russia agreed to renounce war and to protect the Christian religion. The Holy Alliance spoke of "the bonds of a true and indissoluble brotherhood . . . to protect religion, peace, and justice." Russia was able to give some credibility to the alliance with the sheer size of its army. Career diplomats were aware of the hollowness of the Holy Alliance as a treaty arrangement, but it did indicate the willingness of Europe's three eastern autocracies to intervene in the affairs of other states.

The concept of Europe acting as a whole, through a system of periodic conferences, marked the emergence of a new diplomatic era. Conflict, however, was inherent in the commitment of parliamentary governments to open consultation and the need for secrecy in diplomacy. Dynastic regimes sought to intervene in smaller states to buoy up despots. That certainly seemed to be the case in 1822, when European powers met to consider restoring the Bourbon monarchy in Spain. The British, acting as a counterbalance to revolutionary tendencies, refused to cooperate and blocked united action by the Alliance. France took military action on its own in 1823, restored King Ferdinand VII, and abolished the Spanish constitution.

Both in the Congress of Vienna and the system of alliances that succeeded it, European nations aimed to establish a balance of power that recognized legitimate rulers and preserved the peace. The upheaval of the French Revolution and the revolutionary and Napoleonic wars had made clear the interdependence of one nation on another as a guarantee of survival. Europe's statesmen hoped, erroneously as it turned out, that by keeping the peace abroad, domestic peace would follow.

The New European Society

The peace that emerged from the Congress of Vienna did not restore the old order, although it did preserve principles of rule that a property-owning elite held dear. The search for stability, restoration, and the reaction to change characterized national and international affairs after 1815. Social structure and the world of production were undergoing dramatic transformations, and European states had to reckon with the fact that the daily lives of growing numbers of their subjects were transformed between 1815 and 1850. The demands of an international balance of power stood poised against the internal assaults on old social values in new arenas of conflict. Urbanization, industrialization, and economic uncertainties challenged Europeans in new ways in their search for stability.

Urban Miseries

In 1800, two of every one hundred Europeans lived in a city. By 1850, the number of urban dwellers per hundred had jumped to five and was rising rapidly. In England, the shift was more concentrated than the general European pattern. With one of every two people living in a city, England had become an urban society by mid-century. London was the fastest growing city in Europe, followed at some distance by Paris and Berlin. The numbers of smaller urban centers were also multiplying.

Balancing Power in Europe, 1815–1823

May 1814	First Peace of Paris
23 September 1814 to 9 June 1815	Congress of Vienna
26 September 1815	Formation of the Holy Alliance
20 November 1815	Second Peace of Paris; formation of the Quadruple Alliance
November 1818	Quadruple Alliance expands to include France in Quintuple Alliance
1823	French restoration of Bourbon monarchy in Spain

This sketch of a lane in St. Giles, the notorious London slum, was made in the 1840s. Such squalor and overcrowding contributed to the miseries of the working class. Note the pig, which confronts a dog on its scavenging rounds.

Massive internal migration caused most urban growth. People from the same rural areas often lived together in the same urban neighborhoods and even in the same boardinghouses. Irish emigrants crowded together in the "Little Dublin" section of London. Similarly, districts in other cities were set off by regional accents and native provincial dress. Workers from the same hometowns gravitated to their favorite cafes. These social networks helped make the transition from rural to urban life bearable for the tens of thousands of people who poured into Europe's cities in search of jobs and opportunity. Until mid-century, many migrants returned to their rural homes for the winter when work, especially in the building trades, was scarce in the city. Young migrant women who came to the city to work as servants sent money home to support rural relatives, or worked to save a nest egg—or dowry—in order to return

to the village permanently. Before 1850, 20 percent of the workers in London were domestics, and most of them were women.

Despite the support networks that migrants constructed for themselves, the city was not always a hospitable place. Workers were poorly paid and women workers were more poorly paid than men. When working women were cut free of the support of home and family, uncounted numbers were forced into part-time prostitution to supplement meager incomes. More and more women resorted to prostitution as a means of surviving in times of unemployment. It is conservatively estimated that there were 34,000 prostitutes in Paris in 1850 and 50,000 in London. The phenomenon of prostitution indicated changing mores about sexuality in the first half of the nineteenth century. The "angel" of middle-class households and the "whore" of the streets were subjects of fascination in literature. Increased prostitution created an epidemic of venereal diseases, especially syphilis, for which there was no cure until the twentieth century.

Urban crime also grew astronomically, with thefts accounting for the greatest number of crimes. Social reformers identified poverty and urban crowding as causes of the increase in criminal behavior. In 1829 both Paris and London began to create modern urban police forces to deal with the challenges to law and order. Crime assumed the character of disease in the minds of middle-class reformers. Statisticians and social scientists, themselves a new urban phenomenon, produced massive theses on social hygiene, lowerclass immorality, and the unworthiness of the poor. The pathology of the city was widely discussed. Always at the center of the issue was the "social question": the growing problem of what to do with the poor.

The Social Question

State-sponsored work relief expanded after 1830 for the deserving poor: the old, the sick, and children. Ablebodied workers who were idle were regarded as undeserving and dangerous, regardless of the causes of their unemployment. Performance of work became an indicator of moral worth, as urban and rural workers succumbed to downturns in the economic cycle. Those unable to work sought relief, as a last resort, from the state. What has been called "a revolution in government" took place in the 1830s and 1840s, as legislative bodies increased regulation of everything from factories and mines to prisons and schools.

Poverty was not just an urban problem, although it was both more conspicuous and more feared in urban areas. Politicians, social reformers, religious thinkers, and revolutionaries all had different solutions that followed one of two general orientations. There were those who argued, as in the case of the Irish famine, that the government must do nothing to intervene because the problem would correct itself, as Thomas Malthus had predicted forty years earlier, through the "natural" means of famine and death that would keep population from outgrowing available resources and food supplies. The Irish population, one of the poorest in Europe, had indeed doubled between 1781 and 1841, and for Malthusians, the Irish famine was the fulfillment of their vision that famine was the only way to correct overpopulation. Poverty was a social necessity; by interfering with it, this first group insisted, governments could only make matters worse.

A second group contended that poverty was society's problem, and perhaps society's creation, and not a law of nature. Thus, it was the social responsibility of the state to take care of its members. The question of how to treat poverty, or "the social question" as it came to be known among contemporaries, underlay many of the protests and reforms of the two decades before 1850 and fueled the revolutionary movements of 1848. Parliamentary legislation attempted to improve the situation of the poor and especially the working class in the 1830s and 1840s.

In 1833 British reformers turned their attention to the question of child labor. Against the opposition of those who argued for a free market for labor, Parliament passed the Factory Act of 1833, which prohibited the employment of children under nine years of age and restricted the work week of children aged nine to thirteen to forty-eight hours. No child in this age group could work more than nine hours a day. Teenagers between thirteen and eighteen years could work no more than sixty-nine hours a week. By modern standards, these "reformed" workloads present a shocking picture of the heavy reliance on child labor. The British Parliament commissioned investigations, compiled in the "Blue Books," that reported the abusive treatment of men, women, and children in factories. Similar studies existed for French and Belgian industry.

The British legislation marked an initial step in state intervention in the workplace. Additional legislation over the next three decades further restricted children's and women's labor in factories and concerned itself with improvement of conditions in the workplace. At bottom the social question was the question of what was the state's role and responsibility in caring for its citizens.

Smaller Families, Higher Hopes

Industrialization profoundly altered the structure of daily life within the family during the first half of the nineteenth century. Changes affected both middle-class and working-class families, although to varying degrees. With the rise of the state and a growing emphasis on education, the socialization role of the family was gradually transformed by the rise of public institutions. By mid-century population growth was beginning to slow down throughout Europe, as people were choosing to restrict the size of their families. Europeans of earlier times had delayed marriage, practiced birth control, and

This satiric cartoon is one of a series by Robert Cruikshank castigating the English factory system and its treatment of child labor.

RECALLING A CHILDHOOD IN THE FACTORY

■ *In the early 1830s, philanthropists and reformers demanded that the British government do something about the appalling abuses of children laboring in textile factories. In response to public outcry, parliamentary commissions interviewed thousands of women and children workers and compiled a record of horrifying exploitation and abuse.*

These investigations resulted in legislation that limited the work hours of children, provided for inspection of work conditions by state agents, and required that young workers receive educational instruction.

Eliza Marshall, who was eighteen at the time she gave the following testimony before the Factory Inquiry Commission, recalled her childhood in the factory. Crippled by the tasks she performed and beaten frequently by her employer, she endured a grueling life of factory discipline typical of that of legions of children who helped Britain maintain its industrial dominance.

I was turned ten when I began to work from five [a.m.] to nine [p.m.]. My sister was nine. There were older than me at Burgess'. Mr. Warburton picked us out, I suppose, because I was sharp at my work, a good hand: so was my sister. I was forced to go to work. I had no father, and my mother could not keep us without working. My mother is dead now. She died about half a year ago, since I was in London. I worked on at Warburton's till better than a year ago. I worked those hours all the time. We sometimes worked from six [a.m.] to seven [p.m.], but it was mostly from five to nine. He has got nearly two rooms full now: when I left him, there were about fifteen hands or so. I went from there to the Infirmary . . .

It was the work and hours together that hurt me, and always having to stop the flies* with my knee. I could stop it with my hand, but I had to hold it with my knee while I pieced it.† It was having to crook my knee to stop the spindle that lamed me as much as any thing else.

*Cylinders of a carding machine.
†To join together broken threads.

From Great Britain, *Parliamentary Papers*, 1833.

---

employed abortion to limit family size. But the nineteenth century marks the first time in history that the majority of Europeans recognized that having fewer children was a value and acted on it.

Why decisions about limiting family size were made and how they were implemented are among the most intimate and private of questions, whose answers can never really be known. But there is no doubt about the outcome of these decisions: people began having two or three children per family, instead of five or six. Economic motivation appears to have been primary. In the nineteenth century, children had little economic value as laborers with their elimination from the workplace. The hope of a better life for one's progeny required that existing resources be concentrated on fewer children. The middle-class pattern of small families became the domi-

nant one in western Europe in the nineteenth century, as middle-class culture became more self-conscious.

Jane Austen (1775–1817), one of Europe's great novelists, created a picture of middle-class life in nineteenth-century England and of women's place in it. In *Pride and Prejudice* (1813) and *Emma* (1815), parents and guardians wait helplessly on the sidelines, hoping their charges will marry well. Young people, freed from the arranged marriages of the previous century, choose mates on the basis of affection and affinity. The couple is a locus for personal fulfillment. Yet the middle-class family exists in a network of value and status. In Austen's novels families are ranked according to their consumption of furniture, carriages, and pianofortes; the numbers of their servants; and the frequency of their trips to London. Austen chronicles the importance of income for marriage and status in a money-oriented society. The family is the primary arena of consumption.

The privacy of family life intensified with the transfer of paid work to a public workplace. Middle-class Europeans, whether French, German, or British, shared with Austen's families a taste for decorated interiors and material comforts in the home. In Germany, the Biedermeier style, named after a popular furniture-maker, appeared in 1815 and remained popular until mid-century. Biedermeier stressed coziness, intimacy, and domesticity in the furnishing, clothes, and paintings of the German middle class. To its critics the style was sentimental and vulgar. During this era middle-class consumers began collecting on a mass scale. They filled their homes with knickknacks, curios, and mass-produced art. By accumulating these objects, the middle class asserted its right as an arbiter of its own style. At the same time middle-class collectors aped the great aristocratic connoisseurs of a previous age.

A vast gulf separated working-class families from these middle-class consumers. Factory owner and social critic Friedrich Engels (1820–95) left a bleak but accurate account of working-class life in Manchester in *The Condition of the Working Class in England in 1844*. Working women, unsupervised children, and unemployed husbands figured prominently in his brutal tale of misery and immorality. Western culture redefined family life as the seat of solace, comfort, and consumption, but for the majority of the population that ideal remained out of reach.

Reformers confronted the disparities in family life and placed the blame squarely on women's absence from the home. Women had made industrialization possible, as they poured into the British and Continental textile factories and became the primary workforce. Employers found women more adept and more dexterous than men in running the intricate new looms. Women worked for cheaper wages and were generally more docile than men in accepting the routinization of the factory. Men were considered more likely to organize, to riot, and to become rowdy. Women and children worked long hours under dire conditions. The number of women in factories was expanding rapidly in the 1830s and 1840s. The solution to the perceived decline in the working-class family was found in legislation to restrict women from the workplace and return them to the home to care for their husbands and children. Children were an even cheaper workforce than women. Some proponents of child labor argued that the choice was to have children running wild in the streets and unsupervised at home or in the disciplined environment of the factories. The situation at its worst was reflected in one eyewitness account of French silk manufacture. For eighteen hours a day six-year-old girls were harnessed to mechanical wheels to work.

Women's rights, little affected by industrialization, were increasingly disputed in public forums after 1815. In France, the equality of citizens before the law did not extend to women. Women's subservience in marriage was clearly defined: "A husband owes protection to his wife, a wife obedience to her husband." The law preserved a double standard for judging the behavior of women and men. In English law, men could terminate their marriages but their wives had no such access to divorce. Agitation for the right to divorce converged with notorious public scandals over abused married

A bourgeois living room of pre-1848 Vienna. Such rooms were designed to promote the social life and cultural interests of the family unit. There was a musical corner and areas for conversation and reading.

FROM *SENECA FALLS RESOLUTIONS*, NEW YORK, 1848

■ One of the most influential meetings in furthering the claims of women to full participation in civil life occurred at Seneca Falls, New York, in 1848. The women present, many of them active in the antislavery and temperance movements, included Elizabeth Cady Stanton (1815–1902) and Susan B. Anthony (1820–1906). In 1840, eight years before Seneca Falls, Stanton and other abolitionists attended an international slavery convention in London. The exclusion of the women delegates from the floor of the London convention shocked Stanton and her female colleagues and served as a turning point in their own political consciousness. Their resolutions at Seneca Falls, especially regarding the right to vote, influenced burgeoning women's movements in Europe and the United States.

Resolved, That such laws as conflict, in any way, with the true and substantial happiness of woman, are contrary to the great precept of nature and of no validity, for this is "superior in obligation to any other."

Resolved, That all laws which prevent woman from occupying such a station in society as her conscience shall dictate, or which place her in a position inferior to that of man, are contrary to the great precept of nature, and therefore of no force or authority.

Resolved, That woman is man's equal—was intended to be so by the Creator, and the highest good of the race demands that she should be recognized as such.

Resolved, That the women of this country ought to be enlightened in regard to the laws under which they live, that they may no longer publish their degradation by declaring themselves satisfied with their present position, nor their ignorance, by asserting that they have all the rights they want.

Resolved, That inasmuch as man, while claiming for himself intellectual superiority, does accord to woman moral superiority, it is pre-eminently his duty to encourage her to speak and teach, as she has an opportunity, in all religious assemblies.

Resolved, That the same amount of virtue, delicacy, and refinement of behavior that is required of woman in the social state, should also be required of man, and the same transgressions should be visited with equal severity on both man and woman.

Resolved, That the objection of indelicacy and impropriety, which is so often brought against woman when she addresses a public audience, comes with a very ill-grace from those who encourage, by their attendance, her appearance on the stage, in the concert, or in feats of the circus.

Resolved, That woman has too long rested satisfied in the circumscribed limits which corrupt customs and a perverted application of the Scriptures have marked out for her, and that it is time she should move in the enlarged sphere which her great Creator has assigned her.

Resolved, That it is the duty of the women of this country to secure to themselves their sacred right to the elective franchise.

Resolved, That the equality of human rights results necessarily from the fact of the identity of the race in capabilities and responsibilities.

Resolved, therefore, That, being invested by the Creator with the same capabilities, and the same consciousness of responsibility for their exercise, it is demonstrably the right and duty of woman, equally with man, to promote every righteous cause by every righteous means; and especially in regard to the great subjects of morals and religion, it is self-evidently her right to participate with her brother in teaching them, both in private and in public, by writing and by speaking, by any instrumentalities proper to be used, and in any assemblies proper to be held; and this being a self-evident truth growing out of the divinely implanted principles of human nature, any custom or authority adverse to it, whether modern or wearing the hoary sanction of antiquity, is to be regarded as a self-evident falsehood, and at war with mankind.

Resolved, That the speedy success of our cause depends upon the zealous and untiring efforts of both men and women, for the overthrow of the monopoly of the pulpit, and for the securing to woman an equal participation with men in the various trades, professions, and commerce.

women. Critics blamed the decline in sexual mores on women's refusal to "know their place." By the mid-nineteenth century women were organizing to demand equal political rights, political representation, assistance in caring for children, and better living conditions. Through their own newspapers, journals, and pamphlets bourgeois women publicized their political demands for all women. John Stuart Mill, the leading liberal theorist, joined with women reformers in demanding full equality for British women. These movements achieved little in solid reforms before 1850, but they made clear the tensions within the family and within the law.

The growing emphasis on public education added its own special twist to the debate over family life and women's rights. Few agreed with French labor leader Flora Tristan (1801-44) and the utopian reformer Charles Fourier (1772-1837) that women had the capacity and the right to receive an equal education with men. Most argued that women should be educated only to fulfill better their natural responsibilities as mothers. Napoleon's dictum, "The hand that rocks the cradle rules the nation," became the chief justification for educating girls as mothers.

In 1837 in Great Britain, an eighteen-year-old young woman became queen. Reigning until her death in 1901, Victoria gave her name to an age and its morals. Girls became queens of Portugal and Spain. But they, like the young Victoria, were little more than political figureheads, protecting the survival of dynastic claims and contributing little to the growing debate about women's proper place in society. Although the presence of women on European thrones may have provided inspiration for disenfranchised women, it did not affect the broader reality that everywhere women were deprived of the vote and equal protection before the law, that married women could not own property or claim custody of their own children. Victoria, ruler of one of the world's great nations, became the model for domestic bliss. The changing expectations about the emotional rewards of family life, reflected in the publicity of the queen's marriage to Prince Albert of Saxe-Coburg-Gotha in 1840, created a new image of proper womanhood that had little relation to the lives that most women led.

To Western societies that had remained stable, if not stagnant, for centuries, the changes in the first half of the nineteenth century were undoubtedly startling and disruptive. More people than ever before lived in cities, as national populations faced the prospect of becoming urban. Industrialization reshaped the ways people worked, the ways they lived, and the ways they consumed. But change did not mean improvement. Urban congestion brought crime and disease; new factories created the arena for exploitation and misery; and patterns of consumption demonstrated beyond dispute that people were not created equal. New expectations were attached to the family as its size changed and gender roles underwent redefinition. A new European society was in the process of emerging that challenged existing political ideas and demanded new formulations.

The New Ideologies

Early industrialization had been accomplished without a dramatically new technology. Wood, water, wind, and muscle—animal and human—the sources of energy in the preindustrial period, fueled the early stages of industrialization. Practices began to change slowly as crises in energy supply—deforestation and drought, for example—encouraged the use of coal as a more reliable and eventually more efficient fuel. After 1815, steam-driven mechanical power in production and transportation steadily replaced human and animal power. In deference to what it was replacing, the new mechanical force was measured in units of horsepower. The new technology challenged old values; new definitions of worth emerged from the changing world of work. The fixed, castelike distinctions of the old aristocratic world were under attack or in disarray. Western intellectuals struggled with the changes of the new age as they sought to make sense of the way in which Europeans lived, looked at the world, and defined their place in it.

The political and economic upheavals of the first half of the nineteenth century encouraged a new breed of thinkers to search for ways to explain the transformations of the period. Before mid-century Europeans witnessed one of the most intellectually fertile periods in the history of the West. This era gave birth to new ideologies—liberalism, nationalism, romanticism, conservatism, and socialism—that came to shape the ideas and institutions of the present day.

Liberalism

The term *liberal* was first used in a narrow, political sense to indicate the Spanish party of reform that supported the constitution modeled on the French document of 1791. But the term assumed much broader connotations in the first half of the nineteenth century as its appeal spread among the European middle classes. The two main tenets of belief that underlay liberalism were the freedom of the individual and the corruptibility of authority. As a political doctrine, liberalism built on Enlightenment rationalism and embraced the right to vote, civil liberties, legal equality, constitutional government, parliamentary sovereignty, and a free-market economy. Liberals firmly believed that less government was better government and that noninterference would produce a harmonious and well-ordered world. They also believed that human beings were basically good and reasonable and needed freedom in which to flourish. The sole end of government should be to promote that freedom.

No single representative thinker embodied all the tenets of liberal thought, but many shared similar ideas and beliefs. Liberal thinkers tried to make sense of the political conflicts of the revolutionary period and the economic disruptions brought on by industrialization. The Great Revolution at the end of the eighteenth century spawned a vast array of liberal thought in France. Republicans, Bonapartists, and constitutional monarchists cooperated as self-styled "liberals," who shared a desire to preserve the gains of the Revolution while ensuring orderly rule.

Not least influenced by liberal ideas were a variety of political movements in the United States, including those demanding the liberation of slaves and the extension of legal and political rights to women. Abolitionists justified their opposition to slavery both on humanitarian, Christian grounds and on the liberal principles of freedom and equality. Women who were active in antislavery societies extended their liberal crusade against oppression to their own legal and political status.

By the mid-nineteenth century, liberal thinking constituted a dominant strain in British politics. Jeremy Bentham (1748–1832) founded utilitarianism, a fundamentally liberal doctrine that argued for "the greatest happiness of the greatest number" in such works as *Introduction to the Principles of Morals and Legislation.* Bentham believed that government could achieve positive ends through limited and "scientific" intervention. John Stuart Mill (1806–73) forged his own brand of classical liberalism in his treatise *On Liberty* (1859). Mill went beyond existing political analyses to apply economic doctrines to social conditions in *Principles of Political Economy* (1848). He espoused social reform for the poor and championed the equality of women and the necessity of birth control. David Ricardo (1772–1823),

in *Principles of Political Economy and Taxation* (1817), outlined his opposition to government intervention in foreign trade and elaborated his "iron law of wages," which contended that wages would stabilize at the subsistence level. Increased wages would cause the working classes to increase, and the resulting competition in the labor market would drive wages down to the subsistence level.

Nationalism

In its most basic sense, nationalism before 1850 was the political doctrine that glorified the people united against the absolutism of kings and the tyranny of foreign oppressors. The success of the French Revolution

This model prison, called the Panopticon, was designed by Jeremy Bentham, a British social philosopher who believed that government could achieve positive ends through limited and "scientific" intervention. The circular arrangement allowed a centrally located guard to monitor all outside cells.

and the spread of Napoleonic reforms boosted nationalist doctrines, which were most fully articulated on the Continent. In Germany, Johann Gottfried von Herder (1744–1803) rooted national identity in German folk culture. The *Fairy Tales* (1812–14) of the brothers Jacob Ludwig Grimm (1785–1863) and Wilhelm Carl Grimm (1786–1859) had a similar national purpose. The brothers painstakingly captured in print the German oral tradition of peasant folklore. The philosophers Johann Fichte (1762–1814) and Georg Wilhelm Friedrich Hegel (1770–1831) emphasized the importance of the state. There was a new concern with history, as nationalists sought to revive a common cultural past.

In the period between 1830 and 1850, many nationalists were liberals and many liberals were nationalists. The nationalist yearning for liberation meshed with the liberal political program of overthrowing tyrannical rule. Giuseppe Mazzini (1805–72) represented the new breed of liberal nationalist. A less-than-liberal nationalist was political economist Georg Friedrich List (1789–1846), who formulated a statement of economic nationalism to counter the liberal doctrines of David Ricardo. Arguing that free trade worked only for the wealthy and powerful, List advocated a program of protective tariffs for developing German industries. British free trade, he perceived, was merely economic imperialism in disguise. List was one of the few nationalists who did not wholeheartedly embrace liberal economic doctrines. Beyond ideology and political practices, nationalism began to capture the imagination of groups who resented foreign domination. Expanding state bureaucracies did little to tame the centrifugal forces of nationalist feeling and probably exacerbated a desire for independence in eastern and central Europe, especially in the Habsburg-ruled lands.

Romanticism

Unlike liberalism and nationalism, which were fundamentally political ideologies, romanticism designated a variety of literary and artistic movements throughout Europe that spanned the period from the late eighteenth century to the mid-nineteenth century. One could be a nationalist and a romantic or a liberal and a romantic just as easily as one could hold opposite political views and be a follower of romanticism. Above all and in spite of variations, romantics shared similar beliefs and a common view of the world. Among the first romantics were the English poets William Wordsworth (1770–1850) and Samuel Taylor Coleridge (1772–1834), whose collaborative *Lyrical Ballads*

(1798) exemplified the iconoclastic romantic idea that poetry was the result of "the spontaneous overflow of powerful feelings," rather than a formal and highly disciplined intellectual exercise. Romantics in general rebelled against the confinement of classical forms and refused to accept the supremacy of reason over emotions.

By rooting artistic vision in spontaneity, romantics endorsed a concept of creativity based on the supremacy of human freedom. The artist was valued in a new way as a genius through whose insight and intuition great art was created. Intuition, opposed to scientific learning, was endorsed as a valid means of knowing. Building on the work of the eighteenth-century philosopher Immanuel Kant (1724–1804), romanticism embraced subjective knowledge. Inspiration and intuition took the place of reason and science in the romantic pantheon of values.

Germaine de Staël (1766–1817), often hailed as the founder of French romanticism, was an extraordinary woman whose writings influenced French liberal political theory after 1815. De Staël authored histories, novels, literary criticism, and political tracts that opposed what she judged to be the tyranny of Napoleonic rule. She, like many other romantics, was greatly influenced by the writings of Jean-Jacques Rousseau, and through him she discovered that "the soul's elevation is born of self-consciousness." The recognition of the subjective meant for De Staël that women's vision was as essential as men's for the flowering of European culture.

By searching for the self in a historic past, and especially in the Middle Ages, German romantics glorified their collective cultural identity and national origins. Medievalism in Germany was at the heart of *Sturm und Drang* (Storm and Stress), a literary movement founded in the 1770s. A founder of the *Sturm und Drang* movement, Johann Wolfgang von Goethe (1749–1832), hailed as the greatest of modern German writers, inspired generations with his dramatic poem *Faust* (Part I: 1808; Part II: 1832). In the poem, Goethe recounts the traditional legend of a man who sells his soul to the devil in exchange for greater knowledge. Faust, who achieves mystical salvation in the poem's final scene, symbolizes for Goethe the spiritual crisis plaguing European civilization in the early nineteenth century.

The supremacy of emotions over reason found its way into the works of the great romantic composers of the age. Liberation from the forms that dominated the classical era could be heard in the works of French composer Louis Hector Berlioz (1803–69), who set Faust's

Mephistopheles, *an engraving by the French artist Eugène Delacroix for Goethe's* Faust.

damnation to music; Polish virtuoso Frederic Chopin (1810–49), who created lyric compositions for the piano; and Hungarian concert pianist Franz Liszt (1811–86), who composed symphonic poems and Hungarian rhapsodies. Artists such as J. M. W. Turner (1775–1851), the English landscape painter, and Eugene Delacroix (1798–1863), the leader of the French romantic school in painting, shared a rebellious experimentation with color and a rejection of classical conventions and forms.

In the postrevolutionary age of the years between 1815 and 1850, romanticism claimed to be no more than an aesthetic stance in art, letters, and music, a posture that had no particular political intent. Yet its validation of the individual as opposed to the caste or the estate was the most revolutionary of doctrines. The romantics helped shape a new way of looking at the world and helped define a new political consciousness.

Conservatism

Conservatism was not a rejection of political, economic, and social change. Like liberalism, conservatism represented a dynamic adaptation to a social system in transition. In place of individualism, conservatives stressed

the corporate nature of European society; in place of reason and progress, conservatives saw organic growth and tradition. Liberty, argued British statesman Edmund Burke (1729–97) in *Reflections on the Revolution in France* (1790), must emerge out of the gradual development of the old order and not its destruction. On the Continent, conservatives Louis de Bonald (1754–1840) and Joseph de Maistre (1753–1821) defended the monarchical principle of authority against the onslaught of revolutionary events.

Conservatism took a reactionary turn in the hands of the Austrian statesman Prince Klemens von Metternich. The Carlsbad decrees of 1819 are a good example of the "Metternich system" of espionage, censorship, and university repression in central Europe, which sought to eliminate any constitutional or nationalist sentiments that had arisen during the Napoleonic period. The German Confederation approved the decrees against free speech and civil liberties and set up mechanisms to root out "subversive" university students. Students who had taken up arms in the Wars of Liberation (1813–15) against France had done so in hopes of instituting liberal and national reforms. Metternich's system aimed at uprooting these goals. Student fraternities were closed and police became a regular fixture in the university. Political expression was driven underground for at least a decade. Metternich set out to crush liberalism, constitutionalism, and parliamentarianism in central Europe. His goals, although tolerated, were certainly not shared by more liberal regimes such as Great Britain's.

Socialism

Socialism, like other ideologies of the first half of the nineteenth century, grew out of the changes in the structure of daily life and the structure of power. There were as many stripes of socialists as there were liberals, nationalists, and conservatives.

Socialist thinkers in France theorized about alternative societies in which wealth would be more equitably distributed. To Henri de Saint-Simon (1760–1825) the accomplishments and potential of industrial development represented the highest stage in history. In a perfect and just society, productive work would be the basis of all prestige and power. The elite of society would be organized according to the hierarchy of its productive members, with industrial leaders at the top. Like Saint-Simon, the French social theorist Pierre Joseph Proudhon (1809–65) recognized the social value of work. But unlike Saint-Simon, Proudhon refused to accept the dominance of industrial society. Proudhon gained national prominence with his ideas about a just society, free credit, and equitable exchange. In his famous pamphlet, *What Is Property?* (1840), Proudhon answered, "Property is theft." This statement was not, however, an argument for the abolition of private ownership. Proudhon reasoned that industrialization had destroyed workers' rights, which included the right to the profits of their own labor. In attacking "property" in its meaning of profits amassed from the labor of others, Proudhon was arguing for a socialist concept of limited possession—people had the right to own only what they had earned from their own labor—and for a potentially anarchist concept of limited government—people had the right to rule themselves.

At least one socialist believed in luxury. Charles Fourier, an unsuccessful traveling salesman, devoted himself to the study and improvement of society and formulated one of the most trenchant criticisms of industrial capitalism. In numerous writings between 1808 and his death, this eccentric, solitary man put forth his vision of a utopian world organized into units called phalanxes, that took into account the social, sexual, and economic needs of their members. With a proper mix of duties, everyone in the phalanx would work only a few hours a day. In Fourier's scheme, work was not naturally abhorrent, but care had to be taken to match temperaments with tasks. Women and men fulfilled themselves and found pleasure and gratification through work. People would be paid according to their contributions in work, capital, and talent. In Fourier's phalanxes, every aspect of life would be organized communally, although neither poverty nor property would be eliminated. Education would help eliminate discord and rich and poor would learn to live together in perfect harmony.

Charles Fourier's work, along with that of Saint-Simon and Proudhon, became part of the tradition of utopian thinking that can be traced back to Thomas More in the sixteenth century. Because he believed in the ability of individuals to shape themselves and their world, Fourier intended his critique of society to be a blueprint for living. Fourier's followers set up communities in his lifetime. Forty phalanxes were established in the United States alone; because of financial frustrations and petty squabbling, all of them failed. The emancipation of women was an issue acknowledged by socialists as well as liberals. Some social reformers, including Fourier, put the issue of women's freedom at the center of their plans to redesign society.

Intellectuals and reformers hoped with the force of their ideas to reshape the world in which they lived. Yet the new ideologies were themselves a consequence of the changing role of government and the changing practices of daily life. The technology of industrial production informed people's values and required a new way of looking at the world. Liberals, nationalists, romantics, conservatives, and socialists addressed the challenges of a changing economy in a political universe buffeted by democratic ideas. Rather than providing neat answers, ideologies fueled actions, as solutions, often violent, erupted in protest and revolution in the streets.

Protest and Revolution

Few Europeans alive in 1830 remembered the age of revolution from 1789 to 1799. Yet the legends were kept alive from one generation to the next. Secret political organizations perpetuated Jacobin republicanism. Mutual-aid societies and artisan associations preserved the rituals of democratic culture. A revolutionary culture seemed to be budding in the student riots in Germany and in the revolutionary waves that swept across southern and central Europe in the early 1820s. Outside Manchester, England, in August 1819 a crowd of 80,000 people gathered in St. Peter's Field to hear speeches for parliamentary reform and universal male suffrage. The cavalry swept down on them in a bloody slaughter that came to be known as the "Peterloo" massacre, a bitter reference to the Waterloo victory four years before.

The fabric of stability began unraveling throughout Europe beginning in the 1820s, proceeding at varying rates throughout the 1830s and 1840s, and culminating in a Europe-wide explosion of revolutionary action in 1848.

The forces of order reacted to protest with repression everywhere in Europe. In the more industrialized countries of England and France, the army was joined and replaced by the new peacekeeping forces of the police. Yet armed force proved insufficient to contain the demands for political participation and the increased political awareness of whole segments of the population. Workers, the middle class, and women's political organizations no longer expected that elites would solve

A savage satire of the Peterloo Massacre by cartoonist George Cruikshank. One soldier urges the others on by telling them that the more poor people they kill, the less taxes they will have to pay for poor relief.

their problems but now demanded, through the vote, the right to govern themselves.

The Revolutions of 1830

In France the late 1820s was a period of increasing political friction. Charles X (1824–30), the former comte d'Artois, had never resigned himself to the constitutional monarchy accepted by his brother and predecessor, Louis XVIII. When Charles assumed the throne in 1824, he dedicated himself to a true restoration of kingship as it existed before the Revolution. To this end, he realigned the monarchy with the Catholic church and undertook several unpopular measures, including approval of the death penalty for those found guilty of sacrilege. The king's bourgeois critics, heavily influenced by liberal ideas about political economy and constitutional rights, sought increased political power through their activities in secret organizations and in public elections. The king responded to his critics by relying on his ultraroyalist supporters to run the government. In May 1830 the king dissolved the Chamber of Deputies and ordered new elections. The elections returned a liberal majority unfavorable to the king. Charles X retaliated with what proved to be his last political act, the Four Ordinances, in which he censored the press, changed the electoral law to favor his own candidates, dissolved the newly elected Chamber, and ordered new elections.

Opposition to Charles X might have remained at the level of political wrangling and journalistic protest, if it had not been for the problems plaguing the people of Paris. A severe winter in France had driven up food

Revolutions of 1830–1848

In southern Europe, Turkish overlords ruled Greece as part of the Ottoman Empire. The longing for independence smoldered in Greece throughout the 1820s as public pressure to support the Greeks mounted in Europe. Greek insurrections were answered by Turkish retaliations throughout the Ottoman Empire. The sultan of Turkey had been able to call upon his vassal, the pasha of Egypt, to subdue Greece. In response Great Britain, France, and Russia signed the Treaty of London in 1827, pledging intervention on behalf of Greece. In a joint effort, the three powers defeated the Egyptian fleet.

Russia declared war on Turkey the following year, seeking territorial concessions from the Ottoman Empire. Following the Russian victory, Great Britain and France joined Russia in declaring Greek independence. The concerted action of the three powers in favor of Greek independence was neither an endorsement of liberal ideals nor a support of Greek nationalism. The British, French, and Russians were reasserting their commitment made at the Congress of Vienna to territorial stability.

The overthrow of the Bourbon monarch in France served as a model for revolution in other parts of Europe. Following the French lead, in the midst of the Greek crisis the Belgian provinces revolted against the Netherlands. The Belgians' desire for their own nation struck at the heart of the Vienna settlement. Provoked by a food crisis similar to that in France, Belgian revolutionaries took to the streets in August 1830. Belgians protested the deterioration of their economic situation and made demands for their own Catholic religion, their own language, and constitutional rights. Bitter fighting on the barricades in Brussels ensued and the movement for freedom and independence spread to the countryside.

The Great Powers disagreed on what to do. Russia, Austria, and Prussia were all eager to see the revolution crushed. France, having just established the new regime of the July Monarchy, and Great Britain, fearing the involvement of the central and eastern European powers in an area where Britain had traditionally had interests, were reluctant to intervene. A provisional government in Belgium set about the task of writing a constitution. All five great powers recognized Belgian independence, with the proviso that Belgium was to maintain the status of a neutral state.

Russia, Prussia, and Austria were convinced to accept Belgian independence because they were having their own problems in eastern and southern Europe. Revolution erupted to the east in Warsaw, Poland. Driven by

prices by 75 percent. The king underestimated the extent of hardship and the political volatility of the population. Throughout the spring of 1830 prices continued to rise and Charles continued to blunder. In a spontaneous uprising in the last days of July 1830, workers took to the streets of Paris. The revolution they initiated spread rapidly to towns and the countryside, as people throughout France protested the cost of living, hoarding by grain merchants, tax collection, and wage cuts. In "three glorious days" the restored Bourbon regime was pulled down and Charles X fled to England.

The people fighting in the streets demanded a republic, but they lacked organization and political experience. Liberal bourgeois politicians quickly filled the power vacuum. They presented Charles' cousin, the duc d'Orléans, as the savior of France and the new constitutional monarch. This July Monarchy, born of a revolution, put an end to the Bourbon Restoration. Louis-Philippe, the former duc d'Orléans, became "king of the French." The Charter that he brought with him was, like its predecessor, based on restricted suffrage, with property ownership a requisite for voting.

Popular disturbances did not always result in revolution. In Britain, rural and town riots erupted over grain prices and distribution, but no revolution followed. German workers broke their machines to protest low wages and loss of control of the workplace, but no prince was displaced. In Switzerland reformers found strength in the French revolutionary example. Ten Swiss cantons granted liberal constitutions and established universal manhood suffrage, freedom of expression, and legal equality.

'Gentlemen,' says Nicholas I, the bear, to the Polish revolutionaries of 1830, 'I know that you wish to address me; but to spare you from delivering a pack of lies, I desire that you hold your tongues.'

This English cartoon of 1832 is titled "The clemency of the Russian monster." It shows Nicholas I in the guise of a bear with menacing teeth and claws addressing the Poles after crushing their rebellion against Imperial Russian rule.

a desire for national independence, Polish army cadets and university students revolted in November 1830 to demand a constitution. Landed aristocrats and gentry helped establish a provisional government but soon split over how radical reforms should be. Polish peasants refused to support either landowning group. Within the year, Russia brought in 180,000 troops to crush the revolution and reassert its rule over Poland.

In February 1831, the Italian states of Modena and Parma rose up to throw off Austrian domination of northern Italy. The revolutionaries were ineffective against Austrian troops. Revolution in the Papal States resulted in French occupation that lasted until 1838 without serious reforms. Nationalist and republican yearnings were driven underground, kept alive there in the Young Italy movement under the leadership of Giuseppe Mazzini.

Although the revolutions of 1830 are called "the forgotten revolutions" of the nineteenth century, they are important for several reasons. First, they made clear to European states how closely tied together were their fates. The events of 1830 were a test of the Great Powers' commitment to stability and a balance of power in Europe. True to the principles of the Vienna settlements of 1815, European leaders preserved the status quo. Revolutions in Poland and Italy were contained by Russia and Austria without interference from the other powers. Where adaptation was necessary, as in Greece and Belgium, the Great Powers were able to compromise on settlements, although the solutions ran counter to previous policies. Heads of state were willing to use the forces of repression to stamp out protest. The international significance of the revolutions reveals a second important aspect of the events of

1830: the vulnerability of international politics to domestic instability.

Finally, the 1830 revolutions exposed a growing awareness of politics at all levels of European society. If policies in 1830 revealed a shared consciousness of events and shared values among ruling elites, the revolutions disclosed a growing awareness among the lower classes of the importance of politics in their daily lives. In a dangerous combination, workers and the lower classes throughout Europe were politicized, yet they continued to be excluded from political power.

Reform in Great Britain

The right to vote had been an issue of contention in the revolutions of 1830 in western Europe. Only the Swiss cantons enforced the principle of one man, one vote. The July Revolution in France had doubled the electorate, but still only a tiny minority of the population (less than 1 percent) enjoyed the vote. Universal male suffrage had been mandated in 1793 during the Great Revolution but not implemented. This exclusion of the mass of the population from participation in electoral politics was no oversight. Those in power believed that the wealthiest property owners were best qualified to govern, in part because they had the greatest stake in politics and society. One also needed to own property in order to hold office because those who served in parliaments received no salary.

Landowners ruled Britain too. There the dominance of a wealthy elite was strengthened by the geographic redistribution resulting from industrialization. Migration to cities had depleted the population of rural areas. Yet the electoral system did not adjust to these changes: large towns had no parliamentary representation, while dwindling county electorates maintained their parliamentary strength. Areas that continued to enjoy representation greater than that justified by their population were dubbed *rotten* or *pocket* boroughs to indicate a corrupt and antiquated electoral system. In general, urban areas were grossly underrepresented, as the wealthy few controlled county seats. Liberal reformers attempted to rectify the electoral inequalities by reassigning parliamentary seats on the basis of density of population.

Vested interests balked at attempted reforms, and members of Parliament wrangled bitterly. Popular agitation by the lower classes provoked the fear of civil war and helped break the parliamentary deadlock. The Great Reform Bill of 1832 proposed a compromise. Although the vast majority of the population still did not have the vote, the new legislation strengthened the industrial and commercial elite in the towns, enfranchised most of the middle class, opened the way to social reforms, and encouraged the formation of political parties.

In the 1830s new radical reformers, disillusioned with the 1832 Reform Bill because it strengthened the power of a wealthy capitalist class, argued that democracy was the only answer to the problems plaguing British society. In 1838 a small group of labor leaders, including representatives of the London Working Men's Association, an organization of craft workers, drew up a document known as the People's Charter. The single most important demand of the Charter was that all men must have the vote. In addition, Chartists petitioned for a secret ballot, salaries for parliamentary service, elimination of property qualifications to run for office, equal electoral districts, and annual elections.

Chartism blossomed as a communal phenomenon in working-class towns and appeared to involve all members of the family. Women organized Chartist schools and Sunday schools in radical defiance of local church organizations. Many middle-class observers were sure that the moment for class war and revolutionary upheaval had arrived. The government responded with force to the perceived threat of armed rebellion and imprisoned a number of Chartist leaders. The final moment for Chartism occurred in April 1848 when 25,000 Chartist workers, inspired by revolutionary events on the Continent, assembled in London to march on the House of Commons. They carried with them a newly signed petition demanding the enactment of the terms of the Charter. In response, the government deputized nearly 200,000 "special" constables in the streets. These deputized private citizens were London property owners and skilled workers intent on holding back a revolutionary rabble. Tired, cold, and rain-soaked, the Chartist demonstrators disbanded. No social revolution took place in Great Britain, and the dilemma of democratic representation was deferred.

Worker Protest

The word *proletariat* entered European languages before the mid-nineteenth century to describe those workers afloat in the labor pool who owned nothing, not even the tools of their labor, and who were becoming "appendages" to the new machines that dominated production.

The Chartist movement was hated and feared by members of the British Establishment, who saw it as the thin end of a democratic wedge. Here the Chartists march to the House of Commons in 1842, carrying their Great Petition to the Commons.

From the 1820s to the 1850s sporadic but intense outbursts of machine-breaking occurred in continental Europe. Skilled workers, fearing that they would be pulled down into the new proletariat because of mechanization and the increased scale of production, organized in new ways after 1830.

Uprisings and strikes in France increased dramatically from 1831 to 1834 and favored the destruction of the monarchy and the creation of a democratic republic. Many French craft workers grew conscious of themselves as a class and embraced a socialism heavily influenced by their own traditions and contemporary socialist writings. Republican socialism spread throughout France by means of a network of traveling journeymen and tapped into growing economic hardship and political discontent with the July Monarchy. Government repression drove worker organizations underground in the late 1830s, but secret societies proliferated.

Women were an important part of the workforce in the industrializing societies. Working men were keenly aware of the competition with cheaper female labor in the factories. Women formed a salaried workforce in the home, too. In order to produce cheaply and in large quantities, some manufacturers turned to subcontractors for the simpler tasks in the work process. These new middlemen contracted out work like cutting and sewing to needy women, who were often responsible for caring for family members in their homes.

Cheap female labor paid by the piece allowed employers to profit by keeping overhead costs low and by driving down the wages of skilled workers. Trade unions opposed women's work both in the home and in the factories. Women's talents, union leaders explained, were more properly devoted to domestic chores; their accomplishments as paid workers were consistently regarded as inferior in skill and strength. Unions argued that their members should earn a family wage "sufficient to support a wife and children." Unions consistently excluded women workers from their ranks.

In some cases, working women formed their own organizations like that of the Parisian seamstresses who joined together to demand improved working conditions. On the whole, however, domestic workers in the home remained isolated from other working women, and many women in factories feared the loss of their jobs if they engaged in political activism. The wages of Europe's working women remained low, often below the level of subsistence. (See Special Feature, "Fear in Paris," pp. 762–763.)

La Barricade *by Ernest Meissonier, 1848.*

Fear in Paris

At the height of his power, in 1810, Napoleon envisioned Paris as the capital of Europe, a mecca of art, style and learning, "the most beautiful city that ever could exist." He never achieved his dream. Paris in 1840 was certainly a center of fashion and culture, but it was far from the extravagant beauty Napoleon dreamed of. Dark, dirty, ugly, rat-infested slums dominated the "City of Light."

Problems arose because early nineteenth-century Paris was physically a medieval city, yet it housed a modern population. By 1840 Paris held one million people, twice as many as it had only forty years earlier. The fastest growth occurred between 1830 and 1850, when 350,000 new residents were recorded. One out of every two Parisians was not born in the city, but had migrated to it. Paris acted like a magnet, attracting provincials in search of employment and opportunity. The craftsman Martin Nadaud was typical of many immigrants who came to the capital expecting to find its streets literally paved with gold. He found instead raw sewage, inadequate water supplies, overcrowded housing, disease, and poverty. Sixty-five percent of all Parisians were so poor they paid no taxes. Fifty percent officially qualified as "indigents" and were eligible for humiliating and inadequate poor relief.

A bad situation got worse when a cholera epidemic ravaged the city for 189 days in 1832, leaving 18,000 people dead and 30,000 others afflicted. The vast majority of those stricken were from the lower classes. City dwellers knew nothing about the etiology of cholera, but they understood that the poor were dying and the rich were not. To explain their apparent immunity, many bourgeois decided that the cholera epidemic was the fault of the poor, whose decadent lifestyles created the disease and caused it to spread. Moralists railed that godlessness and sexual excess were taking their toll. Outraged bourgeois demanded sanitation—but of a spiritual sort.

If the bourgeoisie blamed the epidemic on immorality, workers attributed it to a conspiracy. The wealthy, they argued, were poisoning the water supply of the poor in order to limit their numbers. Such collective delusions gave rise to fear and general panic. Wealthy bourgeois fled the city to sit out the epidemic in rural peace. Among the lower classes, vigilante groups proliferated for the purpose of eliminating bourgeois villains. Several well-dressed gentlemen who strayed into working-class neighborhoods were executed for no greater offense than carrying suspicious looking bottles that might contain contaminated fluids.

Urban life was further polarized by a rising crime rate that many felt portended the end of civilization. Gangs of homeless youths roamed city streets, fanning bourgeois fears. Gavroche, a character in Victor Hugo's *Les Misérables*, was one such fictional child of the streets who participated in the uprising of 1832. Hugo was sympathetic to the child's plight; many of his bourgeois readers were not. Crime was everywhere. In his Human Comedy, a vast collection of novels and short stories appearing between 1830 and 1850, Honoré de Balzac (1799–1850) created gangsters and thieves who were not only part of the criminal world but who also ran the police, commerce, and finance.

During the July Monarchy social-science studies presented the city as a giant laboratory. Misery was measured. The hair color, height, and place of birth of prostitutes were recorded. Infanticides and suicides were tallied. The studies concluded that poverty caused demoralization, violence, and crime. Reformers argued for low-cost housing, mass sanitation, and lighting. Yet the regime did little to address urban problems. Instead, the government undertook what seemed to many a curious public-works project of building a ring of fortifications around the city of Paris.

As other European cities began dismantling fortifications, Paris was the only city in the nineteenth century to enclose itself behind a fortified wall. Fortifications aggravated urban problems as thousands of workers flocked to the city to compete for the new jobs. Police complained about crime on the work sites and the increase in prostitution that they were unable to control. Fortifying the city played on peoples' fears. Why, it was asked, were troops, supplies, and equipment pulled back from the French-German border and concentrated in the capital? If France feared a foreign war, why was it preparing for one at the expense of its national frontiers?

Public debate raged over the excessive costs of the program. When it was discovered that the gun turrets on the forts could swivel inward and be aimed at the city as well as outward at an invading army, critics were sure they knew what was happening. The government, they charged, was preparing itself for a defensive action against its own capital and against its own citizens. There was reason for suspicion. After 1840 the government relied increasingly on the military as a repressive police force, spurning the National Guard, a citizen militia, as unreliable, and its own municipal police as inefficient. Troops were the monarchy's solution to the problems of law and order. Paris in 1840 had been turned into an armed camp.

The fortifications were never used against Parisians. When the revolution came in February 1848, the troops refused to fire on the people. The problems of the city of Paris were so severe that people from all classes shared an apocalyptic vision. At the end of June 1848, thousands of Parisian bourgeois joined the army in pitched battle against the city's revolutionary workers. Fifteen hundred people died in the fighting. Three thousand more insurgents were ruthlessly put to death. The worst fears of urban life had reached their climax.

The Revolutions of 1848

Europeans had never experienced a year like 1848. Beginning soon after the ringing in of the New Year, revolutionary fervor swept through nearly every European country. By year's end, regimes had been created and destroyed. France, Italy, the German states, Austria, Hungary, and Bohemia were shaken to their foundations. Switzerland, Denmark, and Romania experienced lesser upheavals. Great Britain had survived reformist agitation, and famine-crippled Ireland had endured a failed insurrection. No one was sure what had happened. Each country's conflict was based on a unique mix of issues, but all were connected in their conscious emulation of a revolutionary tradition.

Hindsight reveals warning signs in the two years before the 1848 cataclysm. Beginning in 1846 a severe famine—the last serious food crisis Europe would experience—racked Europe. Lack of grain drove up prices. An increasing percentage of disposable income was spent on food for survival. Lack of spending power severely damaged markets and forced thousands of industrial workers out of their jobs. The famine hurt everyone—the poor, workers, employers, and investors—as recession paralyzed the economy.

The food crisis took place in a heavily charged political atmosphere. Throughout Europe during the 1840s middle and lower classes had intensified their agitation for democracy. Chartists in Great Britain argued for a wider electorate. Bourgeois reformers in France campaigned for universal manhood suffrage. The movement was known as the "banquet" campaign because its leaders attempted to raise money by giving speeches at subscribed dinners. In making demands for political participation, those agitating for the vote necessarily criticized those in power. Freedom of speech and freedom of assembly were demanded as inalienable rights. The food crisis combined with political activism were the ingredients of an incendiary situation.

In addition to a burgeoning democratic culture, growing demands for national autonomy based on linguistic and cultural claims spread through central, southern, and eastern Europe. The revolts in Poland in 1846, although failures, encouraged similar movements for national liberation among Italians and Germans. Even in the relatively homogeneous nation of France, concerns with national mission and national glory grew among the regime's critics. National unity was primarily a middle-class ideal. Liberal lawyers, teachers, and businessmen from Dublin to Budapest to Prague agitated for separation from foreign rule. Austria, with an empire formed of numerous ethnic minorities, had the most to lose. Since 1815, Metternich had been ruthless in stamping out nationalist dissent. By the 1840s national claims were assuming a cultural legitimacy that was difficult to dismiss or ignore.

The events in France in the cold February of 1848 ignited the conflagration that swept Europe. On 22 February bourgeois reformers had staged their largest banquet to date in Paris in support of extension of the vote. City officials became nervous at the prospect of thousands of workers assembling for political purposes and canceled the scheduled banquet. This was the spark that touched off the powder keg. In a spontaneous uprising Parisians demonstrated against the government's repressive measures. Skilled workers took to the streets not only in favor of the banned banquet but also with the hope that the government would recognize the importance of labor to the social order. Shots were fired; a demonstrator was killed. The French Revolution of 1848 had begun.

Events moved quickly. The National Guard, a citizen militia of bourgeois Parisians, defected from Louis-Philippe. Many army troops garrisoned in Paris crossed the barricades to join revolutionary workers. The king attempted some reform, but it was too little and too late. Louis-Philippe fled. The Second Republic was proclaimed at the insistence of the revolutionary crowds on the barricades. The Provisional Government, led by the poet Alphonse de Lamartine (1790–1869), included members of both factions of political reformers of the July Monarchy: moderates who sought constitutional reforms and an extension of the suffrage; and radicals who favored universal manhood suffrage and social programs to deal with poverty and work. Only the threat of popular violence held together this uneasy alliance.

The people fighting in the streets had little in common with the bourgeois reformers who assumed power on 24 February. Workers made a social revolution out of a commitment to their "right to work," which would replace the right to property as the organizing principle of the new society. Only one member of the new Provisional Government was a worker, and he was included as a token symbol of the intentions of the new government. He was known as "Albert, the worker," and was not addressed by his surname, Martin. The government acknowledged the demand of the "right to work" and set up two mechanisms to guarantee workers' relief. First, a commission of workers and employers was created to act as a grievance and bargaining board and settle

questions of common concern in the workplace. Headed by the socialist Louis Blanc (1811–82) and known as the Luxembourg Commission, the worker-employer parliament was an important innovation but accomplished little other than deflecting workers' attention away from the problems of the Provisional Government. The second measure was the creation of "national workshops" to deal with the problems of unemployment in Paris. Workers from all over France poured into Paris with the hope of finding jobs. The workshops, however, had a residency requirement that even Parisians had difficulty meeting. As a result, unemployment skyrocketed. Furthermore, the government was going bankrupt trying to support the program. The need to raise taxes upset peasants in the provinces. National pressure mounted to repudiate the programs of the revolution.

French workers were too weak to dominate the revolution. The government recalled General Louis Cavaignac (1802–57) from service in Algeria to maintain order. In a wave of armed insurrection, Parisian workers rebelled in the "June Days" of 1848. Using troops from the provinces who had no identification with the urban population and employing guerrilla techniques he had mastered in Algeria, Cavaignac put down the uprising. The Second Republic was placed under the military dictatorship of Cavaignac until December, when presidential elections were scheduled.

France was not alone in undergoing revolution in 1848. Long-suppressed desires for civil liberties and constitutional reforms erupted in widespread popular disturbances in Prussia and the German states. Fearing a war with France and unable to count on Austria or Russia for support, the princes who ruled Baden, Württemberg, Hesse-Darmstadt, Bavaria, Saxony, and Hanover followed the advice of moderate liberals and acceded quickly to revolutionary demands. In Prussia, King Frederick William IV (1840–61) preferred to use military force to respond to popular demonstrations. Only in mid-March 1848 did the Prussian king yield to the force of the revolutionary crowds building barricades in Berlin by ordering his troops to leave the city and by promising to create a national Prussian assembly. The king was now a prisoner of the revolution.

Meanwhile, the collapse of absolute monarchy in Prussia gave further impetus to a constitutional movement among the liberal leaders of the German states. The governments of all the German states were invited to elect delegates to a national parliament in Frankfurt. The Frankfurt parliament, which was convened in May 1848, had as its dual charge the framing of a constitution and the unification of Germany. It was composed for the most part of members of the middle class, with civil servants, lawyers, and intellectuals predominating. In spite of the principle of universal manhood suffrage, there was not a single worker among the eight hundred men elected. To most parliamentarians, who were trained in universities and shared a social and cultural identity, nationalism and constitutionalism were inextricably related.

As straightforward as the desire for a German nation appeared to be, it was complicated by two important facts. First, there were non-German minorities living in German states. What was to be done with the Poles, Czechs, Slovenes, Italians, and Dutch in a newly constituted and autonomous German nation? Second, there were Germans living outside the German states under Habsburg rule in Austria, in Danish Schleswig and Holstein, in Posen (Poznan), in Russian Poland, and in European Russia. How were they to be included within the linguistically and ethnically constituted German nation? After much wrangling over a "small" Germany that excluded Austrian Germans and a "large" Germany that included them, the Frankfurt parliament opted for the small-Germany solution in March 1849. The crown of the new nation was offered to the unpredictable Frederick William IV of Prussia (1840–61), head of the largest and most powerful of the German states. Unhappy with his capitulation to the revolutionary crowd in March 1848, the Prussian king refused to accept a "crown from the gutter." He had his own plans to rule over a middle-European bloc but not at the behest of liberal parliamentarians. The attempt to create a German nation crumbled with his unwillingness to lead.

Revolution in Austrian-dominated central Europe was concentrated in three places: Vienna, where German-speaking students, workers, and middle-class liberals were agitating for constitutional reform and political participation; Budapest, where the Magyars, the dominant ethnic group in Hungary, led a movement for national autonomy; and Prague, where Czechs were attempting self-rule. By April 1848, Metternich had fallen from power and the Viennese revolutionaries had set up a constituent assembly. In Budapest, the initial steps of the patriot Lajos Kossuth (1802–94) toward establishing a separate Hungarian state seemed equally solid, as the Magyars defeated Habsburg troops. Habsburg armies were more successful in Prague, where they crushed the revolution in June 1848.

The Habsburg empire was also under siege in Italy, where the Kingdom of the Two Sicilies, Tuscany, and

In this incident from the revolutionary year of 1848, Imperial Austrian troops fire on a Viennese crowd assembled at the convening of the Estates General to petition for their right to a voice in the new social order.

Piedmont declared new constitutions in March 1848. Championed by Charles Albert of Piedmont, Venice and Lombardy rose up against Austria. Nationalist sentiments had percolated underground in the Young Italy movement, founded in 1831 by Giuseppe Mazzini. Mazzini (1805–72), a tireless and idealistic patriot, favored a democratic revolution. In spite of a reputation for liberal politics, Pope Pius IX (1846–78) lost control of Rome and was forced to flee the city. Mazzini became head of the Republic of Rome, created in February 1849.

The French government decided to intervene to protect the pope's interests and sent in troops to defeat the republicans. One of Mazzini's disciples, Giuseppe Garibaldi (1807–82), returned from exile in South America to undertake the defense of Rome. Garibaldi was a capable soldier who had learned the tactics of guerrilla warfare by joining independence struggles in Brazil and Argentina. Although his legion of poorly armed patriots and soldiers of fortune, known from their

attire as the Red Shirts, waged a valiant effort to defend the city from April to June 1849, they were no match for the highly trained French army. French troops restored Pius IX as ruler of the Papal States.

Meanwhile, from August 1848 to the following spring, the Habsburg armies fought and finally defeated each of the revolutions throughout the Austrian Empire. Austrian success can be explained in part because the various Italian groups of Piedmontese, Tuscans, Venetians, Romans, and Neapolitans continued to identify with their local concerns and lacked coordination and central organization. Both Mazzini and Pius IX had failed to provide the focal point of leadership necessary for a successful national movement.

By the fall of 1849, Austria had solved the problems in its own capital and with Italy and Hungary by military dominance. Emperor Ferdinand I (1835–48), whose authority had been weakened irreparably by the overthrow of Metternich, abdicated in favor of his eighteen-year-old nephew, Franz Josef I (1848–1916). Austria understood that a Germany united under Frederick William IV of Prussia would undermine Austrian dominance in central Europe. In 1850 Austrians threatened the Prussians with war if they did not give up their plans for a unified Germany. In November of that year Prussian ministers signed an agreement with their Austrian counterparts in the Moravian city of Olmutz. The convention became known as "the humiliation of Olmutz" because Prussia was forced to accept Austrian dominance or go to war. In every case, military force and diplomatic measures prevailed to defeat the national and liberal movements within the German states and the Austrian Empire.

Europe in 1850

By 1850, a veneer of calm spread over central Europe. In Prussia, the peasantry were emancipated from feudal dues, and a constitution, albeit conservative and based on a three-class system, was established. Yet beneath the surface, there was the deeper reality of Austrian decline and Prussian challenge. The great Habsburg empire needed to call on outside help from Russia to defeat its enemies within. The imperial giant was again on its feet, but for how long? In international relations, Austria's dominance in the German Confederation had diminished, as Prussia assumed greater political and economic power.

The 1848 revolutions spelled the end to the concert of Europe as it had been defined in the peace settlement of 1815. The European powers were incapable of

FROM GIUSEPPE MAZZINI, *YOUNG ITALY* (1832)

■ *Giuseppe Mazzini, an Italian patriot and revolutionary, was the principal theorist of national revolution in Europe in the first half of the nineteenth century. He explained his strong commitment to equality and democratic principles from his readings on the French Revolution of 1789 and from his study of the Latin classics. In 1832 he founded the secret society Young Italy. The goal of this revolutionary group was the unification of Italy under a republican form of government through direct popular action.*

We have beheld Italy—Italy, the purpose, the soul, the consolation of our thoughts, the country chosen of God and oppressed by men, twice queen of the world and twice fallen through the infamy of foreigners and the guilt of her citizens, yet lovely still though she be dust, unmatched by any other nation whatever fortune has decreed; and Genius returns to seek in this dust the word of eternal life, and the spark that creates the future . . .

Young Italy: but we chose this term because the one term seems to marshal before the youth of Italy the magnitude of its duties and the solemnity of the mission that circumstances have entrusted to it, so that it will be ready when the hour has struck to arise from its slumber to a new life of action and regeneration. And we chose it because we wanted to show ourselves, writing it, as what we are, to do battle with raised visors, to bear our faith before us, as the knights of medieval times bore their faith on their shields. For while we pity men who do not know the truth, we despise men who, though they know the truth, do not dare to speak it.

united action to defend established territorial interests. Perhaps France would have provoked united action if it had attempted to extend its revolution throughout Europe as it had done in 1792. Instead, pragmatism prevailed. The British failed to support independence for Hungary, for example, because they feared the consequences for Russian ambitions that would be unchecked with a weaker Austria.

The revolutions of 1848 failed in part because of the irreconcilable split between moderate liberals and radical democrats. The participation of the masses had frightened members of the middle classes who were committed to moderate reforms that did not threaten property. In France, working-class revolutionaries had attempted to replace property with labor. Property triumphed. In the face of more extreme solutions, members of the middle class were willing to accept the increased authority of existing rule as a bulwark against anarchy. In December 1848 Prince Louis Napoleon, nephew of the former emperor, was elected president of the Second Republic by a wide margin. The first truly modern French politician, Louis Napoleon managed to appeal to everyone—workers, bourgeois, royalists, and peasants—by making promises that were vague or unkeepable. Severe repression forced radical protest into

hiding. The new Bonaparte bided his time, apparently as an ineffectual ruler, until the moment in 1851 when he seized absolute power.

Similar patterns emerged elsewhere in Europe. In Germany, the bourgeoisie accepted the dominance of the old feudal aristocracy as a guarantee of law and order. Repressive government, businessmen were sure, would restore a strong economy. The attempts in 1848 to create new nations based on ethnic identities were in shambles by 1850.

Nearly everywhere throughout Europe constitutions had been systematically withdrawn with the recovery of the forces of reaction. With the French and Swiss exceptions, the bid for the extension of the franchise failed. The propertied classes remained in control of political institutions. Radicals willing to use violence to press electoral reforms were arrested, killed, or exiled. The leadership of the revolutionary movements had been decapitated, and there seemed no effective opposition to the rise and consolidation of state power.

The 1848 revolutions have been called a turning point at which modern history failed to turn. Contemporaries wondered how so much action could have produced so

Protest and Revolution

August 1819	"Peterloo" massacre
1824	Charles X assumes French throne
1827	Treaty of London to support liberation of Greece
July 1830	Revolution in Paris; creation of July Monarchy under Louis-Philippe
August 1830	Revolution in Belgium
November 1830	Revolution in Poland
1831–38	Revolutions in Italian states
1831–34	Labor protests in France
1832	Britain's Great Reform Bill
1838	Drawing up of the first People's Charter in Britain
1846	Beginning of food crisis in Europe; revolts in Poland
1846–48	Europe-wide movements for national liberation
February 1848	Revolution in France—first uprising and overthrow of the July Monarchy; proclamation of the Second Republic in France and creation of Provisional Government
March 1848	Uprisings in some German states; granting of a constitution in Prussia
March 1848– June 1849	Revolutions in Italy
April 1848	Revolutions in Vienna, Budapest, Prague
May 1848	Frankfurt parliament; demonstrations in Paris and Vienna
June 1848	Second revolution in Paris, severely repressed by army troops under General Cavaignac
December 1848	Presidential elections in France; Louis Napoleon wins

few lasting results. Yet the perception that nothing had changed was wrong. Conservatives and radicals alike turned toward a new realism in politics. Everywhere governments were forced to adapt to new social realities. No longer could the state ignore economic upheavals and social dislocations if it wanted to survive. Revolutionaries also learned the lesson of repression. The state wielded powerful forces of violence against which nationalists, socialists, republicans, and liberals had all been proven helpless.

SUGGESTIONS FOR FURTHER READING

EUROPE AFTER 1815

* Robert Gildea, *Barricades and Borders, Europe 1800–1914* (Oxford: Oxford University Press, 1987). A synthetic overview of economic, demographic, political, and international trends in European society.

* Harold Nicolson, *The Congress of Vienna: A Study in Allied Unity, 1812–1822* (New York: Viking Press, 1965). Dissects the maneuverings of the Allied diplomats and analyzes their cooperation in reconstructing Europe.

* Alan Sked, *The Decline and Fall of the Habsburg Empire, 1815–1918* (London: Longman, 1989). A revisionist interpretation that demonstrates the strength and viability of Europe's greatest dynasty throughout the nineteenth century.

THE NEW EUROPEAN SOCIETY

* Leonore Davidoff and Catherine Hall, *Family Fortunes: Men and Women of the English Middle Class, 1780–1850* (Chicago: University of Chicago Press, 1991). Through the stories of families during the Industrial Revolution, the authors explain the development of middle-class identity and the role that gender played in the development of property relationships, the construction of family life, and the differentiation of the world of the home from the public world of production.

* Gertrude Himmelfarb, *The Idea of Poverty: England in the Early Industrial Age* (New York: Vintage Books, 1983). Traces the concept of poverty in Britain from the mid-eighteenth to the mid-nineteenth century through inadequate solutions, changing material conditions of industrialism, and new modes of thought and sensibility.

* Joel Mokyr, *Why Ireland Starved: A Quantitative and Analytical History of the Irish Economy, 1800–1850* (London: George Allen & Unwin, 1983). An analysis of the structural factors that produced poverty in prefamine Ireland and a thorough examination of the impact of the famine.

* Redcliffe N. Salaman, *The History and Social Influence of the Potato,* [revised impression edited by J. G. Hawkes] (Cambridge: Cambridge University Press, 1985). The classic study of the potato. A major portion of the work is devoted to the potato famine.

* Louise A. Tilly and Joan W. Scott, *Women, Work and Family* (New York: Holt, Rinehart and Winston, 1978). An overview of

the impact of a wage economy on the family and on women's work.

THE NEW IDEOLOGIES

* Jonathan Beecher, *Charles Fourier: The Visionary and His World* (Berkeley, CA: University of California Press, 1986). An intellectual biography which traces the development of Fourier's theoretical perspective and roots it firmly in the social context of nineteenth-century France.

* Craig Calhoun, *The Question of Class Struggle: Social Foundations of Popular Radicalism During the Industrial Revolution* (Chicago: University of Chicago Press, 1982). Presents popular protest in England in the eighteenth and early nineteenth centuries as the reaction of communities of craftsmen defending their traditions against encroaching industrialization.

* William H. Sewell, Jr., *Work and Revolution in France: The Language of Labor From the Old Regime to 1848* (Cambridge: Cambridge University Press, 1980). Traces nineteenth-century working-class socialism to the corporate culture of Old Regime guilds through traditional values, norms, language, and artisan organizations.

Gareth Stedman Jones, *Languages of Class: Studies in English Working Class History, 1832–1982* (Cambridge: Cambridge University Press, 1983). A series of essays, including topics on working-class culture and Chartism, that examine the development of class consciousness.

* Edward P. Thompson, *The Making of the English Working Class* (New York: Pantheon Books, 1963). Spans the late eigh-teenth to mid-nineteenth centuries in examining the social, political, and cultural contexts in which workers created their own identity and put forward their own demands.

PROTEST AND REVOLUTION

* Maurice Agulhon, *The Republican Experiment, 1848–1852* (Cambridge: Cambridge University Press, 1983). Traces the Revolution of 1848 from its roots to its ultimate failure in 1852 through an analysis of the ideologies of the republicanism of workers, peasants, and the bourgeoisie.

Clive Church, *Europe in 1830: Revolution and Political Change* (London: George Allen and Unwin, 1983). Considers the origins of the 1830 revolutions within a wider European crisis through a comparative analysis of European regions.

* Peter N. Stearns, *1848: The Revolutionary Tide in Europe* (New York: Norton, 1974). Surveys the causes, impact, and legacy of the revolutions in France, Germany, the Habsburg empire, and Italy, which shattered the diplomatic framework established at the Congress of Vienna and served as a transition to a new society.

* Dorothy Thompson, *The Chartists: Popular Politics in the Industrial Revolution* (New York: Pantheon Books, 1984). Thompson demonstrates that Chartism was an extraordinary coalition of women, laborers, artisans, and alehouse keepers, whose goals were transforming public life and forging a new political culture.

* Indicates paperback edition available.

CHAPTER 26

European States and Societies, 1850–1914

THE BIRTH OF THE GERMAN EMPIRE

Secret fancies bubbled in Otto von Bismarck's brain. As he explained in long letters to his wife, he imagined that the Prussian king and German princes crowding round him were pregnant women seized by "strange cravings." In the next moment, he imagined himself a midwife assisting at a momentous birth. In spite of his remarkable train of thought, Otto von Bismarck (1815–98) was not a fanciful man. The birth in his daydream was the proclamation of the German Empire on 21 January 1871. The building was the Versailles Palace outside Paris. As the Prussian statesman stood in the great Hall of Mirrors on that fateful day, surrounded by German aristocrats, he could not forget the years of struggle and planning that preceded this event. His tension and anticipation provoked his birthing fantasies.

The newly established Second Reich, successor to the Holy Roman Empire (962–1806), united the German states into a single nation. The unification process had been a precarious pregnancy, with years of foreign wars and a herculean labor of diplomatic maneuverings. The placid, glossy scene painted by Anton von Werner (1843–1915) hardly suggests Bismarck's violent emotions on this momentous day. This warrior group was the most masculine of gatherings. Look at the painting. The richly marbled and mirrored room, the site of the birth of the German Empire, figures as prominently in the tableau as the uniformed princes and aristocrats, who, with sabers, helmets, and standards raised, cheer the new emperor. The massive mirrors reflect more than this soldier society standing before the long windows of the opposite wall; they reflect a humiliation. This is, after all, the great hall built by Louis XIV at Versailles, one of Europe's greatest palaces, to reflect and glorify the power of absolutist France. Here the kings of France presided over lavish ceremonies and opulent receptions. Here Napoleon I honored his generals, victorious in conquering central Europe. Here not long ago Napoleon III had danced on the parqueted floors with Queen Victoria of Britain. The choice of the Hall of Mirrors as the meeting place for the German princes, who had successfully combined forces to defeat the French Second Empire in only six weeks of war in the fall of 1870, was intended as an assertion of German superiority in Europe.

In less than a decade German unity had been achieved through military victories over Denmark, Austria, and France. The gilded moldings that commemorate the age of the Sun King are matched by the glitter of golden ribbons, medals, buttons, and cuffs of German uniforms, by the soft glow of burnished Prussian helmets. France was about to be stripped of its territories of Alsace and Lorraine; now the French were to be stripped of their dignity, as the Prussian king stands on luxuriant French carpeting to assert his claim. There is an arrogance here in the details on which Werner dwells. The French understood and promised to avenge it.

Look at the painting again. There on the dais is King William I of Prussia, flanked by his son Crown Prince Frederick William and his son-in-law, Frederick I, the Grand Duke of Baden, whose upraised hand signals the cheer for the new emperor. At the foot of the steps, like a loyal retainer, stands the self-described midwife, Otto von Bismarck. Yet there is something amiss here. The new German emperor, the person for whom the event has been orchestrated, stands to one side of the canvas. Bismarck commands its center. If most eyes of the cheering princes turn to the emperor, ours are pulled to the chancellor of the new Reich, who is singled out in his pure white uniform. Werner is telling us that this is the statesman's event, for it is he who has crafted a united Germany. Bismarck got what he wanted: a German empire under the leadership of the Prussian king.

Bismarck understood that symbols forge unity. The artist Werner, too, attends to symbol. In Bismarck's hands, he places both the document proclaiming the empire and his Prussian military helmet. Military victories had ensured Prussian predominance over a united Germany. To Bismarck's left, in profile facing the emperor, stands Count Helmuth von Moltke (1800–91), head of the Prussian General Staff and the man responsible for reorganizing the Prussian army with Bismarck's support. Medals for bravery and service to his sovereign adorn Moltke's chest. With one foot forward, Moltke is a man of action, almost caught in mid-stride, a man ready to move into the future.

Bismarck created this new "state of princes," the German Empire, through "iron and blood"—force and military conquest—and not by democratic means. Conservative state building succeeded in unifying Germany where the liberal ideology of representative government had failed. European states in the second half of the nineteenth century assumed responsibility for social and economic reforms, as class society gave way to mass society.

Building Nations: The Politics of Unification

The revolutions of 1848 had occurred in a period of political experimentation. Radicals enlisting popular support had tried and failed to reshape European states for their own nationalist, liberal, and socialist ends. Governments in Paris, Vienna, Berlin, and a number of lesser states had been swept away as revolutions created a power vacuum but no durable solutions. To fill that vacuum, a new breed of politicians emerged in the 1850s and 1860s, men who understood the importance of the centralized nation-state and the need of reforms from above. They also appreciated the importance of foreign policy successes as a means of furthering domestic programs. Cavour of Italy, Bismarck of Germany, and Louis Napoleon of France shared a new realism about means and ends.

In the 1850s and 1860s those committed to radical transformations worked from within the existing system. When revolutionary goals were achieved, direction came from above. Between 1848 and 1850 national unification had escaped the grasp of liberals and radicals. After 1850 liberal nationalism was subordinated to conservative state building. Military force validated what intellectuals and revolutionaries had not been able to legitimate through ideological claims.

The Crimean War

In 1849 and 1850 Russia had fulfilled its role as policeman of Europe by supporting Austria against Hungary and Prussia. Yet Russia was not merely content to keep the peace; it sought greater power to the south in the Balkans. The narrow straits connecting the Black Sea with the Aegean Sea were controlled by the Ottoman Empire. Russia hoped to benefit from Ottoman weakness caused by internal conflicts and gain control of the straits as an outlet for the Russian fleet to the Mediterranean.

At the center of the hope for Ottoman disintegration lay the "Eastern Question," the term used in the nineteenth century to designate the problems surrounding the European territories controlled by the Ottoman Empire. Each of the Great Powers—including Russia,

Great Britain, Austria, Prussia, and France—hoped to benefit territorially from the collapse of Ottoman control. In 1853 Great Power rivalry over the Eastern Question created an international situation that led to war.

In 1853 the Russian government demanded that the Turkish government recognize Russia's right to protect Greek Orthodox believers in the Ottoman Empire. The Turkish government refused Russian demands, and the Russians ordered troops to enter the Danubian Principalities of Moldavia and Wallachia, which were held by the Turks. In October 1853, the Turkish government, counting on support from Great Britain and France, declared war on Russia.

Russia easily prevailed over its weaker neighbor to the south. In a four-hour battle, a Russian squadron destroyed the Turkish fleet off the coast of Sinope. Tsar Nicholas I (1825–55) drew up the terms of a settlement with the Ottoman Empire and submitted them to Great Britain and France for review. The two western European powers, fearing Russian aggrandizement at Turkish expense, responded by declaring war on Russia on 28 March 1854, the date that marked a new phase in the Crimean War: Great Britain and France joined Turkey and declared war against Russia. The Italian kingdom of Sardinia joined the war against Russia in January 1855, hoping to make its name militarily and win recogni-

tion for its aim to unite Italy into a single nation. Although without explicit economic interests, Great Britain, France, and the Italian state of Sardinia were motivated by ambition, prestige, and rivalry in the Balkans.

British and French troops landed in the Crimea, the Russian peninsula extending into the Black Sea, in September 1854, with the intention of capturing Sevastopol, Russia's heavily fortified chief naval base on the Black Sea. The allies laid siege to the fortress at Sevastopol, which fell only after 322 days of battle on 11 September 1855. The defeated Russians abandoned Sevastopol, blew up their forts, and sank their own ships. Facing the threat of Austrian entry into the war, Russia agreed to preliminary peace terms.

In the Peace of Paris of 1856, Russia relinquished its claim as protector of Christians in Turkey. The British gained the neutralization of the Black Sea. The mouth of the Danube was returned to Turkish control, and an international commission was created to oversee safe navigation on the Danube. The Danubian Principalities were placed under joint guarantee of the powers, and Russia gave up a small portion of Bessarabia. In 1861 the Principalities were united in the independent nation of Romania.

The Crimean War had dramatic and enduring consequences. Russia ceased playing an active role in European affairs and turned toward expansion in central Asia. Its withdrawal opened up the possibility for a move by Prussia in central Europe.

Unifying Italy

The movement to reunite Italy culturally and politically was known as the *Risorgimento*, literally, "resurgence." In 1848, both Giuseppe Mazzini's Young Italy movement and Giuseppe Garibaldi's Red Shirts had sought a united republican Italy achieved through direct popular action. But they had failed. It took a politician of aristocratic birth to recognize that Mazzini's and Garibaldi's model of revolutionary action was doomed against the powerful Austrian military machine. Mazzini was a moralist. Garibaldi was a fighter. But Camillo Benso di Cavour (1810–61), the opportunistic politician, was a realist.

As premier of Sardinia from 1852 to 1859 and again in 1860–61, Cavour was well placed to launch his campaign for Italian unity. The Kingdom of Sardinia, whose principal state was Piedmont, had made itself a focal point for unification efforts. Its king, Carlo-Alberto (1831–49), had stood alone among Italian rulers in opposing Austrian domination of the Italian peninsula in 1848 and

The Crimean War

Unification of Italy

assemblies in Tuscany, Modena, Parma, and the Romagna, wanting to eject their Austrian rulers, voted in favor of union with the Piedmontese. By April 1860 these four areas of central Italy were under Victor Emmanuel II's rule. Sardinia had doubled in size to become the dominant power on the Italian peninsula.

Southern Italians took their lead from events in central Italy and in the spring of 1860 initiated disorders against the rule of King Francis II (1859–61) of Naples. Uprisings in Sicily inspired Giuseppe Garibaldi to return from his self-imposed exile to organize his own army of Red Shirts, known as the Thousand, who liberated Sicily, and then crossed to the Italian mainland to expel Francis II from Naples. Garibaldi next turned his attention to the liberation of the Holy City, where a French garrison protected the pope.

As Garibaldi's popularity as a national hero grew, Cavour became alarmed at the competition in uniting Italy and took secret steps to block the advance of the Red Shirts and their leader. To seize the initiative, Cavour directed the Piedmontese army into the Papal States. After defeating the pope's troops, Cavour's men crossed into the Neapolitan state and scored important victories

1849. Severely defeated by the Austrians, he was forced to abdicate. He was succeeded by his son Victor Emmanuel II (1849–61), who had the good sense to appoint Cavour as his first minister. From the start, Cavour undertook liberal administrative measures that included tax reform, stabilization of the currency, improvement of the railway system, the creation of a transatlantic steamship system, and the support of private enterprise. With these programs Cavour created for Sardinia the dynamic image of progressive change. He involved Sardinia in the Crimean War, thereby securing its status among the European powers.

Most important, however, was his alliance with France against Austria in 1858. The alliance was quickly followed by an arranged provocation against the Habsburg monarchy. Austria declared war in 1859 and was easily defeated by French forces in the battles of Magenta and Solferino. The peace settlement joined Lombardy to the Piedmontese state.

Cavour's approach was not without its costs. His partnership with a stronger power meant sometimes following France's lead, and the need to cajole French support meant enriching France with territorial gain in the form of Nice and Savoy. Sardinia, however, got more than it gave up. In the summer of 1859 revolutionary

In a British cartoon of 1860, Garibaldi surrenders his power to King Victor Emmanuel II. The caption read "Right Leg in the Boot at Last."

against forces loyal to the king of Naples. Cavour proceeded to annex southern Italy for Victor Emmanuel II, using plebiscites to seal the procedure. At this point, Garibaldi yielded his own conquered territories to Sardinia, making possible the declaration of a united Italy under Victor Emmanuel II, who reigned as king of Italy from 1861 to 1878.

The new king of Italy was now poised to acquire Venetia, under Austrian rule, and Rome, ruled by Pope Pius IX, and he devoted much of his foreign policy in the 1860s to these ends. In 1866, when Austria lost a war with Prussia, Italy struck a deal with the victor and gained control of Venetia. When Prussia prevailed against France in 1870, Victor Emmanuel II took over Rome. The boot of Italy, from top to toe, was now a single nation. The pope remained in the Vatican, opposed to an Italy united under King Victor Emmanuel II.

Unifying Germany

In an age of realistic politicians, Otto von Bismarck (1815–98) emerged as the supreme practitioner of *Realpolitik*, the ruthless pursuit by any means, including illegal and violent ones, to advance the interests of a country. Bismarck was a Junker, an aristocratic estate-owner from east of the Elbe River, who entered politics in 1847. In the 1850s, he became aware of Prussia's future in the center of Europe: he saw that the old elites must be allied with the national movement in order to survive.

In 1850 Prussia had been forced to accept Austrian dominance in central Europe or go to war. Throughout the following decade, however, Prussia systematically undermined Austrian power and excluded Austria from German economic affairs. In 1862, at the moment of a crisis provoked by the king over military reorganization, Bismarck became minister-president of the Prussian cabinet and foreign minister. He overrode the parliamentary body, the Diet, by reorganizing the army without a formally approved budget. In 1864 he constructed an alliance between Austria and Prussia for the purpose of invading Schleswig, a predominantly German-speaking territory controlled by the king of Denmark. Within five days of the invasion, Denmark yielded the duchies of Schleswig and Holstein, now to be ruled jointly by Austria and Prussia.

Counting on the neutrality of France and Great Britain, the support of Sardinia, and good relations with Russia, Bismarck promoted a crisis between Austria and

Unification of Germany

Prussia over management of the formerly Danish territories and led his country into war with Austria in June 1866. In this Seven Weeks' War, Austrian forces proved to be no match for the better-equipped and better-trained Prussian army. Bismarck dictated the terms of the peace, excluding Austria from a united, Prussian-dominated Germany. Austria faced further reorganization in 1867 when, in response to pressures from the subject nationalities, the Habsburg Empire transformed itself into a dual monarchy of two independent and equal states under one ruler, who would be both the emperor of Austria and the king of Hungary. In spite of the reorganization, the nationalities problem persisted, and ethnic groups began to agitate for total independence from imperial rule.

Bismarck's biggest obstacle to German unification was laid to rest with Austria's defeat. The south German states continued to resist the idea of Prussian dominance, but growing numbers of people in Baden, Württemberg, Bavaria, and the southern parts of Hesse-Darmstadt recognized the value of uniting under Prussian leadership.

Many French observers were troubled by the Prussian victory over Austria and were apprehensive over what a united Germany might portend for the future of French dominance in Europe. Napoleon III attempted unsuccessfully to contain Prussian ambitions through diplomatic maneuverings. Instead, France found itself stranded without important European allies. In the spring of 1870, Bismarck seized the initiative and provoked a crisis with France. The issue of succession to the Spanish throne provided the pretext. On July 13, 1870, the Prussian king (later Emperor William I) sent a message to Napoleon III reporting a meeting with the French ambassador. Bismarck skillfully edited this "Ems Dispatch" to suggest that the French ambassador had insulted the Prussian king, then leaked news of the incident to the press in both countries.

As a direct result of this contrived misunderstanding, France declared war on Prussia in July 1870. As Bismarck hoped, the southern German princes immediately sided with the Prussian king. Unlike the Germans, who were well prepared for war, the French had not coordinated deployment with the new technology of the railroad. Although French troops had the latest equipment, they were sent into battle without instructions on how to use it. And they were outnumbered almost two to one. All these factors combined to spell disaster for the French. Within a matter of weeks, it was clear that France had lost this Franco-Prussian War. The path was now clear for the declaration of the German Empire in January 1871.

In unifying Germany, Bismarck built on the constitution of the North German Confederation formed in 1867, which guaranteed Prussian dominance. Bismarck used the bureaucracy as a mainstay of the emperor. The new Reichstag—the national legislative assembly—was to be elected by means of universal male suffrage, but it was not sovereign, and the chancellor was accountable only to the emperor.

In the 1860s another crisis in state building was resolved across the Atlantic. The United States cemented political unity through the use of force in its Civil War (1861–65). The president of the United States, Abraham Lincoln (1809–65) mobilized the superior resources of the industrial Northern states against the heavily agrarian, slave-owning South. The United States worked to achieve national unity and territorial integrity in another sense through ongoing expansion westward by eliminating and subduing Native American tribes.

With the emancipation of the slaves, republican democracy appeared to triumph in the United States. Newly created European nation-states followed a different path: plebiscites were manipulated by those in power in Italy and a neo-absolutism emerged in Germany. Yet the Civil War in the United States and the successful bids for unification in Italy and Germany shared remarkable similarities. In all three countries, wars eventually resulted in a single national market and a single financial system without internal barriers. Unified national economies, particularly in Germany and the United States, paved the way for significant economic growth and the expansion of industrial power.

Reforming European Society

Three different models for social and political reform developed in Europe after 1850. In France, the emperor worked through a highly centralized administrative structure and with a valued elite of specialists in order to achieve social and economic transformation.

In Great Britain, reform was fostered through liberal parliamentary democracy. In government by "amateurs," with local rather than a highly centralized administration, British legislation alternated between a philosophy of freedom and one of protection. But reforms were always hammered out by parliamentary means with the support of a gradually expanding electorate.

Finally, Russia offers a third model for reform. Like Britain, Russia had avoided revolution at mid-century and hoped to preserve social peace. Yet the Russian model for reform stands in dramatic contrast to Britain's. Russia was still a semifeudal society in the 1850s. Beginning in the late 1850s, Russia embarked on a radical restructuring of society by autocratic means. Reforms in the three societies had little in common ideologically, but all reflected a commitment to progress and an awareness of the state's role and responsibility in achieving it.

The Second Empire in France, 1852–1870

Under Napoleon III's direction, the Second Empire achieved economic expansion and industrial development. A new private banking system enabled the pooling of investors' resources to finance industrial expansion. Napoleon III and his advisers believed prosperity was the answer to all social problems. Between 1852 and 1860 the government supported a massive program of railroad construction. Jobs multiplied and investment increased. Agriculture expanded as railroad lines opened new markets. The rich got richer but the extreme poverty of the first half of the nineteenth century was shrinking.

PLEBISCITE FOR EMPIRE

■ *Louis Napoleon (1808–73), nephew of the emperor Napoleon (1769–1821), was the surviving male contender who hoped to restore Bonapartist rule to France. After failed attempts to capture public attention during the 1840s, Louis Napoleon entered the race for the presidency of the Second Republic as a dark-horse candidate. In December 1848 he won a resounding victory against a wide field of other contenders by running a successful, modern political campaign in which he promised something to everyone and guaranteed a return to order after the revolutionary upheaval of 1848. So insignificant did he seem as a national leader in comparison to his dynamic uncle that no one really took him seriously, least of all the politicians who sought to undermine him.*

On 2 December 1851, Louis Napoleon engineered a coup d'état by which he seized dictatorial power. A year later, he proclaimed himself Emperor Napoleon III and set out to establish his dynasty and reclaim French imperial glory. In both 1851 and 1852, the Bonapartist ruler used the tool of the plebiscite to manufacture national support for his actions. In the trappings of democracy, the ballot box and universal manhood suffrage, Louis Napoleon presented the people of France with accomplished facts for which they could vote only yes or no. The following resolution, drawn up by the Senate on 7 November 1852, is a good example of how public support for the new regime was orchestrated.

The Senate has deliberated, in conformity with articles 31 and 32 of the constitution, and voted the senatus-consultum whose tenor follows:

1. The imperial dignity is re-established.

Louis-Napoleon Bonaparte is Emperor of the French, under the name of Napoleon III.

2. The imperial dignity is hereditary in the direct and legitimate descendants of Louis-Napoleon Bonaparte, from male to male, by order of primogeniture, and to the perpetual exclusion of women and their descendants. . . .

8. The following proposition shall be presented for the acceptance of the French people in the forms fixed by the decrees of December 2 and 4, 1851.

"The French people wish the re-establishment of the imperial dignity in the person of Louis-Napoleon Bonaparte, with inheritance in his direct descendants, legitimate or adopted, and give to him the right to regulate the order of succession, to the throne within the Bonaparte family, as is provided for by the senatus-consultum of November 7, 1852."

The best single example of the energy and commitment of the imperial regime was the rebuilding of the French capital. Before mid-century Paris was one of the most unsanitary, crime-ridden, and politically volatile capitals in Europe. Within fifteen years it had been transformed into a city of lights, wide boulevards and avenues, monumental vistas, parks, and gardens. Poor districts were cleared to make way for the elegant apartment buildings of the Parisian bourgeoisie. The new housing was too expensive for workers, who were pushed out of Paris to the suburbs. Wide, straight Parisian avenues served as an international model copied in Mexico City, Brussels, Madrid, Rome, Stockholm, and Barcelona between 1870 and 1900.

Just as a new Paris would make France a center of Western culture, Napoleon III intended his blueprint for foreign policy to restore France to its pre-1815 status as the greatest European power. By involving France in both the Crimean War and the war for Italian unification, Napoleon III returned France to adventurous foreign policies, acquired Nice and Savoy from Sardinia, and reversed the settlements of 1815.

French construction of the Suez Canal between the Red Sea and the Mediterranean created tensions with Great Britain, protective of its own dominance in the Mediterranean and the Near East. Nevertheless, the free-trade agreement between the British and the French in 1860 was a landmark in overseas policy and a commitment to liberal economic policies.

The Second Empire's involvement in Mexico was another matter. It was simply a fiasco. The Mexican government had been chronically unable to pay its foreign debts and France was Mexico's largest creditor. Napoleon III hoped that by intervening in Mexican

View of the Champs-Élysées after the rebuilding of Paris. The renovations were carried out under the direction of Baron Georges Haussmann, who was called the "Attila of the straight line" for the ruthless manner in which his pencil cut through city neighborhoods on the map.

affairs he could strengthen ties with Great Britain and Spain, to whom the Mexicans also owed money. With the backing of Mexican conservatives who opposed Mexican president Benito Juárez (1806–72), Napoleon III supported the Austrian archduke Maximilian (1832–67) as emperor of Mexico.

After he was crowned in 1863, the new Mexican emperor struggled to rule in an enlightened manner, but he was stymied from the beginning by his ineptitude and lack of popular support. Following the recall of the 34,000 French troops that, at considerable expense, were keeping Maximilian's troubled regime in place, Maximilian was captured and executed by a firing squad in the summer of 1867. The Mexican disaster damaged the prestige of Napoleon III's regime in the international arena, and in 1870 the humiliatingly rapid defeat of French imperial forces in the Franco-Prussian War ended the experiment in liberal empire.

The Paris Commune of 1871

With the defeat of Napoleon III and his army, the Second Empire collapsed. But even with the capture of the emperor, the city of Paris refused to capitulate. The regime's liberal critics in Paris seized the initiative to proclaim France a republic. In mid-September 1870 two German armies laid siege to a recalcitrant Paris by cutting off its vital supply lines.

Despite food and fuel shortages, the population fought on for four months. The Germans steadily bombarded the city beginning in January 1871. Although Parisians continued to resist through three weeks of

shelling, the rest of France wanted an end to the war. The Germans agreed to an armistice to allow French national elections. French citizens outside Paris repudiated the war and returned an overwhelmingly conservative majority to seek peace. Thus the siege came to an end.

Parisians felt betrayed by the rest of France. Through four months in a besieged city, they had sacrificed, suffered, and died. The war was over but Paris was not at peace. The new national government, safely installed outside Paris at Versailles, attempted in March 1871 to disarm the Parisian citizenry by using army troops. Parisian men, women, and children poured into the streets to protect their cannons and to defend their right to bear arms. In the fighting that followed, the Versailles troops were driven from the city.

The spontaneity of the March uprising was soon succeeded by organization. Citizens rallied to the idea of the city's self-government and established the Paris Commune, as other French cities followed the capital's lead. Parisians were still at war, not against a foreign enemy, but against the rest of France. For seventy-two days, as armed citizens formed their own fighting units, the city council regulated labor relations, and neighborhoods ruled themselves. In May 1871, government troops reentered the city and brutally crushed the Paris Commune. In one "Bloody Week" 25,000 Parisians were massacred and 40,000 others were arrested and tried. Such reprisals inflamed radicals and workers all over Europe. The myth of the Commune became a rallying cry for revolutionary movements throughout the world and inspired the future leaders of the Russian revolutionary state.

The Victorian Compromise

Contemporaries were aware of two facts of life about Great Britain in 1850: first, Britain had an enormously productive capitalist economy of sustained growth; and second, Britain enjoyed apparent social harmony without revolution and without civil war.

The stability and calm were undoubtedly exaggerated. Great Britain at mid-century had its share of serious social problems. British slums rivaled any in Europe. Poverty, disease, and famine ravaged the kingdom. Social protests of the 1840s raised fears of upheavals similar to those in continental Europe. Yet Great Britain avoided a revolution. One explanation for the relative calm lay in Britain's parliamentary tradition, which emphasized liberty as the birthright of English citizens and which was able to adapt to the demands of an industrializing society. Adaptation was slow, but it achieved a compromise among competing social interests. The great compromise of Victorian society was the reconciliation of industrialists' commitment to unimpeded growth with the workers' need for the protection of the state.

As part of a pattern of slow democratization, the Reform Bill of 1832 gave increased political power to the industrial and manufacturing bourgeoisie, who joined a landed aristocracy and merchant class. But the property qualification meant that only 20 percent of the population was able to vote. In 1867, under conservative leadership, a second Reform Bill was introduced. Approval of this bill doubled the electorate, giving the vote to a new urban population of shopkeepers, clerks, and workers. In 1884, farm laborers were enfranchised. Women, however, remained disenfranchised until after World War I.

William Ewart Gladstone (1809–98) was a classical liberal who believed in free enterprise and opposed state intervention. Good government, according to Gladstone, should remove obstacles to talent, competition, and individual initiative but should interfere as little as possible in economy and society. Gladstone's first term as prime minister (1868–74) significantly advanced the British liberal state. Taking advantage of British prosperity, Gladstone abolished tariffs, cut defense expenditures, lowered taxes, and sponsored sound budgets. He furthered the liberal agenda by disestablishing the Anglican church in Ireland in 1869. The church had been the source of great resentment to the vast majority of Irish Catholics, who had been forced to pay taxes to support the Protestant state church.

Gladstone reformed the army and the civil service. His government introduced the secret ballot. Finally, the Liberals stressed the importance of education for an informed electorate and passed an Education Act that aimed to make elementary schooling available to everyone. These reforms added up to a Liberal philosophy, in which government sought to remove restraints on individual freedom, foster opportunity and talent, and attack privilege.

During these years another political philosophy also left its mark on British government. This was conservatism. Under the flamboyant leadership of Benjamin Disraeli (1804–81), the Conservative party, trusting the state to correct and protect, supported state intervention and regulation on behalf of the weak and

This female aboveground coal-mine worker was photographed in 1864 by Arthur J. Munby. Such women, who sorted the coal, had low status and no prospects. They were regarded as "unsexed, immoral Amazons."

disadvantaged. Disraeli sponsored the Factory Act of 1875, which set a maximum of fifty-six hours on the factory work week. The Public Health Act established a sanitary code. The Artisans Dwelling Act defined minimum housing standards. Probably the most important conservative legislation was the Trade Union Act, which permitted picketing and other peaceful labor tactics.

Disraeli championed protection against free trade. Unlike the Liberals, he insisted on the importance of traditional institutions like the monarchy, the House of Lords, and the Church of England. His work in organizing a national party machinery facilitated the adaptation of the parliamentary system to mass politics. His methods of campaigning and building a mass base of support were used by successful politicians regardless of political persuasion.

As the intersecting careers of Gladstone and Disraeli demonstrate, the British model combined free enterprise with intervention and regulation. The clear issues and the clear choices of the two great parties—Liberal and Conservative—dominated parliamentary life after

Political rivals William Gladstone (left) and Benjamin Disraeli prepare to sling mud at each other in a Punch *cartoon.*

mid-century. In polarizing parliamentary politics, they also invigorated it.

The terms *liberal* and *conservative* hold none of the meaning today that they did for men and women in the nineteenth century. Classical liberalism has little in common with its twentieth-century counterpart, which favors an active, interventionist state. Disraeli is a far more likely candidate for the twentieth-century liberal label than is Gladstone, Britain's leading nineteenth-century liberal statesman.

Reform in Russia

In 1850 Russia was an unreformed autocracy, in which the tsar held absolute power. Without a parliament, without a constitution, and without civil liberties for his subjects, the Russian ruler governed through a bureaucracy and a police force. Economically, Russia was a semifeudal agrarian state with a class of privileged aristocrats supported by serf labor on their estates.

For decades—since the reign of Alexander I (1801–25)—the tsars and their advisers realized that they were out of step with developments in western Europe. An awareness was growing that serfdom was uncivilized and morally wrong, as critics compared the Russian practice with the atrocities of American slavery. Among the European powers, only Russia remained a serf-holding nation. Russian serfs were tied to the land and owed dues and labor services in return for the lands they held. Peasant protests mounted, attracting public attention to the plight of the serfs. But in spite of growing moral concern, there were many reasons to resist the abolition of serfdom. How were serf-holders to be compensated for the loss of labor power? What was to be the freed serfs' relationship to the land?

Hesitation about abolition evaporated with the Russian defeat in the Crimean War. The new tsar, Alexander II (1855–81), viewed Russia's inability to repel an invasion force on its own soil as proof of its backwardness. Russia had no railroads and was forced to transport military supplies by carts to the Crimea. It took Moscow three months to provision troops, while the enemy could do so in three weeks. Liberating the serfs would permit a well-trained reserve army to exist without fear of rebellion and also create a system of free labor so necessary for industrial development.

In March 1861 the tsar signed the emancipation edict that liberated 52 million serfs. Serfdom was eliminated in Poland three years later. Alexander II, who came to be known as the "Tsar-Liberator," compromised between

The Force of New Ideas   781

landlord and serf by allotting land to freed peasants, while requiring from the former serfs redemption payments that were spread out over a period of forty-nine years. The peasant paid the state in installments; the state reimbursed the landowner in the form of interest-bearing bonds and redemption certificates. Neither serf nor landholder benefited from these financial arrangements, which kept the former serf under obligation and prevented the landlord from making needed capital improvements.

The tsar introduced a vast array of "Great Reforms"—emancipating the serfs, creating local parliamentary bodies, reorganizing the judiciary, modernizing the army—yet Russia was not sufficiently liberalized or democratized to satisfy the critics of autocracy. Between 1860 and 1870 a young generation of intelligentsia, radical intellectuals who were influenced by the rhetoric of revolution in western Europe, protested against the existing order, traveling from village to village to educate and in some cases to attempt to radicalize the peasants. They paid dearly for what proved to be a fruitless commitment to populism in the mass trials and repression of the late 1870s.

Some of these critics fled into exile to reemerge as revolutionaries in western Europe, where they continued to oppose the tsarist regime and helped shape the tradition of revolution and dissent in Western countries. Other educated men and women who remained in Russia chose violence as the only effective weapon against absolute rule. Terrorists who called themselves "Will of the People" decided to assassinate the tsar; in the "emperor hunt" that followed, numerous attempts were made on the tsar's life. In the end, the Will of the People movement succeeded in its mission. In St. Petersburg in 1881, a terrorist bomb killed Alexander II, the "Tsar-Liberator."

European states engaged with the challenges of social and political reform after 1850 in ways that reflected their own political cultures and their level of social and economic development. The technocratic model of France, the liberal parliamentarianism of Great Britain, and the autocratic reforms in Russia differed ideologically. Yet all three reflected a commitment to progress and awareness of the need to be competitive in an international arena. Reform programs affirmed the state's role in achieving economic growth, national dominance, and social peace. The Paris Commune of 1871 stood as a reminder to Europe and the world that the delicate balance between governmental stability and social reform was easily disrupted and that the specter of revolution had not disappeared from Europe.

The Force of New Ideas

Great thinkers reflect their times; they also shape them. The third quarter of the nineteenth century opened an era especially rich in both the creativity and critical stance that shaped modern consciousness with discoveries in the natural and applied sciences and in the study of the individual and society.

Darwinism

Charles Darwin (1809–82), the preeminent scientist of the age, was a great synthesizer. As a young man, he sailed around the world on the *Beagle* (1831–36), collecting specimens and fossils as the ship's naturalist. His greatest finds were in South America and especially the Galápagos Islands. He spent the next twenty years of his life taking notes of his observations. The result, *On the Origin of Species by Means of Natural Selection* (1859) was a book that changed the world.

Darwin's argument was a simple one: life forms originate in and perpetuate themselves through struggle. The outcome of this struggle was determined by "natural selection," or what came to be known as "survival of the fittest." Better-adapted individuals survived, while others died out. Competition between species and within species produced a dynamic model of organic evolution and progress based on struggle. Darwin did not use the word *evolution* in the original edition, but a positivist belief in an evolutionary process permeated the text. Force explained the past and would guarantee the future, as the fittest survived. The general public found these ideas applicable to a whole range of human endeavors.

In 1871 Darwin himself applied his ideas about the natural world to social organization in his *The Descent of Man.* Using the authority of the natural sciences, Darwin argued for the natural mental inferiority of women in the species. As the weaker being, the female needed male protection, the father of evolution reasoned, thereby increasing her dependence over time and increasing the competition of natural selection among men. The result, Darwin asserted, was inequality between the sexes. Biology became destiny in these "scientific" arguments, which were used by others to foil attempts at equal rights and to exclude women from educational opportunities and professions like medicine and law.

Just as Darwin applied his observations of natural phenomena to the gender differences between men and women, others employed his ideas to justify a hierarchy of races. Social Darwinism, as the nonscientific race theories were collectively known, argued from physical characteristics and skin pigmentation to "natural" racial superiority of the white race and the "natural" racial inferiority of peoples of color. The consequences for society of social Darwinism were grave indeed: just as the authority of science was spuriously invoked to deny women electoral rights, so too did it legitimize arguments of racial superiority and racism in an age of European imperial expansion throughout the world.

Marxism

Karl Marx (1818–83) was an iconoclast. The son of a Prussian lawyer who had converted from Judaism to Christianity, he rejected the study of the law to become a philosopher. As the most brilliant of the young German Hegelians, philosophers heavily influenced by the idealist ideas of Georg Friedrich Hegel (1770–1831), he rebelled against Hegel's idealism and developed his own materially grounded view of society. In 1844, Marx joined forces with Friedrich Engels, a wealthy German businessman whose father owned factories in Manchester, England. Engels authored *The Condition of the Working Classes in England in 1844*, an exposé of the social costs of industrialization that shared Marx's outrage over the economic exploitation of workers.

The philosophy of Marx and Engels was built on a materialist view of society. Human beings were defined not by their souls but by their labor. Labor was a struggle to transform nature by producing commodities useful for survival. Building on this fundamental concept of labor, Marx and Engels saw society as divided into two camps: those who own property and those who do not. For Marx, every social system is divided into classes and carries within it the seeds of its own destruction. In a world of commerce and manufacturing, the capitalist

This illustration by Gustave Doré appeared in The Condition of the Working Classes in England in 1844 *by Friedrich Engels. Small and cramped industrial working-class houses with their tiny, walled backyards are framed by railway lines.*

bourgeoisie exploit labor for low wages; they are the new aristocracy against whom workers will eventually rebel.

Marx was more than an observer: he was a critic of capitalism who espoused revolutionary change. In his masterwork, *Das Kapital*, he presented his brand of socialism, which he called "scientific." Like Darwin, Marx was an evolutionist. He demonstrated that history is the dialectical struggle of classes. Unlike Darwin, he was sure that the workers, awakened to their exploitation, would prevail. His labor theory of value was the wedge he drove into the self-congratulatory rhetoric of the capitalist age. Labor is the source of all value, he argued, and yet the bourgeois employers deny workers the profit of their work by refusing to pay them a decent wage. Instead, they pocket the profits. Workers are separated, or *alienated*, from the product of their labor. But more profoundly, in a capitalist system all workers are alienated from the creation that makes them human; they are alienated from their labor.

Marx inspired a fervent following throughout Europe. Political parties coalesced around Marxist beliefs and programs, and Marxists were beginning to be heard in associations of workers. In London in 1864, they helped found the International Working Men's Association, an organization of workers dedicated to "the end of all class rule." The promise of a common association of workers transcending national boundaries became a compelling idea to those who envisioned the end of capitalism. The force of Marxist ideas mobilized thousands of contemporaries aware of the injustices of capitalism. Few thinkers have left a more lasting legacy than Karl Marx. The legacy survived the fact that much of his analysis rested on incorrect predictions about the increasing misery of workers and the inflexibility of the capitalist system. The force of his ideas derived from their identification of the economic roots of social injustice.

Anarchism

Anarchists, like Marxists, recognized the inherent injustice of the economic and political system, and they shared with Marxists the desire for a revolutionary restructuring of society. However, they spurned the Marxist willingness to organize and to participate in parliamentary politics. Instead of waiting for the alienation of workers to lead to political consciousness, anarchists often favored action here and now. A French anarchist named Ravachol led a band of terrorists who opposed the state and the capitalist economy as the dual enemy that could be destroyed only through individual acts of random physical violence. In 1892 his trial for

bombing and assassination attracted great public attention, bringing to light the intent of anarchists to destroy bourgeois society by sustained and random violence.

Mikhail Bakunin (1814–76), a member of the Russian nobility, became Europe's leading anarchist spokesman. He broke with Marx, whom he considered a "scientific bourgeois socialist" out of touch with the mass of workers. Bakunin's successor in international anarchist doctrine was also a Russian of aristocratic lineage—Prince Petr Kropotkin (1842–1921). Kropotkin joined together communism and anarchism, arguing that goods should be communally distributed, "from each according to his ability, to each according to his needs." Anarchism had special appeal to workers in trades staggering under the blows of industrial capitalism. Calling themselves anarcho-syndicalists, artisans, especially in France, were able to combine local trade union organization with anarchist principles.

The problems of disaffected groups in general intensified before 1914. Anarchists and anarcho-syndicalist workers deplored the centralization and organization of mass society. But anarchism never posed a serious threat to social stability because of the effectiveness of policing in most European states.

The Authority of Science

Imagine a world that discovered how to eliminate the difference between night and day. Imagine further a civilization that could obliterate distance or shrink it. Imagine a people who could see for the first time into solid mass, into their own bodies, and send images through space. These are the imaginings of fable and fantasy that can be traced back to prehistory. But what had always been the stuff of magic became reality between 1880 and 1914. The people of the West used science and technology to reshape the world and their understanding of it.

Science changed the way people thought and the way they lived. It improved the quality of life by defeating diseases, improving nutrition, and lengthening life span. But scientific knowledge was not without its negative costs. Scientific discoveries led to new forces of destruction and challenged morals and religious beliefs. New disciplines claimed to study society scientifically with methods similar to those applied to the study of bacilli and the atom. A traditional world of order and hierarchy gave way to a new reality in which the center was no longer holding and the limits were constantly expanding.

The Natural Sciences. What may seem commonplace at the end of the twentieth century was no less than spectacular at the end of the nineteenth. Scientific discoveries in the last quarter of the century pushed out the frontiers of knowledge. In physics, James Clerk Maxwell (1831–79) discovered the relation between electricity and magnetism. Maxwell showed mathematically that an oscillating electric charge produces an

FROM *THE COMMUNIST MANIFESTO*

■ *The Communist Manifesto* is one of the most important documents in world history, one that, translated into many languages in countless editions, inspired worker organizations throughout Europe in the second half of the nineteenth century and fired the imagination of Communist leaders throughout the world, in Asia, Latin America, Africa, and Europe well into the twentieth century.

The pamphlet, which in its entirety consists of no more than twelve thousand words, was written at the beginning of 1848 by Karl Marx, founder of modern communism, and his collaborator and friend, Friedrich Engels. Their intention was to urge exploited workers throughout Europe to prepare themselves for the coming revolution by uniting across national boundaries. *The Communist Manifesto* is a concise statement of the basic tenets of Marxism. Although mistaken in most of its predictions about the future development of capitalism, it accurately distilled some of the most salient inequities of industrial economies whose remedies, Marx and Engels asserted, could only be found through the revolutionary overthrow of the capitalist system.

BOURGEOIS AND PROLETARIANS*

The history of all hitherto existing society† is the history of of class struggles.

Freeman and slave, patrician and plebeian, lord and serf, guild-master and journeyman, in a word, oppressor and oppressed, stood in constant opposition to one another, carried on an uninterrupted, now hidden, now open fight, a fight that each time ended, either in a revolutionary reconstitution of society at large, or in the common ruin of the contending classes. . . .

The modern bourgeois society that has sprouted from the ruins of feudal society has not done away with class antagonisms. It has but established new classes, new conditions of oppression, new forms of struggle in place of the old ones.

Our epoch, the epoch of the bourgeoisie, possesses, however, this distinctive feature: it has simplified the class antagonisms. Society as a whole is more and more splitting up into two great hostile camps, into two great classes directly facing each other: Bourgeoisie and Proletariat. . . .

The bourgeoisie cannot exist without constantly revolutionizing the instruments of production, and thereby the relations of production, and with them the whole relations of society. Conservation of the old modes of production in unaltered form, was, on the contrary, the first condition of existence for all earlier industrial classes. Constant revolutionizing of production, uninterrupted disturbance of all social conditions, everlasting uncertainty and agitation distinguish the bourgeois epoch from all earlier ones. All fixed, fast-frozen relations, with their train of ancient and venerable prejudices and opinions are swept away, all new-formed ones become antiquated before they can ossify. All that is solid melts into air, all that is holy is profaned, and man is at last compelled to face with sober senses, his real conditions of life, and his relations with his kind.

The need of a constantly expanding market for its products chases the bourgeoisie over the whole surface of the globe. It must nestle everywhere, settle everywhere, establish connexions everywhere. . . .

*By bourgeoisie is meant the class of modern Capitalists, owners of the means of social production and employers of wage labour. By proletariat, the class of modern wage-labourers who, having no means of production of their own, are reduced to selling their labour power in order to live. [*Note by Engels to the English edition of 1888.*]

FROM *THE COMMUNIST MANIFESTO*

The proletariat goes through various stages of development. With its birth begins its struggle with the bourgeoisie. At first the contest is carried on by individual labourers, then by the work-people of a factory, then by the operatives of one trade, in one locality, against the individual bourgeois who directly exploits them. They direct their attacks not against the bourgeois conditions of production, but against the instruments of production themselves; they destroy imported wares that compete with their labour, they smash to pieces machinery, they set factories ablaze, they seek to restore by force the vanished status of the workman of the Middle Ages.

PROLETARIANS AND COMMUNISTS

In what relation do the Communists stand to the proletarians as a whole?

The Communists do not form a separate party opposed to other working-class parties.

They have no interests separate and apart from those of the proletariat as a whole. . . .

You are horrified at our [Communists'] intending to do away with private property. But in your existing society, private property is already done away with for nine-tenths of the population; its existence for the few is solely due to its non-existence in the hands of those nine-tenths. You reproach us, therefore, with intending to do away with a form of property the necessary condition for whose existence is the non-existence of any property for the immense majority of society. . . .

In short, the Communists everywhere support every revolutionary movement against the existing social and political order of things.

In all these movements they bring to the front, as the leading question in each, the property question, no matter what its degree of development at the time.

Finally, they labour everywhere for the union and agreement of the democratic parties of all countries.

The Communists disdain to conceal their views and aims. They openly declare that their ends can be attained only by the forcible overthrow of all existing social conditions. Let the ruling classes tremble at a Communistic revolution. The proletarians have nothing to lose but their chains. They have a world to win.

WORKING MEN OF ALL COUNTRIES, UNITE!

From Karl Marx and Friedrich Engels, *The Communist Manifesto*, 1848.

electromagnetic field and that such a field radiates outward from its source at a constant speed—the speed of light. His theories led to the discovery of the electromagnetic spectrum, comprising radiation of different wavelengths, including X rays, visible light, and radio waves. This discovery had important practical applications for the development of the electrical industry and led to the invention of radio and television. Within a generation, the names of Edison, Westinghouse, Marconi, Siemens, and Bell entered the public realm.

Discoveries in the physical sciences succeeded one another with great rapidity. The periodic table of chemical elements was formulated in 1869. Radioactivity was discovered in 1896. Two years later Marie Curie (1867–1934) and her husband Pierre (1859–1906) discovered the elements radium and polonium. At the end of the century, Ernest Rutherford (1871–1937) identified alpha and beta rays in radioactive atoms. Building on the new discoveries, Max Planck (1858–1947), Albert Einstein (1879–1955), and Niels Bohr (1885–1962) dismantled the classical physics of absolute and determined principles and left in its place modern physics based on relativity and uncertainty. In 1900 Planck propounded a theory that renounced the emphasis in classical physics on energy as a wave phenomenon in favor of a new "quantum theory" of energy as emitted and absorbed in minute, discrete amounts.

In 1905 Albert Einstein formulated his special theory of relativity, in which he established the relationship of mass and energy in the famous equation $E = mc^2$. In 1916 he published his general theory of relativity, a mathematical formulation that created new concepts of space and time. Einstein disproved the Newtonian view of gravitation as a force and instead saw it as a curved field in the time-space continuum created by the presence of mass. At the time no one foresaw that the application of Einstein's theory—that a particle of matter could be converted into a great quantity of energy—would unleash the greatest destructive power in history, the atomic and hydrogen bombs. But Einstein, a pacifist, lived to see these weapons developed in his lifetime.

Although the discoveries in the physical sciences were the most dramatic, the biological sciences too witnessed great breakthroughs. Research biologists dedicated themselves to the study of disease-causing microbes and to the chemical bases of physiology. French chemist Louis Pasteur (1822–95) studied microorganisms to find methods of preventing the spread of diseases in humans, animals, and plants. He developed methods of inoculation to provide protection against anthrax in sheep, cholera in chickens, and rabies in animals and humans. The malaria parasite was isolated in 1880. The control of diseases such as yellow fever improved the quality of life.

Knowledge burst the bounds of disciplines and new fields developed to accommodate new concerns. Research in human genetics, a field that was only beginning to be understood, was initiated in the first decade of the twentieth century. The studies in the crossbreeding of peas carried out in the 1860s by the Austrian botanist Gregor Mendel (1822–84) led to the Mendelian laws of inheritance.

Biological discoveries resulted in new state policies. Public health benefited from new methods of prevention and detection of diseases caused by germs. A professor at the University of Berlin, Rudolf Virchow (1821–1902) discovered the relationship between microbes, sewage, and disease that led to the development of modern sewer systems and pure water for urban populations. Biochemistry, bacteriology, and physiology promoted a belief in social progress through state pro-

grams. After 1900 health programs to educate the general public spread throughout Europe.

This was a time of firsts in other applied fields: airplane flights and deep-sea expeditions, based on technological applications of new discoveries, pushed out boundaries of exploration above the land and below the sea. In 1909, the same year that work began in human genetics, American explorer Robert E. Peary (1856–1920) reached the North Pole. In that year, too, plastic was first manufactured, under the trade name Bakelite. Irish-born British astronomer Agnes Mary Clerke (1842–1907) did pioneering work in the new field of astrophysics. Rutherford proposed a new spatial reality in his theory of the nuclear structure of the atom, which stated that the atom can be divided and that it consists of a nucleus surrounded by electrons revolving around it.

The Social Sciences. Innovations in the social sciences paralleled the drama of discovery in the biological and physical sciences. The "scientific" study of society purported to apply the same methods of observation and experimentation to human interactions. After 1870, sociology, economics, history, psychology, anthropology, and archaeology took shape at the core of new social scientific endeavors.

Archaeology uncovered lost civilizations. Heinrich Schliemann (1822–90), who discovered Troy, and Sir

Robert E. Peary. His claim to the discovery of the North Pole was questioned when Frederick Cook announced that he had reached the pole before Peary. After an investigation, the U.S. Congress upheld Peary's claim.

LADY CONSTANCE LYTTON: A SUFFRAGETTE IN JAIL

■ *British women who agitated for the right to vote suffered for their militancy, as civil disobedience evoked harsh repressive measures from the British government. Previous benevolence toward middle-class female prisoners arrested for attacks on property gave way to a new harshness that included the force-feeding of convicted suffragettes who went on hunger strikes in prison as a form of protest.*

Here Lady Constance Lytton describes her own grueling experience in Walton Gaol, Liverpool, in January 1910. She was forced repeatedly to endure the agony of force-feeding, which damaged her heart and brought on a stroke in early 1912, leaving her in poor health until her death in 1923.

Public outcry against the brutality of force-feeding did not result in the extension of the vote to women. Instead, Parliament passed the Cat and Mouse Act in 1913, whereby imprisoned women who refused to eat were released, then reincarcerated once they had resumed eating and regained their strength. This "cat and mouse" pattern of release and reimprisonment could double or extend indefinitely a three-year sentence served in three-day segments and, for the time being, foiled militant feminist protest behind bars.

[The prison's senior medical officer] urged me to take food voluntarily. I told him that was absolutely out of the question, that when our legislators ceased to resist enfranchising women then I should cease to resist taking food in prison . . . I offered no resistance to being placed in position, but lay down voluntarily on the plank bed. Two of the wardresses took hold of my arms, one held my head and one my feet. One wardress helped to pour the food. The doctor leant on my knees as he stooped over my chest to get at my mouth. I shut my mouth and clenched my teeth. . . . The doctor offered me the choice of a wooden nor steel gag; he explained elaborately, as he did on most subsequent occasions, that the steel gag would hurt and the wooden one not, and he urged me not to force him to use the steel gag. But I did not speak nor open my mouth, so that after playing about for a moment or two with the wooden one he finally had recourse to the steel. He seemed annoyed at my resistance and he broke into a temper as he plied my teeth with the steel implement . . . The pain of it was intense and at last I must have given way for he got the gag between my teeth, when he proceeded to turn it much more than necessary until my jaws were fastened wide apart, far more than they could go naturally. Then he put down my throat a tube which seemed to me much too wide and was something like four feet in length. The irritation of the tube was excessive. I choked the moment it touched my throat until it had got down. Then the food was poured in quickly; it made me sick a few seconds after it was down and the action of the sickness made my body and legs double up, but the wardresses instantly pressed back my head and the doctor leant on my knees. The horror of it was more than I can describe. I was sick over the doctor and wardresses, and it seemed a long time before they took the tube out. As the doctor left he gave me a slap on the cheek, not violently, but, as it were, to express his contemptuous disapproval, and he seemed to take for granted that my distress was assumed. . . . I had been sick over my hair, which, though short, hung on either side of my face, all over the wall near my bed, and my clothes seemed saturated with it, but the wardresses told me they could not get me a change that night as it was too late, the office was shut. I lay quite motionless, it seemed paradise to be without the suffocating tube, without the liquid food going in and out of my body and without the gag between my teeth. Before long I heard the sounds of the forced feeding in the next cell to mine. It was almost more than I could bear, it was Elsie Howey, I was sure. When the ghastly process was over and all quiet, I tapped on the wall and called out at the top of my voice, which wasn't much just then, 'No surrender,' and there came the answer past any doubt in Elsie's voice. 'No surrender.'

From Constance Lytton, *Prisons and Prisoners*, 1914.

Military hospital nursing service brooch showing Florence Nightingale.

A Working Woman

Women have always worked. But how society has valued women's work has changed over time. After 1850 women of all income levels, not just the wealthy, were expected to retire from the workplace when they married. Woman's proper role was caring for her husband and family and watching over her children. Young women worked before they married in order to help parents and to save dowries. Many married women continued to work for wages because they had to; they were too poor to live by society's norms. But mid-nineteenth-century European culture reinforced the idea that woman's place was in the separate domestic sphere of private pleasures and unpaid labor. To be a "public" man was a valued attribution. The same adjective applied to a woman meant she was a harlot.

Yet it is this culture that immortalized Florence Nightingale, a woman who valued what she called "my work" above home and family. She was a single woman in an age when more and more women were making the choice to remain unmarried, but it was also an age in which *spinster* was a term of derision and a sign of failure. Queen Victoria, the most maternal and domestic of queens, hailed her as "an example to our sex" and bestowed on her the British Empire's Order of Merit for her life achievements. Miss Nightingale, as she was known, was widely regarded as the greatest woman of her age, a highly visible and outspoken reformer who deviated from woman's unpaid role as nurturer in the private sphere. How could she be an "example" to the women of her time?

Florence Nightingale was lauded for her work during the Crimean War in organizing hospital care at Scutari, a suburb outside Constantinople (on the Asiatic side of the Bosporus). There she attacked the mismanagement, corruption, and lack of organization characteristic of medical treatment for British soldiers. She campaigned for better sanitation, hygiene, ventilation, and diet, and thanks to her efforts, in 1855 the death rate plummeted from 42 percent to 2 percent. The *London Times* declared, "There is not one of England's prettiest and purest daughters who at the moment stands on as high a pinnacle as Florence Nightingale."

It was a pinnacle not easily scaled. Blocked by her family and publicly maligned, Nightingale struggled against prevailing norms to carve out her occupation. She was the daughter of a wealthy gentry family, and from her father she received a man's classical education. The fashion of the day emphasized woman's confinement to the home: crinolines, corsets, and trains restricted movement and suggested gentility. This was the life of Nightingale's older sister and one that "the Angel of the Crimea" fiercely resisted. Nightingale railed at the inequity of married life: "A man gains everything by marriage: he gains a 'helpmate,' but a woman does not." Her memoirs are filled with what she called her "complaints" against the plight of women.

Nightingale was not a typical working woman. She struck out on her career as a rebel. Because of her wealth, she did not need to work, yet she felt driven to be useful. Her choice of nursing much alarmed her family, who considered the occupation to be on the level with domestic service or even prostitution. Nightingale shattered these taboos. She visited nursing establishments throughout Europe, traveling alone—another feat unheard of for women in her day—and studied their methods and techniques. She conceived of her own mission to serve God through caring for others.

In 1860, Nightingale established a school to train nurses, just as similar institutions were being created to train young women as teachers. These occupations were extensions of the domestic role of women as nurturers in the classroom and at the sickbed.

These new female professions were also poorly paid. Significantly, Florence Nightingale, honored as she was in her lifetime, received no salary for her contributions to the British state. Her work was supported by donations from benefactors and administrative protectors she referred to as her "masters."

Florence Nightingale spent a good part of the last forty-five years of her life in a sickbed suffering from what she called "nervous fever." During this period she wrote incessantly and continued to lobby for her programs, benefiting, one of her biographers claimed, from the freedom to think and write provided by her illness. It may well be true that her invalidism protected her from the claims on her time made by her family and by society. It may also be true that she, like many of her middle-class female contemporaries, experienced debilitation or suffered from hypochondria in direct proportion to the limitations they experienced.

Despite the persistence of political and legal inequalities, women did participate in new occupations justified by their role as nurturers. As helpmeets, women entered a new work sector identi-fied by the adjective *service*. Women were accepted as clerical workers, performing the "housekeeping" of business firms and bureaucracies. Nightingale herself believed that the right to vote was less important than financial independence for women. New occupations labeled as "women's work" were essential to the expansion of industrial society. A healthy and literate population guaranteed a strong citizenry, a strong army, and a strong workforce.

After mid-century, gender differences, socially defined virtues for men and women, hardened. Individualism, competition, and militarism were the values of the world of men. Familial support, nurturance, and healing were female virtues. These were the separate and unequal worlds created by the factory and the battlefield. The virtues of the private sphere were extended into the public world with the creation of new forms of poorly paid female labor. In this sense, Florence Nightingale was not a rebel. This "Lady with the Lamp," whom fever-ridden soldiers called their mother, was another working woman.

Arthur Evans (1851–1941), who began excavations in Crete in 1900, used scientific procedures to reconstruct ancient cultures. Historians, too, applied new techniques to the study of the past. German historian Leopold von Ranke (1795–1886) eschewed a literary form of historical writing that relied on legend and tradition in favor of objective, "scientific" history based on documentation and other forms of material evidence.

The social scientific study of economics came to the aid of businessmen. The neoclassical economic theory of Alfred Marshall (1842–1924) and others recognized the centrality of individual choice in the marketplace, while addressing the problem of overproduction: how can businesses know they have produced enough to maximize profits? Economists concerned with how individuals responded to prices devised a theory of marginal utility, by which producers could calculate costs and project profits based on a pattern of response of consumers to price changes.

"Scientific" psychology developed in a variety of directions. In Leipzig in 1879, Wilhelm Wundt (1832–1920) established the first laboratory devoted to psychological research. From his experiments he concluded that thought is grounded in physical reality. The Russian physiologist Ivan Pavlov (1849–1936) won fame with a series of experiments demonstrating the conditioned reflex in dogs. Sigmund Freud (1859–1939) greatly influenced the direction of psychology with his theory of personality development and the creation of psychoanalysis, the science of the unconscious. Freudian probing of the unconscious was a model greatly at odds with the behavioral perspective of conditioned responses based on Pavlov's work.

Emile Durkheim (1858–1917) is regarded as the founder of modern sociology. In his famous study of suicide as a social phenomenon, Durkheim pitted sociological theory against psychology and argued that deviance was the result not of psychic disturbances but of environmental factors and hereditary forces. Heredity became a general explanation for behavior of all sorts. Everything from poverty, drunkenness, crime, and a declining birth rate could be attributed to biologically determined causes. For some theorists, this reasoning teetered on the edge of racism and ideas about "better blood." Intelligence was now measured for the first time "scientifically" with IQ tests developed at the Sorbonne by the psychologist Alfred Binet (1857–1911) in the 1890s. But the tests did not acknowledge the importance of cultural factors in the development of intelligence, and they scientifically legitimated a belief in natural elites.

Feminism and Politics

Women's emancipation had been a recurrent motif of European political culture throughout the nineteenth century. Yet in the areas of civil liberties, legal equality with men, and economic autonomy, only the most limited reforms had been enacted. The cult of domesticity, important throughout the nineteenth century, assigned women to a separate sphere, that of the home. It recognized women's unique contribution to society as wives and mothers, but it also reinforced the separate and inferior status of women.

In the workplace, European women were paid at best one-third to one-half of what men earned for the same work. In Great Britain, women did not have an equal right to divorce until the twentieth century. In France, the earnings of married women were considered their husband's private property. From the Atlantic to the Urals, women were excluded from economic and educational opportunities (see Special Feature, "A Working Woman," pp. 788–789).

At the end of the nineteenth century, amidst the scientific justification of female inferiority, the "new woman" emerged. This cultural phenomenon, omnipresent in the press, the theater, and in popular works of fiction, rejected the Victorian stereotype of the angel at the hearth and replaced it with the "new woman," a heroic being of intelligence, strength, and sexual desire, in every way man's equal. The Norwegian playwright Henrik Ibsen (1828–1906) created a fictional embodiment of the phenomenon in Nora, the hero of *A Doll's House* (1879), who was typical of the restive spirit for independence among wives and mothers confined to suffocating households and relegated to the status of children.

Women's movements of the period from 1871 to 1914 differed socially and culturally from nation to nation. Yet there is a sense in which the women's political activities constituted an international phenomenon. The rise of political consciousness of women occurred in the most advanced Western countries almost simultaneously and had a predominantly middle-class character. By 1900, sexuality and reproduction were openly connected to discussions of women's rights. But in spite of concerted efforts, women remained on the outside of societies that excluded them from political participation, access to education, and social and economic equality.

Growing numbers of women, primarily from the middle classes, began calling themselves *feminist*, a term coined in France in the 1830s. The new feminists throughout western Europe differed from earlier generations in their willingness to organize mass movements and to appropriate the techniques of interest-group politics. The first international congress of women's rights, held in Paris in 1878, initiated an era of international cooperation and exchange among women's organizations. Women's groups now positioned themselves for sustained political action.

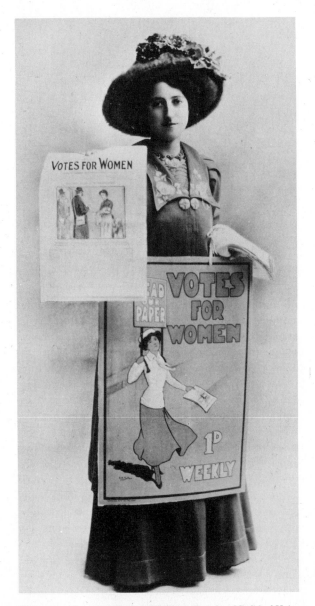

A young member of the National Women's Social and Political Union sells copies of the paper Votes for Women.

Most feminists agitated for the vote as the single most important gain women could achieve in their pursuit of equality. Other feminists thought that the vote for women did not address the real issues of economic, social, and legal oppression. For those feminists who pursued equality at the ballot box, the lessons of the new electoral politics taught them the need to organize and lobby for change. Leaders like Hubertine Auclert (1848–1914) in France and Emmeline Pankhurst (1858–1928) in Great Britain built a mass base of support. Women's organizations, which survived as competing interest groups, formed political alliances, controlled their own newspapers and magazines, and kept their cause before the public eye.

A variety of women's organizations used demonstrations, rallies, and even violent tactics to publicize their cause. No movement operated more effectively in this regard than the Women's Social and Political Union (WSPU), formed in 1903 by a group of eminently respectable middle-class and aristocratic British women. At the center of the movement was Emmeline Pankhurst, a middle-aged woman of frail and attractive appearance, with a will of iron and a gift for oratory. She was joined by her two daughters Christabel (1880–1958), a lawyer by training, and Sylvia (1882–1960), an artist. These three women succeeded in keeping women's suffrage before the British public and brought the plight of British women to international attention.

Mrs. Pankhurst and others advocated violence against personal property to highlight the violence done to women by denying them their rights. Militant women set mailboxes on fire or poured glue and jam over their contents, threw bombs into country houses, and slashed paintings in the National Gallery. These tactics seemed to accomplish little before the war, although they certainly kept the issue of women's suffrage in the public eye until the outbreak of war in 1914.

Those feminists who agitated for social reforms for poor and working-class women parted ways with the militant suffragettes. Sylvia Pankhurst, for example, left her mother and sister to their political battles in order to work for social reform in London's poverty-stricken East End. These feminists were socialists concerned with working-class women's "double oppression" in the home and in the workplace. Working-class women, most notably in Germany, united feminism with socialism in search of a better life.

European women did not easily gain the right to vote. In France and Germany moderate and left-wing politicians opposed extension of the vote to women because they feared that women would strengthen conservative candidates. Many politicians felt that women were not "ready" for the vote and that they should receive it only as a reward—an unusual concept in democratic societies. It was not until 1918 that British women, praised for their wartime efforts, were granted limited suffrage, and not until 1928 that women gained voting rights equal to those of men. Only after war and revolution was the vote extended to other women in the West; Soviet Russia in 1917, Germany in 1918, the United States in 1920, and France at the end of World War II.

The Jewish Question and Zionist Solution

The word *anti-Semitism*, meaning hostility to Jews, was first used in 1879 to give a pseudoscientific legitimacy to bigotry and hatred. Persecution was a harsh reality for Jews in eastern Europe at the end of the nineteenth century. In Russia, Jews could not own property and were restricted to living in certain territories. Organized massacres, or pogroms, in Kiev, Odessa, and Warsaw followed the assassination of Tsar Alexander II in 1881 and occurred again after the failed Russian revolution of 1905. Russian authorities blamed the Jews, perceived as perennial outsiders, for the assassination and the revolution and the social instability that followed them. Pogroms resulted in the death and displacement of tens of thousands of eastern European Jews.

Between 1868 and 1914 two million eastern European Jews migrated westward in search of peace and refuge. Seventy thousand settled in Germany, more in the United States. Another kind of Jewish migration also took place in the nineteenth century—the movement of Jews from rural to urban areas within nations. In eastern Europe Jewish migrations coincided with downturns in the economic cycle, and Jews became scapegoats for the high rates of unemployment and high prices that seemed to follow in their wake. Most Jewish migrants were peddlers, artisans, or small shopkeepers who were seen as threatening to small businesses. Differing in language, culture, and dress, they were seen as alien in every way.

In western Europe Jews considered themselves "assimilated" into their national cultures, identifying with their nationality as much as with their religion. In 1867 Austrian and German Jews were granted full civil rights on the principle that citizens of all religions enjoyed full equality. In France, Jews had been legally emancipated since the end of the eighteenth century. But the west-

Jewish Migration

ern and central European politics of the 1890s had a strong dose of anti-Semitism. Demagogues like Georg von Schönerer (1842–1921) of Austria were capable of whipping up a frenzy of riots and violence against Jews. They did not distinguish between assimilated and immigrant Jewish populations in their irrational denunciations. Western and central European anti-Semitism assumed a new level of virulence at the end of the nineteenth century. Fear of an economic depression united aristocrat and worker alike in blaming a Jewish conspiracy. German anti-Semitism proliferated in the 1880s. "It is like a horrible epidemic," the scholar Theodor Mommsen (1817–1903) observed.

Fear of the Jews was connected with hatred of capitalism. In France and Germany, Jews controlled powerful banking and commercial firms that became the targets of blame in hard times. Upwardly mobile sons of Jewish immigrants entered the professions of banking, trading, and journalism. They were also growing in numbers as teachers and academics. In the 1880s more than half of Vienna's physicians (61 percent in 1881) and lawyers (58 percent of barristers in 1888) were Jewish. Their professional success only heightened tensions and condemnations of Jews as an "alien race." Anti-Semitism served as a violent means of mobilizing mass support, especially among those groups who felt threatened by capitalist concentration and large-scale industrialization.

A Jewish leadership emerged in central and western Europe that treated anti-Semitism as a problem that could be solved by political means. For their generation at the end of the nineteenth century, the assimilation of their fathers and mothers was not the answer. Jews needed their own nation, it was argued, since they were a people without a nation. Zionism was the solution to what Jewish intellectuals called "the Jewish problem." Zion, the ancient homeland of Biblical times, would provide a national territory, and a choice, to persecuted Jews. Zionism became a Jewish nationalist movement dedicated to the establishment of a Jewish state. Although Zionism did not develop mass support in western Europe among assimilated Jews, its program for national identity and social reforms appealed to a large following of eastern European Jews, those directly subjected to the extremes of persecution in Galicia (Poland), Russia, and the Habsburg empire.

Theodor Herzl (1860–1904), an Austrian Jew born in Budapest, was the founder of Zionism in its political form. As a student in Vienna, he encountered discrimination, but his commitment to Zionism developed as a result of his years as a journalist in Paris. There in republican France, he observed the anti-Semitic attacks provoked by scandals surrounding the misappropriation of funds by leading French politicians and businessmen during the failed French attempt to build a Panama canal, and he witnessed the divisive conflict over the Dreyfus Affair in the 1890s. Herzl came to recognize that anti-Semitism was deeply imbedded in European society. He despaired of the ability of corrupt parliamentary governments to solve the problem of anti-Semitism. In *The Jewish State* (1896), Herzl concluded that Jews must have a state of their own. Under his direction, Zionism developed a world organization with the aim of establishing a Jewish homeland in Palestine.

Jews began emigrating to Palestine. With the financial backing of Jewish donors like the French banker Baron de Rothschild, nearly 90,000 Jews had established settlements there by 1914. Calculated to tap a common Jewish identification with an ancient heritage, from the beginning the choice of Palestine as a homeland was controversial, and the problems arising from the choice have persisted through the twentieth century.

Some Jewish critics of Zionism felt that a separate Jewish state would prove that Jews were not good citizens of their respective nation-states and would exacer-

bate hostilities toward Jews as outsiders. Yet Zionism had much in common with the European liberal tradition because it sought in the creation of a nation-state for Jews the solution to social injustice. It learned from other mass movements of the period the importance of a broad base of support. By the time of the First Zionist Congress, held in Basel, Switzerland, in 1897, it had become a truly international movement. But Zionism did not achieve its goals before World War I, and the Jewish state of Israel was not recognized by the world community until 1948.

Advances in the scientific study of the natural world paralleled the development of new theories of social life and social organization. The authority of science cured disease and improved the quality of life for millions. Not all of these new ideas, theories, and applications had happy consequences. The authority of pseudo-scientific beliefs was wielded against excluded groups to justify racist theories and gender differences. Workers, women, and Jews were the targets of exclusionary policies. The force of new ideas placed in flux the world in which Europeans lived, and with it their values and behavior.

Economic Regulation and Mass Politics, *1871–1914*

Between 1871 and 1914, the scale of European life was radically altered. Industrial society had made largeness the norm, as growing numbers of people worked under the same roof. Large-scale heavy industries fueled by new energy sources dominated the economic landscape. Fewer people remained on the land, and those who did stay in the agricultural sector were linked to cities and tied into national cultures by new transportation and communications networks.

Changes in the scale of political life paralleled the rise of heavy industry and the increasing urbanization of European populations. Great Britain experienced the transformation in political organization and social structure before other European nations. But after 1870 changes in politics influenced by the scale of the new industrial society spread to every European country. Mass democracy was on the rise and was pushing aside the liberal emphasis on individual rights valued by parliamentary governments everywhere.

In spite of dramatic changes in politics and society, monarchy remained the dominant form of government.

Although the right to vote was gradually being extended to all men in western Europe, women were excluded from national political participation. Extraparliamentary groups—lobbies, trade unions, and cartels—grew in influence and power and exerted pressure on the political process. The politics of mass society made clear the contradictions inherent in democracy.

Regulating Boom and Bust

Between 1873 and 1895 an epidemic of slumps battered the economies of European nations. These slumps, characterized by falling prices, downturns in productivity, and declining profits, did not strike European nations simultaneously, nor did they affect all countries with the same degree of severity. But they did teach industrialists, financiers, and politicians one important lesson: alternative booms and busts in the business cycle were dangerous and had to be regulated.

Intense economic expansion brought on the steady deflation of the last quarter of the nineteenth century. In the world economy, there was an overproduction of agricultural products, resulting from technological advances in crop cultivation and the low cost of shipping and transport, which had opened up European markets to cheap agricultural goods from North and South America. The drop in food prices affected purchasing power in other sectors and resulted in long-term deflation and unemployment.

Financiers, politicians, and businessmen dedicated themselves to eliminating the boom-and-bust phenomenon, which they considered dangerous. The application of science and technology to industrial production required huge amounts of capital. The two new sources of power after 1880, petroleum and electricity, could be developed only with heavy capital investment. In order to raise the capital necessary for the new heavy industry at the end of the nineteenth century, firms had to look outside themselves to the stock market, banks, or the state. But investors and especially banks refused to invest without guarantees on their capital. The solution they demanded was the elimination of uncertainty through the regulation of markets.

Regulation was achieved through the establishment of *cartels*, agreements among firms in a given industry to fix prices and to establish production quotas, in order to control markets and guarantee profits. For example, all steel producers agreed to fix prices and set quotas. Or they combined vertically by controlling all levels of the production process from raw materials to the finished product.

Firms in Great Britain, falling behind in heavy industry, failed to form cartels and for the most part remained in private hands. But heavy industry in Germany, France, and Austria, to varying degrees, sought regulation of markets through cartels. International cartels appeared that regulated markets and prices across national borders within Europe.

Banks, which had been the initial impetus behind the transformation to a regulated economy, in turn formed consortia to meet the need for greater amounts of capital. A *consortium*, paralleling a cartel, was a partnership among banks, often international in character, in which interest rates and the movement of capital were regulated by mutual agreement.

The state, too, played an important role in directing the economy. Throughout Europe nation-states protected domestic industries by erecting tariff barriers that made foreign goods noncompetitive in domestic markets. Only Great Britain among the major powers stood by a policy of free trade. Europe was split into two tiers—the haves and have-nots: those countries with a solid industrial core and those that had remained unindustrialized. This division had a geographic character, with the north and west of Europe heavily developed and capitalized and the southern and eastern parts of Europe remaining heavily agricultural. For both the haves and have-nots, tariff policies protected established industries and nurtured those industries struggling for existence.

Challenging Liberal England

Great Britain prided itself on the progress achieved by a strong parliamentary tradition based on a homogeneous ruling elite. Aristocrats, businessmen, and financial leaders shared a common educational background in England's elitist educational system, which produced a common outlook and common attitudes toward parliamentary rule regardless of party, and guaranteed a certain stability in policies and legislation.

In the 1880s, issues of unemployment, public health, housing, and education challenged the attitudes of Britain's ruling elite and fostered the advent of an independent working-class politics. Between 1867 and 1885 extension of the suffrage increased the electorate fourfold. Protected by the markets of its empire, the British economy did not experience the roller-coaster effect of recurrent booms and busts after 1873. But after 1900 wages stagnated as prices

A cartoon from a pamphlet published in Britain by the Tariff Reform League in 1903. The tree represents Britain's free-trade policy. The other nations of the world are harvesting the benefits of the British policy.

continued to rise, and workers responded to their distress by supporting militant trade unions.

Trade unions, drawing on a long tradition of working-class associations, were all that stood between workers and the economic dislocation caused by unemployment, sickness, or old age, and beginning in the 1880s and 1890s they flourished. A Scottish miner, James Keir Hardie (1856–1915), attracted national attention as the spokesman for a new political movement, the Labour party, that sought to represent workers in Parliament. In 1892 Hardie was the first independent workingman to sit in the House of Commons. Hardie and his party convinced trade unions to support Labour candidates instead of Liberals in parliamentary elections after 1900. By 1906, the new Labour party had 29 seats in Parliament. Intellectuals now joined with trade unionists in demanding public housing, better public sanitation, municipal reforms, and improved pay and benefits for workers.

After 1906, under threat of losing votes to the Labour party, the Liberal party heeded the pressures for reform. The "new" Liberals supported legislation to strengthen the right of unions to picket peacefully. Led by David Lloyd George (1863–1945), who was chancellor of the exchequer, Liberals sponsored the National Insurance Act of 1911. The act provided compulsory payments to workers for sickness and unemployment benefits.

In order to pay for this new legislation, Lloyd George recognized that Parliament itself had to be renovated. The Parliament Bill of 1911 reduced the Conservative-dominated House of Lords from its status as equal partner with the House of Commons. Commons could and now did raise taxes without the consent of the House of Lords to pay for new programs that benefited workers and the poor. But social legislation did not silence

unions and worker organizations. Between 1910 and 1914, strike waves broke over England. Coal miners, seamen, railroad workers, and dockers protested against stagnant wages and rising prices.

Labour's voice grew more strident. The Trade Unions Act of 1913 granted unions legal rights to settle their grievances with management directly. Only the outbreak of war in 1914 ended the possibility of a general strike by miners, railwaymen, and transport workers. The question of Irish Home Rule also plagued Parliament. In Ulster in northern Ireland army officers of Protestant Irish background threatened to mutiny. In addition, women agitating for the vote shattered parliamentary complacency. The most advanced industrial nation with its tradition of peaceful parliamentary rule had entered the age of mass politics.

Political Struggles in Germany and Austria

During his reign as chancellor of the German Empire (1871–90), Otto von Bismarck repeatedly and successfully blocked the emergence of fully democratic participation in government. Bismarck's objective remained always the successful unification of Germany, and he promoted cooperation with democratic institutions and parties only to enhance that goal.

Throughout the 1870s the German chancellor collaborated with the German liberal parties in constructing the legal codes, the monetary and banking system, the judicial apparatus, and the railroad network that pulled the new Germany together. Bismarck backed German liberals in their antipapal campaign, in which the Catholic church was declared the enemy of the German

Zwischen Berlin und Rom.

Der letzte Zug war mir allerdings unangenehm; aber die Partie ist deshalb noch nicht verloren. Ich habe noch einen sehr schönen Zug in petto!

Das wird auch der letzte sein, und dann sind Sie in wenigen Zügen matt —   wenigstens für Deutschland.

The struggle between Bismarck and the pope is symbolized in this cartoon. Bismarck's chessmen include "Germania," the press, and antimonastic legislation. The pope marshals encyclicals, interdicts, and the Syllabus of Errors.

state. He suspected the identification of Catholics with Rome, which the liberals depicted as an authority in competition with the nation-state. The anti-Church campaign, launched in 1872, was dubbed *Kulturkampf*, "struggle for civilization," because its supporters contended that it was a battle waged in the interests of humanity.

The legislation of the Kulturkampf expelled Jesuits from Germany, removed priests from state service, attacked religious education, and instituted civil marriage. Many Germans grew concerned over the social costs of such widespread religious repression, and the Catholic Center party increased its parliamentary representation by rallying Catholics as a voting bloc.

With the succession of a new pontiff, Leo XIII (1878–1903), Bismarck negotiated a settlement with the Catholic church, cutting his losses and ending the Kulturkampf.

Bismarck's repressive policies also targeted the Social Democratic party, which was committed to a Marxist critique of capitalism and to international cooperation with other socialist parties. In 1878, using the pretext of two attempts on the emperor's life, Bismarck outlawed the fledgling Socialist party. Nevertheless, individual Social Democratic candidates stood for election in this period and learned quickly how to work with middle-class parties in order to achieve electoral successes. By 1890 Social Democrats won the support of 20 percent of the electorate and controlled 35 Reichstag seats in spite of Bismarck's anti-Socialist legislation.

Throughout the 1880s, as his ability to manage Reichstag majorities declined and as Socialist strength steadily mounted, Bismarck grew disenchanted with universal manhood suffrage. Beginning in 1888 the chancellor found himself at odds with the new emperor, William II (1888–1918), over his foreign and domestic policies. The young emperor dismissed Bismarck in March 1890 and abandoned the chancellor's anti-Socialist legislation. The Social Democratic party became the largest Marxist party in the world and by 1914, the largest single party in Germany. During the period when the Social Democratic movement had been outlawed, Bismarck and William II used social welfare legislation to win mass support, including accident insurance, sick benefits, and old-age and disability benefits. But such legislation did not undermine the popularity of socialism, nor did it attract workers away from Marxist programs, as the mounting electoral returns demonstrated.

Unable to defeat social democracy by force or by state-sponsored welfare policies, Bismarck's successors set out to organize mass support. Agrarian and industrial interests united strongly behind state policies. An aggressive foreign policy was judged as the surest way to win over the masses.

In the end the Reichstag failed to defy the absolute authority of Emperor William II, who was served after 1890 by a string of ineffectual chancellors. Despite its constitutional forms, Germany was ruled by a state authoritarianism in which the bureaucracy, the military, and various interest groups exercised influence over the emperor. A high-risk foreign policy that had a mass appeal was one way to circumvent a parliamentary system incapable of decision-making.

In the 1870s the liberal values of the bourgeoisie dominated the Austro-Hungarian Empire. The Habsburg monarchy had adjusted to constitutional government, which was introduced throughout Austria in 1860. Faith in parliamentary government based on a restricted suffrage had established a tenuous foothold. After the setbacks of 1848 and the troublesome decade of the 1860s, when Prussia had trounced Austria and Bismarck had routed the hope of an Austrian-dominated German empire, the Austrian bourgeoisie counted on a peaceful future with a centralized, multinational state dedicated to order and progress.

But by 1900 the urban and capitalist middle class that ruled Austria by virtue of a limited suffrage based on property had lost ground to new groups that were essentially anticapitalist and antiliberal in their outlook. The new groups were peasants, workers, urban artisans and shopkeepers, and the colonized Slavic peoples of the empire. Bourgeois politics and laissez-faire economics had offered little or nothing to these varied groups, who were now claiming the right of participation. Mass parties were formed based on radical pan-Germanic feeling, anticapitalism that appealed to peasants and artisans, hatred of the Jews shared by students and artisans, and nationalist aspirations that attracted the lower middle classes.

The political experiences of Great Britain, Germany, France, and Austria between 1871 and 1914 make clear the common challenges confronting Western parliamentary systems in a changing era of democratic politics. In spite of variations, each nation experienced its own challenge to liberal parliamentary institutions and each shaped its own responses to a new international phenomenon—the rise of the masses as a political force.

Political Scandals and Mass Politics in France

The Third Republic in France had an aura of the accidental about its origins and of the precarious about its existence. Yet appearances were misleading. Founded in 1870 with the defeat of Napoleon III's empire by the Germans, the Third Republic claimed legitimacy by placing itself squarely within the revolutionary democratic tradition. The Third Republic successfully worked toward the creation of a national community based on a common identity of citizens. Compulsory schooling, one of the great institutional transformations of French government in 1885, socialized French children in common values, patriotism, and identification with the nation-state. Compulsory service in the army for the generation of young men of draft age served the same ends of communicating national values to a predominantly peasant population. Technology also accelerated the process of shaping a national citizenry, as railroad lines tied people together and new and better roads shrank distances.

A truly national and mass culture emerged in the period between 1880 and 1914. Two events in particular indicate the extent of the transformation of French political life. The first, the Boulanger Affair, involved the attempt of a French general to seize power. As minister of war, General Georges Boulanger (1837–91) became a hero to French soldiers when he undertook needed reforms of army life. He won over businessmen by leading troops against strikers. Above all, he cultivated the image of a patriot ready to defend France's honor at any cost. But Boulanger was a shallow man whose success was owed to a carefully orchestrated publicity campaign that made him the most popular man in France by 1886.

Boulanger's political potential attracted the attention of right-wing backers, including monarchists who hoped eventually to restore kingship to France. Supported by big-money interests who favored a strength-

ened executive and a weaker parliamentary system, Boulanger undertook a nationwide political campaign, hoping to appeal to those unhappy with the Third Republic and promising vague constitutional reforms. By 1889 Boulanger was able to amass enough national support to frighten the defenders of parliamentary institutions. The charismatic general ultimately failed in his bid for power and fled the country because of allegations of treason. But he left in his wake an embryonic mass

FROM EMILE ZOLA'S *J'ACCUSE*

■ *The central role of the press during the Dreyfus Affair is nowhere more apparent than in the impact of the novelist Emile Zola's (1840–1902) front-page letter to the president of the Third Republic in* Le Figaro, *one of France's leading newspapers, on 13 January 1898.*

J'Accuse was an impassioned appeal to the French nation for justice in which Zola pointed to those truly guilty of betraying France in a cascade of ringing accusations. Zola laid bare the initial mistake of the conviction of an innocent man which was compounded by a cover-up of "outright falsifications" by those at the highest levels of the military. This letter, which was ultimately instrumental in freeing Captain Dreyfus, resulted in Zola's own prosecution for libel.

J'ACCUSE

. . . I accuse Lieutenant-Colonel du Paty de Clam of having been the diabolical artisan of the judicial error, without knowing it, I am willing to believe, and then of having defended his nefarious work for three years throughout the most grotesque and culpable machinations.

I accuse General Mercier of having become an accomplice, out of mental weakness at the least, in one of the greatest iniquities of the century. . . .

I accuse the three handwriting experts, Mssrs. Belhomme, Varinard, and Couard, of having composed deceitful and fraudulent reports, unless a medical examination declares them to be stricken with an impairment of vision or judgment.

I accuse the offices of War of having conducted in the press, particularly in *L'Eclair* and in *L'Echo de Paris,* an abominable campaign designed to mislead public opinion and to conceal their wrongdoing.

Finally, I accuse the first Court Martial of having violated the law in convicting a defendant on the basis of a document kept secret, and I accuse the second Court Martial of having covered up that illegality on command by committing in turn the juridical crime of knowingly acquitting a guilty man.

In bringing these accusations, I am not without realizing that I expose myself in the process to Articles 30 and 31 of the press law of July 29, 1881, which punishes offenses of slander. And it is quite willingly that I so expose myself.

As for those whom I accuse, I do not know them, I have never seen them, I have neither rancor nor hatred for them. They are for me no more than entities, spirits of social malfeasance. And the act that I hereby accomplish is but a revolutionary means of hastening the explosion of truth and justice.

I have but one passion, one for seeing the light, in the name of humanity which has so suffered and which is entitled to happiness. My fiery protest is but the cry of my soul. Let me be brought then before a criminal court and let the investigation be conducted in the light of day!

I am waiting.

movement on the Right that operated outside the channels of parliamentary institutions.

A second crisis began to take shape in 1894 with the controversy surrounding the trial of Captain Alfred Dreyfus (1859–1935) that came to be known simply as "the Affair." Dreyfus was an Alsatian Jewish army officer accused of selling military secrets to the Germans. His trial for treason served as a lightning rod for xenophobia—the hatred of foreigners, especially Germans—and anti-Semitism, the hatred of Jews. Dreyfus was stripped of his commission and honors and sentenced to solitary confinement for life on Devil's Island, a convict colony off French Guiana in South America.

Illegal activities and outright falsifications by Dreyfus' superiors in order to secure a conviction came to light in the mass press and divided the nation. Those who supported Dreyfus's innocence, the pro-Dreyfusards, were for the most part on the Left of the political spectrum and spoke of the Republic's duty to uphold justice and freedom. The anti-Dreyfusards were associated with the traditional institutions of the Catholic church and the army and considered themselves to be defending the honor of France.

Captain Dreyfus, accused of treason, marches with a "guard of dishonor." After Dreyfus was declared innocent, he became a lieutenant colonel in the French army and was enrolled in the Legion of Honor.

European States and Societies, 1850–1871

1853–56	Crimean War
1859	Austria declares war on Kingdom of Sardinia; France joins forces with Italians
1860	Sardinia annexes duchies in central Italy; France gains Nice and Savoy
3 March 1861	Emancipation of Russian serfs
14 March 1861	Kingdom of Italy proclaimed with Victor Emmanuel II as king
1861–65	American Civil War
1863	Maximilian crowned as emperor of Mexico
1865	Prussians and Austrians at war with Denmark
1866	Seven Weeks' War between Austria and Prussia; Italy acquires Venetia
1867	Emperor Maximilian executed
July 1870	Franco-Prussian War begins
2 September 1870	French Second Empire capitulates with Prussian victory at Sedan
20 September 1870	Italy annexes Rome
18 January 1871	German Empire proclaimed
March–May 1871	The Paris Commune

The Affair represented the ability of an individual to seek redress against injustice. On the national level, it represented an important transformation in the nature of French political life. Existing parliamentary institutions had been found wanting. They were unable to cope with the mass politics stirred up by Dreyfus's conviction. The newspaper press vied with parliament and the courts as a forum for investigation and decision making.

The crises provoked by Boulanger's attempt at power and the Dreyfus Affair demonstrated the major role of the press and the importance of public opinion in exerting pressure on the system of government. The Third Republic was never in danger of collapsing but it was transformed. The locus of power in parliament was challenged by pressure groups outside it.

Nothing was small about European economic expansion at the end of the nineteenth century. Heavy industry demanded economies of scale and government became a key part of the process through regulation and state controls. Nor was anything small about the new style of electoral politics. By the end of the nineteenth century a faceless, nameless electorate had become the basis of new political strategies and a new political rhetoric. Just as big business and cartels replaced the small entrepreneurs that had been the cornerstone of early industrialization, so too did mass electoral politics emerge by replacing classes with interest groups and by seeking extraparliamentary forums for their political activities.

Western societies had crossed the threshold into the modern age in the third quarter of the nineteenth century. Strong states from Great Britain to Russia were committed to creating and preserving the conditions of industrial expansion. The machine age, railroads, and metallurgy were spreading industrial development much more widely through western and central Europe than had been possible before 1850. Italians and Prussians, in attempting to join the ranks of nation-states, realized that the goal of a strong nation could be achieved only with industrial development and social reforms. Europeans prided themselves on a future of continued progress. Yet the protests of the excluded and the threat of violence were never far beneath the surface. Modernizing transitions brought in their wake social disruptions, and the force of new ideas not only healed but also divided.

SUGGESTIONS FOR FURTHER READING

BUILDING NATIONS: THE POLITICS OF UNIFICATION

Derek Beales, *The Risorgimento and the Unification of Italy* (London: George Allen & Unwin Ltd., 1982). Drawing a distinction between unification and national revival, Beales situates the period of unification within the larger process of the cultural and political revival.

* Gordon A. Craig, *Germany, 1866–1945* (New York: Oxford University Press, 1978). This synthetic view of German history provides a thorough examination of German unification. Craig analyzes all aspects of imperial development with spe-

cial attention to the institutional framework, its politics, economy, and diplomacy.

James J. Sheehan, *German Liberalism in the Nineteenth Century* (Chicago: University of Chicago Press, 1978). Explores the problems of transferring Western liberalism to Germany by examining the origins of German liberalism, the revolutions of 1848, and the politics of the Bismarckian state.

REFORMING EUROPEAN SOCIETY

* David Pinkney, *Napoleon III and the Rebuilding of Paris* (Princeton: Princeton University Press, 1972). Describes how Paris was transformed into the monumental city that became not only a manifestation of French culture, but also a symbol of European culture as a whole. The planning, financing, and building of Napoleon III's Paris are analyzed, as is the impact of the rebuilding on the city's residents.

* Alain Plessis, *The Rise and Fall of the Second Empire, 1852–1871*, trans. Jonathan Mandelbaum (Cambridge: Cambridge University Press, 1985). Discusses the Second Empire as an important transitional period in French history, when the conflict was between traditional and modern values in political, economic, and social transformations.

H. Seton Watson, *The Russian Empire, 1801–1917* (Oxford: The Clarendon Press, 1967). This narrative history describes the social and economic background of late imperial Russia with attention to intellectual trends and political ideologies.

Jenni Calder, *The Victorian Home* (London: R. T. Batsford, 1977). A cultural and social history of Victorian domestic life in which the author describes both bourgeois and working-class domestic environments.

THE FORCE OF NEW IDEAS

* Bonnie G. Smith, *Ladies of the Leisure Class: The Bourgeoisie of Northern France in the Nineteenth Century* (Princeton, NJ: Princeton University Press, 1981). Explores the impact of industrialization on the lives of bourgeois women in northern France and demonstrates how the cult of domesticity emerged in a particular community.

* Martha Vicinus, *Independent Women: Work and Community for Single Women, 1850–1920* (Chicago: The University of Chicago Press, 1985). Chronicles the choice that Victorian women made to live outside the norms of marriage and domesticity in various communities of women, including sisterhoods, nursing communities, colleges, boarding schools, and settlement houses.

* Steven C. Hause and Anne R. Kenney, *Women's Suffrage and Social Politics in the French Third Republic* (Princeton, NJ: Princeton University Press, 1984). Examines the women's suffrage movement from its origins through its defeat after World War I in the Senate. Aims, tactics, and leadership of the women's movement receive special attention.

* Richard Stites, *The Women's Liberation Movement in Russia: Feminism, Nihilism, and Bolshevism, 1860–1930* (Princeton, NJ: Princeton University Press, 1978). Situates the Russian women's movement within the contexts of both nineteenth-century European feminism and twentieth-century Communist ideology and traces its development from the early

feminists through the rise of the Bolsheviks to power. Includes a discussion of the Russian Revolution's impact on the status of women.

* Stephen Kern, *The Culture of Time and Space, 1880-1918* (Cambridge, MA: Harvard University Press, 1983). Describes how late-nineteenth-century technological advances created new modes of thinking about and experiencing time and space.

Paul Avril, *Anarchist Portraits* (Princeton, NJ: Princeton University Press, 1988). A series of biographies of leading and lesser-known anarchists worldwide who represented key tenets of the anarchist struggle at the end of the nineteenth and the beginning of the twentieth centuries.

Susan Kingsley Kent, *Sex and Suffrage in Britain, 1860-1914* (Princeton, NJ: Princeton University Press, 1987). Provides a useful introduction to the British women's suffrage movement and the relation of the movement to the broader culture. The author argues that the suffragists saw political action as the best way to attain personal power and to redefine Britain's repressive sexual culture.

ECONOMIC REGULATION AND MASS POLITICS, 1871–1914

Michael Burns, *Rural Society and French Politics: Boulangism and the Dreyfus Affair, 1886–1900* (Princeton, NJ: Princeton University Press, 1984). Examines the impact on rural France of two political watersheds of the Third Republic in order to gauge the importance of national politics in nonurban settings.

* Carl E. Schorske, *Fin-de-Siecle Vienna: Politics and Culture* (New York: Alfred A. Knopf, 1980). A series of essays describing the break with nineteenth-century liberal culture in one of Europe's great cities, as artists, intellectuals, and politicians responded to the disintegration of the Habsburg Empire.

* Eugen Weber, *Peasants Into Frenchmen: The Modernization of Rural France* (Stanford, CA: Stanford University Press, 1976). Views the integration of the French peasantry into national political life through agents of change, including the railroads, schools, and the army. The author contends that a national political culture took the place of traditional beliefs and practices between 1870 and 1914 in France.

* Hans-Ulrich Wehler, *The German Empire, 1871-1918* (Leamington Spa: Berg Publishers, 1985). Stresses the institutional continuities of German society and links pre-World War I Germany to the rise of Nazism.

* Michael R. Miller, *The Bon Marché: Bourgeois Culture and the Department Store, 1869-1920* (Princeton, NJ: Princeton University Press, 1981). A social and cultural history of the department store as the creation and reflection of bourgeois culture.

* Martin Wiener, *English Culture and the Decline of the Industrial Spirit, 1850-1980* (Cambridge: Cambridge University Press, 1981). A cultural history of growth and decline from Victoria to Thatcher. By drawing on literature, art, architecture, politics, and economics, the author describes the ambiguous attitude of the elite toward industry and argues that English culture was never conducive to sustained industrial growth.

* Indicates paperback edition available.

CHAPTER 27

Europe and the World, 1870–1914

IMPERIAL FEDERATION — MAP OF THE WORLD SHOWING THE EXTENT OF THE BRITISH EMPIRE IN 1886.
STATISTICAL INFORMATION FURNISHED BY CAPTAIN J. C. R. COLOMB M.P. FORMERLY R.M.A. —— BRITISH TERRITORIES COLOURED RED.

MAPPING THE WORLD AND MEASURING TIME

Before people knew how to write, they drew maps. Yet in 1885 only one-ninth of the land surface of the earth had been surveyed. Within the next decade, however, centuries-old ignorance diminished as cartographers, surveyors, and compilers fanned out around the globe to probe peninsulas and chart continents. By 1900, every continent, including Antarctica, had been explored and its measure taken.

This great leap forward in knowledge did not produce a standardized and uniform map of the world. State officials argued for the primacy of their own national traditions, symbols, colors, and units of measurement, and they blocked attempts at standardization. Mapmakers from Europe and the United States began to gather regularly in international conventions with the goal of devising a uniform map of the world that would satisfy everyone. Their attempts repeatedly failed.

One particular meeting in Paris in 1875 chose the meter, the unit of measurement whose practical application originated in the French Revolution, as the standard measurement for the world map. Supporters argued that it could provide mapmakers with a common language, easily understood and easily divisible. The British countered with yards and miles, unscientifically developed units of measurement to which they had been committed for centuries.

Mapmakers who acknowledged the logic of the meter could not agree on which prototype meter should be taken as standard. Should the meter be measured according to the common method of the movement of a pendulum? If so, gravitation varying from one place to another on the earth's surface would result in different meter lengths. Most agreed that the meter should be measured in reference to the arc of the meridian.

The prime meridian, the place on a map that indicates zero longitude, was itself not a fixed phenomenon. The debate over where the prime meridian should be located is a perfect example of the politics of mapmaking. Unlike the equator, which is midway between the North and South poles, zero longitude can be drawn anywhere. As a result, maps of different national origins located the prime meridian to enhance their own claims to importance. Paris, Philadelphia, and Beijing were just three of the sites for zero longitude on nineteenth-century maps.

Uniformity, the cartographers insisted, would have advantages for everyone. Not least of all, a standardized map would make standardized timekeeping easier. Standard time could be calculated according to zones of longitude. Germany had five different time zones in 1891. In France every city had its own time taken from solar readings. The United States had over two hundred time zones from one coast to the other. In industrial societies with railroad timetables and legal contracts, time had to be controlled and it had to be exact. Time had to be standardized. Specialists proposed that the Royal Observatory in Greenwich, England, was the best place to locate the prime meridian in order to calculate a standard time system. The French balked, insisting on Paris as the only candidate for the designation. In the end, there was compromise. The metric system prevailed as the standard for measurement, and the prime meridian passed through the Royal Greenwich Observatory, where standard time was calculated for most of the globe. All of this was possible for the first time only at the end of the nineteenth century.

In 1891 a young Viennese geographer named Albrecht Penck proposed an international map of the world. Penck's idea was a simple one: to produce a map using standard symbols and colors and omitting political boundaries. Original place names would be used out of respect for local usage. He did not live to see his international map of the world completed, and the disruptions of the twentieth century have slowed its progress. Penck's proposal came up against the harsh realities of mapmaking. Technology had made more accurate knowledge possible. Political wranglings and national pride prevented knowledge from being standardized. A global vision remained subordinate to the limits of national boundaries.

The New Imperialism

The concept of empire was certainly not invented by Europeans in the last third of the nineteenth century. Before 1870 European states had controlled empires. The influence of Great Britain stretched beyond the limits of its formal holdings in India and South Africa. Russia held Siberia and central Asia, and France ruled Algeria and Indochina. Older empires, Spain for example, had survived from the sixteenth century, but as hollow shells. What, then, was new about the "new imperialism" practiced by England, France, and Germany after 1870? In part, the new imperialism was the acquisition of territories on an intense and unprecedented scale. Industrialization created the tools of transportation, communication, and domination that permitted the rapid pace of global empire building. Above all, what distinguished the new imperialism was the domination by the industrial powers over the nonindustrial world. The United States also participated in the new imperialism, less by territorial acquisition and more by developing an "invisible" empire of trade and influence in the Pacific. The forms of imperialism may have varied from nation to nation, but the basically unequal relationship between an industrial power and an undeveloped territory did not.

Only nation-states commanded the technology and resources necessary for the new scale of imperialist expansion. Rivalry among a few European nation-states—notably, Great Britain, France, and Germany—was a common denominator that set the standards by which these nations and other European states gained control of the globe by 1900. Why did the Europeans create vast empires? Were empires built for economic gain, military protection, or national glory? Questions about motives may obscure common features of the new imperialism. Industrial powers sought to take over nonindustrial regions, not in isolated areas but all over the globe. In the attempt, they necessarily competed with one another, successfully adapting the resources of industrialism to the needs of conquest.

The Technology of Empire

For Europeans at the end of the nineteenth century, the world had definitely become a smaller place. Steam, iron, and electricity—the great forces of Western industrialization—were responsible for shrinking the globe. Technology not only allowed Europeans to accomplish tasks and to mass-produce goods efficiently, but it also altered previous understandings of time and space.

Steam, which powered factories, proved equally efficient as an energy source in transportation. Great iron steamships fueled by coal replaced the smaller, slower, wind-powered, wooden sailing vessels that had ruled the sea for centuries. Steam-powered vessels transported large cargoes of people and goods more quickly and more reliably. Iron ships were superior to wood in their durability, lightness, watertightness, cargo space, speed, and fuel economy. For most of the nineteenth century British trading ships and the British navy dominated the seas, but after 1880 other nations, especially Germany, challenged England by building versatile and efficient iron steamers. In a society in which time was money, steamships were important because, for the first time, oceangoing vessels could meet schedules as precisely and as predictably as could railroads. Just as the imperial Romans had used their network of roads to link far-flung territories to the capital, Europeans used sea lanes to join their colonies to the home country.

Until 1850 Europeans ventured no farther on the African continent than its coastal areas. Now the installation of coal-burning boilers on smaller boats permitted navigation of previously uncharted rivers. Steam power made exploration and migration possible and greatly contributed to knowledge of terrain, natural wealth, and resources. Smaller, steam-powered vessels also increased European inland trade with China, Burma, and India.

While technology improved European mobility on water, it also literally moved the land. Harbors were deepened to accommodate the new iron- and then steel-hulled ships. One of the greatest engineering feats of the century was the construction of a hundred-mile-long canal across the Isthmus of Suez in Egypt (see Chapter 19). Completed in 1869, the Suez Canal joined the Mediterranean and Red seas and created a new, safer trade route to the East. No longer did trading vessels have to make the long voyage around Africa's Cape of Good Hope. The Suez Canal was built by the French under the supervision of Ferdinand de Lesseps (1805–94), a diplomat with no technical or financial background who was able to promote construction because of concessions he received from Sa'id Pasha of Egypt. The canal could accommodate ships of all sizes. Great Britain purchased a controlling interest in the Suez Canal in 1875 to benefit its trade with India.

De Lesseps later presided over the initial construction of the Panama Canal in the Western Hemisphere. The combination of French mismanagement, bankruptcy, and the high incidence of disease among work crews enabled the United States to acquire rights to the Panama project and complete it by 1914. Fifty-one miles long, the Panama Canal connected the world's two largest bodies of water, the Atlantic and Pacific oceans, across the Isthmus of Panama by a waterway containing a series of locks. Now the passage from the Atlantic to the Pacific took less than eight hours—much less time than the various overland routes or the voyage around the tip of South America. Both the Suez and Panama canals were built in pursuit of speed. Shorter distances meant quicker travel, which in turn meant higher profits.

Technology also altered time by increasing the speed with which Westerners communicated with other parts of the world. In 1830, for example, it took about two years for a person sending a letter from Great Britain to India to receive a reply. In 1850, steam-powered mail boats shortened the time required for the same round-trip correspondence to about two or three months. But the real revolution in communication came through electricity. Thousands of miles of copper telegraph wire laced countries together; insulated underwater cables linked continents to each other. By the late nineteenth century a vast telegraph network connected Europe to every area of the world. In 1870 a telegram from London to Bombay arrived in a matter of hours, instead of months, and a response could be received back in London on the same day. Faster communications extended power and control throughout empires. Now Europeans could communicate immediately with their distant colonies, dispatching troops, orders, and supplies. This communication network eliminated the problem of overextension that had plagued Roman imperial organization in the third century. For the first time continents discovered by Europeans five centuries earlier were brought into daily contact with the West.

Technological advances in other areas helped foster European imperialism in the nineteenth century. Advances in medicine permitted European men and women to penetrate disease-laden swamps and jungles. After 1850, European explorers, traders, missionaries, and adventurers carried quinine pills. The bitter-tasting derivative of cinchona-tree bark, quinine was discovered to be an effective treatment for malaria. This treatment got its first important test during the French invasion of Algeria in 1830, and it allowed the French to stay healthy enough to conquer that North African country between 1830 and 1847. David Livingstone (1813–73) and Henry M. Stanley (1841–1904) were just two of the many explorers who crossed vast terrains and explored the waterways of Africa, after malaria, the number one killer of Europeans, had been controlled.

Europeans carried the technologies of destruction as well as survival with them into less-developed areas of the world. New types of firearms produced in the second half of the nineteenth century included breech-loading rifles, repeating rifles, and machine guns. The new weapons gave the advantages of both accurate aim and rapid fire. The spears of African warriors and the primitive weaponry of Chinese rebels were no match for sophisticated European arms, which permitted their bearers to lie down while firing and to remain undetected at distances of up to half a mile.

The new technology did not cause the new imperialism. The Western powers used technological advances as a tool for establishing their control of the world. Viewed as a tool, however, the new technology does explain how vast areas of land and millions of people were conquered so rapidly.

Motives for Empire

If technology was not the cause but only a tool, what explains the new imperialism of the late nineteenth century? Were wealthy financiers, searching for high-yielding opportunities for investments, the driving force? Was profit the main motive? Were politicians and heads of state in the game for the prestige and glory that territorial expansion could bring them at home?

There are no easy or simple explanations for the new imperialism. Individuals made their fortunes overseas, and heavy industries like the Krupp firm in Germany prospered with the expansion of state-protected colonies. Yet many colonies were economically worthless. Tunisia and Morocco, acquired for their strategic and political importance, constituted an economic loss for the French, who poured more funds into their administration than they were able to extract. Each imperial power held one or more colonies whose costs outweighed the return. Yet this does not mean that some Europeans were simply irrational in their pursuit of empire or that they were driven by an atavistic desire to recapture the glories of a precapitalist past and willing to incur financial losses to do so.

Economics. The test for economic motivation cannot simply be reduced to a balance sheet of debits and credits because, in the end, an account of state revenues and state expenditures provides only a static picture of the business of empire. Even losses cannot be counted as proof against the profit motive in expansion. In modern capitalism, profits, especially great profits, are often predicated on risks. Portugal and Italy took great risks and failed as players in the game in which the great industrial powers called the shots. Prestige through the acquisition of empire was one way of keeping alive in the game. Imperialism was influenced by business interests, market considerations, and the pursuit of individual and national fortunes. Not by accident did the great industrial powers control the scramble and dictate the terms of expansion. Nor was it merely fortuitous that Great Britain, the nation that provided the model for European expansion, dedicated itself to the establishment of a profitable worldwide network of trade and investment. Above all, the search for investment opportunities, whether railroads in China or diamond mines in South Africa, lured Europeans into a world system that challenged capitalist ingenuity and imagination. Acquiring territory was only one means of protecting investments. But there were other benefits associated with the acquisition of territory that cannot be reduced to economic terms, and those too must be considered.

Geopolitics. Geopolitics, or the politics of geography, is based on the recognition that certain areas of the world are valuable for political reasons. The term, first used at the end of the nineteenth century, described a process well under way in international relations. Statesmen influenced by geopolitical concerns recognized the strategic value of land. Some territory was considered important because of its proximity to acquired colonies or to territory targeted for takeover. France, for example, occupied thousands of square miles of the Sahara to protect its interests in Algeria.

Other territory was important because of its proximity to sea routes. Egypt had significance for Great Britain not because of its inherent economic potential but because it permitted the British to protect access to lucrative markets in India through the Suez Canal. Beginning in 1875, the British purchased shares in the canal. By 1879 Egypt was under the informal dual rule of France and Great Britain. The British used the deterioration of internal Egyptian politics to justify their occupation of the country in 1882. Protected access to India also accounted for Great Britain's maintenance of Mediterranean outposts, its acquisition of territory on the east coast of Africa, and its occupation of territory in southern Asia.

A third geopolitical motive for annexation was the necessity of fueling bases throughout the world. Faster and more reliable than wind-powered vessels, coal-powered ships were, nonetheless, dependent on guaranteed fueling bases in friendly ports of call. Islands in the South Pacific and the Indian Ocean were acquired primarily to serve as coaling stations for the great steamers carrying manufactured goods to colonial ports and returning with foodstuffs and raw materials. Ports along the southern rim of Asia served the same purpose. The

This postcard was issued by Kaiser Wilhelm II—whose cameo is seen in the inset—to celebrate the launching of the S.S. Imperator, *a German warship. The grandiose name, which means "emperor" in Latin, was typical of the superpatriotic propaganda of an imperialistic age.*

need for protection of colonies, fueling ports, and sea-lanes led to the creation of naval bases like those on the Red Sea at Djibouti by the French, in Southeast Asia at Singapore by the British, and in the Hawaiian Islands at Honolulu by the Americans.

In turn, the acquisition of territories justified the increase in naval budgets and the size of fleets. Britain still had the world's largest navy, but by the beginning of the twentieth century, the United States and Germany had entered the competition for dominance of sea-lanes. Japan joined the contest by expanding its navy as a vehicle for its own claims to empire in the Pacific.

The politics of geography was land- as well as sea-based. As navies grew to protect sea-lanes, armies expanded to police new lands. Between 1890 and 1914, military expenditures of Western governments grew phenomenally, with war machines doubling in size. In both its impact on domestic budgets and its protection of markets and trading routes, geopolitics had a strong economic component. Governments became consumers of heavy industry; their predictable participation in markets for armaments and military supplies helped control fluctuations in the business cycle and reduce unemployment at home. A side effect of the growing importance of geopolitics was the increased influence of military and naval leaders in foreign and domestic policy making.

Nationalism. Many European statesmen in the last quarter of the nineteenth century gave stirring speeches about the importance of empire as a means of enhancing national prestige. In his Crystal Palace speech of 1872, Benjamin Disraeli, British prime minister in 1868 and 1874–80, put the challenge boldly to the British:

I appeal to the sublime instinct of an ancient people . . . The issue is not a mean one. It is whether you will be content to be a comfortable England, modelled and moulded upon Continental principles and meeting in due course an inevitable fate, or whether you will be a great country, an imperial country, a country where your sons, when they rise, rise to paramount positions and obtain not merely the esteem of their countrymen but command the respect of the world.

National prestige was not an absolute value but one weighed relatively. Possessing an empire may have meant "keeping up with the Joneses," as it did for smaller countries like Italy. Imperial status was important to a country like Portugal, which was willing to go bankrupt to maintain its territories. But prestige without economic power was the form of imperialism without its substance. Nation-states could, through the acquisition of overseas territories, gain bargaining chips to be played at the international conference table. In this way, smaller nations hoped to be taken seriously in the system of alliances that preserved "the balance of power" in Europe.

Western newspapers deliberately fostered the desire for the advancement of national interests. Newspapers competed for readers, and their circulations often depended on the passions they aroused. Filled with tales calculated to titillate and entertain, and with advertisements promising miracle cures, newspapers wrested foreign policy from the realm of the specialist and transformed politics into another form of entertainment. The drama and vocabulary of sporting events, whose mass appeal as a leisure activity also dates from this era, were now applied to imperialist politics. Whether it was a rugby match or a territorial

JOSEPH CHAMBERLAIN'S SPEECH TO THE BIRMINGHAM RELIEF ASSOCIATION

■ *Joseph Chamberlain (1836–1914) was an English businessman and statesman and, from 1873 to 1876, the mayor of one of Great Britain's leading industrial cities, Birmingham. He was a national advocate for an expansionist colonial policy as the means of keeping his country strong. On 22 January 1894 he spoke before a community group to convince them that British imperialism helped the working class.*

Believe me, if in any one of the places [in Africa] to which I have referred any change took place which deprived us of that control and influence of which I have been speaking, the first to suffer would be the working-men of this country. Then, indeed, we should see a distress which would not be temporary, but which would be chronic, and we should find that England was entirely unable to support the enormous population which is now maintained by the aid of her foreign trade. If the working-men of this country understand, as I believe they do—I am one of those who have had good reason through my life to rely upon their intelligence and shrewdness—if they understand their own interests, they will never lend any countenance to the doctrines of those politicians who never lose an opportunity of pouring contempt and abuse upon the brave Englishmen, who, even at this moment, in all parts of the world are carving out new dominions for Britain, and are opening up fresh markets for British commerce, and laying out fresh fields for British labour. (Applause.) If the Little Englanders[1] had their way, not only would they refrain from taking the legitimate opportunities which offer for extending the empire and for securing for us new markets, but I doubt whether they would even take the pains which are necessary to preserve the great heritage which has come down to us from our ancestors. (Applause.)

When you are told that the British pioneers of civilisation in Africa are filibusters,[2] and when you are asked to call them back, and to leave this great continent to the barbarism and superstition in which it has been steeped for centuries, or to hand over to foreign countries the duty which you are unwilling to undertake, I ask you to consider what would have happened if 100 or 150 years ago your ancestors had taken similar views of their responsibility? Where would be the empire on which now your livelihood depends? We should have been the United Kingdom of Great Britain and Ireland; but those vast dependencies, those hundreds of millions with whom we keep up a mutually beneficial relationship and commerce would have been the subjects of other nations, who would not have been slow to profit by our neglect of our opportunities and obligations. (Applause.)

[1]Britain's anti-imperialists.
[2]A person engaged in a private military action against a foreign government.

From Joseph Chamberlain, M.P., *Foreign & Colonial Speeches*, 1897.

conquest, readers backed the "home" team, disdained the opposition, and competed for the thrill of victory. This marked quite a change for urban dwellers whose grandparents worked the land and did not look beyond the horizon of their home villages. Newspapers forged a national consciousness whereby individuals identified with collective causes they did not fully comprehend. Some observed what was happening with a critical eye, identifying a deep-seated need in modern men and women for excitement in their otherwise dull and dreary lives.

Information conveyed in newspapers shaped opinion, and opinion, in turn, could influence policy. Leaders had to reckon with this new creation of "public opinion." In a typical instance, French newspaper editors promoted feverish public outcry for conquest of the

Congo by pointing out the need to revenge British advances in Egypt. "Colonial fever" was so high in France in the summer of 1882 that French policy makers were pressured to pursue claims in the Congo basin without adequate assessment or reflection. As a result, the French government evicted Belgians and Portuguese from the northern Congo territory and enforced questionable treaty claims rather than risk public censure for appearing weak and irresolute.

Public opinion was certainly influential but it could be manipulated. In Germany, the government often promoted colonial hysteria through the press in order to advance its own political ends. Chancellor Otto von Bismarck used his power over the press to support imperialism and to influence electoral outcomes in 1884. His successors were deft at promoting the "bread and circuses" atmosphere that surrounded colonial expansion in order to direct attention away from social problems at home and to maintain domestic stability.

The printed word was also manipulated in Britain during the Boer War (1899–1902), critics asserted, by business interests to keep public enthusiasm for the war effort high. J. A. Hobson (1858–1940), himself a journalist and theorist of imperialism, denounced the "abuse of the press" in his hard-hitting *Psychology of Jingoism* (1901), which appeared while the war was still being waged. Hobson recognized *jingoism* as the appropriate term for the "inverted patriotism whereby the love of one's own nation is transformed into hatred of another nation, and [into] the fierce craving to destroy the individual members of that other nation."

Certainly jingoism was not a new phenomenon in 1900, nor was it confined to Britain. Throughout Europe a mass public appeared increasingly willing to support conflict to defend national honor. Xenophobia, hatred of foreigners, melded with nationalism, both nurtured by the mass press, to put new pressures on the determination of foreign policy. Government elites, who formerly operated behind closed doors far removed from public scrutiny, were now accountable in new ways to faceless masses. Even in autocratic states like Austria-Hungary, the opinion of the masses was a powerful political force that could destroy individual careers and dissolve governments.

Every nation in Europe had its jingoes, those willing to risk war for national glory. Significantly, the term *jingo* was coined in 1878 during a British showdown with the Russians over Turkey. The sentiment was so strong that "The Russians shall not have Constantinople," that the acceptability of war was set to music:

We don't want to fight,
But, by jingo, if we do,
We've got the men,
We've got the ships,
We've got the money too.

This was the most popular music-hall song in Britain that year, and long after the crisis had faded, the tune and its lyrics lingered.

To varying degrees, all of these factors—economics, geopolitics, and nationalism—motivated the actions of the three great imperialist powers—Britain, France, and Germany—and their less-powerful European neighbors. The same reasons account for the global aspirations of non-European nations like the United States and Japan. None of these powers acted independently—each was aware of what the others were doing and tailored its actions accordingly. Imperialism followed a variety of patterns but always with a built-in component of emulation and acceleration. It was both a cause and a proof of a world system of states in which the actions of one nation affected the others.

The nineteenth-century liberal belief in progress encouraged Europeans to impose their beliefs and institutions on captive millions. After all, industrial society had given Europe the technology, the wealth, and the power to tame nature and dominate the world. Imperialists moralized that they had not only the right but also the duty to develop the nonindustrialized world for their own purposes.

The European Search For Territory and Markets

Most western Europeans who read about the distant regions that their armies and political leaders were bringing under control regarded these new territories as little more than entries on a great tally sheet or as distinctively colored areas on a map. The daily press recorded the numbers of square miles acquired and the names of the peoples occupied, and that was that! Few Europeans looked on imperialism as a relationship of power between two parties and, like all relationships, one influenced by both partners. Fewer still understood or appreciated the distinctive qualities of the conquered peoples.

The areas European imperialism affected varied widely in their political organization. In some parts of Africa large states existed, while elsewhere states were small or even nonexistent. Whatever the situation, however, Europeans, filled with the racist prejudices of the period, considered African governmental institutions too ineffectual to produce the economic change and growth of trade they then wanted. Military takeover and direct rule by European officials seemed the only feasible way to establish empire there and extract the goods and labor they sought. In Asia, on the other hand, societies such as India and China were territorially large and possessed efficient institutions of government dominated by established political hierarchies. Although they were more difficult to conquer, their leaders were more likely to cooperate with the imperial powers because their own interests were often similar to those of the Westerners. In Asia, European empire-builders favored either informal empires, such as in China, or formal but indirect rule, as in India.

The Scramble for Africa: Diplomacy and Conflict

In the mid-1860s a committee of the British Parliament recommended that Britain withdraw from the scattering of small colonies it possessed in West Africa, arguing that they were costly anachronisms in an era of free trade. Just thirty years later, in 1898, the president of France, in commenting on French policies of the previous twenty years, remarked that "We have behaved like madmen in Africa, having been led astray by irresponsible people called the 'colonialists.' " The "mad" event that had altered the political landscape of Africa was the so-called scramble for Africa, a partitioning of Africa that is usually considered as extending from around 1875 to around 1912. By its end, Europeans controlled virtually all Africa.

One cannot detect a single reason for the scramble as it actually took place on the ground. Africa is a large and complex continent, and the reasons for which Europeans pursued specific pieces of African territory were similarly complex. The explanations for the acquisition of a particular colony, therefore, depend largely on the historical context of that particular case. In certain areas, such as the West African Sudanic and Sahara desert zones, ambitious French military men sought to advance their careers by carving out grand colonies. The existence of valuable minerals motivated the scramble for the area now called Zimbabwe, the Zambian/Zairian Copperbelt, and other areas. Along the West African

coast, chronic disputes between traders working in an economy soured by a deterioration in the terms of trade seemed to demand European annexation. Some colonies, such as present-day Uganda and Malawi, were created to please missionaries already working there. Britain took Egypt, and France occupied Djibouti for strategic reasons. And, as often as not, as in Mozambique, Tanzania, Namibia, and Botswana, some Europeans seized areas to keep other Europeans from doing the same thing.

Yet there were also basic historical factors that underlay the scramble as a whole. One was the rapid development after 1870 of pseudoscientific racist ideas asserting that Europeans were a superior race and that Africans were inferior. The writings of Charles Darwin (1809–82) were critical in gaining a broad popular acceptance for the concept of a racial hierarchy governed by natural laws operating within an evolutionist dynamic. This was not merely because Darwin's *Origin of Species* (1859) and *Descent of Man* (1871) legitimated "scientifically" the concept of evolution, but also because he himself explicitly suggested its applicability to humanity. Intellectuals such as Herbert Spencer (1820–1903) quickly took up his suggestion and popularized it as Social Darwinism. According to them, the races of mankind not only occupied distinct positions in a staged sequence of "development" over time, with whites the most advanced and blacks the least so, but were also engaged in a natural conflict or struggle with each other. Social Darwinism's strongest message was that the fittest were destined to prevail, an idea especially welcome to the energetic racists of the later nineteenth century because it could be used to justify as "natural" the wars of imperial expansion upon which they were then embarking.

A second underlying factor was the atmosphere created by an economic downturn in Europe that lasted from 1873 until 1896. This downturn, coupled with Germany's fast rise to economic power during the 1870s and 1880s, was deeply unsettling to many Europeans. Protectionist policies springing from new economic anxieties eroded earlier faith in free trade and many Europeans became keen to acquire African territory just in case it should turn out to be useful in the long run. Even Britain, long the major champion of free trade, became ever more protectionist and imperialistic as the century neared its end.

Historians generally agree that the person who provided the catalyst for the scramble was Leopold II, king of the Belgians (1865–1909). His motive was greed. Early in 1876 Leopold read a report about the Congo

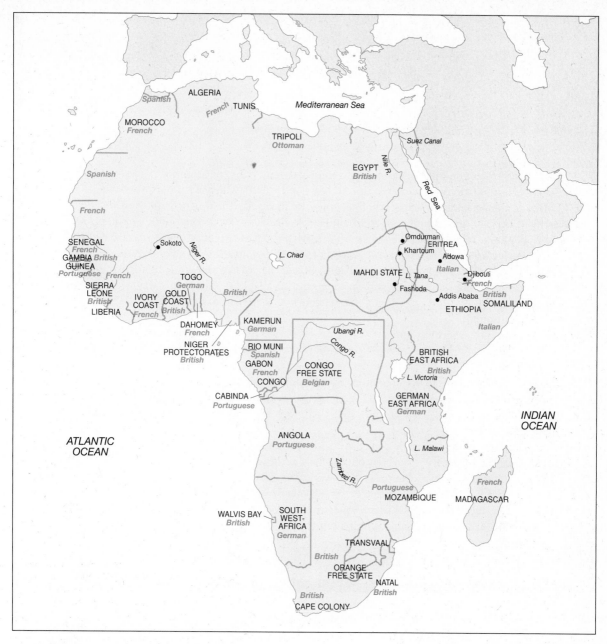

Beginning the Partition of Africa

River basin which claimed that it was "mostly a magnificent and healthy country of unspeakable richness" that could in "from 30 to 36 months begin to repay any enterprising capitalist." Leopold, an ambitious and frustrated king ruling over a small country, went to work at once to acquire this area, one-third the size of the United States, for himself. Cloaking himself in the mantle of philanthropy and asserting that all he desired was to stamp out the remnants of the East African slave trade, he organized the International African Association in late 1876.

His association soon established stations on the region's rivers and robbed the people of much valuable ivory. Meanwhile, Leopold himself skillfully lobbied for formal recognition of his association's right to rule the Congo basin. France and Portugal, also covetous of the

LEOPOLD II OF BELGIUM, SPEECH TO AN INTERNATIONAL CONFERENCE OF GEOGRAPHERS, 12 SEPTEMBER 1876

■ *Leopold II reigned as king of the Belgians from 1865 until his death in 1909. Although the ruler of a small European country, he had vast territorial aspirations in Africa. As the personal ruler of the Congo Free State, Leopold amassed an immense fortune until abuses of African workers forced him to hand over control of what is now Zaire to the Belgian government. In addressing geographers, Leopold evinced some of the goals that made him the architect of the scramble for territory.*

The matter which brings us together today is one most deserving the attention of the friends of humanity. For bringing civilization to the only part of the earth which it has not yet reached and lightening the darkness in which whole peoples are plunged, is, I venture to say, a crusade worthy of this century of progress, and I am glad to find how favourable public opinion is to the accomplishment of this task. We are swimming with the tide. Many of those who have closely studied Africa have come to realise that it would be in the interest of the object they are all seeking to achieve for them to meet and consult together with a view to regulating the course to be taken, combining their efforts and drawing on all available resources in a way which would avoid duplication of effort . . . Among the matters which remain to be discussed, the following may be mentioned:

1. Deciding exactly where to acquire bases for the task in hand . . . on the Zanzibar coast and near the mouth of the Congo, either by means of conventions with chiefs or by purchasing or renting sites from individuals.

2. Deciding on the routes to be successively opened up into the interior, and on the medical, scientific and peace-keeping stations which are to be set up with a view to abolishing slavery, and bringing about good relations between the chiefs by providing them with fair-minded, impartial persons to settle their disputes, and so forth.

3. Setting up—once the task to be done has been clearly defined—a central, international committee with national committees, each to carry out this task in the aspects of it which concern them, to explain the object to the public of all countries, and to appeal to the feeling of charity to which no worthy cause has ever appealed in vain. These are some of the points which seem worthy of your attention. . . . My wish is to serve the great cause for which you have already done so much, in whatever manner you may suggest to me. It is with this object that I put myself at your disposal, and I extend a cordial welcome to you.

area, objected and, after much diplomatic wrangling, an international conference was finally held in Berlin in late 1884 to decide the question. The Berlin Conference was important not only because it yielded the Congo basin to Leopold as the Congo Free State, but also because it laid down the ground rules for the recognition of other colonial claims in Africa. No longer would merely planting a flag in an area be considered adequate to establish sovereignty; instead, the creation of a real presence calculated to produce "economic development" would be needed. If by panicking the European states, Leopold's actions began the scramble,

the Berlin Conference organized and structured it. It is clear, however, in retrospect, that the scramble would have occurred even without Leopold II's greedy intervention.

In dividing Africa, the European states were remarkably cooperative. Although Britain did threaten Portugal with war in 1890 in a dispute about the area around Lake Malawi, and although it appeared for a while that Britain and France were headed toward armed conflict in 1898 over control over the headwaters of the Nile, peaceful diplomatic settlements were always worked out. Deals that traded one piece of territory for another

Contemporary cartoon shows Disraeli buying a controlling interest in the Suez Canal from Egypt. The British lion guards the key to India, the symbol of the canal.

were common and peace was maintained. Africa was not worth a European war.

Yet despite the importance of diplomatic compromise among European states during the scramble, every instance of European expansion in Africa, no matter what its specific motive, was characterized by a readiness to shoot Africans. With Hiram Maxim's invention in 1884 of a machine gun that could fire eleven bullets per second, and with the sale of modern weapons to Africans banned by the Brussels Convention of 1890, the military advantage passed overwhelmingly to the imperialists. As the British poet Hilaire Belloc (1870–1953) tellingly observed,

> Whatever happens, we have got
> The Maxim Gun, and they have not.

The conquest of "them" became more like hunting than warfare. In 1893, for example, in Zimbabwe, fifty Europeans, using only six machine guns, killed 3,000 Ndebele people in under two hours. In 1897, in northern Nigeria, a force of thirty-two Europeans and five hundred African mercenaries defeated the 31,000-man army of the emir of Sokoto. Winston Churchill, reporting on the battle of Omdurman in the Sudan in 1898, summed up well the nature of such warfare:

> The [British] infantry fired steadily and stolidly, without hurry or excitement, for the enemy were far away and the officers careful. Besides the soldiers were interested in the work and took great pains . . . And all the time out on the plain on the other side bullets were shearing through flesh, smashing and splintering bone; blood spouted from

terrible wounds; valiant men were struggling on through a hell of whistling metal, exploding shells, and spurting dust—suffering, despairing, dying.

After five hours of fighting, the number killed were twenty Britons, twenty Egyptian allies, and over 11,000 Sudanese. Technology had made bravery and courage obsolete for the majority of Africans.

Yet not for all. Resistance to European imperialism characterized many areas of Africa. In West Africa, for example, Samory Toure (1830–1900) held out against the French in Guinea and Mali for some two decades. In Somalia, Abdullah Hassan (1864–1920) successfully battled the British for years. In Zimbabwe, revolts by Ndebele and Shona people shook the foundations of British control in 1896–97.

Perhaps the best-known example of such resistance, and one that amply showed the importance of guns in the dynamics of the scramble, occurred in Ethiopia. In the middle of the nineteenth century, the emperor of Ethiopia possessed little more than a grand title. Yet while the empire had broken down into its ethnic and regional components, the dream of a united empire was still alive. It was pursued by the emperors of the time, Amharic-speakers with their political base on the fertile plateau that constituted the heartland of the country. In their successful efforts to rebuild the empire, they relied increasingly on modern weapons imported from Europe and stockpiled.

By the early 1870s, however, the emperor realized that his achievements in rebuilding the empire were endangered not merely by the resistance of those whom he was then trying to force into his empire, but, more ominously, by the outside world, especially by Egypt to the north and the Sudan to the west. The opening of the Suez Canal in 1869 had, furthermore, made the Red Sea and its surrounding areas attractive not only to Egypt but also to European countries eager to ensure their trade routes to Asia. By the end of the 1870s, as the scramble for Africa was seriously getting under way, France, Britain, and Italy all became interested in acquiring land in the region. After Britain occupied Egypt in 1882, France took Djibouti (1884) and Italy seized Eritrea (1885), both on the Red Sea.

The emperor, Menelik II (1889–1913), realized that he could exploit rival European interests in the area by playing off one European power against the others to obtain the weapons he needed for expanding his empire's boundaries. He thus gave certain concessions to France in return for French weapons. Italy, upset at the growing French influence, offered weapons as well,

The Berlin Conference. By the time the conference was held in 1884–1885, the other participants in the scramble for Africa had recognized Leopold II's claim to the Congo.

and Menelik accepted them. Russia and Britain joined in. More and more modern weapons flowed into Ethiopia during the 1870s and 1880s and into the early 1890s, and Menelik steadily strengthened his ability both to suppress internal dissent and to block foreign encroachment.

Then, in the early 1890s, Menelik's strategy of balancing one European power against another began to unravel. In 1889 he had signed the Treaty of Wichale with Italy, granting it certain concessions in return for more arms shipments. Italy then claimed that Ethiopia had thus become an Italian protectorate and moved against Menelik when he objected. By 1896 Italy was ready for a major assault on the Ethiopian army, heady with the confident racism of the time that it could defeat the "primitive" Ethiopians with ease. General Oreste Baratieri (1841–1901), the commander of Italy's 18,000-man army in Eritrea, was wisely cautious, however, understanding that modern weapons functioned no differently when fired by Africans than when fired by Italians. Knowing that Menelik's army of some 100,000 troops had very long supply lines, his strategy was to wait until Menelik could no longer supply his troops with food. Then, he assumed, Menelik's soldiers would simply disappear and the Italians would walk in. But the prime minister of Italy, Francesco Crispi (1819–1901), wanted a quick, glorious victory to enhance his political reputation and ordered Baratieri to send his army into battle at once. Hopelessly outnumbered, the Italians lost over 8,000 men on 1 March 1896 at the decisive battle of Adowa. With its army destroyed and its artillery lost to the Ethiopians, Italy had no choice but to negotiate a peace.

France and Britain soon ratified Italy's acceptance of Ethiopia as a sovereign state with its greatly expanded imperial boundaries. As a consequence of its victory at Adowa—and attesting to the crucial importance of modern weaponry for survival in late-nineteenth-century Africa—Ethiopia was the only African country aside from the United States's quasi-colony of Liberia that Europeans did not occupy in the scramble for Africa. After 1896 Menelik, with his access to modern weapons assured by his country's international recognition, successfully continued his campaigns to extend his control over the Ethiopian empire's subordinate peoples.

Gold, Empire Building, and the Boer War

Europeans were as willing to shoot white Africans as they were black Africans during the scramble as they seized land and resources. In South Africa, for example, the British engaged in a long war over possession of the world's largest supply of gold with a group of white Africans, the Afrikaners, who had developed their own unique identity during the eighteenth and early nineteenth centuries.

After the Great Trek (1837–44), during which a large number of Afrikaners had withdrawn from British control by leaving the Cape Colony, the British had grudgingly recognized the independence of the Orange Free State and the Transvaal, the Afrikaner republics in the interior, in a series of formal agreements. The British complacently believed that the Afrikaners, economically weak and geographically isolated, could never challenge British preeminence in the region. Two events of the mid-1880s shattered their complacence. First, in 1884, Germany, Britain's greatest international competitor, inserted itself into the region by annexing Namibia as part of the scramble. The British, aware that the Germans and the Afrikaners were sympathetic to each other, worried about the German threat to their regional hegemony and economic prospects.

This fear of the Germans was redoubled in 1886 when, in the Transvaal republic, in the Witwatersrand area, the world's largest deposits of gold were discovered. A group of British diamond mine owners who had grown rich exploiting the Kimberley diamond fields after their discovery in 1867 moved in quickly to develop the Witwatersrand's gold, which, because it lay deep in the ground, could be mined only with the investment of

Gender and Culture

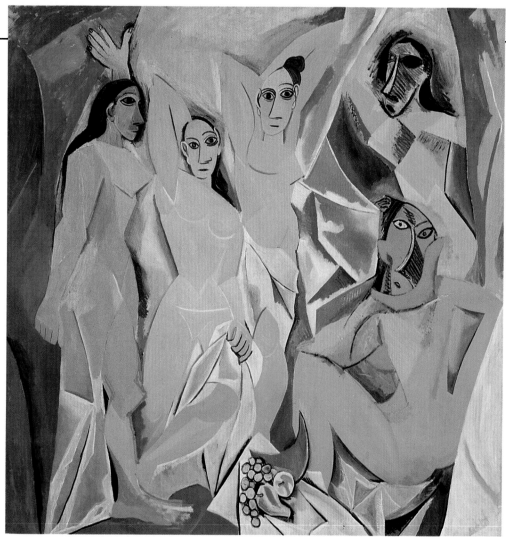

LES DEMOISELLES D'AVIGNON

Figure 1

The limited definition of civilization held by the western world for over a millennium began to broaden in the late nineteenth century. The new cultural disciplines, most notably anthropology and ethnographic studies, postulated that the social structure, habits, beliefs, and products of communities formerly dismissed as primitive or exotic were, in their own way, as complex and evolved as those based in European tradition. The process of revisioning the world view from singular to plural was slow and imperfect, and remains in process today. Two characteristic European institutions—world fairs and public museums—played a central role in this change. The early development of International Exhibitions hosted by

KONGO COUPLE   *Figure 2*

European countries and the United States, from the London Great Exhibition of 1851 to the Chicago Columbian Exposition of 1893, brought material culture from wide ranging sources to a curious public. While such displays may have only engendered awareness, public collections of ethnographic art inspired appreciation and understanding. Objects and costumes provided a point of cultural intersection for Europe, Africa, and the Americas, and the resulting imagery inspired by this contact records the first steps toward a new plurality.

Pablo Picasso encountered African carvings in the ethnographic collections of the Trocadéro in Paris. Fascination with the strength and directness of the non-European aesthetic inspired the young Spanish artist to abandon all traces of traditional form in his work and seek a new expression. His early Cubist works bear the stamp of his personal discovery. In *Les Demoiselles d'Avignon* (1907, France; Figure 1), seen on the preceding page, Picasso used the formula of African carving to simplify the features of the three women on the left. African masks are used to cover the faces of the women on the right. The denial of natural appearance is coupled with the denial of a similar western art convention, the illusion of three-dimensional space. Picasso fragments the planes of the background, and even some of the bodies, breaking them into the jagged slabs that would become the hallmark of Cubism. Picasso knew little about the cultural significance of these masks; he saw them as emblems of primitivism, appropriate for the spirit of danger and mystery he wanted to convey in a portrait of Avignon prostitutes.

The infiltration of western aesthetics into the African view took many forms. This *Kongo Couple* (ca. 1890; Congo and Zaire; Figure 2), for example, encodes the conventional gender construct of the Congo peoples: aggressive male and nurturing female. But the man's modern uniform and weapon, in contrast to the woman's traditional skirt, cuff, and collar, positions him in a new wider world, associating westernization with power and progress.

The Mami Wata cult of west Africa demonstrates another product of cultural intersection. Images of this foreign water spirit, seen here in a painted, Baule wood carving (ca. 1960, Ivory Coast: Figure 3) record the layering of ideas and aesthetics from abroad. Her posture, and her attribute of the coiling snake, has been traced back to a German color lithograph of an East Indian snake charmer, circulated throughout the area in the early 1900s. Her cult has endured through the century, and her image is now associated with more than a dozen cultures from Senegal to Tanzania. Dressed according to modern western standards. Mami Wata's form changes with the times. Her iconography continues to develop.

Cultural and gender references of clothing inform Frida Kahlo's disturbing image *Self-Portrait with Cropped Hair* (1940, Mexico; Figure 4), shown on the following page. Kahlo, born of mixed parentage, was proud of her Mexican roots, and generally dressed in tradi-

BAULE CARVING OF THE FOREIGN WATER SPIRIT   *Figure 3*

SELF-PORTRAIT WITH CROPPED HAIR   *Figure 4*

tional skirts and richly embroidered blouses. Her long, black hair was another emblem of her ethnicity. She wore it in an elaborate upswept coiffure bound with ribbons. But here, Kahlo appears in a dull, masculine suit. The tresses she cut from her own head surround her. By taking on the surface symbols of another gender and another culture, Kahlo comments on her own position in the world. A Mexican woman artist encloses herself in the trappings of the male western art world, gaining recognition, but losing identity. Kahlo reversed Picasso's early act of cultural appropriation, but instead of evoking mystery and danger, she reveals a powerful, but tragic, truth.

large amounts of capital. The best-known of these investors was Cecil Rhodes (1853–1902), a businessman and Cape Colony politician intent upon expanding his wealth through an extension of British power to the north. Rhodes and his colleagues quickly identified Afrikaner governmental policies on agriculture, tariffs, and labor control as major impediments to profitable gold production. Therefore, in 1895, they organized, with the connivance of members of the British government, an attempt to overthrow the Afrikaner government of the Transvaal. This attempt, led by Dr. L. S. Jameson (1853–1917), Rhodes's lieutenant, involved the invasion of the Transvaal by British South African police, and came to be known as the Jameson Raid. It was faultily executed, however, and, to Rhodes's utter humiliation, it failed.

The failure of the Jameson Raid prompted the British government to send a new agent, Alfred Milner (1854–1925), to the area in 1897. An ardent advocate of expanding the British Empire and of keeping German influence in the region to a minimum, and well aware of the importance of gold to Britain's financial position in the world, Milner was determined to push the Afrikaners into uniting with the British in South Africa, either through diplomacy or war. By 1899 it was clear that war was inevitable, and, in October, British demands provoked a declaration of war from the Afrikaners. The British confidently expected to have the war over by Christmas, but the Afrikaners did not cooperate. Skillful Afrikaner leaders carried out a guerrilla war against inept British generals and the so-called Boer War dragged on and on. (See Special Feature, "African Political Heroes and Resistance to the Scramble," pp. 816–817.)

The British eventually sent 350,000 troops to South Africa, but these forces, even when reinforced by thousands of African auxiliaries, could not decisively defeat the 65,000 Afrikaner fighting men. Casualties were high on both sides, not merely from the fighting, but because typhus epidemics broke out in the concentration camps in which the British interned Afrikaner women and children as they pursued their scorched-earth policies in the countryside. By the war's end, 25,000 Afrikaners, 22,000 British imperial troops, and 12,000 Africans had died. Britain had also suffered great international criticism for having treated white Afrikaners as if they were black Africans.

An Ethiopian painting depicting the battle of Adowa. The army of the Ethiopian emperor Menelik II was victorious over the invading Italians. This was the first major victory of an African country over a European power.

The spirit medium Kagubi in captivity.

African Political Heroes and Resistance to the Scramble

A country's political heroes are usually its generals and kings, presidents and statesmen, people of power and accomplishment. Paintings and photographs of them emphasize their grandeur and majesty, reflecting their larger-than-life importance. However, two of contemporary Zimbabwe's heroes—both of whom appear on its postage stamps—are very different. One is a woman of about sixty whose name was Nehanda. The other is a middle-aged man of about forty-five called Kagubi. Both appear unkempt and are barefoot in the reproductions from the photograph taken in jail just before they were executed on 27 April 1898 and buried with utmost secrecy. Although they died almost a century ago, their memory is alive in Zimbabwe, and students are taught about them in their history books. Why?

In 1889 Cecil Rhodes, South African financier and politician, convinced that large deposits of gold existed in Zimbabwe, persuaded the British government to support his efforts to seize Zimbabwe and Zambia. He established a private chartered company known as the British South Africa Company (BSAC) and in 1890 invaded the eastern part of Zimbabwe. The people who lived there were Shona people, and conquering them seemed easy because they were politically fragmented into myriad little states with neither strong chiefs nor a military tradition. So easy was the conquest, indeed, that the settlers came to view the Shona with utter contempt. Soon afterward, in 1893, the BSAC conquered the Ndebele people, to the southwest of the Shona.

One of European imperialism's most frequently stated aims during the scramble for Africa was to bring "civilization" to the peoples of Africa, to "bear the white man's burden" so that Africans could improve their existence. For the Shona and Ndebele, however, Rhodes' agents brought little perceptible civilization but much to be lamented. They soon had a mass of grievances against Rhodes's BSAC. Much of their land was taken. They were forced to work for the settlers for little or no pay. They were compelled to pay taxes. Europeans took African women as concubines. The Africans' grievances grew steadily. Then, in 1896, their cattle herds were almost wiped out by a new disease, rinderpest, which the Italians who were then occupying Eritrea had accidentally imported to Africa in the late 1880s and which was spreading southward. This seemed the last straw.

But then opportunity presented itself. Most of the BSAC police force had gone over the border into the Transvaal to participate in a raid on the Afrikaner state at the end of 1895, and in 1896 they were still languishing in jail. With few police around, the people reasoned, the time was ripe for revolt against the BSAC. Early in 1896, the Ndebele rose in rebellion. The BSAC, with its superior weaponry, defeated them, but in June the Shona also rose. A hundred settlers were slain before the government was aware of what was occurring.

The company could not believe that the disorganized Shona, for whom they had such contempt, were capable of such a rising. But, despite their lack of strong chiefs or a military tradition, they were, and they waged a guerrilla war against the settlers for over fifteen months that almost bankrupted the company's finances. When the company's officials investigated, they were astounded to discover that the uprising, which came to be known as the *Chimurenga*, was being significantly organized and directed by Shona religious leaders known as mediums. These were people who became possessed by spirits of the ancestors and articulated what the ancestors desired the living to do. These people, to the British obscure and ordinary, were able not only to mobilize the attack on the company, but, because of their very lack of notoriety, to sustain it by spying on the company, distributing intelligence as to what company troop movements were taking place, and relaying messages across the countryside.

As a result of the spirit mediums' work, it was not until October 1897 that the company finally ended the rebellion by tracking down its leader, Kagubi, and his colleagues, including the important Nehanda. By then, however, the uprising had attracted so much negative publicity in Britain that the company was brought under greater control from the British government. Many of the abuses that had provoked the people to rebel were curtailed, and a greater regularity of administration was instituted. The Shona had demonstrated to the company that there were limits beyond which the government could not go.

Seven decades later, in the 1970s, the African people again rose up in rebellion, this time against the white settler government of Ian Smith, the political heir to Cecil Rhodes, this time successfully. They called their rebellion the Second *Chimurenga*. When they finally won in the late 1970s, they needed a new group of patriotic heroes from their past about whom to teach in independent Zimbabawe's schools. Two of those chosen were Kagubi and Nehanda, scruffy and unkempt in their photograph to be sure, but remembered as early patriots and martyrs, the memory of whose work against Rhodes and his settlers was able to travel across the years and inspire Zimbabweans during the rebellion of the 1970s.

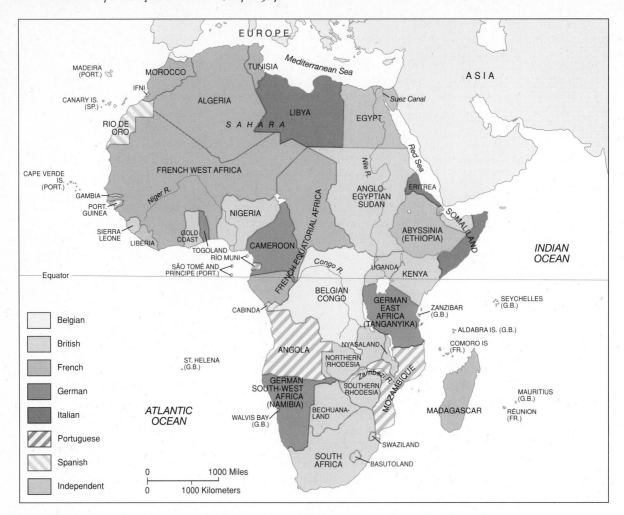

Africa, 1914

In April 1902, the British accepted the conditional surrender of the Afrikaners. The British annexed the Afrikaner republics to the empire and took the opportunity to make the gold industry efficient. But they promised the Afrikaners that no political decisions regarding the majority black African population's political role in a future South Africa would be taken before returning governmental power to the Afrikaners. This crucial concession ensured that segregation would remain the model for race relations in South Africa throughout the twentieth century.

When World War I broke out in 1914, the scramble for Africa was over and the map of the continent was colored in imperial inks. France had secured the larg-est chunk, some four million square miles of mostly tropical forests and deserts. Britain had the second largest empire, richer in minerals and agricultural potential than France's. Germany proudly possessed two West African colonies, Togo and Cameroon, as well as Namibia in southern Africa and Tanganyika in East Africa. Belgium had been forced to assume control over Leopold II's Congo in 1908 after scandals made his continued control unacceptable. Portugal had finally consolidated its feeble hold on Angola, Mozambique, and Portuguese Guinea. Italy had colonies in Libya, Eritrea, and Somalia, while Spain was left with some bits of coast. Only Ethiopia and Liberia were politically independent. Now that they had conquered Africa, the colonial powers had to face the issue of how their new colonies could be made to pay. Now that Africa had been conquered, Africans had to face the issue of how they might regain their political and economic independence.

Imperialism in Asia

The British Parliament proclaimed that on New Year's Day, 1877, Queen Victoria (1837–1901) would add the title of Empress of India to her many honors. India, the great jewel in the imperial crown, was a land Victoria had never seen. The queen's new title, not universally popular in Britain and unnoticed by most famine-stricken Indian peasants, in fact changed nothing about the way the British ruled India. Yet it was more than merely a symbolic assertion of dominance over a country long controlled by the British.

India was the starting point of all British expansion and it stood at the center of British foreign policy. To protect its sea routes to India and to secure its Indian markets, Britain acquired territories and carved out concessions all over the world. Devised by Prime Minister Benjamin Disraeli to flatter an aging monarch, the new title of empress was really a calculated warning to Russia, operating on India's northern frontier in Afghanistan, and to France, busily pursuing its own interests in Egypt.

Formal British rule in India began in 1861 with the appointment of a viceroy, who was assisted by legislative and executive councils. Both of these bodies included some Indian representatives. British rule encountered the four main divisions of the highly stratified Hindu society. At the top were Brahmans, the learned and priestly class, followed by the warriors and rulers, then by farmers and merchants, and finally by the peasants and laborers. On the outside existed the "untouchables," a fifth division intended to perform society's most menial tasks. Rather than disrupt this divisive caste system, the British found it to their advantage to maintain the status quo.

The special imperial relationship, rung in with the new year in 1877, originated in the seventeenth century, when the British East India Company, a joint-stock venture free of government control, began limited trading in Indian markets. The need for regulation and protection firmly established British rule by the end of the eighteenth century. Conquest of the Punjab in 1849 brought the last independent areas under British control. Throughout this period

Britain invested considerable overseas capital in India, and in turn India absorbed one-fifth of total British exports. The market for Indian cotton, for centuries exported to markets in Asia and Europe, collapsed under British tariffs and India became a ready market for cheap Lancashire cotton. The British also exploited India's agriculture, salt, and opium production for profit.

At the end of the eighteenth century, the British traded English wool and Indian cotton for Chinese tea and textiles. But Britain's thirst for Chinese tea grew, while Chinese demand for English and Indian textiles slackened. Britain discovered that Indian opium could be used to balance the trade deficit created by tea. British merchants and local Chinese officials, especially in the entry port of Canton, began to expand their profitable involvement in a contraband trade in opium. The East India Company held a monopoly over opium cultivation in Bengal. Opium exports to China mounted

The Boer War and Queen Victoria. This Dutch caricature is from an album entitled "John Bull in Africa," published in 1900. The war aroused much criticism among the British liberal opposition.

phenomenally: from 200 chests in 1729 to 40,000 chests in 1838. By the 1830s opium was probably Britain's most important crop in world markets. The British prospered as opium was pumped into China at rates faster than tea was flowing out. Chinese buyers began paying for the drug with silver.

Concerned with the sharp rise in addiction, the accompanying social problems, and the massive outflow of silver, the Chinese government reacted. As Chinese officials saw it, they were exchanging their precious metal for British poison. Addicts were threatened with the death penalty. In 1839, the Chinese government destroyed British opium in the port of Canton, touching off the so-called Opium War (1839–42).

Between 1842 and 1895, China fought five wars with foreigners and lost all of them. Defeat was expensive as China had to pay costs to the winners. Before the end of the century, Britain, France, Germany, and Japan had managed to establish major territorial advantages in their "spheres of influence," sometimes through negotiation and sometimes through force. By 1912, over fifty major Chinese ports had been handed over to foreign control as "treaty ports." British spheres included Shanghai, the lower Yangzi, and Hong Kong. France maintained special interests in South China. Germany controlled the Shandong peninsula. Japan laid claim to the northeast.

Spheres of influence grew in importance at the beginning of the twentieth century, when foreign investors poured capital into railway lines, which needed treaty protection from competing companies. Railways necessarily furthered foreign encroachment and opened up new territories to the claims of foreigners. As one Chinese official explained it, the railroads were like scissors that threatened to cut China into many pieces. Foreigners established no formal empires in China, but the treaty ports certainly signaled both informal rule and indisputable foreign dominance.

Treaty ports were centers of foreign residence and trade, where rules of extraterritoriality applied. This meant that foreigners were exempt from Chinese law enforcement and that, although present on Chinese territory, they could be judged only by officials of their own countries. Extraterritoriality, a privilege not just for diplomats but one shared by every foreign national, implied both a distrust of Chinese legal procedures and a cultural arrogance about the superiority of Western institutions. These arrangements stirred Chinese resentment and contributed considerably to growing antiforeignism.

In order to preserve extraterritoriality and maintain informal empires, the European powers appointed civilian representatives known as consuls. Often merchants themselves and, in the beginning, unpaid in their posts, consuls acted as the chieftains of resident merchant communities, judges in all civil and criminal cases, and spokesmen for the commercial interests of the home country. They clearly embodied the commercial intentions of Western governments. Initially they stood outside the diplomatic corps; later they were consigned to its lower ranks. Consuls were brokers for commerce and interpreted the international commercial law being forged. Consulates spread beyond China as Western nations used consuls to protect their own interests. In Africa consuls represented the trading concerns of European governments and were instrumental in the transition to formal rule.

European nations pursued imperialist endeavors elsewhere in Asia, acquired territories on China's frontiers, and took over states that had formerly paid tribute to the Chinese empire. The British acquired Hong Kong (1842), Burma (1886), and Kowloon (1898). The Russians took over the Maritime Provinces in 1858. The French made gains in Indochina (Annam and Tonkin) in 1884 and in 1893 and extended control over Laos (1893) and Cambodia (1884).

The Sino-Japanese War of 1894–95 revealed Japan's intentions to compete as an imperialist power in Asia. The modernized and westernized Japanese army easily defeated the ill-equipped and poorly led Chinese forces. As a result, Japan gained the island of Taiwan. Pressing its ambitions on the continent,

The stacking room in an opium factory in Patna, India. The massive influx of Indian opium destroyed China's economy.

Japan locked horns with Russia over claims to the Liaodong peninsula, Korea, and south Manchuria. Following its victory in the Russo-Japanese War of 1904–05, Japan expanded into all of these areas, annexing Korea outright in 1910. The war sent a strong message to the West about the ease with which the small Asian nation had defeated the Russian giant and contributed to the heightening of anti-imperialist sentiments in China.

Results of a European-Dominated World

Europeans fashioned the world in their own image, but in doing so, Western values and Western institutions underwent profound and unintended transformations. Family values were articulated in an imperialist context, and race emerged as a key factor in culture. The discovery of new lands, new cultures, and new peoples altered the ways in which European women and men regarded themselves and viewed their place in the world. With the rise of new contenders for power, the United States and Japan, and growing criticism about the morality of capitalism, the Western world was not as predictable in 1914 as it had appeared in 1870.

A World Economy

Imperialism produced an interdependent world economic system with Europe at its center. Industrial and commercial capitalism linked together the world's continents in a communications and transportation network unimaginable in earlier ages. As a result,

foreign trade increased from 3 percent of world output in 1800 to 33 percent by 1913. The greatest growth in trade occurred in the period from 1870 to 1914, as raw materials, manufactured products, capital, and men and women were transported across seas and continents by those seeking profits.

Most trading in the age of imperialism still took place among European nations and North America. But entrepreneurs in search of new markets and new resources saw in Africa and Asia opportunities for protected exploitation. Opportunities were not seized but created in nonindustrialized areas of the world, as new markets were shaped to meet the needs of Western producers and consumers. European landlords and managers trained Kenyan farmers to put aside their traditional agricultural methods and to grow more "useful" crops like coffee, tea, and sugar. The availability of cheaper British textiles of inferior quality drove Indian weavers away from their handlooms. Chinese silk producers changed centuries-old techniques to produce silk thread and cloth that was suited to the machinery and mass-production requirements of the French. Non-European producers undoubtedly derived benefits from this new international trading partnership, but those benefits were often scarce. Trade permitted specialization but at the choice of the colonizer, not the colonized. World production and consumption were being shaped to suit the needs of the West.

Capital in search of profits flowed out of the wealthier areas of Europe into the nonindustrialized regions of Russia, the Balkans, and the Ottoman Empire, where capital-intensive expenditures (on railways for instance) promised high returns. Capital investment in overseas territories also increased phenomenally as

A nineteenth-century cartoon entitled "The China Cup Race" depicts imperialist powers lined up to vie for territories in China.

MAJOR WORLD STATES AND COLONIAL POSSESSIONS, 1900

Belgium

France

German Empire

Great Britain

Italy

The Netherlands

Portugal

Spain

United States

Other Independent states

Colonial Holdings, ca. 1914

railroads were built to gain access to primary products. Great Britain maintained its overwhelming dominance in overseas investment with loans abroad greater than those of its five major competitors—France, Germany, Holland, the United States, and Belgium—combined.

The City of London had become the world's banker, serving as the clearinghouse for foreign investment on a global scale. The adoption of gold as the standard for exchange for most European currencies by 1874 further facilitated the operation of a single, interdependent trading and investment system. Britain remained the world's biggest trading nation, with half of its exports going to Asia, Africa, and South America, and the other half to Europe and the United States. But Germany was Britain's fastest-growing competitor, with twice as many exports to Europe and expanding overseas trade by 1914. The United States had recently joined the league of the world's great trading nations and was running a strong third in shares of total trade.

Foreign investments often took the form of loans to governments or to enterprises guaranteed by governments. Investors might be willing to take risks, but they also expected protection, no less so than merchants and industrialists trading in overseas territories. Together trade and investment interests exerted considerable pressure on European states for control through acquisition and concessions. The vast amounts of money involved help explain the expectations of state involvement and the reasons why international competition, rivalry, and instability threatened to lead to conflict and to war.

Race and Culture

The West's ability to kill and conquer as well as to cure was, as one Victorian social observer argued, proof of its cultural superiority. Every colonizing nation had its spokesmen for the "civilizing mission" to educate and to convert African and Asian "heathens." Cultural superiority was only a short step from arguments for racial superiority. Prompted by the United States' involvement in the Philippines, the British poet Rudyard Kipling (1865–1936) characterized the responsibilities of the advanced West as "the white man's burden." The smug and arrogant attitude of his poem about the white man's mission revealed a deep-seated and unacknowledged racism toward peoples considered "half devil and half child."

As discussed earlier in this chapter, views of cultural superiority received support from the scientific work of Herbert Spencer and Charles Darwin. In the 1880s, popularizers applied evolutionary ideas about animal and plant life to the development of human society. Just as animals could be hierarchically organized according to observable differences, so too, it was argued, could the different races of human beings. Race and culture were collapsed into each other. If Westerners were culturally superior, as they claimed, they must be racially superior as well.

Women and Imperialism

Ideas about racial and cultural superiority were not confined to books by pseudoscientists and to discussions among policy makers. Public discussions about marriage, reproduction, motherhood, and childrearing reflected new concerns about furthering "the imperial race," the racial identity of white Westerners. Women throughout Western societies were encouraged by reformers, politicians, and doctors to have more children and instructed to take better care of them. "Children [are] the most valuable of imperial assets," one British doctor instructed his readers. Healthy young men were needed in the colonies, they were told, to defend Western values. State officials paid greater attention to infant mortality at the end of the nineteenth century, set up health programs for children, and provided young women with training in home management, nutrition, and child care. These programs were no coincidence in an age of imperialism. Their rhetoric was explicitly imperialist and often racist in urging women to preserve the quality of the white race.

In "The White Man's Burden," Kipling advised, "Send forth the best ye breed." All over Europe newly formed associations and clubs stressed the need for careful mate selection. In Britain, Francis Galton (1822–1911) founded eugenics, the study of genetics for the purpose of improving inherited characteristics of the race. Imperialism, the propagandists proclaimed, depended on mothers, women who would nurture healthy workers, strong soldiers and sailors, intelligent and capable leaders. High infant mortality and poor health of children were attributed directly to maternal failings and not to environmental factors or poverty. Kaiser William II stressed that German women's attention to the "three Ks"—*Kinder, Küche, Kirche* (children, kitchen, church) would guarantee a race of Germans who would rule the world. British

KARL PEARSON, SOCIAL DARWINISM AND IMPERIALISM

■ *The following is an excerpt from a lecture entitled "National Life From the Standpoint of Science," given by a British professor of mathematics, Karl Pearson (1857–1936), in 1900. Pearson held the first chair in Eugenics at the University of London where he applied statistical methods to the study of heredity and evolution. The term "eugenics" was introduced by Francis Galton, of whom Pearson was a follower. Pearson was heavily influenced by the pseudoscientific assumptions of social Darwinism and combined prejudices about race and nationalism to justify British imperialism as a proof of "survival of the fittest."*

The . . . great function of science in national life . . . is to show us what national life means, and how the nation is a vast organism subject as much to the great forces of evolution as any other gregarious type of life. There is a struggle of race against race and of nation against nation. In the early days of that struggle it was a blind, unconscious struggle of barbaric tribes. At the present day, in the case of the civilized white man, it has become more and more the conscious, carefully directed attempt of the nation to fit itself to a continuously changing environment. The nation has to foresee how and where the struggle will be carried on; the maintenance of national position is becoming more and more a conscious preparation for changing conditions, an insight into the needs of coming environments. . . .

If a nation is to maintain its position in this struggle, it must be fully provided with trained brains in every department of national activity, from the government to the factory, and have, if possible, a *reserve of brain and physique* to fall back upon in times of national crisis . . .

You will see that my view—and I think it may be called the scientific view of a nation—is that of an organized whole, kept up to a high pitch of internal efficiency by insuring that its numbers are substantially recruited from the better stocks, and kept up to a high pitch of external efficiency by contest, chiefly by way of war with inferior races, and with equal races by the struggle for trade-routes and for the sources of raw material and of food supply. This is the natural history view of mankind, and I do not think you can in its main features subvert it . . .

Is it not a fact that the daily bread of our millions of workers depends on their having somebody to work for? that if we give up the contest for trade-routes and for free markets and for waste lands, we indirectly give up our food supply? Is it not a fact that our strength depends on these and upon our colonies, and that our colonies have been won by the ejection of inferior races, and are maintained against equal races only by respect for the present power of our empire? . . .

We find that the law of the survival of the fitter is true of mankind, but that the struggle is that of the gregarious animal. A community not knit together by strong social instincts, by sympathy between man and man, and class and class, cannot face the external contest, the competition with other nations, by peace or by war, for the raw material of production and for its food supply. This struggle of tribe with tribe, and nation with nation, may have its mournful side; but we see as a result of it the gradual progress of mankind to higher intellectual and physical efficiency. It is idle to condemn it; we can only see that it exists and recognise what we have gained by it—civilization and social sympathy. But while the statesman has to watch this external struggle, . . . he must be very cautious that the nation is not silently rotting at its core. He must insure that the fertility of the inferior stocks is checked, and that of the superior stocks encouraged; he must regard with suspicion anything that tempts the physically and mentally fitter men and women to remain childless.

From: Karl Pearson, *National Life from the Standpoint of Science*, 1905.

generals and French statesmen publicly applied similar sentiments to their own countries and stressed that the future depended on the devotion of women to their family obligations.

Some European women participated directly in the colonizing experience. As missionaries and nurses, they supported the civilizing mission. As wives of officials and managers, they were expected to embody the gentility and values of Western culture. Most men who traded and served overseas did so unaccompanied by women. But when women were present in any numbers, as they were in India before 1914, they were expected to preserve the exclusivity of Western communities and to maintain class and status differentiations as a proof of cultural superiority.

Ecology and Imperialism

Ecology, the relationship and adjustment of human groups to their environment, was affected by imperial expansion, which dislocated the societies that it touched. Early explorers had disrupted little as they arrived, observed, and then moved on. The missionaries, merchants, soldiers, and businessmen who came later required that those with whom they came into contact must change their thought and behavior. In some cases, dislocation resulted in material improvements, better medical care, and the introduction of modern technology. For the most part, however, the initial ecological impact of the imperialist was negative. Western men and women carried diseases to people who did not share their immunity. Traditional village life was destroyed in rural India, and African societies disintegrated under the European onslaught. Resistance

"A Dangerous Venture" is the title of this cartoon, which portrays the Russo-Japanese War. The clever Japanese acrobat lures the Russian bear onto a thin bamboo pole stretched over a chasm.

existed everywhere, but only the Ethiopians, defeating the Italians at Adowa in 1896, managed to have any success in keeping out foreigners.

Education of native populations had as its primary goal the improvement of administration and productivity in the colonies. When foreigners ruled indirectly through existing indigenous hierarchies, they often created corrupt and tyrannical bureaucracies that exploited natives. The indirect rule of the British in India was based on a pragmatic desire to keep British costs low.

When Asian and African laborers started producing for the Western market, they became dependent on its fluctuations. Victimized for centuries by the vagaries of weather, they now had to contend with the instability and cutthroat competition of cash crops in world markets. Individuals migrated from place to place in the countryside and from the countryside to newly formed cities. Such migrations necessarily affected family life, with individuals marrying later because they lacked the resources to set up households. The situation paralleled similar disruptions in English society at the beginning of the Industrial Revolution. Women as well as men migrated to find jobs. Many women, cut free of their tribes (as was the case in Nairobi), turned to prostitution, literally for pennies, as a means of survival.

Some European countries used their overseas territories as dumping grounds for hardened and incorrigible convicted criminals. Imitating the earlier example of the British in Australia, the French developed Guiana and New Caledonia as prison colonies in the hope that they could solve their social problems at home by exporting them.

The United States provided another variation on imperial expansion. Its westward drive across the North American continent, beginning at the end of the eighteenth century, established the United States as an imperial power in the Western Hemisphere. By 1848, the relatively young American nation stretched over three thousand miles from one ocean to the other. It had met the opposition and resistance of the Native Americans with armed force, decimated them, and "concentrated" the survivors in assigned territories and, later, on reservations.

At the end of the nineteenth century, the United States, possessing both the people and the resources for rapid industrial development, turned to the Caribbean and the Pacific in pursuit of markets and investment opportunities. By acquiring stepping-stones of islands across the Pacific in the Hawaiian Islands and Samoa, it secured fueling bases and access to lucrative East Asian ports. And by intervening repeatedly in Central America and building the Panama Canal, the United States established its hegemony in the Caribbean by 1914. Growing in economic power and hegemonic influence, the United States had joined the club of imperial powers and was making serious claims against European expansion.

Critiquing Capitalism

Not least significant of the consequences of imperialism was the critique of capitalism it produced. Those who condemned it as exploitative and racist saw imperialism as an expression of problems inherent in capitalism. In 1902, J. A. Hobson (1858–1940) published *Imperialism, A Study*, a work that has remained in print ever since. In the book Hobson argued that underconsumption and surplus capital at home drove Western industrial countries overseas in search of a cure for these economic ills. Rather than solving the problems by raising workers' wages and thereby increasing their consumption power and creating new opportunities for

investment in home markets, manufacturers, entrepreneurs, and industrialists sought higher profits abroad. Hobson considered these business interests "economic parasites," making large fortunes at the expense of national interests.

In the midst of world war, the future leader of the Russian Revolution, Vladimir Ilich Ulyanov (1870–1924), or to use his revolutionary name, Lenin, added his own critique of capitalism. He did not share Hobson's belief that capitalism was merely malfunctioning in its imperialist endeavors. Instead, Lenin argued in *Imperialism, the Highest Stage of Capitalism* (1916) that capitalism is inherently and inevitably imperialistic. Because he was sure that Western capitalism was in the process of effecting its own destruction, Lenin called World War I the final "imperialist war."

Critics, historians, and economists have since pointed out that both works are marred by errors and omissions. Yet they stand at the beginning of almost a century of debate over the morality and economic feasibility of imperialism. Hobson as a liberal and Lenin as a Marxist highlighted the connections between social

George Nathaniel Curzon, viceroy and governor general of India from 1898 to 1905, is shown here meeting with the nizam, the sovereign of Hyderabad, and party in 1900.

problems at home, whether in late Victorian England or in prerevolutionary Russia, and economic exploitation abroad.

Yet if electoral results and the popular press are any indication, Europeans not only accepted but warmly embraced the responsibilities of empire. Criticism of the backwardness of captive peoples prevailed. Victorian social scientist Walter Bagehot (1826–77) told the story of an aged savage who, upon returning to his tribe, informed them that he had "tried civilization for forty years and it was not worth the trouble." No matter how intelligent the judgment of this African might seem with hindsight, the possibility of returning to areas of the world not influenced by the civilization of the West was rapidly disappearing before 1914.

Conflict at Home: The European Balance of Power

In addition to mounting conflicts in colonized areas, European states were locked in a competition within Europe for dominance and control. The politics of geography combined with rising nationalist movements in southern Europe and the Ottoman Empire to create a mood of increasing confrontation among Europe's great powers. The European balance of power so carefully crafted by Bismarck began to disintegrate with his departure from office in 1890. By 1914 a Europe divided into two camps was no longer the sure guarantee of peace that it had been a generation earlier.

The Geopolitics of Europe

The map of Europe had been redrawn in the two decades after 1850. By 1871 Europe consisted of five great powers, known as the Big Five—Britain, France, Germany, Austria-Hungary, and Russia—and a handful of lesser states. The declaration of a German Empire in 1871 and the emergence of Italy with Rome as its capital in 1870 unified numerous disparate states. Although not always corresponding to linguistic and cultural differences among Europe's peoples, national boundaries appeared fixed, with no country aspiring to territorial expansion at the expense of its neighbors. But the creation of the two new national units of Germany and Italy had legitimized nationalist aspirations and the militarism necessary to enforce them.

Under the chancellorship of Otto von Bismarck, Germany led the way in forging a new alliance system based on the realistic assessment of power politics within Europe. In 1873 Bismarck joined together the three most conservative powers of the Big Five—Germany, Austria-Hungary, and Russia—into the Three Emperors' League. Consultation over mutual interests and friendly neutrality were the cornerstones of this alliance. Identifying one's enemies and choosing one's friends in this new configuration of power came in large part to depend on geographic weaknesses. The Three Emperors' League was one example of the geographic imperatives driving diplomacy. Bismarck was determined to banish the specter of a two-front war by isolating France on the Continent.

Each of the Great Powers had a vulnerability, a geographic Achilles' heel. Germany's vulnerability lay in its North Sea ports. German shipping along its only coast could easily be bottlenecked by a powerful naval force. Such an event, the Germans knew, could destroy their rapidly growing international trade. What was worse, powerful land forces could "encircle" Germany. As Britain's century-old factories slowly became obsolete under peeling coats of paint, Germany enjoyed the advantages of a latecomer to industrialization, forced to start from scratch by investing in the most advanced machinery and technology. The German Reich was willing to support industrial expansion, scientific and technological training, and social programs for its workers. Yet as Germany surged forward to seize its share of world markets, it was acutely aware that it was hemmed in on the Continent. Germany could not extend its frontiers the way Russia had to the east. German gains in the Franco-Prussian war in Alsace and Lorraine could not be repeated without risking greater enmity. German leaders saw the threat of encirclement as a second geographic weakness. Bismarck's awareness of these geographic facts of life prompted his engineering of the Three Emperors' League in 1873, two years after the founding of the German Empire.

Austria-Hungary was Europe's second largest landed nation and the third largest in population. The same factors that had made it a great European power—its size and its diversity—now threatened to destroy it. The ramshackle empire of Europe, it had no geographical unity. Its vulnerability came from within, from the centrifugal forces of linguistic and cultural diversity. Weakened by nationalities clamoring for independence

THE SOCIETY OF NATIONAL DEFENSE, SERBIA, 1911

■ *The Society for National Defense (*Narodna Odbrana*) was a secret society formed by Serb nationalists. This group sought the liberation of Slavs through propaganda and subversive activities against Austria-Hungary, which had annexed Bosnia-Herzegovina in 1908. The Society for National Defense was a terrorist group, one of whose members was responsible for the assassination of the Austrian Archduke Ferdinand on June 28, 1914. Here the group spells out its program and speaks of a new kind of nationalism, one that is a "holy cause."*

The Serbian people has endured during its existence many difficult and bitter days. Among these days is September 24, 1908, when Austria-Hungary illegally annexed Bosnia and Herzegovina. This day can be compared to the worst days of our past. It was especially painful for the Serbian people in that it came at a time when more fortunate peoples had already completed their national unification and had created large states, and when culture and freedom were presumed to be at their peak.

At such a time Austria-Hungary oppressed along with other peoples several million Serbs, whom she penalizes and seeks to alienate from us. They may not openly call themselves Serbs, and may not adorn their homes with the Serbian flag; they may not trade freely, cultivate their soil, erect Serbian schools, openly celebrate the feast of the patron saint [Slava], and may not sing of Kossowo or of Prince Marko and Milosch Obilitsch. Only such a state, only an Austria-Hungary, could carry through such an annexation . . .

Today everywhere a new concept of nationalism has become prevalent. Nationalism (the feeling of nationality) is no longer a historical or poetical feeling, but the true practical expression of life. Among the French, Germans, and English, and among all other civilized peoples, nationalism has grown into something quite new; in it lies the concept of bread, space, air, commerce, competition in everything. Only among us is it still in the old form; that is, it is the fruit of spiritual suffering rather than of reasonable understanding and national advantage. If we speak of freedom and union, we parade far too much the phrases "breaking our chains" and "freeing the slaves"; we call far too much upon our former Serbian glory and think too little of the fact that the freeing of subjected areas and their union with Serbia are necessary to our citizens, our merchants, and our peasants on the grounds of the most elementary needs of culture and trade, of food and space. If one were to explain to our sharp-eyed people our national task as one closely connected with the needs of everyday life, our people would take up the work in a greater spirit of sacrifice than is today the case. We must tell our people that the freedom of Bosnia is necessary, not just because of their feeling of sympathy with their brothers who suffer there, but also because of commerce and its connection with the sea; national union is necessary because of the stronger development of a common culture. The Italians welcome the conquest of Tripoli not just because of the glory to be won by the success of their arms, but especially because of the advantage they hope to gain by annexing Tripoli. Our people must adopt a more realistic attitude toward politics. We must show them how we would stand culturally and economically if we were united into one state and were in as favorable a position commercially as that of Timok in relation to the Adriatic . . .

Along with the task of explaining to our people the danger threatening us from Austria, the *Narodna Odbrana* has also the other important tasks of explaining to them, while preserving our holy national memories, this new, healthy, fruitful conception of nationalism, and of convincing them to work for national freedom and unity . . .

All in all, the *Narodna Odbrana* aims through its work to advance upon the enemy on the day of reckoning with a sound, nationally conscious, and internally reconciled Serbian people, a nation of Sokols, rifle clubs, heroes—in fact, the fear and terror of the enemy—reliant front-rank fighters and executors of Serbia's holy cause.

If this succeeds, all will be well for us; woe to us if we fail.

and self-rule and by an unresponsive political system, Austria-Hungary remained backward agriculturally and unable to respond to the industrial challenge of western Europe. It seemed most likely to collapse from social and political pressures.

Another feature must be added to the picture of Europe in the late nineteenth century. To the southeast on the map stood the Ottoman Empire, a great decaying conglomeration that bridged Europe and Asia. Politically feeble and on the verge of bankruptcy, the Ottoman Empire with Turkey at its core comprised a vast array of ethnically, linguistically, and culturally diverse peoples. In the hundred years before 1914, increasing social unrest and nationalist bids for independence had plagued the Ottoman Empire. As was the case with the Habsburgs in Austria-Hungary, the Ottomans maintained power with increasing difficulty over these myriad ethnic groups struggling to be free. The Ottoman Empire, called "the sick man of Europe" by contemporaries, found two kinds of relations sitting at its bedside: those who would do anything to ensure its survival, no matter how weak; and those who longed for and sought to hasten its demise. Fortunately for the Ottoman Empire, its enemies were willing to preserve it in its weakened state rather than see one of the other rival European powers benefit from its collapse.

The Ottomans had already seen parts of their holdings lopped off in the nineteenth century. Britain, ever conscious of its interests in India, had acquired Cyprus, Egypt, Aden, and Sudan from the Ottomans. Germany insinuated itself into Turkish internal affairs and financed the Baghdad Railway in the attempt to link the Mediterranean to the Persian Gulf. Russia acquired territories on the banks of the Caspian Sea and had plans to take Constantinople. But it was the volatile Balkan Peninsula that threatened to upset the European power balance. The Balkans appeared to be a territory that begged for dismemberment. Internally, the Slavs sought independence from their Habsburg and Turkish oppressors. External pressures were equally great, with each of the major powers following its own geopolitical agenda.

The Instability of the Alliance System

The system of alliances formed between and among European states was guided by two realities of geopolitics. The first was the recognition of tension between France and Germany. France had lost its dominance on the Continent in 1870–71, when it was easily defeated by Prussia at the head of a nascent German Empire. With its back to the Atlantic, France faced the smaller states of Belgium, Luxembourg, Switzerland, and Italy, and the industrially and militarily powerful Germany. It had suffered the humiliation of losing territory to Germany—Alsace and Lorraine in 1871—and was well aware of its continued vulnerability. Geopolitically, France felt trapped and isolated and in need of powerful friends as a counterweight to German power.

Honolulu Harbor in 1892. President McKinley defended the annexation of Hawaii by the United States as "manifest destiny."

The second reality guiding alliances was Russia's preoccupation with maintaining free access to the Mediterranean Sea. Russia, clearly Europe's greatest landed power, was vulnerable because it could be landlocked by frozen or blockaded ports. The ice that crippled its naval and commercial vessels in the Baltic Sea drove Russia east through Asia to secure another ice-blocked port on the Sea of Japan at Vladivostok in 1860 and to seek ice-free Chinese ports. Russia was equally obsessed with protecting its warm-water ports on the Black Sea. Whoever controlled the strait of the Bosporus controlled Russia's grain export trade, on which its economic prosperity depended. All diplomatic arrangements, especially after the turn of the century, took into account these two geopolitical realities.

Ostensibly, Russia had the most to gain from the extension of its frontiers and the creation of pro-Russian satellites. It saw that by championing Pan-Slavic nationalist groups in southeastern Europe, it could greatly strengthen its own position at the expense of the two great declining empires, Ottoman Turkey and Austria-Hungary. Russia hoped to draw the Slavs into its orbit by fostering the creation of independent states in the Balkans. A Serbian revolt began in two Ottoman provinces, Bosnia and Herzegovina, in 1874. International opinion pressured Turkey to initiate reforms. Serbia declared war on Turkey on 30 June 1876; Montenegro did the same the next day. Britain, supporting the Ottoman Empire because of its trading interests in the Mediterranean, found itself in a delicate position of perhaps condemning an ally when it received news of Turkish atrocities against Christians in Bulgaria. Prime Minister Disraeli insisted that Britain was bound to defend Constantinople because of British interests in the Suez Canal and India. While Britain stood on the sidelines, Russia, with Romania as an ally, declared war against the Ottoman Empire. The war was quickly over, with Russia capturing all of Armenia, forcing the Ottoman sultan, Abdul Hamid II (1842–1918) to sue for peace on 31 January 1878.

Bismarck, a seemingly disinterested party acting as an "honest broker," hosted the peace conference that met at Berlin. The British succeeded in blocking Russia's intentions for a Bulgarian satellite and keeping the Russians from taking Constantinople. Russia abandoned its support of Serbian nationalism, and Austria-Hungary occupied Bosnia and Herzegovina. The peace concluded at the 1878 Congress of Berlin disregarded Serbian claims, thereby promising continuing conflict over the nationalities question.

The Berlin Congress also marked the emergence of a new estrangement among the Great Powers. Russia felt betrayed by Bismarck and abandoned in its alliance with Germany. Bismarck in turn cemented a Dual Alliance between Austria-Hungary and Germany in 1879 that survived until the collapse of the two imperial regimes in 1918. The Three Emperors' League was renewed in 1881, now with stipulations regarding the division of the spoils in case of a war against Turkey.

In 1882, Italy was asked to join the Dual Alliance with Germany and Austria-Hungary, thus converting it into the Triple Alliance, which prevailed until the Great War of 1914. Germany, under Bismarck's tutelage, signed treaties with Italy, Russia, and Austria-Hungary, and established friendly terms with Great Britain. A new Balkan crisis in 1885, however, shattered the illusion of stable relations.

Hostilities erupted between Bulgaria and Serbia. Russia threatened to occupy Bulgaria, but Austria stepped in to prevent Russian domination of the

This cartoon shows Disraeli successfully negotiating the tightrope of the Congress of Berlin while balancing war and peace. He carries Turkey on his back to safety, as the Ottoman Empire was reestablished in the Balkans.

Balkans, thus threatening the alliance of the Three Emperors' League. Russia was further angered by German unwillingness to support its interests against Austrian actions in the Balkans. Germany maintained relations with Russia in a new Reinsurance Treaty drawn up in 1887, which stipulated that each power would maintain neutrality should the other find itself at war. Bismarck now walked a fine line, balancing alliances and selectively disclosing the terms of secret treaties to nonsignatory countries with the goal of preserving the peace. He was described by his successor as the only man who could keep five glass balls in the air at the same time.

After Bismarck's resignation in 1890, Germany found itself unable to juggle all the glass balls. Germany allowed the arrangement with Russia to lapse. Russia, in turn, allied itself with France in 1894. Also allied with Great Britain, France had broken out of the isolation that Bismarck had intended for it two decades earlier. The Triple Entente came into existence following the Anglo-Russian understanding of 1907. Now it was the Triple Entente of Great Britain, France, and Russia against the Triple Alliance of Germany, Austria-Hungary, and Italy.

There was still every confidence that these two camps could balance each other and preserve the peace. But in 1908–09 the unresolved Balkan problem threatened to topple Europe's precarious peace. Against Russia's objections, Austria-Hungary annexed Bosnia and Herzegovina, the provinces it had occupied since 1878. Russia supported Serbia's discontent over Austrian acquisition of these predominantly Slavic territories that Serbia felt should be united with its own lands. Unwilling to risk a European war at this point, Russia was ultimately forced to back down under German pressure. Germany had to contend with its great geopolitical fear—hostile neighbors, France and Russia, on its western and eastern frontiers.

A third Balkan crisis erupted in 1912 when Italy and Turkey fought over the possession of Tripoli in North Africa. The Balkan states took advantage of this opportunity to increase their holdings at Turkey's expense. This action quickly involved great-power interests once again. A second war broke out in 1913 over Serbian interests in Bulgaria. Russia backed Serbia against Austro-Hungarian support of Bulgaria. The Russians and Austrians prepared for war while the British and Germans urged peaceful resolution. Although hostilities ceased, Serbian resentment toward Austria-Hungary over its frustrated nationalism was greater than ever. Britain, in

The New Imperialism in Africa and Asia

1837–44	Great Trek
1839–42	Opium War
1869	Suez Canal completed
1877	Queen Victoria named Empress of India
1884	Berlin Conference held to regulate imperialism in Africa
1886	Gold discovered in the Transvaal republic
1894–95	Sino-Japanese War
1896	Battle of Adowa
1899–1902	Boer War
1904–05	Russo-Japanese War

its backing of Russia, and Germany, in its support of Austria-Hungary, were enmeshed in alliances that could involve them in a military confrontation.

Great Britain did not share Germany's and Russia's fears of strangulation by blockade. And although the question of Irish home rule was a nationalities problem for Britain, it paled in comparison with Austria-Hungary's internal challenge. As an island kingdom, however, Great Britain relied on imports for its survival. The first of the European nations to become an urban and industrial power, Britain was forced to do so at the expense of its agricultural sector. It could not feed its own people without importing foodstuffs. Britain's geographic vulnerability was its dependence on access to its empire and the maintenance of open sea-lanes. Britain saw its greatest menace coming from the rise of other sea powers—notably Germany.

From the very beginning of the competition for territories and concessions, no European state could act in Africa or Asia without affecting the interests and actions of its rivals at home. The African scramble made clear how interlocking the system of European states was

A Punch *cartoon shows European leaders trying to keep the lid on the simmering kettle of Balkan crises.*

after 1870. The development of spheres of influence in China underlined the value of world markets and international trade for the survival and expansion of Western nations.

A "balance of power" among states guaranteed national security and independence until the end of the nineteenth century. But between 1870 and 1914, industrialization, technology, and accompanying capital formation created vast economic disparities. Conflict and disequilibrium challenged European stability and balance. Ultimately, it was the politics of geography on the European continent, not confrontations in distant colonies, that polarized the European states into two camps. Despite the unresolved conflicts pervading all of these crises, European statesmen prided themselves on their ability to settle disputes through reason and negotiation. The last and final Balkan crisis exploded in the summer of 1914, and with it the myth of rational settlement of differences.

SUGGESTIONS FOR FURTHER READING

THE NEW IMPERIALISM

* Michael W. Doyle, *Empires* (Ithaca, NY: Cornell University Press, 1986). Nineteenth-century imperialism is placed in a broad historical context, which emphasizes a comparative perspective of the European imperial experience.

* Daniel R. Headrick, *The Tools of Empire: Technology and European Imperialism in the Nineteenth Century* (New York: Oxford University Press, 1981). By focusing on technological innovations in the nineteenth century, the author demonstrates how Europeans were able to establish control over Asia, Africa, and Oceania rapidly and at little cost.

Daniel R. Headrick, *The Tentacles of Progress: Technology Transfer in the Age of Imperialism, 1850–1940* (New York: Oxford University Press, 1988). Argues that the transfer of technology to Africa and Asia by the Western imperial powers produced colonial underdevelopment.

THE EUROPEAN SEARCH FOR TERRITORY AND MARKETS

* Winfried Baumgart, *Imperialism: The Idea and Reality of British and French Colonial Expansion, 1880–1914* (New York: Oxford University Press, 1982). Principally concerned with the motives that led to imperial expansion, the author argues that motives were numerous and each action must be studied within its specific social, political, and economic context.

Raymond F. Betts, *The False Dawn: European Imperialism in the Nineteenth Century* (Oxford: Oxford University Press, 1976). Explores the ideology of the empire, as well as the process of cultural transmission through colonial institutions.

* Eric Hobsbawm, *The Age of Empire, 1875–1914* (New York: Pantheon, 1987). A wide-ranging interpretive history of the late nineteenth century, which spans economic, social, political, and cultural developments.

* Thomas Pakenham, *The Scramble for Africa* (New York: Random House, 1991). A narrative history of how Europeans subdivided Africa among themselves.

Ronald Robinson and John Gallagher, with Alice Denny, *Africa and the Victorians: The Official Mind of Imperialism* (London: Macmillan, 1961). A classic, though controversial, analysis of British motivations during the scramble.

G. N. Uzoigwe, *Britain and the Conquest of Africa* (Ann Arbor, MI: University of Michigan Press, 1975). An interpretation of the scramble by an African that disagrees with that of Robinson and Gallagher.

RESULTS OF A EUROPEAN-DOMINATED WORLD

Anna Davin, "Imperialism and Motherhood," *History Workshop* (Spring 1978) No 5: 9–65. Davin's article links imperialism and economic expansion with the increasing intervention of the state into family life. The author offers an analysis of an ideology that focused on the need to increase population in support of imperial aims and that led to the social construction of motherhood, domesticity, and individualism.

Johannes Fabian, *Language and Colonial Power: The Appropriation of Swahili in the Former Belgian Congo* (Cambridge: Cambridge University Press, 1986). Demonstrates how colonial power was exercised in the Belgian Congo through the study of the growth of Swahili as a *lingua franca*. The author pays particular attention to the uses of Swahili in industrial and other work situations.

* Paul B. Rich, *Race and Empire in British Politics* (Cambridge: Cambridge University Press, 1986). An intellectual history of ideas about race in the imperial tradition. Focusing on the years between 1890 and 1970, the author examines the political dimensions of race and race ideology in British society.

CONFLICT AT HOME: THE EUROPEAN BALANCE OF POWER

George F. Kennan, *The Decline of Bismarck's European Order: Franco-Russian Relations, 1875–1890* (Princeton, NJ: Princeton University Press, 1979). A diplomatic history of the origins of the 1894 military alliance between Russia and France, which views the alliance as a critical factor in the breakdown of the European balance of power established by Bismarck's diplomacy.

* Alan Sked, *The Decline and Fall of the Habsburg Empire, 1815–1918* (London: Longman, 1989). An overview of the Habsburg Empire's history from Metternich to World War I. The author interprets the various historiographical debates over the collapse of Habsburg rule. Rather than treating the late empire as a case of inevitable decline, the book examines the monarchy as a viable institution within a multinational state.

* Indicates paperback edition available.

CHAPTER 28

Latin America and Africa to 1914

ANTONIO LÓPEZ DE SANTA ANNA, DICTATOR OF MEXICO

There has been no more controversial figure in Mexican history than Antonio López de Santa Anna (1794–1876). In a career that spanned more than three decades, from the wars of independence through the 1850s, Santa Anna was alternately hero and villain, patriot and traitor. But his personal strengths and weaknesses aside, Santa Anna exemplified in his lifetime the history of an era in Mexico and Latin America. The general and sometimes president symbolized the ambiguities, uncertainties, and continuities of politics in the epoch of independence and its aftermath. Fanny Calderón de la Barca in her famous account, *Life in Mexico*, described Santa Anna as "a gentlemanly, good-looking, quietly dressed, rather melancholy-looking person, with one leg, apparently somewhat of an invalid . . . He has a sallow complexion, fine dark eyes, soft and penetrating, and an interesting expression of face."

Legend swirled around him. Some said he had "a way with women," siring innumerable illegitimate children. Others claimed he was addicted to cockfighting and opium. Perhaps most famous was the story of the leg he lost in defense of the homeland. In 1838, France landed troops at the port of Veracruz in order to collect claims for damages done to the property of its citizens living in Mexico. In a cavalry charge Santa Anna lost his leg below the knee to a French cannonball. In 1842, while serving yet another term as dictator, Santa Anna buried the leg in the cemetery of Santa Paula in Mexico City before an audience of diplomats and luminaries. The occasion was marked with full military honors, including a parade.

Santa Anna was born on 21 February 1794, the son of well-to-do Spanish parents. He chose a military career and saw action as a young officer against the rebel army led by Father Miguel Hidalgo. He spent the 1810s as an officer in the royal army, joining Agustín de Iturbide in 1821 in betraying the royalist army and reaching agreement with the rebels to establish Mexican independence. Two years later, Santa Anna led the republicans against Iturbide, who had established himself as Emperor Agustín I, under the banner of the Plan de Casa Mata. Santa Anna played an important role in politics during the 1820s, first preserving the presidency of Guadalupe Victoria and then seeing to the installation of Vicente Guerrero as president. In 1829 Santa Anna led Mexican forces in the defeat of Spain when it tried to reconquer its former colony. After ousting yet another president, Anastasio Bustamente, in 1832, the general took the reins of government himself. Evidently, he quickly became bored with the daily routine of administration and left it to others. For the next two decades he shuttled in and out of the presidency, back and forth from his large estate Mango de Clavo in the state of Veracruz, near Jalapa.

Santa Anna was at the center of the Mexico's disastrous foreign wars. He captured the Alamo, the famous fort in San Antonio, Texas, in 1836, only to suffer ignominious defeat a few months later at San Jacinto, after which he was captured and humiliated while fleeing in rags. Nonetheless, he recovered from his shame, won a hero's plaudits in 1838, when he lost his limb, and took office as president in 1842.

His greatest defeat lay ahead, for in the midst of the crisis of war in 1846, he took over the defense of Mexico against the invading armies of the United States. Ironically, he was able to return only because the North Americans, mistakenly believing he would bring a quick end to the war, allowed him to slip through their lines. Instead he fought bravely, narrowly missing victory at the battle of Buena Vista on the outskirts of Mexico City. His valiant and bloody resistance temporarily restored his reputation. But the peace treaty that followed ceded half of Mexico's territory to the northern colossus.

There is no better example of the impact of war on Latin America during the nineteenth century than that of the war between Mexico and the United States. Mexico lost an enormous territory with unmeasurable resources; the California gold rush began only two years after the Mexican defeat. Moreover, the devastating loss led to a profound political crisis, which in turn resulted in a terrible civil war between liberals and conservatives (1857–60) and foreign intervention by France from 1861 to 1866.

After years in exile, Santa Anna returned once again in 1853 to establish his harshest regime. The next year he was overthrown for the last time by a coalition of southern peasants and northern liberals, who objected to his centralized rule. The new government not only forced him into exile but also confiscated his properties. Conservatives restored them a few years later, but in 1866 the liberal regime of Benito Juárez declared him a traitor. After an aborted return in 1867, the old general stayed in exile until 1874, when he was granted amnesty. He returned home, and died in 1876.

Santa Anna's career symbolized the complexities of Latin American politics in the post-independence era. He epitomized the uncertain choices that confronted the people of the re-gion, whether they should choose a monarchy or a republic. He began as a monarchist, switched sides in 1821, and then in his later career took on the trappings of royalty in his dictatorship. Further, he illustrated the dilemma between federalists and centralists. Initially he was a federalist, but soon he recognized the impracticality of regionalism and changed to a centralist position. In his first presidency he was a liberal, but he abandoned that stance almost at once. Moreover, Santa Anna was proof of the domination of the military in an era of foreign and civil wars.

The general was probably a political genius. Otherwise, how can we account for his longevity and for his many remarkable comebacks? Until the emergence of Benito Juárez (president of Mexico from 1857 to 1872), Santa Anna was the only leader who had the charisma and ability to unite his nation even for a short period. Despite his catastrophic losses, given the poor weapons, training, and leadership of his armies, it is doubtful that anyone could have done more. Independent Latin America searched for more than half a century for legitimate successors to Iberian colonial rule. Given the geographic, ethnic, and class divisions that plagued them and the daunting economic difficulties that confronted them, the people turned to obtain badly needed leadership from those men who had emerged from the military of the wars of independence. The burdens of colonial rule—regional fragmentation, the wide gap between law and practice, corruption, and economic stagnation—proved too heavy even for men of ability such as Antonio López de Santa Anna.

Latin America, 1700–1870: Independence and Its Aftermath

Latin America participated fully in the enormous economic, political, intellectual, and social changes that transformed the world during the eighteenth and nineteenth centuries: substantial demographic growth, expanding international markets, challenges to monarchical rule, global warfare, rising new classes such as the industrial working class and urban bourgeoisie, and erosion of the place of the peasantry. The age of revolution, as it is sometimes called, not only encompassed the epoch of the American and French revolutions, but included the era of Latin American independence as well.

For two hundred years, the Spanish and Portuguese monarchies maintained a tenuous hold on their Western Hemisphere empires through a combination of the effects of the precipitous decline of the indigenous population during the fifteenth and sixteenth centuries and their own flexible colonial administration. However, in 1700 the Habsburg line, which had ruled Spain since Charles I (1516–56), expired. A Bourbon king, Philip V (1700–46) took the throne (see chapter 18). He and the three monarchs who followed from 1747 to 1808 sought to have Spain compete once again as a great power in the world arena with England and France. The first order of business was to reestablish firm control over their New World empire. The so-called Bourbon reforms they initiated disrupted business as usual in the colonies, alienating important sectors of colonial society, most crucially American-born Spaniards. When combined with events in Europe, such as the overthrow of the Spanish monarchy by Napoleon Bonaparte in 1808, discontent in the colonies led to the independence movements that began in that year. Similar reforms under the Portuguese government of the Marquês de Pombal (1699–1782) also led to discontent in Brazil.

The decades from independence until 1870 produced surprisingly little economic development and political peace. The end of Spanish and Portuguese colonial rule ended the burden of imperial taxation and instituted new ruling groups, but for most of the people life remained a struggle to subsist. Despite their enormous natural resources, Latin American nations stagnated economically until after mid-century as a result of constant foreign and civil wars.

The Bourbon Reforms and the Origins of Independence

Spanish monarchs had maintained their hold on their New World empire because, for the most part, they had let it rule itself. Shattered by the defeat of the famous Armada, sent against England in 1588, and by the death of the last great Habsburg king, Philip II, a decade later, the Spanish monarchy seemed to shrink from its once preeminent position in Europe. In the sixteenth century Spain's kings had fought hard to prevent the emergence of a New World nobility to challenge their power, but the disarray of the monarchy after 1600 allowed the American colonies considerable autonomy. The strongest authority existed in the mining and commercial corridors between the major mining areas, the capital cities, and the principal ports of Peru and New Spain (Mexico). Gradually, through the purchase of colonial offices, sold by a monarchy always desperate for funds, American-born Spaniards, known as *criollos* (creoles), obtained an important role in *audiencias* and local governments. Spaniards sent from the mother country (known as *peninsulares*) to govern the colonies, moreover, established familial and economic ties to local society, which blurred their loyalties.

After 1700 two crucial trends evolved that led to unrest and eventually to the movements that won independence. First, the resurgence of population increased the pressure on land and other resources. Second, Bourbon authoritarianism, manifested most clearly in their drive for increased revenues, alienated a broad spectrum of American society.

The demographic disaster that had struck the Indian population in the fifteenth and sixteenth centuries, which was, perhaps, the most important reason that Spain had ruled so long without serious challenge, reached its lowest point in 1650. The renewed growth of the Indian population and the substantial increase in the number of mixed bloods such as *mestizos* and mulattos multiplied the pressures on colonial economy and society. As the population recovered, the methods of governance needed to adjust to the change. But the feeble Habsburgs could not manage this transformation, and their Bourbon successors were either unable or unwilling to do so.

It is not surprising, then, that after a century and a half of relative peace, the number and seriousness of disturbances and uprisings grew during the eighteenth century. Initially, depopulation had deprived the native peoples of the critical mass to rebel. But after 1650, when the Indian population began its recovery, social

Decisive battle

| 0 | 500 | 1000 Miles |
| 0 | 500 | 1000 Kilometers |

UNITED STATES

ATLANTIC OCEAN

MEXICO

PACIFIC OCEAN

Havana
CUBA (Sp.)
DOMINICAN REP.
GUANAJUATO
Veracruz
HAITI
PUERTO RICO (Br.)
Mexico City
BR. HONDURAS
HONDURAS
JAMAICA (Br.)
Guatemala
Caribbean Sea
GUATEMALA
EL SALVADOR
NICARAGUA
Cartagena
BR. GUIANA
COSTA RICA
PANAMA
Caracas
DUTCH GUIANA
ANTIOQUIA
VENEZUELA
FR. GUIANA
Boyacá
Bogotá
COLOMBIA
Quito
ECUADOR
Amazon R.
PERU
BRAZIL
Bahia
Lima
Ayacucho
La Paz
BOLIVIA
MINAS GERAIS
SÃO PAULO
São Paulo
PARAGUAY
Rio de Janeiro
Paraná R.
RIO GRANDE DO SUL
CHILE
ARGENTINA
Valparaíso
URUGUAY
Santiago
Montevideo
Buenos Aires
Bahaí Blanca
PATAGONIA
FALKLAND/MALVINAS ISLANDS

Inset map:

Disputed by England, Spain and Russia

ATLANTIC OCEAN

VICEROYALTY OF NEW SPAIN

CUBA
HAITI/ST. DOMINIQUE
PUERTO RICO
JAMAICA
Caribbean Sea

VICEROYALTY OF NEW GRANADA
GUIANA

Amazon R.

PACIFIC OCEAN

VICEROYALTY OF PERU
VICEROYALTY OF BRAZIL

ANDES MOUNTAINS

VICEROYALTY OF RIO DE PLATA

AUDIENCIA OF CHILE

Latin America, ca. 1830. Inset map: Latin America, ca. 1700.

tensions increased. During the 1700s there were over one hundred uprisings in the Peruvian countryside and several serious urban riots in Mexico. Other mass upheavals erupted in Ecuador in 1765 and Venezuela in 1795 and 1797. One Peruvian province, Cajamarca, alone experienced thirteen rebellions between 1756 and 1800. Growing impoverishment created unrest. The multiplying population was unable to subsist with gainful employment and often, as a result, turned to crime.

It was at this point of blossoming creole influence and recovering native population that the Bourbons set out to regain an influential place for Spain in Europe, using increased resources to be wrung from the Americas. Reform of the colonial administration in order to generate more revenues, quite contrary to its intent, badly undermined Bourbon rule. New, increased demands for taxes and loans for the monarchy pushed their subjects to the brink of rebellion. In their zeal to enhance revenues, the Bourbons upset the delicate balance of power in the empire between its administration, local elites, and the Church. In order to bring the colonies under stricter control, the Bourbons ended the sale of offices to creoles and sent trusted peninsular bureaucrats to rule in their place, thereby intensifying the rivalry between Iberian and American-born Spaniards. Habsburg flexibility gave way to Bourbon intransigence. Powerful elite families, especially those who lived at the periphery of Spanish rule and who had long enjoyed relative autonomy, deeply resented the intrusion on their prerogatives.

The Bourbon program included increasing the number of administrative units—dividing the region into more viceroyalties, captaincies general, and presidencies, streamlining local rule, and bypassing the Council of the Indies. The Bourbons also, reluctantly, opened American ports, first to trade with ports in Spain other than Seville and Cadiz, then to intercolonial commerce, and eventually to other European nations. The monarchy generated huge revenues by creating government monopolies of tobacco, alcoholic beverages, gunpowder, and salt (which raised their cost to American consumers). The colonial government also took over administration of the sales tax (*alcabala*), which it previously had farmed out to private collectors.

The reforms were often disruptive, as in the case of the notorious *repartimiento de mercancías*, the system that forced Indians to sell their produce cheaply to local crown-appointed officials, who would in turn hoard these staples until shortages arose and then resell them to the very same Indians at exorbitant prices. Local officials also coerced the Indians to buy all their other consumer goods from them at outrageously high prices.

The Bourbons abolished the *repartimiento* in the mid-1780s. But what seemed a sensible reform of an inefficient and corrupt institution in actuality upset the structure of local commerce, adversely affecting merchants, landowners, and Indians. The Indians, dependent on credit, albeit on exploitative terms, were not accustomed to a cash, free-market economy.

The Bourbon reforms exacerbated the growing antipathy between creoles and peninsulares. The division of the white ruling class at a time when the Indian population was reaching a point where renewed, widespread rebellion was possible created a dangerous situation. The creoles saw the barely 100,000 peninsulares in the Americas as obstacles to their access to political offices. The Bourbons did not trust the locals to rule the empire, and after 1750 began to place more and more peninsulares in government positions. The peninsulares' haughty attitude and disdain for Americans increased tensions. To make matters worse, creole taxes paid for the proliferating peninsular bureaucracy.

During the eighteenth century, protests by creoles grew, their grievances usually centering on taxes. But the creoles walked a fine line, not wanting to risk mass uprisings. The first creole outbreaks took place in Paraguay between 1721 and 1735 and in Venezuela between 1739 and 1742. Another occurred in Quito, Ecuador, in 1765. The best-known and most serious revolts burst forth in 1780 in New Granada (Colombia) and in Peru. The uprising in New Granada was over taxes. Poor, mostly mestizo, small farmers staged a series of disturbances, the leadership of which angry creole landowners soon assumed. Indians, trying to reclaim lands usurped by large landowners; *pardo* (mulatto) cowboys, known as *llaneros*, seeking relief against tribute exactions; and even slaves joined the burgeoning cross-class alliance. With the slogan "Long live the king and death to bad government," the horde threatened Bogotá, the capital. The colonial government then negotiated reductions in the new taxes. In moving quickly and successfully to take over leadership of the protests, creoles prevented a more radical upheaval.

Of the numerous rebellions in Peru that marked the eighteenth century, the revolt of Tupac Amarú in 1780 was the most dangerous to the colonial regime. Again, taxes set off the uprising. An educated man who claimed to be a descendant of the Inca royal family, Tupac Amarú (born José Gabriel Condorcanqui—ca. 1742–93) wanted to eliminate the vicious exactions that beset Peruvian Indians. Initially, he tried to bring about reform through the legal system, but frustrated, he resorted to violence. For the first time since the sixteenth

Tupac Amarú, who was recognized by the Spaniards as the legal heir of the Incas, failed to eradicate European rule in Bolivia.

century, shouts of "death to the Spaniards" were heard in Peru. It took the Spaniards a year and a half to regain control. By that time the uprising had cost 100,000 deaths. Peruvian whites had learned a hard lesson. Four decades later they clung to Spanish colonial rule rather than risk unleashing another mass rebellion.

Taxes were badly received, especially by the creoles, because the colonies obtained no appreciable benefit from them. Spain's reentry onto the world stage caused it to be involved in an almost continuous state of war during the eighteenth century. These conflicts badly disrupted colonial commerce and mining. After 1750 the British fleet completely shut off the access of Europe to American ports for long stretches of time. This situation not only curtailed trade, but closed American mines because of the lack of mercury, a mineral crucial in the extraction of silver, the colonies' most important export. Because the Bourbons could not afford even to pay for the protection of their American empire, they established local militias to defend the colonies. These militias proved ineffective against various rebellions in the late 1700s. They did, however, train a generation of creole militia officers who would lead insurgent armies in the fight for independence after 1800.

Unending demands for taxes were accompanied by onerous, forced loans. In 1804, seeking to capitalize on Church wealth, the Spanish crown demanded that it take over all Church charitable funds. Since the capital in these funds was on loan to creole merchants and landowners, the new policy, the *Ley de Consolidación* (Law of Consolidation), hurt the economy of New Spain. The Church had to call in its loans. Many creoles could not repay the principal on their debts and faced ruin if they had to sell their properties to raise the funds. The lower clergy, mostly creoles, also suffered, because their living depended on the interest from these loans. Scandalously, colonial officials, including the viceroy—all of them peninsulares—received commissions on the enormous fortune sent to Spain.

Even the reforms that made sense in the long term—such as reducing tariffs, abolishing the trade monopoly of Cadiz and Seville, and opening up intercolonial trade—alienated some powerful merchants in the short run because they adversely affected their interests. Abolishing tariffs hurt local manufacturing.

The Bourbons, jealously protective of their authority, were willing to oppose the Church if the need arose. In 1767 they expelled the Jesuits from the Spanish empire. This gave the crown the welcome opportunity to confiscate extensive Jesuit landholdings. The monarchy saw the Jesuits as an intolerable threat to its authority. Since many of the Jesuits were creoles, the expulsion caused considerable bitterness in the colonies.

Despite the Bourbon reforms, Spain had no more modern an economy (perhaps less so) than her colonies. What the American settlements needed, such as manufactured goods, Spain (and Portugal) could not provide. The Iberian countries served as transshipment points, not suppliers. England and Holland provided the goods. Spanish and Portuguese merchants merely added to the cost of trade to the colonies.

Portugal, under the leadership of the Marquês de Pombal, who was the virtual dictator during the reign of José I (1750–77), embarked on a similar program of reform after 1750. Pombal merged administrative units, centralized authority, improved tax collection, liberalized trade, and made efforts to increase exports. He continued to restrict Brazil's economic development, strengthening the prohibitions on manufacturing.

Pombal's reforms created far less hostility toward Portuguese rule in Brazil than the Bourbon reforms did in the Spanish colonies. This was the result in part of a renewed export boom in the last years of the century.

Most important, the frightening events of the Haitian revolution made Brazilian creoles cautious, for there were more African slaves in Brazil than anywhere else in the New World.

The revolution in the French colony of Saint Domingue (modern-day Haiti) erupted in the early 1790s (see chapter 22). To American-born whites it served as a frightening lesson that prevented them from pushing too hard for independence. During the early 1790s, white plantation owners in Haiti had divided over political issues. This led to a slave rebellion and a race war in which Haitian whites either fled or perished. The Haitians defeated an attempt by Napoleon to reconquer the island in 1804. Haiti was a warning to all elites, Spanish- or American-born, of the consequences if they lost their grip on the masses. After the constant unrest of the eighteenth century and the revolutions in the United States and France, the white elite, including the angry creoles, swallowed their resentments in fear. When independence came, it was because creoles and peninsulares sought to keep ahead of the situation before it got out of hand. As we will see in the case of Mexico, even preemptory action did not prevent a mass upheaval, but it did keep the social system from being overwhelmed.

By the end of the eighteenth century, only the fear of mass Indian uprisings in Spanish America and slave revolt in Brazil kept the creoles in check. Events would soon transpire to convince them that the burden of colonial rule was so great it made the risk of rebellion worth taking.

The Spanish and Portuguese American Colonies Win Their Independence, 1808–1828

The movements for independence took place in two stages and in four general theaters of war. From 1808 to 1816 several Spanish American colonies declared their independence. They experienced initial military success, but ultimately failed to achieve their separation from Spain when, after the defeat of Napoleon in 1814, Spain sent additional troops to the New World. Moreover, during the first era, creoles pulled back from an alliance with the masses, choosing to remain loyal to colonial rule rather than risk a social upheaval. From 1816 to 1828 all of the nations of Spanish and Portuguese America except Cuba and Puerto Rico won their independence. The instability in both Iberian nations, their unwillingness to compromise with their colonies, and an infusion of foreign support for independence, especially

from the British, proved crucial. The four theaters of war were (1) the northern tier, comprised of Colombia, Venezuela, Ecuador, and Peru; (2) the southern cone, including the Rio de la Plata (Argentina, Paraguay, and Uruguay) and Chile; (3) Mexico; and (4) Brazil.

Events in Europe in 1807 and 1808 precipitated Latin American independence. After cooperating with Napoleon for several years, Spanish king Charles IV (1788–1808) and his chief advisor Manuel de Godoy (1767–1851) permitted the great general to pass through Spain to crush Portugal. Napoleon then decided to take Spain as well. A palace revolution in 1808 toppled Godoy and forced Charles to abdicate in favor of his son Ferdinand VII. The French then induced father and son to abdicate. Napoleon placed his brother Joseph Bonaparte on the throne of Spain. Technically, the change in dynasty broke the bond between Spain and its colonies. With that link eliminated, colonists had to decide whether to support Charles, Ferdinand, the Spanish resistance to the French, or the Bonapartes, or to proclaim their independence.

The Portuguese royal family and court escaped from Lisbon barely two weeks before the French arrived in 1808. Protected by the British fleet, King John VI (1816–26) set up his court in Rio de Janeiro. He eventually made Brazil a coequal kingdom with Portugal.

In 1811 Venezuela was the first South American nation to declare its independence. However, the creoles there were not unified and pardos harbored deep resentments because of longstanding creole discrimination. Spanish authorities had been far more tolerant of people of color than had the creoles. Eventually, the pardo cowboys (*llaneros*) of the interior threw their support to the crown, which reestablished its hold by 1814.

Simón Bolívar (1783–1830), the greatest hero of South American independence, led the movement in Venezuela and Colombia. Well-educated in Europe in the ideas of the Enlightenment, Bolívar returned to his homeland with a mission to free it from Spain's yoke. Initially based in Colombia, in 1813 he led an army into Venezuela that pushed the Spaniards out of Cartagena. But the next year he was overwhelmed by a llanero army led by loyalist Tomás Boves and went into exile in Jamaica.

The first surge of creole nationalism occurred in June 1806, when a British expedition in Argentina tried to take Buenos Aires. The attack was repelled by creole colonists, who pushed aside the cowardly Spanish viceroy when he refused to resist. Six months later a second attempt was turned back. Spanish government had failed in the one area fundamental to its rule of America—the protection of its colonies. The creoles of Argentina acquired a sense that they could fend for themselves and

SIMÓN BOLÍVAR, THE JAMAICA LETTER, 1815

■ *Written in September 1815 from exile after Bolívar's defeat in the first stage of the war of independence, the Jamaica Letter typifies the feeling of American-born creoles that Spanish rule was unjust. This particular passage emphasizes the economic burden of colonial rule.*

Americans today, and perhaps to a greater extent than ever before, who live within the Spanish system occupy a position in society no better than that of serfs destined for labor, or at best they have no more status than that of mere consumers. Yet even this status is surrounded with galling restrictions, such as being forbidden to grow European crops, or to store products which are royal monopolies, or to establish factories of a type the Peninsula itself does not possess. To this add the exclusive trading privileges, even in articles of prime necessity, and the barriers between American provinces, designed to prevent all exchange of trade, traffic, and understanding. In short, do you wish to know what our future held?—simply the cultivation of the fields . . . cattle raising on the broad plains . . . digging in the earth to mine its gold—but even these limitations would never satisfy the greed of Spain. So negative was our existence that I can find nothing comparable in any other civilized society.

that the Spaniards were a burden too heavy to carry any longer.

The Rio de la Plata was the only region that Spain was unable to reconquer between 1814 and 1816. After defeating the British invasion of Buenos Aires in 1806 and 1807, the creoles sharply divided over breaking ties with Spain. A succession of temporary governments ruled until 1816. In Chile similar rivalries among creole factions led to a civil war, which enabled a Spanish army to retake the area in 1814.

In Mexico the divisions between creole and peninsular briefly opened the way for the most fearsome rebellion of all—the independence wars, led by a priest, Father Miguel Hidalgo (1753–1811). In 1808, to prevent creoles from obtaining power, Spaniards staged a coup that ousted the viceroy. Two years later, on September 16, 1810, Hidalgo proclaimed the *Grito de Dolores*, the cry of independence, calling forth his parishioners to overthrow Spanish rule. The masses of rural people rose in a great war of vengeance. Led by creole officers and marching under the banner of the Virgin of Guadalupe, the horde won a number of impressive victories. The rebels sacked the city of Guanajuato, just north of the capital, slaughtering scores of peninsular Spaniards, whom they derisively called *gachupines* (greenhorns).

At its height, the rebel army, comprised of eighty thousand mestizos and Indians, hovered on the outskirts of Mexico City. For reasons that are still unclear, Hidalgo turned his ragtag army from the capital, and

after a few months it dissipated. The Spanish army captured and executed him in July 1811. The upheaval badly frightened the upper classes of New Spain. The rebels were ultimately defeated because creoles found common ground with peninsular Spaniards in order to protect their own class. Despite the defeat of Hidalgo's army, guerrillas, led by another priest, José María Morelos (1765–1815), continued the rebellion in the regions south of Mexico City. At the height of his movement in 1813 Morelos had 9,000 men under arms and control of all of southern Mexico. He too shied away from an attack on the capital and was hunted down in 1815. For the next six years Vicente Guerrero (1783–1831) and Guadalupe Victoria (1789–1843), each of whom would be president of independent Mexico, led scattered guerrilla bands, wearing the mantle of the independence movement.

Thus, the first stage of independence was a failure, although the Spanish were unable to bring Argentina under control. A divided upper class hampered independence in the north and south, and in Mexico class warfare forced Spaniard and creole together despite their differences. The threat of the masses welded a temporary coalition. But Spain did not learn from past mistakes. Rather than seek accommodation with the creoles, successive Spanish governments sought to re-establish authoritarian rule. Reprisals against creoles were often harsh; the viceroy of Colombia once executed five hundred of them.

The success of the second stage of the independence wars built on a combination of Spanish intransigence; the persistence of creole leaders, most notably Bolívar; and the assistance of the British, who had much to gain from open trade with the Spanish colonies. With Bolívar leading a resurgent army in the north of South America and José de San Martín (1778–1850), a former Spanish army officer, at the head of the army in the Rio de la Plata, the Americans ousted the Spaniards from the continent in the decade that followed.

Bolívar returned in 1816, this time winning the support of the same llaneros who had previously defeated him. Their leader, José Antonio Páez (1790–1873) became a dominant force in Venezuelan politics through mid-century. In addition, Bolívar benefited from British aid. British soldiers were the core of his army and British merchants lent him money to pay them. The first decisive battle took place at Boyacá in Colombia in 1819 after Bolívar led a long forced march through the frozen Andes mountains to surprise the Spanish. The liberal revolution in 1820 prevented Spain from sending reinforcement troops to the Americas. Knowing that he would have to eliminate all vestiges of Spanish power in order to ensure independence, Bolívar led his army south through Ecuador and into Peru. In the meantime, San Martín headed another heroic march through the Andes and defeated the Spaniards in Chile. He too moved into Peru, occupying Lima in 1821. After a meeting with Bolívar the next year, San Martín retired from active duty. Bolívar and his lieutenants achieved the final liberation in a series of battles, culminating in the battle of Ayacucho in August 1824.

Independence for Mexico resulted from an agreement between a royalist officer, Agustín de Iturbide (1783–1824), and the guerrilla leaders Guadalupe Victoria and Vicente Guerrero. In their Treaty of the Three Guarantees, they consented to look for a monarch, to maintain the Catholic religion as an integral part of the state, and to end all discrimination against the creoles. In July 1821, the new viceroy, sent too late to quash the arrangement, agreed to Mexican independence.

The most peaceful transition to independence took place in Brazil. After moving his court to Rio de Janeiro in 1808, King John VI proved reluctant to return to Portugal even though the French occupation ended in 1814. For several years he resisted return, but facing the threat of losing his throne, he went back, leaving his son Pedro with advice to lead any separatist movement. Any proclivity on the part of creoles toward independence was helped along by the Portuguese government, which tried to rescind Brazil's status as a co-kingdom. In Jan-

Manuel Hidalgo, a priest from the town of Dolores, led a revolt against the Spanish government in Mexico.

uary 1822 Pedro proclaimed independence and became the first emperor of Brazil.

Politics and Economics in the Age of Caudillos, 1820–1870

Although the American colonies had won their independence, it did not bring profound change for most Latin Americans. The post-independence era reaped the harvest of Iberian colonial rule: regional fragmentation, corrupt and inefficient government, and lack of economic development. As a result, the new nations experienced long periods of political instability that lasted until the last quarter of the nineteenth century, when landed oligarchies consolidated their rule. This half century was marked by a lack of consensus about who should rule, the form of government, and the path toward economic development. Civil and external wars racked the region, exacerbating political instability and causing economic stagnation.

The departure of the Iberians left Latin America fragmented, disoriented, and disrupted. The practicalities of geography and the precedents of Iberian rule broke up the regions into ungovernable units. Regional rivalries—between Buenos Aires and the interior of Argentina, between the northeast and south of Brazil, between Antioquia and Bogotá in Colombia, to name just a few—were critical obstacles to nationhood. When Spanish bureaucrats and merchants fled, much expertise and capital went with them. The gap between law and reality, illustrated in the famous phrase "I obey but do not comply," which had plagued Iberian governance, was a burdensome legacy for the newly independent nations. To make matters worse, they adopted constitutions modeled on those of the United States, England, or France, without sufficient consideration for the practicalities of politics. The lack of investment by colonial governments in roads, schools, and other infrastructure placed the Latin American nations at a disadvantage in economic competition with the rest of the world.

The Iberian social heritage was as heavy a burden as its governance. Its ruling classes practiced discrimination against Indians, mestizos, and mulattos. The gap between rich and poor was enormous. In Brazil slavery flourished. Although economically viable, on the whole it retarded Brazil's development. Slavery created a stratified society based on hostility, fear, and disdain. Prejudice and inequity long survived the end of the actual institution.

In eighteenth-century Spanish America, a genre of painting developed that portrayed various racial mixtures. This portrait shows a mestizo father and his Spanish wife with their daughter, a castizo *(three-fourths white).*

The Catholic church, which had provided a good part of both the spiritual and economic foundations of the colonial regime, underwent considerable change. Its economic strength was badly undermined when the new nations ended the tithe, the ten percent assessment on all income collected by the colonial government on behalf of the Church. It was weakened further when a conflict with new national governments over whether the Church or the state was to assume the power to appoint high Church officials resulted in a large number of vacancies in these posts, creating a leadership vacuum. While Catholicism remained the official religion everywhere, many of the Church's functions in the areas of education and finance came under fire. The role of the Church became one of the most important political issues of the era.

The end of royal authority left open the question of who was to rule. Except for Brazil, where the heir to the Portuguese throne remained to head the new empire, there was no obvious, legitimate successor to the Iberian monarchies. The creoles, who had led the independence movements, had the most obvious claim and, for the most part, they took the reins. Nonetheless, mestizos and mulattos (pardos), who had gained a measure of prominence in the wars of independence and their aftermath, offered a strong challenge.

There was no real agreement about what type of government was appropriate. Latin American nations, with two exceptions, opposed reinstating monarchy. In Brazil, of course, two emperors ruled from 1822 to 1888. Mexico experienced two short episodes: the reign of Agustín I (Iturbide) during the 1820s and that of Maximilian I (1864–67). Each met an unfortunate end. The other nations became republics.

Perhaps the most important conflict arose over the power of the central government. Because colonial administration had concentrated along the principal mining and commercial routes, with only loose oversight in many of the peripheral regions, the ruling classes of these areas had considerable autonomy. There were, moreover, fierce rivalries between different regions, particularly in Mexico, Colombia, Brazil, and Argentina. Centralists, who sought a strong central government, opposed federalists, who sought sovereignty for their provinces or states.

By the mid-nineteenth century the main political battles were fought—sometimes in vicious civil wars—between liberals and conservatives. It is difficult to define them in terms of economic interests, for the two sides often disputed only the spoils of office. However, they disagreed fundamentally about the role of the

Church. Liberals saw it as a crucial impediment to capitalist economic development, holding vast riches from the economy. While it was true that the Church was Latin America's banker and leading landholder, it was not true that it impeded development. In fact the Church was a banker with "easy terms" and low interest rates, often not demanding repayment of principal. If the recipients of its loans squandered the money, the blame could not be the Church's. Further, the Church was also a relatively benign landlord. The conservatives defended the Church and its prerogatives.

Politics was vastly complicated by the legacy of militarism left by the wars of independence and accentuated by the numerous wars during the next seventy years. Mexico was perhaps the hardest hit by the struggle for independence, with almost constant guerrilla warfare from 1810 to 1821. Internecine strife and foreign invasions kept a large number of people under arms. Although the military regularly swallowed up half or more of the national government budget, public safety was constantly threatened by unpaid or unneeded soldiers who in desperation turned to banditry or rebellion. It was said that the stagecoach route from Veracruz to Mexico City was so dangerous that passengers sometimes arrived at their destinations with nothing other than newspapers on their persons, victims of two or three sets of brigands. Domingo Sarmiento (1811–88), the intellectual who later became president of his native Argentina, declared that conditions had deteriorated to such an extent that it had become a struggle between "civilization and barbarism."

The overall structure of Latin American economies with their twin pillars, the mines and large landed estates (*haciendas*), remained intact. Two decades of the wars of independence, however, badly hurt the mining industry, inflicting severe physical damage and disrupting both markets and investment. The long series of civil and external wars that followed independence not only stymied the recovery of mining production, but lessened the dominance of the haciendas. The disruption of domestic and export markets for their products drove down the value of their lands.

The road to economic development was rocky indeed. Geographic fragmentation, poor transportation and communications, and the wide gap between rich and poor inhibited the growth of internal markets. Free trade policies allowed European manufactured goods to overwhelm Latin American artisans and manufacturers. With the exception of Brazilian sugar and Argentine hides, the European market for Latin American staple products awaited the transportation and technical innovations of the second half of the century. Capital for investment was scarce, because many wealthy Spaniards had fled and foreign investors were discouraged by the uncertainties of politics and transportation. A flurry of investment in mining by the British during the 1820s met utter failure. Similarly a rash of loans by European investment houses to new governments were soon in default. Europeans would be wary of Latin American investments until after the 1870s.

In the search for stability the new nations turned first to the heroes of their independence movements, but the centrifugal forces of regional fragmentation and the disruptions of foreign wars overwhelmed them. The most notable example was Simón Bolívar. During the 1820s, a grateful people made him president and virtual dictator. His dream was to unite the northern tier of the continent and to that end he merged Colombia, Ecuador, and Venezuela as Gran Colombia. But the impracticality of ruling these isolated regions as one was quickly evident. By 1830 Gran Colombia was broken in three. Bolívar died disillusioned. The hero of Chilean independence, Bernardo O'Higgins (1778–1842), was soon tossed aside by quarreling creoles. Agustín de Iturbide fell from his throne in less than two years. His co-conspirators Victoria and Guerrero were ignominiously ousted from the presidency before the end of their terms. Antonio José de Sucre (1795–1830), who had liberated Bolivia, served as president of that nation from 1825 to 1828, only to be the victim of an assassination attempt and resign his office in disgust. This despite the fact he had run a model reformist government.

The new nations then turned to a tougher breed of leader, known as the *caudillo*, or strongman, to bring order. These men, some of whom were mestizos or mulattos, often rose through the ranks of the military to lead their nations. Their records remain the subject of lively, if not emotional, controversy to this day. Leaders like Juan Manuel de Rosas (1793–1877), the dictator of Argentina from 1829 to 1852; José de Francia (1766–1840), the harsh dictator of Paraguay; Andrés Santa Cruz (1792–1865), the unifier of Bolivia and Peru; and Antonio López de Santa Anna (1794–1876) of Mexico, who held the presidency no fewer than eleven different times between 1830 and 1855, dominated politics until mid-century.

Rosas rose to power in the wake of the discord in Argentina between Buenos Aires and the interior and river provinces. Buenos Aires sought to unify what is now Argentina under its domination, while the other provinces fought to maintain their autonomy. In 1829 Rosas, as governor of Buenos Aires, reached an agreement by which each province would conduct its own

The port of Buenos Aires in 1858. The city and its surrounding province were independent from the rest of Argentina during the 1850s. After a military defeat, Buenos Aires united with the other Argentine provinces.

domestic affairs, but Buenos Aires was to handle foreign relations. The ruthless Rosas employed his secret police to intimidate his opposition, only relinquishing his hold in 1852, when ousted by a rival caudillo.

Rosas firmly implanted the rule of the landed oligarchy. The dictator led campaigns against the Indians to free the Pampas for exploitation and ownership by the large landowners, known in Argentina as *estancieros*. (The *estanciero* was the equivalent of the owner of the *hacienda*, known as the *hacendado*.)

To the north in Paraguay ruled another controversial dictator, José Gaspar Rodríguez de Francia, who took the reins of that nation in 1816 and held them firmly until his death in 1840. He presided over a unique social revolution, which mandated that creoles marry only Indians, mestizos, or mulattos, in order to eliminate the upper class and hasten equality. He also limited landownership. Most of all, Francia isolated Paraguay from the outside world, hoping to insulate it from the instability that plagued the rest of the region. His successors, Carlos Antonio López (1790–1862) and his son Francisco Solano López (1827–70), ruled in a similar manner until 1870, when a disastrous war with Argentina and Brazil resulted in Francisco's overthrow.

After Sucre abandoned Bolivia in the late 1820s, Andrés Santa Cruz, who had ruled Peru for a short period after Bolívar's departure in 1826, took the reins of government in 1829. Seven years later he engineered the Peru-Bolivian Confederation. But this experiment, like Gran Colombia, was doomed to fail, confronted by regional jealousies and the implacable opposition of Chile, which went to war to prevent unification. Chile won the war and the confederation disintegrated in 1839.

Antonio López de Santa Anna dominated Mexican politics from the 1820s until 1854. He came on the scene as an ally of Iturbide, helped overthrow the emperor, and then for three decades had a hand in numerous

coups and rebellions. Posing alternately as liberal and conservative, Santa Anna seemingly had more than the cat's nine lives. He was in turn a patriot and war hero and then a traitor and incompetent. It was Santa Anna who lost the Texas War in 1836, only to defeat a French invasion at Veracruz a year later. In this conflict, the so-called Pastry War, France sought to recover loans and damage claims by its citizens against the Mexican government; one of the claims was made by a French baker for damages to his shop. Santa Anna returned once again to lead the Mexican army against the United States invasion in 1846, only to lose half the national territory. Despite this national humiliation, Santa Anna served as president one last time, when conservatives, desperate for leadership, recalled him from exile in 1853. He was overthrown in the liberal revolt the next year.

From 1850 to 1875, landed oligarchies, either directly by grasping the reins of an elected government or indirectly by allying with a dictator, began to establish a measure of order. By 1862 Argentina had consolidated under the leadership of General Bartolomé Mitre (1821–1906). In Mexico between 1858 and 1872, Benito Juárez (1806–72) won a civil war on behalf of the liberals against the conservatives and defeated the French intervention that had enthroned Maximilian as emperor (see chapter 26). This laid the groundwork for the dictatorship of Porfirio Díaz (1877–1911) and the first Mexican economic miracle. Brazil survived the abdication of Dom Pedro I in 1829 and the regency that followed. Dom Pedro II ruled with quiet success for four decades until the divisive issues of slavery and regionalism forced him out in 1888. In Chile the presidencies of Manuel Bulnes (1799–1866) and Manuel Montt (1809–80) secured the power of the landed elite.

Although 1870 did not bring the end of foreign wars or internal strife—the War of the Pacific between Chile and Peru (1879–83) and the War of the Thousand Days in Colombia (1898–1900) lay ahead—the foundation for export-led economic development was built. The landed oligarchy, now in control, often allied with foreign investors, ushered in a long period of rapid economic development.

Everyday Life in Nineteenth-Century Latin America

Until well into the twentieth century most Latin Americans were rural people. It is likely that their living and working conditions were much the same at the end of the nineteenth century as they were at the beginning. Most were very poor, struggling for subsistence. Although the new nations had proclaimed freedom, civil rights were restricted to the propertied classes. Ironically, whatever political power—albeit limited for the most part to the local level—and economic autonomy that accrued to the lower classes derived from the disorders of the era. As long as landed oligarchies required the services of lower-class soldiers, the latter obtained a degree of political independence and kept the former from stealing their lands. Despite the end of slavery in most of Spanish America, it remained in Cuba and Brazil. Even when abolished, its heritage of racial discrimination and prejudice endured. Women's roles changed little until industrialization and urbanization at the end of the century disrupted traditional families.

Although there are substantial gaps in our knowledge of the daily existence of the common people in Latin America in the nineteenth century, historians have recently illuminated the lives of country people in Mexico and Argentina and slaves in Brazil, both on plantations and in the cities.

In the Mexican countryside, the hacienda and the village inhabited by Indians or mestizos, existed in uneasy symbiosis, alternately cooperating and warring. To the male village dweller his small plot of land was not only crucial for the subsistence of his family but symbolic of his social status and his manhood. But few village residents could survive solely on the production of their own land. Thus, many worked on the hacienda seasonally to earn money to pay for life's rites of passage, such as weddings, baptisms, funerals, and fiestas. In densely populated regions, the haciendas held the upper hand in the relationship and kept wages low. In sparsely inhabited areas villages often had leverage to obtain better arrangements. In addition to their seasonal employees, the large estates maintained resident workers and sharecroppers. Residents received dwellings, food allotments, wages, and a small plot for their own use. Sharecroppers worked part of the hacienda in return for a percentage of the crop they produced. In each case the availability of labor was the crucial determinant of the arrangements. In northern Mexico, where the population was sparse, wages were high and the situation was more favorable to the workers.

In many regions of Latin America debt peonage was integral to the operation of the hacienda. Employees received advances in their wages in order to purchase necessities at the hacienda store. The hacendado also would lend money for special events such as baptisms. In many cases the debts were too high to ever repay and

A scene painted in 1828 shows a Mexican hacienda owner with his assistants.

were passed from generation to generation. The peon could not leave the hacienda without paying what he owed. In some areas this system amounted to little more than slavery. In other regions, however, peonage was to the advantage of the employee, for it was understood that the debt would not be repaid. In a few instances, the hacienda was in debt to its workers.

The relationship between village and hacienda changed after independence. To the creoles, the protected, communal village landholding delayed the integration of Indians into the new societies and inhibited economic development. The political disruptions that marked the first half century after independence protected the villages, for the resulting economic depression provided no incentive for the ruling classes to dismember communal holdings. It would not be until the last quarter of the century, when the stimulus of the world market for export agriculture enhanced the value of land, that hacendados undertook the widespread expropriation of village lands.

Despite the stagnation of wages and the general lack of improvement in working conditions, in some ways the era from 1820 to 1870 was beneficial for people in the countryside. Political authority, which inevitably oppressed them, was weak, land expropriations halted, and the absence of pressure from the haciendas pro-vided some economic opportunities. Many of the new governments abolished onerous taxes, such as the head tax. This not only liberated Indians from a harsh burden, but freed them from the need to work for wages to pay the taxes. In Peru labor shortages grew so acute that the government reinstated the head tax under a different name in order to force Indians to work in the mines and on the haciendas. There is, moreover, some evidence, though debated, that in some areas rural people enjoyed at least an adequate standard of living in terms of nourishment, both because shortages forced the haciendas to provide sufficient food rations and because food prices stayed relatively steady.

On the southern plains of Argentina and Brazil, the semitropical plains of Venezuela, and the plateaus of northern Mexico, the cowboy, known in these regions as *gauchos, llaneros,* and *vaqueros,* respectively, played a crucial role in the politics and economy of the nineteenth century. Legendary for their skills riding horses and herding cattle, they were also highly valued as soldiers in a time of internecine strife. Though they never went hungry, feeding themselves from the vast wild herds of cattle that roamed the range, the cowboys lived a miserable existence. Nonetheless, as long as they were needed to fight the battles of landowners and politicians, the gauchos maintained their fierce independence. By

DESCRIPTION OF A GAUCHO

■ *The gaucho, or cowboy, became the symbol in Argentine politics of the "barbarism" of the dictator Juan Manuel de Rosas and the civilization of the civilians who sought to unite the country during the mid-nineteenth century. In fact, gauchos were quite useful to the large landowners as soldiers in the numerous factional wars that marred the post-independence era. The gauchos earned their living as hired hands on the estancias, where they gathered wild cattle. In the last years of the century, when landowners began to fence in their herds and when the feisty gauchos became a threat to order and progress, strict laws limited their movements and forced them into day-worker status.*

These men will not fail to astonish one who is not accustomed to see them. They are always dirty; their beards are always uncut; they go barefoot, and even trouserless under the coverall of the poncho. By their manners, ways and clothing one knows their customs, without sensibility and almost without religion. They are called gauchos . . . As it is very easy for them to kill cattle for food, since none lack a horse, bolas, lasso, and knife with which to catch and kill a cow . . . and since they are satisfied to have nothing but roast meat to eat, they work only to acquire the tobacco they smoke and the Paraguayan yerba mate which they drink, ordinarily without sugar and as many times a day as possible. Or they may work to obtain gifts for their sweethearts.

"Hierra en Rincón de Luna—Corrientes," an 1827 lithograph by D'Orbignay showing vaqueros branding cattle. The cowboy way of life was greatly similar throughout the New World.

the end of the century, however, these same masters saw them as impediments to progress, using vagrancy laws to rein them in.

Several of the new nations, such as Mexico (1820s) and Venezuela and Peru (1850s), ended slavery. Many slaves won their freedom by serving in the armies of the wars of independence. The disruptions of war allowed still others to flee the plantations. But in the countries with the largest slave populations, Brazil and Cuba, slavery flourished.

In the period from 1700 to 1850 between 8 and 12 million Africans were brought across the Atlantic against their will to work on the sugar and coffee plantations of Brazil, the sugar plantations of Cuba, and the mines of Mexico, Peru, and Brazil. Ten percent of them died en route. From 1820 to 1850, Brazil imported over 30,000 slaves a year. There were 1.7 million slaves living in Brazil at mid-century. About one-third toiled on coffee plantations, another third worked in other agriculture, and the rest worked as domestics, artisans, and in industry. At the same time there were 4.2 million people of color who were free.

Although plantation owners worked their slaves hard and often treated them badly, slave mortality mirrored that of the general population. Mortality rates for Brazilian slaves were higher than those in the United States, but we can account for this by the difference in overall mortality among the white populations, which was also higher. The most important factor in life expectancy was infant mortality. The life expectancy of an average American-born slave in Latin America was slightly more than twenty years. However, if a slave lived beyond five years, his life expectancy rose to 38.4 years, and for women it was slightly longer.

Despite their lack of freedom, slaves created a society and community for themselves. Like the indigenous peoples of Latin America, they developed a syncretic religion that combined elements of Catholicism and the customs and beliefs of their African homelands. The requirements of their work, of course, governed their lives. Plantation slaves were closely supervised, but urban slaves, some of whom were skilled artisans, often lived semi-autonomously. In some places little village communities grew up within the plantations with marriages and complex kinship groups. In spite of slavery, people of African descent constructed their own cultures and identities.

Although the new nations adopted limited male suffrage and many abolished slavery, the new governments denied women the franchise: they could not hold public office, vote, or testify in a court of law. Patriarchy predominated; women fell under the authority of men both

Latin American Independence and Its Aftermath Timeline

1702–14	The War of the Spanish Succession
1767	Expulsion of Jesuits from Spanish Empire
1780–81	Rebellion of Tupac Amarú II in Peru
1788–1808	Charles IV rules Spain
1792	Haitian revolution
1804	*Ley de Consolidación*
1806–07	English twice attempt to capture Buenos Aires and are repelled
1807	French invade Portugal; court flees to Brazil
1808	French invade Spain; Charles IV and Ferdinand VII abdicate; Joseph Bonaparte king
1810	Argentina and Paraguay independent
1810	Revolt of Father Hidalgo
1811	Venezuelan independence
1816	Spanish in control of colonies except Rio de la Plata
1818–25	Military victories by Bolívar and his generals liberate northern and western South America
1821	Mexican independence
1822	Gran Colombia established
1822	Brazilian independence; Pedro I emperor
1829–36	Andres Santa Cruz presides over Bolivia
1829–52	Juan Manuel Rosas dominates the Rio de la Plata
1830	Gran Colombia collapses; Bolívar retires
1830–43	José Antonio Páez dominates Venezuela
1831	Pedro I abdicates
1836	Santa Cruz unites Peru and Bolivia, sets off war with Chile
1836	Texas independence from Mexico
1841	Pedro II, emperor of Brazil
1846–48	Mexico-U.S. war
1859–61	War of the Reform in Mexico between liberals and conservatives
1859–63	Federalist wars in Venezuela; Civil conflict
1861–72	Benito Juárez president of Mexico
1864	French install Maximilian as emperor of Mexico
1865–68	Peru at war with Spain

inside and outside the home. The double standard of behavior persisted. New labor codes, if anything, increased female subjugation to husbands and fathers. Paths to independence for upper-class women such as had existed in the colonial Church were less likely options.

Most women, of course, lived in the countryside. They worked the "double day," not only in the home but in the fields and as market sellers, shopkeepers, and artisans. Some historians maintain that the development of a market economy during the nineteenth century, which deprived rural families of land, actually increased the independence of women, because it placed more women at the head of households. It appears that most marriages were never formalized by Church or civic authorities.

The seeds of change were planted in the transfer of power from the Habsburgs to the Bourbons at the beginning of the eighteenth century. The new dynasty attempted to regain a central role for Spain on the world stage, financing its efforts by extracting more revenues from its American empire. The Bourbon attempt to tighten and modernize colonial rule adversely affected American-born whites, known as creoles. The fear of mass upheaval from below in an era when the population of long-oppressed indigenous peoples was rising kept creoles from moving toward independence until after 1800, when the cumulative effects of events in Europe made it clear that the contemporary and future burden of colonial rule was too great and merited the risks involved in rebellion against the metropolis. From below, the rising population, not only of Indians but mixed bloods as well, increased the pressures on food and land resources. Numerous popular rebellions marked the eighteenth century.

The wars for independence lasted for nearly two decades. After internal divisions and fear of radical mass upheaval stymied the initial movements, the creole leadership resurged in South America, taking advantage of military and financial help from Great Britain.

Through the turmoil of the independence movements, civil and foreign wars, and economic underdevelopment, Latin American society remained stratified and unequal. The landed oligarchy ruled, virtually unchallenged, though rural uprisings and urban riots sprinkled the century. The average Latin American was certainly no better off in 1870 than 1810, and may very well have been worse off. Ironically, the only circumstance to the advantage of the poor was instability, for in the countryside it created political and economic space for them to own land, to retain political autonomy, and have the possibility of reasonably equitable employment arrangements. This space would shrink drastically after order was established and the export economy ruled triumphant in the latter quarter of the nineteenth century. The profound transformations brought by industrialization and the commercialization of agriculture lay ahead.

Africa, 1807-1914: A Century of Revolution

The nineteenth century was a century of revolutionary change in Africa, with the Africa of 1914 vastly different from that of 1807. Some of these changes originated within the continent itself. For the most part, however, they were sparked by its greater involvement with forces from beyond its shores. The range of such change was broad. The influence of Islam and Christianity grew, eroding the vitality of many earlier religious beliefs and ultimately producing new, uniquely African religious forms. More and more guns were traded into Africa, contributing to a rising scale of violence in many regions. More and more raw materials were obtained from Africa, an innovation that changed the very nature of the societies involved. Toward the end of the century, the European scramble for Africa produced a political revolution that transformed the political landscape of the continent by bringing nearly all of it under European control.

The colonial powers that occupied Africa during the scramble quickly adopted policies calculated to make their new colonies pay and, by so doing, created four new types of economies. European settlers opened farms and ranches in certain areas, while in others the government pressed peasants to produce crops for the world market. Or, people were taken to work as migrant laborers on mines and farms far from their homes. Or, finally, the state compelled people to work on plantations or to produce raw materials for monopolistic concession companies. By 1914, colonial policies and economic realities had combined to impose new patterns of living on virtually all Africans. And while this happened, people throughout the continent considered how they might rid themselves of their unwelcome colonial masters.

The Spread of Islam

In 1914 there were an estimated 70 million Muslims in Africa, the product of a long and complex history of Islamic expansion. Much of this expansion had taken place in the nineteenth century as a consequence of two quite distinct processes. The first of these was a rash of persistent revolutionary outbursts occurring throughout the entire Sudanic zone, to the south of the Sahara. These were linked to mass movements organized into holy wars, or *jihads*, that aimed at suppression of Islamic practices identified as corrupt. The second was the spread of a far less revolutionary form of Islam from the East African coast inland along new trade routes opened up in the nineteenth century by Muslim Swahili traders.

The institutions that gave force to revolutionary Islam in the Sudanic region were *sufi* orders. Sufis were Muslim mystics who were believed to have direct experiences of God. Frequently they became religious teachers and many of them attracted the support of ordinary illiterate people who could not themselves read the Qur'an and who therefore looked to the sufi for spiritual guidance. Sometimes, when a noted sufi died, a successor took his place and a formal "order" was founded, with the deceased sufi's tomb often becoming a holy shrine. These orders had great appeal in Africa because they usually tolerated African spiritual beliefs and practices in a way that the more orthodox Islam of the urban Islamic law courts, schools, and mosques did not. As more rural Africans converted to Islam, the majority of African Muslims came to be members of quasi-theocratic sufi orders that existed side-by-side with the more orthodox Islam that was supported by urban rulers and merchants. With their broad popular support, and

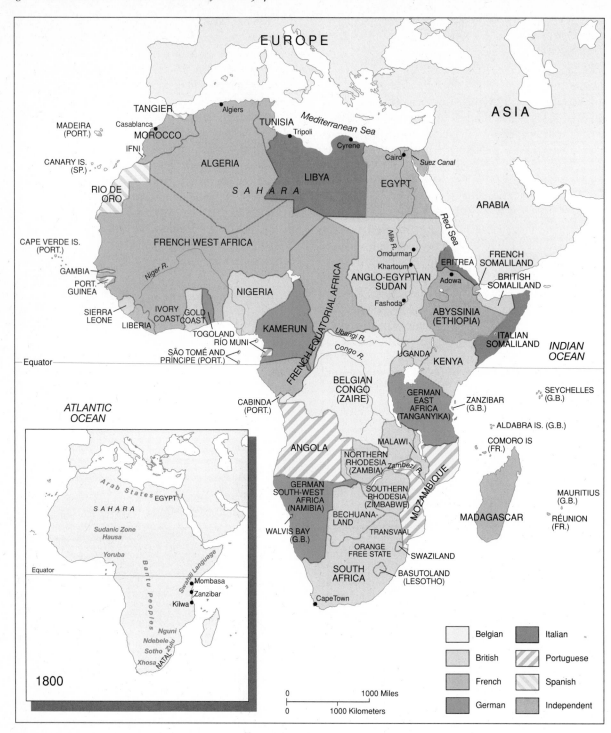

EUROPE

ASIA

TANGIER

Algiers

MADEIRA (PORT.)

Casablanca

MOROCCO

TUNISIA

Tripoli

Mediterranean Sea

IFNI

CANARY IS. (SP.)

ALGERIA

Cyrene

LIBYA

Cairo

Suez Canal

RIO DE ORO

S A H A R A

EGYPT

ARABIA

CAPE VERDE IS. (PORT.)

FRENCH WEST AFRICA

Niger R.

Nile R.

Red Sea

GAMBIA

PORT. GUINEA

NIGERIA

Omdurman

Khartoum

ANGLO-EGYPTIAN SUDAN

ERITREA

FRENCH SOMALILAND

Adowa

BRITISH SOMALILAND

SIERRA LEONE

IVORY COAST

GOLD COAST

LIBERIA

TOGOLAND

RIO MUNI

Fashoda

ABYSSINIA (ETHIOPIA)

ITALIAN SOMALILAND

INDIAN OCEAN

SÃO TOMÉ AND PRÍNCIPE (PORT.)

KAMERUN

Ubangi R.

FRENCH EQUATORIAL AFRICA

UGANDA

KENYA

Equator

Congo R.

CABINDA (PORT.)

BELGIAN CONGO (ZAIRE)

GERMAN EAST AFRICA (TANGANYIKA)

ZANZIBAR (G.B.)

SEYCHELLES (G.B.)

ATLANTIC OCEAN

ALDABRA IS. (G.B.)

COMORO IS (FR.)

ANGOLA

MALAWI

NORTHERN RHODESIA (ZAMBIA)

Zambezi R.

MAURITIUS (G.B.)

GERMAN SOUTH-WEST AFRICA (NAMIBIA)

SOUTHERN RHODESIA (ZIMBABWE)

MOZAMBIQUE

MADAGASCAR

RÉUNION (FR.)

WALVIS BAY (G.B.)

BECHUANA-LAND

TRANSVAAL

ORANGE FREE STATE

SWAZILAND

SOUTH AFRICA

BASUTOLAND (LESOTHO)

Cape Town

Arab States

EGYPT

SAHARA

Sudanic Zone
Hausa

Yoruba

Bantu Peoples

Swahili Language

Mombasa

Zanzibar

Kilwa

Nguni

Ndebele

Sotho

Xhosa

NATAL Zulu

Equator

1800

	Belgian		Italian
	British		Portuguese
	French		Spanish
	German		Independent

0   1000 Miles

0   1000 Kilometers

Africa, ca. 1914. Inset map: Africa, ca. 1800.

with the tradition in the Islamic world of not separating religious and political concerns, the sufi orders had great potential for political action directed against the dominant urban-based elite.

One such order was the Qadiriyya. During the last half of the eighteenth and first decade of the nineteenth centuries the Qadiriyya's leaders vigorously called for a reformed, purified Islam. They preached their message over a wide area of West Africa, from the Sahara desert southward through the Sudanic zone and then along the Niger valley into the forest areas of Nigeria. As it developed, it became more politically charged, criticizing the region's established urban-based political leaders as "pagans" for their failure to follow with sufficient zeal the *shari'a*, or Islamic religious law.

This message, with its clear implications of political revolution, gained the support of pastoralists, who felt oppressed by the heavy taxation that the urban rulers of the region's Hausa states imposed upon them. The man who led the Qadiriyya's reform effort was Usman dan Fodio (1754–1817). He began preaching in Gobir, a small state northeast of the Niger River, around 1775, and he soon gained broad support from the state's pastoralists. For three decades he continued to preach, denouncing the urban elite's alleged abuses of Islamic doctrine. When he learned that Gobir's king was preparing to attack him and his followers, Usman fled, organized his disciples into an effective cavalry, and in 1804 declared a *jihad* ("holy war") against Gobir. By 1808 he had won, slain the king, and founded a new capital for the new state at Sokoto, in Nigeria, beginning a process of Muslim empire building in the region. Emulating Usman dan Fodio and supported by him, other pastoral groups organized successful jihads against the elite of other Hausa states, political movements couched in religious terminology.

From the turmoil of the 1810s and 1820s a new political order grew, with the head of the new state of Sokoto recognized as the representative of Muhammad on earth and paramount over the emirs who ruled other states in the region. Although most West Africans never

A Muslim Rebuts Reasons Given for the *Jihad*, ca. 1810

■ *To justify their jihads against the urban elite, the followers of Usman dan Fodio claimed that their enemies were pagans. The Hausa leader of the state of Bornu, Muhammad al-Amin ibn Muhammad al-Kanami, who was known as a pious and learned Muslim, wrote this letter to rebut charges of "paganism" that had been made against the rulers of Bornu. While he failed to convince them, al-Kanami did manage to rebuff the armies of the jihad's leaders until 1835.*

Tell us therefore why you are frightening us and enslaving our free people. If you say that you have done this because of our paganism, then I say that we are innocent of paganism, and it is far from our compound. If praying and the giving of alms, knowledge of God, fasting in Ramadan and the building of mosques is paganism, what is Islam? These buildings in which we have been standing of a Friday, are they churches or synagogues or fire temples? If they were other than places of worship, then you would not pray in them when you capture them. Is this not a contradiction?

Among the biggest of your arguments for the paganism of the believers generally is the practice of the amirs of riding to certain places for the purpose of making alms-giving there; the uncovering of the heads of free women; the taking of bribes; embezzlement of the property of orphans; oppression in the courts. But these five things do not require you to do the things you are doing . . .

As for uncovering the head in free women, this is also forbidden, and the Qur'an has prohibited it. But she who does it does not thereby become a pagan. It is denial which leads to paganism. Failing to do something while believing in it is rather to be ascribed to disobedience requiring repentance . . .

Since acts of immorality and disobedience without number have long been committed in all countries, then Egypt is like Bornu, only worse. So is Syria and the cities of Islam . . . No age and no country is free from its share of heresy and sin. If, thereby, they all become pagan, then surely their books are useless. So how can you construct arguments based on what they say who are infidel according to you. Refuge from violence and its discord in religion is with God.

adopted the strict Islam for which Usman dan Fodio had hoped, the series of jihads that occurred over the sixty years after 1804 nonetheless did result in a spurt in Islam's missionary efforts and its spread into areas where it had scarcely been known before.

A similar religious reform movement also occurred in the eastern Sudanic zone, along the headwaters of the Nile, although the actual historical circumstances were quite different from those of the western Sudan. Sufi orders had already taken firm root in the eastern Sudan. In the 1820s armies from an imperialist Egypt invaded the area and set up an Egyptian colony. The Egyptians were highly exploitative, vigorously collecting taxes and seizing as slaves girls and boys from the non-Muslim, black peoples of the Nuba Mountains and southern parts of the country. The girls were sent to the households and harems of Egypt and Arabia as servants and concubines, while most of the boys became soldiers in the Egyptian army. Because of the region's lack of natural resources, the slave trade speedily grew to become a central element in its economy.

Sheikh Muhammad al-Amin al-Kanami.

This situation changed in the 1860s, after Isma'il Pasha (1830–95) became ruler of Egypt. Isma'il was dedicated to westernizing his country, and he realized that westernization demanded an end to the Sudanese slave trade. Thus, in 1869, he hired a British explorer, Samuel Baker, and sent him to the Sudan as governor, ordering him to suppress the slave trade. Four years later he dispatched another Briton, Charles George Gordon (1833–85) to continue Baker's work. Gordon declared that trade in ivory, an important commodity in the area, was to be a state monopoly, and that private armies, which had been used to raid for slaves, were to be disbanded. Gordon's army defeated those Sudanese who resisted his orders. The fact that Christian foreigners working for Egyptian imperialists were suppressing the highly lucrative slave and ivory trades deeply offended Sudanese sensibilities, and the resulting economic decline created an explosive political situation.

In mid-1881 Muhammad Ahmad (1848–85), a Sudanese mystic of the Sammaniyya sufi order, proclaimed himself the *Mahdi*, or the long-expected hidden leader of Islam who was expected to appear in times of catastrophe. He called for the purification of local Islam. For the Sudan's poverty-stricken Muslims the Mahdi's religious message had special appeal, for it was also aimed against the occupying Egyptian colonial administration. Within a year the Mahdi had gained the support of a wide range of discontented Sudanese and proclaimed a jihad. By January 1883 he had defeated the demoralized Egyptian forces and had brought large areas of the country under his own control.

In 1884 he extended his conquests to the Red Sea coast, making it clear to the British, who had occupied Egypt in 1882 as part of the scramble for Africa, that the remaining Egyptian forces in the Sudan should be withdrawn at once. General Gordon, deeply committed to ending the slave trade, ignored the order to withdraw and stubbornly remained in Khartoum, the capital. When the local people pledged their allegiance to the Mahdi, Gordon and his troops found themselves besieged. The relief column sent by the British arrived on 18 January 1885, two days after the Mahdi's followers had taken Khartoum and killed Gordon. As the Mahdi prepared for a further extension of his successful jihad, he died. He was replaced by a lieutenant, however, and the campaign to spread reformed Islamic practices continued for the rest of the century, especially against Christian Ethiopia to the south.

While jihads organized by sufi orders spread Islam throughout the Sudanic regions and into the areas to the south, it was also spreading in a more peaceful fashion into eastern and central Africa, carried there by Swahili merchants from the coast trading in ivory and slaves. As in West Africa a thousand years earlier, Africans here discovered that it was far easier to deal with Muslim merchants, to obtain credit from them, and to have business conflicts resolved if they converted to Islam and became subject to Islamic law. As a consequence, many traders and some rulers converted, establishing by 1890 the social base from which widespread conversions of ordinary people were to take place in the twentieth century.

African Innovation in Christianity

In 1914 there were about seven million Christians in Africa, the product of a missionary effort that had truly revolutionary implications for the continent as a consequence of the nature of the Christianity imported to Africa during the nineteenth century. Whether British or Continental, whether Protestant or Roman Catholic, Christianity was similar to Islam in significant ways. Both stressed that religious conversion had to involve far more than a change in religious ideas alone. Both aimed at a person's total conversion. The ideal Christian converts were expected not only to practice Christianity, but to try to live in a European way, to educate their children, to wear Western-style clothes where possible, and to work for their personal economic improvement.

Both Africans and Europeans participated in the effort to spread Christianity in Africa, with Africans who had already converted having special significance in the initial effort in both West Africa and South Africa. In West Africa, Yoruba-speaking Nigerians were in the forefront of this effort. Some of these had been rescued from ships taking them as slaves to the Americas and had been sent to the resettlement colony of Sierra Leone, on the West African coast. Many had converted to Christianity there, received a Western education, and embraced the range of values associated with nineteenth-century Britain. As a sign of their new allegiance, many adopted English names, with Samuel Crowther, James Johnson, and Thomas Macauley all becoming leading Yoruba intellectuals. Many of the intellectuals opened churches and schools, while their entrepreneurial cousins opened trading firms.

In the 1840s many of these Yoruba decided to return to Nigeria, the land of their fathers, to work as missionaries, educators, and merchants to redeem it from the evils of the slave trade and transform it along Western lines. The British supported them, believing that Christianity and commerce could, when combined, help suppress the slave trade. As a result of their work, the inland town of Abeokuta became a world-famous center for mission conversions to Christianity in Africa, with more and more Africans becoming missionaries to their brothers and cousins. In this way, then, Christianity began to spread along the West African coast; and, like Islam, it was especially welcomed by those who aspired to become traders and to live a middle-class existence in the European fashion.

The immigrant Yoruba also played an explicitly political role. Coming from British Sierra Leone, they remained British subjects even after settling in Nigeria. Deeply opposed to the slave trade, they joined European missionaries and traders in requesting that the British government intervene actively against it. Largely as a result of such urgings, in 1851 the British established a consulate at Lagos in an attempt to close off the slave trade with the interior. In subsequent years, a great surge of activity occurred. European merchants arrived to do business. Steamships stopped regularly to pick up produce. The city grew and prospered, drawing from Sierra Leone more and more Yoruba, who came to constitute a westernized African elite that in

Samuel Crowther became an Anglican bishop after he was rescued from a slave ship and converted to Christianity in the resettlement colony of Sierra Leone.

1860 opened both the first secondary school and the first newspaper in the area. In subsequent decades a class of Nigerians dedicated to education, Christianity, and business developed out of this community, acting as vigorous agents of westernization. Ironically, once British colonialism was established, this same group of westernized intellectuals became vigorous opponents of colonial control and advocates for African independence.

Liberated slaves from West Africa were not the only Africans who ardently espoused Christianity in the early nineteenth century. A very similar situation developed during the middle third of the century in South Africa's Eastern Cape region, among the Xhosa-speaking people. The breakdown of Xhosa society as a result of attacks by the British army and a great increase in trade with European merchants made many Xhosa willing to listen to British missionaries. Many converted to Christianity and, like their Yoruba brethren in West Africa, they began to preach both the Gospel and the desirability of adopting Western values. Their work was not restricted to South Africa, as they were crucial in establishing Victorian Christianity as far north as the areas north of the Zambezi River before the end of the century.

Although African catechists remained important in missionary endeavor, the early missionary work of African Christians was speedily overtaken and surpassed by a great expansion of European mission activity after the middle of the nineteenth century. Convinced by the racist propaganda of the time that Africans were "pagans" desperately in need of salvation, and eager to acquire converts for their respective churches, an ever expanding number of European missionaries arrived in Africa seeking converts. Enjoying quinine's protection from malaria and, once colonial control was established, the colonial administrations' political protection, these missionaries built mission stations throughout Africa. Combining medicine, agricultural innovation, and education with their religious message, the missionaries' appeal proved considerable, particularly as the older African religions seemed to have lost much of their relevance in the context of the political upheavals and ecological decline that occurred in the final decades of the nineteenth century. More and more Africans converted, and by the start of the twentieth century the Christian message had begun a period of expanding acceptance which, like Islam's, continues to the present day.

The initial phase of Africans' conversions to Christianity involved the adoption of a whole set of European cultural values. Soon, however, Africans began to bring their own perspectives to the religion and create wholly new forms of Christianity. The core of Christianity's message—that all people were created equal in the eyes of God—was a powerful one in its own right and the inequities of colonialism made it even more obvious. Leading opponents of the colonial system were drawn from the groups of educated Christians produced by the mission churches, with their critiques based on the Christian ideal of equality. Within the churches themselves, this demand for equality frequently prompted secession by blacks who saw that the white missionaries were not adhering to Christian principles. From the 1880s, such secessionists established black versions of the Christian churches in which Africans held leadership roles and that served as political training grounds in much the same way that African-American churches did in the era of American segregation. As a group, these secessionist churches came to be known as "Ethiopianist" churches, named after the successful repulse of Italian colonialism by the Ethiopians under Menelik II at the battle of Adowa in 1896.

Even more important from the point of view of the number of people eventually involved were the churches that came to be known as "Zionist," named after the holy mountain, Zion, near Jerusalem. By the early twentieth century it was clear that Christian mission activity, which had earlier produced a progressive, educated African elite, could not expand to meet the demand for churches everywhere and among all classes of society. For many illiterate and uneducated Africans—and especially for poor women—Zionist churches had great appeal. They were, much like the sufi orders of Muslim Africa, highly incorporative of African religious ideas and social customs, and the Zionists' stress upon healing as the core of their emotional services resonated strongly among the poor and oppressed, who increasingly joined such churches.

By the early twentieth century, then, Africans who were interested in becoming Christians had a wide range of Christian choices available to them. They could become members of ordinary Christian denominations such as the Methodists, Baptists, and Catholics, all of which were still mostly under white leadership. Or, if especially eager to be under black religious guidance, they could join the Ethiopianist churches that were playing an increasing political role in voicing grievances against colonial domination. Or, if the mainline churches and their Ethiopianist versions were either too strict or too Western in approach, there were Zionist churches—tolerant, emotional, and a place to find spiritual shelter and healing within the Christian community.

The Zulu Empire and State Building in Southeast Africa

The nineteenth century revolutions that transformed Africa were not restricted to religion. Great political changes that were not explicitly linked to religion also occurred, often associated with an increase in the size of African political units. Perhaps the best-known example of such change is that associated with the name of Shaka (179?-1828), which had immense impact throughout southeastern Africa and even beyond.

During the last half of the eighteenth century, big men in the northern part of Natal began to expand their power. A new trade in ivory oriented toward the East African coast required large-scale hunting parties that only big men could organize. The most able consolidated their positions and built small states such as Ngwane, Mthethwa, and Ndwandwe. These changes resulted in an increase in tension between the ever more powerful big men and ordinary family leaders over the issue of access to labor. As their power grew, then, the big men instituted changes that gave them greater control over the labor of young men and women. These included the creation of new "regiments" through which young men and women were organized for agricultural work, hunting, and warfare, working for the new states' elites for a specific period of years.

After 1800, these states entered a period of ever greater competition among themselves for several reasons. First, the discovery of fresh sources of ivory in East Africa caused its local price to decrease, in turn provoking local big men to try to maintain their economic position by producing more of it for sale. Then, between 1803 and 1806, competition was increased by a great drought that killed off many of the area's cattle and prompted people to try to rebuild their depleted herds by cattle raiding. Finally, in 1807 the international outlawing of the slave trade north of the Equator gradually created a demand for slaves at southeast African coastal ports as slavers moved their operations from West Africa. This new trade, associated with the importation of guns, proved highly disruptive to local societies by creating opportunities for men with large followings of people to increase their powers and put at risk those who were too weak to resist raiders seeking ivory, cattle, and slaves.

As a result of these competitive pressures, the regiments were used to hunt elephants, to raid for cattle, and even to look for slaves. The state increased the length of time that youths had to serve in the regiments and conflict became chronic throughout Natal. In 1818, after the death of one of the most important of the area's

Shaka, the founder of the Zulu empire.

leaders, a young man of great military skill came to power in Mthethwa. His name was Shaka. Using his army of an estimated 40,000 soldiers, Shaka began to create a new political entity, the Zulu empire, and consolidated many of the changes that had begun earlier in the century. He improved his army, increased the length of time the young were required to spend in military service, and deployed new weapons and tactics. As a result, the Zulu armies became virtually unbeatable.

The wars of empire building continued, and the result was prolonged political instability radiating outward from northern Natal throughout southeastern Africa. This era of instability and conflict came to be known as the *Mfecane*, "the crushing." It produced more than refugees, however. Quite rapidly, where before there had been only small chiefdoms or localized family groupings, large-scale states crystallized out of the unstable conditions as refugees came together to seek safety in numbers. In reaction to the expansion of the Zulu empire, many new states were formed in southern Africa during the 1820s and 1830s. These included Swaziland, founded by Ngwane's leader, Sobhuza Dhlamini; Lesotho, founded by Moshoeshoe in the Caledon River valley; the Ndebele, established by Mzilikazi and later led by him away from the area of conflict to settle in southwest Zimbabwe; and the Gaza state founded in southern Mozambique by Soshangane. Finally, Zwangendaba, a leading general, left the region entirely and took his group on a lengthy sojourn through central and eastern Africa before it fragmented in the 1850s and its people settled in Malawi, Tanzania, and Zambia and established new states there.

These new states had two important characteristics. First, all were what have been called "snowball states," constantly absorbing more and more people to achieve strength through numbers. As a result, family or cultural identification became relatively unimportant, and one's loyalty to the leader was the central test of good citizenship. Second, all the states had highly disciplined armies. Wherever they settled they became threats to their neighbors, whom they raided for slaves, food, and ivory. The creation of these new, relatively large states resulted, therefore, in the spread of violence in the interior of southeast Africa in the decades after 1820.

Arab Settlement and the Militarization of Commerce in East Africa

While these unsettling political changes were taking place in southeastern Africa, similar changes were also beginning along the East African coast and in its hinterland. After decades of jockeying between Portugal, Britain, France, and Holland for dominance over the trade of the Indian Ocean basin, in the mid-seventeenth century new players appeared on the scene. These were Arabs from Oman, on the southeastern coast of Arabia, who were involved in commercial activities in the Indian Ocean. Encouraged by the British, as early as 1650 the Omani Arabs challenged Portugal on the coast of East Africa itself, and in 1696–98 they succeeded in expelling the Portuguese from the entire coast north of Mozambique.

Over the next thirty years the Omani established garrisons at Mombasa, Zanzibar, and Kilwa. Their presence was always shadowy and uncertain, however, as Arabia remained their main concern. Thus, while the East African coast was divided into a vaguely defined Portuguese sphere along the Mozambique coast and a similarly vague Arab sphere to the north, the coastal Swahili cities remained for the most part independent. Then, in the early years of the nineteenth century, the situation changed.

In 1806 Sayyid Sa'id (1791–1856) became sultan of Oman and soon decided to establish greater control over the Swahili cities so that he could dominate the region's growing trade. As a sign of his seriousness, in 1840 he moved his capital from the Omani city of Muscat to Zanzibar, coopting the local Swahili rulers rather than subduing them by force. In effect, Sayyid Sa'id and his successors were true "merchant princes," interested both in enriching themselves through trade and in strengthening the cultural links between the coast and their Arab homeland, not in overt political control.

It was the great increase in trade of two important commodities that had stimulated Sayyid Sa'id's growing interest in East Africa. First, the demand for ivory in India, China, and, especially, Europe—to be made into *objets d'art*, piano keys, and billiard balls—sent the price rocketing. As African ivory was the world's best, merchants sought it in East Africa, an area with huge herds of elephants. Second, after 1810 slaves were also sought in ever-increasing numbers from this area. This increase in demand for slaves was stimulated not only by the British campaign against the slave trade from West Africa that began in 1807 and helped shift the focus of its supply to East Africa, but also by the enlargement of French-owned sugar plantations on Mauritius, Reunion, and other islands in the Indian Ocean and by the establishment of Omani-owned clove plantations on the islands of Pemba and Zanzibar after the 1830s.

The combination of an increase in demand for ivory and slaves along the coast and Sayyid Sa'id's ability to extend credit over an immense geographical area resulted in a rapid spread of trade throughout the interior. In earlier centuries most economic activity had been centered on the coast itself, but in the nineteenth century coastal traders pushed into the deep interior in their quest for ivory and slaves. As elephants became decimated near the coast, they retreated inland, creating a moving frontier of elephant hunting. Initially, slaves were raided from coastal peoples, but as they organized themselves to resist, a slave-raiding frontier also moved into the interior. Sometimes the two frontiers were congruent, sometimes they were separate; but their spread into the interior brought the area into deep contact with the world economy for the first time.

As the two frontiers moved from the coast into the hinterland, competition for ivory and slaves grew. This competition in turn transformed East African society.

This change occurred largely because the increased competition came to be expressed militarily, and for two reasons. The first of these was the arrival in the region of the Ngoni people. The second was the importation into East Africa of large amounts of European weapons.

The Ngoni were highly militarized groups of refugees from the wars associated with the rise of the Zulu empire in South Africa and led by Zwangendaba. Because they spent a long time in East Africa and traveled over a great deal of territory, they had a profound impact upon the region. Equipped with the effective military techniques perfected earlier in South Africa, they found that the easiest way to survive as they traveled was to raid other peoples. Groups of East African peoples that were themselves attacked by the Ngoni had no choice but to adopt many of the outsiders' techniques, if only for reasons of sheer self-defense. The Ngoni intrusion of the 1840s and early 1850s took place just when the

highly competitive ivory-hunting and slave-raiding frontiers were moving westward from the coast for the first time, bringing large numbers of guns into the interior. As most traders dealing in ivory and slaves were too weak to dominate the trade routes themselves, they turned to their natural partners, the region's big men, who were eager to take advantage of the new opportunities to increase their political and economic status. To fulfill their role as partners of the Swahili traders from the coast, these big men adopted the new military strategies that had been brought with the Ngoni refugees from South Africa and established bands of loyal young mercenaries to raid for ivory and slaves. To make their new armies more effective, they armed them with European weapons available from the traders with whom they dealt.

Beginning in the late 1850s, bands of well-armed mercenaries were to be found throughout Tanzania, Uganda, Kenya, Zambia, eastern Zaire, Malawi, and

Elephant tusks being weighed in Zanzibar before being sent to Boston, where the valuable ivory will be made into such items as piano keys.

A Yao slave trader in southern Malawi in the 1860s.

Mozambique. The mercenaries were loyal to their leaders and patrons and they were potent fighting forces. On this military base, ambitious big men speedily increased their power, building up larger and larger states in a region in which states had been generally small. As a consequence of the militarization of commercial competition in the 1850s and afterward, a third frontier—a frontier of violence—came into being, moving in lockstep with the slave-raiding and ivory-hunting frontiers. The old bonds of kinship began to be regularly transcended, although not abolished, by new, stronger bonds between clients and patrons who could protect them. Societies that earlier had been roughly egalitarian on the material level came to be more clearly hierarchical, both in matters of power and in the distribution of material goods.

Clearly, the changes of the nineteenth century distinguished the trajectory of history in East Africa from that in West Africa. While in West Africa the transatlantic slave trade was winding down, in East Africa the slave trade increased steadily into the late 1880s. While in West Africa the production of items such as peanuts and palm oil fostered new peasant and middle classes, in East Africa the trade in the luxury commodities of ivory and slaves increased the power of the established big men who had the manpower needed to produce them. Finally, while in West Africa Christian Africans reinforced the new middle classes and moved the coastal zones toward increased Christianization and an acceptance of Western-type education and literacy, in East Africa Muslim influences were intensified as, under Omani patronage, the Swahili language increasingly came to be spoken and written, Islamic schools established, and Arab influence greatly increased.

When early European explorers and missionaries, already firm in their belief that Africans lacked the ability to govern themselves, ventured into the East African interior during the 1860s and after, they encountered conditions of violence and warfare that confirmed their prejudices. While the reports of violence they made were largely factual, clearly they did not accurately reflect the nature of the area's history over time or as a whole. The situation into which these European outsiders had come was unusual in that it was a period of revolutionary change. But the European visitors did not realize this and assumed that this was the customary way of life there, drawing typically racist conclusions from it. The fact that such disorder existed at the height of the scramble for Africa in the 1880s and 1890s was used as a rationalization for European intervention in the region by Germany, Britain, and Belgium's Leopold II. Ironically, the violence resulting from the process of building new large-scale political structures in East and Central Africa that might in time have withstood European attack was an excuse for their actual takeover by Europeans.

Making Colonies Pay

Once the scramble for Africa was over and African resisters defeated, the new colonial powers had to address the issue of how their new colonies could be made to pay. The dreams of untold wealth that helped spark the scramble soon proved to be only dreams, and the hopes for lucrative markets were shown to have been vain. Africa was not the treasure chest that Europeans had believed. Yet it was an abiding principle of colonial administration at the time that colonies had to pay their own way. Whether they were Belgian or Portuguese, French or British, German or Italian, all European governments quickly moved to wring whatever money could be wrung from the new colonies with the least possible investment in the public sector. If hospitals and schools were to be built, it would be the Christian missions that would do it. If the churches did not, then Africans would have to do without.

By the start of the twentieth century, the colonialists had concluded that there were four possible ways to organize their colonies' economies and societies to meet their goal of making their colonies pay their own way. These early decisions, reinforced after World War I, fundamentally shaped—or misshaped—the African economies in ways that have persisted to the present.

First, in certain areas European settlement was encouraged. Given that late-nineteenth-century Europeans were racially biased against African agricultural methods, the new colonial powers decided that the most attractive areas of Africa should be opened to European settlement. Europeans had long settled in areas with a Mediterranean climate, such as Algeria and South Africa, but now the cool highlands of East Africa, with mountain elevations of up to 11,000 feet, and the Zimbabwean plateau, free from the disease-carrying tsetse fly, attracted settlers who established cattle ranches and farms. By 1914 it was evident that the settlers, although numbering only a few thousand in each colony, were politically important enough and economically promising enough to be allowed to shape the local economic infrastructure and governmental policies to suit them.

In Zimbabwe and Kenya and wherever else Europeans settled the consequence for the majority African population was the subordination of their interests to those of the settlers. Large areas of land were taken from them and made available to Europeans. Taxes were imposed. Agricultural prices were rigged to subsidize settler production. Governmental power was deployed to compel the Africans—men, women, and children—to work for low wages on the settlers' ranches and farms. And, of course, every measure was taken to prevent Africans from participating in economic or political life.

A second approach to shaping African economies occurred in areas that were unsuitable for European settlement but were considered to have the necessary prerequisites for agricultural production, such as decent land, access to transport, and an adequate workforce. In these areas the state stimulated increased peasant production of raw materials needed in the world economy. Thus, along the coastal areas of West Africa, Africans working their own lands produced commodities such as

Changes in East Africa During the Nineteenth Century

1806	Sayyid Sa'id becomes Sultan of Oman
1818	Shaka comes to full power in Natal and begins Zulu empire
1835	Zwangendaba leads Ngoni north of the Zambezi, beginning their long journey through east central Africa
1830s	Clove plantations established on Zanzibar and Pemba
1840	Sayyid Sa'id moves Omani capital to Zanzibar
1860s	Intense Protestant missionary activity in the East African interior
1873	Sultan Barghash signs treaty with Britain promising to end the East African slave trade, but trade continues
1878	Pope Leo XIII approves missionary activity by the White Fathers Order in the East African interior
1882	British occupation of Egypt
1884	Defeat of General Gordon by the Mahdi at battle of Khartoum
1885	Germany proclaims a protectorate over Tanganyika
1886	Britain and Germany agree to a division of the Sultan of Zanzibar's territory between them
1890	Britain declares a protectorate over Zanzibar
1894	Britain formally annexes Uganda
1898	Conflict between France and Britain over Nile headwaters resolved after Fashoda crisis

palm oil and cacao. In the drier areas of the Sudanic zone, the main peasant crops became peanuts and, later, cotton. Cotton was also introduced to the fertile areas of southern Uganda and parts of Malawi. Peasant-produced tobacco became important in Malawi.

While the economies of these areas were not reshaped to benefit European settlers, and while African peasants involved in crop production clearly did not have their lives disrupted to the extent that those living in areas of European settlement did, the workings of the peasant economies were nonetheless gradually rigged to benefit European interests. This was partly accomplished, especially in West Africa, by large European trading houses conspiring to depress prices paid for commodities and, more generally throughout Africa, by massive governmental intervention in the marketplace to nullify the operation of the free market.

The rest of Africa, considered unattractive for European settlement and unsuitable for peasant production, required other approaches. In the operation of a third type of economy, one based on labor migrancy, the state manipulated tax laws to force the men of an area to leave their homes and families for a year or two or five or ten and to journey to places where they could find work. A portion of their earnings was then remitted to their home area and used to pay their taxes and to purchase necessities for their families. The major areas employing such migrant laborers included the great complex of mines in South Africa, which drew men from all over southern Africa, but especially from Zambia, Malawi, Lesotho, Swaziland, and Mozambique; the mines of the

A contemporary cartoon characterizes King Leopold of the Belgians as a monstrous snake crushing the life out of the black population of the Congo Free State.

Zambia and Zairian Copperbelt, which attracted labor from all over central Africa; and areas of agricultural production such as southern Uganda, Zimbabwe, central Mozambique, and the cacao plantations of West Africa, which attracted labor from neighboring areas. At its worst, the Africa of the migrant labor system was an Africa characterized by the absence of up to 70 per cent of its able-bodied men at any one time, by disintegrating village and family life, and by ever increasing poverty affecting the life expectancy of the women and children left behind. These were the true slums of the European empires.

Even these areas, however, were paradises compared with the parts of the continent that came under the fourth, and earliest type, of the colonial economic systems. These were areas in which the state ceded monopolistic concessions to private individuals or companies. In return for the mere promise that they would "develop" their area, they were given the right to exploit the African population pretty much as they wished. In effect, the concession holders took the place of the government. As their purpose was to make profits, their regimes became synonymous with true hells-on-earth where no rights, human or civil, were respected and where nothing was done for the welfare of the African people.

The prototype for the concession system was developed by Leopold II's Congo Free State administration. The state obtained rubber from the people during the 1890s and into the early twentieth century by forcing them to produce it as a form of tax. When they failed to fulfill their quotas, the state's agents amputated people's hands or legs as punishment. The rubber obtained from this system came to be known as "red rubber" because of the blood spilled to produce it. It was only when books such as Joseph Conrad's *Heart of Darkness* (1900) appeared and when opposition groups such as E. D. Morel's Congo Reform Society (1904) were formed that the depths to which Leopold's administration had sunk became known throughout the world. Regrettably however, while publicity and resulting outrage ended Leopold's administration, they did not end the concession system in all of Africa, and this system continued as a means of economic exploitation in large parts of French Equatorial Africa down to World War II and in Portugal's African colonies until the 1960s.

In the calculations of all colonial administrations Africans counted for little except as laborers. Whether the colony was devoted to European settler production, peasant agricultural production, labor migrancy, or concessionary plantation production, the roles assigned to Africans were to work hard, pay their taxes, and keep quiet. As the coercive powers of the state were large, and

CHILD LABOR AND ECONOMIC DEVELOPMENT IN MOZAMBIQUE, CA. 1920

■ *The scramble for Africa was followed by a scramble for African labor as European powers set Africans to work to "develop" the new colonies. In the concession zones that the Portuguese government established in Mozambique, women and children were part of the labor force. Each concession holder had the legal right to force the Africans living within his or her concession, known in Portuguese as* prazos, *to work for wages that he or she set. Because competition for their labor was legally eliminated, Africans were effectively serfs of the concession holder. As a consequence of reports of abuses after World War I, the Portuguese government sent Dr. Guerra Lage to investigate. This is a report of what he found on the Lugella and Lomwe concessions in central Mozambique.*

Lately the agricultural work in the *prazos* has considerably developed: all this work is carried on by women and children. The women and children in the *prazos* are on average compelled to work 120 days in the year. The employees of the *prazo* in order to get the number of labourers which they require compel the native chiefs to bring them a certain number of children and women. They are not given food, which has to come from their homes. If the arrest of the chiefs' wives [to force the chiefs to produce the laborers] gives no result, the police are sent to the native villages and they rob and arrest everybody they find. The adult prisoners, the women and children are compelled to work and receive in payment after thirty days' work one yard of very common calico. All sleep under the same shed.

I saw children under six years of age compelled to work for thirty consecutive days. When a child falls ill, it is not treated nor sent to the native village: only after the father or mother has replaced it by another child is it allowed to go and be treated. I think that children of 6 and 7 years of age are purposely compelled to work, though they can produce almost nothing, in order to compel the parents to replace them, thus succeeding in getting men to work for [a child's wage.] I saw some ten or twelve children, very ill, some with fever, others with very sore eyes, who were notwithstanding compelled to work. At Corue station I saw 12 children, very thin and emaciated who, when cross-questioned by me declared that they were starving because their mothers could not bring them food. The number of children employed in the two *prazos* is over 20,000 (twenty thousand). If the children run away, the mothers are arrested and compelled to work for them; if the mother or father, through any circumstance is not caught, the police go to the kraals and bring the first native they can find and compel him to work, in place of the runaway child.

From translation of a report by Dr. Guerra Lage, Enclosed in Consul General Pyke, Lourenco Marques, to British Foreign Office, 7 August 1926, in F.O. 311/11136, at Public Record Office, London.

---

as the state was quick to deploy them, most Africans had little choice but to conform.

African Reactions to Colonial Rule

Yet Africans were not content to play the game according to colonial rules. Although many had learned from the lopsided battles of the late nineteenth century that without modern weapons, armed opposition to colonial governments was not feasible, some people still rebelled. Such rebellions occurred, for example, in Tanganyika in 1905, in Natal in 1906, in Rwanda in 1912, and in Mozambique in 1917. One of the most notable of these ultimately unsuccessful rebellions was the abortive insurrection organized in 1915 by the Reverend John Chilembwe in southern Malawi against the concession system that operated there. (See Special Feature, "The Black Englishman," pp. 864–865.)

More effective resistance took other forms. One was so-called silent resistance, in which exploited Africans attempted to undermine the economic systems in which they were forced to live by shirking at work, breaking employers' machinery, avoiding paying taxes, and similar covert actions. But such resistance, while locally effective, could not shake colonialism, let alone bring it down.

John Chilembwe with his family.

*T*he "*Black Englishman*"

It was a day in January 1915 in Blantyre, Nyasaland's largest town. As the
photographer read the newspapers, he
recalled that day years before when he
had traveled out to Chiradzulu to take
the picture of that well-known "black
Englishman" who was preaching
nonsense to the natives. He had been a
strange one! Despite the heat of the
Central African afternoon, Chilembwe
had been dressed in a buttoned-up suit,
tie, and starched collar and had a natty

straw hat. His wife, a Congolese woman
whom he had married in the United
States—of all places!—was worse, with
her high-collared, mutton-sleeved dress
that reached all the way to the ground.
Even the child had an overcoat on! This
"black Englishman" seemed to agree
with the old European saw that "clothes
made the man"! But his ambitious aping
of the white man had clearly done him no
good in the long run for he was now dead
and disgraced, and soon he would be a

scarcely remembered footnote to the
history of British colonialism.

John Chilembwe had an interesting, but not happy, life. He was
born in the early 1870s, and his
father was one of the largely Muslim Yao people, who were prominent in the growing ivory and slave
trade to the East Coast. His
mother was a local Mang'anja
woman. As a child he had witnessed raids by Ngoni soldiers in
his home area, and, perhaps as a
result of the insecurity caused by
them, his family moved to be near
the recently opened Scottish
Presbyterian mission at Blantyre.
He learned to speak English after a
fashion, but at age twenty he had
not yet become a Christian.

In early 1893 he heard about a
strange new missionary from
Scotland who had come to Central
Africa by way of Australia. His
name was Joseph Booth and he was
scandalizing local European settlers by telling his African converts
that colonialism was an evil that
violated God's wish that all men
should be equal and that Africa
should be for the Africans, not for
the colonialists. Chilembwe became Booth's servant, and, in 1897,
when Booth went to the United
States to raise money for his
mission, Chilembwe accompanied
him. He decided to attend the
Virginia Theological Seminary and
become a missionary himself,
returning to Africa in 1900 a good
Christian and with highly westernized manners.

He bought land for his mission
at his birthplace, at Chiradzulu,
and named it the Providence
Industrial Mission. Over the next
few years African-American missionaries joined him in his work,
establishing links to the black
community in the United States

that ensured money for his mission's survival. He opened a farm to show neighboring Africans how modern agricultural methods could help them prosper. He succeeded in his work, and by 1912 he had over one thousand parishioners, while some nine hundred students attended his mission school.

But his successes were not enough to make him happy. On the one hand, members of his mission found it difficult to use their new knowledge for their personal advancement because the British planters in southern Malawi did everything they could to keep Africans subordinate. The last thing that settlers wanted was competition in tobacco and coffee production from upwardly mobile Africans. Equally as bad, Chilembwe's neighbors treated their African migrant workers as serfs whom they could abuse and exploit at will. Especially notorious was William Jervis Livingstone, a relative of the great missionary explorer David Livingstone, who ran a huge concession at Magomero. Not only did he treat his workers shamelessly, but he also tried to prevent their children from hearing the Christian Word of God because of its potential for inciting criticism, favoring Muslim chiefs and their Quranic schools. He also successfully used his contacts in

the government to block Chilembwe's efforts to spread his mission beyond Chiradzulu.

Then, in 1914, strange rumors that the Second Coming of Christ was at hand and that the end of the world would soon occur began to circulate, spread throughout all southern Africa by Jehovah's Witnesses. When World War I broke out in August 1914, the accuracy of the rumors seemed confirmed. With many of the British settlers drawn into the war effort against German East Africa (Tanganyika), Chilembwe decided, in January 1915, that it was time to act, announcing to his followers that the "time has come at last to fight against our oppressors."

Three attacks were planned for the night of Saturday, 23 January, including one on Magomero. The main attack on Blantyre was a failure. The other two succeeded only in killing a handful of British settlers, including the hated William Jervis Livingstone. The colonial government swiftly mobilized their forces, arrested and executed the rebels, and snuffed out the uprising. John Chilembwe fled for the Mozambique border. Before reaching it, however, he was shot, and his body was speedily buried in an unmarked grave.

The consequences of the uprising were uneven. On the one

hand, the state realized that abuses of the nature practiced by W. J. Livingstone and his counterparts had to be ended for reasons of preventing more such uprisings. On the other hand, the state tightened its regulations over educated Africans like Chilembwe, people imbued with the vexatious idea derived from Christian doctrine that all men were created equal and who felt that Africa belonged to Africans. Gradually, the memory of Chilembwe faded, although some villagers maintained he had actually escaped and would come back eventually to liberate the country.

After the country's independence from Britain in 1964 the old photograph taken decades before turned out to be useful. When the new government of Malawi decided to issue a stamp to commemorate the fiftieth anniversary of the uprising, they used the photo as the basis for Chilembwe's portrait. The photographer had gotten it all wrong. Chilembwe had become Malawi's national hero—despite his being mocked decades before as a "black Englishman"—and educated Africans like him had mobilized the anticolonial movements that eventually brought independence to colonial territories.

The greatest focal point for resistance turned out to be the Christian mission schools that were established in colonial Africa soon after the scramble, often despite skepticism of officials and hostility from European business interests. Regrettably, Africa was unevenly served by such missions. Many areas of Africa were either ignored almost entirely or served by missionaries who felt that the education of Africans was of little use. Whether by intention or by accident, these areas of missionary neglect tended to be subject to concessionary exploitation, and strong anticolonial voices were slow to be heard in them. Energetic Protestant missionaries, however, introduced advanced education to places such as South Africa, northern Malawi, Uganda, and sections of coastal British and German West Africa well. As early as the 1880s in South Africa, Ghana, and Nigeria, and soon after 1900 elsewhere, African intellectuals began to attack colonialism.

That they could do so was, ironically, a consequence of the nature of some of the colonial societies themselves. While governments and businesses certainly desired to keep Africans subordinate, they did not want Africans to work only as menial laborers. To save money, they wanted to limit the number of Europeans working in the colonial societies, and they were thus willing to rely on educated Africans to serve as clerks and policemen, as telegraph operators and foremen, and in a host of other positions. In effect, opportunities for African advancement opened up in the interstices of oppression, and people educated by the missions and already articulate in their hostility to colonialism moved into these positions of responsibility. It was these people, together with their counterparts in the ranks of the Christian clergy, who mounted the major resistance to colonialism before World War I.

Their anticolonial message was strongly moral and ethical, argued from an explicitly Christian position. It was wrong to discriminate against Africans; it was unchristian to refuse to pay a living wage; it was unethical to break apart families by demanding labor migrancy; it was cynical to preach Christian brotherhood and practice the opposite. Before World War I, however, these men's opposition remained unheeded by the colonial administrations and business interests whose ideologies were still thoroughly racist and whose practices were highly exploitative. Moreover, with their Western education and manners, they were often alienated from the ordinary Africans for whom they claimed to speak. African Christian intellectuals seemed to be voices crying in the wilderness, and, indeed, it was John Chilembwe's deep sense of isolation and frus-

tration that led him to undertake an uprising that he knew was destined to fail.

Yet it would be wrong to underestimate the influence of these men. They were preparing the way for a future, more broadly based opposition to colonialism that reached fruition after World War II. Equally important, they were also laying the foundations for a new middle class of upwardly mobile Africans in places where such a class had not yet been formed during the nineteenth century, especially in southern, eastern, and central Africa. As such, they were positioning themselves to become the eventual heirs of African big men and European settlers, businessmen, and colonial administrators once independence was achieved.

The period between 1807, when Britain outlawed its nationals from participating in the slave trade, and 1914, when World War I broke out and engulfed large areas of Africa in devastation, saw Africa transformed. African economies were first changed by the growth of the "legitimate trade" in West Africa and by the development of long-distance trade routes into the interior in southern and eastern Africa. Then, these economies were changed a second time, after the scramble for Africa, when the new colonialists reshaped them to try to make the colonies pay. African societies were also altered by the growth of new classes with new interests and new hopes. Politically, Europeans had overwhelmed the continent, but by the end of the nineteenth century the new classes of Africans were envisaging a return to African independence. And at the center of the changes was the impressive growth of Islam and Christianity, flexible religions for a changing Africa. After the end of World War I in 1918, the stage was almost set for the drive toward decolonialization.

A stamp issued by Malawi in 1965 commemorates John Chilembwe. Although frustrated and lonely in his opposition to colonialism in 1915, Chilembwe became a hero of independent Malawi.

SUGGESTIONS FOR FURTHER READING

LATIN AMERICA, 1700–1870: INDEPENDENCE AND ITS AFTERMATH

Timothy E. Anna, *The Fall of the Royal Government in Mexico City* (Lincoln, NB: University of Nebraska Press, 1978). Explores the machinations of *peninsulares* and *creoles* in pre-independence Mexico.

Timothy E. Anna, *The Fall of the Royal Government in Peru* (Lincoln, NB: University of Nebraska Press, 1979). Explains the reluctance of Peruvian elites to abandon colonial governance.

Jonathan C. Brown, *A Socioeconomic History of Argentina, 1776–1860* (New York: Cambridge University Press, 1979). A provocative economic history of the era.

David Bushnell, ed., *The Liberator, Simon Bolivar: Man and Image* (New York: Knopf, 1970). Includes selections of Bolívar's writings and excerpts from studies of his life and times.

David Bushnell and Neill Macaulay, *The Emergence of Latin America in the Nineteenth Century* (New York: Oxford, 1988). A comprehensive overview of the half century after independence.

Fanny Calderón de la Barca, *Life in Mexico* (Berkeley, CA: University of California Press, 1982). These are the observations of an Englishwoman who lived in Mexico from 1839 to 1842. The book is notable for its caustic comments about political leaders.

Gabriel García Márquez, *The General in His Labyrinth* (New York: Knopf, 1990). In the absence of a first-rate biography of the Liberator, this novel provides a provocative view.

Richard Graham, *Independence in Latin America* (New York: Knopf, 1972). A brief but comprehensive overview.

Tulio Halperin-Donghi, *The Aftermath of Revolution in Latin America* (New York: Harper and Row, 1973). An opinionated interpretation of the post-independence era.

John Lynch, *Argentine Dictator: Juan Manuel Rosas, 1829–1852* (New York: Oxford University Press, 1981). This is the best biography of the most famous nineteenth-century *caudillo*.

John Lynch, *The Spanish American Revolutions, 1808–1826* (New York: Norton, 1973). A fuller examination of the movements for independence.

Kenneth R. Maxwell, *Conflicts and Conspiracies: Brazil and Portugal, 1750–1808* (New York: Cambridge University Press, 1973). Discusses the origins of creole nationalism in Brazil.

John Leddy Phelan, *The People and the King: The Comunero Revolution in Colombia, 1781* (Madison, WI: University of Wisconsin Press, 1978). Analyzes one of the precursor movements of independence.

Katia M. Queiros Mattoso, *To Be a Slave in Brazil, 1550–1888* (New Brunswick, NJ: Rutgers University Press, 1986). This is an illuminating view of slavery, partly from the slave's point of view.

Nelson Reed, *The Caste War of Yucatan* (Stanford, CA: Stanford University Press, 1964). Relates the history of Mayan resistance to Mexican rule.

A. J. R. Russell-Wood, *From Colony to Nation: Essays on the Independence of Brazil* (Baltimore: Johns Hopkins University Press, 1975). Politics and society at the time of independence.

Antonio López de Santa Anna, *The Eagle: The Autobiography of Santa Anna*, Ann Fears Crawford, ed. (Austin, TX: The State House Press, 1988). This self-defense is not wholly believable, but always entertaining.

John Tutino, *From Insurrection to Revolution in Mexico: Social Bases of Agrarian Violence, 1750–1940* (Princeton, NJ: Princeton University Press, 1986). A provocative examination of why Mexican peasants took up arms, comparing the wars of independence with the revolution one hundred years later.

Richard A. White, *Paraguay's Autonomous Revolution 1810–1840* (Albuquerque, NM: University of New Mexico Press, 1978). Argues that the Francia dictatorship was not as malicious as previously thought and actually made Paraguay among the most progressive nations in the region.

AFRICA, 1807–1914: A CENTURY OF REVOLUTION

David Robinson, *The Holy War of Umar Tal* (Oxford: Clarendon Press, 1985). A scholarly treatment of some of the Western Sudanic zone's nineteenth century *jihads*.

Richard Hill, *Egypt in the Sudan, 1820–1881* (London: Oxford University Press, 1959). An account of Egypt's intervention in the Sudan and the growth of the Nilotic slave trade.

J. F. A. Ajayi, *Christian Missions in Nigeria, 1841–1891* (London: Longman, 1965). An assessment of the growth of Christian missions in Nigeria.

Bengt Sundkler, *Bantu Prophets in South Africa*, 2d ed. (London: Oxford University Press, 1961). The classic discussion of the growth of separatist Christian movements in southern Africa.

* John D. Omer-Cooper, *The Zulu Aftermath* (Evanston, IL: Northwestern University Press, 1966). A still-serviceable history of the impact of Shaka's successful attempt to build a Zulu empire.

Roland Oliver and Gervase Mathew, eds., *History of East Africa*, Vol. I (London: Clarendon Press, 1963). Still the most readable discussion of nineteenth-century East African history.

Frederick Cooper, *Plantation Slavery on the East Coast of Africa* (New Haven, CT: Yale University Press, 1977). How clove production changed East Africa's labor relations.

* Thomas Pakenham, *The Scramble for Africa: The White Man's Conquest of the Dark Continent from 1876 to 1912* (New York: Random House, 1991). A gigantic, but by no means complete, narrative of Africa's struggle with the "New Imperialism."

Leroy Vail and Landeg White, *Capitalism and Colonialism in Mozambique: A Study of Quelimane District* (Minneapolis, MN: University of Minnesota Press, 1980). A fine study of how a concession system worked.

George Shepperson and T. Price, *Independent African: John Chilembwe and the Nyasaland Rising of 1915* (Edinburgh: Edinburgh University Press, 1958). A classic and compelling narrative of the Reverend John Chilembwe's life and times.

* Indicates paperback edition available.

CHAPTER 29

World War I and the Russian Revolution, 1914–1920

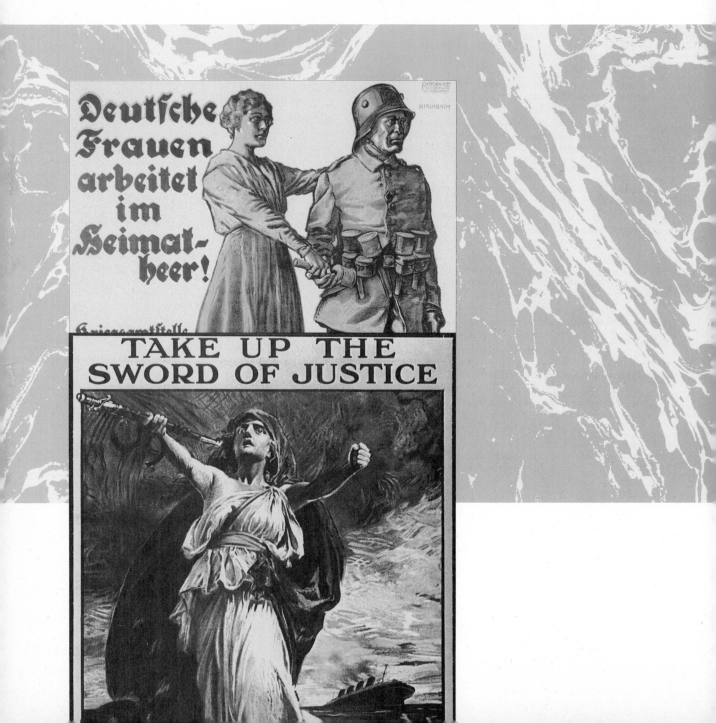

SELLING THE GREAT WAR

Advertising is a powerful influence in modern life. Some suggest it makes us buy goods we do not need. Others insist that advertising is an efficient way of conveying information on the basis of which people make choices. The leaders of European nations discovered the power of advertising in the years of world war from 1914 to 1918. Advertising did not create the Europe-wide conflict that became known as the Great War. Nor did it produce the enthusiasm that excited millions of Europeans when war was declared in 1914. But when death counts mounted, prices skyrocketed, and food supplies dwindled, the frenzy and fervor for the war flagged. Then governments came to rely more heavily on the art of persuasion. Survival and victory required the support and coordination of the whole society. For the first time in history, war had to advertise.

By the early decades of the twentieth century, businessmen had learned that it was not enough to develop efficient technologies and to mass-produce everything from hair oil to corsets—they had to sell their goods to the public. People would not buy goods they did not know about and whose merits they did not understand. Modern advertising pioneered sales techniques that convinced people to buy. Now political leaders came to realize that the advertising techniques of the marketplace could be useful. Governments took up the "science" of selling—not products but the idea of war. It was not enough to have a well-trained and well-equipped army to ensure victory. Citizens had to be persuaded to join, to fight, to work, to save, and to believe in the national war effort. Warring nations learned how to organize enthusiasm and how to mobilize the masses in support of what proved to be a long and bloody conflict.

Look at the poster on the top of the facing page. Here is a dramatic appeal to German women to support war work. A stern soldier whose visage and bearing communicate strength and singleness of purpose is backed up by an equally determined young woman. She is in the act of handing him a grenade as she stands with him, her arm on his shoulder in support, facing the unseen enemy. Grenades hang from his belt and from his left hand, giving us the sense that he is able to enter battle properly armed thanks to this dedicated woman's efforts. The poster is a good representation of the centrality of women's work to the waging of a new kind of war in the twentieth century. The battlefront had to be backed up by a "home front"—the term used for the first time in the Great War—of working men, women, and even children. The poster communicates the dignity and worth that lay in the concerted partnership of soldiers and civilians to defeat the enemy.

Early war posters stressed justice and national glory. Later, as weariness with the war spread, the need for personal sacrifice became the dominant theme. Look at the sad female figure rising from a sea of suffering and death on the bottom of the facing page. The woman, both goddess-like and vulnerable, symbolizes Great Britain. She is making a strong visual plea for action, seeking soldiers for her cause. This appeal for volunteers for the armed forces was unique to Great Britain, where conscription was not established until 1916. Yet the image is typical of every nation's reliance on a noble female symbol to emphasize the justice of its cause. The dark suffering and death in the water, lapping at her robes, are reflected in her eyes. She evinces a fierce determination as she exhorts, "Take up the sword of justice." In February 1915 Germany declared the waters around the British Isles to be a war zone. All British shipping was subject to attack as well as neutral merchant vessels, which were attacked without warning. In May 1915 the *Lusitania* was sunk, taking with it over 1,000 lives, including 128 Americans. The poster frames an illuminated horizon where a ship that is probably the *Lusitania* goes down. We need not read a word to understand the call to arms against the perfidy of an enemy who has killed innocent civilians. The female figure's determined jaw, clenched fist, and outstretched arms communicate the nobility of the cause and the certainty of success.

Civilians had to be mobilized for two reasons. First, it became evident early in the fighting that the costs of the war were high in human lives. Soldiers at the front had to be constantly replenished from civilian reserves. Second, the costs of the war in food, equipment, and productive materials were so high that civilian populations had to be willing to endure great hardships and to sacrifice their own well-being to produce supplies for soldiers at the front. Advertising was used by nations at war to coordinate civilian and military contributions to a common cause.

The European governments proudly "selling" war to their citizens in 1914 expected quick victories and the triumph of their cause. Instead, what they got was a prolonged global war, costly in human life and material destruction, stretching out over four miserable years. Military technology and timetables called the tune in a defensive war fought from the trenches with sophisticated weapons capable of maiming and killing in new ways. Selling the Great War required selectively communicating information and inspiring belief and a commitment to total victory, no matter how high the cost.

The War Europe Expected

In 1914 Europe stood confidently at the center of the world. Covering only 7 percent of the earth's surface, it dominated the world's trade and was actively exporting both European goods and European culture all over the globe. Proud of the progress and prosperity of urban industrial society, Europeans had harnessed nature to transform their environment. They extended their influence beyond the confines of their continent, sure that their achievements marked the pinnacle of civilization.

The values of nineteenth-century liberalism permeated the self-confident worldview of European men and women in 1914. They assumed they could discover the rules that governed the world and use them to fashion a better civilization. Many Europeans took stability and harmony for granted as preconditions for progress. Yet they also recognized the utility of war. In recent times, local confrontations between European states in Africa had been successfully contained in bids for increased territory. While warfare was accepted as an instrument of policy, no one expected or wanted a general war. Liberal values served the goals of limited war, just as they had justified imperial conquest. Statesmen decided there were rules to the game of war that could be employed in the interests of statecraft. Science and technology also served war makers. Modern weapons, statesmen and generals were sure, would prevent a long war. Superiority in armed force became a priority for European states seeking to protect the peace.

The beginning of the modern arms race resulted in "armed peace" as a defense against war. Leaders nevertheless expected and planned for a war, short and limited, in which the fittest and most advanced nation would win. Previous confrontations among European states had been limited in duration and destruction, as in the case of Prussia and France in 1870, or confined to peripheries, as squabbles among the Great Powers in Africa indicated. The alliance system was expected to defend the peace by defining the conditions of war.

As international tensions mounted, the hot summer days of 1914 were a time of hope and glory. The hope was that war, when it came, would be "over by Christmas." The glory was the promise of ultimate victory in the "crusade for civilization" that each nation's leaders held out to their people. When war did come in 1914, it was a choice, not an accident. Yet it was a choice that Europeans did not understand, one whose limits they could not control. Their unquestioned pride in reason and progress that had ironically led them to this war did not survive the four years of barbaric slaughter that followed.

Separating Friends From Foes

At the end of the nineteenth century, the world appeared to be coming together in a vast international network linked by commerce and finance. A system of alliances based on shared interests also connected states to one another. After 1905, the intricate defensive alliances between and among the European states maintained the balance of power between two blocs of nations and helped prevent one bloc from dominating the other. Yet by creating blocs, alliances identified foes as well as friends. On the eve of the war, France, Great Britain, and Russia stood together in the Triple Entente. Since 1882, Germany, Austria-Hungary, and Italy had joined forces in the Triple Alliance. Other states allied with one or the other of these blocs in pacts of mutual interest and protection. Throughout the world, whether in North Africa, the Balkans, or Asia, the power of some states was intended to balance off the power of others. Yet the balance of power did not exist simply to preserve the peace. It existed to preserve a system of independent national societies—nation-states—in a precarious equilibrium. Gains in one area by one bloc had to be offset by compromises in another to maintain the balance. Nations recognized limited conflict as a legitimate means of preserving equilibrium.

The alliance system of blocs reflected the growing impact of public opinion on international relations. Statesmen had the ability to manipulate the newspaper images of allies as good and rivals as evil. But controlling public opinion served to lock policy makers into permanent partnerships and "blank checks" of support for their allies. Western leaders understood that swings in public opinion in periods of crisis could hobble their efforts in the national interest. Permanent military alliances with clearly identified "friends," therefore, took the place of more fluid arrangements.

Although alliances that guaranteed military support did not cause war, they did permit weak nations to act irresponsibly, with the certainty that they would be defended by their more powerful partners. France and Germany were publicly committed to their weaker allies Russia and Austria-Hungary, respectively, in supporting imperialist ambitions in the Balkans from which they themselves derived little direct benefit. Because of treaty commitments, no country expected to face war alone. The interlocking system of defensive alliances was structured to match strength against strength—France against Germany, for example—thereby making

A pre-World War I Spanish cartoon satirizes the militant diplomacy of the era. European nations are playing billiards with cannonballs, the cues are rifles and swords, and the playing field is the map of Europe.

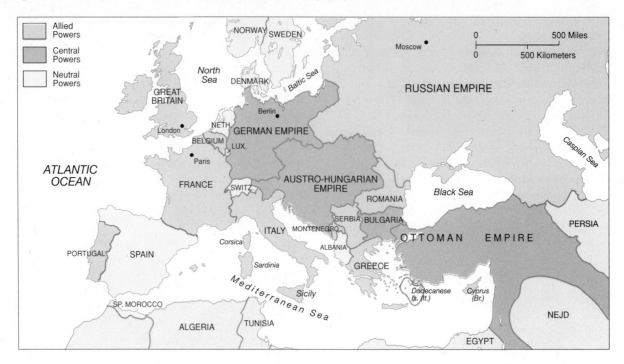

European Alliances on the Eve of World War I

Military Timetables

As Europe soon discovered, military timetables restricted the choices of leaders at times of conflict. The crisis of the summer of 1914 revealed the extent to which politicians and statesmen had come to rely on military expertise and strategic considerations for decisions. Military general staffs assumed increasing importance in state policy making. War planners became powerful, as war was accepted as an alternative to the negotiation of differences. Germany's military preparations are a good example of how war strategy exacerbated crises and prevented peaceful solutions.

Alfred von Schlieffen (1833–1913), the Prussian general and chief of the German General Staff from 1891 to 1905, who developed the war plan, understood little about politics but spent his life studying the strategic challenges of warfare. His war plan was designed to make Germany the greatest power on the Continent. The Schlieffen Plan, which he set before his fellow officers in 1905, was a bold and daring one: in the likely

a prolonged war more likely than would be the case if a weak nation confronted a strong enemy. At base, the alliance system stood as both a defense against war and an invitation to it.

event of war with Russia, Germany would launch a devastating offensive against France. Schlieffen reasoned that France was a strong military presence that would come to the aid of its ally, Russia. Russia, lacking a modern transportation system, could not mobilize as rapidly as France.

Russia also had the inestimable advantage of the ability to retreat into its vast interior. If Germany were pulled into a war with Russia, its western frontier would be vulnerable to France, Russia's powerful ally. The Schlieffen Plan recognized that France must first be defeated in the west before Germany could turn its forces to the task of defeating Russia. The Schlieffen Plan thus committed Germany to a war with France regardless of particular circumstances. Furthermore, the plan, with its strategy of invading the neutral countries of Belgium, Holland, and Luxembourg in order to defeat France in six weeks, ignored the rights of the neutral countries.

Germany was not alone in being driven by military timetables when conflicts arose. Russian military strategists planned full mobilization if war broke out with Austria-Hungary, which was menacing the interests of Russia's ally Serbia. Russia foresaw the likelihood that Germany would come to the aid of Austria-Hungary. Russia knew, too, that because of its primitive railway

Austrian archduke Franz Ferdinand and his wife Sophie leave the Senate House in Sarajevo on 28 June 1914. Five minutes later, Serbian terrorist Gavrilo Princip assassinated the couple.

network it would be unable to mobilize troops rapidly. In order to compensate for this weakness, Russian leaders planned to mobilize *before* war was declared. German military leaders had no choice in the event of full Russian mobilization but to mobilize their own troops immediately and to urge the declaration of war. There was no chance of containing the conflict once a general mobilization on both sides was under way. Mobilization would mean war.

Like the Schlieffen Plan, the French Plan XVII called for the concentration of troops in a single area with the intention of decisively defeating the enemy. The French command, not well informed about German strengths and strategies, designated Alsace and Lorraine for the immediate offensive against Germany in the

event of war. Plan XVII left Paris exposed to the German drive through Belgium called for in the Schlieffen Plan.

Military leaders throughout Europe argued that if their plans were to succeed, speed was essential. Delays to consider peaceful solutions would cripple military responses. Diplomacy bowed to military strategy. When orders to mobilize went out, armies would be set on the march. Like a row of dominoes falling with the initial push, the two alliance systems would be at war.

Assassination at Sarajevo

A teenager with a handgun started the First World War. On 28 June 1914, in Sarajevo, the sleepy capital of the Austro-Hungarian province of Bosnia, Gavrilo Princip

GERMAN WAR AIMS

■ *Theobald von Bethmann Hollweg (1856–1921) was chancellor of Germany from 1909 to 1917. Known as a moderate who did not desire war, he nevertheless drew up a statement of "war aims" in September 1914, a month after the outbreak of hostilities. This chilling document, which he intended to implement once Germany was victorious, was no less than a redrawing of the map of Europe with Germany as supreme power. Bethmann Hollweg's vision of a German-dominated Mitteleuropa was deliberately kept a secret; as he explained to a close colleague, "We are keeping all the cards in our hand hidden from the enemy's eyes."*

BETHMANN-HOLLWEG'S PROVISIONAL NOTES ON THE DIRECTION OF POLICY ON THE CONCLUSION OF PEACE, 9 SEPTEMBER 1914.

[The] general aim of the war [is] security for the German Reich in west and east for all imaginable time. For this purpose France must be so weakened as to make her revival as a great power impossible for all time. Russia must be thrust back as far as possible from Germany's eastern frontier and her domination over the non-Russian vassal peoples broken.

1. France. The military to decide whether we should demand cession of Belfort and western slopes of the Vosges, razing of fortresses and cession of coastal strip from Dunkirk to Boulogne.

The ore-field of Briey, which is necessary for the supply of ore for our industry, to be ceded in any case.

Further, a war indemnity, to be paid in instalments; it must be high enough to prevent France from spending any considerable sums on armaments in the next 15–20 years.

Furthermore: a commercial treaty which makes France economically dependent on Germany, secures the French market for our exports and makes it possible to exclude British commerce from France. This treaty must secure for us financial and industrial freedom of movement in France in such fashion that German enterprises can no longer receive different treatment from French.

2. Belgium. Liège and Verviers to be attached to Prussia, a frontier strip of the province of Luxemburg to Luxemburg.

Question whether Antwerp, with a corridor to Liège, should also be annexed remains open.

At any rate Belgium, even if allowed to continue to exist as a state, must be reduced to a vassal state, must allow us to occupy any militarily important ports, must place her coast at our disposal in

---

(1895–1918), a nineteen-year-old Bosnian Serb, repeatedly pulled the trigger of his Browning revolver, killing the designated heir of the Habsburg throne, Archduke Franz Ferdinand and his wife, Sophie. Princip belonged to the Young Bosnian Society, a group of students, workers, a few peasants, Croats, Muslims, and intellectuals, who wanted to free Slavic populations from Habsburg control. Princip was part of a growing movement of South Slavs struggling for national liberation, who believed they were being held in colonial servitude by Austria-Hungary.

Struggle over control of the Balkans had been a longstanding issue that had involved all the major European powers for decades. As Austria-Hungary's ally since 1879, Germany was willing to support Vienna's showdown in the Balkans as a way of stopping Russian advances in the area. The alliance with Germany gave

Austria-Hungary a sense of security and confidence to pursue its Balkan aims. Germany had its own plans for domination of the Continent and feared a weakened Austria-Hungary would undermine its own position in central Europe. Independent Balkan states to the south and east were also a threat to Germany's plans. German leaders hoped that an Austro-Serbian war would remain localized and would strengthen their ally, Austria-Hungary. While Austria-Hungary had Germany's support, Serbia was backed by a sympathetic Russia that favored nationalist movements in the Balkans. Russia had, in turn, been encouraged by France, its ally by military pact since 1894, to take a firm stand in its struggle with Austria-Hungary for dominance among Balkan nationalities.

The interim of five weeks between the assassination of the Archduke Ferdinand and the outbreak of the war

GERMAN WAR AIMS

military respects, must become economically a German province. Given such a solution, which offers the advantages of annexation without its inescapable domestic political disadvantages, French Flanders with Dunkirk, Calais and Boulogne, where most of the population is Flemish, can without danger be attached to this unaltered Belgium. The competent quarters will have to judge the military value of this position against England.

3. Luxemburg. Will become a German federal state and will receive a strip of the present Belgian province of Luxemburg and perhaps the corner of Longwy.

4. We must create a *central European economic association* through common customs treaties, to include France, Belgium, Holland, Denmark, Austria-Hungary, Poland [sic], and perhaps Italy, Sweden and Norway. This association will not have any common constitutional supreme authority and all its members will be formally equal, but in practice will be under German leadership and must stabilise Germany's economic dominance over Mitteleuropa.

5. The question of colonial acquisitions, where the first aim is the creation of a continuous Central African colonial empire, will be considered later, as will that of the aims to be realised *vis-à-vis* Russia.

6. A short provisional formula suitable for a possible preliminary peace to be found for a basis for the economic agreements to be concluded with France and Belgium.

7. Holland. It will have to be considered by what means and methods Holland can be brought into closer relationship with the German Empire.

In view of the Dutch character, this closer relationship must leave them free of any feeling of compulsion, must alter nothing in the Dutch way of life, and must also subject them to no new military obligations. Holland, then, must be left independent in externals, but be made internally dependent on us. Possibly one might consider an offensive and defensive alliance, to cover the colonies; in any case a close customs association, perhaps the cession of Antwerp to Holland in return for the right to keep a German garrison in the fortress of Antwerp and at the mouth of the Scheldt.

---

was a period of intense diplomatic activity. The assassination gave Austria-Hungary the excuse it needed to bring a troublesome Serbia into line. Austria-Hungary held Serbia responsible for the shootings. Leaders in Vienna had no evidence at the time to justify their allegations of a Serbian conspiracy, but they saw in this event the perfect pretext for military action. On 23 July 1914, Austria-Hungary issued an ultimatum to the small Balkan nation and secretly decided to declare war regardless of Serbia's response. The demands were so severe that, if met, they would have stripped Serbia of its independence. Austria's aim was to destroy Serbia. In spite of a conciliatory, although not capitulatory, reply from Serbia to its ultimatum, Austria-Hungary declared war on the Balkan nation on 28 July 1914. Russia mobilized two days after the Austro-Hungarian declaration of war against Serbia. Germany mobilized in response to the Russian action and declared war on Russia on 1 August and on France on 3 August. France had begun mobilizing on 30 July, when its ally, Russia, entered the war.

Great Britain stood briefly outside the fray in the futile attempt to mediate a settlement in the Austro-Serbian conflict. Britain's dependence on its alliance with France as a means of protecting British sea routes in the Mediterranean meant that Great Britain could not remain neutral once France declared war. The domino effect of the alliance system meant that one by one each of the European nations stood by their friends by declaring war on their foes. On 4 August, after Germany had violated Belgian neutrality in its march to France, Great Britain honored its treaty obligations and declared war on Germany. Great Britain entered the war because it judged that a powerful Germany could use ports on the English Channel to invade the British Isles. Italy alone of the major powers remained for the moment outside the conflict. Although allied with Germany and Austria-Hungary, its own aspirations in the Balkans kept it from fighting for the Austrian cause in 1914.

Self-interest, fear, and ambition motivated the Great Powers in different ways in the pursuit of war. The international diplomatic system that had worked so well to prevent war in the preceding decades now enmeshed European states in interlocking alliances and created a chain reaction. The Austro-Serbian war of July 1914 became a Europe-wide war within a month.

The expectation of a speedy war of decisive victories and domestic glory drove European leaders and their populations to embrace armed conflict as an acceptable means of mediating grievances in 1914. The peace that had been preserved from the end of the nineteenth century to 1914 was a precarious one indeed, predicated as it was on military timetables that planned for war and alliance systems that guaranteed that local disagreements would become international conflicts. The international mechanisms for keeping the peace led directly to war and guaranteed that once war broke out, it would not remain limited and local.

The War Europe Got

Early in the war, the best-laid plans of political and military leaders collapsed. First, Europe got a war that was not limited but one that quickly spread throughout Europe and became global. Switzerland, Spain, the Netherlands, and all of Scandinavia remained neutral, but every other European nation was pulled into the war. In August 1914 Japan cast its lot with the Allies, as the Entente came to be known, and in November the Ottoman Empire joined the Central Powers of Germany and Austria-Hungary. In the following year Italy joined the war, not on the side of its long-term treaty partners, Germany and Austria-Hungary, but on the side of the Allies, with the expectation of benefiting in the Balkans from Austrian defeat. Bulgaria joined Germany and Austria-Hungary in 1915, seeking territory at Serbia's expense. By the time of the United States' entry in 1917, the war had become a world war.

The second surprise for the European powers was that they did not get a preventive war of movement, nor one of short duration. Within weeks, that pattern had given way to what promised to be a long and costly war of attrition. All started as Schlieffen's successors had planned, with German victory in battle after battle. The end seemed near. But in the space of less than a month the war changed in ways that no one had predicted. Technology was the key to understanding the change and to explaining the surprises.

Technology and the Trenches

In the history of nineteenth-century European warfare, armies had relied on mobile cavalry and infantry units whose greatest asset was speed. Rapid advance had been decisive in the Prussian victory over the French in 1870, which had resulted in the formation of the German Empire. Soldiers of the twentieth century were also trained for a moving war, high maneuverability, and maximum territorial conquest. Yet after the first six weeks of battle, soldiers were ordered to do something unimaginable to strategists of European warfare: they were ordered to dig ditches and fight from fixed positions. Soldiers on both sides shoveled out trenches four feet deep, piled up sandbags, mounted their machine guns, and began to fight an unplanned, defensive war.

The front lines of Europe's armies in the west wallowed within the four hundred miles of trenches that ran from the English Channel to the Swiss frontier. The British and French on one side and the Germans on the other fought each other with machine guns and mortars, backed up by heavy artillery to the rear. Strategists on both sides believed they could break through enemy lines. As a result, the monotony of trench warfare was punctuated periodically by infantry offensives in which immense concentrations of artillery caused great bloodshed. Ten million men were killed in this bizarre and deadly combination of old and new warfare. The glamour of battle that attracted many young men disappeared quickly in the daily reality of living in mud with rats and constantly facing death. The British poet Wilfred Owen (1893–1918) wrote shortly before his own death in battle about how the soldier next to him had been shot in the head, soaking Owen in blood: "I shall feel again as soon as I dare, but now I must not."

The invention of new weaponry and heavy equipment had transformed war into an enterprise of increasing complexity. Military and naval staffs expanded to meet new needs of warfare. Old ways persisted. In their bright blue coats and red trousers, French and Belgian infantrymen made easy targets. Outmoded cavalry units

A typical World War I trench. Millions of soldiers lived amid mud, disease, and vermin, awaiting death from enemy shells. After the French army mutiny in 1916, the troops wrung this concession from their commanders: They did not have to charge German machine guns while armed only with rifles.

survived despite more efficient mechanization. The railroad made the mobilization, organization, and deployment of mass armies possible. Specialists were needed to control the new war machines that heavy industry had created.

It has been observed that the spade and the machine gun transformed war. The machine gun was not new in 1914, but its strategic value was not fully appreciated before then. The Maxim machine gun had been used by the British in Africa. But strategists failed to ask how a

weapon of such phenomenal destructive power would work against an enemy equally armed with machine guns instead of spears. Military strategists drew all the wrong conclusions. They continued to plan an offensive strategy when the weaponry developed for massive destruction had pushed them into fighting a defensive war from the trenches. Both sides resorted to concentration of artillery, increased use of poison gas, and unrestricted submarine warfare, in desperate attempts to break the deadlock caused by meeting armed force with force.

British machine gunners wearing gas masks at the battle of the Somme in 1916.

The necessity of total victory drove the Central Powers and the Allies to grisly new inventions. Late in the war, the need to break the deadlock of trench warfare ushered in the airplane and the tank. Neither was decisive in altering the course of the war, although the airplane was useful for reconnaissance and for limited bombing, and the tank promised the means of breaking through defensive lines. Chlorine gas was first used in warfare by the Germans in 1915. "Mustard" gas, which was named for its distinctive smell and which caused severe blistering, was introduced two years later. The Germans were the first to use flamethrowers, especially effective against mechanized vehicles with vulnerable fuel tanks. Barbed wire, invented in the U.S. Midwest to contain farm animals, became an essential aspect of trench warfare as it marked off the no-man's-land between combatants and prevented surprise attacks.

The technology that had been viewed as a proof of progress was now channeled toward engineering new instruments of death. Yet technology itself produced a stalemate. New weapons sometimes produced their antidotes; for example, the invention of deadly gas was followed soon after by gas masks. Each side was capable of matching the other's ability to devise new armaments. Deadlocks caused by technological parity forced both sides to resort to desperate concentrations of men and weaponry that resulted not in decisive battles but in ever escalating casualty rates. Improving their efficiency at killing, the European powers were not finding a way to end the war.

The Battle of the Marne

German forces seized the offensive in the west and invaded neutral Belgium at the beginning of August 1914. The Belgians resisted stubbornly but unsuccessfully. Belgian forts were systematically captured and the capital of Brussels fell under the German advance on 20 August. After the fall of Belgium, German military might swept into northern France with the intention of defeating the French in six weeks.

In the years preceding the war, the German General Staff, unwilling to concentrate all of their troops in the west, had modified the Schlieffen Plan by committing divisions to its eastern frontier. The absence of the full German fighting force in the west did not appreciably slow the German advance through Belgium. Yet the Germans had underestimated both the cost of holding back the French in Alsace-Lorraine and the difficulty of maneuvering German forces and transporting supplies in an offensive war. Eventually, unexpected Russian advances in the east also siphoned off troops from the west. German forces in the west were so weakened by the offensive that they were unable to swing west of Paris, as planned, and instead chose to enter the French capital from the northeast by crossing the Marne River. This shift exposed the German First Army on its western flank and opened up a gap on its eastern flank.

Despite an initial pattern of retreat and a lack of coordination of forces, Allied French and British troops were ready to take advantage of the vulnerabilities in the German advance. In a series of battles between 6 and 10 September 1914 that came to be known as the First Battle of the Marne, the Allies counterattacked and advanced into the gap. The German army was forced to drop back. In the following months each army tried to outflank the other in what has been called "the race to the sea." By late fall it was clear that the battles from the Marne north to the border town of Ypres in northwest Belgium near the English Channel ended an open war of movement on the western front. Soldiers now dug in along a line of battle that changed little in the long three and a half years until March 1918.

The Allies gained a strategic victory in the First Battle of the Marne by resisting the German advance in the fighting that quickly became known as the "miracle" of the Marne. The legend was further enhanced by true stories of French troops being rushed from Paris to the front in taxicabs. Yet the real significance of the Marne lay in the severe miscalculations of military leaders and statesmen on both sides, who had expected a different kind of war. They did not understand the new technology that made a short war unlikely. Nor did they understand the demands that this new kind of warfare would make on civilian populations. Those Parisian taxidrivers foreshadowed how other European civilians would be called upon again and again to support the war in the next four years. The Schlieffen Plan was dead. But it was no more a failure than any of the other military timetables of the Great Powers.

"I don't know what is to be done—this isn't war." So spoke Lord Horatio Kitchener (1850–1916), one of the most decorated British generals of his time. He was not alone in his bafflement over the stalemate of trench warfare at the end of 1914. By that time, Germany's greatest fear, a simultaneous war on two fronts, had become a grim reality. The Central Powers were under a state of siege, cut off from the world by the great battlefront in the west and by the Allied blockade at sea. The rules of the game had changed, and the European powers settled in for a long war.

War on the Eastern Front

War on Germany's eastern front was a mobile war, unlike its western counterpart, because there were relatively fewer men and guns in relation to the vast distances. The Russian army was the largest in the world. Yet it was crippled from the outbreak of the war by inadequate supplies and poor leadership. At the end of August 1914 the smaller German army, supported by divisions drawn from the west, delivered a devastating defeat to the Russians in the one great battle on the eastern front. At Tannenberg, the entire Russian Second Army was destroyed, and about 100,000 Russian soldiers were taken prisoner. Faced with this humiliation, General Aleksandr Vasilievich Samsonov (1859–1914), head of the Russian forces, committed suicide on the field of battle.

The German general Paul von Hindenburg (1847–1934), a veteran of the Franco-Prussian war of 1870, had been recalled from retirement to direct the campaign against the Russians because of his intimate knowledge of the area. Assisted by Quartermaster General Erich Ludendorff (1865–1937), Hindenburg followed the stunning victory of Tannenberg two weeks later with another devastating blow to Russian forces at the Masurian Lakes.

The Russians were holding up their end of the bargain in the Allied war effort, but at great cost. They kept the Germans busy and forced them to divert troops to the eastern front, weakening the German effort to knock France out of the war. In the south the tsar's troops defeated the Austro-Hungarian army at Lemberg in Galicia in September. This Russian victory gave Serbia a temporary reprieve. But by mid-1915 Germany had thrown the Russians back and was keeping Austria-Hungary propped up in the war. By fall Russia had lost most of Galicia, the Polish lands of the Russian empire, Lithuania, and parts of Latvia and Belorussia to the advancing enemy. These losses amounted to 15 percent of its territory and 20 percent of its population. The Russian army staggered, with over one million soldiers taken as prisoners of war and at least as many killed and wounded.

The Russian army, as one of its own officers described it, was being bled to death. Russian soldiers were poorly led into battle or not led at all because of the shortage of officers. Munitions shortages meant that soldiers often went into battle without rifles, armed only with the hope of scavenging arms from their fallen comrades. Despite these difficulties the Russians, under the direction of General Aleksei Brusilov (1853–1926), commander of the Russian armies in the southern part of the eastern front, remarkably managed to throw back the Austro-Hungarian forces in 1916 and almost eliminated Austria as a military power. But this was the last great campaign on the eastern front and Russia's last show of strength in the Great War.

Russia's near destruction of the Austrian army tremendously benefited Russia's allies. In order to protect its partner, Germany was forced to withdraw eight divisions from Italy, alleviating the Allied situation in the Tyrol, and twelve divisions from the western front, providing relief for the French at Verdun and the British at the Somme. In addition, Russia sent troops to the aid of a new member of the Allied camp, Romania, an act which probably further weakened Brusilov's efforts. In response to Brusilov's challenge, the Germans established control over the Austrian army, assigning military command of the coalition to General Ludendorff.

By the summer of 1917, the tsardom had been overthrown and a provisional government ruled Russia. Tens of thousands of Russian soldiers were walking away from the war. Russia withdrew from the war and in March 1918 signed a separate peace by which Germany gained extensive territorial advantages and important supply bases for carrying on the war in the west. To protect these territories and their resources, the Germans had to maintain an army on this front. No longer fighting in

World War I

the east, however, Germany could release the bulk of its forces to fight in the west.

War on the Western Front

Along hundreds of miles of trenches, the French and British tried repeatedly to expel the Germans from Belgium. Long periods of inactivity were punctuated by orgies of heavy bloodletting. The German phrase, "All quiet on the western front," used in military communiqués to describe those periods of silence between massive shellings and infantry attacks, reported only the uneasy calm before the next violent storm.

Military leaders on both sides cherished the dream of a decisive offensive, the breakthrough that would win the war. In 1916 the Allies planned a joint strike at the Somme, a river in northern France flowing west into the English Channel, but the Germans struck first at Verdun, a small fortress city in northeast France. By concentrating great numbers of troops, the Germans

outnumbered the French five to two. As General Erich von Falkenhayn (1861–1922), chief of the General Staff of the German army from 1914 to 1916, explained it, the German purpose in attacking Verdun was "to bleed the French white by virtue of our superiority in guns."

On the first day of battle one million shells were fired. The battlefield was a living hell as soldiers stumbled across corpse after corpse. Against the German onslaught, French troops were instructed to hold out though they lacked adequate artillery and reinforcements. General Joseph Joffre (1852–1931), commander-in-chief of the French army, was unwilling to divert reinforcements to Verdun.

The German troops advanced easily through the first lines of defense. But the French held their position for ten long, horrifying months of continuous mass slaughter from February to December 1916. General Henri Philippe Pétain (1856–1951), a local commander planning an early retirement before the war, bolstered

FROM *ALL QUIET ON THE WESTERN FRONT*

■ *Eye-witness accounts described the horrors of the new trench warfare. But no one captured the war better than the German novelist Erich Maria Remarque (1898–1970), who drew on his own wartime experiences in* All Quiet on the Western Front. *Published in 1928 and subsequently translated into twenty-five languages, this powerful portrayal of the transformation of a schoolboy into a soldier indicts the inhumanity of war and pleads for peace. Stressing the camaraderie of fighting men and sympathy for the plight of the enemy soldier, Remarque also underscored the alienation of a whole generation, the "lost generation" of young men who could not go home again after the war.*

Attack, counter-attack, charge, repulse—these are words, but what things they signify! We have lost a good many men, mostly recruits. Reinforcements have again been sent up to our sector. They are one of the new regiments, composed almost entirely of young fellows just called up. They have had hardly any training, and are sent into the field with only a theoretical knowledge. They do know what a hand-grenade is, it is true, but they have very little idea of cover, and what is most important of all, have no eye for it. A fold in the ground has to be quite eighteen inches high before they can see it.

Although we need reinforcement, the recruits give us almost more trouble than they are worth. They are helpless in this grim fighting area, they fall like flies. Modern trench-warfare demands knowledge and experience; a man must have a feeling for the contours of the ground, an ear for the sound and character of the shells, must be able to decide beforehand where they will drop, how they will burst, and how to shelter from them.

The young recruits of course know none of these things. They get killed simply because they hardly can tell shrapnel from high-explosive, they are mown down because they are listening anxiously to the roar of the big coal-boxes falling in the rear, and miss the light, piping whistle of the low spreading daisy-cutters. They flock together like sheep instead of scattering, and even the wounded are shot down like hares by the airmen.

Their pale turnip faces, their pitiful clenched hands, the fine courage of these poor devils, the desperate charges and attacks made by the poor brave wretches, who are so terrified that they dare not cry out loudly, but with battered chests, with torn bellies, arms and legs only whimper softly for their mothers and cease as soon as one looks at them.

Their sharp, downy, dead faces have the awful expressionlessness of dead children. . . .

I am young, I am twenty years old; yet I know nothing of life but despair, death, fear, and fatuous superficiality cast over an abyss of sorrow. I see how peoples are set against one another, and in silence, unknowingly, foolishly, obediently, innocently slay one another. I see that the keenest brains of the world invent weapons and words to make it yet more refined and enduring. And all men of my age, here and over there, throughout the whole world see these things; all my generation is experiencing these things with me. What would our fathers do if we suddenly stood up and came before them and proffered our account? What do they expect of us if a time ever comes when the war is over? Through the years our business has been killing;—it was our first calling in life. Our knowledge of life is limited to death. What will happen afterwards? And what shall come out of us?

morale by constantly rotating his troops to the point that most of the French army—259 of 330 infantry battalions—saw action at Verdun. Nearly starving and poorly armed, the French stood alone in the bloodiest offensive of the war. Attack strategy backfired on the Germans as their own death tolls mounted.

Pétain and his flamboyant general Robert Georges Nivelle (1856–1924) were both hailed as heroes for fulfilling the instruction to their troops: "They shall not pass." Falkenhayn fared less well and was dismissed from his post. Yet no real winners emerged from the scorched earth of Verdun, where observers could see the nearest thing to desert created in Europe. Verdun was a disaster. The French suffered over one half million total casualties. German casualties were almost as high. A few square miles of territory had changed hands back and forth. In the end, no military advantage was gained. Almost 700,000 lives were lost. The legends of brilliant leadership of Pétain and Nivelle, who both went on to greater positions of authority, and the failed command of Falkenhayn, who retired in disgrace, obscured the real lesson of the battle: an offensive war under these conditions was impossible.

Still, new offensives were devised. The British went ahead with their planned offensive on the Somme in July 1916. For an advance of seven miles, 400,000 British and 200,000 French soldiers were killed or wounded. The American writer F. Scott Fitzgerald (1896-1940), who served as an army officer in World War I, later wrote of the battle of the Somme in his novel *Tender Is the Night* (1934). One of his characters describes a visit to the Somme Valley after the war: "See that little stream. We could walk to it in two minutes. It took the British a whole month to walk to it—a whole empire walking very slowly, dying in front and pushing forward behind. And another empire walked very slowly backward a few inches a day, leaving the dead like a million bloody rugs." German losses brought the total casualties of this offensive to one million men. Despite his experience at Verdun, French general Robert Nivelle planned his own offensive in the Champagne region in spring 1917, sure that he could succeed where others had failed in "breaking the crust." The Nivelle offensive resulted in 40,000 deaths. Nivelle was dismissed. The French army was falling apart, with mutiny and insubordination everywhere.

The British believed they could succeed where the French had fallen. Under General Douglas Haig (1861-1928), the commander-in-chief of British expeditionary forces on the Continent, the British launched an attack in Flanders through the summer and fall of 1917. Known as the Passchendaele offensive, named for the village and ridge in whose "porridge of mud" much of the fighting took place, this campaign resulted in almost 400,000 British soldiers slaughtered for insignificant territorial gain. The Allies and the Germans finally recognized that "going over the top" in offensives was not working and could not work. The war must be won by other means.

This scene, near Passchendaele in 1917, shows a derelict British tank stuck in the notorious mud of Flanders. The incessant bombardments churned up the landscape and contributed to the mud that made the battlefield a hellish morass.

War on the Periphery

Recognizing the stalemate in the west, the Allies attempted to open up other fronts where the Central Powers might be vulnerable. In the spring of 1915 the Allies were successful in convincing Italy to enter the war on their side by promising that it would receive at the time of the peace the South Tyrol and the southern part of Dalmatia and key Dalmatian islands, which would assure Italy's dominance over the Adriatic Sea. By thus capitalizing on Italian antagonism toward Austria-Hungary over control of this territory, the Allies gained 875,000 Italian soldiers for their cause. Although these Italian troops were in no way decisive in the fighting that followed, Great Britain, France, and Russia saw the need to build up Allied support in southern Europe in order to reinforce Serbian attempts to keep Austrian troops beyond its borders. The Allies also hoped that by pulling Germans into this southern front, some relief might be provided for British and French soldiers on the western front.

Germany, in turn, was well aware of the need to expand its alliances beyond Austria-Hungary if it was to compete successfully against superior Allied forces. Trapped as they were to the east and west, the Central Powers established control over a broad corridor stretching from the North Sea through central Europe and down through the Ottoman Empire to the Suez Canal so vital to British interests. In the Balkans, where the war had begun, the Serbs were consistently bested by the Austrians. By late 1915 the Serbs had been knocked out of the war, in spite of allied attempts to assist them. Serbia paid a heavy price in the Great War: it lost one-sixth of its population through war, famine, and disease. The promise of booty persuaded Bulgaria to join Germany and Austria-Hungary. Over the next year and a half, the Allies responded by convincing Romania and then Greece to join them.

The theater of war continued to expand. Although the Ottoman Empire had joined the war in late 1914 on the side of the Central Powers, its own internal difficulties attenuated its fighting ability. As a multinational empire consisting of Turks, Arabs, Armenians, Greeks, Kurds, and other ethnic minorities, it was plagued by Turkish misrule and Arab nationalism. Hence the Ottoman Empire was the weakest link in the chain of German alliances. Yet it held a crucial position. The Turks could block shipping of vital supplies to Russia through the Mediterranean and the Black seas. Coming to the aid of their Russian ally, a combined British and French fleet attacked Turkish forces at the Straits of the Dardanelles in April 1915. In the face of political and military opposition, First Lord of the Admiralty Winston Churchill (1874–1965) supported the idea of opening a new front by sea. Poorly planned and mismanaged, the expedition was a disaster. When the naval effort in the German-mined Straits failed, the British foolishly decided to land troops on the Gallipoli peninsula, which extends from the southern coast of European Turkey. There British soldiers were trapped on the rocky terrain, unable to advance against the Turks, unable to fall back. Gallipoli was the first large-scale attempt at amphibious warfare. The Australian and New Zealand forces (ANZACs) showed great bravery in some of the most brutal fighting of the war. Critics in Britain argued that the only success of the nine-month campaign was its evacuation.

Britain sought to protect its interests in the Suez Canal. Turkish troops menaced the canal effectively enough to terrify the British into maintaining an elaborate system of defense in the area and concentrating large troop reinforcements in Egypt. War with the Ottoman Empire also extended battle into the oil fields of Mesopotamia and Persia. This attempt at a new front was initially a fiasco for the British and Russian forces that threatened Baghdad. The Allies proceeded not only without plans but also without maps. They literally did not know where they were going. Eventually, British forces recovered and took Baghdad in 1917, while Australian and New Zealand troops captured Jerusalem. The tentacles of war spread out, following the path of Western economic and imperial interests throughout the world.

A German submarine takes on supplies at a harbor. The U-boats became widespread military weapons because of their effectiveness in surprise attack. These "iron coffins" were to take a terrible toll on Allied shipping in World War II.

Most surprising of all was the indecisive nature of the war at sea. The great battleships of the British and German navies avoided confrontation on the high seas. The only major naval battle of the Great War, the Battle of Jutland in the North Sea, took place in early 1916. Each side inflicted damage on the other but, through careful maneuvering, avoided a decisive outcome to the battle. Probably the enormous cost of replacing battleships deterred both the British and the Germans from risking their fleets in engagements on the high seas. With the demands for munitions and equipment on the two great land fronts of the war, neither side could afford to lose a traditional war at sea. Instead, the British used their seapower as a policing force to blockade German trade and strangle the German economy.

The German navy, much weaker than the British, relied on a new weapon, the submarine, which threatened to become decisive in the war at sea. Submarines were initially used in the first months of the war for reconnaissance. Their potential for inflicting heavy losses on commercial shipping became apparent in 1915. Undergoing technological improvements throughout the war, U-boats, or *Unterseebooten* as German submarines were called, torpedoed six million tons of Allied shipping in 1917. With cruising ranges as high as 3,600 miles, German submarines attacked Allied and neutral shipping as far away as off the shore of the United States and the Arctic supply line to Russia. German insistence on unrestricted use outraged neutral powers, who considered the Germans in violation of international law. The Germans rejected the requirements of warning an enemy ship and boarding it for investigation as too dangerous for submarines, which were no match for battleships above water. The Allies invented depth charges and mines capable of blowing German submarines out of the water. These weapons, combined with the use of the convoy system in the Atlantic and the Mediterranean, produced a successful blockade and antisubmarine campaign that put an end to the German advantage.

The war that Europe got differed from all previous experiences and expectations of armed conflict. Technological advances, equally matched on both sides, introduced a war of attrition, defensive and prolonged. Nineteenth-century wars that lasted six to eight weeks, were confined to one locale, and were determined by a handful of battles marked by low casualties, had nothing in common with the long, dirty, lice-infested reality of trench warfare. Warring European nations faced enemies to the west, to the east, and on the periphery, with no end in sight to the slaughter.

Adjusting to the Unexpected: Total War

The period from 1914 to 1918 marked the first time in history that the productive activities of entire populations were directed toward a single goal: military victory. The Great War became a war of peoples, not just of armies. Wars throughout history have involved noncombatants caught in the cross fire or standing in the wrong place at the wrong time. But this unexpected war of attrition required civilian populations to adjust to a situation in which what went on at the battlefront transformed life on the home front. For this reason, the Great War became known as history's first *total* war.

Adjusting to the unexpected war of 1914, governments intervened to centralize and control every aspect of economic life. Technology and industrial capacity made possible a war of unimaginable destruction. The scale of production and distribution of war-related materials required for victory was unprecedented. To persuade civilians to suffer at home for the sake of the war, leaders pictured the enemy as an evil villain who must be defeated at any cost. The sacrifice required for a total war made total victory necessary. And total victory required an economy totally geared to fighting the war.

Mobilizing the Home Front

While soldiers were fighting on the eastern and western fronts, businessmen and politicians at home were creating bureaucratic administrations to control wages and prices, distribute supplies, establish production quotas, and, in general, mobilize human and material resources. Just as governments had conscripted the active male population for military service, the Allies and the Central Powers now mobilized civilians of all ages and both sexes to work for the war.

Women played an essential role in the mobilization of the home front. They had never been isolated from the experiences and hardships of war, but they now found new ways to support the war effort. In cities women went to work in munitions factories and war-related industries that had previously employed only men. Women filled service jobs, from firefighters to trolley-car conductors, jobs that were essential to the smooth running of industrial society and that had been left vacant by men. On farms women literally took up the plow, as both men and horses were requisitioned for the war effort.

During World War I, women workers flocked to the munitions plants to take the place of men who had marched off to war. The women above are operating cranes in a shell-filling factory.

By 1918, 650,000 French women were working in war-related industries and in clerical positions in the army. And they had counterparts all over Europe. In Germany, two out of every five munitions workers were women. Women became more prominent in the workforce as a whole, as the case of Great Britain makes clear: there the number of women workers jumped from 250,000 at the beginning of the war to five million by the war's end. Women also served in the auxiliary units of the armed services in the clerical and medical corps in order to free men for fighting at the front. In eastern European nations, women entered combat as soldiers. Although most women were displaced from their wartime jobs with the return of men after the armistice, they were as important to the war effort as men fighting at the front.

In the first months of the war the private sector had been left to its own devices with nearly disastrous re-sults. Shortages, especially of shells, and bottlenecks in production threatened military efforts. Governments were forced to establish controls and to set up state monopolies in order to guarantee the supplies necessary to wage war. In Germany, industrialists Walter Rathenau (1867–1922) and Alfred Hugenberg (1865–1951) worked with the government. By the spring of 1915, they had eliminated the German problem of munitions scarcity. France was in trouble six weeks after the outbreak of the war: it had used up half of its accumulated munitions supplies in the First Battle of the Marne. German occupation of France's northern industrial basin further crippled munitions production. Through government intervention, France improvised and relocated its war industries. The British government got involved in production, too, by establishing in 1915 the first Ministry of Munitions under the direction of David Lloyd George (1863–1945). Distinct from the Ministry of War, the Ministry of Munitions was to coordinate military needs with the armaments industry.

In a war that leaders soon realized would be a long one, food supplies assumed paramount importance. Germany, dependent on food imports to feed its people and isolated from the world market by the Allied blockade, introduced rationing five months after the outbreak of the war. Other Continental nations followed suit. Government agents set quotas for agricultural producers. Armies were fed and supplied at the expense of domestic populations. Great Britain, which enjoyed a more reliable food supply by virtue of its sea power, did not impose food rationing until 1917.

Three factors put food supplies at risk. First, the need for large numbers of soldiers at the front pulled farmers and peasants off the land. The resultant drop in the agricultural workforce meant that land was taken out of production and what remained was less efficiently cultivated. Productivity declined. A second factor was fear of requisitioning and the general uncertainties of war that caused agricultural producers to hoard supplies. What little was available was traded on black markets. Finally, because all European countries depended to some extent on imports of food and fertilizers, enemies successfully targeted trade routes for attack.

Silencing Dissent

The strains of total war were becoming apparent. Two years of sacrificing, scrimping, and, in some areas, starving began to take their toll among soldiers and civilians on both sides. With the lack of decisive victories, war weariness was spreading. Work stoppages and strikes, which had virtually ceased with the outbreak of war in 1914, began to climb rapidly in 1916. Between 1915 and 1916 in France, the number of strikes by dissatisfied workers increased by 400 percent. Underpaid and tired workers went on strike, staged demonstrations, and protested exploitation. Labor militancy also intensified in the British Isles and Germany. Women, breadwinners for their families, were often in the forefront of these protests throughout Europe. Social peace between unions and governments was no longer held together by patriotic enthusiasm for war.

Politicians, too, began to rethink their suspension of opposition to government policies as the war dragged on. Dissidents among European socialist parties regained their prewar commitment to peace. Most Socialists had enthusiastically supported the declarations of war in 1914. By 1916, the united front that political opponents had presented against the enemy was crumbling under growing demands for peace.

In a total war unrest at home guaranteed defeat. Governments knew that all opposition to war policies had to be eliminated. In a dramatic extension of the police powers of the state, both among the Allies and the Central Powers, criticism of the government became treason. Censorship was enforced. Propaganda became more virulent. Those who spoke for peace were no better than the enemy. The governments of every warring nation resorted to harsh measures. Parliamentary bodies were stripped of power, civil liberties were suspended, democratic procedures were ignored. The civilian governments of Premier Georges Clemenceau (1841–1929) in France and Prime Minister Lloyd George in Great Britain resorted to rule by emergency police power to repress criticism. Under Generals von Hindenburg and Ludendorff in Germany, military rule became the order of the day. Nowhere was government as usual possible in total war.

Every warring nation sought to promote dissension from within the societies of its enemies. Germany provided some aid for the Easter Rebellion in Ireland in 1916 in the hope that the Irish demand for independence that predated the war would deflect British attention and undermine fighting strength and morale. Germany also supported separatist movements among minority nationalities in the Russian empire and was responsible for returning the avowed revolutionary V.I. Lenin under escort to Russia in April 1917. The British engaged in similar tactics. The British foreign secretary

Arthur Balfour (1848–1930) worked with Zionist leaders in 1917 in drawing up the Balfour Declaration, which promised to "look with favor" on the creation of a Jewish homeland in Palestine. The British thereby encouraged Zionist hopes among central European Jews, with the intent of creating difficulties for German and Austrian rulers. Similarly, the British encouraged Arabs to rebel against Turks with the same promise of Palestine. Undermining the loyalties of colonized peoples and minorities would be at minimum a nuisance to the enemy. Beyond that, it could erode war efforts from within.

Turning Point and Victory, 1917–1918

For the Allies, 1917 began with a series of crises. Under the hammering of one costly offensive after another, French morale had collapsed and military discipline was deteriorating. A combined German-Austrian force had eliminated the Allied states of Serbia and Romania. The Italians experienced a military debacle at Caporetto and were effectively out of the war.

The year 1917 was "the blackest year of the war" for the Allies. At the beginning of the year, the peril on the sea had increased with the opening of unrestricted U-boat warfare against Allied and neutral shipping. The greatest blow came when Russia, now in the throes of domestic revolution, withdrew. Germany was able to concentrate more of its resources in the west and fight a one-front war. Perhaps more significantly, it was able to utilize the foodstuffs and raw materials of its newly acquired Russian territories to buoy its home front.

Yet in spite of Allied reversals, it was not at all the case that the war was turning in favor of the Central Powers. Both Austria-Hungary and the Ottoman Empire teetered on the verge of collapse, with internal difficulties increasing as the war dragged on. Germany suffered from labor and supply shortages and economic hardship, resulting from the blockade and an economy totally dedicated to waging war.

The war had gone from a stalemate to a state of crisis for both sides. Every belligerent state was experiencing war weariness that undermined civilian and military morale. Pressures to end the war increased everywhere. Attrition was not working. Attacks were not working. Every country suffered on the home front and battlefront from strikes, food riots, military desertions, and mutinies. Defeatism was everywhere on the rise.

The Allies longed for the entry of the United States into the war. Although the United States was a neutral country, it had become an important supplier to the Allies from early in the war. Trade with the Allies had jumped from $825 million in 1914 to $3.2 billion in 1916. American bankers also made loans and extended credit to the Allies to the amount of $2.2 billion. The United States had made a sizable investment in the Allied war effort, and its economy was prospering.

Beginning with the sinking of the *Lusitania* in 1915, German policy on the high seas had incensed the American public. Increased U-boat activity in 1916 led U.S. President Woodrow Wilson (1856–1924) to issue a severe warning to the Germans to cease submarine warfare. The Germans, however, were driven to desperate measures. The great advantage of submarines was in sneak attacks, a procedure against the international rules that required a warning. Germany initiated a new phase of unrestricted submarine warfare on 1 February 1917, when the German ambassador informed the U.S. government that U-boats would sink on sight all ships, including passenger ships, even those neutral and unarmed.

German machinations in Mexico were also revealed on 25 February 1917, with the interception of a telegram from Arthur Zimmermann (1864–1940), the German foreign minister. The telegram communicated Germany's willingness to support Mexico's recovery of "lost territory" in New Mexico, Arizona, and Texas in return for Mexican support of Germany in the event of U.S. entry into the war. U.S. citizens were outraged. On 2 April 1917, Wilson, who had won the presidential election of 1916 on the promise of peace, asked the U.S. Congress for a declaration of war against Germany.

U.S. entry was the turning point in the war, tipping the scales dramatically in favor of the Allies. The United States contributed its naval power to the large Allied convoys formed to protect shipping against German attacks. In a total war, control and shipment of resources had become crucial issues, and it was in these areas that the U.S. entry gave the Allies indisputable superiority. The United States was also able to send "over there" tens of thousands of conscripts fighting with the American Expeditionary Forces under the leadership of General John "Black Jack" Pershing (1860–1948). They reinforced British and French troops and gave a vital boost to morale.

For such a rich nation, however, the help that the United States was able to give was at first very little. The U.S. government was new to the business of coordinating a war effort, but it displayed great ingenuity in

Fighting the Great War

1905	Development of the Schlieffen Plan
28 July 1914	Assassination of Archduke Franz Ferdinand and wife Sophie
28 July 1914	Austria-Hungary declares war on Serbia
30 July–4 August	Germany, Russia, France, and Britain declare war in accordance with system of alliances
August 1914	Germany defeats Russia at battle of Tannenberg
6–10 September 1914	First battle of the Marne
1915	Germany first uses chlorine gas as weapon
April 1915–January 1916	British/French campaign at Gallipoli
May 1915	Sinking of the *Lusitania*
February–December	German offensive at Verdun
July 1916	Allied offensive on the Somme
1917	First use of mustard gas
1 February 1917	Germany opens unrestricted U-boat warfare
2 April 1917	United States enters the war
March 1918	Russia signs separate peace treaty with Germany
21 March 1918	Germany starts Ludendorff offensive
11 November 1918	Armistice
28 June 1919	Treaty of Versailles

creating a wartime bureaucracy that increased a small military establishment of 210,000 soldiers to 9.5 million young men registered before the beginning of summer 1917. By July 1918, the Americans were sending a phenomenal 300,000 soldiers a month to Europe. By the end of the war 2 million Americans had traveled to Europe to fight in the war.

The U.S. entry is significant not just because it provided reinforcements, fresh troops, and fresh supplies to the beleaguered Allies. From a broader perspective, it marked a shift in the nature of international politics: Europe was no longer able to handle its own affairs and settle its own differences without outside help.

U.S. troops, although numerous, were not well trained and they relied on France and Great Britain for their arms and equipment. But the Germans correctly understood that they could not hold out indefinitely against this superior Allied force. Austria-Hungary was effectively out of the war. Germany had no replacements for its fallen soldiers, but it was able to transfer troops from Russia, Romania, and Macedonia to the west. It realized its only chance of victory lay in swift action. The German high command decided on a bold measure: one great, final offensive that would knock the combined forces of Great Britain, France, and the United States out of the war once and for all by striking at a weak point and smashing through enemy lines. The great surprise was that it almost worked.

Known as the Ludendorff offensive, after the general who devised it, the final German push began in March 1918. Secretly amassing tired troops from the eastern front pulled back after the Russian withdrawal, the Germans counted on the element of surprise to enable them to break through a weak sector in the west. On the first day of spring Ludendorff struck. The larger German force gained initial success against weakened British and French forces. Yet in spite of breaches in defense, the Allied line held. Allied Supreme Commander, General Ferdinand Foch (1851–1929), coordinated the war effort that withstood German offensives throughout the spring and early summer of 1918.

The final drive came in mid-July. More than one million German soldiers had already been killed, wounded, or captured in the months between March and July. German prisoners of war gave the French details of Ludendorff's plan. The Germans, now exposed and vulnerable, were placed on the defensive. The German army was rapidly disintegrating. On the other side, tanks, plentiful munitions, and U.S. reinforcements fueled an Allied offensive that began in late September. The German army retreated, destroying property and equipment as it went. With weak political leadership and indecision in Berlin, the Germans held on until early November. The end finally came after four years of war. On 11 November 1918, an armistice signed by representatives of the German and Allied forces took effect.

Thus came to an end a war of slightly more than four years' duration that had consumed the soldiers, matériel, and productive resources of the European nations on both sides. Europeans had prided themselves on representing the pinnacle of civilization against the barbarians of other continents. Yet nothing matched the destructiveness of the Great War. Of the 70 million who were mobilized, about one in eight were killed. Battlefields of scorched earth and mud-filled ditches, silent at last, scarred once-fertile countrysides as grim memorials to history's first total war. Home fronts, too, served as battlefields, with those who demanded peace silenced as traitors. In the end, only the entry of the United States into the war on the side of the Allies brought an end to the human misery and staggering bloodletting. The war to end all wars was over; the task of settling the peace now loomed.

Reshaping Europe: After War and Revolution

In the aftermath of war, the task of the victors was to define the terms of a settlement that would guarantee peace and stabilize Europe. Russia was the ghost at the conference table, excluded from the negotiations because of its withdrawal from the Allied camp in 1917 and its separate peace with Germany in March 1918. The

Allied flags are paraded on Armistice Day in Vincennes, France. The long ordeal was over, but the relief and joy soon faded as the bitterness of the peace terms corroded postwar Europe.

Bolsheviks were dealing with problems of their own following the revolution, including a great civil war lasting through 1920. Much of what happened in the peace settlements reflected the unspoken concern with the challenge of revolution that the new Soviet Russia represented.

A variety of goals marked the peace talks: the idealistic desire to create a better world, the patriotic pursuit of self-defense, the commitment to self-determination of nations, and the fixing of blame for the outbreak of the war. In the end, the peace treaties satisfied none of these goals. Meanwhile, Russia's new leaders carefully watched events in the west, looking for opportunities that might permit them to extend their revolution to central Europe.

Settling the Peace

From January to June 1919, an assembly of nations convened in Paris to draw up the new European peace. Although the primary task of settling the peace fell to the Council of Four—Premier Georges Clemenceau of France, Prime Minister David Lloyd George of Great Britain, Prime Minister Vittorio Emanuele Orlando of Italy, and President Woodrow Wilson of the United States—small states, newly formed states, and non-European states, Japan in particular, joined in the task of forging the peace. The states of Germany, Austria-Hungary, and Soviet Russia were excluded from the negotiating tables where the future of Europe was to be determined.

President Wilson, who captured international attention with his liberal views on the peace, was the central figure of the conference. He was firmly committed to the task of shaping a better world: before the end of the war he had proclaimed the "Fourteen Points" as a guideline to the future peace and as an appeal to the people of Europe to support his policies. Believing that secret diplomacy and the alliance system were responsible for the events leading up to the declaration of war in 1914, he put forward as a basic principle, "open covenants of peace, openly arrived at." Other points included the reduction of armaments, freedom of commerce and trade, self-determination of peoples, and a general association of nations to guarantee the peace that became the League of Nations. The Fourteen Points were, above all, an idealistic statement of the principles for a good and lasting peace. Point 14, which stipulated "mutual guarantees of independence and territorial integrity" through the establishment of League of Nations, was endorsed by the Peace Confer-

Europe After World War I

ence. The League, which the United States refused to join in spite of Wilson's advocacy, was intended to arbitrate all future disputes among states and to keep the peace.

Georges Clemenceau of France represented a different approach to the challenge of the peace, one motivated primarily by a concern for his nation's security. France had suffered the greatest losses of the war in both human lives and property destroyed. In order to prevent a resurgent Germany, Clemenceau supported a variety of measures to cripple it as a military force on the Continent. Germany was disarmed. The territory west of the Rhine River was demilitarized, with occupation by Allied troops to last for a period of fifteen years. With Russia unavailable as a partner to contain Germany, France supported the creation of a series of states in eastern Europe carved out of former Russian, Austrian, and German territory. Wilson supported these new states out of a concern for self-determination of peoples. Clemenceau's main concern was self-defense.

Much time and energy were devoted to redrawing the map of Europe. New states were created out of the lands of three failed empires. Based on self-determination,

Women demonstrating in Petrograd in 1917. Throughout the revolutionary period a variety of Russian women's groups agitated for major reforms in the status of women.

The Women Who Started The Russian Revolution

Women in Russia, like their counterparts all over Europe in 1914, took over new jobs in the workplace as men marched off to war. Four out of every ten Russian workers were women, up from three of ten on the eve of the war. The situation was more dramatic in Petrograd, Russia's capital and principal industrial center, where, by 1917, women constituted 55 percent of the labor force. Russian

working women faced greater hardships than their sisters in the West. Most women workers in Petrograd held unskilled, poorly paid jobs in the textile industries and worked grueling twelve- and thirteen-hour days. They left work only to stand for hours in long breadlines and then returned home to care for their elderly relatives and often sick children. Infant mortality was alarmingly high, with

as many as half of all children dying before the age of three. Factory owners reported that nothing could be done. "The worker mother drudges and knows only need, only worry and grief," one commentator observed. "Her life passes in gloom, without light."

Russia was suffering badly in the war, with over two million soldiers killed by the beginning of 1917. News of disasters at the front reached mothers, wives, and sisters at home in spite of the government's efforts to hide the defeats. In the less than three years since the war had begun, prices had increased 400 percent and transport lines for food and coal had broken down. Bread was the main staple of meager diets. Supplies of flour and grain were not reaching towns and cities. People were starving and freezing to death. Young children were now working eleven-and-a-half hour days in the factories. The situation was dire, and working women knew that something must be done if their families were to survive.

The working women of Petrograd correctly understood that the intolerable state of affairs had come about because the government was unable to control distribution and to ration limited supplies. Carrying a double burden of supporting those at home unable to work and of producing in the factory the armaments essential for the war effort, women workers began demanding that labor organizations take action to alleviate the situation. In the winter of 1916–17, labor leaders advised exhausted and starving workers to be cautious and patient: workers must wait to strike until the time was ripe. Women workers did not agree. On 8 March 1917 (February 23 by the Russian calendar), over 7,000 women went on strike in acknowledgement of International Women's Day, an event initiated in the United States in 1909 to recognize the rights of working women. These striking women were angry, frustrated, hungry, and tired of watching their families starve while their husbands, brothers, and sons were away at the battlefront. The week before, the city had been placed on severe rationing because Petrograd was down to its last few days' supply of flour. Although the principal concern of the striking women was bread, their protest was more than just a food riot. Women left their posts in the textile mills to demand an end to the war and an end to the reign of Tsar Nicholas II. They were responding not to revolutionary propaganda but to the politics of hunger. Singing songs of protest, they marched through the streets to take their cause to the better-paid and more radical male metalworkers. Women appealed to workingmen to join the strike. By the end of the day, 100,000 workers had left their jobs to join demonstrations against the government.

The women did not stop there. They took justice into their own hands and looted bakeries and grocery shops in search of food. In the street demonstrations of the next several days, women and men marched by the thousands, attracting growing support from workers throughout the city and the suburbs. Forty demonstrators were killed when government troops fired into a crowd. Still the women were not deterred. Bolshevik leader Leon Trotsky recalled women's bravery in going up to detachments of soldiers: "More boldly than men, they take hold of the rifles and beseech, almost command: 'Put down your bayonets—join us'" Stories abound of how poor working women persuaded officers and soldiers of the Cossacks, the tsar's privileged fighting force, to lay down their arms. It was rumored that soldiers abandoned the tsar because they would not fire on the crowds of women. A participant in one confrontation reported how women workers stood without flinching as a detachment of Cossacks bore down upon them. Someone in the crowd shouted out that these were the wives and sisters of soldiers at the front. The Cossacks lowered their rifles and turned their horses around. Troops like these, tired of the war, mutinied all over Petrograd. Within four days of the first action taken by women textile operatives, the government had lost the support of Petrograd workers, women and men, and its soldiers, who had joined the demonstrators. The tsar was forced to abdicate. From this point on the Romanov monarchy and the Russian war effort were doomed.

In those first days of protest, the women of Petrograd took action into their own hands, pouring into the streets to call for bread, peace, and the end of tsardom. They rejected autocracy and war in defense of their communities and their families. The eighth of March 1917 was women's day. The Russian Revolution had begun.

Finland, Latvia, Estonia, Lithuania, Poland, Czechoslovakia, Austria, Hungary, and Yugoslavia were all granted status as nation-states. However, the rights of ethnic and cultural minorities were violated in some cases because of the impossibility of redrawing the map of Europe strictly according to the principle of self-determination. In spite of good intentions, every new nation had its own national minority, a situation that held the promise of future troubles.

The Peace Conference produced five separate treaties with each of the defeated nations: Austria, Hungary, Turkey, Bulgaria, and Germany. The treaty signed with Germany on 28 June 1919, known as the Treaty of Versailles because it was signed in the great Bourbon palace, preceded the others in timing and importance. In that treaty, the Allies imposed blame for the war on Germany and its expansionist aims in the famous War Guilt Clause. If the war was Germany's fault, then Germany must be made to pay. Reparations, once the price of defeat, were now exacted as compensation for damages inflicted by a guilty aggressor.

The principle of punitive reparations was included in the German settlement. By 1920 the German people knew that Germany had to make a down payment of $5 billion against a future bill; had to hand over a significant portion of merchant ships, including all vessels of more than 1,600 tons; had to lose all German colonies; and had to deliver coal to neighboring countries. These harsh clauses, more than any other aspect of the peace settlement, came to haunt the Allies in the succeeding decades.

In the end, no nation got what it wanted from the peace settlement. The defeated nations felt that they had been badly abused. The victorious nations were aware of the compromises they had reluctantly accepted. Cooperation among nations was essential if the treaty was to work successfully. It had taken the combined resources of not only France and the British Empire but also Russia with its vast population and the United States with its great industrial and financial might to defeat the power of Germany and the militarily ineffective Austro-Hungarian Empire. A new and stable balance of power depended on the participation of Russia, the United States, and the British Empire. But Russia was excluded from and hostile to the peace settlement, the United States was uncommitted to it, and the British Empire declined to guarantee it. All three Great Powers backed off their European responsibilities at the end of the war. By 1920 all aspects of the treaty, but especially the reparations clause, had been questioned and criticized by the very governments that had written

A German cartoon, titled "The Mask Falls," depicts German reaction to the terms of the Treaty of Versailles and to the Allies' brand of justice.

them and had accepted them. The search for a lasting peace had just begun.

Revolution in Russia, 1917–1920

Every country has its prophets. So too did Russia in 1914 when a now-forgotten former government minister advised Tsar Nicholas II (1894–1917) to avoid war or else face a social revolution. Other advisers prevailed: they said that Russia must go to war because it was a Great Power with interests beyond its borders. But within its empire, the process of modernization was widening social divisions. Nicholas preferred to listen to those who promised that a short, successful war would strengthen his monarchy against the domestic forces of change.

Little did Nicholas know, when he committed Russia to the path of war instead of revolution, that he guaranteed a future of war *and* revolution, that he was delivering his nation up to humiliating defeat in global war and a devastating civil war, and that his own days were numbered, with his fate to be determined at the hands of a Marxist dictatorship.

The Last Tsar. The Romanov dynasty surely needed strengthening. In 1914 Russia was considered backward by the standards of Western industrial society. Russia still recalled a recent feudal past. The serfs had been freed in the 1860s, but the nature of the emancipation exacerbated tensions in the countryside and peasant hunger for land. Russia's limited, rapid industrialization in the 1880s and 1890s was an attempt to catch up with Great Britain, France, and Germany as a world industrial power. But the speed of such change brought with it severe dislocations, especially in the industrial city of Moscow and the capital, St. Petersburg.

Twelve years earlier, in 1905, the workers of St. Petersburg protested hardships due to cyclical downturns in the economy. On a Sunday in January 1905 the tsar's troops fired on a peaceful mass demonstration in front of the Winter Palace, killing and wounding scores of workers, women, and children who were appealing to the tsar for relief. The event, which came to be known as Bloody Sunday, set off a revolution that spread to Moscow and the countryside. In October 1905 the regime responded to the disruptions with a series of reforms that legalized political parties and established the Duma, or national parliament. Peasants, oppressed with their own burdens of taxation and endemic poverty, launched mass attacks on big landowners throughout 1905 and 1906. The government met workers and peasants' demands with a return to repression in 1907. In the half-decade before the Great War, the Russian state stood as an autocracy of parliamentary concessions blended with severe police controls.

What workers had learned in 1905 was the power and the means of independent organization. Factory committees, trade unions, and "soviets," or workers' councils, proliferated. Despite winning a grant of legal status after 1906, unions gained little in terms of ability to act on behalf of their members. Unrest among factory

Russian imperial troops fire on demonstrators outside the Winter Palace in St. Petersburg. The people were asking for better working conditions and a more responsive government. This day, 22 January 1905, is known in Russian history as Bloody Sunday.

workers revived on the eve of the Great War, a period of rapid economic growth and renewed trade-union activity. Between January and July 1914, Russia experienced 3,500 strikes in a six-month period. Although economic strikes were considered legal, strikes deemed political were not. With the outbreak of war, all collective action was banned. Protest stopped, but only momentarily. The tsar certainly weighed the workers' actions in his decision to view war as a possible diversion from domestic problems.

Russia was less prepared for war than any of the other belligerents. Undoubtedly, it had more soldiers than other countries, but it lacked arms and equipment. Problems of provisioning such a huge fighting force placed great strains on the domestic economy and on the workforce. Under government coercion to meet the needs of war, industrial output doubled between 1914 and 1917, while agricultural production plummeted. The tsar, who unwisely insisted on commanding his own troops, left the government in the hands of his wife, the Tsarina Alexandra, a German princess by birth, and her eccentric peasant adviser, Rasputin. Scandal, sexual innuendo, and charges of treason surrounded the royal court. The incompetence of a series of unpopular ministers further eroded confidence in the regime. (See Special Feature, "The Women Who Started the Russian Revolution," pp. 890–891.)

In the end, the war sharpened long-standing divisions within Russian society. Led by exhausted and starving working women, poorly paid and underfed workers toppled the regime in the bitter winter of March 1917. This event was the beginning of a violent process of revolution and civil war. The tsar abdicated, and all public symbols of the tsardom were destroyed. The banner bearing the Romanov two-headed eagle was torn down and in its place the Red Flag flew over the Winter Palace.

Dual Power. With the tsar's abdication, two centers of authority replaced autocracy. One was the Provisional Government, appointed by the Duma and made up of progressive liberals led by Prince Georgi Lvov (1861–1925), prime minister of the new government, who also served as minister of the interior. Aleksandr Kerenski (1881–1970), the only socialist in the Provisional Government, served as minister of justice. The members of the new government hoped to establish constitutional and democratic rule.

The other center of power was the "soviets," committees or councils elected by workers and soldiers, who were supported by radical lawyers, journalists, and intellectuals in favor of socialist self-rule. The Petrograd

Soviet was the most prominent among the councils. (In 1914, the name of St. Petersburg had been changed to the Russian Petrograd). This duality of power was matched by duality in policies and objectives and guaranteed a short-lived and unstable regime.

The problems facing the new regime soon became apparent as revolution spread to the provinces and to the battlefront. Peasants, who made up 80 percent of the Russian population, accepted the revolution and demanded land and peace. Without waiting for government directives, peasants began seizing the land. Peasants tried to alleviate some of their suffering by hoarding what little they had. The food crisis of winter persisted throughout the spring and summer, as breadlines lengthened and prices rose. Workers in cities gained better working conditions and higher wages. But wage increases were invariably followed by higher prices that robbed workers of their gains. Real wages declined.

In addition to the problems of land and bread, the war itself presented the new government with other insurmountable difficulties. Hundreds of thousands of Russian soldiers at the front deserted the war, having heard news from home of peasant land grabs and rumors of a new offensive planned for July. The Provisional Government, concerned with Russia's territorial integrity and its position in the international system, continued to honor the tsar's commitments to the Allies by participating in the war. By spring 1917, six to eight million Russian soldiers had been killed, wounded, or captured. The Russian army was incapable of fighting.

The Provisional Government tried everything to convince its people to carry on with the war. In the summer of 1917, the Women's Battalion of Death, composed exclusively of female recruits, was enlisted into the army. Its real purpose, officials admitted, was to "shame the men" into fighting. The all-female unit, like its male counterparts, experienced high losses: 80 percent of the force suffered casualties. The Provisional Government was caught in an impossible situation: it could not withdraw from the war but neither could it fight. Continued involvement in the lost cause of the war blocked any consideration of social reforms.

While the Provisional Government was trying to deal with the calamities, many members of the intelligentsia, Russia's educated class, who had been exiled by the tsar for their political beliefs, now rushed back from western Europe to take part in the great revolutionary experiment. Theorists of all stripes put their cases

Revolution and Civil War in Russia

before the people. Those in favor of gradual reform debated with those who favored violent revolution the relative merits of various government policies. The months between February and July 1917 were a period of great intellectual ferment. It was the Marxists, or Social Democrats, who had the greatest impact on the direction of the revolution.

The Social Democrats believed that there were objective laws of historical development that could be discovered. Russia's future could be understood only in terms of the present situation in western Europe. Like Marxists in the West, the Russian Social Democrats split over how best to achieve a socialist state. The more moderate Mensheviks (the term means "minority") wanted to work through parliamentary institutions and were willing to cooperate with the Provisional Government. A *smaller* faction—despite its name—calling themselves Bolsheviks (meaning "majority") dedicated themselves to preparation for a revolutionary upheaval. After April 1917, the Bolsheviks refused to work with the Provisional Government and organized themselves to take control of the Petrograd Soviet.

The leader of the Bolsheviks was Vladimir Ilich Ulyanov (1870–1924), best known by his revolutionary name, Lenin. Forty-seven years old at the time of the revolution, Lenin had spent most of his life in exile or in prison. More a pragmatist than a theoretician, he argued for a disciplined party of professional revolutionaries, a vanguard who would lead the peasants and workers in a socialist revolution against capitalism. In contrast to the Mensheviks, he argued that the time was now ripe for a successful revolution, and that it could be achieved through the soviets.

Immediately upon arrival in Petrograd from Switzerland, Lenin threw down the gauntlet to the Provisional Government. In his April Theses, he promised the Russian people peace, land, and bread. The war must be ended immediately, he argued, because it represented an imperialist struggle that was benefiting capitalists. Russia's duty was to withdraw and wait for a world revolution. This was more than rhetoric on Lenin's part. His years in exile in the West and news of mutinies and worker protests convinced him that revolution was imminent. His revolutionary policies on land were little more than endorsements of the seizures already taking

In this Communist poster of 1922 Lenin points to a utopian future as he proclaims, "Let the ruling class tremble before the Communist revolution." The rising sun in the background symbolizes the dawn of the socialist era.

place all over Russia. Even his promises of bread had little substance. But on the whole, the April Theses constituted a clear critique of the policies of the Provisional Government.

Dissatisfaction with the Provisional Government increased as the war dragged hopelessly on and bread lines lengthened. In the midst of these calamities, a massive popular demonstration erupted in July 1917 against the Provisional Government and in favor of the soviets, which excluded the upper classes from voting. The Provisional Government responded with repressive force reminiscent of the tsardom. The July Days were proof of the growing influence of the Bolsheviks among the Russian people. Although the Bolshevik leadership had withdrawn support for the demonstrations at the last moment, Bolshevik rank-and-file party members strongly endorsed the protest. Indisputably, Bolshevik influence was growing in the soviets despite repression and persecution of its leaders. Lenin was forced to flee to Finland.

As a result of the July Days, Kerenski, who had been heading the ministry of justice, was named prime minister and continued the Provisional Government's moderate policies. In order to protect the government from a coup on the right, Kerenski permitted the arming of the Red Guards, the workers' militia units of the Petrograd Soviet. The traditional chasm between the upper and the lower classes was widening as the policies of the Provisional Government conflicted with the demands of the soviets.

Lenin and the Bolsheviks Seize Power.   The second revolution came in November (October in the Russian calendar). This time it was not a spontaneous street demonstration by thousands of working women that triggered the revolution but rather the seizure of the Russian capital by the Red Guards of the Petrograd Soviet. The revolution was carefully planned and orchestrated by Lenin and his vanguard of Bolsheviks, who now possessed majorities in the soviets in Moscow and Petrograd and other industrial centers. Returning surreptitiously from Finland, Lenin moved through the streets of Petrograd disguised in a curly wig and head bandages, watching the Red Guard seize centers of communication and public buildings. The military action was directed by Lev Bronstein, better known by his revolutionary name, Leon Trotsky (1879–1940). The Bolshevik chairman of the Petrograd Soviet, Trotsky used the Red Guard to seize political control and arrest the members of the Provisional Government. Kerenski escaped and fled the city.

The takeover was achieved with almost no bloodshed and was immediately endorsed by an All-Russian Congress of Soviets, which consisted of representatives of local soviets from throughout the nation who were in session amid the takeover of the capital. A Bolshevik regime under Lenin now ruled Russia. Tsar Nicholas II and the royal family were executed by the Bolshevik revolutionaries in July 1918.

The Russian Civil War, 1917–1920.   Lenin immediately set to work to end the war for Russia. After months of negotiation, Russia signed a separate peace with the Germans in March 1918 in the Treaty of Brest-Litovsk. By every measure, the treaty was a bitter humiliation for the new Soviet regime. The territorial losses were phenomenal. In a vast amputation, Russia was reduced to the size of its Muscovite period: it recognized the independence of Ukraine, Georgia, and Finland; it relinquished its Polish territories, the Baltic states, and part of Belorussia to Germany and Austria-Hungary; and it handed over other territories

In this satirical painting, The Pillars of Society, *George Grosz caricatures the society of the Weimar Republic as composed of corrupt judges, petty bourgeoisie, militarists, and hypocritical pacifists.*

on the Black Sea to Turkey. Lenin felt he had no choice: he needed to buy time to consolidate the revolution at home, and he hoped for a socialist revolution in Germany that would soften the enforcement of the terms of the treaty.

The Treaty of Brest-Litovsk was judged a betrayal not only outside Russia among the Allied powers but also inside Russia among some army officers who had sacrificed much for the tsar's war. To these military men, the Bolsheviks were no more than German agents who held the country in their sway. Lacking sufficient organization, unable to coordinate their movements because the Bolsheviks dominated the

country's center, and torn apart by different political goals, the White armies ultimately failed to challenge successfully the Bolshevik hold on the reins of state. But in the three years of civil war between Whites and Reds, the Whites posed a serious threat to Bolshevik policies.

Anti-Bolshevik forces were assisted with materials by the Allies, who intended to keep the eastern front viable. The Allies sent over 100,000 troops and supplies for the purpose of overthrowing the Bolshevik regime by supporting its enemies. Allied support for the White armies came primarily from the United States, Great Britain, France, and Japan and continued beyond the armistice that ended the Great War in 1918. Although Allied support was not crucial to the outcome of the civil war, it played a significant role in shaping Soviet perceptions of the outside world. For generations of Soviet citizens, anti-Bolshevik assistance was viewed as the indication of a hostile and predatory capitalist world intent on destroying the fledgling Soviet state for its own ends.

The civil war had another legacy for the future of the Soviet state. To deal with the anarchy caused by the fratricidal struggle, Lenin had to strengthen the government's dictatorial elements at the expense of its democratic ones. The new Soviet state used state police to suppress all opposition. The dictatorship of the proletariat yielded to the dictatorship of the repressive forces.

In the course of the civil war, Lenin was no more successful than Kerenski and the Provisional Government in solving the problems of food supplies. Human costs of the civil war were high, with over 800,000 soldiers dead on both sides, and 2 million civilian deaths from dysentery and diseases caused by poor nutrition. Industrial production ceased and people fled towns to return to the countryside. In 1920 it seemed Russia could drop no lower. Millions had been killed in war or died from famine. Stripped of territories and sapped of its industrial strength, Russia was a defeated nation. Yet Bolshevik idealism about the success of the proletarian revolution prevailed. No longer sure that a world socialist revolution would come to their aid, Bolshevik leaders set out to build the future.

The Weimar Republic

In September 1918 the leaders of the German High Command, Erich Ludendorff and Paul von Hindenburg, knowing that the German war effort was a lost

PROCLAMATION OF THE "WHITES," 8 JULY 1918

■ *In the summer of 1918 opponents of the Bolsheviks organized their own volunteer army with the hope of destroying the communist Red Army and eliminating Bolshevik rule. This "White Army" included disgruntled military officers who had fought loyally in World War I and felt betrayed by the devastating peace with Germany; republicans who sought the restoration of the moderate democratic rule of the Provisional Government period; a wide variety of political groups on the Right and Left, including Socialist Revolutionaries; and Cossacks, who feared the loss of their lands and privileges under a Bolshevik state. Detachments of workers, students, and intellectuals also rallied to join the counterrevolutionary forces.[1]*

To the Workers and Peasants:

Citizens! The events of the last few days compel all those who love their country and the Russian people, all true defenders of freedom, to take up arms against the Soviet Government and defeat the usurpers who are disguising their nefarious acts by using the name of the people.

The Soviet of People's Commissars has brought ruin to Russia . . . Instead of bread and peace it has brought famine and war. The Soviet of People's Commissars has made of mighty Russia a bit of earth dripping with the blood of peaceful citizens doomed to the pangs of hunger. In the name of the people the self-styled commissars have given the most fertile land to the enemies of Russia—the Austrians and Germans. There have been wrested from us the Ukraine, the Baltic and Vistula regions, the Kuban, the Don, and the Caucasus, which fed and supplied us with bread. That bread now goes to Germany. With that bread they are feeding those who, step by step, are conquering us and with the help of the Bolsheviks are placing us in the power of the German Kaiser. With that bread they are feeding the German army, which is slaughtering our people in cities and villages of the Ukraine, on the banks of the Don, in the mountains of the Caucasus, and in the fields of Great Russia.

The Soviet of People's Commissars is a plaything in the hands of the German Ambassador, Count Mirbach.

The Soviet of People's Commissars dictates decrees in the name of the people but Kaiser Wilhelm writes those decrees. Spurning agreement with the best citizens of the country, the Soviet of People's Commissars is not only in complete accord with the German imperialists but is carrying out unhesitatingly all their orders and demands.

---

cause, decided that a constitutional monarchy must be introduced in Germany. Their intention was to save the throne of Emperor William II and to save themselves by handing the responsibility for the government over to the socialist and liberal politicians who were dedicated to ending the war, getting German soldiers home, and demobilizing the army. Popular uprisings in the navy and in urban areas followed, forcing the emperor to abdicate. In spring 1919, a national assembly meeting in the city of Weimar produced Germany's first democratic constitution. The Weimar Republic was born.

The Weimar Republic was in trouble from the start. Germany's first democracy came into existence saddled with a harsh peace. Many Germans identified the new government with defeat and humiliation. Rumors spread that the German military had never really been defeated and that Communists and Jews now associated with the new government had "stabbed the German army in the back" on the home front. The harsh terms of the Treaty of Versailles compounded the negative image of the Weimar Republic. Lost territory and people, destroyed markets, a vastly reduced military force, and reparations payments were the legacy of the new democratic experiment.

Born of political revolution and social upheaval, the Weimar Republic faced the challenges of establishing

PROCLAMATION OF THE "WHITES," 8 JULY 1918

By its treacherous policy of executing the orders of Count Mirbach the Soviet of People's Commissars forced the rising of the Czechoslovak army, which was marching to the Western front to fight the Germans[1]. . .

The Czechoslovaks are true republicans and serve the same sublime cause that we do. They are making war on the usurpers and will not permit the strangling of liberty. The People's Commissars, having long since betrayed the cause of the working class and knowing that the wrath of the people is terrible, now depend upon the bayonets of the Germans and the duped Letts[2] to save their own lives and to keep in power.

The People's Commissars have brought about a terrible fratricidal war, sending detachments of Red Guards and Letts against the peasants to take their grain. The People's Commissars are arresting and shooting workers who do not agree with their policies, are manipulating the elections, and are strangling all civil liberties . . .

To arms all! Down with the Soviet of People's Commissars! Only by overthrowing it shall we have bread, peace, and freedom! Long live unity and order in Russia! When we put an end to the Soviet power we shall at the same time end civil war and return once more to our former strength and power.

And then the enemies of our country will not be terrifying to us. Down with the hirelings—the People's Commissars and their tools! Long live the coming Constituent Assembly!

Long live the free mighty fatherland!

[1] The "rising" refers to the anti-Bolshevik activities of about 30,000 Czech soldiers, known as the Czech Legion, who were attempting to traverse Soviet territory to reach the port of Vladivostok in order to return by ship to Europe, where they hoped to engage the Central Powers in combat on the Western front. The Czechs hoped, by joining forces with the Allies, to strengthen their claims to nationhood following the war. Czech units joined with Russian Socialist Revolutionaries to set up for a brief time the Volga Republic.

[2] Inhabitants of Latvia.

From James Bunyon, *Intervention, Civil War and Communism in Russia, April–December 1918.*

its legitimacy and maintaining social peace. Yet it lacked a democratic tradition on which to draw. Traditional ruling groups—the Prussian military and agrarian and bureaucratic elites—preserved their power and privileges even as democratic institutions struggled for existence. Political as well as economic power continued to be concentrated in the hands of the privileged elite that had ruled the Second Reich.

By every measure, the Great War was disastrously expensive. Some European nations suffered more than others, but all endured significant losses of life, property, and productive capacity. The cost in human lives was enormous. In western Europe 8.5 million were dead; total casualties amounted to 37.5 million. France lost 20 percent of its men between the ages of twenty and forty-four, Germany lost 15 percent, and Great Britain 10 percent. The war also resulted in huge losses in productive capacity. National economies buckled under the weight of foreign debts and resorted to a variety of methods to bail themselves out, including taxes, loans, and inflations. The people of Europe continued to pay for the war long after the fighting had ended.

The big winner in the war was the United States, now a creditor nation holding billions of dollars of loans

The Russian Revolution

22 January 1905	Bloody Sunday massacre in St. Petersburg sets off unrest in all of Russia
October 1905	Creation of the Duma, the national parliament
July 1914	Russia enters World War I
March 1917	Women's protests in Petrograd trigger first Russian Revolution and abdication of Tsar Nicholas II; creation of the Provisional Government and the soviets
April 1917	Bolsheviks take control of Petrograd
July 1917	Massive demonstrations against Provisional Government lead to repression; Lenin is forced to flee Russia
November 1917	Red Guards and Bolsheviks seize political control in what comes to be known as the October Revolution
March 1918	Russia signs peace treaty with Germany, the Treaty of Brest-Litovsk
July 1918	Tsar Nicholas II and family are executed

to the Allies and operating in new markets established during the war. The shift was not a temporary move but a structural change. The United States now took its place as a Great Power in the international system. The world of 1914 was gone. What was to replace it was still very much in flux. To the east, Russia was engaged in a vast experiment of building a new society. In the west, the absence of war was not peace.

SUGGESTIONS FOR FURTHER READING

THE WAR EUROPE EXPECTED

Marc Ferro, *The Great War, 1914–1918* (London: Routledge & Kegan Paul, 1973). The origins of World War I within a broad social and cultural context. Stressing the importance of an imagined war and patriotism as two factors that precipitated

actual conflict, Ferro shows how the gulf between imagination and reality led to domestic conflict and social unrest once war broke out.

* James Joll, *The Origins of the First World War* (New York: Longman, 1984). In an examination of the decisions that brought about war in 1914, importance is placed on the limited options available to decision makers. The July crisis, the international system, the arms race, domestic politics, the international economy, imperial rivalries, and cultural and psychological factors are considered in terms of their contributions to the outbreak of war.

* Keith Robbins, *The First World War* (Oxford: Oxford University Press, 1984). The major cultural, political, military, and social developments between 1914 and 1918. Includes discussion of the course of the land war and modes of warfare.

THE WAR EUROPE GOT

David Fromkin, *A Peace to End All Peace: Creating the Modern Middle East, 1914–1922* (New York: Henry Holt and Company, 1989). Firmly rooted in newly opened archives, secret communiques, and private correspondence, this study explains how the Middle East of Egypt, Israel, Iran, Turkey, the Arab states of Asia, Soviet Central Asia, and Afghanistan emerged from World War I, told from both the European and the Middle Eastern perspectives.

* Gerd Hardach, *The First World War, 1914–1918* (Berkeley: University of California Press, 1977). Describes the changes in the world economy leading up to the war, the war's impact on trade, wartime monetary and fiscal policies, and the war's impact on labor. Each major power is included in an analysis of wartime economic history.

B. E. Schmitt and H. C. Vedeler, *The World in a Crucible, 1914–1919* (New York: Harper & Row, 1984). A broad survey of the military and political history of World War I; the war is viewed here as a period of revolution in both warfare and politics. Includes considerable discussion of the Russian Revolution and a section on the entry of the United States into European affairs.

* Denis Winter, *Death's Men: Soldiers of the Great War* (London: Penguin, 1979). Not an account of military strategy and battlefield tactics, *Death's Men* goes inside the infantrymen's war to convey the experience of war in the trenches.

ADJUSTING TO THE UNEXPECTED: TOTAL WAR

John Williams, *The Homefronts: Britain, France and Germany, 1914–1918* (London: Constable, 1972). A comparative study of the home fronts, their impact on the course of the war, and the war's impact on civilian life.

J. M. Winter, *The Experience of World War I* (New York: Oxford University Press, 1989). A comprehensive survey of the war in terms of the politics that governed it, its battles from the point of view of the soldiers in the trenches and military leaders, impact on civilians, and its consequences for global history.

RESHAPING EUROPE: AFTER WAR AND REVOLUTION

* Sheila Fitzpatrick, *The Russian Revolution, 1917–1932* (Oxford: Oxford University Press, 1982). An analysis of the

October Revolution of 1917 from the perspective of Stalinist society. The February and October revolutions of 1917, the civil war, and the economic policies of the 1920s are treated as various aspects of a unitary revolutionary movement.

Tsuyoshi Hasegawa, *The February Revolution: Petrograd, 1917* (Seattle: University of Washington Press, 1981). A thorough examination of the effects of World War I on Russian workers, liberals, and revolutionary parties leads to an interpretation of the February Revolution as the outcome of a conflict between the state and civil society. Particular attention is given to events leading to the abdication of the tsar, the establishment of the Provisional Government, and the early stages of the Russian Revolution.

* Temma Kaplan, "Women and Communal Strikes in the Crisis of 1917–1922," in *Becoming Visible: Women in European History,* edited by Renate Bridenthal, Claudia Koonz, and Susan Stuard (Boston: Houghton Mifflin, 1987). Analyzes the nature of female consciousness in the urban working class, comparing Russian women's activities in March 1917 with women's response to crises in Italy, Spain, and Mexico in the same period.

Lars T. Lih, *Bread and Authority in Russia, 1914–1921* (Berkeley: University of California Press, 1990). Focuses on the importance of the food-supply question to explain the origins and development of the Russian Revolution.

Arno J. Mayer, *The Politics and Diplomacy of Peacemaking* (New York: Knopf, 1967). A comprehensive examination of the role of internal political concerns and the foreign policy of the warring nations as well as a thorough analysis of the struggle between Bolshevism, Wilsonian liberalism, and counterrevolution.

*David Stevenson, *The First World War and International Politics* (Oxford: Oxford University Press, 1988). A study of the global ramifications of World War I, this work traces the development of war aims on both sides, the reasons peace negotiations failed, and why compromise proved elusive.

* Indicates paperback edition available.

THE SCREAMS FROM GUERNICA

Rarely does a piece of art scream out. The mural *Guernica* is different. Listen to the painting shown here. It is a painting whose images convey sounds, the shrieks of terror, fear, suffering, and death. There is a chaos of noise here that seems at odds with the drab greys, black, and white, the monochromatic colorlessness of the artist's palette. But no, the lack of color only heightens the noise and allows us to focus on the sound, the screams that come from open mouths of human and beast on the canvas. Death and brutality reverberate throughout the painting. The open mouths of the dead baby's mother, the bull standing behind her, the small bird to the right of the bull, and the wounded horse at the center of the canvas emit fear like projectiles, beak and tongues thrusting forth in pointed daggers.

Pablo Picasso (1881–1973) painted this great mural in May and June 1937 for the Spanish Pavilion of the International Exhibition to be held in Paris. He called it *Guernica* in commemoration of the bombing of the small Basque town in Spain by German planes at the end of April 1937. The destruction of Guernica was an event that shocked the world and devastated the Spanish artist, then living in France. Working in collaboration with the insurgent forces of Francisco Franco (1892–1975), German planes dropped bomb after bomb on the ancient city, destroying it in three and a half hours. Their purpose was to cut off the retreat of loyalist government troops and to terrorize civilians through saturation bombing. Picasso demonstrates vividly that noncombatants, represented by the women and child, were no longer just hapless bystanders but were, in fact, the very targets of indiscriminate killing.

Guernica is a huge canvas, measuring over 11 feet high and 25 feet long. It dwarfs spectators who stand before it, enveloping them in a modern-day apocalypse of contorted bodies. We do not look at war directly in the mural but at the terror it creates in this vision of needless slaughter. Picasso deliberately used the traditional religious symbols of the Madonna and Child and the Pietà as models for his terrifying image of maternity. The lips of the baby, who hangs like a rag doll in the arms of its despairing mother on the far left of the canvas, are sealed in the silence of death. The mother finds her counterpoint in the figure of the limping woman in the right foreground, who drags behind her a wounded arm and a swollen knee. Above her a woman, gaping in disbelief and clutching her breasts in anguish, raises a lamp over the scene. On the far right, a fourth woman, trapped in the flames of a burning building, appears to be exploding upward in terrified petition. On the ground under the horse lies a dead man with his head and arm severed from his body, clutching a broken sword and flower whose petals wait to be picked in his right hand. The presentation of his head as a piece of statuary fallen from its pedestal reinforces the bloodless horror of his death. His left palm is crisscrossed with the lines of fate or perhaps marked with the toil of heavy labor. Suspended over the scene like a huge eye is a naked light bulb, a modern image illuminating the timelessness of the theme of the horror of war.

In one of his rare moments of self-interpretation, Picasso explained to a public eager to grasp the mural's symbolism that the horse whose side is opened by a terrible gash is "the people," victimized by incomprehensible cruelty. The bull is an enigmatic figure symbolizing, Picasso tells us, darkness and brutality. The horned beast appears as a powerful and vulnerable witness to this scene of needless destruction.

Guernica has been hailed as the most significant painting of the twentieth century. Picasso claimed his greatness as an artist derived from his ability to understand his time. In the stripped-down, almost cartoonlike figures of *Guernica*, Picasso presents us with a picture of European society that is brutal and horrible. Here is a condemnation of the modern technological war that targets civilian populations; here

on this horrifying canvas are portrayed the consequences of totalitarianism and the failure of democracy that characterized the European search for stability between 1920 and 1939. Subsequent events made Germany's actions in the Spanish Civil War seem like a dress rehearsal for atrocities against the population centers of Warsaw, Rotterdam, and London and made this canvas seem a prophecy of horrors to come. Some years later, during the Second World War, a Nazi official challenged Picasso with a photograph of the great mural, "So it was you who did this." The artist answered, "No, you did."

International Politics and Economic Nationalism

The armistice that ended World War I in 1918 did not stop the process of social upheaval and transformations challenging attempts to restore order throughout Europe. In 1918 parts of war-torn Europe faced the possibility of revolution. Russia, where revolution had destroyed tsardom, expectantly watched revolutionary developments in countries from the British Isles to eastern Europe. The Bolshevik leaders of Russia's revolution counted on the capitalist system to destroy itself. That did not happen. By 1921, revolutions had been brutally crushed in Berlin, Munich, and Budapest. The Soviets, meanwhile, had won the civil war against the Whites and survived the intervention of the British, French, Japanese, and Americans. But the new Russian regime was diplomatically isolated and in a state of almost total economic collapse.

In 1917–18, the United States had played a significant and central role in the waging of war and in the pursuit of peace. Under U.S. president Woodrow Wilson, who urged his country to guarantee European security and guide Europe's future, the American nation seemed

promising as an active and positive force in international politics. By 1921, however, the United States had retreated to a position, not of isolation, but of selective involvement. With one giant, Russia, devastated and isolated, and the other, the United States, reluctant, Europeans faced an uncertain future.

New Nation-States, New Problems

Before World War I, east central Europe was a region divided among four great empires—the Ottoman, the Habsburg, the Russian, and the German. Under the pressure of defeat those empires collapsed into their component national parts, and when the dust of the peace treaties had settled, the region had been molded into a dozen sovereign states. The victorious Allies hoped that independent states newly created from fragments of empire would buffer Europe from the spread of communism westward and the expansion of German power eastward.

A swath of new independent states cut through the center of Europe. Finland had acquired its independence from Russia in 1917. Estonia, Latvia, and Lithuania, also formerly under Russian rule, comprised the now independent Baltic states. After more than a century of dismemberment among three empires, Poland became a single nation again. Czechoslovakia was carved out of former Habsburg lands. Austria and Hungary shriveled to small independent states. Yugoslavia was pieced together from a patchwork of territories. Romania swelled, fed on a diet of settlement concessions. These new nations assured the victorious powers and especially France that the new political geography of east central Europe would guarantee the peace.

World War I victor nations hoped that these new states would stabilize European affairs; they could not have been more wrong. They erred in three important ways in their calculations. First, many of the new states were internally unstable precisely because of the principle of national self-determination, the idea that nationalities had the right to rule themselves. Honoring

the rights of nationalities was simple in the abstract, but application of the principle proved complicated and at times impossible. Religious, linguistic, and ethnic diversity abounded, and recognizing one nationality often meant ignoring the rights of other ethnic groups. In Czechoslovakia, for example, the Czechs dominated the Slovaks and the Germans even though the Czechs were fewer in number. Ethnic unrest plagued all of eastern Europe. Minority tensions weakened and destabilized the fragile governments.

Second, the struggle for economic prosperity further destabilized the new governments. East central Europe was primarily agricultural and the existence of the great empires had created guaranteed markets. The war disrupted the economy and generated social unrest. The peace settlements only compounded the

Europe in the 1920s

Project for Glass Skyscraper *(1921) by Mies van der Rohe.*

Buildings for the Future

Buildings tell tales. Archaeologists trying to understand other civilizations excavate ancient dwellings in order to reconstruct past lives. Family life, social values, the nature of work, technology, and progress are all embodied in the structures in which people live and work. If future generations had only traces of the buildings of the twentieth century, they would nonetheless hold a key to understanding our civilization and values.

The twentieth-century architecture that we call "modern" was the child born from the union of technology and art in the aftermath of the Great War of 1914–18. In reaction to the horrors of the battlefront, a new generation of architects, many of them ex-soldiers, committed themselves to the creation of buildings as works of art that answered the needs of modern society. Those who followed the lead of the prewar avant-garde disdained imitating past masters. They saw their task as "starting from zero"—that is, striking out in a new direction unencumbered by the cultural baggage of a past that had proven itself to be morally bankrupt. In building for the future, the postwar generation felt that the present must create a new style of its own.

The battle cry for a new architectural style arose from defeated Germany and in particular from a single man, Walter Gropius (1883–1969). In 1919, only a few months after the Treaty of Versailles ended World War I, Gropius, a recent veteran of the front, founded the Bauhaus, a school based on the collaborative efforts of architects, sculptors, artists, and craft workers. The Bauhaus movement stressed the social responsibility of art and an awareness of a new age. As Gropius explained, "This is more than just a lost war. A world has come to an end. We must seek a radical solution to our problems."

The untranslatable term *Bauhaus*, resulting from joining the German words "building" and "house," soon characterized a new movement in the arts and architecture. As director of the Bauhaus until 1928, Gropius attracted some of Europe's leading artists to the school, including the architects Marcel Breuer (1902–81), and Ludwig Mies van der Rohe (1886–1969). Russian abstract artist Vasili Kandinski (1866–1944) and his Swiss colleague Paul Klee (1879–1940) were also members of the teaching staff at the Bauhaus. Characterized by intense activity, exciting experimentation, and enthusiastic collaboration, the men and women who assembled at the Bauhaus pioneered new designs in everything from kitchen utensils and furniture to lighting fixtures and skyscrapers.

Gropius was a utopian dreamer who saw in buildings and in the humble objects of daily life the means of creating human happiness. Beauty in design was defined by the fit between form and function. Rather than rejecting industrial society, Gropius sought a new way of uniting art with it. Unlike other arts and crafts movements, the Bauhaus was willing to make use of the machine to produce for the masses, whether the production was of prefabricated houses or teacups. Gropius knew well that architecture does not move faster than the society it seeks to serve. But he also knew that it must keep pace with the world around it. The school's motto, one that Gropius considered realistic and responsible, proclaimed: "Art and technology—a new unity!"

Pictured here is one of the first Bauhaus models of a skyscraper. Modest by subsequent standards, its thirty-two stories dwarf the traditional building at its base. Steel and glass were expressly used to liberate the structure from supporting walls. With new engineering knowledge about support, loads, stress, and mass, sheer facades of glass opened up inside space to the outside world. Interior walls were eliminated. Gropius admired the new functional factory structures and early skyscrapers in the United States and Canada for their starkness and simplicity and sought to introduce their "majesty" to residential architecture.

The architects of the Bauhaus were in the right place at the right time. Germany needed new buildings, and in the period from 1924 to 1929 the return of economic prosperity allowed them to be built. Under Gropius' direction, working-class apartment blocks with open floor plans, unadorned facades, clean lines, and a stark simplicity spread across the German landscape.

Office buildings of reinforced concrete with little to distinguish them from the new residential housing also mushroomed. By the end of the decade Bauhaus architects had left their mark on German towns and cities. Then, seeking refuge from Hitler (eventually in the United States), Gropius and some of his associates transformed the skylines of America's great cities within a decade. In the second half of the twentieth century, the Bauhaus style of architecture spread throughout the world.

The architects of the Bauhaus changed the appearance of the modern world and with it the twentieth-century experience. Critics who longed for a traditional architecture of decoration and classical emulation judged the Bauhaus style to be barren and ugly. Yet its emphasis on design and function prevailed. The skyscrapers of the twentieth century are products of the lessons of war and technology and the idealistic pursuit of a better world that took shape very visibly in the 1920s.

economic problems of the region. When the Habsburg Empire disintegrated, the Danube River basin ceased to be a cohesive economic unit. New governments were saddled with borders that made little economic sense.

Creating cohesive economic units proved an insurmountable task for newly formed governments and administrations that lacked both resources and experience. Low productivity, unemployment, and overpopulation characterized most of east central Europe. Attempts to industrialize and to develop new markets confronted many obstacles. Much of the land was farmed on a subsistence basis. What agricultural surplus was created was difficult to sell abroad. East central Europeans, including Poles, Czechs, Yugoslavs, and Romanians, all tied to France through military and political commitments, were excluded from western European markets and were isolated economically from their treaty allies. Economic ties with Germany endured in ways that perpetuated economic dependence and threatened future survival.

Finally, common borders produced tensions over territories. The peace settlements made no one happy. Poland quarreled with Lithuania and Czechoslovakia vied with Poland over territorial claims. Poland actually went to war with Russia for six months in 1920 in an effort to reclaim the Ukraine and expand its borders to what they had been more than a century earlier. The Bolsheviks counterattacked and tried to turn the conflict into a revolutionary war to spread communism to central Europe. French military advisers came to the aid of the Poles and turned the Russians back. The Treaty of Riga, signed in March 1921, gave Poland much but not all of the territory it claimed.

Hungary, having lost the most territory in World War I, held the distinction of having the greatest number of territorial grievances against its neighbors—Czechoslovakia, Romania, and Yugoslavia. Yugoslavia made claims against Austria. Bulgaria sought territories controlled by Greece and Romania. Ethnicity, strategic considerations, and economic needs motivated claims for territory. Disputes festered, fed by the intense nationalism that prevented the cooperation necessary for survival.

Germany, the Soviet Union, and Italy further complicated the situation with their own territorial claims against their east central European neighbors. The new German government refused to accept the loss of the "corridor" controlled by Poland that severed East Prussia from the rest of Germany. Nor was Germany resigned to the loss of part of Silesia to Poland. Russia refused to forget its losses to Romania, Poland, Finland, and the Baltic states. Italy, too weak to act on its own,

nevertheless dreamed of expansion into Yugoslavia, Austria, and Albania. The redefined borders of eastern and central Europe produced animosity and the seeds of ongoing conflict. The new states of eastern Europe stood as a picket fence between Germany and Russia, a fence that held little promise of guaranteeing the peace or of making good neighbors.

German Recovery

From defeat, Germany, the most populous nation in western Europe with 60 million people, emerged strong. In 1919 the German people endorsed a new liberal and democratic government, the Weimar Republic, so named for the city in which its constitution had been written. The constitution of the new government was unusually progressive, with voting rights for women and extensive civil liberties for German citizens. Because World War I had not been fought in Germany, German transportation networks and industrial plant had escaped serious damage. Its industry was fed by raw materials and energy resources unsurpassed anywhere in Europe outside Russia. (See Special Feature, "Buildings for the Future," pp. 906–907.)

In east central Europe, Germany had actually benefited from the dismantling of the Habsburg Empire and the removal of Poland and the Baltic states from Russian control. Replacing its formerly large neighbor to the east were weak states potentially susceptible to Germany's influence. Because the governments of east central Europe feared communism, they were not likely to ally with the Soviet state. The existence of the small buffer states left open the possibility of German collaboration with Russia, since the two large nations might be able to negotiate their interests in the area.

On its western frontier, Germany's prospects were not so bright. Alsace and Lorraine had been returned to France. From German territory, a demilitarized zone had been created in the Rhineland. The Saar district was under the protection of League of Nations commissioners, and the Saar coal mines were transferred to French ownership until 1935, when a plebiscite returned the region to Germany. Humiliated and betrayed by the geographic consequences of its defeat, Germany looked to recover its status.

Germany's primary foreign policy goal was revision of the treaty settlements of World War I. German politicians and military leaders perceived disarmament, loss of territory, and payment of reparations as serious obstacles in restoring Germany's position as a great power.

German statesmen sought liberation of the Rhineland from foreign military occupation, return of the Saar basin, and recovery of the Corridor and Upper Silesia from Poland.

German leaders set economic recovery as the basis of their new foreign policy. In 1922, Germany signed the Treaty of Rapallo with Russia, a peacetime partnership that shocked the western powers. Economics motivated the new Russo-German alliance: German industry needed markets and the Russians needed loans to reconstruct their economy. Both states wanted to break out of the isolation imposed on them by the victors of World War I. However, Germany quickly learned that markets in Russia were limited and that hopes for recovery depended on financial cooperation with western Europe and the United States. At the end of 1923, Gustav Stresemann (1878–1929) assumed direction of the German Foreign Ministry and began to implement a conciliatory policy toward France and Britain. By displaying peaceful intentions he hoped to secure American capital for German industry and win the support of the West for the revision of the peace settlement.

Stresemann joined his French and British counterparts, Aristide Briand (1862–1932) and Austen Chamberlain (1863–1937), in fashioning a series of treaties at Locarno, Switzerland, in 1925. In a spirit of cooperation, Germany, France, and Belgium promised never again to go to war against each other and to respect the demilitarized zone that separated them. Britain and Italy "guaranteed" the borders of all three countries and assured the integrity of the demilitarized zone. The treaties initiated an atmosphere of goodwill, a "spirit of Locarno," that heralded a new age of security and nonaggression.

However, Germany did not renounce its ambitions in eastern Europe. Stresemann expected Germany to recover the territory lost to Poland. He also knew that Germany must rearm and expand to the east. From the early 1920s until 1933, Germany secretly rearmed in violation of Versailles treaty agreements. Undercover, it rebuilt its army and trained its soldiers and airmen on Russian territory. In violation of Versailles, Germany planned to be once again a great power with the same rights as other European countries.

France's Search for Security

Having learned the harsh lessons of 1870–71 and 1914–18, France understood well the threat posed by a united, industrialized, and well-armed Germany. During the years immediately following World War I, France deeply distrusted Germany. France had a smaller population at 40 million people and lower industrial production than Germany. France was devastated by the war and Germany was not. But France did have certain advantages in 1921. It had the best-equipped army in the world. Germany was disarmed. The Rhineland was demilitarized and occupied. But France knew that without the support of Great Britain and the United States it could not enforce the Treaty of Versailles and keep Germany militarily weak.

The Americans and the British refused to conclude a long-term peacetime alliance with the French. In search of allies on the Continent, therefore, France committed itself to an alliance in the east with Poland and the Little Entente nations of Czechoslovakia, Romania, and Yugoslavia. Treaties with these four states of east central Europe gave France some security in the event of an attack. But the treaties were also liabilities because France would have to fight to defend east central Europe.

To keep Germany militarily and economically weak, the French attempted to enforce the Treaty of Versailles fully and completely in 1921–23. They were willing to do so alone if necessary. In 1923 the French army invaded the Ruhr district of Germany and occupied it with the intention of collecting reparations payments. But the Ruhr invasion served only to isolate France further from its wartime allies. France depended on loans from American banks to balance its budget, and the Americans disapproved of the French use of military might to enforce the treaty.

In 1924–25, France decided to cooperate with the United States and Great Britain rather than continue a policy of enforcing the treaty alone and attempting to keep Germany weak. France withdrew its army from the Ruhr and some troops from the Rhineland. It agreed to lower German reparations payments. In addition, by signing the Locarno treaties, France cooperated with the Anglo-American policy that rejected the use of military force against Germany and promoted German economic recovery.

French anxiety about security continued. Nothing indicated the nature of this anxiety more clearly than the construction, beginning in the late 1920s, of the Maginot Line, a system of defensive fortifications between Germany and France.

Throughout the 1920s French political leaders tried to engage Great Britain in guaranteeing the security of France and Europe. The British agreed to defend France and Belgium against possible German aggression. They stopped short, however, of promising to defend Poland and Czechoslovakia. After settling this matter at Locarno, Britain largely reverted to its prewar pattern of withdrawing from continental Europe and concentrating its attention on the demands of its global empire.

The United States in Europe

The Treaty of Versailles marked the demise of European autonomy. American intervention had boosted French and British morale during the crucial months of 1917. In providing financial help, ships, troops, and supplies, the United States had rescued the Allied powers. After the war, a balance of power in Europe could not be maintained without outside help. Germany had been defeated, but if it recovered, France and Britain alone would probably not be able to contain it. Security and peace now depended on the presence of the United States to guarantee a stable balance of power in Europe and to defend Western hegemony in the world.

The United States was, however, unwilling to assume a new role as political leader of Europe and mediator of European conflict. It refused to sign a joint peace, arranging instead a separate peace with Germany. It also refused to join the League of Nations. Following the war, the League had been devised as an international body of nations committed, according to Article 10 of its Covenant, to "respect and preserve as against external aggression the territorial integrity and existing political independence" of others. Germany was excluded from membership until 1926; and the USSR (Union of Soviet Socialist Republics) was denied entry until 1934. Otherwise, the League of Nations claimed a global membership. But the absence of U.S. support and the lack of any machinery to enforce its decisions undermined the possibility of the League's long-term effectiveness. Hopes that the international body could serve as a peacekeeper collapsed in 1931 with the League's failure to deal with the crisis of Japanese aggression against Manchuria.

The United States persisted in avoiding political and military obligations in Europe with the idea of protecting its own freedom and autonomy. Instead it sought to promote German economic recovery and reasoned that a peaceful and stable Europe would be reestablished without a real balance of power in Europe and without a commitment from the United States.

Many feared that territorial settlements of the peace held the promise of another war. Even efforts at comprehensive international cooperation like the League of

International Politics

1919	Creation of the League of Nations
1920	War between Poland and Russia
1921	Treaty of Riga
1922	Germany and Russia sign Treaty of Rapallo
1923	French and Belgian troops invade the Ruhr district
1924	Dawes Plan
1925	Locarno Treaties
1928	Kellogg-Briand Pact
1929	Young Plan
October 1929	Collapse of the United States stock market; beginning of the Great Depression
1935	Saar region returned to German control
1936	Germany stations troops in the Rhineland in violation of the Versailles Treaty

Nations did not overcome the problem of competitive nations, nor did the Kellogg-Briand Pact signed by twenty-three nations in 1928. Named for U.S. Secretary of State Frank B. Kellogg (1856–1937) and French foreign minister Aristide Briand, who devised the plan, the pact renounced war. In the atmosphere of the 1920s, a time of hope and caution, the agreement carried all the weight of an empty gesture.

Crisis and Collapse in a World Economy

In 1918 the belligerent nations—winners and losers alike—had big bills on their hands. Although nations at war had borrowed from their own populations through the sale of war bonds, private citizens could not provide all the money needed to finance four years of war. France borrowed from Great Britain. Both Great Britain and France took loans from the United States. When all else failed, belligerent nations could and did print money not backed by productive wealth. Because more money had claims on the same amount of national wealth, the money in circulation was worth less. When the people who had purchased war bonds were then paid off with depreciated currency, they lost real wealth. Inflation had the same effect as taxation. The people had less wealth and the government had less debt.

The United States, for the first time in history the leading creditor nation in the world, had no intention of wiping the slate clean by forgiving war debts. Nor did it intend to accept repayment in less-valuable postwar currencies: loans were tied to gold. Britain, France, and Belgium counted on reparations from Germany to pay their war debts and to rebuild their economies. Reparations were calculated on the basis of the damages Germany had inflicted on the Allies. The postwar Reparations Commission determined that Germany owed the victors 132 billion gold marks ($33 billion) to be paid in annual installments of 2 billion gold marks ($500 million) plus 26 percent of the value of German exports.

For the German people and for German leaders, reparations were an unacceptable, punitive levy that mortgaged the prosperity of future generations. Germany, too, wanted to recover from the years of privation of the war. Substantial reparations payments would have transferred real wealth from Germany to the Allies.

This hopeful cartoon was inspired by the "spirit of Locarno." The artist saw the 1925 Locarno treaties as the long-awaited millennium of European peace. Fourteen years later, the German panzers rolled into Poland.

Transferring wealth would have cut into any increase in the German standard of living in the 1920s, and it would have diminished the investment needed to make the German economy grow.

When French and Belgian troops entered the Ruhr district of Germany in order to exact overdue reparations payments, the German government recommended that German miners, trainmen, and civil servants respond with passive resistance. To pay these idle employees and employers, the German government printed huge amounts of currency. The mark collapsed, and world currencies were endangered. With financial disaster looming, the British and Americans decided to intervene. A plan must be devised that would permit Germany to prosper while funneling payments to France, so dependent on reparations for its own recovery and for its war debt payments to the United States. In 1924, the American banker Charles G. Dawes (1865–1951), along with a group of international financial experts appointed by the Allied governments, devised a solution to the reparations problem. The Dawes Plan aimed to end inflation and restore economic prosperity in Germany by giving Germany a more modest and realistic schedule of payments and by extending a loan from American banks to get payments started.

As important as reparations and war debts are in any understanding of the Western world in the 1920s, they cannot be considered in isolation. Debtor nations, whether Allies paying back loans to the United States or defeated nations paying reparations to the victors, needed to be able to sell their goods in world markets. They saw trade as the principal way to accumulate enough national income to pay back what they owed and to prosper domestically without burying their citizens under a mountain of new taxes.

If trade was to be the stepladder out of the financial hole of indebtedness, open markets and stable currencies were its rungs. A stable Europe would give the United States, it recognized, a market for its own agricultural and industrial products and provide a guarantee for recovery of its loans and investments. Yet the proverbial monkey wrench in a smoothly functioning international economy was the trade policy of the United States. Republican political leaders in the United States insisted on high tariffs to protect domestic goods against imports. But high tariffs prevented Europeans from selling in the United States and earning the dollars they needed to repay war debts.

While blocking imports, the United States planned to expand its own exports to world markets, especially to Europe. The problem for American exporters, however, was the instability of European currencies in the first half of the 1920s. All over Europe governments allowed inflation to rise with the expectation that depreciating currencies would make their goods cheaper in world markets and hence more saleable.

Depreciating European currencies on the one hand meant an appreciating dollar on the other. For the "grand design" of U.S. trade expansion, a strong dollar was no virtue. More and more German marks, British pounds, and French francs had to be spent to purchase American goods. The result was that fewer American exports were sold in European markets. Because two-thirds of Germany's long-term credits came from the United States, Germany's fate was directly linked to the fortunes of American financial centers. Conversely, the soundness of American banks depended on a solvent Germany, which now absorbed 18 percent of U.S. capital exports.

Despite the scaled-down schedule of the Dawes Plan, reparations remained a bitter pill for German leaders and the German public to swallow. In 1929, American bankers devised another plan under the leadership of the American businessman Owen D. Young (1874–1962), chairman of the board of General Electric. Although the Young Plan initially transferred $100 million to Germany, Germans saw the twentieth century stretching before them as year after year of nothing but humiliating reparations payments. To make matters worse, after 1928 American private loans shriveled in Germany, as American investors sought the higher yields of a booming stock market at home.

Europe as a whole made rapid progress in manufacturing production during the second half of the decade, and by 1929 had surpassed its prewar (1913) per capita income. Yet structural weaknesses were present, although they went almost unnoticed. The false security of a new gold standard masked the instability and interdependence of currencies. Low prices prevailed in the agricultural sector, keeping the incomes of a significant segment of the population depressed. But the low rate of long-term capital investment was obscured in the flurry of short-term loans, whose disappearance in 1928 spelled the beginning of the end for European recovery. The protectionist trade policy of the United States conflicted with its insistence on repayment of war debts. Germany's resentment over reparations was in no way alleviated by the Dawes and Young repayment plans. The irresponsibility of American speculation in the stock market pricked the bubble of prosperity. None of these factors operated in isolation to cause the collapse

that began in 1929. Taken together, however, they caused a depression of previously unimagined severity of the international economic system.

The Great Depression

In the history of the Western world the year 1929 has assumed mythic proportions. During one week in October of that year, the stock market in the United States collapsed. This crash set off the Great Depression in an international economic system already plagued with structural problems. It also marked the beginning of a long period of worldwide economic stagnation and depression.

A confluence of factors made Europe and the rest of the world vulnerable to reversals in the American economy. Heavy borrowing and reliance on American investment throughout the 1920s contributed to the inherent instability of European economies. Even Great Britain, itself a creditor, relied on short-term loans; "borrowing

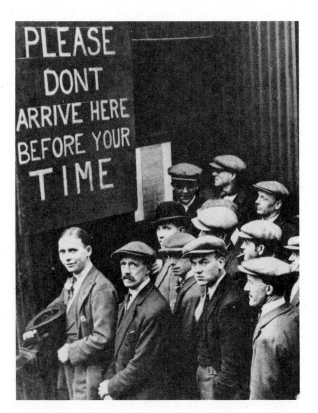

Lining up for the dole in London, 1931. During the Great Depression, private charity and public relief offered hope to the unemployed.

WINIFRED HOLTBY (1898–1935)

■ *Winifred Holtby was a British novelist, journalist, and social reformer who covered European political events throughout the interwar period. In this selection from her writings she chronicles the differential impact that war and depression had on women's lives. Expectations about woman's proper role, whether it be in returning to the "natural" functions of housewife and mother or serving her country in the workplace, were profoundly political and at the center of national politics.*

The effect of the slump upon women's economic position is most obvious, not only in the problems of unemployment among both industrial and professional women, but still more in the bitterness surrounding the question of married women's paid employment, "pin money" office girls, unorganised casual female factory labour, and claims to alimony, maintenance and separation allowances. These are the dilemmas of scarcity. It is here that the shoe pinches when national purchasing power has failed to distribute adequately the products of industry.

During the War, women entered almost every branch of industry and most of the professions. . . . In transport, engineering, chemicals, textiles, tailoring and woodwork, women took the places which, ever since the sorting-out process which followed the first disorganised scramble of the Industrial Revolution, had been reserved to men. They took and they enjoyed them.

Then the men returned, and on demobilisation demanded again the jobs which they had left. The position was not simple.

Some of the men had received promises that their work should be kept for them; but of these, some did not return. Some women surrendered their shovels, lathes and hoes without a grievance. Their work had been "for the duration of the war" and they had no desire to retain it.

But others thought differently. Women, they told themselves, had been excluded from the more highly-skilled and better-paid industrial posts for two or more generations. They had been told that certain processes were beyond their power. It was a lie. During the war they had proved it to be so, by their own skill and efficiency. Why surrender without a word opportunities closed to them by fraud and falsehood? They had as much right to wheel, loom or cash-register as any man. Why then pretend that they were intruders in a world which was as much their own as their brothers'? . . .

After 1928, jobs became not duties which war-time propaganda taught girls that it was patriotic to perform, but privileges to be reserved for potential bread-winners and fathers of families. Women were commanded to go back to the home.

The bitterness began which has lasted ever since—the women keeping jobs and the men resenting it—the men regaining the jobs and the women resenting it. . . .

In Italy, Germany and Ireland a new dream of natural instinctive racial unity was arising, which designed for women a return to their "natural" functions of house-keeping and child-bearing; while in the English-speaking countries a new anti-rational philosophy combined with economic fatalism, militated against the ebullient hopes which an earlier generation had pinned to education, effort, and individual enterprise.

All generalisations are false. In every civilised country are little groups of older women with memories of suffrage struggles, and young women who grew up into the post-war optimism, and whose ideas remain unchanged by the fashions of the hour. It is they who still organise protests against reaction; who in national and international societies defend the political, civil, and economic equality of men and women; who invade new territories of achievement; who look towards a time when there shall be no wrangling over rights and wrongs, man's place and woman's place, but an equal and co-operative partnership, the individual going unfettered to the work for which he is best suited, responsibilities and obligations shared alike.

From Winifred Holtby, *Women and a Changing Civilization,* 1934.

"Passing the Buck," a British cartoonist's view of the ripple effect of Germany's inability to repay war reparations.

short and lending long" proved to be disastrous when loans were recalled. Excessive lending and leniency were fatal mistakes of creditor nations, especially the United States. When in the summer of 1929 American investors turned off the tap of the flow of capital to search for higher profits at home, a precarious situation began to get worse.

A depression is a severe downturn marked by sharp declines in income and production, as buying and selling slow down to a crawl. Depressions were not new in the business cycles of modern economies, but what happened in October 1929 was more serious in its extent and duration than any depression before or since. The bottom was not reached until three years after it began. In 1932 one in four American workers was without a job. One in three banks had closed its doors. People lost their homes, unable to pay their mortgages; farmers lost their land, unable to earn enough to survive. The great prosperity of the 1920s had vanished overnight.

The plight of the United States rippled through world markets. Americans stopped buying foreign goods. The Smoot-Hawley Tariff Act, passed by the U.S. Congress in 1930, created an impenetrable tariff fortress against agricultural and manufactured imports and hampered foreign producers. The major trading na-

tions of the world, including Great Britain, enacted similar protectionist measures. American investment abroad dried up, as the lifelines of American capital to Europe were cut.

European nations tried to stanch the outward flow of capital and gold by restricting the transfer of capital abroad. Nevertheless, large amounts of foreign-owned gold ($6.6 billion from 1931 to 1938) were deposited in American banks. In 1931 President Herbert Hoover supported a moratorium on the payment of reparations and war debts. The moratorium, combined with the pooling of gold in the United States, led to a run on the British pound sterling in 1931 and the collapse of Great Britain as one of the world's great financial centers.

The gold standard disappeared from the international economy, never to return. So too did reparations payments and war debts when the major nations of Europe met without the United States at a special conference held in Lausanne, Switzerland, in 1932. Something else died at the end of the 1920s: confidence in a self-adjusting economy, an "invisible hand" by which the business cycle would be righted. In 1932–33, the Depression, showing no signs of disappearing, reached its nadir and became a global phenomenon. Economic hardship transformed political realities. The Labour cabinet in Great Britain was forced to resign, and a new national government composed of Conservative, Liberal, and Labour leaders was formed to deal with the world economic emergency. Republican government was torn by bitter divisions in France. In the United States the Republican party, which had been in power since 1920, was defeated in 1932. Franklin D. Roosevelt, a Democrat, was elected president in a landslide victory with a mandate to transform the American economy. German democratic institutions were pulled down in favor of fascist dictatorship.

In the decade following the Great War, peace settlements did not promote a stable, international community. Instead, self-determination of peoples created new grounds for national rivalries in eastern Europe, and the lack of any effective means of guaranteeing the peace only exacerbated prewar animosities. The economic interdependence of nation-states through an international system of reparations payments and loans increased the vulnerability of governments to external pressures. With the collapse of world markets and the international finance system in 1929, political stability and international cooperation seemed more elusive than ever.

The Soviet Union's Separate Path

In the decade following war, revolution, and civil war, the Soviet state committed its people to a program of rapid industrial growth in order to ensure its survival as a great power. The costs of Russia's rapid industrialization were wasted resources, enormous human suffering, and millions of lost lives. Lenin's successor, Joseph Stalin (1879-1953), obliged the Soviet people to achieve in a single generation what it had taken Western Europe a century and a half to accomplish.

The Soviet Regime at the End of the Civil War

Echoing Karl Marx, the Bolshevik leader Lenin declared that the revolution and the civil war had been won in the name of "the dictatorship of the proletariat." The hammer and sickle on the Soviet flag represented the united rule of workers and peasants and were symbolic reminders of the commitment to rule from below. But at the end of the civil war in 1921, the Bolsheviks, not the people, were in charge.

The industrial sector, small as it was, was in total disarray by 1921. Famine and epidemics in 1921-22 killed and weakened more people than the Great War and the civil war combined. The countryside had been plundered to feed the Red and White armies. The combination of empty promises and a declining standard of living left workers and peasants frustrated and discontented. Urban strikes and rural uprisings defied short-term solutions. The proletarian revolutionary heroes of 1917 were rejecting the new Soviet regime. The Bolshevik party now faced the task of restoring a country exhausted by war and revolution, its resources depleted, its economy destroyed.

At the head of the Soviet state was Lenin, the first among equals in the seven-man Politburo. The Central Committee of the Communist party decided "fundamental questions of policy, international and domestic," but in reality the Politburo, the inner committee of the Central Committee, held the reins of power.

Among the Politburo seven, three men in particular attempted to leave their mark on the direction of Soviet policy: Leon Trotsky (1879-1940), Nikolai Bukharin (1888-1938), and Joseph Stalin (1879-1953). The great drama of Soviet leadership in the 1920s revolved around how the most brilliant (Trotsky) and the most popular (Bukharin) failed at the hands of the most shrewdly political (Stalin).

The two poles in the debate over the direction of economic development were on one end a planned economy totally directed from above, and on the other an economy controlled from below. In 1920-21 Leon Trotsky, at that time people's commissar of war, favored a planned economy based on the militarization of labor. Trade unions opposed such a proposal and argued for a share of control over production. Lenin, however, favored a proletarian democracy and supported unions organized independently of state control.

The controversy was resolved in the short run at the Tenth Party Congress in 1921, when Lenin chose to steer a middle course between trade-union autonomy and militarization by preserving the unions and at the same time insisting on the state's responsibility for economic development. His primary goal was to stabilize Bolshevik rule in its progress toward socialism. He recognized that nothing could be achieved without the peasants. As a result, Lenin found himself embracing a new economic policy that he termed a "temporary retreat" from Communist goals.

The New Economic Policy, 1921-1928

In 1921 Lenin ended the forced requisitioning of peasant produce, which had been in effect during the civil war. In its place, peasants were to pay a tax in kind, that is, a fixed portion of their yield, to the state. Peasants in turn were permitted to reinstate private trade on their own terms. Party leaders accepted this dramatic shift in economic policy because it held the promise of prosperity, so necessary for political stability. The actions of Lenin to return the benefits of productivity to the economy, combined with those of the peasants to reestablish markets, created the New Economic Policy, or NEP, that emerged in the spring and summer of 1921.

It remained for Nikolai Bukharin to give shape and substance to the economic policy that permitted Russian producers to engage in some capitalist practices. As one of the founding fathers of the Soviet state and the youngest of the top Bolshevik leaders, Bukharin took his place on the Central Committee of the Communist party and on the Politburo as well.

Bukharin set about solving Russia's single greatest problem: how could Russia, crippled by poverty, find enough capital to industrialize? Insisting on the need for long-term economic planning, Bukharin counted on a prosperous and contented peasantry as the mainstay of his policy. Bukharin was also strongly interested in attracting foreign investment to Soviet endeavors as a way of ensuring future productivity.

At base Bukharin appreciated the importance of landholding to Russian peasants and defended a system of individual farms and private accumulation. Agriculture would operate through a market system, and the peasants would have the right to control their own surpluses. Rural prosperity would generate profits that could be used for gradual industrial development. Bukharin's policy stood in stark contrast to Stalin's later plan to feed industry by starving the agricultural sector.

Collective and large-scale farming had to be deferred indefinitely in order to reconcile the peasantry to the state—a policy profoundly at odds with the programs of the Communist state to pull down the capitalist system and establish socialism. In 1924 the tax in kind was replaced with a tax in cash. With this shift the state now procured grain through commercial agencies and cooperative organizations instead of directly from the peasants. The move toward western capitalist models seemed more pronounced than ever to critics of the NEP.

Beginning in 1922 Lenin suffered a series of strokes, which virtually removed him from power by March 1923. When he died on 21 January 1924, the Communist leadership split over the ambiguities of the NEP. The backward nature of agriculture did not permit the kind of productivity that the NEP policy makers anticipated. Cities demanded more food as their populations swelled with the influx of unskilled workers from rural areas. In 1927 peasants held back their grain. The Soviet Union was then experiencing a series of foreign-policy setbacks in the west and in China, and Bolshevik leaders spoke of an active anti-Soviet conspiracy by the capitalist powers, led by Great Britain. The Soviet state lowered the price of grain, thereby squeezing the peasantry. The war scare, combined with the drop in food prices, soon led to an economic crisis.

By 1928 the NEP was in trouble. Stalin, general secretary of the Communist party of the Soviet Union, saw his chance. Under his supervision, the state intervened to prevent peasants from disposing of their own grain surpluses. The peasants responded to requisitioning by hoarding their produce and violent rioting. Bukharin and the NEP were in danger. Stalin exploited the internal crisis and external dangers to eliminate his political rivals. Stalin's rival Trotsky had been expelled from the Communist party in November 1927 on charges that he had engaged in antiparty activities. Banished from Rus-

sia in 1929, he eventually found refuge in Mexico, where he was assassinated in 1940 at Stalin's command.

Bukharin's popularity in the party also threatened Stalin's aspirations. Bukharin was dropped from the Politburo in 1929. Tolerated through the early 1930s, he was arrested in 1937, and tried and executed for alleged treasonous activities the following year. The fate that befell Trotsky and Bukharin was typical of that which afflicted those who stood in the way of Stalin's pursuit of dictatorial control. Stalin was, in a colleague's words, "a grey blur." Beneath his apparently colorless personality, however, was a dangerous man of great political acumen, a ruthless, behind-the-scenes politician who controlled the machinery of the party to his own ends and was not averse to employing violence in order to achieve them.

Stalin's Rise to Power

Joseph Stalin was born Iosif Vissarionovich Dzhugashvili in 1879. His self-chosen revolutionary name, Stalin, means "steel" in Russian and is as good an indication as any of his opinion of his own personality and will. Stalin, the man who ruled the Soviet Union as a dictator from 1928 until his death in 1953, was not a Russian. He was from Georgia, an area between the Black and Caspian seas, and spoke Russian with an accent. Georgia, with its land occupied and its people subjugated by invading armies for centuries, was annexed to the expanding Russian empire in 1801.

As the youngest of four and the only surviving child of Vissarion and Ekaterina Dzhugashvili, Stalin endured a childhood of brutal misery. Vissarion was a poor and often unemployed shoemaker who intended that his son be apprenticed in the same trade. Under his mother's protection, young Iosif received an education and entered a seminary against his father's wishes. Iosif's schooling, extraordinary for someone of his poverty-stricken background, gave him the opportunity to learn about revolutionary socialist politics. At the turn of the century, Georgia had a strong Marxist revolutionary movement that opposed Russian exploitation. Iosif dropped out of the seminary in 1899 to engage in underground Marxist activities, and he soon became a follower of Lenin.

Stalin's association with Lenin kept him close to the center of power after the October Revolution of 1917. First as people's commissar for nationalities (1920-23) and then as general secretary of the Central Committee of the Communist party (1922-53), Stalin showed natural talent as a political strategist. His familiarity with

Leon Trotsky was a loser in the Soviet power struggle that followed the death of Lenin. He was exiled from Russia in 1929, and in 1940 he was assassinated in Mexico on Stalin's orders.

non-Russian nationalities was a great asset in his dealings with the ethnic diversity and unrest in the vast Soviet state. Unlike other party leaders who had lived in exile in western Europe before the revolution, Stalin had little knowledge of the West.

After Lenin's death in 1924, Stalin shrewdly bolstered his own reputation by orchestrating a cult of worship for Lenin. In 1929 Stalin used the occasion of his fiftieth birthday to fashion for himself a reputation as the living hero of the Soviet state. Icons, statues, busts, and images of all sorts of both Lenin and Stalin appeared everywhere in public buildings, schoolrooms, and homes. He systematically began eliminating his rivals, so that he alone stood unchallenged as Lenin's true successor.

The First Five-Year Plan

The cult of Stalin coincided with the first Five-Year Plan (1929–32), which launched Stalin's program of rapid industrialization. Between 1929 and 1937, the period covered by the first two five-year plans, truncated because of their proclaimed success, Stalin laid the foundation for an urban industrial society in the Soviet

Union. By brutally squeezing profits out of the agricultural sector, Stalin managed to increase heavy industrial production between 300 and 600 percent.

Stalin committed the Soviet Union to rapid industrialization as the only way to preserve socialism. The failure of revolutionary movements in western Europe meant that the Soviet Union must preserve "Socialism in one country," the slogan of the political philosophy that justified Stalin's economic plans. Stalin made steel the idol of the new age. The Soviet state needed heavy machinery to build the future. An industrial labor force was created virtually overnight as peasant men and women were placed at workbenches and before the vast furnaces of modern metallurgical plants. The number of women in the industrial workforce tripled in the decade after 1929. The reliability of official indices varied, but there is little doubt that heavy industrial production soared between 1929 and 1932. The Russian people were constantly reminded that no sacrifice could be too great in producing steel and iron.

When he first began to deal with the grain crisis of 1928, Stalin did not intend collective agriculture as a solution. But by the end of 1929 the increasingly repressive measures instituted by the state against the

THE RESULTS OF THE FIRST FIVE-YEAR PLAN

■ Under Joseph Stalin the Soviet Union embarked on rapid industrialization that transformed the peasant-based economy into a leading iron and steel producer. Stalin here chronicles the achievements of a Five-Year Plan that met its goals in four years, achieving what the western industrialized nations took many generations and about 150 years to accomplish. The Soviet leader did not tally the cost in human lives or the impact on the quality of life that such brutal economic transformation entailed.

The fundamental task of the Five-Year Plan was to transfer our country, with its backward, and in part medieval, technique, to the lines of new, modern technique.

The fundamental task of the Five-Year Plan was to convert the USSR from an agrarian and weak country, dependent upon the caprices of the capitalist countries, into an industrial and powerful country, fully self-reliant and independent of the caprices of world capitalism.

The fundamental task of the Five-Year Plan was, in converting the USSR into an industrial country, fully to eliminate the capitalist elements, to widen the front of socialist forms of economy, and to create the economic base for the abolition of classes in the USSR, for the construction of socialist society . . .

The fundamental task of the Five-Year Plan was to transfer small and scattered agriculture to the lines of large-scale collective farming, so as to ensure the economic base for socialism in the rural districts and thus to eliminate the possibility of the restoration of capitalism in the USSR.

Finally, the task of the Five-Year Plan was to create in the country all the necessary technical and economic prerequisites for increasing to the utmost the defensive capacity of the country, to enable it to organize determined resistance to any and every attempt at military intervention from outside, to any and every attempt at military attack from without. . . .

What are the results of the Five-Year Plan in four years in the sphere of *industry?*

Have we achieved victory in this sphere?

Yes, we have. . . .

We did not have an iron and steel industry, the foundation for the industrialization of the country. Now we have this industry.

We did not have a tractor industry. Now we have one.

We did not have an automobile industry. Now we have one.

We did not have a machine-tool industry. Now we have one.

We did not have a big and up-to-date chemical industry. Now we have one.

We did not have a real and big industry for the production of modern agricultural machinery. Now we have one.

We did not have an aircraft industry. Now we have one.

In output of electric power we were last on the list. Now we rank among the first.

In output of oil products and coal we were last on the list. Now we rank among the first.

We had only one coal and metallurgical base—in the Ukraine—which we barely managed to keep going. We have not only succeeded in improving this base, but have created a new coal and metallurgical base—in the East—which is the pride of our country.

peasants had led both to collectivization and to the deportation of *kulaks*, the derisive term for wealthy peasants that literally means "the tight-fisted ones." Stalin achieved forced collectivization by confiscating land and establishing collective farms run by the state. Within a few months, half of all peasant farms were collectivized. By 1938 private land was virtually eliminated. The state set prices, controlled distribution, and selected crops with the intention of ensuring a steady food supply and freeing a rural labor force

THE RESULTS OF THE FIRST FIVE-YEAR PLAN

We had only one center of the textile industry—in the North of our country. As a result of our efforts we will have in the very near future two new centers of the textile industry—in Central Asia and Western Siberia.

And we have not only created these new great industries, but have created them on a scale and in dimensions that eclipse the scale and dimensions of European industry.

And as a result of all this the capitalist elements have been completely and irrevocably eliminated from industry, and socialist industry has become the sole form of industry in the USSR.

And as a result of all this our country has been converted from an agrarian into an industrial country; for the proportion of industrial output, as compared with agricultural output, has risen from 48 per cent of the total in the beginning of the Five-Year Plan period (1928) to 70 per cent at the end of the fourth year of the Five-Year Plan period (1932) . . .

The object of the Five-Year Plan in the sphere of agriculture was to unite the scattered and small individual peasant farms, which lacked the opportunity of utilizing tractors and modern agricultural machinery, into large collective farms, equipped with all the modern implements of highly developed agriculture, and to cover unoccupied land with model state farms . . .

The party has succeeded, in a matter of three years, in organizing more than 200,000 collective farms and about 5,000 state farms specializing mainly in grain growing and livestock raising, and at the same time it has succeeded, in the course of four years, in enlarging the crop area by 21,000,000 hectares.

The party has succeeded in getting more than 60 per cent of the peasant farms, which account for more than 70 per cent of the land cultivated by peasants, to unite into collective farms, which means that we have *fulfilled* the Five-Year Plan *threefold*.

The party has succeeded in creating the possibility of obtaining, not 500,000,000 to 600,000,000 poods[1] of marketable grain, which was the amount purchased in the period when individual peasant farming predominated, but 1,200,000,000 to 1,400,000,000 poods[1] of grain annually.

The party has succeeded in routing the kulaks as a class, although they have not yet been dealt the final blow; the laboring peasants have been emancipated from kulak bondage and exploitation, and a firm economic basis for the Soviet government, the basis of collective farming, has been established in the countryside.

The party has succeeded in converting the USSR from a land of small peasant farming into a land where agriculture is run on the largest scale in the world.

Such, in general terms, are the results of the Five-Year Plan in four years in the sphere of agriculture.

[1]pood—a unit of weight equivalent to 36.1 lbs.

From Joseph Stalin, *Selected Writings,* 1942.

for heavy industry. More as a publicity ploy than a statement of fact, the Five-Year Plan was declared a success after only three years. It was a success in one important sense: it did lay the foundations of the Soviet planned economy, in which the state bureaucracy made all decisions about production, distribution, and prices.

Collectivization meant misery for the 25 million peasant families who suffered under it. At least 5 million peasants died between 1929 and 1932. Collectivization ripped apart the fabric of village life, destroyed families, and sent homeless peasants into exile. Peasants who resisted collectivization retaliated by destroying their own crops and livestock. Rapid industrial development shattered the delicate shells of the lives of millions of people. In attempting to develop an industrial sector overnight, Stalin, as tsars before him, saw that Russia could be carried into the future only on the backs of its peasants.

The Comintern, Economic Development, and the Purges

In addition to promoting its internal economic development, the Soviet Union had to worry about survival in a world-political system composed entirely of capitalist countries. After the Bolshevik revolution in 1917, Lenin had fully expected that other socialist revolutions would follow throughout the world, especially in central and western Europe. These revolutions would destroy capitalism and secure Russia's place in a new world order. But as the prospects for world proletarian revolution evaporated, Soviet leaders sought to protect their revolutionary country from what they saw as a hostile capitalist world. They used diplomacy to this end. The end of the Allied intervention in Russia allowed the Bolshevik state to initiate diplomatic relations with the West, beginning with the Treaty of Rapallo signed with Germany in 1921. By 1924 all the major countries of the world—with the exception of the United States—had established diplomatic relations with the Soviet Union. In 1928 the USSR cooperated in the preparation of a world disarmament conference to be held in Geneva and joined western European powers in a commitment to peace. The United States and the Soviet Union exchanged ambassadors for the first time in 1933.

In addition to diplomatic relations, the Soviet state in 1919 encouraged various national Communist parties to form an association for the purpose of promoting and coordinating the coming world revolution. This Communist International, or Comintern, was based in Moscow and included representatives from thirty-seven countries by 1920. As it became clear that a world revolution was not imminent, the Comintern concerned itself with the ideological purity of its member parties. Under Lenin's direction, the Soviet Communist party determined policy for all the member parties.

Bukharin and Stalin shared a view of the Comintern that prevailed from 1924 to 1929: since the collapse of

A Soviet propaganda poster shows a caricature of the fat capitalist dismissing the Five-Year Plan as "fantasy." Later, the smug capitalist turns green with envy as Soviet industrial might amazes the world.

capitalism was not imminent, the Comintern should work to promote the unity of working classes everywhere and should cooperate with existing worker organizations. In 1929, however, Stalin argued that advanced capitalist societies were teetering on the brink of new wars and revolutions. As a result, the Comintern must seek to sever the ties between foreign Communist parties and social democratic parties in order to prepare for the revolutionary struggle. Stalin purged the Comintern of dissenters, and he decreed a policy of noncooperation in Europe from 1929 to 1933. As a result, socialism in Europe was badly split between Communists and democratic socialists.

The Second Five-Year Plan, announced in 1933, succeeded in reducing the Soviet Union's dependence on foreign imports, especially in the areas of heavy industry, machinery, and metal works. The basic physical plant for armaments production was in place by 1937, and resources continued to be shifted away from consumer goods to heavy industrial development. This industrial development, and the collectivization of agriculture, brought growing urbanization. By 1939 one in three Soviet people were living in cities, compared to one in six in 1926. In his commitment to increased production, Stalin introduced into the workplace incentives and differential wage scales at odds with the principles and programs of the original Bolshevik revolution. Stricter discipline was enforced; absenteeism was punished with severe fines or loss of employment. Workers who exceeded their quotas were rewarded and honored.

Amid this rapid industrialization, Stalin inaugurated the Great Purge, actually a series of purges lasting from 1934 through 1938. Those whom Stalin believed to be his opponents—real and imagined, past, present, and future—were labeled "class enemies." The most prominent of them, including leaders of the Bolshevik revolution who had worked with Stalin during the 1920s, appeared in widely publicized "show trials." They were intimidated and tortured into false confessions of crimes against the regime, humiliated by brutal prosecutors, and condemned to death or imprisonment. Stalin wiped out the Bolshevik old guard, Communist party members whose first loyalty was to the international Communist movement rather than to Stalin himself, and all potential opposition within the Communist party. Probably 300,000 people were put to death, among whom were engineers, managers, technologists, and officers of the army and navy. In addition, 7 million people were placed in labor camps. Stalin now had unquestioned control of the Party and the country.

The purges dealt a severe blow to the command of the army and resulted in a shortage of qualified industrial personnel, slowing industrial growth. The Great Purge coerced the Soviet people to make great sacrifices in the drive for industrialization. It prevented any possible dissension or opposition within the USSR at a time when the "foreign threat" posed by Nazi Germany was becoming increasingly serious.

The human suffering associated with the dislocation and heavy workloads of rapid, coerced industrialization cannot be measured. Planned growth brought with it a top-heavy and often inefficient bureaucracy, and that bureaucracy ensured that the Soviet Union was the most highly centralized of the European states. The growing threat of foreign war meant an even greater diversion of resources from consumer goods to war industries, beginning with the third Five-Year Plan in 1938.

Women and the Family in the New Soviet State

The building of the new Soviet state exacted particularly high costs from women. Soviet women had been active in the revolution from the beginning. Lenin and the Bolshevik leaders were committed to the liberation of women, who, like workers, were considered to be oppressed under capitalism. Lenin denounced housework as "barbarously unproductive, petty, nerve-wracking, stultifying, and crushing drudgery." In its early days the Soviet state pledged to protect the rights of mothers without narrowing women's opportunities or restricting women's role to the family.

The Soviets waged a vigorous campaign against illiteracy. This picture shows Muslim women of the northern Caucasus region learning to read and write. The poster in the background is written in Russian and Arabic script.

THE LAW ON THE ABOLITION OF LEGAL ABORTION, 1936

■ *In his drive to industrialize the Soviet Union as rapidly as possible, Stalin stressed the economic importance of woman's role both as a worker and as a mother. At the height of the Second Five-Year Plan, many women's rights were revoked, including the right to an abortion. The "new Woman" of the revolutionary period gave way to the post-1936 woman, depicted by the state as the perfect mother who matched her husband's productivity in the workplace, ran the household, and raised a large family.*

When we speak of strengthening the Soviet family, we are speaking precisely of the struggle against the survivals of a bourgeois attitude towards marriage, women and children. So-called "free love" and all disorderly sex life are bourgeois through and through, and have nothing to do with either socialist principles or the ethics and standards of conduct of the Soviet citizen. Socialist doctrine shows this, and it is proved by life itself.

The elite of our country, the best of the Soviet youth, are as a rule also excellent family men who dearly love their children. And vice versa: the man who does not take marriage seriously, and abandons his children to the whims of fate, is usually also a bad worker and a poor member of society.

Fatherhood and motherhood have long been virtues in this country. This can be seen at the first glance, without searching enquiry. Go through the parks and streets of Moscow or of any other town in the Soviet Union on a holiday, and you will see not a few young men walking with pink-cheeked, well-fed babies in their arms. . . .

The toilers of our land have paid with their blood for the right to a life of joy, and a life of joy implies the right to have one's own family and healthy, happy children. Millions of workers beyond the frontiers of our land are still deprived of this joy, for there unemployment, hunger and helpless poverty are rampant. Old maids and elderly bachelors, a rare thing in our country, are frequent in the West, and that is no accident.

We alone have all the conditions under which a working woman can fulfil her duties as a citizen and as a mother responsible for the birth and early upbringing of her children.

A woman without children merits our pity, for she does not know the full joy of life. Our Soviet women, full-blooded citizens of the freest country in the world, have been given the bliss of motherhood. We must safeguard our family and raise and rear healthy Soviet heroes!

After the October revolution of 1917, the Bolsheviks passed a new law establishing equality for women within marriage. In 1920 abortion was legalized. New legislation established the right to divorce and removed the stigma from illegitimacy. Communes, calling themselves "laboratories of revolution," experimented with sexual equality. Russian women were enfranchised in 1917, the first women in the major countries to win this right in national elections. The Russian revolution went further than any revolution in history toward the legal liberation of women within such a short span of time.

These advances, as utopian as they appeared to admirers in western European countries, did not deal with the problems faced by the majority of Russian women. Bolshevik legislation did little to address the special economic hardships of peasant and factory women. Although paid maternity leaves and nursing breaks were required by law, these guarantees became a source of discrimination against women workers who were the last hired and first fired by employers trying to limit expenses. Divorce legislation was hardly a blessing for women with children, since men incurred no financial responsibility toward their offspring in terminating a marriage. Even as legislation was being passed in the early days of the new Soviet state, women were losing ground in the struggle for equal rights and independent economic survival.

made illegal. Homosexuality was declared a criminal offense. The family was glorified as the mainstay of the socialist order and the independence of women was challenged as a threat to Soviet productivity. While motherhood was idealized, the Stalinist drive to industrialize could not dispense with full-time women workers.

Women's double burden in the home and workplace became heavier during Stalin's reign. Most Russian women held full-time jobs in the factories or on the farms. They also worked what they called a "second shift" in running a household and taking care of children. In the industrialized nations of western Europe, the growth of a consumer economy lightened women's labor in the home to some extent. In the Soviet Union, procuring the simplest necessities was woman's work that required waiting in long lines for hours. Lack of indoor plumbing meant that women spent more hours hauling water for their families at the end of a working day. In such ways, rapid industrialization exacted its special price from Soviet women.

In the 1920s and 1930s the Soviet search for stability and prosperity took the Soviet Union down a path very different from the states of western Europe. Rejecting an accommodation with a market economy, Stalin committed the Soviet people to planned rapid industrialization that was accomplished through mass repression and great human suffering. Insulated from world markets and the devastation of the Great Depression, the Soviet Union relied on a massive state bureaucratic system to achieve socialism in one country and to make the Soviet state into an industrial giant.

The Promise of Fascism

Throughout western Europe, parliamentary institutions, representative government, and electoral politics offered no ready solutions to the problems of economic collapse and the political upheaval on the Left and the Right. Fascism promised what liberal democratic societies failed to deliver—a way out of the economic and political morass. Ruling by means of dictatorship by a charismatic leader, fascism promised an escape from parliamentary chaos, party wranglings, and the threat of communism. Fascism promised more: by identifying ready enemies, scapegoats for failed economic and

---

The Soviet Union's Separate Path

November 1917	Bolsheviks and Red Guard seize power
1919	Creation of the Communist International (Comintern)
1920	Legalization of abortion and divorce
1921	End of the civil war
1921	Introduction of the New Economic Policy
3 April 1922	Stalin becomes secretary general of the Communist party
21 January 1924	Lenin dies
1924–29	Comintern policy of "Unity of the Working Classes"
1927	Dissatisfied peasants hoard grain
November 1927	Trotsky expelled from Communist party
1928	Stalin introduces grain requisitioning
November 1929	Bukharin expelled from Politburo
1929	Introduction of First Five-Year Plan and the collectivization of agriculture
1929–33	Comintern policy of noncooperation with social democratic parties
1933–37	Second Five-Year Plan
1934–38	Great Purges
1936	Abortion declared illegal
1938	Third Five-Year Plan

By the early 1930s, reforms affecting women were in trouble due in large part to a plummeting birthrate. This decline created special worries for Soviet planners, who forecast doom if the trend was not reversed. In 1936, women's right to choose to end a first pregnancy was revoked. In the following decade all abortions were

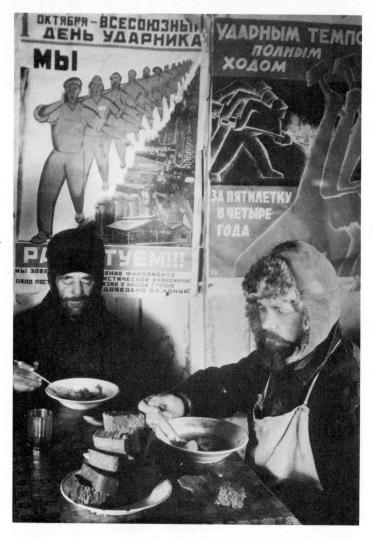

Two Soviet bricklayers enjoy a simple lunch of soup and black bread under a poster that exhorts them to accelerate production. By the end of the second Five-Year Plan in 1937, Soviet industrial production was second in the world.

national ambitions, fascism promised that it held the answer for those who sought protection and security.

The Rise of Dictatorships

Dictatorships became the most prevalent form of government in interwar Europe. Dictatorships appealed to middle classes who feared loss of their property to socialists and loss of their money to the vagaries of international markets. The move toward dictatorship appeared relentless in the interwar period. In 1920, of the twenty-eight states in Europe, twenty-six were parliamentary democracies. By the end of 1940, only five democracies remained: the United Kingdom, Ireland, Sweden, Finland, and Switzerland. The rest of Europe was under dictatorial rule. The European dictatorships of the 1930s displayed a variety of forms. On the Left,

the "dictatorship of the proletariat" in the Soviet Union was in fact a regime driven by the ruthless brutality of Joseph Stalin toward the goal of building socialism. Other dictatorships were on the Right. Italy and Germany each constructed fascist dictatorships that regarded Soviet communism as their mortal enemy. The Soviet Union, in turn, saw fascism as a serious threat.

War and postwar hardships were the catalysts for the emergence of the new mass movements of fascism in Europe. The Great War had created a political vacuum caused by the crisis in liberal values. In condemning the war and its costs, new fascist leaders, who tended to start their political careers as social reformers and even socialists, proposed a radical reformation of the status quo.

Fascism sounded very like socialism. In the Soviet Union, Bolshevik leaders reassured their people that

Europe: Types of Government

Legend:
- Dictatorships by 1938
- Democracies dismantled by dictatorships, 1938–1940
- Remaining democracies in 1940

attention than the fascist experiment in Italy that inspired observers throughout Europe to consider emulation.

Mussolini's Italy

Italy was a poor nation. Although Italy was one of the victorious Allies in World War I, Italians felt that their country had been betrayed by the peace settlement of 1919 by being denied the territory and status it deserved. A recently created electoral system based on universal manhood suffrage had produced parliamentary chaos and ministerial instability. The lack of coherent political programs only heightened the general disapproval with government that accompanied the peace negotiations. People were beginning to doubt the parliamentary regime's hold on the future. It was under these circumstances that the Fascist party, led by Benito Mussolini (1883–1945), entered politics in 1920 by attacking the large Socialist and Popular (Catholic) parties.

Mussolini had begun his prewar political career as a Socialist. The young Mussolini was arrested numerous times for Socialist political activities and placed under state surveillance. An ardent nationalist, he volunteered for combat in World War I and was promoted to the rank of corporal. Injured in early 1917 by an exploding shell detonated during firing practice, he returned to Milan to continue his work as editor of *Il Populo d'Italia* (The People of Italy), the newspaper he founded in 1914 to promote Italian participation in the war.

Mussolini yearned to be the leader of a revolution in Italy comparable to that directed by Lenin in Russia. Although his doctrinal allegiance to socialism was beginning to flag, Mussolini recognized, like Lenin, the power of the printed word to stir political passions. Emphasizing nationalist goals and vague measures of socioeconomic transformation, Mussolini identified a new enemy for Italy—bolshevism. He organized his followers into the Fascist party, a political movement that by utilizing strict party discipline quickly developed its own national network.

Many Fascists were former socialists and war veterans like Mussolini who were disillusioned with postwar government. They dreamed of Italy as a great world power, as it had been in the days of ancient Rome. Their enemies were not only Communists with their international outlook but also the big businesses, which they felt drained Italy's resources and kept its people poor and powerless. Panicky members of the lower middle

socialism was the only way of dealing with the weaknesses and inequities of the world capitalist system laid bare in the world war. In its initial condemnations of the capitalist economy and liberal political institutions and values, fascists employed revolutionary language similar to that of the Left, while manipulating in radically new ways the political symbols of the Right—the nation, the flag, and the army. Fascism promised to steer a course between the uncertainties and exploitation of a liberal capitalist system and the revolutionary upheaval and expropriation of a socialist system. Fascism was ultranationalist, and the use of force was central to its appeal.

The word *fascism* is derived from the Latin *fasces*, the name for the bundle of rods with ax head carried by the magistrates of the Roman Empire. Fascism was rooted in the mass political movements of the late nineteenth century, which emphasized nationalism, antiliberal values, and a politics of the irrational. The electoral successes of the German variant, National Socialism, or nazism, were just beginning in the late 1920s. In the same period, fascist movements were making their appearance in England, Hungary, Spain, and France. But none was more successful and none demanded more classes sought security against the economic uncertainties of inflation and were willing to endorse violence to achieve it. Unions were to be feared because they used strikes to further their demands for higher salaries and better working conditions for their members while other social groups languished. Near civil war erupted as Italian Communists and Fascists clashed violently in street battles in the early 1920s. The Fascists entered the national political arena and succeeded on the local level in overthrowing city governments. In spite of its visibility on the national political scene, the Fascist party was still very much a minority party when Mussolini refused to serve as a junior minister in the new government in 1922.

His refusal to serve as representative of a minority party reflected Mussolini's belief that the Fascists must be in charge. On 28 October 1922, the Fascists undertook their famous March on Rome, which followed similar Fascist takeovers in Milan and Bologna. Mussolini's followers now occupied the capital. This event marked the beginning of the end of parliamentary government and the emergence of Fascist dictatorship and institutionalized violence. Rising unemployment and severe inflation contributed to the politically deteriorating situation that helped bring Mussolini to power.

Destruction and violence, not the ballot box, became fascism's most successful tools for securing political power. *Squadristi*, armed bands of Fascist thugs, attacked their political enemies, both Catholic and Socialist, destroyed private property, dismantled the printing presses of adversary groups, and generally terrorized both rural and urban populations. By the end of 1922, Fascists could claim a following of 300,000 members, who endorsed the new politics of intimidation.

The Fascists achieved their first parliamentary majority by using violent tactics of intimidation to secure votes. One outspoken Socialist critic of Fascist violence, Giacomo Matteotti (1885–1924), was murdered by Mussolini's subordinates. The deed threatened the survival of Mussolini's government as 150 Socialist, Liberal, and Popular party deputies resigned in protest. Mussolini chose this moment to consolidate his position by arresting and silencing his enemies to preserve order. Within two years, Fascists were firmly in control, monopolizing politics, suppressing a free press, creating a secret police force, and transforming social and economic policies. Mussolini destroyed political parties and made Italy into a one-party dictatorship.

In 1925 the Fascist party entered into an agreement with Italian industrialists that gave industry a position of privilege protected by the state in return for its support. Mussolini presented this partnership as the end to class conflict, but in fact it ensured the dominance of capital and the control of labor and professional groups. A corrupt bureaucracy filled with Mussolini's cronies and run on bribes orchestrated the new relationship between big business and the state.

Mussolini, himself an atheist, recognized the importance of the Catholic church in securing his regime. In 1870 when Italy had been unified, the pope was deprived of his territories in Rome. This event, which became known as the "Roman Question," proved to be the source of ongoing problems for Italian governments. In February 1929 Mussolini settled matters with Pope Pius XI in the Lateran Treaty and the accompanying Concordat, which granted to the pope sovereignty over the territory around St. Peter's Basilica and the Vatican. The treaty also protected the role of the Catholic church in education and guaranteed that Italian marriage laws would conform to Catholic dogma.

By 1929 *Il Duce*, or the leader, as Mussolini preferred to be called, was at the height of his popularity and his power. Apparent political harmony had been achieved by ruthlessly crushing fascism's opponents. The agreement with the pope, which restored harmony with the Church, was matched by a new sense of order and accomplishment in Italian society and the economy.

Mussolini's Plans for Empire

In spite of official claims, Fascist Italy had not done well in riding out the Depression. A large rural sector masked the problems of high unemployment by absorbing an urban workforce without jobs. Corporatism, a system of economic self-rule by interest groups, was a sham promoted on paper by Benito Mussolini that had little to do with the dominance of the Italian economy by big business. By lending money to Italian businesses on the verge of bankruptcy, the government acquired a controlling interest in key industries, including steel, shipping, heavy machinery, and electricity.

As fascism failed to initiate effective social programs, Mussolini's popularity plummeted. In the hope of boosting his sagging image, *Il Duce* committed Italy to a foreign policy of imperial conquest. Italy had conquered Ottoman-controlled Libya in North Africa in 1911. Now in the 1930s Mussolini targeted Ethiopia for his expansionist aims and ordered Italian troops to invade that east African kingdom in October 1935. Using poison gas and aerial bombing, the Italian army defeated the native troops of Ethiopian emperor Haile Selassie (1930–74). European democracies, under the pressure of public opinion, cried out against the wanton and unwarranted attack, but Mussolini succeeded in proclaiming Ethiopia an Italian territory.

The invasion of Ethiopia exposed the ineffectiveness of the League of Nations to stop such flagrant violations. Great Britain and France took no action other than to express their disapproval of Italy's conquest. Yet a rift opened up between these two western European nations and Italy. Mussolini had distanced himself from the Nazi state in the first years of the German regime's existence and he was critical of Hitler's plans for rearmament. Now, in light of the disapproval of Britain and France, Mussolini turned to Germany for support. In October 1936, Italy aligned itself with Germany in what Mussolini called the "Rome-Berlin Axis." This alliance was little more than a pledge of friendship. Less than three years later in May 1939, however, Germany and Italy agreed to offer support in any offensive or defensive war; the agreement, known as the Pact of Steel, in fact bound Italy militarily to Germany.

Mussolini pursued other imperialist goals within Europe. The small Balkan nation of Albania entered into a series of agreements with Mussolini beginning in the mid-1920s that made it dependent financially and militarily on Italian aid. By 1933 Albanian independence had been undermined by this "friendship" with its stronger neighbor. In order not to be outdone by Hitler, who was at the time dismantling Czechoslovakia, Mussolini invaded and annexed Albania in April 1939, ending the fiction that Albania was an Italian protectorate.

The Beginnings of the Nazi Movement in Germany

Repeated economic, political, and diplomatic crises of the 1920s buffeted Germany's internal stability. Most Germans considered reparations to be an unfair burden, so onerous that payment should be evaded and resisted in every way possible. The German government did not actually promote inflation in order to avoid paying reparations but it did do so to avoid a postwar recession, revive industrial production, and maintain high employment. But the moderate inflation that stimulated the economy spun out of control into destructive hyperinflation.

The Germans blamed the French with their reparations demands and their invading troops for the eco-

The runaway inflation of the 1920s is dramatized by this photo of a German housewife who is lighting the cooking fire with millions of marks. She declared that it was cheaper to use the worthless currency for kindling than to buy wood with it.

nomic plight of Germany. Rampant inflation had negative repercussions for democracy, as extremist political groups on both right and left attracted growing numbers of followers by blaming the liberal and democratic Weimar Republic. Because of the horrors of inflation, German governments thereafter were committed to balanced budgets. When the Depression hit the German economy in 1929, the fear of a new inflation prevented the government from using deficit spending to bring back prosperity. The Depression in turn contributed to the burgeoning appeal of Hitler and the National Socialists. People grew cynical and defiant through suffering and sought security in extraordinary and extrademocratic solutions.

The fiscal problems of the Weimar Republic obscure the fact that, in the postwar period, Germany experienced real economic growth. German industry advanced, productivity was high, and German workers flexed their union muscles to secure better wages. Weimar committed itself to large expenditures for social welfare programs, including unemployment insurance. By 1930 social welfare was responsible for 40 percent of all public expenditures, compared to 19 percent before the war. All these changes, apparently fostering the well-being of the German people, aggravated the fears of German big businessmen, who resented the trade unions and the perceived trend toward socialism. The lower middle classes also felt cheated and economically threatened by inflation. They were a politically volatile group, susceptible to the antidemocratic appeals of some of Weimar's critics.

Constitutional provisions that allowed for the constant wrangling of a multiparty system divided the Weimar Republic. Political parties formed and destroyed cabinet after cabinet while Germany's real problems remained—the humiliating peace treaty, reparations, and a weak economic structure. As a result, growing numbers of Germans expressed disgust with parliamentary democracy. The Depression dealt a staggering blow to the Weimar Republic in 1929 as American loans were withdrawn and German unemployment skyrocketed. By 1930 the antagonisms among the parties were so great that the parliament was no longer effective in ruling Germany. As chancellor from 1930 to 1932, Centrist leader Heinrich Brüning (1885–1970) attempted to break this impasse by overriding the Weimar constitution. This move opened the door to enemies of the republic, and Brüning was forced to resign.

One man in particular knew how to exploit the Weimar Republic's weaknesses for his own political ends. Adolf Hitler was that man. He denounced the betrayal of reparations. He made a special appeal to Germans who saw their savings disappearing, first in inflation and then in the Depression. He promised a way out of economic hardship and the reassertion of Germany's claim to status as a world power.

Hitler and the Third Reich

Just as Stalin was born a Georgian and not an ethnic Russian, Adolf Hitler (1889–1945) was born an Austrian outside the German fatherland he came to rule. Hitler, the son of a customs agent who worked on the Austrian side of the border with Germany, came from a middle-class family with social pretensions. Aimlessness and failure marked Hitler's early life. Denied admission to architecture school, he took odd jobs to survive. Hitler welcomed the outbreak of war in 1914 that put an end to his self-described sleepwalking. He volunteered imme-

diately for service in the German army. Wounded and gassed at the front, he was twice awarded the Iron Cross for bravery in action.

Hitler later described what he had learned from war in terms of the solidarity of struggle against a common enemy and the purity of heroism. The army provided him with a sense of security and direction. What he learned from the peace that followed was an equally powerful lesson and determined his commitment to a career in politics. Hitler profoundly believed in the stab-in-the-back legend: Germany had not lost the war, he insisted, it had been defeated from within, or stabbed in the back by communists, socialists, liberals, and Jews. The Weimar Republic signed the humiliating Treaty of Versailles and continued to betray the German people by taxing wages to pay reparations. His highly distorted and false view of the origins of the Republic and its policies was the basis for his demand that the "Weimar System" must be abolished and replaced by a Nazi regime.

For his failed attempt to seize control of the Munich municipal government in 1923 in an event that became known as the Beer Hall Putsch because of the locale in which Hitler attempted to initiate "the national revolution," he served nine months of a five-year sentence in prison. There he began writing the first volume of his autobiography, *Mein Kampf* (My Struggle). In this turgid work, he condemned the decadence of western society and singled out for special contempt Jews, Bolsheviks, and middle-class liberals. From his failed attempt to seize power, Hitler learned the important lesson that he could succeed against the German republic only from within, by coming to power legally. By 1928 he had a small party of about 100,000 Nazis. Modifying his anti-capitalist message, Hitler appealed to the discontented small farmers, and tailored his nationalist sentiments to a frightened middle class.

Adolf Hitler became chancellor of Germany in January 1933 by legal, constitutional, and democratic means. The Nazi party was supported by farmers, small businessmen, civil servants, and young people. In the elections of 1930 and 1932, the voters made the Nazi party the largest party in the country—although not the majority one. President Paul von Hindenburg invited Hitler to form a government. Hitler claimed that Germany was on the verge of a Communist revolution, and he persuaded Hindenburg and the Reichstag to consent to a series of emergency laws, which the Nazis used to establish themselves firmly in power. Legislation outlawed freedom of the press and public meetings, and approved of the use of violence against Hitler's political enemies, particularly the Socialists and the Communists. Within two months after Hitler came to office, Germany was a police state and Hitler was a "legal" dictator who could issue his own laws without having to gain the consent of either the Reichstag or the president. After carrying out this "legal revolution" incapacitating representative institutions and ending civil liberties, the Nazis worked to consolidate their position and their power. They abolished all other political parties, established single-party rule, dissolved trade unions, and put their own people into state governments and the bureaucracy.

Many observers at the time considered the new Nazi state to be a monolithic structure, ruled and coordinated from the center. This was not, however, an accurate observation. Hitler actually issued few directives. Policy was set by an often chaotic jockeying for power among rival Nazi factions. Hitler's political alliance with traditional conservative and nationalist politicians, industrialists, and military men helped give the state created by Adolf Hitler, which he called the Third Reich, a claim to legitimacy based on continuity with the past. (The first Reich was the medieval German empire; the second Reich was the German Empire created by Bismarck in 1871.)

The first of the paramilitary groups so important in orchestrating violence to eliminate Hitler's enemies was the SA *(Sturmabteilung)*, or the storm troopers, under Ernst Röhm (1877–1934), who helped Hitler achieve electoral victories by beating up political opponents on the streets and using other thuglike tactics. The SA, also known as Brown Shirts, adopted a military appearance for their terrorist operations. By the beginning of 1934, there were 2.5 million members, vastly outnumbering the regular army of 100,000 soldiers.

Heinrich Himmler (1900–45) headed an elite force of the Nazi party within the SA called the SS (*Schutzstaffel*, or protection squad), a group whose members wore black uniforms and menacing skull-and-crossbones insignia on their caps. Himmler seized control of political policing and emerged as Röhm's chief rival. In 1934 with the assistance of the army, Hitler and the SS purged the SA and executed Röhm, thereby making the SS Hitler's exclusive elite corps, entrusted with carrying out his extreme programs and responsible later for the greatest atrocities of the Second World War.

Hitler identified three organizing goals for the Nazi state: *Lebensraum*, or living space; rearmament; and economic recovery. These goals were the basis of the new

Ranks of seamstresses churn out Nazi flags in 1933 Berlin. The swastika—das Hakenkreuz—was a ubiquitous Nazi symbol that has come to stand for bigotry and religious and racial oppression throughout the world.

foreign policy Hitler forged for Germany. And they served to fuse that foreign policy with the domestic politics of the Third Reich.

Key to Hitler's worldview was the concept of *Lebensraum*, by which he considered it the right and the duty of the German master race to be the world's greatest empire, one that would endure for a thousand years. Hitler first stated his ideals about living space in *Mein Kampf*, where he argued that superior nations had the right to expand into the territories of inferior states. Living space meant for him German domination of central and eastern Europe at the expense of Slavic peoples. The Aryan master race would dominate inferior peoples. Colonies were unacceptable because they weakened rather than strengthened national security; Germany must annex territories within continental Europe. Hitler's primary target was what he called "Russia and her vassal border states."

Hitler continued the secret rearmament of Germany begun by his Weimar predecessors in violation of the restrictions of the Treaty of Versailles. He withdrew Germany from the League of Nations and from the World Disarmament Conference, signaling a new direction for German foreign policy. In 1935 he publicly renounced the Treaty of Versailles and announced that Germany was rearming. The following year he openly defied the French and moved German troops into the Rhineland, the demilitarized security zone that separated the armed forces of the two countries. Hitler also reversed the cooperative relationship his nation had established with the Soviet Union in the 1920s. In

1933 the German state was illicitly spending one billion Reichsmarks on arms. By 1939 annual expenditures to prepare Germany for war had climbed to thirty billion.

Hitler knew that preparation for war meant more than amassing weapons; it also required full economic recovery. One of Germany's great weaknesses in World War I had been its dependence on imports of raw materials and foodstuffs. To avoid a repetition of this problem, Hitler instituted a program of *autarky*, or economic self-sufficiency, by which Germany aimed to produce everything that it consumed. He encouraged the efforts of German industry to develop synthetics for petroleum, rubber, metals, and fats.

The state pumped money into the private economy, creating new jobs and achieving full employment after 1936, an accomplishment unmatched by any other European nation. Recovery was built on armaments as well as consumer products. The Nazi state's concentration of economic power in the hands of a few strengthened big businesses. The victims of corporate consolidation were the small firms that could no longer compete with government-sponsored corporations like the chemical giant I.G. Farben.

In 1936–37 Hitler introduced his Four-Year Plan dedicated to the goals of full-scale rearmament and economic self-sufficiency. Before the third year of the Four-Year Plan, however, Hitler was aware of the failure to develop synthetic products sufficient to meet Germany's needs. But if Germany could not create substitutes, it could control territories that provided fuel, metals, and foodstuffs. Germany had been importing raw materials from southeastern Europe and wielding increasing economic influence over the Balkan countries. Hitler now realized that economic self-sufficiency could be directly linked to the main goal of the Nazi state: *Lebensraum.*

Hitler was, thus, committed to territorial expansion from the time he came to power. He rearmed Germany for that purpose. When economists and generals cautioned him, he refused to listen. Instead he informed them of his commitment to *Lebensraum* and of his intention to use aggressive war to acquire it. He removed his critics from their positions of power and replaced them with Nazis loyal to him.

Propaganda, Racism, and Culture

To reinforce his personal power and to sell his program for the *total state*, Hitler created a Ministry of Propaganda under Joseph Goebbels (1897–1945), a former journalist and Nazi party district leader in Berlin. Goebbels was a master of manipulating emotions in mass demonstrations held to organize enthusiasm for Nazi policies. Flying the flag and wearing the swastika signified identification with the Nazi state. With his magnetic appeal, Hitler inspired and manipulated the devotion of hundreds of thousands of those who heard him speak. Leni Riefenstahl, a young filmmaker working for Hitler, made a documentary of a National Socialist party rally at Nuremberg. In scenes of swooning women and cheering men, her film, called *Triumph of the Will*, recorded the dramatic force of Hitler's rhetoric and his ability to move the German people. Hitler's public charisma masked a profoundly troubled and incomplete individual capable of irrational rage and sick hatred of his fellow human beings. His warped views of the world were responsible for the greatest outrages committed in the name of legitimate power. Yet millions, including admirers in western Europe and the United States, succumbed to his appeal.

Family life, too, was carefully regulated through the propaganda machinery. Loyalty only to the state meant less loyalty to the family. Special youth organizations indoctrinated boys with nationalistic and military values. Hitler Youth comprised 82 percent of all young people in 1939. Organizations for girls were intended to mold them into worthy wives and mothers. Teenage girls were required to join a Nazi organization called Faith and Beauty, which taught them etiquette, dancing, fashion consciousness, and beauty care. Woman's natural function, Hitler argued, was to serve in the home. Education for women beyond the care of home and family was a waste. Adult women had their own organizations to serve the Nazi state. The German Women's Bureau under Gertrud Scholtz-Klink instructed women in their "proper" female duties. In an effort to promote large families, the state paid allowances to couples for getting married, subsidized families according to their size, and gave tax breaks to large families. Abortion and birth control were outlawed and women who sought such measures risked severe penalties and imprisonment.

By 1937 the need for women workers conflicted with the goals of Nazi propaganda. With the outbreak of war in 1939, women were urged to work, especially in jobs like munitions manufacture, formerly held by men. For working women with families, the double burden was a heavy one, as women were required to work long shifts—sixty-hour work weeks were not unusual—for low wages. Many women resisted entering the workforce if they had other income or could live on the cash

ADOLF HITLER ON RACIAL PURITY

■ *The purity of German blood was a recurrent theme in Hitler's speeches and writings from the beginning of his political career. In attacking both liberalism and socialism, Hitler offered racial superiority as the essence of the National Socialist "revolution." This speech, delivered in Berlin on 30 January 1937, lays out his attack on the concept of individual rights and humanity in favor of the folk community.*

The most important plank in the National Socialist program is to abolish the liberal idea of the individual and the Marxist idea of humanity and to substitute for them the folk community rooted in the soil and held together by the bond of common blood. This sounds simple, but it involves a principle which has great consequences.

For the first time and in the first country our people are being taught to understand that, of all the tasks we have to face, the most noble and the most sacred for all mankind is the concept that each racial species must preserve the purity of blood which God has given to it.

The greatest revolution won by National Socialism is that it has pierced the veil which hid from us the knowledge that all human errors may be attributed to the conditions of the time and hence can be remedied, but there is one error that cannot be set right once it has been made by men—that is, the failure to understand the importance of keeping the blood and the race free from intermingling, and in this way to alter God's gift. It is not for human beings to discuss why Providence created different races. Rather it is important to understand the fact that it will punish those who pay no attention to its work of creation. . . .

I hereby prophesy that, just as knowledge that the earth moves around the sun led to a revolutionary change in the world picture, so will the blood-and-race doctrine of the National Socialist movement bring about a revolutionary change in our knowledge. . . . It will also change the course of history in the future.

This will not lead to difficulties between nations. On the contrary, it will lead to a better understanding between them. But at the same time it will prevent the Jews, under the mask of world citizenship, from thrusting themselves among all nations as an element of domestic chaos. . . .

The National Socialist movement limits its domestic activities to those individuals who belong to one people. It refuses to permit those of a foreign race to have any influence whatever on our political, intellectual, or cultural life. We refuse to give any members of a foreign race a dominant position in our national economic system.

In our folk community, which is based on ties of blood, in the results which National Socialism has obtained by training the public in the idea of this folk-community, lies the deepest reason for the great success of our Revolution.

payments they received as the wives of soldiers. At the beginning of 1943, the German people were ordered to make sacrifices for a new era of "total war." Female labor became compulsory and women were drafted into working for the war.

Propaganda condemned everything foreign, including Mickey Mouse, who was declared an enemy of the state in the 1930s. Purging foreign influences meant purging political opponents, especially members of the Communist party, who were rounded up and sent to concentration camps in Germany. Communism was identified as an international Jewish conspiracy to destroy the German Volk, or people. Nazi literature also identified "asocials," those who were considered deviant in any way, including homosexuals, who were likewise to be expelled. Euthanasia was used against the mentally ill and the developmentally disabled in the 1930s. Concentration camps were expanded to contain enemies of the state. Later, when concentration camps became sites of extermination and forced labor, gypsies, homosexuals, criminals, and religious offenders had to wear insignia of different colors to indicate their basis for persecution. The people who received the greatest attention for exclusion from Nazi Germany, and then from Europe, were Jews.

The first measures against the German Jews, their exclusion from public employment and higher education, began almost immediately in 1933. In 1935 the Nuremberg Laws were enacted to identify Jews, to deprive them of their citizenship, and to forbid marriage and extramarital sexual relations between Jews and non-Jews. On the night of 9 November 1938, synagogues were set afire and books and valuables owned by

A propaganda-laden German beer coaster of the Nazi era informs the world that "Who buys from the Jews is a traitor."

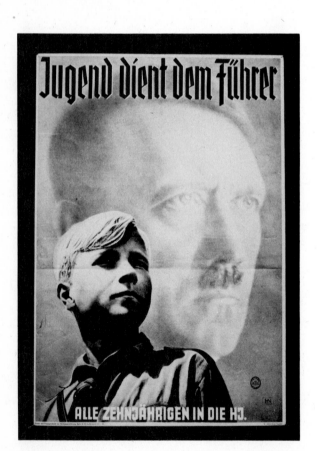

A recruiting poster bearing the slogans "Youth serves the Führer" and "All ten-year-olds in the Hitler Youth" urges young boys to join the paramilitary youth organization.

Jews were confiscated throughout Germany. Jews were beaten, about 91 were killed, and 20,000 to 30,000 were imprisoned in concentration camps. The night came to be called *Kristallnacht*, meaning "night of broken glass," which referred to the Jewish shop windows smashed by the Brown Shirts under orders from Goebbels. The government claimed that *Kristallnacht* was an outpouring of the German people's will. An atmosphere of state-sanctioned hate prevailed.

Racism was nothing new in European culture. Nor was its particular variant, anti-Semitism—hatred of Jews—the creation of the Third Reich. The link the Nazis cultivated between racism and politics was built on cultural precedents. In the 1890s in France and Austria and elsewhere in Europe, anti-Semitism was espoused by political and professional groups that formed themselves around issues of militant nationalism, authoritarianism, and mass politics. Hitler himself was a racist and an anti-Semite, and he placed theories of race at the core of his fascist ideology. "Experts" decided sterilization was the surest way to protect "German blood." In 1933, one of the early laws of Hitler's new Reich decreed compulsory sterilization of "undesirables" in order to "eliminate inferior genes." The Nazi state decided who these "undesirables" were and forced the sterilization of 400,000 men and women.

The Third Reich was a government that delivered on its promises to end unemployment, to improve productivity, to break through the logjam of parliamentary obstacles, and to return Germany to the international arena as a contender for power. Yet Hitler's Nazi state ruled by violence, coercion, and intimidation. With a propaganda machine that glorified the leader and vilified groups singled out as scapegoats for Germany's problems, Hitler undermined democratic institutions and civil liberties in his pursuit of German power.

Democracies in Crisis

Democracies in the 1930s turned in on themselves in order to survive. In contrast to the fascist mobilization of society and the Soviet restructuring of the economy, European democracies took small, tentative steps to respond to the challenges of the Great Depression. Democratic leaders lacked creative vision or even clear policy. Both democratic France and Great Britain were less successful than Nazi Germany in responding to the challenges of the Depression. France paid a high price for parliamentary stalemate and was still severely depressed on the eve of war in 1938–39. Great Britain maintained a stagnant economy and stable politics under Conservative leadership. Internal dissension ripped Spain apart. Its civil war assumed broader dimensions as the Soviet Union, Italy, and Germany struggled over Spain's future, while Europe's democratic nations stood by and accepted defeat.

The Failure of the Left in France

France's Third Republic, like most European parliamentary democracies in the 1930s, was characterized by a multiparty system. Genuine political differences often separated one party from another. The tendency to parliamentary stalemate was aggravated by the Depression and by the increasingly extremist politics on both the Left and the Right in response to developments in the Soviet Union and Germany.

The belief of the French people in a private enterprise economy was shaken by the Great Depression, but no new unifying belief replaced it. Some felt that state planning was the answer; others were sure that state intervention had caused the problem. Distrusting both the New Deal model of the United States and the Nazi response to Depression politics, the Third Republic followed a haphazard, wait-and-see policy of insulating the economy, discouraging competition, and protecting favored interests in both industry and agriculture. Stimulating the economy by deficit spending was considered anathema. Devaluation of the franc, which might have helped French exports, was regarded by policy makers as an unpatriotic act. France stood fast as a bastion of liberal belief in the self-adjusting mechanism of the market and it suffered greatly for it. Party politics worked to reinforce the defensive rather than offensive response to the challenges of depression and a sluggish economy.

In 1936 an electoral mandate for change swept the Left into power. The new premier, Léon Blum (1872–1950), was a Socialist. Lacking the votes to rule with an exclusively Socialist government, Blum formed a coalition of Left and Center parties intent on economic reforms, known as the Popular Front. Before Blum's government could take power, a wave of strikes swept France. Though reluctant to intervene in the economy, the Popular Front nevertheless was pushed into some action. It promised wage increases, paid vacations, and collective bargaining to French workers. The reduced work week of forty hours caused a drop in productivity, as did the short-lived one-month vacation policy. The government did nothing to prevent the outflow of investment capital from France. Higher wages failed to generate increased consumer demand because employers raised prices to cover their higher operating costs.

German rearmament, now publicly known, forced France into rearmament, which France could ill afford. Blum's government failed in 1937, with France still bogged down in a sluggish and depressed economy. The last peacetime government of the 1930s represented a conservative swing back to laissez-faire policies that put the needs of business above those of workers and brought a measure of revival to the French economy.

The radical Right drew strength from the Left's failures. Right-wing leagues and organizations multiplied, appealing to a frightened middle class. The failure of the Socialists, in turn, drove many sympathizers further to the Left to join the Communist party. A divided France could not stand up to the foreign policy challenges of the 1930s posed by Hitler's provocations.

Muddling Through in Great Britain

Great Britain was hard hit by the Great Depression of the 1930s; only Germany and the United States experienced comparable economic devastation. The socialist Labour government of the years 1929 to 1931 under Prime Minister Ramsay MacDonald (1866-1937) was unprepared to deal with the 1929 collapse and lacked the vision and the planning to devise a way out of the morass. It took a coalition of moderate groups from the three parties—Liberal, Conservative, and Labour—to address the issues of high unemployment, a growing government deficit, a banking crisis, and the flight of capital. The National Government (1931-35) was a non-party, centrist coalition whose members included Ramsay MacDonald, retained as prime minister, and Stanley Baldwin (1867-1947), a Conservative with a background in iron and steel manufacturing.

In response to the endemic crisis, the National Government took Britain off the international gold standard and devalued the pound. In order to protect domestic production, tariffs were established. The British economy showed signs of slow recovery, probably due less to these government measures than to a gradual improvement in the business cycle. The government had survived the crisis without resorting to the kind of creative alternatives devised in the Scandinavian countries where, for example, consumer and producer cooperatives provided widespread economic relief. Moderates and classical liberals in Great Britain persisted in defending the nonintervention of the government in the economy, despite new economic theories, such as that of John Maynard Keynes (1883-1946), who urged government spending to stimulate consumer demand as the best way to shorten the duration of the Depression.

In 1932 Sir Oswald Mosley (1896-1980) founded the British Union of Fascists (BUF), consisting of goon squads and bodyguards. The BUF was opposed to free-trade liberalism and communism alike. Mosley developed a corporate model for economic and political life in which interest groups rather than an electorate would be represented in a new kind of parliament. He favored, above all, national solutions by relying on imperial development; he rejected the world of international finance as corrupt.

The BUF shared similarities with European fascist organizations. BUF squads beat up their political opponents and began attacking Jews, especially the eastern European émigrés living in London. The British fascists struck a responsive chord among the poorest working classes of London's East End; at its peak the group claimed a membership of 20,000. Public alarm over increasingly inflammatory and anti-Semitic rhetoric

The Rise of Fascism and Democracy in Crisis

28 October 1922	Italian Fascists' March on Rome
November 1923	Beer Hall Putsch in Munich
1924	Fascists achieve parliamentary majority in Italy
1929	Lateran Treaty between Mussolini and Pope Pius XI
1932	Nazi party is single largest party in German parliament
January 1933	Hitler becomes chancellor of Germany
30 June 1934	Purge of the SA leaves Hitler and the SS in unassailable position
March 1935	Hitler publicly rejects Treaty of Versailles and announces German rearmament
15 September 1935	Enactment of Nuremberg Laws against Jews and other minorities
3 October 1935	Italy invades Ethiopia
1936	Popular Front government elected in Spain
July 1936	Beginning of Spanish Civil War
October 1936	Rome-Berlin Axis Pact, an Italo-German accord
1936-37	Popular Front government in France
27 April 1937	Bombing of the Spanish town of Guernica
9 November 1938	*Kristallnacht* initiates massive violence against Jews
March 1939	Fascists defeat the Spanish Republic
April 1939	Italy annexes Albania
May 1939	Pact of Steel between Germany and Italy

converged with parliamentary denunciation. Popular support for the group was already beginning to erode when the BUF was outlawed in 1936. By this time, anti-Hitler feeling was spreading in Great Britain.

Mosley's response to harsh economic times had proven to be no match for the steady and reassuring strength of Stanley Baldwin's National Government, which seemed to be in control of an improving economic situation. The traditional party system prevailed not because of its brilliant solutions to difficult economic problems but because of the willingness of moderate parliamentarians to cooperate and to adapt, however slowly, to the new need for economic transformation.

The Spanish Republic as Battleground

In 1931 Spain became a democratic republic after centuries of Bourbon monarchy and almost a decade of military dictatorship. In 1936 the voters of Spain elected a Popular Front government. The Popular Front in Spain was more radical than its French counterpart. The property of aristocratic landlords was seized; revolutionary workers went on strike; the Catholic church and its clergy were attacked. This social revolution initiated three years of civil war. On one side were the Republicans, the Popular Front defenders of the Spanish Republic and of social revolution in Spain. On the other side were the Nationalists, those who sought to overthrow the Republic—aristocratic landowners, supporters of the monarchy and the Catholic church, and much of the Spanish army.

The Spanish Civil War began in July 1936 with a revolt against the Republic from within the Spanish army. It was led by General Francisco Franco (1892–1975), a tough, shrewd, and stubborn man, a conservative nationalist allied with the Falange, the fascist party in Spain. The conflict soon became a bloody military stalemate, with the Nationalists led by Franco controlling the more rural and conservative south and west of Spain and the Republicans holding out in the cities of the north and east—Madrid, Valencia, and Barcelona.

Almost from the beginning, the Spanish Civil War was an international event. Mussolini sent ground troops, "volunteers," to fight alongside Franco's forces. Hitler dispatched technical specialists, tanks, and the Condor Legion, an aviation unit, to support the Nationalists. The Germans regarded Spain as a testing ground for new equipment and new methods of warfare, including aerial bombardment. The Soviet Union intervened on the side of the Republic, sending armaments, supplies, and technical and political advisers. Because the

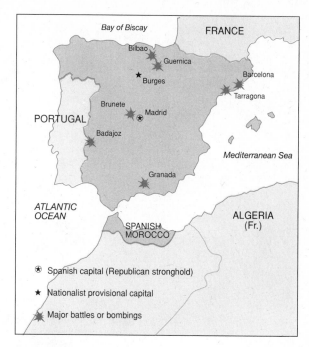

The Spanish Civil War

people of Britain and France were deeply divided in their attitudes toward the war in Spain, the British government stayed neutral, and the government of France was unable to aid its fellow Popular Front government in Spain. Although Americans volunteered to fight with the Republicans, the American government did not prevent the Texas Oil Company from selling 1.9 million tons of oil to Franco's insurgents, nor did it block the Ford Motor Company, General Motors, and Studebaker from supplying them with trucks.

The Spanish government pleaded, "Men and women of all lands! Come to our aid!" In response, 2,800 American volunteers, among them college students, professors, intellectuals, and trade unionists, joined the loyalist army and European volunteers in defense of the Spanish Republic. Britons and antifascist émigrés from Italy and Germany also joined international brigades, which were vital in helping the city of Madrid hold out against the Nationalist generals. The Russians withdrew from the war in 1938, disillusioned by the failure of the French, British, and Americans to come to the aid of the Republicans. Madrid fell to the Nationalists in March 1939. The government established by Franco sent one million of its enemies to prison or concentration camps.

The fragile postwar stability of the 1920s crumbled under the pressures of economic depression, ongoing national antagonisms, and insecurity in the international

Members of the British Union of Fascists kneel to salute the grave of the Unknown Warrior in the courtyard of Westminster Abbey, 1922. The popularity of the BUF declined sharply in the mid-1930s. Oswald Mosley's continued support for Hitler and Nazi Germany led to his imprisonment during World War II.

arena. Europe after 1932 was plagued by the consequences of economic collapse, fascist success, and the growing threat of armed conflict. Parliamentary institutions were fighting and losing a tug-of-war with authoritarian movements. A fascist regime was in place in Italy. Political and electoral defeats eroded democratic and liberal principles in Germany's Weimar Republic. Dictatorships triumphed in Spain and in much of eastern and central Europe. Liberal parliamentary governments were failing to solve the economic and social challenges of the postwar years. In the democratic nations of France, Great Britain, and, during the brief period from 1931 to 1936, Spain, parliamentary institutions appeared to be persevering. But even here, polarization and increasing intransigence on both the Left and the Right threatened the future of democratic politics.

The exclusion of the Soviet Union from Western internationalism both reflected the crisis and exacerbated it. The Bolshevik revolution had served as a political catalyst among workers in the West, attracting them to the possibility of radical solutions. That poten-

tial radicalization aggravated class antagonisms where mass politics prevailed and drove political leaders to seek conservative solutions as a means of stabilizing class politics.

SUGGESTIONS FOR FURTHER READING

INTERNATIONAL POLITICS AND ECONOMIC NATIONALISM

Marshall M. Lee and Wolfgang Michalka, *German Foreign Policy, 1917–1933: Continuity or Break?* (Leamington Spa, England: Berg, 1987). A solid and synthetic treatment of Weimar diplomacy that takes into account the historiographical debates over revisionism and expansion.

* Melvyn P. Leffler, *The Elusive Quest: America's Pursuit of European Stability and French Security, 1919–1933* (Chapel Hill, NC: University of North Carolina Press, 1979). Examines the economic and financial imperatives guiding U.S. foreign policy after World War I and identifies a particular Republican party approach labeled "economic diplomacy." Special attention is paid to European stabilization, French security, and Germany's rehabilitation.

* Joseph Rothschild, *East Central Europe Between the Two World Wars* (Seattle: University of Washington Press, 1983). A balanced survey of interwar developments in Poland, Czechoslovakia, Hungary, Yugoslavia, Romania, Bulgaria, Albania, and the Baltic states, highlighting internal weaknesses and external vulnerabilities. A concluding chapter covers cultural contributions.

* Derek H. Aldcroft, *From Versailles to Wall Street, 1919-1929* (Berkeley, CA: University of California Press, 1977). Traces the recovery of the international economy and the systemic forces of its disintegration in the 1920s, with special attention to such areas as war debts, reparations, the gold standard, the agricultural sector, and patterns of international lending.

* Stephen A. Schuker, *The End of French Predominance in Europe: The Financial Crisis of 1924 and the Adoption of the Dawes Plan* (Chapel Hill, NC: University of North Carolina Press, 1976). Locates the decline of France as a great power in the financial crisis of 1924 and the diplomacy of reparations and examines the domestic bases for French powerlessness.

THE SOVIET UNION'S SEPARATE PATH

* Stephen F. Cohen, *Bukharin and the Bolshevik Revolution: A Political Biography, 1888-1938* (Oxford: Oxford University Press, 1980). This milestone work is a general history of the period as well as a political and intellectual biography of Bukharin, "the last Bolshevik," who supported an evolutionary road to modernization and socialism and whose policies were an alternative to Stalinism.

* Sheila Fitzpatrick, *The Russian Revolution, 1917-1932* (Oxford: Oxford University Press, 1985). Arguing from the premise that the revolutionary upheaval did not end with the Bolshevik seizure of power in November 1917, Fitzpatrick interprets the developments of the 1920s and early 1930s, including the NEP and the first Five-Year Plan, as stages in a single revolutionary process.

* Robert C. Tucker, *Stalin as Revolutionary, 1879-1929: A Study in History and Personality* (New York: Norton, 1973). Traces Stalin's development from his Georgian childhood to his fiftieth year, when he established himself as the new hero of the Soviet state. Tucker uses Freudian terms of analysis in considering Stalin's hero-identification with Lenin.

THE PROMISE OF FASCISM

* Volker R. Berghahn, *Modern Germany: Society, Economy and Politics in the Twentieth Century* (Cambridge: Cambridge University Press, 1987). Considers the particular challenges of rapid industrialization faced by Germany and how they interacted with social tensions and political conflict.

* MacGregor Knox, *Mussolini Unleashed, 1939-1941: Politics and Strategy in Fascist Italy's Last War* (Cambridge: Cambridge University Press, 1982). Argues that Mussolini had a consistent and planned foreign policy in the Mediterranean

and a genuine program for living space in the Mediterranean and the Middle East. In his bid for power and prestige, Mussolini was willing to risk war and short-term instability at home.

Eberhard Kolb, *The Weimar Republic*, trans. P. S. Falla (London: Unwin Hyman, 1988). An introduction to the history of Germany's first republic both as a historic survey and as an examination of the basic problems and trends in research.

* Adrian Lyttelton, *The Seizure of Power: Fascism in Italy, 1919-1929* (New York: Scribners, 1973). Addresses the question of why fascism first took root in Italy.

* Ian Kershaw, *The "Hitler Myth": Image and Reality in the Third Reich* (New York: Oxford University Press, 1987). Examines the power of the "Hitler" myth created by the German Propaganda Ministry, the German people, and Hitler. The myth accounted for the stability of the Third Reich throughout the thirties and in the first years of the war.

* Detlev Peukert, *Inside Nazi Germany: Conformity, Opposition, and Racism in Everyday Life* (New Haven, CT: Yale University Press, 1987). Discusses the informal modes of resistance among the German people.

DEMOCRACIES IN CRISIS

M. S. Alexander and H. Graham, *The French and Spanish Popular Fronts: Comparative Perspectives* (Cambridge: Cambridge University Press, 1989). Contributions by specialists on the interwar period.

Herschel B. Chipp, *Picasso's Guernica: History, Transformations, Meanings* (Berkeley, Los Angeles, London: University of California Press, 1988). Documents the creation of the *Guernica*, rooting it firmly in the context of the Spanish Civil War, and discusses the painting's reception in Spain and abroad.

* John Hiden and Patrick Salmon, *The Baltic Nations and Europe: Estonia, Latvia, and Lithuania in the Twentieth Century* (London and New York: Longman, Inc., 1991). Surveys the development of the Baltic states in this century, discussing Baltic independence, the interwar period, and incorporation into the Soviet Union, as well as renewed efforts toward independence in the Gorbachev era.

* Julian Jackson, *The Popular Front in France: Defending Democracy, 1934-1938* (Cambridge: Cambridge University Press, 1988). The first in-depth study of Leon Blum's government, with a special emphasis on cultural transformation and the legacy of the Popular Front.

Maurice Larkin, *France Since the Popular Front: Government and People, 1936-1986* (Oxford: Clarendon Press, 1988). A work of total history that situates French political developments in the history, traditions, social structure, and economy of France. Separates the legend from the legacy of the Popular Front.

* Indicates paperback edition available.

CHAPTER 31

East Asia Transforms, 1800-1930

Seasons Turn as a Society Changes

Celebrating the burst of beauty brought on by cherry blossoms has been a favorite springtime activity for the Japanese. With their love of nature and appreciation for fleeting moments of pleasure, cherry-blossom viewing is a perfect Japanese pastime. At the bottom of this 1915 lithograph of Ueno Park in Tokyo we see some happy revelers with kerchiefs on their heads and sake jugs across their backs. A woman, perhaps startled by their loud behavior, modestly raises a sleeved hand to her face. Turning the corner we see children on a family outing as they run along a path in the park. In front of them a man in Western coat, tie, and hat contrasts with the more common Japanese robes of both men and women. A few paces behind the man in Western clothes walk two men in Western-style military uniforms—gone are the samurai with their two swords and subdued robes.

Ueno Park itself is a monument to Western notions of public space and urban lifestyles. The old city did not lack for places from which pleasant views of cherry blossoms could be enjoyed; whether along a riverbank or in the garden of a religious temple, Japanese had enjoyed the pleasures of cherry-blossom viewing long before Ueno Park's 1873 opening. But these other spaces began to disappear in the late nineteenth century. More than just a collection of trees and walking paths, Ueno Park boasted the country's first art museum and its first zoo, as well as the first trolley, shown in the picture. In 1898 the bronze statue of Saigō Takamori (1828–77), erected by townspeople grateful for his arranging the peaceful surrender of the Edo castle in 1868, took its commanding position overlooking the train station.

Cherry-blossom viewing at Ueno Park in the early twentieth century was an unmistakably Japanese leisure-time activity, but it took place in a public space created by Japanese acceptance of Western definitions of urban social possibilities. Whether in Japanese or Western-style clothes, early twentieth-century Japanese could enjoy an electric trolley ride as well as group singing and numerous cups of sake under the falling petals of the cherry blossoms.

In September 1923, some of Ueno Park's buildings were destroyed amid the devastation Tokyo suffered when over 1,700 earthquake tremors shook the city to its foundations for three days. Fires that quickly ignited among the many wooden structures contributed to the deaths of thousands of people. But Ueno Park survived as a public space. From the major train station bordering the park, Japanese troops would leave for Manchuria in the 1930s. In the Pacific War that followed, the cherry blossoms enjoyed at Ueno would come to symbolize the *kamikaze* pilots who died in the bloom of their youth.

Following the 1923 earthquakes, the city of Tokyo renewed itself with an increasing variety of architectural styles. Tokyo has become a cosmopolitan center, where Western influences have combined with Japanese sensibilities to create a unique city. From Ueno Park to the city of Tokyo to the country of Japan, the trajectory of change leading through the nineteenth and early twentieth centuries brought the formation of a modern state, new kinds of urban life, and the early stages of industrialization. In this process the Japanese succeeded more fully than any other Asian people in reacting to Western challenges and threats by combining Western models with native sensibilities. Indeed, so great was their success that they began to attack other countries and become a problematic presence facing the rest of Asia, even as they could still be considered an Asian model for successful modern development.

China's Nineteenth-Century Challenges

China's nineteenth-century history turns on the twin axes of domestic rebellion and foreign challenges. At first it appeared that the dynasty might collapse along its domestic axis. Unlike rebellions of previous centuries, those of the mid-nineteenth century attacked far more parts of the empire at the same time. They also reflected a greater diversity of factors—competing ideologies, religious differences, and persistent economic hardships. Through innovative mobilizations of military and financial resources, the Qing state survived the challenges of rebellion. These domestic problems loomed larger at mid-century than European diplomatic demands, which were handled initially according to a model of foreign relations the Chinese had developed in their dealings with Inner Asian peoples. But European attitudes and desires later proved to be more troublesome. It was this axis of foreign relations that would become extremely destructive for the Qing state by the turn of the century.

Opium: Trade, Crisis, and War

In the nineteenth century, the British sold large amounts of opium, the addictive narcotic, to the Chinese, creating one of the worst drug problems the world has known. Opium became Britain's major export to China because the famous British industrial revolution produced nothing the Chinese wanted in exchange for tea, which—under the Canton system of trade—was Britain's major import from China. From 1761, when some 2.5 million pounds of Chinese tea left for Britain, to 1800, when over 23 million pounds were sent, the tea trade grew every year. The absence of any British commodities enjoying equivalent demand in China meant that British ships set sail for Canton (now Guangzhou) with up to 90 percent of their stock in silver. This serious trade imbalance was reduced by the so-called country trade, exchanges conducted by British licensed by their East India Company in India. These country traders sold to the Chinese Indian cotton piece goods, elephant teeth, and most importantly opium.

Opium smoking in China began by the early eighteenth century. At first smokers mixed opium with tobacco, but by the 1760s and 1770s pure opium smoking was practiced. Increasing British opium exports to China fueled an expanding addiction. The Chinese government had outlawed opium sales as early as 1729 by threatening owners of opium dens with the punishment of strangulation. From the 1780s through the 1830s, imperial edicts prohibited opium consumption and imports. By 1813 the problem had extended very close to the imperial throne: opium addicts were discovered among the emperor's bodyguards.

During the next two decades, the Chinese government grew increasingly concerned about British opium imports as the boom in opium dramatically altered China's world balance of payments. After a positive account of $26 million during the first decade of the nineteenth century, China witnessed an outflow of $38 million between 1828 and 1836. For their part, British merchants wished to increase their trade, feeling increasingly confined by Chinese restrictions. They had succeeded in ending the East India Company's monopoly on the British side in 1833, but believed their commercial relations were unfairly limited by Chinese regulations, which allowed foreign trade only with *hong* merchants, merchants specifically licensed to conduct foreign trade in Canton. Despite these restrictions, annual opium imports reached more than 1,820 tons by 1836. In the

LIN ZEXU'S MORAL ADVICE

■ *When Commissioner Lin Zexu was first sent to Canton to deal with the problem of opium, he wrote Queen Victoria making clear to her that the issue of opium was not an economic one of "free trade," but a moral problem stemming from the sinister effects of opium addiction on Chinese society. He explained his intent to hold foreigners to the same laws that governed Chinese behavior, but before implementing his harsh penalties he appealed to the English monarch's conscience and capacity to persuade English traders to give up their commerce in drugs. The Chinese in 1839 were trying to do no more than American officials in their own "war on drugs" a century and a half later. For their efforts, however, they were subjected to a European system of unequal treaties that became its own additional source of outrage in later decades.*

Even though the barbarians may not necessarily intend to do us harm, yet in coveting profit to an extreme, they have no regard for injuring others. Let us ask, where is your conscience? I have heard that the smoking of opium is very strictly forbidden by your country; that is because the harm caused by opium is clearly understood. Since it is not permitted to do harm to your own country, then even less should you let it be passed on to the harm of other countries—how much less to China! . . .

Now we have set up regulations governing the Chinese people. He who sells opium shall receive the death penalty and he who smokes it also the death penalty. Now consider this: if the barbarians do not bring opium, then how can the Chinese people resell it, and how can they smoke it? The fact is that the wicked barbarians beguile the Chinese people into a death trap. How then can we grant life only to these barbarians? He who takes the life of even one person still has to atone for it with his own life; yet is the harm done by opium limited to the taking of one life only? Therefore in the new regulations, in regard to those barbarians who bring opium to China, the penalty is fixed at decapitation or strangulation. This is what is called getting rid of a harmful thing on behalf of mankind . . .

Our Celestial Dynasty rules over and supervises the myriad states, and surely possesses unfathomable spiritual dignity. Yet the Emperor cannot bear to execute people without having first tried to reform them by instruction. Therefore he especially promulgates these fixed regulations. The barbarian merchants of your country, if they wish to do business for a prolonged period, are required to obey our statutes respectfully and to cut off permanently the source of opium. They must by no means try to test the effectiveness of the law with their lives. May you, O King, check your wicked and sift your vicious people before they come to China, in order to guarantee the peace of your nation, to show further the sincerity of your politeness and submissiveness, and to let the two countries enjoy together the blessings of peace.

succeeding decades, several million Chinese became heavy smokers. The associated horrors of the drug traffic, including gangsters and corrupt officials, made the political and social impact of British opium imports increasingly disruptive.

To meet the growing crisis, the Court sent to Canton a distinguished official, Lin Zexu, who had previously served in the capital and various provinces, including a stint as governor general of Hubei and Hunan, where he had launched vigorous anti-opium campaigns. Appointed the Imperial Commissioner for Frontier Defense in December 1838, Lin went to Canton, where he sought to eradicate opium through a campaign of moral suasion and intimidation. His actions precipitated a period of confrontation and hostilities with the British known as the Opium War (1839–42). British military superiority led to a Chinese defeat. The subsequent Treaty of Nanking (Nanjing) included (1) an indemnity of $21 million; (2) opening Canton, Amoy (Xiamen), Fuzhou, Ning-po (Ningbo), and Shanghai to foreign trade; (3) British counsels at each treaty port listed above to provide their own law for foreigners in residence (the principle of extraterritoriality); (4) abolition of the

Photograph of two men in an opium den at Guangzhou. Such photographs and the lurid literature describing them were in great demand in the West and contributed to exotic stereotypes. Less was said about the role of Western merchants in promoting the use of opium by the Chinese.

hong merchant monopoly; (5) low tariffs on imports and exports; (6) recognition in diplomatic rituals of equality between the Chinese and foreign governments; (7) cession of Hong Kong to Britain to become a crown colony.

The Chinese defeat was a deep outrage to the imperial Court. The indemnity and the failure of Chinese principles of foreign relations were painful markers of a changed world. The opium that so aggrieved Chinese officials continued to be imported, and the social problems of addiction continued to spread. To the Chinese, the British rhetoric of free trade and equality in the diplomatic protocols of international relations could hardly mask the bitter realities. The unequal treaties forced them to suffer the continued importation of an abusive narcotic unrelated to the economic superiority Britain claimed to achieve through its new industries. Under the principle of extraterritoriality, growing numbers of Europeans lived in Chinese port cities, but they were exempt from Chinese laws. Treaty ports provided the foundations upon which Europe's unequal relations with China were erected.

For all the difficulties foreigners began to pose in the late 1830s, the Chinese government was able to wedge the Europeans into a limited number of treaty ports. For nearly a half century they did not worry about the dynasty being undermined directly by foreign activities. Far more pressing were the challenges of domestic rebellion.

Rebellions and Recovery

Many of the achievements of the eighteenth-century empire depended upon the determined efforts of officials to support local economies against hardship and disasters. As population expansion increased the influx into poorer parts of the frontier, the government was increasingly unwilling and unable to stabilize conditions. In some remote regions, the state was barely present at all by the late eighteenth century. Problems between the Miao minority ethnic group and the Han Chinese had precipitated a Miao rebellion in central China in the early 1790s. At the same time, a heterodox cult of millenarian Buddhists in the mountainous border region of Sichuan and Hubei were inciting resistance to the imperial government. The Court dispatched troops to suppress the potential sedition. This intervention prompted increased resistance that became known as the White Lotus Rebellion (1795-1804) after the doctrine of millenarian Buddhist beliefs that precipitated the uprising. A massive effort to weed out those who professed these beliefs provoked many who were not particularly religious to rise up to defend themselves against the Qing military intervention. This state effort exhausted the reserves in the central government treasuries, but did little to shake the basic security of the throne. A half century later, however, conflicts pushed the dynasty close to collapse when considerable stretches of territory fell into rebel hands.

The largest rebellion in nineteenth-century world history was the Taiping Rebellion (1850-64), dwarfing in scale even such events as the American Civil War. Millions died as a direct result of the fighting or because of illness or starvation attending the disruption of normal life. The rebellion began in China's remote southwest, where Hakka, a subethnic group of Han Chinese, formed the Society of God Worshippers. Led by Hong Xiuquan, an unsuccessful civil service examination candidate, the group gathered followers and left Guangxi province and headed for the Yangzi River. Hong had a unique view of the world influenced by Christian missionary tracts. During a nervous breakdown following his repeated failure to pass the civil service exams, he

Nineteenth Century Chinese Rebellions

Area of Taiping control, 1854

Area of Taiping control, 1862

Nian core area 1857-1863

Area affected by Nian rebellion1851-1868

Final encirclement of Nian rebels

Area affected by Red Turban rebellion 1854-1857

Area affected by Miao rebellion, 1850-1872

Area affected by Yunnan and Sichuan Muslim rebellion 1855-1878

Area affected by northwestern Muslim rebellion 1863-1874

villages against possible rebel attack. But the mobilization of these new armies and militia only partially explains the state's ultimate triumph in 1864. The Taiping failure stemmed not only from Qing power but also from internal dissension and weakness. Moreover, the Qing state's victory should not obscure the significance of the Taiping challenge. Before their downfall, they controlled part of China's economic heartland for a full decade. Meanwhile, the Qing government faced a host of other challenges.

North of the Taiping in a barren region known as Huaibei (literally "north of the Huai River"), a movement that grew out of indigenous banditry became the Nian Rebellion (1853–68). Lacking any particular ideology, the Nian were largely poor peasants and peddlers who previously engaged in periodic banditry.

dreamed he was speaking to God as the younger brother of Jesus Christ. As a result of this dream, he believed that he had a religious mission to save his people and to establish a new government. The God Worshippers gathered additional disaffected people as they first marched northward to the Yangzi and then turned eastward to the lower Yangzi heartland. On 19 March 1853 they broke through the wall defending Nanjing, the first capital of the Ming dynasty, and established their Taiping Kingdom. In the Taiping vision, society should be constituted as a brotherhood of all men, who lived in harmony achieved through social and economic equality. Though they put forth ambitious blueprints for land redistribution and in principle rejected Confucian ideology and institutions, the Taiping were unable to remake society according to their ideal plans; they implemented a bureaucratic structure and political principles not so very different from those of the Qing dynasty. These parallels, however, did not lessen the Taiping threat to the state.

To meet the Taiping forces, the Qing state created new armies mobilized by major provincial officials and financed by taxes on commerce. To complement the large-scale mobilization of men for major armies, gentry led efforts to create local militia units to defend their

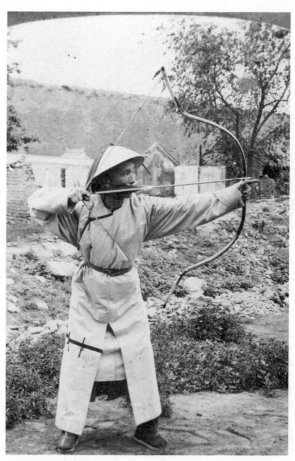

Early Qing dynasty archer. Even after these "banner men" were given modern arms, officers still had to pass examinations in archery and swordsmanship.

The combination of worsening climatic conditions and increasing military pressures stimulated the growth of the Nian. Though they never took over a major city and never proclaimed a capital, the Nian posed a challenge to Qing rule for fifteen years. In addition to these two major rebellions, there was unrest among the Miao in central China between 1850 and 1872 and a far briefer revolt between 1854 and 1857 in south China by a group known as the Red Turbans, who were led by Triad secret societies composed of marginal people, such as bandits, pirates, and smugglers who attacked major cities. In 1854 Red Turban groups attacked Canton under the slogan of restoring the Ming dynasty. Though they failed to take the city, they did take the smaller city of Foshan to the south of Canton and thus challenged urban authorities for two years as they gained control of the countryside from gentry leaders who fled. Through similar kinds of actions in September 1853, the Small Swords Society, composed of Cantonese and Fujianese, stormed Shanghai and held the city until February 1855.

In 1855, a third major rebellion broke out in the southwestern province of Yunnan, spilling over the border into Sichuan, where Han Chinese sought to take away gold and silver mines from Chinese Muslims. Rebel Muslims briefly held the provincial capital in 1863. More importantly, they also occupied the province's major western city of Dali for a full decade. To the northwest in Shanxi and Gansu, another Muslim rebellion broke out in 1863. For more than two decades, between 1855 and 1878, the Qing state faced Moslem unrest in the northwest and southwest. The northwestern Muslim difficulties erupted after a half century in which the Qing had successfully consolidated its control over Inner Asia. Despite the signs of weakness of Qing rule in China proper, the Manchus had done well in Mongolia, Xinjiang, and Tibet.

China's external and domestic problems met on the Inner Asian frontier in the early nineteenth century—rebellion and foreign relations came together in this area that had already contributed so much to the definition of the Qing empire. The principles the Qing would soon

Treaty Ports in China, ca. 1860

employ with the British were first developed in the northwest to deal with the Kokandis, who rose to regional power during the first half of the nineteenth century. Between 1831 and 1835 the Qing made the following set of concessions to Kokand that subsequently would be made to the British between 1842 and 1844: (1) extraterritoriality—foreign-appointed consuls with jurisdiction over their nationals; (2) an indemnity; (3) modest tariffs; (4) most favored nation status, which to the Chinese state meant impartial benevolence; (5) abolition of the hong merchant monopoly system. When granted to the Kokandis, none of these decisions undermined the Chinese belief in their own centrality. Allowing foreigners to manage their own people was a tactical maneuver to diminish burdens on a Qing bureaucracy already stretched thin governing its own subjects; granting economic concessions was a sign of imperial favor that implied no loss of political strength to the Qing state. The initial Qing perspective on relations with foreigners hardly means that the treaties imposed by Europeans were fair, but it does help explain how the Chinese could have so readily agreed to them.

Domestic and Foreign Challenges to the Qing Dynasty

In China's densely populated centers of agricultural and handicraft production, the post-rebellion central state depended on lower-level officials and local elites to establish social order. Missing was the eighteenth-century vision of an empire-wide network of social policies and institutions in which state efforts were especially large in areas lacking well-developed markets and wealthy Confucian elites committed to supporting their locales. Having shifted its organizational and fiscal resources to meet the military challenges of multiple rebellions and uprisings, the state lacked the capacity and perhaps the will to prevent serious social problems from emerging. The Grand Canal Administration no longer dredged and repaired the waterways linking the lower Yangzi to the capital; the Yellow River Administration farmed out the fiscal responsibilities to local administrations along the river, who lacked the resources to maintain embankments by any but the cheapest and least effective means. In the summer of 1876 famine conditions emerged in the northern province of Shandong; by autumn, the crisis spread across north and northwest China. Crops failed and relief ef-

forts were inadequate. The late nineteenth-century state did not meet the political agenda that had created eighteenth-century social order. Official energies had turned to other activities.

Under a movement known in English as "self-strengthening," leading provincial officials spearheaded the establishment of new industries and programs. From 1861 to 1872, government initiatives introduced Western firearms, machines, and scientific knowledge. By the 1870s and 1880s more attention was given to diversifying the economy beyond defense industries. Ships, railroads, mines, and telegraphs were all begun in this period. By the mid 1880s, government programs had expanded to include light industry. Although textile mills under joint official and private management never stimulated broader private industrialization as they did in Meiji Japan, it would be difficult to blame the state for this. A larger limitation than government resources or government will and vision was the paucity of private sector efforts to complement and take advantage of state initiatives.

The Sino-Japanese War of 1894–95, stemming from competition in Korea, marked a key turning point, because in this conflict China lost to an Asian country it had previously considered inferior. Flexing their military and diplomatic muscles, the Japanese imposed an

The Western powers sent troops to China during the Boxer Rebellion to protect the lives and property of their nationals. These African-American U.S. cavalrymen are shown riding down a street in Tianjin.

Noodle break at a portable restaurant in Gangzhou, ca. 1910.

Chinese Food: Cuisine, Culture, and Nutrition

The Chinese culinary tradition has developed sophisticated flavors, aromas, and textures. A wealth of seasonings—including pepper, sesame oil, salted black beans, rice wine, dried fruit skins—combine with a wide variety of vegetables, sea life, and animal meats to form a wide array of dishes. The importance of food in Chinese culture is confirmed by the early presence of food in poetry celebrating banquets for political, ritual, and family occasions. The first Chinese cookbook appeared nearly one thousand years ago. Fine meals are still always prepared at New Year and for major events like weddings, even in poor parts of the countryside.

In eleventh-century China, northern, southern (meaning south of the Yangzi River) and Sichuan cuisines formed the principal categories. Cantonese cuisine, the most common form of Chinese food in the United States because most of the pre-World War II Chinese immigration was from south China, developed a few centuries later. Basic differences between northern and southern cooking begin with staple grains. Northerners rely on wheat and millet for breads and noodles; southerners are more likely to eat rice. Other differences come from the range of spices chosen—more red pepper in Sichuan cuisine, more ginger in Cantonese food; and the relative frequency of stir frying (higher in the south) and steaming (more common in the north). Some ingredients and flavors are of course universal throughout Chinese cuisine, such as soy sauce and vinegar.

Chinese cuisine depends on a range of ingredients more diverse than that found in many Western cooking traditions. These differences led some Westerners of earlier times to consider Chinese cooking as strange, from which it was a short step to the belief that the Chinese diet was a poor one. Adam Smith claimed in *The Wealth of Nations*, "The poverty of the lower ranks of people in China far surpasses that of the most beggarly nations in Europe . . . The subsistence which they find . . . is so scanty that they are eager to fish up the nastiest garbage thrown overboard from any European ship. Any carrion, the carcase of a dead dog or cat, for example, half putrid and stinking, is as welcome to them as the most wholesome food to the people of other countries." While we have no systematic evidence about Chinese diets before the twentieth century, first-hand European observers during the nineteenth century did not always agree with Smith's late eighteenth-century pronounce-

ment. The Scotsman Robert Fortune, a stern critic of many Chinese customs, reported at mid-nineteenth century that "The food of these people is of the simplest kind—namely, rice, vegetables, and a small portion of animal food, such as fish or pork. But the poorest classes in China seem to understand the art of preparing their food much better than the same classes at home. With the simple substances I have named, the Chinese labourer contrives to make a number of very savory dishes, upon which he breakfasts or dines most sumptuously. In Scotland, in former days—and I suppose it is much the same now—the harvest labourer's breakfast consisted of porridge and milk, his dinner of bread and beer, and porridge and milk again for supper. A Chinaman would starve upon such food." Surveys in urban and rural China in the 1920s and 1930s generally found Chinese diets to be balanced and adequate. Where malnourishment occurred, it was due to people having inadequate food, not an unhealthy mix of food.

More troubling than a constantly inadequate food supply, which in the nineteenth and early twentieth centuries probably affected relatively few people, was the disruption of food supplies caused by harvest failure. When poor harvests struck a region two or more years in a row, the difficulties in managing the shortfalls could become acute, especially because the government's capacity to intervene in subsistence matters had declined from its eighteenth-century heights. The rebellions

that covered much of the empire around mid-century exacerbated natural problems of drought and flood to cause serious episodes of subsistence crises. To combat famine, the Chinese relied on manuals with useful information on edible wild plants. To stave off starvation, Chinese peasants turned to a far broader range of "foods" than those conventionally consumed. Probably no other culture in the world has invested as much energy and creativity in inventing different foods and been as willing to consume whatever nature can provide to keep them alive in difficult times.

By the late twentieth century, Chinese migrants carried their cuisines to many corners of the globe. On its travels, Chinese cooking has often been creatively adapted to new environments. New York City sports Cuban Chinese cooking, while at the other end of the social and geographical spectrum of the United States, Chinese cooking has been transformed by California cuisine to create distinctively American additions to the already broad range of Chinese tastes and textures. The galaxy of Chinese food consumed by the several hundred million people making up China, has now been augmented by new constellations created wherever Chinese immigrants have moved. From ornate dishes presented in elegant settings frequented by the wealthy to lunchroom counters with fast food, Chinese cooking has nourished and delighted people across the globe.

indemnity of 200 million taels, equaling twice the total annual revenue of the central government. This massive sum was quickly dwarfed by the indemnity levied by the allied powers at the resolution of the Boxer Uprising (1898–1901). This anti-Christian movement blamed foreign missionaries, with their landownership and connections to local Chinese officials and foreign diplomats, for the rural problems suffered by those not connected to missionaries. The movement gained the tacit support of the Court, which saw in the Boxers' actions a challenge to the foreigners that they could applauddiscreetly from the sidelines. The eight-nation army that marched into Beijing demanded the punishment of both Boxer leaders and the officials who had condoned their presence. They imposed an indemnity of 450 million taels to be paid over 39 years at 4 percent annual interest. To finance the indemnities from the Sino-Japanese War and the Boxer Rebellion, the state raised new taxes and borrowed from foreign banks. The ability of the state to increase revenues was no small achievement, but since most of the resources went directly to financing the indemnities, the new state funds accomplished little good for the country's economy.

Amid the difficulties created by contentious relations with foreign powers, some Chinese officials and intellectuals were deeply impressed by the wealth and power of Western countries. Western science and technology as well as governmental institutions were seen as key elements in European and American successes. Some Chinese, like some Japanese and Vietnamese, came to accept social Darwinism—already popular in Western countries—as a vision of social evolution in which the countries that can adapt and become strong enough will survive. Important Chinese intellectuals such as Yan Fu (1853–1921), a translator of major Western works, and Liang Qichao (1873–1929), an advocate of governmental reform, enjoyed influence throughout Asia.

In 1898 the Chinese state announced a set of governmental reforms that were not in fact implemented during the so-called 100 Days' Reform. Political changes were difficult to make because of serious divisions at the Court between leaders favoring major institutional reform and those officials, led by the Empress Dowager, who defended existing procedures. More serious proposals and actions did not take place until 1905 to 1911 when the government established new ministries, including those for commerce, education, and police, abolishing civil service examinations and other older government organizations.

Provincial assemblies, composed of leading elites, provided forums for the discussion of national issues. Pressure for governmental changes continued—some wanted reforms to transform the government into a constitutional monarchy; a second group favored a revolutionary overthrow of the dynastic system. Momentum for political change grew when the government proposed to buy up the rights to recently built railroads with money supplied by foreign loans. In the opinion of educated elites, these loans would give too much power to foreign interests. The railroad recovery campaign to assure Chinese control mobilized savings from a spectrum of rich and poor alike. Elites who had supported the government now turned to active opposition. Within the government, modern new armies were mobilized in which soldiers and their officers were actively

Jiang Jieshi.

involved in national politics. Some secretly became involved in anti-Qing activities and proved another key opponent of the regime. With both elites and the military turning against the throne, little effective support remained.

The Easy Collapse of the Last Dynasty and Post-Imperial Uncertainties

In a surprisingly swift period of a few months in 1911 the central government lost control over the country. Some provinces were led to declare independence from the Qing by their New Army units, others by provincial assemblies that largely represented an urban-oriented reformist elite. For a political system more than 2,000 years old, its collapse was very sudden and rather quiet. The void created an unstable vacuum. In 1912 a republic was founded with Sun Yat-sen (1866–1925) as the first president. Sun, a revolutionary with a strong south China base and overseas connections, understood that a unified country depended upon support from northern leaders. He therefore deferred immediately to Yuan Shi-kai (1859–1916), a former high military and civilian official under the Qing, who became president.

Before his death in 1916, Yuan attempted to centralize government control and create a viable and believable political system. Unable to imagine a substitute for the imperial system, he made an ill-conceived attempt to revive the system with himself as emperor. This failure was followed by a decade of disunity when China was divided into zones controlled by competing warlords. Politics had degenerated into a contest for control of territory among those possessing military power.

In 1926 an ambitious young general, Jiang Jieshi, or Chiang Kai-shek as he became known in the West, recently having achieved the top position in the Nationalist party (Guomindang, or GMD), launched the final stage of an army drive from south China to the north. Through a mix of alliances and battles, Jiang achieved a superficial national unity in 1927 that would last until the Japanese invasion of 1937. With his base of support in urban China, Jiang Jieshi's major agrarian concern was in fact a military one—to exterminate the Communists.

The Communist party of China (CCP) was founded on 1 July 1921 in Shanghai by urban intellectuals who were influenced by the writings of Karl Marx and by the Russian Revolution of 1917. These demonstrated to Chinese intellectuals how a political revolution could propel a backward country into the forefront of world history. In 1923, under guidance from the Comintern, the Moscow-directed international Communist movement, the CCP formed a united front with the GMD. The two parties shared as a primary goal the reunification of the country in an uneasy alliance that lasted until April 1927, when Jiang reached Shanghai. After workers' strikes had crippled the city, making it easier for him to enter, Jiang staged nighttime raids on Communist strongholds and with the help of the Green Gang, a powerful urban gang that controlled the Shanghai underworld, Jiang smashed the urban bases of the Communist movement. Remnants from Shanghai and other cities fled to the countryside to form a base area in Jiangxi province in central China.

Competing views of the Chinese countryside could easily confuse our understanding of what agrarian living conditions were like at this time. An optimistic view highlights economic improvements occasioned by increased trade, better transport, and more credit. A pessimistic view stresses exploitation of tenants by landlords, the low standards of living, and the danger of subsistence crises. (See Special Feature, "Chinese Food: Cuisine, Culture, and Nutrition," pp. 946–947.) The collapse of farm prices during the Depression in the early 1930s fueled the pessimistic view of the countryside. In fact, both views highlight important features of the varied scene across rural China. Some peasants benefited from expanding trade just as others were no doubt exploited by their landlords. More fundamental than a stress on either the positive or negative features is the fact that China's agrarian system had changed relatively little over the past two centuries. Although marketing had expanded, it could not transform a countryside that organizationally and technologically was very similar to the countryside of Qing China.

No Chinese alive in 1800 could have predicted the dramatic political changes that would take place barely a century later when the last dynasty collapsed. Domestic unrest, though widespread and intense, was defeated by state efforts. The nineteenth-century state could not replicate the successes of eighteenth-century leaders, but bureaucratic and fiscal limitations did not render the government unable to rule. Ultimately it was new foreign challenges that undermined the Qing state's capacity to survive. Cities continued to grow under strong foreign influence in the post-imperial period, but in the countryside no fundamental changes took place. Political changes were more important than economic. Gone was the eighteenth-century state or even a nineteenth-century integrated state. Local governments in some places became more intrusive, exacerbating difficulties that peasants sometimes experienced because elites were no longer encouraged to support local welfare effectively. The Communists would ultimately build their social revolution upon the dissatisfactions peasants suffered economically and politically under Nationalist rule.

The Formation of Japan's Modern State

In stark contrast to the collapse of the Chinese empire and subsequent post-imperial political uncertainties, political leaders in nineteenth-century Japan successfully initiated a wide-ranging set of reforms in the 1870s and 1880s to create a modern state. Following these dramatic political changes came early twentieth-century economic changes that brought forth an ever more important industrial sector, which would experience a sudden spurt of development during World War I. But much of Japan remained rural and not closely connected to this industrialization process. To integrate such people into a society sharing common goals with both urban workers and capitalists, the state embarked upon a program that created a formal empire and expanded informal Japanese influence throughout Asia.

Prelude to the Meiji Restoration

After widespread rural revolts in the 1780s, the countryside remained peaceful until the Tempo era (1830–44), when famine conditions prompted protests on an unprecedented scale, including the 1836 assembly of some 30,000 people gathered to protest food shortages. The chronic problem of crop failures had become more serious because village wealth was becoming increasingly unequal. The few families benefiting from amassing large amounts of land were no doubt less vulnerable to crop failures, but the many more with little or no land faced greater peril. Some landless peasants depended on local farms for wage labor; others migrated to cities in search of jobs. The Tokugawa ideal of a stable rural society based on village communities of relatively equal peasants in a world separate from the cities filled with samurai and merchants was impossible to implement even partially in the nineteenth century. In the cities many samurai faced growing difficulties; morale fell as they were prohibited from engaging in trade, agriculture, or any other means of making a living wage. Their fixed stipends were inadequate in a period of inflation that began in the 1820s, forcing many to depend on loans to survive. Once in debt, their situations worsened.

The eighteenth-century economy had been coordinated by urban-based specialized merchants whose activities were licensed and regulated by domain administrations. Nineteenth-century economic expansion depended on small-scale local merchants tapping underemployed rural labor and new resources diverted from agriculture to rural handicrafts. Neither central

These young samurai from Satsuma, Choshu, and Tosa took part in the overthrow of the Tokugawa shogunate.

SHANGHAI DIARY

■ Japanese anxieties about the potential harm awaiting them at Western hands were fueled by what they observed happening to China. Takasugi Shinsaku (1839–67) was a samurai from Chōshū who recorded the following thoughts in his diary while on a mission to Shanghai in 1862. Although excited by the thought that the Taiping rebels were near at hand, he was dismayed to think of how the Westerners made Shanghai different from what he imagined the capital of Beijing to be like.

May 7. From the land, the sounds of rifles have come echoing and tearing through the dawn sky across which the day has not broken yet. According to everyone I have talked with, this must be the sounds of the rifles with which the Imperial Army and the Taiping rebels are fighting. If they are right, I will be able to see the real fight. I could not hide my excitement. . . . I heard that the place where our ship is anchored is called Shinko. The width of the river has become very narrow and the distance between the banks is only a few *chō.* Muddy water is swiftly flowing. According to a British sailor, the few thousand ships which have been anchored here and the Chinese who live on the land are all using this muddy water as their drinking water. Near dusk, a small ship passed by our ship flying a flag which said "munitional duty." The flurry of the war made me restless . . .

May 21. During the morning, I walked around an antique shop and saw some paintings. I have come to think about the city, Shanghai, all day long today. Here most of the Chinese have become the servants of foreigners. When English and French people come walking, the Chinese give way to them stealthily. Although the main power here is Chinese, it really is nothing but a colony of England and France. Peking is said to be 300 *ri* [1 *ri* = 2.44 miles] away from here—the traditional China of the past must remain there. I really hope that is so. I wonder, what would those Chinese think of if they saw this city? However, turning to the situation in our country and thinking of the case of Japan, we'll have been forewarned—who can be sure the same fate will not visit our country in the future? . . .

May 23. In the morning, I visited the English missionary (Muirhead) with Godai. The missionary has come to Shanghai to propagate the Christian religion. The place where he lives serves both as a church and as a hospital. I heard it is called Shii-in. When Europeans propagate their religion in foreign countries, they always bring a physician with them. At the Shii-in they help to cure people who are down with sickness and then convert them to Christianity. We will have to be prepared for such things too in Japan.

From the diary of Takasugi Shinsaka.

(bakufu) nor local (daimyo) rulers proved able to tap revenues from the economic changes of the early nineteenth century. Chronically overspending by the 1830s, they could not escape permanent indebtedness.

In the 1840s, Japanese leaders called for a defense of Japan against potential Western threats. Some recognized that the Japanese should learn Western armament techniques to defend themselves against possible attacks. By the 1850s the Japanese were particularly concerned about British commercial activities and Russian initiatives in the islands near the northern border. However, Britain was far more interested in China and the Russians in making advances in Manchuria. As a result, it was the United States' Commodore Perry who "opened" Japan in 1853. Through a series of negotiations with the United States, Britain, and Russia, Japan agreed to commercial treaties in 1857 and 1858 that incorporated Japan into the same treaty port system that bound China. The Japanese did manage to have opium imports prohibited, but in virtually all other respects Japan's foreign relations with the West for the next several decades would be on the same diplomatic basis as Western powers were establishing throughout Asia wherever formal colonial power was not installed.

Acceptance of foreign demands for treaty ports inspired heated critiques of the Tokugawa leadership. To meet foreign challenges and domestic problems, some leaders promoted rule by the emperor as an alternative to rule by the bakufu. Reaffirming the emperor's place at the center of Japan's political system gave the domains who challenged bakufu authority an alternative to Tokugawa institutions of rule. Led by the Satsuma and Chōshū domains of southwest Japan, critics proposed that the shogun step down from office to join other great lords on a council to advise the emperor. These leaders feared disorder in the countryside, the cities, and in foreign relations. In January 1868 a coup stripped the Tokugawa shogun of his powers, and returned responsibility for the government to the emperor. An imperial army made up of soldiers from domains "loyal" to the emperor proceeded toward Edo; terms were negotiated in April. The restoration of imperial power had been completed. Now the challenge of creating a modern state in the Meiji era (1868–1912) could be addressed.

Modern State Formation in Japan

The Meiji state came to power with no blueprint for institutional change, nor was there a coherent ideology for rule to displace the combination of Confucianism, Shinto, and Buddhism deployed under the Tokugawa. In 1868 the most pressing problem was creating a set of institutions for central government. By 1869 power and authority rested with the ministers and vice-ministers of six departments—Civil Affairs, Finance, War, Justice, Imperial Household, and Foreign Affairs. The emperor moved to the shogun's former castle in Edo and the city was renamed Tokyo, "eastern capital" because it was east of the old capital of Kyoto. The domains were abolished in 1871 and renamed prefectures. The central government moved to control two key aspects of state administration, fiscal affairs and the military. Tax revenues were channeled to the central government. To cut expenditures, the government had reduced samurai stipends in 1868 and in 1871 allowed samurai to take up other occupations; in 1876 government bonds were dis-

tributed as a one-time payment to replace annual samurai allowances.

Foreign advice and models were reviewed by Japanese officials seeking to create a modern government. With French advice on military organization and training, Japan had an arsenal, ordnance yard, and gunpowder factory established by 1875. In the 1870s the new army mobilized through conscription was kept busy with peasant and samurai unrest. The peasants' issues had little to do with the central government. They concerned rice hoarding, loan foreclosure, and other issues affecting popular welfare. A more serious threat was posed by several samurai uprisings, culminating in the Satsuma rebellion of 1877; samurai were upset by the destruction of their privileges and their inability to influence political developments. The Meiji state survived both peasant and samurai dissatisfaction, putting down unrest with their newly mobilized armies. Having centralized both fiscal and military matters, the Meiji state enjoyed the financial and coercive capacities to rule. But institutions remained to be developed to channel the participation of elites into government.

These institutions were subsequently constructed through the Popular Rights Movement. In 1873 samurai from Tosa spearheaded a proposal to create a constitutional structure. In 1874 they petitioned for the creation of an elected legislature. Government leaders who had traveled to Europe were convinced that a constitution and other institutional changes could make the Japanese state stronger, as well as more similar to European ones and therefore more acceptable to Western powers. The structure of a government was outlined—an assembly with limited powers, having no right to initiate legislation or deny the government money, and a cabinet responsible to the emperor. Representatives went to Europe to learn more about constitutions and concluded that German political traditions were more congenial than British or French. The notion that the monarch represents a more general interest than those of any competing groups confirmed the emperor's central role and the limited participation by others in governmental affairs. Other government reforms were also modeled on foreign examples. The criminal code was drafted under a French adviser, while the drafting of commercial law was shaped by German suggestions. The police, like the military, was shaped by French models. Foreign practices provided inspiration and legitimation for early Meiji reforms, but they were not imitated slavishly. In part, incomplete knowledge precluded their complete reproduction. But more importantly, Japanese officials also faced local concerns

The Tokugawa government sent several embassies to the West to negotiate more favorable treaty terms. This photograph shows such a delegation in Paris in 1862, led by Takeuchi Yasumori.

and were influenced by other considerations. In fact, the similarities between Western and Japanese institutions such as the police or the postal system were often greater initially than they were after a period of innovation. Thus, while foreigners believed that the Japanese were adopting European practices in order to become more like them, the Japanese were in fact forming their own synthesis, which adapted foreign principles to Japanese concerns.

In 1881 the government announced the future formation of a parliament in response to years of pressure by reformers to adopt more Western forms of government. Political parties were formed as adjuncts to bureaucratic factions representing different perspectives on government policies and actions. By 1890 when Japan's parliament, called the Diet, opened, a reaction against Western-style reforms of the 1870s was gathering momentum. Political parties declined in importance as their leaders withdrew and people lost interest in pop-

ular rights. Their greatest political concern was the revision of Japan's unequal treaties. In 1872, Britain denied Japan's first request to revise the unequal treaties. Additional talks in the 1880s produced the same result. Only in the 1893 negotiations did the Japanese persuade the Europeans that they had appropriate legal institutions, making extraterritoriality unnecessary. The first genuinely equal treaty was signed in July 1894. Though the Japanese took more than twenty years to achieve a revision of foreign relations with Europeans, their ultimate success contrasts sharply with the fates of other Asian countries that would labor under unequal treaties well into the twentieth century.

Economic Change and Social Protests

Over the nineteenth century the output of Japan's economy quadrupled. Industry's proportion of total output doubled as the economy began a transition from traditional and agrarian to modern and industrial. Economic changes in the first half of the nineteenth century centered on increased cash cropping and rural industry. Rural traders created new networks of exchange that successfully challenged the older and larger merchants in castle towns. With greater specialization and better use of native technologies, farm output in the 1880s probably climbed above that achieved in the 1860s. Between 1885 and 1920 rapid growth of modern transport, communications, metals, and machinery building signaled the emergence of modern economic growth.

The Meiji state played an important role in these economic changes. In the 1870s the government initiated railways and a postal service as well as subsidies for the shipping industry. In addition the early Meiji state set up model factories in textiles, cement, glass, and bricks; then in the early 1880s it sold these businesses to private entrepreneurs. Between 1897 and 1914 30 to 40 percent of total investment was provided by the state to build the infrastructure in banking, railroads, shipping, postal service, telegraph, electric power, and education. Changes in the modern sector capture the observer's attention most easily. But most of the economy's output before World War I continued to come from traditional activities. The wartime push into modern industrial development raised Japan's GNP by 40 percent between 1914 and 1918. The textile industry's shift to urban factories brought the women already engaged in silk and cotton production into cities, where they lived in company dormitories and worked in dangerous conditions. Like early factory women in Europe, the women in Japan were subjected to strong hierarchical discipline and sexual harassment by both male workers and managers. The development of heavy industry was staffed by men who were initially brought to factories by labor contractors. Managers who wanted to initiate stricter discipline were forced by worker demands for job security, wage security, and fair treatment to improve working conditions.

The countryside also witnessed social and economic changes, creating new forms of protest. Between 1917 and 1931 almost 25,000 rural disputes have been tabulated, more than half of them in the Kinko and Chubu areas, which were heavily commercialized and supplied more than 50 percent of the national rice market. Two groups—upwardly mobile tenants and poor tenants vulnerable to failure—united in common antagonism to landlords and merchants. Their protest movement was later displaced by a popular agrarianism led by educated youth who chose to stay

Japan's Asian Empire

on the farms to improve them. This new agrarianism blamed urban capitalism for rural ills and in the 1930s would be mobilized by the government for a total war effort.

Economic changes in industry and agriculture created social protests and fueled social changes in both urban and rural Japan. To reduce domestic frictions and to support continued economic expansion, the Japanese state embarked upon building an empire.

Japanese Empire

In a short thirty-year period, Japan, initially a small Asian nation of islands subjected to the Western treaty port system, became an expanding imperialist power in its own right. This dramatic display of political power was driven by Japanese anxieties over national security. The Japanese empire differed from European counterparts, which were often developed in response to initiatives by traders, missionaries, and adventurers in far-flung corners of the globe. Japanese colonies were near to the islands and were targeted by the government as

The Sino-Japanese war of 1894 had its roots in disputes over territorial rights in Korea that dated from the seventh century. This Japanese print depicts one of a series of clashes between Chinese and Japanese troops that led to a treaty declaring Korea's "independence." Japan formally annexed Korea fifteen years later.

strategic moves to bolster the nation's immediate security in a Darwinian competition for survival among the world's nations. Japanese leaders not only liberated themselves from Western domination but successfully imitated Western practices to create a formal empire of their own through the defeat of China in the Sino-Japanese War of 1894–95 and the defeat of Russia in the Russo-Japanese War of 1904–05. They welcomed Western indicators of power and prestige, using foreign colonial successes to bolster domestic support for the government. By 1922 the colonial empire had five components: Korea, Taiwan, the Kwantung (now Guandong) leased territory on the Liaodong Peninsula of China, Karafuto (the southern half of Sakhalin Island, shared with Russia), and Nan'yō (the German Micronesian colony taken over by Japan after the German defeat in World War I). The most important components of this empire were Korea and Taiwan.

Japan aimed to establish its rule over Korea through the Sino-Japanese War of 1894–95, during which the Japanese pushed the Chinese out of Korea. They also occupied Liaodong and seized the town of Weihaiwei on the Shandong Peninsula. The army favored pressing its advantage all the way to Beijing, but the navy favored a settlement less troubling to the Westerners. The result-

ing treaty recognized Japanese authority over Taiwan, the Pescadores Islands, and the Liaodong Peninsula. However, the so-called Triple Intervention of Russia, Germany, and France forced the return of the Liaodong Peninsula to China, which then promptly leased it to Russia. In 1905 Japan made Korea a formal protectorate and in 1910 a formal colony. Japanese rule, strict and often cruel, was in the hands of the military and the police. The authoritarian colonial administration that lasted until 1919, deeply resented by the Korean people, was tempered by a decade of so-called "cultural rule" from 1920 to 1930 that permitted some freedoms, removed judicial system abuses, and reduced discrimination in public services for Koreans. By allowing Korean-language publications and easing judicial and political restrictions, the Japanese hoped to co-opt political opposition to their colonial regime. But Korean nationalist sentiments were difficult to rein in; nationalist intellectuals wrote national histories and followed the activities of Chinese nationalist leaders Jiang Jieshi and Mao Zedong. A Korean Communist movement began after the Russian Revolution; Communists and non-Communists joined to form a United Front organization between 1927 and 1929. The Japanese broke up this United Front and repressed the

Communist movement, turning Kim Il Sung, who would later be North Korea's founding father, into a guerrilla leader.

Japanese decisions determined Korean economic development, which until 1930 was aimed at expanding rice production to feed Japan, especially after the 1918 Japanese rice riots. Korean farmers benefited little from increased agricultural production, though Korean landlords enjoyed a prosperity that made them willing collaborators with Japanese colonial rule. Japanese colonial rulers made important investments in infrastructure, which supplied the foundation for Korea's industrialization in metals, machinery, and chemicals. Later Korean leaders also learned how to run an economy under centralized bureaucratic guidance from the Japanese practices in Korea. But resentment and ill will have accompanied Korean admiration for Japanese accomplishments and culture to the present day.

In contrast to Korea's difficult experience with Japanese colonialism, Taiwan's situation was far less painful. The initial military takeover of the island was bloody; casualties included at least 7,000 Japanese and thousands more islanders. But after their entrenchment, the Japanese faced less antagonism because wealthy people opposing Japanese rule could return to mainland China. The colonial administration made efforts to develop the island's social and economic infrastructure through schools, public health facilities, transport, and communications. In economic terms, the colonial government in Taiwan promoted sugar production between 1900 and 1910, laying the foundation for a successful commodity on world markets. Beyond sugar the colonial government helped stimulate commercialized agriculture, made public investment, formed quasi-government monopolies, and supported deficit financing to stimulate social and economic improvements. The Japanese colonial government created the infrastructure necessary for modern economic change without ever abandoning the threat of repression to keep the populace under control.

Japan's administration of its colonies differed among places and changed over time. The conservative policies of the early 1900s gave way to more liberal policies in the 1920s. Policies would change again in the 1930s to a more military focus, complementing the country's buildup for war. Throughout policy shifts and administrative changes, the Japanese position on the colonies was shaped by two independent lines of thinking. First, Japan saw colonial administration very much as an issue of international politics like Western countries did;

strategic and economic concerns shaped decisions in Tokyo. Second, and more distinctly Asian, the Japanese promoted a vision of assimilation, which recognized Japan's bond with its colonies in the Sinitic cultural sphere. Stressing the mystical link between the Japanese people and the imperial house, some leaders claimed that those who came under Japanese rule could also become imperial peoples. This perspective is a distinctly Japanese version of the English "white man's burden" or the French *mission civilisatrice*. It also resonates with the Chinese cultural notion of creating Chinese people by educating them in proper ways of living. But it contrasts with a strongly racialist insistence on Japanese purity that was argued in later decades. Whatever the distinctive elements of Japanese rhetoric creating the Japanese image of how their empire worked, the realities of day-to-day administration in the colonies created the familiar colonial elite with its privileged lifestyle amidst poorer native populations.

Japan's successes in creating a colonial empire made it the equal of major Western powers in international politics by 1930. The Meiji Restoration had created a centralized state able to consolidate domestic control through the formation of a new military and new methods for extracting financial resources. With many government features modeled on Western experiences, Europeans easily saw themselves reflected in these Japanese changes. But becoming accepted in diplomatic circles as an equal partner did not mean that the Japanese envisioned themselves becoming "Western." In Japan, as in the rest of Asia, the central intellectual concern of the first several decades of the twentieth century was how to promote rapid political change and economic development without endorsing social and cultural transformations that made Asian countries mere imitations of Western countries.

Becoming Modern Without Becoming Western

China's twentieth-century post-imperial problems spanned difficulties introduced by the enlarged European world order and challenges rooted in creating and sustaining agrarian social order across a vast territory with a huge population. The persistence of agrarian China necessarily meant that the country's modern trajectory could not trace the arc of changes by European

Student demonstration in Tiananmen Square, Beijing, in 1919. Thousands of students massed to support China's rights in Shandong and to call for "democracy and science."

countries that lost their peasant societies. In Japan, the constant signs of social change fostered critiques and challenges that called into question how Japanese identity would be defined and how changes originating in the West would come to be seen. Not many Chinese or Japanese in the early twentieth century would have considered themselves to be anything other than Chinese or Japanese, but how to be a modern Chinese or Japanese was a most vexing issue.

China's Post-Imperial Search for a New Order

On 4 May 1919 a demonstration of thousands filled the streets of Beijing to protest the Treaty of Versailles concluding World War I. Chinese, expecting the German defeat to mean the return of German leaseholds, were shocked to discover that the Western powers had agreed to allow Japan to take over German interests in China. Initially the demonstration of 4 May was an urban expression of nationalism by students, merchants, and workers, but May Fourth also became the label attached to a movement of intellectual and cultural change. Chinese intellectuals assessed what Western ideas and institutions would best serve China's goal of becoming a country of wealth and power. Motivated most strongly by a desire to save the country, young, urban, educated Chinese pondered the merits of different Western philosophies, political systems, and social practices. Writing in the vernacular language to be more accessible to a broader audience, intellectuals welcomed new styles of literature openly shaped by foreign influences in a variety of new periodicals. Chinese translations of Western literature, history, and social thought made their appearance to excite and challenge China's best young minds with a barrage of information about democracy, capitalism, and socialism.

Facing China's multiple uncertainties in the early 1920s, urban intellectuals focused on a range of political, social, economic, and cultural issues. The complex anxieties generated by competing warlord governments, none of which was strong enough to withstand major foreign pressures from Japan or Western powers, did not inspire much confidence in those searching for a political solution to China's ills. Hu Shi, a Columbia University-trained student of John Dewey's, would become a leading educator and diplomat for the Nationalists. He strongly criticized the false panaceas promised by various totalizing "isms" like socialism and communism. Consistent with his Columbia training, he believed China should seek modest reforms to gradually create a more Western political system. His quiet optimism that small positive steps could lead to gradual and effective change seemed inadequate to many Chinese intellectuals who, as heirs to a Confucian tradition that placed a premium on public service, could affirm a commitment to saving society from its ills without subscribing directly to any Confucian beliefs.

The Russian Revolution of 1917 taught some Chinese intellectuals a dramatic lesson—a backward country could produce a social revolution, putting into power a government committed to rapid industrialization. To Chinese intellectuals Marxism offered a Western critique of Western power, a modern weapon to employ in the war against the influence of foreign capitalists and domestic power holders. But not all vigorous critics of China's weak and vulnerable condition joined the CCP. Many others were inspired to do concrete social research in the Chinese countryside in order to document the ills demanding reform. Their research reports filled new scholarly journals and formed the basis for discussions in China's urban universities of China's agrarian social conditions.

In China's cities, major shifts in popular attitudes accompanied the emergence of new social groups such as students and workers. The nationalism of the May Fourth movement is one such new set of beliefs that spanned social classes. For educated elites, changes in family life—and especially the position of women within and beyond the family—were key issues. China's traditional family system was built on the hierarchical relations of husband over wife and parents over children. China's urban youth found this a confusing and oppressive situation, especially for young women who had fewer educational opportunities and if they did become educated enjoyed fewer options for careers.

Despite the absence of a state able to exercise authority over the entire country, a modern economy established itself in cities. The major center was Shanghai, where both foreign-owned and Chinese factories began to multiply after 1915. Most production in Shanghai was concentrated in light industrial products—textiles, food processing, cigarettes. A second center of industrial growth was in China's northeast in Manchuria, where heavy industry played a larger role. But these new industrial developments did not spill over into the countryside. China's twentieth-century changes—political, economic, social, and cultural—were all largely the products of an urban environment. How they could be linked to the countryside became the concern of some Chinese intellectuals, some of whom chose to reject Western influences whenever they could.

Which Way Forward?

Not everyone in the May Fourth generation of intellectuals embraced Western ideas. Some searched instead for what they could consider a Chinese identity. Intellectuals striving to conserve a Chinese "essence" looked to the high culture, not popular culture, for beliefs they wished to promote. Their notion of a Chinese essence was stripped of any specific historical context; Chinese identity was conceived as an abstract set of "timeless" characteristics with no dynamic of genesis or transformation. Finally, this preservation project identified a national spirit or essence separate from politics and the state. This move protected the survival of a Chinese identity against the possibility of the state's political collapse. At the same time it obscured the intimate relationship that politics and culture had previously shared.

In imperial China for some two thousand years the state defined orthodox belief. Cultural commitments were also political ones because Confucian thought created roles and responsibilities within and beyond government offices. The twentieth-century conservative's failure to preserve this older linkage between politics and culture agreed with liberal perspectives as well, which also advocated a divorce between politics and culture. Central to this shared understanding was a realization that Chinese politics in the post-imperial period was not clearly guided by a coherent vision of how society should work. The inability of intellectuals or officials to fuse politics and culture in urban China of the 1920s and 1930s comes as no surprise. Strategies to

NORA LEAVES HOME

■ *Lu Xun, widely regarded as twentieth-century China's greatest literary voice, was a sharp critic of "traditional" ways, but he was also a sober enough realist to recognize the profound difficulties of transforming society into a better one. In a talk given to the students at Beijing Women's Normal College on 26 December 1923, he confronted the problem of what would happen to Chinese women if, like Nora, the heroine of the Norwegian playwright Henrik Ibsen's* A Doll's House, *they left their husbands or attempted to avoid marriage. Since Ibsen's play ends with Nora leaving the family, we never learn what becomes of her. The possibilities Lu Xun imagines for Chinese "Noras," urban, educated young women of the May Fourth era, are bleak.*

The most painful thing in life is to wake up from a dream and find no way out. Dreamers are fortunate people. If no way out can be seen, the important thing is not to awaken the sleepers.

However, since Nora has awakened it is hard for her to return to the dream world; hence all she can do is to leave. After leaving, though, she can hardly avoid going to the bad or returning. Otherwise the question arises: What has she taken away with her apart from her awakened heart? If she has nothing but a crimson woollen scarf of the kind you young ladies are wearing, even if two or three feet wide it will prove completely useless. She needs more than that, needs something in her purse. To put it bluntly, what she needs is money . . .

Of course money cannot buy freedom, but freedom can be sold for money. Human beings have one great drawback, which is that they often get hungry. To remedy this drawback and to avoid being puppets, the most important thing in society today seems to be economic rights. First, there must be a fair sharing out between men and women in the family; secondly, men and women must have equal rights in society.

Unfortunately I have no idea how we are to get hold of these rights; all I know is that we have to fight for them. We may even have to fight harder for these than for political rights.

Actually, today, if just one Nora left home she might not find herself in difficulties; because such a case, being so exceptional, would enlist a good deal of sympathy and certain people would help her out. To live on the sympathy of others already means having no freedom; but if a hundred Noras were to leave home, even that sympathy would diminish; while if a thousand or ten thousand were to leave, they would arouse disgust. So having economic power in your own hands is far more reliable.

Unfortunately China is very hard to change. Just to move a table or overhaul a stove probably involves shedding blood; and even so, the change may not get made. Unless some great whip lashes her on the back, China will never budge. Such a whip is bound to come, I think. Whether good or bad, this whipping is bound to come. But where it will come from or how it will come I do not know exactly.

And here my talk ends.

replace the connections between politics and culture forged by an agrarian empire in a twentieth-century urban setting are difficult to imagine. But what about the countryside?

The intellectual ferment in China's cities spilled into the countryside in three distinct forms—conservative, liberal, and radical. In north China's Shandong province, Liang Shuming led a conservative effort to rekindle a passion for moral community divorced from formal politics. He called upon intellectuals to recognize a Confucian responsibility for the welfare of the peasants and set out to organize various agricultural and commercial projects to improve peasant livelihoods. His successes attracted Jiang Jieshi, who wanted to make Liang's efforts the model for rural welfare efforts across other parts of Shandong and then the rest of Nationalist China. This bottom-up effort, co-opted by the government, was cut off by the 1937 Japanese invasion.

Crop-watcher's field house, from North China Villages *by Sidney D. Gamble.*

Similarly, efforts by the liberal James Yen, a Yale-educated Christian reformer with wide-ranging ties to foreigners, focused on introducing programs to improve peasant welfare in some north China villages. Through Yen's efforts some of the earliest scientific surveys of village conditions were undertaken, setting standards for research in the Chinese countryside. But better knowledge of the countryside did not lead necessarily to greater improvements. As Marx argued and the Chinese Communists certainly believed, the object of analysis was not simply to understand a bad situation but to change it.

Mao Zedong, leader of the Chinese revolution, gave an assessment of the countryside in 1927 as the formation of peasant associations to challenge landlords and local officials expanded in parts of southern China. He expressed exuberant confidence in the power of the people to protest the exploitation of landlords and local government. The driving logic of the radical approach to the countryside was to transform the social relations that put peasants under multiple forms of oppression. In the 1920s and early 1930s, conservative, liberal, and radical approaches to the countryside in fact shared several common characteristics. First, they all stressed initiatives to improve peasant welfare. Second, none had yet developed a program to link peasant society to the social, political, and economic changes of urban China. The challenge of moving China forward would ultimately depend not simply upon solving agrarian problems, but on joining those rural solutions to rule of China's increasingly impor-tant cities, where modern industries and new social actors—students, workers, capitalists—demanded a new political order.

The Japanese Embrace and Rejection of Western Thought

Japanese leaders understood the importance of Western political ideas and institutions to the formation of their state and to the legitimation of their government and society in Western eyes. At the same time, many were nervous about the changes overtaking Japan and sounded critical warnings against recent developments. In the late 1890s, fears of the socially divisive impact of industrialization led conservative professors at the University of Tokyo to form a society to promote welfare programs inspired by a German perspective on industrialization's ills. The group criticized recent changes from a moral perspective, observing a decadence seeping into society as Japanese virtues were displaced by the pursuit of profit. The views of these conservatives were held in check by the government's 1900 Public Peace Police Law, which gave officials wide authority to shut down labor and socialist organizations.

Some leaders saw Japan's problem not in capitalism but in the arrested political development of Japanese society. What Japan needed, in their view, was more parliamentary progress to wrest authority from the bureaucrats. The 1918 rice riots persuaded many liberals that political rights were insufficient; people demanded economic security as well. The 1920s witnessed a diversity of critiques. Prominent at the beginning were anarchosyndicalist types who fused hopes for political revolution with those for personal liberation. Marxists replaced them as the most potent intellectual force on the left. Japanese Marxism embraced a variety of approaches to Japan's political situation of the 1920s. Some, like Fukumoto Kazuo (1894–1983), were Leninists advocating a secret vanguard party to surreptitiously foment revolution. Others, like Yamakawa Hitoshi (1880–1958), sought a more open challenge to abolish old institutions and democratize politics. Even as the government increasingly cracked down on the Communists, Marxists became a more potent intellectual force. Radicals sought a strong nation-state as they pushed for social revolution.

Western notions of liberal politics could not be adopted fully in Japan because Western liberalism was intimately connected to the concept of individualism. The Japanese individual lacked the private space common in Western cultural expectations; enmeshed in a set of reciprocal obligations and responsibilities formed by family and community, Japanese could not construct an autonomous "private" sphere very easily. The complementary "public" sphere of politically concerned people organized by interest group or class did develop more in Japan than Western notions of a "private" sphere, but without a Western kind of individualism, Japanese liberalism could not resemble Western models very closely. Nevertheless, political changes did take place. Whereas the Meiji government was really a government of former samurai in a ruling structure composed of bureaucrats, generals, and admirals, the Taisho government (1912–25), which was installed after the Meiji emperor's death, included new groups of businessmen, professionals, and landlords whose voices were represented in the Diet. Without sharing much of a Western liberal political philosophy, Japanese leaders were still able to construct a more liberal political structure.

At the same time as the Japanese government made changes inspired by Western models, the intense curiosity about foreign ideas prompted a more ambitious effort to defend the integrity of Japanese culture. This integrity could not be based on some unique Japanese qualities unaffected by foreign influences because Japan had become too heavily involved with foreign ideas, institutions, and countries to have a very large core of "pure" elements. The eighteenth-century nativist reaction to Chinese Confucianism could no longer serve effectively as a model for rejection of Western influences. Though a few searched for a "pure" Japanese essence untainted by foreign influences, many others found Japanese distinctiveness in their society's ability to combine features of East and West. Yet others aimed to reject, violently on occasion, what they considered dangerous Western practices.

Right-wing intellectuals came forward with different statements of a distinctly Japanese path of change. For Kita Ikki (1883–1937), the failure of China's 1911 revolution provided a lesson for the Japanese. Kita believed that China's political failures were due to the absence of a supreme leader; Asian societies, in his view, needed to maintain an imperial principle of authority. Retention of this principle of authority did not contradict other Western-style social or economic changes. Asian political principles could, in Kita's view, be joined to Western-induced economic and social changes. A more inclusive rejection of modern economics and society

came from those like Gondō Seikyō (1868–1937), who promoted an ideal of the Asian agrarian community with local government attached to the people as an alternative to industrial urban society ruled by a bureaucratic state. The intense nationalism inherent in critiques of the West paved the way for the militarism of the 1930s, which would resemble in many ways the fascism of Germany and Italy.

Japanese Popular Culture and Modern Possibilities

Japanese cities, home to new styles of literature and art beginning in the eighteenth century, continued in the nineteenth century to house these cultural pursuits. The Meiji Restoration introduced Western influences

Japanese women of the Meiji era learned Western musical forms and played Western instruments.

DARKNESS OF HUMANITY

Akira Kurosawa is Japan's most famous film director. His vision of human life, its tragedies and its comedies, has taken advantage of traditional Japanese tales, Western stories like Shakespeare's Macbeth, *and contemporary dramas as well as samurai epics. He has shot a movie in Russia and has been financed in recent endeavors by American filmmakers George Lucas and Steven Spielberg. An international success, he was awarded a Lifetime Achievement Award by the Academy of Motion Picture Arts and Sciences in 1990. Yet Kurosawa grew up a Japanese boy, shaped by the events that shaped others of his day. In his autobiography, he recalls the Great Kantō earthquake of 1923, the new islands of mud in the river, the fissures in the roads, and the fires sweeping through Tokyo casting a dim glow in the nights otherwise left dark from the absence of electricity. The atmosphere of terror lurking in the dark destroyed, in his opinion, all sense of reason. It made possible the subsequent persecution of Koreans, a brutal racist attack that gave the young Kurosawa much to contemplate.*

The massacre of Korean residents of Tokyo that took place on the heels of the Great Kantō Earthquake was brought on by demagogues who deftly exploited people's fear of the darkness. With my own eyes I saw a mob of adults with contorted faces rushing like an avalanche in confusion, yelling, "This way!" "No, that way!" They were chasing a bearded man, thinking someone with so much facial hair could not be Japanese.

We ourselves went to look for relatives who had been burned out in the fires around the Ueno district. Simply because my father had a full beard, he was surrounded by a mob carrying clubs. My heart pounded as I looked at my brother, who was with him. My brother was smiling sarcastically. At that moment my father thundered angrily, "Idiots!" They meekly dispersed.

In our neighborhood each household had to have one person stand guard at night. My brother, however, thumbed his nose at the whole idea and made no attempt to take his turn. Seeing no other solution, I took up my wooden sword and was led to a drainage pipe that was barely wide enough for a cat to crawl through. They posted me here and said, "Koreans might be able to sneak in through here."

But there was an even more ridiculous incident. They told us not to drink the water from one of our neighborhood wells. The reason was that the wall surrounding the well had some kind of strange notation written on it in white chalk. This was supposedly a Korean code indication that the well water had been poisoned. I was flabbergasted. The truth was that the strange notation was a scribble I myself had written. Seeing adults behaving like this, I couldn't help shaking my head and wondering what human beings are all about.

From Akira Kurosawa, *Something Like an Autobiography,* 1983.

in taste and fashion as well as political ideas and institutions. By the late nineteenth century, the first department stores in Tokyo heralded new forms of consumerism for the Japanese middle class. As an alternative to the labor-intensive personal service of the dry goods salesperson, who would present and unroll bolts of cloth for each customer individually, the department store displayed a variety of cloth in glass window cases for the growing number of middle-class Japanese who could afford fine textiles.

The countryside lacked the intensity of city life, but rural life also experienced material and cultural changes. Under the Meiji period reforms, farmers were declared the owners of the land they tilled. They were given the right to bear surnames and to ride horses. The Meiji regime dismantled the Tokugawa status distinctions so important to the continuation of the previous social and political order. Crops and goods originating in the West became parts of the Japanese farmer's lifestyle. They began eating beef and drinking beer; they wrote with steel pens and rode on leather saddles. A cold lemonade quenched a Japanese thirst on a hot and humid summer's day, while an evening meal could include tomatoes, green peppers, or Irish potatoes. By the turn of the century horse-drawn public buses appeared in some parts of the countryside and railways cut through valleys and across plains to be seen if not ridden on by farmers living nearby. A few years later electricity began to reach some villages.

The farmer's worldview was also beginning to change in the Meiji and Taisho reigns. Bright sons went on to middle school and occasionally university. Those who returned became school teachers or officials, while others worked for the post office or railways. Conscription took away even more young men to serve in the emperor's army. Through military service and education, new generations of rural Japanese gained a sense of their society beyond the village boundaries. New ideas about social relationships became possible. In an essay in a 1933 local paper, for instance, the author spoke of women's sexual rights, "By which of course I do not mean that women should have the same sexual freedom as men. Rather that women should have the right to expect the same pure chastity of their husbands as society expects of them." These small signs that relations between the sexes would become more equal did little to reduce the hierarchical and authoritarian nature of most social relationships.

Japanese leaders created nationalism on the basis of a preexisting sense of loyalty. Townspeople formed their commitments to emperor and country through reading newspapers and discussing issues with others in coffeeshops and cafes. The settings and instruments for communication could be new and the target, serving the country, could also be new, but the social sentiments and sensibilities of loyalty and obedience were sound traditional Japanese virtues.

Many urban and rural Japanese may have seen their material standards of living improve during the early twentieth century. But how did they view material success? How did they view the purposes and possibilities of politics? How did they synthesize new Western ideas and gadgets with Japanese practices? It is easy for outsiders to assume that the Japanese have gradually adopted Western practices and in the process become more Western. But this simple logic assumes a set of identifications between actions and sentiments and between the origins of habits and their social meanings that may not make sense for the actors themselves. When most men living in Tokyo put on Western suitcoats and ties in the 1930s, did they do this thinking it

made them more "Western"? Not likely. Did the adoption of such forms of dress make them act more "Western"? Not at all. Of course, there were changes in perspectives and attitudes that more closely resembled certain European and American attitudes, but they too could be conceived in terms of creating a new Japanese identity rather than adopting a Western one. Cultural conservatives could worry that Western practices might undermine Japanese customs, but those embracing change did not need to agree with the terms set out by conservatives. They could conceive of a modern Japanese identity distinct from earlier Japanese sensibilities even as they would have rejected being thought of as Western.

Modern economies and modern states all share some common organizational features and follow similar practices. Business firms all have some division of labor, while modern governments all have specialized bureaucracies. But the ways in which people come to see themselves and the world around them as both rapidly change are more difficult to label in universal terms. Postimperial Chinese intellectuals and political leaders had to imagine ways of re-creating rural social order and managing the swiftly changing urban scene amidst genuine uncertainty over the survival of the country as a unified whole. Their early twentieth-century Japanese counterparts achieved far greater success at creating political and economic changes, but these achievements did not mean that other social and cultural changes common in the West would also naturally take place. Becoming modern did not mean no longer being Chinese or Japanese.

International Relations and Political Change in Asia

During the first half of the nineteenth century, strong Asian powers grew even stronger. The Qing increased its control over Inner Asian territories; Vietnam and Siam, predecessor to modern Thailand, enhanced their powers in Southeast Asia. By the end of the nineteenth century, Asian political dynamics looked entirely different. In Inner Asia the Qing government had been permanently weakened. Vietnam had fallen to French colonial rule and Thailand had lost half its territories. Japan became an aggressive power, defeating the Chinese in 1895 and the Russians in 1905, and

European colonials often formed close ties with the princes of conquered territories. Here a Dutch official poses arm-in-arm with the Susuhunan of Surakarta.

through these efforts gained Korea and Taiwan as colonies. The opening decades of the twentieth century found Asia partially subject to the attempts of European governments to achieve a regional balance of their respective powers. But more significant than those efforts would be Japan's growing presence as the region's strongest power.

Southeast Asia, 1800–1870

Vietnam and Thailand, Southeast Asia's most powerful states, gathered additional strength during the first half of the nineteenth century. In Vietnam the rebellion of the Tay-son brothers, begun in 1771, was ended in 1802, to be followed by the Nguyen dynasty (1802–1945). For the first time in history a single Vietnamese state ruled a united country stretching from the Chinese border in the north to the Gulf of Thailand in the south.

Over the next half century, Vietnamese leaders consolidated their territorial control through the continued domestication of Chinese principles and institutions of rule. The adaptation of Chinese institutions to Vietnamese realities was necessarily different from that in China, where a vast agrarian empire contrasted sharply with a far smaller country stretched thinly along a north-south axis. Vietnam, indeed, was never a little China, having a rich separate language, a poetic literature written in Vietnamese characters (called *nom*) as well as in Chinese ones, and different social and legal traditions, which included greater tolerance than in China for female property rights. Furthermore, the Vietnamese economy was not as developed as China's. Instead of groups of individual households, each open to outside commercial influence, Vietnamese villages were usually more closed, with more corporate community identity than those in China. Amid these differences, Vietnamese leaders adopted Chinese power structures, communication processes, civil service examinations, and personnel evaluation procedures.

Thailand was an even larger and more successful state in early nineteenth-century Southeast Asia. Its rice exports to China were bringing in Chinese luxury goods, copper, and silver. Politically the country was expanding its borders, reversing earlier losses to Burma (now Myanmar) and extending its power into Cambodian lands. The country was ruled as a kingdom in which powerful regional families held considerable local authority through patron-client relations and personal contacts. This system was adequate domestically and in dealing with its neighbors, but Thai leaders in the late nineteenth century discovered that changes would become necessary when Europeans asserted themselves.

Long before the nineteenth century, the Europeans had already been well established in several parts of Southeast Asia. In the Philippines, a Spanish presence going back to the mid-sixteenth century had become a limited bureaucratic government with weak ties to the home country; it took the Spanish government two years to get a message to the Philippines, which was under the jurisdiction of the viceroy of Mexico. As part of its power politics back in Europe, Britain occupied Manila for two years from 1762 to 1764. When the Spanish regained control, they decided to promote cash cropping and hoped to see peasants gain a more secure livelihood. The core of the Filipino elite in the 1800s were the offspring of Chinese fathers and "native" (*india*) mothers, able to take advantage of their fathers' commercial resources and their mothers' extended kinship networks. Known as Chinese mestizos, they now linked their identities far more strongly to the Philippines than to China, and were further driven by the stiff trading competition of newly arrived Chinese immigrants to become landowners and members of an increasingly important intelligentsia.

The early alternative to formal colonial rule practiced by the Spanish was the Dutch East India Company in Java, which maintained a kind of overlordship without much intervention into the conduct of affairs in the different regions. Indeed, by the eighteenth century some Javanese even succeeded in domesticating the foreign origins of the Dutch, claiming that the Dutch founder of Batavia had been the son of a wandering foreigner and a princess of west Java! In 1798 the Dutch government took over from the Dutch East India Company. Under Dutch rule a dual economy was developed in which plantations produced sugar and other cash crops for the international trade, while peasants continued with subsistence rice cultivation for themselves. International trade tied Java closely to Holland's economy, but its subsistence sector kept the locals rooted in poverty and misery. As the population of Java exploded from 7 million in 1830 to 42 million in 1930, the difficulties facing many of Java's peasants grew more severe.

The British established themselves along the western coast of the Malay Peninsula. Economically, rubber plantations and mining, especially of tin, attracted European investment. Politically, the British established their power in urban centers. The most important of these was Singapore, a cosmopolitan port with roughly 50 percent Chinese and the balance from all over south and Southeast Asia, including Tamils, Arabs, Javanese, Malays, Bengalis, and others. European presence here as well as in other parts of Southeast Asia would grow, especially after 1870.

European Imperialism in Southeast Asia, 1870–1930

With the Dutch already well-established in Java, France, Great Britain and the United States each established a center of power in Southeast Asia and sought a balance of strength there to complement their global efforts to keep any one of them from getting ahead of the others. The French creation of Indochina was administratively the most complex. Composed of five territories administered separately, only Cochinchina (south Vietnam) was a formal colony; the other four regions were protectorates—Annam (central Vietnam), Tonkin (northern Vietnam), Cambodia, and Laos.

South Vietnam was the first to fall under French domination between 1858 and 1867, with other parts of Indochina following in the next quarter century. French power remained strongest in south Vietnam and weakest in the center where, as in the north, local government was under a combined French and Vietnamese rule. The French approach to colonial rule combined hierarchical administration, economic exploitation, and cultural elitism. They introduced plantation agriculture for coffee and tea; together with rubber, these plantations were concentrated in the southern region of Indochina. Some light industry developed in the north at Hanoi; this economic growth supported its becoming in 1902 the capital of the Indo-Chinese Union.

The French established their dominion in Laos at the expense of Thailand. Self-righteously claiming they were protecting Laos from Thai imperialism, the French precipitated a diplomatic crisis by demanding the whole of Laos after a French officer was killed leading an attack against the Thai. The Thai expected aid from the British who, they anticipated, would naturally wish to defend their own interests in the region against French expansion. Unfortunately for the Thai, however, the British saw French control over Laos as a reasonable part of the regional balance of European power. Britain and France agreed to make the Mekong River the boundary between British Burma and French Laos. Laos, Cambodia, and central Vietnam all stagnated under French colonial rule. While the Mekong Delta in the

French and Spanish troops storm the fortress of Saigon in 1959, on the pretext of protecting Catholicism.

Held in 1830
1831–1870
1871–1900
1901–1940
Maximum Thai suzerainty, 19th century

UPPER BURMA
TONKIN
LOWER BURMA
LAOS
BRITISH
FRENCH
CAMBODIA
ANNAM
THAI
COCHIN-CHINA
SPANISH-AMERICAN (PHILIPPINES)
Sulu
B R I T I S H
Singapore
D U T C H

0   800 Miles
0   800 Kilometers

The Formation of States in Southeast Asia

economic changes would begin in the early 1930s when modern factories were established in the cities through national economic planning.

In the Philippines, Spanish suppression of nationalist sentiments led to increasingly bitter feelings in the 1870s and 1880s. Separate groups of educated and poor people who opposed Spanish rule were unified by the Spanish execution of elite leader José Rizal (1861–96). His martyrdom inspired broadly based resistance. The Spanish exiled another leader, Emilio Aguinaldo (1869–1964), but the United States brought him back when they took control of the Philippines from the Spanish during the Spanish-American War over Cuba. Faced with continued Filipino nationalism, the U.S. then put down Filipino resistance to its new colonial rule. U.S.

south continued to export raw materials and crops, political power became more concentrated in the north in Hanoi.

Thailand was the only country in Southeast Asia to escape direct control by the Western powers. But it still paid a heavy price for the entry of European competition into Southeast Asia, yielding roughly half the territory it once controlled. Moreover, like China and Japan, Thailand had to accept the treaty port system with its controlled tariffs and extraterritoriality. The Thai attempted to revise their government structure to meet the demands of facing foreign powers without forsaking their traditional institutions of Buddhist monarchy and monkhood. In 1912 the government survived domestic unrest when a coup attempt led by Sino-Thai military officers was smashed. The government then joined the allies in World War I, sending 1,300 men to France. At Versailles they urged an end to the treaty port system, but they were rebuffed. Between 1920 and 1926 they recovered tariff autonomy and had extraterritoriality removed. Socially, increased Chinese immigration effectively created a second Thailand in the early twentieth century when Chinese women joined their men. Only 230,000 people in 1825, the Chinese population grew to 792,000 in 1910, jumping from 5 percent to 9.5 percent of the total population. Amidst these demographic changes, modern education introduced other social changes beginning with elites, in particular the royal family, and spreading downward through society. Major

Emilio Aguinaldo, a leader of the Philippine insurgents.

Japan and International Relations in Asia, 1800–1930

1802–1945	Nguyen dynasty in Vietnam establishes first unified rule of entire country
1853–54	Commodore Perry arrives in Japan
1858	Three Japanese ports open to foreign trade—Kanagawa, Nagasaki, and Hakodate
1858	French begin domination of Vietnam
1860	First Japanese foreign mission to the United States
1864	Chōshū rebellion in Japan
1868	Meiji Restoration; imperial rule formally proclaimed
1871	Japanese feudal domains abolished
1873	Conscription begins in Japan
1877	Satsuma rebellion put down
1885	First cabinet formed in Japan
1889	Meiji constitution
1890	First Japanese Diet convenes
1894–95	Sino-Japanese War; Japan awarded Taiwan, Liaodong Peninsula, and rights in Korea
1899	Extraterritoriality ends in Japan
1904–05	Russo-Japanese War; Japanese establish stronger presence in Manchuria as a result
1907	Franco-Japanese Entente, in which Japanese recognize French rule over Indochina in return for French recognition of Japan's gains through war with Russia
1910	Japan annexes Korea
1912	Taishō era in Japan begins
1913	Outer Mongolia and Tibet each declares independence from China
1915	Japan makes Twenty-one Demands on China
1918	Rice riots over inflated prices in Japan
1919	May Fourth protest in China against Treaty of Versailles giving Japan former German leasehold in Shandong
1921	Assassination of Prime Minister Hara Takeshi at Tokyo Station
1922	U.S. Open Door policy replaces treaties guaranteeing spheres of influence
1923	Great Kantō earthquake
1926	Shōwa era begins with reign of Emperor Hirohito

officials believed they were fulfilling a paternalistic mission of preparing the Philippines for eventual independence; the U.S. government therefore thought itself a more noble presence in Southeast Asia than other Western states. But in economic terms American colonialism collaborated with a conservative landowning Filipino oligarchy, whose huge sugar plantations resembled plantation agriculture elsewhere in colonized Southeast Asia. These plantations impeded the development of a more balanced agriculture that could feed the country's population. American colonial rule, like colonial regimes elsewhere in the region, fostered an acute Philippine economic dependency on the colonial power (over 80 percent of Philippine exports went to the U.S. in 1940).

North and Northeast Asia, 1800–1930

The first half of the nineteenth century saw the consolidation of a Chinese presence across much of Inner Asia through the increased migration of Chinese to settle the northwestern and northern frontiers in Gansu, Xinjiang, and Mongolia. With the exception of the extreme northeastern portion of Manchuria, which was lost to Russian advances, the Chinese increased their imperial strength to the north. During the second half of the nineteenth century control over these areas declined as the Qing state confronted rebellions within China proper and both Inner Asian groups and European governments sought to expand their powers. An adventurer from western Central Asia, Ya'quub Beg, attempted to set up an independent emirate in Xinjiang, which the Qing defeated in the 1870s, re-establishing control over all of Xinjiang, except for a northwestern portion taken by the Russians during the rebellion. In 1904 a British invasion of Tibet ignored Qing control there to take over the capital of Lhasa, but two years later, without consulting Tibet, the British signed a convention with the Qing acknowledging Chinese responsibility for Tibet.

The 1911 Revolution diminished Chinese power across Inner Asia. Some peoples, such as the Turkic-speaking populations, were constructing a new ethno-linguistic identity as Uighurs. With Chinese power in eclipse and the potential for growing British and Russian influence in the region, local peoples saw both the opportunity and the need to develop stronger ties among themselves to defend against expanding European powers and against China, should it become powerful again. In 1913 Tibet and Outer Mongolia declared their independence from China. China never recognized Tibetan independence and accepted Outer Mongolia's autonomy only reluctantly because of pressures from Russia and Japan in nearby areas. Separatist feelings were expressed in Inner Mongolia, Gansu, and Qinghai, but Chinese power managed to keep them under formal, if not very effective, control. In the coming warlord years, Muslim warlords held power throughout Qinghai despite continued Han Chinese immigration into the area. The Mongols of Inner Mongolia grew nervous over continued Chinese immigration. Though unhappy with the prospect of increasing Chinese influence, they were also unhappy with the increased Russian presence in the area as refugees from the Russian Revolution came in after 1917. Some Mongolian leaders were therefore attracted to separatist ideas, but their goals were defeated by Jiang Jieshi's 1928 conversion of Inner Mongolia into four new Chinese provinces. China's power in the area, which was never very strong, became increasingly tenuous in the 1930s when Japanese expansion into Manchuria brought Inner Mongolia into their continental sights.

Japan's interests in mainland Asia began during China's Qing dynasty. The first object of Japanese attentions was Manchuria, a logical step once Korea was put firmly under its control in 1910. Following its victory over Russia in the Russo-Japanese War (1904–05), Japan gained the Kwantung (Guandong) leased territory, including Dairen and Port Arthur, and a foothold in southern Manchuria through establishing the South Manchuria Railway Company. When Manchuria came under the warlord leadership of Zhang Zuolin after the 1911 Revo-

lution, the Japanese established close relations with him. These relations became strained as the Nationalists later attempted to reassert Chinese authority in the region in the face of Japanese efforts to expand their economic and military presence. By the 1920s, expansionary continental desires among Japanese leaders embraced not only north and northeast Asia, but Southeast Asia as well. China loomed at the center of these grand ambitions. Could this center hold against the pressures brought on by Japan?

The Fate of China

With its Inner Asian territories gone and its influence in Southeast Asia reduced to nothing, China no longer had much political presence let alone a world order reaching beyond its borders. But nineteenth-century migrations of Chinese to points north and south had extended the sphere of Chinese culture well beyond the state's political control. Ironically, it was the political weakness and economic difficulties of the late imperial empire that motivated Chinese to migrate even as the state had once conceived of ever expanding Chinese settlements as a means to bring more territory into China's world order. The early twentieth-century separation of politics and culture meant that Chinese culture could make a large impact in new areas of Inner Asia and Southeast Asia even as China's political power through these regions declined.

Closer to home, China as a society of nearly half a billion people was guaranteed to survive as a culture, but would China as a political unit continue amid the many uncertainties of the twentieth century? With very little semblance of a national government between 1912 and 1927, China's political future continued to look bleak in 1930. Though Jiang Jieshi had achieved a formal unity of the country, whether he and his fellow Nationalists could create a new kind of state, able to rule China and deal with the outside world effectively, remained to be seen. Certainly Jiang Jieshi's victory in 1927 calmed Western fears of China's strong nationalist sentiments becoming openly anti-imperialist and hostile to foreign interests. What Westerners most feared was the possible influence of the Bolsheviks, whose vision of society they considered a direct challenge. Jiang's massacre of the urban labor movement, which undercut the Communists' social base and sent them fleeing into the countryside, was a popular move with foreign business.

Westerners recognized that in China as in other parts of Asia, the treaty port system was becoming awkward to

China, 1800–1930

1831–35	Qing concessions to Kokandis in Inner Asia
1839–40	Lin Zexu appointed Special Commissioner of Trade in Canton to stop opium trade
1839–42	Opium War between China and Great Britain
1842	Treaty of Nanking, creating the first treaty ports
1843	Hong Kong ceded to Great Britain
1850–64	Taiping Rebellion; capture of Nanjing in 1853
1853–68	Nian Rebellion
1855–78	Moslem rebellions in Yunnan and Gansu
1856–60	Arrow War with Great Britain and France
1862–74	Reign of the Tongzhi emperor, period of self-strengthening
1871	Russian troops occupy Ili region of Xinjiang
1872	First Chinese students sent abroad
1881	China recognizes Japanese occupation of Ryukyu Islands
1884–85	Sino-French War over Annam; establishment of French Indochina
1890	Early industrialization; first modern textile factory established in Shanghai
1894–95	Sino-Japanese War over Korea
1898	100 Days' Reform
1900–01	Boxer Rebellion
1906	Constitutional government proclaimed
1911	Majority of provinces declare independence from Qing
1912	Chinese republic founded with Sun Yat-sen as first president
1915	Japan presents Twenty-one Demands to China
1916–26	Warlord period
1919	May Fourth protest
1921	Chinese Communist party founded in Shanghai
1923–24	United front between Communists (CCP) and Nationalists (GMD)
1925	Sun Yat-sen dies; Jiang Jieshi's power grows
1926	Peasant association movement spreads, especially in Guangdong and Hunan
1926–27	Final stages of northern expeditions that unify China under Nationalist regime
1927	Jiang Jieshi's "White Terror" against Communists
1927–37	Nationalist rule from Nanjing
1928	Mao Zedong and other leaders establish guerrilla base area in Jiangxi province

defend in the face of mounting nationalistic antagonism. But since 1902 Chinese efforts to remove various aspects of the system had repeatedly failed. Finally, the Germans lost extraterritorial rights after World War I, since they were the losers of that conflict. Then, at the 1922 Washington Conference, the U.S. Open Door policy replaced treaties guaranteeing spheres of influence, but treaty port privileges for the great powers remained unchallenged. The Soviets voluntarily renounced their extraterritorial rights in 1924, but the major Western powers kept waiting for assurances that the Chinese could provide the law and order necessary to protect foreign property and persons. The chronically unstable political situation in China did not inspire foreign confidence. Finally in 1943, the U.S. and Britain agreed to do away with extraterritoriality except for the case of Hong Kong; other countries followed suit, ending the system of foreign relations that had plagued China for a century. At the time they finally recognized the end of this treaty port system, Japan had already overrun the most populated and most economically advanced parts of China, diminishing the real impact of these formal changes.

Japan's military invasion of China would not come until 1937, but the desire among some in the Japanese government to establish greater influence on the continent went back to the first decade of the twentieth century. Many important leaders—but by no means all—in Japan considered expansion into continental Asia central to the creation of a powerful and secure Japan. Initially, the Japanese wished to pursue continental expansion within a framework that the European and American powers would accept. Japan had already learned how to trade recognition for imperialist gains with Western countries, obtaining British and American assent to its position in Korea in return for recognizing the British in India and the U.S. in the Philippines. The Franco-Japanese Entente of 1907 traded recognition of French rule over Indochina for France's recognition of Japan's gains through its war with Russia. In the early years of the Chinese republic, the Japanese pushed their interests in China in the form of a draft treaty, known as the infamous Twenty-one Demands. The Japanese proposed in 1915 to take over German interests in Shandong, extend their lease period in Liaodong, receive commercial rights in Manchuria, join the Chinese in joint operations of the Hanyeping coal mines, and limit China's right to cede coastal areas to third powers. The last set of demands, if met, would have turned China politically into another Korea—Japan insisted that the Chinese government employ Japanese advisers in the police, military, and financial administrations, giving them a major role in running China's affairs. The U.S. formally lodged protests over the Japanese intention to compromise Chinese sovereignty. While Japan did not succeed with all its demands, it did expand its leverage over the Chinese government. The 1918 Nishihara loans of 145 million yen (1 yen = U.S. $0.50) established Japanese financial leverage over the Chinese government. European and American powers continued to recognize Japanese interests in Asia, but would not accept all of Japan's moves. At Versailles at the conclusion of World War I and later at the 1922 Washington Conference, Japan's gains were restricted—Japanese troops withdrew from Siberia and Shandong was returned to the Chinese. Western powers created a foreign policy toward China that promoted nonintervention in Chinese domestic affairs. No such restrictions applied to Japanese moves in Manchuria. From the base Japan would establish in Manchuria in 1931, an increasingly strident military, no longer held in check by leaders opposed to territorial aggrandizement, would launch a land invasion of China in 1937 based on a vision of continental expansion with its origins dating from the declining years of China's last dynasty.

Dramatic political, social and economic changes restructured East Asia's two major powers in the nineteenth and early twentieth centuries. China suffered domestic and foreign challenges that ultimately led to the collapse of the final dynasty and ended a two-thousand-year political system. China's world order, which had stretched into Inner Asia and Southeast Asia, fell apart never to be reconstructed. In contrast, Japan underwent a swift political and social transformation. New state organs guided a belligerent foreign policy that inspired a confident nationalism among the common people. Continued economic change and the influx of foreign ideas propelled Japan along a trajectory of modern change. But for neither Japan nor China did the creation of modern traits mean the uncritical and uniformly enthusiastic adoption of Western practices and beliefs. Nowhere in East and Southeast Asia was the future trajectory of political, social, economic, and cultural changes clear. Monumental tragedies would afflict the region in the coming decades before countries would make fresh starts to be transformed anew.

SUGGESTIONS FOR FURTHER READING

CHINA'S NINETEENTH-CENTURY CHALLENGES

* Arthur Waley, *The Opium War Through Chinese Eyes* (Stanford, CA: Stanford University Press, 1968). A revealing account of the Opium War through Chinese documents, assembled into a narrative by one of the foremost translators of Chinese literature.

* John King Fairbank, *Trade and Diplomacy on the China Coast: The Opening of the Treaty Ports, 1842–1854* (Stanford, CA: Stanford University Press, 1969). The classic account of the treaty port system by the founder of modern China studies in the United States.

* Philip Kuhn, *Rebellion and Its Enemies in Late Imperial China* (Cambridge, MA: Harvard University Press, 1971). An influential statement of how officials and elites mobilized military power to oppose the Taiping.

* Mary Wright, *The Last Stand of Chinese Conservatism* (Stanford, CA: Stanford University Press, 1962). The best survey of the full range of policies taken by the Chinese state after defeating the mid-century rebellions.

THE FORMATION OF JAPAN'S MODERN STATE

* Carol Gluck, *Japan's Modern Myths: Ideology in the Late Meiji Period* (Princeton, NJ: Princeton University Press, 1985). A fascinating presentation of the ideology created to support the early Meiji state.

* Edward Seidensticker, *Low City, High City, Tokyo from Edo to the Earthquake: How the Shogun's Ancient Capital Became a Great Modern City* (New York: Knopf, 1983). A pleasant and informative study of urban life in Tokyo during the Meiji and Taisho eras.

D. Eleanor Westney, *Imitation and Innovation: The Transfer of Western Organizational Patterns to Meiji Japan* (Cambridge, MA: Harvard University Press, 1987). A careful and sophisticated analysis of how selected Western institutions were adapted to Japanese conditions by the Meiji state.

Andrew Gordon, *The Evolution of Labor Relations in Japan: Heavy Industry, 1853-1955* (Cambridge, MA: Harvard University Council on East Asian Studies, 1985). An insightful analysis of Japanese industrial development with a stress on factory organization.

BECOMING MODERN WITHOUT BECOMING WESTERN

* Tse-Tsung Chow, *The May Fourth Movement* (Stanford, CA: Stanford University Press, 1967). A rich survey of the intellectual currents of the time.

* Philip Huang, *The Peasant Economy and Social Change in North China* (Stanford, CA: Stanford University Press, 1985). A challenging study of economic change, social relations, and political control in early twentieth-century north China.

Peter Duus and Irwin Scheiner, "Socialism, Liberalism, and Marxism, 1901–1931," and Tetsuo Najita and H. D. Harootunian, "Japanese Revolt Against the West: Political and Cultural Criticism in the Twentieth Century," in Peter Duus, ed., *The Cambridge History of Japan*, Vol. 6, *The Twentieth Century* (Cambridge: Cambridge University Press, 1988). Excellent guides to intellectual positions in early twentieth-century Japan.

INTERNATIONAL RELATIONS AND POLITICAL CHANGE IN ASIA

* David Joel Steinberg, ed., *In Search of Southeast Asia: A Modern History*, rev. ed. (Honolulu: University of Hawaii Press, 1986). Parts II and III consider nineteenth-century political changes before and after European imperialism.

Morris Rossabi, *China and Inner Asia: From 1368 to the Present Day* (London: Thames and Hudson, 1975). Part III considers China's strength in Inner Asia and its subsequent decline.

* James E. Sheridan, *China in Disintegration: The Republican Era in Chinese History, 1912-1949* (New York: The Free Press, 1975). A comprehensive survey of Republican China's precarious situation.

* Indicates paperback edition available.

CHAPTER 32

Global Conflagration: World War II, 1939–1945

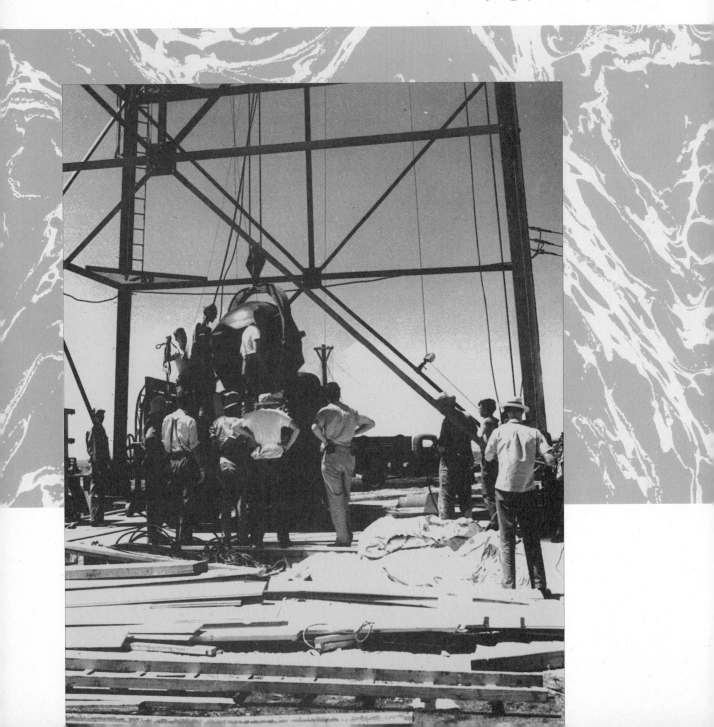

BUILDING BOMBS

Scientists in the twentieth century participate in an international community of ideas and discoveries. In the first half of the twentieth century, as now, academic scientists dedicated themselves to basic research—the pursuit of scientific knowledge for its own sake—and published their findings in scholarly scientific journals read only by specialists in their own fields throughout the world. It was not unusual for public-minded critics to accuse scientists and other academicians of living in an ivory tower, producing work without relevance or social value. For that matter, scientists themselves did not dispute the accusation that they gave little thought to the practical and applied scientific outcomes of their research. The transfer of basic research to useful technology was not a primary motivator for the great discoveries in physics and chemistry in the first half of the twentieth century. Einstein's theory of relativity or Heisenberg's uncertainty principle both merited the Nobel Prize in physics, but seemed to offer little to the average citizen to change the world.

While international in their exchange of information, scientists worked very much within national scientific communities. Because of the demands for interdisciplinary knowledge and highly specialized control, however, scientists began to abandon more individualistic models of doing research in favor of team approaches. In Italy, for example, the creation of a research center at the University of Rome brought together an outstanding and creative research team headed by the physicist Enrico Fermi and dedicated to collaboration on atomic physics. In France, the team led by J. F. Joliot and his wife Irene Curie Joliot, daughter of Nobel physicists Marie and Pierre Curie, trailblazed new direc-tions in atomic physics with their discovery of artificial radioactivity. In 1932 the team of J. D. Cockcroft and E. T. S. Walton attracted public attention by doing the unimaginable: they split the atom, which hitherto had been considered invisible and indivisible. At the time few consid-ered that this accomplishment held more than a curiosity value.

The leading national "factories" in the garnering of Nobel Prizes in the sciences were the United States and Germany. Most of the important theoretical breakthroughs in physics were published first in the German language and spread quickly to research teams of other na-tions, who offered new perspectives and new insights in pushing back the frontier of scientific knowledge. All of this, while interesting, seemed of little value to people concerned with improving depression economies or keeping the world safe from war.

But politics changed everything. The quiet world of the university and research center laboratories appeared to be isolated from the great international political and economic crises of the 1930s, but that was not the case. Begin-ning in 1933, the racial policies directed against the Jews in Germany and Nazi political repres-sion provoked a diaspora of leading chemists and physicists, who fled central Europe for the safer havens of Great Britain and the United States. Enrico Fermi traveled to Stockholm in 1938 to claim his Nobel Prize in physics, but did not return home to Italy. Instead he fled to the United States with his wife Laura, who was Jewish, because he feared for her safety in fascist Italy. Two other refugee scientists, Otto Frisch and Rudolf Peierls, left Germany and settled in Great Britain, where, because of their work on Uranium-235, they were able to persuade the British government to sponsor the first work on atomic weapons.

And here is where the story of science changed. In 1939 German scientists began to consider the possibility of applying all of the accumulated knowledge about atomic physics to the task of building the ultimate weapon, a new kind of bomb with explosive force unimaginable before the discovery of fission in 1939. The Allies feared that Germany would achieve exactly that goal. Building the ultimate bomb required a great commitment of resources and highly coordinated management of science, technology, and military needs. We now know that the German scientific community never really believed that building a massive bomb was possible, nor was it feasible for the Nazi state to dedicate sufficient resources to accomplish the task. German leaders were sure that the war would be long over before such a weapon could be manufactured, and in the meantime they had more pressing needs for weapons creation and production.

The Allies lacked neither resources nor scientific brainpower to address the task. The U.S. government joined forces with the British in an endeavor known by the code name the Manhattan Project. By 1945 the budget of the project, entirely underwritten by the United States government, was estimated to be the equivalent of that of the entire U.S. auto industry. Refugee scientists from central Europe and their British and American colleagues joined together in a collaboration unique in the annals of scientific culture.

The speed with which the scientists of the Manhattan Project moved from basic to applied research was staggering. Plutonium, an artificial material used in the bomb's explosive chain reaction, had to be manufactured. Detonation of a nuclear core was an especially knotty problem, since the materials comprising the bomb had to be compressed to critical volume in less than one-millionth of a second. The head of the Manhattan Project, Robert Oppenheimer, 1904–1967) a physicist who managed the scientific side of the project, spoke of the successive challenges of the production of the atomic bomb as "technically sweet." He explained that the scientists of the Manhattan Project continued to do what they did best— make discoveries, albeit in a highly focused and applied environment. "You go ahead and do it and you argue about what to do about it only after you have had your technical success. This is the way it was with the atomic bomb. I do not think anybody opposed making it; there were some debates about what to do with it after it was made."

The atom bomb resulting from this collaboration changed the world. It is easy to overlook the culture that itself had changed in order to build bombs. Governments entered laboratories as key players in supporting the research agenda; and scientists, perhaps not for the first time but certainly dramatically, were forced to confront the ethical consequences of their actions in a world where now no form of knowledge could be considered innocent.

The Coming of World War II

The years between 1933 and 1939 marked a bleak period in international affairs when the British, the French, and the Americans were unwilling or unable to recognize the dire threat to world peace of Hitler and his Nazi state. The leaders of these countries did not comprehend Hitler's single-minded goal to extend German living space eastward as far as western Russia. They failed to understand the seriousness of the Nazi process of consolidation at home. They took no action against Hitler's initial acts of aggression. The war that began in Europe in 1939 eventually became a great global conflict that pitted Germany, Italy, and Japan—the Axis Powers—against the British Empire, the Soviet Union, and the United States—the Grand Alliance.

Even before war broke out in Europe, there was armed conflict in Asia. The rapidly expanding Japanese economy depended on Manchuria for raw materials and on China for markets. Chinese boycotts against Japanese goods and threats to Japanese economic interests in Manchuria led to a Japanese military occupation of Manchuria and the establishment of the Japanese puppet state of Manchukuo there in 1931-32. When the powers of the League of Nations, led by Great Britain, refused to recognize this state, Japan withdrew from the League. Fearing that the Chinese government was becoming strong enough to exclude Japanese trade from China, Japanese troops and naval units began an undeclared war in China in 1937. Many important Chinese cities—Beijing, Shanghai, Nanjing, Guangzhou, and Hankou—fell to Japanese forces. Relentless aerial bombardment of Chinese cities and atrocities committed by Japanese troops against Chinese civilians outraged Europeans and Americans. The governments of the Soviet Union, Great Britain, and the United States, seeking to protect their own ideological, economic, and security interests in China, gave economic, diplomatic, and moral support to the Chinese government of Jiang Jieshi. Thus, the stage was set for a major military conflict in Asia and in Europe.

Hitler's Foreign Policy and Appeasement

For Hitler, a war against the Soviet Union for living space was inevitable. It would come, he told some of his close associates, in the years 1943-45. However, he wanted to avoid refighting the war that had led to Germany's defeat in 1914-18. World War I was a war fought on two fronts—in the east and in the west. It was a war in which Germany had to face many enemies at the same time, and a war that lasted until German soldiers, civilians, and resources were exhausted. In the next war, Hitler wanted, above all, to avoid fighting Great Britain while battling Russia for living space. He convinced himself that the British would remain neutral if Germany agreed not to attack the British Empire. Would they not appreciate his willingness to abolish forever the menace of communism? Were they not Aryans also?

Beginning in 1938, with the non-Nazi conservatives removed from positions of power in Germany, Hitler alone determined foreign policy. He was becoming increasingly impatient, considering time his greatest enemy. He feared that Germany could fail to achieve its destiny as a world power by waiting too long to act. And he became more aggressive and willing to use military force as he set out to remove the obstacles to German domination of central Europe—Austria, Czechoslovakia, and Poland. In March, he annexed Austria to the German Reich. Many Austrians wished to be united with Germany; others had no desire to be led by Nazis. Using the threat of invasion, he intimidated the Austrian government into legalizing the Nazi party, which brought pro-Nazis into the Austrian cabinet and German troops into the country. Encouraged by his success, Hitler provoked a crisis in Czechoslovakia in the summer of the same year. He demanded "freedom" for the German-speaking people of the Sudetenland area of Czechoslovakia. His main objective, however, was not to protect the Germans of Czechoslovakia but to smash the Czech state, the major obstacle in central Europe to the launching of an attack on living space farther east.

Western statesmen did not understand Hitler's commitment to destroying Czechoslovakia or his willingness to fight a limited war against the Czechs to do so. Hitler did everything possible to isolate Czechoslovakia from its neighbors and its treaty partners. France, an ally of Czechoslovakia, appeared distinctly unwilling to defend it against Germany's menaces. Britain, seeking to avoid a war that the government did not think was necessary and for which the British were not prepared, sent Prime Minister Neville Chamberlain (1869-1940) to reason with Hitler. Believing that transferring the Sudetenland, the German-speaking area of Czechoslovakia, to Germany was the only solution—and one that would redress some of the wrongs done to Germany after World War I—Chamberlain convinced France and Czechoslovakia to yield to Hitler's demands.

Chamberlain's actions were the result of British self-interest. British leaders agreed that their country could not afford another war like the Great War of 1914-18. Defense expenditures had been dramatically reduced in order to devote national resources to improving domestic social services, protecting world trade, and fortifying Britain's global interests. Britain understood well its weakened position in its dominions. In the

World War II

1937	Japanese begin undeclared war on China
March 1938	Germany annexes Austria to the German Reich
29 September 1938	Chamberlain, Daladier, Mussolini, and Hitler meet at Munich conference
May 1939	"Pact of Steel," a military alliance between Italy and Germany
1939	Non-Aggression Pact between Germany and the Soviet Union
1 September 1939	Germany attacks Poland
3 September 1939	Great Britain and France declare war on Germany
April 1940	Germany attacks Denmark and Norway
May 1940	Germany invades the Netherlands, Belgium, and Luxembourg and then France
June 1940	Italy enters the war on the side of Germany
17 June 1940	French Marshal Pétain petitions Germany for an armistice and creates a collaborationist government at Vichy
September 1940	Japan, Germany, and Italy sign Tripartite Pact
September–November 1940	The battle of Britain
22 June 1941	Germany invades the Soviet Union
1941	First extermination camp created in Chelmno, Poland
7 December 1941	Japan attacks Pearl Harbor; the United States declares war on Japan
11 December 1941	Germany declares war on the United States
January 1942	Wannsee Conference, where the Final Solution was planned
10 June 1942	Czech village of Lidice razed.
September 1942	Italian government withdraws from the war
April 1943	Unsuccessful uprising in the Warsaw ghetto
November 1943	Churchill, Roosevelt, and Stalin meet at Teheran Conference
6 June 1944	Allied forces land in northern France
February 1945	Churchill, Roosevelt, and Stalin meet at Yalta
March 1945	American forces march into Germany
30 April 1945	Hitler commits suicide
July and August 1945	Churchill, Truman, and Stalin meet at Potsdam
June 1945	Battle of Midway
6 August 1945	U.S. drops atomic bomb on Hiroshima
2 September 1945	Japan surrenders

British hierarchy of priorities, defense of the British Empire ranked first, above defense of Europe; and Britain's commitment to western Europe ranked above the defense of eastern and central Europe.

Hitler's response to being granted everything he requested was to renege and issue new demands. His desire for war could not have been more transparent, nor could his unwillingness to play by the rules of diplomacy have been clearer. One final meeting was held at Munich to avert war. On 29 September 1938, one day before German troops were scheduled to invade Czechoslova-

kia, Mussolini and the French prime minister, Edouard Daladier (1884–1970), joined Hitler and Chamberlain at Munich to discuss a peaceful resolution to the crisis.

At Munich, Chamberlain and Daladier again yielded to Hitler's demands. The Sudetenland was ceded to Germany and German troops quickly moved to occupy the area. The policy of the British and French was dubbed *appeasement* to indicate the willingness to concede to demands in order to preserve peace. *Appeasement* has become a dirty word in twentieth-century European history, taken to mean weakness and cowardice. Yet

A triumphant Hitler enters Austria in 1938. The union of his native country with the German Reich had long been a cherished goal of the Nazi leader.

Chamberlain was neither weak nor cowardly. His great mistake in negotiating with Hitler was in assuming that Hitler was a reasonable man, who like all reasonable persons wanted to avoid another war.

Chamberlain thought his mediation at Munich had won for Europe a lasting peace—"peace for our time," he reported. The people of Europe received Chamberlain's assessment with a sense of relief and shame—relief over what had been avoided, shame at having deserted Czechoslovakia. In fact, the policy of appeasement further destabilized Europe and accelerated Hitler's plans for European domination. Within months, Hitler cast aside the Munich agreement by annihilating Czechoslovakia. German troops occupied the western, Czech part of the state, including the capital of Prague. The Slovak eastern part became independent and a German satellite. At the same time, Lithuania was pressured into surrendering Memel to Germany, and Hitler demanded that Germany control Gdansk and the Polish Corridor. No longer could Hitler be ignored or appeased. No longer could his goals be misunderstood.

Hitler's War, 1939–1941

In the tense months that followed the Munich meeting and the occupation of Prague, Hitler readied himself for war in western Europe. In order to strengthen his position, in May 1939 he formed a military alliance with Mussolini's Italy, the Pact of Steel. Then, Hitler and Stalin, previously self-declared enemies, shocked the West by joining their two nations in a pact of mutual neutrality, the Non-Aggression Pact of 1939. Opportunism lay behind Hitler's willingness to ally with the Communist state that he had denounced throughout the 1930s. A German alliance with the Soviet Union would, Hitler believed, force the British and the French to back down and to remain neutral while Germany conquered Poland—the last obstacle to a drive for expansion eastward—in a short, limited war. Stalin recognized the failure of the western European powers to stand up to Hitler. There was little possibility, he thought, of an alliance against Germany with the virulently anti-communist Neville Chamberlain. The best Stalin could hope for was that the Germans and the western powers

The Expansion of Nazi Germany

Hitler's war, the war for German domination of Europe, had begun. But it had not begun the way he intended. Great Britain and France, true to their alliance with Poland, and contrary to Hitler's expectations, declared war on Germany on 3 September 1939, even though they were unable to give any help to Poland. In the six months after the fall of Poland, no military action took place between Germany and the Allies, because Hitler postponed offensives in northern and western Europe due to poor weather conditions. This strange interlude that became known as "the phony war" was a period of suspended reality in which France and Great Britain waited for Hitler to make his next move. Civilian morale in France deteriorated among a population that still remembered the death and destruction that France had endured in the Great War. An attitude of defeatism germinated and grew before the first French soldier fell in battle.

With the arrival of spring, Germany attacked Denmark and Norway in April 1940. Then on 10 May 1940, Hitler's armies invaded the Netherlands, Belgium, and Luxembourg. By the third week of May, German mechanized forces were racing through northern France toward the English Channel, cutting off the British and Belgian troops and 120,000 French forces from the rest of the French army. With the rapid defeat of Belgium, these forces were crowded against the Channel and had to be withdrawn from the beaches of Dunkirk. France, with a large and well-equipped army, nevertheless relied on Allied support and was in a desperate situation without it.

In France, the German army fought a new kind of war called *Blitzkrieg*, or lightning war, so named because of its speed. The British and the French had expected the German army to behave much as it had in World War I, concentrating its striking forces in a swing through coastal Belgium and Holland in order to capture Paris. French strategists believed that France was safe because of the hilly and forested terrain they thought was impassable. They also counted on the protection of the fortress wall known as the Maginot Line that France had built in the interwar period. The Maginot Line stretched for hundreds of miles but was useless against mobile tank divisions that outflanked it. With stunning speed, Germany drove its tanks—*Panzers*—through the French defenses at Sedan in eastern France.

The French could have pinched off the advance of the overextended *Panzers*, but the French army, suffering from severe morale problems, collapsed and was in retreat. On 17 June 1940, only weeks after German soldiers had stepped on French soil, Marshal Henri-Philippe Pétain, the great hero of the battle of Verdun

would fight it out while the Soviet Union waited to enter the war at the most opportune moment. As an added bonus, Germany promised not to interfere if the Soviet Union annexed eastern Poland, Bessarabia, and the Baltic republics of Latvia and Estonia.

Finally recognizing Hitler's intent, the British and the French also signed a pact in the spring of 1939, promising assistance to Poland in the event of aggression. Tensions mounted throughout the summer, as Europeans awaited the inevitable German aggression. On 1 September 1939 Germany attacked Poland, which was ill-prepared to defend itself. By the end of the month, in spite of valiant resistance, the vastly outnumbered Poles surrendered. Although the German army needed no assistance, the Russians invaded Poland ten days before its collapse, and Germany and Russia divided the spoils. Almost immediately, Stalin took measures to defend Russia against a possible German attack. The Soviet Union assumed military control in the Baltic states and demanded of Finland territory and military bases from which the city of Leningrad (formerly Petrograd) could be defended. When Finland refused, Russia invaded. In the snows of the "Winter War" of 1939–40, the Finns initially fought the Russian army to a standstill, much to the encouragement of the democratic West. The Finns, however, were eventually defeated in March 1940.

At the Munich Conference in September 1938, British prime minister Neville Chamberlain (left) and French premier Edouard Daladier (second from left) acceded to Hitler's demand for the cession of the Sudetenland from Czechoslovakia. Italian dictator Benito Mussolini stands at the right.

in World War I, petitioned the Germans for an armistice. Three-fifths of France, including the entire Atlantic seaboard, was occupied by the German army and placed under direct German rule. In the territory that remained unoccupied, Pétain created a collaborationist government that resided at Vichy, a spa city in central France, and worked in partnership with the Germans for the rest of the war. Charles de Gaulle (1890–1970), a brigadier general opposed to the armistice, fled to London, where he set up a Free French government in exile.

French capitulation in June 1940 followed Italian entry into the war on the side of Germany in the same month. The British were now alone in a war against the two Axis powers as Germany made plans for an invasion of the British Isles from across the English Channel. To prepare the way, the German air force under Reichsmarshal Hermann Göring (1893–1946) launched a series of air attacks against England—the battle of Britain. The German air force first attacked British aircraft, airfields, and munitions centers and then shifted targets to major population centers like London and industrial cities like Coventry. Between 7 September and 2 November 1940, the city of London was bombed every night, inflicting serious damage on the city and killing 15,000 people.

World War II in Europe

Under the leadership of Winston Churchill, the British resisted these attacks. Churchill had succeeded Chamberlain as prime minister in 1940. He was a master public speaker who, in a series of radio broadcasts, inspired the people of Britain with the historic greatness of the task confronting them—holding out against Nazism until the forces of the overseas British Empire and the United States could be marshaled to liberate Europe. The British Royal Air Force inflicted serious losses on German aircraft while British industry was able to maintain steady production of planes, bombs, and armaments. Civilians endured the nightly destruction and air

raids in what Churchill termed Britain's "finest hour." Recognizing his lack of success in establishing air superiority over the Channel or in breaking the will of the British people, Hitler abandoned the battle of Britain and canceled the invasion.

It was not in Great Britain but in the Balkans that Hitler was able to engage the British enemy and inflict serious losses. The British had a presence in the Greek peninsula, where their air units were deployed to support the valiant resistance of the Greeks against Italian aggression. In his original plans for a limited war, Hitler hoped to establish control over the Balkans by peaceful, diplomatic means. But Mussolini's disastrous attempt to achieve military glory by conquering Greece impelled Hitler to make his own plans to attack Greece. Using Bulgaria as the base of operations, Germany invaded Yugoslavia, whose government had been weakened by a recent military coup. The capital of Belgrade fell in April 1941. Internal ethnic enmity between the Croats and the Serbs led to the mutiny of Croatian soldiers and to the formation of an autonomous Croatian government in Zagreb that was favorably disposed to the Germans.

German troops then crossed the Yugoslav border into Greece. Moving quickly down the Greek mainland, German soldiers captured the capital of Athens on 27 April 1941. German forces then turned their attention to the Greek island of Crete, where fleeing British soldiers sought refuge. In the first mass paratroop attack in history, Crete was rapidly subdued, forcing the British to evacuate to Egypt. The British were routed and experienced humiliating defeat by the German *Blitzkrieg*.

The Balkans were important to Hitler for a number of reasons. Half of Germany's wheat and livestock came from the countries of southeastern Europe. Romanian and Hungarian oilfields supplied Germany's only non-Russian oil. Greece and Yugoslavia were important suppliers of metal ores—including aluminum, tin, lead, and copper—so necessary for industry and the war effort.

The necessity of protecting resources, and especially the oilfields in Romania, also gave the area geopolitical importance for Germany. Hitler was well aware of the strategic significance of controlling the Dardanelles in launching an attack against the Soviet Union. Potentially the British lifeline to its empire could also be cut by control of the eastern Mediterranean.

Collaboration and Resistance

No one nation has ever controlled the Balkans, and Hitler understood that he must rule not by occupation but by collaboration. Some Balkan collaborators joined puppet governments out of an ideological commitment to fascism. They were hostile to communism and believed that Hitler's Nazism was far preferable to Stalin's communism. They saw in the German victory the chance to put their beliefs into practice.

Some governments collaborated with the Germans out of national self-interest. Just as the government of Hungary allied with Germany in the hope of winning back territory lost at the end of World War I, so did Romania ally with Russia. The government of Slovakia

was loyal to the Third Reich because Hitler had given it independence from the Czechs. A German puppet state was set up in the Yugoslav province of Croatia. Other collaborators were pragmatists who believed that by taking political office they could negotiate with the German conquerors and soften the effects of the Nazi conquest on their people. Hitler had little affection for local ideological fascists and sometimes smashed their movements. He preferred to work with local generals and administrators. Pragmatic collaborators often could not or would not negotiate with the German authorities very well. The help they gave in rounding up opponents of Nazi Germany—resistance fighters and Jews—resulted in their punishment after the war.

Resistance against German occupation and collaborationist regimes took many forms. Resisters wrote subversive tracts, distributed them, gathered intelligence information for the Allies, sheltered Jews or other

During the battle of Britain, London buildings near St. Paul's Cathedral crumble under the onslaught of a Nazi air raid.

The Division of France, 1940–1944

required secrecy, moral courage, and great bravery. On the whole, however, the actions of resistance fighters seldom affected military timetables and did little to change the course of the war and Hitler's domination of Europe.

By the middle of 1941 Hitler controlled a vast continental empire that stretched from the Baltic to the Black Sea and from the Atlantic Ocean to the Russian border. The German army occupied territories and controlled satellites, or Hitler relied on collaborationist governments for support. Having destroyed the democracies of western Europe, with the exception of Great Britain, Hitler's armies absorbed territory and marched across nations at rapid speed with technical and strategic superiority. But military conquest was not the only horror that the seemingly invincible Hitler inflicted on European peoples.

Racism and Destruction

enemies of the Nazis, committed acts of sabotage or assassination or other violent acts, and carried on guerrilla warfare against the German army. Resisters ran the risk of endangering themselves and their families, who, if discovered, would be tortured and killed. Resistance movements developed most strongly after the German attack on the Soviet Union in 1941, when the Communist parties of occupied Europe formed the core of the violent resistance against the Nazi regime. Resistance grew stronger when the Germans began to draft young European men for work on German farms and in German factories. Many preferred to go underground rather than to Germany.

One of the great resistance fighters of the Second World War was Josip Broz (1892–1980), alias Tito. He was a Croatian communist and a Yugoslav nationalist. Instead of waiting to be liberated by the Allies, his partisans fought against Italian and German troops. Ten or more German divisions, which might otherwise have fought elsewhere, were tied up combating Tito's forces. He gained the admiration and the support of Churchill, Roosevelt, and Stalin. After liberation, Tito's organization won 90 percent of the vote in the Yugoslav elections, and he became the leader of the country in the postwar era. Resistance entailed enormous risks and

War, as the saying goes, is hell. But the horrors perpetrated in World War II exceeded anything ever experienced in Western civilization. In both the European and Asian theaters of battle, claims of racial superiority were invoked to justify inhuman atrocities. The Germans and Japanese used spurious arguments of racial superiority to fuel their war efforts. In Asia the subjugation of inferior peoples became a rallying cry for conquest. But the Germans and the Japanese were not alone in using racist propaganda. The United States employed racial stereotypes to depict the inferiority of the enemy. They seized the property of Japanese-Americans living on the West Coast and interned them in "relocation" camps.

Nowhere, however, was the use of racism by the state more virulent than in Germany. German racist ideology distorted pseudoscientific theories for the purpose of separating those they deemed racially superior from the racially inferior. Nazis used the term "the master race" to identify those human beings worthy of living; those not worthy were designated "subhuman." Hatred of certain groups fueled both politics and war. Hitler promised the German people a purified Reich of Aryans "free of the Jews" and the racially and mentally inferior. Slavic peoples—Poles and Russians—he designated as subhumans who could be displaced in the search for

Lebensraum and German destiny. With the war in eastern Europe, anti-Semitism changed from a policy of persecution and expropriation in the 1930s into a program of systematic extermination beginning in 1941.

Enforcing Nazi Racial Policies

Social policies erected on horrifying biomedical theories discriminated against a variety of social groups in the Third Reich. Gypsies were a case in point of "outsiders" who were labeled as racially and genetically inferior. Gypsy ancestors had migrated to Germany in the fifteenth century; they originated in the Punjab region of north India and converted to the Christian religion in the course of their travels through Persia, Asia Minor, and the Balkans. As German itinerants with their own language, customs, and lifestyle, they were viewed by many other Germans during the Weimar period as a "nuisance," threatening the morals and hygiene of local communities. Beginning in 1933, police harassment intensified against those identified as gypsies. In 1936 the Nazi bureaucracy expanded to include the Reich Central Office against the Gypsy Nuisance, which assiduously maintained files on gypsies. Gypsies were subject to all racialist legislation and could be sterilized for their "inferiority" without any formal hearing process. In September 1939, even as the war was beginning, high-ranking Nazis planned the removal of 30,000 gypsies to Poland. Over 200,000 German, Russian, Polish, and Balkan gypsies were killed in the course of the war by internment in camps and by systematic extermination. Discrimination against gypsies, however, did not begin with the Nazis, nor did it end with them. Not until 1982 were gypsies officially recognized by the German government as a persecuted group who had been subjected to Nazi genocidal policies. In 1989, as East Germans were welcomed in West Germany, gypsies from East Germany were either summarily deported to Yugoslavia or subject to attacks and discrimination in the newly united Germany.

Nazi racial policies also singled out mixed-race children for special disgrace. Children, born of white German mothers and black fathers, were a consequence of the presence of French colonial troops from Senegal, Morocco, and Malaga, who were among the occupation forces in the Rhineland in the 1920s and 1930s. During both the Weimar Republic and the Nazi regime the press attacked the children of these unions, numbering probably no more than 500 to 800 individuals, as "Rhineland bastards." In 1937, without any legal proceedings, the Nazis sterilized them.

Those suffering from hereditary illnesses were also labeled as a biological threat to the racial purity of the German people. State doctors devised illegitimate medical tests in order to establish who was feebleminded and genetically defective. By treating the society of the Third Reich as one huge laboratory for the production of the racially fit and the "destruction of worthless life," categories were constructed according to subjective criteria that claimed scientific validation. Medical officials examined children, and those judged to be deformed were separated from their families and transferred to special pediatric clinics, where they were either starved to death or injected with lethal drugs. In the summer of 1939, the government organized euthanasia programs for adults and identified 65,000 to 70,000 Germans for death. The government required asylums to rank patients according to their race, state of health, and ability to work. These rankings were used to determine candidates for death. In Poland mental patients were simply shot; in other places they were starved to death. The uncooperative, the sick, and the disabled were purged as racially undesirable.

The category covering the "asocial" was even broader than that covering hereditary illness. Under this designation, criminals, beggars, vagrants, and the homeless could be compulsorily sterilized. Alcoholics, prostitutes, and people with sexually transmitted diseases could be labeled asocial and treated accordingly. These forms of behavior were considered to be hereditary and determined by blood.

Nazi social policies likewise treated homosexuals as "community aliens." The persecution of homosexual men intensified after 1934, when any form of "same-sex immorality" became subject to legal persecution. "Gazing and lustful intention" were left to the definition of the police and the courts. Criminal sentences could involve a term in a concentration camp. But because homosexuality was judged to be a sickness rather than an immutable biological trait, gays did not become the primary object of Nazi extermination policies that began to be enforced against the "biologically inferior." Treatment of homosexuality might involve psychoanalysis, castration, or indefinite incarceration in a concentration camp.

Gay men in Nazi concentration camps during the war were singled out with the badge of a pink triangle. Although it is not clear how many gay men were actually killed by the Nazis, estimates run as high as 200,000.

THE ATROCITY AT LIDICE

■ *Lidice was a small village in Czechoslovakia. The Nazis decided to raze the village to the ground in retaliation for the assassination of Reinhard Heydrich, Nazi head of the Secret Police and the Security Service of the SS. On 10 June 1942 all 173 men of the village were executed by German soldiers and the women and children were deported to concentration camps. Only 15 of Lidice's 104 children survived the war. So outraged was world opinion by this atrocity that memorials were created everywhere and many towns and cities changed their name to Lidice as a commemoration.*

A NAZI OFFICIAL'S REQUEST:

What follows is a letter from a Nazi official by the name of Krumey in charge of the camp at Lodz, Poland, where 88 of Lidice's children had been sent, to his superior, Adolf Eichmann, asking for direction.

"In a telegram dated 17 June 1942 I asked the Commander of the Security Police and the Security Service . . . what was to be done with the Czech children. In the meantime, the Race and Resettlement Office has found seven of the children fit to be Germanized. [Note: these 7 children were adopted by German families.]

   "Since I have no word on further disposition of the children and since the children were transferred here without any luggage, I urgently ask you to decide on the further use of the children."

THE CHILDREN'S PLEA:

A letter addressed to the villagers of Lidice from five of the children in the camps has survived.

"Here it is always cold. We feel homesick for Lidice. We would like to beg you to send us some clothing because we don't own anything beyond what we are wearing, or especially something to eat . . . Do you know anything about our parents? Send the things as soon as possible because we don't know how long we will remain in this place. Let us know what has become of Lidice. Send something that does not go bad for a long time. We are all here, all the children of the town. We don't know where our parents are. Send also some dresses and shoes. Above all, if you can, at least a bit of bread."

Signed Vera, Marenka, Mila, Anicka, and Valek

Officials of the Third Reich singled out gay men rather than lesbian women because their behavior was considered a greater threat to the perpetuation of the German race.

The Destruction of Europe's Jews

Although anti-Semitism was an integral part of Hitler's view of the world, he did not think the peoples of Germany or of Europe were ready for harsh measures against the Jews. In 1933, when the Nazis came to power, they did not have a blueprint for the destruction of Europe's Jews. The anti-Semitic policies of the Third Reich evolved incrementally in the 1930s and 1940s.

After 1938, German civil servants expropriated Jewish property as rightfully belonging to the state. When the war began, Jews were rounded up and herded into urban ghettos in Germany and in the large cities of Poland. For a time the German foreign ministry considered the possibility of deporting the more than three million Jews under German control to Madagascar, an island off the southeast coast of Africa. Until 1941, Nazi policies against the Jews were often uncoordinated and unfocused.

The "Final Solution." Confinement in urban ghettos was the beginning of a policy of concentration that ended in annihilation. After German authorities identified Jews,

Seizing Jews in Warsaw.

seized their property, and confined them to ghettos, they began to implement a step-by-step plan for extermination. There appears to have been no single order from Hitler that decreed what became known to German officials as the "Final Solution"—the total extermination of European Jews. But Hitler's recorded remarks make it clear that he knew and approved of what was being done to the Jews. A spirit of shared purpose permeated the entire administrative system from the civil service through the judiciary. Administrative agencies competed to interpret Hitler's will. SS guards in the camps and police in the streets embraced Hitler's "mission" of destruction. Those involved in carrying out the plan for extermination understood what was meant by the Final Solution and what their responsibilities were for enforcing it. To ensure that the whole process operated smoothly, a planning conference for the Final Solution was held for the benefit of state and party officials at Wannsee, a Berlin suburb, in January 1942. Reinhard Heydrich (1904–42), head of the *Sicherheitsdienst* (SD), or Security Service of the SS, led the conference.

Mass racial extermination began with the German conquest of Poland, where both Jews and non-Jews were systematically killed. It continued when Hitler's army invaded the Soviet Union in 1941. This campaign, known as Operation Barbarossa, set off the mass execution of eastern Europeans declared to be enemies of the Reich. The tactics of the campaign pointed the way to the Final Solution. To the Nazi leadership, Slavs were "subhuman," and by extension, Russian Jews were the lowest of the low, even more despised than German Jews. Nazi propaganda had equated Jews with Communists, and Hitler had used the single word *Judeocommunist* to describe what he considered to be the most dangerous criminal and enemy of the Third Reich, the enemy who must be annihilated at any cost.

The executions were the work of the SS, the elite military arm of the Nazi party. Special mobile murder squads of the SD under Heydrich were organized behind the German lines in Poland and Russia. Members of the army were aware of what the SS squads were doing and participated in some of the extermination

Principal German Concentration Camps and Extermination Camps

measures. In the spring of 1941, Hitler ordered a massive propaganda campaign to be conducted among the armed forces. This campaign indoctrinated the army to believe that the invasion of the Soviet Union was more than a military campaign; it was a "holy war," a crusade that Germany was waging for civilization. SS chief Heinrich Himmler, probably responding to oral orders from Hitler, set about to enforce Hitler's threats with concrete extermination policies. Fearful that the SS would be outstripped by the regular army in Hitler's favor, Himmler exhorted his men to commit the worst atrocities.

Firing squads shot Russian victims en masse, then piled their bodies on top of one another in open graves. Reviewing these procedures for mass killings, Himmler—ever competitive with other Nazi agencies—suggested a more efficient means of extermination that would require less manpower and would enhance the prestige of the SS. As a result, extermination by gas was introduced, using vans whose exhaust fumes were piped into the enclosed cargo areas that served as portable gas chambers. In Poland, Himmler replaced the vans with permanent buildings housing gas chambers using Zyklon B, a gas developed for the purpose by the chemical

firm I.G. Farben. The chambers could annihilate thousands at a time.

The Third Reich began erecting its vast network of death in 1941. The first extermination camp was created in Chelmno, Poland, where 150,000 people were killed between 1941 and 1944. The camps practiced systematic extermination for the savage destruction of those groups deemed racially inferior, sexually deviant, and politically dangerous. The terms *genocide, judeocide,* and *holocaust* have been used to describe the mass slaughter of the Jewish people, most of which took place in five major killing centers in what is now Polish territory—Chelmno, Belzec, Sobibor, Treblinka, and Auschwitz.

Many victims died before ever reaching the camps, transported for days in sealed railroad cars, without food, water, or sanitation facilities. Others died within months as forced laborers for the Reich. People of all ages were starved, beaten, and systematically humiliated. Guards taunted their victims verbally, degraded them physically, and tortured them with false hope. Promised clean clothes and nourishment, camp internees were herded into "showers," which dispensed gas rather than water. Descriptions of life in the camps reveal a systematized brutality and inhumanity on the part of the German, Ukrainian, and Polish guards toward their victims. In all, eleven million people died by the extermination process—six million Jews and almost as many non-Jews, including children, the aged, homosexuals, Slavic slave laborers, Soviet prisoners of war, Communists, members of the Polish and Soviet leadership, various resistance elements, gypsies, and Jehovah's Witnesses.

Work Makes Free. The words *Arbeit Macht Frei* ("Work Makes Free") were emblazoned over the main gate at Auschwitz, the largest of the concentration camps. It was at Auschwitz that the greatest number of persons died in a single place, including more than one million Jews. The healthy and the young were kept barely alive to work. Hard labor, starvation, and disease—especially typhus, tuberculosis, and other diseases that spread rapidly because of the lack of sanitation—claimed many victims.

On entering the camps, the sick and the aged were automatically designated for extermination because of their uselessness as a labor force. Many children were put to work, but some were designated for extermination. Many mothers chose to accompany their children to their deaths to comfort them in their final moments. Pregnant women too were considered useless in the

MANIFESTO OF THE JEWISH RESISTANCE IN VILNA, SEPTEMBER 1943

■ In May 1943, in spite of the valiant resistance of Jewish fighting groups, the Nazi SS destroyed the Warsaw ghetto. In August of the same year, inmates revolted in the concentration camp at Treblinka in the face of insurmountable odds. News of the Warsaw ghetto revolt had spread to the camp, where it inspired Jews to rise up and fight against their captors. Few survived the revolt, although considerable damage was done to the gas chambers, the railway station, and the barracks by the armed inmates. The Jews of the ghetto of Vilna (Vilnius) organized active resistance to the Nazis with the rallying cry, "Jews, we have nothing to lose!"

Offer armed resistance! Jews, defend yourselves with arms!

The German and Lithuanian executioners are at the gates of the ghetto. They have come to murder us! Soon they will lead you forth in groups through the ghetto door.

Tens of thousands of us were despatched. But we shall not go! We will not offer our heads to the butcher like sheep.

Jews, defend yourselves with arms!

Do not believe the false promises of the assassins or believe the words of the traitors.

Anyone who passes through the ghetto gate will go to Ponar! [Death Camp]

And Ponar means death!

Jews, we have nothing to lose. Death will overtake us in any event. And who can still believe in survival when the murderer exterminates us with so much determination? The hand of the executioner will reach each man and woman. Flight and acts of cowardice will not save our lives.

Active resistance alone can save our lives and our honor.

Brothers! It is better to die in battle in the ghetto than to be carried away to Ponar like sheep. And know this: within the walls of the ghetto there are organized Jewish forces who will resist with weapons.

Support the revolt!

Do not take refuge or hide in the bunkers, for then you will fall into the hands of the murderers like rats.

Jewish people, go out into the squares. Anyone who has no weapons should take an ax, and he who has no ax should take a crowbar or a bludgeon!

For our ancestors!

For our murdered children!

Avenge Ponar!

Attack the murderers!

In every street, in every courtyard, in every house within and without the ghetto, attack these dogs!

Jews, we have nothing to lose! We shall save our lives only if we exterminate our assassins.

Long live liberty! Long live armed resistance! Death to the assassins!

Vilna, the Ghetto, September 1, 1943.

forced labor camps and were sent immediately to the "showers." The number of German Jewish women who died in the camps was 50 percent higher than the number of German Jewish men. Starvation diets meant that women stopped menstruating. Because the Nazis worried that women of childbearing age would continue to reproduce, women who showed signs of menstruation were killed immediately. Women who were discovered to have given birth undetected in the camp were killed, as were their infants. Family relations were completely destroyed, as inmates were segregated by sex. It soon became clear that even those allowed to live were only intended to serve the short-term needs of the Nazis.

The Protestant pastor André Trocmé, shown here with his wife Magda, led the people of the village of Le Chambron in rescuing some 5,000 Jewish children from being sent to their deaths.

Resisting Destruction. Could the victims of extermination have effectively resisted? The answer is no. The impossibility of any effective resistance was based on two essential characteristics of the process of extermination. First, the entire German state and its bureaucratic apparatus were involved in the policies, laws, and decrees of the 1930s that singled out victims, while most Germans stood silently by. There was no course of appeal and no place to hide. Those who understood early what was happening and who had enough money to buy their way out emigrated to safer places, including Palestine and the United States. But most countries blocked the entry of German and eastern European refugees with immigration quotas. Neither Britain nor the United States was willing to deal with the mass influx of European Jews. Jews in the occupied countries and the Axis nations had virtually no chance to escape. They were trapped in a society where all forces of law and administration worked against them.

A second reason for the impossibility of effective resistance was the step-by-step nature of the process of extermination, which meant that few understood the final outcome until it was too late. Initially in the 1930s, many German Jews believed that things could get no worse and obeyed the German state as good citizens. Even the policy of removing groups from the ghetto militated against resistance because the hope was that sending 1,000 Jews to "resettlement" would allow 10,000 Jews remaining behind to be saved. The German authorities deliberately controlled information to cultivate this misunderstanding of what was happening.

Isolated instances of resistance in the camps—rioting at Treblinka, for example—only highlight how impossible rebellion was for physically debilitated people in these heavily guarded centers. In April 1943, in the Warsaw ghetto, Jews organized a resistance movement with a few firearms and some grenades and homemade Molotov cocktails. Starvation, overcrowding, and epidemics made Warsaw, the largest of the ghettos, into an extermination camp. As news reached the ghetto that "resettlement" was the death warrant of tens of thousands of Polish Jews, armed rebellion erupted. It did not succeed in blocking the completion of the Final Solution against the Warsaw ghetto the following year when the SS commandant proclaimed, "The Jewish Quarter of Warsaw is no more!" Polish and Russian Jews account for 70 percent of the total Jewish deaths.

Who Knew?

It is impossible that killing on such a scale could have been kept secret. Along with those who ordered extermination operations, the guards and camp personnel involved in carrying out the directives were aware of what was happening. Those who brought internees to the camps, returning always with empty railroad cars, knew it too. People who saw their neighbors disappearing believed for a time that they were being resettled in the east. But as news got back to central and western Europe, it was more difficult to sustain belief in this ruse. People who lived near the camps could not ignore the screams and fumes of gas and burning bodies that permeated the environs of the camps.

Although never publicly announcing its extermination program, the German government convinced its citizens that the policies of the Nazi state could not be judged by ordinary moral standards. The benefits to the

THE WHITE ROSE

■ *Resistance to Hitler's rule in Germany was a limited and isolated phenomenon without any coordinated leadership or mass following. On 22 February 1943, two students at the University of Munich and their professor were executed for distributing pamphlets that criticized Hitler's regime. The students, Sophie and Hans Scholl, were brother and sister and, along with Professor Kurt Huber, they belonged to a small group of students, faculty, scientists, and intellectuals who called their society the White Rose.*

APPEAL TO ALL GERMANS!

The war goes on to its certain conclusion. As in the year 1918, the German Government tries to tell us that the U-boat campaign is succeeding, while in the East our armies are retreating without stopping and in the West an Allied invasion is expected momentarily. America has yet to reach the height of its arming for war, and today it is already armed beyond anything like it in the past. With mathematical certainty Hitler is leading the German people to destruction.

Hitler cannot win the war, he can only prolong it. His guilt and that of those who helped him have already gone beyond the point of no return. A just punishment comes nearer and nearer!

What must the German people do? It sees nothing and it hears nothing. Blinded, it staggers on to its destruction. "Victory at any cost!" are the words written on its banners. "I shall fight to the last man," says Hitler—even though the war has already been lost.

Germans! Do you want yourself and your children to suffer the same fate as the Jews? Do you want to be judged the same way your mis-leader will be judged? Shall we forever be the most hated and rejected people in the world? Separate yourself, therefore, from the National Socialist subhumanity! Show by your deeds that you think otherwise!

This is the beginning of a new War of Liberation. The most decent of our people fight on our side! Tear up the cloak of indifference which you have placed around your hearts! *Decide yourself, before it is too late*!

Don't fall for that National Socialist propaganda that has put the fear of Bolshevism in your bones! Do you really think that the salvation of Germany is bound up for better or worse with National Socialism? A criminal conspiracy cannot possibly win a German victory. Abandon *immediately and in time* anything to do with National Socialism! There is going to be a terrible and just verdict for those who have shown themselves to be cowardly and irresolute.

This war was never a national one. What will be its lesson for us?

The imperialist concept of power, no matter from which side it comes, must have its teeth drawn for all time. One-sided Prussian militarism must never again be allowed to win power. Only in noble cooperation with other Europeans can the ground be prepared for a new political structure. Any centralized power, such as that the Prussian state sought to exercise inside Germany and in Europe, must be stifled in its germinal stage. The future Germany can be only a federal state. Only a sound federal state order can give Europe a new life. Workers must be freed by a rational socialism from their condition of abject slavery. The phantom of an autarchic economy must disappear in Europe. Every single person has the right to the good things of the world!

Freedom of speech, freedom of conscience, protection of the individual from despotism of the criminal power-state, these will be the foundation of the new Europe.

Support the Resistance! Distribute these leaflets!

Rows of dead slave laborers await burial by U.S. troops at Norden-
hausen concentration camp in 1945. They died from starvation,
overwork, and beatings while working on the V-1 and V-2 bombs.

German state were justification enough for the annihilation of eleven million people. Official propaganda successfully convinced millions that the Reich was the supreme good. Admitting the existence of the extermination program carried with it a responsibility on which few acted, perhaps out of fear of reprisals. There were some heroes like Raoul Wallenberg of Sweden, who interceded for Hungarian Jews and provided Jews in the Budapest ghetto with food and protection. The king of Denmark, when informed that the Nazis had ordered Danish Jews to wear the yellow star, stated that he and his family would also wear the yellow star as a "badge of honor." Heroic acts, however, were isolated and rare.

Collaborationist governments and occupied nations often cooperated with Nazi extermination policies. The French government at Vichy introduced and implemented a variety of anti-Jewish measures. All of this was done without German orders and without German pressure. By voluntarily identifying and deporting Jews, the Vichy government sent 75,000 men, women, and children to their deaths.

As the war dragged on for years, internees of the camps hoped and prayed for rescue by the Allies. But such help did not come. The U.S. State Department and the British Foreign Office had early and reliable information on the nature and extent of the atrocities. But they did not act. American Jews were unable to convince President Franklin D. Roosevelt to intercede to prevent the slaughter. Appeals to bomb the gas chambers at Auschwitz and the railroad lines leading to them were rejected by the United States on strategic grounds. Those trying to survive in the camps and the ghettos despaired at their abandonment.

The handful of survivors found by Allied soldiers who entered the camps after Germany's defeat presented a haunting picture of humanity. A British colonel who entered the camp at Bergen-Belsen in April 1945 gave a restrained account of what he found:

> As we walked down the main road of the camp, we were cheered by the internees, and for the first time we saw their condition. A great number were little more than living skeletons. There were men and women lying in heaps on both sides of the track. Others were walking slowly and aimlessly about, vacant expressions on their starved faces.

The sight of corpses piled on top of one another lining the roads, the piles of shoes, clothing, underwear, and gold teeth extracted from the dead shocked those who came to liberate the camps. One of the two survivors of Chelmno summed it up: "No one can understand what happened here."

The Final Solution was a perversion of every value of civilization. The achievements of twentieth-century industry, technology, state, and bureaucracy in the West were turned against millions to create, as one German official called it, murder by assembly line. Mass killing was not prompted by military or security concerns. Nor was the elimination of vital labor power consistent with the needs of the Nazi state. The international tribunal for war crimes that met in 1945 in the German city of Nuremberg attempted to mete out justice to the criminals against humanity responsible for the destruction of eleven million Europeans labeled as demons and racial inferiors. History in the end must record, if it cannot explain, such inhumanity.

Allied Victory

At the end of 1941 the situation appeared grim for the British and their dominions and the Americans who were assisting them with munitions, money, and food.

Hitler had achieved control of a vast land empire covering all of continental Europe in the west, north, south, and center. This empire, which Hitler called his "New Order," included territories occupied and directly administered by the German army, satellites, and collaborationist regimes. It was fortified by alliances with Italy, the Soviet Union, and Japan. Hitler commanded the greatest fighting force in the world, one that had knocked France out of the war in a matter of weeks, brought destruction to British cities, and conquered Yugoslavia in twelve days. Much of the world was coming to fear that the German army was invincible.

Then in June 1941, Hitler's troops invaded the Soviet Union, providing the British with an ally. In December the naval and air forces of Japan attacked American bases in the Pacific, providing the British and the Russians with still another ally. What began as a European war became a world war. This was the war Hitler did not want and which Germany could not win—a long, total war to the finish against three powers with inexhaustible resources—the British Empire, the Soviet Union, and the United States.

The Holocaust

The Soviet Union's Great Patriotic War

Hitler had always considered the Soviet Union Germany's primary enemy. His hatred of communism was all-encompassing: Bolshevism was an evil invention of the Jewish people and a dangerous ideological threat to the Third Reich. The 1939 Non-Aggression Pact with Stalin was no more than an expedient for him. Hitler rebuked a Swiss diplomat in 1939 for failing to grasp the central fact of his foreign policy:

> Everything I undertake is directed against Russia. If those in the West are too stupid and too blind to understand this, then I should be forced to come to an understanding with the Russians to beat the West, and then, after its defeat, turn with all my concentrated force against the Soviet Union.

That is exactly what happened on 22 June 1941 when German armies marched into Russia. They found the large Soviet army totally unprepared for war. In contrast to German soldiers, who had fought in Spain, Poland, and France, Soviet troops had no first-hand battle experience. Nor were they well led. Stalin's purges in the late 1930s removed 35,000 officers from their posts by dismissal, imprisonment, or execution. Many of the men who replaced them were unseasoned in the responsibilities of leadership.

Russian military leaders were sure they would be ready for a European war against the capitalist nations by 1942, and Stalin refused to believe that Hitler would attack the Soviet Union before then. British agents and Stalin's own spies tried to warn him of German plans for an invasion in the spring of 1941. When the Germans did invade Russian territory, Stalin was so overwhelmed that he fell into a depression and was unable to act for days.

On 3 July 1941, in his first radio address after the attack, Stalin identified his nation with the Allied cause: "Our struggle for the freedom of our country will merge with the struggle of the peoples of Europe and America for their independence, for democratic liberties." He accepted offers of support from the United States and Great Britain, the two nations that had worked consistently to exclude the Soviet Union from European power politics since the Bolshevik Revolution in 1917. With France defeated and Great Britain crippled, the future of the war depended on Soviet fighting power and American supplies.

Hitler's invasion of Russia involved three million soldiers from Germany and Germany's satellites, the largest invasion force in history. It stretched along an immense battlefront from the Baltic to the Black Sea. Instead of exclusively targeting Moscow, the capital, the German army concentrated first on destroying Soviet armed forces and capturing Leningrad in the north and the oil-rich Caucasus in the south. In the beginning the German forces advanced rapidly in a *Blitzkrieg* across western Russia, where they were greeted as liberators in the Ukraine. The Germans took 290,000 prisoners of war and massacred tens of thousands of others in their path through the Jewish settlements of western Russia.

Within four months, the German army had advanced to the gates of Moscow, but they concentrated their forces too late. The Red Army rallied to defend Moscow, as thousands of civilian women set to work digging trenches and antitank ditches around the city. The Soviet people answered Stalin's call for a scorched-earth policy by burning everything that might be useful to the advancing German troops. German troops had also burned much in their path, depriving themselves of essential supplies for the winter months ahead. The German advance was stopped, as the best ally of the Red Army—the Russian winter—settled in. The first snow fell at the beginning of October. By early November, German troops were beginning to suffer the harsh effects of an early and exceptionally bitter Russian winter.

Hitler promised the German people that "final victory" was at hand. So confident was Hitler of a speedy and decisive victory that he sent his soldiers into Russia wearing only light summer uniforms. Hitler's generals knew better and tried repeatedly to explain military realities to him. General Heinz Guderian (1888–1954), commander of the tank units, reported that his men were suffering frostbite, tanks could not be started, and automatic weapons were jamming in the subzero temperatures. Back in Germany, the civilian population received little accurate news of the campaign. They began to suspect the worst when the government sent out a plea for woolen blankets and clothing for the troops.

By early December, the German military situation was desperate. The Soviets, benefiting from intelligence information about German plans and an awareness that Japan was about to declare war on the United States, recalled fresh troops from the Siberian frontier and the border with China and Manchuria and launched a powerful counterattack against the poorly outfitted German army outside Moscow. Under the command of General Gyorgi Zhukov (1896–1974), Russian troops, dressed and trained for winter warfare, pushed the Germans back in retreat across the snow-covered ex-

Men and women on a Ukrainian collective farm labor to erect huge antitank traps during the German invasion of the Soviet Union. The steadfast courage of the civilian population contributed greatly to the defeat of Hitler's quest for Lebensraum *in the east.*

panses. By February, 200,000 German troops had been killed, 46,000 were missing in action, and 835,000 were casualties of battle and the weather. Thus, the campaign cost the German army over one million casualties. It probably cost the Soviets twice that number of wounded, missing, captured, and dead soldiers. At the end of the Soviet counterattack in March, the German army and its satellite forces were in a shambles reminiscent of Napoleon's troops, who 130 years earlier had been decimated in the campaign to capture Moscow. An enraged Hitler dismissed his generals for retreating without his permission, and he himself assumed the position of commander-in-chief of the armed forces.

Hitler was not daunted by the devastating costs of his invasion of Russia. In the summer of 1942, he initiated a second major offensive, this time to take the city of Stalingrad. Constant bombardment gutted the city, and the Soviet army was forced into hand-to-hand combat with the German soldiers. But the German troops, once again inadequately supplied and unprepared for the Russian winter, failed to capture the city. The Battle of Stalingrad was over in the first days of February 1943. Of the original 300,000 members of the German Sixth Army, fewer than 100,000 survived to be taken prisoner by the Soviets. Of those, only 5,000 returned to Germany in 1955, when German prisoners of war were repatriated.

The Soviets succeeded by exploiting two great advantages in their war against Germany: the large Soviet population and their knowledge of Russian weather and terrain. There was a third advantage that Hitler ignored: the Soviet people's determination to sacrifice everything for the war effort. In his successive Five-Year Plans, Stalin had mobilized Soviet society with an appeal to fulfill and surpass production quotas. In the summer of 1941, as Hitler's troops threatened Moscow, he used the same rhetoric to appeal to his Soviet "brothers and sisters" to join him in waging "the Great Patriotic War." The Russian people shared a sense of common purpose, sacrifice, and moral commitment in their loyalty to the nation.

The advancing Germans themselves intensified Soviet patriotism by torturing and killing tens of thousands of peasants who might have willingly cooperated against the Stalinist regime. Millions of Soviet peasants joined the Red Army. Young men of high-school age were drafted into the armed forces. Three million women became wage earners for the first time as they replaced men in war industries. Women who remained on the land worked to feed the townspeople and the soldiers. Because the Red Army had requisitioned horses and tractors for combat, grain had to be sown and harvested by hand—and this often meant women's hands. Tens of thousands of Russians left their homes in western Russia to work for relocated Soviet industries in the Urals, the Volga region, Siberia, and Central Asia. More than 20 million Soviet people, soldiers and civilians, men, women, and children, died

Russian villagers search for loved ones among civilians slain by German troops. Noncombatants were frequent victims of the Nazi policy of enslavement or annihilation.

in the course of World War II. In addition to those killed in battle, millions starved as a direct result of the hardships of war. In 1943, food was so scarce that seed for the next year's crops was eaten. One in every three men born in 1906 died in the war. But Soviet resistance did not flag.

The Great Patriotic War had a profound impact on Soviet views of the world and the Soviet Union's place in it. The war left the Soviet people with an enduring fear of invasion. The official falsification of all published maps of the Soviet Union in order to mislead spies and foreign armies was just one indication of the Russian expectation of treachery. (This practice was as recent as 1988.) Today, a visitor to Stalingrad, renamed Volgograd, can still find old tanks in city parks and on streets as reminders of the front line of the Red Army in the Great Patriotic War. Ruins of buildings have been left standing as grim monuments of the need for continued preparedness. The few remaining trees that endured through the war's devastation bear plaques that make of their survival a memorial.

The Soviet Union sacrificed 10 percent of its population to the war effort and incurred well over 50 percent of all the deaths and casualties of the war. Few families escaped the death of members in the defense of the nation. Soviet citizens correctly considered that they had given more than any other country to defeat Hitler. For the Soviet people, their suffering in battle made World War II the Soviet Union's war and their sacrifice made possible the Allied victory. But victory still eluded the Allies in western Europe, where now another nation, the United States, had entered the fray.

The United States Enters the War

Although a neutral power, the United States began extending aid to the Allies after the fall of France in 1940. Since neither Britain nor the Soviet Union could afford to pay the entire costs of defending Europe against Hitler, the United States Congress passed the Lend-Lease Act in 1941. This act authorized President Roosevelt to provide armaments to Great Britain and the Soviet Union without payment. America became "the arsenal of democracy." The United States and Britain sent 4,100 airplanes and 138,000 motor vehicles as well as steel and machinery to the Soviet Union for the campaign of 1943. In all, America pumped $11 billion worth of equipment into the Soviet war effort between 1941 and 1945. Stalin later told Roosevelt that the USSR

PRESIDENT FRANKLIN ROOSEVELT'S REQUEST FOR A DECLARATION OF WAR ON JAPAN

■ *On 7 December 1941 Japanese naval and air forces attacked the American naval base at Pearl Harbor in Hawaii. Most of the U.S. Pacific fleet was moored in Pearl Harbor, and it sustained severe destruction of its naval vessels, battleships, and aircraft. U.S. military and political leaders were taken completely by surprise by the Japanese attack. Roosevelt's declaration of war reflects the outrage over this "infamy." In spite of marked cultural differences between the US and Japanese declaration which followed the next day both the Japanese and the American leaders make clear their reliance on the total support of their people to win the war.*

To the Congress of the United States:

Yesterday, December 7, 1941—a date which will live in infamy—the United States of America was suddenly and deliberately attacked by naval and air forces of the Empire of Japan.

The United States was at peace with that Nation and, at the solicitation of Japan, was still in conversation with its Government and its Emperor looking toward the maintenance of peace in the Pacific. Indeed, one hour after Japanese air squadrons had commenced bombing in Oahu, the Japanese Ambassador to the United States and his colleague delivered to the Secretary of State a formal reply to a recent American message. While this reply stated that it seemed useless to continue the existing diplomatic negotiations, it contained no threat or hint of war or armed attack.

It will be recorded that the distance of Hawaii from Japan makes it obvious that the attack was deliberately planned many days or even weeks ago. During the intervening time the Japanese Government has deliberately sought to deceive the United States by false statements and expressions of hope for continued peace.

The attack yesterday on the Hawaiian Islands has caused severe damage to American naval and military forces. Very many American lives have been lost. In addition American ships have been reported torpedoed on the high seas between San Francisco and Honolulu.

Yesterday the Japanese Government also launched an attack against Malaya.

Last night Japanese forces attacked Hong Kong.

Last night Japanese forces attacked Guam.

Last night Japanese forces attacked the Philippine Islands.

Last night the Japanese attacked Wake Island.

This morning the Japanese attacked Midway Island.

Japan has, therefore, undertaken a surprise offensive extending throughout the Pacific area. The facts of yesterday speak for themselves. The people of the United States have already formed their opinions and well understand the implications to the very life and safety of our Nation.

As Commander-in Chief of the Army and Navy I have directed that all measures be taken for our defense.

Always will we remember the character of the onslaught against us.

No matter how long it may take us to overcome this premeditated invasion, the American people in their righteous might will win through to absolute victory. . . .

With confidence in our armed forces—with the unbounded determination of our people—we will gain the inevitable triumph—so help us God.

I ask that the Congress declare that since the unprovoked and dastardly attack by Japan on Sunday, December seventh, a state of war has existed between the United States and the Japanese Empire.

FRANKLIN D. ROOSEVELT

would have lost the war with Germany without the help of the Americans and the British.

President Roosevelt and his advisers considered Germany, not Japan, to be America's primary target for a future war. Japan nevertheless had been threatening American trade interest in Asia and had embroiled the United States in disputes over Japanese imperialist expansion in the late 1930s. The United States understood Japan to be an aggressive country determined to expand its control over China and Southeast Asia; the U.S. initially opposed this expansion through economic embargoes. The presence of the Soviet Union pressing eastward across Asia coupled with the colonial presences in Asia of Great Britain, France, and the United States, severely constrained Japan's capacity to expand its frontiers and ensure its security. The war in western Europe and the German invasion of the Soviet Union in June 1941 meant that the Japanese could concentrate their attention farther south in China, Indochina, and Thailand. Japan's limited reserves of foreign currency and raw materials made it increasingly vulnerable to economic disruptions. Japanese leaders accepted the necessity of grasping oil and raw materials in Southeast Asia.

In September 1940 Japan joined forces with the Axis Powers of Germany and Italy in the Tripartite Pact, in which the signatories, promising mutual support against aggression, acknowledged the legitimacy of each other's expansionist efforts in Europe and Asia. Japanese-American relations deteriorated following the Japanese invasion of southern Indochina in July 1941. The United States insisted that Japan vacate China and Indochina and reestablish the open door for trade in Asia. The United States knew, however, that it was only a matter of time until Japan attacked U.S. interests but was uncertain about where that attack would take place.

On Sunday morning, 7 December 1941, Japan struck at the heart of the American Pacific Fleet stationed at Pearl Harbor, Hawaii. The fleet was literally caught asleep at the switch: 2,300 people were killed, and eight battleships and numerous cruisers and destroyers were sunk or severely damaged. The attack crippled American naval power in the Pacific as the American navy suffered its worst loss in history in a single engagement. The attack on Pearl Harbor led to the United States' immediate declaration of war against Japan. In President Roosevelt's words, 7 December 1941 was "a date which will live in infamy." In the next three months, Japan captured Hong Kong, Malaya, and the important naval base at Singapore from the British, taking 60,000

The battleship USS West Virginia *in flames at Pearl Harbor. The attack was carried out entirely by carrier-based aircraft—a sign of things to come in naval warfare.*

prisoners. Like their earlier march into China, the Japanese invasion of Southeast Asia moved swiftly to establish control, outstripping the Japanese military's own timetables for advance. In December 1941 the Japanese landed in Thailand and secured immediate agreement for Japanese occupation of strategic spots in the country. They then turned to the Malay peninsula, decisively defeating the British fleet off Malaya and pushing on the ground toward Singapore, which they conquered in February 1942. They conquered British Borneo in January, drove the Dutch from all of Indonesia but New Guinea, pushed American forces in the Philippines into the Bataan peninsula, occupied Burma, and inflicted severe defeats on British, Dutch, and American naval power in East Asia. U.S. general Douglas MacArthur (1880–1964) surrendered the Philippines to the Japanese on 2 January 1942 with the promise to return. With the armies of Germany deep in Russian territory, Australia now faced the threat of a Japanese invasion.

Hitler praised the Japanese government for its action against the British Empire and against the United States and its "millionaire and Jewish backers." Germany, with its armies retreating from Moscow, nevertheless declared war against the United States on 11

JAPAN'S DECLARATION OF WAR

■ *Japan's sense of its mission in East Asia is embodied in Emperor Hirohito's declaration of war against the United States and Great Britain on 8 December 1941, the day after Japanese forces attacked the American fleet in Hawaii. Interestingly, the Japanese declaration speaks of "world peace," and "friendship among nations."*

JAPAN'S DECLARATION OF WAR ON THE UNITED STATES AND GREAT BRITAIN (DECEMBER 8, 1941)

We, by grace of heaven, Emperor of Japan, seated on the Throne of the line unbroken for ages eternal, enjoin upon ye, Our loyal and brave subjects.

We hereby declare war on the United States of America and the British Empire. The men and officers of Our Army and Navy shall do their utmost in prosecuting the war, Our public servants of various departments shall perform faithfully and diligently their appointed tasks, and all other subjects of Ours shall pursue their respective duties; the entire nation with a united will shall mobilize their total strength so that nothing will miscarry in the attainment of our war aims.

To insure the stability of East Asia and to contribute to world peace is the far-sighted policy which was formulated by Our Great Illustrious Imperial Grandsire and Our Great Imperial Sire succeeding Him, and which We have constantly to heart. To cultivate friendship among nations and to employ prosperity in common with all nations has always been the guiding principle of Our Empire's foreign policy. It has been truly unavoidable and far from Our wishes that Our Empire has now been brought to cross swords with America and Britain. More than four years have passed since the government of the Chinese Republic, failing to comprehend the true intentions of Our Empire, and recklessly courting trouble, disturbed the peace of east Asia and compelled Our Empire to take up arms. . . .

Patiently have We waited and long have We endured, in the hope that Our Government might retrieve the situation in peace. But our adversaries, showing not the least spirit of conciliation, have unduly delayed a settlement; and in the meantime, they have intensified the economic and military pressure to compel thereby Our Empire to submission. This trend of affairs would, if left unchecked, not only nullify Our Empire's efforts of many years for the sake of the stabilization of east Asia, but also endanger the very existence of Our nation. The situation being such as it is, Our Empire for its existence and self-defence has no other recourse but to appeal to arms and to crush every obstacle in its path.

The hallowed spirits of Our Imperial Ancestors guarding Us from above, We rely upon the loyalty and courage of Our subjects in Our confident expectation that the task bequeathed by Our Forefathers will be carried forward, and that the sources of evil will be speedily eradicated and an enduring peace immutably established in East Asia, preserving thereby the glory of Our Empire.

The 8th day of the 12th month of the 16th year of Showa.

HIROHITO

December 1941. Hitler, in fact, considered that the United States was already at war with Germany because of its policy of supplying the Allies. Within days the United States, a nation with an army smaller than Belgium's, had gone from neutrality to a war in two theaters. Although militarily weak, the United States was an economic giant, commanding a vast industrial capacity and access to resources. America grew even stronger under the stimulus of war, increasing its production by 400 percent in two years. It now devoted itself to the demands of a total war and the unconditional surrender of Germany and then Japan.

Winning the War in Europe

The Allies did not always share the same strategies or concerns. President Roosevelt and Prime Minister Churchill had already discussed common goals in the summer of 1941 before U.S. entry into the war. The United States embraced the priority of the European war and the postponement of war in the Pacific. Stalin pleaded for the Anglo-Americans to open up a second front against Germany in western Europe in order to give his troops some relief and save Soviet lives. Anglo-American resources were committed to the Pacific in

World War II in the Pacific

order to stop the Japanese advance, and the Americans and the British disagreed as to where a second front in Europe might be opened.

The second front came not in western Europe but in the Mediterranean. After the defeat of France in 1940 and the neutralization of the French navy in the Mediterranean, Italy saw a chance to extend its empire in North Africa. With a large army stationed in Libya, Ethiopia, Eritrea, and Italian Somaliland, Mussolini ordered a series of offensives against the Sudan, Kenya, British Somaliland, and Egypt. Most of the Italian advances had been reversed by the British, and 420,000 Italian troops, including African soldiers, were listed as casualties, compared to 3,100 British troops. Germany, however, having succeeded in invading Greece and Yugoslavia, turned its attention to aiding its Axis partner in trouble. In February 1941 Hitler sent General Erwin Rommel (1891–1944), a master strategist of tank warfare, to help the Italians take control of the Suez Canal by launching a counteroffensive in the North African war. Rommel's Axis troops succeeded in entering Egypt and driving the British east of the Egyptian border, thereby dealing the British a serious setback.

The British were simultaneously securing territories in Syria, Palestine, and Iraq in order to guarantee the oil pipelines of the Gulf for the Allies. Between November 1941 and July 1942 the pendulum swung back and forth between Allied and Axis forces in the Desert War, as the North African campaign came to be known. In August 1942 the Allied forces, now under the command of Bernard Montgomery (1887–1976), launched a carefully planned offensive at El Alamein, and Rommel was forced to retreat to Tunisia.

Now a joint American-British initiative, the first of the war, landed troops in French Morocco and Algeria and advanced into Tunisia, attacking Rommel's Afrika Korps from behind. About 250,000 German and Italian soldiers were taken prisoner, as the Axis powers were decisively defeated in May 1943. Although not a central theater of the war, North Africa did provide British forces with important victories and was a good testing ground for the cooperation of Allied forces.

Because of British interests in the Mediterranean, Churchill insisted on a move from North Africa into Sicily and Italy. This strategy was put into effect in 1942. The Italian government withdrew from the war in September, but German troops carried on the fight in Italy. The Anglo-American invasion of Italy did little to alleviate Russian losses, and the Soviet Union absorbed almost the entire force of German military power until 1944. Stalin's distrust of his allies increased. Churchill, Roosevelt, and Stalin met for the first time in late November 1943 at Teheran, Iran. Roosevelt and Churchill made a commitment to Stalin to open a second front in France within six months. Stalin, in turn, promised to attack Japan in order to aid the United States in the Pacific. The great showdown of the global war was at hand.

On 6 June 1944, Allied troops under the command of the American general Dwight D. Eisenhower (1890–1969) came ashore on the beaches of Normandy in the largest amphibious landing in history. In a daring operation identified by the code name Operation Overlord, 2.2 million American, British, and Free French forces, 450,000 vehicles, and 4 million tons of supplies poured into northern France. Allied forces broke through German lines to liberate Paris in late August. The Germans launched a last-ditch counterattack in late December 1944 in Luxembourg and Belgium. This battle of the Bulge only slowed the Allied advance; in March 1945 American forces crossed the Rhine into Germany. Hitler, meanwhile, refused to surrender and insisted on a fight to the death of the last German soldier. Members of his own High Command had attempted unsuccessfully to assassinate Hitler in July 1944. The final German defeat came in April 1945, when the Russians stormed the German capital of Berlin. Hitler, living in an underground bunker near the Chancellery building, committed suicide on 30 April 1945.

Japanese War Aims and Assumptions

Japan and the United States entered the Pacific war with very different understandings of what was at stake. Initially, the Japanese appealed to Southeast Asian leaders as the liberators of Asian peoples from Western colonialism and imperialism. The approach struck a responsive chord as the Japanese established what they called the Greater East Asia Co-Prosperity Sphere. In November 1943, Burma's leader, Ba Maw, said at the Assembly of the Greater East Asiatic Nations held in Tokyo, "My Asiatic blood has always called to other Asiatics. . . . This is not the time to think with our minds; this is the time to think with our blood, and it is thinking with the blood that has brought me all the way from Burma to Japan." But the passionate and positive welcome Ba Maw extended to the Japanese liberators did not last long. As he bluntly explained in his memoirs, "The brutality, arrogance, and racial pretensions of the Japanese militarists in Burma remain among the

Supplies for the Allied forces pour ashore at the beachheads of Normandy during Operation Overlord in 1944. The invasion began the opening of the second front that Stalin had been urging on the Allies since the German armies thrust into Russia in 1941.

deepest Burmese memories of the war years; for a great many people in Southeast Asia these are all they remember of the war."

The Greater East Asia Co-Prosperity Sphere began in 1940 and lasted until the summer of 1945. This reorganization of east and southeast Asia under Japanese hegemony constituted a redefinition of world geography with Japan at the center. The Japanese fashioned a romanticized vision of the family living in harmony, all members knowing their places and enjoying the complementary division of responsibilities and reciprocities that made family life work smoothly. Behind this pleasant image lurked the reality of a brutal power structure forcing subject peoples to accept massively inferior positions in a world fashioned exclusively for Japanese desires and needs. The Japanese viewed southeast Asia principally as a market for Japanese manufactured goods, a source of raw materials, and a source of profits for Japanese capital invested in mining, rubber, and raw cotton. Plans were made for hydroelectric power and aluminum refining facilities.

Wartime Japanese nakedly displayed their disdain for the people they conquered in southeast Asia. All subject peoples were to bow on meeting a Japanese, while at public assemblies a ritual bow in the direction of the Japanese emperor was required. This practice dismayed southeast Asians such as Indies Muslims or Philippine Catholics, who regarded Japanese emperor worship as pagan and presumptuous. Japanese holidays, like the emperor's birthday, were enforced as Co-Prosperity Sphere holidays, and the calendar was reset to the mythical founding of the Japanese state in 660 B.C.E.

The Japanese were less brazen toward the Chinese in their rhetoric, in part because so much of east Asian civilization had its roots in China. But in spite of more temperate pronouncements in China, Japanese aggression against the Chinese included one of the worst periods of destruction in modern warfare. When the Japanese took over the Nationalist capital of Nanjing in December 1937, 20,000 women were raped, 30,000 soldiers killed, and another 12,000 civilians died in the

These drawings by Japanese atomic bomb survivors are from Unforgettable Fire, *which tells in text and pictures the stories of the horrors they endured.*

The Atomic Wasteland

The sixth of August 1945 was a typical summer day in southwestern Japan. In the city of Hiroshima at 8:15 A.M., people were walking to work, sitting down at office desks, riding buses, weeding gardens, and clearing away breakfast dishes. Suddenly a noiseless flash lit the sky over the city and its environs for miles. A mammoth column of smoke in the shape of a mushroom cloud ballooned up. The United States had dropped history's first atomic bomb.

The explosion had the intensity of a huge blast furnace. In some areas, the brilliant light created by the explosion bleached everything it touched. Near the epicenter of the blast, human bodies were charred to cinders or turned into frightening statues. Flesh melted and bones fused. Buildings were reduced to ashes. Stones bled. The world had never seen a bomb like this. Hiroshima, a city renowned in prewar Japan for its relaxed and agreeable atmosphere, was leveled in an instant by the terrifying force of a single atomic bomb.

More than 78,000 died in Hiroshima on 6 August. By December the number had reached 140,000 as the sickness caused by radiation poisoning continued to take its toll. Rescue workers inhaled the dense dust and became contaminated by radioactivity. Surviving victims often lost their hair and eyebrows, experienced nausea, vomiting, diarrhea, and bleeding. Others suffered from internal hemorrhaging, blindness, chronic weakness, fatigue, and leukemia. Many developed cancers, sometimes years later. The bomb scarred and disfigured. Atomic radiation released by the bomb caused unseen damage by attacking the lungs, heart, bone marrow, and internal organs. It poisoned the lymph glands. It worked unobserved to alter genetic structure, deforming unborn babies and those not yet conceived.

Harry Truman, who became president of the United States on 12 April 1945, following the death of Franklin D. Roosevelt, later spoke of his decision to drop the atomic bomb in order to bring the war to a speedy end. In July 1945 Truman issued an ultimatum to Japan to surrender immediately or face dire consequences. The Japanese ignored the warning. Hiroshima was targeted, according to Truman, in order to make a point to the Japanese, to demonstrate the unimaginable force of this new American weapon. The city was a military center, a major storage and assembly point that supplied the armed forces. Nagasaki, bombed three days after Hiroshima with an experimental plutonium bomb, was targeted as an industrial center and the place where the torpedoes that had destroyed American ships were manufactured.

It is undoubtedly true that the bombings were responsible for the Japanese surrender that followed a few days later. The atomic bomb did bring the Asian war to an immediate end. But critics of the bombings pointed out that Japan was already close to defeat. Secret U.S. intelligence studies that came to light in the 1980s indicate that American leaders knew that Japan had been weakened by intense American incendiary bombing of its cities. Twenty-six square miles of the working-class and industrial section of Tokyo had been burned at the cost of well over 100,000 lives. Many refugees from other Japanese cities had fled to Hiroshima to live with relatives. The Sea of Japan had been heavily mined, cutting off Japan from its armies on the Asian mainland. Some young radical officers of the Japanese army were preparing to kidnap Emperor Hirohito in order to keep him from capitulating. The planned American landing on Japan was expected to be costly. U.S. forces had already suffered over 100,000 casualties in the conquest of the Japanese island of Okinawa in April. Truman and his advisers were now prepared to use any means possible to prevent further American casualties. Defenders of the decision have argued that any responsible American leader would have made the same decision to use the atomic bomb. Modern total wars acquire a life of their own, and desperate nations use the science, technology, and weapons available to them.

In the summer of 1945, General Dwight D. Eisenhower, then the victorious Supreme Allied Commander in the European theater of war, was informed by U.S. Secretary of War Henry L. Stimson of what was about to take place in Hiroshima. Eisenhower voiced his "grave misgivings" based on his "belief that Japan was already defeated and that the dropping of the bomb was completely unnecessary" to end the war. He was not alone among military men in questioning the use of nuclear force on strategic and moral grounds. Strong opposition to nuclear weapons began to surface among scientists working on the bomb. In opposition to many of their colleagues, they warned that the atomic bomb was an undiscriminating weapon that could not pinpoint supply depots and military targets but would destroy entire civilian populations. The peace movement based on banning nuclear weapons actually began among horrified scientists who were aware, before the rest of the world could know, of the terrible force that they had helped to create.

At the Potsdam Conference in July 1945 Stalin had informed President Truman and Prime Minister Winston Churchill that the Soviet Union was about to invade Manchuria, honoring the promise he had made at Teheran in 1943 to join the war against Japan after Germany was defeated. The Soviet Union would now play a role in determining the future of Asia. Truman told Stalin of the powerful new weapon America had developed. Stalin seemed unimpressed. Secretary of War Stimson was aware that the atomic bomb would be an important weapon to have in the American arsenal when the time came to negotiate a postwar world settlement with the Russians. Truman and his advisers, however, never deviated from their insistence that saving the lives of thousands of American and Japanese soldiers was their only consideration in dropping the bomb.

An American observer called the bombing of Hiroshima "the immersion in death." Survivors repeatedly described Hiroshima after the "flash" as what hell must be like. Photographs of the city record the total devastation to buildings and vegetation. Japanese cameramen avoided photographing the devastation to human bodies, believing that what they saw was too horrible to record. Yet the brutality of nuclear war could not be ignored. It has become a central issue of international politics in the second half of the twentieth century. The decision to drop the atomic bomb has had enduring moral and political consequences. On that August morning in 1945, the world had its first terrifying glimpse of the power of total annihilation. In an instant—0.3 second—Hiroshima became an atomic wasteland. The world now lived with the knowledge that it could happen again.

more than six weeks of wanton terror inflicted by Japanese soldiers.

With regard to Westerners, Japanese propaganda avoided labeling them as inferior. In part this reflected Japan's economic and political emulation of the West since the late nineteenth century. Rather than denigrating Western people, the Japanese chose to elevate themselves as a people descended from divine origins. Stressing their unique mythical history gave the Japanese a strong sense of superiority neither intellectual nor physical, but moral. They believed that virtue was on their side in their mission to stop Western expansion in Asia and to take their "proper place" as the leading people in Asia by tyrannizing the Co-Prosperity Sphere.

To achieve their moral superiority, the Japanese government urged their people to "purify" themselves. Although purification rituals occur in the world's great religions, rarely do governments urge people to cleanse their souls. For the average wartime Japanese citizen, purification meant accepting extreme material poverty and scarcities, rejecting foreign influences, and if called upon, dying for the emperor. The Japanese elevation of patriotism to the level of human self-sacrifice lay outside Western sensibilities of the time; to expect the spirit to become more purified made little sense to large numbers of Westerners. A bit more comprehensible perhaps were Japanese wartime views of Americans as

In the last desperate months of the Second World War, the Japanese employed suicide pilots to purposely dive airplanes into U.S. warships. The popular name for such planes and pilots, Kamikaze, came from the "divine wind" that had destroyed the Mongol invasion force in 1281.

beasts for the atrocities that American soldiers committed. The grotesque quality of the American soldiers' desire for war trophies was captured by a *Life* magazine photograph of a blond American young woman holding a Japanese skull sent to her by her GI sweetheart. What *Life* magazine considered "human interest," the Japanese found racist. However reasonable this assessment may be, Japanese impressions of Westerners definitely proved fatally false in another matter. The Japanese assumed that individual selfishness and egoism would make Americans and Europeans incapable of mobilizing for a long fight.

Winning the War in the Pacific

The tide in the Pacific war began to turn when the planned Japanese invasion of Australia was thwarted. Fighting in the jungles of New Guinea, Australian and American troops under the command of General Douglas MacArthur turned back the Japanese army. U.S. Marines did likewise with a bold landing at Guadalcanal and months of bloody fighting in the Solomon Islands. In June 1942, within six months of the attack at Pearl Harbor, American naval forces commanded by Admiral Chester Nimitz (1885–1966) inflicted a defeat on the Japanese navy from which it could not recover. In the battle of Midway, Japan lost four aircraft carriers, a heavy cruiser, over 300 airplanes, and 5,000 men. Midway was the Pacific equivalent of the battle of Stalingrad.

In the summer of 1943, as the Soviet Union launched the offensive that was to defeat Germany, America began to move across the Pacific toward Japan. Nimitz and MacArthur conceived a brilliant plan in which American land, sea, and air forces fought in a coordinated effort. With a series of amphibious landings, they hopped from island to island. Some Japanese island fortresses like Tarawa were taken; others like Truk were bypassed and cut off from Japanese home bases. With the conquest of Saipan in November 1944 and Iwo Jima in March 1945, the United States forces acquired bases from which B-29 bombers could strike at the Japanese home islands. In the summer of 1945, in the greatest air offensive in history, American planes destroyed what remained of the Japanese navy, crippled Japanese industry, and mercilessly firebombed major population centers. The attack ended with the dropping of atomic bombs on the cities of Hiroshima and Nagasaki. (See Special Feature, "The Atomic Wasteland," pp. 1000–1001.) The Japanese government accepted American terms for peace and surrendered unconditionally on 2 September 1945 on the battleship *Missouri* in Tokyo Bay. Four months after the defeat of Germany, the war in Asia was over.

The Fate of Allied Cooperation: 1945

The costs of World War II in terms of death and destruction were the highest in history. Fifty million lives were lost. Most of the dead were Europeans, and most of them were Russians and Poles. The high incidence of civilian deaths distinguished the Second World War from previous wars—well over 50 percent of the dead were noncombatants. Deliberate military targeting of cities explains this phenomenon only in part. The majority of civilian deaths were the result of starvation, enslavement, massacre, and deliberate extermination.

The psychological devastation of continual violence, deprivation, injury, and rape of survivors cannot be measured. Terrorizing citizens became an established means of warfare in the modern age. Another phenomenon not matched in the First World War emerged in 1945: mass rape. The Soviet officer corps encouraged the advancing Russian army in the use of sexual violence against German women and girls. The Russians, brutally treated by Hitler's army, returned the savagery in their advance through eastern and central Europe. Rape became a means of direct retaliation. The Great Patriotic War reached its nadir in central Europe with collective rape as a form of war against civilians. Victorious Japanese soldiers raped Chinese women as part of the spoils of war. Regardless of what country was involved, victorious armies practiced rape against civilian populations as one of the unspoken aspects of conquest.

Material destruction was great. Axis and Allied cities, centers of civilization and culture, were turned into wastelands by aerial bombing. The Germans bombed Rotterdam and Coventry. The British engineered the firebombing of Dresden. The German army destroyed Warsaw and Stalingrad. The United States leveled Hiroshima and Nagasaki. The nations of Europe had been weakened after World War I; after World War II, they were crippled. Europe was completely displaced from the position of world dominance it had held for centuries. The United States alone was undamaged and stronger after the war than before, its industrial capacity and production greatly improved by the war.

What would be the future of Europe? The leaders of the United States, Great Britain, and the Soviet Union—the Big Three as they were called—met three times between 1943 and 1945: first at Teheran; then in February 1945 at Yalta, a Russian Black Sea resort; and finally in July and August 1945 at Potsdam, a suburb of Berlin. They coordinated their attack on Germany and

A JAPANESE POET AT HIROSHIMA

■ *Hara Tamiki (1905–1951) was a Japanese poet who was living in Hiroshima when the atomic bomb exploded there on 6 August 1945. His poem "Glittering Fragments" tells about what he saw. Himself a victim of the bomb's radioactivity, he committed suicide in 1951.*

HARA TAMIKI. *GLITTERING FRAGMENTS*

Glittering fragments
Ashen embers
Like a rippling panorama,
Burning red then dulled.
Strange rhythm of human corpses.
All existence, all that could exist
Laid bare in a flash. The rest of the world
The swelling of a horse's corpse
At the side of an upturned train,
The smell of smouldering electric wires.

Churchill, Roosevelt, and Stalin—the Big Three—at the Yalta Conference. Stalin invoked the Yalta agreements to justify the Soviet Union's control over Eastern Europe after the war.

Japan and discussed their plans for postwar Europe. After Allied victory, the governments of both Germany and Japan would be totally abolished and completely reconstructed. No deals would be made with Hitler or his successors; no peace would be negotiated with the enemy; surrender would be unconditional. Germany would be disarmed and denazified and its leaders tried as war criminals. The armies of the Big Three would occupy Germany, each with a separate zone, but the country would be governed as a single economic unit. The Soviet Union, it was agreed, could collect reparations from Germany. With Germany and Japan defeated, a United Nations organization would provide the structure for a lasting peace in the world.

Stalin expected that the Soviet Union would decide the future of the territories of eastern Europe that the Soviet army had liberated from Germany. This area was vital to the security of the war-devastated Soviet Union; Stalin saw it as a protective barrier against another attack from the west. The Big Three agreed that Romania, Bulgaria, Hungary, Czechoslovakia, and Poland would have pro-Soviet governments. Since Soviet troops occupied these countries in 1945, there was little that the Anglo-Americans could do to prevent Russian

control unless they wanted to go to war against the USSR. Churchill realistically accepted this situation. But, for Americans who took seriously the proclamations of President Roosevelt that their country had fought to restore freedom and self-determination to peoples oppressed by tyranny, Soviet power in eastern Europe proved to be a bitter disappointment.

The presence of Soviet armies in eastern Europe guaranteed that communism would prevail there after 1945. In western Europe the American and British presence fostered the existence of parliamentary democracies. Germany was divided. A similar pattern emerged in Asia. The United States forces of occupation in Japan oversaw the introduction of democratic institutions. The USSR controlled Manchuria. Korea was divided. The celebration of victory after a war in which 50 million people died did not last long. Nor did the Anglo-American cooperation with the Soviet Union endure. With the defeat of Germany and Japan, the United States and the Soviet Union were the undisputed giants in world politics. Two ideological systems stood facing each other suspiciously across a divided Europe and a divided Asia.

SUGGESTIONS FOR FURTHER READING

THE COMING OF WORLD WAR II

* Paul Kennedy, *The Realities Behind Diplomacy: Background Influences on British External Policy, 1865–1980* (London: Allen & Unwin, 1981). Essay dealing with the continuity of appeasement in British foreign policy across two centuries.

* Ian Kershaw, *The Nazi Dictatorship* (London: Edward Arnold, 1985). A fine synthesis of key problems of interpretation regarding the Third Reich. Special attention is paid to the interdependence of domestic and foreign policy and the inevitability of war in Hitler's ideology.

Henry Rousso, *The Vichy Syndrome: History and Memory in France Since 1944* (Cambridge, MA, and London: Harvard University Press, 1991). Examines the collective memories of the French and the way they obscured widespread French collaboration with the Nazis.

* Donald Cameron Watt, *How War Came: The Immediate Origins of the Second World War* (London: Heinemann, 1989). An international historian chronicles the events leading to the outbreak of the war.

RACISM AND DESTRUCTION

* Renate Bridenthal, Atina Grossmann, and Marion Kaplan, eds., *When Biology Became Destiny: Women in Weimar and Nazi Germany* (New York: Monthly Review Press, 1984). A volume of essays pursuing common themes on the relation between sexism and racism in interwar and wartime Germany.

* Raul Hilberg, *The Destruction of the European Jews* (New York: Holmes and Meier, 1985), 3 vols. An exhaustive study of the annihilation of European Jews beginning with cultural precedents and antecedents. Examines step-by-step developments that led to extermination policies and contains valuable appendices on statistics and a discussion of sources.

* Charles S. Maier, *The Unmasterable Past: History, Holocaust, and German National Identity* (Cambridge, MA: Harvard University Press, 1988). A thoughtful discussion of the historical debate over the Holocaust and the comparative dimensions of the event. Especially valuable in placing the Holocaust within German history.

* Michael R. Marrus, *The Holocaust in History* (New York: New American Library, 1987). A comprehensive survey of all aspects of the Holocaust, including the policies of the Third Reich, the living conditions in the camps, and the prospects for resistance and opposition.

Gordon Martel, ed., *Modern Germany Reconsidered, 1870–1945* (London and New York: Routledge, 1992). Leading scholars of modern Germany provide surveys of the important historiographical issues and controversies in modern German history as well as their own interpretations.

ALLIED VICTORY

John Campbell, ed., *The Experience of World War II* (New York: Oxford University Press, 1989). This richly illustrated work provides an overview of the Second World War in both the Asian and European theaters, in terms of origins, events, and consequences.

* Akira Iriye, *The Origins of the Second World War in Asia and the Pacific* (London: Longman, 1987). Examines the events of the 1930s leading up to hostilities in the Pacific theaters with a special focus on Japanese isolation and aggression.

* John Keegan, *The Second World War* (New York: Viking, 1990). Provides a panoramic sweep of "the largest single event in human history," with special attention to warfare in all its forms and the importance of leadership.

* Indicates paperback edition available.

CHAPTER 33

Nationalism and Dependence in the Twentieth Century

NASSER: ARAB HERO AND VISIONARY

Never before in history had there been a funeral of its size. On 1 October 1970, over one million Egyptians flooded into an already overcrowded Cairo to mourn Gamal 'Abd al-Nasser (1918–70), president of Egypt, who had died of a heart attack two days before. An Egyptian radio announcer reported, "Words cannot describe the grief I am seeing," then signed off, overtaken by emotion.

Western observers could not understand this outpouring of grief for a man whose failures seemed to outnumber his accomplishments. Wasn't Nasser's regime one of the most repressive in modern Egyptian history? Didn't his 1967 confrontation with Israel, designed to eliminate the "dagger stuck in the Arab heart," end in humiliation? Didn't the centralized economic planning he promoted have disastrous results? Even the construction of the Aswan High Dam, a pet project designed to ensure a regular water supply from the Nile for cultivators, caused the salinization of once-productive soil and drove ruined peasants to curse his name.

If Nasser's legacy was to be counted in these terms, he would certainly have been more vilified than celebrated. But like other nationalist leaders of his generation—Sukarno of Indonesia, Nehru of India, Jou En-lai of the People's Republic of China, Tito of Yugoslavia—Nasser, a man who rose from provincial middle-class roots to become a world statesman, embodied all the possibilities latent in the new postcolonial world. The failures of Nasser and his cohorts throughout the third world, while perhaps inevitable, must be counted among the great tragedies of the twentieth century.

Nasser, unlike those who had ruled Egypt through mid-century, was "fellahi," of the people. He was born in 1918 in a provincial town in Upper Egypt, the son of a postal clerk. He went to secondary school and military college in Cairo, where he became a lecturer after graduation.

Nasser was in Cairo during the Second World War and witnessed an event that many Egyptians described as the greatest humiliation of national honor since British troops occupied the country in 1882. Fearing that the German successes in the North Africa campaign threatened Britain's position in Egypt, the British representative in Cairo ordered British tanks to surround the palace of the Egyptian king to force the king to dismiss the government and install another government more to British liking.

Disgusted by the shame of this event, Nasser formed a group known as the Free Officers from among his colleagues to promote the Egyptian nationalist cause in the ranks of the army. The incompetence displayed by the Egyptian military and civilian leadership during the First Palestine War in 1948 (in which Nasser was gravely wounded) further convinced him of the need to expunge the corruption that sapped national strength. In July 1952, the Free Officers staged a coup d'etat and within a year deposed the monarchy and declared Egypt a republic. By 1954, Nasser was the undisputed leader of Egypt.

Nasser's vision for Egypt and the Arab world was shared by many Egyptians. He sought to win true Egyptian independence by eliminating the last remnants of British colonial control in the country. He negotiated the withdrawal of British troops from the Suez Canal zone and when, in the wake of his nationalization of the canal, the British, French, and Israelis colluded to reverse the nationalization and overthrow him, he emerged from the crisis a victor in the eyes of most Egyptians and Arabs. The three invading countries were forced to withdraw their forces from Egypt, the canal remained in Egyptian hands, and British prime minister Anthony Eden (1897–1977) retired from the confrontation a broken man.

A hero to the Arab world, Nasser sought to make the Middle East a major player in international politics. He railed against the region's artificial political divisions and promoted pan-Arab unity, spreading his message via the largest radio transmitter in the world. When opposed by other Arab leaders (whom he called "feudalists"), he took his case directly to the Arab masses. "Take the dwarf," he told the Jordanian population, referring to King Hussein, "and hang him from the gates of the British embassy." After making a decision that angered the United States, he announced, "If the Americans don't like it, they can drink from the sea (i.e., go to hell). And if the Mediterranean is not big enough, there is the Red Sea as well."

Like many other third-world nationalists of his time, Nasser refused to be drawn into the Cold War on either side. According to Nasser, Egypt's role in the world was not to be defined by either the United States or the Soviet Union. He therefore advocated a policy of nonalignment between the two superpowers, and he represented Egypt and the Arab world at the Bandung Convention of 1955, the first summit conference of nonaligned leaders.

"The annals of history are full of heroes who carved for themselves great and heroic roles and played them on momentous occasions on the stage," he wrote in his *The Philosophy of the Revolution*.

> History is also charged with great heroic roles which do not find actors to play them on the stage. I do not know why I always imagine that in this region in which we live there is a role wandering aimlessly about seeking an actor to play it. I do not know why this role, tired of roaming about in this vast region which extends to every place around us, should at last settle down, weary and worn out, on our frontiers beckoning us to move, to dress up for it, and to perform it, since there is nobody else who can do so.

Although stung by the failure of Egyptian-Syrian unification and defeat at the hands of Israel in 1967, Nasser remained larger than life. Even Nasser's successor as president of Egypt, Anwar al-Sadat (1918–81), who reversed many of Nasser's policies and who lived most of his life in Nasser's shadow, bitter because he never achieved the same popularity he thought was his due, remarked, "Nasser's death was a tragedy for the Arab world."

Latin America Since 1870: Economic Development and Social Upheaval

The last half of the nineteenth century brought profound changes to Latin America. In almost every major country there was a long period of relative stability, built on an alliance between landed oligarchies and dictators. Responding to market opportunities in industrialized Europe and the United States, often in cooperation with foreign entrepreneurs, Latin American oligarchs constructed burgeoning economies based on the export of agricultural and mineral commodities to these areas. In the short term, economic expansion solidified the hold of the ruling classes. Railroads, for example, enabled governments to master ever wider territories, for they could quickly dispatch soldiers vast distances to enforce their authority. Increased government revenues enlarged bureaucracies. In the long term, however, economic development undermined oligarchical rule, for it created two new classes, the urban middle and working classes; and it alienated an ancient class, the peasantry. The struggles of the former to obtain equal opportunity in both the political and economic spheres and the latter two for social and economic justice tore apart Latin American society after 1900. In Argentina, Brazil, and Chile the so-called "social question" destabilized politics, leading to a pattern of alternating civilian democracies and military dictatorships. In Mexico societal divisions led to a revolution, whose violent phase lasted nearly a decade. The resulting reform was sufficient to formulate a stable political structure since the 1920s. The issues of equity and justice, however, remain throughout Latin America as we approach the turn of a new century.

Latin America and the World Economy

Demand for agricultural commodities for consumers and raw materials for industry created markets for Latin American products in Europe and the United States. Innovations in technology, business management, and finance facilitated the movement of products from Latin America to these markets.

A population explosion in Europe stimulated demand for Latin American products. There was enormous pressure to use land more efficiently. This situation limited extensive agriculture like livestock raising.

Great Britain, for example, did not have enough land to raise sheep to satisfy the demand for mutton for its dinner tables and wool for its textile mills. To increase staple crop production required fertilizers. Moreover, relatively prosperous Europeans wanted not only more beef and mutton, but also luxury items such as bananas and coffee. Latin America responded. The great plains of Argentina, called the Pampas, became a vast supplier of sheep and cattle for the British market. Chilean nitrates and Peruvian guano fertilized the fields of Europe. Central American bananas and Brazilian and Colombian coffee enriched European and North American breakfasts.

Spectacular innovations in technology, management, and finance also spurred economic growth. The widespread use of electricity stimulated the Chilean copper industry. The invention of the automobile created a need for petroleum. Mexico and Venezuela became leading producers of oil. The demand for rubber for automobile tires and conveyor belts caused a boom in the Brazilian Amazon. The refrigerator ship radically changed Argentina, creating a meatpacking industry to slaughter and prepare cattle before shipment to foreign markets. Improvements in communications and transportation extended the export economy into the interior. The railroad was the most crucial technological innovation, for improved transportation and communications united regionally divided countries. The rise of modern corporations, banks, and investment houses transferred the capital surpluses of prosperous Europe and the United States to Latin America to exploit its

Chilean nitrates being loaded aboard ships in the port of Pisagua, ca. 1890.

resources. Foreign investment in transportation, mining, food processing, and manufacturing underwrote Latin American economic development.

Population pressures in Europe and the lure of a better life in the New World induced immigration to Latin America. Italians and Spaniards transformed Argentina. Portuguese, Italians, Germans, and Japanese greatly influenced Brazil.

Economic development through exports profoundly altered the social structure of Latin America. In the cities two new adversarial classes, industrialists and workers, arose. In the countryside, the delicate balance between large and small landowners disintegrated. Large landowners expropriated peasant-owned land made more valuable by commercial agriculture. A new middle class arose from the opportunities presented in the burgeoning cities and expanded government bureaucracies. Large landholders, who had long dominated the region, had to adjust to the challenges of new classes. The upper classes resisted sharing either political and economic influence or opportunity.

The "Golden Age" of the Landed Oligarchy, 1870–1920

Toward the end of the nineteenth century many Latin American nations ended decades of civil war and entered prolonged periods of stability under either a long-term dictatorship or a firm, landowning oligarchy. The greatest of these dictators was Porfirio Díaz (1830–1915), who dominated Mexico from 1877 to 1911. In Chile the great landowners of the Central Valley, in Argentina the cattle barons of the Pampas, and in Brazil coffee plantation owners (*fazenderos*) ran their nations efficiently for their own benefit.

Peace and stability brought spectacular economic growth. During the Díaz dictatorship, Mexico's per capita national income doubled. In the last quarter of the nineteenth century the acreage under cultivation in the Pampas increased by fifteen times, all for export crops. Brazilian coffee production more than tripled.

But there were hints of problems to come. Volatile export markets experienced cycles of boom and bust. The downturns were successively deeper and caused more suffering. Depressions occurred in the early 1890s, 1907, 1920–1921, and 1929. The dislocations caused by these depressions created social unrest, especially among the vulnerable middle classes, whose upward mobility proved precarious, and the working classes, who suffered periodic unemployment.

There were two wars fought over control of export commodities. With valuable nitrate fields at stake, Chile defeated Peru and Bolivia in the War of the Pacific (1879–83), devastating the latter two nations' politics and economy for decades. The United States embarked upon war with Spain in 1898 in part to protect the interests of its citizens in sugar plantations in Cuba.

Prosperity did not guarantee that oligarchies would always agree among themselves. An alliance of disgruntled landowners and military officers overthrew the Brazilian monarchy in 1889. Civil war erupted in Chile in 1890. The turn of the century brought the War of the Thousand Days in Colombia, a vicious conflict during which 100,000 people died.

Social currents eroded the oligarchies' control. They sometimes found themselves divided among the conflicting interests of industrialists and large landowners. An emerging urban middle class sought equality of opportunity both in business and politics. The working class, centered in export-related occupations (miners, railroaders, meatpackers, stevedores), wanted to share in the prosperity of the booming economies. The large influx of immigrants into Argentina added to working-class agitation, for they brought with them from Europe lessons in radical ideology and labor organization. Most important in Mexico, the export economy pushed peasants from their lands as the oligarchy sought to expand commercial agricultural production and to increase the availability of cheap labor.

For the long term, the growth in the strength and influence of the Latin American military would have the most important impact. In the last quarter of the nineteenth century, the oligarchies, funded by export revenues, transformed the ragged guerrilla armies led by charismatic leaders that characterized the fifty years after independence into professionalized armed forces. At first led by the sons of the upper classes, the officer corps after 1900 attracted second-generation immigrants and other members of the middle class who saw the military as a means of upward mobility. Better trained, armed, and paid, the military evolved as a crucial, independent force, one that would soon come to dominate Latin American politics.

The last one-third of the nineteenth century also saw the emergence of the United States as the preeminent economic and political power in Latin America, replacing Great Britain. By the end of World War I, the United States was the region's most important trading partner and investor. Only Argentina escaped its dominance. After the Spanish-American-Cuban War (1898) and the

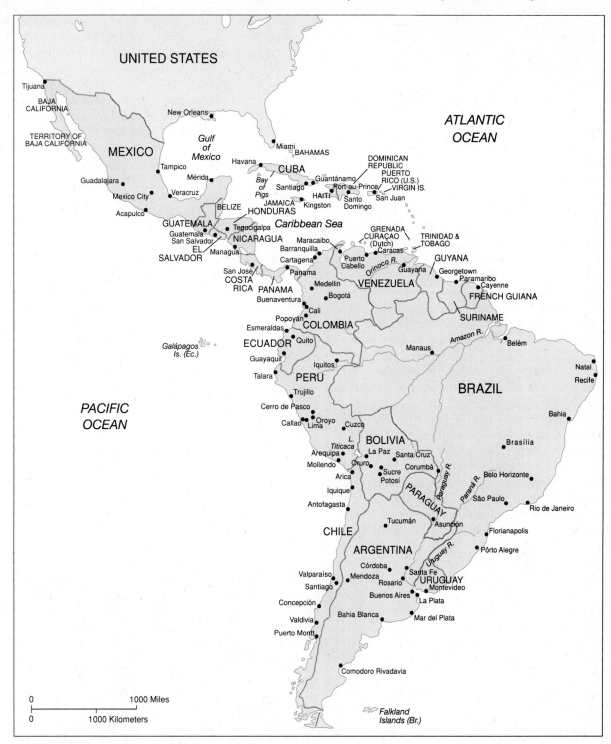

Modern Latin America

completion of the Panama Canal (1914) the United States took upon itself the additional role of policeman of the hemisphere. In order to protect its trade, investments, and canal, the United States regularly meddled and intervened militarily in Mexico and the Caribbean.

The Emergence of the Popular Classes: Populism and Revolution, 1900–1964

As the twentieth century began, access to politics was severely limited. The right to vote depended on literacy, property, or gender. As the middle class grew, its members demanded their fair share of economic opportunity and government offices. Workers clamored for a better life. The crucial question of the first two decades of the new century was how the oligarchy would respond to the demands of the middle and lower classes, whether they would repress their challengers or make concessions to them. In Argentina and Chile, the oligarchies made reluctant concessions. In other countries, like Brazil, the working class did not organize extensively or effectively enough to threaten the oligarchy until after World War II. In Mexico the lower classes participated in a revolution.

There were two critical factors in determining whether or not violent upheaval occurred. One was the role of the middle class. In most countries the middle class sided with the oligarchy because it, too, feared the lower classes. In Mexico, however, the middle class allied with the lower classes because the oligarchy refused them even minimal concessions. The second factor was the ability of the oligarchy to remain united. In most instances it did, but in Mexico the oligarchy split, some joining the revolutionaries.

The large landowners of Argentina at first resisted the demands of the urban middle and working classes. In the second decade of the new century, however, they reached a compromise in which they determined to allow middle-class political participation through the adoption in 1912 of universal male suffrage. The Radical party (*Unión Cívica Radical*), which was comprised of members of the middle class of Argentina's major city, Buenos Aires, and elements of the large landowning class, was the vehicle of this compromise. Led by the eccentric Hipólito Yrigoyen (1852–1933) and run by means of political patronage, much like the urban political machines in the United States at the same time, the Radicals (who were somewhat less than their name implied) elected Yrigoyen as president in 1916. But the ruling class was not willing to include the working class in politics or recognize its economic aspirations. Strikes were brutally repressed. Conservative landowners and the military, dissatisfied with their handling of the depression, overthrew the Radicals in 1930.

The need for attention to the demands of the working class led to the rise of a populist leader, Juan Perón (1895–1974), a colonel in the Argentine army, who won the support of organized labor, industrialists, and elements of the military that rose from the middle class. Perón dislodged the landed oligarchy for nearly ten years, from 1946 to 1955, when he fell to a military coup. This coup began the long cycle of alternating civilian and military regimes that continued through the 1980s.

Zapatistas—*followers of the Mexican revolutionary leader Emiliano Zapata—resting and receiving orders before attacking federal troops.*

THE MEXICAN CONSTITUTION OF 1917: ARTICLE 27

■ *The Mexican Constitution of 1917 was the most radical document of its type at that time. Article 27 provided the basis for the sweeping land reform that took place in spurts from 1917 to 1940. It also reestablished the Mexican nation's ownership of its natural resources (known as subsoil rights).*

Article 27. Ownership of the lands and waters within the boundaries of the national territory is vested originally in the nation, which has had, and has, the right to transmit title thereof to private persons . . .

The Nation at all times shall have the right to impose on private property such limitations as the public interest may demand, as well as to regulate the utilization of natural resources . . . in order to ensure more equitable distribution of public wealth. With this end in view, necessary measures shall be taken to divide up large landed estates; to develp small landed holdings . . . to create new agricultural centers . . . Centers of population which at present either have no lands or water or which do not possess them in sufficient quantities for the needs of their inhabitants, shall be entitled to grants thereof, which shall be taken from adjacent properties . . .

In the nation is vested the direct ownership of all natural resources . . . of all minerals or substances . . . .

This translation of the Constitution and its amendments was published by the Organization of American States in 1972.

Chile followed a somewhat different road from Argentina. After a decade of bloody strikes, many Chileans, seeking compromise, elected Arturo Alessandri (1868–1950) president in 1920. But the oligarchy blocked all progress until 1924, when a group of impatient young military officers ousted him and enacted far-reaching reforms. The slowness of reforms led to the proclamation of a socialist republic in 1932, which lasted twelve days. A Popular Front coalition of working- and middle-class parties governed during the late 1930s and World War II, but the oligarchy continued to thwart meaningful change. No Chilean political party or leader formed as successful a coalition as Juan Perón's in Argentina, for organized labor was not nearly as powerful in Chile.

Unlike in Argentina and Chile, the upper class in Mexico did not form a united front against the lower classes. It fragmented as a result of conflicting economic interests during the depression of 1907. The middle class joined with peasants and workers to overthrow Porfirio Díaz in 1911. Rallying around Francisco I. Madero (1873–1913), a large landholder, the lower classes armed themselves. Their leaders, like Emiliano Zapata (1879–1919), who headed a predominantly peasant

movement in the southern and central part of the country, and Francisco "Pancho" Villa (1878–1923), who headed a heterogeneous movement of northern small landholders, workers, cowboys, and middle class, fought on for nearly a decade of bitter, bloody civil war.

Victory in the upheaval was taken by the middle class, which conceded a considerable number of reforms to the lower classes in return for their support. The Mexican constitution of 1917, which included land redistribution, a progressive labor code, and democratization of the political system, was the most radical document written to that time.

Over the course of the next three decades the revolutionary regime created a single-party state that incorporated the lower classes. Labor unions and peasant leagues cooperated with the national party and in return received land and employment. The greatest wave of reform took place in the late 1930s under the presidency of Lázaro Cárdenas (1895–1970). He distributed 45 million acres to land-hungry peasants.

Demands from below continued, from peasants for more land and from workers for better wages and working conditions. Two strategies evolved to resolve these issues. After mid-century the oligarchies of

Latin America lost much of their coercive power to national militaries. The armed services became the fulcrum of politics, for the most part allying with conservative landowners and industrialists, but on occasion supporting leaders who appealed to the masses. From the 1930s onward, Latin America alternated between cycles of dictatorship and democracy, depending on which side the military and the middle classes chose to ally. In Argentina, Chile, and Brazil the rapid growth of the cities transformed the political base. The urban working and middle classes took on increasingly important roles. It was to the urban masses that populist leaders such as Perón appealed and from whom the conservative military regimes exacted the greatest retribution.

The most successful populist leader was Juan Perón in Argentina, who used his position of secretary of labor in the military government of the mid-1940s to build enormous support among labor organizations in Buenos Aires. Elected president in 1946, Perón redistributed wealth from the landed oligarchy to workers. His wife, Eva Duarte de Perón (1919–52), a beautiful actress, had a charismatic hold on the Argentine masses. But Perón's formula did not last through the economic hard times of the early 1950s. He was overthrown by the military in 1955.

In the 1950s democratic regimes led most of Latin America. But during the 1960s, as a result of growing class conflict and the fear spread by the example of the Cuban Revolution of 1959, democracy gave way to dictatorship. The ruling classes were unwilling to tolerate the possibility of a Communist revolution, and the military and middle class sided with the oligarchy. The formula yielded increasingly brutal right-wing military dictatorships: Brazil in 1964, Argentina in 1966 and 1976, Chile in 1973, and Uruguay in 1973. In the cases of Brazil and Chile, these militaries were closely associated with and received substantial backing from the United States.

Fidel Castro (b. 1927) toppled the dictatorship of Fulgencio Batista (1901–73) in Cuba and stormed onto the international scene on New Year's Day 1959. After two years of consolidating his rule, Castro defied the United States and declared himself and his movement Communist. He vowed to export his revolution throughout Latin America and to create a "New Socialist" Cuba. Castro entered into an alliance with the Soviet Union, which supplied the island with much-needed machinery and arms and a market for Cuba's sugar.

Castro actively fostered revolutionary movements throughout Latin America during the 1960s. The ruling

Soviet premier Nikita Khrushchev (right) has a friendly greeting for Cuban premier Fidel Castro on the floor of the United Nations General Assembly in New York in 1960.

classes in alliance with the military, and often with the support of the United States (which trained Latin American militaries in counterinsurgency and government administration), harshly repressed popular opposition to their regimes.

The Reign of Terror and the Rebirth of Democracy, 1964–1990

The years after World War II brought unprecedented change to Latin America. Advances in disease prevention and treatment, and in agricultural technology (the so-called Green Revolution) created a population explosion. Brazil, with 150 million people in 1990, had doubled its population in just thirty years. Mexico, with 90 million inhabitants, had more than doubled in the same period. The heavy concentration of land ownership in the hands of a small elite combined with the burgeoning population to push millions from rural areas into the cities. The attraction of better employment possibilities and educational and health facilities added a strong pull to this migration. Buenos Aires, Mexico City, and São Paulo came to rank among the largest metropolises in the world.

Latin American elites sought economic development. They chose to industrialize through partnerships between themselves, governments they controlled, and foreign companies. Their plans were threatened by a surge of popular protests during the 1960s. Frightened by Castro's revolution and scattered urban terrorism and determined to compete in the world economy through the maintenance of low wages, the ruling classes of Argentina, Brazil, and Chile, in conjunction with the militaries of these nations, imposed brutal dictatorships.

In a reversal of the roles of a century, Latin American militaries gained the dominant position in the partnership between them and the upper classes. Rearmed and retrained by the United States Alliance for Progress programs, the militaries developed a deepened sense of mission and conviction that theirs was the only institution that had the ability to govern. The middle classes, worried that revolution was at their doorsteps, supported them.

The most tyrannical regimes ruled in Argentina, which between 1976 and 1983 murdered 10,000 people and imprisoned and tortured many more, and in Chile, after the overthrow of the democratically elected socialist government in 1973. In Chile and Brazil (though not in Argentina) the military dictatorships presided over long periods of economic growth. The benefits from this growth were limited to the upper class, however.

The era of brutal repression ended in the 1980s. In Brazil the military eased out of government, discredited by its inability to manage the economy. A humiliating defeat in the Malvinas War in 1983 against Great Britain awakened Argentina from its nightmare. Oppression had not eliminated either the desire of Latin Americans for democracy or their striving for economic and social equity. The collapse of communism in the Soviet Union and Eastern Europe toward the end of the decade eliminated the threat from the left that had long justified the harsh regimes.

The major trouble spot in the 1980s was Central America. The Frente Sandinista de Liberación Nacional, or Sandinistas, ousted long-term dictator Anastasio Somoza (1925–80) in 1978. The United States financed a ten-year "Contra" war against the Sandinistas under presidents Ronald Reagan and George Bush. Nicaraguans themselves voted out the Sandinistas in 1990, tired of economic failure and civil war.

Latin American Wars, 1808–1982

1808–24	Wars of Independence
1829	Mexico war with Spain; invasion quickly repelled
1836	Texas War resulted in independence of Texas from Mexico
1836–39	War between Chile and Bolivia-Peru Confederation
1846–48	Mexico–United States War; Mexico lost one-half its national territory
1859–61	War of the Reform in Mexico between liberals and conservatives
1861	Intervention in Mexico by France, Great Britain, and Spain; latter two withdrew
1862–67	French intervention; French install Maximilian as emperor of Mexico in 1864
1865–70	War between Paraguay and Triple Alliance, consisting of Brazil, Uruguay, and Argentina; Paraguayan population decimated
1879–83	War of the Pacific between Chile and an alliance of Bolivia and Peru
1895–98	Cuban War of Independence
1898–99	Cuban-Spanish-American War ended Spanish colonial rule; United States protectorate lasted until 1934
1899–1903	Thousand Days War; Colombia torn apart by civil war
1910–20	Mexican Revolution ended thirty-four-year dictatorship of Porfirio Díaz
1932–35	Chaco War between Bolivia and Paraguay resulted in bloody defeat for Bolivia
1949–53	La Violencia in Colombia; vicious civil war
1982	Malvinas War

A mural of the figures of the revolution by the Mexican artist Diego Rivera. Influential foreign companies are depicted at the top; in the middle are journalists and intellectuals, along with the two opposing political leaders, Francisco Madero and Porfirio Díaz; at the bottom are the Indian peons.

Society and Culture, 1870 to the Present

Export-led economic development and industrialization profoundly changed Latin America. In the 1990s Latin Americans live mostly in urban areas. Only in Central America and Paraguay are more than half the people engaged in agriculture. Despite the migration from the countryside, there are not enough jobs. Even Brazil and Mexico, which have industrialized to the extent that they can no longer be considered underdeveloped, cannot generate sufficient employment for their citizens. Vast slums have sprung up on the outskirts of all the major cities. Without sanitation, utilities or schools, the *barrios* or *favelas* as they are called, teem

with children, soon to reach unemployable adulthood. Although there have been periods of advancements, such as in Argentina under Perón, the working class has experienced a continual deterioration in its standard of living, most acutely since the mid-1960s. In order to finance development, Latin American nations borrowed heavily abroad in the 1970s, so that by 1990 Latin American nations had compiled national debts totaling more than $400 billion. Brazil and Mexico together accounted for more than half this amount. Repayment of interest and principal absorbed a growing percentage of the national income, allowing little if any investment in industry, agriculture, or public works. Inflation, sometimes reaching the level of 1000 percent a year or more, has destroyed savings and investment, and produced downward mobility among the middle class. Government policies have widened the gap between rich and poor.

Despite the profound transformations in other aspects of Latin American life, the status of women has not greatly improved. In most Latin American nations they did not acquire the vote until the mid-twentieth century. Suffrage, moreover, did not mean equality under the law. Even in such reputedly egalitarian settings as revolutionary Cuba, there has been a notable absence of women among the highest leadership. Women have achieved the presidencies of Argentina, Bolivia, and Nicaragua, although only Violeta Barrios de Chamorro in Nicaragua was elected to the post. Industrialization and urbanization have affected the position of women somewhat in that in some areas like northern Mexico, female workers earn significant wages and have altered the balance of male and female in family structures. Neither phenomenon has raised urban women heads-of-household from their poverty or middle-class women to positions of high responsibility.

Poverty and despair have not, however, destroyed the indomitable spirit of the people. Latin American art and literature have attained the highest pinnacles. Novelists such as the Colombian Gabriel García Márquez (b. 1928), with his mystical tales that skewer the tyrannies of the upper classes in *One Hundred Years of Solitude* and *Autumn of the Patriarch*; Euclides da Cunha (1866–1909), who exposed the brutality of the massacres of Canudos in Brazil in the 1890s in *Rebellion in the Backlands*; and Mariano Azuela (1873–1952), who revealed the real Mexican Revolution in *The Underdogs*, to name but three of dozens, rival all the great literature of the nineteenth and twentieth centuries. The Mexican painter-muralists, David Alfaro Siquieros (1896–1974), Diego Rivera (1886–1957), and Rufino Tamayo (b. 1899), laid bare the Mexican soul.

Despite more than a century of struggle, the "social question" in Latin America remains unanswered. The gap between rich and poor is greater than in 1850 and widening. Only Brazil and Mexico have constructed a substantial manufacturing base that can compete in foreign markets and have begun to develop domestic markets. The entire region continues its dependence on the export of agricultural and mineral products for their economic well-being. Latin American political systems are held in precarious balance by the need of the ruling classes to regain their credibility after decades of brutal rule, and the lower classes fear that too-strident demands will lead to the recurrence of tyranny.

Africa Since 1919: Resistance, Success, and Disillusion

The scramble for Africa both partitioned Africa's territory and amalgamated its peoples. Although colonial borders drawn up in European capitals divided certain peoples between different colonies, the great bulk of the estimated 10,000 African kinship groups, chiefdoms, and states of varying sizes were combined to form some forty new territories ruled from Europe. As the importance of local big men was eclipsed even where they remained a real factor in politics, these new colonies served as the main political stage for Africans. Most educated Africans quickly realized that real political power lay in the colonial capital and in Europe and that opposition to the colonial system had to be organized on a territory-wide basis if it were to be effective.

Political change was not the sole product of the scramble. The twentieth century also saw revolutions in the consciousness of ordinary Africans, with new perspectives fueling the eventual African drive against colonial control. One such change was in the area of religious beliefs. Wider acceptance of Islam and, especially, Christianity helped end locally oriented cultural beliefs and contributed to a growing opposition to colonialism on ethical grounds. Even more important was the growing awareness among both workers and peasants that the labor, tax, and agricultural policies of the colonial regimes were fundamentally worsening their economic welfare. When World War II left the colonial powers too weak and too poor to resist determined efforts to overthrow colonialism, the colonial system's days were numbered. The exceptions to this general trend were the Portuguese, whose neutrality in the war and dictatorial governmental system left them able to resist decolonialization until the mid-1970s, and the white-dominated states of South Africa and Rhodesia (now Zimbabwe), where the growth of highly authoritarian systems of *apartheid* and segregation checked effective resistance until the 1970s.

The "Second Occupation" of Africa

World War I left European nations prostrate economically and deeply indebted to the United States for war loans. Impoverishment prompted the colonial powers to reassess their attitude toward their African territories. Before the war they had been content to make the

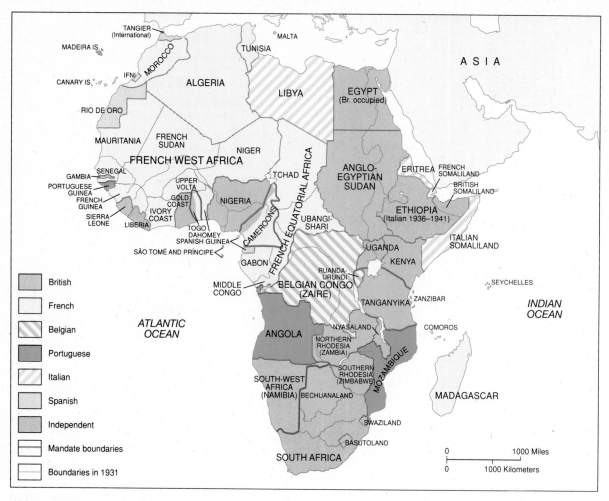

Africa, ca. 1919

colonies pay for their administrative costs. In the years after the war, however, they viewed the colonies as sources for raw materials to be purchased with their own weak currencies instead of obtaining them on the world market with scarce hard currency. They moved to make the colonies of real positive value to themselves.

In what some historians have termed "the second occupation of Africa," the colonial regimes intensified their operations to maximize Africa's benefit to them by increasing pressures on Africans, "occupying" the four types of African economies as they had not done before. In some areas, such as in parts of the Belgian Congo, Mozambique, Angola, and French Equatorial Africa, the state forcibly compelled Africans to grow cotton and other commodities. In others, such as Zimbabwe and Kenya, peasants saw the free market on which they had sold their tobacco, corn, cotton, and other products be-

fore World War I destroyed, as the state's bureaucracy manipulated the market to drive down commodity prices and give European settlers major competitive advantages. West African peasants suffered a similar fate, not from settlers but at the hands of large trading companies that were powerful enough to set prices as they desired. In other areas, such as Mozambique and Malawi, where labor migrancy had come to dominate the economy, tight governmental controls ended free voluntary migrancy and resulted in reduced wages. And in concession areas, concession companies used ever larger amounts of forced labor to increase the production of the crops they wanted. (See Special Feature, "The Power of Words," pp. 1020–1021.)

These interventions in the economy would have angered workers, agriculturalists, and those seeking economic advancement in any case, but they were made

THE FREEDOM CHARTER OF THE
AFRICAN NATIONAL CONGRESS, 1955

■ *In 1955, as part of its efforts to rally increased support behind its opposition to the South African government's policies of apartheid, the African National Congress met at Kliptown and endorsed the Freedom Charter, a document that remains the projected political guide for a South Africa under African National Congress leadership.*

We, the People of South Africa, declare for all our country and the world to know: that South Africa belongs to all who live in it, black and white, and that no government can justly claim authority unless it is based on the will of all the people; that our people have been robbed of their birthright to land, liberty, and peace by a form of government founded on injustice and inequality; that our country will never be prosperous or free until all our people live in brotherhood enjoying equal rights and opportunities; that only a democratic state, based on the will of all the people, can secure to all their birthrights without distinction of colour, race, sex or belief . . .

The national wealth of our country, the heritage of all South Africans, shall be restored to the people. The mineral wealth beneath the soil, the banks and monopoly industry shall be transferred to the ownership of the people as a whole. All other industry and trade shall be controlled to assist the well-being of the people. All people shall have equal rights, to trade where they choose, to manufacture and to enter all trades, crafts and professions.

Restrictions of land ownership on a racial basis shall be ended, and all the land redivided amongst those who work it, to banish famine and land hunger . . . The law shall guarantee to all their right to speak, to organise, to meet together, to publish, to preach, to worship, and to educate their children. The privacy of the house from police raids shall be protected by law. All shall be free to travel without restriction from countryside to town, from province to province, and from South Africa abroad. Pass Laws, permits and all other laws restricting these freedoms shall be abolished.

Excerpts from the Freedom Charter, printed in *Forward to Freedom: Documents of the National Policies of the African National Congress of South Africa.*

even more offensive because they took place at a time of fundamental changes in the world economy that made their impact even more damaging. The first of these changes was the Great Depression. Usually the Depression is seen as starting in late 1929, but collapses in European commodity markets occurred as early as the mid-1920s, putting great pressure on African producers of raw materials. Once the Depression started, many workers were fired and rural Africans were reduced to the deepest poverty that they had known for decades, with many unable to purchase clothing and forced to revert to wearing bark cloth. While the outbreak of World War II and the postwar efforts to rebuild the world economy resulted in a great demand for African raw materials and ended the terrible poverty of the

1930s, a scarcity of imported goods and a great increase in inflation cut the purchasing power of Africans. The economic distress of ordinary Africans in the 1920s was thus continued into the 1940s.

Discontent was not restricted to rural dwellers and unskilled migrant workers. Because the growing colonial economies were also increasingly complex, skilled workers were also needed for work on railways, dock facilities, and in mines. These workers soon discovered, however, that no matter how skilled they became, they could not advance up the employment ladder. Whites held the best jobs, and, by using their political leverage, they blocked African advancement. Realizing their crucially important position in the colonial economies, these workers, beginning in the 1930s,

Young Congolese children carry the flag of the new Republic of Congo around a stadium in Leopoldville on 1 July 1960, the day the Congo formally received its independence from Belgium.

The Power of Words

The initial conquest of Africa involved sizable military expeditions and often resulted in many deaths. After the conquest, however, imperial domination generally took more subtle and ambiguous forms. Language, for example, was an important tool of control as colonialists sought to extract Africa's natural wealth and control millions of Africans through the power of words.

For certain kinds of exploitation, words were not necessary: terror and repression were enough. In the Congo rubber trade, for example, employees of King Leopold II simply blackmailed whole villages to produce "red rubber" until international horror at the atrocities committed stopped them. But for enterprises that required organization and discipline, such as mining and domestic service, communication between the colonized and the colonizer was essential. Hierarchies of power and authority had to be established on the basis of orders

given and orders understood. A shared language was the only way of moving toward sustained economic activity, efficiency, and profitability.

Europeans generally did not impose their own languages on Africans. Because of the racism of the period, most Europeans believed that Africans were incapable of learning European languages well. Nor did they take the time and trouble to learn the numerous languages of the peoples with whom they came into contact, for they doubted that there was anything to be gained by expending such energies. Instead, they used simple pidgin languages such as the South African *Fanagalo* ("Do it this way!"), a language with Zulu vocabulary and Afrikaans syntax, or simplified forms of a real language such as Swahili to communicate.

Particularly instructive is how Swahili, a trade language used in East Africa, was adopted as a *lingua franca*, or common language, in parts of colonial Zaire. Because of

the large number of languages spoken in the region, Europeans were reluctant to learn any one of them because of its limited range. Swahili, like European languages, is, however, not a tonal language and is fairly easy for Europeans to learn. Europeans felt that this easy language could be transplanted from East Africa and spread throughout the Congo basin. Thus, Catholic priests and Protestant missionaries adopted Swahili and produced vocabularies, training manuals, and catechisms in Swahili. Priests were even sent home if they were not properly trained in Swahili. In the same manner, the Belgian government required basic language instruction in Swahili for administrators before they left the home country.

Swahili did not remain restricted to mission stations and government offices, however. Migration from rural areas populated by Africans who could speak Swahili spread the language to newly created urban areas like Elizabethville (Lubumbashi) and into the towns around the Belgian-owned copper mines of colonial Zaire. Unlike European settlers, Africans showed a willingness to learn new languages quickly. Through such urban migration and the encouragement of Belgian overseers, Swahili became the common tongue of growing numbers of workers and urban dwellers.

While Europeans were willing to use Swahili to communicate with the workers, they did not speak the language grammatically. This is an important distinction. Many Europeans had access to vocabularies and used a blunt pidgin Swahili to give orders rather than explain ideas or express feelings. Nouns were limited to concrete objects.

True signs of language mastery—concern for syntax and grammar—were absent from Belgian training manuals. Verbs were listed only in their imperative forms—including the verb for "love," *penda!* Most verbs referred to movements connected with employer-employee relations and domestic and agricultural work.

In much the same way that modern tourists learn enough of a foreign language to order a meal or request the location of the restroom, Belgian managers and work bosses were content to control labor and increase output using narrow language skills that excluded the possibility of any discussion or exchange of ideas. This was true of the British in East Africa as well, in what became Tanzania, Uganda, Kenya, and Zanzibar. Natives identified the limited dialect the British spoke as *kiSetla* Swahili—the dialect of the settlers. The same pattern existed throughout colonial Africa, whether in Portuguese, French, or British areas, or in South Africa.

This situation prevented meaningful communication between European and Africans and reinforced stereotypes of each. Europeans concluded from their limited exchanges that Africans were, at best, childlike and simple and, at worst, idle, thieving, and dishonest. And what did Africans think of the Europeans? Because they possessed the power in the colonial situation, they were exceedingly dangerous. But because they were ignorant of the languages and customs of the people, they might be manipulated if one was lucky. What existed between Africans and Europeans in the colonial situation was, then, a silence borne of ignorance and misunderstanding.

The hierarchy of languages reinforced this silence. In 1908 the Charter of the Belgian Congo specified that French was the official language to be used at all state ceremonies. Africans, however, had no advanced training in French. Elementary French taught in mission schools was intended only to prepare the Congolese to serve their Belgian masters as servants and low-level clerks. Furthermore, all decrees and regulations were to be published in French and Flemish, but not in Swahili or any other African language. As a result, Africans could not read the laws that governed them, although they could hear the laws if they were translated for them into their languages by their own people.

Swahili, promoted by the state as the common language of work, expanded from being spoken by a few hundred people in the mid-nineteenth century in what is now central Zaire to become the language of millions, including entire urban populations and large numbers of rural dwellers. Just as the French language was an effective barrier to Congolese participation in public life, ignorance of Swahili's subtleties effectively excluded Europeans from the private lives and popular customs of the Congolese throughout the twentieth century. Within two generations, the Congolese were also able to use Swahili, encouraged originally as a language of deference and labor, as a bond of common identity and political resistance against their imperial rulers. The language imposed by the conqueror had become the language of potential liberation.

An advertisement published by the Empire Marketing Board of Great Britain in 1927 promotes products of the British African colonies.

staged a series of strikes over the issue. Clearly, a new worker consciousness was emerging. The impact of the Depression and the postwar inflation intensified this consciousness, and in the years after World War II full-scale labor unions were founded in much of Africa, from Senegal and Nigeria in West Africa to Kenya and Zambia in East and Central Africa as well as in South Africa.

It was on the basis of such discontent that the isolated frustrated, Western-educated African intellectuals of the years before World War I began to construct a general, broad-based political consensus directed against colonialism. These graduates of the mission schools knew colonialism was wrong not only because it violated Christian notions of equality, but, more to the point, because it checked their desire to advance as qualified educated people in colonial society. They sought out compatriots who were similarly frustrated and angry, and throughout the British and French African empires formal anticolonial political movements with popular support came into existence during the 1940s. In the Portuguese colonies and the Belgian Congo, police repression and the lack of a substantial group of educated Africans delayed the formation of such movements.

Of great long-term significance, most of these movements adopted the colonial territory itself as the appropriate stage for its activities. Thus they became "nationalist" movements that viewed the colony as a potential new nation. In areas where an ethnic minority had gained a superior niche in colonial society because of greater access to education—Nigeria, Ghana, Togo, Kenya, Uganda, and certain other colonies—ethnically based movements existed, yet such organizations were very much in the minority. Generally, however, the whites who ran the colonial regimes, not fellow Africans, were identified as the main enemy, and virtually all anticolonial sentiments in a territory were unified by the very presence of that enemy.

In the years after World War II, Britain and France, the major colonial powers, speedily realized that to try to retain power in their colonies for much longer would be both risky and costly. African anticolonial movements had become more powerful during the war, and the decolonialization of India, Burma, and Indonesia in the late 1940s convinced their leaders that African territories should follow in their path. Moreover, the United States and the United Nations were ideologically hostile to the retention of the old colonial empires, strongly believing in the desirability of free trade and free peoples, respectively. Finally, colonial wars proved costly both in manpower and resources. France fought a major war against the Algerian people and eventually capitulated, in 1962, because of its costs. While Britain successfully repressed the Mau Mau nationalists in Kenya between 1951 and 1956, it had been a hard fight, and both France and Britain learned that the retention of the colonies would be costly.

As an alternative to repression and war, therefore, the British and the French decided to transfer power to those African leaders whom they identified as "moderates," hoping that they would continue the former relationships between Africa and Europe. Once they had

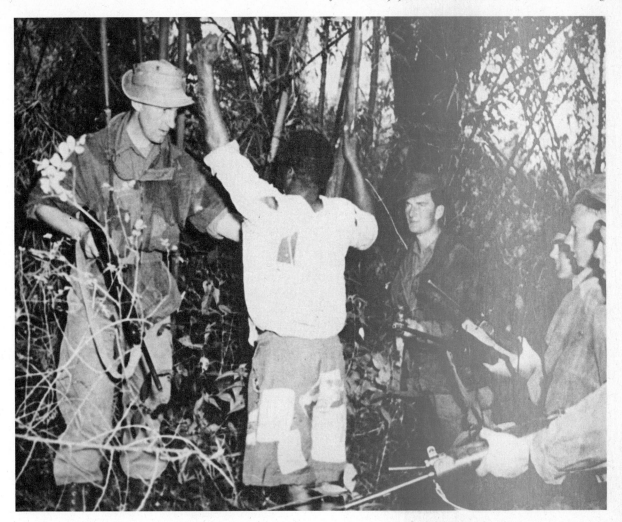

British Royal Irish Fusiliers searching a suspected Mau Mau fighter. Mau Mau *was the European name for a secret political movement that developed in Kenya in the late 1940s to promote independence from colonial rule. The government took action against the movement after its members began committing acts of terrorism in 1952.*

identified the "moderate" leadership in each colony, the colonial governments took quick action to grant independence. The first state in British Africa to gain its independence was Ghana, in 1957. The French colonies followed in rapid order. By 1965 virtually all French and British colonies had become independent.

There were exceptions to the process. In Guinea, for example, the search for the "moderate" leader failed, and the country fell under the leftist rule of Sekou Toure (1922–88). The Belgians left Zaire without having identified a leadership to which they could cede authority, and the result was instability, civil war, and the eventual establishment of a dictatorship under Sese Seko Mobutu (b. 1930). In Zimbabwe the white minority that was led by Ian Smith declared itself independent from Britain in 1966 so that it could sustain its rule over the majority African population. They were successful only until the end of the 1970s, when armed African resistance overcame them. The Portuguese also refused to grant independence to their colonies, but draining wars in Guinea-Bissau, Angola, and Mozambique, coupled with the refusal of the European Economic Community to grant Portugal membership for as long as it retained its colonies, resulted in the overthrow of the government in Portugal in 1974 and the termination of the long-enduring Portuguese empire in 1975.

South Africa Goes in the Opposite Direction

Yet while colonial Africa moved with deliberation toward political independence, the situation in South Africa, one of Africa's most important countries, moved in the opposite direction. After the formation in 1910 of the Union of South Africa from the territories of the Cape Colony, Natal, the Orange Free State, and the Transvaal, political power passed to a coalition of English and Afrikaner South Africans. Economic power remained almost wholly in the hands of the English-speaking white population. Both groups agreed that the proper role for the black majority was as quiet and obedient workers without political rights. After 1910, therefore, intense efforts were made to "keep the Africans in their place" while using underpaid African laborers to develop the white-dominated economy. The notorious Native Land Act of 1913, which split South Africa into two parts—87 percent for the minority whites and 13 percent for the majority blacks—was only one of a host of laws passed to reinforce racial segregation in the country and drive Africans from the land and into the workplace. Although black intellectuals organized the African National Congress (ANC) in 1912 to oppose this process, it remained elitist and weak until the mid-1940s. Only then did the economic importance of the black urban industrial workforce during the demanding years of World War II encourage a new ANC leadership to begin building alliances with black workers and peasants.

During the 1920s the political leadership of the Afrikaners was split between ardent nationalists, led by General J. B. M. Hertzog (1866–1942), who wanted to end South Africa's ties with Britain and establish a republic, and moderates, led by General Jan Smuts (1870–1950), who accepted political links to the British Empire and British economic dominance of the country. The Great Depression was a devastating experience in South Africa as it was elsewhere in Africa. The fact that Afrikaans-speaking whites, less well-educated and less wealthy than the English speakers, suffered great economic hardships fueled support for a new Afrikaner Nationalist Party, led by D. F. Malan (1874–1959), and made improvement of the economic position of Afrikaners one of its central aims. During the late 1930s and into the 1940s Afrikaner support gradually shifted from General Smuts's party to Malan's Nationalists. In the election of 1948 the Nationalists finally triumphed.

Once in power, the Nationalists moved quickly to replace the often ragged system of racial segregation that had characterized South Africa for centuries with a new, far more systematic and ruthless version known as *apartheid* ("apartness"). Under the guidance of the Nationalist Party's ideologue, Hendrik Verwoerd (1901–66), a host of laws were passed during the 1950s that regulated and curtailed contact between whites and blacks at every level of existence. Finally, in 1961, as an end to the process of laying the foundations of apartheid, South Africa left the British Commonwealth and became a republic.

While the Afrikaners were monopolizing political power and increasing their economic power, black Africans were also organizing. Influential African labor unions were established during the war years, and steps were taken to rejuvenate the old African National Congress (ANC) by building alliances between its intellectuals and discontented workers and rural dwellers. Among those in the forefront of this effort were Anton Lembede (1914–47) and Nelson Mandela (b. 1918). By the 1950s the ANC had become a mass organization able to sponsor mass resistance to the apartheid system, and in 1955 it published the Freedom Charter, a blueprint for a post-apartheid South Africa that has remained its basic

African nationalist leader Nelson Mandela addressing a crowd at London's Wembley Stadium in 1990. The head of the African National Congress was imprisoned by the South African government for more than 27 years.

constitution. Government repression of all such resistance increased throughout the 1950s until finally, after the Sharpeville Massacre on 21 March 1960, in which police killed sixty-nine blacks, the state banned resistance of every kind and jailed the leaders of the ANC and other opposition groups.

During the 1960s white South Africans seemed secure in their dominance and black South Africans appeared to be checkmated. The South African government created "Bantustans," homelands for the African population ruled by puppets chosen by the South African authorities, as arenas into which black political ambitions could be channeled, and large numbers of "surplus people" were forcibly removed from white areas of South Africa to them. In the 1970s, however, this domination began to erode. Illegal labor unions began to go out on strike and gain their demands. The new ideology of Black Consciousness, espoused by Steve Biko (1947–77) and advocating black pride, gained many adherents, especially among the young. The ANC's efforts to stigmatize apartheid internationally gradually succeeded, and South Africa became more and more isolated on the international scene as boycotts of South Africa became common. And in 1976 an uprising of students in Soweto, a large African township near Johannesburg, spread throughout the country, showing both South Africa and the world that apartheid's time was strictly limited.

The Afrikaners responded to the developing crisis by naming a new leader, P. W. Botha (b. 1916), who attempted to halt the dissolution of the country by a combination of still more repression and a limited reform of the most egregious aspects of apartheid. Yet resistance intensified in the 1980s. As the international financial community lost confidence in the white racist regime's ability to sustain peace and civil order, investments slowed and the economy faltered. International sanctions against South Africa accelerated its economic decline. Urged on by increasing poverty, in 1986 blacks again rebelled, and this rebellion has not ceased. As a consequence of the country's ever increasing isolation, weakened economy, and persistent black resistance, the government of the new president, F. W. de Klerk (b. 1936), had no choice but to release political prisoners in early 1990 and to begin negotiations with Nelson Mandela to end apartheid and transfer power to the black majority. Opposition from right-wing white opponents of de Klerk's policies, and from black leaders of the Bantustans whom the apartheid regime had created and who disagreed with the ANC's program, have slowed the negotiations and led to escalating violence and

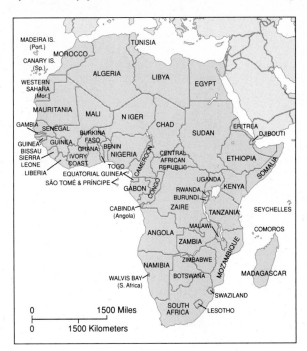

Africa of Nation States

instability even as the structures of apartheid are being dismantled.

Problems of Independence

The transfer of power to African politicians that had taken place in the colonies during the 1960s was, in the long run, not wholly successful. Although the 1960s saw great optimism about the future of Africa, by the 1970s it was clear that things were not going well. The newly independent states of Africa faced a host of problems. One arose from the very nature of the anticolonial movements themselves. For the most part they had been alliances of interest groups representing workers, agriculturalists, and would-be businesspeople and professionals, each with its own particular—and often incompatible—set of goals. Once the colonial enemy had departed from the scene, the movements tended to fragment and fall apart. The resulting political vacuum frequently opened the way for the emergence of strong military leaders who used the coercive mechanisms of the state inherited from colonial times to beat down opposition.

Everywhere in Africa the main aim of the new governments during the 1960s and into the early 1970s was

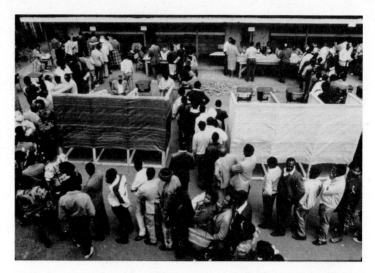

In December 1992, Kenyans wait in line to vote in the country's first multiparty elections to be held in twenty-five years.

the same: "building the nation." With few exceptions, political leaders of all ideological persuasions agreed that building the nation meant total unity and that total unity necessitated suppressing both dissidence and debate. In one country after another one-party regimes came into existence. Some of these were civil and moderate, as Tanzania under Julius Nyerere and Senegal under Leopold Senghor; some were brutal and harsh, as Uganda under Idi Amin and Guinea under Sekou Toure. But all claimed that firm rule was essential and that opposition was unacceptable.

Some initial opposition to the growing power of the state came from the labor unions, but, in almost every case, they were quickly reduced to being mere instruments used to carry forth government labor policies. Some opposition also came from ethnically based movements, which sought to protect privileged positions inherited from colonial days, as in Uganda, or to defend themselves against infringement from the ethnic group in power, as in Rwanda. These were usually also speedily suppressed, although in one case—the Nigerian civil war of the late 1960s—hundreds of thousands of people died from conflict and subsequent famine. And some opposition came from intellectuals who favored open societies, but jail sentences or exile usually ended it. By the 1970s the one-party state had silenced politics throughout most of the continent.

Several factors combined to permit this authoritarianism. First, and most obviously, the new rulers had inherited the police and army established in the colonial period and were willing to use them. Second, and in many ways even more important, chiefs and other big men from the precolonial period were largely discredited by the mid-twentieth century, and their place had

not been taken by nongovernmental institutions. In short, there were few able to challenge the claims of the state. The churches were timid; universities scarcely existed; labor unions had been quickly emasculated; newspapers were under government control; the legal profession was just beginning. And, with only three percent of the African people having had any high-school education at the time of independence in the 1960s, articulate opposition could easily be co-opted or forcibly silenced.

Yet there was a third factor operating as well. This was that the terms of trade between Africa and the world turned against Africa in the early 1970s and produced severe economic strains within African societies. Between the outbreak of World War II in 1939 and the end of the 1960s, the terms of trade were very much in Africa's favor and tended to improve with each passing year. The growing income this situation produced in Africa had made independence seem attractive, appearing to promise adequate funds to "build the nation." By the start of the 1970s, however, the terms of trade began to turn against Africa as a consequence of a glut of raw materials on the world market, the inflation in prices of manufactured goods from the industrial world, and the winding down of the Vietnam War, which had provided a market for African minerals such as copper. The oil crisis of 1973 also severely wounded sub-Saharan African countries' economies (aside from Nigeria, Gabon, and Angola, which produced oil for export), and they plunged into a fiscal whirlpool from which they have never recovered. In this situation, a new slogan, "economic development," replaced "building the nation." It was accepted throughout most of Africa that if economic development were to be achieved in a hostile global economic situation, then strong governments

The Decolonization of Africa

1946	Gold Coast (Ghana) has elected African majority in Legislative Assembly
1947	Britain leaves India and Pakistan
1951	Outbreak of Mau Mau rebellion in Kenya
1955	South African National Congress issues Freedom Charter
1957	Ghana becomes first independent postcolonial African state
1958	France offers French colonies autonomy or full independence; Guinea takes independence
1960	Belgium withdraws abruptly from Belgian Congo; civil war lasting until 1963 follows
1960	Independence of Nigeria
1960	Sharpeville Massacre in South Africa and repression of African opposition
1961	Independence of Tanganyika
1963	Independence of Kenya
1964	Independence of Malawi and Zambia after dissolution of the Federation of Rhodesia and Nyasaland in 1963
1967	Outbreak of Nigerian civil war when Biafra secedes
1974	Overthrow of Portuguese government because of military dissatisfaction with long colonial wars
1975	Independence of Mozambique and Angola from Portugal
1976	Soweto uprising shakes white confidence in South Africa
1977	Death of Steve Biko, Black Consciousness advocate, in South Africa
1980	Zimbabwean Africans gain independence after long guerrilla war against white settler minority
1986	Uprising in South Africa leads to state of emergency
1990	Nelson Mandela released from prison in South Africa

would have to direct the economies with great firmness and without criticism.

Unfortunately, because of corruption or ineptness on the part of the governments, because of the lack of skills or lack of basic resources on the part of the people, because of the distorted economies inherited from colonialism, because of low commodity prices on the world market, and because of often misguided development projects, "economic development" did not take place. Even worse, the sliding economy came to be paralleled by a steady decline in food production, with the decline, adjusted for population growth, running at approximately 0.5 percent per year between 1970 and 1990.

The reasons for this decline in Africa's capability to feed itself are many. The great population growth of Africa since 1900 resulted in too many mouths to feed. The transfer of the best communal land to the status of private real estate to be bought and sold by individuals removed much of the best lands from the system of shifting cultivation that had guaranteed successful agriculture in Africa for millennia. Too much strictly marginal land has consequently been brought under cultivation, with production from it highly difficult to sustain. The migration of tens of millions of people to urban centers has also removed from the countryside people who might otherwise be producing food. The high cost of fertilizer has also injured productivity, as has the importation of cheap foreign grains, usually sent as "foreign aid." So brittle did Africa's rural economy become that when natural disasters occurred—such as the Sahelian drought in the 1970s and the Ethiopian famine of the 1980s—vulnerable rural areas swiftly collapsed.

The failure of one-party states to produce the much-desired economic development became painfully clear in the 1980s. And with the coming of age of ever larger numbers of educated Africans, dissatisfaction with the one-party system that had so ineffectually managed the economy grew rapidly, accelerated by the collapse of the Communist dictatorships of Eastern Europe in the late 1980s. New slogans—"multiparty democracy" and "privatization"—appeared, and claims were made that a greater involvement of more people in governmental decisions and a diminished involvement of the state in economic affairs would produce the economic turnaround so long and so ardently desired. While the ruling establishments of certain one-party states have resisted the new orthodoxy, it has received support from both Western nations and international financial institutions such as the World Bank and the International

Monetary Fund, and it appears likely that they too will soon fall into line now that international loans are contingent upon democratization.

While hard workers, Africans still lack many of the skills needed for a modern economy. The age-old problems of soil management in tropical areas and the presence of the tsetse fly continue to inhibit agricultural production. The population in many parts of the continent is still growing far too fast and, consequently, 50 percent of the population is sixteen years old or younger, placing immense educational and welfare burdens on the state. Africa's economies are still largely shaped by the colonial experience and, dependent on the former colonial powers for markets, are still ill-equipped to cope with the continued depression of the prices paid for raw materials. As a consequence, the heavy burden of international indebtedness prevents most states from making needed investments in infrastructure.

In a remarkably brief period of time, from 1919 to today, Africa passed through four periods, distinct in themselves but interrelated. Between 1919 and 1945 more and more Africans became disenchanted by economic problems caused by local exploitation and fluctuations in the world economy as well as by the oppression inherent in colonialism itself. During the 1940s and 1950s, broad segments of African society organized themselves to end colonialism, efforts not vigorously opposed by Britain and France, the principal colonial powers. The 1960s saw independence and attempts at "nation building" that produced great euphoria but little else. The downturn in Africa's economy that extended from the early 1970s onwards first evoked strongly authoritarian governments bent on expanding the economy, but with their failure, new experiments with free-market economics and multiparty democracy began at the start of the 1990s.

The First World War and the Political Origins of the Modern Middle East

World War I was the most important political event in the history of the modern Middle East. At the beginning of the war, the Ottoman Empire ruled, in law if not in deed, Anatolia (the site of contemporary Turkey), the Fertile Crescent, Egypt, much of the Arabian Peninsula, and North Africa. By the early 1920s, Turkey was an independent republic, the Fertile Crescent had been

divided into separate states under the control of France and Britain, Egypt had evolved from an Ottoman territory and a British protectorate to an independent state, and much of the Arabian Peninsula had been united under the control of the dynasty of Ibn Sa'ud.

In addition to the laying of the foundations for the state system in the Middle East, two other phenomena occurred in the aftermath of the war that had important consequences for the region for the remainder of the century. First, the "Palestine problem" arose for the first time in its modern form, as Jewish immigrants to Palestine clashed with its Arab inhabitants. Second, varieties of nationalism spread throughout the region as the concept of political community was redefined.

War and the Dissolution of the Ottoman Empire

Comparing a map of the Middle East in 1918 with one of the same region in 1914 reveals a striking feature—by 1918 the Ottoman Empire is no longer on the map. Although European powers had nibbled at the edges of the empire during the nineteenth century, the "sick man of Europe" had entered the twentieth century weakened but intact. The concert of European powers had managed both to protect the interests of the individual European nations in the Ottoman Empire and to defuse crisis after crisis through diplomacy. Only once during the century—during the Crimean War (1854–56)—did European nations go to war to resolve a dispute involving the Ottoman Empire.

The end of the concert of Europe in 1914 heralded the end of the Ottoman Empire. On the eve of the First World War, European nations divided themselves into two alliances: Britain, France, and Russia (and later the United States) formed the Entente Powers, while Germany and Austria formed the core of the Central Powers. The Ottoman Empire joined the Central Powers for several reasons, including German political and economic influence in the empire and its traditional hostility to Russia. In addition, the Austrians, anxious to control Ottoman ambitions in the Balkans, actively solicited the empire's participation in the war on their side.

As soon as it became clear that the war would not be over quickly, each of the Entente powers began to maneuver to be in a position to claim the spoils it desired in the Middle East in the event of victory. For Russia, these spoils were obvious: the Russian dream of access to warm-water ports could be realized by laying claim to the Turkish Straits. France claimed to have "historic rights" in the region of the empire that is present-day Syria and Lebanon. France based this claim both on its role as protector of Lebanon's Maronite Christian population (Maronite Christianity is similar to Roman Catholicism) and on its economic interests in the region, such as investments in railroads and in silk production. The British focused on their long-standing obsession with the protection of the sea routes to India and on ensuring postwar security for investment and trade in the region.

Starting in 1915, the Entente powers negotiated a series of secret agreements to confirm their claims and to attract to their alliance other states, such as Italy and Greece. These agreements divided up the territory of the Ottoman Empire without regard for the wishes of the local inhabitants. For example, one of the agreements, known as the Sykes-Picot Agreement (named after the men who negotiated it), divided up most of the Fertile Crescent into zones that would be under direct and indirect British and French control in the aftermath of the war. The same agreement placed Palestine under international control. In a separate agreement, Istanbul and the Turkish Straits were promised to Russia.

Ultimately, the postwar settlement differed from the terms of these secret agreements for five reasons. First, the agreements were both ambiguous and mutually contradictory. According to various interpretations of the wartime agreements and declarations, Palestine, for example, was promised to the French, to international control, to an independent Arab kingdom, and to Zionists (Jewish nationalists). Second, Britain, having launched attacks on the Ottoman Empire in Iraq and along the Mediterranean coast, was the only Entente power with troops occupying the region. This gave the British leverage in postwar negotiations with the other members of the victorious alliance. Third, the Bolsheviks seized power in Russia in 1917 and renounced the claims made by the Tsarist government. Fourth, a nationalist revolt in Turkey prevented the division of Turkish territory in Anatolia. Finally, when the United States entered the war on the side of the Entente powers, President Woodrow Wilson announced his intention to make his "Fourteen Points" the basis of a postwar peace. Indigenous nationalist leaders seized in particular on Wilson's call for an end to secret agreements and the right of the colonized to determine their own future. Thus, when representatives from the Entente powers sat down in Paris to negotiate the final terms of peace, their task proved daunting.

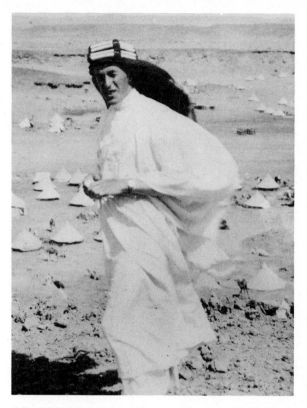

Colonel T.E. Lawrence became famous as Lawrence of Arabia because of his exploits in the cause of Arab independence from the Ottomans during World War I.

State Building by Decree

State building in the Arab Fertile Crescent (present-day Lebanon, Syria, Iraq, Jordan) was initiated in the post-World War I period by victorious European powers rather than by the inhabitants of the region. No Washington or Garibaldi forged nations through wars of national liberation. No Valley Forge became a mythic symbol of nation building. No indigenous Bismarck or Napoleon stirred patriotism through conquest. States in the Fertile Crescent were plotted on maps by diplomats with imperialist ambitions and received their independence slowly, in stages. Thus, patriotic sentiments rarely corresponded to national boundaries, and the Arab population of the region saw the division of the Fertile Crescent into separate nations as debilitating and unnatural.

Although Britain and France played the major role in the creation of states in the Middle East, a third actor was involved as well—the Hashemite family, which administered the Hejaz (western Arabia) in the name of the Ottoman sultan. Before the First World War, the

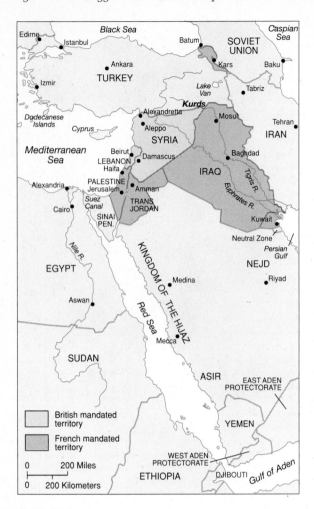

The Fertile Crescent, 1923

the so-called mandate system, the League authorized France to supervise the area of present-day Syria and Lebanon while it awarded the mandate for Palestine and Iraq to Britain. Although the League directed that "the wishes of the communities must be a principal consideration in the selection of the mandatory," those wishes were not taken into account, and the Fertile Crescent was carved up according to the desires of Britain and France.

The population of the Fertile Crescent was never seriously consulted to determine its needs or desires. The French sent an army to Damascus to oust Faisal and to impose thinly disguised colonial control over the population. The French later divided this territory in two—a territory with a large Christian population along the coast, present-day Lebanon, and an inland territory, present-day Syria. In an attempt to restore Faisal to power, Faisal's brother, 'Abdallah (1882–1951), marched north from his home in Mecca. The British now faced two problems—what to do with their wartime ally, Faisal, and what to do about 'Abdallah, who was threatening to make war on their more important wartime ally, France. To distract 'Abdallah, the British divided their Palestine mandate in two and offered him the throne of a territory east of the Jordan River—a territory thus called Transjordan, later simply Jordan. Jordan has been ruled by the descendants of 'Abdallah ever since. At the same time, the British granted to Faisal the throne of a territory created by joining the regions around Basra, Baghdad, and Mosul, creating the nation of Iraq. Thus, the mandate system divided the Fertile Crescent into territories that later became the states of Lebanon, Syria, Jordan, and Iraq. The first three of these states were finally granted their independence in the wake of the Second World War.

While these states eventually won their political independence, the contradictory nature of the mandate system inhibited their full development. The League of Nations, it must be remembered, entrusted the territories of the Ottoman Empire to Britain and France so that the European states could prepare their charges for self-rule. However, Britain and France accepted the mandates so that they could retain control over those areas in which they felt they had vital interests. They thus divided and combined territories into states for their own economic and political interests, rarely considering whether the states they were creating were truly viable. For example, the British carved out Jordan from a desert that contained few economic resources. The territory of Iraq included populations with significant ethnic and religious differences and, as a result,

patriarch of the family, Sharif Husayn (1854–1931), alienated from Ottoman rule, made contact with the British to see if they would support his bid for independence. After the Ottoman Empire joined the Central Powers, the British resumed contact with the sharif. As a result, the sharif authorized the famous "Arab Revolt" led by his son, Emir Faisal (1885–1933), and a bombastic British officer, T. E. Lawrence (1888–1935). At the end of the war, Faisal's troops occupied Damascus.

Faisal tried to assume administrative control over the region centered in present-day Syria. The French, for reasons cited above, opposed Faisal's pretensions. French claims were supported by the League of Nations, which authorized France and Britain to supervise the establishment of governments in the region. Under became notorious for its political instability. Shi'ite Arabs made up the largest group of those living in mandated Iraq, although the ruling elites were Sunni Arabs. The northern area, Mosul, was inhabited by Sunni Kurds who would have preferred self-rule. British policy makers understood this situation and, realizing that Iraqi leaders would have to continue to depend on British assistance to remain in power, granted Iraq independence in 1932, well ahead of the other mandated territories, which were better prepared for independence.

The mandate system had important economic consequences for the region as well. European investors were reluctant to invest in territories over which their governments would eventually have to give up control. In addition, according to the terms under which the League of Nations granted mandates, the emerging nations were not permitted to impose tariffs or trade restrictions. As a result, Europeans maintained a colonial-style system of trade with the region, buying raw materials and agricultural products while dumping finished goods on unprotected markets. Europeans only invested in the sort of infrastructure associated with colonial states, such as transportation networks necessary to send locally produced raw materials to European factories and markets. Thus, the mandate system both stifled and skewed economic growth.

The thinly disguised colonialism that underlay the mandate system and led to the creation of modern Lebanon, Syria, Jordan, and Iraq, diminished the legitimacy of the governments of those states. This lack of legitimacy is one of the reasons for the appeal of pan-Arabism—the yearning for the unity of all Arabs and the obliteration of national boundaries—which exists in the region to this day. It also helps explain the popularity of spokesmen for that doctrine, such as Gamal 'Abd al-Nasser of Egypt.

EGYPTIAN WOMEN TAKE TO THE STREETS

■ *The nationalist movements of the post–World War I period mobilized all segments of the population. The following is a description by the Egyptian nationalist and feminist, Huda Shaarawi, of a demonstration of women held in Cairo.*

No sooner were we approaching Zaghlul's house than British troops surrounded us. They blocked the streets with machine guns, forcing us to stop along with the students who had formed columns on both sides of us.

I was determined the demonstration should resume. When I advanced, a British soldier stepped toward me pointing his gun, but I made my way past him. As one of the women tried to pull me back, I shouted in a loud voice, 'Let me die so Egypt shall have an Edith Cavell' (an English nurse shot and killed by the Germans during the First World War, who became an instant martyr). Continuing in the direction of the soldiers, I called upon the women to follow. A pair of arms grabbed me and the voice of Regina Kayyat rang in my ears. 'This is madness. Do you want to risk the lives of the students? It will happen if the British raise a hand against you.' At the thought of our unarmed sons doing battle against the weaponry of British troops, and of the Egyptian losses sure to occur, I came to my senses and stopped still. We stood still for three hours while the sun blazed down on us. The students meanwhile continued to encourage us, saying that the heat of the day would soon abate. Some of the students departed for the legations of the United States, France, and Italy, announcing that the British had surrounded women in front of Saad Pasha's house. I did not care if I suffered sunstroke—the blame would fall upon the tyrannical British authority—but we stood up to the heat and suffered no harm. The British also brought out Egyptian soldiers armed with sticks.

From Huda Shaarawi, *Harem Years: The Memoirs of an Egyptian Feminist (1879-1924)*.

State Building by Revolution and Conquest

The League of Nations applied the mandate system in the Middle East only in the Fertile Crescent. Outside this region, in Turkey, Egypt, and Persia (called Iran since the 1930s), indigenous nationalist movements and nation builders established states through conquest and anticolonial struggle. These methods facilitated the development of a national identity among the population in each of these states, a national identity that roughly coincided with political boundaries.

World War I had both political and economic consequences for Egypt. In spite of the fact that Britain had occupied Egypt since 1882, Egypt had been legally part of the Ottoman Empire until the First World War. With the outbreak of the war, Britain declared Egypt a protectorate, ending Ottoman sovereignty once and for all. By war's end, however, the British had alienated virtually all segments of the Egyptian population. Large landowners could not market cotton without British interference; the educated were excluded from political power; wartime inflation and conscription devastated the urban poor and peasants.

All that was needed to ignite the tensions between much of the Egyptian population and the British occupiers was a spark. That spark was touched off in November 1918, when a delegation of Egyptian politicians petitioned the British high commissioner in Cairo for permission to go to Paris to represent the Egyptian population at the peace conference. When the British arrested and deported members of this delegation, demonstrations and strikes erupted throughout the country. In response, the British government appointed a commission to investigate the unrest. The commission concluded that British interests could best be maintained in Egypt if Britain gave Egypt conditional independence while retaining control over such governmental functions as defense, foreign policy, and the protection of the Suez Canal. Thus, in 1922, Egypt was granted limited independence. Although Egypt did not achieve full independence until after the Second World War, the 1919 revolution gave the modern Egyptian nation a pantheon of national heroes, political structures, and a founding myth.

In both Turkey and Iran, leaders seeking to centralize their authority and "modernize" their states took power in the wake of the First World War. In Turkey, a military leader, Mustafa Kemal (1881–1938), led a successful campaign against invading Greek and French armies. In the wake of his victory, Mustafa Kemal adopted the name "Ataturk" (father of the Turks), and guided the establishment of a secular Turkish republic that ruled over an undivided Anatolia. In Iran, famine, foreign occupation, and political chaos brought on by the First World War enabled a leader of an elite cavalry unit, Reza Khan (1878–1944), to seize power and establish a dynasty that ruled Iran until 1979.

The changes that Reza Khan, later Reza Shah, and Ataturk imposed on their nations were similar. Indeed, Reza Shah consciously modeled himself on Ataturk. Both leaders sought to restructure their nation's taxation, law, educational system, and military along European lines. Ataturk even oversaw the abolition of the caliphate and a "Latinization" of the Turkish script.

Thus, both Ataturk and Reza Shah might be considered the last in a line of defensive modernizers who ruled in the Middle East from the beginning of the nineteenth century. However, the changes implemented by the former were more successful than those implemented by the latter for two reasons. First, defensive modernization in the Ottoman Empire during the nineteenth century had had a greater impact on society than defensive modernization in Iran. In Turkey, the successor state to the Ottoman Empire, the state had already expanded its role before the First World War and had taken over functions that were still in the hands of nongovernment institutions in Iran. Therefore, the changes in Iran were more novel than those in Turkey and fostered a greater resistance. Second, Ataturk created his state and government through a popular war of national liberation, whereas Reza Shah took power in a coup d'etat and ruled by decree.

Zionism, Palestinian Nationalism, and the Struggle for Palestine

The Arab-Israeli dispute has gone on for such a long time and has been the subject of so much heated debate that it is easy to lose sight of the fundamental issue involved. The dispute had been, simply put, over land: two peoples—Jewish immigrants united by their adherence to the nationalist ideology of Zionism, and Palestinian Arab inhabitants among whom the Zionists settled—have both claimed an exclusive right to inhabit and control a narrow territory on the eastern coast of the Mediterranean Sea, a territory that stretches from Lebanon in the north to the Sinai peninsula in the south.

The Zionist movement was similar to other nationalist ideologies that arose in Europe in the nineteenth

Jewish refugees from Europe arriving in Israel in the late 1940s.

century. Zionist doctrine was formulated in part by a Viennese journalist, Theodor Herzl (1860–1904), who was shocked by anti-Semitism in Europe and believed that Jews could be secure only in their own homeland. Since the first century C.E., when the Jewish people were exiled from Palestine by the Romans, Palestine held an allure for many Jews who lived, often uncomfortably, as a scattered community. Thus, Zionism combined Herzl's call for the establishment of a Jewish national home with the traditional yearning for Palestine.

Herzl participated in the founding of the World Zionist Organization in 1897 to "create for the Jewish people a home in Palestine secured by Public Law." In an effort to enlist worldwide Jewish support for the Entente powers during the First World War, the British government endorsed the Zionist program by issuing the Balfour Declaration. The Balfour Declaration stated, in part, "His Majesty's Government view with favor the establishment in Palestine of a national home for the Jewish people, and will use their best endeavors to facilitate the achievement of this object . . ." This declaration marked a milestone in the efforts that culminated in the creation of the State of Israel.

Jewish immigration to Palestine began even before the issuance of the Balfour Declaration, and continued long after the end of the war. Immigration took place in waves, called "*aliyot*" (sing. *aliya*). The second and third aliyot, which took place during 1904–14 and 1918–23, brought 65,000 Jews to Palestine from Europe and shaped many of the institutions that still exist in Israel.

Influenced by both socialism and romanticism, the new immigrants organized collective and communal farms, a labor federation, and mutual aid societies. They also resurrected the biblical language of Hebrew for use as the national tongue. Perhaps most important for the future of the Middle East was the labor policy of the new immigrants. In part to maintain high wages for the new immigrants, Zionists banned the use of Arab labor. Thus, after the Zionists bought land, often from absentee landlords, they frequently displaced Palestinian farmers, who received little or no compensation.

Nationalist ideologies like Zionism received mass support in Europe before they became widespread in other parts of the world. Therefore, in contrast to the Jewish community in Palestine, which had both a unifying ideology and a centralized administration, the Arab community in Palestine initially possessed neither. It was not until the 1930s, when Jewish immigration to Palestine exploded as a result of anti-Semitism in Europe, that the Palestinians were able to form a Palestine-wide organization, the Arab Higher Committee, to organize a unified resistance to what most Palestinians perceived to be a foreign presence in their midst. By that time, Zionist settlers made up 30 percent of the population.

Tensions between the two communities exploded into violent confrontations, which continued into the post-World War II period. As a result, the British government, which had received the mandate for Palestine from the League of Nations, brought its Palestine problem to the United Nations, the League's successor. In the wake of the United Nations' vote to partition Palestine, a civil war broke out between the Zionist and Palestinian communities, followed by the intervention of surrounding Arab nations on behalf of the Palestinians.

As a result of the Zionist victory in the First Palestine War (1948), Zionists founded the State of Israel, whose borders corresponded to the armistice lines. About 70 percent of the Palestinian population fled from their homes and subsequently were trapped behind cease-fire lines. Many of these Palestinians ended up in refugee camps sponsored by the United Nations, camps that exist to this day in states surrounding Israel.

Besides creating a seemingly intractable refugee problem, the creation of the State of Israel and the four Arab-Israeli Wars (1956, 1967, 1973, 1982) affected the Middle East in other ways as well. The wars created tens of thousands of casualties—25,000 to 30,000 Arab casualties alone in the 1967 war, which lasted merely six days. Valuable national resources have been destroyed or diverted for military expenditures. The conflict has destabilized states as well, provoking coups d'etat in Syria, Iraq, and Egypt and civil wars in Jordan and Lebanon. Finally, the Arab-Israeli conflict has been used to excuse both authoritarian rule in Arab nations and human rights violations by both sides.

The Invention and Spread of Arab Nationalism

Nations do not arise naturally, but are constructed when enough people living in a territory choose to believe that because they share a common language, religion, or history, they should constitute a political community. Before this can occur, previous ties that bound the population to larger or smaller communities must be weakened and superseded by new ones. These preconditions for the rise of nationalism did not emerge in the Middle East until the mid-nineteenth century. It was not until after World War I, however, that political conditions would allow those committed to the idea of a political community based on their identity as Arabs to disseminate nationalist ideas through the population.

Before the late nineteenth and early twentieth centuries, most people in the Middle East were loyal to supernational communities (such as the Islamic umma) and/or subnational communities (such as a quarter of a city). The incorporation of the Middle East into the world economic system and defensive modernization, however, transformed both institutions and social relations, and set the stage for the emergence of popular, nationalist ideologies. This transformation took place through various means. The circulation of newspapers and the standardization of secondary and university-level education facilitated the homogenization of culture. The introduction of new technologies such as railroads, steamboats, tramways, and telephones integrated cities and united town with countryside. The state widened its control and coercive capability, and took responsibility for activities that had previously been left to individuals.

In September 1993, the Israeli government and the Palestine Liberation Organization (PLO)—considered by most Palestinians to be the "sole legitimate representative of the Palestinian people"—formally recognized each other and agreed to a declaration of principles for Palestinian self-rule in Jericho and the Gaza Strip, part of the territory occupied by Israel since the 1967 war. Several factors contributed to this event. Life for Palestinians under Israeli occupation has been difficult. Furthermore, because of the end of the Cold War and their support for the Iraqi invasion of Kuwait in 1990, Palestinians could no longer count on Eastern Bloc or Gulf Arab financial and diplomatic assistance. The Israeli willingness to reach an accord stemmed from the election of a government that was prepared to withdraw from parts of the Occupied Territories, anticipation of the economic benefits of peace, and continued civil unrest and expanded Islamic militancy among Palestinians under occupation. Whether or not a lasting peace between Arabs and Israelis will evolve from these agreements, however, still remains to be seen.

As a result of these changes, a new notion of political community emerged in the Arab Middle East and found its spokesmen among the growing stratum of professionals, trained military officers, and skilled bureaucrats from the Fertile Crescent, particularly the cities of Damascus and Beirut. To many of these individuals, the ideal political community was larger than an individual city or region but smaller than the multiethnic, multilingual Ottoman Empire. As in the case of many European nationalisms, the bond that united this community was common language—Arabic. At first, these "Arabists" advocated constructing their community within a decentralized Ottoman Empire, an empire in which Arab provincial autonomy would allow them to participate in governing. When it became clear that the Ottoman government would not permit decentralization, some of the Arabists joined secret societies that called for Arab independence. During the First World

War, members of these societies linked their fate to that of the Arab Revolt and established contact with Emir Faisal. After the war, many of the members of the secret societies became prominent members of Faisal's government, while others published nationalist newspapers or built educational institutions that propagated nationalist doctrines.

Under Faisal, factional strife became bitter in Syria, pitting those who had fought in the Arab Revolt against those who had remained in Syria during the war, traditional notables against those who identified with the new stratum, those who sought to compromise with the Entente powers who were dividing up the region against those who wanted to wage an armed struggle against them. Contenders for power increasingly looked for support from the urban masses, whom they mobilized for demonstrations and organized into militias. Because of this, they not only increased the numbers of those who participated in politics, but also spread nationalist ideas. As rivals for power sought to win support for their faction, the doctrines of nationalism took on popular themes and symbols, thus becoming genuinely populist.

Popular nationalism spread in other former provinces of the Ottoman Empire as well. In addition to the Egyptian revolt of 1919, a significant segment of the population of Iraq participated in anti-British revolts in 1920. These uprisings mobilized people who had never before participated in politics, fostering a sense of community—a sense of nation—among many of the participants.

With the establishment of the mandate system in the Fertile Crescent, national identities rarely coincided with state boundaries drawn by foreign powers. Syrian nationalists, for example, differed on the boundaries of the ideal national community: while some supported the establishment of a Fertile Crescent nation, others promoted the idea of a political community that would link all Arabic speakers. Still others supported a nation made from the union of Syria and Lebanon. Only after years of nation building, of developing state institutions for education, defense, and administration, were Fertile Crescent states able to foster state patriotisms that could compete with local and regional nationalisms.

As a result of the First World War, the victorious Entente powers replaced the Ottoman Empire with a state system of their own design and conforming to their own needs. The creation of viable national communities within the context of this system would challenge both the leaders and populations of those states throughout the remainder of the century.

The Middle East Since Midcentury

Perhaps the most contentious issue that dominated the politics of the Middle East in the three-quarters of a century that followed the First World War was whether or not states and state institutions that were established principally to conform to the needs of foreign powers would be able to survive and enhance their legitimacy among the populations over which they ruled.

The effort to consolidate modern states led to consequences that would have shocked and confounded the statesmen meeting at the Paris Peace Conference. As a logical outgrowth of the state-building process, segments of the population that had never before been involved in politics—middle-class army officers and their bureaucratic allies—sought to erase all remnants of colonial control and dependency. In the aftermath of the Second World War, they took power in state after state, expanding government power in an effort to reconstruct national communities.

These efforts have been complicated by two related phenomena. First, Western economic growth increased the demand for Middle Eastern oil. The ensuing "oil revolution" defined the economic and political environment in which all Middle Eastern leaders had to operate. Second, the inability of states to fulfill their goals, coupled with social dislocations that came about as a result of the transformation of civic institutions, fostered popular resistance to state power.

Military Revolts Consolidate the State System

The states that emerged in the aftermath of the First World War were either directly created by outside powers or won their sovereignty in an environment largely defined by outside powers. Although most states in the region were independent by midcentury, many of the pre-independence institutions remained intact during the post-independence period. In most countries, a small elite, usually sympathetic to the West, dominated political and social institutions. The West maintained a military presence throughout the region, from the Suez Canal to the Persian Gulf. Governments were inefficient and frequently corrupt. For these reasons, military-led rebellions erupted in state after state in the Middle East: Syria (1949), Egypt (1952), Iraq (1958), North Yemen (1962), and Libya (1969). In all these revolts the army seized power in the name of the disenfranchised and powerless to put an end to the aforementioned ills.

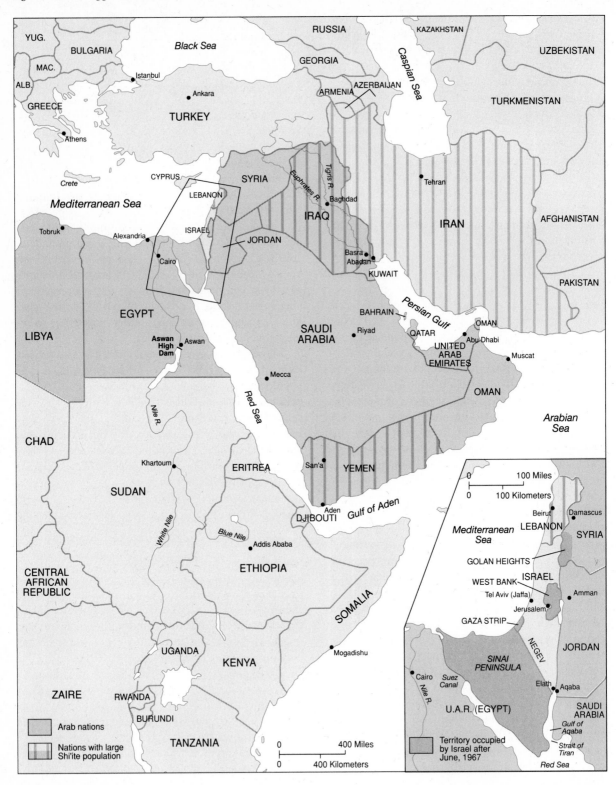

The Modern Middle East

Their rebellions empowered a new, larger layer of society who expanded the authority of the state. The ultimate failure of these revolts has had tragic results for the region.

During the mandate period, both the French and the British relied on local notables and sympathetic rulers to maintain their influence. They did this for several reasons. The economic interests of most notables were compatible with those of the mandatory power; the populations of the mandated territories (and Egypt) who chafed at direct control from Paris or London tolerated indirect control; the competition among notables and between notables and sovereigns precluded unified nationalist movements; and finally, indirect rule was cheaper, an important consideration for governments that had just come out of a world war and could not afford to invest large amounts of money or skilled manpower in foreign expenditures. By fostering indirect rule, the British and French thus ensured weak central authority in the states they left as their legacy in the Middle East.

Even though national politics was the domain of notables and sovereigns, the seeds of change were planted during this period. As a result of the Great Depression of the 1930s, prices for agricultural products collapsed and peasants left their lands and migrated to cities. In the 1940s, cities attracted more peasants and provincials when, as a result of the Second World War, industrial production in the Middle East expanded by 50 percent. Additionally, students, bureaucrats, and army officers moved temporarily or permanently from outlying areas to the new national capitals like Damascus or Baghdad to complete their training or to seek employment. In the process, they strengthened both the ties between provincial centers and the capital and their own national identities.

Middle Eastern society was changing, and the political structure of Middle Eastern states was not able to keep up with the changes. The new states that had been created in the wake of the First World War and achieved their independence over the next thirty years had to establish their authority and legitimacy, eliminate competing centers of power, and remodel their bureaucracies along functional lines. Trained military officers seized power to do these things, which the governing elites and their allies were incapable of doing.

Alongside the structural changes that fostered these rebellions were political causes. The 1948 defeat of Arab forces in the First Palestine War underscored to military officers in Egypt and Syria the incompetence of the ruling elites, whom the officers accused of corruption. The rebels also claimed their actions were opposed to imperialism, to feudalism (as represented by large landowners) and to the treason of which the notables were guilty by their alliances with European powers.

The new leaders crushed all potential rivals, such as independent political parties, trade unions, and the press, and expanded the control of the state over society. The case of Egypt is illustrative. In the wake of the 1952 Free Officers revolt, which led to Gamal 'Abd al-Nasser's eighteen-year presidency, the state became the central organ for economic development. As the result of a clause in the new constitution that guaranteed all university graduates employment in the state sector, the bureaucracy expanded 250 percent. In addition, the government initiated a number of sweeping programs. It built the Aswan High Dam to regulate the flow of the Nile River. It nationalized industry, banks, and even the Suez Canal. It declared a land-reform program aimed at destroying the financial base of the wealthiest landholding notables, redistributing much of their holdings to peasants who joined state-sponsored cooperatives.

Other regimes that took power in the Middle East during this period likewise dramatically expanded the role of the state in society. Through centrally planned economies and unopposed state power, these regimes were able not only to deliver certain benefits to their populations, such as road and school construction, rural electrification, health care and literacy, but also to reshape the constitution and arrangement of social classes in society.

Unfortunately, the cost of these accomplishments was high. Since these regimes claimed to represent the "will of the nation," they repressed their opponents and classified whole layers of society as "enemies of the people." They wasted revenues on prestige projects and money and lives on anti-imperialist wars. As in other parts of the world, centralized economic planning was wasteful and rewarded inefficient state enterprises while sapping initiative and resources from more-productive private ventures.

Over the years, successor regimes overturned many of the economic initiatives undertaken during this period. After Anwar al-Sadat became president of Egypt in the wake of Nasser's death, for example, he initiated a program called *infitah* ("opening up") to encourage foreign investment and private enterprise. Several factors led to this change of course: problems inherent to centralized planning; regional economic and political shifts brought about by the "oil revolution" of the 1970s; and the strengthening of the American position in the region, which came about as a result of the death of

"I AM THE TRAIN OF SADNESS"

■ *Themes of exile and alienation are common in the poetry of the Arab Middle East. Over the course of his lifetime, the Syrian poet Nizar Qabbani (b. 1923), one of the most popular Arab poets in the region, increasingly abandoned his earlier romantic poetry and turned instead to political and social themes.*

I AM THE TRAIN OF SADNESS

I travel on thousands of trains
I saddle my despair
I mount the clouds of my cigarette
In my suitcase
I carry the addresses of my lovers
Who were my lovers of yesterday?

The train's travelling
Faster . . . faster
Chewing on its way
The flesh of distances
Ravaging the fields on its way
Gulping the trees on its way
Licking the feet of the lakes

The inspector asks for my ticket
And my destination
Is there a destination?
No hotel on the earth knows who I am
Nor does it know the addresses of my lovers

I am the train of sadness
I have no platform
To stop at . . . In all my journeys
My platforms slip away
My stations
Slip away from me

From *A Mirror for Autumn*, by Abdullah al-Udhari.

Nasser, the Israeli victory in the 1967 war, and the unprecedented role of the conservative Gulf oil-exporting countries in the regional balance of power.

Nevertheless, before this period, most Middle Eastern states were weak and often illegitimate. They were not a principal focus of loyalty for their populations. The chief legacy of this period was, therefore, the consolidation of strong, activist states that were among the chief architects of late-twentieth-century Middle Eastern social institutions.

Oil Revolutionizes the Middle East

Oil was not an important commodity for the Middle East until the twentieth century, and the revolutionary economic and social changes brought about by the export of oil occurred within the last twenty-five years. Although these changes occurred so recently, they have been momentous. The region became divided between rich and poor—the oil exporters and the labor exporters—as all states in the region became either directly or

*The Aswan High Dam under construction. This huge project
displaced ancient ruins and put an end to the immemorial yearly
flooding of the Nile.*

indirectly dependent on oil. The Gulf region, considered a social and cultural backwater by the more populous and cosmopolitan regions of the Middle East, assumed a new and important role in the inter-Arab balance of power. The Middle East became a prime arena for superpower competition, as the region changed from an area from which wealth was extracted to an area that extracted wealth from the rest of the globe. Thus, the exploitation of oil, similar to the cultivation of cotton in nineteenth-century Egypt, has proven to be both a blessing and a curse for the region.

For more than half a century, the West was able to exploit the oil resources of the Middle East with little interference from, and few benefits for, the states from which that oil was extracted. The shah of Persia granted

the first modern oil concession to a British adventurer, William Knox D'Arcy (1849–1917) in 1901. D'Arcy acquired the right to "obtain, exploit, develop, render suitable for trade, carry away and sell" petroleum and petroleum products from all of Persia in exchange for 20,000 shares of his company and 16 percent of its profits. Several years later, the Ottoman government signed a similar agreement, which allowed the establishment of a consortium called the Turkish Petroleum Company. All the concessions granted in the first thirty years of the twentieth century shared certain characteristics. They were all of long duration, usually from sixty to seventy-five years, and they covered huge areas, such as all of Kuwait or all of Iraq. The consortia had the right to pursue all operations connected with the industry, including exploration, production, refining, transport, and marketing. In return for the concession, the consortia paid royalties and fees. The consortia, not the governments of the oil-producing countries, had a free hand in determining the quantity and price of the output.

The so-called oil revolution, which culminated in the 1970s, was nothing more than a step-by-step whittling down of the these privileges by the countries that owned the oil. For example, not until 1973 did the oil-producing countries win the right to set oil prices themselves; and only in 1975 did the first Persian Gulf oil-producing nations, Kuwait and Dubai, take full control over the consortia operating in their countries.

The idea for an association to represent the common needs of producers—the Organization of Petroleum Exporting Countries (OPEC)—originated in South America, not the Middle East. The government of Venezuela proposed the formation of a producers' association in 1947 to prevent the United States from importing lower-priced Middle Eastern oil to undercut the Latin American nation's production. However, the idea was not implemented until 1960 when, because of a recession in the West, oil companies unilaterally cut prices to stimulate demand. Since at that time the consortia paid oil-producing nations 50 percent of their revenues, a drop in prices meant a drop in the incomes of producing nations. Outraged, representatives from five nations—Venezuela, Kuwait, Saudi Arabia, Iran, and Iraq—agreed on "the unification of the petroleum policies of member countries and the determination of the best means for safeguarding their interests."

The price hike of 1973, which stimulated the influx of enormous wealth into the region, came about as the result of the American devaluation of the dollar in 1971. Since oil was priced in dollars, the devaluation meant that, while oil producers would receive the same

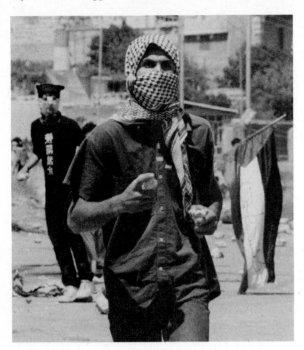

Masked Palestinians clash with Israeli police in Jerusalem in 1990.

number of dollars for a barrel of oil, they would be able to buy fewer commodities with those dollars. Using the Arab-Israeli war as a pretext, OPEC not only seized the right to set oil prices, but Arab members of OPEC ensured higher prices by temporarily decreasing production, thereby limiting supply. As a result, the price of oil jumped 380 percent and wealth flowed back into the region from the industrialized, petroleum-importing world.

The exploitation of oil and the influx of new wealth into the Middle East fostered both new opportunities and new problems for the region on all levels. Even before the price increases of the early 1970s, the United States and the Soviet Union competed for influence in the region. Like Great Britain in the nineteenth century, which sought to protect its route to India from Russian expansion, the United States sought to prevent Soviet expansion into an area whose petroleum resources were vital for Western economies and thus social stability. On the regional level, the enrichment of the oil-exporting states has given them a role in inter-Arab politics disproportionate to their size or previous level of influence. For example, after the 1967 Arab-Israeli War, Saudi Arabia, Kuwait, and Libya (at that time a conservative monarchy) began paying subsidies to the so-called "frontline states" bordering on Israel to

enable them to restock their arsenals. Because the payments were made in quarterly installments, the oil states maintained constant leverage over the foreign policies of Egypt, Jordan, and Syria.

Grants are not the only leverage the oil-producing states have over other states in the region. The oil-exporting states have small populations; Saudi Arabia, for example, has a population of less than ten million. These states must import labor from abroad, from states both within and outside the Middle East. Remittances (money sent home by workers employed abroad) make up an important part of the national income of resource poor, labor rich countries such as Egypt. In 1968, for example, no more than 10,000 Egyptians worked abroad; within ten years, as a result of the oil boom of the 1970s, that number increased to over 500,000.

The migration of labor has had negative as well as positive effects. While employment in the Gulf during boom times may have acted as a safety valve in those poorer Arab states where population growth and the spread of education have far outpaced economic opportunities, labor migrants are not fully integrated into the society of the host countries in which they live for years at a time. Further, the employment of male workers in the Persian Gulf has led to what one social scientist has called the "feminization of the Egyptian family" and a shift in women's roles outside the home, in village or community life.

In addition to labor migration, oil wealth has affected social life in other ways. The conservative oil-producing countries of the Gulf have been forced to balance development, often seen as "Westernization," with the maintenance of the norms of insular societies. In order to attract affluent vacationers from the Gulf area, a new class of entrepreneurs in less conservative non-oil-producing countries such as Egypt and Lebanon have invested in hotels and casinos, while ignoring other, more socially beneficial investment. This emphasis has skewed the economies of such cities as Beirut and Cairo toward the construction industry and tourism, increasing social tensions and widening the gap between rich and poor.

Popular Movements Challenge the States

Over the last decade, Middle Eastern popular movements, frequently using Islamic symbols, have captured the attention of the world. Sometimes these some of these movements have merely attempted to reclaim functions that have been taken over by the state, others have attempted to reconstruct the community in its entirety.

From the time of the first defensive modernizers through the period of military rebellions, the state in the Middle East has increasingly intruded into the lives of the region's inhabitants. States assumed responsibility for education, economic development, medical care, and social welfare. States jealously guarded their authority and destroyed or co-opted all potential rivals for that authority, such as independent trade unions and opposition political parties.

The fact that states were only partially successful ultimately contributed to the undermining of the state's authority. While state-sponsored public health campaigns, hospital construction, etc., decreased infant mortality, increased life expectancy, and spawned some of the highest population growth rates in the world, most states have been unable to keep up with the demands and expectations of this increased population. Unexpected factors, including the collapse of oil prices in the late 1970s, the disastrous effects of centralized economic planning, and the loss of prestige brought about by military defeat at the hands of Israel, reduced the capabilities of states further. Because states successfully crushed their opponents and assumed wide-ranging responsibilities, they became the focus of anger when expectations went unfulfilled.

The sector of the population that has increased most dramatically in the Middle East has been the urban lower classes, made up of unskilled and semiskilled workers and shopkeepers. This sector is dependent on the services provided by the state, such as price supports, and it is quite vulnerable to economic shocks. It is also more likely to be sensitive to Islamic symbols and puritanical status concerns. Therefore, people in this sector are likely to join Islamic movements that seek to restore the values, relationships, or communities of a bygone or mythologized past.

It is necessary to emphasize that there is nothing inherent in Islam that compels militancy. Like all religions, Islam provides its adherents with symbols, informs their values, and fosters institutional structures in which ideas can take physical shape. Thus, Islam does not provide the impulse for militant movements, but rather it acts as the medium in which such movements can and do operate.

States and state institutions founded during the mandate period and expanded in the twenty years

movements have confronted states with revolutionary violence, as in the case of the Iranian Revolution of 1978–79 or the *Intifada* (Palestinian uprising) in the Israeli-occupied West Bank and Gaza Strip. Sometimes these movements have peaceably provided their communities with services, such as health care, education, and emergency relief, as in the case of private voluntary organizations of Egypt. Whatever the form these movements have taken, they all share two characteristics. First, they have emerged in the late twentieth century as a result of both state successes and state failures. Second, they have directly challenged the authority of the state by once again redefining the notion of political community. While following the Second World War are thus in a situation where they must increasingly compete for the loyalty of their populations with non-state rivals. Populist movements have proved to be extremely popular. In Jordan and Algeria, these movements have garnered considerable support when allowed to participate in the electoral process. In Egypt, the state has abdicated to Islamic groups some of the responsibilities it had assumed during the Nasser era. During the 1992 earthquake that devastated sections of Cairo, Islamic groups delivered aid to the stricken areas of the city far quicker and more efficiently than the government.

Militant Islam is not necessarily incompatible with the state system or with nationalism. Popular nationalism, whether in the Middle East or in other parts of the world, has often borrowed symbols and values from religion, and even those groups that advocate the establishment of Islamic governments in the Middle East have organized themselves along national lines. It is therefore likely that, for the remainder of the century, while the post-World War I state system will remain in place, state governments will increasingly be forced to renegotiate the limits of their authority with their populations.

During the second half of the twentieth century, the state system that had been created in the wake of the First World War underwent significant changes. As a result, a new balance between states and the societies they govern is being negotiated, a process likely to define the course of Middle Eastern history through the commencement of the next century.

SUGGESTIONS FOR FURTHER READING

LATIN AMERICA SINCE 1870: ECONOMIC DEVELOPMENT AND SOCIAL UPHEAVAL

Charles Bergquist, *Labor In Latin America* (Stanford, CA: Stanford University Press, 1986). A classic comparative examination of the role of labor in export economies as the crucial element in determining the political paths followed by the four nations under study.

Leslie Bethell, ed., *The Cambridge History of Latin America*, Vols. 4–7 (New York: Cambridge University Press, 198–). A compendium of the most up-to-date scholarly materials.

Fernando Henrique Cardoso and Enzo Faletto, *Dependency and Development in Latin America*, trans. Marjory Mattingly Urquidi (Berkeley, CA: University of California Press, 1979). The most persuasive elucidation of the "dependency" framework for interpreting Latin American history.

Ruth Berins Collier and David Collier, *Shaping the Political Arena* (Princeton, NJ: Princeton University Press, 1991). A brilliant comparative overview of Latin American politics, with its central focus on labor organizations.

Judith Ewell and William H. Beezley, eds., *The Human Condition in Latin America: The Nineteenth Century* (Wilmington, DE: Scholarly Resources, 1989) and *The Human Condition in Latin America: The Twentieth Century* (Wilmington, DE: Scholarly Resources, 1987). Presents insightful, entertaining mini-biographies of people from all walks of life.

Friedrich Katz, *The Secret War in Mexico: Europe, the United States, and the Mexican Revolution* (Chicago: University of Chicago Press, 1981). A monumental work of scholarship that analyzes the causes and course of the Revolution and the crucial involvement of various foreign governments.

Florencia E. Mallon, *The Defense of Community in Peru's Central Highlands* (Princeton, NJ: Princeton University Press, 1983). Discusses the relationship of one local region to the national and international factors of the world market.

AFRICA SINCE 1919: RESISTANCE, SUCCESS, AND DISILLUSION

* Basil Davidson, *Modern Africa: A Social and Political History* (New York: Longman, 1983). An overview of African history after World War I.

Frederick Cooper, *On the African Waterfront: Urban Disorder and Transformation of Work in Colonial Mombasa* (New Haven, CT: Yale University Press, 1987). A stimulating assessment of the rise of workers' consciousness in one important African port.

* Landeg White, *Magomero: Portrait of an African Village* (New York: Cambridge University Press, 1987). A sensitive and subtle discussion of colonialism and independence in a Malawian village.

Leroy Vail, ed., *The Creation of Tribalism in Southern Africa* (Berkeley, CA: University of California Press, 1989). An important collection discussing the building of a new type of consciousness in southern Africa after World War I.

* Buchi Emecheta, *The Joys of Motherhood* (New York: Braziller, 1979). A fine novel describing the life of women in colonial Nigeria.

* Tabitha Kanogo, *Squatters and the Roots of Mau Mau* (Athens, OH: Ohio University Press, 1987). A detailed discussion of the causes of the nationalist movement in colonial Kenya.

* Heribert Adam and Hermann Giliomee, *Ethnic Power Mobilized: Can South Africa Change?* (New Haven, CT: Yale University Press, 1979). A survey of the rise of ethnic politics in South Africa.

* Tom Lodge, *Black Politics in South Africa Since 1945* (New York: Longman, 1983). A detailed discussion of African resistance to *apartheid* since World War II.

* Goran Hyden, *No Shortcuts to Progress: African Development Management in Perspective* (Berkeley, CA: University of California Press, 1983). A highly stimulating assessment of the problems of contemporary African economic development.

*Basil Davidson, *The Black Man's Burden: Africa and the Curse of the Nation-State* (New York: Times Books, 1992). A splendidly written analysis of contemporary African political problems.

THE FIRST WORLD WAR AND THE POLITICAL ORIGINS OF THE MODERN MIDDLE EAST

* M. E. Yapp, *The Near East Since the First World War* (London: Longman, 1991). Good overview of the politics of the Middle East.

* David Fromkin, *A Peace to End All Peace* (New York: Avon Books, 1989). Well-written account of the post-World War I settlements.

* Philip S. Khoury, *Syria and the French Mandate* (Princeton, NJ: Princeton University Press, 1987). An encyclopedic account of life in Syria under French rule.

* Arthur Hertzberg, ed., *The Zionist Idea* (Atheneum, NY: Atheneum, 1959). Collection of source documents on Zionism, prefaced by an excellent introductory essay.

Ann Moseley Lesch, *Arab Politics in Palestine, 1917–1939* (Ithaca, NY: Cornell University Press, 1979). A good history of the origins and evolution of Palestinian Arab nationalism.

* Charles D. Smith, *Palestine and the Arab-Israeli Conflict* (New York: St. Martin's Press, 1992). More detailed than Gerner's book; latest edition describes effects of the "New World Order" on the conflict.

* John Waterbury, *The Egypt of Nasser and Sadat* (Princeton, NJ: Princeton University Press, 1983). Very detailed study of Egyptian economic, social, and political history from 1952 to 1981.

* Daniel Yergin, *The Prize* (New York: Touchstone, 1991). Pulitzer Prize-winning account of the history of the oil industry.

THE MIDDLE EAST SINCE MIDCENTURY

* Alan Richards and John Waterbury, *A Political Economy of the Middle East* (Boulder, CO: Westview Press, 1989). Excellent study of the political economy of the region, arranged thematically.

* Fouad Ajami, *The Arab Predicament* (Cambridge: Cambridge University Press, 1981). Well-told narrative of the effects of the 1967 Arab-Israeli War on Arab thought and letters.

* Kemal H. Karpat, ed., *Political and Social Thought in the Contemporary Middle East* (New York: Praeger Publishers, 1982). Excellent source readings on Arab, Turkish, and Iranian nationalisms.

* Zachary Lockman and Joel Beinin, eds., *Intifada* (Boston: South End Press, 1989). Collection of essays and source documents on all aspects of the *Intifada*, from the changing role of women in the occupied territories to the uprising's international ramifications.

* Roy Mottahedeh, *The Mantle of the Prophet* (New York: Pantheon Books, 1985). Extremely well-written account of the elements that make up the Iranian historical memory, told through the eyes of an Iranian cleric.

* Barbara Freyer Stowasser, ed., *The Islamic Impulse* (Washington, DC: Center for Contemporary Arab Studies, 1987). Possibly the best collection of essays on Islamic populism.

* Indicates paperback edition available.

CHAPTER 34

Recovery and Crisis in Europe, 1945 to the Present

SEX AND DRUGS AND ROCK 'N' ROLL

"I Wanna Hold Your Hand" seems an unlikely anthem for a generation. Yet this song, performed by the British rock group the Beatles, was known around the world in the early 1960s by an entire generation of the young. Youth screamed and swooned and danced to it. Parents and educators screamed, too, but out of fear that "Beatlemania" signaled the decline of the younger generation in Western societies. Adults worried that young people were being caught up in hedonism, sexual pleasure, and mind-numbing drugs, all because of this loud, cacophonous music.

Young people of the fifties and sixties saw the advent of rock 'n' roll differently. Rock 'n' roll emerged as a national phenomenon in the United States in the mid-1950s, firmly rooted in the black music of rhythm and blues. White country and western music was also influential in shaping the new sound. Titles like "Rock Around the Clock," "Shake, Rattle, and Roll," "Keep A-Knockin'," and "Blue Suede Shoes," captured the attention of a generation. The experiences of teenagers were at the center of the new rhythms, confronted in the lyrics and amplified with electric guitars. Rock 'n' roll appealed to the young because it dealt openly with the issues of sex and young love and was aimed at the hypocrisy of the adult white world. Even the sound was revolutionary. It became "the music of the young," something that accentuated their differences from the adult world and their commonalities with each other.

Babies born after World War II began entering adolescence near the end of the 1950s, constituting a new audience for mass entertainment. They were also an important international mass market for music, as popular recordings began selling in the millions for the first time in history on such a scale. Music was now a consumer product. Elvis Presley, a white country blues singer from Memphis, Tennessee, emerged as the greatest figure on the rock 'n' roll scene in the late 1950s. His overt and androgynous sexuality, gyrating hips, and explicit lyrics made him an object of adult fears about loss of control of their children. He quickly developed a worldwide following of devoted fans, who hailed him as "the King" and who continue to honor his memory years after his death.

In the 1960s, British groups such as the Beatles from Liverpool entered the international rock scene. Dubbed "the mop tops" because of their long hair, they were condemned for transgressing sex roles in their appearance. Millions of boys copied their idols as hair became a political issue, a symbol of rebellion. Billboards appeared across the United States that proclaimed, "Beautify America—Get A Haircut!" With the new music came a new style of dressing, what adults saw as a uniform of disrespect for traditional values and parental authority. The British group Rolling Stones, who introduced electronic innovations to rock music, was considered more outrageously sexual, vulgar, and lewd than their countrymen the Beatles. Anti-rock movements cited "specialists" who warned that the new, amplified music caused deafness, drug addiction, and excessive sexual activity.

Although rock music served as a rallying cry for a generation who opposed war and exploitation, its frankness about sexuality did not result in a reformulation of gender roles. Woman's place in rock music was usually as an object of desire. Few of the major rock stars were women. The American artist Janis Joplin was a striking exception. What was known in the rock world as "girl groups"—the Ronettes and the Shangri-Las are two examples—reinforced predominantly male views of sexuality both by their dress and by the lyrics of their songs. The female body was treated as a commodity itself in the fashions associated with the new youth culture, such as the miniskirt and the bikini. Girls and young women were important consumers of the new music and the values it communicated.

Rock music quickly became an international phenomenon, spreading from the United States and Great Britain to appeal to the young throughout the world. Rock stars were the new self-made millionaires, often from working-class backgrounds, who were able to benefit from advertising innovations and mass-marketing techniques in a new age of consumption. The postwar generation that grew into adulthood beginning in the late 1960s shared a common musical culture. Student protest movements spread throughout Europe and the United States, and in the same period rock music gained acceptance as a legitimate and important musical genre. Through radio, television, and the international distribution of recordings, an international youth culture linked European and American youth together with common symbols and a common language of protest.

Reconstructing Europe

When the dust from the last bombs of World War II settled over Europe's cities, millions of survivors found themselves homeless. Millions more returned home to rubble from battlefronts and concentration camps with wounds beyond healing. There were no jobs; there was nothing to eat. The psychological trauma that accompanied such devastation could not be captured in the statistics on physical and human destruction that proved beyond a doubt that this was the most barbaric war in history. There could be no returning to life as normal. Yet for many the war was far gentler than the peace. For these peacetime combatants, often women and children, digging out and surviving were the greatest battles of all.

The Problem: Europe in Ruins

An American observer wrote back to his government in 1947 that "Europe is steadily deteriorating. The political position reflects the economic. One political crisis after another merely denotes the existence of economic distress. Millions of people in the cities are slowly starving." Even the winners were losers as survivors experienced a level of human and material destruction unknown in the history of warfare. Economists judged that Europe would need at least twenty-five years to reestablish its prewar economic capacity. But others feared that even that judgment was optimistic and that Europe would never recover as a world economic power.

Large-scale population movements made matters worse. Displaced persons by the millions moved across Europe. The release of prisoners of war and slave workers imprisoned during the Third Reich strained already weak economies. Germans were expelled from territories that Germany had controlled before the war. Soviet expansionist policies forced others to flee Estonia, Latvia, and Lithuania. Jews who survived the concentration camps resettled outside Europe, primarily in Palestine and the United States.

Industrial production in 1945 was one-third of its 1938 level. Housing shortages existed everywhere. France had lost one-fifth of its housing during the war years; Germany's fifty largest cities had seen two-fifths of their buildings reduced to rubble. Frankfurt, Düsseldorf, Dresden, Warsaw, and Berlin were virtually destroyed. The transportation infrastructure was severely damaged: railways, roads, and bridges were in shambles all over Europe. Communications networks were in disarray. In some cases, industrial plants fared better than urban centers. Yet round-the-clock production schedules had worn out machinery everywhere and replacement parts were nonexistent.

The Soviet Union, having incurred drastic losses in human life and productive capacity, sought security and prosperity through territorial expansion. Above all, it wanted a protective ring of satellite states as security against the western powers. Picking up territory from Finland and Poland, parts of East Prussia and eastern Czechoslovakia, forcibly reincorporating the Baltic states of Estonia, Latvia, and Lithuania, and recovering Bessarabia, the Soviet Union succeeded in acquiring sizable territories. Lacking the capital necessary to finance recovery, the Soviets sought compensation from eastern and central European territories. Behind a protective buffer of satellite states—Poland, East Germany, Czechoslovakia, Hungary, Romania, Bulgaria—Soviet leaders addressed the challenges of economic reconstruction. Yugoslavia and Albania chose to follow a more independent Communist path.

Territorial Gains of the USSR

European agriculture suffered severe reversals in wartime economies and was unable in 1945 to resume prewar production. In general, agricultural production stood at 50 percent of its prewar capacity. Italy suffered greatly, with one-third of its overall assets destroyed. The scarcity of goods converged with ballooning inflation. Black markets with astronomical prices for necessities flourished. Everywhere the outlook was bleak as the nations of Europe made only incremental gains in restoring productive capacity. The solution to the problem of Europe in ruins in the end came not from within but from without.

The Solution: The Marshall Plan

In contrast to the Soviet Union, the United States had incurred relatively light casualties in World War II. Because no fighting took place on the North American continent, U.S. cities, farmlands, and factories were intact. The United States had benefited economically from the conflict in Europe and actually expanded its productivity during the war. In 1945 the United States was producing a full 50 percent of the world's goods and services—a staggering fact to a displaced Great Britain, whose former trade networks were permanently destroyed. Furthermore, the United States held two-thirds of the world's gold. A United States bursting with energy and prosperity was a real threat to the Soviet Union viewing the rubble of its destroyed cities and counting the bodies of its dead.

Despite its wealth, the United States knew that it lacked one important guarantee to secure its growth and its future prosperity: adequate international markets for its goods. World War II actually helped the United States gain the markets it needed by facilitating the success of an international economic policy consistent with U.S. economic goals since 1920. War-torn economies, hungry for capital, no longer opposed U.S. intervention or erected trade barriers against American goods. In both Europe and Japan, the United States intervened to aid reconstruction and recovery.

By the spring of 1947 it was clear to American policy makers that initial postwar attempts to stabilize European economies and promote world recovery were simply not enough. The United States had, earlier in the same year, engineered emergency aid to Turkey and Greece, both objects of Soviet aspirations for control. The aid was extended in an atmosphere of opposition between the United States and the Soviet Union over issues of territorial control in eastern and southern Europe.

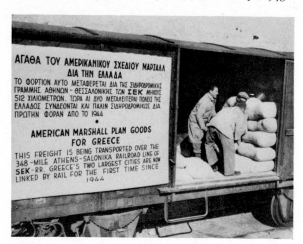

Signs in Greek and English proclaim the mission of a train carrying Marshall Plan goods to Greek cities.

In a bold stroke, on 5 June 1947, Secretary of State George C. Marshall (1880–1959) introduced the European Recovery Act in a commencement address at Harvard University. The legislation, which became popularly known as the Marshall Plan, made available billions of dollars in aid to European states, provided that two conditions were met: (1) the recipient states must cooperate with one another in aligning national economic policies and improving the international monetary system; (2) they must work toward breaking down trade barriers.

Participating countries included Austria, Belgium, Denmark, France, West Germany, Great Britain, Greece, Iceland, Italy, Luxembourg, the Netherlands, Norway, Sweden, Switzerland, and Turkey. Russia and eastern European countries were also eligible for aid under the original formulation. But Russia opposed the plan from the first, wary of U.S. intentions to extend its influence over the nations of eastern Europe. Soviet opposition encouraged members of the U.S. Congress, afraid of a Communist takeover in Europe, to support the plan.

The amount of U.S. aid to Europe was massive. Over $23 billion was pumped into western Europe between 1947 and 1952. American foreign aid restored western European trade and production, while at the same time controlling inflation. Dean Acheson (1893–1971), Marshall's successor as secretary of state, described the plan in terms of "our duty as human beings" but nevertheless considered it "chiefly as a matter of national self-interest."

As significant as the gift of funds to European states undoubtedly was, no less important was the administrative apparatus that American money brought in its wake. In order to expend available monies most effectively and comply with stipulations for cooperation and regulation, the states of western Europe, with the exception of West Germany, resorted to intensified planning and limited nationalization of key industries. Regulation and state intervention dominated the formulation of economic policy. Special attention was given to workers' welfare through unemployment insurance, retirement benefits, public health, and housing policies. European states recognized the need to provide a safety net for their citizens in order to avoid the disastrous depression and stagnation of the 1930s, while attempting to rebuild their shattered economies.

The economic theory of John Maynard Keynes, applied successfully by neutral Sweden to its economic policies during the war, came into vogue throughout Europe in 1945, and the postwar era saw the triumph of Keynesian economics. Keynes favored macroeconomic policies to increase productivity and argued for an active role for government in "priming the pump" of economic growth. The government should be responsible, according to Keynes, for the control and regulation of the economy with the goal of ensuring full employment for its people. Governments could and should check inflation and eliminate boom-and-bust cycles, incurring deficits by spending beyond revenues if necessary.

U.S. foreign aid contributed mightily to the extension of central planning and the growth of the welfare state throughout western Europe. But money alone could not have accomplished the recovery that took place. The chief mechanism for administering Marshall Plan aid was the Office of European Economic Cooperation (OEEC). This master coordinating agency made the requirements for recovery clear. European states had to stabilize their own economies. Cooperation between the public and private sectors was intended to free market forces, modernize production, and raise productivity. Planning mechanisms, including transnational organizations and networks, resulted in the modernization of production and the assimilation of new techniques, new styles of management, and innovative business practices from the United States.

Western European Economic Integration

The Marshall Plan reconciled western Europe with West Germany through economic cooperation, although that was by no means its original purpose. Realizing that

GEORGE C. MARSHALL, THE MARSHALL PLAN, JUNE 1947

■ *In the rituals that are part of graduation ceremonies, guest speakers traditionally address the challenges of the future awaiting graduates. Not many of these commencement addresses change the world. The speech given by U.S. secretary of state George C. Marshall at Harvard University in June 1947 was different. By pledging gifts in aid, the United States helped rebuild war-torn Europe and transform the world's economy.*

The truth of the matter is that Europe's requirements for the next three or four years of foreign food and other essential products—principally from America—are so much greater than her present ability to pay that she must have substantial additional help or face economic, social, and political deterioration of a very grave character.

The remedy lies in breaking the vicious circle and restoring the confidence of the European people in the economic future of their own countries and of Europe as a whole. The manufacturer and the farmer throughout wide areas must be able and willing to exchange their products for currencies the continuing value of which is not open to question.

Aside from the demoralizing effect on the world at large and the possibilities of disturbances arising as a result of the desperation of the people concerned, the consequences to the economy of the United States should be apparent to all. It is logical that the United States should do whatever it is able to do to assist in the return of normal economic health in the world, without which there can be no political stability and no assured peace. Our policy is directed not against any country or doctrine but against hunger, poverty, desperation, and chaos. Its purpose should be the revival of a working economy in the world so as to permit the emergence of political and social conditions in which free institutions can exist. Such assistance, I am convinced, must not be on a piecemeal basis as various crises develop. Any assistance that this Government may render in the future should provide a cure rather than a mere palliative. Any government that is willing to assist in the task of recovery will find full cooperation, I am sure, on the part of the United States Government. Any government which maneuvers to block the recovery of other countries cannot expect help from us. Furthermore, governments, political parties, or groups which seek to perpetuate human misery in order to profit therefrom politically or otherwise will encounter the opposition of the United States.

Department of State Bulletin (June 15, 1947).

Europe as a region needed the cooperation of its member states if it was to contend in world markets, associations dedicated to integration began to emerge alongside economic planning mechanisms. The Council of Europe dealt with the "discussion of questions of common concern and by agreements and common action in economic, social, cultural, scientific, legal, and administrative matters and in the maintenance and further realization of human rights and fundamental freedoms." Although not itself a supranational institution with its own authority, the Council of Europe urged a federation among European states. Britain alone rejected all attempts to develop structures of loose, intergovernmental cooperation.

Belgium, the Netherlands, and Luxembourg were the first European states to establish themselves as an economic unit—the Benelux countries. Internal customs duties were removed among the three states and a common external tariff barrier was erected. The Schuman Plan joined France and West Germany in economic cooperation by pooling all their coal and steel resources beginning in 1950. The creators of the plan, Jean Monnet (1888–1979) and Robert Schuman (1886–1963) of France, saw it as the first step toward the removal of all economic barriers among European states and as a move toward eventual political integration.

In 1951 the Netherlands, Belgium, Luxembourg, France, Italy, and West Germany formed the European

A train carrying iron ore crosses the Franco-Luxembourg border, celebrating the joint community in coal and steel that became effective in 1953. The European Coal and Steel Community was the first step in the economic integration of Europe.

achieved the support of the United States in its transitional period, in which it had fifteen years to accomplish its aims.

While promoting prosperity, European economic unification favored concentration and the emergence of large corporations. Vast individual fortunes flourished under state sponsorship and the rule of the experts. National parliaments were sometimes eclipsed by new economic decision-making organizations that aimed to make western Europe into a single free-trade area. The Soviet Union, too, relied on state planning to foster rapid economic growth, but it was central planning emanating from Moscow with low priority assigned to consumer industries.

The United States found itself playing the role of rich uncle in bankrolling the European recovery. The billions of dollars in American aid pumped into European nations reinforced the political reality that the world was polarizing into two camps, one benefiting from U.S. dollars and the other not. The United States' long-term commitment to promote its own economic interests by helping future trading partners led it also into playing the role of policeman throughout the world. Reconstruction took place in the context of a new kind of global struggle.

Coal and Steel Community (ECSC). While constantly confronting domestic opposition on nationalist grounds, the ECSC succeeded in establishing a "common market" in coal and steel among its member states. In 1957 the same six members created the European Economic Community (EEC) and committed themselves to broadening the integration of markets. This was the beginning of what became known as the Common Market.

The Common Market aimed to establish among its member states a free movement of labor and capital, the elimination of restrictions on trade, common investment practices, and coordinated social-welfare programs. National agricultural interests were to be protected. Great Britain was initially a vocal opponent of the Common Market and continued to defend its own trading relationship with its Commonwealth countries. In 1973 Great Britain became a member of the Common Market and joined with other European nations in defining common economic policies. The EEC meanwhile

Regulating the Cold War

With the cessation of the "hot" war that had ripped Europe apart from 1939 to 1945, Europe and Japan were destroyed, leaving the United States and the Soviet Union as indisputably the two richest and strongest nations in the world. The Soviets understood that they ran a sorry second to American military superiority—the United States was alone in possessing the atomic bomb—and to American wealth, which, measured in GNP, was 400 percent greater than that of the Soviet Union. War had made these two superpowers allies; now the peace promised to make them once again into wary foes. In the three years that followed the war, a new kind of conflict emerged between the two superpower victors, a war deemed "cold" because of its lack of military violence, but a bitter war nonetheless.

The Cold War emerged as an ideological opposition between communism and capitalist democracies, dominated by the two superpowers, the Soviet Union and

NATO countries, 1955

Warsaw Pact countries, 1955

The Cold War

the United States, and affecting the entire globe. Drawing on three decades of distrust, the Cold War was related to the economic and foreign policy goals of both superpowers. Cold War conflict initially developed because of differing Russian and American notions regarding the economic reconstruction of Europe. The Soviet Union realized that American aid to Europe was not a primarily humanitarian program: it was part of an economic offensive in Europe that would contribute to the dominance of American capital in world markets. The United States recognized that the Soviet Union hoped to achieve its own recovery through outright control of eastern Europe. Needing the stability of peace, the Soviets saw in eastern Europe, hostile as the area may have been to forced integration, a necessary buffer against Western competition. The Soviet Union feared U.S. intentions to establish liberal governments and capitalist markets in these states bordering its own frontiers and viewed such attempts as inimical to Soviet interests. For these reasons, Stalin refused to allow free elections in Poland and forcibly annexed neighboring territories that included eastern Finland, the Baltic states, East Prussia, eastern Poland, the Subcarpathian Ukraine (Ruthenia), and Bessarabia. With the excep-

tion of East Prussia, these annexations were all limited to territories that had once been part of tsarist Russia.

Atomic Politics

The nuclear arms race began in earnest during World War II, well before the first atomic bomb was dropped in August 1945. The Germans, the Russians, and the British all had teams exploring the destructive possibilities of nuclear fission during the war. But the Americans had the edge in the development of the bomb. Understanding the political significance of the weapon, Stalin committed the Soviet Union to a breakneck program of development following the war. The result was that the USSR ended the American monopoly in 1949 with the first Soviet atomic bomb. Both countries developed the hydrogen bomb almost simultaneously in 1953. Space exploration by satellite was also deemed important in terms of detection and deployment of bombs, and the Soviets pulled ahead in this area with the launching of the first satellite, *Sputnik 1*, in 1957. Intercontinental ballistic missiles (ICBMs) followed, further accelerating the pace of nuclear armament.

WINSTON CHURCHILL, THE IRON CURTAIN (1946)

■ *Winston Churchill (1874–1965), prime minister of England during World War II, captured the drama of the postwar international order in a speech he delivered in Missouri in 1946. Churchill had long been suspicious of the political motives of the Soviet Union, although he welcomed Stalin as an ally in defeating Hitler. The term that he used,* iron curtain, *described graphically the fate of Europe that many feared, a Europe rigidly divided between East and West, no more than a pawn in the struggle of the superpowers.*

From Stettin in the Baltic to Trieste in the Adriatic, an iron curtain has descended across the Continent. Behind that line lie all the capitals of the ancient states of Central and Eastern Europe. Warsaw, Berlin, Prague, Vienna, Budapest, Belgrade, Bucharest and Sofia, all these famous cities and the populations around them lie in what I must call the Soviet sphere, and all are subject in one form or another, not only to Soviet influence but to a very high and, in many cases, increasing measure of control from Moscow. Athens alone—Greece with its immortal glories—is free to decide its future at an election under British, American and French observation. The Russian-dominated Polish Government has been encouraged to make enormous and wrongful inroads upon Germany, and mass expulsions of millions of Germans on a scale grievous and undreamed-of are now taking place. The Communist parties, which were very small in all these Eastern States of Europe, have been raised to preeminence and power far beyond their numbers and are seeking everywhere to obtain totalitarian control. Police governments are prevailing in nearly every case, and so far, except in Czechoslovakia, there is no true democracy.

The safety of the world requires a new unity in Europe, from which no nation should be permanently outcast. It is from the quarrels of the strong parent races in Europe that the world wars we have witnessed, or which occurred in former times, have sprung. Twice in our own lifetime we have seen the United States, against their wishes and their traditions, against arguments, the force of which it is impossible not to comprehend, drawn by irresistible forces, into these wars in time to secure the victory of the good cause, but only after frightful slaughter and devastation had occurred. Twice the United States has had to send several millions of its young men across the Atlantic to find the war; but now war can find any nation, wherever it may dwell between dusk and dawn. Surely we should work with conscious purpose for a grand pacification of Europe, within the structure of the United Nations and in accordance with its Charter. That I feel is an open cause of policy of very great importance.

In front of the iron curtain which lies across Europe are other causes for anxiety. In Italy the Communist Party is seriously hampered by having to support the Communist-trained Marshal Tito's claims to former Italian territory at the head of the Adriatic. Nevertheless the future of Italy hangs in the balance. Again one cannot imagine a regenerated Europe without a strong France. All my public life I have worked for a strong France and I never lost faith in her destiny, even in the darkest hours. I will not lose faith now. However, in a great number of countries, far from the Russian frontiers and throughout the world, Communist fifth columns are established and work in complete unity and absolute obedience to the directions they receive from the Communist centre. Except in the British Commonwealth and in the United States where Communism is in its infancy, the Communist parties or fifth columns constitute a growing challenge and peril to Christian civilization. These are somber facts for anyone to have to recite on the morrow of a victory gained by so much splendid comradeship in arms and in the cause of freedom and democracy; but we should be most unwise not to face them squarely while time remains.

From *Winston S. Churchill: His Complete Speeches 1897–1963*, ed. Robert Rhodes James 1983.

The atomic bomb and thermonuclear weapons contributed greatly to the shape of Cold War politics. The incineration of Hiroshima and Nagasaki sent a clear message to the world about the power of total annihilation available to those who controlled the bombs. The threat of such total destruction made full and direct confrontation with an equally armed enemy impossible. Both the United States and the Soviet Union, the first two members of the nuclear "club," knew that they had the capability of obliterating their enemy but not before the enemy could respond in retaliation. They also knew that the technology necessary for nuclear arms was available to any industrial power. By 1974 the "nuclear club" included Great Britain, France, the People's Republic of China, and India. These countries joined the United States and the Soviet Union in spending billions every year to expand nuclear arsenals and to develop more sophisticated weaponry and delivery systems.

A new vocabulary transformed popular attitudes and values. "Missile gaps," "deterrence," "first strike," "second strike," "radioactive fallout," and "containment" were all terms that colored popular fears. Citizens in the Soviet Union learned of American weapons stockpiling and American deployment of military forces throughout the world. Americans learned that the Russians had the ability to deliver bombs that could wipe out major U.S. cities. Paranoia on both sides was encouraged by heads of state in their public addresses throughout the fifties. Traitors were publicly tried, while espionage was sponsored by the state.

The first nuclear test-ban treaty, signed in 1963, banned tests in the atmosphere. Arms limitation and nonproliferation were the subjects of a series of conferences between the United States and the Soviet Union in the late 1960s and pointed the way to limitations eventually agreed on in the next decade. The United Nations, created by the Allies immediately following World War II to take the place of the defunct League of Nations, established international agencies for the purpose of harnessing nuclear power for peaceful uses. On the whole, however, the arms race persisted as a key continuity in Cold War politics. The race required the dedication of huge national resources to maintain a competitive stance. Conventional forces were also expanded. With the aim of containing the USSR, the United States entered into a series of military alliances around the world. In order to provide mutual assistance should any member be attacked, the United States joined with Belgium, Britain, Canada, Denmark, France, Iceland, Italy, the Netherlands, Norway, and Portugal in 1949 to form the North Atlantic Organization (NATO). Greece and Turkey became members in 1952, West Germany in 1955, and Spain in 1982. The potential military threat of the Soviet Union in western Europe prompted this peacetime military alliance. The Southeast Asia Treaty Organization (SEATO) in 1954 and the Baghdad Pact of 1955 (known as CENTO in 1959) followed.

The United States strengthened its military presence throughout the period by acquiring 1,400 military bases in foreign countries for its own forces. The Soviet Union countered developments in the West with its own alliances and organizations. In 1949, the USSR established the Council for Mutual Economic Assistance, or Comecon, with bilateral agreements between the Soviet Union and eastern European states. Comecon was Stalin's response to the U.S. Marshall Plan in western Europe. Rather than providing aid, however, Comecon benefited the Soviet Union at the expense of its partners and sought to integrate and control the economies of eastern Europe for Soviet gain. In 1955, Albania, Bulgaria, Romania, Czechoslovakia, Hungary, Poland, and East Germany—all Comecon members—joined with the Soviet Union to form a defensive alliance organization known as the Warsaw Pact. The USSR intended its eastern European allies to serve as a strategic buffer zone against the NATO forces.

In a new kind of global politics the superpowers vied with each other to find partners, especially in formerly colonized areas, to join their camps. By the end of the Second World War, European colonial empires had been weakened or destroyed by the ravages of battle, by occupation, and by neglect. The United States, committed to free and open markets, pushed its advantage at the conclusion of the peace by insisting on the dismantling of the empires of its allies as well as those of its enemies. Nevertheless, decolonization meant continued dependence for many newly formed countries which were no longer directly controlled as colonies but continued to be dominated by the Western capitalist powers and Japan, on whom they relied for their markets and trade.

The Soviets, preoccupied with their own recovery in the years immediately following the war, were in no position to assert a global policy in formerly colonized areas. Soviet leader Joseph Stalin had limited the Soviet Union's foreign involvement following the Second World War to Communist regimes that shared borders with the USSR in eastern Europe and Asia. Stalin's death in 1953 unleashed a struggle for power among the Communist party leadership. It also initiated almost

The signing of the nuclear test ban treaty of 1963. Seated, left to right, are U.S. secretary of state Dean Rusk, Soviet foreign minister Andrei Gromyko, and Lord Home of Great Britain.

immediately a process of de-Stalinization and the beginnings of a thaw in censorship and repression. A growing urban and professional class expected improvements in the quality of life and greater freedoms after years of war and hardship. In 1956, at the Twentieth Party Congress, Nikita Khrushchev (1894–1971), as head of the Communist party, denounced Stalin as incompetent and cruel. After five years of jockeying for power among Stalin's former lieutenants, Khrushchev emerged victorious and assumed the office of premier in 1958. Under Khrushchev, former colonies played an important new role in Soviet Cold War strategies. The Soviet Union abandoned its previous caution and assumed a global role in offering "friendship treaties," military advice, trade credits, and general support for attempts at national liberation in Asia, Africa, and Latin America.

The Two Germanies and the World in Two Blocs

In central Europe, Cold War tensions first surfaced over the question of how to treat Germany. The United States and the Soviet Union had very different ideas about the future of their former enemy. By fostering economic reconstruction in Europe, the United States

counted on a self-supporting and stable German economy transfused with American funds. To the contrary, the Soviet Union, blaming Germany for its extreme destruction, demanded that German resources be siphoned off for Soviet reconstruction.

With Germany's defeat, its territory had been divided into four zones, occupied by American, Soviet, British, and French troops. An Allied Control Commission consisting of representatives of the four powers was to govern Germany as a whole, in keeping with the decisions made at Yalta before the end of the war. As Soviet and American antagonisms over Germany's future deepened, however, Allied rule polarized, with the internal politics of each area determined by the ideological conflicts between communism and capitalist free enterprise.

Allied attempts to administer Germany as a whole faltered and failed in 1948 over a question of economic policy. The zones of the Western occupying forces (the United States, Great Britain, and France), now administered as a single unit, issued a uniform and stable currency that the Russians accurately saw as a threat to their own economic policies in their zone. The Soviets blockaded the city of Berlin which, although behind the frontier of the Russian zone, was being administered in sectors by the four powers and whose western sector promised to become a successful enclave of Western

Nikita S. Khrushchev, Report to the Twentieth Party Congress, February 1956

■ *Like Stalin before him, the Soviet leader Nikita Khrushchev (1894–1971) perceived that the Soviet Union was locked in a worldwide struggle with the United States and Western capitalist nations. The experiences of the Korean War and the escalation of the nuclear arms race prompted him to proceed with wariness in foreign policy. In his now famous speech before the Twentieth Party Congress in February 1956, Khrushchev, as first secretary of the Communist party, accused the United States, England, and France of imperialism and pleaded for the peaceful coexistence of communism and capitalism, confident that, in the end, communism would win the day.*

Soon after the Second World War ended, the influence of reactionary and militarist groups began to be increasingly evident in the policy of the United States of America, Britain and France. Their desire to enforce their will on other countries by economic and political pressure, threats and military provocation prevailed. This became known as the "positions of strength" policy. It reflects the aspiration of the most aggressive sections of present-day imperialism to win world supremacy, to suppress the working class and the democratic and national-liberation movements; it reflects their plans for military adventures against the socialist camp.

The international atmosphere was poisoned by war hysteria. The arms race began to assume more and more monstrous dimensions. Many big U.S. military bases designed for use against the U.S.S.R. and the People's Democracies [East European countries under Soviet control] were built in countries thousands of miles from the borders of the United States. "Cold war" was begun against the socialist camp. International distrust was artificially kindled, and nations set against one another. A bloody war was launched in Korea; the war in Indo-China dragged on for years.

. . . The Leninist principle of peaceful co-existence of states with different social systems has always been and remains the general line of our country's foreign policy. . . . To this day the enemies of peace allege that the Soviet Union is out to overthrow capitalism in other countries by "exporting" revolution. It goes without saying that among us Communists there are no supporters of capitalism. But this does not mean that we have interfered or plan to interfere in the internal affairs of countries where capitalism still exists. . . .

When we say that the socialist system will win in the competition between the two systems—the capitalist and the socialist—this by no means signifies that its victory will be achieved through armed interference by the socialist countries in the internal affairs of the capitalist countries. Our certainty of the victory of communism is based on the fact that the socialist mode of production possesses decisive advantages over the capitalist mode of production. Precisely because of this, the ideas of Marxism-Leninism are more and more capturing the minds of the broad masses of the working people in the capitalist countries, just as they have captured the minds of millions of men and women in our country and the People's Democracies. (*Prolonged applause.*) We believe that all working men in the world, once they have become convinced of the advantages communism brings, will sooner or later take the road of struggle for the construction of socialist society.

Current Soviet Policies II. The Documentary record of the Twentieth Party Congress and its Aftermath, published by *Current Digest of the Soviet Press.*

capitalism. With the support of the people of West Berlin, the United States directed the airlifting of food and supplies into West Berlin for a period of almost a year, defending it as an outpost that must be preserved from the advance of communism. The Russians were forced to withdraw the blockade in the spring of 1949. But the Berlin blockade hardened the commitment on both sides to two Germanies.

The Division of Germany

Two German states came into existence in 1949, their dates of birth separated by less than a month. The Federal Republic of Germany, within the American orbit, was established as a democratic, parliamentary regime. Free elections brought the Christian Democrat Konrad Adenauer (1876–1967) to power as chancellor. The German Democratic Republic was ruled as a single-party state under Walter Ulbricht (1893–1973), who took his direction from the Soviet Union. The division of Germany became a microcosm of the division of the world into two armed camps. With the support of local Communist parties, Soviet-dominated governments were established in Poland, Hungary, Bulgaria, and Romania in 1947. The following year Czechoslovakia was pulled into the Soviet orbit.

Violence erupted in 1953 in East Berlin as workers protested against conditions in the workplace, but it was quickly and effectively suppressed. Among eastern European populations resentful of Soviet control and influence, discontent over collectivization, low wages, and the lack of consumer goods fueled a latent nationalism. Demands for reforms and liberalization in Poland produced riots and changes in Communist party leadership. Wladislaw Gomulka (1905–82), a Communist with a nationalist point of view who had survived Stalin's purges, aimed to take advantage of the power vacuum

created by the departure of Stalinist leaders. Gomulka refused to back down in the face of severe Soviet pressure and the threat of a Soviet invasion to keep him from power. Elected as the first secretary of the Communist party in Poland, Gomulka sought to steer his nation on a more liberal course.

Hungarians followed suit with their demands for diversity and for the withdrawal of Hungary from the Warsaw Pact. On 23 October 1956, inspired by the events in Poland, Hungarians rose up in anger against their old-guard Stalinist rulers. Imre Nagy (1896–1958), a liberal Communist, took control of the government, attempted to introduce democratic reforms, and relaxed economic controls. The Soviets, however, were unwilling to lose control of their sphere of influence in Eastern Bloc nations and to jeopardize their system of defense in the Warsaw Pact. Moscow responded to liberal experimentation in Hungary by sending tanks and troops into Budapest. Brutal repression and purges followed. The Hungarian experience in 1956 made clear that too much change too quickly would not be tolerated by the Soviet rulers and reminded everyone of the realities of Soviet control and its defense priorities in eastern Europe.

East Berlin in the late 1950s and early 1960s posed a particular problem for Communist rule. Unable to compete successfully in wages and standard of living with the western, capitalist sector of the city, East Berlin saw growing numbers of its educated and professional classes commuting or moving to West Berlin to seek better employment. In 1961 the Soviet Union responded to this problem in a fashion that astounded the world: it built a concrete and wire barrier that cordoned off East Berlin, literally turning East Berlin residents into prisoners. The Berlin Wall eventually stretched for 103 miles, with heavily policed crossing points, turrets, and troops and tanks facing each other across the divide that came to symbolize the Cold War.

Attempts at liberalization also met with repression in Czechoslovakia. Early in 1968, Alexander Dubček, Czech party secretary and a member of the younger, educated generation of technocrats, supported liberal reforms in Czechoslovakia. During this time, known as the Prague Spring, Dubček acted on popular desires for nationalism, the end of censorship, and better working conditions. Above all, he led the way to democratic reforms in the political process that would restore rule to the people. Dubček spoke of "socialism with a human face," although, unlike the Hungarians in 1956, he made no move to withdraw his country from the Warsaw Pact or to defy Soviet leadership. Moscow nevertheless feared the erosion of obedience within the Eastern Bloc and the collapse of one-party rule in the Czech state, and sent thousands of tanks and hundreds of thousands of Warsaw Pact troops to Prague and other Czech cities to reestablish control. The Czechs responded with passive resistance.

Alone among eastern European leaders, Marshal Tito of Yugoslavia successfully resisted Soviet encroachment. A partisan leader of the Communist resistance during World War II, Tito ruled Yugoslavia as a dictator after 1945 and refused to accede to Soviet directives to collectivize agriculture and to participate in joint economic ventures.

On numerous occasions in the 1950s and 1960s the Cold War threatened to become hot as the superpowers engaged in a politics of "brinkmanship"—a term coined by the U.S. secretary of state John Foster Dulles (1888–1959) to indicate a confrontationist foreign policy that brought the superpowers repeatedly to the verge of armed conflict. Korea, the Persian Gulf, Egypt, Southeast Asia, Guatemala, and Cuba were important arenas in the development of Cold War antagonisms between the United States and the Soviet Union. Nor was everyone happy within the NATO alliance. General Charles de Gaulle (1890–1970), as president of the French Fifth Republic, rejected the straitjacket of American dominance in western Europe and asserted his country's independent status by exploding the first French atomic bomb in 1960. Refusing to place the French military under an American general who served as Supreme Allied Commander for NATO, de Gaulle completely withdrew France from participation in NATO by 1966. He forged an independent French foreign policy, taking advantage of the loosening of bloc politics around the mid-1960s.

The Eastern Bloc and Recovery

The Soviet economy experienced dramatic recovery after 1945, in spite of the severe damage inflicted on it during the war. The production of steel, coal, and crude oil skyrocketed under state planning, making the Soviet Union second only to the United States in industrial output. Heavy industry was the top priority of Soviet recovery, in keeping with prewar commitments to rapid modernization. In addition, the postwar Soviet economy assumed the new burdens of the development of a nuclear arsenal and an expensive program for the exploration of space. Stalin maintained the Soviet Union on the footing of a war economy, restricted occupational mobility, and continued to rely on forced-labor camps.

The Soviet Union's standard of living remained relatively low in these years when western Europe was undergoing a consumer revolution. In the Soviet Union and throughout the Eastern Bloc countries, women's full participation in the labor force was essential for recovery. In spite of their strong presence in highly skilled sectors like medicine, Soviet and Eastern Bloc women remained poorly paid. Soviet men received higher salaries for the same work on the grounds that they had to support families.

Stalin's successors recognized the need for change, especially with regard to the neglected sectors of agricultural production and consumer products. The Soviet population was growing rapidly, from 170 million in 1939 to 234 million in 1967. Khrushchev promised the Russian people lower prices and a shorter work week but in 1964, when he fell from power, Russians were paying

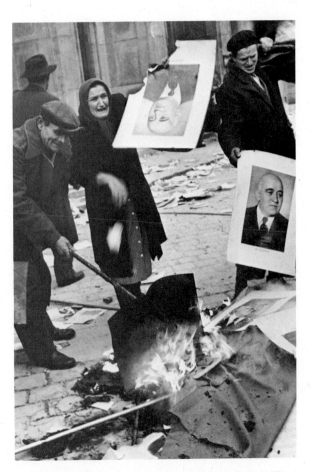

Angry citizens of Budapest rip up portraits of Matyas Rakoski (First Secretary of the Workers' Party) and throw them on a fire during the Hungarian uprising of 1956. The revolt did not bring freedom to Hungary, but it helped cut short the Stalin era in the Soviet Union.

The Cold War

1947	Marshall Plan starts United States aid to European countries
1947	Pro-Soviet governments established in Poland, Hungary, Bulgaria, and Romania
1948	Pro-Soviet government established in Czechoslovakia
1949	Western European states, United States, and Canada form North Atlantic Treaty Organization (NATO)
1949	Federal Republic of Germany and German Democratic Republic established
1949	Soviet Union creates Council for Mutual Economic Assistance (COMECON)
1949	Soviet Union tests its first atomic bomb
1950–53	Korean War, ending with the partition of Korea
1953	United States and Soviet Union develop hydrogen bombs
1956	Hungarian uprising and subsequent repression by Soviet military forces
1957	The Netherlands, Belgium, Luxembourg, France, Italy, and West Germany form the European Economic Community (EEC), also called Common Market.
1957	Soviet Union launches first satellite, *Sputnik 1*
1961	Berlin Wall built
1961–73	United States troops engaged in Vietnam
1962	Cuban missile crisis
1963	Soviet Union and United States sign Nuclear Test-Ban Treaty
1968	Prague Spring uprising in Czechoslovakia, quelled by Soviet Union
1972	Strategic Arms Limitation Treaty between the Soviet Union and the United States

higher prices for their food than before. With a declining rate of development, the Soviet economy lacked the necessary capital to advance the plans for growth in all sectors. Defense spending nearly doubled in the short period between 1960 and 1968.

The nature of planned Soviet growth also exacted heavy costs in the Eastern Bloc countries. Adhering to the Soviet pattern of heavy industrial expansion at the expense of agriculture and consumer goods, East Germany nearly doubled its industrial output by 1955, despite having been stripped of its industrial plant by the Soviet Union before 1948. Czechoslovakia, Bulgaria, Romania, and Yugoslavia all reported significant industrial growth in this period. Yet dislocations caused by collectivization and heavy defense expenditures stirred up social unrest in East Germany, Czechoslovakia, Poland, and Hungary. The Soviet Union responded with some economic concessions but on the whole stressed common industrial and defense pursuits, employing ideological persuasion and military pressure to keep its reluctant partners in line. The slowed growth of the 1960s, the delay in development of consumer durables, and the inadequacy of basic foodstuffs, housing, and clothing were the costs that Eastern Bloc citizens paid for their inefficient and rigid planned economies dedicated to the development of heavy industry. On the positive side, in eastern Europe and the Soviet Union, poverty was virtually eliminated because of state-subsidized housing, health care, and higher education, which were available to all.

The division of the world into two camps framed the recovery of combatant nations dealing with the losses of World War II. The Cold War instilled fear and terror in the populations who lived on both sides of the divide. Yet the Cold War also created the terms for stability following the upheaval of war. It promoted prosperity that preserved the long-term policies of both the United States and the Soviet Union in the twentieth century.

Creating the Welfare State

The welfare state, a creation of the post–World War II era throughout Europe, grew out of the social welfare policies of the interwar period and out of the experiences of the war itself. Welfare programs aimed to protect citizens through the establishment by the state of a decent standard of living available for everyone. In

France, the primary concern of the welfare state was the protection of children and the issue of family allowances. In Great Britain, as in Germany, emphasis was placed on unemployment insurance and health care benefits. Everywhere, however, the welfare state developed a related set of social programs and policies whereby the state intervened in the cycles of individual lives to provide economic support for the challenges of birth, sickness, old age, and unemployment. The student protest and feminist movements of the late 1960s were shaped by the policies and failures of the welfare state and informed a new kind of dissent in western Europe and the United States.

After the phenomenal growth and prosperity of the postwar years, western Europe experienced a new set of harsh realities in the 1970s with skyrocketing oil prices, inflation, and recession. The permanent presence of foreign workers, many of them unemployed or erratically employed in the economic downturns of the 1970s and 1980s, came to be seen as a problem by welfare-state leaders and politicians of the new Right.

The Welfare State and Gender

Despite the different paths toward reconstruction following World War II, every western European nation experienced dramatic increases in total wealth. Per capita income was clearly on the rise through the mid-1960s, and there was more disposable wealth than ever before. Prosperity encouraged new patterns of spending based on confidence in the economy. This new consumerism, in turn, was essential to economic growth and future productivity.

The social programs of the welfare state played an important role in promoting postwar consumption. People began to relax about their economic futures, more secure because of the provisions of unemployment insurance, old-age pensions, and health and accident insurance. In the mid-1950s all over western Europe people began to spend their earnings, knowing that accidents, disasters, and sicknesses would be taken care of by the state. In addition, western Europeans began to buy on credit, spending money they had not yet earned. This, too, was an innovation in postwar markets.

Welfare programs could be sustained only in an era of prosperity and economic growth, since they depended on taxation of income for their funds. Such taxation did not, however, result in a redistribution of wealth. Wealth remained in the hands of a few and became even more concentrated as a result of phenomenal postwar economic growth. In West Germany, for example, 1.7 percent of the population owned 35 percent of the society's total wealth.

Just as the welfare state did not redistribute wealth, neither did it provide equal pay for equal work. In France, women who performed the same jobs as men in typesetting, for example, and who on average set 15,000 keystrokes per hour at the keyboards compared to 10,000 by men, earned 50 percent of men's salaries and held different titles for their jobs. Separate wage scales for women drawn up during the Nazi period remained in effect in West Germany until 1956. The skills associated with occupations performed by women were downgraded, as were their salaries. Women earned two-thirds or less of what men earned throughout western Europe. Welfare state revenues were, in part, a direct result of pay-scale inequities. Lower salaries for women meant higher profits and helped make economic recovery possible.

Social Policies, Family Issues, and Women's Protests

Prewar concerns with a declining birthrate intensified after World War II. In some European countries the birthrate climbed in the years immediately following the war, an encouraging sign to observers who saw in this trend an optimistic commitment to the future after the cessation of the horrors of war. France and the United States, where the birthrates began to climb even before the war was over, deviated from the trajectory. Nearly everywhere throughout Europe, however, the rise in the birthrate was momentary, with the United States standing alone in experiencing a genuine and sustained "baby boom" that lasted until about 1960. On average, women everywhere were having fewer children by choice.

Concurrent with a low birthrate was a renewed emphasis on family life and family values in the postwar years. Those who had lived through the previous twenty years were haunted by the memories of the Great Depression, severe economic hardships, destructive war, and the loss of loved ones. Women and men throughout western Europe and the United States embraced family values and a return to normal life, even if they did not opt for large families. Expectations for improved family life in turn placed new demands on welfare-state programs and on women.

Welfare-state programs aimed at family life differed from country to country as the result of a series of different expectations of women as workers and women as

SIMONE DE BEAUVOIR, *THE SECOND SEX*

■ *Simone de Beauvoir, one of France's leading intellectuals, wrote philosophical treatises, essays, and novels that drew on a wide variety of cultural traditions and synthesized philosophy, history, literary criticism, and Freudian psychoanalysis in her studies of the human condition.* The Second Sex, *which first appeared in French in 1949, has subsequently been translated into many languages and has appeared in numerous editions throughout the world. It served as a call to arms for the feminist movement, provoking debate, controversy, and a questioning of the fundamental gender arrangements of modern society.*

A man never begins by presenting himself as an individual of a certain sex; it goes without saying that he is a man. The terms *masculine* and *feminine* are used symmetrically only as a matter of form, as on legal papers. In actuality the relation of the two sexes is not quite like that of two electrical poles, for man represents both the positive and the neutral, as is indicated by the common use of *man* to designate human beings in general; whereas woman represents only the negative, defining by limiting criteria, without reciprocity. In the midst of an abstract discussion it is vexing to hear a man say: "You think thus and so because you are a woman"; but I know that my only defense is to reply: "I think thus and so because it is true," thereby removing my subjective self from the argument. It would be out of the question to reply: "And you think the contrary because you are a man," for it is understood that the fact of being a man is no peculiarity. A man is in the right in being a man; it is the woman who is in the wrong. It amounts to this: just as for the ancients there was an absolute vertical with reference to which the oblique was defined, so there is an absolute human type, the masculine. Woman has ovaries, a uterus; these peculiarities imprison her in her subjectivity, circumscribe her within the limits of her own nature. It is often said that she thinks with her glands. Man superbly ignores the fact that his anatomy also includes glands, such as the testicles, and that they secrete hormones. He thinks of his body as a direct and normal connection with the world, which he believes he apprehends objectively, whereas he regards the body of woman as a hindrance, a prison, weighed down by everything peculiar to it. "The female is a female by virtue of a certain *lack* of qualities," said Aristotle; "we should regard the female nature as afflicted with a natural defectiveness." And St. Thomas for his part pronounced woman to be an "imperfect man," an "incidental" being. This is symbolized in Genesis where Eve is depicted as made from what Bossuet called "a supernumerary bone" of Adam. . . .

mothers. Many European states implemented official programs to encourage women to have more children and to be better mothers. "Pronatalism," as this policy was known, resulted from an official concern over low birthrates and a decline in family size. Konrad Adenauer, chancellor of West Germany, spoke of "a will to children" as essential for his country's continued economic growth and prosperity. In 1945, Lord Beveridge (1879–1960), the architect of the British welfare system, emphasized the importance of women's role "in ensuring the adequate continuance of the British race" and argued that women's place was in the home as mothers. With the emphasis on larger families—four children was considered "desirable" in En-gland—family allowances calculated by the number of children were tied to men's participation in the workforce; women were defined according to their husband's status. The state welfare system thereby strengthened the financial dependence of English wives on their husbands and rewarded a particular version of family life.

In Great Britain, anxiety over the low birthrate was also tied to the debate over equal pay for women. Opponents of the measure argued that equal pay would cause women to forgo marriage and motherhood and should, therefore, be avoided. There was a consensus about keeping women out of the workforce and paying them less in order to encourage family life.

SIMONE DE BEAUVOIR, *THE SECOND SEX*

Now, woman has always been man's dependent, if not his slave; the two sexes have never shared the world in equality. And even today woman is heavily handicapped, though her situation is beginning to change. Almost nowhere is her legal status the same as man's, and frequently it is much to her disadvantage. Even when her rights are legally recognized in the abstract, long-standing custom prevents their full expression in the mores. In the economic sphere men and women can almost be said to make up two castes; other things being equal, the former hold the better jobs, get higher wages, and have more opportunity for success than their new competitors. In industry and politics men have a great many more positions and they monopolize the most important posts. In addition to all this, they enjoy a traditional prestige that the education of children tends in every way to support, for the present enshrines the past—and in the past all history has been made by men. At the present time, when women are beginning to take part in the affairs of the world, it is still a world that belongs to men—they have no doubt of it at all and women have scarcely any. To decline to be the Other, to refuse to be a party to the deal—this would be for women to renounce all the advantages conferred upon them by their alliance with the superior caste. Man-the-sovereign will provide woman-the-liege with material protection and will undertake the moral justification of her existence; thus she can evade at once both economic risk and the metaphysical risk of a liberty in which ends and aims must be contrived without assistance. Indeed, along with the ethical urge of each individual to affirm his subjective existence, there is also the temptation to forgo liberty and become a thing. This is an inauspicious road, for he who takes it—passive, lost, ruined—becomes henceforth the creature of another's will, frustrated in his transcendence and deprived of every value. But it is an easy road; on it one avoids the strain involved in undertaking an authentic existence. When man makes of woman the *Other*, he may, then, expect her to manifest deep-seated tendencies toward complicity. Thus, woman may fail to lay claim to the status of subject because she lacks definite resources, because she feels the necessary bond that ties her to man regardless of reciprocity, and because she is often very well pleased with her role as the *Other*.

From: *The Second Sex* Simone de Beauvoir, 1952.

Unlike the British system, the French system of *sécurité sociale* defined all women, whether married or single, as equal to men with the same rights of access to welfare programs as men. This policy may well have reflected the particularly strong presence of French women in the workplace historically and the recognition of the importance of women's labor for reconstruction of the economy. As a result, family allowances, pre- and postnatal care, maternity benefits, and child care were provided on the assumption that working mothers were a fact of life. French payments were intended to encourage large families and focused primarily on the needs of children. More and more French women entered the paid labor force after 1945, and they were less financially dependent on their husbands than were their British counterparts.

Both forms of welfare state, the British that emphasized women's role as mothers, and the French that accepted women's role as workers, were based on different attitudes about the nature of gender difference and equality. The women's liberation movements of the late sixties and early seventies found their roots in the contradictions and gender inequities of differing welfare policies.

Women's liberation movements were also rooted in the frustrations of European and American women who participated in the protest movements of the 1960s for civil rights and free expression. Women active in pacifist and antinuclear groups united to "Ban the Bomb," as well as in the anti-Vietnam War movements began to question their place in organizations that did not acknowledge their claims to equal rights, equal pay, and liberation from social oppression. The agenda of protest in the sixties accepted the gender differences reinforced by social policies as normal and natural. Technology allowed women and men to separate pleasure from reproduction but did nothing to alter men's and women's domestic roles. Pleasure was also separated from familial responsibilities, yet the domestic ideal of the woman in the home remained.

During the last quarter of the twentieth century, the lives of Western women reflected dramatic social changes. Women were more educated than ever before. Access to institutions of higher learning and professional schools allowed women to participate in the workforce in the areas of education, law, medicine, and business throughout the world. Women's involvement in the politics of liberation of peoples in the 1960s served to heighten their collective awareness of the disparities between their own situations and the role of men in Western societies: women worked at home without pay; in the workplace women received less than men for the same work.

In this period of increased educational and work opportunities, an international women's movement emerged. International conferences about issues related to women were media events in the 1970s. In 1975 the United Nations Conference on the Decade for Women was convened in Mexico City. On 8 March 1976—International Women's Day—the International Tribunal of Crimes Against Women was convened in Brussels. Modeling the Brussels conference on tribunals like the Nuremberg Commission, which dealt with Nazi atrocities in World War II, feminists from all over the world concentrated on crimes against women for the purpose of promoting greater political awareness and action. Fertility and sexuality were at the center of the new politics of the women's movement, justified in the slogan, "The personal is political." Rape and abortion were problems of international concern. "Sisterhood is powerful!" gave way to a new organizing cry that "International sisterhood is more powerful!"

In Italy women's political action resulted in a new law in 1970 that allowed divorce under very restricted circumstances. Italian feminists used the legal system as a public forum. In France the sale of contraceptives was legalized in 1968. French feminists, like their Italian

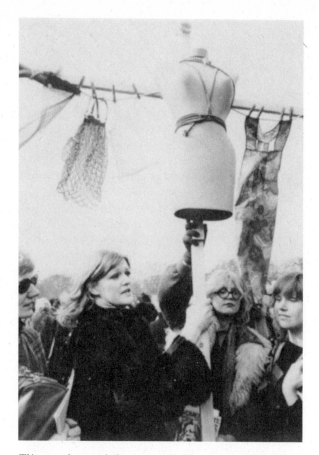

This 1971 photograph shows a women's liberation march in London. The women hold aloft a symbol of the cross they refuse to bear, adorned with the symbols of women's enslavement: shopping bag, washing apron, and a female torso in chains.

counterparts, worked through the courts to make abortion legal: they achieved their goal in 1975.

The feminist movement also created a new feminist scholarship that incorporated women's experiences and perspectives into the disciplines of history, humanities, and the social sciences. Women's studies courses, emphasizing the history of women and their contributions to civilization, became part of university and college curricula throughout Europe and the United States. Reformers also attempted to transform language, which, they argued, had served as a tool of oppression.

The Protests of 1968

Youth culture was created by outside forces as much as it was a self-creation. Socialized together in an expanding educational system from primary school through high school, young people in industrialized societies came to see themselves as a social force. They were also socialized by marketing efforts that appealed to their particular needs as a group.

The prosperity that characterized the period from the mid-fifties to the mid-sixties throughout western Europe provided a secure base for young people intent on criticizing the world of their elders. The young men and women of the 1960s were the first generation to come of age after World War II. Though they had no memory themselves of the destruction of that war, they were reminded daily of the imminence of nuclear destruction in their own lives. The combination of the security of affluence and the insecurity of Cold War politics created a widening gap between the world of decision-making adults and the idealistic universe of the young. To the criticisms of parents, politicians, and teachers, the new generation responded with protests and demands for reform.

Student protest, which began at the University of California at Berkeley in 1964 as the Free Speech movement, by the spring of 1968 had become an international phenomenon that had spread to other American campuses and throughout Europe and Japan. A common denominator of protest, whether in New York, London, or Tokyo, was opposition to the war in Vietnam. Growing numbers of students and intellectuals throughout the world condemned the U.S. presence in Vietnam as an immoral violation of the rights of the Vietnamese people and a violent proof of U.S. imperialism.

Student protesters shared other concerns in addition to opposition to the war in southeast Asia. The growing activism on American campuses was aimed at social reform, student self-governance, and the responsibilities of the university in the wider community. In West Germany, highly politicized radical activists, a conspicuous minority among the students at the Free University of Berlin, directed protest out into the wider society. Student demonstrations met with brutal police repression and violence, and rioting was common.

European students, more than their American counterparts, were also experiencing frustration in the classroom. European universities were unprepared to absorb the huge influx of students in the 1960s. The student-teacher ratio at the University of Rome, for example, was 200 to 1. In Italian universities in general, the majority of over half a million students had no contact with their professors. The University of Paris was similarly overcrowded.

Higher education had been expanded in Europe after World War II to serve the increased needs of a technocratic society. Instead of altering the social structure, as

politically committed student protesters had hoped, mass education served as a certifying mechanism for middle-class students who were being trained for bureaucratic and technical jobs. In France, for example, only 4 percent of university students came from below the middle class. Many of the occupations that students could look forward to were in dead-end service jobs or in bureaucratic posts.

In May 1968 in France, a student protest erupted and spread beyond the university when workers and managers joined students in paralyzing the French economy and threatening to topple the Fifth Republic. Between seven and ten million people went on strike in support of worker and student demands. White-collar employees and technicians joined blue-collar factory workers in the strike. Student demands, based on a thoroughgoing critique of the whole society, proved to be incompatible with the wage and consumption issues of workers. But the unusual if short-lived alliance of students and workers shocked those in power and induced limited reforms.

Student dissent reflected the changing economy of the late 1960s. Inflation, which earlier in the decade had spurred prosperity, was spiraling out of control in the late sixties. In the advanced industrial countries of western Europe and later in the United States, the growth of the postwar period was slowing down. Economic opportunity was evaporating and jobs were being eliminated. One survey estimated that two out three Italian university graduates in 1967 were unable to find a job. The dawning awareness of shrinking opportunities in the workplace, once students had attained their degrees and been properly certified, further aggravated student frustration and dissent.

By the late sixties, universities and colleges provided the forum for expressing their discontent in advanced industrial societies. In their protests, student activists rejected the values of consumer society. The programs and politics of the student protesters aimed to transform the world in which they lived.

A New Working Class: Foreign Workers

Foreign workers played an important role in the industrial expansion of western Europe beginning in the 1950s. Western European nations needed cheap unskilled laborers. Great Britain, France, and West Germany were the chief labor-importing countries, whose economic growth in the fifties and sixties was made

Bob Dylan, "Subterranean Homesick Blues"

■ *The gap between the generations yawned into a gulf as rock music became political in the mid-1960s. Bob Dylan, an American rock performer, introduced folk music to the genre with songs of social protest like "Blowin' in the Wind" and "Only a Pawn in Their Game." Rock music was denounced as a Communist plot, as performers urged their audiences to "Make Love, Not War." Dylan's "Subterranean Homesick Blues" targeted the hypocrisy of his society.*

Subterranean Homesick Blues

Johnny's in the basement
Mixing up the medicine
I'm on the pavement
Thinking about the government

The man in the trench coat
Badge out, laid off
Says he's got a bad cough
Wants to get it paid off
Look out kid
It's somethin' you did
God knows when
But you're doin' it again
You better duck down the alley way
Lookin' for a new friend
The man in the coon-skin cap
In the big pen
Wants eleven dollar bills
You only got ten

Maggie comes fleet foot
Face full of black soot
Talkin' that the heat put
Plants in the bed but
The phone's tapped anyway
Maggie says that many say
They must bust in early May
Orders from the D.A.
Look out kid
Don't matter what you did
Walk on your tip toes
Don't try "No Doz"
Better stay away from those
That carry around a fire hose
Keep a clean nose
Watch the plain clothes
You don't need a weather man
To know which way the wind blows

Get sick, get well
Hang around a ink well

Ring bell, hard to tell
If anything is goin' to sell
Try hard, get barred
Get back, write braille
Get jailed, jump bail
Join the army, if you fail
Look out kid
You're gonna get hit
But users, cheaters
Six-time losers
Hang around the theaters
Girl by the whirlpool
Lookin' for a new fool
Don't follow leaders
Watch the parkin' meters

Ah get born, keep warm
Short pants, romance, learn to dance
Get dressed, get blessed
Try to be a success
Please her, please him, buy gifts
Don't steal, don't lift
Twenty years of schoolin'
And they put you on the day shift
Look out kid
They keep it all hid
Better jump down a manhole
Light yourself a candle
Don't wear sandals
Try to avoid the scandals
Don't wanna be a bum
You better chew gum
The pump don't work
'Cause the vandals took the handles

From "Subterranean Homesick Blues," Bob Dylan (Warner Bros. 1965).

Students riot in Paris in 1968. The student protests of the late 1960s were sparked in part by the war in Vietnam and by disillusionment with the present and uncertainty about the future.

possible by readily available pools of cheap foreign labor. The chief labor-exporting countries included Portugal, Turkey, Algeria, Italy, and Spain, whose sluggish economic performance spurred workers to seek employment opportunities beyond national borders. Great Britain imported workers from the West Indies, Ireland, India, Pakistan, Africa, and southern Europe. Migrant employment was by definition poorly paid, unskilled or semiskilled, manual work. The lot of foreign workers was difficult and sometimes dangerous. Onerous and demanding labor was common. Foreign workers were often herded together in crowded living quarters, socially marginalized, and identified with the degrading work they performed.

Commonly, married men migrated without their families with the goal of earning cash to send home to those left behind. The inability to put down roots hampered assimilation among this sizable percentage of foreign workers. Third and fourth generations of foreign workers born on West German soil, for exam-

ple, were ineligible for citizenship and naturalization. In economic downturns foreign workers were the first to be laid off. Yet their obligations to send money back home to aged parents, spouses, children, and siblings persisted.

Women endured special problems within the foreign workforce. Between 1964 and 1974 the majority of Portuguese immigrants to France came with families, but there was little in the way of social services to support them on their arrival. Dependable child care was either too expensive or unavailable to female workers with children. Increasing numbers of women on their own began migrating to western Europe independently of households and male migrants. Like men, they worked in order to send money back home.

Before 1973 most countries in western Europe, including Great Britain, actively encouraged foreign labor. After that date restrictions became the order of the day. Western governments enforced new conservative policies throughout the 1970s and 1980s aimed at banning

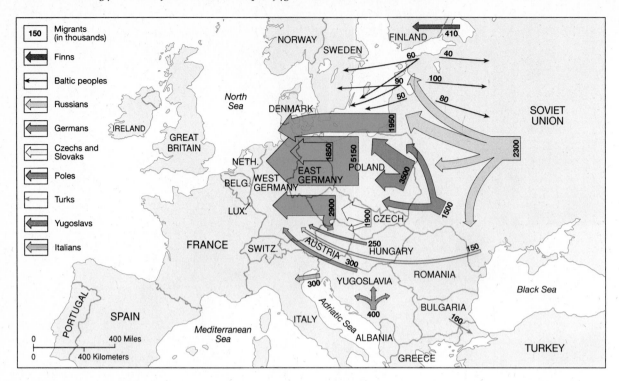

European Migrations After World War II

entry to refugees. Opposition to the presence of foreign workers was often expressed in an ultranationalist rhetoric and usually flared up in economic downturns. Violent incidents became increasingly common.

In 1986 in France the xenophobic National Front campaigned on a platform of "France for the French" and captured 10 percent of the vote in national elections. In 1992 the same party received 16 percent of the vote in regional elections. Racism was out in the open in western European countries that had depended on a foreign labor force for their prosperity. Riots in Great Britain in 1980 and 1981, particularly in the London ghetto of Brixton, were motivated by racial discrimination against blacks, severe cuts in social-welfare spending, and deteriorating working conditions.

On the whole, restrictions failed to achieve what they set out to do—remove foreign workers from western European countries by repatriation. Foreign workers in West Germany learned to get around the restrictions and sent for their families to join them. British laws also had the effect of converting temporary migration by single men into permanent family migrations. In 1977 foreign workers in France were offered cash incentives to return to their home countries, but all to little avail. By

the end of the 1970s there were ten million foreign workers settled in Europe. Their presence heightened racism and overt antagonism from a resurgent extreme Right.

The gains of economic recovery and the promises of a secure future by the welfare state began to unravel in the mid-1960s. Rising expectations were shattered as economic growth slowed and students, women, and workers protested inequities. Foreign workers, so necessary for economic growth because of limited labor pools in Europe, became the scapegoats of racial violence as prosperity stalled. The welfare state, created to protect citizens and to guarantee rights to freedom from economic hardship, began to develop cracks in its facade and many began to question how secure its future really was.

Ending the Cold War

Leonid Brezhnev (1906–82), general secretary of the Communist party and head of the Soviet Union from 1966 to 1982, established a policy whereby the Soviet Union claimed the right to interfere in the internal affairs of its allies in order to prevent counterrevolution.

With the "Brezhnev Doctrine," the Soviets influenced developments in eastern Europe through the next decade. After 1968, rigidity and stagnation characterized the Soviet, East German, and Czechoslovak governments, as well as rule in other east European states.

With repression came protest, at first weak but growing in volume to command international attention in the mid-1970s. Criticism of the Soviet Union by its own citizens was strongly repressed, as was the case for other Eastern Bloc nations. But in the end a strong critique of domestic and foreign policy aims infused movements for reform that undermined communism and repudiated Cold War politics.

Détente: The Soviets and the West

The Nuclear Test Ban Treaty of 1963 inaugurated a period of lessening tension between the Eastern and Western Blocs. By the early 1970s both the United States and the Soviet Union recognized the importance of a rapprochement between the superpowers. The USSR and the United States had achieved nuclear parity: from positions of equality, both sides expressed a willingness to negotiate. The 1970s became a decade of détente, a period of cooperation between the two superpowers. The Strategic Arms Limitation Treaty, known as SALT I, signed in Moscow in 1972, limited defensive antiballistic missile systems.

The refusal in 1979 of the United States to sign SALT II to limit strategic nuclear weapons ushered in "the dangerous decade" of the 1980s, when the possibility of peaceful coexistence seemed crushed. U.S. president Ronald Reagan, during his first term in office, revived traditional Cold War posturing. Nuclear strategists on both sides were once again talking about nuclear war as possible and winnable. Popular concern over the nuclear arms race intensified in the United States, the Soviet Union, and throughout Europe. U.S. plans for the Strategic Defense Initiative (SDI), popularly called the "Star Wars" defense system, promised an escalation in nuclear defense spending in an attempt to end the parity between the United States and the Soviet Union.

On balance, however, East-West relations after 1983 were characterized by less confrontation and more attempts at cooperation between the Soviet Union and the United States. The world political system itself appeared to have stabilized with a diminution of conflict in the three main arenas of superpower competition—the Third World, China, and western Europe. By the end of 1989, leaders in the East and the West declared that the Cold War was over. A new and permanent détente appeared to be now possible.

The Winds of Change in Soviet Society

During the Brezhnev years, dissidence took on new forms in response to state repression. Growing numbers of Soviet Jews sought to emigrate to Israel, in an attempt to escape anti-Semitism within the Soviet Union and to embrace their own religious and cultural heritage. Some of the 178,000 who were allowed to emigrate found their way to western Europe and the United States. In May 1976 a number of Soviet dissidents, many of them Jewish, declared themselves united for the purpose of securing human rights. Some of the leading organizers were charged with anti-Soviet propaganda and given harsh prison sentences, which attracted international attention and brought to an end the isolation of dissidents, who for decades had waged a lonely battle within the Soviet Union for civil liberties, democratic rights, and the end of the nuclear arms race.

The sixties was a period of increasing prosperity in the Soviet Union, as the population became more urban (180 million people lived in cities by mid-1970) and more literate (the majority of the population stayed in school until age 17 or 18). Soviet citizens of the 1960s and 1970s were better fed, better educated, and in better health than their parents and grandparents had been. When people grumbled over food shortages and long lines, the Soviet state reminded its citizens of how far they had come and told them that Soviet economic planning was not a failure.

Shoppers queue outside a Soviet state butcher shop. Long lines for scarce foodstuffs and manufactured goods were a grim reality of Soviet life.

Yet while growth continued throughout the postwar years, the rate of growth was slowing down in the 1970s. Some planners feared that the Soviet Union would never catch up to the economies of the United States, Japan, and West Germany. Soviet citizens were increasingly aware of the sacrifices and suffering that economic development had cost them and of the disparities in the standards of living between the capitalist and Communist worlds. Due to outmoded technology, declining, older industries, severe pollution of the environment, labor imbalances, critical shortages of foodstuffs and certain raw materials, and a significant amount of hidden unemployment in unproductive industries, discontent mounted.

Consumer products were either of poor quality or unavailable. People queued on the average of two hours every day to purchase food and basic supplies. Housing, when it was available, was inadequate, and there were long waiting lists for vacancies. The black market flourished, with high prices on everything from Western blue jeans to Soviet automobiles. People could look around them and see corruption in their ruling elite, who wore Western clothes, had access to material goods not available to the general population, and lived in luxury.

Workers had more disposable income than ever before and that was, ironically, a key to the problem. People had money to spend but little to spend it on. In fact, purchasing power far outstripped supplies. The state system of production, which emphasized quantity over quality, resulted in overproduction of some goods and underproduction of others. The state kept prices low in order to control the cost of living, but low prices did not provide incentives for the production of better-quality goods.

Programs between 1985 and 1988 promised more than they delivered. Modest increases in output were achieved, but people's expectations regarding food and consumer goods were rising faster than they could be met. The Soviet Union did not increase imports of consumer durables or food to meet demand, nor did quality improve appreciably. Rising wages only gave workers more money that they could not or would not spend on Soviet products. The black market was a symbol both of the economic failures of the state and of the growing consumerism of Soviet citizens. Rather than purchase poor-quality goods, Soviets chose to purchase foreign products on the black market at vastly inflated prices.

Although breaking sharply with the economic policies and programs of his predecessors, Soviet leader Mikhail Gorbachev (1931–) candidly warned that there would be no consumption revolution in the near future.

The Big Mac comes to Moscow. McDonald's opened its first Moscow fast-food outlet in 1990, just a few blocks from the Kremlin. Muscovites stood in long lines for milkshakes, fries, and the "Bolshoi Mak."

He set in motion bold plans for increased openness, which he called *glasnost*, and a program of political and economic restructuring, which he dubbed *perestroika*. In place of a controlled economy, Gorbachev proposed a limited open market free of state controls for manufacturing enterprises organized on a cooperative basis and for light industry. He loosened restrictions on foreign trade, encouraged the development of a private service sector, and decentralized economic decision making for agriculture and the service sector. But many of Gorbachev's critics felt that he did not go far or fast enough.

Gorbachev's foreign policy also served his economic goals. Military participation in decision making declined, as state expenditures on defense were decreased. Moscow had always borne larger military costs than Washington. Gorbachev recognized that Cold War defense spending must decline if the Soviet Union was to prosper. Consumer durables had to take the place of weapons on the production lines.

In the late 1980s, grass-roots movements responding to Gorbachev's rhetoric of reform and democracy asserted that they should have a political voice. On coming to power, Gorbachev blamed his predecessors for the Soviet Union's problems, but this defense had its limits, as people began demanding results. Tensions became most apparent over how Communist party rule and centralization could be coordinated with the demands for freedom and autonomy that Gorbachev's own reforms fostered. To gain credibility and backing, Gorbachev supported the formation of new parliamentary bodies and early in 1990 Gorbachev ended the Communist party's constitutional monopoly of power.

New parties proliferated, some defending the old order but many demanding a total break with the past and with Communist ideology and programs. Among Gorbachev's harshest critics was his former ally and supporter, Boris N. Yeltsin (1931–), the former Moscow party leader, who began in 1987 to criticize Gorbachev's caution in implementing reforms. Later, as the popularly elected president of the Russian republic in 1990, Yeltsin called for a true democracy and decisive economic action.

In August 1991, the world watched in shock as a quasi-military council of Communist party hardliners usurped power in order to restore Communist rule and reverse democratic reforms. (See Special Feature, "Television and Revolutions," pp. 1070–1071.) Soviet citizens from the Baltic republics to Siberia protested the takeover, and tens of thousands of Muscovites poured into the streets to defy the tanks and troops of the rebel government. Three people were killed outside Russia's parliament building, which had become a rallying point for the protesters. Meanwhile, Gorbachev

Mikhail Gorbachev (left) and Boris Yeltsin confer at the Russian parliament following the abortive coup of August 1991.

was held prisoner in his vacation home in the Crimea. The timing of the coup was probably determined by the fact that Gorbachev was scheduled to sign a new union treaty with nine of the republics the day following his house arrest.

Boris Yeltsin publicly defied the plotters, rallying popular support behind him, and helping convince Soviet army troops to disobey orders to attack the White House, as the parliament building is called. After only two days, the coup d'état had failed; Gorbachev returned to Moscow and banned the Communist party. Although Gorbachev retained his title of Soviet president, his prestige was seriously damaged by the coup and by the challenge of Yeltsin's new dominance as a popular hero.

The End of the Soviet Union

Central to the vulnerability and collapse of the Soviet Union was its ethnic diversity. In 1979 the Soviet Union listed 102 nationalities in its census. Twenty-two of those nationalities had populations of a million or more people. Gorbachev was caught in the dilemma of supporting the demands for self-determination in eastern European states, yet denying ethnic autonomy in the Soviet republics. For many, the nationalities problem posed the single greatest threat to Gorbachev's regime, even more challenging than the establishment of a free-market economy.

The nationalities problem in the Soviet Union was in fact shaped by the very social forces that brought Gorbachev to power. The three major areas of nationalist conflict within the Soviet Union—Central Asia, Armenia, and the Baltic states—had nursed grievances against the Soviet state since the 1920s. What was different about the protests of the 1980s was the emergence of a new and educated urban elite, formed after World War II, as the driving force behind nationalist reform. Moscow relied on these groups of university-educated and upwardly mobile professionals to further economic reforms. Gorbachev's challenge was to harness nationalist protest without undermining the Party's authority in favor of local organizations. The challenge before him was to make the Party responsible to these new social groups and to local needs.

Ethnic minorities, especially in the Soviet Baltic republics of Latvia, Lithuania, and Estonia, threatened the dominance of Party rule in favor of immediate self-determination. Large-scale riots erupted in Lithuania over demands for nationalist rights. Nationalist awareness was not unprecedented in the Baltic states in the 1980s—but the context of *perestroika* in which nationalist

The corpse of Nicolae Ceaucescu as shown on TV and in newspapers.

Television and Revolutions

Television became the principal means of communicating current events to mass populations in the second half of the twentieth century. It was one of the chief consumer durables purchased by the newly prosperous populations of the United States and Europe beginning in the 1950s. Many intellectuals in the West feared that television, because of its uninspired programming, would dull the sensibilities of the masses and serve as a kind of opiate to cloud political judgment. Yet the role of television in politics was more complex, as events after 1968 made clear.

As East Germans in large numbers began buying televisions in the 1960s and 1970s, they faced a dilemma. Should they heed the prohibition of the East German government against watching West German television programs, whose signals were so easily accessible to them, or should they disobey the law and take advantage of the varied entertainment that West German television afforded? East German leaders feared the "corrupt" and "decadent" images of West Germany that might attract their citizens. The East German head of state, Walter Ulbricht, warned ominously in 1961 that "The enemy of the people stands on the roof." He was talking about television antennas. The East German ban was, however, impossible to enforce. Millions of East German viewers tuned in daily to West German programs and were able to compare the different standards of living in the two German nations and to learn of their own deprivation. The irony of awareness was that as East Germans achieved a higher standard of living and were able to buy more televisions, they became more and more discontented over their relatively low standard of living. Television contributed to rising expectations and the exodus of East Germans to the West.

Television played a central role in the Romanian revolution of 1989, spreading information and encouraging coordinated action throughout the country. One of the first acts of the Bucharest revolutionaries was to seize the headquarters of the state television station in order to transmit their own view of the conflict. When Nicolae and Elena Ceaucescu were executed, the event was videotaped for broadcast to the Romanian nation and the world. In a still heavily rural society undergoing modernization, television provided the essential link between city and countryside. Television promoted concerted action. Simultaneously Romanians in Timósoara, a small city near the Hungarian border, and Bucharest, the nation's capital, espoused the same revolutionary program and adopted the same symbols, as similarly doctored national flags made clear. The new regime governed by means of the television screen.

Politicians on both the Left and the Right used television for political ends. The political utility of television was exploited in France, where 60 percent of the population owned TV sets in 1968. Charles de Gaulle, president of the Fifth Republic, used the medium to appeal directly to the French people against the student-worker revolt that began in Paris in May 1968. Television was decisive in maintaining de Gaulle in power and mobilizing conservatives against the activists.

No one in the late twentieth century was better at grasping the power of the televised image than the Soviet leader Mikhail Gorbachev, who from the very beginning used the small screen to appeal directly to the Soviet people. He carefully cultivated his own image and used television to build a personal power base outside the Communist party. Gorbachev was so successful in creating his own televised publicity that he became a popular figure within the Western capitalist world as

well as within Soviet Bloc countries. Crowds everywhere greeted him with the affectionate nickname "Gorby"; he was as easily recognizable in the streets of New York and Paris as in the streets of Moscow. East European revolutionaries sometimes had difficulty separating his media image from political realities. Romanians chanted his name in public squares as they set about pulling down the communist regime that ruled them.

Above all, television contributed to the revolution in expectations in communist countries in the last quarter of the twentieth century. The contrast between the quality of life in the East and the West became inescapable for many educated east European and Soviet men and women, who had access to travel and to television. Modern video technology did not cause revolutions but it did convey information and provide political platforms. Television also publicized revolutions and, in some cases, sold dreams.

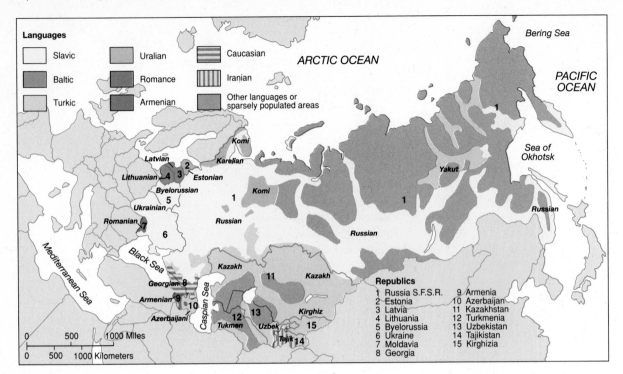

Languages

- Slavic
- Baltic
- Turkic
- Uralian
- Romance
- Armenian
- Caucasian
- Iranian
- Other languages or sparsely populated areas

ARCTIC OCEAN · Bering Sea · PACIFIC OCEAN · Sea of Okhotsk

Komi · Latvian · Karelian · Lithuanian · Estonian · Byelorussian · Komi · Ukrainian · Russian · Yakut · Russian · Romanian · Russian · Mediterranean Sea · Black Sea · Kazakh · Russian · Georgian · Kazakh · Armenian · Caspian Sea · Azerbaijani · Tukmen · Uzbek · Kirghiz · Tajik

Republics

1 Russia S.F.S.R.	9 Armenia
2 Estonia	10 Azerbaijan
3 Latvia	11 Kazakhstan
4 Lithuania	12 Turkmenia
5 Byelorussia	13 Uzbekistan
6 Ukraine	14 Tajikistan
7 Moldavia	15 Kirghizia
8 Georgia	

0 500 1000 Miles
0 500 1000 Kilometers

Republics of the Soviet Union

demands were now being voiced posed a serious challenge to Gorbachev's democratic reforms. In 1988 Estonians demanded the right of veto over any law passed in Moscow. Russians, who were a minority in Estonia, protested attacks and prejudicial treatment at the hands of Estonians.

Endorsing diversity of opinion, individual rights, and freedom as the bases of good government, Gorbachev now had to deal with vocal nationalist awareness in the Baltic states and the republic of Georgia and with outright violence in Azerbaijan. In 1988 tens of thousands of Armenians took to the streets to demand the return of the Armenian enclave of Nagorno-Karabakh, incorporated into Azerbaijan in 1921. In the Azerbaijan capital of Baku, the center of Russia's oil-producing region, demonstrators demanded greater autonomy for their republic and the accountability of their deputies in Moscow. Violence between Azerbaijanis and Armenians resulted in thirty-two deaths and the displacement of tens of thousands. The situation of upheaval climaxed in December 1988 when an earthquake in Armenia killed 25,000 people. Soviet troops were placed in the area, ostensibly to deal with the aftermath of the natural disaster.

In 1986 university students in the central Asian republic of Kazakhstan incited two days of demonstrations and rioting over the removal of a corrupt local leader who was replaced with a Russian. The Soviet government's attempt to clean up politics in the area betrayed a clumsy disregard for ethnic issues and seemed at odds with Gorbachev's commitment to decentralization. Crimean Tatars, who had been exiled in Islamic fundamentalist Kazakhstan since World War II, agitated for return home.

One by one, all fifteen of the Soviet republics proclaimed their independence, following the lead of the breakaway Baltic republics of Estonia, Lithuania, and Latvia. Having failed to agree on a new plan for union, Gorbachev and the leaders of ten republics transferred authority to an emergency State Council in September 1991 until a plan could be devised. By the end of the year the Soviet Union was faced with serious food shortages and was bankrupt, unable to pay its employees and dependent on the financial backing provided by Yeltsin. Rejecting all Soviet authority, Russia, Belarus, and Ukraine joined together in December 1991 to form the Commonwealth of Independent States (CIS). Eight other republics followed their lead. The Soviet Union came to an end on 25 December 1991, with the resignation of Mikhail Gorbachev, who had become a man without a country to rule. Boris Yeltsin moved into Gorbachev's presidential offices at the Kremlin as the president of the new Russian state.

Many issues remained unresolved. The new political organization did not address the endemic problems of economic hardship, and left unanswered the question of who would control the former Soviet Union's vast military machine, including its nuclear arsenal. How would the strong nationalist demands for autonomy accord with the need for cooperation to establish a stable monetary policy, market economies, and effective trade networks? The Soviet Union, which had ruled as a world power for over seven decades, no longer existed. Communism had been totally discredited, but the new nations of the former Soviet Union faced an uncertain future. So did its former allies.

Eastern and Central Europe Since 1968

The recurrent crises over oil prices and the greater hardships inflicted on eastern European consumers fanned the embers of unsettled issues in the 1980s as incidents of protest and resistance began to mount. Poland was especially important to the Soviet Bloc both because it was eastern Europe's most populous country and because of its strategic location. Poland provided a corridor for supplies to the Soviet Union's 380,000 troops in East Germany. In Poland, as in Czechoslovakia, demonstrations against Soviet dominance and one-party rule by the Communists had been brutally repressed. Poland entered the 1970s economically handicapped. In December 1970 the Polish government instituted major price increases for food. Workers spontaneously struck in protest, with demonstrations beginning in the shipyards of Gdansk, the Baltic seaport in northern Poland, and spreading to other cities. The Polish government responded by sending the militia to tear-gas the workers. People were killed and injured but protest was not silenced.

Wladislaw Gomulka, who had been head of the Polish government since 1956, was replaced by Edward Gierek in hopes of improving the economic situation. More protests followed before prices were rolled back and the Soviet Union provided economic aid. Throughout the 1970s one-party rule prevailed, as workers attempted to maintain forms of permanent organization. The Polish government drew loans from abroad for investment in technology and industrial expansion. Resisting raising prices at home, Poland's leaders increased its indebtedness to the West from $2.5 billion in 1973 to $17 billion in 1980. Poland was sinking into the mire of ever higher interest payments that absorbed the country's export earnings. In 1976, however, Gierek could no

longer avoid price increases. A new wave of spontaneous strikes erupted, forcing the government to rescind the increases.

At the beginning of July 1980, in response to price increases, the shipyard workers of Gdansk, solidly organized in a new noncommunist labor union called Solidarity *(Solidarnosc)*, staged a sit-down strike that paralyzed the shipyards. The union, led by a politically astute electrician named Lech Walesa, coordinated their activities from one factory to the next and succeeded in shutting down the entire economy. The government was forced to agree to a series of union-backed reforms known as the Gdansk Accords, which, among other measures, increased civil liberties and acknowledged Solidarity's right to exist.

Within a year Solidarity had an astounding 8 million members out of a population of 35 million. The Catholic church lent important support to those who opposed Communist rule. Dissident intellectuals also cast their lot with the organized workers in demanding reforms. General Wojciech Jaruzelski, who became prime minister in February 1981, was unable to change the situation of shortages appreciably. Jaruzelski attempted to curb the union's demands for democratic government and participation in management by harsh measures: he declared martial law on 13 December 1981 to crack down

Lithuanians in the capital city of Vilnius demonstrated for independence from the Soviet Union throughout the late 1980s.

on the dissidents. The Soviet response was to do nothing. Poland was left to Polish rule.

Martial law in Poland produced military repression. Solidarity was outlawed and Walesa was jailed. The West did not lose sight of him: in 1983 the union leader was awarded the Nobel Peace Prize for his efforts. After years of negotiations and intermittent strikes, Solidarity was legalized once again in 1989. Jaruzelski knew he needed Solidarity's cooperation in order to address dire economic conditions: he agreed to open elections. At the polls, Solidarity candidates soundly defeated the Communist party. Poland was the first country anywhere to turn a Communist regime out of office peacefully.

The great challenge before the new Solidarity government, as for the Communist regime that preceded it, was economic recovery. Inflation drove food prices up at the rate of 50 percent a month. Poland faced the task of earning enough foreign trade credits to alleviate its indebtedness and to justify foreign investment. This was the challenge that Lech Walesa took up when he was elected president of Poland in 1990.

Hungary followed another path in breaking with Soviet rule in the 1970s by experimenting cautiously with free markets and private control. Romania under Nicolae Ceaucescu appeared to be successful in evading its military responsibilities in the Warsaw Pact. It alone of the member states had refused to participate in the Czechoslovak intervention of 1968. The East German government tolerated the Lutheran church's criticism of the Soviet military presence in East Germany in the

1970s. Deviation was not punished by Soviet repression but quietly and carefully pursued in an age colored by Soviet attempts at détente with the West.

Eastern Europe followed the lead of Soviet calls for openness and reform under Gorbachev. In 1988 Gorbachev, speaking before the United Nations, assured the West that he would not prevent eastern European satellites from going their own way: "Freedom of choice is a universal principle," the Soviet head of state declared. Poland's first free elections in forty years were part of a mosaic of protest from which a pattern began to emerge in the spring of 1989. "People power" swept away Communist leaders and ousted the Communist party in Hungary, East Germany, and Czechoslovakia. Hungary opened all of its borders to the West in September 1989. East German vacationers in Hungary poured across the frontiers, creating an international crisis. People wanted freedom of movement and freedom of expression.

The iceberg of communism was melting. But as dictators were replaced by democrats, observers wondered if counterrevolution was waiting in the wings, should the new capitalist experiments fail. Proto-fascist and anti-Semitic groups became more vocal in the early 1990s amidst the economic chaos. Festering ethnic differences erupted in civil war in 1991 in Yugoslavia between the Serbs and secessionist Slovenes and Croats. Serbia, intent on dismembering Bosnia and acquiring most of its territory, espoused "ethnic cleansing" aimed at Bosnia's Muslim minority. Violence, including systematic rape, was aimed at civilian populations forced to

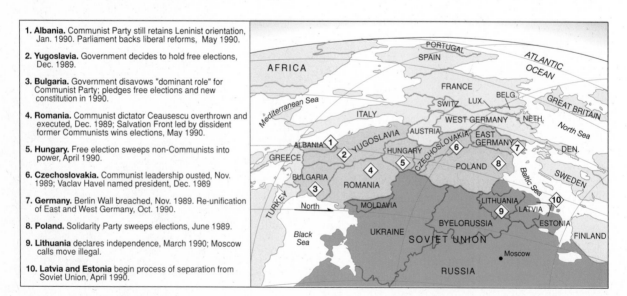

1. **Albania.** Communist Party still retains Leninist orientation, Jan. 1990. Parliament backs liberal reforms, May 1990.

2. **Yugoslavia.** Government decides to hold free elections, Dec. 1989.

3. **Bulgaria.** Government disavows "dominant role" for Communist Party; pledges free elections and new constitution in 1990.

4. **Romania.** Communist dictator Ceaucescu overthrown and executed, Dec. 1989; Salvation Front led by dissident former Communists wins elections, May 1990.

5. **Hungary.** Free election sweeps non-Communists into power, April 1990.

6. **Czechoslovakia.** Communist leadership ousted, Nov. 1989; Vaclav Havel named president, Dec. 1989

7. **Germany.** Berlin Wall breached, Nov. 1989. Re-unification of East and West Germany, Oct. 1990.

8. **Poland.** Solidarity Party sweeps elections, June 1989.

9. **Lithuania** declares independence, March 1990; Moscow calls move illegal.

10. **Latvia and Estonia** begin process of separation from Soviet Union, April 1990.

Events in Eastern Europe 1989–90

A victim of the civil war in Bosnia-Herzegovina wheels a barrow past houses destroyed in the fighting between Bosnian Muslims and Serbian rebels in the town of Gorazde.

flee their homes, creating a challenge to United Nations' attempts at intervention and mediation. Other eastern European states were riddled with ethnic troubles, including the Czechs and Slovaks in Czechoslovakia; the Hungarians and Romanians over the border region of Transylvania; and the Bulgarians and the Turks in Bulgaria. The dawn of a new age of democracy and freedom that seemed to be at hand in eastern Europe in 1989 and 1990 was replaced by the dark reality of racial hatred, war, and the denial of basic freedoms to whole communities.

While eastern Europe was more divided and fragmented than ever in the last decade of the twentieth century, the German states of central Europe appeared to achieve a lasting unification. The German Democratic Republic (East Germany) and the German Federal Republic (West Germany) had developed after 1968 as two separate countries with different social, economic, and political institutions. On the surface, their differences seemed insurmountable. Nevertheless, in spite of the Berlin Wall, West German leaders continued to voice their long-term commitment to reunification, while East German leaders insisted on the independence and autonomy of their state.

In West Germany politics took a new direction in 1969, as an era of social-liberal cooperation between the leftist Social Democrats and the centrist Free Democrats began. Chancellor Willy Brandt, a Social Demo-

crat, was equally committed to liberal domestic reforms and to changes in foreign policy. From the first, he set out to improve relations with eastern Europe and the Soviet Union. While maintaining West Germany's commitment to NATO and western European integration, Brandt pursued a new cooperation with the Soviet Union through a nonaggression pact. Negotiated in 1970, the pact renounced territorial claims and the use of force. A treaty with Poland accepted the status quo of existing borders in return for Polish exit visas for ethnic Germans. Still without the official recognition of East Germany, West Germany agreed to normalized relations in 1972 in the Basic Treaty, which permitted West German citizens easier movement to visit relatives in East Germany. In 1973 both Germanies joined the United Nations.

Succeeding Brandt in 1974, Chancellor Helmut Schmidt, maintained his predecessor's bold foreign policy of *Ostpolitik*, the establishment of cooperative politics with the East, a policy that constituted a clear break with superpower hegemony. A more conservative foreign policy was substituted by the new Christian Democratic chancellor Helmut Kohl, who stressed the importance of individual enterprise and competition and ran a winning campaign with the slogan, "Less State, More Market" in 1982.

West Germany stood in the 1980s as an economic giant, second only in foreign trade to the United States and far ahead of Japan. With its economic opportunities and advanced social welfare programs, West Germany exerted considerable attraction for East Germans. East Germany, too, established itself as an important trading nation—fifteenth in the world in 1975.

Applications for authorized immigration increased in the 1980s, and in 1984 East Germany allowed 30,000 citizens to emigrate to the West. Throughout the late 1980s the emigration rate remained high, with an average exodus of 20,000 a year. With Hungary's refusal to continue to block the passage of East Germans into West Germany, the floodgates were opened and 57,000 East Germans migrated within a matter of weeks. In the face of angry demonstrations, the political leaders of East Germany were forced to resign. The new government opened the Berlin Wall on 9 November 1989, ending all restrictions on travel between East and West. An East Germany with open borders could no longer survive as its citizens poured into the promised land of the West in record numbers. The Federal Republic intervened to assist East Germany in shoring up its badly faltering economy; the West German deutsche mark was substituted for East German currency. Monetary

The Crumbling of the Eastern Bloc

1972	East and West Germany normalize relations with the Basic Treaty
1980	Polish noncommunist labor union Solidarity established, under the leadership of Lech Walesa
1985	Mikhail Gorbachev assumes leadership of the Soviet Communist party, introducing *glasnost* (increased openness) and *perestroika* (political and economic restructuring)
1989	Free elections in Poland lead to the ouster of Communist regime
September 1989	Hungary opens its borders to the West
November 1989	German Democratic Republic lifts travel restrictions between East and West Germany
1990	Boris Yeltsin elected president of the Russian Republic
1990	Gorbachev ends the Communist party's monopoly of power
1990	Lech Walesa elected president of Poland
October 1990	Federal Republic of Germany and German Democratic Republic reunited
December 1991	Eleven former Soviet Republics form Commonwealth of Independent States (CIS); Mikhail Gorbachev resigns and the Soviet Union is dissolved

alization and second-class citizenship, while those of the west worried that their poor cousins from the east would be a brake on the sustained economic expansion that had made West Germany one of the world's leading export economies.

Planning a United Europe

The European Community was created in 1967 by merging the three transnational European bodies: the European Coal and Steel Community; the European

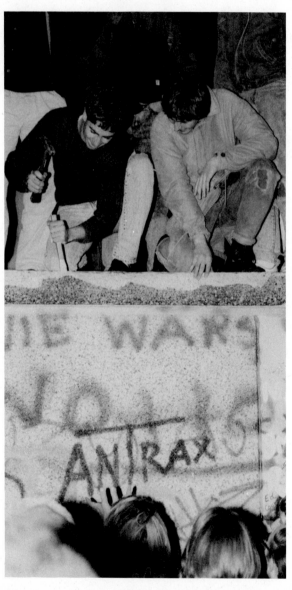

More than any other event, the dismantling of the Berlin Wall in November 1989 has come to symbolize the end of the Cold War.

union prefigured political unification. In October 1990 Germany became a single, united nation once again.

Germans represent the largest nationality in Europe west of Russia. Other Europeans, particularly the French, feared the prospect of a united Germany, although publicly they endorsed the principle of the self-determination of peoples. In addition, western Europeans were troubled by the impact a united Germany might have on plans for European unification in the European Community. Not least of all, Germans themselves feared their new identity as citizens of a single nation: former East Germans were wary about margin-

Economic Community (EEC), or Common Market; and Euratom. It operated with its own commission, parliament, and council of ministers, although it had little real power over the operations of member states. In 1974 a "European Council" was created within the European Community, made up of heads of government who met three times a year for the purpose of furthering European integration.

The oil crisis of the 1970s encouraged isolationism among the members of the EEC and eroded foreign markets, with growing dependence on national suppliers. As the crisis abated, competition and efficiency reemerged as priorities within the European Community. Europeans were well aware that the United States and Japan had surged ahead after the 1973 crisis. They also recognized that the Common Market had been successful in promoting European growth and integration since 1958. They now agreed that integration was the only defense against the permanent loss of markets and dwindling profits. In unity there might be strength, as the aggregate economic indicators for 1987 made clear.

In 1985 the European Community negotiated the Single European Act, which was ratified by the parliamentary bodies of the member nations by 1987. Final steps were initiated to establish a fully integrated market beginning at midnight on 31 December 1992. The twelve members of the European Community intended to eliminate internal barriers and to create a huge open market among the member states with common external tariff policies. In addition, the elimination of internal frontier controls, with a single-format European Community passport, was intended to make travel easier and to avoid shipping delays at frontiers, thereby lowering costs. An international labor market based on standardized requirements for certification and interchangeable job qualifications would result. The easier movement of capital was encouraged to areas where profitability was greatest. All aspects of trade and communication, down to electrical plugs and sockets, had to be standardized. The goal behind the planning was to make the European Community think and act as a single country. Supporters compared it to the fifty individual American states participating in the single U.S. nation.

In 1989 there were 320 million European citizens of the twelve countries of the European Community: the original Common Market six of France, West Germany, Belgium, the Netherlands, Luxembourg, and Italy were joined by Britain, Denmark, and Ireland in 1973, Greece in 1981, and Portugal and Spain in 1986. Plans for Euro-

Europe 1994

pean economic integration moved dramatically forward in October 1991 when the twelve-nation European Community and the seven nations of the European Free Trade Association (EFTA) joined forces to form a new common market to be known as the European Economic Area. The EFTA countries that joined forces with the EC include Austria, Finland, Iceland, Liechtenstein, Norway, Sweden, and Switzerland. Several of the EFTA nations announced plans to join the EC as well. The European Economic Area constituted the world's largest trading bloc, stretching from the Arctic Circle to the Mediterranean and consisting of around 380 million consumers. The nations of the EFTA agreed to abide by the EC's plans for economic integration and adopted the vast array of laws and regulations that governed the European Community.

The European Community plan has had at its core the adoption of a single currency (based on the European Currency Unit, or ECU) by the member nations. Meeting in Maastricht, the Netherlands, in December 1991, the heads of the twelve EC countries agreed that a common currency, the ECU, would replace the national currencies of eligible nations as early as 1997 and no later than 1999. A single central banking system, known as the European Monetary Institute was planned for the purpose of guiding member nations in reducing inflation rates and budget deficits. Economic union would be reinforced by political union, as member states agreed to a common European defense system and common social policies regulating immigration and labor practices. At the end of 1988 President François Mitterrand of France endorsed the goals of the integration: "One currency, one culture, one social area, one environment."

Britain was the most reluctant of the member states at the prospect of European integration, although other European countries began to share with the British their doubts about monetary union and the loss of national sovereignty. In addition to resisting monetary union, the British also expressed cynicism at the 1991 Maastricht negotiations over a Europe-wide social policy affecting working hours, minimum wages, and conditions of employment.

Some planners were wary of the prospect of including all of eastern Europe, whose troubled economies, they feared, would dilute the economic strength of the European Community. Others predicted a fully integrated Europe, including the eastern European nations, by the year 2014. Three of the new regimes—Poland, Czechoslovakia, and Hungary—were admitted with the status of associate members.

The plan for a single European market affected more than just economics. Education, too, faced standardization of curricula and requirements for degrees. There were proposals for a common European history textbook that, in place of national perspectives, would emphasize the values of a single political entity in its discussion of battles, wars, social change, and culture.

Export-producing nations, including Japan and the United States, expressed concerns over "Fortress Europe," that is, Europe as a global trading bloc with a common external tariff policy that would exclude them. The implementation of a united Europe slowed in the mid-1990s, as member nations of the European Community faced economic stagnation, rising unemployment, and resurgent nationalist challenges in the post–Cold War era.

Terrorism and Contemporary Society

Terrorism persisted as a force of political violence in the second half of the twentieth century. The creation of the state of Israel in part of the land of Palestine in 1948 led to conflict between the Israelis and the Palestinian Arabs, who refused to accept the new Jewish state. Israel's Arab neighbors went to war to support the Palestinians but were defeated by Israel in late 1948. Hundreds of thousands of Palestinians became refugees in neighboring Arab states, and Palestinian guerrillas decided that the best way to attack Israel and its protectors was with a global strategy of terrorist violence.

Ejected from Jordan, Palestinian guerrillas set up their headquarters in Syria and Lebanon in order to coordinate their terrorist activities. The first Palestinian highjacking of a passenger plane took place in the summer of 1968. By the late 1970s terrorism had spread to European revolutionaries with political programs that differed from the Palestinians, and terrorist activity intensified with political killings of western European industrial, financial, and judicial leaders.

Terrorism was politically motivated violence performed by groups claiming to represent some greater political cause. Victims were targeted by terrorists not because they merited any punishment themselves but as a means of attracting international attention to the terrorists' cause. Although motivated by different political goals, terrorist groups often formed cooperative networks on an international basis, sharing training, weapons, and information.

In order to succeed—that is, to terrify—terrorism had to be publicized: terrorists relied on media exposure and claimed responsibility for their acts after they had been successfully completed. In September 1972 members of the Palestinian Black September movement kidnapped eleven Israeli athletes at the Olympic Games in Munich. An estimated 500 million people watched in horror as all eleven were slaughtered during an American sports broadcast. In a dramatic televised shoot-out, five of the terrorists also died. Later in the decade OPEC oil ministers were held hostage in Vienna.

A recurrent pattern of terrorism prevailed throughout the 1980s, highlighted by international media coverage. In 1981 a Turkish fascist attempted to kill the pope. In 1983 a Lebanese Shi'ite guerrilla blew up the American marine garrison in Beirut, taking hundreds of American lives along with his own. In October 1985, the cruise ship *Achille Lauro* was highjacked by a Palestinian ultranationalist group. One aged American passenger, confined to a wheelchair, was killed. In 1985, Palestinian terrorists bombed the airports in Vienna and Rome. Middle Eastern terrorists bombed the World Trade Center in Manhattan in 1993.

The Provisional Wing of the Irish Republican Army justified its bombing of Christmas crowds in London with the need to unite Northern Ireland with the independent Irish Republic. Seeing themselves engaged in wars of liberation, revolution, and resistance, terrorists argued that they used the only weapons at their disposal

New York City investigators examine the scene of the bombing in a parking garage below the World Trade Center in February 1993. The blast killed five people and injured 652.

against the great imperialist powers. Plastic explosives in suitcases, nearly impossible to detect by available technology in the 1980s, became the weapon of choice. If all was fair in war—and World War II demonstrated that both sides bombed innocent civilian victims in pursuit of victory—then, terrorists countered, they were fighting the war with the only weapons and in the only arena at their disposal.

By the 1990s terrorism was challenging the tranquility of Europe and the United States in effective ways. One reason for terrorism's success was the vulnerability of advanced industrial societies to random terror. Modern terrorists were able to evade policing and detection. Surveillance has not prevented terrorists from striking at airplanes and cruise ships. In December 1988 hundreds of people died when a Pan American flight was bombed over Lockerbie, Scotland, probably in retaliation for the downing of an Iranian passenger airliner by the U.S. Navy in the Persian Gulf. Yet terrorism accom-

plished little by way of bringing about political change or solutions to problems like the question of a Palestinian homeland in the Middle East.

West European governments often refused to bargain with terrorists. Yet at times European nations have been willing to negotiate for the release of kidnapped citizens. They have also been willing to use violence against terrorists. Israel led the way in creating antiterror squads. In 1976 Israeli commandos succeeded in freeing captives in Entebbe, Uganda. The following year specially trained West German troops freed Lufthansa passengers and crew held hostage at Mogadishu in Somalia on the east coast of Africa. The Arab kidnappers had hoped to bargain for the release of the imprisoned leaders of the Red Army Faction; the West German government refused. In 1986 the United States bombed Libya, long recognized as a training ground for international terrorist recruits, in retaliation for the bombing of a discotheque frequented by American service personnel in West Germany. Israel bombed refugee camps to retaliate against Palestinian nationalists. The goal of this "counterterrorism" was the undermining of support for terrorists among their own people, which made it very similar in tactics and ends to the terrorism it was opposing.

The advanced industrial states of western Europe and the United States were vulnerable to an invisible terrorist enemy who could terrorize populations and incapacitate the smooth functioning of the modern industrial state. More serious threats to stability and demands for some kind of armed response came from the ethnic unrest in central and eastern Europe. Nationalist feelings were intensifying within eastern Europe at the very moment integration appeared to accelerate in the west. Demands for autonomy lay behind the revolutionary events in Poland, the Baltic Soviet states, Hungary, Bulgaria, and Romania. Talk of ethnic purity ominously echoed the despicable racial policies of Nazi Germany. Meanwhile in western Europe, planners spoke of a European Community in which national differences would be muted for the common good.

At the end of the twentieth century Western women and men faced the future filled with uncertainty. Jacques Delors, president of the European Community's Executive Commission, stated simply, "I don't want to live in a Europe that is like it was in 1914." Yet comparisons with Europe on the eve of the Great War seemed salient to some observers. Commentators warned of new nationalist conflicts on the horizon. Social change threatened to wither without producing fruit, as governments cut free of the security of old ways grappled with new political challenges and economic chaos. Yet there was hope, too, as leaders of democratic and former Communist states that had once been enemies spoke of a common European destiny based on security, freedom, and democratic principles.

SUGGESTIONS FOR FURTHER READING

RECONSTRUCTING EUROPE

* Stanley Hoffman and Charles Maier, *The Marshall Plan: A Retrospective* (Boulder, CO: Westview Press, 1984). Based on a commemorative conference held at Harvard University, thirty-five years after George C. Marshall's address at that university, this collection assembles the work of specialists and actual participants in the plan's implementation.
* Michael J. Hogan, *The Marshall Plan: America, Britain, and the Reconstruction of Western Europe* (Cambridgeshire: Cam-

bridge University Press, 1987). A thoroughly researched argument on the continuities of U.S. economic policy in the twentieth century. Hogan counters the interpretation that the Marshall Plan was merely a response to the Cold War.

REGULATING THE COLD WAR

* Franz Ansprenger, *The Dissolution of the Colonial Empires* (London: Routledge, 1989). An analysis of Europe's withdrawal from Asia and Africa following the Second World War, beginning with an examination of post-World War I imperialism.

Charles S. Maier, ed., *The Origins of the Cold War and Contemporary Europe* (New York: Franklin Watts, 1978). A series of essays considering the origins of the Cold War and its impact on the political economy of Europe.

* Charles S. Maier, *In Search of Stability: Explorations in Historical Political Economy* (Cambridgeshire: Cambridge University Press, 1987). Covers a wide variety of issues affecting twentieth-century Europe, including the foundation of American international economic policy after World War II and the conditions for stability in Western Europe after 1945.

* Bruce D. Porter, *The USSR in Third World Conflicts: Soviet Arms and Diplomacy in Local Wars, 1945–1980* (Cambridgeshire: Cambridge University Press, 1984). A case study approach to the Soviet Union's changing postwar policies toward the Third World that centers on local wars in Africa and the Middle East.

CREATING THE WELFARE STATE

* Simone de Beauvoir, *The Second Sex* (New York: Knopf, 1963). The author, one of France's leading intellectuals in the twentieth century, describes the situation of women's lives in the postwar West by placing them within the context of the history and myths governing Western culture.

* J. Bowyer Bell, *Transnational Terror* (Washington, DC: American Enterprise Institute, 1975). Presents a compelling argument about the social revolutionary origins of terror and its threat to Western democracies.

* David Caute, *The Year of the Barricades: A Journey Through 1968* (New York: Harper and Row, 1988). More than its title suggests, this work is an overview of postwar youth culture on three continents. The politics of 1968 is featured, although other topics regarding the counterculture, lifestyles, and cultural ramifications are considered.

* Richard Clutterbuck, *Guerrillas and Terrorists* (London: Faber and Faber, 1977). Clutterbuck considers terrorism as a kind of war rooted in historical experience and global in nature. His purpose is to consider protection against terrorists by examining the roles of the media, the police, and the public.

John R. Gillis, *Youth and History: Tradition and Change in European Age Relations, 1770-Present* (New York: Academic Press, 1981). Connects the history of European youth to broad trends in economic and demographic modernization over the last two hundred years.

* Jane Jenson, "Both Friend and Foe: Women and State Welfare," *Becoming Visible: Women in European History*, edited by Renate Bridenthal, Claudia Koonz, and Susan Stuard (Boston: Houghton Mifflin, 1987). This essay illuminates the mixed

blessing of the welfare state for women after 1945 by focusing on the experiences of women in Great Britain and France.

* Margaret Mead, *Culture and Commitment: The New Relationships Between the Generations in the 1970s* (New York: Columbia University Press, 1978). This series of essays, written by one of America's premier anthropologists, explores the origins and the consequences of the generation gap with special attention to Cold War politics, historical conditions, and technological transformations.

Wolfgang Mommsen and Gerhard Hirschfeld, eds., *Social Protest, Violence and Terror in Nineteenth- and Twentieth-Century Europe* (London: The MacMillan Press Ltd., 1982). Places terrorism within a historical context in Europe over the last century and a half in a series of articles that proceed with a national, case-history approach.

Denise Riley, *War in the Nursery: Theories of the Child and Mother* (London: Virago Press, 1983). Treats social policies of postwar pronatalism within the context of the popularization of developmental and child psychologies in Europe, with special attention to Britain and the United States, and emphasis on the postwar period as a turning point in attitudes toward women and the family.

Richard E. Rubinstein, *Alchemists of Revolution: Terrorism in the Modern World* (New York: Basic Books, 1987). Examines the local root causes of terrorism in historical perspective and argues that it is a social and moral crisis of a disaffected intelligentsia.

* Mary Ruggie, *The State and Working Women: A Comparative Study of Britain and Sweden* (Princeton, NJ: Princeton University Press, 1984). A sociological study comparing the economic status of women in two European welfare states.

ENDING THE COLD WAR

* Stephen F. Cohen, *Rethinking the Soviet Experience: Politics and History Since 1917* (New York: Oxford University Press, 1985). Offers a revisionist analysis of the historiographical debates in Soviet studies with the intention of casting light on contemporary Soviet politics.

* Patrick Cockburn, *Getting Russia Wrong: The End of Kremlinology* (London: Verso, 1989). A Moscow correspondent takes the measure of the politics of the Gorbachev era, while attempting to uncover the shortcomings of Western misconceptions about the Soviet Union.

* Michael Emerson et al., *The Economics of 1992: The E.C. Commission's Assessment of the Economic Effects of Completing the Internal Market* (Oxford: University Press, 1988). A work replete with empirical data that gives a comprehensive assessment of the potential impact of establishing a single internal market in the European Economic Community.

Geoffrey Hosking, *The Awakening of the Soviet Union* (Cambridge, MA: Harvard University Press, 1990). Published in the midst of the dramatic changes taking place in the Soviet Union, this study emphasizes the social bases of reform and the challenges to Soviet leadership.

* Brian McNair, *Images of the Enemy: Reporting the New Cold War* (London: Routledge, 1988). Focuses on the importance of television in conveying the East-West debate to a mass audience in the 1980s. McNair demonstrates that the Soviets learned in the 1980s to manage communication techniques to their own advantage.

* Teresa Rakowska-Harmstone and Andrew Gyorgy, eds., *Communism in Eastern Europe* (Manchester, England: Manchester University Press, 1984). Provides a comprehensive country-by-country approach with consideration of nationalism and shared regional problems.

* Joseph Rothschild, *Return to Diversity: A Political History of East Central Europe* (New York: Oxford University Press, 1989). A historical and analytical survey of Poland, Czechoslovakia, Hungary, Yugoslavia, Romania, Bulgaria, and Albania that appeared just before the great changes that swept eastern Europe in 1989. Rothschild highlights the tensions between nationalist aspirations and communist rule.

Henry Ashby Turner, Jr., *The Two Germanies Since 1945* (New Haven: Yale University Press, 1987). A political history from the postwar division of Germany until 1987 that bridges a period that the author contends was one of increasing involvement and underlying mutual interests between the two nations.

* Adam B. Ulam, *Dangerous Relations: The Soviet Union in World Politics, 1970–1982* (New York: Oxford University Press, 1983). Discusses the making of détente and the relationship between internal developments in the Soviet Union and their impact on foreign policy.

* Indicates paperback edition available.

CHAPTER 35

Asia, 1930 to the Present

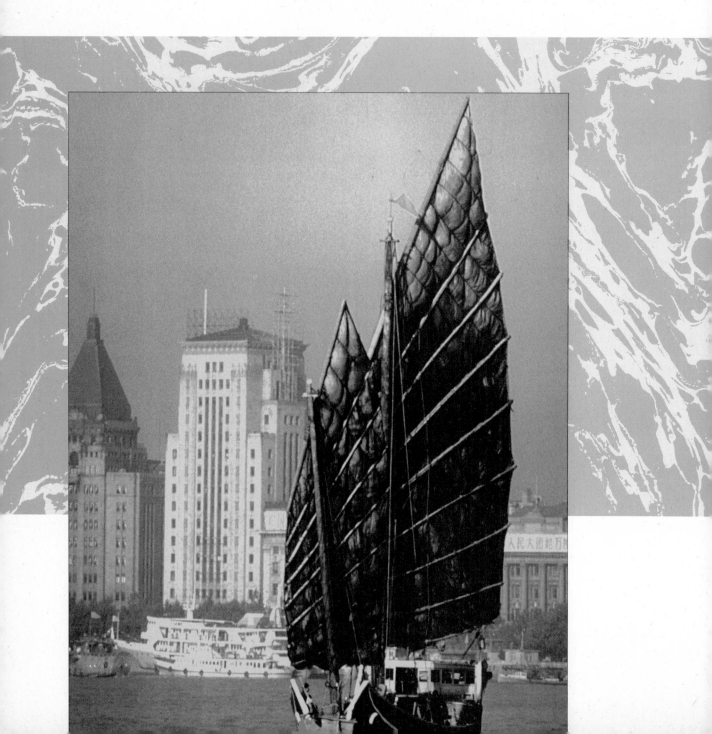

MAKING MODERN CITIES IN ASIA

The transformation of Asian societies in the modern period has begun in the large cities where Asian and Western cultures have collided to create new problems and new possibilities. The Western architecture that dominates the Shanghai skyline is a symbol of the foreigners' earlier dominance of the city. Today these buildings stand behind Chinese junks that worked Yangzi River ports before the Westerners came and that continue to cruise the Shanghai harbor, as this 1980s photograph shows. In coming years the expansion of Shanghai's port facilities promises to accommodate larger ships in greater numbers. Beyond the downtown areas, with their high concentration of foreign influence, a sprawl of mid-rise residential buildings takes over a skyline previously composed of one- and two-story dwellings.

Throughout Asia the twentieth-century connections between cities and the countryside have often been limited. New cultural sensibilities can take decades to reach peasants in remote villages, where they become molded to fit very different social settings. Shanghai's relationships to its hinterland and the rest of China have been difficult and complex. Under the Nationalists, the divide between the city and countryside grew. In Shanghai and other major Chinese cities, economic and political elites created sophisticated banking institutions and new government organizations, while new social groups of students, intellectuals, and workers joined in protests against the growing Japanese threat of the 1930s that culminated in 1936 with Japan's invasion of China. Culturally, Shanghai residents were exposed to a variety of movies, plays, and music in nightclubs that introduced Western notions of entertainment and romantic love. Beneath the comfortable wealth of the foreigners and a small Chinese middle class, the masses of the city labored in poverty. Beneath those fortunate enough to enjoy regular factory jobs, however exhausting and alienating, were the thousands who depended on day labor that was only sometimes available. Urban and rural China belonged to different worlds in a universe of political, social, and cultural uncertainties.

During the early twentieth century, the formal government of Shanghai was divided among the foreigners and the Chinese government. Beneath and apart from the formal governmental offices of both Chinese and foreigners were the gangs that controlled opium, prostitution, and gambling. Shanghai's mysterious and sordid reputation in Hollywood's imagination comes from its underworld, whose leaders extended their power into legitimate businesses and government through personal connections with capitalists and officials. Western awareness of Shanghai grew during World War II when Hitler's march through Europe closed off avenues of escape and drove Jews eastward for China, where many ended up in Shanghai to plan safe passage to another country.

When the People's Republic of China was established in 1949, urban and rural China were formally administered separately, with strict limitations on migration from the countryside to the cities. These policies widened the economic and social breach already separating Shanghai from the countryside. But Chinese policies from the 1950s to the 1970s also repeatedly taxed Shanghai and used the funds raised there to support other less fortunate regions. These policies ignited complaints in Shanghai that they hampered efforts to develop. Now with foreign economic relationships once again a major feature of the Shanghai scene, Shanghai industries and government are raising more resources. But the impacts of increased market activity are not all positive. The city, like other Chinese cities, has become far more open to migration from the countryside, pressuring the overcrowded housing stock with additional people who live on the margins of urban society. Positive signs of individual consumer wealth are balanced by negative cases of economic corruption.

The glistening new foreign ships that make their way into Shanghai's harbor materially connect China's economy with a larger world. They also symbolize the possibilities for cultural and political change. Shanghai is a city that is at once Chinese and foreign in its modern history and in its global future. How the two fit together is a challenge that not only Shanghai continues to confront, but China and the rest of Asia have been facing throughout the twentieth century.

East Asia During the Rise and Fall of Japanese Imperialism, 1930–1952

In 1930, Japan was poised to become the dominant power of Asia. China remained economically weaker and politically somewhat divided. Colonialism had compromised the strength of other, smaller countries. Two decades later, Japan had suffered a thorough defeat in a massive war after having made startling territorial advances throughout Asia between 1937 and 1945. The United States emerged as the principal international force in Asia during the 1950s. But Americans faced a hostile China, where the People's Republic was founded on 1 October 1949. The Chinese went from being a wartime friend to a Cold War foe as the Japanese were transformed from an evil enemy to a junior ally. Beneath these fundamental political realignments, Asian leaders struggled to create domestic order and stable foreign relations.

Chinese Rule and the Imposition of Japanese Puppet Government, 1930–1937

The years 1927 to 1936, when the Nationalists ruled China from their capital in Nanjing, stand out as a positive decade. The Nationalists were not able to improve conditions in the countryside, nor did they welcome Western-style democratic reforms, but compared to the decades preceding and following the so-called Nanjing decade there was at least a measure of political stability. From 1912 to 1927 China had lacked much semblance of any national government, and after 1936 the Japanese invasion destroyed what unity had been achieved by Jiang Jieshi. The Japanese invasion also interrupted a positive trajectory of economic change initiated during the early years of Nationalist rule. Understanding the limitations of economic change in prewar China is essential to understanding the Chinese revolution. Swifter development of a modern economy that benefited peasants might have made peasants less likely to join the Communists against the Nationalists when the Japanese were defeated at the end of World War II in 1945.

Quite separately, the Nationalists would also have stood a better chance of succeeding had they managed to destroy the Communists when they enjoyed vastly superior military strength. Four times between 1930 and 1933, the Nationalist armies encircled Communist base areas, poised to deliver the crushing blow, and four times the Communists managed to escape. The fifth campaign began with 700,000 Nationalist troops counseled by German military advisers. The Communists made a final escape to begin an epic odyssey known as the Long March. The march was composed of several contingents, and the one led by Mao Zedong (1893–1976) crossed 24 rivers and 18 mountain ranges in 11 provinces. Mao's group marched more than 6,000 miles in a little over a year, averaging 17 miles a day, often through very difficult terrain. Altogether, fewer than 40,000 men and women, roughly one-tenth of those who started the journey, reached a remote part of China's northwest called Yanan in northern Shanxi. Some were unable to complete the journey; others died on the way or in the fighting that marked their retreat. The Communists' numbers would be augmented by others who later made their way to Yanan, attracted to the possibilities the Communists promised for a new and better China. Though the Communists survived, they hardly seemed a force to be taken seriously. Indeed, frustration with Jiang Jieshi's pursuit of the Communists when the Japanese loomed as a much more serious danger led to Jiang's house arrest by warlord leader Zhang Xueliang in Xian, who insisted that Jiang turn from the Communists to fight the Japanese. The Nationalists joined the Communists, who had already declared war on Japan, to enter their second period of united front work, which was no more likely to last than the first—if they could first survive the Japanese invasion.

To Japan, Manchuria was the frontier, the rich fertile land to which new settlers could move with the hope of creating a better life. The Japanese army was eager to create a pretext for fighting in order to expand their mainland presence; the civilian government in Japan was more cautious. But the army had its way and began a struggle to take over Manchuria. In March 1932, the Japanese completed their occupation of all of Manchuria, installing a puppet state, Manchukuo, under Pu-Yi, who had been the last Qing emperor of China. Many Japanese justified the takeover of Manchuria as a necessary action to bolster their nation's power against Britain and Russia. These interpretations of Japan's interests in mainland east Asia appealed not only to right-wing military advocates but even to some Japanese Communists, who saw their country's mission on the Asian mainland in a positive light. They believed the Japanese were destined to free China from the control of British and American capital. Establishing Manchukuo was simply the first step in the process. Since ideas of colonial independence were "bourgeois," the proper relationship for Manchukuo, as well as Korea and Taiwan, was to be merged closely in political and economic terms with Japan. Beginning in 1932, factions within the civilian and military bureaucracies in Japan promoted a sense of national crisis to advance their power in government. A split in the military over how best to mobi-

lize for war culminated in the mutiny of some fourteen hundred troops on 26 February 1936. They assassinated the finance minister and other top officials, narrowly missing the prime minister and other major figures. The mutiny was suppressed and the military's energies shifted from domestic reform to a full-scale attack on China.

To the Chinese, once the Manchurian puppet regime was established, the threat of Japan spreading its influence was a source of constant anxiety. Not a day went by without some guerrilla gunfire in Japanese-occupied areas. All-out war began in July 1937 after a small military clash outside Beijing at the Marco Polo Bridge. Rather than resolve the incident diplomatically, both sides maneuvered larger forces into place with the result that Beijing fell after an exchange of fire lasting but one day and night. Japanese troops began to move south. On 13 August Japanese naval units landed in Shanghai, and on 15 August the Chinese general headquarters declared a general mobilization as China and Japan headed into eight years of war.

Communists, Nationalists, and Their Wars, 1937–1949

The Japanese took over the Nationalists' capital twice, first in Nanjing and then in Hankou. Each time they expected the Chinese to surrender; each time the Nationalists picked up their government and headed farther inland. After the fall of Hankou, the Nationalists moved to Chongqing, acknowledging that the Japanese had de facto control over the richest half of the country. Working with a puppet government in Nanjing, the Japanese became enmeshed in a protracted effort to bring China under their rule. By year's end in 1937 the Japanese had already moved 700,000 soldiers into China, but with the continual Chinese retreat the Japanese lacked the personnel to consolidate control and continue pushing the front lines forward. By June 1940, Japanese forces in China numbered 850,000 men, who stayed until 1943 when some were moved out to other theaters of war. But even with all these men, the Japanese could not bring down the Nationalist government. For their part, the Communists worked from their northwest base area to penetrate Japanese lines in north China and to engage in guerrilla actions and sabotage.

Isolated in the northwestern wilderness of Yanan, the Communists made great efforts to promote production and exchange within their base area. The principles

Japanese forces occupied the city of Beijing in July 1937.

they developed there to mobilize peasants to sacrifice for the war effort would shape the Communist perspective on economic development in the 1950s, when enlisting peasant enthusiasm was considered a key ingredient to increasing production. The government in Yanan initiated practical concrete measures. They promoted expanded agricultural production through mutual-aid groups and cooperatives; they promoted small handicraft industries; they scattered activists into the villages to raise production by creating model units; and they promoted trade both within the base area and beyond. Communist successes in working with the peasants of the remote northwest have led some analysts to argue that the countryside joined the Communists out of patriotic desire to defeat the Japanese rather than from any commitment to social revolution. Although the Communists did very well in their base area and the peasants under their rule may well have been motivated by patriotism, those factors alone cannot ex-

plain how and why vastly better armed Nationalist forces were defeated in the civil war that followed Japan's surrender on 14 August 1945.

Following the Japanese retreat, Communist forces began moving across north China. Even before proclaiming their rule over the entire country on 1 October 1949, they began to send work teams into north China villages to begin a revolutionary process of land redistribution that dispossessed the rich and gave everyone some land. Communist confidence in the north China villages was paralleled by the high morale in Communist armies; soldiers were well disciplined and confident under their military leaders. Nationalist armies, in contrast, suffered the low morale of a conscript army lacking any vision of why they were fighting. They were, however, aided by American power, which made a massive sea and air lift of half a million Nationalist troops back to the coastal areas and into Manchuria. But this proved inadequate, and the Communists continued to gain the

ONE PAGE OF A DIARY

■ *In the spring of 1936, advertisements appeared in many Chinese periodicals and newspapers inviting readers to write letters concerning events and issues of concern to them on 21 May. The intent of the editors, who numbered among them some of China's best and most famous writers, was to capture a cross section of educated opinion about the state of the country. One major theme in the letters was the threat posed by the Japanese. Already in control of Manchuria, the Japanese were becoming an increasingly obvious presence in unoccupied parts of China even before they launched their land invasion in 1936. In this excerpted letter, written by a female college student in Taiyuan, the provincial capital of the northern province of Shanxi, the dangers, not of military invasion, but of educated youth without work selling out to the Japanese are raised.*

Recently, this "friendly power" of ours has shown "Kindly Benevolence"[1] by using airplanes to send to Taiyuan "military officers" and "advisers" once every two or three days with all kinds of "secret messages." As all of us looked at the airplane of the "friendly power" going on its mission of "Kindly Benevolence" between the two countries and flying freely through our own air space, our hearts weighed heavy as lead and we felt oppressed . . .

Graduation is near so students are allowed to hold discussions in class about their plans for the future. This is indeed a serious problem. But the entire nation and race have no future. How can an individual have a future! . . .

I've long wanted to look up X, but I've never had the chance. . . .

After he graduated last year from the Economics Department in the Faculty of Law, he couldn't find a job for about a year. Just recently, after expending the energy of nine oxen and two tigers, he found a job as a petty copyist in the headquarters of the Militia for the Promotion of Public Justice.[2] Working more than eight or ten hours a day, he makes a monthly salary of eighteen dollars!

Some time ago, someone advertised in the newspaper saying they wished to hire some sort of "Chinese language teacher." There were no requirements, and the pay was good. "Interested persons please come to Zhengda Hotel for further information."

At that time we already sensed that this advertisement was evil and subversive. Later someone looked into it and discovered that it was indeed the X [Japanese] who were using the term "Chinese language teacher" as a pretext for buying off Chinese traitors. The salary was quite high, but the work was very secretive.

A friend of mine from college had no place to go after graduation. I heard recently that he has become this kind of "Chinese language teacher." Living on the third floor of the Zhengda Hotel, he always carries a big leather case under his arm, travels back and forth in an automobile, and appears to be very prosperous.

So, if you want to be a "good person," then you'll have no rice to eat . . . Therefore, many people who mouth denunciations of Chinese traitors are tempted in their hearts. As people's stomachs shrivel, it is certain that the number of "Chinese language teachers" produced will rise shockingly!

[1] Li Yun used the term "friendly power" sarcastically, implying that Japan was the opposite—an unfriendly power—in China. "Kindly Benevolence" was one of the slogans used in Japanese propaganda at this time.
[2] This was one of hundreds of thousands of organizations by this name which were created by Yan Xishan, a Chinese warlord whose armies controlled Shanxi province between 1912 and 1949.

From Sherman Cochran and Andrew C.K. Hsieh, *One Day in China May 21, 1936.*

upper hand. Jiang Jieshi succeeded in escaping the mainland, taking with him not only many of his soldiers but also valuable art works and U.S. $300 million of his reserve funds. He left behind a war-torn society with hyperinflation rapidly impoverishing and demoralizing those fortunate enough to have salaried jobs. Jiang's invasion of Taiwan was bloody, but he successfully put down resistance to his arrival and established the Republic of China as an island fortress, vowing to take back the mainland and eradicate the Communist "bandits"—a task he had unsuccessfully set himself many times in the past. Jiang's survival would turn on the intervention of the U.S. government, fresh from its successes in the Second World War and groping for a policy to represent its perceived interests in Asia. The United States had to perform some swift rethinking of international politics. After a decade of considering the Japanese to be the Asian enemy and the Chinese as its Asian friends, the U.S. government chose to reverse those roles. But U.S. knowledge of both countries was little better than it had been when the Japanese bombed Pearl Harbor on 7 December 1941 and drew the United States into World War II.

The United States in Asia, 1946–1952

During the Pacific War, the Japanese expressed very high opinions of themselves compared both to other Asians and to Westerners. Americans had their own images of the Japanese. Whereas an effort was made to distinguish "good" and "bad" Germans, all Japanese were considered bad. They were also considered alternately subhuman and superhuman—but never just human. Images of monkey-like Japanese filled wartime cartoons in the U.S. and Great Britain, but once the Japanese scored swift successes in China and Southeast Asia, the Japanese emerged as some superhuman creature, feeding yellow peril fears. The ferocity of U.S. war efforts in the Pacific took on a zeal absent in the European theater, including the unleashing of atomic bombs on Hiroshima on 6 August 1945 and on Nagasaki on 9 August 1945. Coupled with the wartime internment of Japanese Americans as potential spies, the racist component of the U.S. approach to war in Asia appears painfully clear. The tragic loss of life in the Pacific War, including as many as 15 million Chinese and some 2.5 million Japanese, was swiftly followed by the American occupation of Japan, through which the Japanese suddenly came to enjoy a less threatening position in the

American imagination, replaced by the Chinese, who had become not simply a yellow peril but also a red menace.

Two weeks after the Japanese emperor's prerecorded message informed the Japanese people that the war was over, the Supreme Commander for the Allied Powers (SCAP), General Douglas MacArthur, arrived in Japan. His two principal occupation objectives were to prevent Japan from becoming a threat to U.S. security and world peace, and to establish a Japanese government willing to support U.S. objectives as represented in the Charter of the United Nations, preferably a government representing the principles of democratic self-government. Within a month SCAP became the source for a stream of directives to the Japanese caretaker government to implement measures to achieve occupation objectives—a new constitution and new rules for the Diet, cabinet, imperial household, courts, local government, and public services. The previously powerful Home Ministry was divided into ministries of Labor, Health and Welfare, Construction, and Local Autonomy. The police were reorganized and a sweeping land reform for farmers was initiated. An overhaul of education created six years of compulsory primary education followed by three more of secondary education. A new labor union law gave workers the right to organize.

The Japanese government during the early occupation years faced the difficult challenges of implementing occupation commands and defusing resentments and animosities toward the Allies. Facing a war-torn economy suffering serious difficulties, it labored to restore civilian industrial production amid skyrocketing inflation. To deal with the inflation, occupation forces mandated a deflationary program that cost a half million employees their jobs in the public and private sectors.

Once the Korean War began in 1950, occupation policies shifted. The caretaker government formed a Japanese defense agency, implemented policies to regulate labor union activity, and softened antimonopoly measures. Occupation officials reinstated more than 200,000 businessmen in seventy-five holding and trading companies, ending a period of personal hardship and corporate disruption. The Japanese accepted American domination in the immediate postwar years because as losers of the Pacific War their "proper place" had become that of the defeated.

When the Japanese were defeated, their former colony of Taiwan was returned to China. The Nationalist government treated the island as a conquered territory with a harsh and exploitative hand. In February and

March of 1947, Nationalist troops killed thousands of Taiwanese who protested their treatment. In May several thousand more Taiwanese were killed by additional Nationalist troops brought to the island. Finally in 1949, nearly 2 million soldiers and civilians entered Taiwan and ruthlessly destroyed any and all opposition, killing thousands more in the process. The Nationalists were able to establish their rule of the island in part because the Communists could not cross the Formosa Strait, controlled by the U.S. Seventh Fleet since the outbreak of the Korean War.

With the 1945 defeat of the Japanese in Korea, the Allies agreed to have the Russians occupy Korea north of the 38th parallel and the United States occupy the portion south of the 38th parallel. Koreans openly resisted the imposition of yet other foreigners on their country. They were shocked and angry to learn of the Allied decision in autumn 1945 to put Korea under the trusteeship of the United States, Britain, the Soviet Union, and China for five years. Repeated efforts to negotiate a unification of Korea failed because the United States and the Soviet Union each wished to establish a system sympathetic to its foreign policies. Within Korea there was a basic division of political vision between a revolutionary nationalist movement and a conservative movement defending the status quo. In its essence, the Korean War, like the later tragedy in Vietnam, was a civil war that was transformed by world politics. Before the

outbreak of sustained hostilities in July 1950 there had been repeated skirmishes as well as significant guerrilla warfare in South Korea by rebels opposed to the south Korean government. When the war began, North Koreans initially overwhelmed South Korean forces. With a mandate from the U.S.-dominated United Nations, American troops, joined later by soldiers from Britain, France, Canada, Australia, the Philippines, and Turkey, pushed the Communists out of South Korea and advanced toward China. From a U.S. perspective, this reunification would mean a Korea allied with the free world. For the Chinese, however, the advance of hostile U.S. troops toward their border was a dangerous challenge to their survival. The mobilization and deployment of thousands of Chinese troops surprised the Americans, forcing their retreat to the 38th parallel, where an uneasy truce has been maintained ever since.

Japanese ambitions to form a colonial empire, so promising in 1930, were thoroughly crushed by 1945. Four years later the establishment of the People's Republic of China ushered in the first period of national political unity and social stability to last more than a decade since the fall of the Qing dynasty in 1911. The antagonistic relationship of the 1930s and 1940s between China and Japan became insulated in the 1950s by a bipolar world order in which the Chinese became part of the communist block of countries dominated by the Soviet Union, and Japan fell under the influence of Western countries led by the United States. The construction of this postwar world order in Asia was built first upon the collapse of Japan's imperial pretensions and later on the destruction of Western colonial strongholds.

Refugees from the fighting of the Korean War flee to the rear past advancing American troops in July 1950.

The End of Colonialism in South and Southeast Asia

The defeat of the Japanese in World War II briefly created a political vacuum in Southeast Asia. The Western colonial powers—Britain, France, the Netherlands, and the United States—all re-entered the region but met with varying degrees of nationalist opposition. Gradually, and often at great human cost, Western colonialism was destroyed. But American and European political and economic power remained important throughout the region.

Asia, 1930–1952

1930–34	Jiangxi Soviet survives four extermination campaigns
1931	Japanese invade Manchuria; Chinese Soviet Republic formed in Jiangxi
1932	Communists declare war on the Japanese
1932	Puppet state of Manchukuo established as Japanese colony
1933	Japan withdraws from League of Nations
1934	Jiang Jieshi's last "extermination" campaign; the Communists begin their Long March
1935	Mao Zedong achieves undisputed control of CCP; Communist headquarters established in Yanan
1937	Communists and Nationalists agree to cooperate against the Japanese who invade China
1941–45	Pacific War, also known as the Greater East Asia War (Daitooa Sensō)
1945	U.S. atomic bombs destroy Hiroshima and Nagasaki; Japan surrenders; occupation headquarters under General Douglas MacArthur established
1946–1949	Civil war between Communists and Nationalists, ending with Communist victory
1947	Establishment of India and Pakistan as independent countries
1947	New Japanese constitution; MacArthur bans February 1 general strike
1949	People's Republic of China established in Beijing; U.S. and other Western powers recognize Nationalist government on Taiwan
1950	Sino-Soviet friendship pact
1950–53	Korean War
1952	Occupation ends; Japan regains sovereignty

State Making and Nation Building in Southeast Asia

In the Philippines, formal independence was declared in 1946 after complex domestic maneuvering among nationalist groups. The Huks, a peasant nationalist movement with loose Communist affiliations and prestige from having fought the Japanese, won seven seats in the 1946 elections for parliament. The Huk pressed for land reform and social changes and thus posed an awkward political force for the U.S. and the Filipino elites it supported. Huk opposition was smashed by the early 1950s. The U.S. no longer occupied the Philippines as a formal government, but its military and business corporations retained their presence as forces in the country.

In the postwar period, the U.S. presence grew in Thailand. Concerned by the mid-1950s about the potential growth of communism, the U.S. increased its military and economic aid, displacing the British as the Western power with the most influence in the country. Thailand had entered the war-torn 1940s after a decade of political debates over reforming the monarchy. During the 1930s Western political ideas about democracy had enjoyed considerable influence among educated Thais, a prestige that would fade by the Second World War, when the capacity of Western states to deal with economic crises and international tensions seemed inadequate at best. By 1940 an aggressive Asian state like Japan proved a more attractive model to the Thais. When France fell to Germany in 1940, the Thai government pressed for the return of territories in Cambodia and Laos taken by the French to form Indochina. Fighting a full-scale war with the French in 1940–41, they received western Cambodian provinces and territory in Laos. The Japanese supported the Thai efforts and then moved in their own troops as part of their drive to establish control over the region. The Thai government capitulated to Japanese demands that it declare war on the U.S. and Britain. Thai territorial successes lasted only as long as Japanese power was in force. After World War II, the French insisted on the return of Laotian and Cambodian territories as a condition for its support of Thai entry into the United Nations.

In Burma the British role diminished after World War II. In 1948 the country was declared fully independent. But among the Malay states, the British colonial presence was maintained until 1957, when the Federation of Malaya declared its independence. In 1959 Singapore achieved self-rule. For a brief period between 1963 and 1965, Singapore became part of a new and expanded

Modern Southeast Asia

nation-state named Malaysia, which included both Malaya and Singapore and the resource-rich former British Borneo territories of Sarawak and Sabah, across the South China Sea. But the Malays came to fear that the largely Chinese Singapore would challenge the Malays' ethnic political hegemony in Malaysia, and this tension led to Malaysia's divorce from Singapore in 1965.

In the case of Indonesia, a national identity had to be invented for a diverse mix of people. In 1930, the Dutch East Indies embraced a universe of separate indigenous societies—Islamic, Hindu-Buddhist, Christian, and animist. There were villages of rice paddy producers; other people moved every few years seeking new fields to practice slash-and-burn agriculture. Speaking different languages and enjoying distinct cultural traditions, the people had no clear common sense of nationhood. The creation of the cultural idea of Indonesia depended first on accepting the Dutch East Indies as a social reality and then on transforming this identity imposed by a foreign power into a native concept. For educated urban leaders this process began in

the 1920s. But the great masses of peasants lived and died in their traditional political and cultural worlds. On 17 August 1945 Indonesian independence was declared with Japanese encouragement as Japan's military presence in the region was faltering. But the Dutch did not recognize the declaration of independence. They killed many people en route to re-establishing military control over urban areas. They reached an impasse with Indonesian nationalists, who through UN intervention, secured a cease fire and then independence in 1949. Dutch economic interests remained until 1957, when Dutch firms were expelled and their companies nationalized.

The end of colonialism in this part of the world created the opportunities for democratic political systems, but more often than not, military leaders have risen to the top. In Thailand military leaders have frequently disbanded democratic governments and institutions, often in the name of restoring social order. In fact, brutal military suppression of dissent has increased opposition. In the late 1960s student unrest culminated in hundreds of thousands of people in the streets of Bangkok in 1973 demanding an end to military rule. Since 1980 the military leadership has been more divided than before and more tolerant of dissent. In Burma, national integration was difficult to create because of the opposition of ethnic minorities to incorporation into a postcolonial "Burmese" nation-state that ethnic Burmans would inevitably try to dominate. In 1948, rival Communist groups began a civil war against the government. In 1962, after barely a decade of civil government, the army took over and dismantled the previous political system. In 1974 a socialist one-party state was proclaimed. More recently, a pro-democracy party won elections in May 1990 but their leaders remained jailed thereafter in what became known as Myanmar. Through all these changes, the country has remained economically undeveloped, though rich in untapped mineral reserves, and has only recently forged some economic contacts with the rest of the world.

In Indonesia, the institutions of parliamentary democracy were introduced in the mid-1950s but collapsed immediately under the pressures exerted by local army commanders, who engineered a series of coups the government was able to suppress. The Indonesian government was not popular among Western powers in the late 1950s; they had expelled Dutch firms and in the early 1960s developed close ties with the People's Republic of China and hostile relations with Malaysia. In the mid-1960s a return to promoting relations with developed countries attracted Western and Japanese capital.

The Philippines has been no more successful in achieving democratic political institutions despite its close ties to the U.S. Through the 1950s and 1960s there were elections and parties, but these did not prevent the declaration of martial law in 1972, formally in place until 1981. Growing opposition to the widespread government corruption and military abuses brought the Marcos regime down in 1986.

Creating stable nations has sometimes been difficult in Southeast Asia. Even when formal political freedom from a colonial situation went smoothly, other serious challenges confronted new nations. First, the demographic issues of rapid population growth made economic advance more difficult because priority often had to go to meeting basic food supply demands. Second, the civil service bureaucracy, once freed from colonial powers, proved vulnerable to problems of corruption, nepotism, and other forms of favoritism. Third, it was difficult to plan well-rounded economic development to replace the colonial formula of raw materials supplier to industrialized nations in return for manufactured and luxury goods, which largely went to the small number of rich and middle class. Fourth, even with Western efforts to promote democratic institutions, these have proven extremely fragile; military dictatorship has been the most common outcome. Despite these difficulties, impressive economic progress has been made in Indonesia, Malaysia, the Philippines, Singapore, and Thailand, which together formed ASEAN (Association of South East Asian Nations) on 8 August 1967 to promote trade among members and to generate external trade through regional cooperation.

French Indochina: Vietnam, Laos, and Cambodia

The country of Southeast Asia with which the United States has had the most complex and tragic relationship is Vietnam. After World War II, nationalist leaders in Vietnam, inspired by communism, moved to establish independence. The most important Vietnamese nationalist, Ho Chi Minh (1890–1969), was a Communist revolutionary with ties to the USSR since the 1920s and also to the Chinese Communists. In 1941 he organized a patriotic coalition, the Viet Minh, which appealed both to poor peasants and to nationalist intellectuals and acquired its own village-based guerrilla army by the end of 1944. Ho received military aid from the U.S. in fighting the Japanese in Vietnam, and then declared an independent republic in Hanoi in 1945. In the fall of 1945 the French moved with British support to take Saigon and then the countryside in south Vietnam. They succeeded more than a year later. Meanwhile some 180,000 Nationalist Chinese troops were trying to bring the leaders of the Vietnamese Nationalist party back into power from China, where they had been exiled since 1930. To beat back the Vietnamese Nationalist party challenge, Ho negotiated with the French to postpone any fighting with them. But diplomacy with the French ultimately did not work. Seven and a half years of war culminated in a Viet Minh victory at the battle for Dien Bien Phu in May 1954. Through the Geneva Accords of 1954, Viet Minh rule north of the 17th parallel was recognized by the French. South of the 17th parallel a new, non-Communist regime was established under Catholic politician Ngo Dinh Diem (1901–63), in rivalry with Ho's northern republic.

French troops move into the Catholic town of Bui Chu in Vietnam during the war to regain the French colonies in Indochina.

Diem's major patron was the U.S., which did not sign the Geneva Accords and firmly wished to retain the option of forcing a non-Communist reunification of Vietnam. The South Vietnamese regime faced its own domestic difficulties between Catholics and Buddhists. In 1963 Diem was overthrown and assassinated in a U.S.-supported coup. The military took on more civilian power as the U.S. proposed an American-style government with a two-house legislature, presidential executive, and a new constitution. Even with the increasingly massive presence of American troops and commanders in Vietnam in the late 1960s, the U.S. could not defeat the Communist Viet Cong or transplant American democratic institutions. Nor did the secret spread of U.S. bombing missions into Cambodia in 1973 lead to victory. The U.S. government learned slowly and painfully that it lacked any understanding of Vietnam and that its

policies for making the country non-Communist were impractical. After serious domestic criticism and continued failures on the ground, the U.S. government withdrew its troops from Vietnam and the country was finally reunified.

Once political reunification was achieved, the government confronted the challenge of creating a socialist economy throughout the entire country. Immediate plans called for a mixed economy with some government ownership, some collective ownership, joint private-state ownership, private capitalist ownership, and individual ownership. The government leaders placed high priority on science and technology to improve primitive industrial conditions; they targeted heavy industry for construction and growth. But the results were meager because Soviet aid was used unwisely in heavy industry, heavy taxation of collectivized

EBB TIDE, RISING TIDE

■ *After French colonial control over Vietnam had been defeated, the country's future became uncertain. The Viet Minh controlled the north and Diem's regime was installed in the south. How did peasants in South Vietnam view their possibilities? One of those who has tried to understand their impressions is a former refugee relief worker who went back in November 1974 and lived in a village until March 1975 to assemble the story of how people there perceived and experienced the revolution. In the following brief statements, the peasants share with their American friend the ways in which they came to be recruited to the Communist cause and oppose the domestic South Vietnamese regime and its American backers.*

Why did the Viet Minh do so much for us, and then stop? Why did they do so much to make our people into revolutionaries, and then leave us? The Communists are very tricky. They did it because they knew that after a few years living under Mr. Diem and the Americans that we would be stronger revolutionaries than before. Ah, the Communists are very tricky!

I remember in the years right after Viet Cong became active—before Mr. Diem was overthrown—they came at night, usually just a few of them, and made our families listen to their propaganda. Those Viet Cong never threatened us. They never did anything bad to us, but we were a little bit afraid of them, because we did not know anything about them. So we all went, and listened, and usually did not say anything.

Sometimes, also, people who were our friends and who were with the Viet Cong came to our house. Often they would tell us to join them. They said, "We are friends. You should join." They came to our house so often, and it happened to almost everybody here.

During the Viet Minh movement the enemy was very clear. Everybody opposed the French and hated the French, but under Mr. Diem it was not as clear as before.

In other words, the Liberation had to show the people why they had to fight. It had to show them why they as the poor class were being used by the upper class and by the Americans. . . .

From James Walker Trullinger, Jr., *Village at War*, 1980.

peasants sparked passive resistance, and the economy did not forge ties with other Asian economies in the region. The market economy faced serious problems with hoarding and speculation, while the public sector made only modest progress. In the late 1970s, some bad harvests due to poor weather forced the state to implement food rationing. These difficulties appear to have persuaded leaders to push for the socialization of production, which resulted in a mass emigration out of the country and further economic uncertainty. Reforms in the 1980s have begun a process of liberalization with its attendant growth and increasing differentiation of urban and rural income groups. But how the society will develop in the coming years is still unknown.

The fates of Cambodia and Laos have always been tied to the purposes and plans of other people. In the nineteenth century, Cambodia had struggled for survival between the more powerful governments of Vietnam and Thailand before becoming a French protectorate in 1863. In that same period, Laos had shifted from control by Thailand to control by France, without most of the population located in villages experiencing much change in their lives as a result. In the twentieth century, French efforts to break Cambodian and Laotian cultural ties to Thailand led the colonial authorities to promote a Buddhist institute, which was established in Phnom Penh in 1930; another was started in Laos in 1937. These centers shifted local elite attention away from the high culture of Thailand to their own domestic societies.

After the Pacific War, the histories of Cambodia and Laos have remained dominated by outsiders. Cambodian elites, often divided among themselves, pressed the French for independence. Through the 1950s, King Norodom Sihanouk (1922-) skillfully created and when necessary redefined the conditions under which he was leader of the country. Divisions within the country, including the growth of a Communist movement, undermined his authority in the 1960s and he was removed from power in 1970. Cambodia's geopolitical position made it a staging area for Vietnamese Communist actions during the Vietnam War. In the first half of 1973, the U.S. postponed its defeat in Vietnam by dropping more than one hundred thousand tons of bombs on Cambodia. These horrors were compounded by fighting among groups seeking to gain control of the country with different bases of support among outside powers, a process that has been going on through the 1970s, 1980s, and into the 1990s. One of the most tragic periods came between 1975 and 1978, when the Khmer Rouge under Pol Pot sent 3.5 million of their countrymen out of the cities into the countryside in a vain effort to create agricultural self-sufficiency. This fiasco led to widespread malnutrition and disease. Criticism of the regime led to thousands of executions, largely destroying Cambodia's educated classes. The terror unleashed by the Pol Pot regime against its own people led to the deaths of some one million people of a total population of some 7.3 million.

For Laos, the role of outsiders has been even more prominent, to the extent that Laos is basically a creation defined by foreign powers. Just as the French replaced the Thai in the late nineteenth century as the patron of the Lao, the Vietnamese have taken the place of the French since the 1970s.

The Formation of India and Pakistan

The process leading to the formation of independent countries in South Asia differed from the range of Southeast Asian experiences, in part because Britain was the only colonial power on the South Asian subcontinent. Britain's colonial rule began in 1760, and by the twentieth century the British had made institutional changes to introduce urban-educated Indian participation into government.

British rule challenged traditional Indian organization of society along rigid caste lines by opening its courts to all equally, by modifying the private property basis upon which dominant castes asserted their power in the countryside, and by creating new economic opportunities outside the caste-controlled system. But these changes did not penetrate deeply, since British rule in India was superficial and fragile. The leading figure, the viceroy, appointed governors for the provinces, which were in turn governed by popularly elected ministries and the governor. In addition there were some 600 princely states with some 100 million people directly governed by princely rulers under treaty relations with the British; the British represented them in the country's foreign relations, but the princes enjoyed complete domestic control within their jurisdictions.

The diversity beneath British colonial rule went beyond politics to include major religious divisions. The most basic cleavage was between Hindus and Muslims. In addition there were the Sikhs, believers of a composite faith. These divisions, formed by the social changes of earlier centuries, were pieces of the foundation upon which British colonial control was structured. As challenges to colonial rule mounted, these differences would prove important as bases for mobilizing people and for dividing them.

The separation of India and Pakistan in 1947 sparked a two-way mass migration as Hindus from the newly created state of Pakistan fled to India and Muslims left their homes in India to travel to the Muslim state.

The Indian nationalist movement for independence began with the Congress party, which was formed in 1885 with British support as a moderate political force through which the opinions of educated and wealthy Indians could be expressed. After World War I, Mohandas K. Gandhi (1869–1948) began his epic struggle to achieve national independence and unity through nonviolent struggle. By World War II any hopes for a reconciliation between his Congress party leadership and Muslim interests, represented by the Muslim League, were shattered. The final decision to form separate states for the largely Hindi areas and for those with large Muslim populations created India and Pakistan as formally independent countries in 1947. Millions of Hindus, Muslims, and Sikhs who feared they would be living in new states hostile to their faiths abandoned their homes to cross to the other side, where they hoped to find safety. Of some ten million people who migrated in the summer of 1947 to seek security in either India or Pakistan, about one million never reached their destinations alive. But formal independence for India and Pakistan didn't solve the problems of linguistic, religious, and cultural differences resting on a base of mass poverty.

The political trajectories of India and Pakistan since independence have proved surprisingly different. In India, with the exception of the period between July 1975 and March 1977, democratic political institutions have basically been in force. In Pakistan, moments of democratic order have been limited to 1971 to 1973. When East Pakistan broke off to become Bangladesh in 1972, it began as a formal parliamentary democracy but by 1975 had become a government of one-party rule with frequent changes in top power holders. Over time the government in Bangladesh became more overtly Islamic, much as Pakistan has in recent years.

Until the early 1970s Indian democracy was institutionally based on a system that responded to organized political interest groups at different levels of the system. An outgrowth of Gandhi's multiclass alliance that opposed the British, India's democratic institutions became a complex structure of political relationships spanning classes and different locales. But by the late 1960s, after twenty years of rhetoric about equality and participation, there were still no organizational devices to give reality to these political visions. As a result, mass mobilization to attack the propertied classes increasingly pressured the political system for change. In India's federal system, some provinces even came under Communist party control. Prime Minister Indira Gandhi's (1917–84) response to po-

tential turmoil was to centralize authority into her own hands. After democracy was suspended for less than two years in the mid-1970s, India returned to a democratic system, throwing Prime Minister Gandhi and her party out of power.

In recent years political stability and public order throughout South Asia has been challenged by social conflicts that often have an ethnic or communal component. In the 1984 Delhi riots between Sikhs and Hindus, large crowds moved through south Delhi on the afternoon of 31 October upon learning that two Sikh guards had assassinated Indira Gandhi that morning. On the second day, more-organized attacks in poorer sections of the city engaged both Sikhs and non-Sikhs as targets. Gandhi's Congress party mobilized its local supporters as well as thugs who were armed with kerosene. Bus drivers were either coerced or agreed voluntarily to carry rioters to different parts of the city, where they set fires and caused considerable death and destruction.

The independent nations that emerged in Asia after World War II have followed distinct political trajectories into the present. The promotion of democratic institutions competes with the appeal of autocratic military rule. Nationalist sentiments underlie much of the diversity. Throughout Asia, people are anxious to establish for their countries political independence and economic security. But these new countries have not only been vulnerable to international pressures. Tensions among different ethnic groups within both South and Southeast Asian countries are an additional source of fragility. The violence of the late 1980s and early 1990s in Europe along ethnic and cultural lines, in which the assertion of communal identities and group loyalties creates the potential for divisive nationalisms to tear apart existing states, reminds us that the problem is not just an Asian dilemma.

Paths for Development and Change: South Asia and China

The post-World War II experiences of India and China are often compared. India is considered an example of democratic development, while China is taken as an example of socialist development. The political priorities each system has defined have in turn shaped the economic paths of development each society has followed.

South Asia: In Pursuit of Democracy and Development

Economic plans in India during the 1950s aimed to increase per capita income and to make Indian economic growth self-sustaining. To reach this goal, the country needed to diminish its dependence on a few raw materials as its main foreign exports. It also needed to expand its capital goods industry, which in turn meant increasing savings and investment. The overall figures in the 1950s were quite good. Economic output rose 44 percent; agriculture was up 36 percent, with 60 percent of this increase due to expanded cultivation and 40 percent due to higher yields. Industry and mining rose 43 percent; and commerce, transport, and services rose by 57 percent. But in 1960 the economy remained largely an agrarian economy in which many people remained threatened by famine and natural disasters. The vulnerability of the Indian economy to famines and reliance on foreign relief were painfully confirmed in 1966 when $435 million in U.S. loans and credits was necessary.

The "Green Revolution" in the late 1960s and early 1970s raised agricultural productivity in some places, but these changes led to no further dramatic economic changes; rather, they simply made possible the feeding of a continually growing population. More troubling, even if India's food production kept pace with population increases, chronic malnutrition affected a population larger than that of the United States.

Modern South Asia

Recent industrial advances of the 1980s have taken place in an atmosphere of laissez-faire economics in which the government has made little effort to redress the problems of poverty that remain the defining basis of life for hundreds of millions of people. With high infant mortality and low adult life expectancies, many people live without safe drinking water supplies, and the limited availability of elementary education means that many adults remain illiterate. These problems continue to persist despite the fact that India enjoys a rich natural resource base, an educated elite of scientists and engineers who are the core of a middle class that is roughly the same size as the total population of France, and political leaders who are acutely aware of the society's problems. To date at least, pervasive and persistent inequities have proven impossible to eradicate amid a democratic politics that seeks to accommodate very diverse interests and in which the elites—business, rich farmers, and white collar professionals—conceive and execute most of the political plans and possibilities.

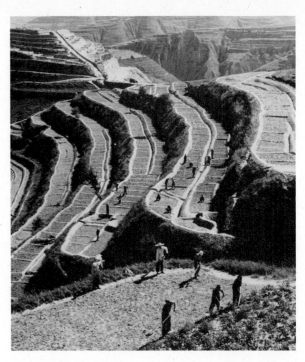

This photograph, taken in September 1962, shows members of the Heifen Commune in China working the terraced fields that transformed a barren terrain into productive agricultural land.

Exploring the Socialist Road: China, 1949–1960

China's path of economic and social change provides several sharp contrasts with India's. Radical changes in the countryside began with land reform in 1949. In contrast with India's land reform in the 1950s, which appears mainly to have benefited those with some land already and done nothing for the landless, China's land reform gave land to all rural households and completely dismantled the landlords and rich peasants as a class. But Mao Zedong and other Chinese leaders were not satisfied with land reform. In order to mobilize and inspire the peasants to produce even larger amounts, the government initiated forms of labor cooperation followed by the pooling of draft animals, and finally implemented the common ownership of land. By 1955 China had a system of rural collectives in which most land and capital belonged to the group, and private property was limited to the land on which a peasant's house stood and a small plot for vegetables.

Throughout the first half of the 1950s agricultural output generally rose, but Mao believed additional gains could be made by pushing the collectivization movement further. He therefore unleashed the Great Leap Forward (1957–59), a movement to create even larger collective groups known as communes. Units of political and economic decision making, communes organized the peasants' work life by assigning them to tasks as part of a collective workforce. The radical organizational changes of the Great Leap Forward disrupted previous farming practices. In combination with bad weather across much of China, poor harvests in 1958 and 1959 led to a massive subsistence crisis in which as many as thirty million people may have died. As a result, the innovations of the Great Leap Forward were dismantled, and Mao Zedong had to step down from day-to-day leadership because of the disasters his plans had helped create. For the next two decades the countryside was organized in smaller collective units with production quotas set by the government. Once peasants delivered their assigned outputs and met their own consumption needs, they could sell surpluses on regulated markets.

In the cities, under separate administration, a process parallel to agricultural collectivization took place in the 1950s, leading to the gradual nationalization of private industries and the initiation of new state-owned industries under centralized ministry management. The government bought out capitalists and retained them as managers of their former factories. China's first five-year plan followed the orthodox Soviet model, stressing construction in heavy industries—metals, machinery, and power—under central ministry control. By 1956, leaders began to doubt the wisdom of concentrating investment in heavy industries located in a few urban centers. During the second half of the 1950s more investment went into creating new industrial bases across the country with a mix of light and heavy industry. Administrative control for some industry was decentralized from ministries in Beijing to provincial officials and administrators beneath them. In part this was an economic move toward developing the entire country rather than only those areas already having some industrial base. But the decision was also a strategic one, to make the country's industrial economy less vulnerable to enemy attack. China's sense of international isolation, already very strong in the 1950s because of the U.S.-led refusal to recognize the Communist regime, became even stronger after the pullout of Soviet advisers in the summer of 1960.

The Chinese government certainly confronted (and even created) problems in the countryside and the cities during the 1950s. But despite these difficulties and the tragic consequences of the Great Leap Forward, China made basic and important advances in both agriculture and industry. By no means a developed or even prosperous society, China in 1960 was at least ahead of where it had been in 1949.

issuing orders and acting like capitalist bullies. He wanted to shake up the leadership and arouse the people to challenge their leaders in order to make them more responsive to popular concerns. He wanted to renew popular dedication to revolution and to view the continued transformation of society as a revolutionary struggle flowing directly from the triumphs of the party in 1949. In fact, however, the Great Proletarian Cultural Revolution (1966–69) plunged the country into a deep abyss of social chaos and political persecution. Schools, factories, and offices were paralyzed by the formation of competing groups of "revolutionary" students and workers opposed to those in power and to each other. Families were painfully split when accusations of political deviations against individual members forced others in the family to support the charges or face damnation along with the accused. Millions suffered great hardship. Some were imprisoned and tortured. Many died.

Given the scale of social disruption, it is surprising the economy did not suffer more seriously. In fact, the rural economy was affected in only minor ways. Urban factories were severely affected, but because so much of the economy remained rural, the society overall did not suffer economically as much as it did during the Great Leap Forward. In fact, the stress on pushing public services into the countryside improved the quality of life there. Modestly trained health care workers, called "barefoot doctors," offered rudimentary services. On

New Successes and New Misfortunes: China, 1960–1976

In the early 1960s, China's economic development was once again guided by a centralized bureaucracy committed to planning and managing the urban and rural economies. Party and government bureaucrats formed a class of privileged officeholders who could wield their power for personal gain. The masses of peasants and workers were certainly better off than previous generations had been during the difficulties and uncertainties of warlords, the Japanese invasion, and civil war, but in Mao Zedong's mind, the boundless energy and enthusiasm of the masses to push forward positive social and economic changes had lost their force. In order to rekindle popular spirits and to criticize the entrenched power of party bureaucrats, Mao orchestrated a remarkable challenge to the very party he led to power barely two decades earlier. Mao was convinced that many party leaders had grown complacent in their jobs and comfortable

Red Guards line up before a giant portrait of Communist leader Mao Zedong in 1966.

balance, however, the Cultural Revolution was a devastating disruption to Chinese society. It shattered millions of lives and destroyed the faith and confidence individuals felt toward their families, fellow workers, neighbors, and the Communist party.

Economic Reforms and Political Tragedies: China Since 1976

The death of Mao Zedong in 1976 gave reformers who sought to develop the economy an opportunity to move against his widow Jiang Qing and three other top leaders who were responsible for the continued rhetoric of revolutionary struggle and policies ill-suited for economic growth. The arrest and jailing of this so-called Gang of Four made possible the emergence of another set of leaders, including many people who had risen from political disgrace in the Cultural Revolution, most prominently Deng Xiaoping (1904-). Reform-minded leaders aimed to regain the enthusiastic support of the people through improving their livelihoods. Under Deng's leadership, dramatic economic reforms took place, first in the countryside and then in the cities.

The dismantling of collective production in the countryside startled most foreign observers, who never expected a return to family farming in China. Not only has agricultural labor productivity risen but even more importantly, surplus agricultural labor has moved into new rural industries, which are often owned by local governments. People who previously were severely underemployed in the villages, a common problem in poor agrarian countries, now gained employment in small industries without leaving the countryside for large urban centers. Rural industries continue to spread and create new sources of income in the countryside.

In the cities, since the early 1980s many factories have enjoyed considerable autonomy regarding investment and production decisions. These management changes, combined with other financial and marketing reforms, have stimulated dramatic industrial growth. Much of the new production is aimed at foreign markets, often produced in joint-venture enterprises where foreign capitalists gain considerable control over wages and worker quality. Foreign influence has not strictly been economic. Chinese youth enjoy new styles of clothes, music, and literature. For old-time Communist leaders these social changes with foreign cultural content create great anxieties over "bourgeois spiritual pol-

lution." Their problem has been to create some viable cultural alternative to Western influences. The old-timers' instinct has been simply to suppress foreign ideas with their political claim to cultural correctness. But many young urban Chinese turn to the songs of rock star Cui Jian, whose loud music with driving rhythms insistently questions social norms and practices. Beneath the lyrics is an implicit criticism of a government that no longer can persuade its young people that it stands for goals worthy of pursuit. This failure hangs heavily over China's future.

For many young urban Chinese and for most foreign observers the economic reforms promised political changes to encourage popular participation in government. The charges of corruption and authoritarian arrogance leveled against top leaders and petty bureaucrats were not themselves so very new. In fact the reform leaders, and even Mao Zedong before them, recognized the political system's vulnerability to the abuse of power by individuals. But the many people critical of the government in the 1970s and 1980s sought different ends. Unlike reformers in power who simply want to punish the evildoers; unlike Mao, who wanted to mobilize the masses to attack the party; and also unlike late imperial officials, who consistently perceived their problems to be those of individual personnel rather than of bureaucratic structures, these critics wanted institutional reforms.

In the late 1970s and early 1980s, advocates of democracy who published critical views of China's political system were jailed, causing concern both within China and among foreigners. Proponents of democratic reforms have repeatedly made two demands—free elections and an independent press. In the spring of 1989, thousands of university students took over Tiananmen Square, where in earlier years parades of People's Liberation Army soldiers proudly marched in front of top leaders on National Day and where thousands upon thousands of people once waved Mao's little red book of collected sayings as they gathered to glimpse their leader during the Cultural Revolution. After weeks of debate and protest, when the students' ranks were swelled by thousands of sympathizers and onlookers, after endless parades with banners representing different workplaces in Beijing demanding political change, and after hunger strikes and intense international attention, the government could no longer bear its inability to defuse the confrontation. Late at night on 3 June 1989, army tanks rolled into Tiananmen Square and fired upon unarmed Chinese civilians, killing and injuring untold numbers. Protests that had already been

A Chinese woman checks the prices of refrigerators in a Beijing department store in 1989. A decade-long consumer spending spree was curtailed by a government austerity program that pushed the economy to the brink of recession.

mounted in other Chinese cities grew more angry when news of the Tiananmen massacre reached them. Since this tragic event that bared to the world the failure of the Chinese government, officials and the people have been struggling to find ways to accept each other. In their search they face persistent questions about the relationship between politics and economics and between material improvements and cultural sensibilities.

While once Indian capitalist democracy and Chinese socialism represented polar alternatives, recent changes have narrowed the gap. Markets play a significant role in China now as well as in India; foreign capital is invested in both countries while exports, especially from China, have increased dramatically. Political leaders in both

countries continue to face the vexing challenges of linking urban and rural sectors and spreading material success throughout the society.

Successful Capitalist Societies and Those Left Behind

Asia in the late twentieth century is a vast region of dramatic contrasts. The clean and efficient world of the Japanese, filled with state-of-the-art factories with robot labor, seems light-years away from the poverty in places like the rural Philippines or rural Indonesia. Yet

IT'S NOT THAT I CAN'T SEE

■ *Cui Jian, a Chinese rock-and-roll singer and composer, is known in the Western newspapers as China's Bob Dylan. Until April 1987 he played the trumpet in the Beijing Philharmonic Orchestra, when he was jailed at the height of the anti-bourgeois liberalism campaign. When he sang a song, "Nothing to My Name," dressed in army and peasant clothes in the style of the Yanan period of the early 1940s, the Beijing Municipal Party Committee found the allusions to the poverty and difficulties of the war years incomprehensible in the relatively prosperous period of the 1980s. They evidently could not comprehend the spiritual and intellectual emptiness against which Cui Jian's music lashes out. Alternately banned and allowed to be played at small gatherings, Cui Jian's music remains available on cassette tapes, and a contract with CBS Records may someday bring his music into the United States. In the following song lyrics, Cui Jian affirms how crazy his society seems to be—the absence of meaningful purpose is an unmistakable attack on the Party's effort to create order and meaning for people.*

It's Not That I Can't See
Never used to know what it meant to take it easy,
Just couldn't see how weird the world was growing.
The future I'd been seeing sure isn't here today,
But now I think I know which way it's going.

Of everything that's said and done,
I can't tell good from bad,
Which year was which, the times I've had.
The things I thought were simple.
Makes me feel like I've been had.
Suddenly it seems as if the world's no place for me.

Twenty years and all I've learnt is patience, holding on.
No wonder all the comrades said my head was in the clouds,
I got myself together, made myself stop dreaming,
Now I'm awake and I can see
This world's as weird as weird can be.

Looking out at all the highrise buildings there
    like fields of rice and wheat,
Looking out and all I see is waves of people
    traffic in the street.
Looking left now right, front, back,
I'm so busy I can't keep track.
This 'n' that, that 'n' this
    the more I see the weirder it is.

Never used to know what it meant to take it easy,
Just couldn't see how weird the world was growing.
The future I'd been seeing sure isn't here today,
But now I think I know which way it's going.

It's not that I can't see,
The world's too weird for me.

It's not that I can't see.
The world's too weird for me.

From Geremie Barmc and John Minford, *Seeds of Fire*, 1989.

Gender and Culture

WOMAN'S WORK IN SILK CULTURE   *Figure 1*

The favored trade goods—silk and porcelain—exported from Asia and distributed in European markets symbolize the western vision of the eastern world. There were no European fabrics or ceramics as fine as Asian silk or porcelain, and the means to produce them were unknown. Asia was seen as a land of luxury and mystery, possessing resources and skills beyond western ingenuity. Eastern goods were the objects of western desire, and the relationship of producer and consumer persisted through the centuries. Although the west did not understand how these products were made or how they were marketed and used in their lands of origin, the demand and appreciation for them persisted well into the modern era. Europe viewed Asia as a willing provider and steady source for fulfillment. In trade relations, as well as in military actions and political negotiations, Europe cast Asia in a feminine role—passive and compliant—asserting its own masculine self-identity. Other misconceptions arose. To the European point of view, Asian government seemed stable and unchanging and its culture seemed monolithic and timeless. Both sides associated western ways with technology and advancement. In the modern era the arts have provided a means for cultural exchange and reciprocity, but these presuppositions, misunderstandings, and gender codes have proved remarkably enduring.

Although products of Asian manufacture had been admired for centuries the strongest influence of eastern art on western artists came shortly after the forced reopening of Japan to western contact in 1854 by Admiral Perry. During the time of Japanese isolation, new technologies in the arts were developed. The multicolored printing method or *Ukiyo-E*, developed in the seventeenth century, combines the subtlety of watercolor painting with the cheap production method of printing. Utamaro was a master of this technique. His specialty was the images of the "Floating World," pictures of pretty women and popular entertainments. The scene of silk weaving (ca. 1802, Japan; Figure 1) portrayed on the preceding page was part of a series of twelve entitled *Woman's Work in Silk Culture*. Each

SYMPHONY IN WHITE NO. 2: THE LITTLE WHITE GIRL   *Figure 2*

THE LETTER

image illustrates an important step in silk production. However, the lovely weavers, with their trailing hair and loosely draped kimonos, were ladies of the "Floating World," and they, rather than silk production, were the real focus of Utamaro's prints.

By the middle of the nineteenth century, *Ukiyo-E* prints were common in Japan, and unpopular series and printer's discards were often used to wrap and cushion porcelains and other fragile objects for shipping. In the 1850s, when trade between Europe and Japan resumed, French and English consumers became as interested in these colorful wrappings as the contents that they protected. American artist James Abbott McNeil Whistler first encountered these prints in Paris, and collected them, and other Asian objects, throughout his lifetime. In *Symphony in White No. 2: The Little White Girl* (1864, America; Figure 2), Whistler uses a blue and white jar, a paper painted fan, and a flowering branch to create an atmosphere of "Japonisme" around a very western sitter. In *The Letter* (1892, America; Figure 3) Mary Cassatt better integrates the styles of east and west. Even her sitter is culturally ambiguous. Although she never mastered the *Ukiyo-E* technique, Cassatt assimilated its compositional characteristics—the flattening of space, the varied use of pattern, the simple blocks of color—revealing a deeper understanding for the Asian aesthetic than is evident in Whistler's use of exotic props.

HAIL THE DEFEAT OF REVISIONISM IN OUR CHINA

Figure 4

A striking example of reverse influence is seen in a contemporary Chinese revolutionary poster. *Hail the Defeat of Revisionism in Our China* (1967, China; Figure 4) typifies the curious persistence of traditional eastern and western perceptions. The vigorous postures of the figures, their muscular proportions and gregarious expressions are western in origin. Similarly, the uniforms and coveralls adopted by Maoist China to eliminate the appearance of class rank, come from the west. In form and technique, this image has a clear western model; this communist poster reminds the viewer of a capitalist advertisement. There is an irony in these selections. To convey a message of strength and assertiveness, the Chinese Cultural Revolution reverted to the age-old dichotomy of masculine/feminine and borrowed its style and iconography from the west.

Japan's relationship to Southeast Asia is comparable to the U.S. relationship with Latin America and the European relationship to Africa.

Japanese Miracles

The Pacific War devastated Japan, destroying one-fourth of the country's wealth. Real GNP fell to half the prewar level. In the immediate postwar period, the priority went to stimulating industrial production. In order to combine existing capital with large numbers of unemployed workers, Japan had to obtain raw-material imports. Once this bottleneck was removed by allowing Japan access to foreign markets, economic recovery proceeded swiftly. By 1955, the level of economic activity had returned to levels achieved before the war. New investment then became necessary in order to expand further and to make Japanese industry more competitive internationally. High investment in industry beginning in the mid-1950s drew upon the bank savings of individual Japanese consumers tapped through indirect financing by Japanese firms.

Part of Japan's successful industrial growth is the result of a unique partnership between government and business. Government and industry leaders agree on the international markets in which Japanese products can become competitive. The particular goods have changed over time as technological advances gathered from abroad and developed at home have continually created new markets—from cameras, to consumer electronics and automobiles, to high-tech computer hardware and scientific instruments—the Japanese have learned to excel in a diverse array of products. The government has played a crucial role in shaping Japan's industrial efforts through special tax treatment for growth industries, subsidies of interest, loans of government funds, use of import quotas, and control over the import of foreign capital. Japanese firms react to the priorities and incentives created by the government; a close alliance between government and business rests upon the sharing of information and a common concern for formulating strategies that create long-run Japanese success in the international marketplace. While American complaints of a so-called "Japan Incorporated"—government and business acting as a single entity—exaggerate and distort the relations between the state and private firms, there is far more long-range strategic planning carried on by business and government than there is in Europe or the United States. The Japanese government acts to speed up

Asia Since 1952

1954	Chinese agricultural cooperative movement
1954	Mutual Defense Agreement between Japan and U.S.
1954	Geneva Accords recognizes Viet Minh rule north of the 17th parallel; a client state of the U.S. is established south of the 17th parallel
1956	Japan enters United Nations
1958	Great Leap Forward and establishment of people's communes in China
1960	Sino-Soviet dispute comes into the open; Soviet advisers withdraw
1966–69	Cultural Revolution creates chaos in China
1967	Formation of ASEAN (Association of South East Asian Nations)
1968	Student turmoil; student occupation of buildings at University of Tokyo
1971	People's Republic replaces Nationalist China at UN
1971	Bangladesh established in former East Pakistan
1973	Paris Agreement facilitates full U.S. withdrawal from Vietnam
1975	Communists secure victory and unite Vietnam
1975	Jiang Jieshi dies on Taiwan
1976	Death of Mao Zedong in China
1977	Deng Xiaoping returns to high office in Beijing
1978–present	Chinese push for economic development, including increased contacts with the West

the information sharing necessary for efficient planning in a competitive global marketplace. The negative dimension of this relationship has been repeatedly exposed in scandals involving government officials receiving money from corporations to reward them for kind treatment.

In the Tiananmen Square student demonstrations of May 1989, students erected a 33-foot-tall replica of the Statue of Liberty called "The Goddess of Democracy."

enterprises that work as subcontractors. According to a 1976 survey, more than 80 percent of the large manufacturing enterprises relied on outside suppliers; almost 60 percent of small and medium manufacturing enterprises had subcontracting relations with large firms rather than producing directly for the market. Because large firms establish long-term relations with their subcontractors, they develop confidence in the consistent quality of the materials they receive and can efficiently adjust production to supply-and-demand conditions without carrying large inventories; they can easily vary their orders with subcontractors instead. The ability of Japanese firms to reduce inventories contributes considerably to their higher labor productivity. The subcontractors and their employees pay the price for the flexibility and efficiency achieved by the major enterprises. Jobs for the subcontractors and therefore employment for their workers fluctuate, which makes them far less secure economically than the members of the large corporations.

Japanese firms generally earn lower profits than American firms and carry larger debt. Their aim is to establish a larger market share in growing fields. Once a

Enterprise management and labor relations in Japan also differ markedly from those in the United States or Europe. Labor-management relations in the major firms have been characterized by lifetime employment, seniority-based wages, and company unions. Enterprises have recruited new school graduates and given them on-the-job training; the investment the company makes in the workers motivates it to keep them rather than simply laying them off during a recession. For their part, Japanese workers have believed in a work ethic uncommon in the recent history of the United States.

Beneath the famous large Japanese multinational firms are a much larger number of small and medium

Kimono-clad Tokyo Stock Exchange staff members and share dealers clap their hands in ceremonies opening the first day of trading for the New Year, 4 January 1993.

DEFINITION OF THE JAPANESE FILM

■ *Donald Richie, a long-time Tokyo resident and an eminent Japanese film critic, has devoted his professional life to explaining Japanese movies to Western audiences. In one of his many perceptive essays, he lays out some basic differences in cultural perspectives that shape attitudes toward cinema and cinematic technique that increase our understanding not simply of Japanese film, but of the society and culture more generally.*

Japanese philosophic tradition sees the individual as an integral part of his world; each man is an extension of the universe.

Nature is complementary to the individual, and one should live in harmony with it.

Things as they are, are the way things should be. Unhappy events are simply accepted because they exist. Japanese art observes *mono no aware*, the transience of all earthly things, a concept popularized by Buddhism and of great importance in any discussion of Japanese aesthetics; it implies not only an acceptance of evanescence but also a mild celebration of that very quality.

The Japanese recognizes his dual nature; he is an individual but he is also a social unit in society. If he must choose between his loyalty to himself and his society, he often sacrifices the former.

The Japanese is limited by his attitude. He finds the average, the normal, even the mediocre reassuring.

The Japanese finds in nature, in his social duties, a sense of belonging to something larger than himself, which paradoxically affirms him as an individual.

In the cinema this creates a feeling for actuality, since the Japanese accept, although perhaps unwillingly the way things naturally are—thus the sense of realism in the Japanese film.

The films are contemplative and fairly slow. They are rambling stories, built like the Japanese house or garden.

The Japanese realize that the only reality is surface reality. They have no sense of hidden reality, no sense of conscience. They are a people without private guilt, though they do have social shame.

This results in films which do not usually contain any strong personal statements, but which do examine the world in precise detail.

Western philosophic tradition views the individual as unique, each man being the center of his personal universe.

Nature is an enemy to be conquered, to be used violently if necessary.

Things as they are, are to be denied; one must always create a better world where things are as they should be.

The Western individual likes to think of himself as a unique personality, not as part of a larger unit. If he must sacrifice his social persona he gladly does so, since such an action affirms his individuality.

The Westerner strives to exceed limitations. He dislikes the average, the mediocre.

The Westerner, with only his idea of himself to sustain him soon falls into cynicism, into disillusion, into various forms of heroics.

In the cinema this creates a feeling for action, because things as they are cannot be accepted. Films are more concerned with plot than with atmosphere or realistic detail.

The films are filled with action and move very quickly. They are tightly plotted, utilitarian, like the American home or skyscraper.

The West refuses to believe that surface reality is the only reality. For this reason Western religions suggest after-life and stress private conscience. Westerners have little sense of social shame but a great sense of private guilt.

This results in films which are strong personal statements but stress little of the world's realistic detail.

From Donald Richie, "A Lateral View" *Japan Times*, 1987.

Oh Sadaharu, Japan's greatest baseball star.

Baseball, the Japanese Way

Baseball was introduced to Japan in 1873 by an American named Horace Wilson, who taught at a Tokyo university. The game was initially played by high-school and college students in kimono and sandals, but the Japanese later adopted the conventional attire of the game. Baseball was a popular collegiate sport from the turn of the century in Japan, but the professional game was not established until 1936, two years after a tour of American major-league players led by Babe Ruth and Lou Gehrig had played some exhibition games.

As a visual spectacle, the game played on the field looks exactly like the game of baseball in the United States. But some differences between the American and Japanese game emerge when visiting American major league teams play exhibitions with Japanese major league teams. Most Americans report on the physical differences of the players—American players are bigger, faster, and stronger. But the physical differences are diminishing. American players who play in Japan—each professional team is allowed two foreign players—say that the best Japanese pitchers could now be number one or two starters on major league American teams. While Oh Sadaharu, the player with the most home runs in the world, would have hit fewer home runs in American ballparks because they are larger, no one doubts that he would have hit a very large number in the U.S.

Penetrating the formal similarities, and more important than the physical differences among players, the spirit and meaning of baseball to Japanese tells us why it is no longer simply an American game when played in Japan. Each year a ten-day national high-school championship tournament in Osaka draws over 400,000 people to the stadium. TV sets in coffee-shops, tea rooms, bars, and family homes are all tuned to the daily coverage from 9:00 A.M. to 6:00 P.M. Tokyo's Big Six University League inspires intense competition; the winner's supporters party wildly in the narrow back alleys and streets of Tokyo's Shinjuku or Ginza districts making a Big Ten football rivalry like Michigan and Ohio State's seem rather subdued. Professional baseball is Japan's most popular spectator sport. TV announcers keep up an endless barrage of information in which speculation about the pitcher and the batter substitutes for the leisurely small talk typical of an American broadcast. Japanese spectators are intensely into the game of baseball. Just what kind of game is it? Why the frenzied pitch of excitement for spectators, not just at World Series time, but at every game and even when they are just watching a routine game on TV at home?

Japanese ballplayers are modern heroes. But they are not admired, as they are in the United States, as distinctive individuals whose skills make them stand out from others and whose sometimes galactic egos and seismic temper tantrums are tolerated because of their greatness. Japanese baseball players live according to a modified samurai code of conduct, which stresses, as did the samurai code, duty and honor; the great Japanese ballplayer always thinks of his team first. He values being a "team player." Beyond contractual obligations, players are expected to show up for early "voluntary" spring training, to arrive early for practice and stay late after practice, to stay in the dugout if taken out of a game early, and to spend free time with the other players. In Japanese baseball there is tremendous stress on form—the

ideal Japanese form is the same for every hitter and for every pitcher. The Japanese player shows a fighting spirit, an absence of materialism (two more good samurai traits), care when speaking with the press, and a constant sense of himself as a role model when off the playing field. Team harmony and spirit are considered crucial ingredients to success.

Baseball's intimate connection to Japanese culture was captured shortly after World War II by a leading Japanese newspaper journalist: "If high-school baseball should become just a game, it would lose its essential meaning. High-school baseball should always remain an education of the heart; the ground a classroom of purity, a gymnasium of morality. Without this spirit, it will lose its eternal value." The fusing of Japanese sensibilities with Western forms finds expression in the professional game, with the discipline at the plate achieved by Oh Sadaharu, Japan's home-run king, through his study of *kendo*, the way of the sword. The samurai's mastery of the sword, like all martial arts in Japan, is not limited to facility with certain physical skills; it is also a state of the mind and the heart. Referring to a conversation

with his hitting "master," or instructor, Oh recalled, "One night Arakawa-san said to me that the real problem we were facing was to apply the Japanese psyche to an American game, and that for me this was especially important, because of my lack of willpower. It was at this point that he first acquainted me with his theories about Zen. I was very absorbed in what he said. Recently, I had read Yoshikawa's *Miyamoto Musashi*. My imagination had been stirred by this account of a legendary samurai who overcame the chaos of his own heart by disciplined training and simple living to become the greatest of swordsmen." Oh Sadaharu perfected his home-run swing through his study of the Japanese sword. He achieved a unity of mind and body through a careful concentration tied to Japanese forms of meditation and reflection.

Reporters were fond of taking Oh's picture in traditional robes with a gleaming sword—the baseball player as samurai. Americans cannot ground their sports heroes so thoroughly in the nation's history. The Japanese, in their game of baseball, have managed to stake out a connection between their past and present as they transform what was once simply an American pastime.

desired market share is achieved, efforts are continuously made to diversify and create new markets rather than be satisfied with what the company presently has achieved. Contrary to stereotypes, Japanese companies have begun since the 1970s and 1980s to invest heavily in research and development. Previously, the Japanese borrowed a large amount of technology; this has led some Americans to believe that the Japanese can copy but cannot invent. This charge is proving false. When a large technology gap existed, the Japanese simply took advantage of advanced technologies. Now that they are on the cutting edge of many information, computer, and bioengineering fields, they invest at least as much as American companies to create new products. Moreover, Japanese firms create consortiums to push new technologies forward, recognizing that no single company can afford the development costs and that they can all benefit from a common advance.

There are clear institutional, organizational, and work ethic reasons why Japanese business has become so successful world-wide. The Japanese military could not succeed in forging an Asian empire, but Japanese business has succeeded in creating Japanese economic dominance in Asia and beyond.

Japanese Social Change and Cultural Sensibilities

The increasingly intimate ties that the Japanese economy has forged with the international marketplace intensify the contact that Japanese have with Western commodities and outlooks on life and leisure. In clothing, Japanese designers take their places alongside those from Paris and New York; Tokyo dresses in Western styles with a quality and elegance to match any European or American city. Yet a Japanese woman will also venture out onto the crowded subways wrapped in layers of rich and smooth silk cloth making up her kimono, her feet covered by white socks and resting in wooden sandals. The two styles can even mix on the same occasion. At many Japanese weddings, which take place at wedding halls where they are tightly scheduled one after another, the bride is presented to the wedding guests in two sets of formal attire—one a kimono, the other a flowing white bridal gown. But neither of these styles is necessarily more "Japanese" than the other. The acceptance of conventions with Western origins does not mean that they remain "Western" to the Japanese who practice them.

In their high cuisine, the Japanese have sustained the visual aesthetic of traditional presentation of their simple but subtle foods. They have also developed a passionate taste for European food; the large Japanese cities have foreign restaurants where owner and chef are often natives of the foreign culture, be it French, Italian, or another of Europe's many regional cuisines. The clean separation of native and foreign that is clear in high cuisines becomes blurred in more popular forms of food. Among the less expensive restaurants are "Chinese-style" restaurants in which food influenced by Chinese cooking has been domesticated into a Japanese style that is at times even more remote from "authentic" cuisine than the Chinese food in the United States. The Japanese domestication of foreign food takes a more unexpected turn in its capacity to transform items of European high cuisine into fast food creations. When the Italian dessert tiramisu became a fad in the Italian restaurants of New York and Tokyo, the Japanese went several steps beyond what Americans could initially have imagined. To make this symbol of foreign taste available to Japanese on a mass-market scale, tiramisu was transformed into a frozen desert available at an American fried chicken chain, taking the place of an ice cream bar or popsicle. Tiramisu then became a sweet vending machine drink and a candy bar. Some time after this commercial flood of attention, tiramisu has found its way into some American bakeries and frozen dessert counters.

Music offers a parallel illustration. Japanese are among the most knowledgeable consumers of classical music, and a number of the major professional performers of Western classical music are Japanese. At the same time, traditional Japanese instruments are still made and played. Bridging the musical gap are innovative performers in jazz, who seek to combine Japanese and Western musical motifs, as well as the more common pop singers, whose music and lyrics adapt the sentiments and sensibilities of American and European songs.

Amid a sophisticated cosmopolitan awareness of fashion, food, and music, many Japanese sustain an affirmation of the symbols of their native culture. The government celebrates the achievements of great craft workers in pottery, textile dyeing, sword making, and kimono silk weaving by proclaiming the very best to be "national living treasures." It gives them stipends to help them survive in a world the economics of which would not include them. At the mundane level of tourism, Japanese always buy gifts to present upon their return home. All regions of Japan have some gift, modest or expensive, for which they are famous; it might be some kind of beanpaste cake, rice wine, or pottery, but a Japanese can always return home with a local Japanese souvenir to present. How different from the United States or other Western countries where even the most famous tourist spots have trinkets produced in foreign countries. Japanese have chosen to reproduce the artifacts of their culture and invest them with meaning; at the same time they have opened their culture to outside influences.

Asia's New Dragons

The Japanese have not been alone in Asia in creating impressive material successes. In the past twenty years, many parts of the Sinitic world have made great strides. A quarter century ago, East Asia produced eight percent of the world's output, while the U.S. and Canada produced nearly one-third. North America now contributes only 28 percent and East Asia has risen to 14 percent. The rise of East Asian economic production is not the result simply of Japanese successes or new developments in the People's Republic. Major actors in East Asia's economic rise are the four dragons that were formerly outposts of the Chinese world order—Korea, Taiwan, Hong Kong, and Singapore. These four were also under colonial administrations of the Japanese or British. Their complex histories contribute to the manner in which each has become a newly industrialized economy.

In Korea a sharp contrast between North and South Korea has emerged in less than two decades. As recently as 1975, per capita GNP was higher in the north than in the south; by 1988, the per capita GNP of the south was three times that of the north. The earlier success of North Korea under Communist leadership came from mobilizing labor and capital for heavy industrialization in the 1950s; professing a strategy of self-reliance, North Korea in fact received substantial Soviet aid in this period. After growth rates slowed down in the 1960s, the North Koreans began importing Western technology in the hopes of creating economic change, but ran into payment difficulties due to insufficient foreign exchange. In the south, massive foreign aid, largely from the U.S., helped set the country on a course of industrialization; in the first phase business stressed the development of industries to produce goods the society would otherwise have to import. Once having achieved its aims, business shifted from this import-substitution strategy to concentrate on export manufactures, moving from textiles through heavy industrial products like cement and steel to automobiles and most recently computers.

This same general outline of industrialization applies to Taiwan as well. In both countries the legacy of Japanese colonialism is an ambivalent blessing. The strong state role in guiding economic development in both countries no doubt owes something to both colonial administrations and the inclinations of political regimes toward authoritarian rule deriving from Confucian pasts.

In Hong Kong and Singapore, British administration over small city-state economies dominated by Chinese has created unusual combinations of English political and Chinese economic traits. Hong Kong stands poised to be returned to the People's Republic in 1997, when the lease granting the New Territories to the British expires. Hong Kong's current political status is the last formal vestige of the unequal treaties begun in the midnineteenth century. Amid political uncertainties, foreign trade and investment continue to grow. The textile industry has left behind part of its sweatshop past as it

The rise of South Korea as an industrial power is epitomized by these rows of Hyundai automobiles awaiting export.

retools with computer-aided designs to leap forward in the world fashion industry. As a major port and Asia's second most important financial center behind Tokyo, Hong Kong can sustain its economic importance after political control is returned to Beijing, unless Chinese administration proves seriously disruptive.

Singapore does not face this set of anxieties. Since splitting off from a Malay federation in 1965, this very small city-state (26 miles long and 14 miles wide), has developed a manufacturing base initially combining foreign (mainly U.S.) investment with cheap local labor in labor-intensive industries for export markets. From this industrialization base, the economy has increasingly shifted into more skilled industries and is training its workforce to enter high-tech fields. Chinese dominate society, accounting for roughly three-quarters of the population; Malays comprise 15 percent and Indians about half that amount. Given this ethnic diversity, the country has four national languages—English, Malay, Mandarin, and Tamil; all people are expected to be at least bilingual. Politically, the leadership has simultaneously sought to create an identity for Singapore Chinese separate from other Chinese and to celebrate Confucian virtues of accepting social hierarchy and the discipline of doing one's job.

The Struggles of Those Left Behind

Beyond these newly industrialized economies of the four dragons of the Pacific Rim, which along with Japan have made the transition to modern forms of material security, and with the exception of China, where dramatic economic progress has been made across diverse settings, few other parts of Asia have enjoyed more than limited success. Thailand has enjoyed considerable growth in Southeast Asia, and India certainly has achieved some modern development in South Asia. But excess population plagues many south Asian and Southeast Asian societies where the population control policies of China—a goal of one child per family, achieved in urban areas only—cannot even be remotely approached. Many people are landless, especially in Bangladesh, Java, and the Philippines. Because they lack any reliable work in the countryside, many stream into the cities to create a vast underclass of people living in primitive conditions, some of whom find employment in the service sector, becoming barbers, cab drivers, waiters, waitresses, and prostitutes. As former colonies of Western countries and Japan, many had economies previously tailored to provide food crops and industrial raw materials. To shift out of this situation has proven painfully difficult.

In a country like Bangladesh, development efforts have in fact not prevented a decline in living standards for most people. In the 1980s the distribution of income was more unequal in both rural and urban areas than it had been at independence in 1971. Poverty appears to have worsened as nutrition has been in decline. Policies aimed at agricultural development without any changes in the system of land tenure or other institutions have failed. In neighboring India, where much more industrial progress can be noted, the failure of those changes to affect the lives of millions of rural poor attests to a similar difficulty in raising the quality of life for peasants in the absence of major institutional changes in the countryside. India's economy remains a dual economy in which the benefits of industrialization have yet to reach most of the people.

In the Communist countries of Vietnam, Cambodia, and Laos, economic development has not progressed very far. Some industrialization has taken place in Vietnam, but their political isolation has been accompanied by an economic isolation, in part created by a U.S. trade embargo. Like their even more isolated neighbor Burma, the Communist countries of Southeast Asia have had a dismal record of economic progress.

Economic conditions in many of the capitalist parts of Southeast Asia are only marginally better than their Communist neighbors. In the Philippines, the failure of land reforms to create a secure basis for poor peasants means that many landless and land-poor peasants continue to struggle to survive. The Philippines in the 1990s has just begun to transform the position it had in the 1960s when it was largely a producer of raw materials for the U.S. economy and a consumer of U.S. manufactured goods, a relationship initially created in the 1930s. Now, international capital in search of cheap labor has begun processing in the Philippines as well as in other parts of Southeast Asia. Conditions in Indonesia combine signs of positive change and indications of persistent problems. Fueled by the rising oil prices of the early 1970s, Indonesia expanded its state-run oil production and used the revenues from this operation to begin financing other industrial development; oil replaced rubber as the major export commodity. But as the government moved to develop its raw materials, it continued to face severe demographic pressures, especially on Java where surplus agricultural populations still struggle for livelihoods. In the best of conditions, most Southeast Asian countries have created some industrial base but have yet to become industrialized economies like the Four Dragons.

Squatters' shacks line up along a river in the shadow of luxury housing in the Philippines.

The basic problem throughout South and Southeast Asia is a vast surplus of labor without sufficient capital to create industrial jobs for them. In Japan, Korea, and Taiwan, industry succeeded in drawing labor out of agriculture; modern inputs into agriculture complemented modern technologies in industry to raise outputs in both industry and agriculture. This combination of changes has not taken place in many parts of South and Southeast Asia. These areas share, with much of Africa, Latin America, and parts of the Middle East, a poverty that contrasts sharply with the material successes of the advanced industrial societies in East Asia, North America, and Western Europe.

Toward a Future World History

In societies where most people enjoy economic prosperity, problems of poverty and social inequities are less pressing than they are in other parts of the world. Some prosperous countries are democracies, where people can give open voice to their concerns and a free press raises public awareness of social issues, making it difficult for governments to ignore such major problems. But many societies lack both developed economies and democratic political institutions. Authoritarian regimes, often under military leadership, rule poor societies through force and fear in many parts of Africa, Asia, and Latin America. The struggle to create political institutions responsive to popular needs and aspirations continues to be waged. Western political developments have long defined a set of norms according to which changes elsewhere are conventionally measured. But the limitations of these systems as well as the inability to export Western institutions wholesale to culturally and historically different settings challenges people to create new alternatives to the politics of the past.

Even in the most optimistic scenarios, formal governments and politics can create only so much change. A profound skepticism of government's capacities as well as its intentions has become common in many political systems. Beyond the world's many different states are a variety of societies subject to patterns of change set in motion by forces stretching back several decades and even centuries. When we look at the status of women, their opportunities continue to grow in advanced industrial societies, but some argue that at current rates of change, women will enjoy economic equity with men in about one thousand years. Yet the challenge is even more forbidding in nonindustrialized parts of the world, where the scarcity of fuel and water can condemn women to walking several hours every day just to gather the basics with which they can prepare the minimal subsistence required to keep their children alive. With such demands, these women cannot afford the luxury of education or entertain realistic desires for a better life.

The global ties creating an integrated world history connect the urban and posturban populations of advanced industrial societies. Beneath the superwealthy and powerful, who themselves jet about the world, are the far larger number of affluent people whose lives are shaped by the commodities and ideas that flow easily through worldwide networks of trade and communication. Many people share a material world made up of the same automobiles, electronic goods, and clothing; they hear many of the same news stories and express similar hopes and anxieties about the future. Theirs is a world quite separate from the millions who face the constant struggle to survive in the small villages that still cover many parts of the globe. Will the future bring a world in which the connections among rich and poor societies will lead to the positive transformations of both?

Social changes across the globe in modern times have given people similar opportunities and difficulties. And yet people's awareness of their shared situations does not mean they consider each other to be so very similar. Dramatically different historical experiences form the cultural resources from which people construct their sense of the present and their relations with each other in local settings and across a global civilization. The affirmation of distinctions in matters of religion, language, cuisine, and dress combine to form a multiplicity of identities. At times, ethnic and religious differences, often tied to differences in economic well-being and access to political power, have ripped apart societies in Asia and Europe.

The integration of the world through human migration heightens social awareness of cultural differences, as people with very different histories enter a shared present. Displacing people to new settings strains the capacities and sensibilities of democratic systems seeking to define agreed-upon principles to accept and reject new immigrants. A society like the United States, founded as an immigrant nation, may have a clearer history upon which to build policies to incorporate new waves of immigrants than many societies in Asia and Europe, but in the U.S., as elsewhere, new immigrants have historically faced discrimination and at times open violence. Will people learn to accept and even celebrate cultural diversity without inviting mutual distrust, fomenting social attacks, and putting forward demands to exclude others?

Beyond the challenges of diverse peoples forming an increasingly interdependent world lie the uncertainties of humankind's relationship with the planet earth. For most of the time human beings have lived on this globe, they have been limited by the resources and energy of the organic world. Only with the Industrial Revolution did people begin to discover ways to unleash the potentials of mineral sources of energy, to create for two centuries seemingly boundless possibilities for additional growth by tapping fossil fuels like coal, oil, and natural gas. But now the costs and dangers of destroying nature are becoming more widely studied and recognized. Decisions to pollute in one country can create acid rain in another. The industrialized world can destroy the ozone shield for everyone. At the same time, countries anxious to industrialize wonder why they should not contribute to the pollution advanced industrialized powers previously created in order to reap material advantages like those already enjoyed by the richer countries.

Different historical trajectories have brought the world's many societies and cultures into increasing contact. The problems and possibilities tackled in the future will be shaped by the distinctive priorities and concerns that people across the globe bring to their understanding of the present. To imagine and to create a desirable future demands an informed understanding of how we have come to reach this point in world history today.

SUGGESTIONS FOR FURTHER READING

EAST ASIA DURING THE RISE AND FALL OF JAPANESE IMPERIALISM, 1930-1952

W. G. Beasley, *Japanese Imperialism, 1894-1945* (Oxford: Oxford University Press, 1987). A systematic and balanced account of Japan's formal and informal empire throughout Asia.

* Elizabeth Perry, *Rebels and Revolutionaries in North China, 1845-1945* (Stanford, CA: Stanford University Press, 1980). An elegant comparison of the Nian Rebellion and the Communist movement in north China.

* John Dower, *War Without Mercy: Race and Power in the Pacific War* (New York: Pantheon, 1986). A sobering analysis of Japanese and U.S. perspectives on the enemy during World War II.

The End of Colonialism in South and Southeast Asia

* David J. Steinberg, ed., *In Search of Southeast Asia: A Modern History*, rev. ed. (Honolulu: University of Hawaii Press, 1987). Parts IV and V survey nationalist movements and the establishment of independence through the region.

Chris Dixon, *South East Asia in the World Economy* (Cambridge: Cambridge University Press, 1991). A sweeping review of Southeast Asian political and economic history that locates the end of colonial rule within a long-term perspective.

* George Rosen, *Democracy and Economic Change in India* (Berkeley, CA: University of California Press, 1967). A clear analysis of Indian society, politics and the economy from independence through the 1950s.

Paths for Development and Change: South Asia and China

Francine R. Frankel, *India's Political Economy, 1947–1977* (Princeton, N.J.: Princeton University Press, 1978). A revealing portrait of how Indian politics shaped economic development for the first three decades of Indian independence.

* Franz Schurmann, *Ideology and Organization in Communist China*, 2nd ed. (Berkeley, CA: University of California Press, for 1971). A systematic analysis of China's political organization and ideology during the 1950s and 1960s.

For autobiographical analyses of the Cultural Revolution years consider any of the three following accounts:

* Liang Heng and Judith Shapiro, *Son of the Revolution* (New York: Vintage Books, 1983).

* Yue Daiyun and Carolyn Wakeman, *To the Storm: The Odyssey of a Revolutionary Chinese Woman* (Berkeley, CA: University of California Press, 1985).

* Gao Yuan, *Born Red: A Chronicle of the Cultural Revolution* (Stanford, CA: Stanford University Press, 1987).

* Harry Harding, *China's Second Revolution: Reform After Mao* (Washington: Brookings Institution, 1987). A balanced assessment of China's political and economic reforms from 1976 to the late 1980s.

Successful Capitalist Societies and Those Left Behind

* Shintaro Ishihara, *The Japan That Can Say No: Why Japan Will Be First Among Equals* (New York: Simon and Schuster, 1991). A controversial view of Japan's strengths and future international policies.

* Donald Richie, *A Lateral View: Essays on Contemporary Japan* (Tokyo: The Japan Times, 1987). A selection of film critic Donald Richie's insightful essays on Japanese culture and society.

* Toshio Watanabe, *Asia: Its Growth and Agony* (Honolulu: East-West Center, 1992). A straightforward account of how some parts of Asia are developing and others are not.

* Indicates paperback edition available.

CREDITS

Chapter 21

Small excerpt on "evil" from Philosophical Dictionary by Voltaire, translated by Peter Gay. Copyright © 1962 by Basic Books, Publishing Co., Inc. Copyright renewed. Reprinted by permission of Basic Books, a division of HarperCollins, Publishers, Inc.

Chapter 22

"What is the Third Estate?" Reprinted with the permission of Macmillan Publishing Company from A Documentary Survey of the French Revolution by John Hall Stewart. Copyright © 1951 by Macmillan Publishing Company, renewed 1979 by John Hall Stewart.
"Declaration of the Rights of Woman and Citizen." Olympe de Gouges, *Declaration of the Rights of Woman and the Female Citizen.* In *Women in Revolutionary Paris 1789- 1795.* Translated by Darline Gay Levy, Harriet Branson Applewhite, and Mary Durham Johnson. (Urbana, IL: University of Illinois Press, 1979), pp. 89-92.

Chapter 23

"Zhang Ying's Advice to His Son." From "Translation of Heng-Ch 'an So-Yen by Chang Ying" in Land and Lineage in China by Hilary J. Beattie. Copyright © 1979 by Cambridge University Press. Reprinted by permission.

Chapter 26

"Plebiscite for Empire." Reprinted with permission of Macmillan Publishing Company from The Constitutions and Other Select Documents Illustrative of the History of France, 1789–1907, edited by Frank Maloy Anderson, 2/e (Russell & Russell, New York, 1967).
"From Emile Zola's *J'Accuse.*" From The Affair: *The Case of Alfred Dreyfus* by Jean-Denis Bredin, translated by Jeffrey Mehlman. Copyright © 1983 by George Braziller, Inc. Reprinted by permission.

Chapter 27

"Leopold II of Belgium, Speech to an International Conference of Geographers, 1876." Excerpts from French Colonialism, 1871–1914: Myths and Realities by Henri Brunschwig. Reprinted by permission of Armand Colin Éditeur.
"The Abuses of Imperialism." Excerpt from E.D. Morel, "The Black Man's Burden." Copyright © 1969 by Monthly Review Press. Reprinted by permission of Monthly Review Foundation.
"The Society of National Defense, Serbia, 1911." Reprinted with permission of Macmillan College Publishing Company from Europe in the 19th Century: A Documentary Analysis of Change and Conflict, Volume II 1870–1914 by Eugene N. Anderson, Stanley J. Pinceti and Donald J. Ziegler. Copyright © 1961 by Macmillan College Publishing Company, Inc.

Chapter 28

Excerpt from "The Jamaica Letter" by Simon Bolivar, translated by David Bushnell in The Liberator, Simon Bolivar. Reprinted by permission.
Excerpts from "The Case Against the Jihad" by Al-Kanami from Nigerian Perspectives by Thomas Hodgkin. Reprinted by permission of Oxford University Press.

Chapter 29

"German War Aims." Reprinted from Germany's Aims in the First World War by Fritz Fischer, by permission of W. W. Norton & Company, Inc. Copyright © 1961 by Droste Verlag und Druckerei GmbH, Dusseldorf. Translation copyright © 1967 by W. W. Norton & Company, Inc. From "Proclamation of the 'Whites' " from Intervention, Civil War and Communism in Russia, April–December 1918 by James Bunyon. Reprinted by permission of Hippocrene Books.

Chapter 30

Excerpt from "The Results of the First Five-Year Plan" from Joseph Stalin, Selected Writings (New York: International Publishers, 1942). Reprinted by permission of International Publishers Company.
Excerpt from "Racial Purity: Hitler Reverts to the Dominant Theme of the National Socialist Program, January 30, 1937" from Hitler's Third Reich edited by Louis L. Snyder. Copyright © 1981 by Louis L. Snyder. Reprinted by permission of Nelson-Hall, Inc.
Excerpt from Winifred Holtby, Women and a Changing Civilization. Copyright 1934 by Bodley Head, Ltd. Selections reprinted by permission of Paul Berry, literary executor for Winifred Holtby.
Excerpt from Rudolph Schlesinger, The Family in The USSR: Documents and Readings. (London: Routledge & Kegan Paul, 1949), pp. 251–254. Reprinted by permission of the publisher.

Chapter 31

"Lin Zexu's Moral Advice." Reprinted by permission of the publishers from China's Response to the West: A Documentary Survey 1839–1923 by Ssu-Yu Teng and John K. Fairbank. Cambridge, Mass.: Harvard University Press. Copyright 1954 by the President and Fellows of Harvard College, © 1982 by Ssu-Yu Teng and John K. Fairbank.
"Shanghai Diary" from The Japan Reader: *Volume I, Imperial Japan* by Jon Livingston, Joe Moore and Felicia Oldfather. Copyright © 1973 by Random House, Inc. Reprinted by permission of Pantheon Books, a division of Random House, Inc.
Excerpts from "What Happens After Nora Leaves Home?" from Silent China, Selected Writings of Lu Xun, edited and translated by Gladys Yang. Copyright © Oxford University Press 1973. Reprinted by permission.

Chapter 32

"Manifesto of the Jewish Resistance in Vilna (September 1943)" from An Anthology of Holocaust Literature, edited by J. Glatstein, I. Knox, and S. Margoshes. Philadelphia: The Jewish Publication Society, 1969, pp. 332–333. Reprinted by permission of the publisher.
"The White Rose." Excerpt from "Opposition: Students of the 'Weisse Rose' Distribute a Leaflet Denouncing Nazism and Pay for It with Their Lives, February 22, 1943" translated by Louis L. Snyder, editor of Hitler's Third Reich. Copyright © 1981 by Louis L. Snyder. Reprinted by permission of Nelson-Hall, Inc.

Excerpts from "Japan's Declaration of War" from World War II: Policy and Strategy by Hans Adolf Jacobsen and Arthur J. Smith, Jr. Reprinted by permission.

Excerpts from "Roosevelt's Request for Declaration of War on Japan" from World War II: Policy and Strategy by Hans Adolf Jacobsen and Arthur J. Smith, Jr. Reprinted by permission.

"Glittering Fragments" by Hara Tamiki (p. 221) from The Penguin Book of Japanese Verse translated by Geoffrey Bownas and Anthony Thwaite (Penguin Books, 1964) translation copyright © Geoffrey Bownas and Anthony Thwaite, 1964. Reprinted by permission of Penguin Books Ltd., Letters translated by Corinner Antezana-Pernet from La Seconda Guerra Mondiale, 6th Edition by Roberto Battaglia. Reprinted by permission.

Chapter 33

"I Am the Train of Sadness" by Qabbani Nizar from New Writing From the Middle East, edited by L. Hamilian and J.D. Yohannan. Copyright © 1969 by Qabbani Nizar, translation copyright © 1974 by Abdullah al-Udhari. Reprinted by permission of The Crossroad Publishing Company.

Excerpt from Harem Years: The Memoirs of an Egyptian Feminist by Huda Shaarawi. Translation copyright © 1986 by Margot Badran from the book Harem Years: The Memoirs of an Egyptian Feminist by Huda Shaarawi. Translated and introduced by Margot Badran. Published by The Feminist Press at The City University of New York. All rights reserved.

Chapter 34

"Winston Churchill, The Iron Curtain (1946)." Excerpt from "The Sinews of Peace" by Winston Churchill from Robert Rhodes James, Winston S. Churchill: His Complete Speeches 1897–1963 Volume VII 1943–1949. Copyright © 1983 by Chelsea House Publishers. Reprinted by permission of Chelsea House Publishers.

"Subterranean Homesick Blues" by Bob Dylan. Copyright © 1965 by Warner Bros. Music, copyright renewed 1993 by Special Rider Music. All rights reserved. International copyright secured. Reprinted by permission.

Excerpts from "Report to the Twentieth Party Congress" by Nikita S. Khrushchev reprinted from Current Soviet Policies II. The Documentary Record of the Twentieth Party Congress and Its Aftermath published by The Current Digest of the Soviet Press, Columbus, Ohio. Used by permission.

Excerpts from The Second Sex by Simone De Beauvoir, translated by H.M. Parshley. Copyright 1952 and renewed 1980 by Alfred A. Knopf, Inc. Reprinted by permission of the publisher.

Chapter 35

Ian Buruma, A Japanese Mirror: *Heroes and Villains of Japanese Culture.* London: Jonathon Cape, Ltd., 1984, p. 147.

Excerpt from "A Definition of the Japanese Film" from A Lateral View: Essays on Culture and Style in Contemporary Japan by Donald Richie (Stone Bridge Press, 1992). Reprinted by permission.

Excerpt from "One Page of a Diary" from One Day in China: May 21, 1936 translated, edited and introduced by Sherman Cochran and Andrew C.K. Hsieh with Janis Cochran. Copyright © 1983 by Yale University. Reprinted by permission of Yale University Press.

PHOTO CREDITS

Positions of the photographs are indicated in the abbreviated form as follows: top (t), bottom (b), center (c), left (l), right (r).

Unless otherwise acknowledged, all photographs are the property of ScottForesman.

Table of Contents
vi Emil Muench
vii American School of Classical Studies at Athens: Agora Excavations
viii Bibliothèque Nationale, Paris
ix The British Library
x Kodansha Ltd., Tokyo
xi The New York Public Library; Astor, Lenox and Tilden Foundations
xii The New York Public Library; Astor, Lenox and Tilden Foundations
xiii Private Collection
xv National Archives of Zimbabwe
xvi Library of Congress
xvii Reuters/Bettmann

Table of Contents (Volume B 1300 to 1800)
vi Kodansha Ltd., Tokyo
vii Mary Evans Picture Library
viii © Photo RMN
ix The New York Public Library; Astor, Lenox and Tilden Foundations

Table of Contents (Volume C 1789 to the Present)
vi Copyright British Museum
vii Historisches Museum der Stadt Wien
ix Historical Pictures/Stock Montage

Bomb Survivors edited by The Japan Broadcasting Association. Copyright © 1977 by NHK. Reprinted by permission by Pantheon Books, a division of Random House, Inc.
1002 U. S. Navy
1004 Franklin D. Roosevelt Library, National Archives and Records Service

Chapter 33
1006 Mourners surrounding the flag-draped coffin of UAR President Gamal Abdel Nasser during his funeral procession. UPI/Bettmann
1012 UPI/Bettmann
1014 AP/Wide World
1016 N.R. Farbman, *Life* Magazine © Time Warner Inc.
1020 UPI/Bettmann
1023 East African Standard Newspapers Ltd.
1024 AP/Wide World
1026 Betty Press/Woodfin Camp & Associates
1029 Trustees of the Imperial War Museum, London
1033 Courtesy of United Jewish Appeal
1039 Ralph Crane, *Life* Magazine © Time Warner Inc.
1040 Reuters/Bettmann

Chapter 34
1044 *The Poster Scene*, 1967. Topham/Image Works
1048 UPI/Bettmann
1050 European Community Information Service
1054 UPI/Bettmann
1057 Erich Lessing/Magnum
1062 UPI/Bettmann
1065 Bruno Barbey/Magnum
1067 Peter Marlow/Magnum
1068 Vlastimir Shone/Gamma-Liaison
1069 DeKeerle/Grochowiak/Sygma
1070 AP/Wide World
1073 Leh/Saukkomaa/Woodfin Camp & Associates
1075 AP/Wide World
1076 AP/Wide World
1079 Reuters/Bettmann

Chapter 35
1082 Shanghai Sampan. Hiroji Kubota/Magnum
1086 UPI/Bettmann
1089 AP/Wide World
1093 UPI/Bettmann
1095 AP/Wide World
1098 UPI/Bettmann
1099 AP/Wide World
1101 AP/Wide World
1104 (l) AP/Wide World; (r) Reuters/Bettmann
1106 Courtesy of *Baseball Magazine Sha*
1109 T. Matsumoto/Sygma
1111 Andy Hernandez/Sygma

Color Essay 1 following page 126
1 Erich Lessing/Art Resource, NY
2 B. Norman/Ancient Art & Architecture Collection
3 TAP Service/National Museum, Athens
4 Hirmer Fotoarchiv, Munich

Color Essay 2 following page 222
1 Scala/Art Resource, NY
2 The Metropolitan Museum of Art, Purchase, Lita Annenberg Hazen Charitable Trust Gift, in honor of Cynthia Hazen and Leon Bernard Polsky, 1982 (1982.220.8)
3 The Board of Trinity College Dublin
4 Scala/Art Resource, NY

Color Essay 3 following page 318
1 Erich Lessing/Art Resource, NY
2 Scala/Art Resource, NY
3 Reproduced by courtesy of the Trustees, The National Gallery, London
4 Reproduced by courtesy of the Trustees, The National Gallery, London

Color Essay 4 following page 414
1 The Granger Collection, New York
2 Scala/Art Resource, NY
3 Derby Museums and Art Gallery
4 Werner Forman/Art Resource, NY

Color Essay 5 following page 590
1 Giraudon/Art Resource, NY
2 Courtesy of The Arthur M. Sackler Museum, Harvard University Art Museums, Private Collection
3 Colorphoto Hans Hinz
4 Reproduced by permission of the Trustees of the Wallace Collection

Color Essay 6 following page 718
1 Bridgeman/Art Resource, NY
2 Royal Academy of Arts, London
3 Erich Lessing/Art Resource, NY
4 Erich Lessing/Art Resource, NY

Color Essay 7 following page 814
1 Pablo Picasso. *Les Desmoiselles d'Avignon*. Paris (June–July 1907). Oil on canvas, 8′ × 7′ 8″. The Museum of Modern Art, New York. Acquired through the Lillie P. Bliss Bequest
2 M. Felix Collection, Brussels. Photo: Dick Beaulieux
3 Private Collection. Photo: Jeffrey Ploskonka
4 Frida Kahlo. *Self Portrait with Cropped Hair*. 1940. Oil on canvas, 15¾ × 11″. The Museum of Modern Art, New York. Gift of Edgar Kaufmann, Jr.

Color Essay 8 following page 1102
1 Kitagawa Utamaro, Japanese, 1753–1806, *Joshoku Kaiko Tewaza Gusa (Women's Work in Silk Culture)*, woodblock print, c. 1802, 38.1 × 25.4 cm, Departmental Funds, 1925.3257, photograph © 1993, The Art Institute of Chicago. All Rights Reserved
2 Tate Gallery, London/Art Resource, NY
3 Library of Congress
4 From *Prop Art: Over 1000 Contemporary Political Posters* by Gary Yanker. Darien House, New York, distributed by New York Graphic Society, 1972. Copyright © 1972 by Gary Yanker

INDEX

Page numbers followed by *t* and *f* indicate tables and figures, respectively. pronunciation guidance is supplied in square brackets, [ ], after difficult words. The symbols used for pronunciation are found in the table below. Syllables for primary stress are *italicized*.

a	act, bat, marry
AY	age, rate
år	air, dare
ä	ah, part, calm
ch	chief, beach
e	edge, set
EE	equal, seat, bee
EER	here, ear
g	give, trigger
h	here
hw	which, when
i	if, big
I	bite, ice
ng	sing
o	ox, hot
O	hope, over
ô	order, ball
oi	oil, joint
oo	book, tour
ou	plow, out
sh	she, fashion
th	thin, ether
u	up, sum
zh	vision, pleasure
uh	*a*lone, syst*e*m, eas*i*ly, gall*o*p, circ*u*s
A	as in French *a*mi
KH	as in German a*ch*, i*ch*
N	as in French bo*n*
OE	as in French d*eu*x
R	as in French *r*ouge
Y	as in German f*ü*hlen

Aachen [*ä* kuhn, *ä* Huhn], 255, 258, 610
Abbas I (Safavid shah), 457, 457*f*, 461*f*, 464
'Abbas [uh *bä, ä* buh], 206
'Abbasid [uh *bas* id, *ab* uh sid] dynasty, 206–207, 211, 443, 445
Abbots, 276, 287
'Abd [ab d] al-Qadir (Algerian shaykh), 578
'Abdallah (Arab leader), 1030
'Abd ar-Rahman III, 206
'Abduh, Muhammad, 589

Abdullah Hassan (Somalian leader), 813
Abeokuta [ä bAY *O* koo tä], 19th-c., 855
Abolition movement
  in British West Africa, 855
  in Great Britain, 560, 565–567, 751
  in United States, 751, 753
Abolition philosophy, and French Revolution, 665, 668
Abraham, 21, 24, 173
Abu Bakr [uh bU *bak* uhr, A bu Bekr], 203–204
Académie des Sciences, 538
Academies, in 18th-century Europe, 635
Academy (Plato's), 88
Achaemenid dynasty, 68
Acheson, Dean [*ach* uh suhn] (U.S. official), 1048
Achille Lauro, highjacking of, 1078
Achilles, 45, 92
Acropolis, 52, 65, 67, 86
Actium [*ak* tEE uhm, *ak* shEE uhm], battle of, 159, 164, 166
Acts of the Apostles, 173
Adam brothers, 623
Adbul Hamid II (Ottoman sultan), 830
Address to the Christian Nobility of the German Nation (Luther), 389
Aden, 417
  19th-c., British acquisition of, 829
Adenauer, Konrad [*ad* n ou uhr] (West German chancellor), 1056, 1060
Adowa, battle of, 814, 815*f*, 825, 856
Adrianople, battle of, 182
Advancement of Learning (Bacon), 538
Advertising, 869–870. *See also* Press; Public opinion
Aeneas, 167 *Aeneid* [i *nEE* id], 167
Aeolians, 49
aeropagus, 66
Aeschylus [*es* ku luhs], 81, 84
Afghanistan, 443, 449, 457, 462, 467. *See also* Ghaznavids; Mahmud of Ghazna
  19th-c., and Russia, 819
  Hellenistic, 96
  and Safavid Empire, 451, 466
Afghans, 447, 464–466
Afonso (Kongolese *maniKongo*), 419
Africa. *See also* East Africa; North Africa; *specific country or group*; West Africa
  15th-16th-c., Catholicism in, 418–419, 421
  15th-17th-c., Portuguese in, 408–424
  17th-c., and European economy, 561–562
  17th-19th-c., relationship with Europe, 560–575

19th-c., 568*f*, 573, 809–818, 821, 825, 851–856
20th-c., *map* 818, 822, 860–863, 866, 1017–1019, 1020–1021, 1065
agricultural/pastoral peoples in, 4–8
"big men" in. *See* Big men
Christianity in, 855–856, 864–866, 1017
climate of, 7
European exploration of, 410–424, 805
European settlers in. *See* Africa, 20th-c., European settlers in; Rhodesia; South Africa; Zambia; Zimbabwe
before European slave trade, economic structure of, 413
Islam in, 193, 211–219
Lower Guinea Coast, *map* 562
map, 4, 414, 852, 1018
Neolithic food-production practices, diffusion of, 4–6
political policies and practices of. *See* Political policies and practices, of Africa; *specific country*
politics of kinship in, 7–8
regional politics in, 8–9
religion in. *See also* Christianity, spread, in Africa; Islam, spread, in Africa
social structure of, 413
sub-Saharan, early civilization in, to 700 c.e., 4–9
African National Congress, 1024–1025
  Freedom Charter of, 1019, 1025
Africans
  in Americas. *See* Llaneros; Pardos; Slaves
  resistance to Portuguese intervention, 424
  Western-educated elite, 855–856, 1022
Afrika Korps, 998
Afrikaner Nationalist Party, 1024
Afrikaners, 569–572, 814–818, 1024–1025
Afterlife, belief in
  Chinese Buddhist, 226
  Egyptian, 18–19
  Han Chinese, 113
  Vedic, 29
Agamemnon, 84
Agincourt, battle of, 297*f*
Agni [*ug* nEE, *ag* nEE] (god), 29
Agora, 52
Agricultural Revolution, 715–717
Agriculture. *See also* Collectivization; Ecology; Famine in Africa, 193, 421
  ancient Andean, 39
  Angkor (Khmer), 242

in Arabia, 200
in Austria, 18th-19th centuries, 735
in Carthage, 135
in China, 105–106, 117, 119–120, 223, 228, 231, 317, 321, 326, 329, 331, 682–683, 683*f*, 688–689, 945
collective, in Soviet Union, interwar period, 916–920
in colonized societies, 19th-c., 825
common farming system, 643
in Communist Yanan, 1086
development of, 3–4
double-cropping system, 128, 698
dry field system, 682
in eastern Europe, 18th-c., 643–644
Egyptian, 16–17, 577–578, 585
enclosed field system, 716–717
in England, 307, 511
equal field system, 228, 233, 245, 247
Etruscan, 137
in Europe, 263, 264*f*, 272–273, 302–303, 510–511, 638–639, 642*f*, 642–644, 643*f*, 714–717, 738, 885, 1047
European philosophy on, 18th-c., 631
fertilizers, 106, 128, 242, 643, 688, 706
flooded-field system, 317
fodder crop system, 716
four-course rotation system, 716
in France, 776
in Germany
in Great Britain
in Greece, 51, 75
Harappan (ancient India), 28
in Holland, 546
in Hungary, 18th-c., 644
Indian, 26, 28, 128
Indian philosophy regarding, 123
in Indonesia, 20th-c., 1091
invention of, in Chinese mythology, 103
in Iraq, 19th-c., 584
in Ireland, 643, 741
in Islamic empires, 207, 441–442, 462
in Japan, 250, 335–336, 340
in Java, 19th-c., 965
in Kenya, 19th-c., 821
in Korea, 244–245
in Latin America, 20th-c., 1009–1010, 1014, 1016
Longshan (ancient Chinese), 31
market, development in Europe, 644, 716–717
Mayan, 39
meadow-floating system, 716
Mesoamerican and ancient South American, 34–35, 41
in Mesopotamia, 9, 12